Bisk Education

CPA Review™

AMERICA'S BEST CPA REVIEW SINCE 1971

S0-BZD-374

GET READY TO
PASS
THE CPA EXAM

SAVE
HUNDREDS
OF DOLLARS!

See coupons at back of book for special offers on VIDEO and ONLINE exam reviews.

▶▶▶ **WITH BISK'S**
ONLINE CPA REVIEW

PASS THE CPA EXAM THE FIRST TIME — GUARANTEED!*

5 EASY STEPS TO EXAM SUCCESS...ONLINE

STEP 1
SELECT YOUR STUDY METHOD
- **Bisk Instructor-Led CPA Review Online** – We bring the classes to you. The hands-on guidance of an instructor-led live review with the flexibility of online learning!
- **Bisk Self-Directed CPA Review** – The self-directed alternative to our instructor-led program with the flexibility to study on your own anytime, anywhere.

STEP 2
UTILIZE THE PERSONAL TRAINER
The Bisk Personal Trainer™ feature analyzes your performance throughout your study session by matching your weakest areas against the most heavily tested exam topics (according to AICPA specifications) and automatically develops an extensive study plan just for you. Featuring practice exams with links to thousands of pages of the most comprehensive textbooks on the market, this powerful learning tool even reevaluates your needs and modifies your study plan after each study session or practice exam!

STEP 3
DIVE INTO THE MULTIMEDIA STUDY CENTER
- Get access to 60+ hours of streaming video lectures online or on CD.
- Electronic flashcards help you drill those difficult concepts. Print them for on-the-go studying.
- Take unlimited practice exams that give you right/wrong answer explanations with links to the related text.

*Call for details

CPAexam.com/2013

STEP 4

RELY ON OUR EXPERT GUIDANCE

Bisk Instructor-Led CPA Review Online allows you to interact with professors and fellow exam candidates via email, message boards and chat rooms. With both our instructor-led and self-directed online review, you get direct access to our editorial and technical support staffs. Plus, customer service personnel will be standing by to help with any other questions you might have!

STEP 5

FIRE UP THE CPA EXAM TEST ENGINE

The CPA Exam Test Engine allows you to practice taking an unlimited number of final exams (formatted just like the real thing) before you sit. Multiple-choice questions feature instant on-screen grading – helping track your study performance from start to finish and ensuring your success on the CPA Exam.

▶▶▶ HUNDREDS OF SIMULATIONS

ENHANCE YOUR CPA REVIEW WITH:

SIMULATION STRATEGIES VIDEO SERIES

Designed to aid candidates in their final preparation for the exam.
- Available by section or as a full set
- Focuses on simulation drills
- Will help to remove any concerns candidates may have regarding simulation questions

HOT • SPOT DVDs

Choose from topic-specific videos to help with specific areas of difficulty. These DVDs focus on the toughest, most challenging and most frequently tested topics. Each is packed with valuable tips, plus a viewer guide so you can follow along.

CPA REVIEW e-BOOKS

Available now at www.CPAexam.com

CALL NOW ▶▶▶ 888-CPA-BISK

Bisk Education

CPA REVIEW™

ONLINE CLASSROOM IS NOW iPAD COMPATIBLE!

GENERAL FEATURES

- Expanded help system
- "Getting Started" section
- Tutorial-based help system
- Print capabilities
- Web-based interface
- Earn up to 12 college credits

STATISTICS FEATURES

- Color-coded statistical analysis by topic and microtopic
- Statistical charts compare all exams taken
- Statistics saved for every question and exam taken
- Summary details for all areas of study

STUDY FEATURES

60+ HOURS OF STREAMING VIDEO

- Hundreds of simulation questions
- Bisk Personal Trainer™ (develops a personalized study plan based on exam performance)
- More than 4,000 actual CPA exam questions
- Ability to mark questions for later reference
- Thousands of pages of embedded text from our four-volume textbook series
- Statistical and Progress Tracking
- Bookmark and booknote capability
- Electronic flashcards

- Custom study (user chooses what to study)
- Study mode with answer explanations
- Super search
- Weekly assignments to help keep students on track
- Study guides included
- Lecture viewer guides
- 60+ hours of streaming video lectures
- Supplemental examples help explain difficult concepts
- Link to your Facebook, LinkedIn accounts or Twitter

TEST FEATURES

UNLIMITED FINAL EXAMS

- Test advisor (guides you through the test-taking process and recommends specific custom tests)
- Unlimited AICPA-based final exams, unique and timed
- More than 4,000 actual CPA Exam questions
- Mirrors the actual exam
- Questions chosen and weighted from topics based on the CPA Exam
- Ability to mark questions for later reference
- AICPA final exam chart

COMMUNICATION FEATURES

BETTER THAN LIVE

- Message boards for threaded discussions*
- Weekly chat sessions with your professor*
- Email interaction for one-on-one communication*
- Class news to keep you up to date
- Link to your Facebook, LinkedIn or Twitter

MORE THAN 4,000 PRACTICE QUESTIONS!

AVAILABLE BY SECTION OR COMPLETE SET

- Financial Accounting & Reporting
- Auditing & Attestation
- Regulation
- Business Environment & Concepts

Bisk Education, Inc. | 9417 Princess Palm Avenue | Tampa, FL 33619-8313
888-CPA-BISK | 813-621-6200 | www.CPAexam.com/2013 | info@CPAexam.com

Microsoft Certified **Solution Provider**

©2012 Bisk Education, Inc. All rights reserved. | SC 198970zbb1 | MCID 18328 | *Available in instructor-led online review only

CPA

Comprehensive Exam Review

Auditing & Attestation

Nathan M. Bisk, JD, CPA

ACKNOWLEDGMENTS

EDITORIAL BOARD

Nathan M. Bisk, JD, CPA
Mortimer M. Caplin, LLB, JSD, LLD
Richard M. Feldheim, MBA, JD, LLM, CPA
William J. Meurer, CPA

Robert L. Monette, JD, CPA
Paul Munter, PhD, CPA
Thomas A. Ratcliffe, PhD, CPA
C. William Thomas, MBA, PhD, CPA

CONTRIBUTING EDITORS

J. Ralph Byington
PhD, CPA
Coastal Carolina University

Anne Keaty
JD
University of Louisiana at Lafayette

Robert L. Monette
JD, CPA
Philadelphia CPA Review

Paul Munter
PhD, CPA
KPMG

Thomas A. Ratcliffe
PhD, CPA
Warren Averett, LLC

C. William Thomas
MBA, PhD, CPA
Baylor University

Mark A. Turner
DBA, CPA, CMA
Texas State University

We wish to thank the American Institute of Certified Public Accountants and other organizations for permission to reprint or adapt the following copyrighted materials:

1. Uniform CPA Examination Questions and Unofficial Answers, Copyright by American Institute of Certified Public Accountants, Inc. All rights reserved. Reprinted with permission.

2. Audit and Accounting Guides, Auditing Procedure Studies, Risk Alerts, Statements of Position, and Code of Professional Conduct, Copyright by American Institute of Certified Public Accountants, Inc. All rights reserved. Reprinted with permission.

3. *The FASB Accounting Standards Codification*® and Statements of Financial Accounting Concepts, Copyright by the Financial Accounting Standards Board, 401 Merritt 7, P.O. Box 5116, Norwalk, CT 06856, are reprinted with permission.

4. GASB Statements, Interpretations, and Technical Bulletins, Copyright by the Governmental Accounting Standards Board, 401 Merritt 7, P.O. Box 5116, Norwalk, CT 06856-5116.

5. Statements on Auditing Standards, Statements on Standards for Consulting Services, Statements on Responsibilities in Personal Financial Planning Practice, Statements on Standards for Accounting and Review Services, Statements on Quality Control Standards, Statements on Standards for Attestation Engagements, and Statements on Responsibilities in Tax Practice, Copyright by American Institute of Certified Public Accountants, Inc. All rights reserved. Reprinted with permission.

6. ISB Standards, Copyright by the Independence Standards Board, 6th Floor, 1211 Avenue of the Americas, New York, NY 10036-8775

7. International Standards on Auditing and *Code of Ethics for Professional Accountants*, Copyright April 2010 by the International Federation of Accountants (IFAC). All rights reserved. Used with permission of IFAC, 545 Fifth Avenue, 14th Floor, New York, NY 10017 USA

© 2012 by NATHAN M. BISK, JD, CPA
Tampa, Florida 33619

FORTY-SECOND EDITION
ALL RIGHTS RESERVED. Reproduction in any form expressly prohibited. Printed in the United States of America.

PREFACE

Our texts provide comprehensive, complete coverage of all the topics tested on all four sections of the CPA Examination, including **Financial Accounting & Reporting, Auditing & Attestation, Regulation,** and **Business Environment & Concepts.** Used effectively, our materials will enable you to achieve maximum preparedness for the Uniform CPA Examination. Here is a brief summary of the **features** and **benefits** that our texts will provide for you:

1. **Unique Objective Question Coverage With Updated AICPA Unofficial Answers**…We explain *why* the multiple-choice alternatives are either right or wrong. Plus, we update the AICPA's unofficial answers to correctly reflect current business and tax laws and AICPA, PCAOB, SEC, IAASB, FASB, GASB, IASB, and other authoritative pronouncements.

2. **Complete Coverage**…No extra materials are required to be purchased. We discuss and explain all important AICPA, PCAOB, SEC, IAASB, FASB, GASB, and IASB pronouncements, as well as the current tax code and UCC content. Our coverage is based on the most recent **AICPA content specification outlines for the Uniform CPA Examination**.

3. **Thousands of Pages of Text**…Including a selection of thousands of recent CPA Examination and exclusive Bisk Education multiple-choice questions, simulations, and written communication tasks with the AICPA's unofficial answers from past CPA examinations. Solving these questions with immediate verification of results instills confidence and reinforces our **SOLUTIONS APPROACH**™ to solving exam questions.

4. **Separate Volumes**…Each volume includes text, multiple-choice questions, and either simulations or written communication tasks with solutions for an entire exam section. There is no need to refer to any other volume.

5. **Detailed Summaries**…We set forth the significant testable concepts in each exam topic. These highly readable summaries are in outline format to facilitate rapid and complete comprehension. The summaries isolate and emphasize topics historically tested by the CPA examiners.

6. **Emphasis on "How to Answer Questions" and "How to Take the Exam"**…We teach you to solve free-response and simulations using our unique and famous **SOLUTIONS APPROACH**™.

7. **Discussion and Development of**…AICPA grading procedures, grader orientation strategies, examination confidence, and examination success.

8. **Information on the Computer-Based Exam**…The Uniform CPA Examination is administered at secure testing centers on computers. See Appendix B for a full discussion of this issue. This edition contains up-to-date coverage, including complete coverage of all exam changes.

9. **Research and Writing Skills**…Each volume contains an appendix to help you brush up on either your research or writing skills for the related section of the exam.

10. **Indexes**…We have included a comprehensively compiled index for easy topic reference in each volume.

11. **Cross-References**…If you do decide to use our other materials, the software uses the same chapter numbering system as the book to allow for easy synchronization between the two formats. Our video programs are also referenced to those same chapters (page B-2).

12. **Practice Exam to Test Your Preparedness**…We include a practice exam to test your exam preparedness. These testing materials are designed to help you identify for concentrated study any exam topic area where you need further study after reviewing each of the chapters.

Our materials are designed for the candidate who previously has studied accounting. Therefore, the rate at which a candidate studies and learns (not merely reads) our material will depend on a candidate's background and aptitude. Candidates who have been out of school for a period of years might need more time to study than recent graduates. The point to remember is that all the material you will need to know to pass the exam is here, except for the professional databases available for free via the AICPA's website (aicpa.org/becomeacpa /cpaexam/forcandidates/howtoprepare/pages/literature.aspx) to candidates with their *Notice to Schedule*. All you need to do is apply yourself and learn this material at a rate that is appropriate to your situation. **As a final thought,** keep in mind that test confidence gained through disciplined preparation equals success.

OUR EDITORIAL BOARD INCLUDES THE NATION'S LEADING CPAs, ATTORNEYS AND EDUCATORS!

The Only CPA Review Texts Developed By Full-Time Experts.

Publisher and Editor-in-Chief
NATHAN M. BISK, JD, CPA (FL), is both an attorney and certified public accountant in the State of Florida. He is a graduate of Franklin and Marshall College and the University of Florida College of Law. He is a member of the AICPA, Florida Institute of Certified Public Accountants, American Association of Attorney-CPAs, Florida Bar, American Bar Association, and American Business Law Association. His background includes public accounting experience at both Ernst & Young and Arthur Andersen & Co. He is a graduate of the two-year JET program of Merrill Lynch, Pierce, Fenner & Smith, Inc. Mr. Bisk has written and taught accounting, auditing, taxation, and business law programs since 1970.

Contributing Editor
ROBERT L. MONETTE, JD, CPA (PA), is a specialist in continuing professional education and nationally recognized as an expert on the CPA exam. He is an entrepreneur with extensive experience in business acquisitions. His background includes experience in statistical sampling, EDP auditing, financial statement analysis, and taxation. Mr. Monette also has taught CPA Review in Boston, New York, New Jersey, and Philadelphia, where he has helped tens of thousands of candidates become CPAs. He is one of the expert instructors on Bisk Education's CPA Review video series and has appeared as an expert commentator in several Bisk Education CPE programs. Mr. Monette earned an undergraduate degree from Bentley College and a law degree from Villanova University.

Contributing Editor
PAUL MUNTER, PhD, CPA, is currently a partner in the Department of Professional Practice—Audit with KPMG. Previously, he served as KPMG Professor and Chairman of the Department of Accounting at the University of Miami in Coral Gables, Florida. Dr. Munter also served as the Academic Fellow in the Office of the Chief Accountant at the US Securities and Exchange Commission from 2002-2003 where he worked on many of the Commission's Sarbanes-Oxley initiatives and rule-making activities.

Consulting Editor
MORTIMER M. CAPLIN, LLB, JSD, LLD, is a Senior Partner with the Washington, D.C. law firm of Caplin & Drysdale. He is a former IRS Commissioner, and served as a member of the President's Task Force on Taxation. He is a recipient of the Alexander Hamilton Award (the highest award conferred by the Secretary of the Treasury) "for outstanding and unusual leadership during service as US Commissioner of Internal Revenue." For more than 30 years, Mr. Caplin has been in private practice with his present law firm, and has served as Adjunct Professor for the University of Virginia Law School. He is a nationally acclaimed author of numerous articles on tax and corporate matters.

YOU WILL LEARN FROM OUR OUTSTANDING EXPERTS... WITHOUT LEAVING YOUR HOME OR OFFICE.

Consulting Editor
RICHARD M. FELDHEIM, MBA, JD, LLM, CPA (NY), is a New York CPA as well as an attorney in New York and Arizona. He holds a Master's in Tax Law from New York University Law School. Mr. Feldheim is a member of the AICPA, New York State Society of CPAs, American Bar Association, New York State Bar Association, and Association of the Bar of the City of New York. His background includes practice as both a CPA with Price Waterhouse & Co. and as a Senior Partner with the Arizona law firm of Wentworth & Lundin. He has lectured for the AICPA, the Practising Law Institute, Seton Hall University, and the University of Arizona.

Consulting Editor
THOMAS A. RATCLIFFE, PhD, CPA (TX), serves as the senior accounting and auditing technical advisor for Warren Averett, LLC, as well as advising and consulting for six different associations of CPA firms throughout the country. Dr. Ratcliffe has served as a member of the Auditing Standards Board (ASB) during the development of the clarified and converged auditing and quality control standards. He also has served on the Audit Issues Task Force, the AICPA Council, AICPA Accounting and Review Services Committee, and the Private Company Financial Reporting Committee. Dr. Ratcliffe is the primary contributing author to the AICPA Guide for Compilation and Review Engagements. He is a member of the Auditing Panel for The Journal of Accountancy. Dr. Ratcliffe has received numerous research and teaching awards throughout his career, including the Alabama Society of CPAs Outstanding Professional Educator award, which since was renamed in his honor.

Consulting Editor
WILLIAM J. MEURER, CPA (FL), is former Managing Partner for both the overall operations in Central Florida and the Florida Audit and Business Advisory Services sector of Arthur Andersen LLP. During his 35-year career with the firm, Mr. Meurer developed expertise in several industries, including high technology, financial services, real estate, retailing/distribution, manufacturing, hospitality, professional services, and cable television. A graduate of Regis University, Mr. Meurer is a member of both the American Institute of CPAs and the Florida Society of CPAs.

Consulting Editor
C. WILLIAM THOMAS, MBA, PhD, CPA (TX), is J.E. Bush Professor and former chairman of the Department of Accounting and Business Law at Baylor University. He is a member of the AICPA, the Texas Society of CPAs, the Central Texas Chapter of CPAs, and the American Accounting Association, where he is past Chairperson for the Southwestern Regional Audit Section. In addition, he has received recognition for special Audit Education and Curriculum projects he developed for Coopers & Lybrand. His background includes public accounting experience with KPMG Peat Marwick.

CHANGE ALERTS

Government Auditing Standards, 2011 Revision; issued 12/2011

In December 2011, the Comptroller General of the United States issued the 2011 revision of *Government Auditing Standards* (GAGAS). The 2011 GAGAS is effective for performance audits beginning on or after December 15, 2011. Coverage of this guidance applicable to performance audits is included in this edition. It is effective for financial audits and attestation engagements for periods ending on or after December 15, 2012. Coverage of this guidance applicable to financial audits and attestation engagements is **not** included in this edition as it is not eligible to be tested until the July-August 2013 exam window. Early implementation is not permitted. (Chapter 9)

SQCS 8, *A Firm's System of Quality Control (Redrafted)*, (QC 10A); issued 11/2010

In November 2010, the Auditing Standards Board of the American Institute of Certified Public Accountants (AICPA) issued Statement on Quality Control Standards (SQCS) 8, *A Firm's System of Quality Control (Redrafted)*. SQCS 8 is applicable to a CPA firm's system of quality control for its accounting and auditing practice as of January 1, 2012. (Chapter 14)

CSO Update; approved 10/1/2011

In October 2011, the AICPA Board of Examiners approved changes to the CPA Examination Content Specification Outlines (CSO) for all four exam sections. The new CSO is effective beginning with the January-February 2013 exam window. According to the AICPA, the changes include general improvements for clarity; the removal of redundancies; a reference review and update; and general editorial updates. Please see the third section of Appendix B of this textbook for the new AUD CSO.

The AICPA Auditing Standards Board's Clarity Project

The goal of the Clarity Project (also known as the Clarification and Convergence Project) is to redraft and recodify US generally accepted auditing standards for nonpublic companies—nonissuers—to make them easier to understand and apply as well as to converge with International Standards on Auditing (ISA) while avoiding unnecessary conflict with Public Company Accounting Oversight Board audit standards.

In October 2011, the Auditing Standards Board of the AICPA issued Statement on Auditing Standards (SAS) 122, *Statements on Auditing Standards: Clarification and Recodification*, effective for audits of financial statements for periods ending on or after December 15, 2012. The result is a recodification which reorders, and in some cases, regroups GAAS topics into new AU-C sections.

Coverage of clarified standards (SAS 122-126—SAS 126 was the latest to be issued when we went to press) is **not** included in this edition as they are not eligible to be tested until the July-August 2013 exam window.

Our coverage of the clarified standards will be included in a Bisk Education updating supplement to this, our 42nd edition. A release date has not yet been set for the 42 series updating supplement that will include them, but it will probably be available for download from our CPA Review website (cpaexam.com/support.asp) during mid-June 2013. Please see our 41 series updating supplement available now for download from the same location for more information about the Clarity Project.

Editor note: Please see the change alerts preceding the chapters indicated above for more information and when these new pronouncements are/were eligible to be tested. Accounting and auditing pronouncements are eligible to be tested on the CPA Examination in the testing window beginning six months after a pronouncement's *effective* date, unless early application is permitted. When early application is permitted, a new pronouncement may be tested in the window beginning 6 months after the *issue* date. In this case, *both* the previous and the new pronouncement can be tested until the previous pronouncement has been superseded.

AUDITING & ATTESTATION

VOLUME II of IV

TABLE OF CONTENTS

The editors strongly advise candidates to download *The Uniform CPA Examination Candidate Bulletin / Information for Applicants* from the AICPA's website (aicpa.org). (You will need to go to the "For Candidates" section within the exam area of their site to find the instructions to download it.) It is the official handbook for exam candidates—it covers exam requirements, candidate responsibilities, and other important information. Candidates should read the "Foreword: Getting Started" and "Appendix B: Exam Preparation Tips" sections of this volume for help with devising a study plan. It's also important to keep the extent of the exam's coverage of the various topics in mind while studying. The AICPA's content specification outline, which includes the approximate percentage of total exam questions associated with each area in their outline, is included in the "Appendix B: Exam Preparation Tips" section.

QUICK TEXT REFERENCE

....

....

....

....

....

....

....

The editors strongly recommend that candidates read the entire "Foreword: Getting Started," "Appendix B: Exam Preparation Tips," and "Appendix C: Research Skills" sections of this volume. The references on this page are intended only for conveniently relocating selected parts of the volume. Add items to this list that you find yourself revisiting frequently.

FOREWORD: GETTING STARTED

Step One: **Read Sections One and Three of the Exam Preparation Tips Appendix**

The first section of this volume's "Appendix B: Exam Preparation Tips" material is designed to familiarize you with the exam. It includes an overview of the exam and other valuable information. You can avoid wasting time due to possible misconceptions by learning about the exam.

The AICPA's content and skill specification outline (CSO/SSO) for the AUD exam section is included in the third section. Make sure you are aware of the areas covered by the exam. The CSO includes the approximate percentage of total exam questions associated with each area.

Step Two: **Review the Exam Tutorial and Sample Test on the AICPA's Website**

The tutorial is a guided tour of the exam. It demonstrates the functionality of question types, tools, resources, and navigation found in the Uniform CPA Examination. The tutorial does not contain actual exam content.

The sample tests (one for each exam section) provide candidates with a preview of the exam experience. It is a functional replica of the exam and gives you the opportunity to become familiar with the exam's format in an interactive environment. (You should familiarize yourself with the exam functionality demonstrated in the tutorial *before* you review the sample tests.) The sample test software allows you to answer each type of test question that appears on the exam.

The tutorial and sample tests are **not** available at test centers—thorough familiarity with the exam's functionality, format, and directions is required *before* you report to a test center.

Aicpa.org/becomeacpa/cpaexam/forcandidates/tutorialandsampletest is the website address.

Step Three: **Estimate Your Strengths and Weaknesses**

The typical exam candidate has recently or nearly completed a university's 5-year accounting program with above average grades in accounting and other business courses. Most candidates' first language is English. Consider your background and how it differs from this. You should also consider other factors. For example, if you work in a specialized area of accounting such as tax preparation, you may need to spend more time reviewing the auditing topics. Additionally, if you have already taken any exam section, analyze your performance to help determine how to refine your efforts for the remaining exam sections.

Step Four: **Develop a Personalized Study Plan**

Develop your personalized study plan based on your analysis of your strengths and weaknesses. See our sample study plan at the end of this section. This plan entails a minimum of 20 hours of study per week. This level of intensity should increase during the final weeks before the exam. If you cannot allot this many hours per week, you may need to start studying sooner. Use this plan as a benchmark—make any adjustments needed for your background and fine-tune it as you progress.

There are also sample study plans on our website for candidates preparing to sit for 2 exam sections during the same testing window. Go to cpaexam.com and click on "EXAM INFO" on the menu bar to locate these plans.

How to Find 20 Hours a Week to Study

Most candidates have many other demands on their time. Consequently, your first reaction may be, "I don't have 20 hours a week to devote to studying for the CPA exam." We can show you how to find the time that you need. Begin by preparing a chart with each column as a day of the week and each line as an hour of the day.

1. Keeping in mind what you consider to be a typical week, first mark the time you know you won't be able to study. For example, mark an "X" in each block which represents time you normally sleep, have a class, work, or some other commitment. Be realistic.

2. Next, put a "C" in each block that represents commuting time, an "M" (meal) in each block that represents when you normally eat, and an "E" in each block that represents when you exercise.

3. Now pick one hour each day to rest and relax and give yourself a break—write "R & R" in one block for each day. Do not skip this step. By taking a break, you will study more efficiently and effectively.

4. Write "S" in the remaining blocks. Count these study blocks. Are there 20? If not, count your "C," "M," and "E" blocks; these blocks can be used to gain additional study time by using Bisk Education CPA Review video programs. For example, you may be able to watch video lectures a second time while eating or exercising to gain valuable review time.

5. If you still do not have 20 study blocks, you have several options: (1) reprioritize and make a block that has an "X" in it available for study time; (2) concentrate on fewer exam sections; or (3) start your regimen sooner—study more weeks so you can decrease the number of hours per week.

How to Allocate Your Weeks

Develop your overall study plan. As discussed at the beginning of this step, you may want to start with our sample study plan at the end of this section. The time allocated to each chapter is based on the amount and difficulty of the material and how heavily the content is tested on the exam (refer to the AUD AICPA content specification outline in the third section of this volume's "Appendix B: Exam Preparation Tips").

Keep in mind that our sample study plan was developed for the typical candidate as defined in "Step Three" of this section. You should customize this plan based on your degree of comfort with the exam and the estimated level of your knowledge of each chapter's content.

These are the number of weeks needed to complete each of our sample plans for candidates preparing for one exam section at a time:

Auditing & Attestation (AUD)	7	Regulation (REG)	6
Financial Accounting & Reporting (FAR)	8	Business Environment & Concepts (BEC)	4

Exam Scheduling Strategies

Most candidates spread taking the exam over two or more exam windows. Candidates who sit for all four sections during one window usually either want to pass it quickly or must travel to a test center from a great distance. Sitting for one exam section per window is the best means of ensuring a passing score; however, you must weigh this against a much more protracted commitment of your time.

Sitting for two exam sections per window obviously halves the number of windows. It also takes advantage of the synergy resulting from studying one exam section with or soon after another. You can arrange a separation of several weeks between sittings by scheduling one exam section near the beginning of a two-month testing window and the second near the end of the same window.

Another approach to consider is sitting for only one section during your first window to get a realistic idea of the preparation needed given your particular circumstances. Once you have the experience of one exam section behind you, sitting for multiple exam sections in the next window will be facilitated by the study habits you will have developed.

Step Five: Read the Rest of the Exam Preparation Tips Appendix

The second section of this volume's "Appendix B: Exam Preparation Tips" covers test-taking strategies and the exam's scoring conventions. It explains our Solutions Approach™, an approach that will help you maximize your score.

Step Six: Integrate Your Review Materials

In this step, we demonstrate how to integrate the Bisk Education CPA Review products to optimize the effectiveness of your study plan. Find the section that corresponds to the package of materials you purchased.

If you purchased our software, you should go through all of the software tutorials prior to beginning intensive study. Each one is only a few minutes long, but is loaded with valuable information. There is simply no better way to get the most from the software.

Videos

The Hot•Spot™ and Simulation Strategies videos are designed to supplement the other study materials. These videos have content similar to the video lectures included with the Bisk CPA Review Online and Classic™ courses, but they are not exactly the same.

Each Hot•Spot™ video concentrates on a few topics. Use them to help you study the areas that are most troubling for you.

Designed to round out your study program, the Simulation Strategies videos focus on answering simulations as opposed to concentrating on content.

These videos also contain exam tips and techniques that will help you to learn the material needed to pass the exam. The video titles are listed on page B-2. Also see the video study tips in "Step Seven" of this section.

If you would like more information about these or any of our products discussed next, please contact a representative (855-300-9392) or visit our website (cpaexam.com).

Bisk CPA Review Online or Classic™

Our most comprehensive review package—our online course—provides the discipline and learning experience of a classroom setting with the convenience of self-study. Access to the class site lasts for about four months and is available until the close of the exam window. During seven weeks of this time—the duration of the course's guided study plan—a faculty advisor is available to answer questions about exam content. Candidates have the option of enrolling in a course in which the faculty advisor is available immediately or one in which this feature is delayed for about 4 weeks for those who prefer some study time prior to this period. The course includes video lectures, weekly assignments, our comprehensive CPA exam review textbook, and powerful software study tools not available elsewhere. We strongly recommend that candidates working full time take no more than two sections of the online course concurrently.

The Bisk CPA Review Classic™ is the CD-based alternative to the online course. It includes the same video lectures, weekly assignments, our comprehensive CPA exam review textbook, and powerful software study tools, but there is no faculty advisor and it is not web-based.

By studying with and successfully completing one of these packages, you can become eligible to qualify for Bisk Education's money-back guarantee. (Certain restrictions and preparation requirements apply—refer to the instructions received with your materials or call a representative at 800-280-9718 for details.)

Information about integrating materials is available on the online course's website or in the materials that ship with the Classic™.

The study plans included with these packages generally work better for candidates with this material than the study plan designed for candidates without this material (the sample plan at the end of this section).

These and our other comprehensive packages are intended for those candidates who want to make sure they pass the exam the *first* time.

Bisk Textbook & CPA Review Software

This comprehensive self-study review package is also designed for the serious CPA candidate. This combination allows you to use the book to study when you do not have access to a computer.

By using the software, you can become eligible to qualify for Bisk Education's money-back guarantee. (Refer to the instructions included with the software or call a representative at 800-280-9718 to learn how to qualify.)

In chapters where you are strong:

1. Answer all the multiple-choice questions using the Bisk CPA Review Software (software).

2. Read the sections of the chapter that correspond to your weak areas.

3. Using the software, answer the multiple-choice questions you previously answered incorrectly. Move on to the next chapter if you answer 70% or more correctly. If you answer less than 70% correctly, treat this as one of your "weak" chapters (see next section).

4. Answer at least one simulation.

In chapters where you are weak:

1. Read the chapter.

2. Reread the sections of the chapter that correspond to your weak areas.

3. Using the software, answer all the multiple-choice questions for this chapter. Move on to the next chapter if you answer 70% or more correctly. If you answer less than 70% of the questions correctly, review the areas where you are weak and then answer the questions that you answered incorrectly. Allocate more time than you originally budgeted, if necessary.

4. Answer at least one simulation.

Bisk Textbook

This route is available for candidates who have a strong preference for hard copy; however, bear in mind that the exam is administered only via a computer.

In chapters where you are strong:

1. Answer all the multiple-choice questions for that chapter. Using the performance-by-topics worksheet in the textbook (located after the multiple-choice answers), analyze your strong and weak areas.

2. Read the sections of the chapter that correspond to your weak areas.

3. Answer the multiple-choice questions that you previously answered incorrectly. Move on to the next chapter if you answer 70% or more correctly If you answer less than 70% correctly, treat this as one of your "weak" chapters (see next section).

4. Answer at least one simulation.

In chapters where you are weak:

1. Read the chapter.

2. Reread the sections of the chapter that correspond to your weak areas.

3. Answer the multiple-choice questions and score yourself using the performance-by-topics worksheet in the textbook (located after the multiple-choice answers). Move on to the next chapter if you answer 70% or more correctly. If you answer less than 70% of the questions correctly, review the areas where you are weak and then answer the questions that you answered incorrectly. Allocate more time than you originally budgeted, if necessary.

4. Answer at least one simulation.

Step Seven: Use These Helpful Hints as You Study

♦ MAKE NOTES AND/OR HIGHLIGHT WHILE READING CHAPTERS OR WATCHING LECTURES.

You will find these notes very useful for weekly reviews and your final review.

♦ USE THE VIDEO LECTURES EFFECTIVELY.

Watch the video lectures in an environment without distractions. Be prepared to take notes and answer questions just as if you were attending a live class. Frequently, the instructors will have you stop the program to work questions on your own. Be sure to do this rather than just watching the instructor work out the solution.

Intersperse reading text, answering questions, and watching video programs to suit your particular learning style as well as your strengths and weaknesses. We suggest that you try the following approaches if you are not sure what will work best for you:

- If a topic is one of your weak areas, watch the related video before reading the chapter. After reading the chapter, watch the video again and then answer the questions. (Skip the second viewing of the video if you are somewhere in-between weak and strong in an area.)

- If a topic is one of your strong areas, read the chapter before watching the video. After watching the video, answer the questions.

Consider watching select lectures repeatedly while you are exercising. Repetition will help you to memorize and retain key concepts. It also will reinforce your reading and question drill. The more times that you listen to a lecture, the more familiar you will become with the material and the easier it will be for you to recall it during the exam.

- MAKE FLASH CARDS.

Make flash cards for topics that are heavily tested or are giving you trouble. By making your own flash cards, you learn during their creation plus you can tailor them to your individual learning style.

You will find these very useful for weekly reviews and your final review.

Keep them handy so you can review them at opportune times, for example, while you are waiting in line, so you can turn nonproductive time into valuable study time.

Put flash cards on information you know aside and replace them with new material as you progress through your study plan. Review your complete set during the last two weeks before the exam.

- DO NOT MARK QUESTION ANSWERS IN THE BOOK.

Do not circle the answers to multiple-choice questions or fill in the blanks on any simulations. You should work every multiple-choice question and simulation at least twice and you do not want to influence later answers by knowing how you previously answered.

Retain and date your answer sheets to facilitate tracking your progress.

- NOTE QUESTIONS YOU ANSWER INCORRECTLY OR MERELY GUESSED CORRECTLY.

This will serve as a reminder to answer these questions again at a later time.

- SPEND YOUR WEEKLY REVIEW TIME EFFECTIVELY. DURING EACH WEEKLY REVIEW:

Answer the multiple-choice questions and simulations that you previously answered incorrectly or merely guessed correctly. This is particularly important if you moved on to the next chapter with a score at the minimum 70% suggested in "Step Six" of this section. You need to increase that score to a *minimum* of 75% during your weekly review activities to be ready for the exam. How high do you need to increase it? A cushion to assure that you pass the exam is preferable. How big that cushion needs to be depends on your personal tolerance for risk.

Review your flash cards and notes.

Step Eight: Implement Your Study Plan

This is it! You are primed and ready. You have decided which study tools will work best for you and you know how to use them. Your goal is to obtain a passing score (75) or better on each exam section. Therefore, you should concentrate on learning new material and reviewing old material only to the extent that it helps you reach this goal. Utilize the personalized study plan you developed in "Step Four" of this section so that you do not fall behind. Adjust it when necessary if you need more time in one chapter or less time in another. (Refer to the AUD AICPA content specification outline in the third section of this volume's "Appendix B: Exam Preparation Tips" to make sure that the adjustment is warranted.) Above all else, remember that passing the exam is an attainable goal. Good luck!

Supplement to Step Four: Sample Study Plan

The time allocated by the following plan to each chapter is based on the amount and difficulty of the material and how heavily the content is tested on the exam (refer to the AUD AICPA content specification outline in the third section of this volume's "Appendix B: Exam Preparation Tips").

The editors strongly recommend that candidates develop a personalized study plan. Modify this plan based on your study habits, available time, and level of knowledge of each chapter's content.

There are also sample study plans on our website for candidates preparing to sit for 2 exam sections during the same testing window. Go to cpaexam.com and click on "EXAM INFO" on the menu bar to locate these plans.

AUD Sample Study Plan

		Hours
Week 1:	Read *Getting Started* and *Exam Preparation Tips* sections; review	
	AICPA exam tutorial and AUD sample test	3
	Chapter 1–Standards & Related Topics	4
	Chapter 2–Planning	10
	Chapter 3–Internal Control	3
Week 2:	Chapter 3–Internal Control	7
	Chapter 4–Evidence & Procedures	10
	Chapter 5–Audit Programs	3
Week 3:	Chapter 5–Audit Programs	4
	Weekly review: weeks 1–2	2
	Chapter 6–Audit Sampling	6
	Chapter 7–Auditing IT Systems	5
	Chapter 8–Reports on Audited Financial Statements	3
Week 4:	Chapter 8–Reports on Audited Financial Statements	7
	Weekly review: weeks 1–3 and check for *updating supplement	3
	Chapter 9–Government Auditing	4
	Chapter 10–Other Auditing Standards	6
Week 5:	Weekly review: weeks 1–4 and check for *updating supplement	3
	Chapter 11–Other Types of Reports	6
	Chapter 12–Accounting & Review Services	8
	Chapter 13–Attestation Engagements	3
Week 6:	Chapter 13–Attestation Engagements	4
	Weekly review of weeks 1–5 and check for *updating supplement	3
	Chapter 14–Accountants' Professional Responsibilities	10
	Practice research skills (see Appendix C)	3
Week 7:	Review areas in which you still feel weak & revisit AICPA exam tutorial and	
	AUD sample test	6
	Take practice exam under exam conditions (see page A-1)	4
	Do final review and check for *updating supplement	10

*UPDATING SUPPLEMENTS

Bisk Education's updating supplements are small publications available from either customer service representatives or our CPA Review website (cpaexam.com/content/support.asp). The editors recommend checking our website for new supplements at least once a month and again a week before your exam. Version 42 updating supplements are appropriate for candidates with the 42nd edition. Information from supplements of earlier editions (through the version 41 series) has been incorporated into this edition. Supplements are issued only as appropriate information becomes available and is eligible to be tested.

CHAPTER 1

STANDARDS & RELATED TOPICS

CHAPTER 1

STANDARDS & RELATED TOPICS

I. Audit Function Overview

A. Responsibilities

1. **Independent Auditor** The independent auditor is responsible for performing an audit in accordance with generally accepted auditing standards (GAAS).

   The objective of the audit is the expression of an opinion as to whether, in all material respects, the financial position, results of operations, and cash flows are presented fairly in conformity with generally accepted accounting principles (GAAP).

   The auditor's responsibility to express an opinion on the financial statements based on the audit is stated explicitly in the introductory paragraph of the auditor's report.

2. **Management** Management is responsible for the fair presentation of the financial statements in conformity with GAAP, even if the statements are prepared or audited by CPAs. Financial statements are management's representations of the effects of transactions and events on the organization's financial position and results of operations.

   Management is also responsible for establishing and maintaining effective internal control and developing accounting policies.

3. **Users** Financial statement users should recognize that the accounting process necessitates the use of estimates and evaluations that affect the fairness of the financial statements. They also should understand the meaning and significance of the auditor's report.

B. Audit Function
The auditor independently accumulates and evaluates audit evidence of an economic entity for the purpose of reporting on the degree of correspondence between the information produced and the established criteria (e.g., GAAP).

Exhibit 1 ▶ Comparison of Financial Accounting & Auditing

Note that financial accounting is a **process of aggregation.** Individual transactions are first recorded in journals; subsequently, the data in journals are classified in ledgers; and finally, the data in ledgers are summarized in the financial statements.

1. **Vouching** Did the transactions summarized in the financial statements actually occur? The auditor makes this determination by vouching items from the financial statements back to the accounts and ultimately to the original transaction documents. This is a downward process in Exhibit 1.

2. **Tracing** Have all transactions that occurred during the period been recorded properly in the accounts and summarized in the financial statements? (Are the financial statements complete?) The auditor makes this determination by tracing items from original transaction documents to the accounts and ultimately to the financial statements. This is an upward process in Exhibit 1.

C. Audit Process Steps

1. **Establish Understanding With Client** The auditor should establish an understanding with the client regarding the engagement services, including the objectives, scope, and limitations of the engagement, as well as the auditor's and management's responsibilities.

   The auditor should document the understanding in an engagement letter.

2. **Obtain Understanding of the Entity & Its Environment, Including Internal Control** The auditor should perform risk assessment procedures to obtain this understanding. The nature, extent, and timing of these procedures depend on the size and complexity of the entity as well as the auditor's previous experience with the entity, if any.

   This process should include a discussion among the audit team concerning the susceptibility (risk) of the financial statements to material misstatements.

3. **Assess the Risk of Material Misstatement (RMM)** The auditor will identify and evaluate the RMM at the financial statement and *relevant assertion* levels. This will include identifying risks and potential misstatements, as well as considering the materiality and probability of potential misstatements.

   In representing that the financial statements are fairly presented in conformity with GAAP, management implicitly or explicitly makes assertions regarding the recognition, measurement, presentation, and disclosure of information in the financial statements and related disclosures. *Relevant assertions* are assertions that have a meaningful bearing on whether an account is fairly stated. For example, valuation may not be relevant to a cash account unless currency translation is involved; however, assertions as to existence and completeness are always relevant. (For more information about relevant assertions see the section of Chapter 4 on the use of assertions in obtaining audit evidence.)

4. **Design & Perform Procedures to Address the RMM** The auditor uses the knowledge provided by the understanding of the entity and its environment and the assessed RMM in determining the nature, extent, and timing of further audit procedures. Further audit procedures include testing the operating effectiveness of controls and substantive procedures.

   While tests of controls are optional, substantive procedures are required for all relevant assertions related to each material class of transactions, account balance, and disclosure.

5. **Evaluate Audit Evidence** Based on procedures performed, the auditor analyzes the accumulated audit evidence to determine whether the assessments of the RMM at the relevant assertion level are still appropriate. The auditor may need to reevaluate the planned audit procedures to obtain sufficient appropriate audit evidence to support the opinion on the financial statements.

6.   **Form Opinion & Issue Audit Report**   The audit report will describe the scope of the audit and state the auditor's conclusion regarding the fairness of the financial statements and related disclosures.

Before issuing the audit report, the lead audit partner will perform a final review of the workpapers to ensure that the appropriate type of opinion will be expressed.

For public companies (issuers), there must also be an engagement quality review and concurring approval of issuance. The objective of the engagement quality reviewer is to perform an evaluation of the significant judgments made by the engagement team and the related conclusions reached in forming the overall conclusion on the engagement and in preparing the engagement report to determine whether to provide concurring approval of issuance. (See Chapter 14 for more information.)

D.   **Definitions**

1.   **Financial Statement Audit**   This is the audit discussed above and throughout the remainder of this text unless otherwise indicated. Its objective is to express an opinion on the fairness, in all material respects, with which the financial statements present the organization's financial position, results of operations, and cash flows in conformity with GAAP.

2.   **Compliance Audit**   The purpose of this type of audit is to evaluate an organization's compliance with a defined set of specifications. Common examples include Internal Revenue Service audits to determine whether a taxpayer has complied with applicable provisions of the Internal Revenue Code; audits of governmental units to verify their compliance with applicable state and federal regulations; and verification audits by a CPA to determine a client's compliance with the provisions of a bond or loan indenture.

3.   **Operational Audit**   These audits, usually performed by internal auditors, evaluate the efficiency and effectiveness of some part of an organization in achieving its specific goals in relation to the general goals of an organization. This type of audit involves an evaluation of operating procedures and methods, and usually requires the auditor to issue a report to management recommending ways to improve efficiency and/or effectiveness. A common example would be a review by government auditors to determine the effectiveness and continued utility of specific government-funded programs. This type of audit usually is not concerned with financial information.

4.   **Audit Program (Plan)**   This is a detailed list of audit procedures to be performed to satisfy audit objectives. Informally, sometimes this phrase refers to the substantive tests for a particular account or transaction cycle.

5.   **External Auditors**   These are independent CPAs who provide a professionally competent evaluation (audit) of the financial statements of a client. Consistent with their external audit and advisory responsibilities, CPAs are certified and licensed by the individual states or territories in which they practice. The terms *CPA* and *auditor* frequently are used interchangeably. In this text, unless otherwise indicated, the term *auditor* signifies a CPA who is independent of the client.

Exhibit 2 ▶ Important Characteristics of Audits & Auditors

Independence	Auditors represent neither the financial statement preparers (management) nor the financial statement users (investors, creditors, etc.).
Materiality	An audit is directed toward the discovery of material misstatements or omissions in the financial statements. Materiality involves professional judgment and is influenced by the auditor's perception of the needs of a reasonable person relying on the financial statements. Materiality judgments are made in light of the surrounding circumstances and involve both quantitative and qualitative considerations.
Selective Testing	Auditors base their opinions on selective testing; they rarely examine all of the items in an individual account or in the financial statements.
Audit Risk	Audit risk is a key consideration in an audit. Audit risk is a function of both the risk that the financial statements prepared by management are materially misstated and the risk that the auditor will not detect the misstatement. The auditor should perform the audit to reduce audit risk to a low enough level that is appropriate, in the auditor's judgment, to allow the expression of an opinion on the financial statements or if circumstances require, a disclaimer of an opinion. An auditor's report provides reasonable, not absolute, assurance as to whether the financial statements adhere to the established criteria. This is because audit risk cannot be eliminated due to the nature of audit evidence and the characteristics of fraud.
Overall Opinion	The auditor's opinion relates to the financial statements taken as a whole as stated in the fourth reporting standard. *Taken as a whole* can apply to a complete set of financial statements or to an individual financial statement. (An auditor may express an unqualified opinion on one of the financial statements and a different type of opinion or a disclaimer on another, if warranted.)
Presentation	An audit is concerned with financial statement presentation; it is not concerned with the effectiveness of management, or the advisability of investing in the client.

6. **Internal Auditors** Internal auditors work full time for an organization or entity. Some internal auditors perform financial statement audits, while others perform compliance or operational audits. Internal auditors are not independent in the same sense as an external auditor, so they cannot issue an audit report for stockholders or other interested outside parties. For an internal audit function to be effective, it is important that it be directed to a level of the organization that is above the level being audited. Optimally, if the internal auditors report to the audit committee of the board of directors, the internal audit function is organizationally independent from any particular area of the company.

7. **Governmental Auditors** These are auditors who work for the federal, state, or local government. Two of the most commonly mentioned are the following:

   a. **Government Accountability Office (GAO) Auditors** GAO auditors conduct audits for Congress. While they do a considerable number of compliance audits, they also perform an increasing amount of operational-type audit work.

   b. **Internal Revenue Agents** These are auditors who conduct compliance audits for the Internal Revenue Service.

8. **Those Charged With Governance** The term *those charged with governance* refers to the person(s) with responsibility for overseeing the strategic direction of the entity and obligations related to the accountability of the entity, including overseeing the entity's financial reporting process. This term includes the board of directors and the audit committee.

9. **Audit Committee** This is a special committee formed by the client's board of directors to assist in oversight responsibilities. In general, responsibilities include monitoring the financial

reporting process and related internal controls as well as communicating with internal and external auditors.

II. Generally Accepted Auditing Standards (GAAS)

A. Codification of Professional Standards

The American Institute of Certified Public Accountants' (AICPA's) Codification of Professional Standards is a copyrighted topical codification of Statements on Auditing Standards (SAS) and other standards. The codification abbreviations are used throughout this text along with section numbers. The codification is segregated into broad areas of interest, typically by type of service, as follows:

1. US Auditing Standards [AU]

2. Attestation Standards [AT]

3. Accounting & Review Services [AR]

4. Code of Professional Conduct [ET]

5. Bylaws of the American Institute of Certified Public Accountants [BL]

6. Consulting Services [CS]

7. Quality Control [QC]

8. Peer Review [PR]

9. Tax Services [TS]

10. Personal Financial Planning [PFP]

11. Continuing Professional Education [CPE]

B. Applicability of Professional Standards

1. **Issuers** As a result of the passage of the Sarbanes-Oxley Act of 2002 (Act), auditing and related professional practice standards to be used in the performance of and reporting on audits of the financial statements of public companies are now established by the Public Company Accounting Oversight Board (PCAOB) and approved by the Securities and Exchange Commission (SEC).

   The term *public companies* is a general reference to the entities subject to the securities laws. The Act refers to these companies as *issuers*. (Accordingly, *nonissuers* are those entities not subject to the Act or the rules of the SEC.)

   The PCAOB adopted, on an initial, transitional basis, the professional standards of auditing, attestation, quality control, ethics, and independence issued by the AICPA that were in existence on April 16, 2003.

   Editor note: See Chapter 10 for more information about auditing standards and related rules issued by the PCAOB; there are also references throughout this text to pertinent differences between the standards for nonissuers vs. issuers.

2. **Nonissuers** Nonissuers are those entities not subject to the Act or the rules of the SEC. For audits of nonissuers, the preparation and issuance of audit reports must be conducted in accordance with the AICPA Code of Professional Conduct and the standards promulgated by the AICPA Auditing Standards Board (ASB).

C.   Observations on GAAS (AU 150)
An independent auditor is required to plan, conduct, and report the results of an audit in accordance with GAAS. The standards provide measures of quality of the auditor's performance and audit objectives.

Exhibit 3 ▶ Generally Accepted Auditing Standards Mnemonic

T	Training
I	Independence
P	Performance (due professional care)
S	Supervision & planning
E	Entity & its environment, including internal control
E	Evidence
A	Accounting basis (GAAP or OCBOA)
C	Consistency
D	Disclosure
E	Express an opinion

1.   **Foundation** The concepts of *materiality* and *audit risk* underlie the application of GAAS, especially the standards of fieldwork and reporting. Materiality and audit risk need to be considered when determining the nature, extent, and timing of audit procedures to be performed, as well as evaluating the results of those procedures. (See Exhibit 2.)

2.   **Statements on Auditing Standards** SAS are detailed statements issued by the Auditing Standards Board (ASB) of the AICPA. These statements are the primary body of GAAS.

Auditing standards are not the same as auditing procedures.

a.   **Procedures** Procedures relate to the acts to be performed; for example, the confirmation of a predetermined number of accounts receivable. Auditing procedures will vary from engagement to engagement.

b.   **Standards** Standards provide the objectives that audit procedures are to attain and measures of the quality of procedures to be performed. Auditing standards do not vary from engagement to engagement.

3.   **Professional Requirements (AU 120)** The SAS contain professional requirements along with related guidance. There are two kinds of requirements:

a.   **Unconditional Requirements** The auditor is required to comply with an unconditional requirement in all cases in which the requirement applies. The words *must* or *is required* indicate an unconditional requirement.

b.   **Presumptively Mandatory Requirements** The auditor is also required to comply with a presumptively mandatory requirement in all cases in which the requirement applies. However, in rare circumstances, the auditor may depart from such a requirement provided the auditor documents the justification for the departure and how the alternative procedures performed were sufficient to achieve the objectives of that requirement. The word *should* indicates a presumptively mandatory requirement.

If a SAS provides that a procedure or action is one that the auditor *should consider*, the consideration of the procedure or action is presumptively required; however, carrying out the procedure or action is not.

c.   **Explanatory Material** Explanatory material within a SAS provides further explanation and guidance on the professional requirements; it does **not** impose requirements. The words *may*, *might*, and *could* are used to describe actions and procedures included in explanatory material.

D. General Standards

The general standards are personal in nature. They relate to the qualifications of the auditor and the quality of the work performed. They apply alike to the areas of fieldwork and reporting.

1. **Technical Training & Proficiency** The auditor must have adequate technical training and proficiency to perform the audit.

2. **Independence** The auditor must maintain independence in mental attitude in all matters relating to the audit.

3. **Due Professional Care** The auditor must exercise due professional care in the performance of the audit and the preparation of the report.

E. Standards of Fieldwork

Audit documentation should be sufficient to show that the standards of fieldwork have been observed.

1. **Adequate Planning & Supervision** The auditor must adequately plan the work and must properly supervise any assistants.

2. **Understanding the Entity & Its Environment** The auditor must obtain a sufficient understanding of the entity and its environment, including its internal control, to assess the risk of material misstatement of the financial statements whether due to error or fraud, and to design the nature, extent, and timing of further audit procedures.

3. **Sufficient Appropriate Audit Evidence** The auditor must obtain sufficient appropriate audit evidence by performing audit procedures to afford a reasonable basis for an opinion regarding the financial statements under audit.

F. Standards of Reporting

1. **Accounting in Conformity With GAAP** The auditor must state in the auditor's report whether the financial statements are presented in accordance with generally accepted accounting principles (GAAP).

2. **Consistency** The auditor must identify in the auditor's report those circumstances in which such principles have not been consistently observed in the current period in relation to the preceding period.

3. **Adequate Informative Disclosure** When the auditor determines that informative disclosures are not reasonably adequate, the auditor must so state in the auditor's report.

4. **Expression of Opinion** The auditor must either express an opinion regarding the financial statements, taken as a whole, or state that an opinion cannot be expressed, in the auditor's report. When the auditor cannot express an overall opinion, the auditor should state the reasons therefor in the auditor's report. In all cases where an auditor's name is associated with financial statements, the auditor should clearly indicate the character of the auditor's work, if any, and the degree of responsibility the auditor is taking, in the auditor's report.

III. General Standards

A. Training & Proficiency of the Independent Auditor (AU 210)
An auditor must be proficient in accounting and auditing. This requires academic training and professional experience. Training is an ongoing process that includes remaining current with new developments taking place in business and finance as well as in the accounting profession.

Exhibit 4 ▶ The First General Standard

The auditor must have adequate technical training and proficiency to perform the audit.

B. Independence (AU 220)
The attitude implied by independence is that of judicial impartiality or fairness toward clients and others who rely upon the independent auditor's report. The auditor's objective is to ensure that the general public maintains confidence in the independence of the auditor. Independence in attitude also implies the auditor is without bias towards the client.

The SEC also has adopted independence requirements for auditors who report on financial statements filed with it that differ from the AICPA requirements in some respects. The restrictions imposed by the Sarbanes-Oxley Act of 2002 also apply, as discussed in Chapter 10.

Exhibit 5 ▶ The Second General Standard

The auditor must maintain independence in mental attitude in all matters relating to the audit.

1. **Disclose** The auditors of publicly owned companies (issuers) must disclose, in writing, to those charged with governance, all relationships between the auditor (and its related entities) and the client entity (and its related entities) that may be considered to bear on independence. Auditors of nonissuers may determine, in certain situations, that it is appropriate to communicate this same information.

2. **Confirm** The auditor must confirm in writing, in conjunction with SEC filings, that the auditor is independent of the client entity according to the federal securities statutes.

3. **Discuss** The auditors of issuers must discuss the auditor's independence with those charged with governance.

C. Due Care in the Performance of Work (AU 230)
Each person within an independent auditor's organization has the responsibility to exercise due care and adhere to the standards of fieldwork and reporting. This responsibility necessitates critical review by supervisors of the work done and judgment exercised by those assisting in the audit.

Exhibit 6 ▶ The Third General Standard

The auditor must exercise due professional care in the performance of the audit and the preparation of the report.

1. **Professional Skepticism** Due professional care requires the auditor to exercise professional skepticism. Professional skepticism is an attitude that includes a questioning mind and a critical assessment of audit evidence.

2. **Reasonable Assurance** In exercising due care, the auditor must plan and perform the audit to obtain sufficient appropriate audit evidence so that audit risk will be limited to a low level. The high, but not absolute, level of assurance that is intended to be obtained by the auditor is expressed in the auditor's report as obtaining reasonable assurance about whether the financial statements are free of material misstatement (whether caused by error or fraud).

3. **Fraud** An auditor commits a type of fraud if the auditor alleges possessing the degree of skill commonly possessed by other auditors when that is not the case.

4. **Not Infallible** Due care does not guarantee infallibility in either performance or in matters of pure judgment.

IV. Communications Between Predecessor & Successor Auditors (AU 315)

A. Overview

AU 315 provides guidance relating to communications between the predecessor and successor auditors when a change in auditors has taken place or is in process.

Editor note: Generally, the requirements of this guidance do *not* apply when the most recently audited financial statements are more than two years prior to the beginning of the period to be audited by the successor auditor.

1. **Predecessor Auditor** A predecessor auditor may have either reported on the most recently audited financial statements or been engaged to perform, but did not complete an audit and has either resigned or been terminated. A predecessor auditor can also be an auditor who previously reported on financial statements that a client wants reaudited.

    A CPA who performed a review or compilation, instead of an audit, is *not* a predecessor auditor.

2. **Successor Auditor** A successor auditor is one who has provisionally accepted an engagement or has been asked to make a proposal for an engagement.

B. Communications

The successor has the responsibility to initiate the communication. Either written or oral communication is permissible. The information communicated should be kept confidential, regardless of whether or not the successor accepts the engagement.

1. **Before Successor Accepts Engagement** The successor auditor should attempt certain communications **before** accepting the engagement.

    a. **Permission** The AICPA Code of Professional Conduct precludes an auditor from disclosing confidential information without the client's consent, so the successor must ask the prospective client to authorize the predecessor to respond to the successor's inquiries.

    b. **Refusal** If a prospective client refuses to permit the predecessor to respond or limits the response, the successor auditor should inquire as to the reasons and consider the implications of that refusal in deciding whether to accept the engagement.

    c. **Inquiries** These inquiries should relate to matters that will help the successor to decide whether to accept the engagement. Matters covered by inquiries should include:

        (1) **Integrity of Management** Information that might bear on the integrity of management

        (2) **Disagreements** Disagreements with management on accounting principles, auditing procedures, or other significant matters

        (3) **Fraud or Illegal Acts** Communications to those charged with governance regarding fraud and illegal acts by the client

        (4) **Internal Control Weaknesses** Communications regarding significant deficiencies and material weaknesses in internal control

    (5)   **Reason for Change in Auditors** The predecessor's understanding of the reasons for the change in auditors.

    d.   **Response** The predecessor should respond promptly and fully. If the predecessor decides not to respond fully—due to unusual circumstances such as impending litigation—the predecessor should clearly state that a limited response is being given. The successor should consider the implications of receiving a limited response in deciding whether to accept the engagement.

2.   **Review of Workpapers** There are other advisable communications between the auditors that do not have to occur prior to acceptance of the engagement—timing is more flexible for these matters. These are mainly concerned with assisting the successor with planning the audit; evaluating the reliability of opening balances; and evaluating the consistency of application of accounting principles. Such matters involve the successor's review, with the client's authorization, of the predecessor's workpapers. Items of interest would include those of continuing accounting or auditing significance. Some examples are matters regarding contingencies, analysis of balance sheet accounts, and documentation of internal control. Ultimately, the predecessor determines what workpapers the successor may review or copy.

3.   **No Reference to Predecessor in Audit Report** The successor's review of the predecessor's work may affect the nature, extent, and timing of the predecessor's audit procedures with respect to the opening balances and consistency of accounting principles. However, the audit procedures as well as the opinion the successor auditor reaches, are solely that auditor's responsibility. The successor should not make any reference to the predecessor's work or report as a basis, in part, for the successor's own opinion.

4.   **Revision** During the course of the audit, the successor may become aware of information that leads to a belief that the financial statements reported on by the predecessor may require revision. The successor should ask the client to arrange for the three parties to meet to resolve the matter. If the client refuses to meet or if the successor is not satisfied with the resolution, the auditor should evaluate any possible implications this has for the current engagement and whether to resign. The successor auditor may also want to consider consulting an attorney.

Registration Process

To sit for the exam, candidates must apply to the appropriate board of accountancy or its exam administrator. (Some boards contract with an exam administrator to handle candidate applications.) Once a board or its exam administrator determines that a candidate is eligible to sit for the exam, they inform the National Association of State Boards of Accountancy (NASBA) and NASBA adds the candidate to its database. With a national database, NASBA is able to ensure that no candidate can sit for the same exam section more than once during the same exam window. NASBA then sends Prometric a notice to schedule (NTS). (The exam is given at test centers operated by Prometric.) When you receive your NTS you can make your appointment with Prometric to sit for the exam.

Candidates may select any available date during the open window. If taking the exam on a particular day is important to you, it is advisable to schedule it at least 45 days in advance. **No appointment can be made fewer than 5 days (10 days, if you have been approved for special testing accommodations) in advance of a desired test date**. Your NTS will have an expiration date which is set by your board. After the expiration date, you must reapply and pay the fees again.

If any medical conditions exist or other special testing accommodations are needed, candidates must supply their information to their board or its exam administrator during the application process in order to obtain their approval so the information can be included on their NTS. Ordinarily, candidates may not bring anything into the exam room—including prescription medications.

See the ***Uniform CPA Examination Candidate Bulletin / Information for Applicants*** for more information. To download a copy, visit the exam portion of the AICPA's website (aicpa.org) or NASBA's (nasba.org).

CHAPTER 1—STANDARDS & RELATED TOPICS

Problem 1-1 MULTIPLE-CHOICE QUESTIONS

1. Which of the following statements is correct concerning an auditor's responsibilities regarding financial statements?

    a. An auditor may not draft an entity's financial statements based on information from management's accounting system.
    b. The adoption of sound accounting policies is an implicit part of an auditor's responsibilities.
    c. An auditor's responsibilities for audited financial statements are confined to the expression of the auditor's opinion.
    d. Making suggestions that are adopted about an entity's internal control environment impairs an auditor's independence. (R/03, AUD, #8, ID: 7630)

2. Which of the following best describes what is meant by the term generally accepted auditing standards (GAAS)?

    a. Procedures to be used to gather evidence to support financial statements
    b. Measures of the quality of the auditor's performance
    c. Pronouncements issued by the Auditing Standards Board
    d. Rules acknowledged by the accounting profession because of their universal application (11/91, AUD, #9, ID: 7485)

3. GAAS require the auditor to document in the workpapers the justification for a departure from a presumptively mandatory requirement. What language indicates a presumptively mandatory requirement?

    a. "must" or "is required"
    b. "could"
    c. "may consider"
    d. "should" (Editors, ID: 8263)

4. The second standard of fieldwork requires the auditor to obtain an understanding of

    a. Internal control
    b. The internal audit function
    c. The entity and its environment, including internal control
    d. The control environment (Editors, ID: 8261)

5. The third general standard requires that due care is to be exercised in the performance of an audit. This standard is ordinarily interpreted to require

    a. Thorough review of the existing safeguards over access to assets and records
    b. Limited review of the indications of employee fraud and illegal acts
    c. Objective review of the adequacy of the technical training and proficiency of firm personnel
    d. Critical review of the judgment exercised at every level of supervision (5/95, AUD, #23, ID: 5641)

6. An auditor strives to achieve independence in appearance in order to

    a. Maintain public confidence in the profession
    b. Become independent in fact
    c. Maintain an unbiased mental attitude
    d. Comply with the generally accepted auditing standards of fieldwork (Editors, ID: 20)

7. Because an audit in accordance with generally accepted auditing standards is influenced by the possibility of material misstatements, the auditor should conduct the audit with an attitude of

    a. Objective judgment
    b. Conservative advocacy
    c. Professional responsiveness
    d. Professional skepticism (Editors, ID: 213)

8. Which of the following categories is included in generally accepted auditing standards?

    a. Standards of review
    b. Standards of planning
    c. Standards of fieldwork
    d. Standards of evidence

    (R/07, AUD, #1, ID: 8373)

9. An independent auditor must have which of the following?

    a. A pre-existing and well-informed point of view with respect to the audit
    b. Technical training that is adequate to meet the requirements of a professional
    c. A background in many different disciplines
    d. Experience in taxation that is sufficient to comply with generally accepted auditing standards

    (R/10, AUD, #3, ID: 89455)

10. Before accepting an audit engagement, a successor auditor should make specific inquiries of the predecessor auditor regarding

    a. Specialized accounting principles of the client's industry
    b. The competency of the client's internal audit staff
    c. The uncertainty inherent in applying sampling procedures
    d. Disagreements with management as to auditing procedures

    (5/95, AUD, #2, amended, ID: 5620)

11. In auditing the financial statements of Star Corp., Land discovered information leading Land to believe that Star's prior year's financial statements, which were audited by Tell, require substantial revisions. Under these circumstances, Land should

    a. Notify Star's audit committee and stockholders that the prior year's financial statements cannot be relied on
    b. Request Star to arrange a meeting among the three parties to resolve the matter
    c. Notify Tell about the information and make inquiries about the integrity of Star's management
    d. Request Star to reissue the prior year's financial statements with the appropriate revisions

    (5/95, AUD, #18, amended, ID: 5636)

12. A successor auditor should make specific and reasonable inquiries of the predecessor auditor prior to accepting the engagement regarding the predecessor's

    a. Understanding of the reasons for the change in auditors
    b. Methodology used in applying sampling techniques
    c. Opinion on subsequent events that have occurred since the balance sheet date
    d. Perception of the competency and reliance on the client's internal audit function

    (R/05, AUD, #37, amended, ID: 7832)

13. Before accepting an engagement to audit a new client, a CPA is required to obtain

    a. An understanding of the prospective client's industry and business
    b. A management representation letter
    c. A preliminary understanding of the prospective client's control environment
    d. The prospective client's consent to make inquiries of the predecessor auditor

    (5/97, AUD, #2, amended, ID: 6391)

14. A successor auditor should request the new client to authorize the predecessor auditor to allow a review of the predecessor's

	Engagement letter	*Working papers*
a.	Yes	Yes
b.	Yes	No
c.	No	Yes
d.	No	No

(R/03, AUD, #10, ID: 7632)

15. Ordinarily, the predecessor auditor permits the successor auditor to review the predecessor's working paper analyses relating to

	Contingencies	Balance sheet accounts
a.	Yes	Yes
b.	Yes	No
c.	No	Yes
d.	No	No

(11/98, AUD, #19, ID: 6710)

16. A successor auditor's inquiries of the predecessor auditor prior to accepting the engagement should include questions regarding

a. The predecessor's evaluation of audit risk and judgment about materiality
b. Subsequent events that occurred since the predecessor's audit report was issued
c. The predecessor's understanding as to the reasons for the change in auditors
d. The predecessor's knowledge of accounting matters of continuing significance

(R/09, AUD, #8, amended, ID: 8808)

17. Before accepting an audit engagement, a successor auditor should make specific inquiries of the predecessor auditor regarding the predecessor's

a. Opinion of any subsequent events occurring since the predecessor's audit report was issued
b. Communications to those charged with governance regarding fraud and illegal acts by clients
c. Awareness of the consistency in the application of GAAP between periods
d. Evaluation of all matters of continuing accounting significance

(Editors, ID: 4666)

18. Before accepting an engagement to audit a new client, a CPA is required to obtain

a. An assessment of fraud risk factors likely to cause material misstatements
b An understanding of the prospective client's industry and business
c. The prospective client's signature to a written engagement letter
d. The prospective client's consent to make inquiries of the predecessor auditor

(R/11, AUD, #10, amended, ID: 9910)

SIMULATION

Problem 1-2 SIMULATION: Research

Why is inquiry by the successor auditor of the predecessor auditor considered necessary?

| | § | | | (ID: 9200) |

_____

Solution 1-1 MULTIPLE-CHOICE ANSWERS

GAAS

1. (c)   The auditor's responsibility for the financial statements audited is confined to the expression of an opinion on them. The auditor may make suggestions about the form or content of the financial statements or draft them, in whole or in part, based on information from management during the performance of the audit; however, the financial statements are management's responsibility. Management, not the auditor, is responsible for adopting sound accounting policies. The audit of financial statements requires CPAs to review many aspects of an organization's activities and procedures. Consequently, they can advise clients of needed improvements in internal control and make constructive suggestions on financial, tax, and other operating matters without impairing their independence.   (ID: 7630)

2. (b)   GAAS provide a measure of audit quality and the objectives to be achieved in an audit. Auditing procedures are the acts performed during an audit to comply with GAAS. GAAS are issued by the AICPA's Auditing Standards Board, but that does not describe what is meant by the term. GAAS must be followed by CPAs per the AICPA's Code of Professional Conduct, not because they are rules acknowledged by the accounting profession due to their universal application.   (ID: 7485)

3. (d)   The word *should* indicates a presumptively mandatory requirement. The auditor is required to comply with a presumptively mandatory requirement in all cases in which the requirement applies; however, in rare circumstances, the auditor may depart from such a requirement provided the auditor documents in the workpapers the justification for the departure and how the alternative procedures performed achieved the objectives of that requirement. If a SAS includes a procedure that the auditor *should consider*, the consideration of the procedure is presumptively required, while carrying out the procedure is not. The words *must* or *is required* indicate an unconditional requirement. The auditor is required to comply with an unconditional requirement in all cases in which the requirement applies. The words *may, might,* and *could* are used to describe procedures included in explanatory material in the standards. Explanatory material is intended to be descriptive rather than imperative.   (ID: 8263)

4. (c)   The second standard of fieldwork states: "The auditor must obtain a sufficient understanding of the entity and its environment, including its internal control, to assess the risk of material misstatement of the financial statements whether due to error or fraud, and to design the nature, timing, and extent of further audit procedures."   (ID: 8261)

5. (d)   The third general standard states, "The auditor must exercise due professional care in the performance of the audit and the preparation of the report." The exercise of due care requires critical review at every level of supervision of the work done and the judgment exercised by those assisting in the audit. Safeguards over assets and records and review of indications of fraud and illegal acts are internal control issues. Objective review of the adequacy of the training and proficiency of personnel is a quality control issue.   (ID: 5641)

6. (a)   It is of utmost importance to the profession that the general public maintain confidence in the independence of independent auditors. Public confidence would be impaired by evidence that independence was actually lacking, and it might also be impaired by the existence of circumstances which reasonable people might believe likely to influence independence.   (ID: 20)

7. (d)   Due professional care requires the auditor to exercise professional skepticism. Professional skepticism is an attitude that includes a questioning mind and a critical assessment of audit evidence.   (ID: 213)

8. (c)   Standards of fieldwork is one of the three categories of the ten generally accepted auditing standards (GAAS). The other two categories are general standards and standards of reporting.   (ID: 8373)

9. (b)   The first general standard states that the auditor must have adequate technical training and proficiency to perform the audit. The attainment of that proficiency begins with the auditor's formal education and extends into the auditor's subsequent experience. The independent auditor must undergo technical training that is adequate to meet the requirements of a professional. The other answer alternatives are not requirements.   (ID: 89455)

Predecessor & Successor Auditors

10. (d)   Prior to the acceptance of an engagement, a successor should ask about disagreements with management as to accounting principles, auditing procedures, or other significant matters. Other matters subject to inquiry that will assist the successor auditor in determining whether to accept the engagement should include information that might bear on the integrity of management; the predecessor's communications to those charged with governance regarding fraud and illegal acts by the client; the predecessor's communications to management and those charged with governance regarding significant deficiencies and material weaknesses in internal control; and the predecessor's understanding of the reasons for the change in auditors. The auditor would use other sources for learning specialized accounting principles of the client's industry and the inherent uncertainty in applying sampling procedures. The competency of the client's internal audit staff should be an evaluation made by the current auditor.   (ID: 5620)

11. (b)   If during an audit, the successor auditor becomes aware of information that leads the auditor to believe the financial statements reported on by the predecessor auditor may require revision, the successor auditor should request the client to arrange a meeting among the three parties to resolve the matter. If the client refuses or if the successor is not satisfied after the meeting, the successor auditor should evaluate any implications on the current engagement and whether resignation from the engagement is appropriate as well as consider consulting with an attorney in determining an appropriate course of action.   (ID: 5636)

12. (a)   A successor should ask about the predecessor's understanding of the reasons for the change in auditors. Other matters subject to inquiry should include information that might bear on the integrity of management; disagreements the predecessor had with management as to accounting principles, auditing procedures, or other significant matters; the predecessor's communications to those charged with governance regarding fraud and illegal acts by the client; and the predecessor's communications to management and those charged with governance regarding significant deficiencies and material weaknesses in internal control. Appropriate inquiries should help the successor to decide whether to accept the engagement. The other answer alternatives do not meet this objective. Additionally, the nature, extent, and timing of the audit work performed and the conclusions reached are matters solely for the successor auditor's judgment.   (ID: 7832)

13. (d)   The successor auditor should request permission from the prospective client to make an inquiry of the predecessor auditor prior to final acceptance of the engagement. Except as permitted by the Rules of the Code of Professional Conduct, an auditor is precluded from disclosing confidential information obtained in the course of an engagement unless the client specifically consents. Thus, the successor auditor should ask the prospective client to authorize the predecessor auditor to respond fully to the successor auditor's inquiries. If a prospective client refuses to permit the predecessor auditor to respond or limits the response, the successor auditor should inquire as to the reasons and consider the implications of that refusal in deciding whether to accept the engagement. The other answers describe activities that are not required *prior* to the acceptance of an engagement. Editor note: If an auditor does not possess an understanding of the client's industry and business prior to the acceptance of the engagement, the auditor must have the ability to gain it.   (ID: 6391)

14. (c)   The successor auditor should request that the client authorize the predecessor auditor to allow a review of the predecessor auditor's working papers. It is customary in such circumstances for the predecessor auditor to be available to the successor auditor and make available for review certain working papers. The predecessor auditor should determine which working papers are to be made available for review and which may be copied. The predecessor auditor should ordinarily permit the successor auditor to review working papers, including documentation of planning, internal control, audit results, and other matters of continuing accounting and auditing significance, such as the working paper analysis of balance sheet accounts, and those relating to contingencies. While, in a broad sense, an engagement letter could be considered part of the predecessor's working papers, as the predecessor's engagement letter could shed little light on the previous audit, there is little point in a successor reviewing it.   (ID: 7632)

15. (a)   The working papers the predecessor would ordinarily make available would include analysis of balance sheet accounts and those relating to contingencies.   (ID: 6710)

16. (c)   A successor auditor's inquiries of the predecessor auditor should include questions regarding the predecessor's understanding as to the reasons for the change in auditors. The purpose of the inquiries is to assist the successor auditor in determining whether to accept the engagement. (The other answer alternatives

do not directly relate to that.) Other matters subject to inquiry for this purpose are information that might bear on the integrity of management; disagreements with management as to accounting principles, auditing procedures, or other similarly significant matters; communications to those charged with governance regarding fraud and illegal acts by clients; and communications to management and those charged with governance regarding significant deficiencies and material weaknesses in internal control. An auditor should not accept an engagement until the appropriate communications with the predecessor auditor have been evaluated. The predecessor's evaluation of audit risk and judgment about materiality would have limited if any value for the current audit; additionally, these are matters of judgment that are the sole responsibility of the successor auditor. Subsequent events that occurred since the predecessor's audit report was issued would generally not be appropriate subject matter for successor inquiries. The successor would have better access to information about such events than the predecessor would because after the date of the predecessor's report, an auditor (the predecessor) has no obligation to make any further or continuing inquiry or perform any other auditing procedures with respect to the audited financial statements covered by that report, unless new information which may affect the report comes to the predecessor's attention. The question did not indicate that was the case. The predecessor's knowledge of accounting and auditing matters of continuing significance (as revealed by the successor's auditor's review of the predecessor's workpapers) may be of interest to the successor auditor as evidence about opening balances and consistency or for purposes of planning the engagement. The timing of communications for these purposes is more flexible, i.e., they do not have to occur prior to acceptance of the engagement.   (ID: 8808)

17. (b)   The successor auditor should make specific and reasonable inquiries of the predecessor regarding matters that will assist the successor in determining whether to accept the engagement. Such matters should include the predecessor's communications to those charged with governance regarding fraud and illegal acts by clients. Other matters subject to inquiry for this purpose are information that might bear on the integrity of management; disagreements with management as to accounting principles, auditing procedures, or other similarly significant matters; communications to management and those charged with governance regarding significant deficiencies and material weaknesses in internal control; and the predecessor's understanding as to the reasons for the change in auditors. Subsequent events would be covered in the successor's audit period. The predecessor's knowledge of accounting and auditing matters of continuing significance and consistency of GAAP (as revealed by the successor's auditor's review of the predecessor's workpapers) may be of interest to the successor; however, the timing of communications regarding the review of the predecessor's workpapers is more flexible, i.e., they do not have to occur prior to acceptance of the engagement.   (ID: 4666)

18. (d)   The successor auditor should request permission from the prospective client to make an inquiry of the predecessor auditor prior to final acceptance of the engagement. Except as permitted by the Rules of the Code of Professional Conduct, an auditor is precluded from disclosing confidential information obtained in the course of an engagement unless the client specifically consents. Thus, the successor auditor should ask the prospective client to authorize the predecessor auditor to respond fully to the successor auditor's inquiries. If a prospective client refuses to permit the predecessor auditor to respond or limits the response, the successor auditor should inquire as to the reasons and consider the implications of that refusal in deciding whether to accept the engagement. The other answers describe activities that are not required *prior* to the acceptance of an engagement. Editor note: If an auditor does not possess an understanding of the client's industry and business prior to the acceptance of the engagement, the auditor must have the ability to gain it.   (ID: 9910)

PERFORMANCE BY TOPICS

Each category below parallels a topic covered in Chapter 1. Record the number and percentage of questions you answered correctly in each topic.

GAAS			Predecessor & Successor Auditors		
Question #	Correct	√	Question #	Correct	√
1			10		
2			11		
3			12		
4			13		
5			14		
6			15		
7			16		
8			17		
9			18		
# Questions	9		# Questions	9	
# Correct			# Correct		
% Correct			% Correct		

Solution 1-2 SIMULATION ANSWER: Research

AU	§	315	07

(ID: 9200)

.07   Inquiry of the predecessor auditor is a necessary procedure because the predecessor auditor may be able to provide information that will assist the successor auditor in determining whether to accept the engagement. The successor auditor should bear in mind that, among other things, the predecessor auditor and the client may have disagreed about accounting principles, auditing procedures, or similarly significant matters.

CHAPTER 2

PLANNING

CHAPTER 2

PLANNING

I. Planning & Supervision (AU 311)

A. Appointment of the Independent Auditor

Exhibit 1 ▶ The First Standard of Fieldwork

The auditor must adequately plan the work and must properly supervise any assistants.

1. **Early Appointment** An early appointment is advantageous. It allows the auditor to plan the audit prior to the balance sheet date.

2. **Appointment Near Year-End** Before accepting an engagement near or after the close of the accounting period, the auditor should consider whether it will be possible to perform an adequate audit that will support an unqualified opinion. If not, the auditor should discuss with the potential client the possibility of either a qualified opinion or a disclaimer of an opinion due to the scope limitation.

B. Understanding With the Client

The auditor should establish an understanding with the client regarding the objectives, scope, and limitations of the services to be performed and document it in an engagement letter to the client. The letter should also delineate the responsibilities of the auditor versus those of management. Such an understanding reduces the chance that either party will misinterpret the needs or expectations of the other.

1. **Engagement Letter Requirements** The engagement letter should generally include the following matters.

    a. The objective of the audit is the expression of an opinion on the financial statements.

    b. Management's responsibilities include:

    (1) The entity's financial statements as well as the selection and application of accounting policies

    (2) Establishing and maintaining effective internal control over financial reporting

    (3) Designing and implementing programs and controls to prevent and detect fraud

    (4) Identifying and ensuring compliance with applicable laws and regulations

    (5) Making all financial records and related information available to the auditor

    (6) Providing the auditor with a letter at the conclusion of the engagement that confirms certain representations made during the audit

    (7) Adjusting the financial statements to correct material misstatements

    (8) Affirming to the auditor in the representation letter that the effects of any uncorrected misstatements aggregated by the auditor during the current engagement and pertaining to the latest period presented are immaterial, both individually and in the aggregate, to the financial statements taken as a whole.

     c.   The auditor is:

          (1)   Responsible for conducting the audit in accordance with GAAS

          (2)   Responsible for obtaining an understanding of the entity and its environment, including its internal control, sufficient to assess the risk of material misstatement (RMM) of the financial statements and to design the nature, extent, and timing of further audit procedures

          (3)   Not required to search for significant deficiencies in internal control; however, the auditor is responsible for ensuring that those charged with governance are aware of any significant deficiencies that come to the auditor's attention

     d.   The engagement letter should also communicate the following about the nature of an audit.

          (1)   GAAS require the auditor to obtain reasonable rather than absolute assurance about whether the financial statements are free of material misstatement, whether caused by error or fraud; consequently, a material misstatement may remain undetected.

          (2)   An audit is not designed to detect error or fraud that is immaterial to the financial statements.

          (3)   An audit is not designed to provide assurance on internal control or to identify significant deficiencies in internal control.

          (4)   If, for any reason, the auditor is unable to complete the audit or is unable to form an opinion, the auditor may decline to express an opinion or issue a report.

  2.   **Optional** The engagement letter may also include other matters such as: overall audit strategy; involvement of specialists, internal auditors, and/or predecessor auditors; fees and billing; liability issues; access to the auditor's workpapers; and any additional services to be provided.

C. **Planning**

Planning involves the development of an overall strategy for the expected conduct, organization, and staffing of the audit.

The nature, extent, and timing of planning vary with the size and complexity of the entity and the auditor's experience with and knowledge of the entity and its environment, including internal control.

The auditor must plan the audit to be responsive to the assessment of the RMM.

Planning begins with engagement acceptance and continues throughout the audit because evidence gathered may require the revision of the overall audit strategy. The auditor should document any significant changes to the overall audit strategy.

  1.   **Preliminary Engagement Activities** The auditor should perform the following procedures at the beginning of the audit engagement. (Performance of these procedures should also be part of a CPA firm's system of quality control—see Chapter 14.)

     a.   **Procedures**

          (1)   Procedures regarding both the continuance of the client relationship and the specific audit engagement

          (2)   Evaluation of the auditor's compliance with ethical requirements, including independence

b. **Purpose** The purpose of performing these preliminary engagement activities is to consider any events or circumstances that may either adversely affect the auditor's ability to plan and perform the audit engagement to reduce audit risk to an acceptably low level or may pose an unacceptable level of risk to the auditor. These preliminary quality control activities help ensure that:

(1) The auditor maintains the required independence and capability to perform the audit

(2) There are no issues with management's integrity

(3) There are no misunderstandings with the client regarding the terms of the engagement

2. **Overall Audit Strategy** In establishing the overall audit strategy, the auditor should:

a. **Characteristics That Define Scope** Determine the characteristics of the engagement that define its scope, such as the basis of reporting, industry-specific reporting requirements, and the locations of the entity.

b. **Reporting Objectives / Required Communications / Deadlines** Determine the reporting objectives of the engagement to plan the timing of the audit and the nature of required communications, such as deadlines for interim and final reporting as well as key dates for expected communications with management and those charged with governance.

c. **Key Factors That Define the Focus of an Audit** Consider the important factors that will determine the focus of the audit team's efforts, such as:

(1) Determination of materiality levels

(2) Preliminary identification of areas where there may be higher RMM

(3) Preliminary identification of material locations and account balances

(4) Evaluation of whether the auditor plans to perform tests of controls to obtain evidence regarding the operating effectiveness of internal control

(5) Identification of any recent significant developments regarding the entity's financial reporting or concerning other relevant matters within the entity or its industry

d. **Examples of Matters to Consider** In establishing the overall audit strategy, the auditor may consider the following matters:

(1) **Scope of Engagement**

- Basis of reporting, including any need to reconcile to another basis of reporting

- Industry-specific reporting requirements

- Expected audit coverage, including the number and locations to be included

- Nature of the control relationships between a parent and its subsidiaries that determine how the group is to be consolidated

- Extent to which locations are audited by other auditors

- Nature of the subsidiaries or divisions to be audited, including need for specialized knowledge

- Reporting currency to be used, including any need for currency translation

- Statutory or regulatory audit requirements

- Availability of internal auditors and the extent of the auditor's potential reliance on their work

- Entity's use of service organizations

- Expected use of audit evidence obtained in prior audits

- Effect of IT on audit procedures

- Coordination of the expected coverage and timing of the audit work with any reviews of interim financial information and the effect on the audit of the information obtained during such reviews

- Discussion of matters that may affect the audit with firm personnel responsible for performing other services for the entity

- Availability of client personnel and data

(2)   Reporting Objectives, Timing & Communications Required

- Entity's timetable for reporting, including interim periods

- Organization of meetings with management and those charged with governance to discuss the nature, extent, and timing of the audit work

- Discussion with management and those charged with governance regarding the expected type and timing of reports to be issued and other communications

- Discussion with management concerning the expected communications on the status of audit work throughout the engagement and the expected deliverables resulting from the audit procedures

- Communication with auditors of other locations regarding the expected types and timing of reports as well as other communications

- Expected nature and timing of communications among audit team members, including team meetings and timing of the review of work performed

- Whether there are any other expected communications with third parties, including any statutory or contractual reporting responsibilities arising from the audit

(3)   Scope of the Audit

- Setting materiality for planning purposes

- Setting and communicating materiality for auditors of other locations

- Reconsidering materiality as audit procedures are performed during the course of the audit

- Identifying the material locations and account balances

- Audit areas where there is a higher RMM

- Effect of the assessed RMM at the overall financial statement level on scope, supervision, and review

- Selection of the audit team and the assignment of audit work to the team members, including assignment of experienced members to areas where there may be higher RMM

- Engagement time budgeting

- Manner in which the auditor emphasizes to team members the need to maintain a questioning mind and to exercise professional skepticism in gathering and evaluating audit evidence

- Results of previous audits that involved evaluating the operating effectiveness of internal control, including the nature of identified weaknesses and actions taken to address them

- Management's commitment to the design and operation of internal control

- Volume of transactions, which may be a factor in determining whether it is more effective for the auditor to rely on internal control

- Importance attached to internal control throughout the entity

- Significant business developments, including changes in IT, business processes, and key management as well as acquisitions, mergers, and divestments.

- Significant industry developments

- Significant accounting changes

- Other significant relevant developments

3. **Audit Plan** Once the audit strategy has been established, the auditor will be able to develop a more detailed audit plan (set of audit programs) that addresses the matters identified in the audit strategy (specific audit objectives). Although the auditor develops the audit strategy before beginning the audit plan, these two planning phases are not necessarily discrete or sequential because changes in one will often result in adjustments to the other. The auditor should document any changes to the original audit plan.

   The audit plan documents the nature, extent, and timing of audit procedures that are expected to reduce audit risk to an acceptably low level by obtaining sufficient appropriate audit evidence.

   The audit plan should include:

   a. **Risk Assessment Procedures** A description of the nature, extent, and timing of planned risk assessment procedures sufficient to assess the RMM. This may occur early in the audit process.

   b. **Further Audit Procedures** A description of the nature, extent, and timing of further audit procedures at the relevant assertion level for each material class of transactions, account balance, and disclosure; these will include any planned tests of controls and all substantive procedures.

      The planning of specific further audit procedures depends on the outcome of the risk assessment procedures. Also, the auditor may begin to perform some further audit procedures before the planning of others is completed.

   c. **Other Procedures** A description of other audit procedures to be performed in order to comply with GAAS.

4. **Determining Involvement of Specialists** The auditor should consider whether specialized skills are needed in performing the audit.

   a. **Responsibilities** If the use of a specialist is planned, the auditor should determine whether that professional will effectively function as a member of the audit team. For example, a tax practitioner or a professional with valuation skills employed by the audit firm may be used to perform audit procedures as part of the audit team. If such a professional is part of the audit team, the auditor's responsibilities for supervising that professional are equivalent to those for other assistants.

b. **Information Technology (IT) Specialists** In determining whether an IT professional is needed on the audit team, the auditor should consider such factors as the:

(1) Complexity of the entity's systems and IT controls and the manner in which they are used in conducting the entity's business

(2) Significance of changes made to existing systems or the implementation of new systems

(3) Extent to which data is shared among systems

(4) Extent of the entity's participation in electronic commerce

(5) Entity's use of emerging technologies

(6) Significance of audit evidence that is only available in electronic form

D. **Communication**
The auditor is required to communicate with those charged with governance an overview of the planned scope and timing of the audit.

E. **Supervision**
Supervision involves directing assistants in accomplishing the audit objectives and subsequently determining whether those objectives were accomplished. The extent of supervision required will vary depending on the complexity of the subject matter, the qualifications of the persons performing the work, and other factors or circumstances.

1. **Communication Between Auditor & Assistants**

a. **Responsibilities / Audit Objectives** Assistants should be informed of their responsibilities and the objectives of the audit procedures they are to perform in sufficient detail.

b. **Significant Accounting & Auditing Questions** The assistants should be instructed to bring significant accounting and auditing questions to the attention of the auditor with final responsibility for the audit.

c. **Report Difficulties** Assistants should be directed to report difficulties encountered in performing the audit, such as missing documents or resistance from client personnel in providing access to information or in responding to inquiries.

d. **Material Misstatement / Fraud Discussion** The auditor with final responsibility for the audit should discuss with members of the audit team the susceptibility of the entity's financial statements to material misstatement due to error or fraud, with special emphasis on fraud. The purpose of the discussion is to help the audit team members to understand the entity and its environment, including control and how the entity's risks may affect the audit. The discussion should emphasize the need to maintain a questioning mind and to exercise professional skepticism in gathering and evaluating evidence.

2. **Review Assistants' Work** The work performed by each assistant should be reviewed to

a. **Confirm Performance / Documentation** Be sure it was performed and documented adequately and

      b.   **Confirm Consistency With Audit Report** Evaluate whether the results obtained are consistent with the conclusions to be presented in the audit report.

  3.   **Disagreements** Both the auditor and the assistants should be aware of the procedures to be followed when differences of opinion arise on accounting and auditing issues. The procedures should allow assistants to document their disagreements with the conclusions reached if, after appropriate consultation, assistants believe it necessary to disassociate themselves from the issue's resolution. The basis for the resolution should also be documented.

II. Audit Risk & Materiality in Conducting an Audit (AU 312)

Audit risk and materiality affect the application of GAAS and should be considered together in designing the nature, extent, and timing of audit procedures and evaluating the results of those procedures.

A. Nature of Audit Risk

Audit risk is the risk that an auditor may unknowingly fail to appropriately modify the opinion on financial statements that are materially misstated. The existence of audit risk is acknowledged in the auditor's standard report by the statement that the auditor obtains reasonable [not absolute] assurance about whether the financial statements are free of material misstatement. The auditor should plan the audit so that audit risk will be reduced to a low level that is appropriate, in the auditor's judgment, for expressing an opinion on the financial statements.

The auditor should consider audit risk in relation to the:

- Relevant assertions regarding individual account balances, classes of transactions, and disclosures
- Overall financial statement level

B. Nature of Materiality

  1.   **Nature** Some matters are important for the fair presentation of financial statements, while others are not. The auditor plans and performs the audit to obtain reasonable assurance that material misstatements, whether caused by error or fraud, are detected.

  2.   **Auditor's Judgment / Reasonable Person Standard** The auditor's materiality judgments involve both quantitative and qualitative considerations and the auditor's perception of the needs of users of the financial statements. A misstatement is material if it is one that would change or influence the judgment of a reasonable person relying on the financial statements.

  3.   **Financial Statement User Profile** An auditor of financial statements considers the needs of users in general (as a group) rather than the needs of specific users. Users are assumed to:

      a.   Have an appropriate knowledge of business and economic activities and accounting practices

      b.   Have a willingness to study the information in the financial statements with appropriate diligence

      c.   Understand that financial statements are prepared and audited to levels of materiality

      d.   Recognize the uncertainties inherent in the measurement of amounts based on the use of estimates, judgment, and the consideration of future events

      e.   Make appropriate economic decisions on the basis of the information in the financial statements

C. **Nature & Causes of Misstatements**
There are two types of misstatements.

1. **Known Misstatements** These are misstatements specifically identified during the audit arising from the incorrect selection or misapplication of accounting principles or misstatements of facts.

2. **Likely Misstatements**

   a. **Unreasonable Estimates** Likely misstatements arise from differences between management's and the auditor's judgment concerning accounting estimates. The difference between an estimate in the financial statements that the auditor considers unreasonable or inappropriate and the closest reasonable estimate should be treated by the auditor as a likely misstatement.

   b. **Extrapolation From Evidence** The auditor may also determine that misstatements are likely to exist based on an extrapolation from audit evidence, for example, the projection of the results of a sample to the relevant population. (When an auditor uses audit sampling to test a relevant assertion for an account balance or a class of transactions, the auditor should project the amount of known misstatements identified in the sample to the items in the balance or class from which the sample was selected. That projected misstatement, along with the results of other substantive procedures, contributes to the auditor's assessment of likely misstatement in the balance or class.)

3. **Causes of Misstatements** Misstatements result from errors or fraud. This distinction affects the auditor's response to misstatements. The auditor has no responsibility to plan the audit to detect immaterial misstatements. However, if misstatements due to fraud are detected, the auditor should consider the implications for the integrity of management and employees and the possible effects on other aspects of the audit even if the misstatements are not material.

   a. **Errors** Errors are unintentional mistakes of amounts or disclosures in financial statements.

   b. **Fraud** Fraud is an intentional act involving the use of deception to obtain an unjust or illegal advantage committed by employees, management, those charged with governance, or third parties. There are two types of fraudulent misstatements that are relevant in an audit of financial statements (for more information, see the section on fraud in this chapter). They are misstatements arising from:

      (1) Fraudulent financial reporting

      (2) Misappropriation of assets (theft)

D. **Financial Statement Level Considerations**

1. **Purposes** The auditor must consider audit risk and determine a materiality level for the financial statements taken as a whole for the purposes of

   a. Determining the extent and nature of risk assessment procedures

   b. Identifying and assessing the RMM

   c. Determining the nature, extent, and timing of further audit procedures; and

   d. Evaluating whether the financial statements taken as a whole are presented fairly.

2. **Pervasive Risks** The auditor should consider RMM that relate pervasively to the financial statements taken as a whole and potentially affect many relevant assertions. Risks of this nature often relate to the entity's control environment and are not necessarily identifiable with specific assertions at the account balance, class of transactions, or disclosure level. Such risks may be especially relevant to the consideration of the risk of fraud.

3. **Considerations for Developing Audit Responses** In developing responses to RMM at the overall financial statement level, the auditor should consider:

   a. The knowledge, skill, and ability of personnel assigned significant engagement responsibilities

   b. Whether a specialist is needed

   c. The appropriate level of supervision of assistants

4. **Multiple Locations / Components** The auditor should consider the extent to which audit procedures should be performed at selected locations or components. The factors an auditor should consider regarding the selection of a particular location or component include the:

   a. Nature and amount of assets and transactions

   b. Degree of centralization of records or information processing

   c. Effectiveness of the control environment, particularly with respect to management's direct control over the exercise of authority delegated to others and its ability to effectively supervise activities at a particular location

   d. Frequency, timing, and scope of the entity's monitoring activities

   e. Judgments about materiality of a particular component or location

   f. Risks associated with the location or component, such as political or economic instability

E. **Individual Account Balance, Class of Transactions & Disclosure Level Considerations**

1. **Risk / Materiality Relationship** There is usually an inverse relationship between audit risk and materiality considerations at this level. The risk that relevant assertions related to a particular account balance, class of transactions, or disclosure could be misstated by a very large amount may be very low, but the risk that it could be misstated by a small amount may be very high.

2. **Auditor Response to Risk / Materiality Judgments** Everything else being equal, a decrease in either the acceptable level of audit risk or the perceived materiality level of an account balance, class of transactions, or disclosure would require the auditor to do one or more of the following.

   a. Select a more effective auditing procedure (nature).

   b. Increase the extent of a particular auditing procedure (extent).

   c. Perform auditing procedures closer to the year-end (timing).

3. **Materiality** In planning the nature, extent and timing of audit procedures for a specific account balance, class of transactions, or disclosure, the auditor is concerned with detecting misstatements that could be quantitatively material when aggregated with misstatements in other balances, classes, or disclosures to the financial statements taken as a whole.

(Although the auditor should also be alert for misstatements that could be qualitatively material, it is generally not practical to design audit procedures to detect them.)

4. **Audit Risk Components** The risk that relevant assertions related to account balances, classes of transactions, or disclosures are misstated has two components: inherent risk and control risk. The combination of these two risks is known as the risk of material misstatement (RMM). The RMM combined with the auditor's detection risk make up audit risk. These components may be assessed in quantitative terms (such as percentages) or nonquantitative terms (such as high, medium, or low).

The general relationship between audit risk and its components is expressed in the following model. This is not a mathematical formula nor does it include all factors that may influence the assessment of audit risk. The standard setters included it because they thought this form of representation might prove useful.

Exhibit 2 ▶ Audit Risk Model

$$AR = RMM \times DR \quad \text{or} \quad AR = (IR \times CR) \times (AP \times TD)$$

where:

AR	=	Audit Risk	IR	=	Inherent Risk
RMM	=	Risk of Material	CR	=	Control Risk
		Misstatement	AP	=	Substantive Analytical Procedures Risk
DR	=	Detection Risk	TD	=	Tests of Details Risk

a. **Risk of Material Misstatement (RMM)** The RMM (consisting of inherent risk and control risk) is the risk that the relevant assertions related to account balances, classes of transactions, or disclosures contain misstatements that could be material to the financial statements when aggregated with other misstatements. The RMM rests within the entity, independent of the audit.

The auditor should assess the RMM at the relevant assertion level as a basis for further audit procedures. This assessment is not a precise measurement of risk—it is a judgment. The auditor should make the assessment by performing:

- Risk assessment procedures to obtain an understanding of the entity and its environment, including its internal control; and

- Tests of controls, where appropriate, to obtain evidence about their operating effectiveness.

(1) **Inherent Risk (IR)** Inherent risk is the susceptibility of a relevant assertion to a material misstatement, assuming there are no related controls. Some items pose more risk simply due to their nature, for example, cash has a lot of inherent risk because it is more susceptible to theft than most items. Complex calculations have more inherent risk than simple calculations. Accounts consisting of estimates that are subject to significant measurement uncertainty have more inherent risk than do accounts consisting of relatively routine, factual data. External factors that give rise to business risk can influence inherent risk, for example, technological developments could make a particular product obsolete, causing inventory to be more susceptible to overstatement.

(2) **Control Risk (CR)** Control risk is the risk that a material misstatement that could occur in a relevant assertion will not be prevented or detected on a timely basis by the entity's internal controls. This risk is a function of the effectiveness of the design and operation of internal controls related to the preparation of the financial statements. Some control risk will always exist because of the inherent limitations of any entity's internal control system. These include breakdowns in controls that can occur due to human fallibility or circumvention of controls either by collusion or inappropriate management override.

b. **Detection Risk (DR)** It is the risk that the auditor will not detect a material misstatement that exists in a relevant assertion. It is nearly always present to some degree because an auditor rarely examines 100 percent of an account balance or class of transactions. Detection risk is also a function of the effectiveness of an auditing procedure and its application by the auditor, i.e., the auditor can select an inappropriate procedure, misapply a procedure, or misinterpret the audit results.

(1) Detection risk relates to substantive procedures. It can be broken down (disaggregated) into the additional components of tests of details risk (TD) and substantive analytical procedures risk (AP).

(2) Detection risk is managed by the auditor's response to the RMM. It should bear an inverse relationship to the RMM, i.e., if the auditor perceives an increase in the RMM, the auditor should accept less detection risk. Conversely, the lower the RMM, the greater the detection risk than can be accepted by the auditor.

Accordingly, the level of detection risk also has an inverse relationship with the amount of substantive testing needed. If the auditor decreases the acceptable level of detection risk, more substantive testing will be in order and vice versa. *However, the auditor should perform substantive procedures for all relevant assertions related to all material account balances, classes of transactions, and disclosures regardless of the level of risk.*

And there is a direct relationship between the RMM and the amount of substantive testing needed.

Exhibit 3 ▶ Risk Relationships

Inherent Risk and Control Risk (RMM)	Acceptable Level of Detection Risk	Substantive Tests
Increase	Decrease	Increase
Decrease	Increase	Decrease

c. **How the RMM & Detection Risk Differ** Inherent risk and control risk (RMM) differ from detection risk in that they are the entity's risks and exist independently of the audit, whereas detection risk relates to the auditor's procedures and can be altered by adjusting the nature, extent, and timing of substantive procedures. Thus, the auditor assesses inherent risk and control risk (RMM).

F. **Determining Materiality When Planning the Audit**

1. **Financial Statement Level** The auditor should determine a materiality level for the financial statements taken as a whole when establishing the overall audit strategy. Determining a materiality level for the financial statements taken as a whole helps the auditor identify and assess the RMM as well as plan the nature, extent, and timing of further audit procedures.

a. **Benchmarks** Determining materiality is a matter of professional judgment. The auditor may apply a percentage to a chosen benchmark to aid in determining overall materiality. Depending on the nature and circumstances of the entity, appropriate benchmarks might include: total revenues, gross profit, and other categories of reported income. For asset-based entities (e.g., an investment fund), an appropriate benchmark might be net assets.

When identifying an appropriate benchmark, the auditor may consider the following factors.

(1) The elements of the financial statements (e.g., assets, liabilities, etc.) and the financial statement measures defined by GAAP (e.g., financial position), or other specific requirements

(2) Whether there are financial statement items, for the particular entity, that users tend to focus on

(3) The nature of the entity and the industry in which it operates

(4) The size of the entity, nature of its ownership, and the way it is financed

b. **Considerations** In determining materiality, the auditor should consider (1) prior periods' financial results and financial positions, (2) the period-to-date financial results and financial position, and (3) budgets or forecasts for the current period. The auditor should take into account any significant changes in the entity's circumstances (e.g., a significant business acquisition) and relevant changes in the economy or the industry in which the entity operates. For example, if an auditor usually determines materiality for a specific entity based on a percentage of profit, but there are circumstances that gave rise to an exceptional increase in profit, the auditor may conclude that a normalized profit figure based on past results is a more appropriate benchmark.

2. **Misstatements of Lesser Amounts** The materiality level determined for the financial statements taken as a whole is not a threshold below which identified misstatements are always considered to be immaterial.

a. **Specific Circumstances** When establishing the overall audit strategy the auditor should consider whether specific circumstances of the entity may cause misstatements of particular items to be considered material by users of the financial statements even if they are below the determined materiality level. The views of management and those charged with governance may be helpful to the auditor in gaining or confirming an understanding of user needs.

Factors to consider when identifying such items include:

(1) Whether accounting standards, laws, or regulations affect users' expectations regarding the measurement or disclosure of certain items (for example, related party transactions or compensation of management or those charged with governance)

(2) The key disclosures in relation to the industry and the entity's environment (for example, research and development costs for a pharmaceutical company)

(3) Whether attention is focused on the financial performance of a particular subsidiary or division that is separately disclosed in the consolidating financial statements (for example, a newly acquired business)

b. **Tolerable Misstatement Determination**

(1) **Definition** When planning a test of details, tolerable misstatement (or tolerable error) is the maximum monetary misstatement that the auditor is willing to accept in a particular account balance or class of transactions.

(2) **Purpose** The auditor normally sets the levels of tolerable misstatement lower than the materiality level. In doing so, the auditor acknowledges the possibility that some misstatements of lesser amounts could, when aggregated, result in the material misstatement of the financial statements.

Setting the tolerable misstatement for a specific audit procedure at less than the financial statement materiality level allows the auditor to use it as a tool to design the audit so that tolerable misstatement, combined for all of the tests in the audit, does not exceed materiality for the financial statements. (See Chapter 6, *Audit Sampling*, for more information on tolerable misstatement.)

3. **Changes in Materiality** During the audit, the auditor may become aware of additional factors that change the auditor's judgment about materiality. Thus, when evaluating audit findings, the auditor may use a different level of materiality than that used for planning purposes. If the auditor decides to lower the level of materiality, the auditor should reconsider the related levels of tolerable misstatement and the appropriateness of the nature, extent, and timing of further audit procedures.

4. **Documentation Requirements** The auditor should document the levels of materiality and tolerable misstatement, including any changes, and the basis on which those levels were determined.

G. **Communication of Misstatements to Management & Those Charged With Governance**

1. **Communication to Management** The auditor must communicate all nontrivial misstatements (distinguishing between known and likely ones) to the appropriate level of management on a timely basis.

   a. **Request Correction of Known Misstatements** The auditor should request that management record the adjustments needed to correct all of these known misstatements, including the effect of prior period misstatements.

   b. **Investigate Likely Misstatements** The auditor should request that management investigate the likely misstatements.

      (1) If the auditor evaluates the amount of likely misstatement from a sample in an account balance, class of transactions, or disclosure as material, either individually or in aggregate with other misstatements, the auditor should request management to examine the entire population to find any additional corrections needed.

      (2) If the auditor has identified a likely misstatement involving differences in estimates, the auditor should request management to review the assumptions and methods used in developing management's estimate.

      (3) If an analytical procedure indicates that a misstatement might exist, but not its approximate amount, the auditor should request management to investigate and, if necessary, should expand audit procedures to determine whether a misstatement exists.

   In all cases, after management's investigation is completed, the auditor should reevaluate the amount of likely misstatement which may include performing additional audit procedures.

   c. **Documentation Requirements** The auditor should document all nontrivial known and likely misstatements identified by the auditor during the audit that have been corrected by management.

   d. **No Correction** If management decides not to correct some or all of the known and likely misstatements, the auditor should obtain an understanding of management's reasons and should take that into account when considering the qualitative aspects of the entity's accounting practices and the implications for the auditor's report. (See the following section—H.—for further coverage on uncorrected misstatements.)

2. **Communication to Those Charged With Governance** The auditor should communicate with those charged with governance significant findings from the audit which include the following matters regarding misstatements.

    a. **Material Corrected Misstatements** Material corrected misstatements that were brought to the attention of management should be communicated to those charged with governance. The auditor may also communicate other corrected immaterial misstatements, such as frequently recurring immaterial misstatements that may indicate a particular bias in the preparation of the financial statements.

    b. **Uncorrected Misstatements**

        (1) The auditor should communicate uncorrected misstatements and the effect that they may have on the auditor's opinion, and request their correction. In communicating the effect that material items may have on the auditor's opinion, the auditor should communicate them individually. Where there are a large number of small uncorrected misstatements, the auditor may communicate the number and overall monetary effect, rather than the details of each one.

        (2) The auditor should discuss the implications of a failure to correct known and likely misstatements, if any, considering qualitative as well as quantitative aspects, including possible implications in relation to future financial statements. The auditor should also communicate the effect of uncorrected misstatements related to prior periods on the relevant classes of transactions, account balances or disclosures, and the financial statements as a whole.

    (See the following section—H.—for further coverage on uncorrected misstatements.)

    c. **Significant Deficiencies and Material Weaknesses** AU 325, *Communicating Internal Control Related Matters Identified in an Audit*, (covered in Chapter 3) requires the auditor to communicate, in writing, to management and those charged with governance, significant deficiencies and material weaknesses identified in an audit. (Material misstatements often indicate that there are significant deficiencies and/or material weaknesses in internal control.)

H. Evaluating Uncorrected Misstatements

In evaluating whether the financial statements are presented fairly, the auditor must consider the effects, both individually and in the aggregate, of all uncorrected known and likely misstatements. In making this evaluation, in relation to particular classes of transactions, account balances, and disclosures, the auditor should consider the size and nature of the misstatements and the particular circumstances of their occurrence, and determine the effect of such misstatements on the financial statements taken as a whole.

There are both quantitative and qualitative considerations as to whether misstatements are material. As a result of the interaction of quantitative and qualitative considerations in materiality judgments, misstatements of relatively small amounts that come to the auditor's attention could have a material effect on the financial statements. For example, an illegal payment of an otherwise immaterial amount could be material if there is a reasonable possibility that it could lead to a material contingent liability or a material loss of revenue.

1. **Quantitative Evaluation**

    a. **Individually** Before considering the aggregated effect, the auditor should consider each uncorrected misstatement separately to evaluate:

        • Its effect in relation to the relevant individual account balances, classes of transactions, or disclosures, including whether materiality levels for particular items of lesser amounts due to specific circumstances of the entity have been exceeded

- Whether it is appropriate to offset misstatements, for example, misstatements of items within the same account balance

- The effect of misstatements related to prior periods on the current period's financial statements—in prior periods, misstatements may not have been corrected by the entity because they did not cause those financial statements to be materially misstated

b.   Aggregate Effect

(1)   Method of Aggregation Uncorrected misstatements should be aggregated in a manner that allows the auditor to determine whether, in relation to individual amounts, subtotals, or totals in the financial statements, they materially misstate the financial statements taken as a whole.

(2)   Prior Period Misstatements The auditor should include the effect of uncorrected prior period misstatements on the current period's financial statements.

(3)   Calculation of Likely Misstatement of an Estimate The difference between an estimate in the financial statements that the auditor considers unreasonable or inappropriate and the closest reasonable estimate should be treated by the auditor as a likely misstatement. The closest reasonable estimate may be a range of acceptable amounts or a precisely determined amount. In the case where the auditor determines a range of acceptable amounts, if management's recorded estimate falls within that range; no difference would be aggregated as a likely misstatement by the auditor. However, if management's recorded estimate falls outside the auditor's range, the difference between the recorded amount and the amount at the closest end of the auditor's range would be aggregated as a likely misstatement.

(4)   Use of Estimates to Manipulate Earnings The auditor should evaluate whether the aggregated differences between estimates supported by audit evidence and those included in the financial statements, while individually reasonable, indicate a possible bias on the part of management, if when considered as a whole, their effect is to increase income. In these circumstances, the auditor should reconsider whether other recorded estimates reflect a similar bias and should perform additional audit procedures that address those estimates. Or if estimates are clustered at one end of the acceptable range in the prior year and at the other end in the current year, it may be that management is using the swing to manipulate earnings to conform to expectations. The auditor should consider whether these conditions should be communicated to those charged with governance.

(5)   Undetected Misstatements If the auditor concludes that the effects of uncorrected misstatements, individually or in the aggregate, do not cause the financial statements to be materially misstated, they could still be materially misstated due to further misstatements remaining undetected. As the aggregate misstatements approach materiality, the risk that the financial statements may be materially misstated also increases; consequently, the auditor should also consider the effect of undetected misstatements in concluding whether the financial statements are fairly stated.

(6)   Consider Revision of Audit Strategy The auditor should consider whether the overall audit strategy and the audit plan need to be revised if the nature of misstatements and the circumstances of their occurrence are indicative that other misstatements may exist that, when aggregated with identified misstatements, could be material. The auditor should not assume that a misstatement is an isolated occurrence.

2. **Qualitative Evaluation** The following qualitative factors to consider are only examples, thus this is not a complete list nor are all of these likely to be present in all audits. Additionally, the existence of any circumstances such as these does not necessarily lead to a conclusion that the misstatement is material.

- The potential effect of the misstatement on trends, especially trends in profitability

- A misstatement that changes a loss into income or vice versa

- The potential effect of the misstatement on the entity's compliance with loan covenants, other contractual agreements, and regulatory provisions

- The existence of statutory or regulatory reporting requirements that affect materiality thresholds

- The misstatement masks a change in earnings or other trends, especially in the context of general economic and industry conditions

- A misstatement that has the effect of increasing management's compensation, for example, by satisfying the requirements for the award of bonuses or other forms of incentive compensation

- The sensitivity of the circumstances surrounding the misstatement, for example, the implications of misstatements involving fraud and possible illegal acts, violations of contractual provisions, and conflicts of interest

- The significance of the financial statement element affected by the misstatement, for example, a misstatement affecting recurring earnings as contrasted to one involving a nonrecurring charge or credit, such as an extraordinary item

- The effects of misclassifications, for example, misclassification between operating and nonoperating income or recurring and nonrecurring income items or a misclassification between fund-raising costs and program activity costs in a not-for-profit organization

- The significance of the misstatement relative to reasonable user needs, for example, earnings to investors and the equity amounts to creditors

- The definitive character of the misstatement, for example, the precision of an error that is objectively determinable as contrasted with a misstatement that unavoidably involves a degree of subjectivity through estimation, allocation, or uncertainty

- The motivation of management with respect to the misstatement, for example, (1) an indication of a possible pattern of bias by management when developing and accumulating accounting estimates, (2) a misstatement precipitated by management's continued unwillingness to correct weaknesses in the financial reporting process, or (3) the intentional decision not to follow GAAP

- The cost of making the correction; it may not be cost-beneficial for the client to develop a system to calculate a basis to record the effect of an immaterial misstatement; on the other hand, if management appears to have developed a system to calculate an amount that represents an immaterial misstatement, it may reflect a motivation of management as noted above

- The existence of offsetting effects of individually significant but different misstatements

- The likelihood that a misstatement that is currently immaterial may have a material effect in future periods because of a cumulative effect

- The risk that possible additional undetected misstatements would affect the auditor's evaluation

3. **Documentation Requirements** The auditor should document

- A summary of uncorrected misstatements, other than those that are trivial, related to known and likely misstatements

- The auditor's conclusion as to whether uncorrected misstatements, individually or in aggregate, do or do not cause the financial statements to be materially misstated, and the basis for that conclusion

III. Understanding the Entity & Its Environment (AU 314)

A. Second Standard of Fieldwork

Exhibit 4 ▶ The Second Standard of Fieldwork

> The auditor must obtain a sufficient understanding of the entity and its environment, including its internal control, to assess the risk of material misstatement of the financial statements whether due to error or fraud, and to design the nature, timing, and extent of further audit procedures.

B. Risk Assessment Procedures

The auditor should perform risk assessment procedures to gain an understanding of the entity and its environment, including its internal control. The nature, extent, and timing of these procedures depend on the circumstances of the engagement, such as the size and complexity of the entity as well as the auditor's experience with the entity. The auditor may choose to perform risk assessment procedures concurrently with tests of controls and/or substantive procedures. These procedures include:

1. **Inquiries** The auditor is required to make inquiries of management and others within the entity. Much of the information needed can be obtained from management and those responsible for financial reporting. However, inquiries of others within the entity, such as internal auditors, and other employees with different levels of authority, may be useful in providing the auditor with different perspectives in identifying RMM.

2. **Analytics** The auditor should apply analytics in planning the audit to assist in understanding the entity and its environment as well as to identify areas that may represent specific risks. In performing analytics as risk assessment procedures, the auditor should develop expectations about plausible relationships that are reasonably expected to exist. When comparison of those expectations with recorded amounts or ratios reveals unusual or unexpected relationships, the auditor should consider those results in identifying RMM. However, when analytics use data aggregated at a high level, the results of those analytics may provide only a broad initial indication about whether a material misstatement exists. Accordingly, the auditor should consider the results of such analytics along with other information gathered in identifying the RMM.

3. **Observation & Inspection** Observation and inspection may support inquiries of management and others as well as provide information about the entity and its environment. Such procedures ordinarily include:

   a. Observation of entity activities and operations

   b. Inspection of documents (such as business plans and strategies), records, and internal control manuals

   c. Reading reports prepared by management (such as quarterly management reports and interim financial statements), those charged with governance (such as minutes of board of directors' meetings), and internal audit

   d. Visits to the entity's premises

    e.   Tracing transactions through the information system relevant to financial reporting (as part of a walk-through)

4.   Prior Period Information If the auditor uses information about the entity and its environment obtained in prior periods, the auditor should determine whether changes have occurred that may affect the relevance of such information in the current audit. Previous experience with the entity contributes to the understanding of the entity. For example, procedures performed in previous audits ordinarily provide information about the entity's organizational structure, business, and controls, as well as past misstatements and whether they were corrected on a timely basis. However, such information may be irrelevant due to changes in the entity or its environment. The auditor should make inquiries and perform other appropriate audit procedures, such as walk-throughs, to determine whether changes have occurred.

5.   Fraud Risk The auditor should specifically assess the RMM due to fraud and consider that assessment in designing audit procedures. The results of the fraud risk assessment provide only a broad initial indication about whether a material misstatement due to fraud may exist. Therefore, the auditor should consider the results of the fraud risk assessment along with other information gathered in identifying the RMM.

6.   Other Information The auditor also should consider other relevant information such as that obtained from the auditor's client acceptance or continuance process, or, where practicable, experience gained on other engagements performed for the entity.

C.   Audit Team Discussion

The audit team should discuss the susceptibility of the financial statements to material misstatement. This discussion may be held concurrently with the required fraud risk discussion.

1.   Objective The objective of this discussion is to gain a better understanding of the potential for material misstatements resulting from fraud or error in the specific areas assigned to the audit team, and to understand how the results of procedures performed may affect other aspects of the audit, including decisions about the nature, extent, and timing of further audit procedures.

2.   Topics The discussion is an opportunity for more experienced team members to share their insights based on their knowledge of the entity. It is also a time for the team members to exchange information about the entity's business risks as well as to discuss how and where the financial statements may be susceptible to material misstatement due to error or fraud. There should be an emphasis on the need to exercise professional skepticism throughout the engagement, to be alert to indications of material misstatement due to fraud or error, and to be rigorous in following up on such indications. Additional critical issues to be discussed include: areas of significant audit risk; areas susceptible to management override of controls; unusual accounting procedures used; important control systems; materiality at the financial statement and account level; and how materiality will be used to determine the extent of testing. The application of GAAP in light of the entity's accounting policies also should be addressed.

D.   Areas of Understanding

The auditor should obtain an understanding of the entity and its environment in the following areas:

1.   Industry, Regulatory & Other External Factors This includes:

    a.   Industry conditions, such as competitors, supplier and customer relationships, and technological developments

    b.   The regulatory environment, including relevant accounting pronouncements, the legal and political environment, and environmental requirements pertaining to the entity, among other matters

    c.   Other external factors, such as general economic conditions

2. **Nature of the Entity** This refers to the entity's operations, ownership, governance, types of investments, organizational structure, and financing. Understanding the nature of an entity enables the auditor to understand the entity's classes of transactions, account balances, and disclosures to be expected.

   a. **Complex Structures** The existence of subsidiaries or other components gives rise to additional RMM such as: consolidation difficulties; the allocation of goodwill to subsidiaries, and its impairment; whether investments are joint ventures, subsidiaries, or investments accounted for using the equity method; and whether special-purpose entities are accounted for appropriately.

   b. **Related Parties** It is important to understand the relationships between the owners, management, and other key personnel as well as their relations with other people or entities to determine whether related-party transactions have been identified and accounted for appropriately.

3. **Objectives, Strategies & Related Business Risks** In response to industry, regulatory and other internal and external factors, the entity develops objectives (overall plans for the entity) and strategies to achieve those objectives.

   a. **Business Risks** Business risks result from significant conditions, events, actions, or inactions that could interfere with the entity's ability to achieve its objectives and execute its strategies. Inappropriate objectives and strategies also represent business risks. Not all business risks give rise to RMM; however, most business risks will affect the financial statements in some way either immediately or in the future. Long-term consequences may need to be considered when assessing going concern issues; for example, a decline in the industry may affect the entity's ability to continue as a going concern. The auditor does not, however, have a responsibility to identify or assess all business risks.

   b. **Sources** As part of internal control, management usually identifies business risks and develops approaches to address them. However, smaller entities often do not set their objectives and strategies, or manage the related business risks, through formal plans or processes; therefore, there may not be any documentation of such matters. In such cases, the auditor may use inquiries of management and observation to obtain an understanding of how the entity responds to such matters.

4. **Measurement & Review of the Entity's Financial Performance** Review of performance measures highlights aspects of the entity's performance that management and others consider important. Whether external or internal, such performance measures create pressures on the entity that could motivate management to take actions that either improve the business performance or misstate the financial statements. Internally generated information used by management may include key performance indicators; budgets; variance analysis; subsidiary, divisional, departmental, or other level performance reports; as well as comparisons of the entity's performance with that of competitors. External information, such as analysts' reports and credit rating agency reports, may be obtained from the client or websites.

5. **Internal Control** The auditor should obtain an understanding of the five components of internal control by performing risk assessment procedures to evaluate the design and implementation of relevant controls. The auditor's knowledge should be sufficient to:

   a. Identify types of potential misstatements

   b. Consider factors that affect the RMM

   c. Design tests of controls, when applicable, and substantive procedures

E. Documentation

1. **Discussion** The auditor should document the discussion concerning the susceptibility of the financial statements to material misstatement due to error or fraud, including:

   a. How and when the discussion took place

   b. The subject matter discussed

   c. Who participated in the discussion

   d. Significant decisions regarding planned responses at the financial statement and relevant assertion levels

2. **Understanding** The auditor also should document:

   a. Key elements of the understanding obtained regarding each of the five aspects outlined above, including each of the five components of internal control

   b. The sources of information from which the understanding was obtained

   c. The risk assessment procedures performed

IV. Service Organizations (AU 324)

The guidance for service auditors in AU 324 has been superseded by AT 801, *Reporting on Controls at a Service Organization,* which is covered in Chapter 13. The AICPA decided that the guidance for service auditors should be moved to the attestation standards because the examination conducted by service auditors is not an audit of financial statements.

The AICPA has redrafted AU 324 as part of its Clarity Project. (The redrafted guidance for user auditors is not effective until audits of financial statements for periods ending on or after December 15, 2012 and thus, is eligible to be tested beginning with the July-August 2013 exam window. See this volume's page vi for information on the Clarity Project.) The AICPA has stated that, during the interim period, the superseded guidance for service auditors currently in AU 324 will not be deleted because they believe the guidance for user auditors can be gleaned without deleting the guidance for service auditors and the guidance for both is too intertwined.

A. Overview

AU 324 provides guidance on the factors an auditor considers when auditing the financial statements of an entity that uses a service organization to process certain transactions. This section also provides guidance for auditors who issue reports on the processing of transactions by a service organization for use by other auditors.

1. **User Organization** The entity that has engaged a service organization and whose financial statements are being audited.

2. **Service Organization** The entity (or a segment of an entity) that provides services to the user organization that are part of the user organization's information system.

B. Service Auditor

A service auditor reports on controls of a service organization that may be relevant to a user organization's internal control as it relates to an audit of financial statements. The service auditor is responsible for the representations in his or her report and for exercising due care in the application of procedures that support those representations. The service auditor's work should be performed in accordance with GAAS general standards and the relevant fieldwork and reporting standards.

1. **Independence** The service auditor should be independent from the service organization; however, the service auditor is **not** required to be independent from each user organization.

2. **Engagement** The type of engagement to be performed and the related report to be prepared should be established by the service organization. The service auditor may issue either of the following types of reports:

    a. **Reports on Controls Placed in Operation** The auditor reports on whether the controls were (1) suitably designed to achieve specified objectives and (2) placed in operation as of a specific date.

    b. **Reports on Controls Placed in Operation & Tests of Operating Effectiveness** Like the report previously discussed, the auditor reports on whether such controls were (1) suitably designed to achieve specified objectives and (2) placed in operation as of a specific date. The auditor also reports on whether the controls that were tested were operating with sufficient effectiveness to provide reasonable, but not absolute, assurance that the related objectives were achieved during the period specified.

C. User Auditor

The user auditor reports on the financial statements of the user organization (an entity that has engaged a service organization). The user auditor's understanding of the user organization's internal control obtained during the planning phase of an audit and assessment of the risk of material misstatement (RMM) may encompass a service organization's controls whose services are part of the entity's information system. (This guidance is applicable to the audit of the financial statements of an entity that obtains services from another organization that are part of its information system.) Information about the nature of the services provided by a service organization may be available from a wide variety of sources, such as user manuals; system overviews; technical manuals; the contract between the user organization and the service organization; and reports by service auditors, internal auditors, or regulatory authorities on the service organization's controls.

1. **Client's System** A service organization's services are part of an entity's information system if they affect any of the following:

    a. The classes of transactions in the entity's operations that are significant to the entity's financial statements

    b. The procedures, both automated and manual, by which the entity's transactions are initiated, authorized, recorded, processed, and reported from their occurrence to their inclusion in the financial statements

    c. The related accounting records, whether electronic or manual, supporting information, and specific accounts in the entity's financial statements involved in initiating, recording, processing, and reporting the entity's transactions

    d. How the entity's information system captures other events and conditions that are significant to the financial statements

    e. The financial reporting process used to prepare the entity's financial statements, including significant accounting estimates and disclosures.

Service organizations that provide such services include, for example, bank trust departments that invest and service assets for employee benefit plans or for others; mortgage bankers that service mortgages for others; and application service providers that provide packaged software applications and a technology environment that enables customers to process financial and operational transactions. This guidance may also be relevant to situations in which an organization develops, provides, and maintains the software used by client organizations. This guidance is **not** intended to apply to situations in which the services provided are limited to executing client organization transactions that are specifically authorized by the client, such as the processing of checking account transactions by a bank or the execution of securities transactions by a broker.

2. **Significance** The significance of the service organization's controls to those of the user organization depends on the nature of the services provided by the service organization in two primary areas.

   a. The nature and materiality of the transactions it processes for the user organization

   b. The degree of interaction between its activities and those of the user organization.

3. **Additional Procedures** If the user auditor believes that the service auditor's report or other available information may not be sufficient to assess the RMM, the user auditor may consider contacting the service organization, through the user organization, to obtain specific information or request that a service auditor be engaged to perform procedures that will supply the necessary information. Alternatively, the user auditor may visit the service organization and perform such procedures. If the user auditor is unable to obtain sufficient audit evidence to achieve his or her audit objectives, the user auditor should qualify his or her opinion or disclaim an opinion on the financial statements because of a scope limitation.

4. **Audit Evidence** A service auditor's report on controls placed in operation at the service organization should be helpful in providing a sufficient understanding to assess the RMM of the user organization. Such a report, however, is **not** intended to provide any evidence of the operating effectiveness of the relevant controls that would allow the user auditor to reduce the assessed level of control risk as low or moderate. Such audit evidence should be derived from one or more of the following:

   a. Tests of the user organization's controls over the activities of the service organization

   b. A service auditor's report on controls placed in operation *and* tests of operating effectiveness, or a report on the application of agreed-upon procedures that describes relevant tests of controls

   c. Appropriate tests of controls performed by the user auditor at the service organization

5. **Use of Service Auditor's Report** The user organization may establish effective controls over the service organization's activities that may be tested and that may enable the user auditor to reduce the assessed level of control risk as low or moderate for some or all of the relevant assertions. However, a user auditor may find that controls relevant to assessing control risk as low or moderate for particular assertions are applied only at the service organization. In this case, if the user auditor decides to use a service auditor's report (that is, a report on controls placed in operation *and* tests of operating effectiveness, or an agreed-upon procedures report), instead of performing the tests at the service organization himself or herself, the user auditor should consider the extent of the evidence provided by the report about the effectiveness of controls for those assertions.

   The user auditor remains responsible for evaluating the evidence presented by the service auditor and for determining its effect on the assessment of control risk at the user organization.

   The user auditor should consider:

   a. The service auditor's reputation—the user auditor should make inquiries concerning the service auditor's professional reputation

   b. The nature, source, and interrelationships among the evidence

   c. The period covered by the tests of controls

   d. Whether the specific tests of controls and results in the service auditor's report are relevant to assertions that are significant in the user organization's financial statements (because the report may be intended to satisfy the needs of several different user auditors)

6. **Reference** The user auditor should not make reference to the report of the service auditor as a basis, in part, for his or her own opinion on the user organization's financial statements. The service auditor's report is used in the audit, but the service auditor is not responsible for examining any portion of the financial statements as of any specific date or for any specified period. Thus, there cannot be a division of responsibility for the audit of the financial statements.

V. Consideration of Fraud in a Financial Statement Audit (AU 316)

A. Fraud Overview

1. **Responsibilities**

   a. **Management & Those Charged With Governance** It is management's responsibility to design and implement programs and controls to prevent, deter, and detect fraud. Management and those charged with governance should set the proper "tone at the top" for the entity.

   b. **Auditor**

      (1) **Reasonable Assurance** The auditor has a responsibility to plan and perform the audit to obtain reasonable assurance about whether the financial statements are free of material misstatement, whether caused by error or fraud. Because absolute assurance is not attainable, even a properly designed and executed audit may not detect a material misstatement resulting from fraud.

      (2) **Focus on Misstatements of Financial Statements** Auditors do not make legal determinations of whether fraud has occurred—the auditor is interested in acts that result in a material misstatement of the financial statements.

2. **Fraud Characteristics** Fraud is primarily differentiated from error by whether the resulting misstatement in the financial statements is intentional or unintentional. Fraud is an intentional act that causes a misstatement. Misstatements due to fraud are difficult to detect because fraud is usually concealed.

   a. **Types of Misstatements** There are two types of misstatements relevant to an auditor's consideration of fraud—those arising from fraudulent financial reporting and the misappropriation of assets.

      (1) **Fraudulent Financial Reporting** Misstatements arising from fraudulent financial reporting are intentional misstatements or omissions of amounts or disclosures in financial statements designed to deceive financial statement users. It may be accomplished by:

      - Manipulation, falsification, or alteration of accounting records or supporting documents from which financial statements are prepared

      - Misrepresentation in or intentional omission from the financial statements of events, transactions, or other significant information

      - Intentional misapplication of accounting principles relating to amounts, classification, manner of presentation, or disclosure

      Material misstatements due to fraudulent financial reporting often result from an overstatement of revenues (for example, through premature revenue recognition or recording fictitious revenues) or an understatement of revenues (for example, through improperly shifting revenues to a later period). Therefore, the auditor should ordinarily presume that there is a RMM due to fraud relating to revenue recognition. If an auditor finds this not to be the case, the auditor should document the reasons supporting this conclusion.

    (2) Misappropriation of Assets Misstatements arising from misappropriation of assets involve the theft of an entity's assets where the effect causes the financial statements to be misstated. It can be accomplished in various ways—including embezzling receipts, stealing assets, or causing an entity to pay for goods or services that have not been received. It is sometimes referred to as defalcation.

  b. **Attributes** The auditor should consider the following attributes of the RMM due to fraud to identify whether and how a risk is relevant to the audit.

    (1) Type Whether it involves fraudulent financial reporting or misappropriation of assets

    (2) Significance Whether it is of a magnitude that could result in a possible material misstatement of the financial statements

    (3) Likelihood The likelihood that it will result in a material misstatement in the financial statements

    (4) Pervasiveness Whether the potential risk is pervasive to the financial statements as a whole or specifically related to a particular assertion, account, or class of transactions

  c. **Conditions Conducive to Fraud** Three conditions generally are present when fraud occurs. (See the section on fraud risk factors within the *Assessment of the Risk of Material Misstatement Due to Fraud* section of this chapter for examples of circumstances or events that can create these conditions.)

    (1) Incentive / Pressure Management or other employees have an incentive or are under pressure, which provides a reason to commit fraud.

    (2) Opportunity Circumstances exist—for example, the absence of controls, ineffective controls, or the ability of management to override controls—that provide an opportunity for a fraud to be perpetrated.

    (3) Attitude / Rationalization Those involved are able to rationalize committing a fraudulent act.

B. **Assessment of the Risk of Material Misstatement Due to Fraud**

  1. **Professional Skepticism** Due professional care requires the auditor to exercise professional skepticism. The auditor should conduct the engagement with a mindset that recognizes the possibility that a material misstatement due to fraud could be present, regardless of any past experience with the entity or the auditor's belief about management's honesty and integrity. The auditor should be aware that management is often in the best position to perpetrate fraud. Such an attitude is demonstrated by designing audit procedures to obtain more reliable evidence for certain account balances and classes of transactions and/or the related assertions; and obtaining corroboration of management's assertions or representations from independent sources.

  2. **Audit Team Discussion About the RMM Due to Fraud** Members of the audit team should have a brainstorming session which includes the auditor with final responsibility for the audit. The discussion should cover how and where the financial statements may be susceptible to fraud; how management could perpetrate and conceal fraudulent financial reporting; and how assets could be misappropriated. Factors affecting the entity that could create the three conditions conducive to fraud (see preceding section) should be covered. Management override of controls should also be considered. Finally, the team should plan a response to the entity's susceptibility to fraud.

How and when this discussion occurred should be documented. The record should include the names of the participants and the subject matter discussed.

Communication among the audit team members about the RMM due to fraud should continue throughout the audit.

3. **Obtaining Information to Identify the RMM Due to Fraud**

   a. **Inquiries of Those Charged With Governance** The auditor should inquire directly of those charged with governance regarding their views about the risks of fraud and whether they have knowledge of any fraud or suspected fraud affecting the entity. If the audit committee is charged with the oversight of the entity's assessment of fraud and the controls established to mitigate those risks, the auditor should obtain an understanding of how the audit committee fulfills that responsibility.

   b. **Inquiries of Management** The auditor should inquire of management as to the risks of fraud and how they are addressed. This should include

      (1) Whether management has knowledge of any fraud or suspected fraud affecting the entity

      (2) Whether management is aware of any allegations of fraud or suspected fraud received from employees, former employees, analysts, regulators, etc.

      (3) Management's understanding about the risks of fraud in the entity, including any specific fraud risks the entity has identified or account balances or classes of transactions for which a risk of fraud may be likely to exist

      (4) Programs and controls to mitigate specific fraud risks the entity has identified, or that otherwise help to prevent, deter, and detect fraud, and how management monitors those programs and controls and reports on them to those charged with governance

      (5) For an entity with multiple locations, the nature and extent of monitoring of these, and whether there are any among them for which a risk of fraud may be more likely to exist

      (6) Whether and how management communicates to employees its views on business practices and ethical behavior

   c. **Inquiries of Others** The auditor should inquire of others within the entity about the existence or suspicion of fraud.

      (1) Internal auditors should be asked whether they have performed any procedures to detect fraud, and if these resulted in the discovery of any fraud, how management responded to their findings.

      (2) The auditor should use professional judgment to determine those others within the entity to whom inquiries should be directed and the extent of such inquiries. To make this determination, the auditor should consider those who may have additional knowledge about or be able to corroborate risks of fraud identified in the discussions with management or those charged with governance.

      An example of others the auditor may approach include employees involved in the handling of complex or unusual transactions. Talking with in-house legal counsel is also often helpful. And to gain additional perspective, the auditor may wish to talk with personnel in operations or at least **not** involved in the financial reporting process.

d. **Analytical Procedure Results** The auditor should consider any unusual or unexpected relationships, particularly those involving revenue accounts, that have been identified in performing analytical procedures during the planning of the audit. However, because analytical procedures generally use data aggregated at a high level, their results should be considered along with other evidence.

e. **Fraud Risk Factors** The auditor should consider evidence that indicates the existence of the three conditions that are conducive to fraud (covered earlier in this section—incentives or pressures to perpetrate fraud; opportunities to carry out the fraud; and attitudes or rationalizations to justify a fraudulent action). All three do not need to be evident for the auditor to conclude there may be risks. Circumstances or events that can create these conditions are known as fraud risk factors. Fraud risk factors do not necessarily indicate the existence of fraud, but they are often present where fraud exists.

(1) **Examples of Risk Factors Relating to Misstatements Due to Fraudulent Financial Reporting**

• **Incentives / Pressures**

• Financial stability or profitability is threatened by economic, industry, or entity operating conditions, such as or as indicated by (1) a high degree of competition or market saturation, accompanied by declining margins; (2) a high vulnerability to rapid changes, such as changes in technology, product obsolescence, or interest rates; (3) significant declines in customer demand and increasing business failures in either the industry or overall economy; (4) operating losses making the threat of bankruptcy, foreclosure, or hostile takeover imminent; (5) recurring negative cash flows from operations and an inability to generate cash flows from operations while reporting earnings and earnings growth; (6) rapid growth or unusual profitability, especially compared to that of other companies in the same industry; or (7) new accounting, statutory, or regulatory requirements.

• Excessive pressure exists for management to meet the requirements or expectations of third parties due to (1) profitability or trend level expectations of investment analysts, institutional investors, significant creditors, or other external parties (particularly expectations that are unduly aggressive or unrealistic), including expectations created by management in, for example, overly optimistic press releases or annual report messages; (2) the need to obtain additional debt or equity financing to stay competitive—including financing of major research and development or capital expenditures; (3) a marginal ability to meet exchange listing requirements or debt repayment or other debt covenant requirements; or (4) perceived or real adverse effects of reporting poor financial results on significant pending transactions, such as business combinations or contract awards.

• Information available indicates that management's or those charged with governance's personal financial situation is threatened by the entity's financial performance arising from (1) significant financial interests in the entity; (2) significant portions of their compensation (for example, bonuses, stock options, and earn-out arrangements) being contingent upon achieving aggressive targets for stock price, operating results, financial position, or cash flow; or (3) personal guarantees of debts of the entity.

- There is excessive pressure on management or operating personnel to meet financial targets set up by those charged with governance or management, including sales or profitability incentive goals.

- **Opportunities**

  - The nature of the industry or the entity's operations provides opportunities to engage in fraudulent financial reporting that can arise from (1) significant related-party transactions not in the ordinary course of business or with related entities not audited or audited by another firm; (2) a strong financial presence or ability to dominate a certain industry sector that allows the entity to dictate terms or conditions to suppliers or customers that may result in inappropriate or nonarm's-length transactions; (3) assets, liabilities, revenues, or expenses based on significant estimates that involve subjective judgments or uncertainties that are difficult to corroborate; (4) significant, unusual, or highly complex transactions, especially those close to period end that pose difficult "substance over form" questions; (5) significant operations located or conducted across international borders in jurisdictions where differing business environments and cultures exist; or (6) significant bank accounts or subsidiary or branch operations in tax-haven jurisdictions for which there appears to be no clear business justification.

  - There is ineffective monitoring of management as a result of (1) domination of management by a single person or small group (in a nonowner-managed business) without compensating controls; or (2) ineffective oversight over the financial reporting process and internal control by those charged with governance.

  - There is a complex or unstable organizational structure, as evidenced by (1) difficulty in determining the organization or individuals that have controlling interest in the entity; (2) overly complex organizational structure involving unusual legal entities or managerial lines of authority; or (3) high turnover of senior management, counsel, or board members.

  - Internal control components are deficient as a result of (1) inadequate monitoring of controls, including automated controls and controls over interim financial reporting (where external reporting is required); (2) high turnover rates or employment of ineffective accounting, internal audit, or information technology staff; or (3) ineffective accounting and information systems, including situations involving significant deficiencies or material weaknesses in internal control.

- **Attitudes / Rationalizations**

  - Ineffective communication, implementation, support, or enforcement of the entity's values or ethical standards by management or the communication of inappropriate values or ethical standards

- Nonfinancial management's excessive participation in or preoccupation with the selection of accounting principles or the determination of significant estimates

- Known history of violations of securities laws or other laws and regulations, or claims against the entity, its senior management, or board members alleging fraud or violations of laws and regulations

- Excessive interest by management in maintaining or increasing the entity's stock price or earnings trend

- A practice by management of committing to analysts, creditors, and other third parties to achieve aggressive or unrealistic forecasts

- Management failing to correct known significant deficiencies or material weaknesses in internal control on a timely basis

- An interest by management in employing inappropriate means to minimize reported earnings for tax-motivated reasons

- Recurring attempts by management to justify marginal or inappropriate accounting on the basis of materiality

- The relationship between management and the current or predecessor auditor is strained, as exhibited by (1) frequent disputes with the current or predecessor auditor on accounting, auditing, or reporting matters; (2) unreasonable demands on the auditor, such as unreasonable time constraints regarding the completion of the audit or the issuance of the auditor's report; (3) formal or informal restrictions on the auditor that inappropriately limit access to people or information or the ability to communicate effectively with those charged with governance; or (4) domineering management behavior in dealing with the auditor, especially involving attempts to influence the scope of the auditor's work or the selection or continuance of personnel assigned to or consulted on the audit engagement.

(2)   **Examples of Risk Factors Relating to Misstatements Due to Misappropriation of Assets**

- **Incentives / Pressures**

    - Personal financial obligations may create pressure on management or employees with access to cash or other assets susceptible to theft to misappropriate those assets.

    - Adverse relationships between the entity and employees with access to cash or other assets susceptible to theft may motivate those employees to misappropriate those assets. For example, adverse relationships may be created by (1) known or anticipated future employee layoffs; (2) recent or anticipated changes to employee compensation or benefit plans; or (3) promotions, compensation, or other rewards inconsistent with expectations.

- **Opportunities**

    - Certain characteristics or circumstances may increase the susceptibility of assets to misappropriation. For example, opportunities to misappropriate assets increase when there are (1) large amounts of cash on hand or processed; (2) inventory items that are small in size, of high value, or in high demand; (3) easily convertible assets, such as bearer bonds, diamonds, or computer chips; or (4) fixed assets that are small in size, marketable, or lacking observable identification of ownership.

- Inadequate internal control over assets may increase the susceptibility of misappropriation of those assets. For example, misappropriation of assets may occur because there is / are (1) inadequate segregation of duties or independent checks; (2) inadequate management oversight of employees responsible for assets, for example, inadequate supervision or monitoring of remote locations; (3) inadequate job applicant screening of employees with access to assets; (4) inadequate record keeping with respect to assets; (5) an inadequate system of authorization and approval of transactions (for example, in purchasing); (6) inadequate physical safeguards over cash, investments, inventory, or fixed assets; (7) a lack of complete and timely reconciliations of assets; (8) a lack of timely and appropriate documentation of transactions, for example, credits for merchandise returns; (9) a lack of mandatory vacations for employees performing key control functions; (10) inadequate management understanding of information technology, which enables information technology employees to perpetrate a misappropriation; or (11) inadequate access controls over automated records, including controls over and review of computer systems event logs.

- **Attitudes / Rationalizations**

  - Disregard for the need for monitoring or reducing risks related to misappropriations of assets

  - Disregard for internal control over misappropriation of assets by overriding existing controls or by failing to correct known internal control deficiencies

  - Behavior indicating displeasure or dissatisfaction with the company or its treatment of the employee

  - Changes in behavior or lifestyle that may indicate assets have been misappropriated

f. **Other Information Gained Throughout the Audit** Information from reviews of interim financial statements or from procedures relating to the acceptance and continuance of clients and engagements may be helpful in assessing the RMM due to fraud. Inherent risks of assertions or those identified at the account balance or class of transaction level should also be considered in relation to the RMM due to fraud.

The auditor's assessment of the RMM due to fraud should be ongoing throughout the audit. Conditions may be identified during fieldwork that change or support a judgment regarding the assessment of the risks, such as discrepancies in the accounting records; conflicting or missing audit evidence; and problematic or unusual relationships between the auditor and management.

g. **Consideration of the Entity's Controls That Address Fraud** The auditor should consider whether such programs and controls mitigate the identified RMM due to fraud or whether specific control deficiencies may exacerbate the risks.

h. **Final Review** At or near the completion of fieldwork, the auditor should evaluate whether the accumulated results of auditing procedures and other observations affect the assessment of the RMM due to fraud made earlier in the audit. This evaluation primarily is a qualitative matter based on the auditor's judgment. Such an evaluation may provide further insight about the RMM due to fraud and whether there is a need to perform additional or different audit procedures. As part of this evaluation, the auditor with final responsibility for the audit should ascertain that there has been appropriate communication with the other audit team members throughout the audit regarding information or conditions indicative of RMM due to fraud.

C.   Response to the Risk of Material Misstatement Due to Fraud

1.   **Overall Response** Judgments about the RMM due to fraud have an overall effect on how the audit is conducted.

a.   **Assignment of Personnel & Supervision** The knowledge, skill, and ability of personnel assigned significant engagement responsibilities should be commensurate with the auditor's assessment of the RMM due to fraud.

b.   **Accounting Principles** The auditor should consider management's selection and application of significant accounting principles, particularly those related to subjective measurements and complex transactions, to determine if their collective application indicates a bias that may create such a material misstatement of the financial statements.

c.   **Predictability of Auditing Procedures** The auditor should incorporate an element of unpredictability in the selection of auditing procedures from year to year—for example, performing substantive tests of selected account balances and assertions not otherwise tested due to their materiality or risk, adjusting the timing of testing from that otherwise expected, using differing sampling methods, and performing procedures at different locations or at locations on an unannounced basis.

2.   **Responses Involving the Nature, Extent, & Timing of Audit Procedures** The auditing procedures performed in response to identified RMM due to fraud will vary depending upon the types of risks identified and the account balances, classes of transactions, and related assertions that may be affected. These procedures may involve both substantive tests and tests of the operating effectiveness of the entity's programs and controls. However, because management may have the ability to override controls that otherwise appear to be operating effectively, it is unlikely that audit risk can be reduced to an appropriately low level by performing only tests of controls.

The auditor's responses to address specifically identified RMM due to fraud may include changing the nature, extent, and timing of auditing procedures in the following ways.

a.   **Nature** The nature of auditing procedures may need to be changed to obtain evidence that is more reliable or to obtain additional corroborative information. Also, physical observation or inspection of certain assets may become more important.

b.   **Extent** The extent of the procedures applied should reflect the assessment of the RMM due to fraud. For example, increasing sample sizes or performing analytical procedures at a more detailed level may be appropriate.

c.   **Timing** The timing of substantive tests may need to be modified. For example, the auditor might conclude that substantive testing should be performed at or near the end of the reporting period.

3.   **Responses to Further Address the Risk of Management Override of Controls** Management is in a unique position to perpetrate fraud because of its ability manipulate accounting records and prepare fraudulent financial statements by overriding established controls. By its nature, management override of controls can occur in unpredictable ways. Accordingly, in addition to overall responses and responses that address specifically identified RMM due to fraud, further audit procedures should be performed to address the risk of management override of controls. The results of these procedures should be documented. These include:

a.   **Examining Journal Entries** Material misstatements of financial statements due to fraud often involve the manipulation of the financial reporting process by recording inappropriate or unauthorized journal entries; or making adjustments to amounts reported in the financial statements that are not reflected in formal journal entries, such as through consolidating adjustments, report combinations, and reclassifications. Accordingly, the auditor should examine journal entries and other adjustments for evidence of possible material misstatement due to fraud. The selection of the appropriate journal entries should be based on the auditor's understanding and the nature of the entity's financial reporting process and influenced by the assessment of the effectiveness of the related controls. Other selection factors include the characteristics of the journal entries and the nature and complexity of the affected accounts. Special attention should be paid to journal entries processed outside of the normal course of business.

b.   **Reviewing Accounting Estimates for Biases** Fraudulent financial reporting often is accomplished through intentional misstatement of accounting estimates. The auditor should consider whether differences between estimates supported by the audit evidence and those included in the financial statements, even if they are individually reasonable, indicate a possible bias, in which case the auditor should reconsider the estimates taken as a whole.

The auditor should also compare current year estimates to the prior year's to determine (with the aid of hindsight) if there are indications of bias. The significant accounting estimates selected for testing should include those that are based on highly sensitive assumptions or are otherwise significantly affected by judgments made by management.

c.   **Evaluating the Business Rationale for Significant Unusual Transactions** The auditor should gain an understanding of the business rationale for such transactions and whether that rationale (or the lack thereof) suggests that the transactions may have been entered into to engage in fraudulent financial reporting or conceal misappropriation of assets.

4.   **Withdrawal** The auditor may conclude that it would not be practicable to design auditing procedures that sufficiently address the RMM due to fraud. In that case, withdrawal from the engagement with communication to the appropriate parties may be an appropriate course of action.

D.   Evaluation of Evidence

1.   **Immaterial Misstatements Due to Fraud** Even if the misstatements due to fraud are not material to the financial statements, the auditor should evaluate the implications for the integrity of management and employees and the possible effects on other aspects of the audit. The auditor should reevaluate the assessment of the RMM due to fraud and its resulting impact on the nature, extent, and timing of the tests of balances or transactions and the assessment of the effectiveness of controls if control risk was assessed below the maximum.

2.   **Material Misstatements Due to Fraud** If the auditor believes that the misstatement could be material, the auditor should:

a.   **Obtain Additional Evidence** Attempt to obtain additional audit evidence to determine whether material fraud has occurred or is likely to have occurred

b.   **Effect on Financial Statements & Audit Report** If fraud has occurred, determine its effect on the financial statements and the audit report

c.   **Impact on Other Aspects of the Audit** Consider the implications for other aspects of the audit

      d.   **Discuss with Management & Those Charged With Governance** Discuss the matter and the approach for further investigation with a level of management that is at least one level above those involved, and with senior management and those charged with governance

      e.   **Legal Counsel** If appropriate, suggest that the client consult with legal counsel

3.   **Withdrawal** The auditor's consideration of the RMM and the results of audit tests may indicate such a significant RMM due to fraud that the auditor should consider withdrawing from the engagement and communicating the reasons for withdrawal to those charged with governance. Whether to withdraw may depend on the implications about the integrity of management and the diligence and cooperation of management or the board of directors in investigating the circumstances and taking appropriate action. The auditor may wish to consult with legal counsel when considering withdrawal from an engagement.

E.   **Communications**

1.   **Those Charged With Governance & Management** The appropriate level of management should be informed whenever the auditor detects evidence of possible fraud, even if the matter is insignificant.

The auditor should report any fraud involving senior management or fraud causing a material misstatement of the financial statements directly to those charged with governance. The auditor should reach an agreement with those charged with governance about the nature and extent of communications regarding fraud by lower level employees.

If the auditor's assessment of the RMM due to fraud has identified risks that have continuing control implications that could represent significant deficiencies or material weaknesses in internal control the auditor is required to communicate those, in writing, to management and those charged with governance.

2.   **Outside Parties** The auditor's ethical and legal obligations regarding confidentiality generally preclude the auditor from the disclosure of possible fraud to outside parties unless the matter is reflected in the audit report; however, there are exceptions. In the following circumstances, an auditor may need to disclose information. The auditor may want to consult with legal counsel beforehand.

      a.   To comply with legal and regulatory requirements

      b.   To a successor auditor making inquiries in accordance with GAAS

      c.   In response to a subpoena

      d.   To a funding agency or other specified agency in accordance with requirements for the audits of entities that receive governmental financial assistance

F.   **Documentation**
The auditor should document:

1.   The discussion among engagement personnel in planning the audit regarding the susceptibility of the entity's financial statements to material misstatement due to fraud, including how and when the discussion occurred, the audit team members who participated, and the subject matter discussed

2.   The procedures performed to identify and assess the RMM due to fraud

3.   Specific RMM due to fraud that were identified, and a description of the auditor's response to those risks

4. If the auditor has not identified, in a particular circumstance, improper revenue recognition as a RMM due to fraud, the reasons supporting the auditor's conclusion

5. The results of the procedures performed to further address the risk of management override of controls

6. Other conditions and analytical relationships that caused the auditor to believe that additional auditing procedures or other responses were required and any further responses the auditor concluded were appropriate, to address such risks or other conditions

7. The nature of the communications about fraud made to management, those charged with governance, and others

VI. Assessing the Risk of Material Misstatement (AU 314 continued)

A. Steps
The auditor should identify and evaluate the RMM at the relevant assertions level as well as at the financial statement level. More specifically, the auditor should:

1. **Identify Risks** Identify risks throughout the process of obtaining an understanding of the entity and its environment, including related internal controls, as well as while considering the classes of transactions, account balances, and disclosures in the financial statements.

2. **Identify Potential Misstatements** Relate the identified risks to types of potential misstatements that could occur at the relevant assertion level.

3. **Consider Materiality** Consider whether any identified risks are so significant that they could cause a material misstatement of the financial statements.

4. **Consider Probability** Consider the probability that identified risks will cause a material misstatement of the financial statements.

B. Support
The auditor should use the information gathered from risk assessment procedures, including the audit evidence obtained in evaluating the design and implementation of controls, as evidence to support the risk assessment. The auditor should use the risk assessment to determine the nature, extent, and timing of further audit procedures. If the risk assessment is based on an expectation that controls are operating effectively to prevent or detect material misstatements, the auditor should test the operating effectiveness of controls that have been determined to be suitably designed to prevent or detect material misstatements.

C. Pervasiveness
The auditor should determine whether the identified risks relate to specific relevant assertions related to classes of transactions, account balances, and disclosures, or whether they are more pervasive and relate to the financial statements taken as a whole. For example, a weak control environment creates risks that are not likely to be confined to specific assertions, but rather relate to the financial statements as a whole.

D. Significant Risks
The auditor should use professional judgment to determine which identified risks are *significant risks* that require special audit consideration. The auditor should consider inherent risk to determine whether the nature of the risk, the materiality of the potential misstatement including the likelihood of multiple misstatements, and the probability of occurrence are such that they require special audit consideration.

1. **Nature** In considering the nature of identified risks, the auditor should consider the following:

   a. Whether the risk is a risk of fraud

    b.   Whether the risk is related to recent significant economic, accounting, or other developments and, therefore, requires specific attention

    c.   The complexity of transactions

    d.   Whether the risk involves significant transactions with related parties

    e.   The degree of subjectivity involved in the measurement of financial information related to the risks, especially those involving a wide range of measurement uncertainty

    f.   Whether the risk involves significant nonroutine or unusual transactions that are outside the normal course of business

2.   **Nonroutine Transactions** Nonroutine transactions are transactions that are unusual, either due to size or nature, and therefore, occur infrequently.

The RMM related to nonroutine transactions may be greater when the following circumstances are involved:

    a.   Greater management intervention to specify accounting treatment

    b.   Greater manual intervention for data collection and processing

    c.   Complex calculations or accounting principles

    d.   Difficult implementation of effective controls over the risks due to the nature of the transaction

    e.   Significant related-party transactions

3.   **Judgmental Matters** Judgmental matters may include the development of accounting estimates for which there is significant measurement uncertainty.

The RMM related to judgmental matters requiring the development of accounting estimates may be greater when the following matters are involved:

    a.   Accounting principles for estimates or revenue recognition are subject to different interpretations

    b.   Required judgment is subjective, complex, or requires assumptions about the effects of future events

E.   **Risks Requiring Tests of Controls**
The auditor should identify those risks for which it is not possible or practicable to obtain sufficient audit evidence from substantive procedures alone. Such risks may concern routine transactions that are often highly automated with little or no manual intervention. In these cases, audit evidence may be available only in electronic form; therefore, its appropriateness and sufficiency often depend on the operating effectiveness of controls over its completeness and accuracy.

F.   **Risk Assessment Revision**
The auditor's assessment of the RMM is based on audit evidence available; therefore, as additional audit evidence is obtained, this risk assessment may need to be revised during the course of the audit. For example, in performing tests of controls, the auditor may obtain audit evidence that controls are not operating effectively. Also, while performing substantive procedures, the auditor may detect more misstatements than is consistent with the auditor's original risk assessment. Thus, in these circumstances, the auditor should modify the assessment and adjust further audit procedures accordingly.

G. **Documentation**
The auditor should document:

1. The assessment of the RMM at the financial statement and relevant assertion levels

2. The basis for that assessment

3. Significant risks identified and related controls evaluated

4. Risks identified that require tests of controls to obtain sufficient audit evidence (when substantive procedures alone are not adequate) and the related controls evaluated

VII. Responding to Assessed Risks (AU 318)

A. **Financial Statement Level**
The auditor should develop overall responses to address the assessed RMM at the financial statement level. Some responses to consider include:

1. **Professional Skepticism** More emphasis on the need to maintain professional skepticism in gathering and evaluating audit evidence

2. **Assignments** Assignment of more experienced staff or those with specialized skills or the use of specialists

3. **Supervision** Increase supervision

4. **Unpredictability** Incorporation of more unpredictable elements in further audit procedures

5. **General Changes** General changes to the nature, extent, or timing of further audit procedures; an example of this would be to perform substantive procedures at the end of the period instead of at an interim date in response to weaknesses in the control environment; other general changes may include seeking more extensive audit evidence from substantive procedures, modifying the nature of audit procedures to obtain more persuasive audit evidence, or increasing the number of locations to be included in the audit scope

B. **Relevant Assertion Level**
The auditor should design and perform further audit procedures whose nature, extent, and timing are responsive to the assessed RMM at the relevant assertion level. In designing further audit procedures, the auditor should consider such matters as: the significance of the risk; the probability that a material misstatement will occur; the characteristics of the class of transactions, account balance, or disclosure involved; the nature of specific controls, including whether they are manual or automated; and whether the auditor expects to obtain audit evidence to determine if the entity's controls are effective in preventing or detecting material misstatements.

1. **Audit Approach** Performing substantive procedures alone may be appropriate for specific relevant assertions and risks; hence, the auditor may ignore the effect of controls. This may be because risk assessment procedures have not identified any effective controls relevant to the assertion or because testing the operating effectiveness of controls would not be efficient. However, the auditor must be satisfied that performing only substantive procedures for specific assertions would be effective in reducing detection risk to an acceptably low level. A combined approach using both tests of controls and substantive tests is often most effective.

    a. Regardless of the audit approach selected, the auditor should design and perform substantive procedures for all relevant assertions related to each material class of transactions, account balance, and disclosure. Also, analytical procedures alone may not be sufficient in some instances.

    b.   Sometimes small entities do not have many control activities that can be identified by the auditor. In these circumstances, further audit procedures will most likely consist primarily of substantive procedures.

2.   **Nature** The nature of procedures refers to whether they are tests of controls or substantive procedures as well as their type (i.e., inspection, observation, inquiry, confirmation, recalculation, reperformance, or analytical procedures). The nature of audit procedures is the most important consideration in responding to assessed risks.

    a.   **Appropriateness** Some audit procedures are more appropriate for some assertions than others. For example, in relation to revenue, tests of controls may be more appropriate to test the completeness assertion, whereas substantive procedures may more appropriate to test the occurrence assertion.

    b.   **Basis** The selection of audit procedures should be based on the risk assessment; thus, the higher the risk, the more reliable and relevant the audit evidence should be. This will affect the type and combination of audit procedures. The auditor should consider both the inherent risk and control risk of each class of transactions, account balance, or disclosure. For example, if the auditor determines that there is low inherent risk regardless of the related controls; substantive analytical procedures alone may provide sufficient appropriate audit evidence. Alternatively, if the auditor expects there is low control risk because an entity has effective controls and the auditor intends to design substantive procedures based on the operating effectiveness of those controls, then the auditor should perform tests of controls also.

3.   **Timing** This refers to when audit procedures are performed as well as the period or date for which the audit evidence is applicable.

    a.   **Interim Date** The auditor may perform further audit procedures at an interim date or at the end of the period. The higher the RMM, the more effective it may be to perform substantive procedures nearer to, or at, the period end. It may also be effective to perform audit procedures at unpredictable times. However, while performing audit procedures at an interim date, the auditor may detect significant issues at an early stage of the audit. This will give management more time to resolve such issues or the auditor more time to adjust the audit approach to address such issues. If the auditor performs tests of controls or substantive procedures at an interim date, the auditor will need to consider the additional evidence for the remaining period that is necessary.

    b.   **Period End** Certain procedures can be performed only at or after period end such as agreeing the financial statements to the accounting records.

    c.   **Additional Considerations** The auditor also should consider the following factors when planning the timing of audit procedures:

        (1)   The control environment

        (2)   When relevant information is available, for example, electronic files may only be available for a short amount of time

        (3)   The nature of the risk, for example, if there is a risk of overstatement of revenues to meet earnings expectations by subsequent creation of false sales agreements, the auditor may examine contracts available on the date of the period end

        (4)   The period or date to which the audit evidence will relate

4.   **Extent** This refers to the quantity of a specific audit procedure to be performed; for example, a sample size or the number of observations of a control activity may vary. Generally, the extent of audit procedures should increase as the RMM increases.

The extent of an audit procedure is a matter of professional judgment. In making this judgment, the auditor should consider:

a.   Tolerable misstatement

b.   Assessed RMM

c.   Degree of assurance the auditor plans to obtain

C.   **Documentation**
The auditor should document:

1.   Overall responses to address the assessed risks of misstatement at the financial statement level

2.   Nature, extent, and timing of the further audit procedures

3.   Connection of those procedures with the assessed risks at the relevant assertion level

4.   Results of the audit procedures

5.   Conclusions reached concerning the use of audit evidence about the operating effectiveness of controls that was obtained in a prior audit

VIII. Illegal Acts by Clients

A.   **Illegal Acts**
Illegal acts are defined as violations of laws or governmental regulations by management or employees acting on behalf of an entity. Illegal acts by clients do not include personal misconduct by the entity's personnel unrelated to their business activities.

1.   **Focus on Effect on the Financial Statements** Illegal acts vary considerably in their relation to the financial statements. Generally, the further removed an illegal act is from the events and transactions ordinarily reflected in financial statements, the less likely the auditor is to become aware of the act or to recognize its possible illegality. Generally, the auditor leaves the determination of the legality of an act to an expert qualified to practice law or to a court of law.

2.   **Direct vs. Indirect Effect on the Financial Statements**

a.   **Direct Effect** The auditor considers laws and regulations that have a direct and material effect on the determination of financial statement amounts, for example, tax laws. The nature of the auditor's responsibility to detect and report misstatements resulting from illegal acts having a direct and material effect on the financial statements is the same as that for misstatements caused by error or fraud.

b.   **Indirect Effect** Entities may be affected by many other laws or regulations, including those related to securities trading, occupational safety and health, food and drug administration, environmental protection, equal employment, and price-fixing or other antitrust violations. Generally, these laws and regulations relate more to an entity's operating aspects than to its financial and accounting aspects, and their financial statement effect is indirect. Their indirect effect is normally the result of the need to disclose a contingent liability because of the allegation or determination of illegality.

Normally, an audit in accordance with GAAS does not include audit procedures specifically designed to detect illegal acts. If information comes to the auditor's attention that provides evidence concerning the existence of possible illegal acts that could have a material indirect effect on the financial statements, the auditor should apply audit procedures specifically directed to ascertaining whether an illegal act has occurred. However, because of the characteristics of "indirect effect" illegal acts, an audit made in accordance with GAAS provides no assurance that illegal acts will be detected or that any contingent liabilities that may result will be disclosed.

3. **Red Flags** In applying audit procedures, the auditor may encounter information (or "red flags") that may raise a question concerning possible illegal acts, such as the following:

   a. Unauthorized or improperly recorded transactions

   b. Investigation by a governmental agency

   c. Large payments for unspecified services to consultants

   d. Excessive sales commissions or agents' fees

   e. Unusually large cash payments

   f. Unexplained payments to government officials or employees

   g. Failure to file tax returns

   h. Forced discontinuance of operations in a foreign country

4. **Relation to Financial Statements** The auditor normally considers only those laws and regulations having a direct and material effect on the financial statement amounts. The auditor is required to consider illegal acts that could have a direct and material effect on the financial statements (e.g., violations of tax law) and consider that in the design of substantive tests.

   a. **Indirect** An entity may be affected by many laws or regulations relating more to its operating aspects than to the financial statements. An auditor ordinarily does not have sufficient basis for recognizing possible violations of laws and regulations (for example, shipping regulations for tractor-trailers or maritime vessels).

   b. **Notification** The auditor may not become aware of illegal acts that could have an indirect effect on the financial statements unless the client discloses such information, or there is evidence of a governmental agency investigation or enforcement proceeding in the records normally inspected in an audit. Examples would include price-fixing, equal employment violations, and occupational safety and health violations.

B. **Procedures**
Normally, an audit conducted in accordance with GAAS does not include procedures specifically designed to detect illegal acts. During the course of an audit, however, other audit procedures may bring illegal acts to the auditor's attention. Such procedures may include the following: reading minutes; inquiring of client's management and legal counsel concerning litigation, claims, and assessments; and performing substantive tests of details of transactions or balances. The auditor also should make inquiries of management concerning the client's compliance with laws and regulations, and the client's policies to prevent illegal acts. The auditor should obtain written representations from management concerning the absence of violations or possible violations of laws or regulations whose effects must be considered for disclosure in the financial statements or as a basis for recording a loss contingency.

1. **Possible Illegal Act** If a possible illegal act has occurred, the auditor should obtain an understanding of the act, the circumstances under which it occurred, and sufficient information to evaluate its effect on the financial statements. The auditor may wish to consult with the client's legal counsel or other specialists regarding the possible illegal act and its effects, and additional procedures may be applied, if necessary, to obtain further understanding of the acts.

2. **Additional Procedures** Additional audit procedures may include the following:

a. Examining supporting documents, such as invoices, canceled checks, and agreements, and comparing them with accounting records

b. Confirming significant information concerning the matter with the other party to the transaction or with intermediaries, such as banks or lawyers

c. Determining whether the transaction has been authorized properly

d. Considering whether other similar transactions or events may have occurred, and applying procedures to identify them

C. Financial Statement Effect
When an illegal act has occurred, the auditor should consider both the quantitative and qualitative materiality of the act on the financial statements as well as the implications for other aspects of the audit, such as the reliability of representations of management. The illegal act may involve contingent liabilities that must be disclosed. The auditor should consider whether material revenue or earnings are derived from transactions involving illegal acts, or if illegal acts create significant unusual risks associated with material revenue or earnings.

D. Communication With Those Charged With Governance
The auditor should ascertain that those charged with governance are adequately informed about illegal acts that come to the auditor's attention. The communication should describe the act, the circumstances, and the effect on the financial statements. If senior management is involved in an illegal act, the auditor should communicate directly with those charged with governance. The communication may be written or oral. If oral, it should be documented. The auditor need not communicate inconsequential matters.

E. Audit Report
If the client refuses to accept the audit report as modified, the auditor should withdraw from the engagement and indicate the reasons for doing so in writing to the audit committee or board of directors.

1. **Not Disclosed** If the auditor concludes that an illegal act having a material effect on the financial statements has occurred, and the act has not been accounted for or disclosed properly, the auditor should express a qualified opinion or an adverse opinion, depending on the materiality.

2. **Scope Limitation** If the auditor is precluded by the client from obtaining sufficient audit evidence to determine whether an illegal act that could be material has, or is likely to have, occurred, (i.e., a scope limitation), the auditor should disclaim an opinion on the financial statements.

F. Other Considerations
The auditor may decide that withdrawal is necessary when the client does not take remedial action that the auditor considers necessary, even when the illegal act is not material to the financial statements.

1. **Management Integrity** The auditor should consider the implications of an illegal act in relation to other aspects of the audit, particularly the reliability of management representations.

2. **Outside Parties** The auditor may wish to consult with legal counsel before discussing illegal acts with outside parties. Disclosure of illegal acts to outside parties may be necessary in certain circumstances, such as

a. When the entity reports an auditor change under the appropriate securities law on Form 8-K; also see the information on the Private Securities Litigation Reform Act of 1995 below

b. To an auditor making inquiries in accordance with AU 315, *Communications Between Predecessor and Successor Auditors*

c. In response to a subpoena

d. To a funding agency or other specified agency in accordance with requirements for the audits of entities that receive governmental financial assistance

3. **Private Securities Litigation Reform Act of 1995** Auditors must include procedures that are designed to:

- Provide reasonable assurance of detecting illegal acts that would have a direct and material effect on the financial statements

- Identify related-party transactions that are material to the financial statements or otherwise require disclosure in the financial statements

- Evaluate an issuer's ability to continue as a going concern during the ensuing fiscal year

a. **Report by the Auditor to the Issuer** An auditor who becomes aware of possible illegal activities (whether or not perceived to have a material effect on the financial statements) should inform management and assure that those charged with governance are adequately informed. If the illegal act has a material effect on the financial statements and management has not taken appropriate remedial action, and thus, departure from a standard audit report or resignation from the engagement is warranted, the auditor should report this directly to those charged with governance of the issuer.

b. **Notification of the SEC** The issuer is required to notify the SEC no later than 1 business day after the receipt of such a report and furnish the auditor with a copy of the notice sent to the SEC. If the issuer fails to notify the SEC thusly, the auditor must furnish a copy of the report to the SEC no later than 1 business day following such failure to receive notice even if the auditor has resigned from the engagement.

4. **Foreign Corrupt Practices Act of 1977 (FCPA)**

a. **Antibribery Provisions** The antibribery provisions of the FCPA make it illegal for a US person or company, and any foreign company or person acting while in the United States, to bribe a foreign government official for the purpose of obtaining or retaining business. Companies are subject to a fine of up to $2 million while individuals are subject to a maximum fine of $100,000 and up to 5 years imprisonment. Moreover, under the Alternative Fines Act, these fines may actually be quite higher—the actual fine may be up to twice the benefit that the defendant sought to obtain by making the corrupt payment. Fines imposed on individuals cannot be paid by their employers. In addition, civil penalties may be imposed.

b. **Required Accounting Provisions** The FCPA also requires companies whose securities are listed in the United States (issuers registered with the SEC) to maintain records, which, in reasonable detail, accurately and fairly reflect the transactions and dispositions of assets of the company. It also requires issuers to maintain a system of internal accounting control sufficient to provide reasonable assurance that:

(1) Transactions are executed in accordance with management's authorization

(2) Transactions are recorded as necessary to permit preparation of financial statements in conformity with GAAP (or other criteria applicable to such statements) and to maintain accountability for assets

(3) Access to assets is restricted to those authorized by management

(4) The recorded accountability for assets is reconciled to existing assets at reasonable intervals and appropriate action is taken for any discrepancies

These accounting provisions are designed to act in tandem with the FCPA's anti-bribery provisions to prevent slush funds (accounts used to make illegal payments) or the misrepresentation of expenses. The FCPA does **not** require the auditor to issue a special report on internal control.

G. **Responsibilities in Other Circumstances**
An auditor may accept an engagement that entails, by agreement with the client, a greater responsibility for detecting illegal acts than a typical audit. For example, an auditor may be engaged to test and report on compliance with specific government regulations.

IX. **Communication With Those Charged With Governance (AU 380)**

A. **Definitions**

1. **Those Charged With Governance** Persons with responsibility for overseeing the strategic direction of the entity and obligations related to the accountability of the entity are defined as those charged with governance. This includes overseeing the financial reporting process. (The term *those charged with governance* encompasses the terms *board of directors* and *audit committee*.)

2. **Management** Those responsible for achieving the objectives of the entity and who have the authority to establish policies and make decisions by which those objectives are to be pursued are termed management. Their responsibilities include the financial statements and the system of internal control over financial reporting.

B. **Matters to Be Communicated to Those Charged With Governance**
Matters related to the financial statements that are significant and relevant to the responsibilities of those charged with governance in overseeing the financial reporting process must be communicated by the auditor. However, communication by the auditor does not relieve management of their responsibility to communicate matters of interest to those charged with governance.

1. **GAAS** The auditor should communicate the auditor's responsibilities under GAAS, including that:

a. **Opinion** The auditor is responsible for forming and expressing an opinion about whether the financial statements that have been prepared by management with the oversight of those charged with governance are presented fairly, in all material respects, in conformity with GAAP.

b. **Responsibilities** The audit does not relieve either management or those charged with governance of their responsibilities.

c. **Independence** The auditor may determine that it is appropriate to communicate circumstances or relationships that in the auditor's professional judgment may reasonably be thought to bear on independence and that the auditor gave significant consideration to in reaching the conclusion that independence has not been impaired.

2. **Overview** An overview of the planned scope and timing of the audit should be communicated. The auditor must exercise professional judgment in determining the nature and extent of this communication. For example, communicating the nature and timing of specific audit procedures may make them too predictable.

3. **Significant Findings** The auditor should communicate significant findings from the audit, including:

   a. The auditor's views about qualitative aspects of the entity's significant accounting practices, including accounting policies, accounting estimates, and financial statement disclosures

   b. Significant difficulties, if any, encountered during the audit

   c. Uncorrected misstatements, other than those the auditor believes are trivial, if any

   d. Disagreements with management, if any

   e. Other findings or issues, if any, arising from the audit that are, in the auditor's professional judgment, significant and relevant to those charged with governance regarding their oversight of the financial reporting process

   And, unless all of those charged with governance are involved in managing the entity, the auditor also should communicate:

   f. Material, corrected misstatements that were brought to the attention of management as a result of audit procedures

   g. Representations the auditor is requesting from management

   h. Management's consultations with other accountants

   i. Significant issues, if any, arising from the audit that were discussed, or the subject of correspondence, with management

C. **The Communication Process**
It is important that the communication process be effective and two-way, so the auditor should communicate with those charged with governance the form, timing, and expected general content of the communications. If the two-way communication is not adequate, the auditor should consider the effect, if any, on the auditor's assessment of the RMM. The auditor must exercise professional judgment as to whether the communication is oral or in writing.

D. **Documentation**
The auditor should document matters communicated orally and retain those in writing.

CHAPTER 2—PLANNING

Problem 2-1 MULTIPLE-CHOICE QUESTIONS

1. An auditor's engagement letter should include a statement regarding

   a. Management's responsibility to provide certain written representations to the auditor
   b. Conditions under which the auditor may modify the preliminary judgment about materiality
   c. Internal control activities that would reduce the auditor's assessment of control risk
   d. Materiality matters that could modify the auditor's preliminary assessment of fraud risk

   (R/05, AUD, #35, amended, ID: 7830)

2. An auditor is required to establish an understanding with a client regarding the services to be performed for each engagement. This understanding generally includes

   a. The auditor's responsibility for determining the preliminary judgments about materiality and audit risk factors
   b. Management's responsibility for identifying mitigating factors when the auditor has doubt about the entity's ability to continue as a going concern
   c. The auditor's responsibility for ensuring that the audit committee is aware of any significant deficiencies and material weaknesses that come to the auditor's attention
   d. Management's responsibility for providing the auditor with an assessment of the risk of material misstatement due to fraud

   (R/06, AUD, #12, ID: 8130)

3. During the initial planning phase of an audit, a CPA most likely would

   a. Identify specific internal control activities that are likely to prevent fraud
   b. Evaluate the reasonableness of the client's accounting estimates
   c. Discuss the timing of the audit procedure with the client's management
   d. Inquire of the client's attorney as to whether any unrecorded claims are probable of assertion

   (5/98, AUD, #2, ID: 7798)

4. An auditor should design the written audit plan (or program) so that

   a. All material transactions will be selected for substantive testing.
   b. Substantive tests prior to the balance sheet date will be minimized.
   c. The audit procedures selected will achieve specific audit objectives.
   d. Each account balance will be tested under either tests of controls or tests of transactions.

   (5/95, AUD, #16, amended, ID: 5634)

5. Which of the following procedures would an auditor most likely include in the initial planning of a financial statement audit?

   a. Obtaining a written representation letter from the client's management
   b. Examining documents to detect illegal acts having a material effect on the financial statements
   c. Considering whether the client's accounting estimates are reasonable in the circumstances
   d. Determining the extent of involvement of the client's internal auditors   (11/94, AUD, #1, ID: 5074)

6. Prior to commencing fieldwork, an auditor usually discusses the general audit strategy with the client's management. Which of the following details do management and the auditor usually agree upon at this time?

   a. The specific matters to be included in the communication with the audit committee
   b. The minimum amount of misstatements that may be considered to be significant deficiencies and material weaknesses
   c. The schedules and analyses that the client's staff should prepare
   d. The effects that inadequate controls may have over the safeguarding of assets

   (R/06, AUD, #7, ID: 8125)

7. The audit work performed by each assistant should be reviewed to determine whether it was adequately performed and to evaluate whether the

    a. Audit has been performed by persons having adequate technical training and proficiency as auditors.
    b. Auditor's system of quality control has been maintained at a high level.
    c. Results are consistent with the conclusions to be presented in the auditor's report.
    d. Audit procedures performed are approved in the professional standards.

        (11/91, AUD, #5, ID: 2273)

8. The in-charge auditor most likely would have a supervisory responsibility to explain to the staff assistants

    a. That immaterial fraud is not to be reported to the client's audit committee
    b. How the results of various auditing procedures performed by the assistants should be evaluated
    c. Why certain documents are being transferred from the current file to the permanent file
    d. What benefits may be attained by the assistant's adherence to established time budgets

        (5/95, AUD, #7, amended, ID: 5625)

9. A difference of opinion regarding the results of a sample cannot be resolved between the assistant who performed the auditing procedures and the in-charge auditor. The assistant should

    a. Accept the judgment of the more experienced in-charge auditor
    b. Refuse to perform any further work on the engagement
    c. Document the disagreement and ask to be disassociated from the resolution of the matter
    d. Notify the client that a serious audit problem exists   (Editors, ID: 209)

10. An auditor is required to establish an understanding with a client regarding the services to be performed for each engagement. This understanding generally includes

    a. Management's responsibility for errors and the illegal activities of employees that may cause material misstatement
    b. The auditor's responsibility for ensuring that the audit committee is aware of any significant deficiencies that come to the auditor's attention
    c. Management's responsibility for providing the auditor with an assessment of the risk of material misstatement due to fraud
    d. The auditor's responsibility for determining preliminary judgments about materiality and audit risk factors   (R/99, AUD, #6, amended, ID: 6822)

11. Which of the following statements would **least** likely appear in an auditor's engagement letter?

    a. Fees for our services are based on our regular per diem rates, plus travel and other out-of-pocket expenses.
    b. During the course of our audit we may observe opportunities for economy in, or improved controls over, your operations.
    c. Our engagement is subject to the risk that material errors or irregularities, including fraud and defalcations, if they exist, will not be detected.
    d. After performing our preliminary analytical procedures we will discuss with you the other procedures we consider necessary to complete the engagement.   (5/95, AUD, #3, ID: 5621)

12. An auditor's engagement letter should include

    a. Management's acknowledgment of its responsibility for maintaining effective internal control
    b. The auditor's preliminary assessment of the risk factors relating to misstatements arising from fraudulent financial reporting
    c. A reminder that management is responsible for illegal acts committed by employees
    d A request for permission to contact the client's lawyer for assistance in identifying litigation, claims, and assessments   (R/02, AUD, #3, amended, ID: 7093)

13. A document in an auditor's working papers includes the following statement:

    "Our audit is subject to the inherent risk that material errors and fraud, including defalcations, if they exist, will not be detected. However, we will inform you of fraud that comes to our attention, unless it is inconsequential."

    The above passage is most likely from a(an)

    a. Comfort letter
    b. Engagement letter
    c. Letter of audit inquiry
    d. Representation letter   (R/03, AUD, #12, ID: 7634)

14. The element of the audit planning process most likely to be agreed upon with the client before implementation of the audit strategy is the determination of the

    a. Evidence to be gathered to provide a sufficient basis for the auditor's opinion
    b. Procedures to be undertaken to discover litigation, claims, and assessments
    c. Pending legal matters to be included in the inquiry of the client's attorney
    d. Timing of inventory observation procedures to be performed   (5/95, AUD, #1, ID: 5619)

15. Which of the following procedures would an auditor most likely include in the initial planning phase of a financial statement audit?

    a. Obtain an understanding of the entity's risk assessment process
    b. Identify specific internal control activities designed to prevent fraud
    c. Evaluate the reasonableness of the entity's accounting estimates
    d. Perform cutoff tests of the entity's sales and purchases   (11/98, AUD, #18, amended, ID: 6709)

16. Audit programs should be designed so that

    a. Most of the required procedures can be performed as interim work.
    b. Inherent risk is assessed at a sufficiently low level.
    c. The auditor can make constructive suggestions to management.
    d. The audit evidence gathered supports the auditor's conclusions.   (11/94, AUD, #16, ID: 5089)

17. Which of the following factors would a CPA ordinarily consider in the planning stage of an audit engagement?

        I. Financial statement accounts likely to contain a misstatement
        II. Conditions that require extension of audit tests

    a. I only
    b. II only
    c. Both I and II
    d. Neither I nor II   (R/02, AUD, #12, ID: 7102)

18. Which of the following circumstances would permit an independent auditor to accept an engagement after the close of the fiscal year?

    a. Issuance of a disclaimer of opinion as a result of inability to conduct certain tests required by generally accepted auditing standards due to the timing of acceptance of the engagement
    b. Assessment of control risk below the maximum level
    c. Receipt of an assertion from the preceding auditor that the entity will be able to continue as a going concern
    d. Remedy of limitations resulting from accepting the engagement after the close of the end of the year, such as those relating to the existence of physical inventory   (R/08, AUD, #20, ID: 8626)

19. Which of the following statements most likely would be included in an engagement letter from an auditor to a client?

    a. The CPA firm will provide absolute assurance about whether the financial statements are free of material misstatement.
    b. The CPA firm is responsible for ensuring that the client complies with applicable laws.
    c. The CPA firm will involve information technology specialists in the performance of the audit.
    d. The CPA firm will adjust the financial statements to correct misstatements before issuing a report.

    (R/09, AUD, #34, ID: 8834)

20. Prior to, or in conjunction with, the information-gathering procedures for an audit, audit team members should discuss the potential for material misstatement due to fraud. Which of the following best characterizes the mind-set that the audit team should maintain during this discussion?

    a. Presumptive
    b. Judgmental
    c. Criticizing
    d. Questioning

    (R/11, AUD, #19, ID: 9919)

21. Inherent risk and control risk differ from detection risk in that inherent risk and control risk are

    a. Functions of the client and its environment, while detection risk is not
    b. Changed at the auditor's discretion, while detection risk is not
    c. Considered at the individual account-balance level, while detection risk is not
    d. Elements of audit risk, while detection risk is not

    (Editors, ID: 2810)

22. On the basis of audit evidence gathered and evaluated, an auditor decides to increase the assessed level of control risk from that originally planned. To achieve an overall audit risk level that is substantially the same as the planned audit risk level, the auditor would

    a. Decrease substantive testing
    b. Decrease detection risk
    c. Increase inherent risk
    d. Increase materiality levels

    (11/94, AUD, #10, ID: 5083)

23. The acceptable level of detection risk is inversely related to the

    a. Assurance provided by substantive tests
    b. Risk of misapplying auditing procedures
    c. Preliminary judgment about materiality levels
    d. Risk of failing to discover material misstatements

    (5/91, AUD, #26, ID: 44)

24. Which of the following would an auditor most likely use in determining the auditor's preliminary judgment about materiality?

    a. The results of the initial assessment of control risk
    b. The anticipated sample size for planned substantive tests
    c. The entity's financial statements of the prior year
    d. The assertions that are embodied in the financial statements

    (11/97, AUD, #10, ID: 6573)

25. Prior to commencing fieldwork, an auditor usually discusses the general audit strategy with the client's management. Which of the following matters does the auditor and management agree upon at this time?

    a. The appropriateness of the entity's plans for dealing with adverse economic conditions.
    b. The determination of the fraud risk factors that exist within the client's operations.
    c. The control weaknesses to be included in the communication with the audit committee.
    d. The coordination of the assistance of the client's personnel in data preparation.

    (R/07, AUD, #10, ID: 8382)

26. An auditor's engagement letter most likely would include a statement that

    a. Lists potential control deficiencies discovered during the prior-year's audit.
    b. Explains the analytical procedures that the auditor expects to apply.
    c. Describes the auditor's responsibility to evaluate going-concern issues.
    d. Limits the auditor's responsibility to detect errors and fraud.   (R/07, AUD, #11, amended, ID: 8383)

27. An audit supervisor reviewed the work performed by the staff to determine if the audit was adequately performed. The supervisor accomplished this by primarily reviewing which of the following?

    a. Checklists
    b. Working papers
    c. Analytical procedures
    d. Financial statements   (R/07, AUD, #23, ID: 8395)

28. The risk that an auditor will conclude, based on substantive tests, that a material error does **not** exist in an account balance when, in fact, such error does exist is referred to as

    a. Sampling risk
    b. Detection risk
    c. Nonsampling risk
    d. Inherent risk   (11/91, AUD, #7, ID: 2275)

29. When an auditor increases the assessed level of control risk because certain control activities were determined to be ineffective, the auditor most likely would increase the

    a. Level of detection risk
    b. Extent of tests of details
    c. Level of inherent risk
    d. Extent of tests of controls   (R/05, AUD, #4, ID: 7799)

30. Which of the following audit risk components may be assessed in nonquantitative terms?

	Control risk	Detection risk	Inherent risk
a.	Yes	Yes	No
b.	Yes	No	Yes
c.	Yes	Yes	Yes
d.	No	Yes	Yes

    (5/95, AUD, #10, ID: 5628)

31. Which of the following would an auditor most likely use in determining the auditor's preliminary judgment about materiality?

    a. The anticipated sample size of the planned substantive tests
    b. The entity's annualized interim financial statements
    c. The results of the internal control questionnaire
    d. The contents of the management representation letter   (5/95, AUD, #11, ID: 5629)

32. Detection risk differs from both control risk and inherent risk in that detection risk

    a. Exists independently of the financial statement audit
    b. Can be changed at the auditor's discretion
    c. Arises from risk factors relating to fraud
    d. Should be assessed in nonquantitative terms   (R/08, AUD, #11, ID: 8617)

33. In a financial statement audit, inherent risk is evaluated to help an auditor assess which of the following?

    a. The internal audit department's objectivity in reporting a material misstatement of a financial statement assertion it detects to the audit committee
    b. The risk that the internal control system will not detect a material misstatement of a financial statement assertion
    c. The risk that the audit procedures implemented will not detect a material misstatement of a financial statement assertion
    d. The susceptibility of a financial statement assertion to a material misstatement assuming there are no related controls (R/09, AUD, #33, ID: 8833)

34. An auditor finds several errors in the financial statements that the client prefers not to correct. The auditor determines that the errors are not material in the aggregate. Which of the following actions by the auditor is most appropriate?

    a. Document the errors in the summary of uncorrected errors, and document the conclusion that the errors do **not** cause the financial statements to be misstated
    b. Document the conclusion that the errors do **not** cause the financial statements to be misstated, but do **not** summarize uncorrected errors in the working papers
    c. Summarize the uncorrected errors in the working papers, but do **not** document whether the errors cause the financial statements to be misstate
    d. Do **not** summarize the uncorrected errors in the working papers, and do **not** document a conclusion about whether the uncorrected errors cause the financial statements to be misstated (R/10, AUD, #21, ID: 9371)

35. Which of the following underlies the application of generally accepted auditing standards, particularly the standards of fieldwork and reporting?

    a. Internal control
    b. Sufficient appropriate evidence
    c. Audit risk and materiality
    d. Quality control (Editors, ID: 15)

36. Which of the following is a definition of control risk?

    a. The risk that a material misstatement will not be prevented or detected on a timely basis by the client's internal controls.
    b. The risk that the auditor will not detect a material misstatement.
    c. The risk that the auditor's assessment of internal controls will be at less than the maximum level.
    d. The susceptibility of material misstatement assuming there are no related internal controls, policies, or procedures. (R/11, AUD, #17, ID: 9917)

37. Which of the following statements is correct regarding internal control?

    a. A well-designed internal control environment ensures the achievement of an entity's control objectives.
    b. An inherent limitation to internal control is the fact that controls can be circumvented by management override.
    c. A well-designed and operated internal control environment should detect collusion perpetrated by two people.
    d. Internal control is a necessary business function and should be designed and operated to detect all errors and fraud. (R/11, AUD, #31, ID: 9931)

38. The auditor's analysis of specific problem accounts receivable and recent trends in bad-debt write-offs as a percent of sales cause the auditor to conclude that the allowance for doubtful accounts should be between $130,000 and $160,000. Management's estimate for the allowance is $126,000. Which amount should be aggregated as a likely misstatement?

    a. $126,000
    b. None
    c. $ 4,000
    d. $ 19,000 (Editors, ID: 89461)

39. Which of the following procedures would an auditor most likely perform in planning a financial statement audit?

    a. Inquiring of the client's legal counsel concerning pending litigation
    b. Comparing the financial statements to anticipated results
    c. Searching for unauthorized transactions that may aid in detecting unrecorded liabilities
    d. Examining computer generated exception reports to verify the effectiveness of internal controls

    (5/95, AUD, #4, amended, ID: 5622)

40. When obtaining an understanding of the entity and its environment, including its internal control, the auditor is required to document

    I. The discussion concerning the susceptibility of the financial statements to material misstatement
    II. The risk assessment procedures performed

    a. I only
    b. II only
    c. Both I and II
    d. Neither I nor II

    (Editors, ID: 8266)

41. In planning an audit of a new client, an auditor most likely would consider the methods used to process accounting information because such methods

    a. Influence the design of internal control
    b. Affect the auditor's preliminary judgment about materiality levels
    c. Assist in evaluating the planned audit objectives
    d. Determine the auditor's acceptable level of audit risk

    (11/94, AUD, #7, amended, ID: 5080)

42. The primary objective of procedures performed to obtain an understanding of the entity and its environment, including its internal control, is to provide an auditor with

    a. Knowledge necessary to assess the risk of material misstatement and design further audit procedures
    b. An evaluation of the consistency of application of management's policies
    c. A basis for modifying tests of controls
    d. Audit evidence to use in assessing inherent risk

    (Editors, ID: 5642)

43. Which of the following statements is correct concerning analytical procedures used in planning an audit engagement?

    a. They often replace the tests of controls that are performed to assess control risk.
    b. They usually use financial and nonfinancial data aggregated at a high level.
    c. They usually involve the comparison of assertions developed by management to ratios calculated by an auditor.
    d. They are often used to develop an auditor's preliminary judgment about materiality.

    (R/11, AUD, #29, ID: 9929)

44. The significance of the controls of the service organization to those of the user organization depend primarily on

    a. The auditor's assessment of the user organization's control risk
    b. The nature and materiality of the transactions it processes for the user organization and the degree of interaction between its activities and those of the user organization
    c. The degree of reliance the user auditor plans to place on the work of the service auditor
    d. Whether sufficient and appropriate evidence can be obtained to determine the operating effectiveness of the controls at the service organization

    (Editors, ID: 9272)

45. In considering whether to use the service auditor's report, the user auditor should make inquiries concerning the service auditor's professional reputation. All of the following are acceptable sources for this **except for**

    a. The AICPA
    b. Other practitioners
    c. The service auditor's published *vita*
    d. Bankers and other credit grantors (Editors, ID: 9273)

46. An auditor is auditing a mutual fund company that uses a transfer agent to handle accounting for shareholders. Which of the following actions by the auditor would be most efficient for obtaining information about the transfer agent's internal controls?

    a. Review reports on internal control placed in operation and its operating effectiveness produced by the agent's own auditor.
    b. Review prior year workpapers to determine whether the number of transactions processed by the agent has materially increased.
    c. Perform an audit on the internal control function of the agent.
    d. Perform tests of controls on a sample of the audited firm's transactions through the agent.
    (R/08, AUD, #27, ID: 8633)

47. Green, CPA, is auditing the financial statements of Ajax Co. Ajax uses the DP Service Center to process its payroll. DP's financial statements are audited by Blue, CPA, who recently issued a report on DP's policies and procedures regarding the processing of other entity's transactions. In considering whether Blue's report is satisfactory for Green's purposes, Green should

    a. Make inquiries concerning Blue's professional reputation
    b. Assess control risk at the maximum level
    c. Review the audit programs followed by Blue
    d. Perform tests of controls at the DP Service Center (R/10, AUD, #9, ID: 9359)

48. Which of the following statements describes why a properly designed and executed audit may **not** detect a material misstatement in the financial statements resulting from fraud?

    a. Audit procedures that are effective for detecting an unintentional misstatement may be ineffective for an intentional misstatement that is concealed through collusion.
    b. An audit is designed to provide reasonable assurance of detecting material errors, but there is no similar responsibility concerning fraud.
    c. The factors considered in assessing control risk indicated an increased risk of intentional misstatements, but only a low risk of unintentional errors in the financial statements.
    d. The auditor did not consider factors influencing audit risk for account balances that have effects pervasive to the financial statements taken as a whole. (11/91, AUD, #10, amended, ID: 2278)

49. Which of the following factors most likely would heighten an auditor's concern about the risk of fraudulent financial reporting?

    a. Large amounts of liquid assets that are easily convertible into cash
    b. Low growth and profitability as compared to other entities in the same industry
    c. Financial management's participation in the initial selection of accounting principles
    d. An overly complex organizational structure involving unusual lines of authority
    (R/01, AUD, #3, ID: 7018)

50. Which of the following circumstances most likely would cause an auditor to suspect that there are material misstatements in an entity's financial statements?

    a. The entity's management places no emphasis on meeting publicized earnings projections
    b. Significant differences between the physical inventory count and the accounting records are not investigated
    c. Monthly bank reconciliations ordinarily include several large outstanding checks
    d. Cash transactions are electronically processed and recorded, leaving no paper audit trail
    (R/03, AUD, #7, ID: 7629)

51. If the business environment is experiencing a recession, the auditor most likely would focus increased attention on which of the following accounts?

    a. Purchase returns and allowances
    b. Allowance for doubtful accounts
    c. Common stock
    d. Noncontrolling interest of a subsidiary purchased during the year   (R/06, AUD, #23, ID: 8141)

52. Which of the following circumstances would an auditor most likely consider a risk factor relating to misstatements arising from fraudulent financial reporting?

    a. Several members of management have recently purchased additional shares of the entity's stock.
    b. Several members of the board of directors have recently sold shares of the entity's stock.
    c. The entity distributes financial forecasts to financial analysts that predict conservative operating results.
    d. Management is interested in maintaining the entity's earnings trend by using aggressive accounting practices.   (R/06, AUD, #37, ID: 8155)

53. Disclosure of possible fraud to parties other than a client's senior management and its audit committee ordinarily is not part of an auditor's responsibility. However, to which of the following outside parties may a duty to disclose that possible fraud exists?

	To the SEC when the client reports an auditor change	To a successor auditor when the successor makes appropriate inquiries	To a funding agency from which the client receives governmental financial assistance
a.	Yes	Yes	No
b.	Yes	No	Yes
c.	No	Yes	Yes
d.	Yes	Yes	Yes

    (5/90, AUD, #55, amended, ID: 163)

54. Which of the following statements reflects an auditor's responsibility for detecting errors and fraud?

    a. An auditor is responsible for detecting employee errors and simple fraud, but not for discovering fraud involving employee collusion or management override.
    b. An auditor should plan the audit to detect errors and fraud that are caused by departures from GAAP.
    c. An auditor is not responsible for detecting errors and fraud unless the application of GAAS would result in such detection.
    d. An auditor should design the audit to provide reasonable assurance of detecting errors and fraud that are material to the financial statements.   (5/95, AUD, #15, amended, ID: 5633)

55. Which of the following circumstances most likely would cause an auditor to suspect that there are material misstatements in an entity's financial statements?

    a. Senior financial management participates in the selection of accounting principles and the determination of significant estimates.
    b. Supporting accounting records and files that should be readily available are not produced promptly when requested.
    c. Related-party transactions take place in the ordinary course of business with an entity that is audited by another CPA firm.
    d. Senior management has an excessive interest in upgrading the entity's information technology capabilities.   (R/05, AUD, #31, ID: 7826)

56. Which of the following procedures would an auditor most likely perform during the overall review stage of an audit of an entity's financial statements?

    a. Obtain assurance from the entity's attorney that all material litigation has been disclosed in the financial statements
    b. Verify the clerical accuracy of the entity's proof of cash and its bank cutoff statement
    c. Determine whether inadequate provisions for the safeguarding of assets have been corrected
    d. Consider whether the results of audit procedures affect the assessment of the risk of material misstatement due to fraud
    (R/01, AUD, #12, ID: 7027)

57. Which of the following statements is correct concerning an auditor's responsibility to report fraud?

    a. The auditor is required to communicate to the client's audit committee all minor fraudulent acts perpetrated by low-level employees, even if the amounts involved are inconsequential.
    b. The disclosure of material management fraud to principal stockholders is required when both senior management and the board of directors fail to acknowledge the fraudulent activities.
    c. Fraudulent activities involving senior management of which the auditor becomes aware should be reported directly to the SEC.
    d. The disclosure of fraudulent activities to parties other than the client's senior management and its audit committee is not ordinarily part of the auditor's responsibility.
    (R/05, AUD, #14, ID: 7809)

58. Which of the following characteristics most likely would heighten an auditor's concern about the risk of material misstatement arising from fraudulent financial reporting?

    a. There is a lack of interest by management in maintaining an earnings trend.
    b. Computer hardware is usually sold at a loss before being fully depreciated.
    c. Management had frequent disputes with the auditor on accounting matters.
    d. Monthly bank reconciliations usually include several large checks outstanding.
    (R/07, AUD, #48, ID: 8420)

59. Which of the following situations represents a risk factor that relates to misstatements arising from misappropriation of assets?

    a. A high turnover of senior management
    b. A lack of independent checks
    c. A strained relationship between management and the predecessor auditor
    d. An inability to generate cash flow from operations
    (R/08, AUD, #40, ID: 8646)

60. If **not** already performed during the overall review stage of the audit, the auditor should perform analytical procedures relating to which of the following transaction cycles?

    a. Payroll
    b. Revenue
    c. Purchasing
    d. Inventory
    (R/10, AUD, #46, ID: 9396)

61. Which of the following analytical procedures most likely would be used during the planning stage of an audit?

    a. Comparing current year to prior year sales volumes
    b. Reading the financial statements and notes and considering the adequacy of evidence
    c. Comparing the current year ratio of aggregate salaries paid to the number of employees to the prior year's ratio
    d. Reading the letter from the client's attorney and considering the threat of litigation
    (R/11, AUD, #42, ID: 9942)

62. When assessing the risk of material misstatement, an auditor is required to document

    I. The basis for the assessment
    II. Significant risks identified and the related controls that were evaluated

    a. I only
    b. II only
    c. Both I and II
    d. Neither I nor II   (Editors, ID: 8265)

63. Regardless of the assessed level of control risk, an auditor would perform some

    a. Tests of controls to determine the effectiveness of internal control policies
    b. Analytical procedures to verify the design of internal control procedures
    c. Substantive tests to restrict detection risk for significant transaction classes
    d. Dual-purpose tests to evaluate both the risk of monetary misstatement and preliminary control risk
                                                            (11/93, AUD, #23, ID: 4260)

64. After obtaining an understanding of the entity and its environment and assessing the risk of material misstatement, an auditor decided to perform tests of controls. The auditor most likely decided that

    a. It would be efficient to perform tests of controls that would result in a reduction in planned substantive tests.
    b. Additional evidence to support a further reduction in control risk is not available.
    c. An increase in the assessed level of control risk is justified for certain financial statement assertions.
    d. There were many internal control weaknesses that could allow errors to enter the accounting system.
                                                    (5/95, AUD, #33, amended, ID: 5651)

65. As the acceptable level of detection risk increases, an auditor may

    a. Increase the assessed level of control risk
    b. Change the assurance provided by tests of controls by using a larger sample size than planned
    c. Change the timing of substantive tests from year-end to an interim date
    d. Change the nature of substantive tests from a less effective to a more effective procedure
                                                    (11/92, AUD, #10, amended, ID: 2944)

66. An auditor may decide to perform only substantive procedures for specific assertions because the auditor believes

    a. Control policies and procedures are unlikely to pertain to the assertions.
    b. The entity's control environment, monitoring, and control activities are interrelated.
    c. Sufficient audit evidence to support the assertions is likely to be available.
    d. More emphasis on tests of controls than substantive tests is warranted.
                                                    (11/93, AUD, #21, amended, ID: 4258)

67. An auditor uses the assessed risk of material misstatement to

    a. Evaluate the effectiveness of the entity's internal control policies and procedures
    b. Identify transactions and account balances where inherent risk is at the maximum
    c. Indicate whether materiality thresholds for planning and evaluation purposes are sufficiently high
    d. Determine the acceptable level of detection risk for financial statement assertions
                                                    (5/94, AUD, #24, amended, ID: 4689)

68. Which of the following explanations best describes why an auditor may decide to reduce tests of details for a particular audit objective?

    a. The audit is being performed soon after the balance sheet date.
    b. Audit staff are experienced in performing the planned procedures.
    c. Analytical procedures have revealed **no** unusual or unexpected results.
    d. There were many transactions posted to the account during the period.   (R/10, AUD, #36, ID: 9386)

69. An audit client sells 15 to 20 units of product annually. A large portion of the annual sales occur in the last month of the fiscal year. Annual sales have not materially changed over the past five years. Which of the following approaches would be most effective concerning the timing of audit procedures for revenue?

    a. The auditor should perform analytical procedures at an interim date and discuss any changes in the level of sales with senior management.
    b. The auditor should inspect transactions occurring in the last month of the fiscal year and review the related sale contracts to determine that revenue was posted in the proper period.
    c. The auditor should perform tests of controls at an interim date to obtain audit evidence about the operational effectiveness of internal controls over sales.
    d. The auditor should review period-end compensation to determine if bonuses were paid to meet earnings goals. (R/10, AUD, #39, ID: 9389)

70. Which of the following information discovered during an audit most likely would raise a question concerning possible illegal acts?

    a. Related-party transactions, although properly disclosed, were pervasive during the year.
    b. The entity prepared several large checks payable to cash during the year.
    c. Material internal control weaknesses previously reported to management were not corrected.
    d. The entity was a campaign contributor to several local political candidates during the year. (11/97, AUD, #13, ID: 6576)

71. Which of the following procedures would **least** likely result in the discovery of possible illegal acts?

    a. Reading the minutes of the board of directors' meetings
    b. Making inquiries of the client's management
    c. Performing tests of details of transactions
    d. Reviewing an internal control questionnaire (R/05, AUD, #25, ID: 7820)

72. When an auditor becomes aware of a possible illegal act by a client, the auditor should obtain an understanding of the nature of the act to

    a. Evaluate the effect on the financial statements
    b. Determine the reliability of management's representations
    c. Consider whether other similar acts may have occurred
    d. Recommend remedial actions to the audit committee (11/92, AUD, #4, ID: 2938)

73. If information comes to an auditor's attention that implies the existence of possible illegal acts that could have a material, but indirect effect on the financial statements, the auditor should next

    a. Apply audit procedures specifically directed to ascertaining whether an illegal act has occurred
    b. Seek the advice of an informed expert qualified to practice law as to possible contingent liabilities
    c. Discuss the evidence with the client's audit committee, or others with equivalent authority and responsibility
    d. Report the matter to an appropriate level of management at least one level above those involved (Editors, ID: 172)

74. An auditor who discovers that a client's employees paid small bribes to municipal officials most likely would withdraw from the engagement if

    a. The payments violated the client's policies regarding the prevention of illegal acts.
    b. The client receives financial assistance from a federal government agency.
    c. Documentation that is necessary to prove that the bribes were paid does not exist.
    d. Management fails to take the appropriate remedial action. (R/00, AUD, #6, ID: 6931)

75. Under the Private Securities Litigation Reform Act of 1995, Baker, CPA, reported certain uncorrected illegal acts to Supermart's board of directors. Baker believed that failure to take remedial action would warrant a qualified audit opinion because the illegal acts had a material effect on Supermart's financial statements. Supermart failed to take appropriate remedial action and the board of directors refused to inform the SEC that it had received such notification from Baker. Under these circumstances, Baker is required to

    a. Withhold an audit opinion until Supermart takes appropriate remedial action
    b. Deliver a report concerning the illegal acts to the SEC within one business day
    c. Notify the stockholders that the financial statements are materially misstated
    d. Resign from the audit engagement within ten business days   (R/99, AUD, #4, ID: 6820)

76. An auditor would most likely question whether a client has committed illegal acts if the client has

    a. Been forced to discontinue operations in a foreign country
    b. Been an annual donor to a local political candidate
    c. Disclosed several subsequent events involving foreign operations in the notes to the financial statements
    d. Failed to correct material weaknesses in internal control that were reported after the prior year's audit
    (Editors, ID: 189)

77. Jones, CPA, is auditing the financial statements of XYZ Retailing Inc. What assurance does Jones provide that direct effect illegal acts that are material to XYZ's financial statements, and illegal acts that have a material, but indirect, effect on the financial statements, will be detected?

	Direct effect illegal acts	*Indirect effect illegal acts*
a.	Reasonable	None
b.	Reasonable	Limited
c.	Limited	None
d.	Limited	Limited

    (5/94, AUD, #6, amended, ID: 4671)

Items 78 and 79 are based on the following:

During the annual audit of Ajax Corp., a publicly held company, Jones, CPA, a continuing auditor, determined that illegal political contributions had been made during each of the past seven years, including the year under audit. Jones notified the board of directors about the illegal contributions, but they refused to take any action because the amounts involved were immaterial to the financial statements.

78. Jones should reconsider the intended degree of reliance to be placed on the

    a. Letter of audit inquiry to the client's attorney
    b. Prior years' audit programs
    c. Management representation letter
    d. Preliminary judgment about materiality levels   (11/94, AUD, #12, ID: 5085)

79. Since management took no action, Jones should

    a. Report the illegal contributions to the Securities and Exchange Commission
    b. Issue an "except for" qualified opinion or an adverse opinion
    c. Disregard the political contributions since the board of directors were notified and the amounts involved were immaterial
    d. Consider withdrawing from the engagement or dissociating from any future relationship with Ajax Corp
    (Editors, ID: 7487)

80. Which of the following statements is correct regarding the auditor's consideration of the possibility of illegal acts by clients?

    a. The auditor has a responsibility to plan and perform the audit to obtain reasonable assurance that no illegal acts have been committed by clients.
    b. The auditor's training, experience, and understanding of the client should be used to provide a basis for the determination as to whether illegal acts have occurred.
    c. If specific information concerning an illegal act comes to the auditor's attention, the auditor should apply audit procedures specifically directed to ascertaining whether an illegal act has occurred.
    d. If an illegal act has occurred, the auditor should express a qualified opinion or an adverse opinion on the financial statements taken as a whole. (R/07, AUD, #50, ID: 8422)

81. Which of the following information that comes to an auditor's attention most likely would raise a question about the occurrence of illegal acts?

    a. The exchange of property for similar property in a nonmonetary transaction
    b. The discovery of unexplained payments made to government employees
    c. The presence of several difficult-to-audit transactions affecting expense accounts
    d. The failure to develop adequate procedures that detect unauthorized purchases
    (R/10, AUD, #5, ID: 9355)

82. During the audit of a new client, the auditor determined that management had given illegal bribes to municipal officials during the year under audit and for several prior years. The auditor notified the client's board of directors, but the board decided to take no action because the amounts involved were immaterial to the financial statements. Under these circumstances, the auditor should

    a. Add an explanatory paragraph emphasizing that certain matters, while **not** affecting the unqualified opinion, require disclosure
    b. Report the illegal bribes to the municipal official at least one level above those persons who received the bribes
    c. Consider withdrawing from the audit engagement and disassociating from future relationships with the client
    d. Issue an "except for" qualified opinion or an adverse opinion with a separate paragraph that explains the circumstances (R/10, AUD, #30, ID: 9380)

83. Which of the following matters would an auditor most likely communicate to an entity's audit committee?

    a. A list of negative trends that may lead to working capital deficiencies and adverse financial ratios
    b. The level of responsibility assumed by management for the preparation of the financial statements
    c. Difficulties encountered in achieving a satisfactory response rate from the entity's customers in confirming accounts receivables
    d. The effects of significant accounting policies adopted by management in emerging areas for which there is no authoritative guidance (R/02, AUD, #5, ID: 7095)

84. An auditor's communication with the audit committee is required to include the

    a. Basis for the auditor's preliminary judgment about materiality
    b. Justification for the auditor's selection of sampling methods
    c. Discussion of disagreements with management about matters that significantly impact the entity's financial statements
    d. Assessment of the quality of the entity's earnings as compared to the previous year
    (R/05, AUD, #39, ID: 7834)

85. An auditor would **least** likely initiate a discussion with a client's audit committee concerning

    a. The methods used to account for significant unusual transactions

    b. The maximum dollar amount of misstatements that could exist without causing the financial statements to be materially misstated

    c. Indications of fraud and illegal acts committed by a corporate officer that were discovered by the auditor

    d. Disagreements with management as to accounting principles that were resolved during the current year's audit   (5/95, AUD, #19, ID: 5637)

86. In identifying matters for communication with an entity's audit committee, an auditor most likely would ask management whether

    a. The turnover in the accounting department was unusually high.

    b. It consulted with another CPA firm about accounting matters.

    c. There were any subsequent events of which the auditor was unaware.

    d. It agreed with the auditor's assessed level of control risk.   (5/96, AUD, #6, ID: 6238)

87. Which of the following matters is an auditor **not** required to communicate to an entity's audit committee?

    a. Significant adjustments arising from the audit that were recorded by management

    b. The basis for the auditor's conclusions about the reasonableness of management's sensitive accounting estimates

    c. The level of responsibility assumed by the auditor under generally accepted auditing standards

    d. The degree of reliance the auditor placed on the management representation letter   (R/03, AUD, #15, ID: 7637)

88. Which of the following disagreements between the auditor and management do **not** have to be communicated by the auditor to those charged with governance?

    a. Disagreements regarding management's judgment about accounting estimates for goodwill

    b. Disagreements about the scope of the audit

    c. Disagreements in the application of accounting principles relating to software development costs

    d. Disagreements of the amount of the LIFO inventory layer based on preliminary information   (R/10, AUD, #41, ID: 9391)

Problem 2-2 SIMULATION: Audit Risk

Company

The year under audit is year 2. Scott, Inc. (Scott) is a manufacturer of handmade glycerin soap and candles. The company has been in business for 15 years and has its headquarters in Yorba Linda, California.

Marketing

Scott is divided into two divisions, which serve the major markets for the company's products. One division focuses on sales to department stores. The other division focuses on placing company products in small specialty shops. Currently, each division generates about half of Scott's revenues and net income.

Management

Management realized it must strictly control all costs to make its overall operations more efficient. As a result, Scott announced that it would make a series of restructuring changes as of the end of year 2 as part of its overall business plan. During year 2, the company issued long-term debt with complex financial covenants. The debt was incurred to purchase property, plant and equipment. The company also issued additional common stock during year 2.

Senior management at the company experienced significant turnover in recent years. The CEO has been with the company for only one year. The CEO was hired from a major competitor after the previous CEO left to take a position with a large manufacturing company in the Northeast. In another management change, the company's CFO retired, and the current CFO was hired only six months ago. The new CFO was an audit manager from the predecessor audit firm.

Engagement

For year 2, Scott switched audit firms. There have been no internal disagreements over accounting issues in any of the prior three years.

Based on the information in Scott's profile, determine whether each of the factors below would be likely to increase audit risk or have no impact on audit risk.

Factors	Impact on Audit Risk	
	Increases Audit Risk	No Impact
1. The company has begun to focus on a strategic advertising plan so it may expand its market into other states.		
2. During year 2, management issued additional long-term debt with complex financial covenants.		
3. Scott is divided into two divisions, which serve the major markets of the company's products.		
4. The new CFO was an audit manager from the predecessor audit firm.		

(ID: 9201)

_____

Problem 2-3 SIMULATION: Risk of Material Misstatement

Green, CPA, is considering audit risk at the financial statement level in planning the audit of National Federal Bank (NFB) Company's financial statements for the year ended December 31, year 1. Audit risk at the financial statement level is influenced by the risk of material misstatement, which may be indicated by a combination of factors related to management, the industry, and the entity. In assessing such factors, Green has gathered the following information concerning NFB's environment.

NFB is a federally insured bank that has been consistently more profitable than the industry average by marketing mortgages on properties in a prosperous rural area, which has experienced considerable growth in recent years. NFB packages its mortgages and sells them to large mortgage investment trusts. Despite recent volatility of interest rates, NFB has been able to continue selling its mortgages as a source of new lendable funds.

Based only on the information above, determine whether each of the factors below *increases* or *decreases* the risk of material misstatement.

Factors	Effect on Risk of Material Misstatement
1. Governmental regulation over the banking industry is extensive.	
2. NFB operates profitably in growing prosperous area.	
3. Overall demand for the industry's product is high.	
4. Interest rates have been volatile recently.	
5. The availability of funds for additional mortgages is promising.	

(ID: 9202)

Problem 2-4 SIMULATION: Risk of Material Misstatement

Edwards, CPA, is considering audit risk at the financial statement level in planning the audit of Middleton Bank financial statements for the year ended December 31, year 1. Audit risk at the financial statement level is influenced by the risk of material misstatement, which may be indicated by a combination of factors related to management, the industry, and the entity. In assessing such factors, Edwards has gathered the following information concerning Middleton Bank's environment.

Middleton Bank's board of directors is controlled by Smith, the majority stockholder, who also acts as the chief executive officer. Management at the bank's branch offices has authority for directing and controlling Middleton Bank's operations and is compensated based on branch profitability. The internal auditor reports directly to the chairman of the board's audit committee. The Accounting Department has experienced little turnover in personnel during the five years Edwards has audited Middleton Bank.

Based only on the information above, determine whether each of the factors below *increases* or *decreases* the risk of material misstatement.

Factors	Effect on Risk of Material Misstatement
1. The principal shareholder is also the chief executive officer and controls the board of directors.	
2. Branch management is compensated based on branch profitability.	
3. The internal auditor reports directly to the chairman of the board's audit committee.	
4. The Accounting Department has experienced little turnover in personnel recently.	
5. Middleton Bank is a continuing audit client.	

(ID: 9203)

Problem 2-5 SIMULATION: Risk of Material Misstatement

Howard, CPA, is considering audit risk at the financial statement level in planning the audit of Oak Bank financial statements for the year ended December 31, year 1. Audit risk at the financial statement level is influenced by the risk of material misstatement, which may be indicated by a combination of factors related to management, the industry, and the entity. In assessing such factors, Howard has gathered the following information concerning Oak Bank's environment.

Oak Bank's formula consistently underestimates the allowance for loan losses, but its controller has always been receptive to Howard's suggestions to increase the allowance during each engagement.

During year 1, Oak Bank opened a branch office in a suburban town thirty miles from its principal place of business. Although this branch is not yet profitable due to competition from several well-established local banks, management believes that the branch will be profitable by year 3.

Also, during year 1, Oak Bank increased the efficiency of its accounting operations by installing a new, sophisticated computer system.

Based only on the information above, determine whether each of the factors below *increases* or *decreases* the risk of material misstatement.

Factors	Effect on Risk of Material Misstatement
1. Management fails to establish proper procedures to provide reasonable assurance of reliable accounting estimates.	
2. Management has been receptive to Howard's suggestions relating to accounting adjustments.	
3. Oak Bank recently opened a new branch office that is not yet profitable.	
4. Oak Bank recently installed a new sophisticated computer system.	

(ID: 9204)

———————————

Problem 2-6 SIMULATION: Research

What authoritative reference recognizes that although fraudulent journal entries often are made at the end of a reporting period, the auditor should consider whether there is a need to test journal entries throughout the reporting period under audit?

[   ] § [   ] [   ]   (ID: 9205)

_____

Problem 2-7 SIMULATION: Research

What authoritative reference states that the discussion among the audit team about the susceptibility of the entity's financial statements to material misstatements can be held concurrently with the discussion about the susceptibility of the financial statements to fraud?

[   ] § [   ] [   ]   (ID: 9217)

_____

Solution 2-1 MULTIPLE-CHOICE ANSWERS

Planning & Supervision

1. (a)   The AICPA's sample engagement letter states, "At the conclusion of our audit, we will request certain written representations from you about the financial statements and matters related thereto." Auditors generally do not discuss preliminary judgments about materiality or fraud risk with the client. Internal control activities that would reduce the auditor's assessment of control risk generally would be discussed later in the audit, when the auditor has greater familiarity with the internal controls in place, typically when making recommendations to improve internal controls. (ID: 7830)

2. (c)   The understanding with the client generally includes the auditor's responsibility for communicating significant deficiencies and material weaknesses, if the auditor becomes aware of any. Preliminary judgments about materiality and audit risk factors are not required to be understood by the client. It is the auditor's responsibility to identify mitigating factors when there is going concern doubt as well as to assess the risk of material misstatement due to fraud. (ID: 8130)

3. (c)   In the planning phase of an audit a CPA most likely would coordinate with client personnel, requiring a discussion of the timing of audit procedures, such as a physical count of inventory. An auditor would identify specific internal control activities that are likely to prevent fraud during the review of internal control or when fraud factors are discovered. An auditor would evaluate the reasonableness of a client's accounting estimates and inquire of a client's attorney regarding unrecorded claims when collecting evidence. (ID: 7798)

4. (c)   The auditor should prepare a written audit plan (or program). The audit plan should detail the nature, extent, and timing of the audit procedures that are necessary to accomplish the objectives of the audit. All material transactions and all account balances are not required to be tested in all circumstances. Minimizing substantive tests prior to the balance sheet date is not required. (ID: 5634)

5. (d)   Of the procedures listed, an auditor is most likely to determine the extent of involvement of the client's internal auditors in the initial planning of a financial statement audit. A written representation letter from the client's management is usually obtained at the end of an audit, not the beginning. Examining documents and considering the reasonableness of estimates are procedures that are done during the audit. (ID: 5074)

6. (c)   Among other procedures performed during the planning of the audit, the auditor may discuss the general audit strategy concerning the type, scope, and timing of the audit with the entity's management, audit committee, or board of directors, as well as coordinate any assistance of the entity's personnel in data preparation that is needed. (ID: 8125)

7. (c)   The work performed by each assistant, including the audit documentation, should be reviewed to determine whether it was adequately performed and documented and to evaluate the results, relative to the conclusions to be presented in the auditor's report. The question pertains to the first standard of fieldwork which encompasses the need for reviewing assistants' work, not the first general standard (auditor's qualifications). The quality control standards do not state that quality control must be maintained at a high level, rather, a firm is to establish and maintain a system of quality control to provide it with reasonable assurance that the firm and its personnel comply with professional standards and applicable regulatory and legal requirements; and reports issued by the firm are appropriate in the circumstances. The standards are guidelines for auditing procedures which are applied based on the auditor's professional judgment. (ID: 2273)

8. (b)   The auditor should inform assistants of their responsibilities and the objective(s) of the audit procedures they are to perform. This would also serve to inform them of the basis of how the results of the audit procedures should be evaluated. It is very unlikely that staff assistants would report to the client's audit committee. Answers c. and d. are less vital duties than audit procedure evaluation. (ID: 5625)

9. (c)   Procedures should enable an assistant to document his or her disagreement with the conclusions reached if, after appropriate consultation, the assistant believes it necessary to become disassociated from the resolution of the matter. An assistant can disagree with the in-charge auditor—the matter should be addressed in some manner. An assistant is not precluded from working on the audit if the assistant has a difference of opinion concerning auditing or accounting issue(s). The assistant should not, on his or her own, notify the client that a serious audit problem exists. (ID: 209)

10. (b) The auditor is responsible for ensuring that those charged with governance are aware of any significant deficiencies that come to the auditor's attention. Management is unlikely to take responsibility for errors and illegal activities of employees. The auditor assesses the risk of material misstatement due to fraud. The auditor's preliminary judgments about materiality and audit risk factors generally are not discussed with the client. (ID: 6822)

11. (d) In an engagement letter, the firm and the client indicate their mutual understanding and agree to the nature and terms of the engagement. Answer a. would be included as part of the terms of the engagement. Answer b. would be included to indicate the nature of the services the client could expect in the engagement. Answer c. would be included to establish the mutual understanding of some of the limitations inherent in an audit due to less than 100% testing of all accounts. The auditor would usually not outline to the client the specific procedures to be performed during the audit. (ID: 5621)

12. (a) An understanding with the client regarding an audit of the financial statements generally includes a statement that management is responsible for establishing and maintaining effective internal control over financial reporting. An engagement letter should document this understanding. At the point at which an engagement letter usually is sent, the auditor typically has not performed any assessment of risk factors relating to misstatements arising from any circumstances. Management's liability for employee acts is not a part of audit engagement terms. It is appropriate for the client to understand the auditor will request permission to contact the client's lawyer for assistance in identifying litigation, claims, and assessments; however, this permission typically is requested separately from the engagement letter. (ID: 7093)

13. (b) An understanding with the client regarding an audit of the financial statements generally includes the following matters. The auditor is responsible for conducting the audit in accordance with generally accepted auditing standards. Those standards require that the auditor obtain reasonable rather than absolute assurance about whether the financial statements are free of material misstatement, whether caused by error or fraud. Accordingly, a material misstatement may remain undetected. Also, an audit is not designed to detect error or fraud that is immaterial to the financial statements. If, for any reason, the auditor is unable to complete the audit or is unable to form or has not formed an opinion, he or she may decline to express an opinion or decline to issue a report as a result of the engagement. These matters should be communicated in the form of an engagement letter. A comfort letter is provided to an underwriter by an auditor; typically an auditor informs the client of fraud, not the underwriter. A letter of audit inquiry is sent to a third party such as a vendor, customer, or attorney; typically an auditor informs the client of fraud, not third parties such as these. A representation letter is addressed by management to the auditor; management is unlikely to use the phrase *our audit*. (ID: 7634)

14. (d) The element of the audit planning process most likely to be agreed upon with the client before implementation of the audit strategy is the timing of inventory observation procedures to be performed. Evidence to be gathered to provide a sufficient basis for the auditor's opinion is solely a matter of auditor judgment. The procedures to be undertaken to discover litigation, claims, and assessments are determined by the auditor. Pending legal matters to be included in the inquiry of the client's attorney are more likely to be discussed after implementation of the audit strategy. (ID: 5619)

15. (a) Gaining an understanding of the entity and its environment, including internal control, is the first of these four procedures to be performed in an audit. The entity's risk assessment process is part of its internal control. The auditor identifies specific activities designed to prevent fraud when considering relying on internal control. The other two options are substantive procedures. (ID: 6709)

16. (d) The primary purpose of the audit is to gather sufficient evidence to support the auditor's conclusions. The design of the audit program has no effect on inherent risk. Procedures *may* be performed prior to the balance sheet date only if the effectiveness of interim work is not likely to be impaired. Suggestions to management are secondary considerations in an audit. (ID: 5089)

17. (c) Planning involves the development of an overall strategy for the expected conduct, organization, and staffing of the audit. The auditor must plan the audit to be responsive to the assessment of the risk of material misstatement. In establishing the overall audit strategy, the auditor should consider the important factors that will determine the focus of the audit team's efforts, such as (1) determination of appropriate materiality levels, (2) preliminary identification of areas where there may be a higher risk of material misstatement, (3) preliminary identification of material locations and account balances, (4) evaluation of whether the

auditor plans to perform tests of controls, and (5) identification of recent significant entity-specific, industry, financial reporting, or other relevant developments. (ID: 7102)

18. (d)   Remedy of limitations resulting from accepting the engagement after the close of the end of the year, such as those relating to the existence of physical inventory would permit the auditor to accept such an engagement. Although early appointment is preferable, an auditor may accept an engagement near or after the close of the fiscal year. The taking of the inventory could be postponed or failing that, another could be taken for the auditor to observe. If the auditor believes that circumstances are such that acceptance after the close of the fiscal year would preclude an unqualified opinion, the auditor should discuss the possible necessity of a qualified or disclaimer of opinion with the client. This is an example of when candidates need to choose the best answer on the exam. It is much more likely that an auditor would accept an engagement after the close of the client's fiscal year if the determination was made that the resultant limitations could be remedied. The assessment of control risk below the maximum level cannot be determined prior to the acceptance of an engagement and is also not relevant to the issue of whether to accept the engagement after the close of the fiscal year. An auditor cannot rely on a predecessor auditor's assertion about a client's ability to continue as a going concern, setting aside the unlikelihood of receiving such a communication. Further, this is not relevant to the issue of whether to accept the engagement after the close of the fiscal year. (ID: 8626)

19. (c)   The statement most likely to be included in an engagement letter from an auditor to a client is that the CPA firm will involve information technology specialists in the performance of the audit. Involvement of specialists or internal auditors, if applicable, is something the auditor may choose to include in the letter. The engagement letter should include a statement that the auditor will obtain reasonable (not absolute) assurance about whether the financial statements are free of material misstatement, whether caused by error or fraud; accordingly a material misstatement may remain undetected. The letter should state that management (not the auditor) is responsible for identifying and ensuring that the entity complies with the laws and regulation applicable to its activities. The letter should also state that management (not the auditor) is responsible for adjusting the financial statement to correct material misstatements. (ID: 8834)

20. (d)   The auditor with final responsibility for the audit should communicate with members of the audit team regarding the susceptibility of the entity's financial statements to material misstatement due to error or fraud, with special emphasis on fraud. The discussion should emphasize the need to maintain a questioning mind and to exercise professional skepticism in gathering and evaluating evidence throughout the audit. The terms *judgmental* and *criticizing* are too extreme. A presumptive mind-set in the context of an audit would mean supposing (assuming) conclusions before gathering evidence which is nearly the opposite of the appropriate questioning mind-set. (ID: 9919)

Audit Risk & Materiality

21. (a)   Inherent risk is the susceptibility of an assertion to a material misstatement, assuming that there are no related controls. Control risk is the risk that a material misstatement that could occur in an assertion will not be prevented or detected on a timely basis by the entity's internal control. Detection risk is the risk that the auditor will not detect a material misstatement that exists in an assertion. Thus, inherent risk and control risk are functions of the client and its environment while detection risk is not. Inherent risk and control risk differ from detection risk in that they exist independently of the audit of financial statements, whereas detection risk relates to the auditor's procedures and can be changed at the auditor's discretion. All of the elements of audit risk should be considered in relation to individual account balances, classes of transactions and disclosures; and at the overall financial statement level. Inherent risk, control risk, and detection risk are all a part of audit risk. (ID: 2810)

22. (b)   Detection risk has an inverse relationship to control risk. Therefore, if an auditor decides to increase the assessed level of control risk from the originally planned level, in order to achieve an equivalent overall level of risk, the detection risk must be decreased. (ID: 5083)

23. (a)   Detection risk relates to the substantive audit procedures and is managed by the auditor's response to the risk of material misstatement. For a given level of audit risk, detection risk should bear an inverse relationship to the risk of material misstatement at the relevant assertion level. The greater the risk of material misstatement, the less the detection risk that can be accepted by the auditor. Conversely, the lower the risk of material misstatement, the greater the detection risk that can be accepted by the auditor. However, the auditor

should perform substantive procedures for all relevant assertions related to material classes of transactions, account balances, and disclosures. The risk of misapplying audit procedures is a part of detection risk. The acceptable level of detection risk is unrelated to the preliminary judgment about materiality levels. The risk of failing to discover material misstatements during an audit is detection risk. (ID: 44)

24. (c)   In determining materiality, the auditor should consider, among other things, prior-periods' financial results and financial positions. Materiality impacts the evaluation of the alternative answers, rather than the reverse. (ID: 6573)

25. (d)   Planning involves the development of an overall strategy for the expected conduct, organization, and staffing of the audit. To consider the appropriateness of the entity's plans for dealing with adverse economic conditions effectively, the auditor should be familiar with the entity and the conditions it is likely to encounter; such familiarity is enhanced by fieldwork. The fraud risk factors that exist within the client's operations and the control weaknesses to be included in the communication with the audit committee are unlikely to be known prior to commencing fieldwork. (ID: 8382)

26. (d)   The engagement letter documents the understanding with the client regarding the services to be performed for each engagement. The understanding should include the objectives of the engagement, management's responsibilities, the auditor's responsibilities, and limitations of the engagement. Matters that should be communicated in the form of an engagement letter include a statement that the auditor is responsible for conducting the audit in accordance with GAAS. Those standards require that the auditor obtain reasonable rather than absolute assurance about whether the financial statements are free of material misstatement, whether caused by error or fraud. Accordingly, a material misstatement may remain undetected. Also, an audit is not designed to detect error or fraud that is immaterial to the financial statements. Potential control deficiencies typically would not be mentioned. The analytical procedures that the auditor expects to apply would be documented in the audit plan, not the engagement letter. The engagement letter could describe the auditor's responsibility to evaluate going-concern issues, but it is not required to be included. (ID: 8383)

27. (b)   The work performed by each assistant, including the audit documentation, should be reviewed to determine whether it was adequately performed and documented and to evaluate the results, relative to the conclusions to be presented in the auditor's report. Checklists, worksheets documenting analytical procedures, and financial statements are each a part of working papers; a review of only one of these parts most likely would be insufficient. (ID: 8395)

28. (b)   Detection risk is the risk that the auditor will not detect a material misstatement that exists in an assertion. Inherent risk is the susceptibility of an assertion to a material misstatement assuming that there are no related controls. Sampling risk arises from the possibility that, when a test of controls or a substantive test is restricted to a sample, the auditor's conclusions may be different from the conclusions the auditor would reach if the test were applied in the same way to all items in the account balance or class of transactions. Nonsampling risk includes all the aspects of audit risk that are not due to sampling. (ID: 2275)

29. (b)   As the assessed level of control risk increases, the acceptable level of detection risk decreases. To decrease detection risk, an auditor changes the nature, extent, or timing of tests of details. To decrease detection risk, an auditor increases the extent of test of details. The level of inherent risk doesn't change, although an auditor may change the assessment of the level of inherent risk. As inherent risk is the susceptibility of an assertion to misstatement, assuming no related internal controls, the assessment of inherent risk level rarely changes due to a change in control risk. Increased testing of controls that the auditor already has determined to be ineffective provides no benefit. (ID: 7799)

30. (c)   All three components of audit risk (control risk, detection risk, and inherent risk) may be assessed in quantitative terms, such as percentages, or nonquantitative terms, such as high, medium, or low risk. (ID: 5628)

31. (b)   In determining materiality, the auditor should consider (1) prior-periods' financial results and financial positions, (2) the period-to-date financial results and financial position, and (3) budgets or forecasts for the current period. The auditor should take into account any significant changes in the entity's circumstances and relevant changes in the economy or the industry in which the entity operates. The anticipated sample size of the planned tests and the internal control questionnaire are, if anything, dependent on materiality, not vice versa.

The contents of the management representation letter are not always known during the planning stages of the audit. (ID: 5629)

32. (b) Detection risk differs from control risk and inherent risk in that it can be changed at the auditor's discretion. Detection risk, control risk, and inherent risk make up audit risk. *Detection risk* is the risk that the auditor will not detect a misstatement that exists in a relevant assertion. It is a function of an audit procedure's effectiveness and how the auditor applies the procedure. Accordingly, it can be changed at the auditor's discretion. *Control risk* is the risk that a misstatement that could occur in a relevant assertion will not be prevented or detected on a timely basis by the entity's internal control. *Inherent risk* is the susceptibility of a relevant assertion to a misstatement assuming that there are no related controls. Thus, inherent risk and control risk, rather than detection risk, are the entity's risks, i.e., they exist independently of the audit and cannot be changed at the auditor's discretion. Detection risk arises from the fact that the auditor does not examine 100 percent of an account balance or a class of transactions and other factors (which include the possibility that an auditor might select an inappropriate audit procedure, misapply an appropriate audit procedure, or misinterpret the audit result) rather than from fraud risk factors. All three risks can be assessed in quantitative terms, such as percentages, or nonquantitative terms, such as high, medium, or low risk. (ID: 8617)

33. (d) Inherent risk is the susceptibility of a relevant financial statement assertion to a misstatement that could be material, either individually, or when aggregated with other misstatements, assuming that there are no related controls. If the auditor decides it would be efficient to consider how the internal auditors' work might affect the nature, extent, and timing of audit procedures, the auditor should assess the competence and objectivity of the internal auditors. This evaluation affects detection risk, not inherent risk. The risk that the internal control system will not prevent or detect a material misstatement on a timely basis is control risk, not inherent risk. The effectiveness of an audit procedure or its application by the auditor is detection risk, not inherent risk. (ID: 8833)

34. (a) If a client prefers not to correct several errors in the financial statements that are not material in the aggregate, the auditor should document the errors in the summary of uncorrected errors, and document the conclusion that the errors do not cause the financial statements to be misstated. (ID: 9371)

35. (c) Audit risk and materiality underlie the application of GAAS, especially the standards of fieldwork and reporting, and are reflected in the standard audit report. An understanding of internal control and sufficient appropriate evidence are requirements of GAAS, but do not affect the application of the standards of fieldwork and reporting as pervasively as audit risk and materiality. Quality control standards relate to the conduct of a firm's audit practice as a whole; GAAS relate to the conduct of individual audit engagements. A system of quality control provides a firm with reasonable assurance that its personnel will comply with GAAS. GAAS and quality control are related and a firm's quality control affects the conduct of audit engagements, but it does not have as direct and pervasive an effect on the application of the standards of fieldwork and reporting as audit risk and materiality. Further, deficiencies or noncompliance with a firm's system of quality control do not, in and of themselves, indicate that a particular audit engagement was not performed in accordance with GAAS. (ID: 15)

36. (a) Control risk is the risk that a misstatement that could occur in a relevant assertion and that could be material, either individually or when aggregated with other misstatements, will not be prevented or detected on a timely basis by the entity's internal control. The risk that the auditor will not detect a material misstatement is detection risk, not control risk. The risk that the auditor's assessment of internal controls will be at less than the maximum level is not a risk—the use of risk assessment procedures and tests of controls may appropriately result in such a conclusion. The susceptibility of material misstatement assuming there are no related internal controls, policies, or procedures is inherent risk, not control risk. (ID: 9917)

37. (b) An inherent limitation to internal control is the fact that controls can be circumvented by management override. Other limitations inherent to internal control include human failures such a faulty decision making and simple errors or mistakes. Additionally, controls can be circumvented by the collusion of two or more people. A well-designed internal control system does not ensure the achievement of an entity's control objectives nor can it be designed and operated to detect all errors and fraud; it only provides the entity with reasonable, not absolute, assurance due to these inherent limitations. (ID: 9931)

38. (c) The difference between the estimate for the allowance for doubtful accounts and the closest reasonable estimate should be treated by the auditor as a likely misstatement. When the auditor determines a range of

acceptable amounts, if management's recorded estimate falls outside the auditor's range, the difference between the recorded amount and the amount at the closest end of the auditor's range would be aggregated as a likely misstatement. The closest end of the auditor's range to management's estimate of $126,000 is $130,000. Thus, the difference of $4,000 should be aggregated as a likely misstatement by the auditor. If management's recorded estimate had fallen within the auditor's range (between $130,000 and $160,000), no difference would be aggregated. (ID: 89461)

Entity & Its Environment

39. (b) The purpose of applying analytical procedures in planning the audit, for example, comparing recorded amounts to anticipated results, is to assist the auditor in planning the nature, extent, and timing of auditing procedures that will be used to obtain audit evidence for account balances or classes of transactions. Inquiry of the client's legal counsel is an audit procedure that would be performed near the end of the audit engagement. Answer c. is a substantive audit procedure that would be performed later in the audit engagement to support management's assertion of completeness. The auditor determines whether controls have been placed in operation, i.e., whether the entity is using the control, as part of the understanding of internal control necessary to plan the audit. Answer d. is an example of testing the operating effectiveness of a control. Whether a control has been placed in operation at a point in time is different from its operating effectiveness over a period of time. The auditor evaluates the operating effectiveness of controls as part of assessing control risk. (ID: 5622)

40. (c) The auditor should document both the discussion among the audit team regarding the susceptibility of the entity's financial statements to material misstatement and the risk assessment procedures performed. (ID: 8266)

41. (a) The auditor should obtain sufficient knowledge about the accounting system because the methods influence the design of internal control. Materiality levels, audit objectives, and an auditor's acceptable level of audit risk are independent of the methods used to process accounting information. (ID: 5080)

42. (a) The second standard of fieldwork states, "The auditor must obtain a sufficient understanding of the entity and its environment, including its internal control, to assess the risk of material misstatement of the financial statements whether due to error or fraud, and to design the nature, timing, and extent of further audit procedures." The other choices are intermediate considerations. (ID: 5642)

43. (b) Auditors generally perform analytical procedures that use data aggregated at a high level to assist in planning the nature, extent, and timing of other audit procedures. The objective is to identify such things as the existence of unusual transactions and events; and amounts, ratios, and trends that might indicate matters that have financial statement and audit planning ramifications. This is an instance where an alternative response is also a true statement, but it is not the best answer. One could argue that an auditor may compare current and past financial results and financial positions to determine what is normal for an entity when setting materiality limits for the financial statements taken as a whole when planning the audit; however, the answer they usually use financial and nonfinancial data aggregated at a high level in the planning stage is the best answer to this question because it is generally more likely to be the case than the use of analytical procedures to develop a preliminary judgment about materiality. Or to be more pragmatic, GAAS specifically stress the concept described in the correct answer. Analytical procedures are not used to replace tests of controls. Analytical procedures can be used as substantive tests to obtain audit evidence (which is not part of the planning stage) about particular assertions related to account balances or classes of transactions. Substantive analytical procedures often involve the comparison of expectations developed by the auditor (not assertions developed by management) to recorded amounts or ratios developed from recorded amounts to achieve an audit objective related to a particular assertion made by management. (ID: 9929)

Service Organizations

44. (b) The significance of the controls of the service organization to those of the user organization depend primarily on the nature and materiality of the transactions it processes for the user organization and the degree of interaction between its activities and those of the user organization. The other answer alternatives do not speak to the question's premise—the significance to the controls to the user organization. The other answer alternatives deal more with their significance to the auditor, thus b. is the best answer. (ID: 9272)

45. (c)   All of the answer alternatives are appropriate sources for making inquiries as to the professional reputation and standing of the other auditor except for the service auditor's *vita*. The nature of the information on the other auditor's *vita* is what the user audit would be seeking to corroborate by making the inquiries to the other appropriate sources. (ID: 9273)

46. (a)   The most efficient method to obtain information about the transfer agent's internal control would be to review reports on internal control placed in operation and its operating effectiveness produced by the agent's own auditor. Answers c. and d. describe methods of obtaining information that are not as efficient as answer a. While a significant increase in the number of transactions processed may bear on the planning of the audit procedures, it doesn't reveal any information about internal controls. (ID: 8633)

47. (a)   In considering whether the report issued by Blue, a service auditor, is satisfactory, Green should make inquiries concerning Blue's professional reputation. The question does not give enough information to determine if Green should assess control risk at the maximum level and it is not relevant to the consideration of whether the service auditor's report is satisfactory for the user auditor's purposes. Green would perform tests of controls at the service organization to obtain audit evidence of the operating effectiveness of relevant controls that would allow Green to assess control risk—the service auditor's report does not provide such evidence; it helps in providing a sufficient understanding of the controls of the service organization. Green might review the audit programs followed by Blue to gain a better understanding of the controls of the service organization, but the guidance specifically directs the user auditor to consider the professional reputation of the service auditor for the determination of whether the report is satisfactory. (ID: 9359)

Errors & Fraud

48. (a)   Due to the characteristics of fraud, even a properly designed and planned audit may not detect a material misstatement resulting from fraud. Audit procedures that are effective for detecting unintentional misstatements may be ineffective for detecting intentional misstatements concealed through collusion. (ID: 2278)

49. (d)   An overly complex organizational structure as an operating characteristic is a risk factor of fraudulent financial reporting. (ID: 7018)

50. (b)   Failure to investigate discrepancies between physical inventory count and accounting records reveals, at best, a careless attitude, even if such discrepancies are due to innocent errors. Undue emphasis by management on meeting publicized earnings projections indicates a questionable control environment; the opposite attitude rarely indicates a problem. Monthly bank reconciliations with large outstanding checks and cash transactions processed and recorded electronically without paper documentation are often part of normal proper operations. (ID: 7629)

51. (b)   The auditor should take into consideration such specific conditions in identifying areas of the financial statements that are especially susceptible to misstatement. The allowance for doubtful accounts may increase substantially in a recession; therefore, the auditor most likely would focus increased attention on this account due to its susceptibility to understatement during a recession. In declining economic conditions, the client may be tempted to overstate accounts receivable by understating the allowance for doubtful accounts. Answers a., c., and d. are not likely to be affected by a recession. (ID: 8141)

52. (d)   The fact that management is interested in maintaining the entity's earnings trend by using aggressive accounting practices indicates that management may have an incentive to engage in fraudulent financial reporting also. Stock transactions of management or the board of directors are not ordinarily considered fraud risk factors. Aggressive financial forecasts as opposed to conservative financial forecasts would be considered a fraud risk factor. (ID: 8155)

53. (d)   Disclosure of possible fraud to parties other than the client's senior management and its audit committee ordinarily is not part of the auditor's responsibility, and ordinarily would be precluded by the auditor's ethical or legal obligation of confidentiality unless the matter is reflected in the auditor's report. The auditor should recognize, however, that in the following circumstances a duty to disclose outside the client may exist: (a) when the entity reports an auditor change under the appropriate securities law on Form 8-K, (b) to a successor auditor when the successor makes inquiries in accordance with AU 315, (c) in response to a subpoena, and (d) to a funding agency or other specified agency in accordance with requirements for the audits of entities that receive governmental financial assistance. (ID: 163)

54. (d) The auditor has a responsibility to plan and perform the audit to obtain reasonable assurance about whether the financial statements are free of material misstatements, whether caused by error or fraud.

(ID: 5633)

55. (b) When supporting accounting records and files that should be readily available are not produced promptly when requested, it suggests either a hostile staff (poor control environment) or a poor information and communication system. Senior financial management should participate in the selection of accounting principles and determination of significant estimates. Related-party transactions do not, in themselves, indicate misstatements. Management's excessive interest in updating the IT capabilities may lead to poor financial performance by the entity, but not necessarily misstatements in the financial statements. (ID: 7826)

56. (d) Auditors should obtain assurance from the entity's attorney, verify clerical accuracy, and determine whether inadequate asset safeguards are corrected during the evidence gathering stage of the audit. Considering whether audit results affect the assessment of fraud risk is an overall review stage procedure. (ID: 7027)

57. (d) The auditor must inform the audit committee directly regarding fraud possibly concerning senior management or causing a material misstatement of the financial statements. The auditor may need to disclose information: when legal and regulatory compliance requirements exist; to a successor auditor; in response to a subpoena; or to a funding agency or other specific agency in accordance with requirements for the audits of entities that receive financial assistance from a governmental agency. Typically, the auditor reports directly to the SEC only when the audit committee fails to do so. (ID: 7809)

58. (c) A strained relationship between management and auditors is one of the risk factors of fraud due to fraudulent financial reporting. A lack of interest in maintaining an earnings trend tends to reduce the risk of fraud due to fraudulent financial reporting. It may be in an entity's best interest to sell computer hardware before it is depreciated fully. The mere existence of outstanding checks of any amount in monthly bank reconciliations is a normal occurrence. (ID: 8420)

59. (b) A lack of independent checks or inadequate segregation of duties is one of the risk factors associated with misstatements arising from misappropriation of assets. The other answer alternatives are risk factors relating to misstatements arising from fraudulent financial reporting. (ID: 8646)

60. (b) If not already performed during the overall review stage of the audit, the auditor should perform analytical procedures relating to revenue with the objective of identifying unusual or unexpected relationships involving revenue accounts that may indicate a material misstatement due to fraudulent financial reporting. (ID: 9396)

61. (a) The analytical procedure most likely to be used during the planning stage of the audit is comparing current year to prior year sales volumes. Comparing the current year ratio of aggregate salaries paid to the number of employees to the prior year's ratio is the next best answer. Analytical procedures used in planning the audit generally use data aggregated at a high level which is true of both of these answers. However, in planning the audit, the auditor should also perform analytical procedures relating to revenue with the objective of identifying unusual or unexpected relationships that may indicate a material misstatement due to fraudulent financial reporting. Thus, it is the more likely of the two procedures. The other two answer alternatives do not describe analytical procedures. (ID: 9942)

Assessing & Responding to RMM

62. (c) The auditor should document: (1) the assessment of the risk of material misstatement at the financial statement and relevant assertion levels; (2) the basis for that assessment; (3) significant risks identified and related controls evaluated; as well as (4) risks identified that require tests of controls to obtain sufficient audit evidence and the related controls evaluated. (ID: 8265)

63. (c) Regardless of the assessed risk of material misstatement, the auditor should design and perform substantive procedures for all relevant assertions related to each material class of transactions, account balance, and disclosure. The auditor should perform tests of controls when the auditor's risk assessment includes an expectation of the operating effectiveness of controls or when it is not possible or practicable to reduce detection risk at the relevant assertion level to an acceptably low level with audit evidence obtained from substantive procedures alone. Analytical procedures are required to be used in the planning stage of the audit

(and in the final review stage); however, they would not be performed to verify the design of internal control procedures. A dual-purpose test is a procedure that is designed to test both the operating effectiveness of the control(s) and details of the same transaction; this is efficient, but not required. (ID: 4260)

64. (a) The auditor's assessment of the identified risks at the relevant assertion level provides a basis for considering the appropriate audit approach for designing and performing further audit procedures. In some cases, the auditor may determine that performing only substantive procedures is appropriate for specific relevant assertions and risks. In those circumstances, the auditor may exclude the effect of controls from the relevant risk assessment. This may be because the auditor's risk assessment procedures have not identified any effective controls relevant to the assertion or because testing the operating effectiveness of controls would be inefficient. If evidence is not available, tests of controls are not performed. As the assessed level of control risk increases, the auditor is less likely to test controls. If the auditor is aware of many internal control weaknesses, the assessed level of control risk will be high, and controls will not be tested. (ID: 5651)

65. (c) As the risk of material misstatement decreases, which consists of inherent risk and control risk, detection risk increases; therefore, the auditor may decrease the assurance obtained from substantive procedures by altering their nature, extent, and timing. Answers b. and d. would tend to increase assurance obtained from procedures performed. (ID: 2944)

66. (a) In some cases, the auditor may determine that performing only substantive procedures is appropriate for specific relevant assertions and risks. In those circumstances, the auditor may exclude the effect of controls from the relevant risk assessment. This may be because the auditor's risk assessment procedures have not identified any effective controls relevant to the assertion or because testing the operating effectiveness of controls would be inefficient. (ID: 4258)

67. (d) The auditor should design and perform further audit procedures whose nature, extent, and timing are responsive to the assessed risk of material misstatement at the relevant assertion level. Detection risk is a function of the effectiveness of an auditing procedure and its application by the auditor; therefore, the assessed risk of material misstatement will determine the acceptable level of detection risk and hence the appropriate audit procedures to be performed. The effectiveness of internal control, inherent risk, and materiality thresholds are all factors that help the auditor assess the risk of material misstatement. (ID: 4689)

68. (c) Analytical procedures have revealed no unusual or unexpected results is the explanation that best describes why an auditor may decide to reduce tests of details for a particular audit objective. The auditor may determine that performing only substantive analytical procedures may be sufficient to reduce the planned level of detection risk to an acceptably low level. The other answer explanations are not factors. (ID: 9386)

69. (b) The most effectively timed audit procedure for revenue would be to inspect transactions occurring in the last month of the fiscal year and review the related sales contracts to determine that revenue was posted in the proper period. Audit procedures should be in synch with the flow of the transactions being tested. This approach will allow the best evidence to be obtained because the most relevant information will be available during the last month, rather than an interim date. A review of period-end compensation for bonuses paid which are based on revenue is not an audit procedure to test revenue. (ID: 9389)

Illegal Acts by Clients

70. (b) Large cash payments are unusual in normal, legal business practice. Cash transactions have the attribute of anonymity, which is useful for hiding illegal acts. Properly disclosed related party transactions and contributions to several local candidates, in and of themselves, do not suggest the occurrence of illegal acts. Internal control procedures are subject to cost/benefit constraints. An entity may appropriately decide that a major weakness is too costly to alleviate. (ID: 6576)

71. (d) Management and other employees are unlikely to implicate themselves in wrongdoing on an internal control questionnaire that they know is designed expressly for audit purposes. Reading the minutes of the board of directors' (BOD) meetings, making inquiries of the client's management, or performing tests of details of transactions is more likely to reveal possible illegal acts. Minutes of the BOD meetings are recorded with considerable BOD scrutiny and over a long period. Close scrutiny makes it difficult to falsify minutes. Also, wrongdoers might not think to falsify minutes sufficiently far enough in advance of possible illegal acts to mask motivations or opportunities for performing illegal acts. Inquiries of the client's management can target issues

raised during those same inquiries. Also, body language, voice tone, and other intangibles noticed during a face-to-face discussion may indicate possible illegal acts to an alert interviewer. Tests of details of transactions may reveal unauthorized or improperly recorded transactions, investigation by a governmental agency, large payments for unspecified service to consultants, excess commissions, or agents' fees, unusually large cash payments, or other "red flags." (ID: 7820)

72. (a)   When the auditor becomes aware of information concerning a possible illegal act, the auditor should obtain an understanding of the nature of the act, the circumstances in which it occurred, and sufficient other information to evaluate the effect on the financial statements. Obtaining an understanding of the act will not necessarily affect the reliability of management's representations. Consideration of whether other similar acts may have occurred is an additional procedure used, if necessary, by the auditor to obtain further understanding of the nature of the acts. It would not be considered until after the auditor determined the effect of the act on the financial statements. While the occurrence of illegal acts will be communicated to the audit committee, the auditor will not necessarily recommend remedial actions. (ID: 2938)

73. (a)   If information comes to the auditor's attention that provides evidence concerning possible illegal acts that could have a material indirect effect on the financial statements, the auditor should apply audit procedures specifically directed to determining whether an illegal act has occurred. Only after determining that an illegal act has occurred would the auditor contemplate the steps in the alternatives. (ID: 172)

74. (d)   If management fails to take appropriate remedial action when informed of illegal acts, management's integrity and representations may be questionable. The auditor should consider withdrawal if illegal payments do not violate the client's policies. If the client receives financial assistance from the government, the discovery of illegal acts may increase the auditor's reporting responsibilities. It is not in employees' interests to document their illegal acts, so it would not be surprising that documentation might not exist. (ID: 6931)

75. (b)   An auditor who becomes aware of possible illegal activities shall inform the entity's management. If the auditor concludes that the illegal act has a material effect on the financial statements and management has not taken appropriate remedial actions, and departure from a standard report seems reasonable, the auditor shall directly report this to the board of directors. The entity is required to notify the SEC no later than 1 business day after receipt of such report. If the entity fails to notify the SEC within 1 business day, the auditor must notify the SEC within 1 business day. (ID: 6820)

76. (a)   Forced discontinuance of operations in a foreign country may indicate illegal acts. Annual donations to a local politician generally are not illegal. Management may elect not to correct material weaknesses if the cost of correction would exceed the benefit. Disclosure of subsequent events generally would not cause the auditor to question whether illegal acts have occurred. (ID: 189)

77. (a)   The auditor's responsibility to detect and report misstatements resulting from illegal acts having a direct material effect on the financial statements is the same as that for misstatements caused by error or fraud. (The auditor should plan and perform the audit to obtain reasonable assurance about whether the financial statements are free of material misstatement, whether caused by error or fraud.) Due to the nature of illegal acts, an audit made in accordance with generally accepted auditing standards provides no assurance that illegal acts that could have an indirect material effect on the financial statements will be detected or any contingent liabilities that may result will be disclosed. (ID: 4671)

78. (c)   The auditor should consider the implications of an illegal act in relation to other aspects of the audit, particularly the reliability of representations of management. (ID: 5085)

79. (d)   The auditor may conclude that withdrawal is necessary when the client does not take the remedial action that the auditor considers necessary in the circumstances even when the illegal act is not material to the financial statements. (ID: 7487)

80. (c)   If a possible illegal act has occurred the auditor should obtain an understanding of the act, the circumstances under which it occurred, and sufficient information to evaluate its effect on the financial statements. Normally, an audit conducted in accordance with GAAS does not include procedures specifically designed to detect illegal acts not having a direct and material effect on the financial statements. An auditor's training, experience, and understanding of the client probably would be insufficient to provide a basis of the

determination as to whether illegal acts have occurred; consultation with legal counsel or other specialists may be necessary. Not all illegal acts would require an auditor to express a qualified opinion or an adverse opinion on the financial statements taken as a whole. (ID: 8422)

81. (b) The discovery of unexplained payments made to government employees would most likely raise a question about the occurrence of illegal acts. The exchange of property for similar property in a nonmonetary transaction is not an indicator of an illegal act. Failure to develop adequate procedures that detect unauthorized purchases and difficult-to-audit expense account transactions are causes for concern, but they are not as strong an indicator of a possible illegal act as unexplained payments to government officials. (ID: 9355)

82. (c) The auditor should consider withdrawing from the audit engagement and disassociating from future relationships with the client when the client does not take the remedial action that the auditor considers necessary even when the illegal act is not material to the financial statements. Adding an explanatory paragraph to a standard report is not an option when an illegal act has occurred and a client refuses to take remedial action. A qualified or adverse opinion would be in order if the effect on the financial statements was material and the act had not been accounted for or disclosed properly—the questions states that the amounts were immaterial to the financial statements. Disclosure of an illegal act to parties other than the client's senior management and those charged with governance is not ordinarily part of the auditor's responsibility, and such disclosure would be precluded by the auditor's ethical or legal obligation of confidentiality, unless the matter affects the opinion on the financial statements. However, in the following circumstances a duty to notify parties outside the client may exist: (1) when the entity reports an auditor change under the appropriate securities law on Form 8-K; (2) to a successor auditor when the successor makes inquiries in accordance with AU 315, *Communications Between Predecessor and Successor Auditors*; (3) in response to a subpoena; or (4) to a funding agency or other specified agency in accordance with requirements for the audits of entities that receive financial assistance from a government agency. The question does not indicate that any of these special circumstances exist; further, no guidance exists that calls for reporting to officials at least one level above persons who received the bribe. (ID: 9380)

Communication With Those Charged With Governance

83. (d) The auditor should inform the audit committee of selection of or changes in significant accounting policies, whether or not they pertain to emerging areas for which there is no authoritative guidance or to everyday transactions. The auditor is not responsible for financial analysis, such as a list of negative trends. Management's responsibility for financial statements is the same for every company; further, it is redundant to repeat it in communications to the audit committee when it is included in the audit report. The auditor reports difficulties working with management, not customers, to the audit committee. (ID: 7095)

84. (c) The auditor must inform the audit committee of any disagreements, whether or not resolved, with management about matters that, individually or in the aggregate, could have a significant impact on the financial statements. The auditor rarely discusses either the basis for the auditor's judgment about materiality or justification for sampling methods selection with the client's management or audit committee. The auditor must discuss the auditor's judgment about the quality of a public company's accounting principles and underlying estimates in the financial statements with the audit committee, not the quality of earnings. (ID: 7834)

85. (b) While the amount of misstatements that would be material may be discussed with the audit committee, the auditor must report both the methods used to account for significant unusual transactions and disagreements with management, whether or not satisfactorily resolved. The auditor also has the responsibility to report significant deficiencies and material weaknesses. An indication of fraud and illegal acts is an example of a possible significant deficiency or material weakness. (ID: 5637)

86. (b) In some cases, management may decide to consult with other accountants about auditing and accounting matters. When the auditor is aware that such consultation has occurred, the auditor should discuss with the audit committee his or her views about significant matters that were the subject of such consultation. The rate of turnover being too high and the auditor's assessed level of control risk are judgments of the auditor. The question of subsequent events would be less likely to be discussed than accounting consultations when an auditor is identifying matters for communication with an entity's audit committee. (ID: 6238)

87. (d) The auditor should inform the audit committee about adjustments arising from the audit that could, in the auditor's judgment, either individually or in the aggregate, have a significant effect on the entity's financial

reporting process. The auditor should determine that the audit committee is informed about the process used by management in formulating particularly sensitive accounting estimates and about the basis for the auditor's conclusions regarding the reasonableness of those estimates. In order for the audit committee to understand the nature of the assurance provided by an audit, the auditor should communicate the level of responsibility assumed for these matters under generally accepted auditing standards. (ID: 7637)

88. (d) Disagreements [between the auditor and management] of the amount of the LIFO inventory layer based on preliminary information do not have to be communicated by the auditor to those charged with governance. Disagreements do not include differences of opinion based on incomplete facts or preliminary information that are later resolved. Although the correct answer did not indicate it was later resolved, the other answer alternatives did not indicate that they were based on incomplete or preliminary information. (ID: 9391)

PERFORMANCE BY TOPICS

Each category below parallels a topic covered in Chapter 2. Record the number and percentage of questions you answered correctly in each topic.

Planning & Supervision

Question #	Correct	√
1		
2		
3		
4		
5		
6		
7		
8		
9		
10		
11		
12		
13		
14		
15		
16		
17		
18		
19		
20		

Questions　　20

Correct　　_____
% Correct　　_____

Audit Risk & Materiality

Question #	Correct	√
21		
22		
23		
24		
25		
26		
27		
28		
29		
30		
31		
32		
33		
34		
35		
36		
37		
38		

Questions　　18

Correct　　_____
% Correct　　_____

Entity & Its Environment

Question #	Correct	√
39		
40		
41		
42		
43		

Questions　　5

Correct　　_____
% Correct　　_____

Service Organizations

Question #	Correct	√
44		
45		
46		
47		

Questions　　4

Correct　　_____
% Correct　　_____

Errors & Fraud

Question #	Correct	√
48		
49		
50		
51		
52		
53		
54		
55		
56		
57		
58		
59		
60		
61		

Questions　　14

Correct　　_____
% Correct　　_____

Assessing & Responding to RMM

Question #	Correct	√
62		
63		
64		
65		
66		
67		
68		
69		

Questions　　8

Correct　　_____
% Correct　　_____

Illegal Acts by Clients

Question #	Correct	√
70		
71		
72		
73		
74		
75		
76		
77		
78		
79		
80		
81		
82		

Questions　　13

Correct　　_____
% Correct　　_____

Communication With Those Charged With Governance

Question #	Correct	√
83		
84		
85		
86		
87		
88		

Questions　　6

Correct　　_____
% Correct　　_____

Solution 2-2 SIMULATION ANSWER: Audit Risk

Factors	Impact on Audit Risk	
	Increases Audit Risk	**No Impact**
1. The company has begun to focus on a strategic advertising plan so it may expand its market into other states.		✓
2. During year 2, management issued additional long-term debt with complex financial covenants.	✓	
3. Scott is divided into two divisions, which serve the major markets of the company's products.		✓
4. The new CFO was an audit manager from the predecessor audit firm.	✓	

Explanations

1. It is not likely that an advertising plan will increase audit risk.

2. Audit risk is increased. The auditor will need to focus more attention on the complex financial covenants to determine whether there have been any violations and whether they need to be disclosed in the financial statements.

3. It is not likely that having two divisions that serve different markets will increase audit risk. This is an example of a customary business practice.

4. Audit risk is increased. When a company hires its prior audit firm's audit manager as its CFO the current auditors must consider whether the audit manager exercised an appropriate level of skepticism during the audit process prior to leaving the audit firm. (ID: 9201)

Solution 2-3 SIMULATION ANSWER: Risk of Material Misstatement

Factors	Effect on Risk of Material Misstatement
1. Governmental regulation over the banking industry is extensive.	Decreases
2. NFB operates profitably in growing prosperous area.	Decreases
3. Overall demand for the industry's product is high.	Decreases
4. Interest rates have been volatile recently.	Increases
5. The availability of funds for additional mortgages is promising.	Decreases

Explanations

Decreases

1. Regulation over the industry creates more accountability, thus risk is decreased.

Decreases

2. Profitability reduces the pressures that can increase risks, for example, the risk of fraudulent financial reporting by management tasked with achieving profitable results, so risk is decreased.

Decreases

3. High demand for the industry's product, like profitability, reduces the pressures that can increase risks, so risk is decreased.

Increases

4. Having to constantly react to volatile interest rates increases risk because more judgment is needed and error rates usually increase under these conditions.

Decreases

5. The availability of funds allows the industry to meet the high demand for its products, thereby increasing stability, so risk is decreased. (ID: 9202)

Solution 2-4 SIMULATION ANSWER: Risk of Material Misstatement

Factors	Effect on Risk of Material Misstatement
1. The principal shareholder is also the chief executive officer and controls the board of directors.	Increases
2. Branch management is compensated based on branch profitability.	Increases
3. The internal auditor reports directly to the chairman of the board's audit committee.	Decreases
4. The Accounting Department has experienced little turnover in personnel recently.	Decreases
5. Middleton Bank is a continuing audit client.	Decreases

Explanations

Increases

1. Risk is increased if management's or those charged with governance's personal financial situation is tied to that of the entity. Risk is also increased when too much control rests with one individual.

Increases

2. Risk is increased when management's compensation is based on profitability goals due to increased pressure to falsify results.

Decreases

3. Risk is decreased when the internal auditor reports to such an officer with the status to ensure broad audit coverage and adequate consideration of, and action on, findings and recommendations of the internal auditor.

Decreases

4. Risk is decreased when the accounting department has low turnover because error rates are usually lower.

Decreases

5. Risk is decreased because a continuing auditor usually has more knowledge of the entity.   (ID: 9203)

_____

Solution 2-5 SIMULATION ANSWER: Risk of Material Misstatement

Factors	Effect on Risk of Material Misstatement
1. Management fails to establish proper procedures to provide reasonable assurance of reliable accounting estimates.	Increases
2. Management has been receptive to Howard's suggestions relating to accounting adjustments.	Decreases
3. Oak Bank recently opened a new branch office that is not yet profitable.	Increases
4. Oak Bank recently installed a new sophisticated computer system.	Increases

Explanations

Increases

1. Risk is increased if management doesn't have proper procedures in place to provide reasonable assurance of reliable accounting estimates because results will usually be more inconsistent and less accurate.

Decreases

2. Risk is decreased when management is receptive to the auditor's recommendations.

Increases

3. Risk is increased when a company expands and particularly so if the new venture is unprofitable. This creates pressures which increase risk.

Increases

4. Risk is increased when a new computer system is installed because until it is fully tested under actual conditions the degree of its reliability is unknown. (ID: 9204)

—————————————

Solution 2-6 SIMULATION ANSWER: Research

AU	§	316	62	(ID: 9205)

.62   Because fraudulent journal entries often are made at the end of a reporting period, the auditor's testing ordinarily should focus on the journal entries and other adjustments made at that time. However, because material misstatements in financial statements due to fraud can occur throughout the period and may involve extensive efforts to conceal how it is accomplished, the auditor should consider whether there also is a need to test journal entries throughout the period under audit.

_____

Solution 2-7 SIMULATION ANSWER: Research

AU	§	314	14	(ID: 9217)

.14   The members of the audit team, including the auditor with final responsibility for the audit, should discuss the susceptibility of the entity's financial statements to material misstatements. This discussion could be held concurrently with the discussion among the audit team that is specified by section 316 to discuss the susceptibility of the entity's financial statements to fraud. When the entire engagement is performed by a single auditor, the auditor should consider and document the susceptibility of the entity's financial statements to material misstatements. In these circumstances, the auditor should consider other factors that may be necessary in the engagement, such as personnel possessing specialized skills.

_____

CHAPTER 3

INTERNAL CONTROL

CHAPTER 3

INTERNAL CONTROL

I. Overview

A. Definition
Internal control is a process—effected by those charged with governance, management and other personnel—designed to provide reasonable assurance about the achievement of the entity's objectives with regard to reliability of financial reporting, effectiveness and efficiency of operations, and compliance with applicable laws and regulations. Internal control consists of five interrelated components.

B. Components of Internal Control

Exhibit 1 ▶ Components of Internal Control Mnemonic

C	**C**ontrol Activities
R	**R**isk Assessment
I	**I**nformation & Communication Systems
M	**M**onitoring
E	Control **E**nvironment

1. **Control Activities** Control activities are those policies and procedures established to provide reasonable assurance that management decisions are executed. Control activities may have various objectives and are found at several levels. Control activities relevant to an audit are categorized as practices that relate to the following:

   a. **Performance Reviews** This includes reviewing and analyzing the actual performance of the entity; relating different sets of data (operating or financial) to one another, while analyzing the relationships and investigative and corrective actions; as well as comparing internal data with external information and reviewing functional or activity performance.

   b. **Information Processing** Controls are performed to check accuracy, completeness, and authorization of transactions. The two broad groupings of information systems control activities are application controls and general controls.

   c. **Physical Controls** These involve physical security of assets, including limited access to assets and records; authorization for access to computer programs and data files; and periodic counting and comparison with amounts shown on control records.

   d. **Segregation of Duties** Incompatible functions place employees in the position to both perpetrate and conceal errors or fraud in the normal course of their duties. Therefore, a well designed plan of organization separates the duties of authorization, record keeping, and custody of assets.

2. **Risk Assessment** For financial reporting purposes, risk assessment is an entity's (not an auditor's) identification, analysis, and management of risks relevant to the preparation of financial statements that are presented fairly in conformity with GAAP. Risks relevant to financial reporting include external and internal events that may occur and adversely affect an entity's ability to process and report financial data consistent with management's assertions.

3. **Information & Communication** This refers to the identification, retention, and transfer of information in a timely manner enabling personnel to execute their responsibilities.

    a. **Information** The quality of information impacts management's capacity to make decisions to direct the entity's activities and prepare financial statements. The information system of concern to the auditor, including the accounting system, is composed of the procedures and records established to record, process, summarize, and report transactions as well as maintain accountability for the corresponding assets, liabilities, and equity.

    b. **Communication** Communication includes establishing individual duties and responsibilities relating to internal control and making them known to involved personnel.

4. **Monitoring** Monitoring is a process that evaluates the quality of internal control performance over time. Monitoring also includes initiating appropriate corrective actions. The process is achieved through separate evaluations or ongoing activities. Customer complaints and other external communication may indicate areas of concern.

    a. **Management** Monitoring is a responsibility of management. Management must monitor internal control to consider whether it is being implemented as planned and that it is modified appropriately as changes occur. Internal auditors, or personnel with similar duties, may contribute to monitoring.

    b. **Necessity** Monitoring is necessary, due to the tendency of internal control to break down over time.

5. **Control Environment** The control environment is the foundation for all other components of internal control. It sets the tone of an organization that influences the control consciousness of its people. In other words, it establishes the overall attitude, awareness, and actions of the board of directors, management, employees, and others concerning the importance and emphasis of internal control in the entity. The following elements make up the control environment:

    a. Communication and enforcement of integrity and ethical values

    b. Management's commitment to competence

    c. Participation of those charged with governance

    d. Management's philosophy and operating style

    e. Organizational structure

    f. Methods of assigning authority and responsibility

    g. Human resource policies and practices

II. Understanding of Internal Control (AU 314 continued)

A. General Considerations

1. **Responsibility** It is management's responsibility to establish and maintain internal control.

2. **Perspective** The classification of internal control into five components establishes a framework for evaluation of an entity's internal control, but it is not necessarily how the entity implements internal control. The auditor's main concern is whether, and how, a specific control prevents, detects, and corrects material misstatements in relevant assertions, rather than its classification into any particular component.

3. **Accounting Policies** The auditor should obtain an understanding of the entity's selection and application of accounting policies and should consider whether they are appropriate and consistent with GAAP, or an other comprehensive basis of accounting (OCBOA), as well as accounting policies used in the industry. The understanding should include: the methods used to account for significant and unusual transactions; the effect of significant accounting policies in controversial or emerging areas that lack authoritative guidance; and changes in accounting policies. The auditor should also identify new financial reporting standards or regulations applicable to the entity and consider when and how the entity will adopt them.

4. **Inherent Limitations** Inherent limitations exist with respect to the effectiveness of an entity's internal control. The best designed and operated system of internal control can provide only reasonable assurance regarding accomplishment of control objectives.

   a. **Errors (Inadvertent)** Mistakes may occur in the application of certain policies and procedures due to misunderstanding of instructions or personal carelessness.

   b. **Fraud (Intentional)** Controls can be circumvented by collusion or management override. The potential for override of controls by management depends on the control environment to a great extent.

5. **Smaller Entities** The extent of segregation of duties may be limited in smaller entities due to fewer employees. However, even in a very small entity, it can be practicable to implement some degree of segregation of duties or other form of simple but effective controls for vital areas. For example, if adequate segregation of duties is not possible, management can provide more oversight of incompatible activities.

6. **Identifying Internal Controls** The auditor should identify the controls that are likely to prevent or detect and correct material misstatements in specific relevant assertions. Generally, the auditor gains an understanding of controls and relates them to relevant assertions in the context of processes and systems in which they exist. This is useful because individual control activities do not usually address a specific risk by themselves.

7. **Relationship** Controls can be directly or indirectly related to an assertion. The more indirect the relationship, the less effective that control may be in reducing control risk for that assertion.

8. **Auditability** The auditor's understanding of internal control may cause concerns about the auditability of an entity's financial statements. Doubts as to the integrity of management may cause the auditor to conclude that an audit cannot be completed. Also, the condition and reliability of the entity's records may cause concern regarding the sufficiency of audit evidence available. In such cases, the auditor may need to consider a qualified opinion or disclaimer of opinion. However, some circumstances may require the auditor to withdraw from the engagement.

B. **Relevance**

There is a direct relationship between an entity's *objectives* and the internal controls *components* it implements. The auditor need consider only the objectives and related controls relevant to the audit. Not all categories of objectives and related controls are relevant to a financial statement audit. Even though internal control components may apply to the entire entity or to only a portion of its divisions or operations, it might not be essential for the auditor to obtain an understanding of internal control concerning all of an entity's divisions and operations.

1. **Relevant Controls** Controls, including those that pertain to the entity's ability to produce financial statements for external use in accordance with GAAP, or OCBOA, are relevant to the audit. It is not necessary to assess all controls related to assessing the risks of material misstatement. This is a matter of professional judgment. However, the auditor should evaluate the design and implementation of related controls for all *significant risks* and for risks that substantive procedures alone do not provide sufficient audit evidence.

When using professional judgment to decide which controls should be assessed, the auditor should consider the circumstances, the applicable component, and factors such as:

a. Materiality

b. The size of the entity

c. The nature of the entity's business, including its organization and ownership characteristics

d. The diversity and complexity of its operations

e. Its applicable legal and regulatory requirements

f. The nature and complexity of the systems that are part of the entity's internal control, including the use of service organizations

2. **Significant Risks** *Significant risks* are risks that require special audit consideration (see Chapter 2). Therefore, the auditor should evaluate the design and implementation of related controls for all *significant risks.* However, risks related to significant nonroutine or judgmental matters are less likely to be subject to routine controls. This means the auditor will need to consider how management responds to the risks and whether appropriate control activities have been implemented to address the risks. Appropriate control activities may consist of a review of assumptions by senior management or experts; formal processes for estimations; or approval by the audit committee, or equivalent.

3. **Other Risks Requiring Tests of Controls** The auditor should obtain an understanding of controls over those risks for which it is not possible or practicable to obtain sufficient audit evidence from substantive procedures alone. Such risks may concern routine transactions that are often highly automated with little or no manual intervention. In such cases, audit evidence may be available only in electronic form; therefore, its appropriateness and sufficiency often depend on the operating effectiveness of controls over its completeness and accuracy.

4. **Partially Relevant Controls** Controls pertaining to data the auditor uses to apply or evaluate auditing procedures such as those related to the operations and compliance objectives or the completeness and accuracy of information may also be relevant to the audit. For example, an auditor may use production statistics in analytical procedures. Also, controls related to compliance with tax laws may have a direct and material effect on the financial statements.

5. **Irrelevant Controls** Some controls such as those concerned with adherence to health and safety regulations or the effectiveness, economy, and efficiency of certain management decision-making processes (the appropriate price to charge for its products, etc.) are irrelevant to the audit and do not need to be considered.

6. **Overlapping Controls** Internal control over safeguarding assets to reduce unauthorized procurement, use, or disposition of assets may involve controls related to both financial reporting and operations objectives. For example, use of a lockbox system for collecting payments or passwords for restricted access to payroll records may be relevant to the audit; while controls reducing raw material waste in production usually are irrelevant to the audit.

C. **Depth of Understanding**
Obtaining an understanding of internal control consists of evaluating the design and implementation of controls.

1. **Design** To evaluate the design of a control, the auditor should consider whether the control, individually or in combination with other controls, is able to effectively prevent or detect and correct material misstatements.

2. **Implementation** To evaluate the implementation of a control means to determine whether a control is actually being used by the entity. In determining whether to consider implementation of a control, the auditor should first consider the design of the control. If the control is designed improperly, it may represent a material weakness in the entity's internal control; therefore, the auditor should consider whether to communicate this to those in charge of governance and management.

3. **Procedures** The auditor should perform risk assessment procedures (covered in Chapter 2) to obtain an understanding of internal control. More specifically, procedures to obtain evidence about the design and implementation of controls may include:

   a. Inquiring of entity personnel; inquiries alone are not sufficient to evaluate the design and implementation of a control

   b. Observing the application of specific controls

   c. Inspecting documents and reports

   d. Tracing transactions relevant to financial reporting through the information system

4. **Sufficiency** Obtaining this understanding is not sufficient to serve as testing the operating effectiveness of controls, unless there is some automation that provides for the consistent operation of the control. For example, obtaining audit evidence about the implementation of a manual control at a point in time does not provide audit evidence about the operating effectiveness of the control at other times during the period under audit. However, because IT processing is inherently consistent generally, procedures to determine implementation of an automated control may serve as a test of that control's operating effectiveness.

D. **Understanding of Components of Internal Control**

1. **Control Environment** The auditor should obtain sufficient knowledge of the control environment to understand management's and the board of directors' attitude, awareness, and actions concerning the control environment. The auditor should concentrate on the implementation of controls rather than the form, because appropriate controls may exist but not be enforced. In evaluating the design of the entity's control environment, the auditor should consider all elements of the control environment and how they are incorporated. The responsibilities of the board of directors and its committees, particularly the audit committee, are extremely important.

2. **Risk Assessment** The auditor should obtain sufficient familiarity of the client's risk assessment process to discern how management evaluates risks relevant to financial reporting objectives and elects actions to mitigate those risks. In evaluating the design and implementation of the entity's risk assessment process, the auditor should consider how management identifies business risks relevant to financial reporting, determines the significance of those risks, assesses the probability of their occurrence, and elects actions to mitigate them. An entity's perspective when assessing risk differs from the auditor's evaluation of audit risk. The entity seeks to identify, evaluate, and manage risks that impact the entity's objectives. The auditor evaluates risks to assess the potential for material misstatement of the financial statements.

3. **Information & Communication** The auditor should obtain a sufficient understanding of the process the entity employs to communicate duties, responsibilities, and material matters pertaining to financial reporting. The auditor's understanding of communication also includes communications between management and the board of directors, particularly the audit committee, as well as external communications pertaining to financial reporting matters, such as those with regulatory authorities.

The auditor should obtain sufficient knowledge about the information system pertaining to financial reporting to understand the following:

a. The classes of transactions in the entity's operations that are significant to the financial statements and how those transactions originate within the entity's business processes.

b. The procedures by which transactions are initiated, authorized, recorded, processed, and reported in the financial statements as well as how incorrect processing of transactions is resolved.

c. The accounting records, supporting information, and specific accounts in the financial statements involved in the processing and reporting of transactions.

d. How the information system captures events and conditions, other than classes of transactions, that are significant to the financial statements.

e. The financial reporting process used to prepare the entity's financial statements, including significant accounting estimates and disclosures.

4. **Control Activities** The process of obtaining an understanding of control activities usually overlaps with obtaining knowledge of other components. The understanding gained regarding the existence of control activities while considering other components will indicate if additional understanding of control activities is warranted. Audit planning does **not** demand knowledge of control activities related to every account balance, transaction class, or disclosure component in the financial statements.

5. **Monitoring** The auditor should obtain sufficient understanding of the major types of activities the entity employs to monitor internal control pertaining to financial reporting, including the manner in which those activities are used to take appropriate corrective actions. The auditor also should obtain an understanding of the sources of information used in monitoring activities, as well as management's basis for determining that the sources are reliable. If management assumes, without a basis for that assumption, that data produced from the entity's information system is reliable, errors may exist that could potentially lead management to incorrect conclusions.

E. Documentation
The auditor should document the following regarding the understanding of internal control: (a) key elements of the understanding obtained regarding the five components of internal control; (b) the sources of information from which the understanding was obtained; and (c) the risk assessment procedures performed. The form and extent of documentation is influenced by the size and complexity of the entity, as well as the nature of the entity's internal control. For a large, complex entity, this may include flowcharts, questionnaires, or decision tables. For a small, simple entity, a memorandum may be sufficient.

F.   **Tools**

1.   **Flowchart Approach** An internal control flowchart is a sequential, graphic representation of a portion of a company's internal control system. It shows the segregation of functions, document flows, controls, etc.

Exhibit 2 ▶ Common Flowchart Symbols

DOCUMENT: Paper documents and reports of all kinds, e.g., sales invoices, purchase orders, employee paychecks, and computer-prepared error listings.

COMPUTER OPERATION/PROCESS: Execute defined operations resulting in some change in the information or the determination of flow direction, e.g., checking customer's credit limit.

MANUAL OPERATION: Off-line process that is performed manually, e.g., preparing a three-part sales invoice or manually posting to customer accounts.

MANUAL INPUT: Represents input entered manually at the time of processing, e.g., using a keyboard.

INPUT/OUTPUT: General input/output symbol, e.g., general ledger, can be used regardless of the type of medium or data.

MAGNETIC TAPE: Input/output function in which the medium is magnetic tape, e.g., master payroll data file.

DISPLAY: Input/output device in which the information is displayed at the time of processing for human use, e.g., display customer number.

ONLINE STORAGE: Storage that is connected to and under the control of the computer, e.g., disk, drum, magnetic tape, etc.

OFF-LINE STORAGE: Any off-line storage of information regardless of the medium on which the information is recorded. This includes filing documents such as sales invoices and purchase orders. An "A" signifies an alphabetic file, an "N" is for a numeric file, and a "D" indicates a file organized by date.

OFF-PAGE CONNECTOR: Designates entry to or exit from a page. For example, it can be used to indicate sending a copy of an invoice to a customer.

ANNOTATION: Provides additional information.

DECISION: Determines next action. Used in program flowcharts, e.g., is A = B?

a.   **Advantages** The internal control flowchart shows the steps required and the flow of documents from person to person in carrying out the functions depicted. Therefore, overlooking controls existing between functions or departments is less likely to occur. Another advantage is that the flowchart clearly communicates the structure. The use of a flowchart is especially useful in the evaluation of electronic IT systems because it avoids much of the terminology that would be present in a narrative. Finally, its construction by the auditor requires a complete understanding of the structure.

b. **Disadvantage** It may be more time consuming to construct a flowchart rather than to fill out an internal control questionnaire.

2. **Questionnaire Approach** An internal control questionnaire is simply an enumeration of the matters to be investigated in the auditor's consideration of internal control. It should be designed by persons who are fully conversant with the problems of internal control and who have experience in the kind of structure being reviewed.

a. **Sample Questions** While the size and scope of internal control questionnaires will vary, some possible questions for an accounts receivable system are as follows:

(1) Are the following functions performed by employees other than accounts receivable bookkeepers?

(a) Handling cash and maintaining cash records

(b) Opening incoming mail

(c) Credit and collection

(d) Review and mailing of statements to customers

(2) Are the accounts receivable ledgers unavailable to the cashier?

(3) Are the subsidiary ledgers regularly balanced with the control accounts?

(4) Are the subsidiary ledgers occasionally balanced with the control accounts by someone other than the accounts receivable bookkeepers?

(5) Are aged trial balances of accounts receivable regularly prepared and submitted for executive approval?

(6) Are statements sent at regular intervals to all customers?

b. **Advantages** One advantage of the internal control questionnaire is that it is easy to complete. Another advantage is that the comprehensive list of questions provides assurance that relevant points will be covered. Also, weaknesses are obvious because they are usually the "no" answers.

c. **Disadvantage** A possible problem is that if the questionnaire is too general, it may not be adequate to evaluate an entity's internal control.

3. **Narrative (Memorandum) Approach** The auditor determines what the prescribed system of internal control is, and then writes it out in the auditor's own words.

a. **Advantages** The narrative is tailor-made for each engagement. Another advantage is that it requires a detailed analysis of the client's internal control because the auditor must thoroughly understand the structure in order to describe it.

b. **Disadvantages** The narrative approach is very time consuming. It does not have built-in safeguards to prevent the auditor from overlooking some aspect of internal control—weaknesses are not always obvious and might not be detected by this approach.

III. **Tests of Controls (AU 318 continued)**

A. **General Requirements & Considerations**

The auditor should perform tests of controls when: (1) the auditor's risk assessment includes an expectation of the operating effectiveness of controls or (2) when it is not possible or practicable to reduce detection risk at the relevant assertion level to an acceptably low level with audit evidence obtained from substantive procedures alone.

1. **Testing Operating Effectiveness** Tests of the operating effectiveness of controls are performed only on those controls determined to be capable of preventing or detecting a material misstatement.

2. **Operating Effectiveness vs. Implementation** Testing the operating effectiveness of controls is not the same as obtaining audit evidence that controls have been implemented. When performing risk assessment procedures, the auditor obtains evidence of implementation by determining that relevant controls exist and that the entity is using them. When performing tests of controls, the auditor obtains evidence that controls are operating effectively. This includes obtaining audit evidence about (a) how controls were applied at relevant times during the period under audit, (b) the consistency with which they were applied, and (c) by whom or by what means they were applied. If substantially different controls were used at different times during the period under audit, the auditor should consider each separately.

3. **Concurrent Performance** The auditor may determine that it is efficient to test the operating effectiveness of controls at the same time as evaluating their design and implementation. Even though some risk assessment procedures may not have been specifically designed as tests of controls, they may serve as tests of controls if they provide audit evidence about the operating effectiveness of controls. Nevertheless, the auditor will need to evaluate the sufficiency of the audit evidence provided by those audit procedures.

B. **Nature**

The auditor should select procedures to obtain assurance about the operating effectiveness of controls. As the planned level of assurance increases, the more reliable or extensive audit evidence should be. When the audit approach consists primarily of tests of controls, the auditor should obtain a higher level of assurance about the operating effectiveness of controls. Tests of the operating effectiveness of controls generally include: (1) inquiries of appropriate entity personnel; (2) inspection of documents, reports, or electronic files, indicating performance of the control; (3) observation of the application of the control; and (4) reperformance of the application of the control by the auditor.

1. **Combination of Procedures** The auditor should use a combination of audit procedures to obtain sufficient appropriate audit evidence concerning the operating effectiveness of controls; inquiry alone is not sufficient. Typically, inquiry combined with inspection or reperformance provides more assurance than inquiry combined with observation only. Also, because an observation pertains to only the point in time at which it is made, the auditor should supplement an observation with inquiries of entity personnel and may also need to inspect documentation regarding the operation of such controls at other times during the period under audit.

2. **Design** In designing tests of controls, the auditor should consider the need to obtain audit evidence concerning the operating effectiveness of controls directly related to relevant assertions as well as other indirect controls on which these controls depend. For example, the auditor should consider controls related to the accuracy and completeness of information when other controls depend on that information to operate effectively. Such controls may be IT general and application controls.

3. **Dual-Purpose Tests** The auditor may design a test of controls to be performed concurrently with a test of details on the same transaction. Because the objectives of the tests are different, the auditor should carefully consider the design and evaluation of such tests in order to

accomplish both objectives. For example, the auditor may examine an invoice to determine whether it has been approved and to provide substantive evidence of a transaction. Furthermore, when performing such tests the auditor should consider whether the extent (e.g., sample size) of substantive procedures should be increased from that originally planned if controls are found to be ineffective.

4. **Results of Substantive Procedures** The lack of misstatements detected by substantive procedures does not provide audit evidence that related controls are effective. On the other hand, misstatements detected by substantive procedures should be considered when assessing the operating effectiveness of related controls. When a material misstatement is detected by the auditor that was not identified by the entity, it should be regarded as at least a significant deficiency and a strong indicator of a material weakness in internal control.

C. **Extent**
The auditor should design tests of controls to obtain sufficient appropriate audit evidence that the controls are operating effectively throughout the period of reliance. In determining the extent of tests of controls, the auditor may consider the following factors:

1. The frequency of performance of the control during the period.

2. The length of time the auditor is relying on the operating effectiveness of the control.

3. The relevance and reliability of the audit evidence to be obtained in supporting that the control prevents, or detects and corrects, material misstatements at the relevant assertion level.

4. The extent to which audit evidence is obtained from tests of other controls related to the relevant assertion.

5. The extent to which the auditor plans to rely on the operating effectiveness of the control to reduce substantive procedures. The extent of tests of controls should increase as the auditor increases reliance on the operating effectiveness of controls.

6. The expected deviation from the control. The extent of tests of controls should increase as the expected deviation rate increases. However, the rate of expected deviation may be so high as to indicate that the performance of tests of controls will not be sufficient to reduce the control risk at the relevant assertion level.

D. **Timing**
The timing of tests of controls depends on the auditor's objective and the period of reliance on those controls.

1. **Reliance** The auditor should test controls at a point in time, or throughout the period, depending on when the auditor intends to rely on those controls. For example, evidence relating to only a point in time may be sufficient when testing controls over the counting of physical inventory at the end of the period. However, this may be insufficient if the auditor needs evidence concerning a period of time. In this case, the auditor also should perform tests that provide evidence that the control operated effectively at relevant times during the period. For example, the operation of a control embedded in a computer program may be tested at a particular point in time; then the auditor may perform tests of general controls pertaining to the modification and use of that computer program to obtain evidence concerning the consistent operation of the control during the audit period.

2. **Interim Tests** When the auditor performs tests of controls during an interim period, the auditor should determine what additional audit evidence should be obtained for the remaining period.

    a. **Considerations** In determining the additional evidence needed, the auditor should consider: (1) the significance of the assessed risks of material misstatement at the relevant assertion level, (2) the specific controls that were tested during the interim period, (3) the amount of audit evidence obtained concerning the operating effectiveness of those controls, (4) the length of the remaining period, (5) the extent to which the auditor intends to reduce further substantive procedures based on the reliance of controls, and (6) the control environment.

b. **Significant Changes** The auditor should obtain audit evidence about the nature and extent of any significant changes in internal control, including changes in the information system, processes, and personnel that occur in the remaining period.

c. **Examples** Additional audit evidence may be obtained by extending the testing of the operating effectiveness of controls to the remaining period, or by testing the entity's monitoring of controls.

3. **Prior Audit Evidence** If the auditor plans to use prior period audit evidence about the operating effectiveness of controls, the auditor should obtain audit evidence concerning whether there have been changes in those controls since the prior audit.

a. **Controls With Changes** If the auditor plans to rely on controls that have changed since they were last tested, the auditor should test the operating effectiveness of such controls in the current audit.

b. **Controls Without Changes** If the auditor plans to rely on controls that have not changed since they were last tested, the auditor should test the operating effectiveness of such controls at least once every three years. This rule does not apply to controls that mitigate a significant risk. Generally, as the risk of material misstatement or the reliance on controls increases, the time that is allowed to elapse should decrease.

c. **Considerations** In considering whether it is appropriate to use prior period audit evidence concerning the operating effectiveness of controls and the amount of time that may elapse before retesting a control, the auditor should consider:

(1) The effectiveness of other components of internal control, including the control environment, the entity's monitoring of controls, and the entity's risk assessment process.

(2) The risks arising from the characteristics of the control, including whether controls are manual or automated.

(3) The effectiveness of IT general controls.

(4) The effectiveness of the control and its application by the entity, including the nature and extent of deviations in the application of the control from tests of operating effectiveness in prior audits.

(5) Whether the lack of a change in a particular control poses a risk due to changing circumstances.

(6) The risk of material misstatement and the extent of reliance on the control.

d. **Substantial Reliance on Prior Audits** If the auditor uses audit evidence obtained in prior audits for several controls, the auditor should plan to test a sufficient portion of the controls in each audit period, so that at a minimum, each control is tested at least every third audit.

e. **Controls Mitigating Significant Risks** While the auditor should *consider* information obtained in prior audits in designing tests of controls, the auditor should **not** *rely* on prior audit evidence concerning the operating effectiveness of controls intended to mitigate a significant risk. If the auditor plans to rely on the operating effectiveness of such controls, the auditor should test the operating effectiveness of those controls in the current period.

IV. Communicating Internal Control Related Matters Identified in an Audit of Financial Statements (AU 325)

A. Overview

AU 325 provides guidance on communicating matters related to an entity's internal control over financial reporting identified in an audit of financial statements; it is applicable whenever an auditor expresses or disclaims an opinion on financial statements.

It is **not** the auditor's duty to search for deficiencies in internal control. However, the auditor may notice deficiencies as a consequence of performing audit procedures.

B. Definitions

1. **Deficiency in Internal Control** A *deficiency in internal control* exists when the design or operation of a control does not allow management or employees, in the normal course of performing their assigned functions, to prevent or detect and correct misstatements on a timely basis.

   a. **Design** A deficiency in *design* exists when a control necessary to meet the control objective is missing or an existing control is not properly designed so that even if the control operates as designed, the control objective would not be met.

   b. **Operation** A deficiency in *operation* exists when a properly designed control does not operate as designed or the person performing the control does not possess the necessary authority or competence to perform the control effectively.

2. **Significant Deficiency** A *significant deficiency* is a deficiency, or combination of deficiencies in internal control, that is less severe than a material weakness, yet important enough to merit attention by those charged with governance.

3. **Material Weakness** A *material weakness* is a deficiency, or combination of deficiencies in internal control, such that there is a reasonable possibility that a material misstatement of the entity's financial statements will not be prevented, or detected and corrected on a timely basis.

C. Evaluating Deficiencies in Internal Control

The auditor must evaluate deficiencies in internal control and determine whether they are significant deficiencies or material weaknesses. In making this determination, the auditor should consider the likelihood and magnitude of a possible misstatement. Thus, the significance of a deficiency in internal control depends on the potential for a misstatement, not on whether a misstatement actually has occurred.

1. **Risk Factors** Risk factors that affect whether there is a reasonable possibility that a deficiency will cause a misstatement to occur include: the nature of the financial statement accounts, classes of transactions, disclosures, and assertions involved; the susceptibility of the item to loss or fraud; the subjectivity, complexity, or degree of judgment required to determine the amount involved; the effect other controls or deficiencies have on the control; and possible future consequences of the deficiency.

2. **Multiple Deficiencies in Internal Control** Multiple deficiencies in internal control that affect the same account balance or disclosure increase the likelihood of misstatement and may, in combination, constitute a significant deficiency or material weakness, even though such deficiencies are individually insignificant. Therefore, the auditor should evaluate individual deficiencies in internal control that affect the same account balance, disclosure, relevant assertion, or component of internal control, to determine whether they collectively result in a significant deficiency or material weakness.

3. **Compensating Controls** The auditor may consider the possible mitigating effects of effective compensating controls that have been tested and evaluated as part of the audit. A compensating control is a control that limits the severity of a deficiency in internal control and keeps it from rising to the level of a significant deficiency or, in some instances, a material weakness. However, it does not eliminate the deficiency.

4. **Indicators of Material Weaknesses** Indicators of material weaknesses include: Identification of fraud, whether or not material, carried out by senior management; restatement of previously issued financial statements to correct a material misstatement due to error or fraud; identification by the auditor of a material misstatement that would not have been detected by the entity's internal controls; and ineffective oversight of the entity's financial reporting and internal control by those charged with governance.

D. **Communication**

Deficiencies in internal control that are identified and determined to be significant deficiencies or material weaknesses must be communicated in writing to management and those charged with governance in every audit. This requirement includes significant deficiencies and material weaknesses that were previously communicated to management and those charged with governance that have not yet been remediated.

1. **Timing** The required written communication is best made by the report release date (the date the auditor grants the entity permission to use the auditor's report in connection with the financial statements), but should be made no later than 60 days after the report release date.

   In some circumstances, early communication to management or those charged with governance may be important due to the significance of an issue or the need for timely follow-up action. Therefore, the auditor may decide to communicate certain identified significant deficiencies and material weaknesses *during* the audit. Such matters do not have to be communicated in writing initially; however, even if they are remediated during the audit, they must be included in the final required written communication.

   Editor note: PCAOB standards (for issuers) require that the written communication be made prior to the issuance of the audit report on the financial statements.

2. **Known Deficiencies** The existence of certain significant deficiencies or material weaknesses may already be known to management and may represent a conscious decision to accept the risk because of cost or other considerations. The auditor's responsibility to communicate significant deficiencies and material weaknesses exists regardless of management's decisions.

3. **Required** The written communication should:

   a. State that the purpose of the auditor's consideration of internal control was to express an opinion on the financial statements, but not to express an opinion on the effectiveness of the entity's internal control over financial reporting (ICFR).

   b. State that the auditor is not expressing an opinion on the effectiveness of internal control.

   c. State that the auditor's consideration of internal control was not designed to identify all deficiencies in internal control that might be significant deficiencies or material weaknesses.

   d. Include the definition of the terms *material weakness* and, where relevant, *significant deficiency.*

   e. Identify the matters that are considered to be significant deficiencies and those that are considered to be material weaknesses.

Editor note: PCAOB standards (for issuers) require that the written communication *clearly distinguish* between those matters considered to be significant deficiencies and those considered to be material weaknesses.

f.   State that the communication is intended solely for the information and use of management, those charged with governance, and others within the organization and is not intended to be and should not be used by anyone other than these specified parties. If an entity is required to furnish such auditor communications to a governmental authority, specific reference to such governmental authorities may be made.

Exhibit 3 ▶ Illustrative Written Communication

In planning and performing our audit of the financial statements of ABC Company (the "Company") as of and for the year ended December 31, 20XX, in accordance with auditing standards generally accepted in the United States of America, we considered the Company's internal control over financial reporting (internal control) as a basis for designing our auditing procedures for the purpose of expressing our opinion on the financial statements, but not for the purpose of expressing an opinion on the effectiveness of the Company's internal control. Accordingly, we do not express an opinion on the effectiveness of the Company's internal control.

Our consideration of internal control was for the limited purpose described in the preceding paragraph and was not designed to identify all deficiencies in internal control that might be significant deficiencies or material weaknesses and, therefore, there can be no assurance that all deficiencies, significant deficiencies, or material weaknesses have been identified. However, as discussed below, we identified certain deficiencies in internal control that we consider to be material weaknesses [*and other deficiencies that we consider to be significant deficiencies*].

A deficiency in internal control exists when the design or operation of a control does not allow management or employees, in the normal course of performing their assigned functions, to prevent, or detect and correct misstatements on a timely basis. A material weakness is a deficiency, or a combination of deficiencies, in internal control, such that there is a reasonable possibility that a material misstatement of the entity's financial statements will not be prevented, or detected and corrected on a timely basis. [*We consider the following deficiencies in the Company's internal control to be material weaknesses:*]

[*Describe the material weaknesses that were identified.*]

[*A significant deficiency is a deficiency, or combination of deficiencies, in internal control that is less severe than a material weakness, yet important enough to merit attention by those charged with governance. We consider the following deficiencies in the Company's internal control to be significant deficiencies:*]

[*Describe the significant deficiencies that were identified.*]

This communication is intended solely for the information and use of management, [*identify the body or individuals charged with governance*], others within the organization, and [*identify any specified governmental authorities*] and is not intended to be and should not be used by anyone other than these specified parties.

4.   **Optional** The auditor may include additional statements in the required written communication regarding the general inherent limitations of internal control or the specific nature and extent of the auditor's consideration of internal control during the audit.

Additionally, nothing precludes the auditor from communicating other matters (orally or in writing) that the auditor believes to be of potential benefit to the entity. For example, the auditor could make recommendations for operational or administrative efficiency, or for improving internal control. The auditor could also communicate information about deficiencies in internal control that are not significant deficiencies or material weaknesses. If these matters are communicated orally, the auditor should document the communication.

5. **No Material Weaknesses Identified** The auditor may issue a communication indicating that no *material weaknesses* were identified during the audit of the financial statements for the client to submit to governmental authorities. However, the auditor should **not** issue a written communication stating that no *significant deficiencies* were identified during the audit.

6. **Management's Response** Management may wish or be required by a regulator to prepare a written response to the auditor's communication. If such a response is included in a document containing the auditor's written communication, the auditor may add a paragraph to the auditor's written communication disclaiming an opinion on such information.

V. Internal Control Objectives & Procedures for Specific Transaction Cycles

A. Objectives of Internal Control
A well-designed internal control should ensure five objectives.

1. **Authorization** The starting point for establishing accounting control of transactions is appropriate authorization. Obtaining reasonable assurance of appropriate general or specific authorization requires independent evidence that authorizations are issued by persons acting within the scope of their authority and that transactions conform with the terms of the authorizations.

2. **Validity** Controls should provide reasonable assurance relative to the validity or existence of assets and liabilities at a given date and whether recorded transactions have occurred during a given period.

3. **Proper Recording** The objective of internal control with respect to the proper recording of transactions encompasses several sub-objectives. These include the following:

   a. **Completeness** Transactions are not omitted from the accounting records.

   b. **Valuation** Transactions are recorded at the actual amounts at which they transpired.

   c. **Classification** Transactions are classified in the appropriate accounts.

   d. **Timing** Transactions are recorded in the accounting period in which they occurred. Additionally, they are recorded as promptly as practicable when recording is necessary to maintain accountability.

4. **Accountability & Comparison** The accountability objective of internal control is to assure the availability of information necessary to follow assets from the time of their acquisition until their disposition. This requires maintaining records for accountability of assets and periodic comparison of these records with the related assets. The purpose of comparing recorded accountability with assets is to determine whether the actual assets agree with the recorded accountability. Consequently, it is related closely to the above discussion of proper recording of transactions.

5. **Protection & Limited Access** Controls should provide adequate protection of assets. Such protection is facilitated through segregation of incompatible functions and requires that access to assets be limited to authorized personnel. Access to assets includes both direct physical access and indirect access through documents that authorize use or disposition of assets.

B. Source Documents & Accounting Records
To determine the correct test of an internal control or to identify an internal control weakness, you must understand how source documents and accounting records relate to each other and what type of internal controls should exist.

1. **Segregation** Remember that authorization of a transaction, recording of the transaction, and custody of the related asset should all be separated. If any person or department was responsible for more than one of these functions, an internal control weakness would exist. For example, in the payroll function:

      a.   The Personnel Department should authorize pay rates (authorization).

      b.   The Timekeeping Department should prepare attendance and timekeeping data (record keeping).

      c.   The Payroll Department prepares the payroll (record keeping).

      d.   The Treasurer's Department prepares the payroll checks and distributes them to employees (custody).

2.   **Tracking** Source documents should be prenumbered and controlled so that they all can be accounted for.

3.   **Reconciliation** Subsidiary ledgers should be reconciled to general ledgers.

4.   **Perspective** When considering a question about testing an internal control, first determine what is being asked.

      a.   Tracing from a source document to the recorded entry tests the completeness assertion by looking for understatements.

      b.   Vouching from a recorded entry to the source document tests the existence assertion by looking for overstatements.

C.   **Policies & Procedures Within Transaction Cycles**
This section examines the five transaction cycles more closely by relating specific internal control policies and procedures within the cycles to the objectives of internal control. Additionally, for each control, an audit test of controls is suggested to evaluate the effectiveness of the policies and procedures.

    1.   **Transaction Cycles** Internal control objectives can be analyzed based on specific business activities or logical groups of transactions. Groupings of similar transactions or functions of an entity are known as transaction cycles. Dividing the audit into transaction cycles is known as the cycle approach. The cycle approach combines similar transactions with the ledger balances that result from those transactions. This is more efficient than treating each account balance as a separate segment. Although classification is somewhat arbitrary, the following is representative of the cycles of most businesses:

      a.   Sales, Receivables & Cash Receipts Cycle

      b.   Purchases, Payables & Cash Disbursements Cycle

      c.   Inventory & Production Cycle

      d.   Personnel & Payroll Cycle

      e.   Property, Plant & Equipment Cycle

    2.   **Universal Procedures** Several internal control policies and procedures are common to most, if not all, transaction cycles. Listed in the Appendix at the end of this chapter are general internal control questions that can be asked for most of the transaction cycles indicated. These questions are presented in this format to help you become familiar with the general questions. Specific internal control questions applicable to the individual transaction cycles are included under the transaction cycle titles in the Appendix of this chapter. Questions generally should be worded to require a yes or no answer.

3. Sales, Receivables & Cash Receipts Cycle

Objective	Internal Control	Test of Controls
Authorization	Credit approval occurs before shipment is authorized.	Examine appropriate document for approval.
	Existence of a cash discount policy.	Discuss policy with management. Review sales orders for evidence of compliance.
	Approval of cash discounts and adjustments.	Examine remittance advices for proper approval.
	Sales prices are from authorized price list or executed contract.	Compare sales invoice prices to appropriate price list or contract.
Validity	Prenumbered sales invoices.	Account for numerical sequence of sales invoices.
	Sales are supported by authorized shipping documents and approved customer orders.	Examine supporting bills of lading and customer orders.
	Monthly statements are mailed to customers.	Observe mailing of statements.
	Independent follow-up of customer complaints.	Examine customer correspondence files.
	Separation of the functions of cash handling and record keeping.	Observation. Discuss with management and review employee job descriptions.
	Shipment is acknowledged by Shipping Department.	Examine acknowledgment on sales order copy.
Proper Recording	Shipping documents are prenumbered (Completeness).	Accounting for numerical sequence of shipping documents. Trace documents to recording of sales and accounts receivable subsidiary ledger.
	A chart of accounts is used and is adequate (Classification).	Review adequacy and use of proper accounts. Examine sales documents to determine if sales transactions are properly classified.
	Cash receipts are recorded immediately and deposited on a daily basis (Timing).	Observation. Trace totals to duplicate deposit slips.
	Sales invoices and credit memoranda are prenumbered (Completeness).	Account for numerical sequence of sales invoices and credit memoranda.
	Internal verification of invoice preparation and posting (Valuation, Completeness, Classification).	Observation. Discuss policy with management.

Objective	Internal Control	Test of Controls
Accountability and Comparison	Independent reconciliation of bank statements.	Observation. Review bank reconciliation.
	Cash register totals are verified by persons not having access to cash or cash records.	Examine documentation of verification.
	Cash receipts are recorded immediately to establish accountability.	Observe the cash receiving process.
	A list of checks is prepared as the mail is opened.	Observation. Compare check listing total to duplicate deposit slip.
Protection and Limited Access	Persons receiving or otherwise handling cash are bonded.	Discuss with management. Review appropriate documentation of bonding.
	Checks are immediately endorsed.	Observation.
	Separation of cash handling and record keeping functions.	Observation. Discuss with management and review employee job descriptions.

4. Purchases, Payables & Cash Disbursements Cycle

Objective	Internal Control	Test of Controls
Authorization	Appropriate approval is required for all purchases.	Examine supporting documentation for indication of approval (purchase requisition and order).
	Payment approval required before check signing.	Observation. Examine documentation for indication of approval.
	Authorized signatures on checks. Two signatures on large checks.	Select a sample of large disbursements from the cash disbursements journal and examine the correlating canceled checks for two signatures.
Validity	Purchases are supported by purchase requisition, purchase order, receiving report, and vendor invoice.	Examine supporting documentation of vouchers.
	Documentation is canceled to prevent reuse.	Examine documentation for indication of cancellation.
	Receiving reports are prenumbered.	Account for numerical sequence of receiving reports.
	Receiving reports are required before approval of invoice for payment.	Discuss policy with management. Observation. Compare payment approval and receiving report dates.
Proper Recording	Vouchers are prenumbered (Completeness).	Account for numerical sequence of vouchers.
	Internal verification of vendor invoice amounts and calculations. (Valuation).	Examine invoice copy for indication of clerical accuracy verification.
	Transactions are recorded as soon as possible after receiving goods. (Timing).	Compare purchases journal dates to receiving report and invoice dates. (Observation).

Objective	*Internal Control*	*Test of Controls*
Proper Recording (cont'd)	Purchase orders are prenumbered (Completeness).	Account for numerical sequence of purchase orders.
	A chart of accounts is used and is adequate (Classification).	Review adequacy and use of proper accounts. Examine sales documents to determine if sales transactions are properly classified.
Accountability and Comparison	Independent reconciliation of bank statement.	Observation. Review bank reconciliation.
	Checks are signed only with appropriate support, by the treasurer, and the treasurer mails the checks.	Observation. Examine canceled check signatures.
	Monthly suppliers' statements are compared to accounts payable.	Examine statements for indication of agreement.
	Receiving Department examines quantity and quality of merchandise upon receipt.	Examine copies of receiving reports and purchase orders for indication of goods received.
	Accountability is established for unused and voided checks.	Discuss policy with management.
Protection and Limited Access	Separation of functions between accounts payable and custody of signed checks.	Observation. Review employee job descriptions.
	Checks are prenumbered.	Account for numerical sequence of checks.
	Mechanical check protector is used.	Examine check copies for evidence of check protector use.
	Separation of Purchasing Department functions from receiving and record keeping.	Observation. Review employee job descriptions.
	Physical control of unused checks is properly and securely maintained.	Observation. Discuss policy with management.

5. Inventory & Production Cycle

Objective	*Internal Control*	*Test of Controls*
Authorization	Movement of inventory items is authorized by requisitions.	Examine requisitions for indication of approval. Inquire of client personnel.
	Inventory purchases are appropriately authorized.	Select a sample of recorded purchases and vouch to documents authorizing purchase.
	Write-offs and write-downs of obsolete inventory are appropriately authorized.	Examine appropriate documentation for indication of authorization.
Validity	Receiving prepares prenumbered receiving reports.	Account for numerical sequence of receiving reports.
	Payment for inventory is approved only after verification of quantity and prices of vendor invoice.	Examine documentation for indication of verification.
Proper Recording	Merchandise receiving reports are matched with vendor invoices (Valuation, Completeness).	Examine vendor invoice copy for indication of agreement with receiving report.
	Purchase orders are prenumbered (Completeness).	Account for numerical sequence of purchase orders.
	Shipping or transfer reports are prenumbered (Completeness).	Account for numerical sequence of reports.
	Movement of inventory items is accounted for on a timely basis by authorized requisitions (Timing, Completeness, Classification).	Compare dates recorded for shipping reports of transferor with receiving report and requisition data of Receiving Department.
	Clerical accuracy of vendor invoices is checked prior to payment (Valuation).	Examine invoice for indication of accuracy check.
Accountability and Comparison	Receiving Department indicates description and quantity of inventory received on prenumbered receiving reports.	Examine receiving reports.
	Perpetual inventory records maintained for large dollar value items.	Review inventory records. Discuss policy with management.
	Periodic comparison made between inventory records and physical inventory.	Review inventory records for indication of agreement with physical count.
Protection and Limited Access	Inventory is stored under the control of a custodian. Access is limited.	Observation. Discuss procedures with management and custodian.
	Inventory purchasers and handlers are bonded.	Review appropriate documentation of bonding.
	Inventory records are maintained separate from the functions of shipping, receiving, and custody.	Observation.

Objective	Internal Control	Test of Controls
Protection and Limited Access (cont'd)	Physical safeguards against theft and fire exist.	Examine physical safeguards.
	Insurance coverage on inventory is adequate.	Review insurance policies.

6. Personnel & Payroll Cycle

Objective	Internal Control	Test of Controls
Authorization	Employment is authorized before hiring.	Review hiring policies and verify the hiring authorization of a sample of employees.
	Payment rates (including commissions and bonuses) and hours to be worked are authorized at the appropriate levels.	Examine approval for rates or union contracts and approval for hours to be worked.
	Deduction authorizations are obtained for each payroll deduction.	Review personnel file for authorizations.
	Personnel Department authorizes all changes to payroll master file.	Review change authorizations for sample of changes made during the year.
	Authorized signature(s) required on payroll checks.	Examine payroll checks for evidence of appropriate signature(s).
Validity	Time clock is used to record time worked by employees.	Observation.
	Department head or foreman approves and signs time cards.	Examine time cards for indication of approval.
	A paymaster (with no other payroll responsibilities) distributes payroll checks.	Observation. Discuss policy with management.
	Personnel Department keeps personnel files on each employee.	Review personnel files.
	Terminations are properly documented.	Review personnel files.
Proper Recording	Accounting procedures require recording payroll transactions as timely as possible (Timing).	Compare time card dates with recording date and paycheck dates for proper timing.
	Job time tickets are reconciled to time clock cards.	Examine job time tickets for indication of reconciliation and/or approval.
	An adequate chart of accounts is maintained including appropriate payroll accounts (Classification).	Review adequacy and use of proper accounts.
	Calculation and amounts of payroll are internally verified. (Completeness, Valuation).	Examine indication of internal verification.

Objective	*Internal Control*	*Test of Controls*
Proper Recording (cont'd)	Account classification of payroll-related transactions is internally verified (Classification).	Review reconciliation of monthly payroll with labor distribution.
Accountability and Comparison	Independent reconciliation of bank statement for imprest payroll account.	Observation. Review reconciliation of bank statement.
	Unclaimed payroll checks are returned to a person responsible for their custody (e.g., internal audit).	Discuss policy with management. Observe distribution of paychecks. Inquire of client personnel.
	Accountability is established for unused and voided payroll account checks.	Discuss policy with management and personnel responsible for check accountability (Observation).
Protection and Limited Access	Separation of personnel, payroll, and timekeeping functions.	Observation. Discuss functions with management.
	Use of a separate imprest payroll account.	Review separate documentation such as bank statements.
	Payroll checks are prenumbered.	Account for numerical sequence of payroll checks.
	Treasurer signs payroll checks.	Observation. Examine canceled payroll checks.

7. Property, Plant & Equipment Cycle

Objective	*Internal Control*	*Test of Controls*
Authorization	Authorization is required for all purchases over a certain amount.	Discuss policy with management. Review documentation of a sample of large purchases for indication of approval.
Validity	Major purchases require authorization by the board of directors.	Examine documentation of major purchases for approval by board. Review minutes of board meetings.
	Movements or sales of equipment have prior approval.	Examine appropriate documentation for existence of approval.
	Abandonments are reported to Accounting Department by foremen.	Discuss abandonment policy with management and foremen.
	Purchases are supported by appropriate authorizations, purchase order, receiving report, and vendor invoice.	Examine acquisition files for supporting documentation.
	Policies exist for classification of fixed assets, including a policy for expensing or capitalizing items (Classification).	Examine written policies. Vouch a selected sample of capitalized and expensed disbursements for compliance with policies.
	Policies exist for asset life estimations and depreciation tables used (Valuation, Timing).	Review written policies. Discuss with management. Vouch a sample of items for compliance with policies.

Objective	*Internal Control*	*Test of Controls*
Validity (cont'd)	Depreciation charges are recorded in subsidiary ledgers and amounts are internally verified periodically (Valuation, Completeness).	Examine subsidiary ledgers for appropriate depreciation charges and evidence of internal verification.
	Accounting procedures require timely recording of purchases and associated depreciation (Timing).	Compare receiving report dates, invoice dates, and recording dates for appropriate timing.
Accountability and Comparison	Subsidiary ledgers exist and are used.	Verify the existence of subsidiary ledgers and review entry detail for appropriateness.
	The responsibility for small tools is assigned to individual foremen.	Review tool responsibility with management and foremen. Examine the internal verification of the existence of tools.
	Internal verification is performed to examine existence and condition of fixed assets on a periodic basis.	Discuss policy with internal audit. Examine records for indication of verification.
Protection and Limited Access	Equipment has identification numbers to protect against loss.	Examine assets for existence of identification numbers.
	Insurance coverage on property, plant, and equipment is adequate.	Review insurance policies for adequacy of coverage.
	Physical safeguards are available for protection of assets from fire and theft (e.g., fire extinguishers, burglar alarms, etc.).	Examine physical safeguards for adequacy.

VI. General Internal Control Questionnaires

A. Control Environment

This questionnaire's objective is to determine if responsibilities are defined and authority is assigned to specific individuals to permit identification of whether persons are acting within the scope of their authority.

Management Philosophy and Operating Style

1. Does management have clear objectives in terms of budget, profit, and other financial and operating goals?

2. Are policies

    a. Clearly written?

    b. Communicated throughout the entity?

    c. Actively monitored?

3. Does management adequately consider the effects of taking business risks?

Organizational Structure

1. Is the organization of the entity clearly defined in terms of lines of authority and responsibility?

2. Does the entity have a current organization chart?

3. Are policies and procedures for authorization of transactions established at adequately high levels?

Audit Committee

1. Does the board of directors have an audit committee?

2. Does the audit committee take an active role in overseeing the entity's accounting and financial reporting policies and practices?

3. Does the audit committee

    a. Hold regular meetings?

    b. Appoint members with adequate qualifications?

    c. Adequately assist the board in meeting its fiduciary responsibilities?

    d. Assist the board in maintaining a direct line of communication with the internal and external auditors?

Methods of Assigning Authority and Responsibility

1. Does the entity have code of conduct and conflict of interest requirements?

2. Are employees given job descriptions which delineate specific duties, reporting relationships, and constraints?

3. Has the entity developed computer systems documentation which indicates procedures for authorizing transactions and approving systems changes?

Management Control Methods

1. Are there regular meetings of the board of directors and are minutes of such meetings prepared on a timely basis?

2. Does the entity have in place planning and reporting systems that

    a. Identify variances from planned performance?

    b. Communicate variances to the appropriate management level?

    c. Adequately investigate variances?

    d. Allow management to take appropriate and timely corrective action?

3. Has the company established a records retention policy and made arrangements for the storage of the information?

Internal Audit Function

1. Does the entity have an internal audit function?

2. If the entity has an internal audit function

    a. Are internal auditors independent of the activities they audit?

    b. Is the internal audit function adequately staffed?

    c. Do internal auditors document internal control and perform tests of controls?

    d. Do internal auditors perform substantive tests of the details of transactions and account balances?

    e. Do internal auditors document the planning and execution of their work?

    f. Do the internal auditors render written reports on their findings and conclusions?

    g. Are internal auditors' reports submitted to the board or to a similar committee?

3. Does management take timely action to correct conditions reported by internal auditors?

Personnel Policies and Procedures

1. Are employees adequately trained?

2. Is performance systematically evaluated?

3. Does the entity dismiss employees on a timely basis for critical violations of control policies?

4. Are employees in positions of trust bonded?

5. Are employees required to take mandatory vacations?

6. Is access to records limited to authorized persons?

B. **Accounting System**
    This questionnaire's objective is to determine if accounting policies and procedures are determined in accordance with management's authorization.

    *   Access to the accounting and financial records is limited to minimize opportunity for errors and fraud, and to provide reasonable protection from physical hazards.

- Accounting entries are initiated and approved in accordance with management's authorization.
- Accounting entries are appropriately accumulated, classified, and summarized.
- The general ledger and related records permit preparation of financial statements in conformity with GAAP.
- Financial statements with related disclosures are prepared and released in accordance with management's authorization.
- Individuals at appropriate levels consider reliable information in making estimates and judgments required for preparation of the financial statements and related disclosures.

General Accounting

1. Does the entity have adequate written statements and explanations of its accounting policies and procedures, such as

   a. Chart of accounts?

   b. Assignment of responsibilities and delegation of authority?

   c. Explanations of documentation and approval requirements for various types of transactions and journal entries?

2. Is access to the general ledger and related records restricted to those who are assigned general ledger responsibilities?

3. Is appropriate insurance coverage maintained (such as loss of records coverage and fidelity bonding of employees in positions of trust) in accordance with management's authorization?

4. Are all journal entries reviewed and approved?

5. Are all journal entries explained and supported?

6. Are individuals who review and approve journal entries independent of initiation of the entries they are authorized to approve?

Preparation of Financial Statements

1. Are the general ledger accounts arranged in orderly groupings which are conducive to efficient statement preparation?

2. Are there adequate instructions and procedures for

   a. Assignment of specific preparation and review responsibilities?

   b. Accumulation of information on intercompany transactions?

   c. Accumulation of information for footnote disclosure?

3. Are estimates and adjustments to provide valuation allowances reviewed and approved by appropriate levels in the organization independent of the persons originating the estimates and adjustments?

4. Are procedures adequate for the review and comparison of working papers to source data, and comparison of elimination and reclassification entries to those made in prior periods?

5. Are financial statements subjected to overall review and comparisons with the prior period and with budgeted amounts by appropriate levels of management?

VII. Transaction Cycle Internal Control Questionnaires

A. Revenue & Receivables

This questionnaire's objectives are to determine if the types of goods and services provided, the manner in which they will be provided, and the customers to which they will be provided are in accordance with management's authorization.

- The prices and other terms of sales are established in accordance with management's authorization.
- Credit terms and limits are established.
- Goods delivered and services provided are based on orders which have been approved.
- Deliveries of goods and services result in preparation of accurate and timely billings.
- Sales related deductions and adjustments are made in accordance with management's authorization.

1. Are sales orders approved before shipment?

2. Do approved sales orders record the terms of sales in detail?

3. Are unfilled sales commitments periodically reviewed?

4. Is current information on prices, discounts, sales taxes, freight, warranties, and returned goods clearly communicated to the sales and billing personnel (i.e., approved sales catalogs, manuals, and price lists)?

5. Is the credit of prospective customers investigated before it is extended to them?

6. Is there a periodic review of credit limits?

7. Are shipping documents prepared for all shipments?

8. Are goods shipped based on documented sales orders which have been approved?

9. Are shipping documents subjected to

   a. Timely communication to persons who physically perform the shipping function?

   b. Timely communication to persons who perform the billing function?

10. Are quantities of goods shipped verified by double counting or comparison with counts by common carriers?

11. Are shipping documents compared with billings to determine that all goods shipped are billed and accounted for?

12. Are sales invoices prepared for all shipments of goods?

13. Are sales invoices

   a. Matched with approved sales orders?

   b. Matched with shipping documents?

14. Are credit memos

   a. Prenumbered and accounted for?

   b. Matched with applicable receiving reports for returns?

c.   Approved by a responsible employee independent of the person preparing the credit memo?

15.   Are monthly statements reviewed and mailed by a responsible employee who is independent of the accounts receivable and cash functions?

16.   Is an aging schedule of past due accounts prepared monthly?

17.   Is there documentation of review and analysis of accounts receivable balances for determining valuation allowances and any specific balances to be written off?

18.   Are valuation allowances and write-offs approved?

B.   Cash Receipts

This questionnaire's objectives are to determine if access to cash receipts records, accounts receivable records, and billing and shipping records is controlled to prevent the interception and theft of unrecorded cash receipts or theft of recorded cash receipts.

- Detailed transaction and account balance records are reconciled with control accounts and bank statements at least monthly for the timely detection and correction of errors.
- All cash receipts are recorded at the correct amounts in the period in which received and are classified and summarized properly.

1.   Does the person who opens the mail

a.   Place restrictive endorsements on all checks received so they are for deposit only?

b.   List all remittances and prepare totals daily?

c.   Forward all remittances to the person who prepares and makes a daily bank deposit?

2.   Are currency receipts forwarded daily to the person who prepares the daily bank deposit?

3.   Is a summary listing of daily currency receipts forwarded to a person independent of physical handling of remittances and accounts receivable?

4.   Are each day's receipts deposited intact daily?

5.   Are all employees who handle receipts adequately bonded?

6.   Does company policy prohibit the cashing of any accommodation checks (payroll, personal) out of collections?

7.   Are bank charge-backs received directly from the bank and investigated by a person independent of the physical handling of collections and posting of accounts receivable subsidiary ledgers?

8.   Are entries to the cash receipts journal compared with

a.   Duplicate deposit slips authenticated by the bank?

b.   Deposits per the bank statement?

c.   Listings prepared when the mail is opened?

9.   Is information from remittance documentation adequate for the accurate posting of credits to individual accounts receivable subsidiary records or accounts such as investment income, rents, and sales of property?

10. Are details of collections posted to subsidiary accounts receivable records by a person independent of the general ledger functions, physical handling of collections, and receipt and investigation of bank charge-backs?

C. **Purchases & Accounts Payable**
This questionnaire's objectives are to determine if the types of goods and services to be obtained, the manner in which they are obtained, the vendors from which they are obtained, the quantities to be obtained, and the prices and terms initiated and executed are in accordance with management's authorization.

- Adjustments to vendor accounts and account distributions are made in accordance with management's authorization.
- All goods and services received are accounted for accurately and on a timely basis.
- Only authorized goods and services are accepted and paid for.
- Amounts payable for goods and services received are recorded at the correct amounts in the appropriate period and classified properly.
- Access to purchasing, receiving, and accounts payable records is controlled to prevent or detect duplicate or improper payments.

1. Are written purchase orders used for all commitments and do those orders include the vendor description, quantity, quality, price, terms, and delivery requirements for the goods or services ordered?

2. Is there a record of open purchase commitments?

3. Are open purchase orders periodically reviewed and investigated?

4. Are goods received inspected for condition and independently counted for comparison with the applicable purchase order?

5. Are receiving reports prepared promptly for all goods received?

6. Do receiving reports provide for recording of

   a. Description, quantity, and acceptability of goods?

   b. Date on which the goods or services are received?

   c. Signature of the individual approving the receipt?

7. Are receiving reports subjected to

   a. Accounting for all receiving reports used?

   b. Distribution for timely matching of copies with purchase orders and vendor invoices?

8. Is control established over all invoices received?

9. Are duplicate invoices stamped or destroyed as a precaution against duplicate payment?

10. Are vendors' invoices, prior to payment, compared in detail to purchase orders and receiving reports?

11. Are all available discounts taken?

12. Are there procedures for periodic review and investigation of unprocessed invoices, unmatched purchase orders, and receiving reports to provide for follow-up and proper accruals, and to result in a proper cutoff for financial reporting purposes?

13. Are vendors' statements reviewed for, and proper follow-up made of, overdue items?

D.   **Payroll**

This questionnaire's objectives are to determine if employees are hired and retained only at rates and benefits determined by management's authorization.

- Payroll withholdings and deductions are based on evidence of appropriate authorization.
- Compensation is made only to company employees at authorized rates and for services rendered.
- Gross pay, withholdings, deductions, and net pay are computed correctly using authorized rates and properly authorized withholding exemptions and deductions.
- Payroll costs and related liabilities are accumulated, classified, and summarized correctly in the accounts in the proper period.
- Comparisons are made of personnel, payroll, and work records at reasonable intervals for timely detection and correction of errors.
- Net pay and related withholdings and deductions are remitted to the appropriate employees when due.
- Functions are assigned so that no single individual is in a position to both perpetrate and conceal errors and fraud in the normal course of their duties.
- Access to personnel and payroll records is limited.

1.   Are all new hires, rates of pay and changes thereto, changes in position, and terminations based on written authorizations by management's criteria?

2.   Are appropriate written authorizations obtained from employees for all payroll deductions and withholding exemptions?

3.   Are personnel files maintained on individual employees which include appropriate written authorizations for rates of pay, payroll deductions, and withholding exemptions?

4.   Are methods for determining premium pay rates for matters such as overtime, night shift work, and employee benefits determined in accordance with management's authorizations?

5.   Do employees who perform the payroll processing function receive timely notification of wage and salary rate changes, new hires, changes in position, terminations, and changes in authorized deductions and withholding exemptions?

6.   Is there an adequate chart of accounts for determining account distributions for wages and related taxes and controlling liabilities for payroll deductions and taxes withheld?

7.   Are clerical operations in the preparation of payrolls verified by re-performance or reconciliation with independent controls over source data?

8.   Are piece rate records reconciled with production records, or salary commission records reconciled with recorded sales, or total production hours reconciled with production statistics?

9.   Are payroll checks drawn on a separate imprest account, and are deposits equal to the amount of net pay?

10.   Is responsibility for custody and follow-up of unclaimed wages assigned to a responsible person independent of personnel, payroll processing, and cash disbursement functions?

11.   Are procedures adequate to result in timely and accurate preparation and filing of payroll tax returns and payment of accumulated withholdings and related accrued taxes?

12.   Are personnel and payroll records reasonably safeguarded (locked file cabinets, work areas with limited access)?

E. **Cash Disbursements**

This questionnaire's objectives are to determine if functions are assigned so that no single individual is in a position to both perpetrate and conceal errors or fraud in the normal course of their duties.

- Disbursements are made only for expenditures incurred in accordance with management's authorization.
- Adjustments to cash accounts are made only in accordance with management's authorizations.
- Disbursements are recorded at correct amounts in the appropriate period and are classified properly in the accounts.
- Access to cash and disbursement records is restricted to minimize opportunities for irregular or erroneous disbursements.
- Comparison of detail records, control accounts, and bank statements are made at reasonable intervals for detection and appropriate disposition of errors or fraud.

1. Are bank accounts and check signers authorized by the board of directors?

2. Are approved supporting documents presented with the checks to the check signer?

3. Is a mechanical check protector used to inscribe amounts on checks to protect against alteration?

4. Are supporting documents for checks canceled to avoid reuse?

5. Are signed checks independently mailed directly after signing without being returned to persons involved in the invoice processing, check preparation, and recording functions?

6. Are all voided checks retained and mutilated?

7. Are there written policies that prohibit making checks payable to cash or bearer, and signing blank checks?

8. Are dual signatures required for large disbursements, and are the signers independent of one another?

9. If a check-signing machine is used, are the keys, signature plate, and operation of the signing machine under control at all times of the official whose signature is on the plate? Are employees who have custody of them independent of voucher and check preparation functions, and are they denied access to blank checks?

10. If cash funds are maintained on the premises, they should be kept on an imprest basis; and

    a. Are they kept in a safe place?

    b. Are they reasonable in amount?

    c. Are they controlled by one custodian?

    d. Are disbursements supported by vouchers?

    e. Are vouchers approved with management's authorization?

    f. Are cash funds on a surprise basis counted by someone other than the custodian?

    g. Is the custodian independent of cash receipts?

    h. Does the custodian have no access to accounting records?

    i. Are reimbursements of the cash fund remitted by checks made payable to the order of the custodian?

11. Are old outstanding checks investigated, controlled, and their proper disposition arranged?

F. **Inventory & Cost of Sales**

This questionnaire's objectives are to determine if all production activity and accounting therefore is determined in accordance with management's general or specific authorizations.

- Resources obtained and used in the production process and completed results are recorded accurately on a timely basis.
- Transfer of finished products to customers and other dispositions such as sales of scrap are recorded accurately.
- Inventory, production costs, and costs of sales are accumulated and classified in the accounts to maintain accountability for costs and permit preparation of statements in conformity with GAAP.
- Inventory is protected from unauthorized use or removal.
- Recorded balances of inventory are substantiated and evaluated at reasonable intervals by comparison with quantities on hand.

1. Are production goals and schedules based on accompanying sales forecasts?

2. Are methods and materials to be used based upon product engineering plans and specifications?

3. Does the company have budgeted inventory levels and predetermined reorder points authorized by management?

4. Does the company have policies for identification and disposition of excess or obsolete inventory?

5. Are all adjustments to inventory and cost of sales made in accordance with management's authorizations?

6. Are all dispositions of obsolete or excess inventory approved?

7. Does the chart of accounts provide adequate general ledger control accounts and subsidiary detail for the accumulation and classification of costs of materials, direct labor, and overhead?

8. Is access to the detailed inventory records and control accounts limited to persons responsible for their maintenance, oversight, and internal audit?

9. Are there physical safeguards against theft, fire, and flooding?

10. Is insurance coverage of the inventory maintained and reviewed periodically for adequacy?

11. Do detailed written inventory procedures and instructions exist that have been approved and are they adequately communicated to the persons who perform the physical counts?

12. Are inventory physical counts performed by persons whose duties do not include the physical custody and detailed record keeping of inventory or maintenance of control accounts?

13. Are differences in physical counts and detailed records investigated?

14. Are adjustments of the inventory detail records and control accounts given prior approval by management?

15. Are dispositions of obsolete or excess inventories made in accordance with criteria authorized by management?

G. Property, Plant & Equipment

This questionnaire's objectives are to determine if additions and related accumulation of depreciation, retirements, and dispositions of property, plant, and equipment (PPE) are made in accordance with management's authorization.

- Transactions involving PPE and depreciation are recorded, accumulated, and classified accurately in detail and in control accounts to maintain accountability for the assets.
- PPE are reasonably safeguarded from loss.

1. Are work order forms approved by management for property additions?

2. Are contracts and agreements signed by individuals in accordance with appropriately documented designation by the board of directors?

3. Are detailed records maintained for PPE indicating a description of the assets; their location, cost, acquisition date, date of service, depreciable life, and method of depreciation used?

4. Are PPE insured and coverage reviewed periodically for additions, disposals, and adequacy?

5. Is there a written capitalization/expense policy for PPE purchases?

H. Stockholders' Equity & Capital Accounts

This questionnaire's objectives are to determine if capital transactions are authorized and approved in conformity with the entity's governing document (corporate charter, partnership agreement).

- Transactions and obligations are recorded promptly and accurately.
- Access to records, agreements, and negotiable documents is permitted only in accordance with management's authorization.
- Records, agreements, and documents are subjected to adequate physical safeguards and custodial procedures.
- Dividends are disbursed accurately and in conformity with decisions of the board of directors.

1. Are authorizations and approvals for specific capital transactions appropriately recorded?

2. Are two officials authorized by the board required to sign and countersign stock certificates?

3. Are all stock certificates prepared and approved before issuance within management's authorization?

4. Are appropriate control records maintained for each class of stock on information such as number of shares authorized, issued and outstanding, and the number of shares subject to options, warrants, and conversion privileges?

5. Are timely detailed records maintained on specific stock certificates issued and outstanding for each class of capital stock and the identity of holders of record and the number of shares for each certificate?

6. Are detailed stock certificate records reconciled at reasonable intervals with the control records and the general ledger?

7. Are reconciliations of detailed records with the control records and general ledger performed by persons independent of custody of unissued stock certificates, maintenance of the detailed records, and cash functions?

8. Are unissued stock certificates, reacquired certificates, and detailed stockholder records subject to reasonable physical safeguards?

9. Are stock certificates prenumbered so that all certificates (unissued, issued, and retired) may be accounted for?

10. Are retired stock certificates examined for proper endorsement and effectively canceled by a person whose duties do not include maintenance of the detailed stockholder records?

11. Are treasury stock certificates registered in the name of the company and recorded to be readily distinguished from other outstanding shares?

12. Are dividends declared recorded in the minutes of the board of directors meetings?

13. Do procedures result in an accurate cutoff and accurate listing of stockholders as of the record date?

14. Are total dividends disbursed reconciled to total outstanding shares as of the record date?

———————————

VIII. Appendix: General Internal Control Questions

General Control Questions	Cash Receipts	Cash Disbursements	Payroll
1. Are forms used that are prenumbered?	Prenumbered Receipts, Cash Register tapes by date	Prenumbered Checks	Prenumbered Payroll Checks
2. Is adequate control maintained of unissued forms to prevent misuse?	Unused Blank Receipts controlled	Unused Blank Checks controlled	Unused Blank Payroll Checks controlled
3. Are policies and procedures in place for the authorization of transactions?	Remittance listing prepared by designated mail opener.	Check signers authorized by board of directors. Authorization for bank accounts to be maintained.	Payroll approved in writing by responsible employee prior to issuance of paychecks.
4. Is approval of transaction obtained prior to processing?	Comparison of remittance listing and validated deposit slip before processing.	Invoice matched to approved receiving report and approved purchase order. Disbursements and bank transfers approved.	Supervisor reviews and approves time cards.
5. Is a proper segregation of duties maintained to reduce potential errors and fraud?	Employee responsible for preparing remittance lists independent of billing, cash disbursement, and general ledger functions. Employee making deposit independent of cash disbursement, billing, and general ledger functions.	Employee performing bank reconciliation independent of invoice processing, cash disbursements, cash receipts, petty cash, and general ledger functions.	Payroll checks signed by treasurer. Payroll checks distributed by person independent of personnel, payroll preparation, time—keeping, and check preparation.
6. Are all prenumbered forms accounted for?	Detail Cash Receipts Journal	Outstanding check list maintained.	Payroll Journal, Outstanding check list maintained.
7. Is a detailed record of transactions maintained?	Cash Receipts Journal	Check Register, Cash Disbursements Journal	Payroll Journal
8. Are periodic (monthly, annual) reconciliations made between source documents, quantities on hand, subsidiary ledgers, and the general ledger?	Trace cash receipts journal total to bank statement and/or validated deposit slips.	Bank reconciliations, Cash Disbursements Journal reconciled to general ledger.	Time card hours reconciled to job time tickets.
9. Is access to assets and/or accounting records limited?	Mail received by same person daily who is independent of cash, billings, general ledger and shipping functions.	Bank statement received directly by person who will reconcile.	Payroll records and Personnel files kept in locked file cabinets.
10. Are transactions and source documents checked for clerical accuracy?	Remittance list footed and agreed to validated deposit slip.	Checks compared to approved invoice and supporting documents before signing. Discounts, if available, have been taken.	Time card totals checked by supervisor.
11. Is there a proper cutoff of transactions for accurate reporting?	Bank reconciliations are prepared and approved on a timely basis.	Bank reconciliations are prepared and approved on a timely basis.	Bank reconciliations are prepared and approved on a timely basis.

Inventory	Cost of Sales	Fixed Assets	Accounts Receivable	Accounts Payable
Prenumbered: Shipping Documents, Purchase Orders, Receiving Reports	Prenumbered Inventory Requisitions	Prenumbered Purchase Orders	Prenumbered Invoices	Prenumbered Vouchers
Unused Purchase Orders, Receiving Reports, Shipping Documents controlled.	Unused Inventory Requisitions controlled.	Unused Purchased Orders controlled	Unused Invoices controlled	Unused Vouchers controlled
Purchases made in accordance with vendor acceptability. Customer Acceptance/Terms of Sale, credit clearance all preestablished.	Pre-established overhead rates, requisition processing controls	Additions/Retirements have authorization in Board of Directors meeting minutes.	Invoices prepared from approved shipping reports and matching vendor purchase orders.	Authorization by Board of Directors for large purchases (contracts).
Approved purchase order, Approved inventory requisitions, sales orders approved before shipment	Inventory requisitions, overhead rate changes and personnel rate changes are properly approved.	Approval of additions and retirements in writing; Board minutes, manager approval.	Approval noted on invoice.	Invoices and supporting documents approved before payment.
Credit, Sales, Shipping, Billing, Collections, receiving, and general accounting all independent of one another.	Authority to approve inventory requisitions assigned to employees independent of physical custody, and maintenance of inventory records and inventory control accounts.	Responsibility for physical custody assigned to employees independent of maintaining detailed property records and general ledger functions.	Individual responsible for accounts receivable function is independent of cash and general ledger functions.	Vendors' invoices processed by employee independent of purchasing, receiving, shipping, and cash functions.
Purchase Orders, Shipping Documents, Receiving Reports	Work Orders, Inventory Requisitions	Physical asset identi-fication plates numbered consecutively	Numbered sales invoices properly filed.	Numbered vouchers and Purchase Orders maintained in open, pending, or paid files.
Shipment Log, Receiving Log, Purchases Journal	Work-in-Process and Finished Goods journals	Detailed listing of fixed assets maintained	Sales Invoice Register	Purchases Journal and Accounts Payable Subsidiary Ledger maintained
Inventory physically counted annually. Inventory detail records and control accounts reconciled to physical count. Perpetual records reconciled to general ledger and physical counts.	Cost accounting system reconciled to general ledger.	Detailed records of assets compared to actual PPE on hand, and reconciled to general ledger.	Accounts receivable subsidiary ledger reconciled to general ledger control account.	Accounts payable sub-sidiary ledger reconciled with general ledger control account.
Finished goods and merchandise are restricted so that withdrawals are based on approved sales orders.	Releases from storage of raw materials and supplies based upon approved requisitions.	Physical controls such as fences, burglar alarms, fire alarms, security guards, and requisitioning procedures for the use of portable equipment.	Passwords used on computer system limiting data entry to designated individuals.	Passwords used on computer system limiting data entry to designated individuals.
Receiving Reports, Shipping Documents, Purchase Orders	Inventory Requisitions checked	Invoices compared to approved purchase order and totals including taxes and freight are checked for reasonableness.	Sales Invoices	Vendors' Invoices
Inventory received included, goods on consignment included, goods sold but not shipped excluded from inventory totals.	See Inventory	Cash receipts and dis-bursements checked and compared to bank reconciliation for cutoff.	Shipping documents and related billings compared for proper cutoff.	Receiving reports or service dates and vendor invoices compared prior to recording.

The CPA Examination

The exam is designed as a licensing requirement to measure the technical competence of CPA candidates. Although licensing occurs at the state or territory level (usually by a board of accountancy), the exam is uniform at all sites and has national acceptance. Passing the exam in one jurisdiction generally allows a candidate to obtain a reciprocal certificate or license in another jurisdiction if they meet that jurisdiction's other requirements.

Boards of accountancy also rely upon other means to ensure that candidates possess the necessary technical and character attributes, including background checks, interviews, letters of reference, affidavits of employment, ethics exams, and educational requirements. Each board's contact information is on the website of the National Association of State Boards of Accountancy (www.nasba.org).

It is to your advantage to take the exam as soon as possible after completing the formal education requirements because it is essentially an academic exam that tests the breadth of material covered by a good accounting curriculum. The exam emphasizes the body of knowledge and entry-level skills required for the practice of public accounting.

We recommend that most candidates study for two exam sections at once because there are synergies to be gained. All sections of the exam share some common subjects (particularly Financial Accounting & Reporting and Auditing & Attestation); so as you study for one section, you are also studying, in part, for the others. This advice may not apply to all candidates. Some candidates with full-time jobs and other responsibilities may find that studying for just one exam section at a time is best for them.

More helpful exam information is included in "Appendix B: Exam Preparation Tips."

CHAPTER 3—INTERNAL CONTROL

Problem 3-1 MULTIPLE-CHOICE QUESTIONS

1. Proper segregation of duties reduces the opportunities to allow persons to be in positions to both

   a. Journalize entries and prepare financial statements
   b. Record cash receipts and cash disbursements
   c. Establish internal controls and authorize transactions
   d. Perpetuate and conceal errors and fraud   (11/94, AUD, #26, amended, ID: 5099)

2. Which of the following is **not** a component of an entity's internal control?

   a. Control risk
   b. Control activities
   c. The information and communication systems
   d. The control environment   (Editors, ID: 86)

3. Which of the following are considered control environment factors?

	Detection risk	*Personnel policies and practices*
a.	Yes	Yes
b.	Yes	No
c.	No	Yes
d.	No	No

   (11/94, AUD, #29, ID: 5102)

4. Which of the following is a management control method that most likely could improve management's ability to supervise company activities effectively?

   a. Monitoring compliance with internal control requirements imposed by regulatory bodies
   b. Limiting direct access to assets by physical segregation and protective devices
   c. Establishing budgets and forecasts to identify variances from expectations
   d. Supporting employees with the resources necessary to discharge their responsibilities
       (11/95, AUD, #6, ID: 5955)

5. Which of the following events most likely would indicate the existence of related parties?

   a. Granting stock options to key executives at favorable prices
   b. High turnover of senior management and members of the board of directors
   c. Failure to correct internal control weaknesses on a timely basis
   d. Selling real estate at a price significantly different from appraised value   (R/06, AUD, #41, ID: 8159)

6. Proper segregation of duties reduces the opportunities to allow any employee to be in a position to both

   a. Journalize cash receipts and disbursements and prepare the financial statements
   b. Monitor internal controls and evaluate whether the controls are operating as intended
   c. Adopt new accounting pronouncements and authorize the recording of transactions
   d. Record and conceal fraudulent transactions in the normal course of assigned tasks
       (R/06, AUD, #40, ID: 8158)

7. The overall attitude and awareness of an entity's board of directors concerning the importance of internal control usually is reflected in its

   a. Computer-based controls
   b. System of segregation of duties
   c. Control environment
   d. Safeguards over access to assets   (5/95, AUD, #25, amended, ID: 5643)

8. In an audit of financial statements, an auditor's primary consideration regarding an internal control policy or procedure is whether the policy or procedure

    a. Reflects management's philosophy and operating style
    b. Affects management's financial statement assertions
    c. Provides adequate safeguards over access to assets
    d. Enhances management's decision-making processes   (11/94, AUD, #28, ID: 5101)

9. Proper segregation of functional responsibilities in an effective internal control structure calls for separation of the functions of

    a. Authorization, payment, and recording
    b. Authorization, recording, and custody
    c. Custody, execution, and reporting
    d. Authorization, execution, and payment   (Editors, ID: 92)

10. Which of the following situations most likely could lead to an embezzlement scheme?

    a. The accounts receivable bookkeeper receives a list of payments prepared by the cashier and personally makes entries in the customers' accounts receivable subsidiary ledger.
    b. Each vendor invoice is matched with the related purchase order and receiving report by the vouchers payable bookkeeper who personally approves the voucher for payment.
    c. Access to blank checks and signature plates is restricted to the cash disbursements bookkeeper who personally reconciles the monthly bank statement.
    d. Vouchers and supporting documentation are examined and then canceled by the treasurer who personally mails the checks to vendors.   (R/09, AUD, #18, ID: 8818)

11. Which of the following factors is most relevant when an auditor considers the client's organizational structure in the context of control risk?

    a. Management's attitude toward information processing and accounting departments
    b. The organization's recruiting and hiring practices
    c. Physical proximity of the accounting function to upper management
    d. The suitability of the client's lines of reporting   (R/09, AUD, #45, ID: 8845)

12. Which of the following is **not** a component of internal control?

    a. Control environment
    b. Control activities
    c. Inherent risk
    d. Monitoring   (R/11, AUD, #18, ID: 9918)

13. Which of the following most likely would **not** be considered an inherent limitation of the potential effectiveness of an entity's internal control?

    a. Incompatible duties
    b. Management override
    c. Mistakes in judgment
    d. Collusion among employees   (5/94, AUD, #22, amended, ID: 4687)

14. Which of the following auditor concerns most likely could be so serious that the auditor concludes that a financial statement audit cannot be conducted?

    a. The entity has no formal written code of conduct.
    b. The integrity of the entity's management is suspect.
    c. Procedures requiring segregation of duties are subject to management override.
    d. Management fails to modify prescribed controls for changes in conditions.   (11/95, AUD, #4, ID: 5953)

15. Which of the following factors would most likely be considered an inherent limitation to an entity's internal control?

    a. The complexity of the information processing system
    b. Human judgment in the decision making process
    c. The ineffectiveness of the board of directors
    d. The lack of management incentives to improve the control environment   (R/06, AUD, #18, ID: 8136)

16. Which of the following factors would **least** likely affect the extent of the auditor's consideration of the client's internal controls?

    a. The amount of time budgeted to complete the engagement
    b. The size and complexity of the client
    c. The nature of specific relevant controls
    d. The auditor's prior experience with client operations   (R/06, AUD, #20, ID: 8138)

17. An auditor would most likely be concerned with internal control policies and procedures that provide reasonable assurance about the

    a. Methods of assigning production tasks to employees
    b. Appropriate prices the entity should charge for its products
    c. Efficiency of management's decision-making process
    d. Entity's ability to process and summarize financial data   (Editors, ID: 2303)

18. In obtaining an understanding of an entity's internal control in a financial statement audit, an auditor is **not** obligated to

    a. Determine whether the control procedures have been implemented
    b. Perform procedures to understand the design of the internal control policies
    c. Document the understanding of the entity's internal control
    d. Search for significant deficiencies in the operation of the entity's internal control
        (11/93, AUD, #19, amended, ID: 4256)

19. In obtaining an understanding of an entity's internal control, an auditor is required to obtain knowledge about the

	Operating effectiveness of policies and procedures	*Design of policies and procedures*
a.	Yes	Yes
b.	No	Yes
c.	Yes	No
d.	No	No

        (5/93, AUD, #12, amended, ID: 3908)

20. When obtaining an understanding of an entity's internal control, an auditor should concentrate on the implementation of the procedures because

    a. The procedures may be operating effectively but may not be documented.
    b. Management may implement procedures whose costs exceed their benefits.
    c. The procedures may be so inappropriate that no reliance is contemplated by the auditor.
    d. Management may establish appropriate procedures but not enforce compliance with them.
        (5/94, AUD, #21, amended, ID: 4686)

21. An auditor should obtain sufficient knowledge of an entity's accounting system to understand the

    a. Safeguards used to limit access to computer facilities
    b. Process used to prepare significant accounting estimates
    c. Procedures used to assure proper authorization of transactions
    d. Policies used to detect the concealment of fraud   (5/94, AUD, #20, amended, ID: 4685)

22. When considering internal control, an auditor should be aware of the concept of reasonable assurance, which recognizes that

    a. Internal control policies and procedures may be ineffective due to mistakes in judgment and personal carelessness.
    b. Adequate safeguards over access to assets and records should permit an entity to maintain proper accountability.
    c. Establishing and maintaining internal control is an important responsibility of management.
    d. The cost of an entity's internal control should not exceed the benefits expected to be derived.

    (5/95, AUD, #26, amended, ID: 5644)

23. Which of the following auditor concerns most likely could be so serious that the auditor concludes that a financial statement audit cannot be performed?

    a. Management fails to modify prescribed internal controls for changes in information technology.
    b. Internal control activities requiring segregation of duties are rarely monitored by management.
    c. Management is dominated by one person who is also the majority stockholder.
    d. There is a substantial risk of intentional misapplication of accounting principles.

    (R/02, AUD, #9, ID: 7099)

24. Which of the following procedures most likely would provide an auditor with evidence about whether an entity's internal control activities are suitably designed to prevent or detect material misstatements?

    a. Reperforming the activities for a sample of transactions
    b. Performing analytical procedures using data aggregated at a high level
    c. Vouching a sample of transactions directly related to the activities
    d. Observing the entity's personnel applying the activities   (5/97, AUD, #4, ID: 6393)

25. Which of the following is an inherent limitation in internal control?

    a. Incompatible duties
    b. Lack of segregation of duties
    c. Faulty human judgment
    d. Lack of an audit committee   (R/07, AUD, #5, ID: 8377)

26. Which of the following factors most likely would cause a CPA to decide **not** to accept a new audit engagement?

    a. The CPA's lack of understanding of the prospective client's internal auditor's computer-assisted audit techniques
    b. Management's disregard of its responsibility to maintain an adequate internal control environment
    c. The CPA's inability to determine whether related party transactions were consummated on terms equivalent to arm's-length transactions
    d. Management's refusal to permit the CPA to perform substantive tests before the year-end

    (R/00, AUD, #3, ID: 6928)

27. Which of the following is an inherent limitation of internal controls?

    a. Judgmental sampling
    b. Collusion
    c. Segregation of duties
    d. Employee peer review   (R/08, AUD, #15, ID: 8621)

28. Which of the following represents an inherent limitation of internal controls?

    a. Bank reconciliations are not performed on a timely basis.
    b. The CEO can request a check with no purchase order.
    c. Customer credit checks are not performed.
    d. Shipping documents are not matched to sales invoices.   (R/09, AUD, #36, ID: 8836)

29. An audit client failed to maintain copies of its procedures manuals and organizational flowcharts. What should the auditor do in an audit of financial statements?

    a. Issue a qualified opinion on the basis of a scope limitation.
    b. Document the auditor's understanding of internal controls.
    c. Assess control risk at the maximum level.
    d. Restrict the auditor's responsibility to assess the effectiveness of controls in the audit engagement letter. (R/08, AUD, #33, ID: 8639)

30. Which of the following factors is most likely to affect the extent of the documentation of the auditor's understanding of a client's system of internal controls?

    a. The industry and the business and regulatory environments in which the client operates
    b. The degree to which information technology is used in the accounting function
    c. The relationship between management, the board of directors, and external stakeholders
    d. The degree to which the auditor intends to use internal audit personnel to perform substantive tests (R/10, AUD, #8, ID: 9358)

31. An auditor is concerned about a policy of management override as a limitation of internal control. Which of the following tests would best assess the validity of the auditor's concern?

    a. Matching purchase orders to accounts payable
    b. Verifying that approved spending limits are **not** exceeded
    c. Tracing sales orders to the revenue account
    d. Reviewing minutes of board meetings (R/10, AUD, #33, ID: 9383)

32. Which of the following should an auditor do when control risk is assessed at the maximum level?

    a. Perform fewer substantive tests of details.
    b. Perform more tests of controls.
    c. Document the assessment.
    d. Document the control structure more extensively. (R/11, AUD, #43, ID: 9943)

33. The objective of tests of details of transactions performed as tests of controls is to

    a. Monitor the design and use of entity documents such as prenumbered shipping forms
    b. Determine whether internal controls have been implemented
    c. Detect material misstatements in the account balances of the financial statements
    d. Evaluate whether internal control procedures operated effectively (11/94, AUD, #42, amended, ID: 5115)

34. Which of the following types of evidence would an auditor most likely examine to determine whether internal control policies and procedures are operating as designed?

    a. Gross margin information regarding the client's industry
    b. Confirmations of receivables verifying account balances
    c. Client records documenting the use of computer programs
    d. Anticipated results documented in budgets or forecasts (11/95, AUD, #11, amended, ID: 5958)

35. Audit evidence concerning segregation of duties ordinarily is best obtained by

    a. Performing tests of transactions that corroborate management's financial statement assertions
    b. Observing the employees as they apply control procedures
    c. Obtaining a flowchart of activities performed by available personnel
    d. Developing audit objectives that reduce control risk (5/93, AUD, #10, ID: 3906)

36. Which of the following statements is correct concerning the use of prior audit evidence regarding the operating effectiveness of controls?

   a. If the auditor plans to rely on controls that have changed since they were last tested, the auditor should test those controls at least once every three years.
   b. If the auditor uses prior audit evidence for several controls, the auditor should test a sufficient portion of them in each audit so that each is tested every third audit.
   c. If the auditor plans to rely on controls that have not changed since they were last tested, the auditor should test those controls at least every other year.
   d. If the auditor plans to rely on controls that mitigate a significant risk, those controls should be tested at least every other year.   (Editors, ID: 8267)

37. Which of the following audit techniques ordinarily would provide an auditor with the **least** assurance about the operating effectiveness of an internal control activity?

   a. Inquiry of client personnel
   b. Inspection of documents and reports
   c. Observation of client personnel
   d. Preparation of system flowcharts   (R/05, AUD, #15, ID: 7810)

38. After testing a client's internal control activities, an auditor discovers a material weakness in the operation of a client's internal controls. Under these circumstances the auditor most likely would

   a. Issue a disclaimer of opinion about the internal controls as part of the auditor's report
   b. Increase the assessment of control risk and increase the extent of substantive tests
   c. Issue a qualified opinion of this finding as part of the auditor's report
   d. Withdraw from the audit because the internal controls are ineffective
                      (R/07, AUD, #3, amended, ID: 8375)

39. The ultimate purpose of assessing control risk is to contribute to the auditor's evaluation of the risk that

   a. Specific internal control activities are not operating as designed.
   b. The collective effect of the control environment may not achieve the control objectives.
   c. Tests of controls may fail to identify activities relevant to assertions.
   d. Material misstatements may exist in the financial statements.   (R/07, AUD, #30, ID: 8402)

40. A client maintains a large data center where access is limited to authorized employees. How may an auditor best determine the effectiveness of this control activity?

   a. Inspect the policy manual establishing this control activity.
   b. Ask the chief technology officer about known problems.
   c. Observe whether the data center is monitored.
   d. Obtain a list of current data center employees.   (R/08, AUD, #10, ID: 8616)

41. When an auditor plans to rely on controls that have changed since they were last tested, which of the following courses of action would be most appropriate?

   a. Test the operating effectiveness of such controls in the current audit
   b. Document that reliance and proceed with the original audit strategy
   c. Inquire of management as to the effectiveness of the controls
   d. Report the reliance in the report on internal controls   (R/10, AUD, #34, ID: 9384)

42. An auditor has identified the controller's review of the bank reconciliation as a control to test. In connection with this test, the auditor interviews the controller to understand the specific data reviewed on the reconciliation. In addition, the auditor verifies that the bank reconciliation is properly prepared by the accountant and reviewed by the controller as evidenced by their respective sign-offs. Which of the following types of audit procedures do these actions illustrate?

    a. Observation and inspection of records
    b. Confirmation and reperformance
    c. Inquiry and inspection of records
    d. Analytical procedures and reperformance   (R/11, AUD, #16, ID: 9916)

43. Which of the following is true regarding significant deficiencies and material weaknesses in an audit of financial statements?

    a. Auditors must search for them.
    b. Auditors must communicate them to management and those charged with governance.
    c. They must be included in the financial statements.
    d. They must be disclosed in the notes to the financial statements.
                            (R/06, AUD, #24, amended, ID: 8142)

44 Which of the following is **least** likely to indicate the existence of a material weakness in internal control?

    a. Fraud on the part of senior management
    b. Previously issued financial statements were restated to reflect the correction of a material misstatement due to error or fraud
    c. Those charged with governance exercise ineffective oversight of the entity's financial reporting and internal control
    d. There is substantial doubt about the entity's ability to continue as a going concern.   (Editors, ID: 9037)

45. Which of the following statements is correct concerning an auditor's required communication of significant deficiencies and material weaknesses identified during an audit of financial statements?

    a. A significant deficiency previously communicated during the prior year's audit that remains uncorrected causes a scope limitation.
    b. An auditor should perform tests of controls on significant deficiencies before communicating them to the client.
    c. An auditor's written communication on deficiencies in internal control should include a restriction on the use of the communication.
    d. An auditor should communicate significant deficiencies after tests of controls, but before commencing substantive tests.   (11/94, AUD, #45, amended, ID: 5118)

46. Which of the following statements should **not** be included in a written communication regarding significant deficiencies and material weaknesses identified in an audit of financial statements?

    a. The auditor's consideration of internal control was not designed to identify all deficiencies in internal control that might be significant deficiencies or material weaknesses.
    b. There were no significant deficiencies identified during the audit.
    c. A material weakness is a deficiency, or combination of deficiencies, in internal control, such that there is a reasonable possibility that a material misstatement of the entity's financial statements will not be prevented, or detected and corrected on a timely basis.
    d. The purpose of the auditor's consideration of internal control was to express an opinion on the financial statements, but not to express an opinion on the effectiveness of the entity's internal control.
                            (Editors, ID: 2957)

47. A deficiency in internal control exists when misstatements of the financial statements may occur and not be prevented, detected, or corrected on a timely basis by

    a. Outside consultants who issue a special-purpose report on internal control
    b. Management or employees in the normal course of performing their assigned functions
    c. Management when reviewing interim financial statements and reconciling account balances
    d. An independent auditor during the testing of controls phase of the consideration of internal control

    (Editors, ID: 7489)

48. Which of the following factors should an auditor consider in evaluating the severity a deficiency in internal control to determine if it should be communicated to management and those charged with governance, i.e., that it is a significant deficiency or a material weakness?

       I. Magnitude of the potential misstatement
       II. Likelihood of the misstatement

    a. I only
    b. II only
    c. Both I and II
    d. Neither I nor II

    (Editors, ID: 7105)

49. An auditor's written communication regarding significant deficiencies and material weaknesses identified during a financial statement audit should

    a. Include a brief description of the tests of controls performed in searching for significant deficiencies and material weaknesses
    b. Indicate that the purpose of the auditor's consideration of internal control was to express an opinion on the financial statements but not to express an opinion on the effectiveness of the entity's internal control
    c. Include a paragraph describing management's assertion concerning the effectiveness of internal control
    d. Indicate that the deficiencies should be disclosed in the annual report to the entity's shareholders

    (11/95, AUD, #35, amended, ID: 5982)

50. Which of the following actions should the auditor take in response to discovering a deviation from the prescribed control procedure?

    a. Make inquiries to understand the potential consequence of the deviation
    b. Assume that the deviation is an isolated occurrence without audit significance
    c. Report the matter to the next higher level of authority within the entity
    d. Increase sample size of tests of controls

    (R/09, AUD, #21, ID: 8821)

51. Which of the following documents are examples of audit evidence generated by the client?

    a. Customer purchase orders and bank statements
    b. Shipping documents and receiving reports
    c. Vendor invoices and packing slips
    d. Bills of lading and accounts receivable confirmations

    (R/08, AUD, #4, ID: 8610)

52. Which of the following describes a weakness in accounts payable procedures?

    a. The accounts payable clerk files invoices and supporting documentation after payment.
    b. The accounts payable clerk manually verifies arithmetic on the vendor invoice.
    c. The accounts payable system compares the receiving report to the vendor invoice.
    d. The accounts payable manager issues purchase orders.

    (R/09, AUD, #7, ID: 8807)

53. An auditor's tests of controls for completeness for the revenue cycle usually include determining whether

    a. Each receivable is collected subsequent to the year-end.
    b. An invoice is prepared for each shipping document.
    c. Each invoice is supported by a customer purchase order.
    d. Each credit memo is properly approved.

    (R/09, AUD, #37, ID: 8837)

54. Evidence concerning the proper segregation of duties for receiving and depositing cash receipts ordinarily is obtained by

   a. Completing an internal control questionnaire that describes the control activities
   b. Observing the employees who are performing the control activities
   c. Performing substantive tests to verify the details of the bank balance
   d. Preparing a flowchart of the duties performed and the entity's available personnel

   (R/08, AUD, #3, ID: 8609)

55. Which of the following procedures most likely would **not** be an internal control procedure designed to reduce the risk of errors in the billing process?

   a. Comparing control totals for shipping documents with corresponding totals for sales invoices
   b. Using computer programmed controls on the pricing and mathematical accuracy of sales invoices
   c. Matching shipping documents with approved sales orders before invoice preparation
   d. Reconciling the control totals for sales invoices with the accounts receivable subsidiary ledger

   (11/94, AUD, #36, ID: 5109)

56. Tracing shipping documents to prenumbered sales invoices provides evidence that

   a. No duplicate shipments or billings occurred.
   b. Shipments to customers were properly invoiced.
   c. All goods ordered by customers were shipped.
   d. All prenumbered sales invoices were accounted for.   (5/95, AUD, #32, ID: 5650)

57. Proper authorization of write-offs of uncollectible accounts should be approved in which of the following departments?

   a. Accounts receivable
   b. Credit
   c. Accounts payable
   d. Treasurer   (11/94, AUD, #35, ID: 5108)

58. Which of the following controls most likely would be effective in offsetting the tendency of sales personnel to maximize sales volume at the expense of high bad debt write-offs?

   a. Employees responsible for authorizing sales and bad debt write-offs are denied access to cash.
   b. Shipping documents and sales invoices are matched by an employee who does not have authority to write off bad debts.
   c. Employees involved in the credit-granting function are separated from the sales function.
   d. Subsidiary accounts receivable records are reconciled to the control account by an employee independent of the authorization of credit.   (5/92, AUD, #45, ID: 2798)

59. Which of the following internal controls most likely would reduce the risk of diversion of customer receipts by an entity's employees?

   a. A bank lockbox system
   b. Prenumbered remittance advices
   c. Monthly bank reconciliations
   d. Daily deposit of cash receipts   (11/95, AUD, #12, ID: 5959)

60. An auditor who uses a transaction cycle approach to assessing control risk most likely would test control activities related to transactions involving the sale of goods to customers with the

   a. Collection of receivables
   b. Purchase of merchandise inventory
   c. Payment of accounts payable
   d. Sale of long-term debt   (R/06, AUD, #26, ID: 8144)

61. Management's emphasis on meeting projected profit goals most likely would significantly influence an entity's control environment when

    a. Internal auditors have direct access to the entity's board of directors.
    b. A significant portion of management compensation is represented by stock options.
    c. External policies established by parties outside the entity affect accounting policies.
    d. The audit committee is active in overseeing the entity's financial reporting policies.

    (R/06, AUD, #42, ID: 8160)

62. Which of the following procedures would an auditor most likely perform to test controls relating to management's assertion about the completeness of cash receipts for cash sales at a retail outlet?

    a. Observe the consistency of the employees' use of cash registers and tapes
    b. Inquire about employees' access to recorded but undeposited cash
    c. Trace the deposits in the cash receipts journal to the cash balance in the general ledger
    d. Compare the cash balance in the general ledger with the bank confirmation request

    (11/97, AUD, #15, ID: 6578)

63. Which of the following fraudulent activities most likely could be perpetrated due to the lack of effective internal controls in the revenue cycle?

    a. Merchandise received is not promptly reconciled to the outstanding purchase order file.
    b. Obsolete items included in inventory balances are rarely reduced to the lower of cost or market value.
    c. The write-off of receivables by personnel who receive cash permits the misappropriation of cash.
    d. Fictitious transactions are recorded that cause an understatement of revenue and overstatement of receivables. (R/06, AUD, #44, ID: 8162)

64. Sound internal control procedures dictate that immediately upon receiving checks from customers by mail, a responsible employee should

    a. Add the checks to the daily cash summary
    b. Verify that each check is supported by a prenumbered sales invoice
    c. Prepare a duplicate listing of checks received
    d. Record the checks in the cash receipts journal (5/95, AUD, #30, ID: 5648)

65. Which of the following procedures concerning accounts receivable would an auditor most likely perform to obtain audit evidence to support the operating effectiveness of a control?

    a. Observing an entity's employee prepare the schedule of past due accounts receivable
    b. Sending confirmation requests to an entity's principal customers to verify the existence of accounts receivable
    c. Inspecting an entity's analysis of accounts receivable for unusual balances
    d. Comparing an entity's uncollectible accounts expense to actual uncollectible accounts receivable

    (5/96, AUD, #2, amended, ID: 6234)

66. To determine whether internal control relative to the revenue cycle of a wholesaling entity is operating effectively in minimizing the failure to prepare sales invoices, an auditor most likely would select a sample of transactions from the population represented by the

    a. Sales order file
    b. Customer order file
    c. Shipping document file
    d. Sales invoice file

    (R/05, AUD, #20, ID: 7815)

67. Employers bond employees who handle cash receipts because fidelity bonds reduce the possibility of employing dishonest individuals and

a. Protect employees who make unintentional errors from possible monetary damages resulting from their errors.
b. Deter dishonesty by making employees aware that insurance companies may investigate and prosecute dishonest acts.
c. Facilitate an independent monitoring of the receiving and depositing of cash receipts.
d. Force employees in positions of trust to take periodic vacations and rotate their assigned duties.

(5/90, AUD, #35, ID: 73)

68. Which of the following fraudulent activities most likely could be perpetrated due to the lack of effective internal controls in the revenue cycle?

a. Fictitious transactions may be recorded that cause an understatement of revenues and an overstatement of receivables.
b. Claims received from customers for goods returned may be intentionally recorded in other customers' accounts.
c. Authorization of credit memos by personnel who receive cash may permit the misappropriation of cash.
d. The failure to prepare shipping documents may cause an overstatement of inventory balances.

(11/97, AUD, #14, ID: 6577)

69. For the most effective internal control, monthly bank statements should be received directly from the banks and reviewed by the

a. Cash disbursements accountant
b. Cash receipts accountant
c. Controller
d. Internal auditor

(Editors, ID: 111)

70. Which of the following best represents a key control for ensuring sales are properly authorized when assessing control risks for sales?

a. The separation of duties between the billing department and the cash receipts approval department
b. The use of an approved price list to determine unit selling price
c. Copies of approved sales orders sent to the shipping, billing, and accounting departments
d. Sales orders are sent to the credit department for approval

(R/08, AUD, #6, ID: 8612)

71. An auditor is determining if internal control relative to the revenue cycle of a wholesaling entity is operating effectively in minimizing the failure to prepare sales invoices. The auditor most likely would select a sample of transactions from the population represented by the

a. Cash receipts file
b. Shipping document file
c. Customer order file
d. Sales invoice file

(R/08, AUD, #30, ID: 8636)

72. Which of the following internal control procedures is **not** usually performed in the vouchers payable department?

a. Matching the vendor's invoice with the related receiving report
b. Approving vouchers for payment by having an authorized employee sign the vouchers
c. Indicating the asset and expense accounts to be debited
d. Accounting for unused prenumbered purchase orders and receiving reports

(11/94, AUD, #40, ID: 5113)

73. For effective internal control, the Accounts Payable Department generally should

    a. Stamp, perforate, or otherwise cancel supporting documentation after payment is mailed
    b. Ascertain that each requisition is approved as to price, quantity, and quality by an authorized employee
    c. Obliterate the quantity ordered on the Receiving Department copy of the purchase order
    d. Establish the agreement of the vendor's invoice with the receiving report and purchase order

    (11/95, AUD, #30, ID: 5977)

74. When the shipping department returns nonconforming goods to a vendor, the purchasing department should send to the accounting department the

    a. Unpaid voucher
    b. Debit memo
    c. Vendor invoice
    d. Credit memo

    (11/92, AUD, #16, ID: 2950)

75. To provide assurance that each voucher is submitted and paid only once, an auditor most likely would examine a sample of paid vouchers and determine whether each voucher is

    a. Supported by a vendor's invoice
    b. Stamped "paid" by the check signer
    c. Prenumbered and accounted for
    d. Approved for authorized purchases

    (5/95, AUD, #34, ID: 5652)

76. The authority to accept incoming goods in receiving should be based on a(an)

    a. Vendor's invoice
    b. Materials requisition
    c. Bill of lading
    d. Approved purchase order

    (5/93, AUD, #17, ID: 3913)

77. In testing controls over cash disbursements, an auditor most likely would determine that the person who signs checks also

    a. Reviews the monthly bank reconciliation
    b. Returns the checks to accounts payable
    c. Is denied access to the supporting documents
    d. Is responsible for mailing the checks

    (11/95, AUD, #29, ID: 5976)

78. Which of the following questions would most likely be included in an internal control questionnaire concerning the completeness assertion for purchases?

    a. Is an authorized purchase order required before the receiving department can accept a shipment or the vouchers payable department can record a voucher?
    b. Are purchase requisitions prenumbered and independently matched with vendor invoices?
    c. Is the unpaid voucher file periodically reconciled with inventory records by an employee who does not have access to purchase requisitions?
    d. Are purchase orders, receiving reports, and vouchers prenumbered and periodically accounted for?

    (5/92, AUD, #46, ID: 2799)

79. Which of the following questions would an auditor most likely include on an internal control questionnaire for notes payable?

    a. Are assets that collateralize notes payable critically needed for the entity's continued existence?
    b. Are two or more authorized signatures required on checks that repay notes payable?
    c. Are the proceeds from notes payable used for the purchase of noncurrent assets?
    d. Are direct borrowings on notes payable authorized by the board of directors?

    (11/93, AUD, #32, ID: 4269)

80. Mailing disbursement checks and remittance advices should be controlled by the employee who

    a. Matches the receiving reports, purchase orders, and vendors' invoices
    b. Signs the checks last
    c. Prepares the daily voucher summary
    d. Agrees the check register to the daily check summary   (5/93, AUD, #18, ID: 3914)

81. Which of the following internal control procedures is **not** usually performed in the treasurer's department?

    a. Verifying the accuracy of checks and vouchers
    b. Controlling the mailing of checks to vendors
    c. Approving vendors' invoices for payment
    d. Canceling payment vouchers when paid   (11/93, AUD, #27, ID: 4264)

82. Which of the following controls would be most effective in assuring that recorded purchases are free of material errors?

    a. The Receiving Department compares the quantity ordered on purchase orders with the quantity received on receiving reports
    b. Vendors' invoices are compared with purchase orders by an employee who is independent of the Receiving Department
    c. Receiving reports require the signature of the individual who authorized the purchase
    d. Purchase orders, receiving reports, and vendors' invoices are independently matched in preparing vouchers   (11/90, AUD, #51, ID: 7491)

83. Which of the following events occurring in the year under audit would most likely indicate that internal controls utilized in previous years may be inadequate in the year under audit?

    a. The entity announced that the internal audit function would be eliminated after the balance sheet date.
    b. The audit committee chairperson unexpectedly resigned during the year under audit.
    c. The chief financial officer waived approvals on all checks to one vendor to expedite payment.
    d. The frequency of accounts payable check runs was changed from biweekly to weekly.   (R/05, AUD, #48, ID: 7843)

84. To provide assurance that each voucher is submitted and paid only once, an auditor most likely would examine a sample of paid vouchers and determine whether each voucher is

    a. Stamped *paid* by the check signer
    b. Returned to the vouchers payable department
    c. Supported by a vendor's invoice and purchase order
    d. Prenumbered and accounted for   (R/08, AUD, #12, ID: 8618)

85. An auditor generally tests the segregation of duties related to inventory by

    a. Personal inquiry and observation
    b. Test counts and cutoff procedures
    c. Analytical procedures and invoice recomputation
    d. Document inspection and reconciliation   (5/95, AUD, #31, ID: 5649)

86. Sound internal control procedures dictate that defective merchandise returned by customers should be presented initially to the

    a. Accounts receivable supervisor
    b. Receiving clerk
    c. Shipping department supervisor
    d. Sales clerk   (5/93, AUD, #20, ID: 3916)

87. Which of the following internal control procedures most likely would prevent direct labor hours from being charged to manufacturing overhead?

    a. Periodic independent counts of work in process for comparison to recorded amounts
    b. Comparison of daily journal entries with approved production orders
    c. Use of time tickets to record actual labor worked on production orders
    d. Reconciliation of work-in-process inventory with periodic cost budgets   (5/94, AUD, #32, ID: 4697)

88. Which of the following internal control procedures most likely would be used to maintain accurate inventory records?

    a. Perpetual inventory records are periodically compared with the current cost of individual inventory items
    b. A just-in-time inventory ordering system keeps inventory levels to a desired minimum
    c. Requisitions, receiving reports, and purchase orders are independently matched before payment is approved
    d. Periodic inventory counts are used to adjust the perpetual inventory records

    (5/94, AUD, #33, ID: 4698)

89. The objectives of the internal control for a production cycle are to provide assurance that transactions are properly executed and recorded, and that

    a. Production orders are prenumbered and signed by a supervisor.
    b. Custody of work in process and of finished goods is properly maintained.
    c. Independent internal verification of activity reports is established.
    d. Transfers to finished goods are documented by a completed production report and a quality control report.

    (11/93, AUD, #28, amended, ID: 4265)

90. In obtaining an understanding of a manufacturing entity's internal control concerning inventory balances, an auditor most likely would

    a. Analyze the liquidity and turnover ratios of the inventory
    b. Perform analytical procedures designed to identify cost variances
    c. Review the entity's descriptions of inventory policies and procedures
    d. Perform test counts of inventory during the entity's physical count

    (11/95, AUD, #32, amended, ID: 5979)

91. Which of the following most likely would be an internal control procedure designed to detect errors and fraud concerning the custody of inventory?

    a. Periodic reconciliation of work in process with job cost sheets
    b. Segregation of functions between general accounting and cost accounting
    c. Independent comparisons of finished goods records with counts of goods on hand
    d. Approval of inventory journal entries by the storekeeper

    (5/91, AUD, #29, amended, ID: 7492)

92. What is the most likely course of action that an auditor would take after determining that performing substantive tests on inventory will take less time than performing tests of controls?

    a. Assess control risk at the minimum level
    b. Perform both tests of controls and substantive tests on inventory
    c. Perform only substantive tests on inventory
    d. Perform only tests of controls on inventory

    (R/07, AUD, #47, ID: 8419)

93. An auditor most likely would **not** rely on controls if the payroll department supervisor is responsible for

    a. Examining authorization forms for new employees
    b. Comparing payroll registers with original batch transmittal data
    c. Authorizing payroll rate changes for all employees
    d. Hiring all subordinate payroll department employees

    (5/94, AUD, #29, amended, ID: 4694)

94. The purpose of segregating the duties of hiring personnel and distributing payroll checks is to separate the

    a. Human resources function from the controllership function
    b. Administrative controls from the internal accounting controls
    c. Authorization of transactions from the custody of related assets
    d. Operational responsibility from the record keeping responsibility

    (11/93, AUD, #30, ID: 4267)

95. In determining the effectiveness of an entity's policies and procedures relating to the existence or occurrence assertion for payroll transactions, an auditor most likely would inquire about and

a. Observe the segregation of duties concerning personnel responsibilities and payroll disbursement
b. Inspect evidence of accounting for prenumbered payroll checks
c. Recompute the payroll deductions for employee fringe benefits
d. Verify the preparation of the monthly payroll account bank reconciliation   (11/95, AUD, #31, ID: 5978)

96. Which of the following is a control procedure that most likely could help prevent employee payroll fraud?

a. The personnel department promptly sends employee termination notices to the payroll supervisor.
b. Employees who distribute payroll checks forward unclaimed payroll checks to the absent employees' supervisors.
c. Salary rates resulting from new hires are approved by the payroll supervisor.
d. Total hours used for determination of gross pay are calculated by the payroll supervisor.

(11/95, AUD, #15, ID: 5962)

97. Which of the following circumstances most likely would cause an auditor to suspect an employee payroll fraud scheme?

a. There are significant unexplained variances between standard and actual labor cost.
b. Payroll checks are disbursed by the same employee each payday.
c. Employee time cards are approved by individual departmental supervisors.
d. A separate payroll bank account is maintained on an imprest basis.   (11/95, AUD, #50, ID: 5997)

98. Which of the following departments most likely would approve changes in pay rates and deductions from employee salaries?

a. Personnel
b. Treasurer
c. Controller
d. Payroll   (11/93, AUD, #31, ID: 4268)

99. Which of the following procedures represents a weakness in internal controls for payroll?

a. The payroll clerk distributes signed payroll checks. Undistributed checks are returned to the payroll department.
b. The accounting department wires transfers funds to the payroll bank account. The transfer is based on totals from the payroll department summary.
c. The payroll department prepares checks using a signature plate. The treasurer supervises the process before payroll checks are distributed.
d. The payroll department prepares checks. The chief financial officer signs the payroll checks.

(R/05, AUD, #36, ID: 7831)

100. Which of the following activities performed by a department supervisor most likely would help in the prevention or detection of a payroll fraud?

a. Distributing paychecks directly to department employees
b. Setting the pay rate for department employees
c. Hiring employees and authorizing them to be added to payroll
d. Approving a summary of hours each employee worked during the pay period

(R/10, AUD, #32, ID: 9382)

101. Which of the following flowcharts indicates that new equipment transactions and the old equipment file have been used to prepare equipment labels, prepare a printed equipment journal, and generate a new equipment file?

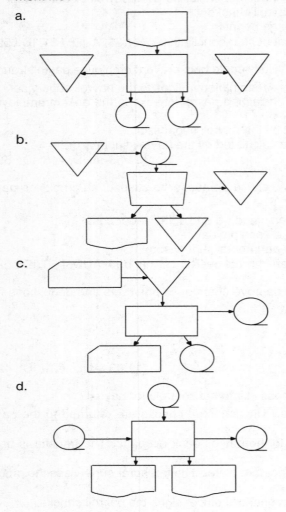

a.

b.

c.

d.

(Editors, ID: 7490)

102. Equipment acquisitions that are misclassified as maintenance expense most likely would be detected by an internal control procedure that provides for

a. Segregation of duties of employees in the accounts payable department
b. Authorization by the board of directors of significant equipment acquisitions
c. Investigation of variances within a formal budgeting system
d. Independent verification of invoices for disbursements recorded as equipment acquisitions

(11/93, AUD, #34, amended, ID: 4271)

103. Which of the following internal control procedures most likely would justify a reduced assessed level of control risk concerning property, plant and equipment acquisitions?

a. Periodic physical inspection of property, plant and equipment by the internal audit staff
b. Comparison of current year property, plant and equipment account balances with prior year actual balances
c. The review of prenumbered purchase orders to detect unrecorded trade-ins
d. Approval of periodic depreciation entries by a supervisor independent of the accounting department

(5/93, AUD, #21, ID: 3917)

104. Which of the following questions would an auditor **least** likely include on an internal control questionnaire concerning the initiation and execution of equipment transactions?

    a. Are requests for major repairs approved at a higher level than the department initiating the request?
    b. Are prenumbered purchase orders used for equipment and periodically accounted for?
    c. Are requests for purchases of equipment reviewed for consideration of soliciting competitive bids?
    d. Are procedures in place to monitor and properly restrict access to equipment?

        (11/94, AUD, #41, ID: 5114)

105. Which of the following controls would an entity most likely use in safeguarding against the loss of marketable securities?

    a. An independent trust company that has no direct contact with the employees who have record keeping responsibilities has possession of the securities.
    b. The internal auditor verifies the marketable securities in the entity's safe each year on the balance sheet date.
    c. The independent auditor traces all purchases and sales of marketable securities through the subsidiary ledgers to the general ledger.
    d. A designated member of the board of directors controls the securities in a bank safe-deposit box.

        (11/92, AUD, #22, ID: 2956)

106. When an entity uses a trust company as custodian of its marketable securities, the possibility of concealing fraud most likely would be reduced if the

    a. Trust company has no direct contact with the entity employees responsible for maintaining investment accounting records.
    b. Securities are registered in the name of the trust company, rather than the entity itself.
    c. Interest and dividend checks are mailed directly to an entity employee who is authorized to sell securities.
    d. Trust company places the securities in a bank safe-deposit vault under the custodian's exclusive control.

        (5/94, AUD, #34, ID: 4699)

107. Which of the following controls would a company most likely use to safeguard marketable securities when an independent trust agent is **not** employed?

    a. The investment committee of the board of directors periodically reviews the investment decisions delegated to the treasurer.
    b. Two company officials have joint control of marketable securities, which are kept in a bank safe-deposit box.
    c. The internal auditor and the controller independently trace all purchases and sales of marketable securities from the subsidiary ledgers to the general ledger.
    d. The chairman of the board verifies the marketable securities which are kept in a bank safe-deposit box, each year on the balance sheet date.

        (11/95, AUD, #16, ID: 5963)

108. Which of the following procedures most likely would give the greatest assurance that securities held as investments are safeguarded?

    a. There is no access to securities between the year-end and the date of the auditor's security count.
    b. Proceeds from the sale of investments are received by an employee who does not have access to securities.
    c. Investment acquisitions are authorized by a member of the Board of Directors before execution.
    d. Custody of investment securities is assigned to an outside agent such as a brokerage house, and access to securities requires the signatures and presence of two designated officials.

        (5/93, AUD, #22, amended, ID: 3918)

Problem 3-2 SIMULATION: Revenue & Accounts Receivable Internal Control Procedures

Field, CPA, is auditing the financial statements of Miller Mailorder, Inc. (MMI) for the year ended January 31, year 1. Field has compiled a list of possible errors and fraud that may result in the misstatement of MMI's financial statements.

For each possible error and fraud listed, select one internal control procedure from the list that, if properly designed and implemented, most likely could assist MMI in preventing or detecting the errors and fraud.

Each response in the list of internal control procedures may be selected once, more than once, or not at all.

Possible Errors & Fraud	Internal Control Procedure
1. Invoices for goods sold are posted to incorrect customer accounts.	
2. Goods ordered by customers are shipped, but are not billed to anyone.	
3. Invoices are sent for shipped goods, but are not recorded in the sales journal.	
4. Invoices are sent for shipped goods and are recorded in the sales journal, but are not posted to any customer account.	
5. Credit sales are made to individuals with unsatisfactory credit ratings.	
6. Goods are removed from inventory for unauthorized orders.	
7. Goods shipped to customers do not agree with goods ordered by customers.	
8. Invoices are sent to allies in a fraudulent scheme and sales are recorded for fictitious transactions.	

Internal Control Procedures

A. Shipping clerks compare goods received from the warehouse with the details on the shipping documents.

B. Approved sales orders are required for goods to be released from the warehouse.

C. Monthly statements are mailed to all customers with outstanding balances.

D. Shipping clerks compare goods received from the warehouse with approved sales orders.

E. Customer orders are compared with the inventory master file to determine whether items ordered are in stock.

F. Daily sales summaries are compared with control totals of invoices.

G. Shipping documents are compared with sales invoices when goods are shipped.

H. Sales invoices are compared with the master price file.

I. Customer orders are compared with an approved customer list.

J. Sales orders are prepared for each customer order.

K. Control amounts posted to the accounts receivable ledger are compared with control totals of invoices.

L. Sales invoices are compared with shipping documents and approved customer orders before invoices are mailed.

M. Prenumbered credit memos are used for granting credit for goods returned.

N. Goods returned for credit are approved by the supervisor of the Sales Department.

O. Remittance advices are separated from the checks in the mailroom and forwarded to the Accounting Department.

P. Total amounts posted to the accounts receivable ledger from remittance advices are compared with the validated bank deposit slip.

Q. The cashier examines each check for proper endorsement.

R. Validated deposit slips are compared with the cashier's daily cash summaries.

S. An employee, other than the bookkeeper, periodically prepares a bank reconciliation.

T. Sales returns are approved by the same employee who issues receiving reports evidencing actual return of goods.

(ID: 9215)

Problem 3-3 SIMULATION: Revenue Cycle Internal Controls Flowchart

The accompanying flowchart depicts part of a client's revenue cycle. Some of the flowchart symbols are labeled to indicate control procedures and/or records. For each symbol labeled 1 through 13, select from the answer list the procedure or record it represents.

Flowchart Symbol No.	Procedure or Record Letter	Flowchart Symbol No.	Procedure or Record Letter
#1		#8	
#2		#9	
#3		#10	
#4		#11	
#5		#12	
#6		#13	
#7			

Answer List

Operations and control procedures	Documents, journals, ledgers, and files
A. Enter shipping data	P. Shipping document
B. Verify agreement of sales order and shipping document	Q. General ledger master file
	R. General journal
C. Write off accounts receivable	S. Master price file
D. To warehouse and Shipping Department	T. Sales journal
E. Authorize account receivable write-off	U. Sales invoice
F. Prepare aged trial balance	V. Cash receipts journal
G. To Sales Department	W. Uncollectible accounts file
H. Release goods for shipment	X. Shipping file
I. To Accounts Receivable Department	Y. Aged trial balance
J. Enter price data	Z. Open order file
K. Determine that customer exists	
L. Match customer purchase order with sales order	
M. Perform customer credit check	
N. Prepare sales journal	
O. Prepare sales invoice	(ID: 9216)

_____

Problem 3-4 SIMULATION: Research

Regardless of the assessed risk of material misstatement, the auditor should design and perform substantive procedures for all relevant assertions related to each material class of transactions, account balance, and disclosure. What authoritative reference lists the substantive procedures related to the financial reporting process that the auditor should include? cess that the auditor should include?

[   ] § [   ]   [   ]   (ID: 89462)

Solution 3-1 MULTIPLE-CHOICE ANSWERS

Components of Internal Control

1.   (d)   Assigning different people the responsibilities of authorizing transactions, recording transactions, and maintaining custody of assets is intended to reduce the opportunities to allow any person to be in a position to both perpetrate and conceal errors or fraud in the normal course of their duties. Answers a. and b. list tasks that are record keeping. Answer c. lists tasks that are both authorization.   (ID: 5099)

2.   (a)   Internal control consists of five interrelated components: control environment, risk assessment, information and communication systems, control activities, and monitoring. Control risk is one of the three components of audit risk.   (ID: 86)

3.   (c)   The control environment sets the tone of an organization, influencing the control consciousness of its people. Factors include management's philosophy and operating style, personnel policies and practices, etc. Detection risk is an element of audit risk, not a factor of the control environment.   (ID: 5102)

4.   (c)   Performance reviews is a category of control activities that includes reviewing and analyzing actual performance versus budgets, forecasts, and prior-period performance.   (ID: 5955)

5.   (d)   Selling real estate at a price considerably different from its appraised value may indicate the existence of related parties. Granting stock options to key executives at favorable prices is a common method of compensation. While high turnover of senior management and members of the board of directors may be a cause for concern, it usually does not provide indications of related parties. Failure to correct internal control weaknesses is often due to cost/benefit considerations.   (ID: 8159)

6.   (d)   The purpose of segregation of duties is to eliminate incompatible functions. Incompatible functions place persons in the position to both perpetrate and conceal errors or fraud in the normal course of their duties. Therefore, a well designed plan of organization separates the duties of authorization, record keeping, and custody of assets. The tasks in answer a. are both record keeping duties. The tasks in answer b. are both internal control functions. The tasks in answer c. are both authorization duties.   (ID: 8158)

7.   (c)   The auditor should obtain sufficient knowledge of the control environment to understand the attitudes, awareness, and actions of those charged with governance concerning the entity's internal control and its importance in achieving reliable financial reporting. Computer-based controls, the system of segregation of duties, and safeguards over access to assets are day-to-day details with which board members are unlikely to have as much influence (unless they are also officers).   (ID: 5643)

8.   (b)   In an audit of financial statements, an auditor's primary consideration is whether, and how, a specific control prevents, or detects and corrects, material misstatements in relevant assertions related to classes of transactions, account balances, or disclosures. Management's philosophy and operating style are elements of the control environment that would influence policies and procedures, but are not the auditor's primary consideration. Whether controls provide adequate safeguards over access to assets is not relevant to all controls (as is answer b.) nor is it the auditor's primary consideration. And again, the enhancement of management's decision-making processes is not an auditor's primary consideration.   (ID: 5101)

9.   (b)   Incompatible functions are those that place any person in a position to both perpetrate and conceal errors or fraud in the normal course of their duties. Therefore, a well-designed plan of organization separates the duties of authorization, record keeping, and custody of assets.   (ID: 92)

10.   (c)   Access to blank checks and signature plates is restricted to the cash disbursements bookkeeper who personally reconciles the monthly bank statement is the situation that most likely could lead to an embezzlement scheme. Bank reconciliations should not be prepared by persons who sign checks or keep the records for receipts or disbursements. This is an example of incompatible functions which place a person in the position to both perpetrate and conceal errors or fraud in the normal course of their duties. The duties of authorization, record keeping, and custody of assets should be separated. Additionally, bank reconciliations should not be done by persons with responsibility for handling cash receipts. The other answer alternatives are examples of appropriate duties/control practices.   (ID: 8818)

11. (d) Control risk is a function of the effectiveness of the design and operation of internal control in achieving a company's objectives relevant to the preparation of the financial statements. One of the five components of internal control is the control environment. One of the elements of the control environment is a company's organizational structure. As it provides the framework for accomplishing the company's objectives, a relevant organizational structure includes considering key areas of authority and responsibility and appropriate (suitable) lines of reporting. The key to selecting the best answer was to determine which was most related to a company's organizational structure. Management's attitude and recruiting and hiring practices are not directly related to organizational structure, as is the case with lines of reporting. The physical proximity of the accounting function to upper management could be completely unrelated to organizational structure. (ID: 8845)

12. (c) Inherent risk is not one of the components of internal control; rather, along with control risk it is a component of the risk of material misstatement. Internal control consists of five interrelated components: (1) control environment; (2) risk assessment; (3) information and communication systems; (4) control activities; and (5) monitoring. (ID: 9918)

Understanding of Internal Control

13. (a) While incompatible duties can be segregated and therefore controlled, the possibility of management override and collusion among employees to circumvent controls will still exist. Mistakes in judgment also cannot be controlled. (ID: 4687)

14. (b) Concerns about the integrity of the entity's management may be so serious as to cause the auditor to conclude that the risk of management misrepresentations in the financial statements is such that an audit cannot be conducted. Answers a., c., and d. should be considered by the auditor but are not necessarily serious enough to raise an auditability question. (ID: 5953)

15. (b) Human judgment in the decision making process is usually considered an inherent limitation because mistakes may occur in the application of certain policies and procedures due to misunderstanding of instructions or personal carelessness. The complexity of the information processing system is not in itself an inherent limitation; it is the incorrect use of the complex system by humans that causes the majority of errors. The ineffectiveness of the board of directors and the lack of management incentives to improve the control environment are correctible weaknesses in internal control; they are not inherent. (ID: 8136)

16. (a) The nature, extent, and timing of procedures the auditor chooses to perform in the consideration of internal control will vary depending on the size and complexity of the entity, previous experience with the entity, the nature of the specific controls used by the entity including the entity's use of IT, the nature and extent of changes in systems and operations, and the nature of the entity's documentation of specific controls. (ID: 8138)

17. (d) Ordinarily, controls that are relevant to an audit pertain to the entity's objective of preparing financial statements that are fairly presented in conformity with generally accepted accounting principles, including the management of risk that may give rise to a risk of material misstatement in those financial statements. (ID: 2303)

18. (d) While the auditor should be alert to significant deficiencies, the auditor is not obligated to search for them. Obtaining an understanding of internal control involves evaluating the design of a control and determining whether it has been implemented. This understanding should be documented. (ID: 4256)

19. (b) Obtaining an understanding of internal control consists of evaluating the design and implementation of controls. This is not the same as testing the operating effectiveness of controls. The auditor only tests the operating effectiveness of controls when: (1) the auditor's risk assessment includes an expectation of the operating effectiveness of controls or (2) when it is not possible or practicable to reduce detection risk at the relevant assertion level to an acceptably low level with audit evidence obtained from substantive procedures alone. (ID: 3908)

20. (d) When obtaining an understanding of an entity's internal control, an auditor should concentrate on the implementation of procedures because management may establish appropriate procedures but not enforce compliance with them. Depending on the size of the entity, written policies may not be necessary. The implementation of procedures whose costs exceed their benefits would not affect the auditor's assessment of the performance of control procedures. An auditor should consider the design (appropriateness) of a control in determining

whether to consider its implementation, thus as the question asks the reason for the auditor's concentration on the implementation of controls, an inappropriate control is not directly related to the question.   (ID: 4686)

21.   (b)   The information system relevant to financial reporting objectives, which includes the accounting system, consists of the procedures and records established to authorize, process, and report an entity's transactions. The auditor should obtain sufficient knowledge of the information system, including the related business processes relevant to financial reporting, to understand the financial reporting process used to prepare the entity's financial statements, including significant accounting estimates and disclosures. Safeguards used to limit access to computer facilities, procedures used to assure proper authorization of transactions, and policies used to detect the concealment of fraud are all examples of control policies and procedures.   (ID: 4685)

22.   (a)   Internal control, no matter how well designed and operated, can provide an entity with reasonable, but not absolute, assurance about achieving an entity's objectives. The likelihood of achievement is affected by limitations inherent to internal control. These include the realities that human judgment in decision making can be faulty and that breakdowns in internal control can occur because of human failures such as simple errors or mistakes. While answers b., c., and d. are generally true statements, they are not included in the concept of reasonable assurance.   (ID: 5644)

23.   (d)   Concerns about the integrity of the entity's management may be so serious as to cause the auditor to conclude that the risk of management misrepresentations in the financial statements is such that an audit cannot be conducted. Answers a., b., and c. may be considerations, but are not necessarily so serious as to cause an auditor to question whether the entity can be audited.   (ID: 7099)

24.   (d)   Observing the entity's personnel applying the activities provides evidence about the design and implementation of internal control activities. Entity personnel may have trouble implementing poorly designed activities. Reperformance alone would not provide evidence about whether and how the activities are actually performed. The procedures in answers b. and c. might detect misstatements, but would not provide much information about internal controls.   (ID: 6393)

25.   (c)   Internal control, no matter how well designed and operated, can provide an entity with reasonable, but not absolute, assurance about achieving an entity's objectives. The likelihood of achievement is affected by limitations inherent to internal control. These include the realities that human judgment in decision making can be faulty. An inherent quality is part of the very nature of something and thus is not considered alterable as are incompatible duties, lack of segregation of duties or the lack of an audit committee.   (ID: 8377)

26.   (b)   Management's carelessness regarding an adequate internal control environment may make it improbable that an auditor will be able to collect sufficient appropriate audit evidence to form an opinion. An auditor need not understand the internal auditor's techniques, particularly before accepting an engagement. The auditor merely needs to determine if related party transactions are properly disclosed, not whether they occur similarly to arm's-length transactions. Performing substantive tests at year-end is adequate if all records are available.   (ID: 6928)

27.   (b)   Collusion is an inherent limitation of any system of internal control. An internal control system, no matter how well designed and operated, cannot give an entity absolute assurance that its objectives will be met because any system has inherent limitations. Other inherent limitations of internal control are faulty human judgment, human failures that lead to errors or mistakes, and inappropriate management override of controls. Judgmental sampling is part of the application of an auditing procedure; not an inherent limitation of internal control. Segregation of duties and employee peer reviews are examples of controls; not inherent limitations.   (ID: 8621)

28.   (b)   One of the inherent limitations of internal control is inappropriate management override of internal control. An example of this would be if the CEO can request a check with no purchase order. The other answer alternatives describe weaknesses in internal control, but they are not inherent limitations. Inherent limitations are intrinsic—no matter how well designed and operated, internal control can only provide an entity with reasonable, not absolute, assurance.   (ID: 8836)

29.   (b)   The auditor should document key elements of the auditor's understanding of internal control regardless of the client's records. The client's failure to do so does not constitute a scope limitation; necessitate

that the auditor assess control risk at the maximum level; nor restrict the auditor's responsibility to assess the effectiveness of controls. (ID: 8639)

30. (b) The degree to which information technology (IT) is used in the accounting function is most likely to affect the extent of the documentation of the auditor's understanding of a client's system of internal control. The form and extent of documentation are influenced by the nature, size, and complexity of the entity and its environment, including its internal control, and the availability of information from the entity and the specific audit methodology and technology used in the course of the audit. An entity's use of IT may affect any of the five components of internal control relevant to the achievement of the entity's financial reporting, operations, or compliance objectives, and its operating units or business functions. The use of IT also affects the fundamental manner in which transactions are initiated, authorized, recorded, processed, and reported. And an entity's mix of manual and automated controls varies with the nature and complexity of the entity's use of IT. Documentation of the understanding of a complex information system in which a large volume of transactions are electronically initiated, authorized, recorded, processed, or reported may include flowcharts, questionnaires, or decision tables. For an information system making limited or no use of IT or for which few transactions are processed, documentation in the form of a memorandum may be sufficient. The effect on the internal control system of an entity of the other answer alternatives is not as pervasive, thus their impact on the extent of the documentation of the auditor's understanding of it is less. (ID: 9358)

31. (b) Verifying that approved spending limits are not exceeded would best assess the validity of the auditor's concern about a policy of management override because It is management's responsibility to authorize expenditures. Irregularities which might be discovered by matching purchase orders to accounts payable or tracing sales orders to revenue accounts might not involve management. Undetected management override of controls would not be described in minutes of board meetings. (ID: 9383)

32. (c) Assessed risks and the basis for those assessments should be documented whether or not control risk is assessed at the maximum level. There is a direct relationship between control risk and substantive testing, thus if control risk is high the auditor should perform more, not fewer, substantive tests of details. If the auditor assesses control risk at the maximum level there is no point in performing more tests of controls. Documenting a control structure more extensively because it is not functioning well is nonsensical. (ID: 9943)

Tests of Controls

33. (d) The auditor may design a test of controls to be performed concurrently with a test of details on the same transaction. The objective of tests of controls is to evaluate whether a control operated effectively. Answer a. would be a substantive test rather than a test of controls. Answer b. is an objective of obtaining an understanding of an entity's internal control. Answer c. is the objective of substantive procedures. (ID: 5115)

34. (c) When a client has documentation regarding the use of computer programs, it is an effective internal control. Answer b. is a substantive procedure. Answers a. and d. are analytical procedures. (ID: 5958)

35. (b) Audit evidence is more reliable when it is obtained directly by the auditor rather than evidence obtained indirectly or by inference. Performing tests of transactions tests segregation of duties from the past which may not be operating currently. A flowchart reflects the ideal operating conditions of the company, established at a point in time, which may not be representative of the actual processing procedures being performed. Audit objectives cannot in themselves reduce control risk. (ID: 3906)

36. (b) When the auditor determines that it is appropriate to use audit evidence obtained in prior audits for a number of controls, the auditor should plan to test a sufficient portion of the controls in each audit period, so that at a minimum, each control is tested at least every third audit. If the auditor plans to rely on controls that have changed since they were last tested, the auditor should test those controls in the current audit. If the auditor plans to rely on controls that have not changed since they were last tested, the auditor should test those controls at least every three years. If the auditor plans to rely on controls that mitigate a significant risk, those controls should be tested in the current period. (ID: 8267)

37. (d) The CPA examiners generally recognize four types of tests of internal controls to determine the degree of operating effectiveness: inquiries of appropriate entity personnel, inspection of documents and reports, observation of the application of specific internal control policies and procedures, and re-performance of the application of the policy or procedures by the auditor. System flowcharts may document the auditor's understanding

of internal control, but flowchart preparation provides little assurance about the documented activity's operating effectiveness. (ID: 7810)

38. (b) An audit is a cumulative and iterative process. As the auditor performs planned audit procedures, the audit evidence obtained may cause the auditor to modify the nature, extent, or timing of other planned audit procedures. In particular, the risk assessment may be based on an expectation that controls are operating effectively. If, after testing a client's internal control activities, the auditor discovers a material weakness in the operation of a client's internal controls, the auditor most likely would increase the assessment of control risk and increase the extent of substantive procedures in order to obtain more audit evidence rather than withdraw from the audit. In an audit of financial statements, the auditor is not required to perform procedures to identify deficiencies in internal control or to express an opinion on the effectiveness of the entity's internal control. (ID: 8375)

39. (d) The purpose of an audit is to express an opinion on the financial statements; an auditor assesses control risk as part of an evaluation of the likelihood that material misstatements exist in the financial statements. (ID: 8402)

40. (c) Observation of the application of the control, i.e., whether the data center is monitored to limit access, yields the most reliable audit evidence about the effectiveness of this control. The control may not be practiced as it is described in the policy manual. Inquiry of the chief technology officer does not provide as reliable evidence as the auditor's observation of the control's application. Obtaining a list of current data center employees by itself does not provide evidence of the effectiveness of the control's application. (ID: 8616)

41. (a) When an auditor plans to rely on controls that have changed since they were last tested, the auditor should test the operating effectiveness of such controls in the current audit. Changes may affect the relevance of the audit evidence obtained in prior periods, thus it may no longer be a basis for continued reliance. (ID: 9384)

42. (c) The question describes inquiries and inspection of records. It describes the auditor interviewing the controller (making inquiries) and inspecting the records (the verification that the reconciliation was properly prepared and included appropriate sign-offs) after the procedure had taken place, so it was not observation. A confirmation, which is a specific type of inquiry, is the process of obtaining and evaluating a direct communication from a third party in response to a request for information about a particular item—this was not described. The auditor did not perform the control procedure (the reconciliation) so it wasn't reperformance. And no analytical procedures are described. (ID: 9916)

Communicating Internal Control Related Matters

43. (b) If the auditor finds significant deficiencies or material weaknesses as a consequence of performing audit procedures in an audit of financial statements, the auditor is required to communicate them in writing to management and those charged with governance. It is not the auditor's duty to search for them or to express an opinion on the effectiveness of internal control. They are not required to be included in the financial statements or disclosed in the notes to the financial statements. (ID: 8142)

44. (d) Answers a. – c. are listed as indicators of material weaknesses by the standard setters. Their list also includes the identification by the auditor of a material misstatement of the financial statements in circumstances that indicate that the misstatement would not have been detected by the entity's internal control. Substantial doubt about the entity's ability to continue as a going concern does not indicate the existence of a material weakness in internal control. (ID: 9037)

45. (c) The written communication regarding significant deficiencies and material weaknesses identified during an audit of financial statements should include a restriction on its use. Significant deficiencies do not create scope limitations; management may have made a conscious decision to accept the degree of risk due to cost or other considerations. The auditor is not required to perform tests of controls on significant deficiencies; however, performing tests of controls in an audit may reveal significant deficiencies. For a nonissuer, the required written communication is best made by the audit report release date, but should be made no later than 60 days after this date. For an issuer, it must be made prior to the issuance of the audit report. In some circumstances, the auditor may decide to communicate certain identified significant deficiencies and material weaknesses during the audit; however these should ultimately be included in the formal final written communication even if remediated during the audit. (ID: 5118)

46. (b) The auditor should not issue an written communication stating that no significant deficiencies were identified during an audit. The other answer alternatives are all examples of items that should be included in the written communication regarding significant deficiencies and material weaknesses identified during an audit of financial statements. (ID: 2957)

47. (b) A deficiency in internal control exists when the design or operation of a control does not allow management or employees, in the normal course of performing their assigned functions, to prevent, detect, or correct misstatements on a timely basis. (ID: 7489)

48. (c) The severity of a deficiency in internal control is dependent on the magnitude of the potential misstatement that could result from the deficiency or deficiencies and whether there is a reasonable possibility (the likelihood) that the entity's controls will fail to prevent, or detect and correct a misstatement of an account balance or disclosure. It's also important to note that whether a misstatement actually occurred is not relevant to the determination of a control deficiency's severity. (ID: 7105)

49. (b) The written communication regarding significant deficiencies and material weaknesses identified during a financial statement audit should (1) include a statement that indicates that the auditor's consideration of internal control was to express an opinion on the financial statements, but not to express an opinion on the effectiveness of the entity's internal control; (2) state that the auditor is not expressing an opinion on the effectiveness of internal control; (3) state that the auditor's consideration of internal control was not designed to identify all deficiencies in internal control that might be significant deficiencies or material weaknesses; (4) include the definition of the terms "material weakness" and, where relevant, "significant deficiency"; (5) identify the matters that are considered to be significant deficiencies and those that are considered to be material weaknesses; and (6) state that the communication is intended solely for the information and use of management, those charged with governance, and others within the organization and is not intended to be and should not be used by anyone other than these specified parties. (If an entity is required to furnish the auditor's written communication to a governmental authority, a specific reference to the governmental authority may be made.) (ID: 5982)

50. (a) When deviations from prescribed controls are discovered the auditor should make inquiries to understand the potential consequences of the deviation. The auditor should never assume that a deviation is an isolated occurrence without audit significance. Answers c. and d. may or may not be determined to be appropriate actions after the auditor has gained an understanding of the potential consequences. (ID: 8821)

Source Documents & Accounting Records

51. (b) Shipping documents (records of goods shipped by the client) and receiving reports (records of goods received by the client) are generated by the client. Customer purchase orders and bank statements are generated externally by the client's customers and the client's financial institutions, respectively. Vendor invoices and packing slips (records of goods shipped to the client) are generated externally by the client's vendors. Bills of lading (records of receipt of goods by a shipper) are generated externally usually by common carriers used by the client. Accounts receivable confirmation requests are sent out by the auditor or the client; the confirmations are completed (generated) by the client's customers and returned directly to the auditor by the client's customers. (ID: 8610)

52. (d) If the accounts payable manager issues purchase orders, incompatible functions of authorization and record keeping are combined creating a weakness in internal control. A person should not be in the position to both perpetrate and conceal errors or fraud in the normal course of their duties, thus the duties of authorization, record keeping, and custody of assets should be separated. The other answer alternatives describe appropriate internal controls. (ID: 8807)

53. (b) When testing for completeness for the revenue cycle, the auditor is checking to see that all sales have been recorded. Tracing ("up the house") from a shipping document to an invoice tests that goods that were shipped were also invoiced. The auditor would also need to confirm that the invoice was recorded. Testing receivables to see if they were collected subsequent to the year-end is done to determine if there was proper cutoff. Checking to see that each invoice is supported by a customer purchase order and that credit memos are properly authorized is testing for occurrence (validity). (ID: 8837)

Policies & Procedures Within Transaction Cycles

54. (b)   The best way to obtain evidence about the proper segregation of duties is by observing the employees who are performing the control activities. Procedures to verify the details of the bank balance, if they included examining signatures on deposit slips, could indicate which employees prepared the deposits, but this would not provide conclusive evidence as to which employees actually collected (physically handled) the receipts. Flowcharts and internal control questionnaires speak more to the effectiveness of the design rather than the operation of this control, but even if they are based on inquiries about the operation of the control, they do not provide as high a degree of evidence as simply actually observing who does what.   (ID: 8609)

Revenue & Receivables Cycle

55. (d)   Answers a. – c. are all controls applicable to the billing process. Answer d. is a control used *after* the billing process.   (ID: 5109)

56. (b)   Tracing from shipping documents to sales invoice provides evidence that shipments to customers were properly invoiced.   (ID: 5650)

57. (d)   The treasury department is independent of record keeping and custodial functions for accounts receivable. Incompatible functions are those that place any person in a position to both perpetrate and conceal errors or fraud in the normal course of their duties. Therefore, a well-designed plan of organization separates the duties of authorization, record keeping, and custody of assets. Answer a. would not separate the authorization and record keeping functions. Credit authorization and write-off of accounts by the same department could allow for an employee defalcation scheme. The A/P department would not have adequate information to make such a recommendation which could result in error or fraud concealment.   (ID: 5108)

58. (c)   The most effective control in offsetting the tendency of sales personnel to maximize sales volume at the expense of high bad debt write-offs would be the segregation of duties of those employees involved in credit-granting and sales functions. If this segregation exists, credit-granting employees should help to screen out those potential customers likely to result in high bad-debt write-offs.   (ID: 2798)

59. (a)   A bank lockbox system assures accountability control as cash enters the client's cash receipts system. Answers b. – d. are controls imposed after cash is captured in the system.   (ID: 5959)

60. (a)   The cycle approach combines similar transactions with the ledger balances that result from those transactions. Receivables result from the sale of goods; therefore, it is logical and more efficient to test these items together.   (ID: 8144)

61. (b)   Management's emphasis on meeting projected profit goals most likely would significantly influence the control environment when a significant portion of management compensation is represented by stock options because it provides an incentive to commit fraud. Answers a., c., and d. would mitigate this risk factor.   (ID: 8160)

62. (a)   Assertions about completeness are tested by testing whether or not all cash is recorded. If employees consistently use cash registers and tapes, it is likely that all cash is recorded. Inquiry about employees' access to undeposited recorded cash, comparing the cash receipts journal to the general ledger, and comparing the cash balance in the general ledger with the bank confirmation request, only test assertions about *recorded* cash.   (ID: 6578)

63. (c)   Segregation of duties prevents an employee from committing fraud and subsequently concealing it. Proper segregation of duties separates the functions of record keeping, custody and authorization. Answers a. and b. are not necessarily fraudulent activities. Fictitious transactions that overstate receivables also tend to overstate revenue, not understate it.   (ID: 8162)

64. (c)   By immediately recording the receipt of the checks, the employee provides evidence of the existence of cash. While the procedures in answers a., b., and d. are appropriate, preparing a duplicate listing of the checks is of immediate concern.   (ID: 5648)

65. (a)   Observation of an entity's preparation of a schedule is a test of a control. Confirmation requests, inspection of an analysis of accounts receivables, and comparison of an entity's uncollectible accounts expense to actual uncollectible accounts receivables are all substantive procedures.   (ID: 6234)

66. (c) For each shipment, there should be a sales invoice. If the auditor selects a sample of transactions from the shipping document file and does not find corresponding sales invoices, the auditor knows the controls are ineffective. For each sales order and customer order, there may or may not be a sales invoice, depending on whether the product was shipped. When testing to see if there is a failure to produce sales invoices, by selecting a sample from the sales invoice file, an auditor would guarantee to get only transactions where this failure did not occur. (ID: 7815)

67. (b) In addition to indemnification in case of loss, fidelity bonds provide a psychological deterrent to employees considering defalcations. The insurance company's investigation before an employee is bonded tends to discourage those with intentions of committing defalcations from accepting jobs requiring bonds. A further deterrent is the employee's knowledge that the insurance company will prosecute in an effort to recover a loss, whereas an employer might forego prosecution. (ID: 73)

68. (c) One of the most effective means of detecting or preventing fraud is the segregation of duties involving authorization, custody, and record keeping. Authorization of credit memos by personnel who receive cash (custody) is not segregation of duties. The recording of fictitious transactions and failure to prepare shipping documents resulting in an overstatement of inventory likely would be discovered during reconciliations. Return claims applied to inappropriate accounts likely would be discovered by customers when monthly statements are issued. (ID: 6577)

69. (d) Internal verifications of cash balances generally should be made monthly. Recorded cash on hand and petty cash balances should be compared with cash counts and recorded bank balances should be reconciled to balances shown on bank statements. These verifications should be made by personnel who are not otherwise involved in executing or recording cash transactions to maintain a segregation of functions. The cash receipts accountant, the cash disbursements accountant, and the controller should not reconcile the monthly statements as they are involved in the executing or recording of cash transactions. (ID: 111)

70. (d) Sending sales orders to the credit department for approval is a key control for ensuring that sales are properly authorized. Although the billing and cash receipts departments should be separate (to reduce the opportunity for any one person to both perpetrate and conceal fraud or errors in the normal course of their duties), their separation does not impact whether sales are properly authorized. Use of an approved price list is a control to ensure the accuracy of sales transactions rather than proper authorization. The receipt of approved sales orders by the shipping, billing, and accounting departments occurs after the fact. (ID: 8612)

71. (b) The auditor should make the selection from the shipping document file. Attempting to match shipping documents to invoices would reveal goods shipped that were not invoiced. The cash receipts file contains evidence of payments, so it would be highly unlikely to discover payments received from customers who weren't billed. The customer order file would be a workable but inefficient choice by the auditor because normally goods are not invoiced until they are shipped, so it would involve checking shipping documents as well to confirm the sale. The sales invoice file would not be used because the auditor is looking for sales that were not invoiced. (ID: 8636)

Disbursements Cycle

72. (d) Accounting for unused purchase orders and receiving reports by the same department does not provide sufficient segregation of duties for the authorization, custody, and reporting functions of an effective internal control system. The lack of segregation of these items could result in an employee defalcation scheme. Answers a. – c. each represent a procedure that is usually performed in the vouchers payable department. (ID: 5113)

73. (d) The agreement of the documents will verify that the goods were ordered (purchase order), received (receiving report), and the company has been billed (vendor's invoice). The individual signing the checks, not accounts payable, should stamp, perforate, or otherwise cancel the supporting documentation. The purchasing department, not accounting, is involved with the approval of purchase requisitions and blanking out the quantity ordered on the receiving department copy of the purchase order. (ID: 5977)

74. (b) When the shipping department returns nonconforming goods to a vendor, the purchasing department should send a debit memo to the accounting department. This enables the accounting department to make the appropriate adjustment to the vendor's account. Answers a. and c. are incorrect because the accounting

department would have no use for the unpaid voucher and the vendor invoice. A credit memo would be provided by the vendor, not by the purchasing department. (ID: 2950)

75. (b) By immediately stamping "paid" on the paid voucher, the check signer prevents the voucher from being paid again. While each of the items in answers a., c., and d. is a recommended practice, none prevent the voucher from being paid again. (ID: 5652)

76. (d) A good internal control system will include the segregation of duties, such as the comparison of an approved purchase order to items received. Answers a. and c. represent documentation included with the order as it is received, without any indication of authorization. Answer b. represents a form used when goods and materials are taken from inventory to be used or shipped. (ID: 3913)

77. (d) A control for cash disbursements is for the person who signs the checks to compare them to supporting documents, cancel the documents, and to mail the checks. The person who signs checks should have access to the supporting documents in order to validate their legitimacy. Reconciliation of the monthly bank statement is a control that should be done by a person independent of cash transactions. Checks should not be returned or given to anyone with cash disbursement responsibilities. (ID: 5976)

78. (d) Assertions about completeness deal with whether all transactions and accounts that should be presented in the financial statements are so included. One step in assuring this is the periodic reconciliation of prenumbered purchase orders, receiving reports, and vouchers. (ID: 2799)

79. (d) Approved borrowings by the board of directors indicate that transactions must be approved before the recording and custody functions can take place. This is also performed by a party independent of the recording and custody functions. (ID: 4269)

80. (b) Good internal controls require that the person who last signs the checks keep control of them until they are mailed. Answers a., c., and d. do not provide sufficient segregation of duties for the authorization, custodial, and reporting functions of an effective internal control system. (ID: 3914)

81. (c) Incompatible functions are those that place any person in a position to both perpetrate and conceal errors or fraud in the normal course of their duties. Therefore, a well-designed plan of organization separates the duties of authorization, record keeping, and custody of assets. The treasurer generally would perform the other procedures. (ID: 4264)

82. (d) The most effective controls over recorded purchases occur when supporting forms such as purchase orders, receiving reports, and vendor invoices are compared independently for agreement. For good control, the Receiving Department should not know the quantity ordered. Answer b. is a step in the right direction, but does not encompass as many independent comparisons as does answer d. Answer c. is an example of incompatible functions. Assets should not be checked in and recorded by the person who authorized their purchase. (ID: 7491)

83. (c) The chief financial officer's willingness to override the internal controls reveals a management philosophy that values meeting goals higher than working within established procedures. Little time would be saved by adhering to approval procedures at most entities, indicating, at best, poor organization regarding the transactions. Elimination of the internal audit function, in itself, doesn't indicate that controls are now inadequate, although this is a second-best answer. As the audit committee chair is unlikely to have been in a position to commit a disreputable act with regard to the entity under audit, the chair's resignation probably doesn't indicate personal misconduct. If an audit committee chair resigned in protest of entity misconduct, the chair likely would have informed the auditor directly of the reasons for the resignation. Check-run frequency rarely effects the quality of internal controls. (ID: 7843)

84. (a) The voucher and all supporting documents should be canceled (stamped paid) by the check signer to avoid duplicate payments. The return of the voucher to the vouchers payable department provides no control to prevent it from being paid more than once. Confirmation that each voucher is supported by a vendor's invoice and purchase order provides evidence that the payment is based on a valid purchase, but would not stop a duplicate payment. Prenumbering and accounting for vouchers allows confirmation that all vouchers were recorded and should allow the discovery of a duplicate payment, but it would not prevent it. (ID: 8618)

Inventory & Production Cycle

85. (a) To test for appropriate segregation of duties, the auditor observes and makes inquiries. The procedures in answers b – d. are not applicable to testing for segregation of duties. (ID: 5649)

86. (b) For sound internal controls, all receipts for goods, including returned goods or materials, should be handled by the receiving clerk. Receiving reports should be prepared for all items received. Employees who have recording responsibilities should not also have custody of the related assets. (ID: 3916)

87. (c) Use of time tickets indicates the amount of actual labor employed during the day on a given job. An internal control procedure requiring the use of charging the actual time to the job in progress would help prevent mistakes in the recording of direct and indirect labor. Answers a. and d. would indicate variances after improperly charging direct labor to factory overhead, but would be poor preventative measures. Answer b. would have no effect on identifying misposted direct labor. (ID: 4697)

88. (d) Assertions about existence or occurrence deal with whether assets or liabilities of the entity exist at a given date and whether recorded transactions have occurred during a given period. Periodically comparing goods on hand with perpetual inventory records would assist in identifying potential errors. Answer a. addresses the valuation of the inventory. Answer b. would not identify variances in actual inventory compared to recorded amounts. Answer c. represents examples of controls necessary for the proper segregation of duties in purchasing inventory. (ID: 4698)

89. (b) Controlling the access to assets is an important objective of proper inventory control. The other answer alternatives are procedures for satisfying inventory control objectives—not actual internal control objectives. (ID: 4265)

90. (c) To obtain an understanding of a manufacturer's internal control concerning inventory balances, an auditor would review the entity's descriptions of inventory policies and procedures. Analyzing inventory ratios, performing cost variance analytical procedures, and performing inventory test counts are substantive procedures. (ID: 5979)

91. (c) An independent comparison of finished goods records with counts of goods on hand is designed to detect errors and fraud concerning inventory custody as it provides an independent reconciliation of the two amounts. Answers a. and b. do not consider the inventory itself nor inventory custody. The storekeeper should not be able to approve inventory journal entries because he or she has custody of the assets. (ID: 7492)

92. (c) An auditor need consider only the objectives and related controls relevant to the audit. An auditor performs tests of the design and operation of internal controls to determine if the auditor may rely upon them. If the auditor has determined that it will take less time to perform substantive tests than it will to perform tests of controls, there is no reason to assess control risk or perform any tests of controls on inventory. Control risk may be assessed at a minimum level only after testing controls and finding them strong. (ID: 8419)

Personnel & Payroll Cycle

93. (c) Incompatible functions are those that place any person in a position to both perpetrate and conceal errors or fraud in the normal course of their duties. Therefore, a well-designed plan of organization separates the duties of authorization, record keeping, and asset custody. Authorizing payroll rate changes for all employees would be incompatible with record keeping. Examining authorization forms for new employees is not the same as authorization; therefore, the payroll department supervisor would only be in control of record keeping. While hiring all subordinate payroll department employees would not be a compatible function with record keeping, it is not as serious as authorizing pay rate changes for all employees. (ID: 4694)

94. (c) Incompatible functions are those that place any person in a position to both perpetrate and conceal errors or fraud in the normal course of their duties. A well-designed organization plan separates authorization, record keeping, and asset custody. (ID: 4267)

95. (a) Observing the segregation of duties concerning personnel responsibilities and payroll disbursement is a common audit procedure relating to the existence or occurrence assertion for payroll transactions. Inspecting evidence of accounting for prenumbered payroll checks would provide evidence related to the completeness

assertion. Recomputing the payroll deductions for employee fringe benefits would provide evidence related to the valuation and the rights and obligations assertions. An auditor would likely review payroll checks and bank reconciliations to determine that all checks were cashed as part of obtaining evidence for the existence or occurrence assertion and not just verify the preparation of the monthly payroll account bank reconciliation. (ID: 5978)

96. (a) By promptly notifying the payroll supervisor of employee terminations, the personnel department would avoid a terminated employee from continuing to be paid. Unclaimed payroll checks should be forwarded to the Treasurer's office. Salary rates should be controlled in the personnel office. Total hours should be determined and approved prior to getting to the payroll department. Although answers c. and d. are good controls, they would not prevent employee payroll fraud. (ID: 5962)

97. (a) Significant unexplained variances between standard and actual labor cost could cause an auditor to suspect a payroll fraud scheme. Payroll checks disbursed by the same employee each payday (as long as that person has no other payroll responsibilities), employee time cards being approved by individual departmental supervisors, and a separate payroll bank account maintained on an imprest basis are proper internal control procedures. (ID: 5997)

98. (a) The authorization of a transaction, its record keeping, and the custody of the related asset should all be separated. In a payroll function, the treasurer's department prepares and distributes payroll checks to employees (custody), the controller reviews the payroll, and the payroll department prepares the payroll (record keeping). (ID: 4268)

99. (a) An important internal control is the separation of the duties of authorization, record keeping, and custody. As the payroll department prepares the payroll (record keeping) and has custody of the related assets, a payroll clerk is in a position to both perpetrate and conceal misappropriation of assets. Having the accounting department wire transfer funds (authorization) based on total from a payroll summary (record keeping) may be unusual, but the two mentioned types of duties are separated. With the treasurer supervises the use of a signature plate (custody) by the payroll department to prepare checks (record keeping), segregation of duties is maintained. With the chief financial officer signing checks (custody) prepared by the payroll department (record keeping), segregation of duties is maintained. (ID: 7831)

100. (d) Having the department supervisor approve a summary of hours each employee worked during the pay period would be most likely to help in the prevention or detection of a payroll fraud. The other answer alternatives are examples of improper segregation of duties. (ID: 9382)

PP&E Cycle

101. (d) The requirement is to find the flowchart indicating two forms of input (new transactions and the old file) being processed to generate three forms of output (labels, printed journal, and a new file). Answer a. shows only one input with four forms of output. Answer b. represents a manual process while the facts indicate that a printed journal is to be generated. Answer c. shows a punched card as one of the output items when labels, a printed journal, and a new file should be represented in the output. (ID: 7490)

102. (c) The investigation of variances within a formal budgeting system would identify any unusual and unanticipated fluctuations in the repair and maintenance accounts when asset acquisitions are recorded there incorrectly. The segregation of duties is a good control; however, answer a. would not ensure that equipment acquisitions were not misclassified. Answer b. would not prevent the recording of an acquisition to the repair and maintenance accounts, nor would it serve to identify misclassifications. Answer d. would not ensure that equipment purchases were recorded properly because these invoices only represent those acquisitions which are already properly recorded as fixed assets. (ID: 4271)

103. (a) The periodic inspection of physical equipment and comparison to the accounting records by the internal auditor (who does not participate in the acquisition or disposal process) may allow for a reduction in the scope of the auditor's tests of asset acquisitions. The comparison of account balances and entries is an analytical procedure that would highlight unusual and unanticipated fluctuations; however, it would not indicate acquisitions that were not approved. The review of prenumbered purchase orders would indicate trade-ins or retirements of fixed assets in exchange for new assets; thus, there would be no change in the quantity of fixed assets on hand. (ID: 3917)

104. (d) The procedures in place to monitor and properly restrict access to equipment would more likely be observed by the auditor than be part of a questionnaire, as this is very important. Answer a. represents the authorization function of the control structure, which would be included on the internal control questionnaire. Answer b. represents a procedure to test the accounting and recording function of the control structure, which the auditor would include in an internal control questionnaire. Requests for competitive bids reduce the possibility of an individual's personal gain at the expense of the business in unusual and material transactions.

(ID: 5114)

Investing Cycle

105. (a) Of the choices given, the strongest internal control in safeguarding against the loss of marketable securities would be the use of an independent trust company that has no direct contact with the employees who have record keeping responsibilities. The fact that only the trust company has access to the securities should prevent unauthorized entity personnel with record keeping responsibility from conspiring or colluding to misappropriate securities. In determining appropriate controls in safeguarding an asset against loss, the auditor would start with those controls involving access to the asset in question. Neither verifying the securities in the safe nor tracing all purchases and sales provides evidence as to who has access to, or custody of, the marketable securities. Allowing just one person access to an asset enables the individual to take the asset without being discovered.

(ID: 2956)

106. (a) The fact that only the trust company has access to the securities should prevent unauthorized entity personnel with record keeping responsibility from conspiring or colluding to misappropriate the securities. Trust company employees or management potentially could sell or otherwise mismanage the assets. Answers c. and d. put custody and record keeping functions in the hands of one party which could result in unauthorized transactions.

(ID: 4699)

107. (b) A bank safe-deposit box with two company officials in control of the assets provides strong physical control over the securities. Answers a. and c. would not safeguard the physical marketable security. Answer d. does not provide for dual control throughout the year, as is preferred.

(ID: 5963)

108. (d) Custody of investment securities usually is maintained on company premises or assigned to an outside agent such as a brokerage house. Good controls dictate that at least two officers should sign for, and be present to access, these investments to prevent unauthorized sales. Having no access to securities between the year-end and the date of the auditor's security count provides no guarantee that unauthorized access to the investments during the time period indicated did not occur. Having proceeds from the sale of investments received by an employee who does not have access to securities and investment acquisitions authorized by a member of the Board of Directors before execution are good controls, but do not address the physical control of the assets.

(ID: 3918)

PERFORMANCE BY TOPICS

Each category below parallels a topic covered in Chapter 3. Record the number and percentage of questions you answered correctly in each topic.

Components of Internal Control

Question #	Correct	√
1		
2		
3		
4		
5		
6		
7		
8		
9		
10		
11		
12		
# Questions	12	
# Correct		
% Correct		

Understanding of Internal Control

Question #	Correct	√
13		
14		
15		
16		
17		
18		
19		
20		
21		
22		
23		
24		
25		
26		
27		
28		
29		
30		
31		
32		
# Questions	20	
# Correct		
% Correct		

Tests of Controls

Question #	Correct	√
33		
34		
35		
36		
37		
38		
39		
40		
41		
42		
# Questions	10	
# Correct		
% Correct		

Communicating Internal Control Related Matters

Question #	Correct	√
43		
44		
45		
46		
47		
48		
49		
50		
# Questions	8	
# Correct		
% Correct		

Source Documents & Accounting Records

Question #	Correct	√
51		
52		
53		
# Questions	3	
# Correct		
% Correct		

Policies & Procedures Within Transaction Cycles

Question #	Correct	√
54		
# Questions	1	
# Correct		
% Correct		

Revenue & Receivables Cycle

Question #	Correct	√
55		
56		
57		
58		
59		
60		
61		
62		
63		
64		
65		
66		
67		
68		
69		
70		
71		
# Questions	17	
# Correct		
% Correct		

Disbursements Cycle

Question #	Correct	√
72		
73		
74		
75		
76		
77		
78		
79		
80		
81		
82		
83		
84		
# Questions	13	
# Correct		
% Correct		

Inventory & Production Cycle

Question #	Correct	√
85		
86		
87		
88		
89		
90		
91		
92		
# Questions	8	
# Correct		
% Correct		

Personnel & Payroll Cycle

Question #	Correct	√
93		
94		
95		
96		
97		
98		
99		
100		
# Questions	8	
# Correct		
% Correct		

PP&E Cycle

Question #	Correct	√
101		
102		
103		
104		
# Questions	4	
# Correct		
% Correct		

Investing Cycle

Question #	Correct	√
105		
106		
107		
108		
# Questions	4	
# Correct		
% Correct		

Solution 3-2 SIMULATION ANSWER: Revenue & Accounts Receivable Internal Control Procedures

Possible Errors & Fraud	Internal Control Procedure
1. Invoices for goods sold are posted to incorrect customer accounts.	C
2. Goods ordered by customers are shipped, but are not billed to anyone.	G
3. Invoices are sent for shipped goods, but are not recorded in the sales journal.	F
4. Invoices are sent for shipped goods and are recorded in the sales journal, but are not posted to any customer account.	K
5. Credit sales are made to individuals with unsatisfactory credit ratings.	I
6. Goods are removed from inventory for unauthorized orders.	B
7. Goods shipped to customers do not agree with goods ordered by customers.	D
8. Invoices are sent to allies in a fraudulent scheme and sales are recorded for fictitious transactions.	L

1. C   The error of posting a customer's invoice to the wrong account would be detected when a monthly statement was received, indicating a balance due, when no payment is owed.

2. G   Before goods are shipped from the warehouse, an employee should determine that a valid sales invoice exists that matches the shipping documents and actual shipment being made. This would prevent shipments being made that have not been invoiced.

3. F   To prevent having unrecorded sales, the company should make a comparison each day of the total sales invoices with the daily sales summaries. This comparison would detect differences between the total sales made vs. recorded.

4. K   Unrecorded accounts receivable would be prevented by comparing the control total of sales invoices to the control total amount posted to the accounts receivable ledger. Any differences would indicate possible errors in the recording function and require a reconciliation, which would detect unposted customer sales.

5. I   Requiring employees to use an approved customer list before making credit sales to customers would prevent the company from allowing sales to be made to uncreditworthy customers.

6. B   An internal control procedure that would prevent goods being removed from the warehouse when a *bona fide* sale does not exist would be the requirement that an approved sales order be received in the warehouse before the goods could be released from the warehouse.

7. D   If shipping clerks compare the order received from the warehouse to the approved customer sales order before shipment, this would prevent the error of shipping the wrong goods to customers.

8. L   The company would be able to prevent a fraudulent sales scheme where sales were recorded for fictitious transactions if certain control procedures were in place. For example, requiring an employee not in the Sales Department to compare customer sales invoices to shipping documents and approved customer orders before invoices were recorded and sent would prevent other than *bona fide* sales transactions from being recorded.

(ID: 9215)

Solution 3-3 SIMULATION ANSWER: Revenue Cycle Internal Controls Flowchart

1. M   Before preparing a sales order, the Computer Processing Department should perform a credit check to determine that the sale will be made to a creditworthy customer. This information may be obtained from the customer credit file or from outside sources.

2. Z   Once the sales order has been prepared, it will be recorded and placed in the open order file.

3. L   This manual operation represents the process of matching customer purchase orders with sales orders for agreement.

4. B   This manual operation represents matching the shipping document with the sales order for agreement.

5. H   Once the shipping document and sales order have been matched, the goods will be released for shipment.

6. S   In order to prepare the customer bill, the computerized billing program will retrieve the shipping data from the shipping file and enter the price data from the master price file.

7. O   Once the shipping data and price data have been retrieved and the sale to the customer generated, the sales invoice will be prepared.

8. U   This document represents the duplicate copy of the sales invoice generated by the computerized billing program.

9. I   One copy of the sales invoice will be sent to the customer, and another copy will be sent to the Accounts Receivable Department as support for the entry to the accounts receivable ledger—to be held until remittance is made by the customer.

10. Q   The Computer Processing Department will (daily, weekly, or monthly) update the master files, such as the accounts receivable ledger, the inventory master file, the sales transaction file, and the general ledger master file.

11. N   The computer processing department will prepare, based upon the update program, an accounts receivable ledger, an aged trial balance, a general ledger transaction summary, and a sales journal.

12. T   This output function represents the sales journal which was generated by the computerized update program for the day, week, or month, depending upon the frequency of report generation established by management.

13. Y   This output report represents the aged trial balance generated by the computerized update program, which combined information from the general ledger master file, the sales transaction file, and the inventory master file.   (ID: 9216)

Solution 3-4 SIMULATION ANSWER: Research

AU	§	318	52	(ID: 89462)

    .52   The auditor's substantive procedures should include the following audit procedures related to the financial statement reporting process:

- Agreeing the financial statements, including their accompanying notes, to the underlying accounting records; and

- Examining material journal entries and other adjustments made during the course of preparing the financial statements.

The nature and extent of the auditor's examination of journal entries and other adjustments depend on the nature and complexity of the entity's financial reporting system and the associated risks of material misstatement.

CHAPTER 4

EVIDENCE & PROCEDURES

CHAPTER 4

EVIDENCE & PROCEDURES

I. **Audit Evidence (AU 326)**

A. **Concept of Audit Evidence**

Exhibit 1 ▶ The Third Standard of Fieldwork

> The auditor must obtain sufficient appropriate audit evidence by performing audit procedures to afford a reasonable basis for an opinion regarding the financial statements under audit.

    1. **Definition** *Audit evidence* is all the information used by the auditor in arriving at the conclusions on which the audit opinion is based, including the information contained in the accounting records underlying the financial statements and other information. This includes evidence obtained from audit procedures performed during the audit and may include evidence obtained from other sources, such as prior audits and quality control procedures for client acceptance and continuance.

    2. **Sources** Audit evidence should be obtained through testing the accounting records. However, because accounting records alone do not provide sufficient appropriate audit evidence, the auditor should obtain other audit evidence. This may consist of:

        a. Minutes of meetings

        b. Confirmations from third parties

        c. Industry analysts' reports

        d. Comparable data about competitors (benchmarking)

        e. Controls manuals

        f. Information obtained through other audit procedures

        g. Information developed by or available to the auditor that permits the auditor to reach conclusions through valid reasoning

    3. **Accounting Records** Accounting records generally include:

        a. Records of initial entries and supporting records, such as checks and records of electronic fund transfers

        b. Invoices

        c. Contracts

        d. General and subsidiary ledgers, journal entries, and other adjustments to the financial statements that are not reflected in formal journal entries

        e. Records such as worksheets and spreadsheets supporting cost allocations, computations, reconciliations, and disclosures

B.   Sufficient Appropriate Audit Evidence
The auditor should consider the sufficiency and appropriateness of audit evidence to be obtained when assessing risks and designing further audit procedures.

1.   **Sufficiency & Appropriateness** *Sufficiency* measures the quantity of audit evidence. *Appropriateness* measures the quality of audit evidence, that is, its relevance and reliability. The quantity of audit evidence needed is affected by the risk of misstatement. This means as risk increases, audit evidence required increases. The quantity also is affected by the quality of such evidence. This means as the quality of evidence increases, the quantity of evidence may be able to be decreased. However, merely obtaining more audit evidence may not compensate for audit evidence of lower quality. The auditor should exercise professional judgment and professional skepticism in evaluating the sufficiency and appropriateness of audit evidence to support the audit opinion.

   a.   **Relevance** Certain audit procedures may provide relevant audit evidence pertaining to some assertions and not others. The auditor can not substitute audit evidence related to a specific assertion for evidence concerning another assertion; that is, the evidence must be relevant to the assertion it supports.

   b.   **Reliability** The reliability of audit evidence is dependent on its source, nature, and the circumstances under which it is obtained. While recognizing that exceptions may exist, the following generalizations can be made:

      (1)   Audit evidence is more reliable when it is obtained from knowledgeable independent sources outside the entity.

      (2)   Internally generated audit evidence is more reliable when the related internal controls are effective.

      (3)   Audit evidence obtained directly by the auditor is more reliable than evidence obtained indirectly or by inference.

      (4)   Audit evidence is more reliable when it exists in documentary form (paper, electronic, or other medium).

      (5)   Audit evidence provided by original documents is more reliable than audit evidence provided by photocopies or facsimiles.

2.   **Accuracy & Completeness** The auditor should obtain audit evidence about the accuracy and completeness of information produced by the entity's information system when that information is used in performing audit procedures. For example, if the auditor uses data obtained from the entity's information system in performing analytical procedures, the auditor should obtain audit evidence concerning the accuracy and completeness of that data.

3.   **Corroborative Evidence** The auditor ordinarily obtains more assurance from consistent audit evidence obtained from different sources or of a different nature than from items of audit evidence considered individually. For example, corroborating information obtained from a source independent of the entity may increase the assurance the auditor obtains from a management representation.

4.   **Cost Constraints** The relationship between the cost of obtaining audit evidence and the usefulness of the information may be considered. However, the degree of difficulty or expense involved in testing a particular item is not, by itself, a valid basis for omitting the procedure for which there is no appropriate alternative.

5.   **Persuasive Evidence** The auditor may need to rely on audit evidence that is persuasive rather than conclusive. However, to obtain reasonable assurance, the auditor must not be satisfied with audit evidence that is less than persuasive.

C.   **Use of Assertions in Obtaining Audit Evidence**

1.   **Nature of Assertions** Assertions are representations made by management that are embodied in the financial statements being audited. Assertions used by the auditor fall into the following categories:

a.   **Classes of Transactions & Events** The following assertions are relevant to classes of transactions and events:

(1)   **Occurrence** Transactions and events that have been recorded have occurred and pertain to the entity.

(2)   **Completeness** All transactions and events that should have been recorded have been recorded.

(3)   **Accuracy** Amounts and other data relating to recorded transactions and events have been recorded appropriately.

(4)   **Cutoff** Transactions and events have been recorded in the correct accounting period.

(5)   **Classification** Transactions and events have been recorded in the proper accounts.

b.   **Account Balances** The following assertions are relevant to ending account balances:

(1)   **Existence** Assets, liabilities, and equity interests actually exist.

(2)   **Rights & Obligations** The entity holds or controls the rights to assets, and liabilities are the obligations of the entity.

(3)   **Completeness** All assets, liabilities, and equity interests that should have been recorded have been recorded.

(4)   **Valuation & Allocation** Assets, liabilities, and equity interests are included in the financial statements at appropriate amounts and any resulting valuation or allocation adjustments are recorded appropriately.

c.   **Presentation & Disclosure** The following assertions are relevant to the presentation and disclosure in the financial statements:

(1)   **Occurrence and Rights & Obligations** Disclosed events and transactions have occurred and pertain to the entity.

(2)   **Completeness** All disclosures that should have been included in the financial statements have been included.

(3)   **Classification & Understandability** Financial information is appropriately presented and described and disclosures are clearly expressed.

(4)   **Accuracy & Valuation** Financial and other information are disclosed fairly and at appropriate amounts.

2.   **Relevant Assertions** The auditor should use relevant assertions in assessing risks by considering the different types of potential misstatements that may occur, and then designing further audit procedures that are responsive to the assessed risks. To identify relevant assertions, the auditor should determine the source of likely potential misstatements in each significant class of transactions, account balance, and presentation and disclosure.

Relevant assertions are assertions that have a meaningful bearing on whether the account is fairly stated. For example, valuation may not be relevant to the cash account unless currency translation is involved; however, existence and completeness are always relevant. Similarly, valuation may not be relevant to the gross amount of the accounts receivable balance but is relevant to the related allowance accounts. In determining whether a particular assertion is relevant, the auditor should evaluate:

a.   The nature of the assertion

b.   The volume of transactions or data related to the assertion

c.   The nature and complexity of the systems by which the entity processes and controls information supporting the assertion

D.   **Audit Procedures for Obtaining Audit Evidence**

1.   **Procedures** The auditor should obtain audit evidence to draw reasonable conclusions on which to base the opinion by performing the following procedures:

a.   **Risk Assessment Procedures** Obtain an understanding of the entity and its environment, including its internal control, to assess the risk of material misstatement at the financial statement and relevant assertion levels. Risk assessment procedures must be supplemented by tests of controls, when necessary, and substantive procedures.

b.   **Tests of Controls** When necessary, or when the auditor has determined to do so, test the operating effectiveness of controls in preventing or detecting material misstatements at the relevant assertion level. Tests of controls are necessary in two circumstances. When the auditor's risk assessment includes an expectation of the operating effectiveness of controls, the auditor should test those controls to support the risk assessment. Also, when the substantive procedures alone do not provide sufficient appropriate audit evidence, the auditor should perform tests of controls to obtain audit evidence about the operating effectiveness of IC.

c.   **Substantive Procedures** Substantive procedures detect material misstatements at the relevant assertion level through tests of details and substantive analytical procedures. The auditor should design and perform substantive procedures for all relevant assertions related to each material class of transactions, account balance, and disclosure regardless of the assessed risk of material misstatement.

2.   **Types of Procedures** The following procedures, or combinations of them, may be used as risk assessment procedures, test of controls, or substantive procedures, depending on the context in which they are applied: (a) inspection of records or documents; (b) inspection of tangible assets; (c) observation; (d) inquiry; (e) confirmation; (f) recalculation; (g) reperformance; or (h) analytics.

E. **Evaluating Audit Evidence (AU 318 continued)**

1. **Risk Assessments** The auditor should determine, based on audit evidence obtained, whether the risk assessments at the relevant assertion level are still appropriate.

2. **Planned Audit Procedures** As an audit is a cumulative and iterative process, audit evidence obtained during the audit may cause the auditor to change the nature, extent, or timing of other planned audit procedures. Such evidence may indicate that risk assessments need to be revised. In this case, the auditor should reevaluate the planned audit procedures based on the revised risk assessments for all or some relevant assertions.

   a. **Deviations From Controls** If deviations are detected in testing the operating effectiveness of controls, the auditor should make specific inquiries to understand these deviations and their potential consequences. The auditor also should consider whether any detected misstatements change the auditor's judgment of the effectiveness of related controls. Furthermore, the auditor should determine whether: (1) reliance on the controls is appropriate based on the tests of controls performed, (2) additional tests of controls are necessary, or (3) the potential risks need to be addressed using substantive procedures.

   b. **Fraud or Error** The auditor cannot assume that an instance of fraud or error is an isolated occurrence; thus, the auditor should consider how that instance affects the assessed risk of material misstatement. The auditor should determine whether audit risk has been reduced to an appropriately low level and whether the nature, extent, and timing of audit procedures need to be reconsidered.

3. **Developing an Opinion** The auditor should use professional judgment to conclude whether sufficient appropriate audit evidence has been obtained to reduce the risk of material misstatement in the financial statements to an appropriately low level. The auditor should evaluate all relevant audit evidence, regardless of whether it supports or contradicts the relevant assertions, when developing an opinion on the financial statements. If the auditor is unable to obtain sufficient appropriate audit evidence, the auditor should express a qualified opinion or a disclaimer of opinion.

II. **Internal Audit Function (AU 322)**

A. **Role of External vs. Internal Auditor**
An external auditor usually will perform financial audits to enable the auditor to attest to the fairness of an entity's financial statements. Internal auditors also may perform financial audits as well as procedural and operational audits beyond the scope of the external audit. Therefore, a comprehensive internal audit program may be more detailed and cover more areas than an independent auditor's program.

1. **External Auditor** The auditor maintains independence from the entity to fulfill the responsibility to obtain sufficient appropriate audit evidence matter to provide a reasonable basis for the opinion on the entity's financial statements.

2. **Internal Auditor** Internal auditors maintain objectivity with respect to the activity being audited to fulfill the responsibility for providing analyses, evaluations, recommendations, and other information to the entity's management and board of directors or to others with equivalent authority.

B. **Obtaining an Understanding & Making an Assessment of Internal Audit Function**
When obtaining an understanding of internal control, the auditor should obtain an understanding of the internal audit function sufficient to identify those internal audit activities that are relevant to planning the audit.

1. **Procedures** The auditor ordinarily should make inquiries of appropriate management and internal audit personnel about the internal auditors

    a. Organizational status within the entity

    b. Application of professional standards

    c. Audit plan, including the nature, extent, and timing of audit work

    d. Access to records

    e. Whether there are limitations on the scope of their activities

2. **Relevance** Internal audit activities relevant to an audit of the entity's financial statements are those that provide evidence about the design and effectiveness of internal control policies and procedures that pertain to the entity's ability to record, process, summarize, and report financial data consistent with the assertions embodied in the financial statements, or that provide direct evidence about potential misstatements of such data. The following procedures help the auditor assess the relevancy of internal audit activities: (a) considering knowledge from prior year audits, (b) reviewing how the internal auditors allocate their audit resources to financial or operating areas in response to their risk assessment process, and (c) obtaining detailed information about the scope of internal audit activities.

3. **Consideration of Internal Auditors' Work** The auditor may conclude that some of the internal auditors' activities are relevant to the audit and that it would be efficient to consider how the internal auditors' work might affect the nature, extent, and timing of audit procedures. In that case, the auditor should assess the competence and objectivity of the internal auditors in light of the intended effect of the internal auditors' work on the audit.

    a. **Competence** The auditor should obtain information about the following.

        (1) Education level and professional experience of the internal auditors

        (2) Professional certification and continuing education of the internal auditors

        (3) Audit policies, programs and procedures

        (4) Practices regarding assignment of internal auditors

        (5) Supervision and review of internal auditors' activities

        (6) Quality of working paper documentation, reports, and recommendations

        (7) Evaluation of internal auditors' performance

    b. **Objectivity** The auditor should obtain information about the following.

        (1) **Organizational Status of Head of Internal Audit** The organizational status of the internal auditor responsible for the internal audit function, i.e., whether

            (a) The position reports to an officer of sufficient status to ensure broad audit coverage and adequate consideration of, and action on, the findings and recommendations of the internal auditors

(b) The position has direct access and reports regularly to those charged with governance

(c) Those charged with governance oversee employment decisions regarding the position

(2) Policies Policies to maintain internal auditor's objectivity, including policies prohibiting internal auditors from auditing areas where

(a) Relatives are employed in important or audit-sensitive positions

(b) Internal auditors were recently assigned or are scheduled to be assigned after working in internal audit

4. **Effectiveness of Internal Auditors' Work** Involves determining whether the scope of work is appropriate; audit programs are adequate; working papers adequately document work performed, including evidence of supervision and review; conclusions are appropriate; and reports are consistent with the results of the work performed.

C. **Direct Assistance**
Internal auditors may assist the auditor in obtaining an understanding of internal control or in performing tests of controls or substantive tests. If the internal auditors provide direct assistance, the auditor should inform the internal auditors of their responsibilities, the objectives of the procedures, and matters that may affect the nature, extent, and timing of audit procedures.

1. **Supervision** The external auditor should assess the internal auditors' competence and objectivity, and supervise, review, evaluate, and test the work performed. The external auditor should test the internal auditors' work by examining some of the controls, transactions, or balances that the internal auditors examined, or similar evidence not actually examined by the internal auditors.

2. **Guidance** The internal auditors also should be informed of the need to bring all significant accounting and auditing issues identified to the external auditor's attention.

3. **Extent** As the materiality of the financial statement amounts increases and either the RMM or degree of subjectivity increases, the need for the external auditor instead of the internal auditors to perform the tests of the assertions increases.

III. **Management Representations (AU 333)**

A. **Purpose**
In order to comply with GAAS, the auditor must obtain certain written representations from management. These are part of the audit evidence but are not a substitute for the application of auditing procedures.

Written representations (1) confirm the oral representations that were given explicitly or implicitly to the auditor during the engagement; (2) serve as documentation of the continuing appropriateness of the representations; and (3) reduce the possibility of misunderstandings.

1. **Complementary Evidence** The auditor frequently obtains written representations from management to complement other auditing procedures. In many cases, the auditor performs procedures specifically designed to obtain evidence about a matter that is also the subject of a representation. An example of this is related-party transactions.

2. **Additional Audit Evidence** Sometimes auditing procedures are limited to inquiries. In these cases, the auditor obtains written representations from management to provide additional audit evidence. An example of this would be if a client plans to discontinue a line of business and the auditor cannot obtain sufficient information using other auditing procedures

to corroborate management's plans. In this case, the auditor would ask for a written representation to provide evidence of management's intent.

3. **Contradictory Evidence** In cases where management representations are contradicted by other audit evidence, the auditor should investigate the circumstances and consider the reliability of the representations being made. Based on the circumstances, the auditor should consider whether reliance on management's representations relating to other aspects of the financial statements is appropriate and justified.

4. **Update** An updating management representation letter should state (a) whether any information has come to management's attention that would cause them to believe that any of the previous representations should be modified, and (b) whether any events have occurred subsequent to the balance sheet date of the latest financial statements reported on by the auditor that would require adjustment to or disclosure in those financial statements.

    An auditor should obtain updating representation letters from management in the following circumstances:

    a. **Reissuance** When a predecessor auditor is requested by a former client to reissue the report on the financial statements of a prior period that are to be presented on a comparative basis with audited financial statements of a subsequent period.

    b. **SEC Filings** When performing subsequent events procedures in connection with filings under the Securities Act of 1933.

B. **Required Representations**
    Written representations from management must be obtained for all financial statements and periods covered by the auditor's report. For example, when comparative financial statements are presented, the written representations obtained at the completion of the most recent audit should address all periods being presented. Representations specifically required for all audits are noted in the sample representation letter in Exhibit 2.

    1. **Adapt** The specific written representations obtained by the auditor depend on the circumstances of the particular engagement and the nature and basis of the financial statement presentation (e.g., whether the financial statements are based on GAAP or OCBOA). The representation letter should be tailored to include additional appropriate representations from management relating to matters specific to the entity's business or industry.

    2. **Duration** If current management was not present during all periods covered by the auditor's report, the auditor should still obtain written representations from current management on all such periods.

    3. **Subsidiary** If the independent auditor performs an audit of the financial statements of a subsidiary, but does not audit those of the parent company, the auditor may want to obtain representations from management of the parent company concerning matters that may affect the subsidiary (for instance, related-party transactions or the parent company's intention to provide continuing financial support to the subsidiary).

    4. **Address** The written representations should be addressed to the auditor.

    5. **Dates** The representations should be made as of the date of the auditor's report. If the auditor *dual dates* the report, the auditor should consider whether obtaining additional representations relating to the subsequent event is appropriate.

    6. **Signatures** The letter should be signed by those members of management with overall responsibility for financial and operating matters whom the auditor believes are responsible for and knowledgeable about (directly or through others in the organization) the matters covered by the representations. Such members of management normally include the chief executive officer and chief financial officer (or others with equivalent positions in the entity).

In certain circumstances, the auditor may want to obtain written representations from other individuals. For example, the auditor may want to obtain written representations about the completeness of the minutes of the meetings of stockholders, directors, and committees of directors from the person responsible for keeping such minutes.

Exhibit 2 ▶ Management Representation Letter

[*Date*]

To [*Independent Auditor*]

We are providing this letter in connection with your audit(s) of the [*identification of financial statements*] of [*name of entity*] as of [*dates*] and for the [*periods*] for the purpose of expressing an opinion as to whether the [*consolidated*] financial statements present fairly, in all material respects, the financial position, results of operations, and cash flows of [*name of entity*] in conformity with accounting principles generally accepted in the United States of America. We confirm that we are responsible for the fair presentation in the [*consolidated*] financial statements of financial position, results of operations, and cash flows in conformity with generally accepted accounting principles.

Certain representations in this letter are described as being limited to matters that are material. Items are considered material, regardless of size, if they involve an omission or misstatement of accounting information that, in the light of surrounding circumstances, makes it probable that the judgment of a reasonable person relying on the information would be changed or influenced by the omission or misstatement.

We confirm, to the best of our knowledge and belief, [*as of (**date of auditor's report**)*,] the following representations made to you during your audit(s).

1. The financial statements referred to above are fairly presented in conformity with accounting principles generally accepted in the United States of America.

2. We have made available to you all

    a. Financial records and related data

    b. Minutes of the meetings of stockholders, directors, and committees of directors, or summaries of actions of recent meetings for which minutes have not yet been prepared

3. There have been no communications from regulatory agencies concerning noncompliance with or deficiencies in financial reporting practices.

4. There are no material transactions that have not been properly recorded in the accounting records underlying the financial statements.

5. We believe that the effects of the uncorrected financial statement misstatements summarized in the accompanying schedule are immaterial, both individually and in the aggregate, to the financial statements taken as a whole.

6. We acknowledge our responsibility for the design and implementation of programs and controls to prevent and detect fraud.

7. We have no knowledge of any fraud or suspected fraud affecting the entity involving

    a. Management

    b. Employees who have significant roles in internal control

    c. Others where the fraud could have a material effect on the financial statements

8. We have no knowledge of any allegations of fraud or suspected fraud affecting the entity received in communications from employees, former employees, analysts, regulators, short sellers, or others.

9. The company has no plans or intentions that may materially affect the carrying value or classification of assets and liabilities.

10. The following have been properly recorded or disclosed in the financial statements:

    a. Related-party transactions, including sales, purchases, loans, transfers, leasing arrangements, and guarantees, and amounts receivable from or payable to related parties

    b. Guarantees, whether written or oral, under which the company is contingently liable

    c. Significant estimates and material concentrations known to management that are required to be disclosed in accordance with Financial Accounting Standards Board (FASB) *Accounting Standards Codification* (ASC) 275, *Risks and Uncertainties*. [*Significant estimates are estimates at the balance sheet date that could change materially within the next year. Concentrations refer to volumes of business, revenues, available sources of supply, or markets or geographic areas for which events could occur that would significantly disrupt normal finances within the next year*.]

11. There are no

    a. Violations or possible violations of laws or regulations whose effects should be considered for disclosure in the financial statements or as a basis for recording a loss contingency

    b. Unasserted claims or assessments that our lawyer has advised us are probable of assertion and must be disclosed in accordance with FASB ASC 450, *Contingencies*

    c. Other liabilities or gain or loss contingencies that are required to be accrued or disclosed by FASB ASC 450

12. The company has satisfactory title to all owned assets, and there are no liens or encumbrances on such assets nor has any asset been pledged as collateral.

13. The company has complied with all aspects of contractual agreements that would have a material effect on the financial statements in the event of noncompliance.

[Add additional representations that are unique to the entity's business or industry.]

To the best of our knowledge and belief, no events have occurred subsequent to the balance sheet date and through the date of this letter that would require adjustment to or disclosure in the aforementioned financial statements.

_____
[*Name of Chief Executive Officer and Title*]

_____
[*Name of Chief Financial Officer and Title*]

    C.   **Materiality**
Management's representations may be limited to matters that are considered either individually or collectively material to the financial statements, provided management and the auditor have reached an understanding on materiality for this purpose. Materiality may be different for different representations. A discussion of materiality may be included explicitly in the representation letter, in either qualitative or quantitative terms. Materiality considerations would not apply to those representations that are not directly related to amounts included in the financial statements. In addition, because of the possible effects on other aspects of the audit, materiality would not be relevant with respect to knowledge of fraud or suspected fraud involving management or those employees who have significant roles in internal control.

D.   Scope Limitation
Management's refusal to furnish written representations constitutes a limitation on the scope of the audit sufficient to preclude an unqualified opinion and ordinarily is sufficient to cause an auditor to disclaim an opinion on the financial statements or withdraw from the engagement.   Further, the auditor should consider the effects of the refusal on the reliability of other management representations.

1.   **Qualified Opinion** Based on the nature of the representations not obtained or the circumstances of the refusal, the auditor may conclude that a qualified opinion is appropriate.

2.   **Audit Procedures Restricted** If the auditor is precluded from performing procedures that are necessary in the circumstances with respect to a matter that is material to the financial statements, even though management has given representations concerning the matter, there is a limitation on the scope of the audit.   In this case, the auditor should qualify or disclaim an opinion.

IV. Analytics (AU 329)

A.   Overview
Analytics, or analytical procedures, consist of evaluations of financial information made by a study of plausible relationships among both financial and nonfinancial data.   The procedures range from simple comparisons to complex models.   To utilize analytics effectively, the auditor must understand financial relationships and have knowledge of the client and its industry.

1.   **Purpose**

   a.   To assist the auditor in **planning** the nature, extent, and timing of substantive tests. (This is **required** by GAAS.) Analytics should focus on enhancing the auditor's understanding of the client's business and the transactions and events that have occurred since the last audit date, and identifying areas that may represent specific risks relevant to the audit.   Analytical procedures used in planning the audit generally use financial data aggregated at a high level; however, sometimes relevant nonfinancial data is considered as well.

   b.   As a substantive test to obtain audit evidence about particular assertions related to account balances or classes of transactions.   (**Not** required by GAAS, but commonly used.)

   c.   As an overall **review** of the financial information in the final review stage of the audit. (This also is **required** by GAAS.)

2.   **Expectations** Analytics involve comparisons of recorded amounts, or ratios developed from recorded amounts, to expectations developed by the auditor.   The auditor develops expectations by identifying relationships that reasonably are expected to exist from understanding the client and the industry in which the client operates.   The following are examples of sources of information for developing expectations:

   a.   Financial information for comparable prior periods giving consideration to known changes

   b.   Anticipated results; for example, budgets or forecasts including extrapolations from interim data

   c.   Relationships among elements of financial information within the period

   d.   Information regarding the industry in which the client operates; for example, gross margin information

   e.   Relationships of financial information with relevant nonfinancial information

3. **Benford's Law** Application of Benford's Law is an example of a complex analytical procedure. Benford's Law is a numerical probability theory establishing the frequency of the appearance of digits in naturally occurring sets of numbers. A common assumption is that in a sample of numbers from any population, all numbers have an equal probability of appearing. Many people do not create convincing dummy data sets because they are unaware of the unequal probability of the appearance of numbers 1 through 9. Benford's Law predicts the following approximate frequencies of occurrence as first digits: 1, 30%; 2, 18%; 3, 12%; 4, 10%; 5, 8%; 6, 7%; 7, 6%; 8, 5%; and 9, 4%. (The law predicts more, but that level of detail is beyond this discussion.) Large and varied populations of numbers adhere more closely to the distribution predicted by Benford's Law than small samples.

Exhibit 3 ▶ Benford's Law

A manager's ceiling for invoice approval is $5,000. Anomalies in the occurrence of 5, 6, 7, 8, and 9 as first digits would be expected. A higher than expected level of occurrence of 4 as a first digit (i.e., invoices at $4,001 to $4,999) suggest that purchases were intentionally divided into component parts to avoid higher level approval procedures. If 4 occurs more frequently than expected, the manager's spending warrants further scrutiny.

a. Seemingly divergent sets of numbers (such as utility bills of a given region, numbers on a newspaper page, and sport statistics) all adhere to Benford's Law. Computer software based on Benford's Law is a powerful device for detecting financial errors (including those due to software bugs), as well as fraud.

b. False positives do occur. Innocent anomalies can be created by "unnatural" external factors. Thresholds and ceilings are some factors that may cause anomalies. For instance, an HMO's fee schedule can create clustering, and hence, noncompliant number repetition, in a medical office's billing.

B. **Used in Overall Review**
Analytics are used in the overall review stage to assist the auditor in assessing conclusions reached and in evaluating the overall financial statement presentation. The overall review generally would include reading the financial statements and notes and considering the adequacy of evidence gathered in response to unusual or unexpected balances identified in planning the audit or in the course of the audit, and unusual or unexpected balances or relationships that were not identified previously. The results of an overall review may indicate that additional evidence may be needed. Also, use of analytics in the overall review helps the auditor in the going concern assessment.

C. **Used as Substantive Tests**
The auditor's reliance on substantive tests to achieve an audit objective related to a particular assertion (management representation) may be derived from tests of details, from analytics, or from a combination of both.

1. **Effectiveness & Efficiency** The expected effectiveness and efficiency of an analytical procedure in identifying potential misstatements depends on, among other things, the nature of the assertion, the plausibility and predictability of the relationship, the availability and reliability of the data used to develop the expectation, and the precision of the expectation. For example, the auditor may use inventory turnover figures to evaluate inventory salability.

2. **Significant Differences** In planning the analytical procedures used as substantive tests, the auditor should consider the amount of difference from the expectation that can be accepted without further investigation. The auditor should evaluate significant unexpected differences. If an explanation for a difference cannot be obtained, the auditor should obtain sufficient evidence about the assertion by performing other audit procedures to determine whether the difference is likely to be a misstatement.

D. Plausibility, Predictability & Precision

A basic premise underlying the application of analytics is that plausible relationships among data reasonably may be expected to exist and continue in the absence of known conditions to the contrary. The expectation should be precise enough to provide the desired level of assurance that differences that may be potential material misstatements, individually or when aggregated with other misstatements, would be identified for the auditor to investigate. The auditor's identification and consideration of factors that significantly affect the amount being audited and the level of detail of data used to develop expectations affect the precision of the expectations. Greater detail of data increases reliability of expectations. For example, using monthly amounts generally will be more effective than annual amounts.

1. Relationships are more predictable in a stable environment, while relationships in a dynamic environment lose predictability.

2. Relationships involving income statement accounts usually are more predictable than those involving only balance sheet accounts because income statement accounts represent transactions over a period, while balance sheet accounts represent amounts as of a point in time.

E. Reliability

The reliability of the data used by the auditor to develop expectations should be appropriate for the desired level of assurance from the analytical procedures. The auditor should assess the reliability of the data by considering the source of the data and the conditions under which it was gathered. The following factors influence the auditor's consideration of the reliability of data:

1. Whether the data was obtained from independent sources outside the entity or from sources within the entity

2. Whether sources within the entity were independent of those who are responsible for the amount being audited

3. Whether the data was developed under a reliable system with adequate controls

4. Whether the data was subjected to audit testing in the current or prior year

5. Whether the expectations were developed using data from a variety of sources

V. Using a Specialist's Work (AU 336)

A. Decision to Use a Specialist's Work

The auditor is not expected to have the expertise of a person trained for, or qualified to engage in, the practice of another profession or occupation. An auditor may encounter complex or subjective matters that may require special skill or knowledge and require using the work of a specialist to obtain appropriate audit evidence. Examples of the types of matters that might require the auditor to use the work of a specialist include:

1. **Valuation** Valuation (for example, special-purpose inventories, high-technology materials or equipment, pharmaceutical products, complex financial instruments, real estate, restricted securities, works of art, and environmental contingencies)

2. **Physical Characteristics** Determination of physical characteristics relating to quantity on hand or condition (for example, quantity or condition of minerals, mineral reserves, or materials stored in stockpiles)

3. **Specialized Techniques** Determination of quantities or amounts derived by using specialized techniques or methods (for example, actuarial determinations for employee benefits obligations and disclosures, and determination of insurance loss reserves)

4. **Interpretation** Interpretation of technical requirements, regulations, or agreements (for example, the potential significance of contracts or other legal documents, or legal title to property)

B. **Selection**
The auditor should evaluate the professional qualifications of the specialist to determine that the specialist possesses the necessary skill or knowledge in the particular field.

1. **Definition** A specialist is a person (or firm) possessing special skill or knowledge in a particular field other than accounting or auditing. Specialists include, but are not limited to, actuaries, appraisers, engineers, environmental consultants, and geologists. Additionally, an attorney engaged in situations other than to provide services to a client concerning litigation, claims, or assessments is considered a specialist.

2. **Considerations**

   a. The professional certification, license, or other recognition of competence

   b. The reputation and standing of the specialist in the views of peers and others

   c. The specialist's experience in the type of work under consideration

3. **Engaged by Management** Management may engage or employ a specialist and the auditor may use that specialist's work as audit evidence in performing substantive tests to evaluate material financial statement assertions. Alternatively, management may engage a specialist employed by the auditor's firm to provide advisory services.

4. **Engaged by Auditor** The auditor may engage a specialist and use that specialist's work as audit evidence in performing substantive tests to evaluate material financial statement assertions.

C. **Understanding**
The auditor should obtain an understanding of the nature of the work performed or to be performed by the specialist. This understanding should cover the following:

1. **Appropriateness, Objectives & Scope of the Specialist's Work** The appropriateness of using the specialist's work for the intended purpose.

2. **Specialist's Relationship to Client** The auditor should evaluate circumstances that might impair the objectivity of the specialist. Such circumstances include situations in which the client has the ability (through employment, family relationship, or otherwise) to control, directly or indirectly, or significantly influence the specialist.

   a. **No Relationship** The specialist's work usually will provide the auditor with greater assurance when there is no relationship.

   b. **Relationship** The auditor should assess the risk that the specialist's objectivity might be impaired. If the relationship might impair the specialist's objectivity, the auditor should perform additional procedures or engage another specialist.

3.   **Methods Used**   The appropriateness and reasonableness of methods and assumptions used and their application are the responsibility of the specialist.

    a.   The auditor should obtain an understanding to determine whether the findings are suitable for corroborating the assertions in the financial statements.   The auditor should consider whether the specialist's findings support the related assertions in the financial statements and make appropriate tests of data provided to the specialist.

    b.   Ordinarily, the auditor would use the work of the specialist unless the auditor believes that the findings are unreasonable, in which case, the auditor should apply additional procedures.

4.   Comparison of methods or assumptions with those used in preceding period

5.   Form & content of a specialist's findings

D.   Auditor's Conclusions
If the auditor determines that the specialist's findings support the related assertions in the financial statements, the auditor may reasonably conclude that sufficient appropriate audit evidence has been obtained.

1.   **Indeterminate**   If there is a material difference between the specialist's findings and the assertions in the financial statements, the auditor should apply additional procedures.   If the auditor is unable to resolve the matter, the auditor should obtain the opinion of another specialist, unless it appears that the matter cannot be resolved.   A matter that has not been resolved ordinarily will cause the auditor to qualify the opinion or disclaim an opinion.

2.   **Disagreement**   The auditor may conclude that the assertions in the financial statements are not in conformity with GAAP.   In that event, the auditor expresses a qualified or adverse opinion.

E.   Effect on Audit Report
Normally, the auditor should not refer to the work or findings of the specialist.   Such a reference might be misunderstood to be a qualification of the auditor's opinion or a division of responsibility, neither of which is intended.   Further, there may be an inference that the auditor making such reference performed a more thorough audit than an auditor not making such reference.   Reporting alternatives are:

1.   **Unqualified Opinion, Standard Report**   No reference to the specialist

2.   **Unqualified Opinion, Explanatory Paragraph Added to Report**   Refer to specialist in explanatory paragraph **only** if doing so will help clarify the reason for the explanatory paragraph.

3.   **Qualified Opinion or Disclaimer**   Scope limitation, the auditor is unable to obtain sufficient appropriate audit evidence—no reference to the specialist

4.   **Qualified or Adverse Opinion**   Auditor concludes there is a departure from GAAP—refer to specialist in explanatory paragraph only if doing so will help clarify the reason for the qualification or adverse opinion.

VI. Inquiry of Client's Lawyer (AU 337)

A. Accounting

Management has the responsibility to adopt policies and procedures that will identify, evaluate, and account for litigation, claims, and assessments as a basis for the preparation of financial statements in conformity with GAAP.

B. Auditing

The auditor should obtain audit evidence relating to (1) the existence of a condition or circumstances indicating an uncertainty as to the possible loss arising from litigation, claims, and assessments, (2) the period in which the underlying cause for legal action occurred, (3) the degree of probability of an unfavorable outcome, and (4) the amount or range of the potential loss.

Editor note: The standards of financial accounting and reporting for loss contingencies, including those arising from litigation, claims, and assessments, are set forth in Financial Accounting Standards Board (FASB) *Accounting Standards Codification* (ASC) 450, *Contingencies*.

1. **Procedures** Management is the primary source of information, accordingly the auditor should perform the following procedures.

    a. Inquire of and discuss with management the client's policies and procedures for identifying, evaluating, and accounting for litigation, claims, and assessments.

    b. Obtain from management a description and evaluation of litigation, claims, and assessments that existed at the balance sheet date and during the period from the balance sheet date to the date management furnishes the information, including an identification of those matters referred to legal counsel. Further, the auditor should obtain assurance, in writing, that the client disclosed all matters that are required to be disclosed by FASB ASC 450, *Contingencies.*

    c. Examine documents that relate to litigation, claims, and assessments, including correspondence and invoices from lawyers.

    d. Obtain assurance from management, ordinarily in writing, that it has disclosed all unasserted claims the lawyer has advised them are probable of assertion and must be disclosed in accordance with FASB ASC 450, *Contingencies*. With the client's permission, the auditor should inform the lawyer that the client has given the auditor this assurance.

    e. Other audit procedures performed for different purposes (e.g., reading the minutes of the board of directors meetings, sending bank confirmations, reading contracts and loan agreements, and inspecting documents for guarantees by the client) may also disclose possible litigation, claims, and assessments.

Exhibit 4 ▶ Sample Inquiry Letter to Legal Counsel

In connection with an audit of our financial statements at (balance sheet date) and for the (period) then ended, management of the Company has prepared, and furnished to our auditors (name and address of auditors), a description and evaluation of certain contingencies, including those set forth below involving matters with respect to which you have been engaged and to which you have devoted substantive attention on behalf of the Company in the form of legal consultation or representation. These contingencies are regarded by management of the Company as material for this purpose (management may indicate a materiality limit if an understanding has been reached with the auditor). Your response should include matters that existed at (balance sheet date) and during the period from that date to the date of your response.

Pending or Threatened Litigation (excluding unasserted claims)

[Ordinarily the information would include the following: (1) the nature of the litigation, (2) the progress of the case to date, (3) how management is responding or intends to respond to the litigation (for example, to contest the case vigorously or to seek an out-of-court settlement), and (4) an evaluation of the likelihood of an unfavorable outcome and an estimate, if one can be made, of the amount or range of potential loss.] Please furnish to our auditors such explanation, if any, that you consider necessary to supplement the foregoing information, including an explanation of those matters as to which your views may differ from those stated and an identification of the omission of any pending or threatened litigation, claims, and assessments or a statement that the list of such matters is complete.

Unasserted Claims and Assessments (considered by management to be probable of assertion, and that, if asserted, would have at least a reasonable possibility of an unfavorable outcome)

[Ordinarily management's information would include the following: (1) the nature of the matter, (2) how management intends to respond if the claim is asserted, and (3) an evaluation of the likelihood of an unfavorable outcome and an estimate, if one can be made, of the amount or range of potential loss.] Please furnish to our auditors such explanation, if any, that you consider necessary to supplement the foregoing information, including an explanation of those matters as to which your views may differ from those stated.

We understand that whenever, in the course of performing legal services for us with respect to a matter recognized to involve an unasserted possible claim or assessment that may call for financial statement disclosure, if you have formed a professional conclusion that we should disclose or consider disclosure concerning such possible claim or assessment, as a matter of professional responsibility to us, you will so advise us and will consult with us concerning the question of such disclosure and the applicable requirements of Financial Accounting Standards Board *Accounting Standards Codification* 450, *Contingencies*. Please specifically confirm to our auditors that our understanding is correct.

Please specifically identify the nature of and reasons for any limitation on your response.

2. **Letter of Audit Inquiry to Client's Lawyer** The auditor should request the client's management to prepare a letter of inquiry to those lawyers consulted by them concerning litigation, claims, and assessments; however, the letter should be mailed by the auditor and the lawyer should respond directly to the auditor.

    Editor note: The auditor requests that management prepare the letter because an auditor ordinarily does not possess legal skills and, therefore, cannot make legal judgments concerning information coming to the auditor's attention.

    This letter is the auditor's primary means of corroborating the information furnished by management. Corroboration may also be provided by information from inside legal counsel. However, audit evidence from inside counsel is not a substitute for information that outside counsel refuses to furnish.

a. **Contents** The matters that should be covered in a letter of audit inquiry include, but are not limited to, the following.

   (1)   Identification of the company, subsidiaries, and audit date

   (2)   A list (or a request that the lawyer prepare a list) that describes and evaluates pending or threatened litigation, claims, and assessments with which the lawyer has been substantially involved; the lawyer is asked either to furnish the following information or, if furnished my management, to comment where the lawyer's views differ from management's:

   (a)   A description of the matter, progress to date, and the action the company plans to take

   (b)   An evaluation of the likelihood of an unfavorable outcome and, if possible, an estimate of the amount or range of the potential loss

   (c)   If management prepared the list, an identification of any missing items or a statement that the list is complete

   (3)   A list that describes and evaluates unasserted claims and assessments that management considers to be probable of assertion and that, if asserted, would have at least a reasonable probability of an unfavorable outcome (with which the lawyer has been substantially involved). The lawyer is requested to comment on those matters where the lawyer's views concerning the description or evaluation of the matter differ from those stated by management.

   (4)   A statement that management understands that it will be notified by the lawyer when an unasserted claim or assessment requiring financial statement disclosure per the Financial Accounting Standards Board (FASB) *Accounting Standards Codification* (ASC) 450, *Contingencies* comes to the attention of the lawyer. Additionally, it is management's understanding that the lawyer will consult with the client concerning the disclosure and applicable requirements of FASB ASC 450. The lawyer is requested to confirm this understanding.

   (5)   A request that the lawyer specifically identify the nature of and reasons for any limitation on the response.

b. **Materiality** No inquiry needs to be made concerning matters not considered material as long as the client and the auditor have reached an understanding on the limits of materiality for this purpose.

c. **Conference** If the client's lawyers provide the auditor with a response to any matters in a conference, the auditor should document the information received.

d. **Change of Lawyers** If there has been a change or resignation of lawyers, the auditor should consider the need to inquire about the reasons for the change. (Lawyers may be required to resign when clients fail to follow their advice on financial accounting and reporting for litigation, claims, and assessments.)

e. **Dates** The client's letter should specify the date by which the lawyer's response should be sent to the auditor and also should request the lawyer to specify the effective date of the response. (If the lawyer's response does not specify an effective date, the auditor can assume it is the date of the response.) The latest date of the period covered by the lawyer's response (the "effective date") should be as close as possible to the date of the auditor's report. Consequently, specifying the effective date of the lawyer's response to reasonably approximate the expected date of the auditor's report will in most instances eliminate the need for an updated response from the lawyer.

3. **Lawyer's Response Appropriately Limited** The lawyer may limit the response to those matters that the lawyer had been involved with substantially and that are considered to be material provided the lawyer and the auditor have agreed on what will be considered material. Such limitations are not limitations on the scope of the audit.

4. **Other Limitations on a Lawyer's Response** A lawyer may be unable to respond (form a conclusion) concerning the likelihood of an unfavorable outcome or the amount or range of potential loss due to inherent uncertainties. Under these circumstances, the auditor must look to the guidance in AU 508, *Reports on Audited Financial Statements,* regarding an uncertainty which is not susceptible of reasonable estimation, to determine the effect of the lawyer's response, if any, on the audit report.

    Editor note: If, after considering the existing conditions and available evidence, the auditor concludes that sufficient audit evidence supports management's assertion that a reasonable estimate cannot be made and the required disclosures are included in the financial statements, an unqualified opinion ordinarily is appropriate.

5. **Inquiry of Lawyer Prohibited by Client** The refusal of a client to allow necessary communications with a lawyer is a scope limitation that usually results in a disclaimer of opinion.

6. **Refusal of Lawyer to Respond** The refusal of a lawyer to furnish the information requested in an inquiry letter is a limitation on the scope of the audit that is sufficient to preclude an unqualified opinion if not satisfactorily resolved.

VII. Audit Documentation (AU 339)

A. Overview

Auditors should prepare and maintain audit documentation, or working papers. Working papers' form and content are designed to meet the circumstances of a particular audit. Audit documentation is the principal record of procedures applied, evidence obtained, and conclusions reached by the auditor. The quantity, type, and content of audit documentation are matters of professional judgment. Audit documentation serves two main purposes. It provides the principal support for (1) the opinion expressed, or disclaimer of opinion, and (2) the representation in the auditor's report that the audit was performed in accordance with US GAAS.

1. **Additional Objectives** Audit documentation serves a number of other purposes:

    a. Assists planning and performance of the audit

    b. Assists new auditors to an engagement and review the prior year's documentation to understand the work performed as an aid in planning and performing the current engagement

    c. Assists supervision and review

    d. Demonstrates accountability for procedures performed, evidence examined, and conclusions reached

    e. Maintains a record of matters of continuing significance to future audits

    f. Enables quality control reviews, and inspections (peer reviews)

    g. Assists successor auditors who review a predecessor auditor's workpapers

2. **Tick Marks** Auditors often use a mark to refer the reader of a schedule or other working paper to a note that is applicable to more than one item on the working paper. In this way, a note only has to be written once, rather than each time it is applicable. Thus, these "tick marks" merely are abbreviated notes. There is no industry-wide standard for tick marks, so

a legend indicating what each mark signifies (similar to a map legend) is important for complete documentation.

3. **Ownership**   Audit documentation is the property of the auditor.

4. **Confidentiality**   The auditor has an ethical, and possibly legal, obligation to maintain the confidentiality of client information.   Reasonable procedures to prevent unauthorized access to audit documentation should be adopted.

5. **Documentation Completion Date**   The auditor should complete the final audit file on a timely basis, but within 60 days following the report release date.

6. **Retention**   The auditor should adopt procedures to retain audit documentation for a period sufficient to satisfy legal or regulatory requirements, and to meet practice needs.   However, such period should be at least 5 years from the report release date.   Under the provisions of the Sarbanes-Oxley Act of 2002, sufficient documentation to support the opinion expressed in the audit report of a public company must be retained for seven years.   Items that do not need to be retained include: superseded drafts of workpapers or financial statements, notes that reflect incomplete or preliminary thinking, previous copies of documents corrected for errors, and duplicates of documents.   After the documentation completion date the auditor must not delete or discard any documentation from the final audit file before the end of the specified retention period.   Also, the auditor must appropriately document any additions to the audit file after the documentation completion date.

B. **Form, Content & Extent**
The form, content, and extent of workpapers depend on the particular circumstances of the audit, audit methodology, and tools used.   Workpapers should include, for example, audit programs, analyses, memoranda, summaries of significant findings or issues, letters of confirmation and representation, checklists, abstracts or copies of important documents, correspondence (including e-mail) of significant findings or issues, and schedules of work performed.   Important documents may include significant contracts or agreements if they are needed for an experienced auditor to understand the work performed and conclusions reached.

1. **Experienced Auditor**   Audit documentation should be sufficient to enable an experienced auditor, with no prior connection to the audit, to understand:

    a.   The nature, extent, and timing of procedures performed

    b.   The results of procedures and the evidence obtained

    c.   The conclusions reached on significant matters

    d.   That the accounting records reconcile with the financial statements or other information being reported on

2. **Oral Explanations**   On their own, oral explanations do not constitute sufficient support for the audit work performed or the conclusions reached.   However, they may be used to clarify or explain information contained in the audit documentation.

3. **Significant Findings or Issues**   The auditor should document significant findings or issues, actions taken to address them, and the basis for final conclusions.   The auditor should document any discussions, including responses, with management or others within the entity about significant findings or issues on a timely basis.   If the auditor identifies evidence that contradicts or is inconsistent with the auditor's final conclusions concerning a significant finding or issue, the auditor should document how the contradictory or inconsistent evidence was addressed in forming the conclusion.

4. **Nature & Extent** Considerations regarding the form, content, and extent of documentation:

a. The nature of the auditing procedures performed

b. The identified risk of material misstatement associated with the assertion, or account or class of transactions, including disclosures

c. The extent of judgment involved

d. The significance of the evidence obtained to the assertion being tested

e. The nature and extent of exceptions identified

f. The need to document a conclusion, or its basis, if not readily determinable from the workpapers

5. **Identification of Preparer & Reviewer** In documenting the nature, extent, and timing of audit procedures performed, the auditor should record:

a. Who performed the procedures and the date they were completed

b. Who reviewed the workpapers and the date of such review

VIII. Related Parties (AU 334)

A. **Accounting Considerations**
Related-party transactions should be disclosed adequately and properly in conformity with GAAP. Recognition should be given to their economic substance rather than merely their legal form. Examples of related-party transactions include parent-subsidiary transactions and transactions among subsidiaries of a common parent. Transactions between related parties are considered related-party transactions even if they are not given accounting recognition (e.g., a parent providing free services to a subsidiary). Transactions that may indicate the existence of related-party transactions include the following:

1. **Loans** Borrowing or lending money without charging interest or at an interest rate significantly different from current market rates or making loans without scheduled repayment terms

2. **Sales** Selling real estate at a price considerably different from its appraised value or exchanging property for similar property in a nonmonetary transaction

B. **Audit Procedures**
The auditor should be aware of the possible existence of such transactions and of any common ownership or management control relationships and may decide there is a need for additional procedures to determine their existence in certain cases. The auditor should be aware that business structure and operating style occasionally are designed deliberately to obscure related-party transactions. The auditor should gain an understanding of management and the business in order to evaluate the possible existence of related-party transactions. Related-party transactions should **not** be assumed to be outside of the normal course of business unless there is applicable evidence.

1. **Motivating Condition Examples**

a. Lack of sufficient working capital or credit to continue in business

b. An urgent desire for a favorable earnings record to support the company's stock price

c. An overly optimistic earnings forecast

d. Significant litigation, especially between stockholders and management

e.   Excess capacity or a declining industry with a large number of business failures

f.   Dependence on a single (or a relatively few) products, customers, or transactions for the ongoing success of the business

g.   Significant dangers of obsolescence from operating in a high technology industry

2.   **Determining Existence of Related Parties**   The auditor should test material transactions between related parties and the client. To discover the existence of less obvious relationships, the auditor may apply one or more specific procedures, such as the following:

a.   Evaluation of the company's procedures for identifying and properly accounting for related-party transactions.

b.   Request of appropriate management personnel the names of all related parties and inquire whether any transaction occurred with these parties during the period (should be documented in the management representation letter).

c.   Review the workpapers from prior years for the names of known related parties. Inquire of the predecessor, principal, or other auditors of related parties as to their knowledge of existing relationships.

d.   Determine the names of all pensions and trusts established for the benefit of employees and the names of their officers and trustees. They will be considered related parties if managed by or under the trusteeship of the client's management.

e.   Review SEC filings, etc., for the names of related parties and for other businesses in which officers and directors occupy directorship or management positions. Review stockholder listings of closely held companies to identify principal stockholders.

f.   Review the period's material investment transactions to determine if any related-party transactions were created.

3.   **Identifying Material Related-Party Transactions**   The following procedures may help the auditor identify material transactions with known related parties or that may indicate previously undetermined relationships:

a.   Provide the names of related parties to the audit staff so they can watch for transactions with those parties.

b.   Review the minutes of the board of directors' meetings (and other executive or operating committees) to see if any material transactions were authorized or discussed.

c.   Review proxy and other material filed with the SEC and comparable data filed with other regulatory agencies for information about material transactions with related parties.

d.   Review conflict-of-interests statements obtained by the company from its management.

e.   Review the extent and nature of transactions with major customers, suppliers, borrowers, and lenders for indications of previously undisclosed relationships.

f.   Consider whether transactions are occurring, but are not being recorded, such as receiving or providing accounting, management, or other services at no charge or a major stockholder absorbing corporate expenses.

g.   Review the accounting records for large, unusual, or nonrecurring transactions or balances. Special attention should be paid to transactions that are recognized at or near the end of the reporting period.

h.   Review confirmations of compensating balance arrangements for indications that balances are maintained for or by related parties.

      i.   Review invoices from law firms that have performed regular or special services.

      j.   Review confirmations of loans receivable and payable for indications of guarantees. When guarantees are indicated, determine their nature and the relationships, if any, of the guarantors to the reporting entity.

   4.   **Examining Transactions** Once related-party transactions have been identified, the auditor should apply whatever procedures considered necessary to obtain reasonable satisfaction as to their purpose, nature, and effect on the financial statements. In extending inquiry beyond the range of management, the auditor should perform the following:

      a.   Obtain an understanding of the business purpose of the transaction.

        (1) Examine pertinent documents such as invoices, contracts, and receiving and shipping documents.

        (2) Determine whether appropriate officials have approved the transaction.

        (3) Test the amounts to be disclosed (or considered to be disclosed) in the financial statements for reasonableness.

        (4) Consider having intercompany balances audited on the same date. The auditors then would exchange relevant information.

        (5) Inspect or confirm the transferability and value of collateral.

      b.   Perform additional procedures needed to fully understand the particular transaction.

        (1) Confirm the amounts and terms of the transactions (including guarantees) with the other parties.

        (2) Inspect evidence that is in the possession of other parties to the transaction.

        (3) Confirm or discuss significant information with such intermediaries as banks, guarantors, or attorneys.

        (4) If there is reason to believe that transactions lacking substance were conducted with any unfamiliar customers, businesses, etc., the auditor should refer to trade journals, credit agencies, etc., to verify the lack of substance.

        (5) Obtain information on the financial capability of the other parties with respect to material uncollected balances, guarantees, and other obligations.

C.   **Disclosure**

The auditor must evaluate the sufficiency and appropriateness of evidence concerning related parties. This evaluation involves all the information available so that, using professional judgment, the auditor can determine the adequacy of the related-party disclosures.

1.   **Difficulty** Unless a transaction with a related party is of a routine nature, it generally is **not** possible to determine whether a particular transaction would have taken place had the parties not been related. As a result, it is quite difficult to determine if the terms were equivalent to those that prevail in arm's-length transactions.

2.   **Representation** If the financial statements contain a representation that a material transaction was carried out at arm's-length bargaining and the representation is unsubstantiated by management, the auditor should, depending upon the materiality of the unsubstantiated representations, express a qualified or adverse opinion due to a departure from GAAP.

CHAPTER 4—EVIDENCE & PROCEDURES

Problem 4-1 MULTIPLE-CHOICE QUESTIONS

1. The best primary audit evidence regarding year-end bank balances is documented in the

   a. Standard bank confirmations
   b. Interbank transfer schedule
   c. Bank reconciliations
   d. Bank deposit lead schedule   (Editors, ID: 146)

2. Which of the following procedures would provide the most reliable audit evidence?

   a. Inquiries of the client's internal audit staff held in private
   b. Inspection of prenumbered client purchase orders filed in the Vouchers Payable Department
   c. Analytical procedures performed by the auditor on the entity's trial balance
   d. Inspection of bank statements obtained directly from the client's financial institution
   (5/93, AUD, #26, ID: 3922)

3. Which of the following presumptions is correct about the reliability of audit evidence?

   a. Information obtained indirectly from outside sources is the most reliable audit evidence.
   b. To be reliable, audit evidence should be convincing rather than persuasive.
   c. Reliability of audit evidence refers to the amount of corroborative evidence obtained.
   d. An effective internal control structure provides more assurance about the reliability of audit evidence.
   (11/94, AUD, #47, amended, ID: 5120)

4. The most reliable procedure for an auditor to use to test the existence of a client's inventory at an outside location would be to

   a. Observe physical counts of the inventory items
   b. Trace the total on the inventory listing to the general ledger inventory account
   c. Obtain a confirmation from the client indicating inventory ownership
   d. Analytically compare the current-year inventory balance to the prior-year balance
   (R/06, AUD, #21, ID: 8139)

5. An auditor scans a client's investment records for the period just before and just after the year-end to determine that any transfers between categories of investments have been properly recorded. The primary purpose of this procedure is to obtain evidence about management's financial statement assertions of

   a. Rights and obligations, and existence or occurrence
   b. Valuation and allocation, and rights and obligations
   c. Existence or occurrence, and classification
   d. Classification, and valuation and allocation   (R/05, AUD, #29, amended, ID: 7824)

6. A client uses a suspense account for unresolved questions whose final accounting has not been determined. If a balance remains in the suspense account at year-end, the auditor would be most concerned about

   a. Suspense debits that management believes will benefit future operations
   b. Suspense debits that the auditor verifies will have realizable value to the client
   c. Suspense credits that management believes should be classified as "Current liability"
   d. Suspense credits that the auditor determines to be customer deposits   (11/96, AUD, #13, ID: 6365)

7. An entity's income statements were misstated due to the recording of journal entries that involved debits and credits to an unusual combination of expense and revenue accounts. The auditor most likely could have detected this misstatement by

    a. Tracing a sample of journal entries to the general ledger
    b. Evaluating the effectiveness of internal control policies and procedures
    c. Investigating the reconciliations between controlling accounts and subsidiary records
    d. Performing analytical procedures designed to disclose differences from expectations

    (11/94, AUD, #14, amended, ID: 5087)

8. An auditor may achieve audit objectives related to particular assertions by

    a. Performing analytical procedures
    b. Adhering to a system of quality control
    c. Preparing auditor working papers
    d. Increasing the level of detection risk

    (11/95, AUD, #38, ID: 5985)

9. In addition to evaluating the frequency of deviations in tests of controls, an auditor should also consider certain qualitative aspects of the deviations. The auditor most likely would give broader consideration to the implications of a deviation if it was

    a. The only deviation discovered in the sample
    b. Identical to a deviation discovered during the prior year's audit
    c. Caused by an employee's misunderstanding of instructions
    d. Initially concealed by a forged document

    (11/95, AUD, #26, ID: 5973)

10. Which of the following circumstances most likely would cause an auditor to suspect that material misstatements exist in a client's financial statements?

    a. The assumptions used in developing the prior year's accounting estimates have changed.
    b. Differences between reconciliations of control accounts and subsidiary records are not investigated.
    c. Negative confirmation requests yield fewer responses than in the prior year's audit.
    d. Management consults with another CPA firm about complex accounting matters.

    (R/02, AUD, #7, ID: 7097)

11. Which of the following types of audit evidence is the most persuasive?

    a. Prenumbered client purchase order forms
    b. Client work sheets supporting cost allocations
    c. Bank statements obtained from the client
    d. Management representation letter

    (5/95, AUD, #39, amended, ID: 5657)

12. Which of the following circumstances most likely would cause an auditor to consider whether material misstatements exist in an entity's financial statements?

    a. Management places little emphasis on meeting earnings projections.
    b. The board of directors makes all major financing decisions.
    c. Significant deficiencies previously communicated to management are not corrected.
    d. Transactions selected for testing are not supported by proper documentation.

    (11/94, AUD, #13, amended, ID: 5086)

13. Which of the following procedures would yield the most appropriate evidence?

    a. A scanning of trial balances
    b. An inquiry of client personnel
    c. A comparison of beginning and ending retained earnings
    d. A recalculation of bad debt expense

    (R/06, AUD, #25, ID: 8143)

14. An auditor observes the mailing of monthly statements to a client's customers and reviews evidence of follow-up on errors reported by the customers. This test of controls most likely is performed to support management's financial statement assertions of

	Classification and understandability	Existence or occurrence
a.	Yes	Yes
b.	Yes	No
c.	No	Yes
d.	No	No

(R/06, AUD, #1, ID: 8119)

15. At the conclusion of an audit, an auditor is reviewing the evidence gathered in support of the financial statements. With regard to the valuation of inventory, the auditor concludes that the evidence obtained is not sufficient to support management's representations. Which of the following actions is the auditor most likely to take?

a. Consult with the audit committee and issue a disclaimer of opinion
b. Consult with the audit committee and issue a qualified opinion
c. Obtain additional evidence regarding the valuation of inventory
d. Obtain a statement from management supporting their inventory valuation (R/07, AUD, #22, ID: 8394)

16. The auditor's inventory observation test counts are traced to the client's inventory listing to test for which of the following financial statement assertions?

a. Completeness
b. Rights & obligations
c. Valuation or allocation
d. Classification & understandability (R/07, AUD, #24, amended, ID: 8396)

17. After making inquiries about credit granting policies, an auditor selects a sample of sales transactions and examines evidence of credit approval. This test of controls most likely supports management's financial statement assertion(s) of

	Rights and obligations	Valuation and allocation
a.	Yes	Yes
b.	Yes	No
c.	No	Yes
d.	No	No

(R/07, AUD, #31, ID: 8403)

18. Which of the following procedures would an auditor most likely perform in auditing the statement of cash flows?

a. Reconcile the amounts included in the statement of cash flows to the other financial statements' amounts
b. Vouch a sample of cash receipts and disbursements for the last few days of the current year
c. Reconcile the cutoff bank statement to the proof of cash to verify the accuracy of the year-end cash balance
d. Confirm the amounts included in the statement of cash flows with the entity's financial institution

(R/07, AUD, #36, ID: 8408)

19. According to the third standard of fieldwork, which of the following terms identifies a requirement for audit evidence?

a. Appropriate
b. Adequate
c. Reasonable
d. Disconfirming (R/09, AUD, #30, ID: 8830)

20. Which of the following procedures is considered a test of controls?

    a. An auditor reviews the entity's check register for unrecorded liabilities.
    b. An auditor evaluates whether a general journal entry was recorded at the proper amount.
    c. An auditor interviews and observes appropriate personnel to determine segregation of duties.
    d. An auditor reviews the audit workpapers to ensure proper sign-off.   (R/10, AUD, #10, ID: 9360)

21. Which of the following factors most likely would lead a CPA to conclude that a potential audit engagement should not be accepted?

    a. There are significant related-party transactions that management claims occurred in the ordinary course of business.
    b. Internal control activities requiring the segregation of duties are subject to management override.
    c. Management continues to employ an inefficient system of information technology to record financial transactions.
    d. It is unlikely that sufficient appropriate evidence is available to support an opinion on the financial statements.   (R/06, AUD, #43, amended, ID: 8161)

22. The work of internal auditors may affect the independent auditor's

    I.   Procedures performed in obtaining an understanding of internal control
    II. Procedures performed in assessing the risk of material misstatement
    III. Substantive procedures performed in gathering direct evidence

    a. I and II only
    b. I and III only
    c. II and III only
    d. I, II, and III   (11/95, AUD, #53, amended, ID: 6000)

23. In assessing the competence and objectivity of an entity's internal auditor, an independent auditor **least** likely would consider information obtained from

    a. Discussions with management personnel
    b. External quality reviews of the internal auditor's activities
    c. Previous experience with the internal auditor
    d. The results of analytical procedures   (11/94, AUD, #68, ID: 5141)

24. In assessing the competence of an internal auditor, an independent CPA most likely would obtain information about the

    a. Quality of the internal auditor's working paper documentation
    b. Organization's commitment to integrity and ethical values
    c. Influence of management on the scope of the internal auditor's duties
    d. Organizational level to which the internal auditor reports   (R/99, AUD, #16, ID: 6832)

25. In assessing the competence of a client's internal auditor, an independent auditor most likely would consider the

    a. Internal auditor's compliance with professional internal auditing standards
    b. Client's policies that limit the internal auditor's access to management salary data
    c. Evidence supporting a further reduction in the assessed level of control risk
    d. Results of ratio analysis that may identify unusual transactions and events.   (R/06, AUD, #9, ID: 8127)

26. For which of the following judgments may an independent auditor share responsibility with an entity's internal auditor who is assessed to be both competent and objective?

	Assessment of inherent risk	*Assessment of control risk*
a.	Yes	Yes
b.	Yes	No
c.	No	Yes
d.	No	No

    (5/96, AUD, #3, ID: 6235)

27. During an audit an internal auditor may provide direct assistance to an independent CPA in

	Obtaining an understanding of internal control	Performing tests of controls	Performing substantive tests
a.	No	No	No
b.	Yes	No	No
c.	Yes	Yes	No
d.	Yes	Yes	Yes

(5/95, AUD, #60, amended, ID: 5678)

28. Miller Retailing, Inc., maintains a staff of three full-time internal auditors who report directly to the controller. In planning to use the internal auditors to provide assistance in performing the audit, the independent auditor most likely will

a. Place limited reliance on the work performed by the internal auditors
b. Decrease the extent of the tests of controls needed to support the assessed level of detection risk
c. Increase the extent of the procedures needed to reduce control risk to an acceptable level
d. Avoid using the work performed by the internal auditors   (5/90, AUD, #28, ID: 157)

29. In assessing the objectivity of internal auditors, the independent CPA who is auditing the entity's financial statements most likely would consider the

a. Internal auditing standards developed by The Institute of Internal Auditors
b. Tests of internal control activities that could detect errors and fraud
c. Materiality of the accounts recently inspected by the internal auditors
d. Results of the tests of transactions recently performed by the internal auditors

(R/02, AUD, #18, ID: 7108)

30. In assessing the competence of internal auditors, an independent CPA most likely would obtain information about the

a. Influence of management on the scope of the internal auditors' duties
b. Policies limiting internal auditors from communicating with the audit committee
c. Quality of the internal auditors' working paper documentation
d. Entity's ability to continue as a going concern for a reasonable period of time

(R/08, AUD, #8, ID: 8614)

31. Which of the following factors most likely would assist an independent auditor in assessing the objectivity of the internal auditor?

a. The organizational status of the director of internal audit
b. The professional certifications of the internal audit staff
c. The consistency of the internal audit reports with the results of work performed
d. The appropriateness of internal audit conclusions in the circumstances   (R/08, AUD, #34, ID: 8640)

32. When assessing the competence of the internal auditors, an independent CPA should obtain information about the

a. Organizational level to which the internal auditors report
b. Quality of the internal auditors' working paper documentation
c. Policies prohibiting internal auditors from auditing sensitive matters
d. Internal auditors' preliminary assessed level of control risk   (R/09, AUD, #41, ID: 8841)

33. When assessing internal auditors' objectivity, an independent auditor should

   a. Consider the policies that prohibit the internal auditors from auditing areas where they were recently assigned.
   b. Review the internal auditors' reports to determine that their conclusions are consistent with the work performed.
   c. Verify that the internal auditors' assessment of control risk is comparable to the independent auditor's assessment.
   d. Evaluate the quality of the internal auditors' working paper documentation and their recent audit recommendations. (R/11, AUD, #33, ID: 9933)

34. During a financial statement audit an internal auditor may provide direct assistance to the independent CPA in performing

	Tests of Controls	Substantive tests
a.	Yes	Yes
b.	Yes	No
c.	No	Yes
d.	No	No

(R/11, AUD, #34, ID: 9934)

35. The company being audited has an internal auditor that is both competent and objective. The independent auditor wants to assign tasks for the internal auditor to perform. Under these circumstances, the independent auditor may

   a. Allow the internal auditor to perform tests of internal controls.
   b. Allow the internal auditor to audit a major subsidiary of the company.
   c. Not assign any task to the internal auditor because of the internal auditor's lack of independence
   d. Allow the internal auditor to perform analytical procedures, but not be involved with any tests of details. (R/11, AUD, #44, ID: 9944)

36. A purpose of a management representation letter is to reduce

   a. Audit risk to an aggregate level of misstatement that could be considered material
   b. An auditor's responsibility to detect material misstatements only to the extent that the letter is relied on
   c. The possibility of a misunderstanding concerning management's responsibility for the financial statements
   d. The scope of an auditor's procedures concerning related-party transactions and subsequent events (5/93, AUD, #32, ID: 3928)

37. When considering the use of management's written representations as audit evidence about the completeness assertion, an auditor should understand that such representations

   a. Complement, but do not replace, substantive tests designed to support the assertion
   b. Constitute sufficient evidence to support the assertion when considered in combination with the assessment of control risk
   c. Replace the assessment of control risk as evidence to support the assertion
   d. Are not part of the audit evidence considered to support the assertion (Editors, ID: 218)

38. Key Co. plans to present comparative financial statements for the years ended December 31, year 7, and year 8, respectively. Smith, CPA, audited Key's financial statements for both years and plans to report on the comparative financial statements on May 1, year 9. Key's current management team was not present until January 1, year 8. What period of time should be covered by Key's management representation letter?

   a. January 1, year 7, through December 31, year 8.
   b. January 1, year 7, through May 1, year 9.
   c. January 1, year 8, through December 31, year 8.
   d. January 1, year 8, through May 1, year 9. (R/99, AUD, #26, amended, ID: 6842)

39. For which of the following matters should an auditor obtain written management representations?

    a. Management's cost-benefit justifications for not correcting internal control weaknesses
    b. Management's knowledge of future plans that may affect the price of the entity's stock
    c. Management's compliance with contractual agreements that may affect the financial statements
    d. Management's acknowledgment of its responsibility for employees' violations of laws
    (R/99, AUD, #25, ID: 6841)

40. Which of the following matters most likely would be included in a management representation letter?

    a. An assessment of the risk factors concerning the misappropriation of assets
    b. An evaluation of the litigation that has been filed against the entity
    c. A confirmation that the entity has complied with contractual agreements
    d. A statement that all material internal control weaknesses have been corrected
    (R/06, AUD, #46, ID: 8164)

41. To which of the following matters would materiality limits **not** apply in obtaining written management representations?

    a. The availability of minutes of stockholders' and directors' meetings
    b. Losses from purchase commitments at prices in excess of market value
    c. The disclosure of compensating balance arrangements involving related parties
    d. Reductions of obsolete inventory to net realizable value   (5/95, AUD, #66, ID: 5684)

42. To which of the following matters would materiality limits **not** apply when obtaining written client representations?

    a. Violations of state labor regulations
    b. Disclosure of line-of-credit arrangements
    c. Information about related-party transactions
    d. Instances of fraud involving management   (R/06, AUD, #6, ID: 8124)

43. A scope limitation sufficient to preclude an unqualified opinion always will result when management

    a. Prevents the auditor from reviewing the working papers of the predecessor auditor
    b. Engages the auditor after the year-end physical inventory is completed
    c. Requests that certain material accounts receivable not be confirmed
    d. Refuses to acknowledge its responsibility for the fair presentation of the financial statements in conformity with GAAP   (R/00, AUD, #16, ID: 6941)

44. Which of the following statements ordinarily is **not** included among the written client representations made by the chief executive officer and the chief financial officer?

    a. "Sufficient audit evidence has been made available to the auditor to permit the issuance of an unqualified opinion."
    b. "There are no unasserted claims or assessments that our lawyer has advised us are probable of assertion and must be disclosed."
    c. "We have no plans or intentions that may materially affect the carrying value or classification of assets and liabilities."
    d. "No events have occurred subsequent to the balance sheet date that would require adjustment to, or disclosure in, the financial statements."   (R/06, AUD, #4, ID: 8122)

45. Which of the following expressions most likely would be included in a management representation letter?

    a. No events have occurred subsequent to the balance sheet date that require adjustment to, or disclosure in, the financial statements.

    b. There are no significant deficiencies identified during the prior-year's audit of which the audit committee of the board of directors is unaware.

    c. We do not intend to provide any information that may be construed to constitute a waiver of the attorney-client privilege.

    d. Certain computer files and other required audit evidence may exist only for a short period of time and only in computer-readable form. (R/05, AUD, #6, amended, ID: 7801)

46. In obtaining written representations from management, materiality limits ordinarily would apply to representations related to

    a. Amounts concerning related-party transactions

    b. Irregularities involving members of management

    c. The availability of financial records

    d. The completeness of minutes of directors' meetings (R/09, AUD, #26, ID: 8826)

47. Which of the following management roles would typically be acknowledged in a management representation letter?

    a. Management has the responsibility for the design of controls to detect fraud.

    b. Management communicates its views on ethical behavior to its employees.

    c. Management's knowledge of fraud is communicated to the audit committee.

    d. Management's compensation is contingent upon operating results. (R/10, AUD, #16, ID: 9366)

48. Which of the following would **not** be considered an analytical procedure?

    a. Estimating payroll expense by multiplying the number of employees by the average hourly wage rate and the total hours worked

    b. Projecting an error rate by comparing the results of a statistical sample with the actual population characteristics

    c. Computing accounts receivable turnover by dividing credit sales by the average net receivables

    d. Developing the expected current year sales based on the sales trend of the prior five years (5/95, AUD, #48, ID: 5666)

49. Analytical procedures used in planning an audit should focus on

    a. Reducing the scope of tests of controls and substantive tests

    b. Providing assurance that potential material misstatements will be identified

    c. Enhancing the auditor's understanding of the client's business

    d. Assessing the adequacy of the available audit evidence (5/95, AUD, #8, ID: 5626)

50. An auditor compares annual revenues and expenses with similar amounts from the prior year and investigates all changes exceeding 10%. This procedure most likely could indicate that

    a. Fourth quarter payroll taxes were properly accrued and recorded, but were not paid until early in the subsequent year.

    b. Unrealized gains from increases in the value of available-for-sale securities were recorded in the income account for trading securities.

    c. The annual provision for uncollectible accounts expense was inadequate because of worsening economic conditions.

    d. Notice of an increase in property tax rates was received by management, but was not recorded until early in the subsequent year. (R/06, AUD, #28, ID: 8146)

51. An auditor discovered that a client's accounts receivable turnover is substantially lower for the current year than for the prior year. This may indicate that

    a. Obsolete inventory has not yet been reduced to fair market value.
    b. There was an improper cutoff of sales at the end of the year.
    c. An unusually large receivable was written off near the end of the year.
    d. The aging of accounts receivable was improperly performed in both years. (R/06, AUD, #45, ID: 8163)

52. Which of the following ratios would an engagement partner most likely calculate when reviewing the balance sheet in the overall review stage of an audit?

    a. Quick assets/current assets
    b. Accounts receivable/inventory
    c. Interest payable/interest receivable
    d. Total debt/total assets   (11/96, AUD, #14, ID: 6366)

53. An auditor most likely would apply analytical procedures in the overall review stage of an audit to

    a. Enhance the auditor's understanding of subsequent events
    b. Identify auditing procedures omitted by the staff accountants
    c. Determine whether additional audit evidence may be needed
    d. Evaluate the effectiveness of the internal control activities   (R/06, AUD, #39, ID: 8157)

54. Which of the following nonfinancial information would an auditor most likely consider in performing analytical procedures during the planning phase of an audit?

    a. Turnover of personnel in the Accounting Department
    b. Objectivity of audit committee members
    c. Square footage of selling space
    d. Management's plans to repurchase stock   (5/97, AUD, #3, ID: 6392)

55. An auditor's analytical procedures most likely would be facilitated if the entity

    a. Segregates obsolete inventory before the physical inventory count
    b. Uses a standard cost system that produces variance reports
    c. Corrects material weaknesses in internal control before the beginning of the audit
    d. Develops its data from sources solely within the entity   (11/95, AUD, #41, ID: 5988)

56. An auditor's analytical procedures performed during the overall review stage indicated that the client's accounts receivable had doubled since the end of the prior year. However, the allowance for doubtful accounts as a percentage of accounts receivable remained about the same. Which of the following client explanations most likely would satisfy the auditor?

    a. The client liberalized its credit standards in the current year and sold much more merchandise to customers with poor credit ratings.
    b. Twice as many accounts receivable were written off in the prior year than in the current year.
    c. A greater percentage of accounts receivable were currently listed in the "more than 90 days overdue" category than in the prior year.
    d. The client opened a second retail outlet in the current year and its credit sales approximately equaled the older, established outlet.   (R/03, AUD, #1, ID: 7623)

57. Which of the following comparisons would an auditor most likely make in evaluating an entity's costs and expenses?

    a. The current year's accounts receivable with the prior year's accounts receivable
    b. The current year's payroll expense with the prior year's payroll expense
    c. The budgeted current year's sales with the prior year's sales
    d. The budgeted current year's warranty expense with the current year's contingent liabilities
                                                            (11/97, AUD, #17, ID: 6580)

58. Analytical procedures performed during an audit indicate that accounts receivable doubled since the end of the prior year. However, the allowance for doubtful accounts as a percentage of accounts receivable remained about the same. Which of the following client explanations would satisfy the auditor?

    a. A greater percentage of accounts receivable are listed in the "more than 120 days overdue" category than in the prior year.
    b. Internal control activities over the recording of cash receipts have been improved since the end of the prior year.
    c. The client opened a second retail outlet during the current year and its credit sales approximately equaled the older outlet.
    d. The client tightened its credit policy during the current year and sold considerably less merchandise to customers with poor credit ratings. (R/06, AUD, #15, ID: 8133)

59. For all audits of financial statements made in accordance with generally accepted auditing standards, the use of analytical procedures is required to some extent

	In the planning stage	As a substantive test	In the review stage
a.	Yes	No	Yes
b.	No	Yes	No
c.	No	Yes	Yes
d.	Yes	No	No

(11/90, AUD, #22, ID: 141)

60. An auditor's decision either to apply analytical procedures as substantive tests or to perform tests of transactions and account balances usually is determined by the

    a. Availability of data aggregated at a high level
    b. Auditor's familiarity with industry trends
    c. Timing of tests performed after the balance sheet date
    d. Relative effectiveness and efficiency of the tests (11/92, AUD, #31, amended, ID: 2965)

61. To be effective, analytical procedures in the overall review stage of an audit engagement should be performed by

    a. The staff accountant who performed the substantive auditing procedures
    b. The managing partner who has responsibility for all audit engagements at that practice office
    c. A manager or partner who has a comprehensive knowledge of the client's business and industry
    d. The CPA firm's quality control manager or partner who has responsibility for the firm's peer review program (R/01, AUD, #10, ID: 7025)

62. Analytical procedures performed in the overall review stage of an audit suggest that several accounts have unexpected relationships. The results of these procedures most likely would indicate that

    a. Fraud exists among the relevant account balances.
    b. Internal control activities are not operating effectively.
    c. Additional tests of details are required.
    d. The communication with the audit committee should be revised. (5/97, AUD, #9, amended, ID: 6398)

63. The accounts receivable turnover ratio increased significantly over a two-year period. This trend could indicate that

    a. The accounts receivable aging has deteriorated.
    b. The company has eliminated its discount policy.
    c. The company is more aggressively collecting customer accounts.
    d. Customer sales have substantially decreased. (R/05, AUD, #47, ID: 7842)

64. Analytical procedures performed in the final review stage of an audit generally would include

    a. Reassessing the factors that assisted the auditor in deciding on preliminary materiality levels and audit risk
    b. Considering the adequacy of the evidence gathered in response to unexpected balances identified in planning
    c. Summarizing uncorrected misstatements specifically identified through tests of details of transactions and balances
    d. Calculating projected uncorrected misstatements estimated through audit sampling techniques

    (R/05, AUD, #18, ID: 7813)

65. Which one of the following tend to be most predictable for purposes of analytical procedures applied as substantive tests?

    a. Data subject to audit testing in the prior year
    b. Transactions subject to management discretion
    c. Relationships involving income statement accounts
    d. Relationships involving balance sheet accounts

    (5/92, AUD, #20, amended, ID: 2773)

66. An auditor compares current annual revenues and expenses with those of the prior year and investigates all changes exceeding 10%. By this procedure the auditor would be most likely to learn that

    a. An increase in property tax rates has not been recognized in the client's accrual.
    b. The client changed its capitalization policy for small tools in the current year.
    c. Fourth quarter payroll taxes were not paid.
    d. The current provision for uncollectible accounts is inadequate because of worsening economic conditions.

    (Editors, ID: 7493)

67. Which of the following factors would most likely influence an auditor's consideration of the reliability of data when performing analytical procedures?

    a. Whether the data were developed in a computerized or a manual accounting system
    b. Whether the data were prepared on the cash basis or in conformity with GAAP
    c. Whether the data were developed under a system with adequate controls
    d. Whether the data were processed in an online system or a batch entry system

    (R/07, AUD, #16, ID: 8388)

68. Which of the following is an analytical procedure that an auditor most likely would perform when planning an audit?

    a. Confirming bank balances with the financial institutions
    b. Scanning accounts receivable for amounts over credit limits
    c. Recalculating inventory extensions of physical inventory counts
    d. Comparing the current-year account balances for conformity with predictable patterns

    (R/07, AUD, #25, ID: 8397)

69. Which of the following procedures would a CPA most likely perform in the planning stage of a financial statement audit?

    a. Obtain representations from management regarding the availability of all financial records
    b. Communicate with the audit committee concerning the prior year's audit adjustments
    c. Make inquiries of the client's attorney regarding pending and threatened litigation and assessments
    d. Compare recorded financial information with anticipated results from budgets and forecasts

    (R/07, AUD, #42, ID: 8414)

70. Which of the following is an analytical procedure that an auditor most likely would perform when planning an audit?

    a. Confirming a sample of accounts payable
    b. Scanning payroll files for terminated employees
    c. Comparing current year balances to budgeted balances
    d. Recalculating interest expense based on notes payable balances   (R/09, AUD, #13, ID: 8813)

71. When performing analytical procedures in the planning stage, the auditor most likely would develop expectations by reviewing which of the following sources of information?

    a. Unaudited information from internal quarterly reports
    b. Various account assertions in the planning memorandum
    c. Comments in the prior year's management letter
    d. The control risk assessment relating to specific financial assertions   (R/09, AUD, #31, ID: 8831)

72. Analytical procedures used in the planning phase of an audit should focus on

    a. Documenting the risk factors relating to the susceptibility of assets to misappropriation
    b. Identifying the internal control activities that could reduce the assessed level of control risk
    c. Discovering uncorrected misstatements that should be communicated to the audit committee
    d. Enhancing the auditor's understanding of the transactions and events that have occurred since the last audit   (R/09, AUD, #43, ID: 8843)

73. Which of the following is an analytical procedure that an auditor most likely would perform during the final review stage of an audit?

    a. Comparing each individual expense account balance with the relevant budgeted amounts and investigating any significant variations
    b. Testing the effectiveness of internal control procedures that appear to be suitably designed to prevent or detect material misstatements
    c. Reading the financial statements and considering whether there are any unusual or unexpected balances that were not previously identified
    d. Calculating each individual expense account balance as a percentage of total entity expenses and comparing the results with industry averages   (R/09, AUD, #1, ID: 8801)

74. Which of the following ratios would an engagement partner most likely consider in the overall review stage of an audit?

    a. Total liabilities/net sales
    b. Accounts receivable/inventory
    c. Cost of goods sold/average inventory
    d. Current assets/quick assets   (R/09, AUD, #47, ID: 8847)

75. Which of the following most likely would cause an auditor to consider whether a client's financial statements contain material misstatements?

    a. Management did not disclose to the auditor that it consulted with other accountants about significant accounting matters.
    b. The chief financial officer will not sign the management representation letter until the last day of the auditor's fieldwork.
    c. Audit trails of computer-generated transactions exist only for a short time.
    d. The results of an analytical procedure disclose unexpected differences.   (R/09, AUD, #9, ID: 8809)

76. An auditor's decision whether to apply analytical procedures as substantive tests usually is determined by the

    a. Availability of documentary evidence that should be verified
    b. Extent of accounting estimates used in preparing the financial statements
    c. Precision and reliability of the data used to develop expectations
    d. Number of transactions recorded just before and just after the year-end   (R/09, AUD, #32, ID: 8832)

77. Auditors try to identify predictable relationships when applying analytical procedures. Relationships involving transactions from which of the following accounts most likely would yield the highest level of evidence?

    a. Interest expense
    b. Allowance for doubtful accounts
    c. Accounts receivable
    d. Accounts payable   (R/08, AUD, #35, ID: 8641)

78. A test of a payroll system involved comparing an individual's number of overtime hours a week with an average of weekly overtime during a similar period in a prior year and evaluating the results. This is an example of what type of test?

    a. Range test
    b. Detail test
    c. Category test
    d. Reasonableness test   (R/09, AUD, #12, ID: 8812)

79. An auditor's analytical procedures indicate a lower than expected return on an equity method investment. This situation most likely could have been caused by

    a. An error in recording amortization of the excess of the investor's cost over the investment's underlying book value
    b. The investee's decision to reduce cash dividends declared per share of its common stock
    c. An error in recording the unrealized gain from an increase in the fair value of available-for-sale securities in the income account for trading securities
    d. A substantial fluctuation in the price of the investee's common stock on a national stock exchange
                                                                     (R/10, AUD, #12, ID: 9362)

80. Analytical procedures are most appropriate when testing which of the following types of transactions?

    a. Payroll and benefit liabilities
    b. Acquisitions and disposals of fixed assets
    c. Operating expense transactions
    d. Long-term debt transactions   (R/10, AUD, #29, ID: 9379)

81. When applying analytical procedures during an audit, which of the following is the best approach for developing expectations?

    a. Considering unaudited account balances and ratios to calculate what adjusted balances should be
    b. Identifying reasonable explanations for unexpected differences before talking to client management
    c. Considering the pattern of several unusual changes without trying to explain what caused them
    d. Comparing client data with client-determined expected results to reduce detailed tests of account balances   (R/10, AUD, #44, ID: 9394)

82. A primary objective of analytical procedures used in the final review stage of an audit is to

    a. Identify account balances that represent specific risks relevant to the audit
    b. Gather evidence from tests of details to corroborate financial statement assertions
    c. Detect fraud that may cause the financial statements to be misstated
    d. Assist the auditor in evaluating the overall financial statement presentation   (R/11, AUD, #1, ID: 9901)

83. Which of the following activities is an analytical procedure an auditor would perform in the final overall review stage of an audit to ensure that the financial statements are free from material misstatement?

    a. Reading the minutes of the board of directors' meetings for the year under audit
    b. Obtaining a letter concerning potential liabilities from the client's attorney
    c. Comparing the current year's financial statements with those of the prior year
    d. Ensuring that a representation letter signed by management is in the file   (R/11, AUD, #12, ID: 9912)

84. Which of the following statements is correct concerning an auditor's use of the work of a specialist?

    a. The auditor need not obtain an understanding of the methods and assumptions used by the specialist.
    b. The auditor may not use the work of a specialist in matters material to the fair presentation of the financial statements.
    c. The reasonableness of the specialist's assumptions and their applications are strictly the auditor's responsibility.
    d. The work of a specialist who has a contractual relationship with the client may be acceptable under certain circumstances.
    (11/95, AUD, #54, ID: 6001)

85. In using the work of a specialist, an auditor may refer to the specialist in the auditor's report if, as a result of the specialist's findings, the auditor

    a. Becomes aware of conditions causing substantial doubt about the entity's ability to continue as a going concern.
    b. Desires to disclose the specialist's findings, which imply that a more thorough audit was performed.
    c. Is able to corroborate another specialist's earlier findings that were consistent with management's representations.
    d. Discovers significant deficiencies in the design of the entity's internal control that management does not correct.
    (5/95, AUD, #62, amended, ID: 5680)

86. An auditor intends to use the work of an actuary who has a relationship with the client. Under these circumstances, the auditor

    a. Is required to disclose the contractual relationship in the auditor's report
    b. Should assess the risk that the actuary's objectivity might be impaired
    c. Is not permitted to rely on the actuary because of a lack of independence
    d. May communicate this matter to management as a control deficiency
    (R/07, AUD, #40, amended, ID: 8412)

87. Which of the following statements is correct concerning an auditor's use of the work of an actuary in assessing a client's pension obligations?

    a. The auditor is required to understand the objectives and scope of the actuary's work.
    b. The reasonableness of the actuary's assumptions is strictly the auditor's responsibility.
    c. The client is required to consent to the auditor's use of the actuary's work.
    d. If the actuary has a relationship with the client, the auditor may not use the actuary's work.
    (R/09, AUD, #14, ID: 8814)

88. In using the work of a specialist, an auditor may refer to the specialist in the auditor's report if, as a result of the specialist's findings, the auditor

    a. Desires to disclose the specialist's findings, which imply that a more thorough audit was performed
    b. Makes suggestions to management that are likely to improve the entity's internal control
    c. Corroborates another specialist's findings that were consistent with management's assertions
    d. Adds an explanatory paragraph to the auditor's report to emphasize an unusually important subsequent event
    (R/08, AUD, #46, ID: 8652)

89. An auditor who uses the work of a specialist may refer to the specialist in the auditor's report if the

    a. Auditor believes that the specialist's findings are reasonable in the circumstances.
    b. Specialist's findings support the related assertions in the financial statements.
    c. Auditor modifies the report because of the difference between the client's and the specialist's valuations of an asset.
    d. Specialist's findings provide the auditor with greater assurance of reliability about management's representations.
    (R/09, AUD, #46, ID: 8846)

90. The scope of an audit is **not** restricted when an attorney's response to an auditor as a result of a client's letter of audit inquiry limits the response to

   a. Matters to which the attorney has given substantive attention in the form of legal representation
   b. An evaluation of the likelihood of an unfavorable outcome of the matters disclosed by the entity
   c. The attorney's opinion of the entity's historical experience in recent similar litigation
   d. The probable outcome of asserted claims and pending or threatened litigation

   (11/90, AUD, #19, ID: 138)

91. The primary source of information to be reported about litigation, claims, and assessments is the

   a. Client's lawyer
   b. Court records
   c. Client's management
   d. Independent auditor

   (11/93, AUD, #39, ID: 4276)

92. A lawyer's response to an auditor's inquiry concerning litigation, claims, and assessments may be limited to matters that are considered individually or collectively material to the client's financial statements. Which parties should reach an understanding on the limits of materiality for this purpose?

   a. The auditor and the client's management
   b. The client's audit committee and the lawyer
   c. The client's management and the lawyer
   d. The lawyer and the auditor

   (R/99, AUD, #24, ID: 6840)

93. "In connection with an audit of our financial statements, management has prepared, and furnished to our auditors a description and evaluation of certain contingencies." The foregoing passage most likely is from a(an)

   a. Audit inquiry letter to legal counsel
   b. Management representation letter
   c. Audit committee's communication to the auditor
   d. Financial statement footnote disclosure

   (R/05, AUD, #22, ID: 7817)

94. If a client will **not** permit inquiry of outside legal counsel, the auditor's report ordinarily will contain a(an)

   a. Adverse opinion
   b. Disclaimer of opinion
   c. Unqualified opinion with a separate explanatory paragraph
   d. Qualified opinion

   (R/05, AUD, #1, ID: 7796)

95. The primary reason an auditor requests letters of inquiry be sent to a client's attorneys is to provide the auditor with

   a. The probable outcome of asserted claims and pending or threatened litigation
   b. Corroboration of the information furnished by management about litigation, claims, and assessments
   c. The attorneys' opinions of the client's historical experiences in recent similar litigation
   d. A description and evaluation of litigation, claims, and assessments that existed at the balance sheet date

   (11/94, AUD, #66, ID: 5139)

96. Which of the following is an audit procedure that an auditor most likely would perform concerning litigation, claims, and assessments?

   a. Request the client's lawyer to evaluate whether the client's pending litigation, claims, and assessments indicate a going concern problem
   b. Examine the legal documents in the client's lawyer's possession concerning litigation, claims, and assessments to which the lawyer has devoted substantive attention
   c. Discuss with management its policies and procedures adopted for evaluating and accounting for litigation, claims, and assessments
   d. Confirm directly with the client's lawyer that all litigation, claims, and assessments have been recorded or disclosed in the financial statements

   (11/95, AUD, #55, ID: 6002)

97. Which of the following statements extracted from a client's lawyer's letter concerning litigation, claims, and assessments most likely would cause the auditor to request clarification?

    a. "I believe that the plaintiff will have problems establishing any liability."
    b. "I believe that this action has only a remote chance in establishing any liability."
    c. "I believe that the plaintiff's case against the company is without merit."
    d. "I believe that the company will be able to defend this action successfully." (R/06, AUD, #38, ID: 8156)

98. A client's lawyer is unable to form a conclusion about the likelihood of an unfavorable outcome of pending litigation because of inherent uncertainties. If the litigation's effect on the client's financial statements could be material, the auditor most likely would

    a. Issue a qualified opinion in the auditor's report because of the lawyer's scope limitation
    b. Withdraw from the engagement because of the lack of information furnished by the lawyer
    c. Disclaim an opinion on the financial statements because of the materiality of the litigation's effect
    d. Add an explanatory paragraph to the auditor's report because of the uncertainty

    (5/95, AUD, #64, ID: 5682)

99. Which of the following factors most likely would cause a CPA to decline to accept a new audit engagement?

    a. The CPA does not understand the entity's operations and industry.
    b. Management acknowledges that the entity has had recurring operating losses.
    c. The CPA is unable to review the predecessor auditor's working papers.
    d. Management is unwilling to permit inquiry of its legal counsel. (R/07, AUD, #12, ID: 8384)

100. Which of the following procedures would an auditor most likely perform regarding litigation?

    a. Confirm directly with the clerk of the court that the client's litigation is properly disclosed.
    b. Discuss with management its policies and procedures for identifying and evaluating litigation.
    c. Inspect the legal documents in the client's lawyer's possession regarding pending litigation.
    d. Confirm the details of pending litigation with the client's adversaries' legal representatives.

    (R/08, AUD, #37, ID: 8643)

101. Which of the following procedures would an auditor most likely perform to assist in the evaluation of loss contingencies?

    a. Checking arithmetic accuracy of the accounting records
    b. Performing appropriate analytical procedures
    c. Obtaining a letter of audit inquiry from the client's lawyer
    d. Reading the financial statements, including footnotes (R/08, AUD, #9, ID: 8615)

102. An auditor requests a client to send letters of audit inquiry to attorneys who have been consulted concerning litigation, claims, and assessments. The primary reason for this request is to obtain

    a. The attorneys' assurance that litigation, claims, and assessments that are probable of assertion are properly accounted for
    b. Corroboration of the information furnished by management concerning litigation, claims, and assessments
    c. A description of litigation, claims, and assessments that have a reasonable possibility of unfavorable outcomes
    d. The opinion of an expert whether any loss contingencies are possible, probable, or remote

    (R/08, AUD, #14, ID: 8620)

103. A client is a defendant in a patent infringement lawsuit against a major competitor. Which of the following items would **least** likely be included in the attorney's response to the auditor's letter of inquiry?

    a. A description of potential litigation in other matters or related to an unfavorable verdict in the patent infringement lawsuit
    b. A discussion of case progress and the strategy currently in place by client management to resolve the lawsuit
    c. An evaluation of the probability of loss and a statement of the amount or range of loss if an unfavorable outcome is reasonably possible
    d. An evaluation of the ability of the client to continue as a going concern if the verdict is unfavorable and maximum damages are awarded   (R/08, AUD, #45, ID: 8651)

104. Which of the following procedures most likely would assist an auditor to identify litigation, claims, and assessments?

    a. Inspect checks included with the client's cutoff bank statement
    b. Obtain a letter of representations from the client's underwriter of securities
    c. Apply ratio analysis on the current year's liability accounts
    d. Read the file of correspondence from taxing authorities   (R/09, AUD, #39, ID: 8839)

105. What is an auditor's primary method to corroborate information on litigation, claims, and assessments?

    a. Examining legal invoices sent by the client's attorney
    b. Verifying attorney-client privilege through interviews
    c. Reviewing the response from the client's lawyer to a letter of audit inquiry
    d. Reviewing the written representation letter obtained from management   (R/10, AUD, #15, ID: 9365)

106. Which of the following statements extracted from a client's lawyer's letter concerning litigation, claims, and assessments most likely would cause the auditor to request clarification?

    a. "We believe that the possible liability to the company is nominal in amount."
    b. "We believe that the action can be settled for less than the damages claimed."
    c. "We believe that the plaintiff's case against the company is without merit."
    d. "We believe that the company will be able to defend this action successfully."
    (R/11, AUD, #4, ID: 9904)

107. Which of the following sets of information does an auditor usually confirm on one form?

    a. Accounts payable and purchase commitments
    b. Cash in bank and collateral for loans
    c. Inventory on consignment and contingent liabilities
    d. Accounts receivable and accrued interest receivable   (11/95, AUD, #40, ID: 5987)

108. Which of the following is **not** required documentation in an audit in accordance with generally accepted auditing standards?

    a. A written engagement letter formalizing the level of service to be rendered
    b. A flowchart depicting the segregation of duties and authorization of transactions
    c. A written audit program describing the necessary procedures to be performed
    d. Written representations from management   (Editors, ID: 2321)

109. In creating lead schedules for an audit engagement, a CPA often uses automated workpaper software. What client information is needed to begin this process?

    a. Interim financial information such as third quarter sales, net income, and inventory and receivables balances
    b. Specialized journal information such as the invoice and purchase order numbers of the last few sales and purchases of the year
    c. General ledger information such as account numbers, prior-year account balances, and current-year unadjusted information
    d. Adjusting entry information such as deferrals and accruals, and reclassification journal entries

    (5/98, AUD, #11, ID: 6628)

110. In performing a count of negotiable securities, an auditor records the details of the count on a security count worksheet. What other information is usually included on this worksheet?

    a. An acknowledgment by a client representative that the securities were returned intact
    b. An analysis of realized gains and losses from the sale of securities during the year
    c. An evaluation of the client's internal control concerning physical access to the securities
    d. A description of the client's procedures that prevent the negotiation of securities by just one person

    (R/00, AUD, #12, ID: 6937)

111. Which of the following factors would **least** likely affect the quantity and content of an auditor's working papers?

    a. The condition of the client's records
    b. The assessed risk of material misstatement
    c. The nature of the auditor's report
    d. The content of the representation letter

    (11/94, AUD, #73, amended, ID: 5146)

112. The permanent (continuing) file of an auditor's working papers most likely would include copies of the

    a. Lead schedules
    b. Attorney's letters
    c. Bank statements
    d. Debt agreements

    (11/95, AUD, #60, ID: 6007)

113. The audit working paper that reflects the major components of an amount reported in the financial statements is the

    a. Interbank transfer schedule
    b. Carryforward schedule
    c. Supporting schedule
    d. Lead schedule

    (11/91, AUD, #52, ID: 2320)

114. An auditor ordinarily uses a working trial balance resembling the financial statements without footnotes, but containing columns for

    a. Cash flow increases and decreases
    b. Audit objectives and assertions
    c. Reclassifications and adjustments
    d. Reconciliations and tick marks

    (11/94, AUD, #72, ID: 5145)

115. "There are no violations or possible violations of laws or regulations whose effects should be considered for disclosure in the financial statements or as a basis for recording a loss contingency." The foregoing passage most likely is from a (an)

    a. Client engagement letter
    b. Report on compliance with laws and regulations
    c. Management representation letter
    d. Attestation report on an entity's internal control

    (11/94, AUD, #64, amended, ID: 5137)

116. Which of the following statements is most accurate regarding sufficient and appropriate documentation?

    a. Accounting estimates are **not** considered sufficient and appropriate documentation.
    b. Sufficient and appropriate documentation should include evidence that the audit working papers have been reviewed.
    c. If additional evidence is required to document significant findings or issues, the original evidence is **not** considered sufficient and appropriate and therefore should be deleted from the working papers.
    d. Audit documentation is the property of the client, and sufficient and appropriate copies should be retained by the auditor for at least five years. (R/10, AUD, #45, ID: 9395)

117. Which of the following procedures most likely could assist an auditor in identifying related-party transactions?

    a. Performing tests of controls concerning the segregation of duties
    b. Evaluating the reasonableness of management's accounting estimates
    c. Reviewing confirmations of compensating balance arrangements
    d. Scanning the accounting records for recurring transactions (R/05, AUD, #16, ID: 7811)

118. When auditing related-party transactions, an auditor places primary emphasis on

    a. Ascertaining the rights and obligations of the related parties
    b. Confirming the existence of the related parties
    c. Verifying the valuation of the related-party transactions
    d. Evaluating the disclosure of the related-party transactions (5/95, AUD, #68, ID: 5686)

119. An auditor searching for related-party transactions should obtain an understanding of each subsidiary's relationship to the total entity because

    a. The business structure may be deliberately designed to obscure related-party transactions.
    b. Intercompany transactions may have been consummated on terms equivalent to arm's-length transactions.
    c. This may reveal whether particular transactions would have taken place if the parties had not been related.
    d. This may permit the audit of intercompany account balances to be performed as of concurrent dates. (Editors, ID: 185)

120. After determining that a related-party transaction has, in fact, occurred, an auditor should

    a. Add a separate paragraph to the auditor's standard report to explain the transaction
    b. Perform analytical procedures to verify whether similar transactions occurred, but were not recorded
    c. Obtain an understanding of the business purpose of the transaction
    d. Substantiate that the transaction was consummated on terms equivalent to an arm's-length transaction (11/94, AUD, #69, ID: 5142)

121. An auditor most likely would modify an unqualified opinion if the entity's financial statements include a footnote on related-party transactions

    a. Disclosing loans to related parties at interest rates significantly below prevailing market rates
    b. Describing an exchange of real estate for similar property in a nonmonetary related-party transaction
    c. Stating that a particular related-party transaction occurred on terms equivalent to those that would have prevailed in an arm's-length transaction
    d. Presenting the dollar-volume of related-party transactions and the effects of any change in the method of establishing terms from prior periods (5/93, AUD, #44, ID: 3940)

122. Which of the following most likely would indicate the existence of related parties?

    a. Writing down obsolete inventory just before year-end
    b. Failing to correct previously identified internal control structure deficiencies
    c. Depending on a single product for the success of the entity
    d. Borrowing money at an interest rate significantly below the market rate (11/92, AUD, #40, ID: 2974)

123. Which of the following events **least** likely would indicate the existence of related-party transactions?

    a. Making a loan with no scheduled date for the funds to be repaid
    b. Maintaining compensating balance arrangements for the benefit of principal stockholders
    c. Borrowing funds at an interest rate significantly below prevailing market rates
    d. Writing off obsolete inventory to net realizable value just before year-end   (R/09, AUD, #22, ID: 8822)

124. When determining whether related-party transactions have been properly accounted for in the financial statements, the auditor should be most concerned that

    a. The transactions represent the appropriate legal form
    b. The method of accounting for the transactions reflects that related parties are involved
    c. The financial statements recognize the substance of the transactions
    d. All related parties have been identified   (Editors, ID: 9269)

125. Which of the following steps should an auditor perform first to determine the existence of related parties?

    a. Examine invoices, contracts, and purchasing orders
    b. Request a list of related parties from management
    c. Review the company's business structure
    d. Review proxy and other materials filed with the SEC   (R/10, AUD, #6, ID: 9356)

_____

Problem 4-2 SIMULATION: Audit Procedure and Purpose

For each of the descriptions of procedures in column a of the table below, select the audit procedure performed from the selection list for column b and then indicate in column c whether it was a substantive procedure or a test of controls. Selections may be used once, more than once, or not at all.

a	b	c
Description of Procedure	**Audit Procedure Performed**	**Classification of Audit Procedure**
1. Examined sales invoices to see if they were initialed by the credit manager indicating credit approval.		
2. Compared this year's expenses with last year's expenses and investigated unusual fluctuations.		
3. Requested responses directly from customers.		
4. Questioned management about subsequent events.		
5. Observed the accounting clerk record the daily deposit of cash receipts.		
6. Examined invoices to support additions to the fixed asset account during the year.		
7. Agreed sales invoices to credit files to determine whether the customer had a credit file and had been approved for credit.		
8. Asked the accounting manager how often cash is deposited and by whom.		

Selection List of Audit Procedures Performed

A. Analytical procedure	F. Monitoring
B. Confirmation	G. Observation
C. Disclosure	H. Recalculation
D. Inquiry	I. Reperformance
E. Inspection	

Selection List of Classifications of Audit Procedure

A. Substantive procedures	B. Tests of controls

(R/11, AUD, ID: 9833)

Problem 4-3 SIMULATION: Documentation

For each of the following unrelated statements, questions, excerpts, and comments taken from various parts of an auditor's working paper file, select the most likely source from the list of sources. A source may be used once, more than once, or not at all.

Excerpts From Working Papers	Source
1. During our audit we discovered evidence of the company's failure to safeguard inventory from loss, damage, and misappropriation.	
2. The company considers the decline in value of equity securities classified as available-for-sale to be temporary.	
3. Was the difference of opinion on the accrued pension liabilities that existed between the engagement personnel and the actuarial specialist resolved in accordance with firm policy and appropriately documented?	
4. Our audit is designed to provide reasonable assurance of detecting misstatements that, in our judgment, could have a material effect on the financial statements taken as a whole. Consequently, our audit will not necessarily detect all misstatements that exist due to error, fraudulent financial reporting, or misappropriation of assets.	
5. There have been no communications from regulatory agencies concerning noncompliance with or deficiencies in financial reporting practices.	
6. Nothing came to our attention that caused us to believe that at October 31, year 1, there was any change in the capital stock, increase in long-term debt, or decrease in consolidated net current assets or stockholders' equity as compared with the amounts shown in the September 30, year 1 unaudited condensed consolidated balance sheet.	
7. It is our opinion that the possible liability to the company in this proceeding is nominal in amount.	
8. As discussed in Note 4 to the financial statements, the company experienced a net loss for the year ended July 31, year 1, and is currently in default under substantially all of its debt agreements. In addition, on September 25, year 1, the company filed a prenegotiated voluntary petition for relief under Chapter 11 of the U.S. Bankruptcy Code. These matters raise substantial doubt about the company's ability to continue as a going concern.	
9. During the year under audit, we were advised that management consulted with Better & Best, CPAs. The purpose of this consultation was to obtain another CPA firm's opinion concerning the company's recognition of certain revenue that we believe should be deferred to future periods. Better & Best's opinion was consistent with our opinion, so management did not recognize the revenue in the current year.	
10. The company believes that all material expenditures that have been deferred to future periods will be recoverable.	

List of Sources

A. Practitioner's report on management's assertion about an entity's compliance with specified requirements

B. Auditor's communications on significant deficiencies

C. Audit inquiry letter to legal counsel

D. Lawyer's response to audit inquiry letter

E. Audit committee's communication to the auditor

F. Auditor's communication to the audit committee (other than with respect to significant deficiencies)

G. Report on the application of accounting principles

H. Auditor's engagement letter

I. Letter for underwriters

J. Accounts receivable confirmation request

K. Request for bank cutoff statement

L. Explanatory paragraph of an auditor's report on financial statements

M. Partner's engagement review notes

N. Management representation letter

O. Successor auditor's communication with predecessor auditor

P. Predecessor auditor's communication with successor auditor

(ID: 9218)

_____

Problem 4-4 SIMULATION: Documentation

For each of the following unrelated statements, questions, excerpts, and comments taken from various parts of an auditor's working paper file, select the most likely source from the list of sources. A source may be used once, more than once, or not at all.

Excerpts From Working Papers	Source
1. Our use of professional judgment and the assessment of audit risk and materiality for the purpose of our audit mean that matters may have existed that would have been assessed differently by you. We make no representation as to the sufficiency or appropriateness of the information in our working papers for your purposes.	
2. Indicate in the space provided below whether this information agrees with your records. If there are exceptions, please provide any information that will assist the auditor in reconciling the difference.	
3. Blank checks are maintained in an unlocked cabinet along with the check-signing machine. Blank checks and the check-signing machine should be locked in separate locations to prevent the embezzlement of funds.	
4. Our audit cannot be relied upon to disclose significant deficiencies in the design or operation of internal control. Nevertheless, we will communicate to you all significant deficiencies and potential areas for improvement that we become aware of during the course of our audit.	
5. The timetable set by management to complete our audit was unreasonable considering the failure of the company's personnel to complete schedules on a timely basis and delays in providing necessary information.	
6. Several employees have disabled the anti-virus detection software on their PCs because the software slows the processing of data and occasionally rings false alarms. The company should obtain anti-virus software that runs continuously at all system entry points and that cannot be disabled by unauthorized personnel.	
7. In connection with an audit of our financial statements, management has prepared, and furnished to our auditors, a description and evaluation of certain contingencies.	
8. The company has no plans or intentions that may materially affect the carrying value or classification of assets and liabilities.	
9. In planning the sampling application, was appropriate consideration given to the relationship of the sample to the audit objective and to preliminary judgments about materiality levels?	

List of Sources

A. Practitioner's report on management's assertion about an entity's compliance with specified requirements

B. Auditor's communications on significant deficiencies

C. Audit inquiry letter to legal counsel

D. Lawyer's response to audit inquiry letter

E. Audit committee's communication to the auditor

F. Auditor's communication to the audit committee (other than with respect to significant deficiencies)

G. Report on the application of accounting principles

H. Auditor's engagement letter

I. Letter for underwriters

J. Accounts receivable confirmation request

K. Request for bank cutoff statement

L. Explanatory paragraph of an auditor's report on financial statements

M. Partner's engagement review notes

N. Management representation letter

O. Successor auditor's communication with predecessor auditor

P. Predecessor auditor's communication with successor auditor

(ID: 9220)

_____

Problem 4-5 SIMULATION: Ratios

Analytical procedures are evaluations of financial information made by a study of plausible relationships among financial and nonfinancial data. Understanding and evaluating such relationships is essential to the audit process. The following financial statements were prepared by Holiday Manufacturing Co. for the year ended December 31, year 2. Also presented are various financial statement ratios for Holiday as calculated from the prior year's financial statements. Sales represent net credit sales. The total assets, receivables, and inventory balances at December 31, year 2, were the same as at December 31, year 1.

Holiday Manufacturing Co.
Balance Sheet
December 31, Year 2

Assets		Liabilities and Capital	
Cash	$ 240,000	Accounts payable	$ 160,000
Receivables	400,000	Notes payable	100,000
Inventory	600,000	Other current liabilities	140,000
Total current assets	$1,240,000	Total current liabilities	$ 400,000
Plant and equipment—net	760,000	Long-term debt	350,000
		Common stock	750,000
		Retained earnings	500,000
Total assets	$2,000,000	Total liabilities and capital	$2,000,000

Holiday Manufacturing Co.
Income Statement
Year Ended December 31, Year 2

Sales		$3,000,000
Cost of goods sold		
Material	$800,000	
Labor	700,000	
Overhead	300,000	1,800,000
Gross margin		$1,200,000
Selling expenses	$240,000	
General and administrative expenses	300,000	540,000
Operating income		$ 660,000
Less interest expense		40,000
Income before taxes		$ 620,000
Less federal income taxes		220,000
Net income		$ 400,000

Each of the following represents a financial ratio that the auditor calculated during the prior year's audit. For each ratio, calculate the current year's ratio from the financial statements presented and select the answer from the list. Calculations should be rounded, if necessary, to the same number of places as the prior year's ratios.

	Ratio	Year 2	Year 1
1.	Current ratio		2.5
2.	Quick ratio		1.3
3.	Accounts receivable turnover		5.5
4.	Inventory turnover		2.5
5.	Total asset turnover		1.2
6.	Gross margin percentage		35%
7.	Net operating margin percentage		25%
8.	Times interest earned		10.3
9.	Total debt to equity percentage		50%

List of Ratio Calculations

A. 0.6	H. 3.1	O. 13%	V. 67%
B. 0.7	I. 4.5	P. 22%	
C. 1.0	J. 5.0	Q. 28%	
D. 1.5	K. 7.5	R. 33%	
E. 1.6	L. 10.0	S. 38%	
F. 2.0	M. 15.5	T. 40%	
G. 3.0	N. 16.5	U. 60%	

(ID: 9221)

Problem 4-6 SIMULATION: Financial Statement Analysis

Each of the following items represent an auditor's observed changes, independent of each other, in certain financial statement ratios or amounts from the prior year's ratios or amounts. For each observed change, select the most likely explanation or explanations from the accompanying list.

Auditor's Observed Changes	Explanations
1. Allowance for doubtful accounts increased from the prior year, but allowance for doubtful accounts as a percentage of accounts receivable decreased from the prior year. (3 explanations)	
2. Long-term debt increased from the prior year, but interest expense increased a larger-than-proportionate amount than long-term debt. (1 explanation)	
3. Operating income increased from the prior year although the entity was less profitable than in the prior year. (2 explanations)	
4. Gross margin percentage was unchanged from the prior year although gross margin increased from the prior year. (1 explanation)	

Explanations

A. Items shipped on consignment during the last month of the year were recorded as sales.

B. A significant number of credit memos for returned merchandise that were issued during the last month of the year were not recorded.

C. Year-end purchases of inventory were overstated by incorrectly including items received in the first month of the subsequent year.

D. Year-end purchases of inventory were understated by incorrectly excluding items received before the year-end.

E. A larger percentage of sales occurred during the last month of the year, as compared to the prior year.

F. A smaller percentage of sales occurred during the last month of the year, as compared to the prior year.

G. The same percentage of sales occurred during the last month of the year, as compared to the prior year.

H. Sales increased at the same percentage as cost of goods sold, as compared to the prior year.

I. Sales increased at a greater percentage than cost of goods sold increased, as compared to the prior year.

J. Sales increased at a lower percentage than cost of goods sold increased, as compared to the prior year.

K. Interest expense decreased, as compared to the prior year.

L. The effective income tax rate increased, as compared to the prior year.

M. The effective income tax rate decreased, as compared to the prior year.

N. Short-term borrowing was refinanced on a long-term basis at the same interest rate.

O. Short-term borrowing was refinanced on a long-term basis at lower interest rates.

P. Short-term borrowing was refinanced on a long-term basis at higher interest rates.

(ID: 9222)

Problem 4-7 SIMULATION: Substantive Tests

For each of the following audit objectives, select the substantive test that would most likely provide support for the objective. A substantive test may be used once, more than once, or not at all.

Part a:

Objective	Substantive Tests
1. Verify existence of accounts receivable.	
2. Determine that inventory balance is accurately stated.	

Selection List

A. Perform tests of subsequent cash receipts after the balance sheet date.

B. Review and assess an aging schedule of accounts receivable.

C. Compare recognized revenue to related industry statistics.

D. Tour the storage facility for inventory to determine adequacy of security controls.

E. Perform shipping cutoff procedures.

F. Review payments to vendors subsequent to year-end.

Part b:

An auditor has chosen to increase attention on the financial statement assertion of valuation. Procedures that might be used in an audit are listed below. From the following list, choose the two procedures that would be most appropriate to perform in an audit that is giving increased attention to the valuation assertion. Only **two** procedures may be chosen.

Selection List

A. Observing the client count the physical inventory

B. Testing shipping and receiving cutoff procedures

C. Obtaining confirmation from lenders regarding inventories pledged under loan agreements

D. Examining paid vendors' invoices

E. Obtaining confirmation of inventories at locations outside the entity

F. Examining an analysis of inventory turnover

G. Tracing test counts recorded during the physical inventory observation to the inventory listing

(ID: 9224)

_____

Problem 4-8 SIMULATION: Analytics

Pacific Gourmet, Inc. and Subsidiary
Consolidated Balance Sheets
December 31, Year 2 and Year 1

	Year 2	Year 1
Assets		
Current assets		
Cash and cash equivalents	$ 54,280,000	$ 42,500,000
Receivables - net	12,000,000	10,000,000
Inventory	12,000,000	10,000,000
Other current assets	7,000,000	5,000,000
Total current assets	85,280,000	67,500,000
Property, plant and equipment - net	23,000,000	25,000,000
Other assets	30,000,000	30,000,000
Total assets	$138,280,000	$122,500,000
Liabilities and Stockholders' Equity		
Current liabilities		
Accounts payable	$ 23,000,000	$ 20,000,000
Current portion of long-term debt	1,000,000	1,000,000
Other current liabilities	965,000	1,000,000
Total current liabilities	24,965,000	22,000,000
Long-term debt	13,000,000	14,000,000
Total liabilities	37,965,000	36,000,000
Stockholders' equity		
Common stock	100,000	100,000
Additional paid-in capital	9,900,000	9,900,000
Retained earnings	90,315,000	76,500,000
Total Stockholders' equity	100,315,000	86,500,000
Total liabilities and stockholders' equity	$138,280,000	$122,500,000

Pacific Gourmet, Inc. and Subsidiary
Consolidated Income Statements
For the Years Ended December 31, Year 2 and Year 1

	Year 2	Year 1
Sales	$100,850,000	$ 95,600,000
Cost of goods sold	55,000,000	42,500,000
Gross profit on sales	45,850,000	53,100,000
Expenses		
Selling expenses	17,600,000	15,000,000
General and administrative	6,015,000	5,000,000
Interest expense	1,120,000	1,200,000
Total expense	24,735,000	21,200,000
Income before taxes	21,115,000	31,900,000
Provision for income taxes	7,300,000	7,500,000
Net income	$ 13,815,000	$ 24,400,000

Pacific Gourmet, Inc. and Subsidiary
Consolidated Statement of Cash Flows
For the Year Ended December 31, Year 2

Cash flows from operating activities:	
Net income (loss)	$13,815,000
Adjustments to reconcile net income (loss) to cash provided by (used for) operating activities	
Depreciation	1,500,000
Changes in certain assets and liabilities:	
Decrease (increase) in receivables	(2,000,000)
Decrease (increase) in inventory	(2,000,000)
Decrease (increase) in other current assets	(2,000,000)
Increase (decrease) in accounts payable	3,000,000
Increase (decrease) in other current liabilities	(35,000)
Net Cash provided by (used for) operating activities	12,280,000
Cash flows from investing activities:	
Proceeds from sales of property, plant and equipment	500,000
Net cash provided by (used for) investing activities	500,000
Cash flows from financing activities:	
Principal payments on long-term debt	(1,000,000)
Net cash provided by (used for) financing activities	(1,000,000)
Net increase (decrease) in cash and cash equivalents	11,780,000
Cash and cash equivalents at beginning of year	42,500,000
Cash and cash equivalents at end of year	$54,280,000

Part a:

Use the data in Pacific Gourmet's financial statements to calculate for year 2 the analytical ratios indicated in the table below to 2 decimal places. (For turnover ratios, year-end balances should be used. All calculations are based on a 365-day year.)

Ratio	Year 2	Year 1
1. Current ratio		3.07
2. Return on equity		28.21%

Part b:

The table below presents several ratios that were considered significant in the current and prior year's audits of Pacific Gourmet. Compare the values for each ratio. Then select the most likely explanation for the analytical results. An explanation may be used once, more than once or not at all. (You should not recalculate ratios. Turnover ratios are based on average balances.)

Ratio	Year 2	Year 1	Explanations
1. Days sales in accounts receivable	40	39	
2. Operating profit margin	22.05%	34.62%	

Explanations

A. Credit terms were restricted on several large accounts during the current year.

B. Operating expenses increased at a higher rate than sales revenue.

C. Sales revenue increased at a higher rate than operating expenses.

D. A smaller percentage of sales occurred during the last month of the year, as compared to the prior year.

E. A larger percentage of sales occurred during the last month of the year, as compared to the prior year.

F. Sales increased as compared to the prior year.

(ID: 9223)

_____

Problem 4-9 SIMULATION: Ratios

The following financial statements were prepared by Feiler Hardware for the year ended December 31, year 2. Sales represent net credit sales. The total assets, the receivables, and inventory balances at December 31, year 2, were the same as at December 31, year 1.

Feiler Hardware
Balance Sheet
December 31, Year 2

Assets		Liabilities and Capital	
Cash	$ 60,000	Accounts payable	$ 40,000
Receivables	100,000	Notes payable	25,000
Inventory	150,000	Other current liabilities	35,000
Total current assets	$310,000	Total current liabilities	$100,000
Plant and equipment—net	190,000	Long-term debt	87,500
		Feiler, Capital	312,500
Total assets	$500,000	Total liabilities and capital	$500,000

Feiler Hardware
Income Statement
Year Ended December 31, Year 2

Sales		$750,000
Less Cost of goods sold		450,000
Gross margin		$300,000
Selling expenses	$60,000	
General and administrative expenses	75,000	135,000
Operating income		$165,000
Less interest expense		10,000
Income before taxes		$155,000
Less federal income taxes		55,000
Net income		$100,000

Each of the following represent financial ratios calculated from the prior year's financial statements. For each ratio, calculate the current year's ratio from the financial statements presented. Calculations should be rounded, if necessary, to the same number of places as the prior year's ratios.

	Ratio	Year 2	Year 1
1.	Current ratio		2.5
2.	Quick ratio		1.3
3.	Accounts receivable turnover		9.0
4.	Inventory turnover		1.5

(ID: 9225)

Problem 4-10 SIMULATION: Analytics

Analytical procedures are evaluations of financial information made by a study of plausible relationships among financial and nonfinancial data. Understanding and evaluating such relationships are essential to the audit process. For each observed change, select the most likely explanations from the accompanying list.

Observed Changes	Explanations
1. Inventory turnover increased substantially from the prior year. (3 explanations)	
2. Accounts receivable turnover decreased substantially from the prior year. (3 explanations)	

Explanations

A. Items shipped on consignment during the last month of the year were recorded as sales.

B. A significant number of credit memos for returned merchandise that were issued during the last month of the year were not recorded.

C. Year-end purchases of inventory were overstated by incorrectly including items received in the first month of the subsequent year.

D. Year-end purchases of inventory were understated by incorrectly excluding items received before the year-end.

E. A larger percentage of sales occurred during the last month of the year, as compared to the prior year.

F. A smaller percentage of sales occurred during the last month of the year, as compared to the prior year.

G. The same percentage of sales occurred during the last month of the year, as compared to the prior year.

H. Sales increased at the same percentage as cost of goods sold, as compared to the prior year.

I. Sales increased at a greater percentage than cost of goods sold increased, as compared to the prior year.

J. Sales increased at a lower percentage than cost of goods sold increased, as compared to the prior year.

(ID: 9226)

Problem 4-11 SIMULATION: Research

While preparing the auditor's report, the audit assistant believes that the auditor's report can never reference the findings of a specialist. The audit manager disagrees. Which citation in the professional standards supports the audit manager's position?

[   ] § [   ]   [   ]   (R/10, AUD, ID: 89454)

Problem 4-12 SIMULATION: Analytics

You are the audit manager assigned to Joe's Office Supply. Based on substantive test work, the staff auditor has proposed the journal entries below to be presented to the client. Assume all proposed journal entries are valid and material.

For each journal entry, indicate its effect (*increased*, *decreased*, or had *no impact*) on the ratios in columns D, E, and F.

A	B	C	D	E	F
Proposed Journal Entry	**Debit**	**Credit**	**Earnings per Share**	**Days Sales in Accounts Receivable**	**Gross Profit**

1. Sales reported after year-end that should have been reported before year-end:
 	
Cost of sales
Accounts receivable
    Sales
    Inventory
	
	90
	100
		
		100
		90			

2. Error in adjusting entry:
 	
Cost of sales
PP&E
Utilities expense
Cash
    Sales
    Accrued expenses
    Inventory
    Interest expense
	
	45
	45
	12
	10
		
		45
		12
		45
		10			

3. To record current and deferred income taxes:
 	
Income tax expense-current
Deferred tax asset
    Income tax expense-deferred
    Deferred tax liability
    Income tax payable
	
	50
	15
		
		10
		5
		50			

(R/10, AUD, ID: 89451)

Problem 4-13 SIMULATION: Analytics

The year under audit is year 2. Duke, Inc. (Duke) is a manufacturing company. Duke experienced record prof-itability in year 1 and management anticipated that year 2 would be another banner year. However, sales declined in year 2 because of regional economic conditions related to a recent recession, and the financial results for year 2 did not meet management's expectations. Sales for year 2 decreased 5% compared to year 1 and gross profit also declined due to increases in manufacturing costs. Management, after reviewing its operations for year 2, recognized that its sales growth had slowed in the past several years and its manufacturing costs had increased.

Duke, Inc.
Consolidated Balance Sheets
December 31, Year 2 and Year 1

	Year 2	Year 1
Assets		
Current assets		
Cash and cash equivalents	$ 3,385,000	$ 6,620,000
Receivables—net	2,964,000	3,124,000
Inventory	3,158,000	3,016,000
Other current assets	639,000	1,379,000
Total current assets	10,146,000	14,139,000
Property, plant and equipment—net	25,900,000	22,000,000
Other assets	800,000	800,000
Total assets	$36,846,000	$36,939,000
Liabilities and Stockholders' Equity		
	Year 2	Year 1
Current liabilities		
Current portion of long-term debt	$ 1,200,000	$ 1,200,000
Accounts payable	3,300,000	11,200,000
Other current liabilities	516,000	1,459,000
Total current liabilities	5,016,000	13,859,000
Long-term debt	19,500,000	16,500,000
Total liabilities	24,516,000	30,359,000
Stockholders' equity		
Common stock	7,280,000	3,280,000
Retained earnings	5,050,000	3,300,000
Total stockholders' equity	12,330,000	6,580,000
Total liabilities and stockholders' equity	$36,846,000	$36,939,000

Duke, Inc.
Consolidated Income Statements
For the Years Ended December 31, Year 2 and Year 1

	Year 2	Year 1
Sales	$19,672,000	$20,730,000
Cost of goods sold	12,197,000	12,231,000
Gross profit on sales	7,475,000	8,499,000
Other operating expenses		
Selling expenses	1,978,000	2,151,000
General administrative	1,377,000	1,248,000
Total other operating expenses	3,355,000	3,399,000
Income from operations before interest expense	4,120,000	5,100,000
Interest expense	1,250,000	1,300,000
Income before taxes	2,870,000	3,800,000
Provision for income taxes	1,120,000	1,520,000
Net income	$ 1,750,000	$ 2,280,000

Duke, Inc.
Consolidated Statements of Cash Flows
For the Years Ended December 31, Year 2 and Year 1

	Year 2	Year 1
Cash flows from operating activities:		
Net income (loss)	$ 1,750,000	$ 2,280,000
Adjustments to reconcile net income (loss) to cash provided by (used for) operating activities:		
Depreciation and amortization	2,000,000	1,900,000
Changes in certain assets and liabilities:		
Decrease (increase) in receivables	160,000	76,000
Decrease (increase) in inventory	(142,000)	(116,000)
Decrease (increase) in other current assets	740,000	
Decrease (increase) in other assets		
Increase (decrease) in accounts payable	(7,900,000)	760,000
Increase (decrease) in other current liabilities	(943,000)	500,000
Net cash provided by (used for) operating activities	(4,335,000)	5,400,000
Cash flows from investing activities:		
Purchase of property, plant and equipment	(5,900,000)	(2,900,000)
Net cash provided by (used for) investing activities	(5,900,000)	(2,900,000)
Cash flows from financing activities:		
Proceeds from issuance of long-term debt	4,200,000	
Principal payments on long-term debt	(1,200,000)	(1,100,000)
Proceeds from issuance of common stock	4,000,000	
Net cash provided by (used for) financing activities	7,000,000	(1,100,000)
Net increase (decrease) in cash and cash equivalents	(3,235,000)	1,400,000
Cash and cash equivalents at beginning of year	6,620,000	5,220,000
Cash and cash equivalents at end of year	$ 3,385,000	$ 6,620,000

The table below presents some ratios that were considered significant in the current and prior year's audit of Duke. Compare the values for each ratio. Then select the most likely explanation for the analytical results. An explanation may be used once, more than once, or not at all. (You should **not** recalculate ratios.)

Ratio	Year 2	Year 1	Explanations
1. Debt to equity	1.99	4.61	
2. Gross profit percentage	38.00%	41.00%	

Selection List

A. Sales decreased as compared to the prior year.

B. Manufacturing costs increased during the year at a greater rate than sales increased.

C. Proceeds from the sale of stock and issuance of debt were used to pay payables on a more current basis.

D. Capital stock was issued during the year.

E. The company may have accumulated excess and obsolete inventory.

F. Manufacturing cost decreased less than sales decreased during the year.

(ID: 9227)

_____

Problem 4-14 SIMULATION: Audit Procedures

During the year 1 audit of Numbaro Co., the auditor performed various procedures.

For each of the audit procedures listed below, select the type of audit procedure, if any, that the auditor performed. A type of audit procedure may be selected once, more than once, or not at all.

Audit Procedures	Type of Audit Procedures
1. During the physical inventory count, the auditor requested that certain material containers be opened to ensure they were not empty.	
2. During a site visit to a branch warehouse, the auditor noted unauthorized personnel have access to the inventory.	
3. The auditor obtained a copy of the company's accounting manual and read the section on inventory to prepare for the physical inventory observation.	
4. The auditor sent a letter to the company's outside attorney accompanied by management's request for information concerning pending or threatened litigation, claims, and assessments.	
5. The auditing firm's computer assisted audit specialist obtained an electronic billing file from the company and checked the accuracy of the summarized billings file.	
6. The auditor obtained the company's aging of accounts receivable and independently created the aging of certain accounts.	
7. The auditor scanned the repairs and maintenance account for unusually large amounts.	

Selection List for Types of Audit Procedures	
Analytical	Inspection
Certifying	Monetizing
Compliance	Observation
Confirmation	Recalculation
Guaranteeing	Reperformance
Inquiry	Valuation

(R/10, AUD, ID: 89452)

Problem 4-15 SIMULATION: Attorney Letters

The following situations represent excerpts from the responses to audit inquiries of external legal counsel of XYZ Co. during the annual audit of year 1. For each excerpt, select the most appropriate audit response related to the financial statements in the audit response (financials) column. Then, in the audit response (report) column, select whether the auditor's report or the attorney's legal response letter needs to be updated; or if it is appropriately dated. Each excerpt is independent. Responses may be used once, more than once, or not at all.

- The client's year-end is December 31, year 1
- The anticipated audit report date is February 15, year 2
- All amounts are material to the financial statements

Situations	Audit Response	
	Financials	Report
1. Letter dated February 14, year 2: "I advise you that at and since December 31, year 1, I have not been engaged to give substantive attention to, or represent XYZ Co. in connection with any pending or threatened litigation, claims, or assessments, nor am I aware of any loss contingencies. No amounts were due to this office for services provided at December 31, year 1."		
2. Letter dated January 21, year 2: "I advise you that at and since December 31, year 1, I have not been engaged to give substantive attention to, or represent XYZ Co. in connection with any pending or threatened litigation, claims, or assessments, nor am I aware of any loss contingencies. There were fees outstanding of $3,675 due to this office for services provided at December 31, year 1."		
3. Letter dated February 26, year 2: "I advise you that at and since December 31, year 1, I have not been engaged to give substantive attention to, or represent XYZ Co. in connection with any pending or threatened litigation, claims, or assessments, except as follows: K. Bowt v. XYZ Co.: This matter commenced in December, year 1. The plaintiff alleges discrimination relating to his termination on November 17, year 1. The company intends to defend this case vigorously. At this time, we are unable to evaluate the likelihood of an unfavorable outcome or estimate the amount or range of potential loss.		
4. Letter dated March 16, year 2: "I advise you that at and since December 31, year 1, I have not been engaged to give substantive attention to, or represent XYZ Co. in connection with any pending or threatened litigation, claims, or assessments, except as follows: J. Myers v. XYZ Co.: This matter commenced in March, year 2. The plaintiff alleges discrimination relating to his termination on November 17, year 1. The company intends to defend this case vigorously. At this time, we are unable to evaluate the likelihood of an unfavorable outcome. The plaintiff is demanding $50,000.		
5. Letter dated January 10, year 2: "I advise you that at and since December 31, year 1, I have not been engaged to give substantive attention to, or represent XYZ Co. in connection with any pending or threatened litigation, claims, or assessments, except as follows: R. Brown v. XYZ Co.: This matter commenced in November, year 1. The plaintiff alleges discrimination relating to his termination on March 17, year 1. The case was tentatively settled for $35,000, which will be covered by XYZ's insurance carrier.		

Situations	Audit Response	
	Financials	**Report**
6. Letter dated January 20, year 2: "I advise you that at and since December 31, year 1, I have not been engaged to give substantive attention to, or represent XYZ Co. in connection with any pending or threatened litigation, claims, or assessments, except as follows: L. Peep v. XYZ Co.: This matter commenced in November, year 1. The plaintiff alleges discrimination relating to his termination on March 17, year 1. The case was tentatively settled for $35,000.		

Selection List for Audit Responses (Financials)	
A. Disclosure in the notes to the financial statements relating to nature of litigation, but no amount disclosed	D. Potential litigation settlement accrued in financial statements
B. Disclosure in the notes to the financial statements relating to nature of litigation, including loss amount	E. Potential litigation settlement not accrued in financial statements, amount disclosed in the notes to the financial statements
C. No impact on financial statements or the notes to the financial statements	F. Verify amount due attorney is recorded in financial statements

Selection List for Audit Responses (Report)
Legal response is appropriately dated
Update report date
Update legal response

(R/10, AUD, ID: 89453)

Solution 4-1 MULTIPLE-CHOICE ANSWERS

Audit Evidence

1. (a) The bank confirmations provide the best primary evidence of the year-end bank balance. In an audit engagement, the best evidence is from an independent third party. If no confirmation is present, a bank reconciliation would provide primary evidence. Neither a bank deposit lead schedule nor an interbank transfer schedule is primary evidence by itself. (ID: 146)

2. (d) Audit evidence is more reliable when it is obtained from independent sources outside the entity. Answers a., b., and c. are examples of auditing procedures performed on information obtained from within the entity. (ID: 3922)

3. (d) Audit evidence that is generated internally is more reliable when the related controls imposed by the entity are effective. Information obtained directly, not indirectly, from outside sources would provide the most reliable evidence. The auditor may find it necessary to rely on audit evidence that is persuasive rather than conclusive. The reliability of audit evidence refers to its source and nature and is dependent on the individual circumstances under which it is obtained. (ID: 5120)

4. (a) The independent auditor's direct personal knowledge, obtained through physical examination, observation, computation, and inspection, is more persuasive than information obtained indirectly. (ID: 8139)

5. (d) Classification concerns whether financial information is appropriately presented in the proper accounts within the financial statements. Valuation and allocation deals with whether assets, liabilities, and equity interests are valued properly and any resulting valuation or allocation adjustments are appropriately recorded. When accounting for investments, the classification has an impact on the appropriate method of valuation in the financial statements. Rights and obligations concerns whether, at a given date, recorded assets indeed represent rights of the entity and liabilities represent obligations. Reviewing investment records regarding transfers between categories (internal documents) provides little evidence that ownership rights in the investments still exists at the balance sheet date, that the investment is not pledged as loan collateral, that the investments exist at the balance sheet date, or that an external transaction involving the investment occurred during the period. (ID: 7824)

6. (a) Suspense debits that management believes will benefit future operations are assets. The auditor is most concerned that assets are not overstated and that liabilities are not understated. Suspense debits that the auditor verifies will have realizable value to the client are, insofar as the auditor knows, correct. Thus, for these items, there would be no overstatement. The other two answer options contain items that, if incorrect, would overstate liabilities. (ID: 6365)

7. (d) Performing analytical procedures designed to disclose differences from expectations would be the most likely way to detect unusual entries. The other answers are not as likely to detect journal entries with unusual combinations of accounts. (ID: 5087)

8. (a) One of the uses of analytics is as a substantive test to obtain audit evidence about particular assertions. In the process of achieving objectives, auditors adhere to a system of quality control, prepare working papers, and may possibly increase the level of detection risk; however, none of these actually cause the auditor to achieve audit objectives. (ID: 5985)

9. (d) Evidence that a deviation was covered up in a fraudulent manner would require the auditor to consider the implications of the deviation more closely. Answers a., b., and c. give no causes for added concern. (ID: 5973)

10. (b) Unreconciled differences between control and subsidiary accounts indicate a disregard for common accounting safeguards. Assumptions used in developing estimates should change with changing circumstances. A lower response rate for negative confirmation requests indicates fewer customer account misstatements. Consultation with a CPA firm about complex accounting matters often indicates conscientious accounting and reporting. (ID: 7097)

11. (c)   Despite being handled by the client, bank statements originate outside the entity and, therefore, are the most persuasive of the choices. Both purchase orders and work sheets originate within the client. Management's representation letter only documents the client's oral representations.   (ID: 5657)

12. (d)   The auditor most likely would consider whether material misstatements exist when transactions selected for testing are not supported by proper documentation. Reduced emphasis on meeting earnings projections would be a factor decreasing the likelihood of earnings overstatements and assets (the most frequent misstatement). Having the board of directors make major financing decisions would decrease the incentive for management to use questionable reporting by reducing the amount of management's responsibility. Significant deficiencies previously communicated to management may not have been corrected because of an unfavorable cost-benefit relationship.   (ID: 5086)

13. (d)   Appropriate evidence is both valid and relevant. The validity of audit evidence is highly dependent upon the circumstances under which it is obtained. The independent auditor's direct personal knowledge, obtained through physical examination, observation, computation, and inspection, is more persuasive than information obtained indirectly.   (ID: 8143)

14. (c)   The existence or occurrence assertions concern whether assets or liabilities exist as of the financial statement date and whether recorded transactions actually occurred during a reporting period. Even though this is a test of controls, this procedure also provides evidence that customers' balances actually exist. The presentation and disclosure assertions concern proper classification, description, and disclosure in the financial statements.   (ID: 8119)

15. (c)   Evidence obtained during an audit may cause the auditor to change the nature, extent, or timing of other planned audit procedures. A disclaimer of opinion or a qualified opinion would be issued if the auditor could not obtain sufficient evidence; there is no indication that that is the case in this situation. A statement from management supporting their inventory valuation is merely another management representation and likely would be an insufficient substitute for additional audit procedures.   (ID: 8394)

16. (a)   Tracing the auditor's inventory observations test counts to the client's inventory listings is testing to see if all assets that should have been recorded have been recorded, i.e., completeness. Rights and obligations would be concerned with, for example, whether the inventory was pledged as collateral or under contract to be sold for other than market value. Valuation or allocation would be concerned with, for example, the value assigned to the inventory and whether its historical cost is under market value as of the balance sheet date. Classification and understandability would be concerned with, for example, whether the inventory was appropriately in short-term assets.   (ID: 8396)

17. (c)   If credit is granted in accordance with policies, there is a greater chance that accounts receivable are correctly valued as allowance account amounts are based on the assumption that those policies are followed. Confirming that credit is granted in accordance with policies provides little evidence as to the rights and obligations connected with those sales.   (ID: 8403)

18. (a)   Reconciling the amount included in the statement of cash flows to other statements is a basic procedure. Relationships among elements of financial information within the period are one source of expectations regarding relationships that reasonably are expect to exist. The other procedures generally are involved in auditing the balance in the cash accounts, not necessarily the statement of cash flows.   (ID: 8408)

19. (a)   The third standard of fieldwork states: "The auditor must obtain sufficient appropriate audit evidence by performing audit procedures to afford a reasonable basis for an opinion regarding the financial statements under audit."   (ID: 8830)

20. (c)   An auditor interviewing and observing appropriate personnel to determine segregation of duties is considered a test of controls. Reviewing the check register for unrecorded liabilities and evaluating a journal entry are examples of tests of details of classes of transactions, account balances—substantive procedures. Reviewing the audit workpapers is an example of a quality control procedure performed by an audit firm to ensure the quality of its engagement performance—tests of controls refer to tests of the client's internal control system.   (ID: 9360)

21. (d) If sufficient appropriate evidence is not available to support an opinion on the financial statements, then an audit cannot be performed. In the absence of evidence to the contrary, transactions with related parties should not be assumed to be outside the ordinary course of business. Further, established accounting principles ordinarily do not require them to be accounted for on a different basis because related parties are involved; however, the auditor must be satisfied that disclosure is adequate. Their existence, in and of itself, would not preclude the performance of an audit. Many internal control activities are subject to management override. The cost of a new efficient information system may outweigh its benefits. (ID: 8161)

Internal Auditors

22. (d) The internal auditors' work may affect the nature, timing, and extent of the audit, including: procedures the auditor performs when obtaining an understanding of the entity's internal control structure; procedures the auditor performs when assessing risk; and substantive procedures the auditor performs. (ID: 6000)

23. (d) Answers a., b., and c. are all items the auditor considers in assessing the internal auditor's competence and objectivity. (ID: 5141)

24. (a) The quality of internal auditors' documentation reflects on their competence. The other answers are concerned with objectivity. (ID: 6832)

25. (a) In assessing competence and objectivity, the auditor usually considers information obtained from previous experience with the internal audit function, from discussions with management personnel, and from a recent external quality review, if performed, of the internal audit function's activities. The auditor may also use professional internal auditing standards as criteria in making the assessment. (ID: 8127)

26. (d) The responsibility to report on the financial statements rests solely with the independent auditor. Because the auditor has the ultimate responsibility to express an opinion on the financial statements, judgments about assessments of inherent and control risks, the materiality of misstatements, the sufficiency of test performed, the evaluation of significant accounting estimates, and other matters affecting the auditor's report should always be those of the auditor. (ID: 6235)

27. (d) In performing an audit, the auditor may request direct assistance from the internal auditors including assistance in obtaining an understanding of internal control or in performing tests of controls or substantive tests. (ID: 5678)

28. (a) If the independent auditor decides that the work performed by internal auditors may have a bearing on his or her own procedures, the independent auditor should assess the competence and objectivity of internal auditors and evaluate their work. When assessing the internal auditor's objectivity, the auditor should determine the organizational status of the internal auditor responsible for the internal audit function. In this case, the independent auditor would place limited reliance on the work performed by the internal auditors because the internal auditors report to the controller and, thus, may be reluctant to report weaknesses in the controller's activities. The independent auditor performs tests of controls to assess the level of control risk and then will use the work of the internal auditors, if appropriate, to decrease the substantive tests. The auditor is not precluded from using the work of internal auditors as long as the auditor is satisfied with their competence and objectivity. (ID: 157)

29. (a) Considering professional standards and whether internal auditors meet them provides an indication regarding their objectivity. Neither the tests of activities that could detect errors and fraud, materiality of recently inspected accounts, nor the results of tests performed by internal auditors influence an internal auditor's objectivity. An internal auditor may concentrate appropriately on compliance testing, rather than tests of errors and fraud. The accounts to be audited may be selected by people other than the auditors. A biased internal auditor conceivably might be unusually careful in work performed just before the external audit. (ID: 7108)

30. (c) The assessment of the competence of internal auditors by the auditor should include obtaining information about the quality of working paper documentation, reports, and recommendations. Information about the influence of management on the scope of the internal auditor's duties and the policies limiting their communication with the audit committee bear on the assessment of their objectivity rather than their competence. Information about the entity's ability to continue as a going concern would not reflect on the competence of the internal auditors. (ID: 8614)

31. (a)   When assessing the internal auditors' objectivity, the auditor should obtain information about such factors as the organizational status of the director of the internal audit function. The professional certifications of the internal audit staff is a factor to consider when assessing their competence; not their objectivity. Answers c. and d. are factors to consider when developing evaluation procedures for testing the effectiveness of internal auditors' work rather than their objectivity.   (ID: 8640)

32. (b)   When assessing the competence of internal auditors, one of the factors a CPA should consider is the quality of the internal auditors' working paper documentation, reports, and recommendations. The organizational level to which they report is an indicator of their objectivity, not their competence. Answer c. is a nonsense answer. Obviously, you would not want to bar internal auditors from auditing sensitive matters. However, a policy prohibiting them from auditing areas where relatives are employed in important or audit-sensitive positions is a measure of their objectivity, but again, not their competence. The evaluation of internal auditors' preliminary assessed level of control risk would be an indicator of their competence because monitoring the performance of an entity's controls is one of internal audit's major responsibilities. However, it is more likely that an independent CPA would obtain information about this matter to assess the relevance of internal audit activities. The best, in this case, the most clear-cut answer, is b.   (ID: 8841)

33. (a)   When assessing the internal auditors' objectivity, the auditor should obtain information about such factors as the organizational status of the internal auditor responsible for the internal audit function, including whether the internal auditor reports to an officer of sufficient status to ensure broad audit coverage and adequate consideration of, and action on, the findings and recommendations of the internal auditors; whether the internal auditor has direct access and reports regularly to those charged with governance; and whether those charged with governance oversee employment decisions related to the internal auditor. The auditor should also obtain information about the client's policies prohibiting internal auditors from auditing areas where relatives are employed in important or audit-sensitive positions and where internal auditors were recently assigned or are scheduled to be assigned on completion of responsibilities in the internal audit function. Reviewing the internal auditor's reports to determine that their conclusions are consistent with the work performed is not done to assess objectivity; it is done to evaluate the effectiveness of their work. The auditor would not verify that the internal auditor's assessment of control risk was comparable to that of the auditor—the auditor has the ultimate responsibility to express an opinion on the financial statements; thus, judgments about assessments of inherent and control risks, the materiality of misstatements, the sufficiency of tests performed, the evaluation of significant accounting estimates, and other matters affecting the auditor's report should always be those of the auditor. The evaluation of the quality of the internal auditors' working paper documentation and their recent audit recommendations is not done to assess their objectivity; it is done to assess their competence.   (ID: 9933)

34. (a)   In performing the audit, the auditor may request direct assistance from the internal auditors. This direct assistance relates to work the auditor specifically requests the internal auditors to perform to complete some aspect of the auditor's work. For example, internal auditors may assist the auditor in obtaining an understanding of internal control or in performing tests of controls or substantive tests.   (ID: 9934)

35. (a)   Internal auditors may assist the auditor in obtaining an understanding of internal control or in performing tests of controls or substantive tests which include both analytical procedures and tests of details. When direct assistance is provided, the auditor should assess the internal auditors' competence and objectivity and supervise, review, evaluate, and test the work performed by internal auditors to the extent appropriate in the circumstances. An auditor should not allow an internal auditor to be responsible for the audit of a major subsidiary of the company—the responsibility to report on the financial statements rests solely with the auditor and unlike the situation in which the auditor uses the work of other independent auditors, this responsibility cannot be shared with the internal auditors. Independence is, of course, not possible for an internal auditor, but they are expected to be objective.   (ID: 9944)

Management Representations

36. (c)   Written representations from management reduce the possibility of a misunderstanding concerning management's responsibility for the financial statements. The auditor does not reduce audit risk or the scope of procedures performed based on representations made in the management representation letter. A representation letter does not reduce the auditor's responsibility to detect material misstatements in the audit.   (ID: 3928)

37. (a) During an audit, management makes many representations to the auditor in response to specific inquiries or through the financial statements. Such representations from management are part of the audit evidence the independent auditor obtains, but they are not a substitute for the application of those auditing procedures necessary to afford a reasonable basis for an opinion regarding the financial statements under audit. Written representations from management ordinarily confirm representations given to the auditor, indicate and document the continuing appropriateness of such representations, and reduce the possibility of misunderstanding concerning the matters that are the subject of the representations. (ID: 218)

38. (b) If comparative financial statements are reported on, the written representations obtained at the completion of the most recent audit should address all periods being reported on. The representations should be made as of the date of the auditor's report. If current management was not present during all periods covered by the auditor's report, the auditor should nevertheless obtain written representations from current management on all such periods. (ID: 6842)

39. (c) Compliance with aspects of contractual agreements that may affect the financial statements is a matter ordinarily included in management representations. Management's justifications for not correcting control weaknesses are primarily of concern to the audit committee, not the auditor. Generally, the auditor is not concerned with forecasts of the entity's stock price. Management is unlikely to acknowledge any responsibility for employees' violations of laws—merely responsibility for having reasonable controls in place. (ID: 6841)

40. (c) Compliance with contractual agreements that may affect the financial statements is a matter ordinarily included in management representations. It is the auditor's responsibility to assess the risk factors concerning the misappropriation of assets. An evaluation of the litigation that has been filed against the entity is a matter to be covered in a lawyer's response to a letter of audit inquiry. Management is not required to correct all material internal control weaknesses. (ID: 8164)

41. (a) Management's representations may be limited to matters that are considered material. Materiality limitations would not apply to those representations that are not directly related to amounts included in the financial statements, such as the availability of minutes of stockholders' and directors' meetings. Answers b., c., and d. relate directly to amounts in the financial statements and, thus, materiality limits would apply. (ID: 5684)

42. (d) Because of the possible effects of fraud and the importance of management integrity on other aspects of the audit, materiality limits do not apply with respect to fraud involving management. This means that no incident involving management fraud may be ignored no matter how minor it may seem. Some instances of answers a., b., and c. may not be significant enough to matter. (ID: 8124)

43. (d) An unqualified opinion requires written management representations. Alternative procedures may be used when the client prevents the auditor from reviewing the predecessor's working papers, engages the auditor after the year-end physical inventory is completed, or requests that certain material A/R not be confirmed. (ID: 6941)

44. (a) Management is required to make all financial records and related data available to the auditor. It is up to the auditor to gather sufficient audit evidence to support the opinion on the financial statements. The other three statements are required to be included in the management representation letter. (ID: 8122)

45. (a) The last paragraph of the AICPA's illustrative management representation letter states: "To the best of our knowledge and belief, no events have occurred subsequent to the balance sheet date and through the date of this letter that would require adjustment to, or disclosure in, the aforementioned financial statements." The auditor, not management, is responsible for reporting significant deficiencies to the audit committee. Statements regarding the attorney-client privilege generally are made by attorneys, not client management. That certain computer files may exist only for a short period of time is more appropriately noted at the beginning of the audit; a management representation letter should be dated as of the date of the auditor's report. (ID: 7801)

46. (a) Materiality limits ordinarily would apply to management representations related to amounts concerning related-party transactions. Materiality considerations would not apply to those representations that are not directly related to amounts included in the financial statements such as the availability of financial records or the completeness of minutes of directors' meetings. Other items of this nature are management's acknowledgement of its responsibility for the fair presentation of financial statements in conformity with GAAP and communications from regulatory agencies concerning noncompliance with or deficiencies in financial reporting practices. Nor

would materiality apply to irregularities involving members of management because of the possible effects of fraud on other aspects of the audit. (ID: 8826)

47. (a) That management has the responsibility for the design of controls to detect fraud is a role that would typically be acknowledged in a management representation letter. None of the other answers would typically be included. (ID: 9366)

Analytics

48. (b) Analytical procedures consist of evaluations of financial information made by a study of plausible relationships among both financial and nonfinancial data. Projecting an error rate is not such an evaluation. (ID: 5666)

49. (c) The purpose of applying analytical procedures in planning the audit is to assist in planning the nature, timing, and extent of auditing procedures that will be used to obtain audit evidence for specific account balances or classes of transactions. To accomplish this, the analytical procedures used in planning the audit should focus on enhancing the auditor's understanding of the client's business and the transactions and events that have occurred since the last audit date. Consideration of reductions in the scope of test of controls and substantive tests occurs after the auditor understands the client's business. The audit as a whole provides reasonable assurance that potential material misstatements will be identified. Assessing the adequacy of available audit evidence can occur only after examination of audit evidence, not in the planning stage. (ID: 5626)

50. (b) This procedure would most likely provide indications of any material improper entries in the revenue and expense accounts. This procedure would not indicate when something was paid. The auditor did not expect much change as the question states that similar amounts from the prior year were used as the expectation to compare. That is, if the auditor did not consider increased property taxes or a change in uncollectible accounts in his or her expectation, then those changes that should have been recorded, but weren't, would not be detected. (ID: 8146)

51. (b) If the client did not properly cutoff sales at the end of the year, then A/R would be overstated as well as sales. A/R turnover equals net credit sales divided by average net accounts receivable. Therefore, if net credit sales is overstated and average net receivables is overstated disproportionately, the turnover would be lower than expected when compared to the prior year. Answers a. and d. would not affect A/R turnover. A/R turnover would increase if a large receivable were written off near the end of the year. (ID: 8163)

52. (d) The overall review of the audit is concerned with the big picture. The other answer options are analytical procedures that likely are performed during earlier stages, or not at all. (ID: 6366)

53. (c) Analytics are used in the overall review stage to assist the auditor in assessing conclusions reached and in evaluating the overall financial statement presentation. The overall review generally would include reading the financial statements and notes and considering the adequacy of evidence gathered in response to unusual or unexpected balances. The results of these procedures may indicate that additional evidence may be needed. Procedures to achieve the objectives in answers a. and d. would be performed before the overall review stage. The auditor would examine the workpapers to determine if any procedures were omitted. (ID: 8157)

54. (c) Analytics are concerned with plausible relationships. The square footage of selling space might be used to compared retail revenues and expenses to industry figures and prior year performance. Personnel turnover and objectivity of audit committee members are concerned with the control environment. Management plans are considered when evaluating the control environment, valuation, and disclosure. (ID: 6392)

55. (b) The use of a standard cost system that produces variance reports allows the auditor an opportunity to compare the output from the standard cost system with the financial information presented by management. Segregating obsolete inventory before the physical inventory count would likely facilitate inventory procedures, but not necessarily the analytical procedures. The auditor should assess the reliability of the data by considering the source of the data and the conditions under which it was gathered. Stronger internal controls and independent sources enhance the reliability of data used in analytics, but b. is the best answer. (ID: 5988)

56. (d) Increased sales to comparable customers would double accounts receivable (A/R) without a change in the allowance for doubtful accounts as a percentage of A/R. The client should increase this percentage if it

has more customers with poor credit ratings. With no other changes, if twice as many A/R were written off previously or if more A/R are old, it suggests the current write-offs are inadequate. (ID: 7623)

57. (b)   Analytics involve evaluations of information made by a study of plausible relationships. The relationship between two consecutive years' payroll expenses is related more closely than warranty expense and contingent liabilities. A/R and sales are not the primary accounts likely to be examined in evaluating an entity's costs and expenses. (ID: 6580)

58. (c)   Increased sales to comparable customers would double accounts receivable (A/R) without a change in the allowance for doubtful accounts as a percentage of A/R. The allowance for doubtful accounts as a percentage should increase if a greater percentage of A/R is overdue this year. Improved internal control over cash receipts would tend to decrease accounts receivable balances. The allowance for doubtful accounts as a percentage should decrease if the client has less customers with poor credit ratings. (ID: 8133)

59. (a)   GAAS require that analytics are to be used to some extent in all audits in the planning of the audit and in the final review stages. The use of analytics as a substantive test is not mandated, but it should be noted that analytics can be more effective or efficient than tests of details for achieving certain substantive testing objectives. (ID: 141)

60. (d)   The auditor's reliance on substantive tests to achieve an audit objective related to a particular assertion may be derived from tests of details, from analytical procedures, or from a combination of both. The decision about which procedure or procedures to use to achieve a particular audit objective is based on the auditor's judgment on the expected effectiveness and efficiency of the available procedures. An auditor's decision whether to apply analytics or to perform tests of transactions and account balances is not determined solely by the availability of data aggregated at a high level, the auditor's familiarity with industry trends, or the timing of tests performed after the balance sheet date. (ID: 2965)

61. (c)   Understanding financial relationships is essential to evaluating the results of analytics and usually requires knowledge of the client and the industry. The staff accountant may not be objective regarding his or her own work and may have limited industry knowledge. It would not be practicable for the managing partner who has responsibility for all audit engagements at that practice office to perform this procedure for all audits. A firm's quality control manager is not a member of the engagement team and, thus, may not participate in this manner in the engagement. (ID: 7025)

62. (c)   Unexpected relationships discovered through analytics indicate additional investigation is appropriate. To assume that fraud exists in the relevant accounts or to revise communications with the audit committee without further investigation would be an over-reaction. Analytics are a substantive test, not a test of internal control. (ID: 6398)

63. (c)   A basic premise underlying the application of analytics is that plausible relationships among data reasonably may be expected to exist and continue in the absence of known conditions to the contrary. The accounts receivable (A/R) turnover formula is net credit sales divided by average net A/R. A/R turnover is a measure of how many times in a year an entity collects its A/R. If the ratio increased, either average net A/R decreased or net credit sales increased. An increase in collections results in decreased average net A/R. The A/R aging is said to have deteriorated when collection times lengthen, an unusual circumstance if average net A/R decreased in proportion to sales. The elimination of a discount policy might decrease sales, but its relative impact on net credit sales and average net A/R is not known; in the absence of information to the contrary, assume that this did not have a significant impact on the ratio. A decrease in net credit sales would decrease the ratio. (ID: 7842)

64. (b)   The final review stage of the audit provides an overall review of financial information in light of the audit opinion expressed. A final consideration of the adequacy of evidence is appropriate for this stage. Factors that determined the preliminary materially and audit risk levels would have been reassessed before arriving at final materially and audit risk levels. Summarizing specified uncorrected misstatements and calculating projected uncorrected misstatements estimated through sampling techniques is done before deciding on an audit opinion. (ID: 7813)

65. (c)   As higher levels of assurance are desired from analytical procedures, more predictable relationships are required to develop the expectation. Relationships involving income statement accounts tend to be more

predictable than relationships involving only balance sheet accounts because income statement accounts represent transactions over a period of time, whereas balance sheet accounts represent amounts as of a point in time. Relationships involving transactions subject to management discretion are sometimes less predictable.

(ID: 2773)

66. (b) A comparison of revenues and expenses with those of the prior year is likely to reveal a change in the capitalization policy for small tools. For instance, if tools costing less than $25 formerly were expensed and the policy is changed to $100, this is likely to show a substantial increase in the amount of tools expensed during the period. Answer c. concerns a liability account (payroll taxes payable), not a revenue or expense account. Failure to recognize the property tax increase would make the account balances comparable and so the auditor would not investigate.

(ID: 7493)

67. (c) The following factors influence the auditor's consideration of the reliability of data for purposes of achieving audit objectives: whether the data was obtained from independent sources outside the entity or from sources within the entity; whether sources within the entity were independent of those who are responsible for the amount being audited; whether the data was developed under a reliable system with adequate controls; whether the data was subjected to audit testing in the current or prior year; and whether the expectations were developed using data from a variety of sources. Whether the data was processed in an IT system or in a manual accounting system, whether the data was prepared on the cash basis or in conformity with GAAP, and whether the data was processed in an online system or a batch entry system generally would not influence the auditor's consideration of the reliability of data for purposes of analytics.

(ID: 8388)

68. (d) Analytics involve comparisons of recorded amounts or ratios developed from recorded amounts to expectations developed by the auditor. Comparing current year account balances for conformity with predictable patterns assists the author's understanding of the client's business and events that have occurred since the last audit date and identifies areas that may represent specific risks relevant to the audit. Confirming bank balances with financial institutions, scanning accounts receivable for amounts over credit limits, and recalculating inventory extensions of physical inventory counts generally are not considered analytics.

(ID: 8397)

69. (d) The auditor is required to perform analytics in the planning stage of the audit. These procedures assist the auditor in planning the nature, extent, and timing of substantive tests; thus, they should focus on enhancing the auditor's understanding of the client's business and the transactions and events that have occurred since the last audit and identifying areas that may represent specific risks relevant to the audit. Analytics involve comparisons of recorded amounts or ratios developed from recorded amounts to expectations developed by the auditor. Comparison of recorded financial information with anticipated results from budgets and forecasts is appropriate for this planning stage. Representations from management are dated the same date as the auditor's report. Communication regarding the prior year's audit adjustments typically occurs near the end of the audit for that year. Inquiry of the client's attorney tends to occur after the planning stage, as part of the substantive tests.

(ID: 8414)

70. (c) The analytical procedure that an auditor most likely would perform when planning an audit is comparing current year balances to budgeted balances. Recalculating interest expense based on notes payable balances is an analytical procedure, but not one that would generally be performed during the planning phase. Analytical procedures used in planning the audit generally use data aggregated at a high level. The other answers are examples of tests of details, not analytical procedures.

(ID: 8813)

71. (a) The purpose of analytics in the planning stage of the audit is to assist in planning the audit procedures that will be used to obtain audit evidence for specific account balances or classes of transactions. To accomplish this one of the things the auditor should focus on is the transactions and events that have occurred since the last audit date. The unaudited information from internal quarterly reports would be the best source of information for developing expectations. Expectations, in this context, are the auditor's predictions of recorded accounts or ratios. The effectiveness of analytical procedures depends on developing expectations that can reasonably be expected to identify unexpected relationships. Account assertions in the planning memorandum would not provide the needed data to develop such expectations. The auditor is interested in transactions and events that have occurred since the last audit date, so comments in the prior year's management letter would have limited usefulness and, again, would probably not include data needed to derive expectations. Control risk affects the reliability of data and, thus, the precision of the expectation, but it would not be considered a source for developing expectations.

(ID: 8831)

72. (d)   Analytical procedures used in the planning phase of an audit should focus on enhancing the auditor's understanding of the client's business and the auditor's understanding of the transactions and events that have occurred since the last audit, and identifying areas that may represent specific risks relevant to the audit. The other answers do not describe activities that would occur during the planning phase of an audit.   (ID: 8843)

73. (c)   The objective of analytical procedures used in the final review stage of the audit is to assess the conclusions reached and evaluate the overall financial statement presentation. It would generally include reading the financial statements and notes and considering the adequacy of the evidence gathered in response to unusual or unexpected balances identified and any unusual or unexpected balances or relationships that were not previously identified. Comparing each individual expense account balance with the relevant budgeted amounts and investigating any significant variations; and calculating each individual expense account balance as a percentage of total entity expenses and comparing the results with industry averages are analytical procedures that would be performed during the course of the audit (used as substantive procedures), not during the final review stage. Analytical procedures are not applicable to tests of controls.   (ID: 8801)

74. (c)   An engagement partner would most likely consider cost of goods sold/average inventory in the overall review stage of an audit. Known as inventory turnover, it measures the number of times inventory is acquired and sold during a period and is thus used as an indicator of the efficiency of the operations of a company. The other answers are not meaningful financial statement analysis calculations.   (ID: 8847)

75. (d)   An auditor would most likely consider the possibility that a client's financial statements contained material misstatements if the results of an analytical procedure disclosed unexpected differences. An auditor should evaluate significant unexpected differences. If an explanation for the difference cannot be obtained, the auditor should design further audit procedures to determine whether the difference is a likely misstatement. Whenever an auditor becomes aware that management has consulted with other accountants about significant accounting matters (whether or not this was disclosed to the auditor by management) the auditor should discuss with those charged with governance the auditor's views about those same matters. Whether this would cause the auditor to consider that the financial statements might be materially misstated would depend on the circumstances. The delivery of the management representation letter is an issue that should be explained to the client during the initial stage of the planning stage of the audit and documented in an engagement letter along with other understandings with the client. The representations should be dated as of the date of the auditor's report. (The reference to completion of fieldwork is based on superseded guidance.) At any rate, the CFO is not refusing to sign and although such representations are part of the audit evidence, they complement, rather than serve as a substitute for, other audit procedures; thus, any issue with them would be less of a concern regarding material misstatements than an unexpected difference disclosed by analytical procedures. Audit trails of computer-generated transactions existing for a short time are not an indication of a material misstatement. The auditor should be aware of the client's record retention policies and either arrange to test the transactions during their existence or develop alternative auditing procedures.   (ID: 8809)

76. (c)   The decision about which procedure to use (analytics or tests of details, or a combination) is based on the auditor's judgment of their effectiveness and efficiency in identifying potential misstatements in the given situation. The effectiveness and efficiency of analytical procedures is based on the nature of the assertion; the plausibility and predictability of the relationship; the availability and reliability of the data used to develop expectations; and the precision of the expectation. The other answers are not relevant considerations.   (ID: 8832)

77. (a)   Relationships involving income statement accounts, such as interest expense, tend to be more predictable than relationships involving only balance sheet accounts because income statement accounts represent transactions over a period of time, whereas balance sheet accounts represent amounts as of a point in time.   (ID: 8641)

78. (d)   This question describes an analytical procedure known as a reasonable test which is a comparison of an estimated amount, calculated by the use of relevant financial and nonfinancial information, with a recorded amount.   (ID: 8812)

79. (a)   A lower than expected return on an equity method investment most likely could have been caused by an error in recording amortization of the excess of the investor's cost over the investment's underlying book value. The investee's decision to reduce cash dividends would increase the expected carrying amount of the investment under the equity method. Marketable securities (available-for-sale or trading securities) are not

accounted for using the equity method. A fluctuation in the market price of the investee's common stock would not affect investments accounted for using the equity method. (ID: 9362)

80. (c) Analytical procedures are most appropriate when testing operating expense transactions. Relationships involving income statement accounts tend to be more predictable than relationships involving only balance sheet accounts because income statement accounts represent transactions over a period of time, whereas balance sheet accounts represent amounts as of a point in time. (ID: 9379)

81. (b) When applying analytical procedures during an audit, the best approach for developing expectations is to identify reasonable explanations for unexpected differences before talking to client management. This allows a more objective approach. Data from unaudited account balances and ratios are less likely to be reliable than data that has been audited. It is nonsensical to consider a pattern of several unusual changes without trying to explain what caused them. Comparing client data with client-determined expected results to reduce detailed tests of account balances is the substitution of the client's judgment for the auditor's judgment which is always inappropriate. (ID: 9394)

82. (d) The objective of analytical procedures used in the overall review stage of an audit is to assist the auditor in assessing the conclusions reached and in the evaluation of the overall financial statement presentation. GAAS require that analytical procedures be applied to some extent for assisting the auditor in planning the nature, extent, and timing of other auditing procedures and as an overall review of the financial information in the final review stage of the audit. Analytical procedures can be, but are not required to be, used as a substantive test during an audit to gather evidence about particular assertions related to account balances or classes of transactions. Identifying account balances that represent specific risks relevant to the audit or detecting fraud that may cause the statements to be misstated are objectives of analytics during the planning, not the final review, stage of the audit. Gathering evidence from tests of details to corroborate financial statement assertions is an objective of using analytical procedures as a substantive test. (ID: 9901)

83. (c) Only comparing the current year's financial statements with those of the prior year is a description of an analytical procedure. Although analytics involve evaluations of financial information made by a study of plausible relationships among both financial and nonfinancial data, the other answers which refer to nonfinancial information do not describe a review of relationships of financial information with relevant nonfinancial information. Additionally, obtaining a letter from the client's attorney and reading the minutes of the board of director's meetings should be done prior to the final review stage. (ID: 9912)

Using a Specialist's Work

84. (d) When a specialist does not have a relationship with the client, the specialist's work usually will provide the auditor with greater assurance of reliability. However, the work of a specialist having a relationship to the client may be acceptable under certain circumstances. The appropriateness and reasonableness of methods and assumptions used and their application are the responsibility of the specialist. The auditor should obtain an understanding of the methods or assumptions used by the specialist, and evaluate whether the specialist's findings support the related assertions in the financial statements. An auditor may encounter complex or subjective matters potentially material to the financial statements. Such matters may require special skill or knowledge that, in the auditor's judgment, require using the work of a specialist. (ID: 6001)

85. (a) The auditor may decide to add explanatory language to a standard report or depart from an unqualified opinion. Reference to and identification of the specialist may be made in the auditor's report if such reference will facilitate an understanding of the reason for the explanatory paragraph or the departure from the unqualified opinion. If, as a result of the use of a specialist, the auditor concludes that conditions exist that cause substantial doubt about the entity's ability to continue as a going concern and the auditor believes a reference to the specialist will facilitate an understanding of the reason for the reference to this conclusion, the auditor may refer to the specialist in the auditor's report. Disclosure of the specialist's findings, implying that a more thorough audit was performed, is not appropriate. If a specialist's findings are consistent with management's representations and corroborate another specialist's earlier findings, there would be no need to disclose the findings of the specialist for the reasons above. Internal control is generally not a matter that would require the use of a specialist. (ID: 5680)

86. (b) An auditor may use the work of a specialist who has a relationship with the client, but must assess the risk that the specialist might not be objective. If the relationship might impair the specialist's objectivity, the

auditor should perform additional procedures or engage another specialist. Normally, an auditor should not refer to the work or findings of the specialist. In expressing an unqualified opinion, the auditor may refer to the specialist in an explanatory paragraph only if doing so will help clarify the reason for the explanatory paragraph. If there is a material departure from GAAP, the auditor may refer to the specialist in an explanatory paragraph only if doing so will help clarify the reason for the qualified or adverse opinion. Control deficiencies result from the client's actions or inactions, not the auditor's actions. (ID: 8412)

87. (a) The auditor should obtain an understanding of the nature of the work performed by a specialist, such as an actuary. This understanding should include the objectives and scope of the specialist's (actuary's) work. The appropriateness and reasonableness of methods and assumptions used and their application are the responsibility of the specialist, not the auditor. The client is not required to consent to the auditor's use of the actuary's work; the auditor decides if there are matters that require special skill or knowledge and, thus, require using the work of a specialist to obtain appropriate audit evidence. Naturally, the auditor enjoys greater assurance of reliability if a specialist does not have a relationship with the client, however, if the auditor can attain satisfaction that the specialist's objectivity will not be impaired, such a specialist can be acceptable. (ID: 8814)

88. (d) The auditor may, as a result of the report or findings of the specialist, decide to add explanatory language to a standard report (for example, to emphasize an unusually important subsequent event) or depart from an unqualified opinion. Reference to and identification of the specialist may be made in the auditor's report if the auditor believes such reference will facilitate an understanding of the reason for the explanatory paragraph or the departure from the unqualified opinion. Otherwise, the auditor should **not** refer to the work or findings of the specialist. Such a reference might be misunderstood to be a qualification of the auditor's opinion or a division of responsibility, neither of which is intended. Further, there may be an inference that the auditor making such reference performed a more thorough audit than an auditor not making such reference. (ID: 8652)

89. (c) An auditor who uses the work of a specialist may refer to the specialist in the auditor's report if the auditor modifies the report because of the difference between the client's and the specialist's valuations of an asset and the auditor believes such reference will facilitate the understanding of the reason for the modification. The modification may take the form of either the addition of an explanatory paragraph to a standard report or the departure from an unqualified opinion. If the auditor believes that the specialist's findings are reasonable in the circumstances, ordinarily the auditor would use the findings, but this does not speak to whether a reference in the auditor's report is appropriate because there is no indication of whether the findings support the related assertions in the financial statements and, thus, do or do not require modification of the auditor's report. If the specialist's findings support the related assertions in the financial statements or provide the auditor with greater assurance of reliability about management's representations, it follows that the auditor will be able to conclude that sufficient appropriate audit evidence has been obtained. As no modification of the auditor's report is needed as a result of the specialist's findings, no reference should be made to the specialist because it could be misinterpreted as either a qualification or a division of responsibility. (Editor note: This question is an example of when candidates must choose the best answer. The other answers are clearly wrong and answer c. is at least partially correct.) (ID: 8846)

Inquiry of Client's Lawyer

90. (a) A lawyer may limit the response to matters to which the lawyer has given substantive attention in the form of legal consultation or representation. Answers b., c., and d. are sufficient to cause a scope limitation.
(ID: 138)

91. (c) As the events or conditions that should be considered in accounting for and reporting litigation, claims, and assessments are matters within the direct knowledge, and often control of, an entity's management, that management is the primary source of information about such matters. Although a letter of audit inquiry to the client's lawyer is the auditor's primary means of obtaining corroboration of the information furnished by management concerning litigation, claims, and assessments, it is not the primary means of obtaining that information.
(ID: 4276)

92. (d) A lawyer's response may be limited to matters that are considered individually or collectively material to the financial statements provided the lawyer and auditor have reached an understanding on the limits of materiality for this purpose.
(ID: 6840)

93. (a)   The passage is a quote from a sample inquiry letter to legal counsel. It is rare to refer to "our auditors" in a letter to that auditor; it is more likely that a third party is being addressed using this language. Management's representation letter states that the financial statements are presented fairly in conformity with GAAP and that, "there are no…other liabilities or gain or loss contingencies that are required to be accrued or disclosed…." That information was furnished to auditors generally is inappropriate for footnotes to financial statement.   (ID: 7817)

94. (b)   When restrictions that significantly limit the scope of the audit are imposed by the client, ordinarily the auditor should disclaim an opinion on the financial statements.   (ID: 7796)

95. (b)   The letter of inquiry to the client's attorney is the primary means the auditor has to obtain corroboration of information furnished by management concerning litigation, claims, and assessments. The terms mentioned in answers a. and c. might be covered by the attorney, but are not the primary reasons the auditor makes the request. The items in answer d. normally are furnished by management (or management may request that the attorney prepare the description and evaluation); they are not the primary reason that the auditor sends a letter of inquiry.   (ID: 5139)

96. (c)   As the events that should be considered in the financial accounting for and reporting of litigation, claims, and assessments are matters within the direct knowledge and, often, control of management of an entity, management is the primary source of information about such matters. Accordingly, the independent auditor's procedures should include inquiry and discussion with management concerning the policies and procedures adopted for identifying, evaluating, and accounting for litigation, claims, and assessments. A letter of audit inquiry to the client's lawyer is the auditor's primary means of obtaining corroboration of the information furnished by management concerning litigation, claims, and assessments. However, the lawyer does not evaluate the client's ability to continue as a going concern or whether all litigation, claims, and assessments have been recorded or disclosed in the financial statements. Examination of documents in the client's lawyer's possession is an atypical procedure.   (ID: 6002)

97. (a)   Only the statement in answer a. would require further clarification. The statements in answers b., c., and d. clearly indicate the probability of an unfavorable outcome.   (ID: 8156)

98. (d)   When a client's lawyer is unable to form a conclusion about the likelihood of an unfavorable outcome of pending litigation because of inherent uncertainties and the effect on the financial statements could be material, the auditor ordinarily will conclude that an explanatory paragraph should be added to the report.   (ID: 5682)

99. (d)   The refusal of a client to allow necessary communications with a lawyer is a scope limitation that usually results in a disclaimer of opinion; knowing that an audit could not be performed, a CPA could not accept the engagement. A CPA need not understand a client's operations and industry when accepting an engagement if the CPA reasonably can expect to gain an appropriate understanding. Recurring operating losses do not prohibit audit completion. An inquiry of the predecessor auditor is a necessary procedure because the predecessor auditor may be able to provide information that will assist the successor auditor in determining whether to accept the engagement. However, the review of the predecessor auditor's working papers assists the successor auditor in the planning of the engagement. The successor auditor may initiate this after accepting the engagement. Furthermore, although the predecessor auditor should ordinarily permit the successor auditor to review the working papers, the extent, if any, to which a predecessor auditor permits access to working papers, is a matter of judgment.   (ID: 8384)

100. (b)   The auditor's procedures should include a discussion with management about the policies and procedures adopted for identifying, evaluating, and accounting for litigation, claims, and assessments. The events or conditions that should be considered in the financial accounting for and reporting of litigation, claims, and assessments are matters within the direct knowledge and, often, control of management of an entity. Accordingly, management is the primary source of information about such matters. It is the auditor's responsibility to conclude whether the client's litigation is properly disclosed. The auditor requests the client's attorney's opinion on this, not the clerk of the court. The clerk of the court would not have the information needed. The auditor would examine documents in the client's possession; not the lawyer's possession. The auditor would not likely inspect documents in the client's lawyer's possession due to confidentiality considerations. If the attorney's response does not provide enough information, the auditor would arrange a conference with the attorney rather than request documentation. It would not be appropriate for the auditor to contact the client's adversaries' legal representatives.   (ID: 8643)

101. (c)   Loss contingencies include those arising from litigation, claims and assessments. A letter of inquiry to the client's lawyer is the auditor's primary means of corroboration of the information furnished by management about such matters. The financial statements (including footnotes), which may include accrual or disclosure of loss contingencies, are part of the information furnished by management. Performing appropriate analytical procedures and checking the arithmetic accuracy of the accounting records are not likely to provide information about the evaluation of loss contingencies. (ID: 8615)

102. (b)   The primary reason for a letter of audit inquiry to the client's attorneys is to obtain corroboration of the information furnished by management concerning litigation, claims, and assessments. The attorney's legal expertise is sought by the auditor, not the assurance that matters are properly accounted for. The letter of inquiry should address two lists; one comprised of pending or threatened litigation, claims, and assessments; and the other, unasserted claims and assessments that would, if asserted, have a reasonable possibility of an unfavorable outcome. The pending matters list is not limited to those that management believes have a reasonable possibility of an unfavorable outcome. And although an attorney's response does include addressing the description of matters and the evaluation of their likely outcome, the primary reason for the auditor's request is to corroborate management's information. The attorney is asked to evaluate the likelihood of an unfavorable outcome, not give an opinion using the terms *possible*, *probable* or *remote*. (ID: 8620)

103. (d)   An auditor would not seek an evaluation of the client's ability to continue as a going concern from an attorney regardless of the cause of the client's financial difficulties; that is the auditor's responsibility and does not involve legal expertise. Answers a., b., and c. would be likely to be covered in the client's attorney's response to a letter of audit inquiry. (ID: 8651)

104. (d)   Management is the primary source of information about litigation, claims and assessments, however, most audits include other procedures (usually for other purposes) that may also assist the auditor in identifying such matters. These include reading minutes of meetings of stockholders, directors, and appropriate committees held during and subsequent to the period being audited; reading contracts, loan agreements, leases, and correspondence from taxing or other governmental authorities, and similar documents; obtaining information concerning guarantees from bank confirmation forms, and inspecting other documents for possible guarantees by the client. Answers a. and b. could possibly reveal evidence of litigation, claims, and assessments, but correspondence from taxing authorities is a more likely source. Applying ratio analysis on the current year's liability accounts is the least likely procedure of the answers to disclose such information. (ID: 8839)

105. (c)   An auditor's primary method to corroborate information on litigation, claims, and assessments is to review the response from the client's lawyer to a letter of audit inquiry. Verifying attorney-client privilege would not provide information about litigation, claims, and assessments. Examining legal invoices does not provide as much evidence about the substance (nature) of the litigation, claims, and assessments as the attorney's letter. Reviewing management's written representations is an incorrect response because management cannot corroborate its own information. (ID: 9365)

106. (b)   The letter requests the attorney to provide an evaluation of the likelihood of an unfavorable outcome and an estimate, if one can be made, of the amount or range of potential loss concerning litigation, claims, and assessments. The statement that it is the attorney's belief that the action can be settled for less than the damages claimed begs for a follow-up question (clarification) as to whether an estimate of how much less can be made; the other answers are definitive responses. (ID: 9904)

Audit Documentation

107. (b)   A standard confirmation request sent to a financial institution at which the client has both a checking or savings account and a loan would include requests on one form regarding the cash balance and the loan balance and, in addition, a description of the loan collateral. While confirmation of accounts receivable is a generally accepted auditing procedure, confirmation of accounts payable is not. It generally is used only in cases of suspected fraud, sloppy or missing records, or suspected understatements. An entity holding inventory on consignment generally would not have information related to contingent liabilities. Accrued interest receivable most likely would be related to notes receivable rather than accounts receivable. (ID: 5987)

108. (b)   The auditor is required to document his or her understanding of the entity's internal control. However, the form and extent of documentation is influenced by the size and complexity of the entity, as well as

the nature of the entity's controls. Therefore, a flowchart depicting the segregation of duties and authorization of transactions is not necessarily required. Answers a., c., and d. are required in all audits. (ID: 2321)

109. (c) Lead schedules generally summarize information, such as a summary of all cash accounts with debits and credits summarized into major categories and information about beginning and ending balances. (ID: 6628)

110. (a) A physical count of assets that could be stolen readily (negotiable securities or gems, for instance) should include acknowledgement that the assets are again in the client's custody, if they are handled by the auditor. Sold securities would not be counted, so an analysis of realized gains and losses is not related closely to a count. An evaluation of control policies concerning physical access or negotiation generally would be documented with other control evaluations, not with substantive tests. (ID: 6937)

111. (d) The matters noted in answers a., b., and c. would all have a significant impact on the quantity and content of the auditor's working papers. While the content of the representation letter may affect the quantity and content of the auditor's workpapers, the effect is minimal. (ID: 5146)

112. (d) Permanent files contain items of continuing interest, such as debt agreements, internal control flowcharts, and articles of incorporation. The other items are of temporary interest only. (ID: 6007)

113. (d) Workpapers for each asset, liability, and equity account begin with a lead schedule summarizing the account's balance per the general ledger, and then showing adjusting and reclassification entries, and the final balance per audit. The lead schedule also includes the auditor's conclusion about whether the account is stated fairly. (ID: 2320)

114. (c) Working trial balances contain reclassification and adjustments columns. The items in answers a., b., and d. are included in the audit workpapers, but are not included in the working trial balance. (ID: 5145)

115. (c) The management representation letter should address that there are no violations or possible violations of laws or regulations whose effects should be considered for disclosure in the financial statements or as a basis for recording a loss contingency. (ID: 5137)

116. (b) Sufficient and appropriate documentation should include evidence that the audit working papers have been reviewed. It should be clear who reviewed specified elements of the audit work performed and when. Accounting estimates are an example of the significant findings or issues that should be documented along with the actions taken to address them and the basis for the final conclusions reached. If additional evidence is required to document significant findings or issues, the original evidence should not be deleted. Audit documentation is the property of the auditor, not the client. Note: The retention period of at least five years from the report release date is correct for nonissuers—it is seven years for issuers. After the documentation completion date, the auditor must not delete or discard audit documentation before the end of the specified retention period; any time prior to this date, the auditor may make changes to delete superseded or incorrect material. (ID: 9395)

Related Parties

117. (c) Business structure and operating style occasionally are designed deliberately to obscure relationships. Because compensating balance arrangements and nonmonetary transactions obscure the form of transactions, they are suspect. Compensating balance arrangements involve related parties more often than the other answer options. Segregation of duties applies whether the parties to a transaction are related or not. Reasonable and unreasonable accounting estimates both exist with and without related parties present. Entities frequently have recurring transactions with independent entities. (ID: 7811)

118. (d) An auditor should place primary emphasis on evaluating the adequacy of the disclosure of the related-party transactions. The other answers are among the possible procedures used to evaluate the adequacy of related-party disclosures. (ID: 5686)

119. (a) When searching for related-party transactions, the auditor should obtain an understanding of each subsidiary's relationship to the total entity because business structure and operating style are occasionally deliberately designed to obscure related-party transactions. Answers b., c., and d. are not reasons for an auditor to obtain an understanding of each subsidiary's relationship to the total entity. (ID: 185)

120. (c) After identifying related-party transactions, the auditor should obtain an understanding of the business purpose of the transactions. The other answers are all procedures that may be performed later. (ID: 5142)

121. (c) Except for routine transactions, it will generally not be possible to determine whether a particular transaction would have taken place if the parties had not been related, or assuming it would have taken place, what the terms and manner of settlement would have been. Accordingly, it is difficult to substantiate representations that a transaction was consummated on terms equivalent to those that prevail in arm's-length transactions. If such a representation is included in the financial statements and the auditor believes that the representation is unsubstantiated by management, the auditor should express a qualified or adverse opinion because of a departure from GAAP, depending on materiality. The disclosure of loans below market value is additional support for items included in the financial statements. Describing the exchange of real estate or presenting the dollar volume of related-party transactions and any changes in the method of establishing terms from prior periods are all typical disclosure items that should be included in the financial statements for them to be in conformity with GAAP. (ID: 3940)

122. (d) Transactions that because of their nature may be indicative of the existence of related parties include borrowing or lending on an interest-free basis or at a rate of interest significantly above or below market rates prevailing at the time of the transaction; selling real estate at a price that differs significantly from its appraised value; exchanging property for similar property in a nonmonetary transaction; and making loans with no scheduled terms for when or how the funds will be repaid. (ID: 2974)

123. (d) The event that is the least likely indicator of the existence of related-party transactions is the writing off obsolete inventory to net realizable value just before year-end. A company should have policies and procedures in place to do this and it would be considered by an auditor searching for related-party transactions. The other three answers are indicators of the existence of related-party transactions. (ID: 8822)

124. (c) The auditor should be aware that the substance of a particular transaction could be significantly different from its form and that financial statements should recognize the substance of particular transactions rather than merely their legal form. Established accounting principles ordinarily do not require transactions with related parties to be accounted for on a basis different from that which would be appropriate if the parties were not related—generally, the auditor should view related-party transactions within the framework of existing pronouncements. The identification of related parties relates more to the disclosure concern rather than the auditor's review for their proper accounting. (ID: 9269)

125. (b) One of the first steps an auditor should perform to determine the existence of related parties is to request a list of related parties from management. Reviewing proxy and other material filed with the SEC is a close second choice, but it is usually best to start with inquiries to management and then corroborate those results with the SEC and other regulatory agencies. Reviewing the company's business structure should be done to determine the scope of work to be performed with respect to possible transactions with related parties rather than determining their existence. Examining invoices, contracts, and purchase orders would be done after related-party transactions have been identified rather than to determine their existence. It would be done to obtain satisfaction or evidence concerning the purpose, nature, and extent of related-party transactions and their effect on the financial statements. (ID: 9356)

PERFORMANCE BY TOPICS

Each category below parallels a topic covered in Chapter 4. Record the number and percentage of questions you answered correctly in each topic.

Audit Evidence

Question #	Correct	√
1		
2		
3		
4		
5		
6		
7		
8		
9		
10		
11		
12		
13		
14		
15		
16		
17		
18		
19		
20		
21		

Questions   21

Correct   _____
% Correct   _____

Internal Auditors

Question #	Correct	√
22		
23		
24		
25		
26		
27		
28		
29		
30		
31		
32		
33		
34		
35		

Questions   14

Correct
% Correct

Management Representations

Question #	Correct	√
36		
37		
38		
39		
40		
41		
42		
43		
44		
45		
46		
47		

Questions   12

Correct   _____
% Correct   _____

Analytics

Question #	Correct	√
48		
49		
50		
51		
52		
53		
54		
55		
56		
57		
58		
59		
60		
61		
62		
63		
64		
65		
66		
67		
68		
69		
70		
71		
72		
73		
74		
75		
76		
77		
78		
79		
80		
81		
82		
83		

Questions   36

Correct   _____
% Correct   _____

Using a Specialist's Work

Question #	Correct	√
84		
85		
86		
87		
88		
89		

Questions   6

Correct   _____
% Correct   _____

Inquiry of Client's Lawyer

Question #	Correct	√
90		
91		
92		
93		
94		
95		
96		
97		
98		
99		
100		
101		
102		
103		
104		
105		
106		

Questions   17

Correct   _____
% Correct

Audit Documentation

Question #	Correct	√
107		
108		
109		
110		
111		
112		
113		
114		
115		
116		

Questions   10

Correct   _____
% Correct   _____

Related Parties

Question #	Correct	√
117		
118		
119		
120		
121		
122		
123		
124		
125		

Questions   9

Correct   _____
% Correct   _____

Solution 4-2 SIMULATION ANSWER: Audit Procedure and Purpose

a	b	c
Description of Procedure	**Audit Procedure Performed**	**Classification of Audit Procedure**
1. Examined sales invoices to see if they were initialed by the credit manager indicating credit approval.	E. Inspection	B. Test of controls
2. Compared this year's expenses with last year's expenses and investigated unusual fluctuations.	A. Analytical procedure	A. Substantive procedures
3. Requested responses directly from customers.	B. Confirmation	A. Substantive procedures
4. Questioned management about subsequent events.	D. Inquiry	A. Substantive procedures
5. Observed the accounting clerk record the daily deposit of cash receipts.	G. Observation	B. Test of controls
6. Examined invoices to support additions to the fixed asset account during the year.	E. Inspection	A. Substantive procedures
7. Agreed sales invoices to credit files to determine whether the customer had a credit file and had been approved for credit.	I. Reperformance	B. Test of controls
8. Asked the accounting manager how often cash is deposited and by whom.	D. Inquiry	B. Test of controls

1. E. Inspection; B. Test of controls

Inspection consists of examining records or documents, whether internal or external, in paper form, electronic form or other media. In this case, the auditor inspected the sales invoices for evidence of authorization by the credit manager. Approval of sales by the credit manager is a control to prevent credit sales to customers who have not been approved for credit. This procedure tested that control.

2. A. Analytical procedure; A. Substantive procedures

Analytical procedures consist of evaluations of financial information made by a study of plausible relationships among both financial and nonfinancial data. Analytical procedures also encompass the investigation of identified fluctuations and relationships that are inconsistent with other relevant information or deviate significantly from predicted amounts. They range from simple comparisons, like this example, to the use of complex models. The comparison of expenses between years and the investigation of unusual fluctuations was used as a substantive procedure performed to detect material misstatements in expenses for the assertions of completeness and accuracy.

3.   B. Confirmation; A. Substantive procedures

Confirmation, which is a specific type of inquiry, is the process of obtaining and evaluating a direct communication from a third party in response to a request for information about a particular item affecting financial statement assertions. It was used as a substantive test of details of the assertions of completeness, existence, and accuracy of the customers' accounts.

4.   D. Inquiry; A. Substantive procedures

Inquiry consists of seeking information of knowledgeable persons, both financial and nonfinancial, inside or outside of the entity. Inquiries can be formal written inquiries or informal oral inquiries. The auditor should consider the reasonableness and consistency of the responses in light of the results of other procedures and the auditor's knowledge of the entity and its industry—evaluating responses to inquiries is an integral part of the inquiry process. Inquiry by itself does not provide sufficient appropriate audit evidence to detect misstatements or to test the operating effectiveness of controls; thus, auditors complement inquiries with other procedures to corroborate the responses received. This inquiry was used as a substantive procedure to test the assertion of the completeness of disclosures regarding type two subsequent events and other assertions, depending on the nature of the event, regarding type one events.

5.   G. Observation; B. Test of controls

Observation consists of looking at a process or procedure being performed by others. Observation provides audit evidence about the performance of a process or procedure, but is limited to the point in time at which the observation takes place and by the fact that the act of being observed may affect how the process or procedure is performed. Depositing cash receipts on a daily basis is a control. This procedure tested that control.

6.   E. Inspection; A. Substantive procedures

Inspection consists of examining records or documents, whether internal or external, in paper form, electronic form or other media. In this case, the auditor inspected the invoices to see if they provided evidence for the additions to the fixed asset account.

7.   I. Reperformance; B. Test of controls

Reperformance is the auditor's independent execution of procedures or controls that were originally performed as part of the entity's internal control, either manually or through the use of computer-assisted audit techniques (CAAT). Investigating a customer's credit worthiness and approving a credit sale by reference to the customer's resulting credit file is a control to prevent credit sales to customers who have not been approved for credit. This procedure tested that control.

8.   D. Inquiry; B. Test of controls

Inquiry consists of seeking information of knowledgeable persons, both financial and nonfinancial, inside or outside of the entity. Inquiries can be formal written inquiries or informal oral inquiries. The auditor should consider the reasonableness and consistency of the responses in light of the results of other procedures and the auditor's knowledge of the entity and its industry—evaluating responses to inquiries is an integral part of the inquiry process. Inquiry by itself does not provide sufficient appropriate audit evidence to detect misstatements or to test the operating effectiveness of controls; thus, auditors complement inquiries with other procedures to corroborate the responses received. This inquiry was used as a test of the controls over the deposit of cash receipts.

(ID: 9833)

Solution 4-3 SIMULATION ANSWER: Documentation

Excerpts From Working Papers	Source
1. During our audit we discovered evidence of the company's failure to safeguard inventory from loss, damage, and misappropriation.	B
2. The company considers the decline in value of equity securities classified as available-for-sale to be temporary.	N
3. Was the difference of opinion on the accrued pension liabilities that existed between the engagement personnel and the actuarial specialist resolved in accordance with firm policy and appropriately documented?	M
4. Our audit is designed to provide reasonable assurance of detecting misstatements that, in our judgment, could have a material effect on the financial statements taken as a whole. Consequently, our audit will not necessarily detect all misstatements that exist due to error, fraudulent financial reporting, or misappropriation of assets.	H
5. There have been no communications from regulatory agencies concerning noncompliance with or deficiencies in financial reporting practices.	N
6. Nothing came to our attention that caused us to believe that at October 31, year 1, there was any change in the capital stock, increase in long-term debt, or decrease in consolidated net current assets or stockholders' equity as compared with the amounts shown in the September 30, year 1 unaudited condensed consolidated balance sheet.	I
7. It is our opinion that the possible liability to the company in this proceeding is nominal in amount.	D
8. As discussed in Note 4 to the financial statements, the company experienced a net loss for the year ended July 31, year 1, and is currently in default under substantially all of its debt agreements. In addition, on September 25, year 1, the company filed a prenegotiated voluntary petition for relief under Chapter 11 of the U.S. Bankruptcy Code. These matters raise substantial doubt about the company's ability to continue as a going concern.	L
9. During the year under audit, we were advised that management consulted with Better & Best, CPAs. The purpose of this consultation was to obtain another CPA firm's opinion concerning the company's recognition of certain revenue that we believe should be deferred to future periods. Better & Best's opinion was consistent with our opinion, so management did not recognize the revenue in the current year.	F
10. The company believes that all material expenditures that have been deferred to future periods will be recoverable.	N

1. B

The auditor's communication to the audit committee regarding significant deficiencies includes a description of the conditions noted.

2. N

Management is a knowledgeable source of the company's viewpoint, beliefs, intentions, and occurrence of events.

3. M

An auditor's review notes include reminders of select conditions to allow a double check to ensure that all matters are resolved appropriately.

4. H

Appropriate places for disclaimers are the engagement letter and post-engagement reports. The statement speaks of the audit in the future ("Consequently, our audit will not…") from the perspective of the auditor.

5. N

Management is a knowledgeable source of the company's viewpoint, beliefs, intentions, and occurrence of events.

6. I

Letters to underwriters may contain negative assurance, which is used in few instances, certainly not in a report on significant deficiencies. A practitioner's report on a management assertion would not be discussing stock-holder's equity in relation to previous unaudited financial statements; it would discuss the practitioner's work in relation to management's assertion.

7. D

An opinion regarding liability related to a proceeding is usually from a lawyer in response to an audit inquiry letter. The management representation letter usually has a less specific statement of all possible liabilities being included in the financial statements as appropriate. These are the two parties most likely to be knowledgeable about proceedings related to the client.

8. L

The phrases *substantial doubt* and *ability to continue as a going concern* are required in the auditor's report when there is a going concern uncertainty.

9. F

The auditor's communication to the audit committee should include any disagreements, whether or not resolved, with management about matters that, individually or in the aggregate, could have a significant impact on the financial statements.

10. N

Management is a knowledgeable source of the company's viewpoint, beliefs, intentions, and occurrence of events.

(ID: 9218)

————————————

Solution 4-4 SIMULATION ANSWER: Documentation

Excerpts From Working Papers	Source
1. Our use of professional judgment and the assessment of audit risk and materiality for the purpose of our audit mean that matters may have existed that would have been assessed differently by you. We make no representation as to the sufficiency or appropriateness of the information in our working papers for your purposes.	P
2. Indicate in the space provided below whether this information agrees with your records. If there are exceptions, please provide any information that will assist the auditor in reconciling the difference.	J
3. Blank checks are maintained in an unlocked cabinet along with the check-signing machine. Blank checks and the check-signing machine should be locked in separate locations to prevent the embezzlement of funds.	B
4. Our audit cannot be relied upon to disclose significant deficiencies in the design or operation of internal control. Nevertheless, we will communicate to you all significant deficiencies and potential areas for improvement that we become aware of during the course of our audit.	H
5. The timetable set by management to complete our audit was unreasonable considering the failure of the company's personnel to complete schedules on a timely basis and delays in providing necessary information.	F
6. Several employees have disabled the anti-virus detection software on their PCs because the software slows the processing of data and occasionally rings false alarms. The company should obtain anti-virus software that runs continuously at all system entry points and that cannot be disabled by unauthorized personnel.	B
7. In connection with an audit of our financial statements, management has prepared, and furnished to our auditors, a description and evaluation of certain contingencies.	C
8. The company has no plans or intentions that may materially affect the carrying value or classification of assets and liabilities.	N
9. In planning the sampling application, was appropriate consideration given to the relationship of the sample to the audit objective and to preliminary judgments about materiality levels?	M

　　1.　P

The client, a CPA performing a review, and a successor auditor are most likely to be the external viewers of workpapers. Typically, each successor will try to view a predecessor's workpapers, but the opposite will be rare. A client is the most atypical user of the three. Further, there is no answer option with a communication regarding the client or reviewer viewing the workpapers.

　　2.　J

A confirmation request seeks an indication of agreement between provided information with another's records. The language in this statement is more suitable to an accounts receivable confirmation (a relatively straightforward matter of matching amounts) than an inquiry of legal counsel (a relatively complex matter requiring the judgment by counsel, and, thus, a more complex letter of inquiry).

　　3.　B

The auditor's communication to the audit committee regarding significant deficiencies includes a description of the conditions noted.

　　4.　H

The statement speaks of the future ("…we will communicate to you….") from the perspective of the auditor. It is most likely that an auditor would send this message to management. The appropriate place for this disclaimer is in the engagement letter.

5. F

The auditor's communication to the audit committee should include any serious difficulties encountered in dealing with management related to the performance of the audit.

6. B

The auditor's communication to the audit committee regarding significant deficiencies includes a description of the conditions noted.

7. C

This statement is from the entity's management ("our financial statements") to a party (other than the auditor) who is knowledgeable about the company's contingent liabilities. In connection with audits, lawyers frequently are asked to provide their opinion of contingent liabilities related to the services that they provide to clients.

8. N

Management is a knowledgeable source of the company's viewpoint, beliefs, intentions, and occurrence of events.

9. M

An auditor's review notes include reminders to check on issues where mistakes have a relatively high probability of being made.

(ID: 9220)

_____

Solution 4-5 SIMULATION ANSWER: Ratios

	Ratio	Year 2	Year 1
1.	Current ratio	H. 3.1	2.5
2.	Quick ratio	E. 1.6	1.3
3.	Accounts receivable turnover	K. 7.5	5.5
4.	Inventory turnover	G. 3.0	2.5
5.	Total asset turnover	D. 1.5	1.2
6.	Gross margin percentage	T. 40%	35%
7.	Net operating margin percentage	P. 22%	25%
8.	Times interest earned	N. 16.5	10.3
9.	Total debt to equity percentage	U. 60%	50%

1. H

The current ratio is total current assets divided by total current liabilities. ($1,240,000 / $400,000 = 3.1)

2. E

The quick (or acid-test) ratio is cash plus marketable securities plus net receivables divided by current liabilities. [($240,000 + $400,000) / $400,000 = 1.6]

3. K

Accounts receivable turnover is net credit sales divided by average net receivables. {$3,000,000 / [($400,000 + $400,000) / 2] = 7.5}

4. G

Inventory turnover is cost of goods sold divided by average inventory. {$1,800,000 / [($600,000 + $600,000) / 2] = 3.0}

5. D

Total asset turnover is sales divided by total assets. ($3,000,000 / $2,000.000 = 1.5)

6. T

Gross margin percentage is the gross margin divided by sales, expressed as a percentage. ($1,200,000 / $3,000,000 = 0.4 = 40%)

7. P

Net operating margin percentage is operating income divided by sales, expressed as a percentage. [($660,000 / $3,000,000 = .22 = 22%)]

8. N

Times interest earned is income before income taxes and interest charges divided by interest charges. ($660,000 / $40,000 = 16.5)

9. U

Total debt to equity percentage is total liabilities divided by owners' equity, expressed as a percentage. [($400,000 + $350,000) / ($750,000 + $500,000) = 0.6 = 60%]

(ID: 9221)

Solution 4-6 SIMULATION ANSWER: Financial Statement Analysis

Auditor's Observed Changes	Explanations
1. Allowance for doubtful accounts increased from the prior year, but allowance for doubtful accounts as a percentage of accounts receivable decreased from the prior year. (3 explanations)	A, B, E
2. Long-term debt increased from the prior year, but interest expense increased a larger-than-proportionate amount than long-term debt. (1 explanation)	P
3. Operating income increased from the prior year although the entity was less profitable than in the prior year. (2 explanations)	L, P
4. Gross margin percentage was unchanged from the prior year although gross margin increased from the prior year. (1 explanation)	H

1. A, B, E

The allowance for doubtful accounts as a percentage of accounts receivable will decrease when the allowance for doubtful accounts decreases proportionately less than the accounts receivable does or when accounts receivable increases. Due to recording consignment items shipped during the last month as sales, accounts receivable is overstated. Due to not recording a significant number of credit memos for returned merchandise, accounts receivable is overstated. However, these occurrences do not impact the allowance for doubtful accounts. A larger percentage of sales occurring during the last month of the year, as compared to the prior year, increases the amount in accounts receivable. This increases average accounts receivable, as compared to last year, without increasing the allowance for doubtful accounts, as compared to last year.

2. P

An increase in the interest rate is the only explanation for the larger-than-proportionate increase in interest expense.

3. L, P

Operating income does not include interest or income tax expense; the rates for these apparently increased.

4. H

Percentages measure proportional changes. The items being compared must have changed proportionately if the percentage did not change. (ID: 9222)

Solution 4-7 SIMULATION ANSWER: Substantive Tests

Part a:

Objective	Substantive Tests
1. Verify existence of accounts receivable.	A
2. Determine that inventory balance is accurately stated.	E

1. A

Performing tests of subsequent cash receipts after the balance sheet date would help verify the existence of accounts receivable since they should have been paid by then if they were valid balances. False accounts receivable would not be paid.

2. E

Performing shipping cut-off procedures would help determine that the inventory balance is accurately stated because to include inventory that was shipped before the end of the year would overstate the inventory balance.

Part b:

Answers: D, F

Examining paid vendors' invoices would allow the auditor to determine whether liabilities are valued accurately in the financial statements. Also, examining an analysis of inventory turnover would allow the auditor to determine whether there may be slow moving or obsolete inventory. (ID: 9224)

_____

Solution 4-8 SIMULATION ANSWER: Analytics

Part a:

Ratio	Year 2	Year 1
1. Current ratio	3.42	3.07
2. Return on equity	13.77%	28.21%

1. 3.42

The current ratio equals current assets divided by current liabilities (85,280,000/24,965,000).

2. 13.77%

Return on equity equals net income divided by average stockholder's equity. Editor's Note: Be careful to follow directions. This problem specifies that for turnover ratios, year-end balances should be used (13,815,000 / 100,315,000).

Part b:

Ratio	Year 2	Year 1	Explanations
1. Days sales in accounts receivable	40	39	E
2. Operating profit margin	22.05%	34.62%	B

1. E

Days sales in accounts receivable equals 360 days divided by receivables turnover. Receivables turnover equals net credit sales divided by average net receivables. If a larger percentage of sales occurred during the last month of the year, average receivables would increase which would then decrease receivables turnover, thereby increasing days sales in accounts receivable.

2. B

Operating profit margin equals operating profit divided by total sales revenue. Operating profit equals gross profit minus operating expenses. Therefore, if operating expenses increase at a higher rate than sales revenue, then operating profit would decrease more than sales revenue would increase, thereby decreasing operating profit margin. (ID: 9223)

_____

Solution 4-9 SIMULATION ANSWER: Ratios

Ratio	Year 2	Year 1
1. Current ratio	3.1	2.5
2. Quick ratio	1.6	1.3
3. Accounts receivable turnover	7.5	9.0
4. Inventory turnover	3.0	1.5

1. 3.1

The current ratio is total current assets divided by total current liabilities. ($310,000 / $100,000 = 3.1)

2. 1.6

The quick (or acid-test) ratio is cash plus marketable securities plus net receivables divided by current liabilities. [($60,000 + $100,000) / $100,000 = 1.6]

3. 7.5

Accounts receivable turnover is net credit sales divided by average net receivables. {$750,000 / [($100,000 + $100,000) / 2] = 7.5}

4. 3.0

Inventory turnover is cost of goods sold divided by average inventory. {$450,000 / [($150,000 + $150,000) / 2] = 3.0}   (ID: 9225)

Solution 4-10 SIMULATION ANSWER: Analytics

Observed Changes	Explanations
1. Inventory turnover increased substantially from the prior year. (3 explanations)	A, B, D
2. Accounts receivable turnover decreased substantially from the prior year. (3 explanations)	A, B, E

1. A, B, D

Inventory turnover is cost of goods sold divided by average inventory. When cost of goods sold is overstated, this ratio will increase. Due to recording consignment items shipped during the last month as sales, the cost of goods sold is overstated. Due to not recording a significant number of credit memos for returned merchandise, the cost of goods sold is overstated. When average inventory is understated, this ratio will increase. The incorrect exclusion of inventory received before year-end, caused average inventory to be understated.

2. A, B, E

Accounts receivable turnover is net credit sales divided by average net receivables. This ratio will decrease when net credit sales decreases or average net receivables increases. Due to recording consignment items shipped during the last month as sales, sales and accounts receivable are both overstated by the same amount. However, proportionately, accounts receivable increases more than net credit sales, decreasing the ratio. Due to not recording a significant number of credit memos for returned merchandise, sales and accounts receivable are disproportionately overstated. A larger percentage of sales occurring during the last month of the year, as compared to the prior year, increases the amount in accounts receivable. This increases average accounts receivable, as compared to last year, without increasing sales, as compared to last year.   (ID: 9226)

Solution 4-11 SIMULATION ANSWER: Research

AU	§	336	16	(ID: 89454)

16. The auditor may, as a result of the report or findings of the specialist, decide to add explanatory language to his or her standard report or depart from an unqualified opinion. Reference to and identification of the specialist may be made in the auditor's report if the auditor believes such reference will facilitate an understanding of the reason for the explanatory paragraph or the departure from the unqualified opinion.

Solution 4-12 SIMULATION ANSWER: Analytics

A	B	C	D	E	F
Proposed Journal Entry	**Debit**	**Credit**	**Earnings per Share**	**Days Sales in Accounts Receivable**	**Gross Profit**

1. Sales reported after year-end that should have been reported before year-end:
Cost of sales
Accounts receivable
    Sales
    Inventory
	
	90
	100
	
		100
		90
			Increase	Increase	Increase

2. Error in adjusting entry:
Cost of sales
PP&E
Utilities expense
Cash
    Sales
    Accrued expenses
    Inventory
    Interest expense
	
	45
	45
	12
	10
		
		45
		12
		45
		10
			Decrease	Decrease	No Impact

3. To record current and deferred income taxes:
Income tax expense-current
Deferred tax asset
    Income tax expense-deferred
    Deferred tax liability
    Income tax payable
	
	50
	15
		
		10
		5
		50
			Decrease	No Impact	No Impact

Ratios:

Earnings per Share
$$\frac{\text{Net Income} - \text{Preferred Dividends}}{\text{Average Number of Common Shares Outstanding}}$$

Days Sales in Accounts Receivable
$$\frac{\text{Net Accounts Receivable}}{\text{Net Sales} / 360}$$

Gross Profit
$$\text{Net Sales-Cost of Sales}$$

1. Earnings per Share: Increase

   The increase in sales increased net income so the earnings per share ratio would increase.

   Days Sales in Accounts Receivable: Increase

   Accounts receivable increased proportionately more than sales per day increased so the days sales in accounts receivable ratio would increase.

   Gross Profit: Increase

   Sales increased more than the cost of sales so the gross profit ratio would increase.

2. Earnings per Share: Decrease

   The increase in expense decreased net income so the earnings per share ratio would decrease.

   Days Sales in Accounts Receivable: Decrease

   Accounts receivable did not change and sales per day increased so the days sales in accounts receivable ratio would decrease.

Gross Profit: No impact

Sales and cost of sales increased by the same amount so there was no change in the gross profit ratio.

3. Earnings per Share: Decrease

The increase in taxes decreased net income so the earnings per share ratio would decrease.

Days Sales in Accounts Receivable: No impact

The accounts that changed are not used in the calculation of this ratio.

Gross Profit: No impact

The accounts that changed are not used in the calculation of this ratio. (ID: 89451)

___

Solution 4-13 SIMULATION ANSWER: Analytics

Ratio	Year 2	Year 1	Explanations
1. Debt to equity	1.99	4.61	D
2. Gross profit percentage	38.00%	41.00%	F

1. D

The debt to equity ratio equals total liabilities divided by shareholder's equity. Therefore, if capital stock was issued during the year, equity would increase, thereby decreasing the ratio.

2. F

Gross profit percentage equals sales less the cost of goods sold divided by sales. If manufacturing cost decreased less than sales decreased during the year, then the numerator would decrease more in proportion to the denominator, thereby decreasing the percentage. (ID: 9227)

___

Solution 4-14 SIMULATION ANSWER: Audit Procedures

Audit Procedures	Type of Audit Procedures
1. During the physical inventory count, the auditor requested that certain material containers be opened to ensure they were not empty.	Inspection
2. During a site visit to a branch warehouse, the auditor noted unauthorized personnel have access to the inventory.	Observation
3. The auditor obtained a copy of the company's accounting manual and read the section on inventory to prepare for the physical inventory observation.	Inspection
4. The auditor sent a letter to the company's outside attorney accompanied by management's request for information concerning pending or threatened litigation, claims, and assessments.	Inquiry
5. The auditing firm's computer assisted audit specialist obtained an electronic billing file from the company and checked the accuracy of the summarized billings file.	Recalculation
6. The auditor obtained the company's aging of accounts receivable and independently created the aging of certain accounts.	Reperformance
7. The auditor scanned the repairs and maintenance account for unusually large amounts.	Analytical

(ID: 89452)

___

Solution 4-15 SIMULATION ANSWER: Attorney Letters

Situations	Audit Response	
	Financials	**Report**
1. Letter dated February 14, year 2: "I advise you that at and since December 31, year 1, I have not been engaged to give substantive attention to, or represent XYZ Co. in connection with any pending or threatened litigation, claims, or assessments, nor am I aware of any loss contingencies. No amounts were due to this office for services provided at December 31, year 1."	No impact on financial statement or footnotes	Legal response is appropriately dated
2. Letter dated January 21, year 2: "I advise you that at and since December 31, year 1, I have not been engaged to give substantive attention to, or represent XYZ Co. in connection with any pending or threatened litigation, claims, or assessments, nor am I aware of any loss contingencies. There were fees outstanding of $3,675 due to this office for services provided at December 31, year 1."	Verify amount due attorney is recorded in financial statements	Update legal response
3. Letter dated February 26, year 2: "I advise you that at and since December 31, year 1, I have not been engaged to give substantive attention to, or represent XYZ Co. in connection with any pending or threatened litigation, claims, or assessments, except as follows: K. Bowt v. XYZ Co.: This matter commenced in December, year 1. The plaintiff alleges discrimination relating to his termination on November 17, year 1. The company intends to defend this case vigorously. At this time, we are unable to evaluate the likelihood of an unfavorable outcome or estimate the amount or range of potential loss.	Disclosure in footnotes relating to nature of litigation, but no amount disclosed	Update report date
4. Letter dated March 16, year 2: "I advise you that at and since December 31, year 1, I have not been engaged to give substantive attention to, or represent XYZ Co. in connection with any pending or threatened litigation, claims, or assessments, except as follows: J. Myers v. XYZ Co.: This matter commenced in March, year 2. The plaintiff alleges discrimination relating to his termination on November 17, year 1. The company intends to defend this case vigorously. At this time, we are unable to evaluate the likelihood of an unfavorable outcome. The plaintiff is demanding $50,000.	Disclosure in footnotes relating to nature of litigation, but no amount disclosed	Update report date
5. Letter dated January 10, year 2: "I advise you that at and since December 31, year 1, I have not been engaged to give substantive attention to, or represent XYZ Co. in connection with any pending or threatened litigation, claims, or assessments, except as follows: R. Brown v. XYZ Co.: This matter commenced in November, year 1. The plaintiff alleges discrimination relating to his termination on March 17, year 1. The case was tentatively settled for $35,000, which will be covered by XYZ's insurance carrier.	Potential litigation settlement not accrued in financial statements; amount disclosed in footnote	Update legal response
6. Letter dated January 20, year 2: "I advise you that at and since December 31, year 1, I have not been engaged to give substantive attention to, or represent XYZ Co. in connection with any pending or threatened litigation, claims, or assessments, except as follows: L. Peep v. XYZ Co.: This matter commenced in November, year 1. The plaintiff alleges discrimination relating to his termination on March 17, year 1. The case was tentatively settled for $35,000.	Potential litigation settlement accrued in financial statements	Update legal response

1. Audit Response (Financials):   No impact on financial statements or notes to the financial statements

   The attorney reported no activity.

   Audit Response (Report):   Legal response is appropriately dated

   The date of the attorney's response and the release date of the audit report are only one day apart.

2. Audit Response (Financials):   Verify amount due attorney is recorded in financial statements

   The attorney's response included the balance of fees outstanding, but no pending litigation, claims, or assessments.

   Audit Response (Report):   Update legal response

   The date of the attorney's response (January 21, year 2) is not close enough to the release date of the auditor's report (February 15, year 2).

3. Audit Response (Financials):   Disclosure in notes to financial statements relating to nature of litigation, but no amount disclosed

   The attorney described pending litigation whose underlying cause was an event that existed at the date of the financial statements, but is unable to evaluate the likelihood of an unfavorable outcome or estimate the amount or range of the potential loss.

   Audit Response (Report):   Update report date

   The attorney's response is dated after the release date of the auditor's report, thus the report would need to be updated.

4. Audit Response (Financials):   Disclosure in notes to financial statements relating to nature of litigation, but no amount disclosed

   The attorney described pending litigation whose underlying cause was an event that existed at the date of the financial statements, but is unable to evaluate the likelihood of an unfavorable outcome.

   Audit Response (Report):   Update report date

   The attorney's response is dated after the release date of the auditor's report, thus the report would need to be updated.

5. Audit Response (Financials):   Potential litigation settlement not accrued in financial statements; amount disclosed in notes to financial statements

   The attorney's response described a tentative settlement of a claim (covered by the XYZ Company's insurance carrier) whose underlying cause was an event that existed at the date of the financial statements.

   Audit Response (Report):   Update legal response

   The date of the attorney's response (January 10, year 2) is not close enough to the release date of the auditor's report (February 15, year 2).

6. Audit Response (Financials):   Potential litigation settlement accrued in financial statements

   The attorney's response described a tentative settlement of a claim whose underlying cause was an event that existed at the date of the financial statements.

   Audit Response (Report):   Update legal response

   The date of the attorney's response (January 20, year 2) is not close enough to the release date of the auditor's report (February 15, year 2).   (ID: 89453)

COMPUTER-BASED TESTING (CBT) FORMAT

The exam is offered only in English and only in a CBT format. The AICPA provides a tutorial and sample tests (aicpa.org/becomeacpa/cpaexam/forcandidates/tutorialandsampletest) on their website. You must review these before the exam because neither is available at the test centers. The AICPA recommends reviewing the tutorial before the sample tests. Exposure to both will allow you to become familiar with how to navigate through the exam and gain exposure to the exam's directions. The time you spend with these materials will prevent you from losing any points on the exam due to unfamiliarity with the CBT system. View the tutorial and take the sample test right before you begin studying for an exam section and then again a week before the exam.

CHAPTER 5

AUDIT PROGRAMS

CHAPTER 5

AUDIT PROGRAMS

I. Substantive Procedures (AU 318 continued)

A. Overview

Substantive procedures, or tests, are designed to detect material misstatements at the relevant assertion level; they include tests of details of classes of transactions, account balances, and disclosures as well as analytical procedures. Substantive procedures should be designed to be responsive to the assessment of the risk of material misstatement with the objective of obtaining sufficient appropriate audit evidence to achieve the planned level of assurance at the relevant assertion level.

1. **Required** Due to the judgment involved in the auditor's risk assessment and inherent limitations in internal control, the auditor should design and perform substantive procedures for all relevant assertions related to each material class of transactions, account balance, and disclosure.

2. **Specific Procedures Required** The following audit procedures related to the financial statement reporting process are required in all audits:

   a. Agreeing the financial statements, including their accompanying notes, to the underlying accounting records.

   b. Examining material journal entries and other adjustments made during the course of preparing the financial statements. The nature and extent of these procedures depend on the nature and complexity of the entity's financial reporting system and the assessed risk of material misstatement.

3. **Significant Risks** The auditor should perform substantive procedures that are specifically responsive to significant risks identified in the auditor's risk assessment process as needing special audit consideration. For example, if the auditor determines that management is under pressure to meet earnings expectations, there may be a risk that management is inflating sales by improperly recognizing revenue related to sales agreements with terms that preclude revenue recognition or by invoicing sales before shipment. In these circumstances, the auditor may, for example, design external written confirmation requests not only to confirm outstanding amounts, but also to confirm the details of the sales agreements, including date, any rights of return, and delivery terms. Also, the auditor may find it effective to supplement such external written confirmations with inquiries of nonfinancial personnel in the entity regarding any changes in sales agreements and delivery terms.

B. Nature

The auditor should plan substantive procedures to be responsive to the planned level of detection risk. In some cases, analytics may be sufficient to reduce the planned level of detection risk to an acceptably low level, for example, when the auditor's risk assessment has been reduced by obtaining audit evidence from testing the operating effectiveness of controls. On the other hand, the auditor may determine that tests of details only are appropriate, or that a combination of analytics and tests of details is most responsive to the assessed risks. The determination of which substantive procedures are most appropriate to obtain the planned level of detection risk is affected by whether the auditor has obtained audit evidence about the operating effectiveness of controls to reduce control risk.

Exhibit 1 ▶ Substantive Tests Mnemonic

C	Confirm
O	Observe
R	Retrace (Trace)
V	Vouch
A	Analytics
I	Inquire
R	Recompute

1. **Tests of Details** Tests of details are ordinarily more appropriate to obtain audit evidence regarding certain relevant assertions about account balances. The auditor should design tests of details responsive to the assessed risk with the objective of obtaining sufficient appropriate audit evidence to achieve the planned level of assurance at the relevant assertion level.

   a. **Tests of Transactions** These tests are performed to determine whether the entity's transactions are recorded and summarized correctly in the accounting records. Many of these tests can be performed simultaneously with the tests of controls (i.e., dual-purpose tests).

   b. **Tests of Balances** These tests are concerned primarily with monetary misstatements in the account balances. Tests of balances relate to individual accounts, whereas the tests of transactions relate to the different transaction cycles.

2. **Analytical Procedures** Analytics generally are more applicable to large volumes of transactions that tend to be predictable over time. The following matters should be considered when designing substantive analytical procedures:

   a. The suitability of using substantive analytical procedures, given the assertions.

   b. The reliability of the data (internal or external) from which the expectation of recorded amounts or ratios is developed. The auditor should consider testing the controls, if any, over the entity's preparation of information to be used. Alternatively, the auditor may consider whether the information was subjected to audit testing in the current or prior period.

   c. Whether the expectation is sufficiently precise to identify the possibility of a material misstatement at the desired level of assurance.

   d. The amount of any difference in recorded amounts from expected values that is acceptable.

C. **Extent**
As the risk of material misstatement increases, the acceptable level of detection risk decreases; this means, the extent of substantive procedures must increase. Therefore, if the auditor has obtained satisfactory evidence regarding the operating effectiveness of controls to reduce the risk of material misstatement, substantive tests may be reduced as the acceptable level of detection risk increases.

D. **Timing**

1. **Interim Testing** When substantive procedures are performed at an interim date, the auditor should perform further substantive procedures or a combination of substantive procedures and tests of controls covering the remaining period to provide a reasonable basis for extending the audit conclusions to the end of the period. Interim testing increases the risk that misstatements existing at the period end will not be detected. This risk increases as the length of the remaining period increases.

   a. **Factors to Consider** In considering whether to perform substantive procedures at an interim date, the auditor should consider such factors as:

      (1) The control environment and other relevant controls

      (2) The availability of information at a later date that is necessary for the auditor's procedures

      (3) The objective of the substantive procedure

      (4) The assessed risk of material misstatement (RMM)

      (5) The nature of the class of transactions or account balance and relevant assertions

      (6) The auditor's ability to reduce the risk that misstatements existing at the end of the period will not be detected

   b. **Misstatements** If misstatements are detected at the interim date, the auditor should consider modifying the risk assessment and the planned nature, extent, or timing of audit procedures covering the remaining period. The auditor may determine that it is necessary to extend or reperform the original procedure at the balance-sheet date.

   c. **Remaining Period** The auditor may compare and reconcile ending balances with balances at the interim date to identify amounts that appear unusual, investigate such amounts, and perform substantive procedures to test the remaining period. When planning to perform analytics with respect to the remaining period, the auditor should consider whether the amount, relative significance, and composition of an ending balance are reasonably predictable. The auditor also should consider whether the entity's procedures for analysis, adjustment, and cutoff of such balances at interim dates are appropriate. Furthermore, the auditor should consider whether the financial reporting system will provide sufficient information to permit investigation of: (1) significant unusual transactions or entries; (2) other causes of significant fluctuations, or expected fluctuations that did not occur; and (3) changes in the composition of classes of transactions or account balances.

2. **Period End** To best address certain identified risks of material misstatement, such as the risk of fraudulent financial reporting, the auditor may need to perform substantive procedures at or near the end of the reporting period. Procedures to extend audit conclusions from an interim date to the period-end may not be effective.

3. **Prior Period** Substantive audit evidence from a prior audit is not sufficient for reducing detection risk to an acceptably low level in the current audit. In order for such evidence to be used in the current period as substantive audit evidence, the audit evidence and the related subject matter must not change fundamentally. The auditor must perform procedures to establish the continuing relevance of the audit evidence. An example of substantive audit evidence obtained in a prior period that may be relevant in the current period is audit evidence substantiating the purchase cost of a building.

4.   Coordination of Procedures In planning the timing of procedures, the auditor should consider the coordination of related audit procedures. This includes, for example: (a) coordinating the audit procedures applied to related-party transactions and balances; (b) coordinating the testing of interrelated accounts and accounting cutoffs; and (c) maintaining temporary audit control over assets that are readily negotiable and simultaneously testing such assets.

E.   Review of Audit Evidence

Exhibit 2 ▶ Audit Evidence Review Mnemonic

C	Calculations by auditor
A	Analytics
D	Documents (authoritative)
S	Subsequent events
C	Client statements
R	Records (subsidiary)
I	Internal control
P	Physical evidence
T	Third-party statements

1.   Calculations by Auditor For example, the auditor may recompute a tax liability or depreciation. In addition to verifying the amount in the financial records, this procedure also contributes to the auditor's understanding of the summarization of the data in the financial statements.

2.   Analytics The interrelationships among the various data are investigated to provide evidence of reasonable presentation in the financial statements. For example, the auditor may examine the ratio of interest expense to long-term debt, the ratio of accounts receivable to sales, and the gross profit ratios for a period of several years. Alternatively, the auditor may match several associated accounts and audit the data simultaneously (e.g., purchases and accounts payable, accounts receivable and sales).

3.   Authoritative Documents Documents such as vendor's invoices, time cards, receiving reports, and purchase orders provide support for recording transactions in journals and are used to authorize transactions.

a.   Preparation In general, documents prepared by third parties are a better form of evidence than those prepared by the client.

b.   Circulation In general, documents used by third parties are a better form of evidence than those used only by the client.

c.   Internal Control Authoritative documents prepared under strong internal control are generally considered better evidence than those prepared under weak internal control.

4. **Subsequent Events** The occurrence of events subsequent to the financial statement date is especially important evidence regarding cutoff work on year-end balances. An important use of subsequent evidence is the search for unrecorded liabilities. In analyzing the cash disbursements made after the year-end, the auditor is looking for items that were a liability at year-end but that were not recorded and disclosed in the financial statements.

Exhibit 3 ▶ Subsequent Events Discovery Mnemonic

M	Management representation letter
I	Inquiry
R	Read minutes / interim financial statements
A	Asset / liability valuation
C	Cutoff
L	Legal letters

5. **Client's Statements** The auditor frequently must rely on statements made by the client. The client's explanations must be evaluated as to the treatment of various items and as to the reasoning that supports certain judgmental decisions.

6. **Subsidiary Records** Subsidiary records add to the audit evidence supporting the financial statement generation process. Subsidiary ledgers for accounts receivable, inventory, and fixed assets are examples of this type of evidence.

7. **Internal Control** Can be thought of as a form of audit evidence because the auditor considers internal control in reaching conclusions concerning the fairness of the financial statements. The strength of internal control affects the nature, extent, and timing of the procedures that will be performed. Therefore, under strong internal control, the auditor may require less audit evidence than under weak internal control.

8. **Physical Evidence** Examples include counting cash, counting inventory, and observing fixed assets such as buildings and machines.

9. **Third-Party Statements** Statements by third parties are strong types of evidence because they are prepared by independent parties. Examples include accounts receivable confirmations, confirmations from insurance brokers concerning the status of various insurance policies, confirmations of the number of shares outstanding from registrars, and confirmations of account balances by banks.

II. **Standardized Audit Procedures**

A. **General Audit Procedures**
The following are frequently used audit procedures. Because they are in general form, each procedure in an audit program should specify the account balance or transaction to which it applies (e.g., vouch sales journal entries to the bills of lading).

1. Obtain an understanding of the entity and its environment, including internal control to assess the risk of material misstatement in order to ascertain the nature, extent, and timing of further audit procedures to be applied.

2. Evaluate whether transactions are properly recorded in conformity with GAAP.

3. Reconcile detail records and data with the general ledger.

4. Confirm and observe for proper segregation of duties in actual practice.

5. Test posting from the journals to the ledgers.

6. Compare an account's beginning balance with the ending balance from the previous period.

7. Scan the accounts for unusual items.

8. Investigate unusual items.

9. Test for proper authorizations.

10. Vouch (i.e., examine) source documents.

11. Inquire about significant accounts and events.

12. Test for adequate disclosures.

13. Foot and cross-foot.

14. Test for interrelationships between certain accounts and between certain amounts (i.e., perform analytics).

15. Recalculate significant figures.

16. Review cutoff dates.

17. Examine subsequent events.

18. Make inquiries of client personnel.

19. Obtain written representations from management.

20. Read the minutes of the board of directors' meetings and committee meetings of the board.

21. Make inquiries of the client's attorney.

Exhibit 4 ▶ Standardized Audit Procedures Mnemonic

T	TRACING	Follow transaction from supporting documentation to accounting records
R	RECONCILE	Account for difference between two amounts
A	ANALYZE	Search for unexpected trends or the lack of expected deviations
F	FOOT	Recompute column totals within financial statements and individual accounts
I	INSPECT	Physically confirm the existence of assets such as stock certificates
C	CONFIRM	Confirmation of certain account balances with third parties
C	CONSIDER	Entity & its environment, including internal control
I	INQUIRE	Make inquiries of client management and employees
V	VOUCHING	Examine documentation that supports entries in the accounting records
I	INVESTIGATE	Look for cause of detected fraud discovered in testing
C	COUNT	Physical count of inventories on hand and fixed assets owned
S	SUBSEQUENT EVENTS	Events occurring after the year-end that may have an effect on the financial statements

B.   Guidelines for Tracing & Vouching
Exam questions frequently require determination of the purpose of tracing or vouching given documents through the accounting process.

1.   **Tracing From Source Documents to Ledgers** Provides evidence of completeness (i.e., all transactions are recorded and the ledger accounts are not understated). This is indicated by the upward arrow in Exhibit 5.

2.   **Vouching From Ledgers to Source Documents** Provides evidence of existence or occurrence (i.e., all transactions summarized in the ledgers actually occurred, the ledgers contain no unsupported entries, and ledger balances are not overstated). This is indicated by the downward arrow in Exhibit 5.

Exhibit 5 ▶ Tracing & Vouching Guidelines

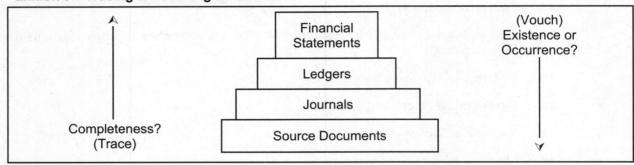

C.   Fair Value Measurements & Disclosures (AU 328)

1.   **Overview** AU 328, *Auditing Fair Value Measurements & Disclosures*, provides guidance for auditing financial statement components and related disclosures that are required by GAAP to be measured at fair value. Fair value measurements (FVM) may occur both when a transaction is initially recorded and later for changes in value. In the absence of observable market prices, GAAP requires fair value to be based on the best information available. The estimation of fair value may be achieved through the use of a valuation method.

2.   **Management Responsibilities** Management is responsible for making the FVM and disclosures included in the financial statements. This includes:

a.   Establishing an accounting and financial reporting process for determining FVM and disclosures

b.   Selecting and preparing the valuation method

c.   Identifying and supporting the significant underlying assumptions used

d.   Ensuring both the presentation and disclosures are in accordance with GAAP

3.   **Obtaining an Understanding of Entity's Process & Assessing Risk** The auditor should obtain an understanding of the entity's process for determining FVM and disclosures and of the relevant controls sufficient to assess the risk of material misstatement. The auditor should then develop an effective audit approach, i.e., determine the nature, extent, and timing of the audit procedures. Generally, more complex FVM requirements impose a greater risk of material misstatement. When obtaining this understanding, an auditor may consider:

a.   Controls over the process

b.   Expertise and experience of the people involved

c.   Role of information technology

d.   Types of accounts or transactions requiring FVM or disclosures

e.   Extent of the reliance on a service organization to either provide the measurement or the data that supports it

f.   Extent to which specialists are used

g.   Significant assumptions (including the process to develop and apply them) and related supporting documentation

h.   Process to monitor changes in assumptions

i.   Integrity of change controls and security procedures for valuation models and relevant information systems, including approval processes

j.   Controls over the consistency, timeliness, and reliability of the data used in valuation models

4.   **Conformity With GAAP**   The auditor should evaluate whether the FVM and disclosures in the financial statements are in conformity with GAAP.

  a.   If relevant, the auditor should evaluate management's intent and ability to carry out specific courses of action. The auditor may consider:

   (1)   Management's past history of carrying out its stated intentions with respect to assets or liabilities

   (2)   Written plans and other documentation, for example, budgets or minutes

   (3)   Management's stated reasons for the selection of a particular course of action

   (4)   Management's ability to carry out a particular course of action given the entity's economic circumstances or contractual commitments or restraints

  b.   When a valuation method is used (because there are no observable market prices), the auditor should evaluate its appropriateness. This would involve a discussion with management about their rationale for selecting the valuation method. The auditor considers:

   (1)   Whether management has sufficiently evaluated and appropriately applied the criteria, if any, provided by GAAP to support the selected method

   (2)   Whether the valuation method is appropriate given the nature of the item being valued and in relation to the business, industry, and environment of the entity

   (3)   In cases where management considered methods with a wide range of values, how they investigated the reasons for the differences

  c.   The auditor should evaluate whether the entity's method for determining FVM is consistently applied, and if so, whether the consistency is appropriate considering possible changes in the environment or accounting principles.

5.   **Engaging a Specialist**   The auditor may have the ability to perform the audit related to fair values or may decide to use a specialist. If a specialist is to be used, the auditor should consider whether the specialist's understanding of the definition of fair value and the method the specialist will use is consistent with those of management and is in conformity with GAAP. The auditor should follow the guidance in AU 336, *Using the Work of a Specialist,* (see Chapter 4) to obtain an understanding of the assumptions and the methods used by the

specialist and if the auditor considers the findings to be unreasonable, should apply additional procedures.

6. **Audit Procedures & Evaluation of Results** FVM can vary widely and can be associated with very different levels of risk of material misstatement, thus audit procedures can vary significantly in nature, extent, and timing. Substantive tests may involve (a) testing management's significant assumptions, the valuation model, and the underlying data; (b) developing independent fair value estimates for corroborative purposes; or (c) reviewing subsequent events and transactions.

   The auditor should evaluate the sufficiency and appropriateness of the FVM audit evidence obtained as well as its consistency with other audit evidence. The auditor's evaluation of whether the FVM and disclosures are in conformity with GAAP is performed in the context of the financial statements taken as a whole.

7. **Testing Management's Significant Assumptions, the Valuation Model & the Underlying Data**

   a. The auditor evaluates whether (1) management's assumptions are reasonable and reflect, or are not inconsistent with, market information; (2) the FVM was determined using the appropriate model; and (3) management used relevant information that was reasonably available at the time.

   b. Where applicable, the auditor should evaluate whether the significant assumptions used by management, taken individually or as a whole, provide a reasonable basis for the FVM and disclosures in the financial statements. Assumptions are frequently interdependent and therefore need to be internally consistent.

   c. Management must exercise judgment to identify the assumptions that are significant. The auditor focuses on the significant assumptions identified by management. Generally, significant assumptions cover matters that materially affect the FVM and may include those that are:

      (1) Sensitive to variation or uncertainty in amount or nature

      (2) Susceptible to misapplication or bias

   d. To be considered reasonable, assumptions need to be reliable and consistent with:

      (1) The general economic environment, the economic environment of the specific industry, and the entity's economic circumstances

      (2) Existing market information

      (3) The plans of the entity, including what management expects will be the outcome of specific objectives and strategies

      (4) If appropriate, assumptions made in prior periods

      (5) Experience of, or previous conditions experienced by, the entity to the extent currently applicable

      (6) Other matters related to the financial statements (e.g., assumptions about other accounting estimates)

      (7) If applicable, the risk associated with cash flows, including the potential variability in the amount and timing of the cash flows and the related effect on the discount rate

e. **Valuation Model** For items valued using a valuation model, the auditor is not an appraiser, i.e., the auditor does substitute his or her judgment for that of management. The auditor reviews the model and evaluates its reasonableness and appropriateness.

f. **Data** The auditor tests the data to evaluate whether it is accurate, complete and relevant; and whether the FVM has been properly determined using such data and management's assumptions.

8. **Developing independent Fair Value Estimates for Corroborative Purposes** When performing substantive procedures, the auditor may make an independent estimate to corroborate FVM, either using management's assumptions or the auditor's own. In the latter case, the auditor should still take management's assumptions into account. The understanding of management's assumptions helps to ensure that the auditor's independent estimate includes consideration of all significant variables. It also helps the auditor to evaluate any significant difference between the two estimates.

9. **Reviewing Subsequent Events & Transactions** Events and transactions that occur after the balance sheet date but before the date of the auditor's report may provide audit evidence regarding management's FVM as of the balance sheet date. When using a subsequent event or transaction to substantiate a FVM, the auditor considers only those events or transactions that reflect circumstances existing at the balance sheet date.

10. **Disclosures** Disclosure of fair value information is an important aspect of financial statements. Often fair value disclosure is required because of the relevance to users in the evaluation of the entity's performance and financial position. The auditor obtains sufficient appropriate evidence that the method of estimation and significant assumptions used are adequately disclosed in accordance with GAAP. If an item contains a high degree of measurement uncertainty, the auditor assesses whether the disclosures are sufficient to inform users of such uncertainty.

11. **Management Representations** The auditor generally should obtain written representations from management regarding the reasonableness of significant assumptions, including whether they appropriately reflect management's intent and ability to carry out specific courses of action where relevant to the use of FVM or disclosures. Management representations about fair values may include representations about:

a. The appropriateness of the measurement methods, including related assumptions, used by management in determining fair value and the consistency in application of the methods.

b. The completeness and adequacy of disclosures related to fair values.

c. Whether subsequent events require adjustment to the FVM and disclosures included in the financial statements.

12. **Communication With Those Charged With Governance** The auditor should determine that those charged with governance are informed about the process used by management in formulating particularly sensitive accounting estimates, including FVM estimates, and about the basis for the auditor's conclusions regarding the reasonableness of those estimates. For example, the auditor should consider communicating the:

a. Nature of significant assumptions used in FVM

b. Degree of subjectivity involved in the development of the assumptions

c. Relative materiality of the items being measured at fair value to the statements as a whole

The auditor should follow the guidance in AU 380, *The Auditor's Communication With Those Charged With Governance*, as to the nature and form of the communication. (See Chapter 2.)

III. Audit Programs

A. Cash

The audit procedures in Exhibit 6 generally are performed during the audit of cash accounts to obtain supporting evidence of the objectives.

1. **Audit Objectives' Focus** To ensure (a) there are adequate internal control policies and procedures over cash, (b) all cash that should be in the custody of the client is (existence), (c) all of the cash in custody of the client is recorded properly (completeness), and (d) the cash in the custody of the client is disclosed properly in the financial statements.

2. **Subfunctions** Subfunctions for cash include (a) accounts receivable, (b) accounts payable, (c) cash sales, and (d) general ledger accounting.

3. **Kiting** This is the practice whereby an employee who is embezzling funds makes a transfer of funds from a bank account in one bank to a bank account in another bank near the end of the period. The transfer is effected through the use of a check and, therefore, does not show up as a withdrawal from the first bank until the check clears. It is listed as a deposit in transit on the receiving bank's books but not as an outstanding check on the disbursing bank's books. As a result, the overall cash balance is temporarily overstated at the balance sheet date and the embezzlement is not detected.

Example 1 ▶ Kiting

Allen Richards is the bookkeeper for Diversified Inc. Diversified has two bank accounts—one in the First Federal Bank and another in the Fourth National Bank. On a hot tip from Allen's investment broker, Allen writes himself a $5,000 check on the First Federal account, makes no entry, and purchases stock in STCG Inc. Shortly thereafter, STCG Inc. is subjected to SEC investigation and all trading in its stock is frozen. As the end of the year nears, Allen's predicament remains unchanged. To cover the defalcation, Allen writes a $5,000 check on the Fourth National account on December 31 and deposits it in the First Federal account on the same day. Furthermore, he makes no entry in the cash disbursements journal and fails to list the check as outstanding on the year-end bank reconciliation. The check will not show up as a decrease in the Fourth National account until it clears, so that account will still reflect the same account balance without the check deduction, and the First Bank will reflect the $5,000 deposited as of December 31. The money "appears" to be in both accounts, when in reality, only due to the delay in transaction posting, it is not.

Exhibit 6 ▶ Sample Program for Cash

Procedures	Assertions*
1. Prepare proof of cash—to ascertain that all recorded receipts have been deposited in the bank	Existence
2. Account for all check numbers—to determine whether there are any missing or outstanding checks that might cause the cash balance to be overstated	Completeness
3. Obtain and review or prepare a year-end bank reconciliation—to accurately determine the client's actual cash position at the close of the period	Completeness
4. Obtain a bank cutoff statement directly from the bank—to ascertain whether the items on the year-end reconciliation have cleared the bank and, therefore, were valid. Bank cutoff statements generally are requested for one to two weeks after year-end. After finishing this procedure, the cutoff bank statement is given to the client. This procedure is useful for detecting kiting between account balances.	Completeness Cutoff

5. Investigate any checks made to cash or bearer—to determine the propriety of the disbursement

Rights & Obligations

6. Trace a sample of entries in the cash receipts journal to the A/R subsidiary ledger, duplicate deposit ticket, and general ledger—to determine whether the cash is stated accurately

Valuation & Allocation Completeness

7. Simultaneously count all cash on hand—to ensure that no cash is counted more than once (coordinate with count of marketable securities on hand)

Existence

8 Investigate NSF checks and other debit memos—because these may be an indication of the covering up of a cash shortage

Existence

9. Prepare a schedule of bank transfers around year-end—to help detect kiting

Existence

10. Confirm the existence of year-end bank balances of the following:

Existence Rights & Obligations

   a. Amounts on deposit
   b. Direct liabilities
   c. Contingent liabilities on notes discounted
   d. Other direct or contingent liabilities
   e. Other security agreements

11. Determine If any cash is restricted—so that the restricted balance is classified properly on the balance sheet, and requirements of compensating balance agreements are disclosed properly

All Presentation & Disclosure Assertions

* Note that many procedures may test multiple assertions. This program is not intended to be a complete presentation. See Chapter 4 for details on assertions.

B. Accounts Receivable (AU 330) & Sales

The procedures (and the purpose behind each procedure) in Exhibit 7 generally are performed during the audit of accounts receivable and sales to obtain supporting evidence of the objectives.

1. **Audit Objectives' Focus** To ascertain: (a) adequate internal control policies and procedures exist; (b) all sales and receivables that should be recorded are properly recorded (completeness); (c) only sales and receivables that should be recorded are recorded (existence); and (d) accounts receivable are presented at approximate realizable value

2. **Subfunctions** After the audit objectives for an audit area are specified, they should be broken into subfunctions. For accounts receivable and sales, possible subfunctions include (a) credit granting, (b) billing, (c) shipping, (d) cash receipts, (e) detailed ledger bookkeeping, and (f) general ledger accounting

3. **Broad Outline of Audit Program for Accounts Receivable & Sales**

   a. **Interim Work** Possibilities include (1) obtaining an understanding of the internal control (may include walking through a transaction, inquiry, and observation), and (2) performing tests of controls as to operating effectiveness

   b. **Year-End Work: Sales** (1) Analytics (including ratio and trend analysis), (2) review sales cutoff and consignment sales, and (3) review sales returns and allowances and sales discounts

   c. **Year-End Work: Accounts Receivable** (1) Review aged trial balance, (2) confirm accounts receivable by positive and/or negative confirmations, and (3) review the bad debts allowance and expense

4. **Confirmation of Accounts Receivable (AU 330)** Confirmation of accounts receivable is a generally accepted auditing procedure. Thus, there is a presumption that the auditor will perform it unless one of the following is true:

- Accounts receivable are immaterial to the financial statements.

- The use of confirmations would be ineffective.

- The auditor's combined assessed level of inherent and control risk is low, and the assessed level, in conjunction with the evidence expected to be provided by analytical procedures or other substantive tests of details, is sufficient to reduce audit risk to an acceptably low level for the applicable financial statement assertions. (In many situations, both confirmation of accounts receivable and other substantive tests of details are necessary to reduce audit risk to an acceptably low level.)

If confirmations in an examination of accounts receivable are **not** requested, the auditor must document the reason.

a. **Auditor's Responsibility** Confirmation requests always should be mailed by the auditor. In addition, the auditor's firm should receive all requests directly. These procedures diminish the possibility that the confirmation requests could be altered by the client, either during the mailing process or upon receipt.

b. **Extent & Method of Confirmation** The extent and method of confirmation is determined by the auditor after considering (1) the effectiveness of internal control; (2) the possibility of disputes, inaccuracies, and fraud in the accounts; (3) the expected degree of cooperation by the debtor; (4) the probability that the debtor will be able to confirm the amounts involved; and (5) the materiality of the amounts involved. A combination of the two forms may be appropriate, with the positive form used for large balances and the negative form for small balances.

c. **Subject of Confirmation** Confirmations may deal with the account balance or with individual items. The latter are useful when the customer may not be in a position to confirm the total account balance owed to the client. This occurs frequently when sales or contracts are made with governmental agencies.

d. **Positive Form of Confirmation Request** Requests a response concerning whether or not the customer is in agreement with the client's records. A positive request also may be blank, requesting the recipient to indicate balances and furnish other information. Use of the blank form provides a greater degree of assurance about the information confirmed because some respondents may sign a "completed" confirmation without verifying it. However, because the blank form requires more effort on the part of the recipient, there may be a lower response rate.

The positive form is preferable when individual account balances are relatively large or when there is reason to believe that a substantial number of the accounts may be disputed or that errors and/or fraud exist.

- **Nonresponse** Generally, nonresponse requires the use of follow-up requests such as additional mailings or telephone calls. In cases where there is still no response to requests dealing with significant accounts, alternative procedures should be used to obtain adequate evidence. These additional procedures may involve the examination of documents such as subsequent cash receipts, sales invoices, and shipping documents.

   e.   **Negative Form of Confirmation Request** Requests a response only in cases where the customer disagrees with the stated balance.

The negative form is useful when the assessed level of control risk is low, when a large number of small balances are involved, and when the auditor has no reason to believe the persons receiving the requests are unlikely to give them consideration.

- **Nonresponse** An inherent weakness in the negative form is that a nonresponse does not necessarily mean that the balance is accurate. Rather, a nonresponse may have nothing to do with the correctness or incorrectness of the balance. The response form may simply have not been returned by the debtor or may have been lost en route from the debtor to the auditor.

   f.   **Use of Electronic Confirmations** The transmission or receipt of electronic confirmations is not precluded by GAAS. Confirmations obtained electronically can be considered to be reliable audit evidence if the auditor is satisfied that (a) the electronic confirmation process is secure and properly controlled, (b) the information obtained is a direct communication in response to a request, and (c) the information is obtained from a third party who is the intended respondent.

5.   **Lapping** One of the most common types of fraud in connection with accounts receivable is lapping. Lapping occurs when a cashier conceals the theft of cash by stealing one customer's payment and then covering the theft by applying the next customer's payment received to the first customer's account and so on. The cashier may replace the stolen cash—ending the need to lap accounts—before the theft is discovered. In other cases, if inadequate segregation of duties allows the cashier to do so, the cashier may instead write off a customer's account equal to the amount of the cash stolen. This also ends the thief's need to lap accounts.

Lapping is made possible through either bad internal control (i.e., having the same employee handle both the cash and the accounts receivable records) or collusion. In order to detect a lapping scheme, the auditor must compare the name, amounts, and dates shown on the customers' remittance advices with entries in the cash receipts journal and the related deposit slips.

Example 2 ▶ Lapping

Georgia Thomas is the bookkeeper for Farley Fabrics (a retail cloth distributor), and her duties consist of receiving the checks from the customers and recording the payments in the A/R subsidiary ledger. On January 8th, Georgia hears the president talk about a one-time purchase of a unique fabric by Colin's Casuals. She also hears that Colin's is going to make a $640 purchase. The next day, Colin's Casuals submits its order for that $640 of fabric. With all of this in mind, Georgia embezzles $640 of that day's payments received from Mama's Moo Moos and Jabba's Jammies (both of whom are regular customers of Farley). Georgia makes no entries in the accounts. Five days later, Colin's Casuals pays its bill, and Georgia credits the payments to Mama's and Jabba's accounts. Colin does no more business with Farley and, at the end of the year, Georgia writes off Colin's receivable as uncollectible.

Exhibit 7 ▶ Sample Program for A/R & Sales

Procedures	Assertions*
1. Compare a sample of shipping documents to the related sales invoices—to discover orders that have been shipped, but not billed	Completeness
2. Reconcile a sample of cash register tapes and sales tickets with the sales journals—so that evidence is gathered that shows that all sales have been recorded, and recorded accurately	Completeness Accuracy
3. Perform analytics—for example, a gross profit test, to determine that all sales have been recorded and classified correctly; investigate any unexpected fluctuations	Completeness Classification
4. Review sales discount procedures and documentation—to determine that discounts were granted only for payments received within the discount period	Accuracy
5. Vouch debits in individual A/R accounts to sales invoices—to determine whether the sales actually occurred	Occurrence Rights & Obligations
6. Review sales and receipts occurring near year-end—to ascertain that such transactions were recorded in the proper time period and were valid transactions	Cutoff Occurrence
7. Test foot the sales journal and reconcile with postings to the general ledger—to find out if the sales figures were brought forward accurately	Accuracy
8. Vouch debit entries in the allowance for doubtful accounts to individual accounts and original write-off authorizations—so that it can be determined that such write-offs were reflected properly in the accounts and were authorized	Valuation & Allocation
9. Prepare or obtain an aged A/R schedule—to (a) help identify accounts that should be written off, (b) determine the reasonableness of the bad-debt expense and allowance for doubtful accounts, and (c) aid the confirmation of A/R	Valuation & Allocation
10. Recalculate and review bad-debt expense and allowance—for reasonableness of expense and adequacy of the allowance	Valuation & Allocation
11. Examine cash receipts after the balance sheet date—to provide evidence of collectability at the balance sheet date	Valuation & Allocation
12. Confirm A/R on a test basis—to verify the existence and accuracy of the account balances and that the receivables are the rights of the company	Existence Accuracy Rights & Obligations
13. Examine all aspects of a sample of sales transactions—to determine whether the internal control procedures are being applied properly (i.e., perform tests of controls directed toward operating effectiveness); this procedure includes the following: a. Comparing the sales invoice with the customer's purchase order b. Checking for proper credit approval c. Comparing prices on sales invoice with those on price list; ascertaining the propriety of discounts granted to purchasers d. Recomputing extensions and footings e. Checking the recording in the sales journal and the posting of the sale in the A/R subsidiary ledger	Occurrence Accuracy
14. Review loan agreements—for pledging of accounts and agreements, for any factoring of accounts, and for disclosure purposes	All Presentation & Disclosure Assertions

* Note that many procedures may test multiple assertions. This program is not intended to be a complete presentation. See Chapter 4 for details on assertions.

C.   **Inventory (AU 331 & 901)**
      The audit procedures in Exhibit 8 typically are performed during the audit of the inventory account to obtain supporting evidence of the objectives.

1.   **Audit Objectives' Focus** To ascertain (a) the inventory exists and the client owns it (existence and rights), (b) it is priced correctly, (c) the quantities shown are reasonable (rights), (d) the computations used to arrive at the inventory dollar amounts are accurate (valuation), and (e) there is adequate disclosure in the financial statements

2.   **Subfunctions** Subfunctions for inventory include (a) purchasing, (b) receiving, (c) storing, (d) processing, (e) shipping, (f) detailed bookkeeping, and (g) general ledger accounting

3.   **Evidence for Inventories (AU 331)** The observation of the taking of the inventory is a generally accepted auditing procedure (although not a standard). Therefore, if an observation is not performed, the auditor must document the reason.

      a.   **Periodic Inventory** When the client determines its inventory quantities entirely by means of a physical count at or near the balance sheet date, the auditor ordinarily must be present at the count. The auditor should use suitable observations, tests, and inquiries to become satisfied that the method of accounting for inventory is effective and that the client's claims as to the quantities and physical condition are reliable.

      b.   **Perpetual Inventory System** When a good perpetual inventory system is maintained in which the client periodically compares the inventory records with the physical counts, the auditor should observe the counting and comparing. However, this can be done either during the period (assuming an adequate system of internal control over inventory and the assessed level of control risk is low) or at or after the end of the period.

      c.   **Advanced Methods** Some companies have developed highly effective inventory methods (using statistical sampling) that make annual counts of each item of inventory unnecessary. In these cases, the auditor must be present at such partial countings as considered necessary. The auditor also must be satisfied that the inventory method will produce results that are comparable to those that would be obtained by a physical inventory. If the inventory plan is based on statistical sampling, the auditor must be satisfied that the plan has statistical validity and is properly applied, and that the resulting precision and reliability are statistically reasonable.

      d.   **Sufficient Audit Evidence** Tests of the accounting records are not sufficient evidence as to current inventories. Rather, the auditor always will have to make or observe some physical counts of the inventory, apply appropriate tests to the intervening transactions, and review any client counts and procedures relating to the physical inventory.

      e.   **Auditor Has Not Audited Prior Inventories** When auditing financial statements covering the current period and one or more periods for which the auditor has not observed or made some physical counts of prior inventories, the auditor must be satisfied as to the prior period's inventory through the results of appropriate tests. These tests might include tests of prior transactions, review of prior record counts, and gross profit tests. An example of this type of situation would be the first audit of a new client who has beginning inventory.

      f.   **Inventories Held in Public Warehouses (AU 901)** In some cases, inventories are held in public warehouses or by other outside custodians. In these situations, direct written confirmation from the custodian is acceptable when the inventory is not material. When the amounts are substantial, relative to current or total assets, the auditor should undertake one or more of the following procedures: (1) test the owner's control procedures for investigating the warehouse and evaluating its performance; (2) obtain an independent accountant's report on the warehouse's control procedures relevant to custody of goods and, if applicable, pledging of receipts; (3) apply alternative procedures at the warehouse to gain reasonable assurance that information received from the warehouse is reliable; (4) observe physical counts wherever reasonable and practicable; and finally (5) obtain confirmations from lenders in cases where warehouse receipts have been pledged as collateral.

g. **Outside Inventory-Taking Firm (AU 9508)** Some companies (e.g., retail stores, hospitals, and automobile dealers) use outside firms of nonaccountants who specialize in the taking of physical inventories to count, list, price, and subsequently compute the total dollar amount of the inventory. While the use of an outside firm ordinarily will reduce the work, it is not, by itself, a satisfactory substitute for the auditor's observation or taking of physical counts. In this situation, the auditor's primary concern will be to evaluate the effectiveness of the outside firm's procedures. Therefore, the auditor would (1) examine its inventory program, (2) observe its procedures and controls, (3) make or observe some physical counts of the inventory, (4) recompute calculations of the submitted inventory on a test basis, and (5) apply appropriate tests to the intervening transactions.

Exhibit 8 ▶ Sample Program for Inventory

Procedures	Assertions*
1. Account for the numerical sequence of inventory purchase requisitions—to ascertain that none are missing, thereby helping to assure that no unauthorized purchases were made	Completeness
2. Trace a sample of receiving reports for inventory to the perpetual inventory records—to determine that all shipments were reflected properly in the accounts; (this cutoff test must be performed at the inventory observation date and at the balance sheet date, if different)	Completeness Cutoff
3. Perform analytics on cost of goods sold—to determine if significant fluctuations exist that would necessitate an audit investigation; perform procedures to test turnover and compare gross margin of current year with that of prior year to test for overstatement or understatement	Completeness
4. Account for inventory tags and count sheets—to verify the inventory has been accounted for completely	Completeness
5. Trace test counts of inventory items from the floor to the client's inventory listing—to ensure all items of inventory have been counted and included	Completeness
6. Vouch a sample of inventory requisitions to customer or department order—so that evidence is obtained that all requisitions are valid	Rights & Obligations
7. Review purchase and sales cutoffs—to ascertain that ending inventory is valued properly and that the inventory transactions are recorded in the proper time period	Cutoff Rights & Obligations
8. Review inventory on consignment (as both consignee and consignor)—to determine the inventory actually owned by the client	Rights & Obligations
9. Confirm inventory held at public warehouses and with third parties—to identify other inventory actually owned by the client	Rights & Obligations Existence
10. Test pricing method used by the client—so that the proper inventory value is attained	Valuation & Allocation
11. Apply lower-of-cost-or-market rule—so that the proper inventory value and any losses are recognized and disclosed	Valuation & Allocation
12. Perform analytics—such as, gross profit percentage calculations, inventory turnover ratios, and number of days sales in inventory ratio analysis	Valuation & Allocation

In addition, inventory audit procedures for a manufacturing client could include the following:

13.	Test cost accumulation process—so that the ending inventory and cost-of-goods-sold are valued properly	Valuation & Allocation
14.	Review the overhead allocations and rates—for accuracy when compared with actual experience	Valuation & Allocation
15.	Vouch a sample of additions to perpetual inventory to supporting receiving reports—to assure that the recorded inventory actually was received	Existence
16.	Physical inventory: observe the physical count—to become satisfied that the counting methods are effective and the client's representations are reliable	Existence
17.	Physical inventory: trace client's physical counts to perpetual records and inventory sheets—to test the completeness of perpetual records	Completeness
18.	Physical inventory: vouch the validity of the perpetual records and inventory sheets against the physical count—to determine that items in perpetual records exist and quantities are correct	Existence
19.	Physical inventory: test inventory sheet and perpetual record computation for clerical accuracy—thereby helping to ascertain that the inventory is valued properly and quantities are correct	Valuation & Allocation
20.	Physical inventory: make random test counts—to assure that the counts made by the client are accurate; test counts of inventory items also should be traced to client's inventory sheets and to client's final inventory compilation report	Existence
21.	Review purchase and sales commitments—to determine whether there is a need to accrue a loss and disclose its relevant facts	Completeness of Disclosures
22.	Determine whether any inventory has been pledged—to assure that such facts are disclosed properly in the financial statements	All Presentation & Disclosure Assertions

* Note that many procedures may test multiple assertions. This program is not intended to be a complete presentation. See Chapter 4 for details on assertions.

D.   Fixed Assets

The procedures in Exhibit 9 normally are performed during the audit of fixed assets to obtain supporting evidence of the objectives.

1.   Audit Objectives' Focus   To (a) ascertain the adequacy of internal control policies and procedures over fixed assets, (b) verify the existence and ownership of the fixed assets, and (c) ascertain the adequacy of valuation and disclosure of the fixed assets in the financial statements

2.   Subfunctions   Subfunctions for fixed assets include (a) depreciation, (b) financing, (c) detailed ledger bookkeeping, and (d) general ledger accounting

Exhibit 9 ▶ Sample Program for Fixed Assets

	Procedures	Assertions*
1.	Trace from fixed assets to the property, plant and equipment subsidiary ledger—to determine that the assets are recorded	Completeness
2.	Obtain or prepare an analysis of the repair and maintenance expense account—to consider if any items should be classified as capital expenditures	Classification
3.	Review rental revenue and property tax expense—by obtaining a map of rented and leased property; this procedure will help determine the accuracy of the rental revenue and tax expense accounts by exposing all the client's real property, thereby enabling a thorough evaluation	Accuracy

4.	Verify the client's ownership of the assets—by examining titles to the fixed assets	Rights & Obligations
5.	Review lease agreements—for determining whether assets should be capitalized	Classification
6.	Reconcile the property, plant and equipment subsidiary ledger with the general ledger—to determine that the accounting for property, plant and equipment transactions was consistent	Valuation & Allocation
7.	Recalculate the accounting for retirements of fixed assets	Valuation & Allocation
8.	Review depreciation methods—for consistency with prior periods	Valuation & Allocation
9.	Review useful lives—for appropriateness and consistency with prior periods	Valuation & Allocation
10.	Recalculate depreciation computations	Valuation & Allocation
11.	Vouch from the property, plant and equipment subsidiary ledger to the fixed assets—to determine that the assets actually exist	Existence
12.	Vouch acquisitions to purchase orders or contracts approved by appropriate personnel	Existence
13.	Review loan agreements—to verify any loans collateralized by property or equipment for proper disclosure	All Presentation & Disclosure Assertions

* Note that many procedures may test multiple assertions. This program is not intended to be a complete presentation. See Chapter 4 for details on assertions.

E.   Investments (AU 332)

1.   **Audit Objectives** Audit objectives include: (a) to ascertain the adequacy of internal control policies and procedures; (b) to ascertain whether investments are accounted for in conformity with GAAP; (c) to ascertain the adequacy of financial statement disclosure; (d) to determine whether a loss in value of such investments should be considered as temporary or permanent; and (e) to obtain evidence as to their existence by inspection and/or confirmation.

2.   **Subfunctions** Subfunctions for long-term investments include (a) financing, (b) cash, (c) detailed ledger bookkeeping, and (d) general ledger accounting.

3.   **Special Knowledge** The auditor may need special skill or knowledge (or to use the work of specialists) to plan and perform auditing procedures for certain assertions about derivatives and securities, for example:

   a.   A derivative may have complex features that require the auditor to have special knowledge to evaluate the measurement and disclosure of the derivative in conformity with GAAP—features embedded in contracts or agreements may require separate accounting as a derivative, and complex pricing structures may increase the complexity of the assumptions used in estimating the fair value of a derivative.

   b.   Identifying controls placed in operation by a service organization that provides services to an entity that are part of the entity's information system for derivatives and securities, which may require that the auditor have an understanding of the operating characteristics of entities in a certain industry

4.   **Evidence** The auditor is concerned with gathering sufficient appropriate audit evidence pertaining to their existence, ownership, and cost, as well as their carrying amounts, or valuation, on the balance sheet.

   a.   Evidence of their existence, ownership, and cost can be obtained from the accounting records and documents of the investor. In the case of securities, such evidence can be corroborated through inspection or, when appropriate, confirmation from an independent custodian. In the case of loans, bonds, and similar debt obligations, evidence should be corroborated through written confirmation from the debtor or trustee.

b. Evidence of their carrying amount and income and losses attributable to them can be obtained from the following sources:

(1) **Audited Financial Statements** Audited financial statements generally provide sufficient audit evidence, when the statements have been audited by an independent auditor, regarding equity in underlying net assets and results of operation of investee, as well as corroboration of investments in bonds and other debt instruments.

Editor note: There may be a time lag in reporting between the date of the financial statements of the investor and that of the investee. If a time lag has a material effect on the entity's financial statements, the auditor should determine whether the entity's management has properly considered the lack of comparability.

(2) **Unaudited Financial Statements** Unaudited financial statements do not provide sufficient evidence. The investor's auditor may utilize the investee's auditor to apply auditing procedures to unaudited statements, thereby obtaining sufficient evidence.

(3) **Market Quotations** Quoted market prices for derivatives and securities listed on national exchanges or over-the-counter markets are available from sources such as financial publications, the exchanges, the National Association of Securities Dealers Automated Quotations System (NASDAQ), or pricing services based on sources such as those. Quoted market prices obtained from those sources are generally considered to provide sufficient evidence of the fair value of the derivatives and securities.

If quoted market prices are **not** available, estimates of fair value frequently can be obtained from broker-dealers or other third-party sources based on proprietary valuation models or from the entity based on internally or externally developed valuation models. The auditor should understand the method used in developing the estimate. The auditor may also determine that it is necessary to obtain estimates from more than one pricing source.

Editor note: If the derivative or security is valued by the entity using a valuation model, the auditor does **not** function as an appraiser and is **not** expected to substitute his or her judgment for that of the entity's management. In this situation, the auditor should obtain evidence supporting management's assertions about fair value determined by performing further procedures, for example, calculating the value using a model developed by the auditor or a specialist to develop an independent expectation to corroborate the reasonableness of the value calculated by the entity; assessing the reasonableness and appropriateness of the model; or comparing the fair value with subsequent or recent transactions.

(4) **Published Dividend Records** These provide the strongest evidence supporting dividends earned on marketable equity securities.

5. **Valuation** Tests of valuation assertions should be designed according to the valuation method used for the measurement or disclosure. GAAP requires the use of several possible methods including cost, the investee's financial results (including but not limited to the equity

method of accounting), or fair value. GAAP may also call for recognition of gains and/or losses prior to their realization.

a. The accounting model will differ depending on the type of security, the nature of the transaction, management's objectives related to the security, and the type of entity. For derivatives, the accounting for the unrealized gain or loss will depend upon whether hedge accounting is appropriate and, if so, the type of hedge. For debt securities, the accounting will depend upon management's investment intention, i.e., held-to-maturity, trading, or available-for-sale.

b. When quoted prices are not readily available, a significant amount of judgment will be needed to properly evaluate the sufficiency of the evidential matter for the valuation assertion.

For securities which are not subject to mark-to-market accounting, there is the additional issue of determining whether an impairment loss for a decline in fair value should be recognized because it is other than temporary. Determinations of whether losses are other than temporary often involve estimating the outcome of future events. Accordingly, judgment is required in determining whether factors exist that indicate that an impairment loss has been incurred at the end of the reporting period. Examples of such factors include:

(1) Fair value is significantly below cost and

- The decline is attributable to adverse conditions specifically related to the security or to specific conditions in an industry or in a geographic area

- The decline has existed for an extended period of time

- Management does not possess both the intent and the ability to hold the security for a period of time sufficient to allow for any anticipated recovery in fair value

(2) The security has been downgraded by a rating agency

(3) The financial condition of the issuer has deteriorated

(4) Dividends have been reduced or eliminated, or scheduled interest payments have not been made

(5) The entity recorded losses from the security subsequent to the end of the reporting period

6. **Factors That Increase Inherent Risk Assessment for Assertions**

a. When a derivative is intended by management to be a hedge for exposure to changes in fair value, inherent risk is increased due to the possibility of other than expected changes in market conditions rendering the hedge ineffective and thus, accounting for it as a hedge is no longer in accordance with GAAP

b. Derivatives or securities with complex features

c. When there is no exchange of cash in the initial transaction for a derivative or security, inherent risk is increased because the instrument may not be identified (recorded)

d. When an entity lacks experience with the derivative or security

e. When a derivative is an embedded feature of an agreement, inherent risk is increased because it is less likely to be identified

    f.   When external factors affect the assertion:

        (1)   Credit risk (issuer defaults)

        (2)   Market risk (fair value decreases)

        (3)   Basis risk (ineffective hedging activities; basis risk is the difference between the fair value of the hedged item and the fair value of the hedging derivative)

        (4)   Legal risk (performance by one or both parties to the derivative or security is precluded by a legal or regulatory action)

    g.   When new forms of derivatives are developed before interpretive guidance (applicable GAAP) is available

    h.   When the entity places significant reliance on external expertise for guidance/valuation, inherent risk is increased because management may be unable to appropriately challenge the specialist's methodology or assumptions

    i.   When GAAP requires developing subjective assumptions about future conditions

7.   **Examples of Internal Controls for Entities With Extensive Derivative Transactions**

    a.   Monitoring by a control staff that is fully independent of derivatives activities

    b.   Derivatives personnel to obtain, prior to exceeding limits, at least oral approval from members of senior management who are independent of derivatives activities

    c.   Senior management to properly address limit excesses and divergences from approved derivatives strategies

    d.   The accurate transmittal of derivatives positions to the risk measurement systems

    e.   The performance of appropriate reconciliations to ensure data integrity across the full range of derivatives, including any new or existing derivatives that may be monitored apart from the main processing networks

    f.   Derivatives traders, risk managers, and senior management to define constraints on derivatives activities and justify identified excesses

    g.   Senior management, an independent group, or an individual that management designates to perform a regular review of the identified controls and financial results of the derivatives activities to determine whether controls are being effectively implemented and the entity's business objectives and strategies are being achieved

    h.   A review of limits in the context of changes in strategy, risk tolerance of the entity, and market conditions

8.   **Service Organizations** A service organization's services are part of an entity's information system for derivatives and securities if they affect any of the following:

    •   How the entity's derivatives and securities transactions are initiated

    •   The accounting records, supporting information, and specific accounts in the financial statements involved in the processing and reporting of the entity's derivatives and securities transactions

    •   The accounting processing involved from the initiation of those transactions to their inclusion in the financial statements, including electronic means used to transmit, process, maintain, and access information

- The process the entity uses to report information about derivatives and securities transactions in its financial statements, including significant accounting estimates and disclosures

Examples of such services include the initiation of the purchase or sale of equity securities by a service organization acting as investment adviser or manager; services that are ancillary to holding an entity's securities, for example, collecting dividend and interest income and distributing that income to the entity or maintaining records of securities transactions for the entity; and a pricing service providing fair values of derivatives and securities through paper documents or electronic downloads that the entity uses to value its derivatives and securities for financial statement reporting.

Examples of services that would not be part of an entity's information system include the holding of an entity's securities or the execution by a securities broker of trades that are initiated by either the entity or its investment adviser.

9. **Control Risk** If the auditor plans to assess control risk at less than maximum for one or more assertions about derivatives and securities, the auditor should identify specific controls relevant to the assertions that are likely to prevent or detect material misstatements and that have been placed in operation by either the entity or the service organization, and gather audit evidence about their operating effectiveness.

Editor note: Confirmations of balances or transactions from a service organization do not provide audit evidence about its controls.

10. **Substantive Procedures** The auditor should use the assessed levels of inherent risk and control risk for assertions about derivatives and securities to determine the nature, timing, and extent of the substantive procedures. And, of course, the provision by a service organization of services that are part of an entity's information system may affect the nature, extent, and timing of the auditor's substantive procedures.

11. **Hedging Activities** The auditor should gather audit evidence to determine whether management complied with the hedge accounting requirements of GAAP, including designation and documentation requirements. In addition, the auditor should gather audit evidence to support management's expectation at the inception of the hedge that the hedging relationship will be highly effective and its periodic assessment of the ongoing effectiveness of the hedging relationship.

12. **Management Representations** The auditor ordinarily should obtain written representations from management confirming aspects of management's intent and ability that affect assertions about derivatives and securities, such as its intent and ability to hold a debt security until its maturity or to enter into a forecasted transaction for which hedge accounting is applied. In addition, the auditor should consider obtaining written representations from management confirming other aspects of derivatives and securities transactions that affect assertions about them.

Exhibit 10 ▶ Sample Program for Investments (Derivatives and Securities)

Procedures	Assertions*
1. Confirmation with the issuer of the security	Existence or Occurrence Valuation (cost method)
2. Confirmation with the holder of the security, including securities in electronic form, or with the counterparty to the derivative	Existence or Occurrence
3. Confirmation of both settled and unsettled transactions with the broker-dealer or counterparty	Existence or Occurrence

4. Physical inspection of the security or derivative contract; inspect securities on hand and compare serial numbers with those shown in previous year's working papers—will help identify any undisclosed sales or purchases of investments; coordinate with cash count to prevent substitution

    Existence or Occurrence

5. Read executed partnership or similar agreements

    Existence or Occurrence

6. Inspect underlying agreements and other forms of supporting documentation, in paper or electronic form, for the following: amounts reported; evidence that would preclude the sales treatment of a transfer; and unrecorded repurchase agreements

    Existence or Occurrence
    Rights & Obligations
    Valuation (cost method)

7. Inspect supporting documentation for subsequent realization or settlement (or any activity) after the end of the reporting period

    Existence or Occurrence
    Completeness

8. Perform analytics—by comparing dividends, interest and other investment income with those of prior years to ascertain the reasonableness of the completeness of recorded investment income, calculate the percentage of accrued investment income to total investments, and estimate total accrued income based on current investments

    Completeness
    Existence or Occurrence

9. Request the counterparty to a derivative or the holder of a security to provide information about it (confirm significant terms), such as whether there are any side agreements or agreements to repurchase securities sold

    Completeness
    Rights & Obligations

10. Obtain or prepare an account analysis for the long-term investment and related revenue or loss accounts to establish the accuracy of the individual debits and credits occurring during the year and prove the validity of the year-end balance in the accounts

    Completeness

11. Request counterparties or holders who are frequently used, but with whom the accounting records indicate there are presently no derivatives or securities, to state whether they are counterparties to derivatives with the entity or holders of its securities

    Completeness

12. Inspect financial instruments and other agreements to identify embedded derivatives

    Completeness

13. Compare previous and current account detail to identify assets that have been removed from the accounts and test those items further to determine that the criteria for sales treatment have been met

    Completeness

14. Read other information, such as minutes of meetings of the board of directors or finance, asset/liability, investment, or other committees to obtain evidence about completeness or about rights and obligations, such as pledging of securities as collateral or selling securities with a commitment to repurchase them

    Completeness
    Rights & Obligations

15. Test calculations of premium and discount amortization

    Valuation (cost method)

16. Read financial statements/audit report of investee companies and read their interim financial information and make inquiries to identify subsequent events and transactions that are material to the entity's financial statements

    Valuation (equity method)

17. Evaluate management's conclusion about the need to recognize an impairment loss for a decline in the security's fair value below its carrying amount that is other than temporary

    Valuation (equity method)

18. Investigate material transactions between entity and the investee

    Valuation (equity method)

19. Determine fair value of securities on the balance sheet date

    Valuation (fair value method)

20. Inquire of management and review loan documents as to possible pledging of securities for appropriate disclosure purposes; if the collateral is an important factor in evaluating the fair value and collectability of the security, the auditor should obtain evidence regarding the existence, fair value, and transferability of such collateral as well as the investor's rights to the collateral	Valuation (fair value method)
21. Examine financial presentation of long-term investments to determine whether GAAP is followed	Presentation & Disclosure
22. Evaluate whether management's stated intent to buy and hold an investment is supported by actual activities and the entity's ability to do so	Classification

* Note that many procedures may test multiple assertions. This program is not intended to be a complete presentation. See Chapter 4 for details on assertions.

F. Accounts Payable, Purchases & Other Liabilities

The audit procedures in Exhibit 11 commonly are performed during the audit of the A/P, purchasing, and other liability accounts to obtain supporting evidence of the objectives.

1. **Audit Objectives' Focus** To ensure: (a) there are adequate internal control policies and procedures over payables and purchases; (b) all transactions that should be recorded are recorded (completeness); (c) those transactions that are recorded are recorded properly (valuation); and (d) the financial statement presentation is adequate (disclosure and obligation)

2. **Subfunctions** Subfunctions for payables and purchases include (a) purchasing, (b) receiving, (c) payment, (d) detailed ledger bookkeeping, and (e) general ledger accounting

Exhibit 11 ▶ Sample Program for Short-Term Liabilities

<div align="center">Procedures</div>	Assertions*
1. Perform search for unrecorded liabilities—to ascertain that all payables have been recorded in the proper period; performed, at the balance sheet date, in the following areas:	Completeness Cutoff Classification
a. Unmatched invoices and unbilled receiving reports	
b. Significant payments subsequent to the end of the period may indicate liabilities that existed at the end of the period	
c. Invoices received after the end of the period may have been for goods received at, or before, the end of the period	
d. Customer deposits recorded as credits to A/R	
e. Unbilled professional fees at the end of the period under audit	
f. Perform inventory receiving cutoff test	
2. Perform analytics—to assess the reasonableness of balances; compare the average number of days purchases in accounts payable at the end of the current year to prior years; compare purchases divided by payables to payables divided by total current liabilities for the current and prior years; compare payables and purchases to budgeted or forecasted amounts	Completeness
3. Vouch the paid check and invoice from the vendor to the receiving report— to determine if any payments were made for goods that were not received	Existence
4. Review the cutoff of purchases, returns, and disbursements—to determine that transactions are recorded in the proper periods	Cutoff
5. Recalculate the extensions and footings on customer invoices—to determine whether such invoices were priced and computed accurately	Accuracy Valuation & Allocation

	Procedures	Assertions
6.	Trace vendor invoices to voucher register and checks to check register—to determine that all payables and related disbursements were recorded properly	Valuation & Allocation
7.	Foot voucher register and trace to general ledger—to substantiate the entries in the general ledger	Valuation & Allocation
8.	Reclassify debit balances as receivables and review for collectability	Valuation & Allocation
9.	Recalculate other (accrued) liabilities—to test computations for reasonableness and consistent treatment when compared to prior years; examples include property and income taxes, commissions, profit-sharing and pension plans, and warranties	Valuation & Allocation
10.	Vouch purchase requisitions of a sample of purchase orders—to determine if any unrequested purchases were made	Existence
11.	Confirm A/P balances with vendors—although not a generally accepted audit procedure, confirm in cases of suspected fraud, sloppy or missing records, or suspected understatements	Completeness
12.	Inspect copies of notes and other agreements	Existence
13.	Review purchase commitments—to determine whether there are any losses to be accrued and/or disclosed	Completeness

* Note that many procedures may test multiple assertions. This program is not intended to be a complete presentation. See Chapter 4 for details on assertions.

G. Payroll

The audit procedures in Exhibit 12 usually are performed during the audit of the payroll accounts to obtain supporting evidence of the objectives.

1. **Audit Objectives' Focus** To (a) ascertain the adequacy of internal control over payroll, (b) verify that all employees included in the payroll actually exist and work for the client (existence), (c) verify the accuracy of the payroll computations (valuation), and (d) ascertain the adequacy of disclosure in the financial statements.

2. **Subfunctions** Subfunctions for payroll include (a) personnel, (b) production, (c) detailed ledger bookkeeping, and (d) general ledger accounting.

Exhibit 12 ▶ Sample Program for Payroll

	Procedures	Assertions*
1.	Review time reports and piecework or commission records—to determine that such reports and records agree with production records	Completeness
2.	Examine payroll cutoff—to determine that wages were reported in the proper time period	Cutoff
3.	Review accounting for unclaimed wages—to ascertain that they are being classified properly	Classification Rights & Obligations
4.	Verify payroll deductions—to ascertain that they are computed appropriately and that they agree with withholding authorizations	Valuation & Allocation
5.	Analyze officers' compensation—to determine if authorization is proper	Rights & Obligations
6.	Recompute payroll register—to determine its accuracy	Accuracy Valuation & Allocation
7.	Vouch items from the payroll register to employee time cards—to verify employees worked the number of hours for which pay was computed	Occurrence
8.	Observe the use of time clocks by employees—to be assured that each employee punches only one time card	Valuation & Allocation Occurrence

Procedures	Assertions
9. Review the results of audits of related pension and profit-sharing plans	Valuation & Allocation
10. Perform analytics—to determine reasonableness of balances; calculate ratios to determine whether accounts relate to each other in the manner expected; if relationships vary significantly from expected results, additional substantive tests of account balances may be necessary; compare payroll expenses with prior periods and investigate differences to determine the accuracy and validity of the expense	Valuation & Allocation Accuracy
11. Review payroll checks and bank reconciliations—to determine that all checks were cashed	Existence
12. Review the payroll register—to determine if all payroll transactions were recorded	Completeness
13. Examine personnel records—to determine that a name, salary rate, and job position all exist for each employee on the payroll	Existence
14. On a surprise basis, observe the distribution of paychecks—to determine that every name on the company payroll is that of a bona fide employee	Existence
15. Review related tax expense and liability, unemployment insurance, and other payroll deduction accounts—to determine accuracy and proper classification in the financial statements	Accuracy & Valuation Classification

* Note that many procedures may test multiple assertions. This program is not intended to be a complete presentation. See Chapter 4 for details on assertions.

H. Long-Term Liabilities

The audit procedures in Exhibit 13 normally are performed during the audit of long-term liabilities to obtain supporting evidence of the objectives.

1. **Audit Objectives' Focus** To (a) ascertain the adequacy of internal control policies and procedures over long-term liabilities; (b) verify that all long-term liabilities are recorded properly (existence and obligation); (c) verify that interest expense is computed correctly and that other contractual obligations are satisfied (valuation); and (d) ascertain the adequacy of disclosure of long-term liabilities in the financial statements

2. **Subfunctions** Subfunctions for long-term liabilities include (a) financing, (b) fixed assets, (c) cash, (d) detailed ledger bookkeeping, and (e) general ledger accounting.

Exhibit 13 ▶ Sample Program for Long-Term Liabilities

Procedures	Assertions*
1. Obtain or prepare an account analysis for the long-term debt, discount, premium, and related interest accounts—allows the auditor to:	Accuracy Completeness
a. Verify the payment or other disposition of the debt listed as outstanding at the beginning of the period	
b. Establish the accuracy of the individual debits and credits occurring during the year	
c. Prove the validity of the year-end balance in the accounts	
2. Perform analytics—compare current amortization amounts to prior actual and current budget amounts; compare current interest costs to prior actual and current budget amounts; compare current and noncurrent debt obligations to prior actual and current budget amounts	Completeness
3. Review bank confirmation—for indication of loans and other commitments, including any unrecorded debt	Completeness Rights & Obligations
4. Review cutoff—to determine that transactions recorded at the end of the year are recorded in the proper period	Cutoff

5.	Verify interest computations and amortization of premiums and/or discounts—to determine whether such amounts were disclosed properly and accurately; also aids in the discovery of undisclosed liabilities	Valuation & Allocation Accuracy Completeness
6.	Confirm with creditor the transactions of the period and compliance with the contractual provisions—provides evidence that the transactions actually occurred and that the transactions were carried out properly (e.g., deposits into a sinking fund)	Occurrence Rights & Obligations
7.	Review contractual provisions and supporting documents of long-term debt—to determine that details of the debt instruments correspond to those in the account analysis and that such details are disclosed accurately in the financial statements; supporting documents include note and loan agreements, bond indentures, and lease agreements	All Presentation & Disclosure Assertions

* Note that many procedures may test multiple assertions. This program is not intended to be a complete presentation. See Chapter 4 for details on assertions.

I.   Stockholders' Equity

The audit procedures in Exhibit 14 normally are performed during the audit of stockholders' equity to obtain supporting evidence of the objectives.

1.   Audit Objectives' Focus To (a) ascertain the adequacy of internal control over stock transactions, stock certificates, receipts and payments; (b) verify that the transactions are authorized properly and comply with applicable regulations; (c) verify that the transactions are recorded in conformity with GAAP; and (d) ascertain the adequacy of disclosure of stockholders' equity in the financial statements

2.   Subfunctions Subfunctions for stockholders' equity include (a) financing, (b) cash, (c) detailed ledger bookkeeping, and (d) general ledger accounting.

Exhibit 14 ▸ Sample Program for Stockholders' Equity

Procedures	Assertions*
1. Obtain or prepare an account analysis for all accounts—to outline the historical picture of corporate capital and any changes to corporate capital	Completeness
2. Account for all certificate numbers—to determine that no unauthorized securities were issued during the period	Completeness
3. Perform analytics—by computing the return on stockholders' equity, the book value per share, and the dividend payout ratio and comparing them to those of prior years; compare current year dividend amounts and balances for common and preferred stock and additional paid-in capital to those of prior years	Completeness
4. Vouch all retirements of securities—to ascertain that no certificates were reissued fraudulently	Rights & Obligations
5. Review compliance with stock option plans and other restrictions on capital stocks—allows the auditor to do the following: a. Determine the adequacy of disclosure with respect to these arrangements b. Verify the number of shares issued during the year through conversion or exercise of convertible stocks and bonds, stock options, and stock warrants c. Ascertain whether the shares held in reserve exceed the shares authorized, but unissued d. Determine that the call provisions of preferred stock are carried out accurately	All Presentations & Disclosure Assertions

6. Review minutes of board of directors' meetings—to verify that stock and dividend transactions have been authorized properly	Rights & Obligations
7. Account for all proceeds from security issues—to determine whether the transactions were accounted for in accordance with underwriting contracts, state stock issuance permits, and SEC registration statements	Valuation & Allocation
8. Analyze treasury stock transactions—to determine that such transactions were authorized properly and recorded in conformity with GAAP	Accuracy Valuation & Allocation
9. Reconcile subsidiary ledger with general ledger control account—to establish the amount of outstanding stock and to rule out the possibility of an over-issuance of shares	Valuation & Allocation
10. Reconcile dividend distributions and verify dividend calculations—to ascertain the accurate dividend amount and to discover any declared, but yet unpaid, dividends	Accuracy Completeness
11. Confirm shares outstanding with registrar—to ascertain whether the corporate records are accurate and that stock is issued in accordance with the authorization of the board of directors and the articles of incorporation	Accuracy Existence
12. Analyze the retained earnings account—to determine whether it is disclosed accurately in the financial statements, and determine the amount of any restrictions on retained earnings that result from loans, other agreements, or state law	All Presentation & Disclosure Assertions
13. Analyze prior-period adjustments—to ascertain whether they are valid and are treated properly in the financial statements and determine the amount of any restrictions on retained earnings that result from loans, other agreements, or state law	All Presentation & Disclosure Assertions

* Note that many procedures may test multiple assertions. This program is not intended to be a complete presentation. See Chapter 4 for details on assertions.

J. Accounting Estimates (AU 342)

  1. **Audit Objectives' Focus** To determine if (a) all accounting estimates that could be material to the financial statements have been developed, (b) the estimates are reasonable, and (c) the estimates are in conformity with GAAP and are disclosed properly

      a. Accounting estimates are used when the measurement of some amounts or the valuations of some accounts is uncertain pending the outcome of future events.

      b. Estimates also are used when relevant data concerning events that have occurred already cannot be accumulated on a timely, cost-effective basis.

  2. **Developing Accounting Estimates** Management is responsible for establishing the process for preparing accounting estimates. Generally this consists of:

      a. Identifying situations that require accounting estimates

      b. Identifying relevant factors

      c. Accumulating relevant, sufficient, and reliable data on which to base the estimate

      d. Developing assumptions based on management's judgment of the most likely circumstances and events

      e. Determining estimated amounts based on the assumptions

      f. Determining the estimate is presented in conformity with applicable accounting principles and that disclosure is adequate

3. **Internal Control**   Internal control may reduce the risk of material misstatements of accounting estimates. Some relevant features of internal control include:

    a.   Management communication of the need for proper accounting estimates

    b.   Accumulation of relevant, sufficient, and reliable data on which to base an accounting estimate

    c.   Preparation of estimates by qualified personnel

    d.   Adequate review and approval of accounting estimates by appropriate levels of authority

    e.   Comparison of prior accounting estimates with subsequent results to assess the reliability of the process used to develop estimates

    f.   Consideration by management of whether the resulting accounting estimate is consistent with the operational plans of the entity

4. **Evaluating Accounting Estimates**   The auditor must evaluate the reasonableness of accounting estimates and consider them with an attitude of professional skepticism. The auditor should develop an independent expectation of the estimate based on knowledge of the entity and its industry.

    a.   In evaluating the reasonableness of an estimate, the auditor normally concentrates on key factors and assumptions that are

        (1)   Significant to the accounting estimate

        (2)   Sensitive to variations

        (3)   Deviations from historical patterns

        (4)   Subjective and susceptible to misstatement and bias

    b.   To determine whether management has identified all accounting estimates that could be material to the financial statements, the auditor should evaluate information regarding the following: changes made or planned in the entity's business; changes in the method of accumulating information; litigation, claims, and assessments; minutes of meetings; and regulatory or examination reports.

    c.   The auditor should understand how management develops estimates and the historical experience of the entity in making past estimates. Management's process of developing accounting estimates should be reviewed and tested. The auditor should consider performing the following procedures:

        (1)   Identify controls over the preparation of accounting estimates and supporting data that may be useful in the evaluation.

        (2)   Identify the sources of data and factors that management used and consider whether such data and factors are relevant, reliable, and sufficient for the purpose.

        (3)   Evaluate whether the assumptions are consistent with each other, the supporting data, historical data, and industry data.

        (4)   Consider whether changes in business or industry may cause other factors to become significant.

(5)   Consider whether there are additional factors that should be evaluated.

(6)   Evaluate historical data used to develop assumptions to assess whether data is comparable and consistent with data of the period being audited.

———————————————

CHAPTER 5—AUDIT PROGRAMS

Problem 5-1 MULTIPLE-CHOICE QUESTIONS

1. The objective of tests of details of transactions performed as substantive tests is to

   a. Comply with generally accepted auditing standards
   b. Attain assurance about the reliability of the accounting system
   c. Detect material misstatements in the financial statements
   d. Evaluate whether management's policies and procedures operated effectively

   (11/95, AUD, #51, ID: 5998)

2. Which of the following procedures would an auditor **least** likely perform before the balance sheet date?

   a. Confirmation of accounts payable
   b. Observation of merchandise inventory
   c. Assessment of control risk
   d. Identification of related parties

   (5/95, AUD, #73, ID: 5691)

3. An auditor confirmed accounts receivable as of an interim date, and all confirmations were returned and appeared reasonable. Which of the following additional procedures most likely should be performed at year-end?

   a. Send confirmations for all new customer balances incurred from the interim date to year-end
   b. Resend confirmations for any significant customer balances remaining at year-end
   c. Review supporting documents for new large balances occurring after the interim date, and evaluate any significant changes in balances at year-end
   d. Review cash collections subsequent to the interim date and the year-end   (R/05, AUD, #45, ID: 7840)

4. An auditor plans to apply substantive tests to the details of asset and liability accounts as of an interim date rather than as of the balance sheet date. The auditor should be aware that this practice

   a. Eliminates the use of certain statistical sampling methods that would otherwise be available
   b. Presumes that the auditor will reperform the tests as of the balance sheet date
   c. Should be especially considered when there are rapidly changing economic conditions
   d. Potentially increases the risk that errors that exist at the balance sheet date will not be detected

   (R/06, AUD, #8, ID: 8126)

5. Which of the following procedures would an auditor most likely perform in obtaining evidence about subsequent events?

   a. Determine that changes in employee pay rates after year-end were properly authorized
   b. Recompute depreciation charges for plant assets sold after year-end
   c. Investigate changes in long-term debt occurring after year-end
   d. Inquire about payroll checks that were recorded before year-end but cashed after year-end

   (5/95, AUD, #65, amended, ID: 5683)

6. An auditor compared the current year gross margin with the prior year gross margin to determine if cost of sales is reasonable. What type of audit procedure was performed?

   a. Test of transactions
   b. Analytical procedures
   c. Test of controls
   d. Test of details

   (R/06, AUD, #22, ID: 8140)

7. Which of the following procedures would an auditor most likely perform in auditing the statement of cash flows?

   a. Compare the amounts included in the statement of cash flows to similar amounts in the prior year's statement of cash flows
   b. Reconcile the cutoff bank statements to verify the accuracy of the year-end bank balances
   c. Vouch all bank transfers for the last week of the year and first week of the subsequent year
   d. Reconcile the amounts included in the statement of cash flows to the other financial statements' balances and amounts
                                              (5/95, AUD, #56, ID: 5674)

8. In testing the existence assertion for an asset, an auditor ordinarily works from the

   a. Financial statements to the potentially unrecorded items
   b. Potentially unrecorded items to the financial statements
   c. Accounting records to the supporting evidence
   d. Supporting evidence to the accounting records
                                            (11/90, AUD, #17, ID: 136)

9. In determining whether transactions have been recorded, the direction of the audit testing should be from the

   a. General ledger balances
   b. Adjusted trial balance
   c. Original source documents
   d. General journal entries
                                            (5/95, AUD, #57, ID: 5675)

10. Tracing copies of computer-prepared sales invoices to copies of the corresponding computer-prepared shipping documents provides evidence that

   a. Shipments to customers were properly billed.
   b. Entries in the accounts receivable subsidiary ledger were for sales actually shipped.
   c. Sales billed to customers were actually shipped.
   d. No duplicate shipments to customers were made.
                                            (R/06, AUD, #27, ID: 8145)

11. In which of the following circumstances is substantive testing of accounts receivable before the balance sheet date most appropriate?

   a. The client has a new sales incentive program in place.
   b. Internal controls during the remaining period are effective.
   c. There is a high turnover of senior management.
   d. It is a first engagement of a new client.
                                            (R/07, AUD, #26, ID: 8398)

12. Before applying principal substantive tests to an entity's accounts receivable at an interim date, an auditor should

   a. Consider the likelihood of assessing the risk of incorrect rejection too low
   b. Project sampling risk at the maximum for tests covering the remaining period
   c. Ascertain that accounts receivable are immaterial to the financial statements
   d. Assess the difficulty in controlling the incremental audit risk
                                            (R/07, AUD, #41, ID: 8413)

13. Which of the following procedures would an auditor most likely perform prior to the balance sheet date?

   a. Review subsequent events
   b. Perform search for unrecorded liabilities
   c. Send inquiry letter to client's legal counsel
   d. Review detail and test significant travel and entertainment expenses
                                            (R/08, AUD, #32, ID: 8638)

14. On receiving a client's bank cutoff statement, an auditor most likely would trace

    a. Prior year checks listed in the cutoff statement to the year-end outstanding checks
    b. Deposits in transit listed in the cutoff statement to the year-end bank reconciliation
    c. Checks dated after year-end listed in the cutoff statement to the year-end outstanding checks
    d. Deposits recorded in the cash receipts journal after year-end to the cutoff statement

    (R/02, AUD, #8, ID: 7098)

15. The usefulness of the standard bank confirmation request may be limited because the bank employee who completes the form may

    a. Not believe that the bank is obligated to verify confidential information to a third party
    b. Sign and return the form without inspecting the accuracy of the client's bank reconciliation
    c. Not have access to the client's cutoff bank statement
    d. Be unaware of all the financial relationships that the bank has with the client

    (11/95, AUD, #45, ID: 5992)

16. Which of the following characteristics most likely would be indicative of check kiting?

    a. High turnover of employees who have access to cash
    b. Many large checks that are recorded on Mondays
    c. Low average balance compared to high level of deposits
    d. Frequent ATM checking account withdrawals

    (R/02, AUD, #17, ID: 7107)

17. The primary purpose of sending a standard confirmation request to financial institutions with which the client has done business during the year is to

    a. Detect kiting activities that may otherwise not be discovered
    b. Corroborate information regarding deposit and loan balances
    c. Provide the data necessary to prepare a proof of cash
    d. Request information about contingent liabilities and secured transactions   (5/93, AUD, #34, ID: 3930)

18. Which of the following cash transfers results in a misstatement of cash at December 31, 20X1?

	Disbursement Date		Receipt Date	
	per books	per bank	per books	per bank
a.	12/31/X1	01/05/X2	12/31/X1	01/04/X2
b.	01/04/X2	01/11/X2	01/04/X2	01/04/X2
c.	12/31/X1	01/04/X2	12/31/X1	12/31/X1
d.	01/04/X2	01/05/X2	12/31/X1	01/04/X2

Bank Transfer Schedule

(R/07, AUD, #8, ID: 8380)

19. An auditor most likely would limit substantive audit tests of sales transactions when control risk is assessed as low for the occurrence assertion concerning sales transactions and the auditor has already gathered evidence supporting

    a. Opening and closing inventory balances
    b. Cash receipts and accounts receivable
    c. Shipping and receiving activities
    d. Cutoffs of sales and purchases

    (11/95, AUD, #46, ID: 5993)

20. An auditor observed that a client mails monthly statements to customers. Subsequently, the auditor reviewed evidence of follow-up on the errors reported by the customers. This test of controls most likely was performed to support management's financial statement assertion(s) of

	Classification and understandability	Rights and obligations
a.	Yes	Yes
b.	Yes	No
c.	No	Yes
d.	No	No

(R/02, AUD, #11, amended, ID: 7101)

21. Which of the following internal control procedures most likely would deter lapping of collections from customers?

    a. Independent internal verification of dates of entry in the cash receipts journal with dates of daily cash summaries
    b. Authorization of write-offs of uncollectible accounts by a supervisor independent of credit approval
    c. Segregation of duties between receiving cash and posting the accounts receivable ledger
    d. Supervisory comparison of the daily cash summary with the sum of the cash receipts journal entries

    (5/93, AUD, #14, ID: 3910)

22. An auditor suspects that a client's cashier is misappropriating cash receipts for personal use by lapping customer checks received in the mail. In attempting to uncover this embezzlement scheme, the auditor most likely would compare the

    a. Dates checks are deposited per bank statements with the dates remittance credits are recorded.
    b. Daily cash summaries with the sums of the cash receipts journal entries.
    c. Individual bank deposit slips with the details of the monthly bank statements.
    d. Dates uncollectible accounts are authorized to be written off with the dates the write-offs are actually recorded.

    (11/95, AUD, #28, ID: 5975)

23. In evaluating the adequacy of the allowance for doubtful accounts, an auditor most likely reviews the entity's aging of receivables to support management's financial statement assertion of

    a. Existence
    b. Valuation and allocation
    c. Completeness
    d. Rights and obligations

    (5/93, AUD, #29, amended, ID: 3925)

24. An auditor discovered that a client's accounts receivable turnover is substantially lower for the current year than for the prior year. This may indicate that

    a. Fictitious credit sales have been recorded during the year.
    b. Employees have stolen inventory just before the year-end.
    c. The client recently tightened its credit-granting policies.
    d. An employee has been lapping receivables in both years.

    (R/02, AUD, #19, ID: 7109)

25. Which of the following most likely would be detected by an auditor's review of a client's sales cutoff?

    a. Shipments lacking sales invoices and shipping documents
    b. Excessive write-offs of accounts receivable
    c. Unrecorded sales at year-end
    d. Lapping of year-end accounts receivable

    (5/92, AUD, #25, ID: 2778)

26. An auditor selects a sample from the file of shipping documents to determine whether invoices were prepared. This test is performed to satisfy the audit objective of

    a. Accuracy
    b. Completeness
    c. Existence
    d. Control

    (Editors, ID: 7494)

27. An auditor most likely would review an entity's periodic accounting for the numerical sequence of shipping documents and invoices to support management's financial statement assertion of

    a. Occurrence
    b. Rights and obligations
    c. Valuation and allocation
    d. Completeness

    (5/93, AUD, #27, amended, ID: 3923)

28. Which of the following audit procedures would an auditor most likely perform to test controls relating to management's assertion concerning the completeness of sales transactions?

a. Verify that extensions and footings on the entity's sales invoices and monthly customer statements have been recomputed

b. Inspect the entity's reports of prenumbered shipping documents that have not been recorded in the sales journal

c. Compare the invoiced prices on prenumbered sales invoices to the entity's authorized price list

d. Inquire about the entity's credit granting policies and the consistent application of credit checks

(5/94, AUD, #27, ID: 4692)

29. An auditor's purpose in reviewing credit ratings of customers with delinquent accounts receivable most likely is to obtain evidence concerning management's assertions about

a. Valuation and allocation

b. Classification and understandability

c. Existence

d. Rights and obligations

(11/94, AUD, #50, amended, ID: 5123)

30. If the objective of an auditor's test of details is to detect a possible understatement of sales, the auditor most likely would trace transactions from the

a. Sales invoices to the shipping documents

b. Cash receipts journal to the sales journal

c. Shipping documents to the sales invoices

d. Sales journal to the cash receipts journal

(R/08, AUD, #16, ID: 8622)

31. Under which of the following circumstances would the use of the blank form of confirmations of accounts receivable most likely be preferable to positive confirmations?

a. The recipients are likely to sign the confirmations without devoting proper attention to them.

b. Subsequent cash receipts are unusually difficult to verify.

c. Analytical procedures indicate that few exceptions are expected.

d. The combined assessed level of inherent risk and control risk is low.

(11/98, AUD, #23, ID: 6714)

32. When an auditor does not receive replies to positive requests for year-end accounts receivable confirmations, the auditor most likely would

a. Inspect the allowance account to verify whether the accounts were subsequently written off

b. Increase the assessed level of detection risk for the valuation and completeness assertions

c. Ask the client to contact the customers to request that the confirmations be returned

d. Increase the assessed level of inherent risk for the revenue cycle

(5/95, AUD, #46, ID: 5664)

33. Which of the following statements would an auditor most likely add to the negative form of confirmation of accounts receivable to encourage timely consideration by the recipients?

a. "This is not a request for payment; remittances should not be sent to our auditors in the enclosed envelope."

b. "Report any differences on the enclosed statement directly to our auditors; no reply is necessary if this amount agrees with your records."

c. "If you do not report an differences within 15 days, it will be assumed that this statement is correct."

d. "The following invoices have been selected for confirmation and represent amounts that are overdue."

(R/99, AUD, #19, ID: 6835)

34. Which of the following strategies most likely could improve the response rate of the confirmation of accounts receivable?

    a. Including a list of items or invoices that constitute the account balance
    b. Restricting the selection of accounts to be confirmed to those customers with relatively large balances
    c. Requesting customers to respond to the confirmation requests directly to the auditor by fax or e-mail
    d. Notifying the recipients that second requests will be mailed if they fail to respond in a timely manner
    (R/00, AUD, #11, ID: 6936)

35. In confirming accounts receivable, an auditor decided to confirm customers' account balances rather than individual invoices. Which of the following most likely would be included with the client's confirmation letter?

    a. An auditor-prepared letter explaining that a nonresponse may cause an inference that the account balance is correct
    b. A client-prepared letter reminding the customer that a nonresponse will cause a second request to be sent
    c. An auditor-prepared letter requesting the customer to supply missing and incorrect information directly to the auditor
    d. A client-prepared statement of account showing the details of the customer's account balance
    (R/99, AUD, #18, ID: 6834)

36. In auditing accounts receivable, the negative form of confirmation request most likely would be used when

    a. The total recorded amount of accounts receivable is immaterial to the financial statements taken as a whole.
    b. Response rates in prior years to properly designed positive confirmation requests were inadequate.
    c. Recipients are likely to return positive confirmation requests without verifying the accuracy of the information.
    d. The combined assessed level of inherent risk and control risk relative to accounts receivable is low.
    (11/97, AUD, #19, ID: 6582)

37. An independent auditor asked a client's internal auditor to assist in preparing a standard financial institution confirmation request for a payroll account that had been closed during the year under audit. After the internal auditor prepared the form, the controller signed it and mailed it to the bank. What was the major flaw in this procedure?

    a. The internal auditor did not sign the form.
    b. The form was mailed by the controller.
    c. The form was prepared by the internal auditor.
    d. The account was closed, so the balance was zero.
    (R/05, AUD, #5, ID: 7800)

38. To reduce the risks associated with accepting e-mail responses to requests for confirmation of accounts receivable, an auditor most likely would

    a. Request the senders to mail the original forms to the auditor
    b. Examine subsequent cash receipts for the accounts in question
    c. Consider the e-mail responses to the confirmations to be exceptions
    d. Mail second requests to the e-mail respondents
    (5/98, AUD, #12, ID: 6629)

39. Hemp, CPA, is auditing the financial statements of a small rural municipality. The receivable balances represent residents' delinquent real estate taxes. Internal control at the municipality is weak. To determine the existence of the accounts receivable balances at the balance sheet date, Hemp would most likely

    a. Send positive confirmation requests
    b. Send negative confirmation requests
    c. Inspect the internal records such as copies of the tax invoices that were mailed to the residents
    d. Examine evidence of subsequent cash receipts
    (Editors, ID: 178)

40. An auditor decides to use the blank form of accounts receivable confirmation rather than the positive form. The auditor should be aware that the blank form may be less efficient because

    a. Subsequent cash receipts need to be verified.
    b. Statistical sampling may not be used.
    c. A higher assessed level of detection risk is required.
    d. More nonresponses are likely to occur.   (R/03, AUD, #18, ID: 7640)

41. The confirmation of customers' accounts receivable rarely provides reliable evidence about the completeness assertion because

    a. Many customers merely sign and return the confirmation without verifying its details.
    b. Recipients usually respond only if they disagree with the information on the request.
    c. Customers may not be inclined to report understatement errors in their accounts.
    d. Auditors typically select many accounts with low recorded balances to be confirmed.
       (11/95, AUD, #39, ID: 5986)

42. Which of the following statements is correct concerning the use of negative confirmation requests?
    a. Unreturned negative confirmation requests rarely provide significant explicit evidence.
    b. Negative confirmation requests are effective when detection risk is low.
    c. Unreturned negative confirmation requests indicate that alternative procedures are necessary.
    d. Negative confirmation requests are effective when understatements of account balances are suspected.
       (5/95, AUD, #45, ID: 5663)

43. Which of the following strategies most likely could improve the response rate of the confirmations of accounts receivable?

    a. Restrict the selection of accounts to be confirmed to those customers with large balances
    b. Include a list of items or invoices that constitute the customers' account balances
    c. Explain to customers that discrepancies will be investigated by an independent third party
    d. Ask customers to respond to the confirmation requests directly to the auditor by fax
       (R/07, AUD, #35, ID: 8407)

44. The blank form of accounts receivable confirmations may be **less** efficient than the positive form because

    a. Shipping documents need to be inspected.
    b. Recipients may sign the forms without proper investigation.
    c. More nonresponses to the requests are likely to occur.
    d. Subsequent cash receipts need to be verified.   (R/09, AUD, #5, ID: 8805)

45. During the confirmation of accounts receivable, an auditor receives a confirmation via the client's fax machine. Which of the following actions should an auditor take?

    a. Not accept the confirmation and select another customer's balance to confirm
    b. Not accept the confirmation and treat it as an exception
    c. Accept the confirmation and file it in the working papers
    d. Accept the confirmation but verify the source and content through a telephone call to the respondent
       (R/10, AUD, #37, ID: 9387)

46. When an auditor decides to confirm accounts receivable balances rather than individual invoices, it most likely would be beneficial to include with the confirmations

    a. Copies of the client's shipping documents that support the account balances
    b. Lists of the customers' recent payments that the client has already recorded
    c. Client-prepared statements of account that show the details of the account balances
    d. Copies of the customers' purchase orders that support the account balances
       (R/11, AUD, #7, ID: 9907)

47. To measure how effectively an entity employs its resources, an auditor calculates inventory turnover by dividing average inventory into

   a. Net sales
   b. Cost of goods sold
   c. Operating income
   d. Gross sales   (11/95, AUD, #42, ID: 5989)

48. While observing a client's annual physical inventory, an auditor recorded test counts for several items and noticed that certain test counts were higher than the recorded quantities in the client's perpetual records. This situation could be the result of the client's failure to record

   a. Purchase discounts
   b. Purchase returns
   c. Sales
   d. Sales returns   (5/95, AUD, #52, ID: 5670)

49. When auditing inventories, an auditor would **least** likely verify that

   a. The financial statement presentation of inventories is appropriate.
   b. Damaged goods and obsolete items have been properly accounted for.
   c. All inventory owned by the client is on hand at the time of the count.
   d. The client has used proper inventory pricing.   (5/93, AUD, #28, ID: 7495)

50. An auditor most likely would inspect loan agreements under which an entity's inventories are pledged to support management's financial statement assertion of

   a. Completeness of disclosures
   b. Valuation of inventory
   c. Existence of inventory
   d. Completeness of inventory   (5/95, AUD, #40, amended, ID: 5658)

51. A client maintains perpetual inventory records in both quantities and dollars. If the assessed level of control risk is high, an auditor would probably

   a. Increase the extent of tests of controls of the inventory cycle
   b. Request the client to schedule the physical inventory count at the end of the year
   c. Insist that the client perform physical counts of inventory items several times during the year
   d. Apply gross profit tests to ascertain the reasonableness of the physical counts
                                                                      (11/94, AUD, #58, ID: 5131)

52. Which of the following audit procedures probably would provide the most reliable evidence concerning the entity's assertion of rights and obligations related to inventories?

   a. Inspect the open purchase order file for significant commitments that should be considered for disclosure
   b. Inspect agreements to determine whether any inventory is pledged as collateral or subject to any liens
   c. Select the last few shipping advices used before the physical count and determine whether the shipments were recorded as sales
   d. Trace test counts noted during the entity's physical count to the entity's summarization of quantities
                                                              (5/92, AUD, #17, amended, ID: 2770)

53. Which of the following auditing procedures most likely would provide assurance about a manufacturing entity's inventory valuation?

   a. Testing the entity's computation of standard overhead rates
   b. Obtaining confirmation of inventories pledged under loan agreements
   c. Reviewing shipping and receiving cutoff procedures for inventories
   d. Tracing test counts to the entity's inventory listing   (11/94, AUD, #48, ID: 5121)

54. To gain assurance that all inventory items in a client's inventory listing schedule are valid, an auditor most likely would trace

   a. Inventory tags noted during the auditor's observation to items listed in the inventory listing schedule
   b. Inventory tags noted during the auditor's observation to items listed in receiving reports and vendors' invoices
   c. Items listed in the inventory listing schedule to inventory tags and the auditor's recorded count sheets
   d. Items listed in receiving reports and vendors' invoices to the inventory listing schedule

   (5/95, AUD, #53, ID: 5671)

55. An auditor selected items for test counts while observing a client's physical inventory. The auditor then traced the test counts to the client's inventory listing. This procedure most likely obtained evidence concerning management's assertion of

   a. Rights and obligations
   b. Completeness
   c. Existence
   d. Valuation

   (5/94, AUD, #41, amended, ID: 4706)

56. Which of the following procedures would an auditor most likely perform to obtain assurance that slow-moving and obsolete items included in inventories are properly identified?

   a. Testing shipping and receiving cutoff procedures
   b. Confirming inventories at locations outside the entity's premises
   c. Examining an analysis of inventory turnover
   d. Tracing inventory observation test counts to perpetual listings

   (R/05, AUD, #9, ID: 7804)

57. In auditing a manufacturing entity, which of the following procedures would an auditor **least** likely perform to determine whether slow-moving, defective, and obsolete items included in inventory are properly identified?

   a. Test the computation of standard overhead rates
   b. Tour the manufacturing plant or production facility
   c. Compare inventory balances to anticipated sales volume
   d. Review inventory experience and trends

   (R/06, AUD, #34, ID: 8152)

58. An auditor most likely would make inquiries of production and sales personnel concerning possible obsolete or slow-moving inventory to support management's financial statement assertion of

   a. Valuation and allocation
   b. Rights and obligations
   c. Existence
   d. Classification and understandability

   (5/95, AUD, #43, amended, ID: 5661)

59. To obtain assurance that all inventory items in a client's inventory listing are valid, an auditor most likely would trace

   a. Inventory tags noted during the auditor's observation to items listed in receiving reports and vendors' invoices
   b. Items listed in receiving reports and vendors' invoices to the inventory listing
   c. Inventory tags noted during the auditor's observation to items in the inventory listing
   d. Items in the inventory listing to inventory tags and the auditor's recorded count sheets

   (R/07, AUD, #46, ID: 8418)

60. As part of the process of observing a client's physical inventories, an auditor should be alert to

   a. The inclusion of any obsolete or damaged goods
   b. Any change in the method of pricing from prior years
   c. The existence of outstanding purchase commitments
   d. The verification of inventory values assigned to goods in process

   (R/09, AUD, #23, ID: 8823)

61. Under which of the following conditions may an auditor's observation procedure for inventory be performed during or after the end of the period under audit?

    a. When the client maintains periodic inventory records
    b. When the auditor finds minimal variations in client records and test counts in prior periods
    c. When total inventory has **not** varied more than 5% in the last five years
    d. When well-kept perpetual inventory records are checked by the client periodically by comparisons with physical counts
    (R/10, AUD, #13, ID: 9363)

62. Which of the following procedures would be most appropriate for testing the completeness assertion as it applies to inventory?

    a. Scanning perpetual inventory, production, and purchasing records
    b. Examining paid vendor invoices
    c. Tracing inventory items from the tag listing back to the physical inventory quantities
    d. Performing cutoff procedures for shipping and receiving
    (R/10, AUD, #31, ID: 9381)

63. The purpose of tracing a sample of inventory tags to a client's computerized listing of inventory items is to determine whether the inventory items

    a. Represented by tags were included on the listing
    b. Included on the listing were properly counted
    c. Represented by tags were reduced to the lower of cost or market
    d. Included in the listing were properly valued
    (R/11, AUD, #11, ID: 9911)

64. A portion of a client's inventory is in public warehouses. Evidence of the existence of this merchandise can most efficiently be acquired through which of the following methods?

    a. Observation
    b. Confirmation
    c. Calculation
    d. Inspection
    (R/11, AUD, #39, ID: 9939)

65. An auditor analyzes repairs and maintenance accounts primarily to obtain evidence in support of the audit assertion that all

    a. Noncapitalizable expenditures for repairs and maintenance have been recorded in the proper period.
    b. Expenditures for property and equipment have been recorded in the proper period.
    c. Noncapitalizable expenditures for repairs and maintenance have been properly charged to expense.
    d. Expenditures for property and equipment have not been charged to expense.
    (11/94, AUD, #62, ID: 5135)

66. Which of the following explanations most likely would satisfy an auditor who questions management about significant debits to the accumulated depreciation accounts?

    a. The estimated remaining useful lives of plant assets were revised upward.
    b. Plant assets were retired during the year.
    c. The prior year's depreciation expense was erroneously understated.
    d. Overhead allocations were revised at year-end.
    (11/95, AUD, #49, ID: 5996)

67. In auditing intangible assets, an auditor most likely would review or recompute amortization and determine whether the amortization period is reasonable in support of management's financial statement assertion of

    a. Valuation and allocation
    b. Existence
    c. Completeness
    d. Rights and obligations
    (5/95, AUD, #41, amended, ID: 5659)

68. When there are numerous property and equipment transactions during the year, an auditor who plans to assess control risk at a low level usually performs

    a. Analytical procedures for property and equipment balances at the end of the year
    b. Analytical procedures for current year property and equipment transactions
    c. Tests of controls and limited tests of current year property and equipment transactions
    d. Tests of controls and extensive tests of property and equipment balances at the end of the year
    (11/95, AUD, #27, amended, ID: 5974)

69. A weakness of internal control over recording retirements of equipment may cause an auditor to

    a. Inspect certain items of equipment in the plant and trace those items to the accounting records
    b. Review the subsidiary ledger to ascertain whether depreciation was taken on each item of equipment during the year
    c. Trace additions to the "other assets" account to search for equipment that is still on hand but no longer being used
    d. Select certain items of equipment from the accounting records and locate them in the plant
    (11/95, AUD, #34, ID: 5981)

70. An auditor's principal objective in analyzing repairs and maintenance expense accounts is to

    a. Determine that all obsolete property, plant, and equipment assets were written off before the year-end
    b. Verify that all recorded property, plant, and equipment assets actually exist
    c. Discover expenditures that were expensed but should have been capitalized
    d. Identify property, plant, and equipment assets that cannot be repaired and should be written off
    (R/07, AUD, #19, ID: 8391)

71. An analysis of which of the following accounts would best aid in verifying that all fixed assets have been capitalized?

    a. Cash
    b. Depreciation expense
    c. Property tax expense
    d. Repairs and maintenance
    (R/07, AUD, #28, ID: 8400)

72. An auditor usually tests the reasonableness of dividend income from investments in publicly-held companies by computing the amounts that should have been received by referring to

    a. Dividend record books produced by investment advisory services
    b. Stock indentures published by corporate transfer agents
    c. Stock ledgers maintained by independent registrars
    d. Annual audited financial statements issued by the investee companies   (11/96, AUD, #11, ID: 6363)

73. In testing long-term investments, an auditor ordinarily would use analytical procedures to ascertain the reasonableness of the

    a. Completeness of recorded investment income
    b. Classification between current and noncurrent portfolios
    c. Valuation of marketable equity securities
    d. Existence of unrealized gains or losses in the portfolio   (5/93, AUD, #31, ID: 3927)

74. In establishing the existence and ownership of a long-term investment in the form of publicly-traded stock, an auditor should inspect the securities or

    a. Correspond with the investee company to verify the number of shares owned
    b. Inspect the audited financial statements of the investee company
    c. Confirm the number of shares owned that are held by an independent custodian
    d. Determine that the investment is carried at the fair market value
    (11/94, AUD, #49, amended, ID: 5122)

75. When a client engages in transactions involving derivatives, the auditor should

    a. Develop an understanding of the economic substance of each derivative
    b. Confirm with the client's broker whether the derivatives are for trading purposes
    c. Notify the audit committee about the risks involved in derivative transactions
    d. Add an explanatory paragraph to the auditor's report describing the risks associated with each derivative
    (R/06, AUD, #13, ID: 8131)

76. An auditor usually determines whether dividend income from publicly-held investments is reasonable by computing the amounts that should have been received by referring to

    a. Stock ledgers maintained by independent registrars
    b. Dividend records on file with the SEC
    c. Records produced by investment services
    d. Minutes of the investee's board of directors
    (R/06, AUD, #17, ID: 8135)

77. An auditor's inquiries of management disclosed that the entity recently invested in a series of energy derivatives to hedge against the risks associated with fluctuating oil prices. Under these circumstances, the auditor should

    a. Perform analytical procedures to determine if the derivatives are properly valued
    b. Examine the contracts for possible risk exposure and the need to recognize losses
    c. Confirm the marketability of the derivatives with a commodity specialist
    d. Document the derivatives in the auditor's communication with the audit committee
    (R/06, AUD, #30, ID: 8148)

78. To satisfy the valuation assertion when auditing an investment accounted for by the equity method, an auditor most likely would

    a. Inspect the stock certificates evidencing the investment
    b. Examine the audited financial statements of the investee company
    c. Review the broker's advice or canceled check for the investment's acquisition
    d. Obtain market quotations from financial newspapers or periodicals   (11/91, AUD, #44, ID: 2312)

79. In confirming with an outside agent, such as a financial institution, that the agent is holding investment securities in the client's name, an auditor most likely gathers evidence in support of management's financial statement assertions of existence and

    a. Valuation and allocation
    b. Rights and obligations
    c. Completeness
    d. Classification and understandability
    (5/95, AUD, #44, amended, ID: 5662)

80. In establishing the existence and ownership of long-term investments in the form of publicly-traded stock, an auditor most likely would inspect the securities or

    a. Correspond with the investee company to verify the number of shares owned
    b. Confirm the number of shares owned that are held by an independent custodian
    c. Apply analytical procedures to the dividend income and investments accounts
    d. Inspect the cash receipts journal for amounts that could represent the sale of securities
    (R/07, AUD, #37, ID: 8409)

81. An auditor is testing the reasonableness of dividend income from investments in publicly-held companies. The auditor most likely would compute the amount that should have been received and recorded by the client by

    a. Reading the details of the board of directors' meetings
    b. Confirming the details with the investee companies' registrars
    c. Electronically accessing the details of dividend records on the Internet
    d. Examining the details of the client's most recent cutoff bank statement   (R/09, AUD, #42, ID: 8842)

82. Which of the following procedures would an auditor most likely perform in searching for unrecorded liabilities?

    a. Trace a sample of accounts payable entries recorded just before year-end to the unmatched receiving report file
    b. Compare a sample of purchase orders issued just after year-end with the year-end accounts payable trial balance
    c. Vouch a sample of cash disbursements recorded just after year-end to receiving reports and vendor invoices
    d. Scan the cash disbursements entries recorded just before year-end for indications of unusual trans-actions
    (11/95, AUD, #47, ID: 5994)

83. An auditor traced a sample of purchase orders and the related receiving reports to the purchases journal and the cash disbursements journal. The purpose of this substantive audit procedure most likely was to

    a. Identify unusually large purchases that should be investigated further
    b. Verify that cash disbursements were for goods actually received
    c. Determine that purchases were properly recorded
    d. Test whether payments were for goods actually ordered
    (11/95, AUD, #48, ID: 5995)

84. Which of the following is a substantive test that an auditor most likely would perform to verify the existence and valuation of recorded accounts payable?

    a. Investigating the open purchase order file to ascertain that prenumbered purchase orders are used and accounted for
    b. Receiving the client's mail, unopened, for a reasonable period of time after the year-end to search for unrecorded vendor's invoices
    c. Vouching selected entries in the accounts payable subsidiary ledger to purchase orders and receiving reports
    d. Confirming accounts payable balances with known suppliers who have zero balances
    (5/93, AUD, #36, ID: 3932)

85. An auditor suspects that certain client employees are ordering merchandise for themselves over the Internet without recording the purchase or receipt of the merchandise. When vendors' invoices arrive, one of the employees approves the invoices for payment. After the invoices are paid, the employee destroys the invoices and the related vouchers. In gathering evidence regarding the fraud, the auditor most likely would select items for testing from the file of all

    a. Cash disbursements
    b. Approved vouchers
    c. Receiving reports
    d. Vendors' invoices
    (R/01, AUD, #4, ID: 7019)

86. To determine whether accounts payable are complete, an auditor performs a test to verify that all merchandise received is recorded. The population of documents for this test consists of all

    a. Payment vouchers
    b. Receiving reports
    c. Purchase requisitions
    d. Vendor's invoices
    (11/93, AUD, #26, ID: 4263)

87. In auditing accounts payable, an auditor's procedures most likely would focus primarily on management's assertion of

    a. Existence
    b. Classification and understandability
    c. Completeness
    d. Valuation and allocation
    (11/93, AUD, #37, amended, ID: 4274)

88. Cooper, CPA, performs a test to determine whether all merchandise for which the client was billed was received. The population for this test consists of all

    a. Merchandise received
    b. Vendors' invoices
    c. Receiving reports
    d. Canceled checks
    (Editors, ID: 195)

89. Which of the following procedures would best detect a liability omission by management?

    a. Inquiry of senior support staff and recently departed employees
    b. Review and check mathematical accuracy of financial statements
    c. Review articles of incorporation and corporate bylaws
    d. Review purchase contracts and other legal documents
    (R/08, AUD, #2, ID: 8608)

90. Which of the following tests of details most likely would help an auditor determine whether accounts payable have been misstated?

    a. Examining reported purchase returns that appear too low
    b. Examining vendor statements for amounts **not** reported as purchases
    c. Searching for customer-returned goods that were **not** reported as returns
    d. Reviewing bank transfers recorded as cash received from customers
    (R/10, AUD, #38, ID: 9388)

91. An auditor most likely would extend substantive tests of payroll when

    a. Payroll is extensively audited by the state government.
    b. Payroll expense is substantially higher than in the prior year.
    c. Overpayments are discovered in performing tests of details.
    d. Employees complain to management about too much overtime.
    (5/94, AUD, #49, ID: 4714)

92. An auditor vouched data for a sample of employees in a payroll register to approved clock card data to provide assurance that

    a. Payments to employees are computed at authorized rates.
    b. Employees work the number of hours for which they are paid.
    c. Segregation of duties exists between the preparation and distribution of the payroll.
    d. Internal controls relating to unclaimed payroll checks are operating effectively.
    (5/95, AUD, #37, ID: 5655)

93. When control risk is assessed as low for assertions related to payroll, substantive tests of payroll balances most likely would be limited to applying analytical procedures and

    a. Observing the distribution of paychecks
    b. Footing and cross-footing the payroll register
    c. Inspecting payroll tax returns
    d. Recalculating payroll accruals
    (5/95, AUD, #54, ID: 5672)

94. An auditor reviews the reconciliation of payroll tax forms that a client is responsible for filing in order to

    a. Verify that payroll taxes are deducted from employees' gross pay
    b. Determine whether internal control activities are operating effectively
    c. Uncover fictitious employees who are receiving payroll checks
    d. Identify potential liabilities for unpaid payroll taxes
    (R/02, AUD, #14, ID: 7104)

95. Which of the following payroll control activities would most effectively ensure that payment is made only for work performed?

    a. Require all employees to record arrival and departure by using the time clock
    b. Have a payroll clerk recalculate all time cards
    c. Require all employees to sign their time cards
    d. Require employees to have their direct supervisors approve their time cards
    (R/10, AUD, #7, ID: 9357)

96. In auditing long-term bonds payable, an auditor most likely would

    a. Perform analytical procedures on the bond premium and discount accounts
    b. Examine documentation of assets purchased with bond proceeds for liens
    c. Compare interest expense with the bonds payable amount for reasonableness
    d. Confirm the existence of individual bondholders at year-end   (11/94, AUD, #60, ID: 5133)

97. An auditor's program to examine long-term debt most likely would include steps that require

    a. Comparing the carrying amount of the debt to its year-end market value
    b. Correlating interest expense recorded for the period with outstanding debt
    c. Verifying the existence of the holders of the debt by direct confirmation
    d. Inspecting the accounts payable subsidiary ledger for unrecorded long-term debt
                                                                          (5/91, AUD, #8, ID: 127)

98. In auditing a client's retained earnings account, an auditor should determine whether there are any restrictions on retained earnings that result from loans, agreements, or state law. This procedure is designed to corroborate management's financial statement assertion of

    a. Valuation and allocation
    b. Occurrence
    c. Completeness of disclosures
    d. Rights and obligations   (11/98, AUD, #22, amended, ID: 6713)

99. The primary responsibility of a bank acting as registrar of capital stock is to

    a. Ascertain that dividends declared do not exceed the statutory amount allowable in the state of incorporation
    b. Account for stock certificates by comparing the total shares outstanding to the total in the shareholders subsidiary ledger
    c. Act as an independent third party between the board of directors and outside investors concerning mergers, acquisitions, and the sale of treasury stock
    d. Verify that stock is issued in accordance with the authorization of the board of directors and the articles of incorporation   (5/91, AUD, #32, ID: 133)

100. An auditor usually obtains evidence of stockholders' equity transactions by reviewing the entity's

    a. Minutes of board of directors meetings
    b. Transfer agent's records
    c. Canceled stock certificates
    d. Treasury stock certificate book   (R/99, AUD, #21, ID: 6837)

101. When a company's stock record books are maintained by an outside registrar or transfer agent, the auditor should obtain confirmation from the registrar or transfer agent concerning the

    a. Amount of dividends paid to related parties
    b. Expected proceeds from stock subscriptions receivable
    c. Number of shares issued and outstanding
    d. Proper authorization of stock rights and warrants   (R/06, AUD, #2, ID: 8120)

102. In performing tests concerning the granting of stock options, an auditor should

    a. Confirm the transaction with the Secretary of State in the state of incorporation
    b. Verify the existence of option holders in the entity's payroll records or stock ledgers
    c. Determine that sufficient treasury stock is available to cover any new stock issued
    d. Trace the authorization for the transaction to a vote of the board of directors
                                                                          (11/94, AUD, #61, ID: 5134)

103. Which of the following procedures most likely would assist an auditor in determining whether management has identified all accounting estimates that could be material to the financial statements?

    a. Inquire about the existence of related-party transactions
    b. Determine whether accounting estimates deviate from historical patterns
    c. Confirm inventories at locations outside the entity
    d. Review the lawyer's letter for information about litigation   (R/02, AUD, #4, ID: 7094)

104. In evaluating the reasonableness of an entity's accounting estimates, an auditor normally would be concerned about assumptions that are

    a. Susceptible to bias
    b. Consistent with prior periods
    c. Insensitive to variations
    d. Similar to industry guidelines   (5/97, AUD, #6, ID: 6395)

105. In evaluating an entity's accounting estimates, one of the auditor's objectives is to determine whether the estimates are

    a. Prepared in a satisfactory control environment
    b. Consistent with industry guidelines
    c. Based on verifiable objective assumptions
    d. Reasonable in the circumstances   (R/06, AUD, #48, ID: 8166)

106. Which of the following procedures would an auditor ordinarily perform first in evaluating the reasonableness of management's accounting estimates?

    a. Review transactions occurring prior to the completion of fieldwork that indicate variations from expectations
    b. Compare independent expectations with recorded estimates to assess management's process
    c. Obtain an understanding of how management developed its estimates
    d. Analyze historical data used in developing assumptions to determine whether the process is consistent   (R/05, AUD, #26, ID: 7821)

107. In evaluating the reasonableness of an entity's accounting estimates, an auditor most likely concentrates on key factors and assumptions that are

    a. Stable and not sensitive to variation
    b. Objective and not susceptible to bias
    c. Deviations from historical patterns
    d. Similar to industry guidelines   (R/08, AUD, 1438A, #43, ID: 8649)

108. Which of the following statements is correct regarding accounting estimates?

    a. The auditor's objective is to evaluate whether accounting estimates are reasonable in the circumstances.
    b. Accounting estimates should be used when data concerning past events can be accumulated in a timely, cost-effective manner.
    c. An important accounting estimate is management's listing of accounts receivable greater than 90 days past due.
    d. Accounting estimates should not be used when the outcome of future events related to the estimated item is unknown.   (R/09, AUD, #10, ID: 8810)

SIMULATIONS

Problem 5-2 SIMULATION: Kiting

The information below was taken from the bank transfer schedule prepared during the audit of Fox Co.'s financial statements for the year ended December 31, year 1. All checks are dated and issued on December 30, year 1.

Check No.	Bank Accounts		Disbursement Date		Receipt Date	
	From	To	Per Books	Per Bank	Per Books	Per Bank
1	National	Federal	Dec. 30	Jan. 4	Dec. 30	Jan. 3
2	County	State	Jan. 3	Jan. 2	Dec. 30	Dec. 31
3	Federal	American	Dec. 31	Jan. 3	Jan. 2	Jan. 2
4	State	Republic	Jan. 2	Jan. 2	Jan. 2	Dec. 31

A. Which two checks might indicate kiting?

B. Which two checks illustrate deposits/transfers in transit at December 31, year 1?   (ID: 9229)

———————————

Problem 5-3 SIMULATION: Audit Procedures for Errors & Fraud

The following items represent possible errors and fraud that an auditor suspects are present. The accompanying list of audit procedures represents procedures that the auditor would consider performing to gather evidence concerning possible errors and fraud. For each item, select one or two procedures, as indicated, that the auditor most likely would perform to gather evidence in support of that item.

Possible Errors and Fraud	Audit Procedures
1. The auditor suspects that a kiting scheme exists because an Accounting Department employee who can issue and record checks seems to be leading an unusually luxurious lifestyle. (Select only 1 procedure)	
2. The auditor suspects that the controller wrote several checks and recorded the cash disbursements just before the year-end but did not mail the checks until after the first week of the subsequent year. (Select only 1 procedure)	
3. The entity borrowed funds from a financial institution. Although the transaction was properly recorded, the auditor suspects that the loan created a lien on the entity's real estate that is not disclosed in its financial statements. (Select only 1 procedure)	
4. The auditor discovered an unusually large receivable from one of the entity's new customers. The auditor suspects that the receivable may be fictitious because the auditor has never heard of the customer and because the auditor's initial attempt to confirm the receivable has been ignored by the customer. (Select only 2 procedures)	
5. The auditor suspects that fictitious employees have been placed on the payroll by the entity's payroll supervisor, who has access to payroll records and to the paychecks. (Select only 1 procedure)	
6. The auditor suspects that selected employees of the entity received unauthorized raises from the entity's payroll supervisor, who has access to payroll records. (Select only 1 procedure)	

List of Audit Procedures

A. Compare the details of the cash receipts journal entries with the details of the corresponding daily deposit slips.

B. Scan the debits to the fixed asset accounts and vouch selected amounts to vendors' invoices and management authorization.

C. Perform analytical procedures that compare documented authorized pay rates to the entity's budget and forecast.

D. Obtain the cutoff bank statement and compare the cleared checks to the year-end bank reconciliation.

E. Prepare a bank transfer schedule.

F. Inspect the entity's deeds to its real estate.

G. Make inquiries of the entity's attorney concerning the details of real estate transactions.

H. Confirm the terms of borrowing arrangements with the lender.

I. Examine selected equipment repair orders and supporting documentation to determine the propriety of the charges.

J. Send requests to confirm the entity's accounts receivable on a surprise basis at an interim date.

K. Send a second request for confirmation of the receivable to the customer and make inquiries of a reputable credit agency concerning the customer's creditworthiness.

L. Examine the entity's shipping documents to verify that the merchandise that produced the receivable was actually sent to the customer.

M. Inspect the entity's correspondence files for indications of customer disputes or for evidence that certain shipments were on consignment.

N. Perform edit checks of data on the payroll transaction tapes.

O. Inspect payroll check endorsements for similar handwriting.

P. Observe payroll check distribution on a surprise basis.

Q. Vouch data in the payroll register to documented authorized pay rates in the Human Resources Department's files.

R. Reconcile the payroll checking account and determine if there were unusual time lags between the issuance and payment of payroll checks.

S. Inspect the file of prenumbered vouchers for consecutive numbering and proper approval by an appropriate employee.

T. Determine that the details of selected prenumbered vouchers match the related vendor's invoices.

U. Examine the supporting purchase orders and receiving reports for selected paid vouchers.   (ID: 9230)

———————————

Problem 5-4 SIMULATION: Audit Procedures for Long-Term Debt

American Manufacturers, Inc.
Long-Term Debt
October 31, Year 20X1

Lender	Interest rate	Payment terms	Collateral	Balance 10/31/X0	Current year borrowings	Current year reductions	Balance 10/31/X1	Interest paid to	Accrued interest payable 10/31/X1	Comments
▲ First National Bank	10%	Interest only on last day of each quarter; principal due in full on 9/30/X3	Manufacturing equipment	500,000 ■	200,000 ◆ 3/31/X1	(100,000) ✪ 6/30/X1	600,000 √	9/30/X1	5,000 ✖	[1]
▲ Second State Bank	9%	$10,000 principal plus interest due on the 1st of each month; due in full on 1/1/X4	First mortgage on production facilities	380,000 ■	0	(110,000) +	270,000 √★	9/30/X1	2,025 ✖	[2]
▲ Third Savings & Loan	12%	$5,000 principal plus interest due on the 15th of each month; due in full on 10/15/X3	Second mortgage on production facilities	180,000 ■	0	(60,000)	120,000 ★★	10/15/X1	600	[3]
▲ A. Clark, majority stockholder	0%	Due in full 10/31/X3	Unsecured	700,000 ■	0	(200,000) 10/28/X1	500,000 √		0	[4]
				1,760,000	200,000	(470,000)	1,490,000 ●		7,625 ●	

[1] First National confirms that interest payments are current and agrees with account balance.

[2] Monthly payment for $12,025 was mailed on 11/3/X1; Second State agrees with account balance.

[3] Third Savings & Loan claims 10/15/X1 payment wasn't received as of 11/5/X1; adjusting entry proposed to increase accrued interest payable.

[4] Borrowed additional $200,000 from Clark on 11/5/X1; need to investigate reborrowing just after year-end and consider imputed interest on 0% stockholder loan.

The items to be answered represent tick marks (symbols) that indicate procedures performed or comments documented in auditing the long-term debt account of American Manufacturers, Inc.

Select, from the accompanying lists of procedures/comments, the procedure/comment that the auditor most likely performed/documented at each point of the audit where a tick mark was made on the working papers. Select only one procedure/comment for each item. Assume that the working papers foot and cross-foot.

Tick Marks	Procedure/Comment
1. ▲	
2. ▣	
3. ♦	
4. ✪	
5. ✚	
6. √	
7. ★	
8. ✳	
9. •	
10. ✕	

List of Procedures/Comments

A. Confirmed, without exception.

B. Confirmed, with exception.

C. Traced amount to prior year's working papers.

D. Traced amount to current year's trial balance and general ledger.

E. Does not recompute correctly.

F. Tested reasonableness of calculations.

G. Agreed to canceled checks and lender's monthly statements.

H. Agreed to canceled check and board of directors' authorization.

I. Agreed interest rate, terms, and collateral to note & loan agreement.

J. Agreed to loan agreement, validated bank deposit ticket, and board of directors' authorization.

K. Reclassification entry proposed for current portion of long-term debt.

(ID: 9231)

_____

Problem 5-5 SIMULATION: Audit Procedures for Property, Plant & Equipment

American Manufacturers, Inc.
Property, Plant & Equipment and Accumulated Depreciation
October 31, Year 20X1

Property, Plant & Equipment

Account	Balance 10/31/X0		Additions		Disposals		Other		Balance 10/31/X1	
Land	650,000	➢	70,000	↕	0		0		720,000	→
Buildings	3,270,000	➢	230,000	✓	0		(30,000)	⊗	3,470,000	→
Equipment	1,750,000	➢	90,000	<	(12,000)	↔	0		1,828,000	→
Fixtures	850,000	➢	200,000	✓	0		30,000	⊗	1,080,000	→
	6,520,000		590,000		(12,000)		0		7,098,000	

Accumulated Depreciation

Account	Depreciation Rate	Method	Balance 10/31/X0		Provision		Disposal	Balance 10/31/X1	
Land									
Buildings	5%	SL	1,144,500	➢	168,500	⌐	0	1,313,000	→
Equipment	10%	SL	700,000	➢	179,500	⌐	(12,000)	867,500	→
Fixtures	15%	SL	510,000	➢	144,750	⌐	0	654,750	→
			2,354,500		492,750		(12,000)	2,835,250	

The items to be answered represent tick marks (symbols) that indicate procedures performed or comments documented in auditing the Property, Plant & Equipment and Accumulated Depreciation accounts of American Manufacturers, Inc. During the year under audit, American Manufacturers purchased new computers directly from wholesalers and constructed an addition to one of its buildings. The company's employees also refurbished the fixtures of several older buildings.

Select, from the accompanying lists of procedures/comments, the procedure/comment that the auditor most likely performed/documented at each point of the audit where a tick mark was made on the working papers. Select only one procedure/comment for each item. Assume that the working papers foot and cross-foot.

Tick Marks	Procedure/Comment
1. ➢	
2. ↕	
3. ✓	
4. <	
5. ↔	
6. ⊗	
7. →	
8. ⌐	

List of Procedures/Comments

A. Does not recompute correctly.

B. Tested reasonableness of calculation.

C. Traced amount to current year's trial balance and general ledger.

D. Reclassification entry for fixtures erroneously recorded as buildings.

E. Reclassification entry for buildings erroneously recorded as fixtures.

F. Traced amount to prior year's working papers.

G. Sold six fully-depreciated computers to employees; no audit procedures necessary.

H. Confirmed, with exception.

I. Confirmed, without exception.

J. Examined supporting vendors' invoices, canceled checks, asset subsidiary ledger and board of directors' minutes of meetings authorizing transactions.

K. Examined supporting work orders and engineers' reports, canceled checks, asset subsidiary ledger, and board of directors' minutes of meetings authorizing transactions.

L. Examined supporting deed and purchase contract, canceled checks, asset subsidiary ledger, and board of directors' minutes of meeting authorizing transactions. (ID: 9232)

Problem 5-6 SIMULATION: Accounts Receivable (AR) Confirmations

The auditor requested the company's aged accounts receivable schedule listing the total amount owed by each customer as of December 31, year 2. The audit team sent the following positive confirmation requests to a sample of the company's customers.

Confirmation Letters

February 15, year 3

Chip Technology
500 E. Fifth Street
Cincinnati, OH 45202

Re: Balance at December 31, year 2 - $95,000

Dear Sirs:

As of December 31, year 2, our records indicate that you have a balance due to our company in the amount listed above. Please complete and sign the bottom portion of this letter, and return the entire letter to our auditors, Whisp, LLP, P.O. Box 100, Cleveland, Ohio 44115.

A stamped, self-addressed envelope is enclosed for your convenience.

Sincerely,

_____
        Jim Johnston
Company Controller

The above balance is [ ] Correct

[X] Incorrect
(show amount) $92,000

If incorrect, please provide information that could help to reconcile your account.

Recipient's Comment: Our records indicate that check #45998 for $3,000 was mailed on December 24, year 2.

Sue Smith	AP Supervisor	3/2/year 3
Signature	Title	Date

Auditor's note to file:

Per discussion with the controller, this customer's payment was received on December 28, but was not processed until January 4.

February 15, year 3

BiCon Semiconductor
8700 West Ave.
Rockland, KY 46009

Re: Balance at December 31, year 2 - $66,700

Dear Sirs:

As of December 31, year 2, our records indicate that you have a balance due to our company in the amount listed above. Please complete and sign the bottom portion of this letter, and return the entire letter to our auditors, Whisp, LLP, P.O. Box 100, Cleveland, Ohio 44115.

A stamped, self-addressed envelope is enclosed for your convenience.

Sincerely,

_____
        Jim Johnston
Company Controller

The above balance is [ ] Correct

[ ] Incorrect
(show amount) _____

If incorrect, please provide information that could help to reconcile your account.

Recipient's Comment: *Blank*

Signature	Title	Date

Auditor's note to file:

This confirmation was returned by the postal service as "return to sender—no such addressee at this location." This was the second attempt to reach the customer.

February 15, year 3

Whistler's Computer Warehouse
700 – 800 Adams St.
Newport, CT 11223

Re: Balance at December 31, year 2 - $120,050

Dear Sirs:

As of December 31, year 2, our records indicate that you have a balance due to our company in the amount listed above. Please complete and sign the bottom portion of this letter, and return the entire letter to our auditors, Whisp, LLP, P.O. Box 100, Cleveland, Ohio 44115.

A stamped, self-addressed envelope is enclosed for your convenience.

Sincerely,

_____Jim Johnston_____
Company Controller

The above balance is ☐ Correct

☒ Incorrect
(show amount) $118,050

If incorrect, please provide information that could help to reconcile your account.

Recipient's Comment: The materials from invoice #145 were returned on December 12, year 2.

Warren C. Worth	AP Supervisor	2/25/year 3
Signature	Title	Date

Auditor's note to file:

Firm confirmed this with the A/R supervisor.

February 15, year 3

Digital Digits
15 8th Ave.
Washington, OR 78899

Re: Balance at December 31, year 2 - $2,000,000

Dear Sirs:

As of December 31, year 2, our records indicate that you have a balance due to our company in the amount listed above. Please complete and sign the bottom portion of this letter, and return the entire letter to our auditors, Whisp, LLP, P.O. Box 100, Cleveland, Ohio 44115.

A stamped, self-addressed envelope is enclosed for your convenience.

Sincerely,

_____Jim Johnston_____
Company Controller

The above balance is ☐ Correct

☒ Incorrect
(show amount) $2,760,000

If incorrect, please provide information that could help to reconcile your account.

Recipient's Comment: In addition, we have invoices #A1768 ($360,000) & A1769 ($400,000), but I'm not sure when they are from.

Darlene Dunham	AP Supervisor	3/5/year 3
Signature	Title	Date

Auditor's note to file:

Blank.

February 15, year 3

Rockford's
37 73rd Street
Leder, VA 39281

Re: Balance at December 31, year 2 - $1,288,698

Dear Sirs:

As of December 31, year 2, our records indicate that you have a balance due to our company in the amount listed above. Please complete and sign the bottom portion of this letter, and return the entire letter to our auditors, Whisp, LLP, P.O. Box 100, Cleveland, Ohio 44115.

A stamped, self-addressed envelope is enclosed for your convenience.

Sincerely,

_____Jim Johnston_____
Company Controller.

The above balance is   [X] Correct

                        [   ] Incorrect
                              (show amount) $_____

If incorrect, please provide information that could help to reconcile your account.

| Recipient's Comment: Please be aware that as of March 1, we are changing our name to Richards' Service and Support. |

Signature   Title   Date

Auditor's note to file:

| *Blank* |

February 15, year 3

Jungle Applications
1200 East End Drive
Richelieu, KY 18998

Re: Balance at December 31, year 2 - $40,000

Dear Sirs:

As of December 31, year 2, our records indicate that you have a balance due to our company in the amount listed above. Please complete and sign the bottom portion of this letter, and return the entire letter to our auditors, Whisp, LLP, P.O. Box 100, Cleveland, Ohio 44115.

A stamped, self-addressed envelope is enclosed for your convenience.

Sincerely,

_____Jim Johnston_____
Company Controller

The above balance is   [   ] Correct

                        [   ] Incorrect
                              (show amount) $_____

If incorrect, please provide information that could help to reconcile your account.

| Recipient's Comment: Sorry for the inconvenience, but our A/P system is unable to confirm balances unless we have purchase order numbers. |

Julie Ashton   AP Supervisor   2/26/year 3
Signature   Title   Date

Auditor's note to file:

| *Blank* |

Review the confirmations and subsequent comments at the bottom of each confirmation and determine the action required for each one. Select the best action to follow from the selection list below. Choose only one action per confirmation. An action may be used once, more than once, or not at all.

Customer	Action Required
1. Chip Technology	
2. BiCon Semiconductor	
3. Whistler's Computer Warehouse	
4. Digital Digits	
5. Rockford's	
6. Jungle Applications	

Selection List

A. Exception noted; propose adjustment and request that the controller post it to the accounting records.	D. Verify by examining shipping documents and subsequent cash collections.
B. Send a second request for confirmation to the customer.	E. Verify that additional invoices noted on confirmation pertain to the subsequent year.
C. Trace to open sales order detail as of December 31, year 2.	F. Not an exception, no further audit work deemed necessary.

(R/11, AUD, 9832)

Problem 5-7 SIMULATION: Audit Procedures for Errors & Fraud

The following items represent possible errors and fraud that an auditor suspects are present. The accompanying list of audit procedures represents procedures that the auditor would consider performing to gather evidence concerning possible errors and fraud. For each item, select one or two procedures, as indicated, that the auditor most likely would perform to gather evidence in support of that item.

Possible Errors and Fraud	Audit Procedures
1. The entity's cash receipts of the first few days of the subsequent year were properly deposited in its general operating account after the year-end. However, the auditor suspects that the entity recorded the cash receipts in its books during the last week of the year under audit. (Select only 1 procedure)	
2. The auditor suspects that vouchers were prepared and processed by an Accounting Department employee for merchandise that was neither ordered nor received by the entity. (Select only 1 procedure)	
3. The details of invoices for equipment repairs were not clearly identified or explained to the Accounting Department employees. The auditor suspects that the bookkeeper incorrectly recorded the repairs as fixed assets. (Select only 1 procedure)	
4. The auditor suspects that a lapping scheme exists because an Accounting Department employee who has access to cash receipts also maintains the accounts receivable ledger and refuses to take any vacation or sick days. (Select only 2 procedures)	
5. The auditor suspects that the entity is inappropriately increasing the cash reported on its balance sheet by drawing a check on one account and not recording it as an outstanding check on that account, and simultaneously recording it as a deposit in a second account. (Select only 1 procedure)	
6. The auditor suspects that the entity's controller has overstated sales and accounts receivable by recording fictitious sales to regular customers in the entity's books. (Select only 2 procedures)	

List of Audit Procedures

A. Compare the details of the cash receipts journal entries with the details of the corresponding daily deposit slips.

B. Scan the debits to the fixed asset accounts and vouch selected amounts to vendors' invoices and management authorization.

C. Perform analytical procedures that compare documented authorized pay rates to the entity's budget and forecast.

D. Obtain the cutoff bank statement and compare the cleared checks to the year-end bank reconciliation.

E. Prepare a bank transfer schedule.

F. Inspect the entity's deeds to its real estate.

G. Make inquiries of the entity's attorney concerning the details of real estate transactions.

H. Confirm the terms of borrowing arrangements with the lender.

I. Examine selected equipment repair orders and supporting documentation to determine the propriety of the charges.

J. Send requests to confirm the entity's accounts receivable on a surprise basis at an interim date.

K. Send a second request for confirmation of the receivable to the customer and make inquiries of a reputable credit agency concerning the customer's creditworthiness.

L. Examine the entity's shipping documents to verify that the merchandise that produced the receivable was actually sent to the customer.

M. Inspect the entity's correspondence files for indications of customer disputes or for evidence that certain shipments were on consignment.

N. Perform edit checks of data on the payroll transaction tapes.

O. Inspect payroll check endorsements for similar handwriting.

P. Observe payroll check distribution on a surprise basis.

Q. Vouch data in the payroll register to documented authorized pay rates in the Human Resources Department's files.

R. Reconcile the payroll checking account and determine if there were unusual time lags between the issuance and payment of payroll checks.

S. Inspect the file of prenumbered vouchers for consecutive numbering and proper approval by an appropriate employee.

T. Determine that the details of selected prenumbered vouchers match the related vendor's invoices.

U. Examine the supporting purchase orders and receiving reports for selected paid vouchers.   (ID: 9233)

_____

Problem 5-8 SIMULATION: Financial Statement Assertions for Investments

Larkin, CPA, has been engaged to audit the financial statements of Vernon Distributors, Inc., a continuing audit client, for the year ended September 30, year 1. After obtaining an understanding of Vernon's internal control, Larkin assessed the risk of material misstatement as high for all financial statement assertions concerning investments.

Larkin prepared a partial audit program of substantive procedures listed in the table below.

Identify the primary financial statement assertion relative to investments that would be addressed by each of the procedures. An assertion may be used once, more than once, or not at all.

Audit Procedures	Primary Assertion
1. Obtain positive confirmation as of the balance sheet date of the investments held by any independent custodian.	
2. Determine that income from investments has been properly recorded as accrued or collected by reference to published sources, by computation, and by tracing to recorded amounts.	
3. For investments in nonpublic entities, compare carrying value to information in the most recently available audited financial statements.	
4. Determine that all transfers between trading and available-for-sale portfolios have been properly authorized and recorded.	
5. Determine that any other-than-temporary decline in the price of an investment has been properly recorded.	

Financial Statement Assertions

A. Presentation & disclosure

B. Existence

C. Contingency disclosure

D. Monetary adjustments

E. Occurrence & rights & obligations

F. Completeness

G. Classes of transactions

H. Valuation & accuracy & allocation

I. Account balances

J. Classification & understandability

(ID: 9234)

_____

Problem 5-9 SIMULATION: Research

What authoritative reference provides guidance on auditing inventories held by outside custodians?

§   (ID: 9235)

_____

Problem 5-10 SIMULATION: Research

What authoritative reference provides guidance regarding the circumstances in which an auditor does **not** request the confirmation of accounts receivable during an audit?

| | § | | | | (ID: 9219) |

Solution 5-1 MULTIPLE-CHOICE ANSWERS

Substantive Procedures

1. (c)   In selecting particular substantive procedures to achieve audit objectives, an auditor considers, among other things, the risk of material misstatement of the financial statements. Omitting a test of details of transactions in some situations would not be a violation of auditing standards. Attaining assurance about the reliability of the accounting system and evaluating whether management's policies and procedures operated effectively are objectives of tests of controls. (ID: 5998)

2. (a)   While the confirmation of accounts receivable and the other answers are common audit procedures, confirmation of accounts payable is an extended procedure and usually occurs under unusual conditions. The greater the combined level of risk, the greater the assurance that the auditor needs from substantive tests related to a financial statement assertion. In these situations, the auditor might use confirmation procedures rather than or in conjunction with tests directed toward documents or parties within the entity. In a low risk situation, review of post balance sheet date payments to vendors may adequately substantiate the accounts payable balance. (ID: 5691)

3. (c)   The lack of misstatements at the interim date would not cause the auditor to increase the assessment of control risk. The auditor most likely would review supporting documents for new large balances and evaluate significant changes in year-end balances. Without an increase in the assessment of control risk, additional extensive procedures, such as sending confirmations to new customers and reviewing subsequent cash collections are unlikely. If the auditor planned to resend confirmations for any customer balances remaining at year-end when interim confirmations returned from these same customers appeared reasonable, it is unlikely that the auditor would plan to confirm accounts receivable as of an interim date. (ID: 7840)

4. (d)   Applying principal substantive tests to the details of an asset or liability account as of an interim date rather than as of the balance sheet date potentially increases the risk that misstatements that may exist at the balance sheet date will not be detected by the auditor. Performing substantive tests at an interim date does not eliminate the use of any sampling techniques. The auditor would only need to consider reperforming substantive tests, as of the balance sheet date, if misstatements are detected at the interim date. Asset and liability accounts should be examined as of the balance sheet date if there are rapidly changing economic conditions. (ID: 8126)

5. (c)   The auditor should perform other auditing procedures with respect to the period after the balance sheet date for the purpose of ascertaining the occurrence of subsequent events that may require adjustment or disclosure including investigating changes in long-term debt after year-end. Other procedures are applied to transactions occurring after the balance sheet date for the purpose of assurance that proper cutoffs have been made, and for the purpose of obtaining information to aid in the evaluation of the assets and liabilities as of the balance sheet date. Answers a., b., and d. would not provide evidence about subsequent events as a. is a test of controls and b. and d. are not common procedures. (ID: 5683)

6. (b)   Analytics involve comparisons of recorded amounts, or ratios developed from recorded amounts, to expectations developed by the auditor. The auditor develops expectations by identifying relationships that reasonably are expected to exist from understanding the client and the industry in which the client operates. In this case, the auditor expected the current year's gross margin to be comparable to the prior year's gross margin. Tests of transactions are test of details that involves other types of procedures such as tracing and vouching to determine whether transactions were recorded correctly. Tests of controls evaluate the effectiveness of the design and operation of policies and procedures in preventing or detecting material misstatements. (ID: 8140)

7. (d)   A reconciliation between the amounts included in the cash flow statement and other financial statements would be a procedure the auditor would perform because the cash flow statement amounts are a result of the transactions reflected in and the changes in balances on the other financial statements. Relationships between current year and prior year amounts due do not necessarily exist as can be expected on the balance sheet and income statement. This procedure would provide more audit evidence in the overall review stage of the audit for the balance sheet and income statement. Answer b. is a procedure an auditor would perform in auditing the cash balance on the balance sheet. Answer c. is a procedure the auditor would perform in auditing the cash balance on the balance sheet. (ID: 5674)

8. (c)   In testing the existence assertion for an asset, the auditor would start with the accounting records themselves to determine that the assets recorded on the client's books do exist. Further evidence of the asset existence would then be found in the supporting evidence.   (ID: 136)

9. (c)   To determine whether transactions have been recorded (completeness), procedures include tracing from supporting documentation (original source documents) to accounting records. Testing from general ledger balances, the adjusted trial balance, and general journal entries (vouching) would provide evidence of existence or occurrence.   (ID: 5675)

10. (c)   Vouching from sales invoices to copies of the corresponding shipping document provides evidence that sales billed to customers were actually shipped (occurrence). Tracing from the shipping documents to the corresponding sales invoices would provide evidence that shipments to customers were properly billed and that no duplicate shipments were made (completeness). Vouching from the accounts receivable subsidiary ledger to the shipping documents would provide evidence that those entries were actually shipped and are valid (occurrence).   (ID: 8145)

11. (b)   The higher the risk of material misstatement, the more effective it may be to perform substantive procedures nearer to, or at, the period end. If the auditor performs test of controls or substantive procedures at an interim date, the auditor needs to consider the additional evidence for the reminder of the period, including the control environment. Effective internal controls allow the auditor greater confidence in such evidence than ineffective controls. A new sales incentive program may provide increased motivation for employees to inflate sales numbers, and hence, accounts receivable; any new program provides increased potential for errors or fraud. A high turnover of senior management is a risk factor of fraud due to fraudulent financial reporting. A first engagement of a new client tends to increase the risk that something will be overlooked due to the unfamiliarity with the client's operations. Editor's Note: While one could argue that interim testing of A/R would be appropriate for a new client, in order that audit staff have additional time to investigate unusual items and, if significant issues are found, more time for management and the auditor to address such issues; however, the examiners instruct candidates to select the best answer.   (ID: 8398)

12. (d)   When substantive procedures are performed at an interim date, the auditor should perform further substantive procedures or a combination of substantive procedures and tests of controls covering the remaining period to provide a reasonable basis for extending the audit conclusions to the end of the period. Interim testing increases the risk that misstatements existing at the period end will not be detected. Evaluations of inappropriate assessments of risk would not be a factor in deciding whether interim testing would be appropriate. Sampling risk need not necessarily be projected at the maximum for tests covering the remaining period. Whether or not substantive tests of accounts receivable may be performed at an interim date does not hinge on whether the balance is material to the financial statements.   (ID: 8413)

13. (d)   The review of travel and entertainment expenses can be done prior to the balance sheet date; however, when substantive procedures are performed at an interim date, the auditor should perform further audit procedures to cover the remaining period that provide a reasonable basis for extending the audit conclusion from the interim date to the balance sheet date. Various phases of an audit are completed during the subsequent period that extends from after the balance sheet date to the date of the audit report. These include the other answers: review of subsequent events (self-explanatory), the search for unrecorded liabilities, and inquiry of the client's legal counsel. Certain procedures are applied to transactions occurring after the balance sheet date such as the examination of data to assure that proper cutoffs have been made and the examination of data that would provide information to aid the auditor in the evaluation of the assets and liabilities as of the balance sheet date. These procedures would include the search through these post balance sheet transactions for evidence of liabilities that existed at the balance sheet date, but were not recorded. The attorney's response should include coverage of as much of this subsequent period as possible, i.e., have an effective date (the latest date of the period covered by the response) as close to the date of the auditor's report as practicable. Note: As a practical matter, an auditor may choose to send an initial request to the attorney earlier in the audit, so that the completion of the audit is not delayed, with the understanding that an update will be needed close to the report date.   (ID: 8638)

Cash

14. (a) An auditor compares prior year checks listed in the cutoff statement compared to the year-end outstanding checks to make sure that all year-end outstanding checks were handled correctly on the bank reconciliation. Deposits in transit are listed on the bank reconciliation, not on the cutoff statements; once on the cutoff statement, they cease to be in transit. Checks dated after year-end in the cutoff statement should not be listed as outstanding at year-end. Checks and deposits dated after year-end merely provide information about liabilities or assets available at year-end. (ID: 7098)

15. (d) The AICPA Standard Form to Confirm Account Balance Information With Financial Institutions is designed to substantiate information that is stated on the confirmation request; the form is not designed to provide assurance that information about accounts not listed on the form will be reported. The bank employee completing the form may be unaware of all the financial relationships that the client has with the bank and the request may not ask specifically about all the financial relationships, thus the usefulness of the confirmation in providing evidence for financial statement assertions may be limited. Responding to bank confirmation requests is a normal activity for a bank. It would be unlikely that a bank employee would not believe that the bank is obligated to verify confidential information to the third party, especially as the confirmation request is signed by the client authorizing the bank to release the information to the auditor. The bank would not have access to the client's bank reconciliation and thus would not inspect its accuracy. The bank does have access to the client's cutoff bank statements, but that information is not used by the bank to confirm year-end balances. (ID: 5992)

16. (c) One would expect a high account balance with a high deposit level. A kiting scheme involves drawing a check on one account to inflate the balance in another; it usually requires careful attention by a trusted perpetrator who is familiar with the operation, and especially, knows the time for checks to clear. This would tend not to be the situation with high turnover. An ATM withdrawal is posted quickly, reducing the time lag necessary for kiting. Kiting would not tend to produce large checks on any one particular day of the week, unless the perpetrator had an unusual work pattern. (ID: 7107)

17. (b) When audit evidence can be obtained from independent sources outside an entity, it provides greater assurance of reliability for the purposes of an independent audit than that secured solely within the entity. Answers a., c., and d. represent audit procedures that may be performed and evidence that can be obtained as a by-product of receiving the standard confirmation; however, they do not represent the primary purpose for obtaining the confirmation. (ID: 3930)

18. (d) This bank transfer results in an overstatement of cash at December 31. The receipt of the transfer was recorded in the books on December 31, thus increasing that bank account's cash balance on that date. However, the disbursement of the transfer was not recorded in the books until January 4; thus, that bank account's cash balance was not decreased until after the financial statement date. The bank transfers indicated in answers a., b., and c. do not result in a misstatement of cash. The books recorded the disbursement and receipt of each of these bank transfers in the same fiscal year. (ID: 8380)

A/R & Sales

19. (b) When the auditor has already gathered evidence supporting cash receipts and accounts receivable, the same evidence would support sales. Thus, having already gathered this evidence and having assessed control risk as low for the existence or occurrence assertion regarding sales transactions, the auditor most likely would conclude that he or she has substantial evidence for sales and would limit substantive tests of sales transactions. Evidence supporting opening and closing inventory balances, shipping and receiving activities, and cutoffs of sales and purchases would give only limited information regarding sales. (ID: 5993)

20. (c) This procedure helps ensure that the accounts receivable (a right to payment) amount is correct, but not that it is reported or disclosed appropriately and clearly. Classification and understandability is an assertion about presentation and disclosure. (ID: 7101)

21. (c) The segregation of custody and reporting is an important internal control that is most likely to deter a lapping scheme. Authorization of write-offs by a supervisor is a good control but would not in itself prevent an employee from misappropriating accounts receivable collections because the supervisor is unfamiliar with the accounts, as indicated in the question, and would, therefore, not be aware of customers who are delinquent in

their payments. Answers a. and d. are examples of good internal controls but would not by themselves uncover a lapping scheme. (ID: 3910)

22. (a) Lapping involves the theft of one customer's payment and subsequently crediting the customer with payment made by another customer. Future remittances may be deposited but would be credited to the account from which funds were stolen, thus comparison of remittance dates would detect the scheme. Answers b., c., and d. occur after the theft and would not show differences to pursue. (ID: 5975)

23. (b) Valuation and allocation is the assertion that assets, liabilities, and equity interests are included in the financial statements at appropriate amounts and any resulting valuation or allocation adjustments are appropriately recorded. Answer a. deals with whether assets, liabilities, or equity interests exist at a given date. Answer c. deals with whether all transactions, accounts, and disclosures that should be presented in the financial statements are so included. Answer d. deals with whether assets are the rights of the entity and liabilities are the obligations of the entity. (ID: 3925)

24. (a) A/R turnover is the number of times that the A/R balance is collected during the year. Fictitious sales increase A/R, but leave collections the same, so A/R turnover decreases. A/R turnover would be unaffected by current inventory levels. Tightening credit-granting policies would tend to increase A/R turnover. Lapping receivables in two years would result in both years' receivables being misstated, but unless the volume of lapped amounts changed, turnover would not be affected. (ID: 7109)

25. (c) In general, cutoff tests are used to detect unrecorded transactions at the end of the period. In this question, the auditor would most likely detect unrecorded sales for the year by reviewing a sales cutoff to determine that sales were recorded in the period in which title to the goods passed to the customer. Such a review would not reveal shipments lacking invoices, excessive write-offs of accounts receivable, or lapping of year-end accounts receivable. (ID: 2778)

26. (b) This test is performed to satisfy the audit objective of completeness. The primary purpose of this objective is to establish whether all transactions that should have been recorded by the client are included in the accounts. (ID: 7494)

27. (d) Assertions about completeness deal with whether all transactions, accounts, and disclosures that should be presented in the financial statements are included. Periodically accounting for the numerical sequence of documents and invoices helps ensure that all entries affecting those accounts have been recognized and posted. Answer a. deals with whether recorded transactions have actually occurred and pertain to the entity. Answer b. deals with whether assets are the rights of the entity and liabilities are the obligations of the entity. Answer c. deals with whether assets, liabilities, and equity interests have been included in the financial statements at appropriate amounts. (ID: 3923)

28. (b) Assertions about completeness deal with whether all transactions, assets, liabilities, equity interests and disclosures that should be presented in the financial statements are included. Inspecting the entity's reports of prenumbered shipping documents that have not been recorded in the sales journal will help the auditor determine whether all transactions have been accounted for. Answer a. is a clerical test for accuracy. Answer c. relates to management's assertion of accuracy and valuation. Answer d. is a test of controls for authorization of credit prior to the sale being approved. (ID: 4692)

29. (a) Valuation and allocation deal with whether assets, liabilities, and equity interests are included in financial statements at appropriate amounts. If the bad debt allowance account is too low, net accounts receivable would be too high, and the assets would, therefore, be overstated. (ID: 5123)

30. (c) To discover understated (unrecorded) sales, the auditor would most likely trace transactions from shipping documents to sales invoices. This would reveal orders that have been shipped, but not billed and is an example of testing for completeness. Vouching from sales invoices to shipping documents (the opposite direction) is a test to substantiate that sales are not overstated (verify their occurrence or existence). Comparing entries between the cash receipts journal and the sales journal would verify that the entries were posted correctly, but it would not locate an unrecorded sale. Note: The sales and cash receipts journals are often combined in one journal. (ID: 8622)

A/R Confirmations

31. (a) Blank A/R confirmations request that the customers supply the amount owed, if any. By having the customers provide the information, the auditor increases the likelihood that customers did examine their records. Positive confirmations have the amount that the customers owe provided by the client, typically invoice-by-invoice. The invoice-by-invoice form simplifies verifying subsequent cash receipts as compared to a single sum owed. Negative confirmations request the customer to return the confirmation, with corrections, only if their records differ. They usually are used if the combined assessed level of inherent risk and control risk is low, i.e., if few exceptions are expected. (ID: 6714)

32. (c) Nonresponse to positive requests for accounts receivable confirmations generally requires the use of follow-up requests, such as additional mailings or telephone calls. It is appropriate that the auditor ask the client to contact the customers. In cases where there is still no response to requests dealing with significant accounts, alternative procedures should be used to obtain adequate evidence. These additional procedures may involve the examination of documents such as subsequent cash receipts, sales invoices, and shipping documents. While nonresponse increases risks associated with the audit, it is the auditor's responsibility to apply alternative procedures to keep the risks within acceptable levels. (ID: 5664)

33. (c) Answer c. clearly states the consequences of the client's customer's actions and informs the customer of the deadline. Answer b. omits any indication of a deadline. While informing the client's customers that the confirmation request is not a payment request may be included in the letter, it only informs the client's customers what not to do—rather than the desired action. Amounts on A/R confirmation requests represent all owed amounts, not just those that are overdue. (ID: 6835)

34. (a) Providing additional information may make the task of confirming debts appear easier to the client's customers' employees, resulting in a response getting prepared and approved, rather than indefinitely waiting in a stack for a supervisor to examine and then approve. Customers with large balances may have the worse response rate. The use of fax or e-mail may impact the response time, but probably not the response rate. The threat of a second request will probably have no more positive impact than the first request had, and may annoy the client's customers. (ID: 6936)

35. (d) The client prepares account confirmation requests. To maintain customer goodwill, an indication that a nonresponse will cause a second request should be avoided. A nonresponse to a positive confirmation request generates further inquiries, not an assumption that a balance is correct. (ID: 6834)

36. (d) Negative confirmations are used when the auditor can tolerate a high level of detection risk, i.e., when the combined assessed level of inherent risk and control risk relative to accounts receivable is low. Negative confirmations provide less persuasive evidence than positive confirmations because the auditor is unable to determine if a lack of response is due to customer agreement or lack of delivery of the request for confirmation, etc. If the total recorded amount of accounts receivable is immaterial to the financial statement taken as a whole, confirmations of any kind would be unlikely. If response rates in prior years were inadequate, the auditor is more likely to consider other procedures rather than a type of confirmation for which response rates cannot be determined. If recipients are likely to return positive confirmations requests without verifying the accuracy of the information, it is unlikely they would have greater inclination to verify the accuracy of the information for negative confirmations. (ID: 6582)

37. (b) Confirmation requests always should be mailed by the auditor and be returned directly to the auditor's place of business. This is to diminish the possibility that the confirmation request could be altered by the client, either during the mailing process or upon receipt. The internal auditor need not sign the form. It is not inappropriate to get confirmations for closed accounts. The internal auditor may prepare confirmation requests. (ID: 7800)

38. (a) The original forms are the (signed) evidence that the auditor first sought. A/R confirmations are more timely and complete evidence than subsequent cash receipts. Accounts may not be paid rapidly or in single payments. Considering e-mail responses as exceptions is unreasonably harsh. Second requests generally would gain the same response as the first requests. (ID: 6629)

39. (a) The positive (confirmation) form is preferable when individual account balances are relatively large or when there is reason to believe that there may be a substantial number of accounts in dispute or with errors

or fraud. In this case, errors or fraud are likely since internal controls are weak. Negative confirmations are used when the assessed level of control risk is low. With weak internal controls, the auditor needs to obtain third party verification. (ID: 178)

40. (d) Blank confirmations merely ask for a balance owed, whereas regular positive confirmations include the amount that the customer owes provided by the client, either listed by invoice or as a single sum. Providing additional information may make the task of confirming debts appear easier to the client's customers' employees, resulting in a response getting prepared and approved, rather than indefinitely waiting in stacks for a supervisor to assign, examine, and then approve. (ID: 7640)

41. (c) The A/R and sales audit objective related to the completeness assertion is to ascertain that all sales and receivables that should be recorded are properly recorded. Customers may not be inclined to report understatement errors in their accounts, and thus not all the sales and receivables that should be recorded are necessarily recorded. It is not as likely that customers will merely sign and return the confirmation without verifying its details; the accounts they are verifying represent liabilities to them. It is more likely that the customers will not return forms. A nonresponse could mean that the intended recipient did not receive the request, has misplaced or not processed the request, or has returned the request but it was delayed or lost in transit. Auditors typically confirm few accounts with low recorded balances and a high percentage of accounts with large balances. (ID: 5986)

42. (a) Unreturned negative confirmations do not provide explicit evidence. Negative confirmations may be effective when the combined assessed level of inherent and control risk is low. Alternative procedures are used for unreturned positive confirmations. The auditor would be more likely to use positive confirmations, which provide more persuasive evidence, if understatements are suspected. (ID: 5663)

43. (b) By including a list of items or invoices that constitute the customers' account balances, the auditor makes it easier for the customers to respond, irrespective of how the customers' records are organized; this tends to increase the response rate. Neither restricting the selection of accounts to be confirmed to those customers with large balances nor explaining to customers that discrepancies will be investigated by an independent third party will likely have much impact on the response rate. (Furthermore; most customers understand that an auditor is independent and is the one investigating discrepancies.) If anything, asking customers to respond to the request by fax may slow or decrease the response rate, as this may be cumbersome for some customers. (ID: 8407)

44. (c) The blank form of accounts receivable confirmation does not include the amount or other information; the recipients are requested to provide it. This form may provide a greater degree of assurance about the information confirmed, however it may be less efficient than the other positive form because more nonresponses to the requests are likely to occur due to the extra effort required of the recipients. Neither inspection of shipping documents or verification of subsequent cash receipts are dictated by the use of the blank form; however, they may be part of the alternative procedures the auditor uses if the response rate to the confirmation process is too low. That recipients may sign the forms without proper investigation is an issue with the other type of positive confirmation that includes the amounts and/or other information. Editor note: The blank form is a type of positive confirmation. The question indicates that it is not which may have been why the examiners released this question. They may not intend to use it again for this reason. (ID: 8805)

45. (d) The receipt (acceptance) of electronic confirmations, for example by facsimile or e-mail, is not precluded by GAAS; however, such responses involve risks relating to reliability because proof of origin and knowledge of the respondent may be difficult to establish and alterations may be difficult to detect. In some cases, the auditor may determine that it is appropriate to address the risks related to the reliability of the information received electronically by directly contacting the purported sender. Also, in this case, the auditor received the confirmation indirectly (the client's fax machine) which is a factor that may indicate increased risk. (ID: 9387)

46. (c) The inclusion of client-prepared statements (that show the details of the account balance) with the confirmation requests would most likely prove beneficial, i.e., improve the response rate. Copies of shipping documents or purchase orders would not be as beneficial as a detailed statement tied to the actual account balance. Shipping documents often do not include the cost of the goods shipped. Lists of the customer's recent payments that the client has already recorded would not be included in the account balance and thus, are irrelevant—the purpose of the confirmation process is to confirm unpaid amounts. Prices included on purchase

orders are generated by the client's customers rather than the client and thus may not be current or include applicable or correct discounts. Also, individual purchase orders may include items that were back-ordered by your client and thus not yet billed, i.e., not part of the current account balance.   (ID: 9907)

Inventory

47.   (b)   The formula for inventory turnover is cost of goods sold divided by average inventory. Cost of goods sold includes only inventory related expenses and thus is the best value to use to compare to average inventory to calculate inventory turnover. Net sales, operating income, and gross sales are all based on the prices charged the customers, not the actual costs to the company for the goods that were sold, and thus are not as closely related to the costs associated with inventory.   (ID: 5989)

48.   (d)   Physical counts of inventory items higher than the recorded quantities in perpetual inventory records could be the result of the failure to record sales returns in the books when sales return items were returned to inventory. Failure to record purchase discounts would have nothing to do with the recorded quantities in the records. Failure to record purchase returns and sales would result in the physical counts being lower than the quantities in the perpetual records.   (ID: 5670)

49.   (c)   When auditing inventory, the auditor needs to obtain evidence supporting management's assertions about presentation and disclosure, answer a., and valuation, answers b. and d. It would not be unusual for the client to have inventory out on consignment or held in a warehouse beyond the client's premises. Also, some of the inventory items could be in transit at the inventory date. The auditor needs to obtain confirmation or perform other auditing procedures to support management's assertions as to the existence and valuation of these assets, but the assets would not necessarily need to be on hand.   (ID: 7495)

50.   (a)   The valuation, existence, and completeness of the inventory are not in question. The inventory is collateral for a loan; disclosure is the issue.   (ID: 5658)

51.   (b)   Normally, when perpetual inventory records are well-kept and physical count comparisons are made on a regular basis, an auditor may perform inventory observation during or after the end of the period being audited. An auditor would probably request that the physical inventory count be done at year-end if the auditor does not have much confidence in the ability of the internal controls to detect errors when control risk is high.
                                    (ID: 5131)

52.   (b)   Inspecting agreements to determine whether any inventory is pledged as collateral or subject to any liens would provide the accountant with evidence concerning the assertions about rights and obligations which deal with whether assets are the rights of the entity and liabilities are the obligations of the entity.   (ID: 2770)

53.   (a)   The procedure in answer a. helps provide assurance about valuation of inventory. The procedures in answers b., c., and d. provide assurance regarding existence.   (ID: 5121)

54.   (c)   To gain assurance that all items in a client's inventory listing schedule are valid, an auditor most likely would trace items listed in the listing schedule to inventory tags and the auditor's recorded count sheets. To trace the inventory tags to the listing schedule and to trace items listed in receiving reports and vendors' invoices to the listing schedule would provide assurance that all the inventory items are on the schedule, but would not give assurance that all of the items on the schedule are valid; some items on the schedule may not exist. Tracing tags to receiving reports and vendors' invoices does not involve the inventory listing schedule and thus does not provide any assurances related to the listing schedule.   (ID: 5671)

55.   (b)   Assertions about completeness deal with whether all transactions, accounts, and disclosures that should be presented in the financial statements are so included. By tracing from the inventory floor to the records, the auditor is checking for completeness. Answer a. would deal with the rights to the inventory which would be evidenced by vendor invoices. Answer c. would be tested by vouching or going from the inventory list to the floor to identify the assets are in existence. Answer d. would be tested by multiplying the inventory count of an item by its cost based on a vendor's invoice.   (ID: 4706)

56.   (c)   Inventory turnover ratios measure the speed with which inventory is purchased or made and subsequently sold. Slow-moving and obsolete items have low turnover ratios. Slow-moving and obsolete items are unlikely to be shipped or received. Existence at locations outside the entity's premises occurs with slow-moving,

obsolete, and current items. Slow-moving, obsolete, and current items may all be traced easily to inventory observation test counts to perpetual listings.
(ID: 7804)

57. (a) Testing the computation of standard overhead rates would not help identify any slow-moving, defective, or obsolete inventory. While touring the plant or production facility, the auditor may actually see these types of items. In comparing inventory balances to anticipated sales volume and reviewing inventory experience and trends, the auditor may become aware of an excessive inventory balance that may indicate that these types of items have not been properly accounted for.
(ID: 8152)

58. (a) The cost of obsolete or slow-moving inventory may have to be written down; this affects the valuation assertion. Rights, obligations, existence, classification, and understandability are not affected by obsolete or slow-moving items.
(ID: 5661)

59. (d) To test that all items in the inventory listing are valid, the auditor would work from the inventory listing to the tags. An auditor would be unlikely to work directly from inventory tags to receiving reports and vendor invoices, or vice versa, without an intermediate step—as these documents don't reference each other, this process would be awkward; moreover, neither of these procedures would test the items in the inventory listing. Working from inventory tags to the inventory listing tests that all items on tags are included in the inventory listing (completeness).
(ID: 8418)

60. (a) As part of the process of observing a client's physical inventories, an auditor should be alert to the inclusion of any obsolete or damaged goods. The other answers are auditing considerations for inventories, but they do not directly relate to the observation of the client's physical count of inventory quantities. (ID: 8823)

61. (d) When well-kept perpetual inventory records are checked by the client periodically by comparisons with physical counts, an auditor's observation procedures for inventory may be performed either during or after the end of the period under audit. When a client maintains periodic inventory records, the physical count required is normally made at the balance sheet date or very close to it. Minimal variation in client records and test counts in prior periods or lack of significant variation in the last five years are not sufficient justification for leaving the observation of inventories to after the end of the period under audit.
(ID: 9363)

62. (d) Performing cutoff procedures for shipping and receiving would be the best test for the completeness assertion as it applies to inventory. The completeness assertion means that all transactions that should have been recorded have been recorded. Many procedures test multiple assertions, so candidates must select the best answer—some of the other answers are better tests of other assertions. Scanning perpetual inventory, production, and purchasing records tests accuracy. Examining paid vendor invoices tests accuracy and occurrence. Tracing inventory items from the tag listing back to the physical inventory quantities tests accuracy and existence.
(ID: 9381)

63. (a) The purpose of tracing a sample of inventory tags to a client's computerized listing of inventory items is to determine whether the inventory items represented by the tags were included on the listing. It is a way of testing the assertion of completeness. The other answers are objectives that would not be accomplished by the procedure as described in the question.
(ID: 9911)

64. (b) If inventories are in the hands of public warehouses or other outside custodians, the auditor ordinarily would obtain direct confirmation in writing from the custodian. If such inventories represent a significant proportion of current or total assets (which this question did not indicate was the case), to obtain reasonable assurance with respect to their existence, the auditor should apply one or more of the following procedures that the auditor considers necessary in the circumstances: (1) test the owner's procedures for investigating the warehouse and evaluating the warehouse's performance; (2) obtain an independent accountant's report on the warehouse's control procedures relevant to custody of goods and, if applicable, pledging of receipts, or apply alternative procedures at the warehouse to gain reasonable assurance that information received from the warehouse is reliable; (3) observe physical counts of the goods, if practicable and reasonable; and/or (4) if warehouse receipts have been pledged as collateral, confirm with lenders pertinent details of the pledged receipts (on a test basis, if appropriate).
(ID: 9939)

Fixed Assets

65. (d)   The repairs and maintenance expense accounts are analyzed by an auditor in obtaining evidence regarding the completeness of fixed assets, since there is the possibility that items were expensed that should have been capitalized. (ID: 5135)

66. (b)   When plant assets are retired, the accumulated depreciation account is debited for the amount of depreciation that has been recorded for those assets, which could be a satisfactory explanation for significant debits to this account. When the estimated remaining useful life of a plant asset is revised upward, the calculation for current and future depreciation is revised to reflect the new estimate of remaining useful life; accumulated depreciation is not affected. If the prior year's depreciation expense was erroneously understated, a correction would require a credit, not a debit, to accumulated depreciation. Revisions in overhead allocations would not affect the accumulated depreciation accounts. (ID: 5996)

67. (a)   Amortization allocates the cost of the intangible to the periods in which the benefit is received and yields an appropriate valuation of the intangible in those periods. Amortization is not relevant to the existence, completeness, or rights and obligations assertions. (ID: 5659)

68. (c)   The auditor should perform tests of controls when the auditor's risk assessment includes an expectation of the operating effectiveness of controls (control risk is low) or when substantive procedures alone do not provide sufficient appropriate audit evidence. Regardless of the audit approach selected, the auditor should design and perform substantive procedures for all relevant assertions related to each material class of transactions, account balance, and disclosure because effective internal controls generally reduce, but do not eliminate, risk of material misstatement, tests of controls reduce, but do not eliminate, the need for substantive procedures. (ID: 5974)

69. (d)   A weakness in internal control over recording retirements of equipment most likely would result in assets that have been retired continuing to be carried in the accounting records. Tracing from the records to the actual assets would be an audit procedure designed to detect such errors. Tracing equipment in the plant to the accounting records would only provide evidence about equipment not yet retired. Depreciation is applied to assets carried on the books and thus depreciation would continue to be taken on retired equipment erroneously still on the books. A review of depreciation would not of itself indicate that certain equipment had been retired. Additions to the "other assets" account would be newly acquired other assets rather than retired equipment and would not likely give any evidence about retired equipment. (ID: 5981)

70. (c)   By reviewing the repairs and maintenance expense accounts, an auditor may uncover transactions that involve assets that should be capitalized rather than expensed. The repairs and maintenance expense accounts are not involved in the write-off of obsolete assets. Property, plant and equipment (PP&E) that cannot be repaired would not tend to involve transactions in the repairs and maintenance expense accounts either. To verify that all recorded PP&E assets exist, an auditor would tend to inspect the assets themselves against the listings in the PP&E accounts, rather than review expense accounts. (ID: 8391)

71. (d)   By reviewing the repairs and maintenance expense accounts, an auditor may uncover transactions that involve assets that should be capitalized rather than expensed. Analysis of depreciation expense accounts would not reveal the existence of assets that should be capitalized, but are not; all entries to these accounts are due to assets being capitalized already. It is less likely that an asset would be involved in the calculation of property tax and yet not be capitalized than it is that an asset would be expensed in the repair and maintenance account; if the entity prepares a property tax report, it probably would be prepared based on the listing of capital assets. (ID: 8400)

Investments

72. (a)   Investment advisory services have an interest in having accurate records of dividends and are ordinarily independent of the audit client. Stock indentures and stock ledgers may not have dividend records. Annual audited investee financial statements may not be timely available. (ID: 6363)

73. (a)   Analytical tests as a source of information for developing expectations include analysis of the relationships among elements of financial information within the period. The reasonableness of answers b., c., and d. cannot be analytically determined due to the nature of the assertions. (ID: 3927)

74. (c)   In the case of investments in the form of securities (such as stocks, bonds, and notes), existence and ownership can be corroborated by inspection of the securities, or by written confirmation from an independent custodian of securities on deposit, pledged, or in safekeeping. Shares owned and signed over to new owners or purchased from other investors would not always be made known to the issuing company on a timely basis. Inspecting the financial statements of the investee company would not indicate the number of shares owned and who the owners are. Answer d. would provide evidence about the valuation assertion.   (ID: 5122)

75. (a)   The auditor will need to understand the economic substance of each derivative in order to evaluate the application of GAAP. The client's broker would not be knowledgeable about management's classification of derivatives. The audit committee should already be aware of the risks involved in derivative transactions. The risks associated with each derivative would not be appropriate to include in the auditor's report.   (ID: 8131)

76. (c)   Published dividend records provide the strongest evidence supporting dividends earned on publicly-held investments. Answers a., b., and d. are not common procedures.   (ID: 8135)

77. (b)   The auditor is required to design procedures to obtain reasonable assurance of detecting misstatements of assertions about derivatives and securities. When designing such procedures, the auditor should consider the inherent risk and control risk for these assertions. Analytical procedures would not provide sufficient evidence to determine the valuation of any investment. The auditor does not need to confirm the marketability of a derivative nor inform the audit committee of them.   (ID: 8148)

78. (b)   The valuation assertion for an investment accounted for by the equity method can generally be satisfied by referring to the audited financial statements of the investee company.   (ID: 2312)

79. (b)   An auditor confirms with an outside agent that the agent is holding investment securities in the client's name to support the existence and rights and obligations assertions. The auditor would check valuation with a listing of market values. Completeness would not be confirmed, as an entity might have more than one agent or have some securities in transit. Classification and understandability is an assertion about presentation and disclosure and would depend, in part, on the nature of the securities, not that they are being held.

(ID: 5662)

80. (b)   Confirmation from a third-party custodian provides evidence as to the existence and ownership of securities. In the event of a sale close to the period end, an investee company might not yet be aware of a sale unrecorded in the audit client books; further, if the investment is held by a custodian, the investee company might not realize the audit client has an ownership interest. In the event of a sale close to the period end, analytics applied to the dividend income and investment accounts would not necessarily detect an unrecorded sale. A sale of stolen securities most likely would not appear in the cash receipts journal.   (ID: 8409)

81. (c)   Published dividend records provide the strongest evidence supporting dividends earned on marketable equity securities.   (ID: 8842)

A/P, Purchases & Other Liabilities

82. (c)   In searching for unrecorded liabilities, the auditor would most likely vouch a sample of cash disbursements recorded just after year-end to receiving reports and vendor invoices to ascertain that payables had been recorded in the proper period. Tracing a sample of accounts payable entries recorded just after (not just before) year-end to the year-end unmatched receiving report file, comparing a sample of purchase orders issued just before (not just after) year-end with the year-end accounts payable, and scanning the cash disbursements entries recorded just after (not just before) year-end for indications of unusual transactions may also aid in the detection of unrecorded liabilities.   (ID: 5994)

83. (c)   Tracing a sample of purchase orders and the related receiving reports to the purchases journal and the cash disbursements journal provides evidence to determine that purchases were properly recorded. Although during this audit procedure the auditor might identify unusually large purchases that should be investigated further, this would not be the prevailing purpose of this substantive audit procedure. To verify that cash disbursements were for goods actually received would require vouching from the cash disbursements journal to the receiving reports. To test whether payments were for goods actually ordered would require vouching from the cash disbursements journal to the purchase orders.   (ID: 5995)

84. (c) In order to verify the existence and valuation of the accounts payable account, the auditor should go to the source documents. These would include purchase orders and receiving reports. Answer a. pertains to the completeness assertion and whether or not management has included all obligations in the account. Answer b. is not a standard auditing procedure but deals with determining whether management has included all obligations for the rights and obligations assertion for the account. Answer d. also pertains to determining whether or not there are any unrecorded obligations of the company not recorded in the account. (ID: 3932)

85. (a) When internal control dictates that each cash disbursement be accompanied by an approved voucher and supported by a prenumbered purchase order and a prenumbered receiving report, the auditor would select items for testing from the population of all cash disbursements (canceled checks). If the auditor were to consider populations made up of all approved vouchers, receiving reports, or invoices, the canceled checks that did not have supporting documentation would not be discovered. (ID: 7019)

86. (b) To verify that all merchandise received is recorded, the auditor would trace from the receiving reports to the related records. Payment vouchers, purchase requisitions, and vendor's invoices would not provide evidence that the related merchandise was actually received. (ID: 4263)

87. (c) Completeness deals with whether all transactions, assets, liabilities, and equity interests that should have been recorded have been recorded. Completeness also pertains to whether all disclosures that should have been included in the financial statements have been included. Because liabilities have the inherent risk of being understated, substantive tests and tests of controls are directed towards determining that all liabilities of the company as of the balance sheet date are properly included. (ID: 4274)

88. (b) The objective of the auditor's test is to determine whether all merchandise for which the client was billed was received. The population for this test consists of all vendor's invoices (bills for merchandise). The auditor would select a sample of vendor's invoices and then trace them to supporting receiving reports to assure that the merchandise for which the client was billed was received. (ID: 195)

89. (d) This is an instance of testing for completeness, i.e., that all transactions and events that should have been recorded have been recorded. The best test for this would be to trace (review) information contained in source documents (purchase contracts and other legal documents) to the financial statements. Inquiry is not as effective as this tracing procedure. Reviewing the financial statements for mathematical accuracy would not detect an unrecorded liability; this would only provide evidence about recorded liabilities. A company's articles of incorporation and corporate bylaws generally do not contain liability information and they would prove an even less likely source of evidence of recent omissions. (ID: 8608)

90. (b) Examining vendor statements for amounts not reported as purchases is the test of details that would most likely help an auditor determine whether accounts payable have been misstated. The vendor statements are directly related to amounts that should be recorded as accounts payable. Cash received from customers and customer-returned goods are related to sales and accounts receivable, not accounts payable. The examination of reported purchase returns would not reveal evidence of unrecorded purchase returns. (ID: 9388)

Payroll

91. (c) Finding overpayments while performing tests of details may cause the auditor to increase the assessed risk of material misstatement. Generally, as the risk of material misstatement increases, the acceptable level of detection risk decreases; this means, the extent of substantive procedures must increase. Answer a., b., and d. do not necessarily increase the risk of material misstatement. (ID: 4714)

92. (b) To test for the appropriate number of hours worked, the auditor examines clock card data. To test for answer a., the auditor checks personnel records. To test for answers c. and d., the auditor uses inquiries and observation. (ID: 5655)

93. (d) Substantive tests of payroll balances when control risk is assessed as low most likely would be limited to applying analytical procedures and recalculating payroll accruals to assure the accuracy of the payroll liabilities. Observing the distribution of paychecks, recomputing the payroll register and inspecting payroll tax returns would be of greater importance if control risk related to payroll was assessed as high. In such a case,

these procedures would be required to assure the accuracy and other assertions related to payroll accounts.
(ID: 5672)

94. (d)   When reviewing payroll tax form reconciliations, an auditor is concerned with unrecorded liabilities. Analytics or review of the calculation process would be better to determine accuracy in the deductions calculation. The effective operation of internal control is determined by tests of controls. Observing check distribution, rather than reconciling tax forms, would bring fictitious employees to light. (ID: 7104)

95. (d)   Requiring employees to have their direct supervisors approve their time cards would most effectively ensure that payment is made only for work performed. The other answers are good controls, but they are not as effective for this purpose. In most cases, the direct supervisor witnesses the actual work performed. Requiring employees to use a time clock improves accuracy and validity of amounts recorded. Having a payroll clerk recalculate the time cards also improves accuracy. Requiring employees to sign their time cards allows verification of employee existence and improves accuracy. (ID: 9357)

Long-Term Liabilities

96. (c)   One of the audit objectives of long-term liabilities is to verify that interest expense is correctly computed and that other contractual obligations are satisfied. The auditor would most likely compare interest expense with the bonds payable amount to see if it is reasonable, and thereby test valuation. This could also aid discovery of undisclosed liabilities. (ID: 5133)

97. (b)   An auditor's program to examine long-term debt should include a step where the auditor reconciles interest expense with debt outstanding during the year (period). This step would provide information as to the completeness and valuation of the account balance. The auditor is not concerned with the year-end market value of the debt. The auditor would not verify the existence of the holders of the debt by direct confirmation. Outstanding balances, terms, and conditions are confirmed with the credit grantor or independent trustee. The search for unrecorded liabilities would generally be made by scanning cash disbursements made in the period following the balance sheet date. Also, the accounts payable subsidiary ledger would not likely provide evidence as to long-term liabilities. (ID: 127)

Stockholders' Equity

98. (c)   Restrictions on retained earnings should be disclosed in the financial statements. Restrictions would not impact the valuation, allocation, or occurrence of retained earnings. Rights and obligations pertain to assets and liabilities, not retained earnings. (ID: 6713)

99. (d)   The primary responsibility of a registrar of capital stock is to verify that securities are properly issued, recorded, and transferred. (ID: 133)

100. (a)   One of the auditor's objectives in the examination of owners' equity is to determine that all transactions during the year affecting owners' equity accounts were properly authorized and recorded. In the case of a corporation, changes in capital stock accounts should receive formal advance approval by the board of directors. A transfer agent's records show detail about the owners of the stock, and do not focus on the total outstanding. Canceled stock certificates and a treasury stock certificate book are less reliable than the minutes, as they would be updated only after the transaction is complete. (ID: 6837)

101. (c)   The auditor will need to confirm the shares issued and outstanding with the registrar to ascertain whether the corporate records are accurate and that stock is issued in accordance with the authorization of the board of directors and the articles of incorporation. Confirming the amount of dividends paid to related parties is not a common procedure. The auditor would obtain confirmations from subscribers to determine the expected proceeds from stock subscriptions receivable. Proper authorization of stock rights and warrants would be verified through reading the minutes of the board of directors' meetings. (ID: 8120)

102. (d)   One of the primary objectives in testing related to Stockholders' Equity and Capital accounts is to verify that capital transactions are appropriately authorized and approved. The granting of stock options would require board of director approval because it could affect the number of shares outstanding. (ID: 5134)

Accounting Estimates

103. (d)   Inquiries about related-party transactions and inventories at external locations are not focused on accounting estimates. Accounting estimates appropriately change with changes in circumstances; further, determining deviation from historical patterns doesn't indicate that all accounting estimates are identified. Unresolved litigation is a frequent reason for accounting estimates, due to the uncertainty in the litigation outcome.

(ID: 7094)

104. (a)   Assumptions that are susceptible to bias provide an opportunity for the overstatement of assets and income and understatement of liabilities. Assumptions that meet the criteria of the other answers offer less scope for creative accounting.

(ID: 6395)

105. (d)   The auditor's objectives in evaluating an entity's accounting estimates are to ensure (1) all accounting estimates that could be material to the financial statements have been developed, (2) the estimates are reasonable, and (3) the estimates are in conformity with GAAP and are disclosed properly.

(ID: 8166)

106. (c)   Of the answers, the auditor first would learn how management developed its estimates. Then, the auditor would compare the current process to previous estimate development to gain evidence regarding consistency. After evaluating management's estimate process, the auditor considers whether there are factors that the auditor's estimates failed to take into account. Then, the auditor would be ready to compare management's and the auditor's estimates. Reviewing variations from expectations may occur after the period end, when the client finishes its preaudit financial statements, while the other answers could commence at an interim date.

(ID: 7821)

107. (c)   In evaluating the reasonableness of an estimate, the auditor normally concentrates on key factors and assumptions that are deviations from historical patterns; sensitive to variations (not stable and insensitive to variations); subjective and susceptible to misstatement and bias (not the opposite); and, of course, significant to the accounting estimate. The auditor would expect the estimates to be consistent with industry guidelines, so estimates that did not conform would bear more scrutiny to obtain evidence that the variation was reasonable under the circumstances.

(ID: 8649)

108. (a)   The auditor's objective when evaluating accounting estimates is to determine if all accounting estimates that could be material to the financial statements have been developed; are reasonable in the circumstances; and are presented in conformity with GAAP and are properly disclosed. The opposite is true of alternatives "b" and "d", i.e., accounting estimates should be used when data concerning past events can**not** be accumulated in a timely, cost-effective manner; and accounting estimates **should** be used when the measurement of some amounts or the valuation of some accounts is uncertain, pending the outcome of future events. Obviously, there is no need to use an estimate for accounts receivable greater than 90 days past due or any other account / amount that can be readily calculated using actual data

(ID: 8810)

_____

PERFORMANCE BY TOPICS

Each category below parallels a topic covered in Chapter 5. Record the number and percentage of questions you answered correctly in each topic.

Substantive Procedures

Question #	Correct	√
1		
2		
3		
4		
5		
6		
7		
8		
9		
10		
11		
12		
13		

Questions   13

Correct   _____
% Correct   _____

Cash

Question #	Correct	√
14		
15		
16		
17		
18		

Questions   5

Correct   _____
% Correct   _____

A/R & Sales

Question #	Correct	√
19		
20		
21		
22		
23		
24		
25		
26		
27		
28		
29		
30		

Questions   12

Correct   _____
% Correct   _____

A/R Confirmations

Question #	Correct	√
31		
32		
33		
34		
35		
36		
37		
38		
39		
40		
41		
42		
43		
44		
45		
46		

Questions   16

Correct   _____
% Correct   _____

Inventory

Question #	Correct	√
47		
48		
49		
50		
51		
52		
53		
54		
55		
56		
57		
58		
59		
60		
61		
62		
63		
64		

Questions   18

Correct   _____
% Correct   _____

Fixed Assets

Question #	Correct	√
65		
66		
67		
68		
69		
70		
71		

Questions   7

Correct   _____
% Correct   _____

Investments

Question #	Correct	√
72		
73		
74		
75		
76		
77		
78		
79		
80		
81		

Questions   10

Correct   _____
% Correct   _____

**A/P, Purchases &
Other Liabilities**

Question #	Correct	√
82		
83		
84		
85		
86		
87		
88		
89		
90		

Questions   9

Correct   _____
% Correct   _____

Payroll

Question #	Correct	√
91		
92		
93		
94		
95		

Questions   5

Correct   _____
% Correct   _____

Long-Term Liabilities

Question #	Correct	√
96		
97		

Questions   2

Correct   _____
% Correct   _____

Stockholders' Equity

Question #	Correct	√
98		
99		
100		
101		
102		

Questions   5

Correct   _____
% Correct   _____

Accounting Estimates

Question #	Correct	√
103		
104		
105		
106		
107		
108		

Questions   6

Correct   _____
% Correct   _____

Solution 5-2 SIMULATION ANSWER: Kiting

A.   2, 4

The term kiting refers to the practice of transferring cash between or among various bank accounts, with recording of the cash receipt (deposit) being made on a timely basis, while the recording of the disbursement (withdrawal) is delayed. Thus, for a period of time, the amount of the check could appear in two different accounts simultaneously. In this question, note that the receipt of check #2 was recorded (per the books) at 12/30, while the disbursement was not recorded (per the books) until 1/3. Also, note that check #4 (written from State Bank) was received by the bank on 12/31 but was not recorded on the Fox Co.'s books until 1/2.

B.   1, 3

Deposits/transfers in transit refer to checks which have been recorded on the entity's books but have not yet cleared the bank. In this question, note that checks #1 and #3 were disbursed (per books) at the end of December, but were not received by the bank until early January.   (ID: 9229)

Solution 5-3 SIMULATION ANSWER: Audit Procedures for Errors & Fraud

1.   E

Preparing a bank transfer schedule would permit the auditor to determine whether a kiting scheme exists.

2.   D

Obtaining a cutoff bank statement and comparing the cleared checks to the year-end bank reconciliation would provide some evidence that checks were not mailed until after the first week of the subsequent year.

3.   H

Confirming loan terms with a lender would reveal that lender's lien on the real estate.

4.   K, L

Sending a second confirmation request and making inquiries of a reputable credit agency would provide evidence of the customer's existence and credit worthiness. Examining the shipping documents assists the auditor to determine whether merchandise was actually shipped to the customer.

5.   P

A surprise observation of the distribution of payroll checks would provide evidence that the new employees exist and are currently working.

6.   Q

Vouching data in the payroll register to authorized pay rates in the human resource files would permit the auditor to determine whether rate increases are properly authorized.   (ID: 9230)

Solution 5-4 SIMULATION ANSWER: Audit Procedures for Long-Term Debt

1. I

A mark next to the lenders' names is most likely to indicate that the information in the next 3 columns is accurate. This mark is unlikely to relate to a dollar balance as it is not positioned closely to any numbers.

2. C

Material beginning balances are generally traced to the prior year's working papers.

3. J

Increased borrowings should be processed with the board of directors' authorization, should correspond to the loan agreement, and their disposition should be traceable. These are all items of interest to an auditor.

4. H

As the loan to First National Bank has the principal due in 20X3, any payment before that date should have specific authorization by the board of directors. The auditor would also likely examine the canceled check(s) associated with this transfer.

5. G

The repayments did not agree to the board of directors (BOD) authorization. [Assume the BOD authorized payment of the full $120,000 ($10,000 × 12 months), based on the terms of the loan.] Confirmation of receipt of the $110,000 is obtained from the monthly statement that the bank issues. The auditor also would likely examine the canceled check(s) associated with this transfer.

6. A

The comments column shows that two of the three lenders with this mark in the ending balance column agrees with the account balance. The third doesn't show a dispute about the amount. The lender without this mark does have a comment about a dispute.

7. K

This mark is next to the two loans that have required payments due in the next year.

8. B

This mark is next to the one loan that has a dispute between the lender and the audit client.

9. D

The total long-term debt and the total accrued interest payable are likely to be entire, separate accounts in the trial balance and general ledger. It is reasonable to trace accounts to the current year financial statements (via the trial balance etc.) after examining them.

10. F

It is normal for the auditor to recompute interest accruals and check the reasonableness of the client's interest accrual.

(ID: 9231)

———————————

Solution 5-5 SIMULATION ANSWER: Audit Procedures for Property, Plant & Equipment

1.   F

Material beginning balances are generally traced to the prior year's working papers.

2.   L

Documentation for additions to PP&E generally is examined in an audit. Deeds and purchase contracts would be appropriate documents to examine for a land purchase.

3.   K

Documentation for additions to PP&E generally is examined in an audit. Work orders and engineers' reports would be appropriate documents to examine for constructed assets.

4.   J

Documentation for additions to PP&E generally is examined in an audit. Vendors' invoices would be appropriate documents to examine for purchased assets.

5.   G

As the disposals are fully depreciated and of relatively small amount, procedures may not be necessary.

6.   D

An amount is removed from buildings and added to fixtures, but the net for PP&E is zero.

7.   C

The individual categories of PP&E and accumulated depreciation are likely to be entire, separate accounts in the trial balance and general ledger. It is reasonable to trace accounts to the current year financial statements (via the trial balance etc.) after auditing them.

8.   B

The provision for accumulated depreciation can be easily checked against the PP&E accounts, as the rate and method for each category is known.   (ID: 9232)

_____

Solution 5-6 SIMULATION ANSWER: Accounts Receivable (AR) Confirmations

1. A

The client should adjust the accounting records to reflect the receipt of the payment during year 2.

2. D

The auditor should perform the additional audit procedures described, i.e., examining shipping documents and subsequent cash receipts to confirm the accounting records are correct because two attempts to reach the customer failed.

3. A

The client should adjust the accounting records to reflect the return of the materials.

4. E

The auditor should perform the additional audit procedures described, i.e., examining the invoices noted on the confirmation to confirm they pertain to the subsequent year and thus, the accounting records are correct.

5. F

There is no exception so no action is required.

6. D

The auditor should perform the additional audit procedures described, i.e., examining shipping documents and subsequent cash receipts to confirm the accounting records are correct. The simulation did not offer supplying the purchase order numbers to the customer on a second request as an option.   (ID: 9832)

————————————

Solution 5-7 SIMULATION ANSWER: Audit Procedures for Errors & Fraud

1. A

Comparing the details of the cash receipts journal entries with the corresponding daily deposit slips would permit the auditor to determine whether the receipts were properly recorded.

2. U

Examining the purchase orders and receiving reports for selected vouchers would permit the auditor to determine whether the merchandise was ordered and received by the entity.

3. B

Vouching fixed asset accounts debits to the vendors' invoices would permit the auditor to determine whether equipment repairs had been misclassified as fixed assets.

4. A, J

Comparing the details of cash receipts journal entries with the corresponding daily deposit slips and confirming the entity's accounts receivable on a surprise basis would permit the auditor to determine whether a lapping scheme exists.

5. E

Preparing a bank transfer schedule would permit the auditor to determine whether cash is being inappropriately increased by drawing an unrecorded check on one account and simultaneously recording a deposit in a second account.

6. J, L

Confirming the entity's accounts receivable on a surprise basis would permit the auditor to determine whether sales to those customers were genuine. Examining the shipping documents would permit the auditor to determine whether merchandise was actually shipped to those customers. (ID: 9233)

Solution 5-8 SIMULATION ANSWER: Financial Statement Assertions for Investments

Primary Assertion	Explanation
1. B. Existence	To determine that the custodian holds the securities as identified in the confirmation.
2. F. Completeness	To determine that all income and related collections from the investments are properly recorded.
3. H. Valuation & accuracy & allocation	To determine that the market or other value of the investments is fairly stated.
4. J. Classification & understandability	To determine that the financial statement presentation and disclosure of investments is in conformity with generally accepted accounting principles consistently applied.
5. H. Valuation & accuracy & allocation	To determine that the market or other value of the investments is fairly stated and the loss is properly recognized and recorded. (ID: 9234)

Solution 5-9 SIMULATION ANSWER: Research

AU	§	331	14

(ID: 9235)

.14 If inventories are in the hands of public warehouses or other outside custodians, the auditor ordinarily would obtain direct confirmation in writing from the custodian. If such inventories represent a significant proportion of current or total assets, to obtain reasonable assurance with respect to their existence, the auditor should apply one or more of the following procedures as he [*sic*] considers necessary in the circumstances.

a. Test the owner's procedures for investigating the warehouseman [*sic*] and evaluating the warehouseman's [*sic*] performance.

b. Obtain an independent accountant's report on the warehouseman's [*sic*] control procedures relevant to custody of goods and, if applicable, pledging of receipts, or apply alternative procedures at the warehouse to gain reasonable assurance that information received from the warehouseman [*sic*] is reliable.

c. Observe physical counts of the goods, if practicable and reasonable.

d. If warehouse receipts have been pledged as collateral, confirm with lenders pertinent details of the pledged receipts (on a test basis, if appropriate).

———————————

Solution 5-10 SIMULATION ANSWER: Research

AU	§	330	34

(ID: 9219)

34. For the purpose of this section, *accounts receivable* means

(a) The entity's claims against customers that have arisen from the sale of goods or services in the normal course of business, and

(b) A financial institution's loans.

Confirmation of accounts receivable is a generally accepted auditing procedure. As discussed in paragraph .06, it is generally presumed that evidence obtained from third parties will provide the auditor with higher-quality audit evidence than is typically available from within the entity. Thus, there is a presumption that the auditor will request the confirmation of accounts receivable during an audit unless one of the following is true:

• Accounts receivable are immaterial to the financial statements.

• The use of confirmations would be ineffective.

• The auditor's combined assessed level of inherent and control risk is low, and the assessed level, in conjunction with the evidence expected to be provided by analytical procedures or other substantive tests of details, is sufficient to reduce audit risk to an acceptably low level for the applicable financial statement assertions. In many situations, both confirmation of accounts receivable and other substantive tests of details are necessary to reduce audit risk to an acceptably low level for the applicable financial statement assertions.

———————————

CHAPTER 6

AUDIT SAMPLING

CHAPTER 6

AUDIT SAMPLING

I. Overview

A. Definition

AU 350 defines audit sampling as the application of an audit procedure to less than 100 percent of the items within an account balance or class of transactions (the population) with the intent of drawing conclusions about the population based on the results of the sample. The third standard of fieldwork requires sufficient appropriate audit evidence to be obtained through audit procedures to afford a reasonable basis for an opinion on the financial statements. The use of sampling relates to this standard. There are two general approaches to audit sampling: statistical and nonstatistical. Both require the auditor to use professional judgment.

1. **Effective** The underlying principle of sampling is that the results of a sample yield information about the population from which the sample was taken. Sampling, therefore, can be looked upon as an effective and efficient method of gathering audit evidence.

2. **Efficient** Without sampling procedures, an auditor would examine every item comprising an account balance or every transaction occurring within a class of transactions. The cost would (a) be prohibitive due to the amount of time required to perform the examination and (b) far outweigh the benefit obtained. Sampling provides the auditor with a means of obtaining information, but at a much lower cost.

3. **Sufficient** The sufficiency of audit evidence is determined by the size and design of an audit sample (among other factors).

   a. **Size** Depends on both the objectives and efficiency of the sample.

   b. **Design** Relates to the efficiency of the sample; for example, one sample is more efficient than another if it achieves the same objectives with a smaller sample size.

4. **Appropriate** The appropriateness of audit evidence is determined by auditor judgment—not the design and evaluation of an audit sample.

B. Types of Sampling

1. **Attributes Sampling** In the auditor's consideration of internal control, tests are performed on the client's internal control policies and procedures in order to determine the degree to which the client's employees have complied (i.e., tests of controls). These tests involve the determination of the rate of occurrence of some characteristic (i.e., attribute), in a population. The attribute of interest is frequently a deviation from the particular control procedure. Thus, the auditor takes a sample from the population, computes the deviation rate in the sample, and draws conclusions about the true population deviation rate.

2. **Variables Sampling** In performing the tests of details of transactions and account balances (i.e., substantive tests), the auditor is concerned with the dollar amounts reported in the financial statements. Thus, the auditor draws a sample from the population of interest, determines the proper dollar value of the items sampled, and makes inferences, based upon projection of the sample results to the population, about the fairness of the amounts reported in the financial statements.

3. **Dual-Purpose Sampling** In some circumstances, the auditor may design a test that will be used for dual purposes—tests of controls and substantive testing. A dual-purpose sample is

a sample that is designed to both test the operating effectiveness of an identified control and test whether the recorded monetary amounts of a transaction are correct.

    a.   **Low Risk Factor** Generally, the auditor who plans to use this type of sample believes that there is an acceptably low risk that the rate of deviations from prescribed internal controls in the population is greater than the tolerable rate.

    b.   **Size** The size of the sample should be the larger of the samples that would have been designed for the two separate purposes.

C. Uncertainty

The concept of a *reasonable basis for an opinion* suggests some degree of uncertainty or audit risk. The theory of sampling is well established in auditing practice because it is unusual to find instances where 100 percent of the items need to be examined for each account balance and class of transactions.

    1.   **Circumstances** There are some situations in which the surrounding factors do not justify the acceptance of any amount of sampling risk, and, therefore, *all* related data is examined.

    2.   **Audit Risk** The uncertainty inherent in applying audit procedures is referred to as audit risk. Audit risk involves uncertainties due to both sampling and nonsampling risks.

        a.   **Sampling Risk** Sampling risk results from the possibility that if a test is restricted to a sample, the conclusions reached may be different than the conclusions that would have resulted if the entire population was examined. The smaller the sample size is, the greater the sampling risk becomes; thus sampling risk varies inversely with sample size.

        b.   **Nonsampling Risk** Nonsampling risk includes all aspects of audit risk not due to sampling. Nonsampling risk can be reduced by adequate planning and supervision of audit work and adherence to quality control standards. Examples of nonsampling risks include:

            (1)   Failure to select appropriate audit procedures for a given objective.

            (2)   Failure to recognize misstatements, thus making a procedure ineffective.

D. Assessing Sampling Risk

The judgment of the auditor should be used to assess sampling risk.

    1.   **Audit Risk Model** Because the acceptable level of audit risk is a matter of professional judgment, the audit risk model is not intended to be a mathematical formula including all factors that may influence the determination of audit risk. However, the model may be useful for planning appropriate risk levels for audit procedures to achieve the desired audit risk.

Exhibit 1 ▶ Audit Risk Model

$AR = RMM \times DR$ or $AR = (IR \times CR) \times (AP \times TD)$
AR = The allowable audit risk that monetary misstatements equal to tolerable misstatements might remain undetected for the account balances, class of transactions, or disclosures for the related relevant assertions after the auditor has completed all audit procedures deemed necessary.
RMM = The risk (consisting of inherent risk and control risk) that the relevant assertions related to account balances, classes of transactions, or disclosures contain misstatements that could be material to the financial statements when aggregated with other misstatements.
IR = **Inherent risk** is the susceptibility of a relevant assertion to a material misstatement, assuming there are no related internal control policies or procedures.
CR = **Control risk** is the risk that a material misstatement that could occur in a relevant assertion will not be prevented or detected on a timely basis by the entity's controls.

DR = The risk that the auditor will not detect a material misstatement that exists in a relevant assertion.

AP = The auditor's assessment of the risk that analytical procedures and other relevant substantive tests will not detect misstatements that could occur in an assertion equal to tolerable misstatement, given that such misstatements are not detected by internal controls.

TD = The allowable risk of incorrect acceptance that tests of details will not detect misstatements equal to tolerable misstatement, given that such misstatements are not detected by internal controls or analytical procedures and other relevant substantive procedures.

2. **Subjective Assessments** The auditor can compute TD mathematically, if the auditor first assigns an acceptable audit risk (AR) and subjectively quantifies the risk of material misstatement (RMM) and the risk that analytical procedures and other relevant substantive test will not detect misstatements (AP). To compute TD, the model must be restated as TD = AR/(RMM × AP).

Example 1 ▶ Audit Risk Model Use

Assume the auditor is planning a sampling application to test a client's accounts receivable voucher register. If AR = .05 and the auditor has subjectively assessed RMM and AP equal to 50% and 30%, respectively, then the auditor can use the model to compute an appropriate level of risk of incorrect acceptance (sampling risk).

$$TD = AR/(RMM \times AP)$$
$$TD = 0.05/(0.5 \times 0.3)$$
$$TD = 0.33 \text{ (or 33\%)}$$

3. **Tests of Internal Control** The auditor is concerned with two aspects of sampling risk while performing tests of controls.

a. **Risk of Assessing Control Risk Too Low** The risk that the assessed level of control risk based on the sample is less than the true operating effectiveness of the internal control policy or procedure.

b. **Risk of Assessing Control Risk Too High** The risk that the assessed level of control risk based on the sample is greater than the true operating effectiveness of the internal control policy or procedure.

Exhibit 2 ▶ Risk for Tests of Control Procedures

Auditor's Assessment of Control Risk Is	Client's Control Risk Is	
	Less Than Maximum	Maximum
Less than Maximum Level	Correct Decision (1)	Incorrect Decision (2)
Maximum Level	Incorrect Decision (3)	Correct Decision (4)

(2) Assessing Control Risk Too Low (effectiveness)
(3) Assessing Control Risk Too High (efficiency)

4.   **Substantive Tests of Details** The auditor is concerned with two aspects of sampling risk while performing substantive tests.

Exhibit 3 ▶ **Risk for Substantive Tests**

Indication of Sample Results	Client's Book Value Is	
	Fairly Stated	Not Fairly Stated
Accept Book Value	Correct Decision (5)	Incorrect Decision (6)
Reject Book Value	Incorrect Decision (7)	Correct Decision (8)

(6)   Incorrect Acceptance (effectiveness)
(7)   Incorrect Rejection (efficiency)

a.   **Risk of Incorrect Acceptance (Beta Risk)** The risk that the sample supports the conclusion that the recorded account balance is not misstated materially, when in fact, it is misstated materially.

b.   **Risk of Incorrect Rejection (Alpha Risk)** The risk that the sample supports the conclusion that the recorded account balance is misstated materially, when in fact, it is not misstated materially.

5.   **Efficiency & Effectiveness** The risk of incorrect rejection and the risk of assessing control risk too high relate to the efficiency of the audit. Thus, if the auditor assesses control risk too high, additional substantive tests will be performed beyond what is necessary. The risk of incorrect acceptance and the risk of assessing control risk too low relate to the effectiveness of the audit in the detection of existing material misstatements. This potentially could result in materially misstated financial statements from not expanding substantive audit tests to a necessary level.

E.   **Sample Selection**
Items for sampling should be chosen in such a way that the sample can be representative of the population. The auditor should ensure that all items have an opportunity to be selected. Commonly used selection procedures include: haphazard sampling, random sampling, systematic sampling, stratified sampling, block sampling, and probability-proportional-to-size sampling. Note that block sampling does not meet the requirements for a representative sample.

F.   **Tests of Internal Controls**
Sampling applies to tests of controls when the auditor needs to decide whether a rate of deviation is equal to or less than a tolerable rate. However, sampling does not apply to risk assessment procedures performed to obtain an understanding of internal control. Furthermore, sampling concepts may not apply to some tests of controls such as the following: (1) tests of automated application controls (generally these are tested only once or a few times when effective IT general controls are present); (2) analyses of controls for determining appropriate segregation of duties or other analyses that do not examine documentary evidence of performance; (3) tests of certain documented controls or analyses of the effectiveness of security and access controls; or (4) tests directed toward obtaining audit evidence about the operation of the control environment or accounting system.

1.   **Planning Sample** The auditor should take the following judgmental factors into consideration when planning samples for tests of controls:

a.   **Relationship** The relationship of the sample to the objective of the test of controls.

b. **Tolerable Rate of Deviations** The maximum, or tolerable, rate of deviations from prescribed internal control policies and procedures that would support the auditor's assessed level of control risk. The tolerable rate is assessed by considering the relationship of procedural deviations to (1) the assessed level of control risk and (2) the degree of assurance desired by the auditor related to the audit evidence in the sample.

c. **Allowable Risk** The auditor's allowable risk of assessing control risk too low. When the degree of assurance desired by the sample is high, the auditor should allow for a low level of sampling risk (that is, the risk of assessing control risk too low).

d. **Characteristics** Characteristics of the population, that is, the items comprising the account balance or class of transactions of interest

e. **Size** The auditor uses professional judgment to relate the following factors in determining a sample size for a test of controls: (1) the tolerable rate of deviation from the tested control, (2) the likely rate of deviations, and (3) the allowable risk of assessing control risk too low.

2. **Performance & Evaluation** In performing audit procedures on items included in a sample and in evaluating sample results, the auditor should repeat the same steps that are outlined for substantive testing. However, for tests of controls, if the auditor is unable to perform all tests on a selected item, it is considered a deviation. If the auditor concludes that the sample results do not support the assessed level of control risk for an assertion, the auditor should reevaluate the nature, timing, and extent of substantive procedures based on a revised consideration of the assessed level of control risk.

G. **Substantive Tests of Details**

1. **Planning Sample** The auditor should consider the audit objectives to be achieved and decide on the procedure(s) to be applied that will achieve those objectives. The auditor should consider the following factors in planning a sample for a substantive test of details:

a. **Relationship** The relationship of the sample to the relevant audit objectives, i.e., the population being sampled should be appropriate for the audit objective.

b. **Materiality** Preliminary judgments of materiality levels

c. **Allowable Risk** Auditor's allowable risk of incorrect acceptance

d. **Characteristics** Characteristics of the population, that is, the items comprising the account balance or class of transactions of interest. The auditor may be able to reduce the needed sample size by separating the population into relatively homogenous groups on the basis of some characteristic related to the specific audit objective. (For example, dividing accounts receivable into several groups based on the size of the individual account balances.)

e. **Tolerable Misstatement** How much monetary misstatement in the related account balance may exist when combined with misstatements that may be found in other tests without causing the financial statements to be misstated materially. This is called the tolerable misstatement or tolerable error for the sample. Tolerable misstatement should usually be set for a particular audit procedure at less than financial statement materiality so that when the results of all audit procedures are aggregated, the required overall assurance will be attained.

f. **Size** The required sample size for a test of details is influenced by (1) the tolerable misstatement and expected misstatement, (2) the audit risk, (3) the characteristics of the population, (4) the assessed risk of material misstatement (RMM), and (5) the assessed risk for other substantive procedures related to the same assertion. Statistical sampling involves the use of tables or formulas to compute sample sizes based on these factors while nonstatistical sample sizes depend on the auditor's professional judgment in relating these factors.

2. **Performance** Procedures that are appropriate to the particular audit objective should be applied to each sample item. If certain selected sample items cannot be examined, the auditor's treatment of these unexpected items will depend upon their effect on the auditor's evaluation of the sample. If the auditor's evaluation of the sample results would not be altered by considering those unexamined items to be misstated, it is not necessary to examine the items. However, if considering those unexamined items to be misstated would lead to a conclusion that the balance or class contains material misstatements, the auditor should consider alternative procedures, and should consider whether the inability to examine the items has implications in relation to (a) assessing the risks of material misstatement due to fraud, (b) the assessed level of control risk the auditor expects to be supported, or (c) the degree of reliance on management representations.

3. **Evaluation** The auditor compares total projected misstatement with the tolerable misstatement.

   a. **Judgment** The auditor's judgment is a necessary factor in this evaluation for both statistical and nonstatistical sampling.

   b. **Quality** In addition to the evaluation of the frequency and amounts of monetary misstatements, consideration should be given to the qualitative aspects of the misstatements. Specifically, the auditor considers the nature and cause of the misstatement and the possible relationship of the misstatement to other phases of the audit.

   c. **Aggregate** When the auditor evaluates whether the financial statements taken as a whole may be misstated materially, projected misstatement results for all audit sampling applications and all known misstatements from nonsampling applications should be considered in the aggregate along with other relevant audit evidence.

H. Statistical Sampling

Statistical sampling is based on the assumption that, within a given confidence level and allowance for sampling risk, a randomly selected sample of items from a population will reflect the same characteristics that occur in the population. Therefore, auditors may draw valid conclusions based on data derived from a relatively small sample of the total population.

1. **Similarities** Both statistical and nonstatistical sampling involve examining less than the whole body of data to express a conclusion about the total body of data. Both methods involve audit judgment in planning and performing a sampling procedure and evaluating the results of the sample. Both provide sufficient appropriate audit evidence. Also, the audit procedures involved in examining the selected items in a sample generally do not depend on the sampling approach used.

2. **Distinguishing Feature** A properly designed nonstatistical sampling application can provide results that are as effective as those from a properly designed statistical sampling application. The distinguishing feature of statistical sampling methods as opposed to nonstatistical methods is that the user is able to provide a mathematical measurement of the degree of uncertainty that results from examining only part of a population. That is, statistical sampling allows an auditor to measure sampling risk.

3. **Sampling Approach** Statistical or nonstatistical approaches can provide sufficient audit evidence. The auditor must choose between statistical and nonstatistical sampling. This choice primarily is a cost/benefit consideration.

   a. **Selection** Because either can provide sufficient audit evidence, the auditor chooses between statistical or nonstatistical sampling after considering their relative cost and effectiveness in the specific situation.

b. **Advantages** Statistical sampling helps to (1) design efficient samples, (2) measure the sufficiency of audit evidence, and (3) evaluate sample results.

4. **Risks** If audit sampling (either nonstatistical or statistical) is used, some sampling risk is always present. One benefit of statistical sampling is that it uses the laws of probability to measure sampling risk.

5. **Sample Sizes** Another benefit of statistical sampling is that it provides a model for determining sample size while explicitly recognizing relevant factors such as the risk of assessing control risk too low, tolerable misstatement, and the expected population deviation rate. With nonstatistical sampling, on the other hand, the auditor implicitly recognizes the relevant factors while determining the sample size based on her/his own judgment and experience.

6. **Costs** Statistical sampling might involve additional costs for (a) training auditors, (b) designing individual samples to meet the statistical requirements, and (c) selecting the items to be examined. For example, if the individual balances comprising an account balance to be tested are not maintained in an organized pattern, it might not be cost effective for an auditor to select items in a way that would satisfy the requirements of a properly designed statistical sample.

II. Classical Sample Selection Methods

A. Judgmental (Haphazard) Sampling

The auditor uses professional judgment to decide how many and which items should be included in the sample (i.e., the items included in the sample are selected without any conscious bias and without any special reason for including or omitting items from the sample).

1. **Description** It does **not** consist of sampling units selected in a careless manner; rather, the sample is selected in a manner the auditor expects to be representative of the population. For example, the auditor decides to select 100 accounts from a population of 1,000 accounts based on the auditor's judgment as to how many and which specific accounts should be included in the sample.

2. **Use** While haphazard sampling is useful for nonstatistical sampling, it is not used for statistical sampling because it does not allow measurement of the probability of selecting the combination of sampling units.

B. Random Number Sampling

The auditor may select a random sample by matching random numbers generated by a computer or selected from a random number table with, for example, document numbers. With this method, every item in the population has the same probability of being selected as every other item in the population, and every sample has the same probability of being selected as every other sample of the same size.

1. **Replacement** With random number and other sample selection methods, the auditor may sample with or without replacement (i.e., with or without replacing an item in the population after its value or attribute has been selected). Sampling with replacement may result in the appearance of a particular item in the sample more than once. In practice, auditors generally choose the without replacement approach.

2. **Use** This approach is useful for both statistical and nonstatistical sampling.

C. Systematic Sampling

For this method, the auditor determines a uniform interval by dividing the number of physical units in the population by the sample size. A random number is selected as a starting point for the first interval, and one item is selected throughout the population at each of the uniform intervals from the starting point (every nth item). For example, if the auditor wishes to select 100 items from a population of 20,000 items, the uniform interval is every 200th item. First the auditor selects a random starting point (a random number from 1 to 200) and then selects every 200th item from the random start, including the random start item.

1. **Description** Because a random start is used, the systematic method provides a sample that allows every sampling unit in the population an equal chance of being selected. If the population is arranged randomly, systematic selection essentially is the same as random number selection. However, unlike random number sampling, this method may not always give every possible combination of sampling units the same probability of being selected. For example, a population of employees on a payroll for a construction company might be organized by teams, each team consisting of a crew leader and nine other workers. A selection of every tenth employee will list either every crew leader or no crew leaders, depending on the random start. No combination would include both crew leaders and other employees. In these circumstances, the auditor may consider using a different sample selection method such as random selection or making a systematic selection with multiple starts. For example, in the case related to payroll cited above, the auditor could use an interval of 50 rather than 10. This would require that the auditor select 5 different random starting points and move through the population 5 different times.

2. **Use** This method is useful for both statistical and nonstatistical sampling.

D. **Stratified Sampling**
The population is divided into groups, called strata, according to some common characteristic, and then random sampling is applied to each stratum. For example, the auditor may divide the client's accounts receivable into three strata—those with balances of $2,000 and above, those with balances between $500 and $2,000, and those with balances of $500 and below. The auditor might positively confirm the whole population of accounts with balances of $2,000 and above, positively confirm a random sample of the accounts with balances between $500 and $2,000, and negatively confirm a random sample of those accounts with balances of $500 and below. The primary objective of stratified sampling is to decrease the effect of variance in the total population thereby reducing sample size.

1. **Mean-Per-Unit** The mean-per-unit (MPU) method is a classical variables sampling technique that uses the sample average to project the total population dollar value by multiplying the sample average by the number of items in the population. A smaller sample size can be obtained by stratifying a highly variable population into segments. These segments then will have a minimum of variability within segments and variability between segments will be eliminated. As a result, the total sample size of all combined segments will be less. This is accomplished without a loss of reliability or precision. Therefore, stratified MPU sampling may be more efficient than unstratified MPU because it usually produces an estimate having the desired level of precision, with a smaller sample size.

2. **Use** This approach can be used for both statistical and nonstatistical sampling. It is particularly useful in reducing the overall sample size when the auditor is using the MPU approach on populations that include sampling units (such as individual customer receivable balances) that have a wide range of dollar values.

E. **Block Sampling**
A block sample consists of selecting contiguous transactions. For example, a block sample from a population of all vouchers processed for the year 20X8 might be all vouchers processed on February 3, May 17, and July 19, 20X8. This sample includes only three sampling units out of 250 business days because the sampling unit, in this case, is a period of time rather than an individual transaction. A sample with so few blocks generally is not adequate to reach a reasonable audit conclusion. Although a block sample might be designed with enough blocks to minimize this limitation, using such samples might be inefficient. If an auditor decides to use a block sample, special care should be exercised to control sampling risk in designing that sample. Block sampling should not be used with statistical sampling approaches. Block sampling is often used to evaluate changes in control procedures by examining all transactions at that time.

III. Attributes Sampling

A. Operating Effectiveness of Internal Control Policies & Procedures

The attribute of interest normally is a control procedure. For example, the auditor may be concerned with estimating the percentage of purchase orders that do not have proper authorization.

1. **Deviation Rate** In performing tests of controls, the auditor frequently is interested in determining the rate of deviation from prescribed internal control policies and procedures. The sampling plan generally used in this situation is attribute sampling.

   Tests of Controls → Attribute Sampling → Deviation Rate

2. **Impact** A weakness in internal control does not necessarily mean that there will be a misstatement in the financial statements. If a material misstatement occurs and is not detected by internal controls or substantive tests, only then will the financial statements be misstated.

3. **Tolerable Rate** The auditor should determine the maximum rate of deviations from the prescribed internal control policy and procedure that s/he would be willing to accept without altering the planned assessed level of control risk. This is referred to as the tolerable rate.

B. Methods

1. **Sequential Sampling** The sample is selected in several steps, with each step conditional on the results of previous steps.

2. **Attribute Estimation Method** A sample is selected and its attribute error rate is determined. This rate serves as an estimate of the error rate in the population and allows the auditor to make statistical statements about the population attribute error rate.

3. **Acceptance Sampling Method** A special case of estimation of attributes. An acceptance sampling table, which utilizes the population size, sample size, and number of errors found in the sample, is used to make a statistical statement that the error rate in the population is not greater than a specified error rate. For example, based on sample results, an auditor may obtain 95-percent confidence that the actual error rate in the population does not exceed 8 percent.

4. **Discovery Sampling Method** A special case of acceptance sampling. The objective is to attain a specified level of confidence that if the error rate in the population is at least a certain percentage the sample will include at least one instance of failure to comply with the control procedure being audited. For example, discovery sampling can be used to determine how large a sample needs to be for the auditor to have 95-percent confidence that, if the error rate in the population is 1 percent or higher, the auditor's sample will include at least one example of an error. What if a sample of the determined size is selected and no error found? The auditor then has 95-percent confidence that the error rate in the population is less than 1 percent.

   • Discovery sampling frequently is used when the auditor expects an extremely low error rate, usually zero. It often is used in testing for critical problems such as forgery. If a forgery is found, the auditor would discontinue sampling and investigate further.

C. Steps

The following general steps are appropriate for attributes sampling in tests of compliance with prescribed internal control procedures:

1. **Determine Objective** In a compliance test of control procedures, the objective is to compare the actual deviation rate to the tolerable rate. It should be remembered that the purpose of the test is to provide reasonable assurance that internal controls are operating in an effective manner.

2.   **Determine Tolerable Rate** This is the maximum rate of deviations from the prescribed internal control procedure (i.e., maximum misstatement rate) that the auditor is willing to accept without altering the assessment of control risk on the particular internal control procedure and is a judgmental decision. Therefore, the tolerable rate is a function of both the expected level of control risk and the degree of assurance desired. Thus, an increase in the tolerable rate would allow a reduction in sample size. If, after performing the sampling application, the auditor finds that the rate of deviations from the prescribed control procedure is close to or exceeds the tolerable rate, the auditor normally would decide that there is an unacceptably high risk that the deviation rate for the population exceeds the tolerable rate. In such cases, the auditor should consider modifying the assessed level of control risk.

3.   **Determine Confidence (Reliability) Level** This is a judgmental decision that quantifies the level of sampling risk that the auditor is willing to accept. The auditor's willingness to accept sampling risk is determined, to a large extent, by the nature of the other tests that the auditor intends to perform that would complement the test of controls.

4.   **Determine Expected Population Deviation Rate** This is the expected rate of occurrence of deviations from the prescribed internal control procedure (i.e., the expected error rate). The expected population deviation rate should not exceed the tolerable rate. If prior to testing, the auditor believes that the actual deviation rate is higher than the tolerable rate, the auditor generally omits testing of that control procedure and either seeks to obtain assurance by testing other relevant internal controls, or assesses control risk at the maximum level for the related financial statement assertion. The auditor estimates the expected population deviation rate, considering such factors as results of the prior years' tests and the overall control environment. Prior years' results should be considered in light of changes in the entity's internal controls and changes in personnel.

5.   **Consider Effect of Population Size** When a sample is small in relation to the population, the population size has little or no effect on the determination of an appropriate sample size. If the sample size is greater than 10 percent of the population size, which rarely is the case, a finite population correction factor may be used. However, the finite population correction factor tends to decrease the sample size. Therefore, most auditors ignore the factor because any error in sample size that results will be on the conservative side.

6.   **Determine Method of Selecting Sample** The sample should be representative of the population, and all items should have a chance of being selected. The various methods for selecting samples are discussed in Section III.B.

7.   **Compute Sample Size** Sample sizes can be computed by the use of formulas, computer software, and sample size tables. Consideration should be given to the following when determining sample size:

    a.   **Assessing Control Risk Too Low** As discussed earlier, there is an inverse relationship between the risk of assessing control risk too low and sample size.

    b.   **Tolerable Deviation Rate** The maximum rate of deviation from a prescribed control policy or procedure that the auditor is willing to accept without modifying the planned level of control risk.

Exhibit 4 ▶ Sample Size When Other Factors Are Changed

Increase in	Effect on Sample Size
Population	Slight increase for increased populations, generally little or no effect
Tolerable rate	Decrease
Expected deviation rate	Increase

When Sample Size Is Changed	
Sample Size	Increase in
Decrease	Risk of assessing control risk too low

Table 1 ▶ Tolerable Rate

	5% Risk of Assessing Control Risk Too Low (with number of expected errors in parentheses)										
Expected Population Deviation Rate	2%	3%	4%	5%	6%	7%	8%	9%	10%	15%	20%
0.00%	149(0)	99(0)	74(0)	59(0)	49(0)	42(0)	36(0)	32(0)	29(0)	19(0)	14(0)
.25	236(1)	157(1)	117(1)	93(1)	78(1)	66(1)	58(1)	51(1)	46(1)	30(1)	22(1)
.50	*	157(1)	117(1)	93(1)	78(1)	66(1)	58(1)	51(1)	46(1)	30(1)	22(1)
.75	*	208(2)	117(1)	93(1)	78(1)	66(1)	58(1)	51(1)	46(1)	30(1)	22(1)
1.00	*	*	156(2)	93(1)	78(1)	66(1)	58(1)	51(1)	46(1)	30(1)	22(1)
1.25	*	*	156(2)	124(2)	78(1)	66(1)	58(1)	51(1)	46(1)	30(1)	22(1)
1.50	*	*	192(3)	124(2)	103(2)	66(1)	58(1)	51(1)	46(1)	30(1)	22(1)
1.75	*	*	227(4)	153(3)	103(2)	88(2)	77(2)	51(1)	46(1)	30(1)	22(1)
2.00	*	*	*	181(4)	127(3)	88(2)	77(2)	68(2)	46(1)	30(1)	22(1)
2.25	*	*	*	208(5)	127(3)	88(2)	77(2)	68(2)	61(2)	30(1)	22(1)
2.50	*	*	*	*	150(4)	109(3)	77(2)	68(2)	61(2)	30(1)	22(1)
2.75	*	*	*	*	173(5)	109(3)	95(3)	68(2)	61(2)	30(1)	22(1)
3.00	*	*	*	*	195(6)	129(4)	95(3)	84(3)	61(2)	30(1)	22(1)
3.25	*	*	*	*	*	148(5)	112(4)	84(3)	61(2)	30(1)	22(1)
3.50	*	*	*	*	*	167(6)	112(4)	84(3)	76(3)	40(2)	22(1)
3.75	*	*	*	*	*	185(7)	129(5)	100(4)	76(3)	40(2)	22(1)
4.00	*	*	*	*	*	*	146(6)	100(4)	89(4)	40(2)	22(1)
5.00	*	*	*	*	*	*	*	158(8)	116(6)	40(2)	30(2)
6.00	*	*	*	*	*	*	*	*	179(11)	50(3)	30(2)
7.00	*	*	*	*	*	*	*	*	*	68(5)	37(3)

* Sample size is too large to be cost-effective for most audit applications.

NOTE: This table assumes a large population.

Example 2 ▶ Use of Table 1 to Determine Sample Size

The auditor would like to assess control risk at below the maximum level. In this case, in order to do this, the auditor must have 95% confidence that the actual population deviation rate (i.e., the percentage of vouchers that are paid without being approved) is not greater than 6%. Therefore, the tolerable rate is 6%; i.e., the auditor will be able to assess control risk at below the maximum level as long as the auditor can conclude with 95% confidence that not more than 6% of the unpaid vouchers lack approval. Based on the error rate observed in last year's sample, the auditor expects a population deviation rate of only 1.50% this year. Using Table 1, 103 vouchers should be examined to yield the desired confidence about the population error rate.

8. **Select & Audit Sample Items** Audit procedures should be applied to the items in the sample to determine deviations from the prescribed control procedures previously identified. Deviations should be grouped according to whether they are occurring with some regularity or are isolated events. In cases where selected items cannot be examined, they should be counted as deviations from control procedures. This occurs, for example, when documentation used

to test for the procedures has been misplaced, lost, or destroyed. A voided item generally would be replaced by another randomly selected item, if it was voided properly.

9.   **Evaluate Sample Results** The results of the sample must be analyzed in order to make an inference about the population error rate. This can be done by formula, but most often is accomplished by tables or computer programs based on the appropriate formula.

Table 2 ▶ Actual Number of Deviations Found

Statistical Sample Results Evaluation Upper Limit at 5% of Assessing Control Risk Too Low										

Sample Size	0	1	2	3	4	5	6	7	8	9	10
25	11.3	17.6	*	*	*	*	*	*	*	*	*
30	9.5	14.9	19.6	*	*	*	*	*	*	*	*
35	8.3	12.9	17.0	*	*	*	*	*	*	*	*
40	7.3	11.4	15.0	18.3	*	*	*	*	*	*	*
45	6.5	10.2	13.4	16.4	19.2	*	*	*	*	*	*
50	5.9	9.2	12.1	14.8	17.4	19.9	*	*	*	*	*
55	5.4	8.4	11.1	13.5	15.9	18.2	*	*	*	*	*
60	4.9	7.7	10.2	12.5	14.7	16.8	18.8	*	*	*	*
65	4.6	7.1	9.4	11.5	13.6	15.5	17.4	19.3	*	*	*
70	4.2	6.6	8.8	10.8	12.6	14.5	16.3	18.0	19.7	*	*
75	4.0	6.2	8.2	10.1	11.8	13.6	15.2	16.9	18.5	20.0	*
80	3.7	5.8	7.7	9.5	11.1	12.7	14.3	15.9	17.4	18.9	*
90	3.3	5.2	6.9	8.4	9.9	11.4	12.8	14.2	15.5	16.8	18.2
100	3.0	4.7	6.2	7.6	9.0	10.3	11.5	12.8	14.0	15.2	16.4
125	2.4	3.8	5.0	6.1	7.2	8.3	9.3	10.3	11.3	12.3	13.2
150	2.0	3.2	4.2	5.1	6.0	6.9	7.8	8.6	9.5	10.3	11.1
200	1.5	2.4	3.2	3.9	4.6	5.2	5.9	6.5	7.2	7.8	8.4

* Over 20 percent

NOTE: This table presents upper limits as percentages. This table assumes a large population.

a.   The first step in the evaluation of the results is tabulating the number of deviations found and comparing this to the number of deviations expected to occur using the sample size determined from the above table. The expected number of deviations is the parenthetical number found next to each sample size. In cases where the deviations found are less than the number that would be expected (the parenthetical number), it can be assumed that the risk of assessing control risk too low and the allowance for sampling risk is not more than the tolerable rate.

b.   When the actual deviations are more than those that would be expected according to the parenthetical number in Table 1, the auditor can calculate the maximum deviation rate in the population using a table similar to Table 2. Table 2 is for evaluating sample results for a 5-percent risk of assessing control risk too low or a 95-percent confidence level.

c.   No one table can accommodate an evaluation of every possible size and number of deviations, and the auditor often will need to use other references to find appropriate tables. In cases where a particular sample size does not appear in a table, it is a good idea to be conservative by using the next smaller sample size shown.

> **Example 3 ▶ Table 2 Use**
>
> Only one error is discovered from the 103 sample items selected in Example 2. Use of Table 2, reveals that there is no corresponding sample size for 103 items, so the next lowest (100 sample size) is used. The intersection of the sample size and the number of deviations found reveals the maximum population deviation rate in this case is 4.7%. This maximum population deviation rate is less than the tolerable rate of 6%, so it can be concluded that within a 95% reliability level, the control is functioning as required.

10. **Reach Overall Conclusion** The auditor uses professional judgment to reach an overall conclusion about the effect of the evaluation of the test of controls on the nature, timing, and extent of planned substantive tests. If the sample results, along with other relevant audit evidence, support the assessed level of control risk, the auditor generally does not need to modify planned substantive tests. If the sample results do not support the assessed level of control risk, the auditor ordinarily either would perform tests of controls on other relevant internal controls for which control risk can be assessed at below the maximum level, or assess control risk at a higher, or the maximum, level and modify the nature, timing, and/or extent of substantive testing. In addition to the evaluation of the frequency and amounts of monetary misstatements, consideration should be given to the qualitative aspects of the misstatements. These would include the nature and cause of the misstatements. For example, were there differences in principle or applications or differences due to misunderstanding of instructions or carelessness? Also, consideration should be given to the possible relationship of the misstatements to other phases of the audit.

11. **Document Sampling Procedure** Documentation might include such items as follows: (a) a description of the prescribed control procedure being tested; (b) the objectives of the test, including the relationship to planned substantive testing; (c) the definition of the population and sampling unit; (d) the definition of the deviation condition (i.e., what is considered a deviation from prescribed internal control policies and procedures); (e) the rationale for the confidence level, the tolerable rate, and the expected population deviation rate used in the application; (f) the method of sample size determination; (g) the method of sample selection; (h) a description of the sampling procedure performed and a listing of compliance deviations identified in the sample; and (i) the evaluation of the sample and a summary of the overall conclusion.

IV. Classical Variables Sampling

A. Substantive Tests of Details
The auditor performs substantive tests either to detect misstatements or to obtain evidence about the validity and propriety of the accounting treatment of transactions and balances. In substantive testing, the auditor is interested primarily in dollar amounts. An example of a substantive test is the use of a sample from the accounts receivable subsidiary ledger to estimate the balance in the control account. The traditional method of performing substantive tests of details is by variables sampling.

Substantive Tests → Variables Sampling → Dollar Amount

B. Methods

1. **Simple Extension (Mean-Per-Unit Approach)** A method of estimating variables in which the auditor finds the average audited value for the items in the sample and then estimates the population value by multiplying the average sample value by the size of the population. For example, if the mean of a sample of 50 accounts is calculated to be $100 and there are 1,000 accounts in the population, the total value of the 1,000 accounts would be estimated at $100,000 [i.e., ($100 per account) × (1,000 accounts)] plus or minus an allowance for sampling error that is determined statistically. Note that the auditor needs to know the audited values of the items in the sample but does not need to know their book values.

2. **Difference Estimation** The auditor first finds the average difference between the audited value and the book value of the items in the sample. This average difference is then multiplied by the size of the population in order to estimate the difference between the book value of the population and its actual value. For example, if the average difference between the book value and audited value for each account in a sample of 100 accounts is $10 and if there are 10,000 accounts in the population, the auditor will estimate that there is a $100,000 difference between the book value of the population and the actual value (i.e., $10 × 10,000 accounts) plus or minus an allowance for sampling risk that is determined statistically. The interval, so determined, then is compared against the precision required (i.e., against the amount of acceptable difference) in order to decide if the account appears to be stated reasonably.

3. **Ratio Method** The auditor uses sample results to estimate the ratio of audited value to book value. This ratio then is applied to the population to estimate the actual value. Ratio estimation should be used when each population item has a book value, an audited value may be ascertained for each sample item, and differences occur frequently. For example, if the auditor finds that the average ratio of audited value to book value for the sample is 1.05 and if the book value for the population is $100,000, the actual value for the population can be estimated to be $105,000 (i.e., 1.05 × $100,000) plus or minus an allowance for sampling risk.

C. **Steps**
The following general steps are appropriate in substantive tests of details:

1. **Determine Objectives** It is important for the auditor to specify the purpose of the test because this will determine the population of the test. For example, the purpose may be to prove the existence of an account balance or to show that the account is complete.

2. **Define Population** The auditor must match the objectives of the test to the appropriate population. The population is made up of the account balances or class of transactions of interest to the auditor. Defining the population involves consideration of the individual sampling units of the entire population, whether the entire population is available to be picked, and the identification of those items that are individually significant. Those items that are individually significant may be accounts that are large enough to exceed the level of tolerable deviation by themselves. These would not be included in the population available for sampling, but should be tested separately.

3. **Determine Confidence Level** The confidence level for the auditor's substantive tests generally will vary inversely with the assessed level of control risk (i.e., the stronger the internal control is judged to be, the lower the assessed level of control risk, thereby affecting the extent of substantive tests). The confidence level for a particular substantive test is a matter of judgment, but the auditor should consider the overall confidence level in making the determination. This confidence level is related to the auditor's assessment of sampling risk.

4. **Determine Expected Standard Deviation of Population or Expected Amount of Misstatement Directly in Dollar Value** This also is a matter of judgment, frequently based on the prior year's audit or on the results of a small pilot sample. As expected misstatement increases, a larger sample size is required.

5. **Determine Tolerable Misstatement** The tolerable misstatement is the maximum monetary misstatement that may exist when combined with misstatements that may be found in other tests without causing the financial statements to be misstated materially. This is a judgmental value which should relate closely to the auditor's preliminary estimates of materiality levels. As tolerable misstatement increases, sample size decreases.

6. **Select Method of Audit Sampling** These can be either statistical or nonstatistical. If statistical sampling is used, either PPS or classical variables techniques would be used.

7. **Determine Sample Size** Compute the sample size by using a sample size table, formula, or software. The sample size formula for substantive testing is illustrated in Exhibit 5.

Exhibit 5 ▶ Substantive Testing Sample Size Formula

$$n = \frac{c^2 \times s^2 \times N^2}{A^2} = \frac{c^2 \times s^2}{a^2}$$

Where:

n = Size of the sample

c = Confidence (reliability) coefficient; this is the number of standard deviations that corresponds to the selected confidence level.

s = Standard deviation of the population (usually the standard deviation of a small pilot sample or the standard deviation found in previous years)

N = Size of the population

A = Population allowance for sampling error (tolerable misstatement less expected amount of misstatement)

a = Allowance for sampling error per population item

Exhibit 6 ▶ Summary of Sampling Factor Relationships

Decrease in	Effect on Sample Size
Confidence (reliability) coefficient	Decrease
Tolerable misstatement	Increase
Expected standard deviation of the population	Decrease

Sample Size	Decrease in
Increase	Risk-Incorrect Acceptance
Increase	Risk-Incorrect Rejection

8. **Inspection** Select and audit the sample items.

Example 4 ▶ Sample Size

An auditor wishes to apply statistical sampling as part of substantive testing of the accounts receivable control account. The account has a book value of $500,000 and is composed of 5,000 individual accounts. The auditor determines that 90% confidence is necessary in the results of substantive testing for this account. The auditor sets total allowance for sampling error (precision) at $40,000. Next, the auditor takes a small pilot sample in order to estimate the standard deviation of the population. The pilot sample has a standard deviation of $40. The number of standard deviations corresponding to 90% for a normal distribution is 1.64.

N	=	5,000	A	=	$40,000
c	=	1.64	s	=	$40
a	=	$40,000/5,000 = $8			

Required: Calculate the sample size.

Solution: Substituting the information into the sample size formula and solving the equation gives the following:

$$n = \frac{(1.64)^2 \ (\$40)^2}{(\$8)^2} = 67.24 \approx 68 \ accounts$$

The auditor should take a random sample of 68 accounts from the population of 5,000 accounts receivable in order to have 90% confidence that the inference based on the sample results will be within $40,000 of the true (actual) value of accounts receivable. That is, if a population of 5,000 accounts actually has a standard deviation of $40, 90% of the possible samples of 68 accounts will yield estimates that are within $40,000 of the actual value of accounts receivable.

---

9. **Evaluate Sample Results** The auditor computes the actual sampling error (precision) and confidence level attained by the sample.

 a. Estimate the population value (multiply the sample mean by the population size).

 b. Compute the actual sampling error (i.e., precision) by solving the sample size formula for A.

$$A = \frac{c \times s \times N}{\sqrt{n}}$$

 c. Compute the actual confidence level by solving the sample size formula for c.

$$c = \frac{A \times \sqrt{n}}{s \times N}$$

Example 5 ▸ Computation of Sampling Error

The auditor selects a sample of 68 accounts as described in Example 4. The auditor would audit these accounts to determine the actual value of each account, then compute the average audited balance. Assume that the average audited balance is $95 per account. The estimated population value is $475,000 ($95 × 5,000 accounts). If the standard deviation of the sample is assumed to be $40, we can compute the actual sampling error (precision) as follows:

$$A = \frac{c \times s \times N}{\sqrt{n}} = \frac{(1.64)\,(\$40)\,(5,000)}{\sqrt{68}} = \$39,775 \approx \$40,000$$

And the confidence level coefficient as follows:

$$c = \frac{A \times \sqrt{n}}{s \times N} = \frac{\$40,000 \times \sqrt{68}}{(\$40)\,(5,000)} = 1.649 \approx 1.65$$

The auditor can rely on the results of the test, with 90% confidence, yielding an estimated value for accounts receivable that differs from the true value by no more than $40,000.

10. **Reach Overall Conclusion** The auditor should project the results of the sample to the population from which the sample was taken before evaluating the results of the sample. The client may adjust the book value of the account to correct the misstatements actually found in the sample and any misstatements discovered in any 100 percent-examined items. The total projected misstatement after the book value has been adjusted should be compared with the tolerable misstatement. If the auditor considers the projected misstatement unacceptable, the auditor should take appropriate action (for example, performing other substantive tests on the account). Note that the auditor also considers the qualitative aspects of misstatements (i.e., misstatements in amount vs. misapplication of accounting principle, or errors vs. fraud) in reaching an overall conclusion.

11. **Document Sampling Procedure** Documentation might include the following: (a) the objectives of the test and a description of other audit procedures related to those objectives; (b) the definition of the population and the sampling unit, including how the auditor considered completeness of the population; (c) the definition of a misstatement; (d) the rationale for the risk

of incorrect acceptance, the risk of incorrect rejection, the tolerable misstatement, and the expected population deviation amount used in the application; (e) the audit sampling technique used; (f) the method of sample selection; (g) a description of the performance of the sampling procedure and a listing of misstatements identified in the sample; and (h) the evaluation of the sample and a summary of the overall conclusion.

V. Probability-Proportional-to-Size Sampling

A. Distinguishing Features
Probability-proportional-to-size sampling (PPS) is a form of variables sampling that uses attribute sampling theory for substantive testing. The sampling unit is not an individual account or transaction, but an individual dollar in an account balance (or another logical unit). PPS sampling has two unique properties.

1. Stratification The audit population is stratified automatically by monetary value.

2. Overstatements Larger dollar amounts have a higher probability of being selected. Therefore, overstatements are more likely to be detected than understatements. Hence, PPS sampling is most appropriate when an auditor desires testing for material overstatements. PPS sampling is ineffective in searching for unrecorded items. (The probability of an item being selected is directly proportional to its recorded dollar value.)

Example 6 ▶ PPS Sampling

| X Co.'s account receivable balance is $2,000,000 | The population is 2,000,000 |
| Customer Y has a balance of $120,000 | The sampling unit is 1 |

Required: Figure the probability that Customer Y has of being selected.

Solution: Customer Y has a 6% chance of being selected (120,000 / 2,000,000 = 6%).

3. Select Sample Items Systematic sampling selection is used most often. Audit procedures then are employed to determine the value of each sample item.

4. Sample Size Sample sizes in low-error environments tend to be relatively small because their approach does not use standard deviations (which tend to be large in most credit environments) in determining sample size.

5. Other Advantages This method also reduces audit work because several dollars selected will appear in the same sample item (for example, a customer's account balance) and, therefore, the same audit procedures often determine the audited value of more than one sample item. Also, this approach does not require a high number of errors to be observed in the sample for the results to be statistically valid, as is the case with Difference Estimation and Ratio Estimation.

B. Disadvantages
An understatement is less likely to be discovered than an overstatement because those accounts with higher dollar values have a greater chance of being selected. Therefore, PPS sampling generally is considered inappropriate for liability accounts. Also, special consideration must be given to zero and negative balance accounts which usually are excluded from the PPS sample. A third disadvantage occurs when the population has a high expected misstatement rate; the auditor then must obtain sample sizes larger than those required by classical variables sampling.

C. Determining Sample Size
Requires that the auditor determine a reliability factor for overstatement errors, a tolerable rate, and an expected error rate.

1. Reliability Factor for Overstatement Errors Can be determined from tables after specifying the expected number of overstatement errors and the risk of incorrect acceptance. The auditor controls the risk of incorrect acceptance by specifying the risk level for the sampling plan. As PPS sampling is most appropriate when no errors are expected, zero is the appropriate estimate for the number of overstatement errors. The risk of incorrect acceptance is a matter of professional judgment; with PPS sampling, it represents an auditor's risk that book value is not overstated materially when material monetary overstatements exist.

Table 3 ▶ Reliability Factors for Errors of Overstatement

Number of Over-statement Errors	Risk of Incorrect Acceptance								
	1%	5%	10%	15%	20%	25%	30%	37%	50%
0	4.61	3.00	2.31	1.90	1.61	1.39	1.21	1.00	.70
1	6.64	4.75	3.89	3.38	3.00	2.70	2.44	2.14	1.68
2	8.41	6.30	5.33	4.72	4.28	3.93	3.62	3.25	2.68
3	10.05	7.76	6.69	6.02	5.52	5.11	4.77	4.34	3.68
4	11.61	9.16	8.00	7.27	6.73	6.28	5.90	5.43	4.68
5	13.11	10.52	9.28	8.50	7.91	7.43	7.01	6.49	5.68
6	14.57	11.85	10.54	9.71	9.08	8.56	8.12	7.56	6.67
7	16.00	13.15	11.78	10.90	10.24	9.69	9.21	8.63	7.67
8	17.41	14.44	13.00	12.08	11.38	10.81	10.31	9.68	8.67
9	18.79	15.71	14.21	13.25	12.52	11.92	11.39	10.74	9.67
10	20.15	16.97	15.41	14.42	13.66	13.02	12.47	11.79	10.67
11	21.49	18.21	16.60	15.57	14.78	14.13	13.55	12.84	11.67
12	22.83	19.45	17.79	16.72	15.90	15.22	14.63	13.89	12.67
13	24.14	20.67	18.96	17.86	17.02	16.32	15.70	14.93	13.67
14	25.45	21.89	20.13	19.00	18.13	17.40	16.77	15.97	14.67
15	26.75	23.10	21.30	20.13	19.24	18.49	17.84	17.02	15.67
16	28.03	24.31	22.46	21.26	20.34	19.58	18.90	18.06	16.67
17	29.31	25.50	23.61	22.39	21.44	20.66	19.97	19.10	17.67
18	30.59	26.70	24.76	23.51	22.54	21.74	21.03	20.14	18.67
19	31.85	27.88	25.91	24.63	23.64	22.81	22.09	21.18	19.67
20	33.11	29.07	27.05	25.74	24.73	23.89	23.15	22.22	20.67

Example 7 ▶ Table 3 Use

The auditor's risk of incorrect acceptance for Co. X is 5% and the number of overstatement errors is 0. The reliability factor for errors of overstatement is 3.00.

2. **Tolerable Rate** The tolerable rate (or tolerable error) is the maximum monetary error that may exist in an account balance without causing the financial statements to be misstated materially. Thus, tolerable error in PPS sampling is related closely to the auditor's planned level of materiality. The sampling interval and the sample size can be determined using the formulas in Exhibit 7.

Exhibit 7 ▶ PPS Sampling Interval & Sample Size

$$n = \frac{c^2 \times s^2 \times N^2}{A^2} = \frac{c^2 \times s^2}{a^2}$$

$$Sampling\ Interval = \frac{Tolerable\ Misstatement}{Reliability\ Factor\ for\ the\ Error\ of\ Overstatement}$$

$$Sample\ Size = \frac{Population}{Sampling\ Interval}$$

Example 8 ▶ Sampling Interval & Sample Size

Using the same assumptions as Example 7, the population is 2,000,000 and the tolerable misstatement is $60,000.

Required: Figure the sampling interval and the sample size.

Solution: The sampling interval is $20,000. (60,000 / 3.00 = 20,000)

The sample size is 100. (2,000,000 / 20,000 = 100)

3. **Expected Error Rate** If some errors are expected, the sample interval can be computed by determining the expected error rate. In cases where the expected error rate is not shown on the table, the auditor would use the sample size for the next higher percentage. If the tolerable rate percentage is not found it would be appropriate to select the sample size for the next smaller percentage shown. This follows the accounting convention of conservatism.

Exhibit 8 ▶ PPS Expected Error Rate

$$n = \frac{c^2 \times s^2 \times N^2}{A^2} = \frac{c^2 \times s^2}{a^2}$$

$$Expected\ Error\ Rate\ = \frac{Expected\ Misstatements}{Population}$$

Example 9 ▶ Sampling Interval & Sample Size

Using the same assumptions as Example 7, we determine that the expected misstatement for Co. X is $10,000 based on our prior experience with the client. The population is 2,000,000. Our expected error rate is .005 (10,000 / 2,000,000 = .005). The tolerable rate has been determined to be 3%. (This example is unrelated to Example 8.)

Required: Figure the sampling interval and the sample size.

Solution: Using Table 1, our sample size is 157.

The sampling interval is then computed by dividing the population by the sample size. (2,000,000 / 157 = 12,739)

D. **Evaluate Sample Results**

Misstatements from the sample should be projected to the population to calculate an allowance for sampling risk. This allowance for sampling risk is a calculation with an incremental allowance for projected errors (misstatements). If the sample contains less than 100-percent errors, the formula for determining the upper limit is as in Exhibit 9.

Exhibit 9 ▶ PPS Upper Limit for Misstatements

Upper limit for errors (misstatements)	=	Projected errors (misstatements)	+	Basic precision	+	Incremental allowance for projected errors (misstatements)

1. **Upper Limit for Misstatements** The upper limit on misstatement is calculated by adding the projected misstatement, the basic precision, and the incremental allowance for projected errors.

   a. Projected misstatements are calculated for each sample item depending on whether the recorded book value is less than or greater than the sampling interval. If less than, the difference between the recorded value and the audited value is divided by the recorded value to arrive at a percentage error known as tainting. The projected misstatement is the tainting percentage multiplied by the sampling interval.

b. Basic precision is calculated by multiplying the reliability factor by the sampling interval.

c. An incremental allowance for projected misstatement is calculated using only those errors in logical units less than the sampling interval. These are ranked from highest to lowest (in terms of tainting percentage), considering the incremental changes in reliability factors for the actual number of errors found.

2. **Comparison** Finishing the evaluation procedure involves comparing the upper limit on errors to the previously estimated tolerable error. If the upper limit on misstatements is less than the tolerable misstatement, such as above, it can be concluded that the total population is not misstated by an amount greater than the originally estimated tolerable misstatement, at the specified risk of incorrect acceptance.

a. If the upper limit on misstatements is greater than the tolerable misstatement, then the sample results do not support the conclusion that the population is not misstated by more than the tolerable misstatement. This may occur if the population was not represented by the sample, the sample was too small due to an excessively low expectation of misstatement, or if the population itself was misstated.

b. In cases where the recorded book value is greater than the sampling interval, the projected misstatement is equal to the actual error.

c. If no errors are found, both the projected errors and the incremental allowance for projected errors would be zero. Therefore, the auditor could conclude that the recorded amount of accounts is not overstated by more than the tolerable error estimated earlier because the only factor with a value other than zero would be the basic precision.

Example 10 ▶ Evaluating Sample Results

Audit procedures reveal four errors. The projected misstatement total is calculated first, followed by the other two components of the upper limits, precision, and the incremental allowance for projected misstatement.

a. Projected Misstatement:

(1) Book value	(2) Audited value	(3) Tainting % (1) – (2) / (1)	(4) Sampling interval	(5) Projected error (3) × (4)
$ 500	$ 450	0.10	$12,739	$1,274
11,000	10,340	0.06	12,739	764
5,700	5,625	0.013	12,739	166
25,350	23,350	—	—	2,000
				$4,204

b. Basic precision: 3 × $12,739 = $38,217

c.   Incremental allowance:

(1) Projected error	(2) Reliability factor (from table)	(3) Incremental change in reliability factor (from table) (increment–1)	(4) Incremental allowance (3) × (1)
$1,274	4.75	0.75 [1]	$ 956
764	6.30	0.55 [2]	420
166	7.76	0.46 [3]	76
			$1,452

[1] $4.75 - 3.00 - 1.00 = 0.75$ [2] $6.30 - 4.75 - 1.00 = 0.55$ [3] $7.76 - 6.30 - 1.00 = 0.46$

d.   Overall conclusion:

Projected misstatement	$ 4,204
Precision	38,217
Incremental allowance	1,452
Upper limit	$43,873

In this example, it can be concluded that the audited sample supports the conclusion that the population is not misstated by more than the tolerable misstatement.

_____

VI. Appendix: Sampling Terms

allowance for sampling error (precision; sampling error) A measure of the closeness of a sample estimate to the corresponding population characteristic for a specified sampling risk.

alpha risk See risk of incorrect rejection and risk of assessing control risk too high.

attribute Any characteristic that is either present or absent. In tests of controls directed toward operating effectiveness, the presence or absence of evidence of the application of a specified internal control policy or procedure is sometimes referred to as an attribute.

attributes sampling A statistical procedure based on estimating whether the rate of occurrence of a particular attribute in a population exceeds a tolerable rate.

audit sampling The application of an audit procedure to less than 100 percent of the items within an account balance or class of transactions for the purpose of evaluating some characteristic of the balance or class.

beta risk See risk of incorrect acceptance and risk of assessing control risk too low.

block sample (cluster sample) A sample consisting of contiguous transactions.

classical variables sampling A sampling approach that measures sampling risk using the variation of the underlying characteristic of interest. This approach includes methods such as mean-per-unit, ratio estimation, and difference estimation.

confidence level (reliability level) The complement of the applicable sampling risk (see risk of incorrect acceptance, risk of assessing control risk too low, risk of incorrect rejection, and risk of assessing control risk too high). In practice, the confidence level is often set equal to the complement of the risk of incorrect rejection (i.e., to the complement of the alpha risk).

difference estimation A classical variables sampling technique that uses the total difference between audited values and individual book values to estimate the total dollar error in a population and an allowance for sampling error.

dollar-unit sampling See probability-proportional-to-size sampling.

expected population deviation rate An anticipation of the deviation rate in the entire population. It is used in determining an appropriate sample size for an attributes sample.

haphazard sample A sample consisting of sampling units selected by the auditor without any special reason for including or omitting particular items.

mean-per-unit method A classical variables sampling technique that uses the sample average to project the total population dollar value by multiplying the sample average by the number of items in the population.

nonsampling risk All aspects of audit risk not due to sampling.

nonstatistical sampling A sampling technique for which the auditor considers sampling risk in evaluating an audit sample without using statistical theory to measure that risk.

population (field; universe) The items comprising the account balance or class of transactions, or a portion of that balance or class of interest. The population excludes individually significant items of which the auditor has decided to examine 100 percent or other items that will be tested separately.

precision See allowance for sampling errors.

probability-proportional-to-size (PPS) sampling (Dollar-unit sampling; CMA sampling) A variables sampling procedure that uses attributes theory to express a projection of the error in a population in dollar amounts.

random sample A sample drawn so that every combination of the same number of items in the population has an equal probability of selection.

ratio estimation A classical variables sampling technique that uses the ratio of audited values to book values in the sample to estimate the total dollar value of the population and an allowance for sampling error.

reliability level See confidence level.

risk of assessing control risk too high The risk that the assessed level of control risk based on the sample is greater than the true operating effectiveness of the internal control policies or procedures.

risk of assessing control risk too low The risk that the assessed level of control risk based on the sample is less than the true operating effectiveness of the internal control policies or procedures.

risk of incorrect acceptance (beta risk; type II misstatement) The risk that the sample supports the conclusion that the recorded account balance is not materially misstated when it is, in fact, materially misstated.

risk of incorrect rejection (alpha risk; type I misstatement) The risk that the sample supports the conclusion that the recorded account balance is materially misstated when, in fact, it is not.

sample Items selected from a population to reach a conclusion about the population.

sampling risk The risk that the auditor's conclusion based on a sample may be different from the conclusion the auditor would reach if the test were applied in the same way to the entire population. For tests of controls, sampling risk is the risk of assessing control risk too high or too low. For substantive testing, sampling risk is the risk of incorrect acceptance or rejection.

sequential sampling A sampling plan for which the sample is selected in several steps, with each step conditional on the results of the previous steps.

standard deviation A measure of the dispersion among the respective values of a particular characteristic as measured for all items in the population for which a sample estimate is developed.

statistical sampling Audit sampling that uses the laws of probability for selecting and evaluating a sample from a population for the purpose of reaching a conclusion about the population.

stratification Division of the population into relatively homogeneous groups.

systematic sampling A method of drawing a sample in which every nth item is drawn from one or more random starts.

tolerable misstatement An estimate of the maximum monetary misstatement that may exist in an account balance or class of transactions when combined with misstatements that may be found in other tests without causing the financial statements to be materially misstated.

tolerable rate The maximum population rate of deviations from a prescribed control procedure that the auditor will tolerate without modifying the nature, timing, or extent of substantive testing.

variables sampling Statistical sampling that reaches a conclusion on the monetary amounts of a population.

CHAPTER 6—AUDIT SAMPLING

Problem 6-1 MULTIPLE-CHOICE QUESTIONS

1. Which of the following courses of action would an auditor most likely follow in planning a sample of cash disbursements if the auditor is aware of several unusually large cash disbursements?

   a. Set the tolerable rate of deviation at a lower level than originally planned
   b. Stratify the cash disbursements population so that the unusually large disbursements are selected
   c. Increase the sample size to reduce the effect of the unusually large disbursements
   d. Continue to draw new samples until all the unusually large disbursements appear in the sample

   (11/94, AUD, #55, ID: 5128)

2. In confirming a client's accounts receivable in prior years, an auditor found that there were many differences between the recorded account balances and the confirmation replies. These differences, which were not misstatements, required substantial time to resolve. In defining the sampling unit for the current year's audit, the auditor most likely would choose

   a. Individual overdue balances
   b. Individual invoices
   c. Small account balances
   d. Large account balances

   (5/95, AUD, #49, ID: 5667)

3. An auditor is determining the sample size for an inventory observation using mean-per-unit estimation, which is a variables sampling plan. To calculate the required sample size, the auditor usually determines the

	Variability in the dollar amounts of inventory items	Risk of incorrect acceptance
a.	Yes	Yes
b.	Yes	No
c.	No	Yes
d.	No	No

   (R/99, AUD, #20, ID: 6836)

4. The risk of incorrect acceptance and the likelihood of assessing control risk too low relate to the

   a. Allowable risk of tolerable misstatement
   b. Preliminary estimates of materiality levels
   c. Efficiency of the audit
   d. Effectiveness of the audit

   (11/95, AUD, #19, ID: 5966)

5. An auditor may decide to increase the risk of incorrect rejection when

   a. Increased reliability from the sample is desired.
   b. Many differences (audit value minus recorded value) are expected.
   c. Initial sample results do not support the planned level of control risk.
   d. The cost and effort of selecting additional sample items is low.

   (11/92, AUD, #38, ID: 2972)

6. The diagram below depicts an auditor's estimated maximum deviation rate compared with the tolerable rate, and also depicts the true population deviation rate compared with the tolerable rate.

	True state of population	
Auditor's estimate based on sample results	Deviation rate is less than tolerable rate	Deviation rate exceeds tolerable rate
Maximum deviation rate is less than tolerable rate	I.	III.
Maximum deviation rate exceeds tolerable rate	II.	IV.

As a result of tests of controls, the auditor assesses control risk too low and thereby decreases substantive testing. This is illustrated by situation

a. I
b. II
c. III
d. IV   (11/95, AUD, #17, ID: 5964)

7. As a result of tests of controls, an auditor assessed control risk too low and decreased substantive testing. This assessment occurred because the true deviation rate in the population was

a. Less than the risk of assessing control risk too low, based on the auditor's sample
b. Less than the deviation rate in the auditor's sample
c. More than the risk of assessing control risk too low, based on the auditor's sample
d. More than the deviation rate in the auditor's sample   (5/95, AUD, #28, ID: 5646)

8. Given random selection, the same sample size, and the same precision requirement for the testing of two unequal populations, the risk of assessing control risk too low on the smaller population is

a. Higher than assessing control risk too low for the larger population
b. Indeterminate relative to assessing control risk too low for the larger population
c. Lower than assessing control risk too low for the larger population
d. The same as assessing control risk too low for the larger population   (Editors, ID: 7498)

9. An auditor may use a systematic sampling technique with a start at any randomly selected item when performing a test of controls with respect to control over cash receipts. The biggest disadvantage of this type of sampling is that the items in the population

a. Must be systematically replaced in the population after sampling
b. May occur in a systematic pattern, thus destroying the sample randomness
c. Must be recorded in a systematic pattern before the sample can be drawn
d. May systematically occur more than once in the sample   (Editors, ID: 0267)

10. While performing a test of details during an audit, an auditor determined that the sample results supported the conclusion that the recorded account balance was materially misstated. It was, in fact, not materially misstated. This situation illustrates the risk of

a. Assessing control risk too high
b. Assessing control risk too low
c. Incorrect rejection
d. Incorrect acceptance   (5/94, AUD, #43, ID: 4708)

11. The purpose of tracing a sample of inventory tags to a client's computerized listing of inventory items is to determine whether the inventory items

a. Represented by tags were included on the listing
b. Included on the listing were properly counted
c. Represented by tags were reduced to the lower of cost or market
d. Included in the listing were properly valued (R/11, AUD, #11, ID: 9911)

12. As a result of sampling procedures applied as tests of controls, an auditor incorrectly assesses control risk higher than appropriate. The most likely explanation for this situation is that

a. The deviation rate in the auditor's sample is less than the tolerable rate, but the deviation rate in the population exceeds the tolerable rate.
b. The deviation rate in the auditor's sample exceeds the tolerable rate, but the deviation rate in the population is less than the tolerable rate.
c. The deviation rates of both the auditor's sample and the population exceed the tolerable rate.
d. The deviation rates of both the auditor's sample and the population are less than the tolerable rate. (R/09, AUD, #27, ID: 8827)

13. An auditor discovers that an account balance believed not to be materially misstated based on an audit sample was materially misstated based on the total population of the account balance. This is an example of which of the following sampling types of risks?

a. Incorrect rejection
b. Incorrect acceptance
c. Assessing control risk too low
d. Assessing control risk too high (R/11, AUD, #45, ID: 9945)

14. Which of the following would be a consideration in planning a sample for a test of subsequent cash receipts?

a. Preliminary judgments about materiality levels
b. The amount of bad debt write-offs in the prior year
c. The size of the intercompany receivable balance
d. The auditor's allowable risk of assessing control risk is too low (R/10, AUD, #11, ID: 9361)

15. When performing a substantive test of a random sample of cash disbursements, an auditor is supplied with a photocopy of vendor invoices supporting the disbursements for one particular vendor rather than the original invoices. The auditor is told that the vendor's original invoices have been misplaced. What should the auditor do in response to this situation?

a. Increase randomly the number of items in the substantive test to increase the reliance that may be placed on the overall test
b. Reevaluate the risk of fraud, and design alternate tests for the related transactions
c. Increase testing by agreeing more of the payments to this particular vendor to the photocopies of its invoices
d. Count the missing original documents as misstatements, and project the total amount of the error based on the size of the population and the dollar amount of the errors (R/10, AUD, #20, ID: 9370)

16. As a result of tests of controls, an auditor assesses control risk too high. This incorrect assessment most likely occurred because

a. Control risk based on the auditor's sample is less than the true operating effectiveness of the client's control activity.
b. The auditor believes that the control activity relates to the client's assertions when, in fact, it does not.
c. The auditor believes that the control activity will reduce the extent of substantive testing when, in fact, it will not.
d. Control risk based on the auditor's sample is greater than the true operating effectiveness of the client's control activity. (Editors, ID: 8393)

17. An advantage of statistical sampling over nonstatistical sampling is that statistical sampling helps an auditor to

    a. Eliminate the risk of nonsampling errors
    b. Reduce the level of audit risk and materiality to a relatively low amount
    c. Measure the sufficiency of the audit evidence obtained
    d. Minimize the failure to detect errors and fraud   (11/95, AUD, #44, amended, ID: 5991)

18. In statistical sampling methods used in substantive testing, an auditor most likely would stratify a population into meaningful groups if

    a. Probability-proportional-to-size (PPS) sampling is used.
    b. The population has highly variable recorded amounts.
    c. The auditor's estimated tolerable misstatement is extremely small.
    d. The standard deviation of recorded amounts is relatively small.   (5/95, AUD, #50, ID: 5668)

19. Using statistical sampling to assist in verifying the year-end accounts payable balance, an auditor has accumulated the following data:

	Number of accounts	Book balance	Balance determined by the auditor
Population	4,100	$5,000,000	?
Sample	200	$ 125,000	$150,000

    Using the ratio estimation technique, the auditor's estimate of year-end accounts payable balance would be

    a. $6,150,000
    b. $6,000,000
    c. $5,125,000
    d. $5,050,000   (Editors, ID: 7496)

20. The expected population deviation rate of client billing misstatements is 2%. The auditor has established a tolerable rate of 3%. In the review of client invoices the auditor should use

    a. Stratified sampling
    b. Discovery sampling
    c. Variable sampling
    d. Attribute sampling   (Editors, ID: 0266)

21. Which of the following sampling methods would be used to estimate a numerical measurement of a population, such as a dollar value?

    a. Attributes sampling
    b. Stop-or-go sampling
    c. Variables sampling
    d. Random-number sampling   (11/94, AUD, #54, ID: 5127)

Items 22 and 23 are based on the following:

An auditor desired to test credit approval on 10,000 sales invoices processed during the year. The auditor designed a statistical sample that would provide 1% risk of assessing control risk too low (99% confidence) that not more than 7% of the sales invoices lacked approval. The auditor estimated from previous experience that about 2½% of the sales invoices lacked approval. A sample of 200 invoices was examined and 7 of them were lacking approval. The auditor then determined the achieved upper precision limit to be 8%.

22. In the evaluation of this sample, the auditor decided to increase the level of the preliminary assessment of control risk because the

    a. Tolerable rate (7%) was less than the achieved upper precision limit (8%)
    b. Expected deviation rate (7%) was more than the percentage of errors in the sample (3½%)
    c. Expected deviation rate (2½%) was less than the tolerable rate (7%)
    d. Achieved upper precision limit (8%) was more than the percentage of errors in the sample (3½%)

                     (11/90, AUD, #59, amended, ID: 0250)

23. The allowance for sampling risk was

    a. 5½%
    b. 4½%
    c. 3½%
    d. 1%

                     (11/90, AUD, #60, ID: 0251)

24. What is an auditor's evaluation of a statistical sample for attributes when a test of 50 documents results in 3 deviations if tolerable rate is 7%, the expected population deviation rate is 5%, and the allowance for sampling risk is 2%?

    a. Modify the planned assessed level of control risk because the tolerable rate plus the allowance for sampling risk exceeds the expected population deviation rate
    b. Accept the sample results as support for the planned assessed level of control risk because the sample deviation rate plus the allowance for sampling risk exceeds the tolerable rate
    c. Accept the sample results as support for the planned assessed level of control risk because the tolerable rate less the allowance for sampling risk equals the expected population deviation rate
    d. Modify the planned assessed level of control risk because the sample deviation rate plus the allowance for sampling risk exceeds the tolerable rate   (5/92, AUD, #54, ID: 2807)

25. An auditor who uses statistical sampling for attributes in testing internal controls should reduce the planned reliance on a prescribed control when the

    a. Sample rate of deviation plus the allowance for sampling risk equals the tolerable rate.
    b. Sample rate of deviation is less than the expected rate of deviation used in planning the sample.
    c. Tolerable rate less the allowance for sampling risk exceeds the sample rate of deviation.
    d. Sample rate of deviation plus the allowance for sampling risk exceeds the tolerable rate.

                     (11/95, AUD, #25, ID: 5972)

26. Which of the following statements is correct about the sample size in statistical sampling when testing internal controls?

    a. The auditor should consider the tolerable rate of deviation from the controls being tested in determining sample size.
    b. As the likely rate of deviation decreases, the auditor should increase the planned sample size.
    c. The allowable risk of assessing control risk too low has no effect on the planned sample size.
    d. Of all the factors to be considered, the population size has the greatest effect on the sample size.

                     (R/06, AUD, #16, ID: 8134)

27. Which of the following statements is correct concerning the auditor's use of statistical sampling?

    a. An auditor needs to estimate the dollar amount of the standard deviation of the population to use classical variables sampling.
    b. The selection of zero balances usually does not require special sample design considerations when using PPS sampling.
    c. A classical variables sample needs to be designed with special considerations to include negative balances in the sample.
    d. An assumption of PPS sampling is that the underlying accounting population is normally distributed.
    (Editors, ID: 0265)

28. Which of the following statements is ordinarily correct about the sample size in statistical sampling when testing controls?

    a. The expected population deviation rate has little effect on determining the sample size.
    b. As the population size doubles, the sample size should also double.
    c. As the tolerable deviation rate increases, the sample size should also increase.
    d. The population size has little effect on the sample size.
    (R/11, AUD, #30, ID: 9930)

29. Which of the following statements is correct concerning statistical sampling in tests of controls?

    a. As the population size increases, the sample size should increase proportionately.
    b. Deviations from specific internal control procedures at a given rate ordinarily result in misstatements at a lower rate.
    c. There is an inverse relationship between the expected population deviation rate and the sample size.
    d. In determining tolerable rate, an auditor considers detection risk and the sample size.
    (11/94, AUD, #27, ID: 5100)

30. An auditor established a $60,000 tolerable misstatement for an asset with an account balance of $1,000,000. The auditor selected a sample of every twentieth item from the population that represented the asset account balance and discovered overstatements of $3,700 and understatements of $200. Under these circumstances, the auditor most likely would conclude that

    a. There is an unacceptably high risk that the actual misstatements in the population exceed the tolerable misstatement because the total projected misstatement is more than the tolerable misstatement.
    b. There is an unacceptably high risk that the tolerable misstatement exceeds the sum of actual overstatements and understatements.
    c. The asset account is fairly stated because the total projected misstatement is less than the tolerable misstatement.
    d. The asset account is fairly stated because the tolerable misstatement exceeds the net of projected actual overstatements and understatements.
    (R/00, AUD, #13, ID: 6938)

31. The likelihood of assessing control risk too high is the risk that the sample selected to test controls

    a. Does not support the auditor's planned assessed level of control risk when the true operating effectiveness of internal control justifies such an assessment
    b. Contains misstatements that could be material to the financial statements when aggregated with misstatements in other account balances or transactions classes
    c. Contains proportionately fewer monetary errors or deviations from prescribed internal control structure policies or procedures than exist in the balance or class as a whole
    d. Does not support the tolerable error for some or all of management's assertions
    (11/94, AUD, #33, amended, ID: 5106)

32. For which of the following audit tests would an auditor most likely use attribute sampling?

    a. Selecting accounts receivable for confirmation of account balances
    b. Inspecting employee time cards for proper approval by supervisors
    c. Making an independent estimate of the amount of a LIFO inventory
    d. Examining invoices in support of the valuation of fixed asset additions
    (5/96, AUD, #4, ID: 6236)

33. An auditor is selecting vouchers for testing an entity's internal control activities related to the proper approval of vouchers before checks are prepared. The auditor is matching random numbers with voucher numbers to determine which vouchers to inspect. If a random number matches a voided voucher, that voucher ordinarily would be replaced by another voucher in the random sample if the voided voucher

   a. Cannot be located in the voucher file
   b. Represents a dollar amount that is material
   c. Indicates a deviation from the prescribed activity
   d. Has been properly voided   (R/03, AUD, #14, ID: 7636)

34. Samples to test internal control procedures are intended to provide a basis for an auditor to conclude whether

   a. The control procedures are operating effectively.
   b. The financial statements are materially misstated.
   c. The risk of incorrect acceptance is too high.
   d. Materiality for planning purposes is at a sufficiently low level.   (5/91, AUD, #40, amended, ID: 0246)

35. An auditor should consider the tolerable rate of deviation when determining the number of check requests to select for a test to obtain assurance that all check requests have been properly authorized. The auditor should also consider

	The average dollar value of the check requests	*The allowable risk of assessing control risk too low*
a.	Yes	Yes
b.	Yes	No
c.	No	Yes
d.	No	No (R/99, AUD, #17, ID: 6833)

36. Which of the following factors is (are) considered in determining the sample size for a test of controls?

	Expected deviation rate	*Tolerable deviation rate*
a.	Yes	Yes
b.	No	No
c.	No	Yes
d.	Yes	No (11/95, AUD, #33, ID: 5980)

37. In determining the number of documents to select for a test to obtain assurance that all sales returns have been properly authorized, an auditor should consider the tolerable rate of deviation from the control activity. The auditor should also consider

   I.   The likely rate of deviations
   II. The allowable risk of assessing control risk too high

   a. I only
   b. II only
   c. Both I and II
   d. Either I or II   (11/97, AUD, #16, amended, ID: 6579)

38. In performing tests of controls over authorization of cash disbursements, which of the following statistical sampling methods would be most appropriate?

   a. Variables
   b. Stratified
   c. Ratio
   d. Attributes   (5/93, AUD, #25, ID: 3921)

39. For which of the following audit tests would a CPA most likely use attribute sampling?

    a. Identifying entries posted to incorrect accounts
    b. Estimating the amount in an expense account
    c. Evaluating the reasonableness of depreciation expense
    d. Selecting receivables for confirmation of account balances   (R/07, AUD, #34, ID: 8406)

40. In attribute sampling, a 25% change in which of the following factors will have the smallest effect on the size of the sample?

    a. Tolerable rate of deviation
    b. Number of items in the population
    c. Degree of assurance desired
    d. Planned assessed level of control risk   (R/09, AUD, #48, ID: 8848)

41. Which of the following most likely would be an advantage in using classical variables sampling rather than probability-proportional-to-size (PPS) sampling?

    a. An estimate of the standard deviation of the population's recorded amounts is not required.
    b. The auditor rarely needs the assistance of a computer program to design an efficient sample.
    c. Inclusion of zero and negative balances generally does not require special design considerations.
    d. Any amount that is individually significant is automatically identified and selected.

                                                                            (5/93, AUD, #43, ID: 3939)

42. When using classical variables sampling for estimation, an auditor normally evaluates the sampling results by calculating the possible error in either direction. This statistical concept is known as

    a. Precision
    b. Reliability
    c. Projected error
    d. Standard deviation   (5/91, AUD, #18, ID: 0244)

43. The use of the ratio estimation sampling technique is most effective when

    a. The calculated audit amounts are approximately proportional to the client's book amounts
    b. A relatively small number of differences exist in the population
    c. Estimating populations whose records consist of quantities, but not book values
    d. Large overstatement differences and large understatement differences exist in the population

                                                                            (5/95, AUD, #51, ID: 5669)

44. When planning a sample for a substantive test of details, an auditor should consider tolerable misstatement for the sample. This consideration should

    a. Be related to the auditor's business risk
    b. Not be adjusted for qualitative factors
    c. Be related to the auditor's determination of materiality
    d. Not be changed during the audit process   (5/90, AUD, #51, amended, ID: 0255)

45. An auditor examining inventory most likely would use variables sampling rather than attributes sampling to

    a. Identify whether inventory items are properly priced
    b. Estimate whether the dollar amount of inventory is reasonable
    c. Discover whether misstatements exist in inventory records
    d. Determine whether discounts for inventory are properly recorded   (R/05, AUD, 0380A, #21, ID: 7816)

46. Which of the following characteristics most likely would be an advantage of using classical variables sampling rather than probability-proportional-to-size (PPS) sampling?

    a. The selection of negative balances requires no special design considerations.
    b. The sampling process can begin before the complete population is available.
    c. The auditor need not consider the preliminary judgments about materiality.
    d. The sample will result in a smaller sample size if few errors are expected.   (R/07, AUD, #32, ID: 8404)

47. Hill has decided to use probability-proportional-to-size (PPS) sampling, sometimes called dollar-unit sampling, in the audit of a client's accounts receivable balances. Hill plans to use the following PPS sampling table:

TABLE
Reliability Factors for Errors of Overstatement

Number of overstatement misstatements	Risk of incorrect acceptance				
	1%	5%	10%	15%	20%
0	4.61	3.00	2.31	1.90	1.61
1	6.64	4.75	3.89	3.38	3.00
2	8.41	6.30	5.33	4.72	4.28
3	10.05	7.76	6.69	6.02	5.52
4	11.61	9.16	8.00	7.27	6.73

Additional Information:

Tolerable misstatement (net of effect of expected misstatement)	$ 48,000
Risk of incorrect acceptance	20%
Number of misstatements allowed	1
Recorded amount of accounts receivable	$480,000
Number of accounts	360

What sample size should Hill use?

    a. 120
    b. 108
    c.   60
    d.   30   (Editors, ID: 7497)

48. Which of the following statements is correct concerning probability-proportional-to-size (PPS) sampling, also known as dollar-unit sampling?

    a. The sampling distribution should approximate the normal distribution.
    b. Overstated units have a lower probability of sample selection than units that are understated.
    c. The auditor controls the risk of incorrect acceptance by specifying that risk level for the sampling plan.
    d. The sampling interval is calculated by dividing the number of physical units in the population by the sample size.   (5/91, AUD, #17, ID: 0243)

49. Which of the following is the primary objective of probability-proportional-to-size (PPS) sample?

    a. To identify overstatement errors
    b. To increase the proportion of smaller-value items in the sample
    c. To identify items where controls were not properly applied
    d. To identify zero and negative balances   (R/09, AUD, #40, ID: 8840)

Problem 6-2 SIMULATION: PPS Sampling

An auditor has decided to use probability-proportional-to-size (PPS) sampling, sometimes called dollar-unit sampling, in the audit of a client's accounts receivable balance. Few, if any, misstatements of account balance overstatement are expected. The auditor plans to use the following PPS sampling table.

TABLE
Reliability Factors for Errors of Overstatement

Number of overstatements misstatements	Risk of incorrect acceptance				
	1%	5%	10%	15%	20%
0	4.61	3.00	2.31	1.90	1.61
1	6.64	4.75	3.89	3.38	3.00
2	8.41	6.30	5.33	4.72	4.28
3	10.05	7.76	6.69	6.02	5.52
4	11.61	9.16	8.00	7.27	6.73

Calculate the sampling interval and the sample size Edwards should use given the following information:

Tolerable misstatement	$ 15,000
Risk of incorrect acceptance	5%
Number of misstatements allowed	0
Recorded amount of accounts receivable	$300,000

(ID: 9209)

_____

Problem 6-3 SIMULATION: Projected Misstatement in a PPS Sample

Calculate the total projected misstatement if the following three misstatements were discovered in a PPS sample:

	Recorded amount	Audit amount	Sampling interval	
1st misstatement	$ 400	$ 320	$1,000	
2nd misstatement	500	0	1,000	
3rd misstatement	3,000	2,500	1,000	(ID: 9210)

_____

Problem 6-4 SIMULATION: Research

What authoritative reference provides guidance to an auditor on choosing between statistical and nonstatistical sampling?

	§			(ID: 9211)

Solution 6-1 MULTIPLE-CHOICE ANSWERS

Audit Sampling

1. (b)   In planning a sample of cash disbursements, if the auditor is aware of several unusually large cash disbursements, the auditor will most likely stratify the sample to include the unusually large disbursements. By stratifying the sample, the auditor will decrease the effect of the variances in the total population, and, therefore, be able to reduce the number of items in the sample.   (ID: 5128)

2. (b)   It is easiest to reconcile differences and for customers to research the auditor's questions on an individual invoice level. The designation of a sampling unit depends on the type of applied auditing procedures. The auditor considers which sampling unit leads to the most efficient and effective application, given the circumstances. In the case of a high number of expected differences in amounts for accounts receivable confirmations, if the auditor selects the customer balance as a sampling unit, the auditor may need to test each individual transaction supporting that balance in the event of a contradictory report from the customer.   (ID: 5667)

3. (a)   With the mean-per-unit method, stratification of a highly variable population into segments allows an auditor to use a smaller sample size. Thus, variability in the dollar amounts of inventory items is considered. The risk of incorrect assessment has an inverse relationship with sample size.   (ID: 6836)

4. (d)   The risk of incorrect acceptance and the risk of assessing control risk too low relate to the effectiveness of an audit in detecting an existing material misstatement. If the auditor incorrectly accepts an account as being materially accurate or incorrectly concludes that control risk is below the maximum, additional procedures that may detect this incorrect conclusion are either eliminated or reduced and the audit would prove ineffective in detecting misstatements. Answers a. and b. are incorrect because of an inappropriate combination of terms. In a., risk should relate to exceeding tolerable misstatement levels. In b., materiality is judged, not estimated, and related to tolerable misstatement. Audit efficiency is related to the risk of incorrect rejection or the risk of assessing control risk as too high.   (ID: 5966)

5. (d)   The risk of incorrect rejection is the risk that the auditor will conclude that an account balance is materially misstated when, in fact, it is not. When this error occurs, the auditor will generally extend her/his audit procedures and would eventually discover that the original conclusion of a material misstatement was incorrect. The cost of this mistake is the cost of the additional procedures that were necessary to discover that the original conclusion was erroneous. If, however, the cost and effort of those additional procedures is low, the auditor may well decide to use a high risk of incorrect rejection because doing so will reduce original sample size. If the desired results are achieved with the original small sample, overall audit cost will be lowered. If an incorrect rejection occurs, however, the incremental cost incurred would not be excessive. An increase in the desired reliability would likely result in a decrease (not increase) in the risk of incorrect rejection. The number of differences expected should have no bearing on the risk of incorrect rejection specified. The "risk of incorrect rejection" is not a concept associated with tests of controls. "Risk of underreliance" would be the corresponding risk that is associated with control testing.   (ID: 2972)

6. (c)   When the auditor's estimate based on the sample results indicates that the maximum deviation rate is less than the tolerable rate and the true state of the population shows that the deviation rate exceeds the tolerable rate, the auditor assesses control risk too low and does not plan sufficient substantive testing. Answer b. is an example of the auditor assessing control risk higher than necessary and, thereby increasing substantive testing. Answers a. and d, represent correct audit decisions regarding controls and planned substantive evidence.   (ID: 5964)

7. (d)   If the sample deviation rate is lower than the true deviation rate in the population, the auditor mistakenly assesses control risk too low. The result is that detection risk is allowed to rise too high and substantive testing is decreased.   (ID: 5646)

8. (c)   The risk of assessing control risk too low is the risk that the assessed level of control risk based on the sample is less than the true operating effectiveness of the control. All things being equal, a sample taken from a smaller population will be more representative of the population than a sample of the same size taken from a larger population. Thus, the risk that the sample taken from the smaller population will yield a result

different from the result obtained had the entire population been examined, is *lower* than such a risk inherent in sampling from a larger population. (ID: 7498)

9. (b) When using the systematic sampling technique, the auditor determines a uniform interval by dividing the number of physical units in the population by the sample size. A random number is selected as a starting point for the first interval, and one item is selected throughout the population at each of the uniform intervals from the starting point. The randomness of the sample can be destroyed if the items in the population occur in a systematic pattern. For example, a population of employees on a payroll for a construction company might be organized by teams; each team consists of a crew leader and nine other workers. A selection of every tenth employee will list either every crew leader or no crew leaders, depending on the random start. No combination would include both crew leaders and other employees. (ID: 0267)

10. (c) The risk of incorrect rejection is the risk that the sample supports the conclusion that the recorded account balance is materially misstated when it is not materially misstated. The risk of assessing control risk too high is the risk that the assessed level of control risk based on the sample is greater than the true operating effectiveness of the control. The risk of assessing control risk too low is just the opposite. The risk of incorrect acceptance is the risk that the sample supports the conclusion that the recorded account balance is not materially misstated when it is materially misstated. (ID: 4708)

11. (a) The purpose of tracing a sample of inventory tags to a client's computerized listing of inventory items is to determine whether the inventory items represented by the tags were included on the listing. It is a way of testing the assertion of completeness. The other answer alternatives are objectives that would not be accomplished by the procedure as described in the question. (ID: 9911)

12. (b) The tolerable rate is the maximum rate of deviation from the prescribed internal control policies and procedures that would support the auditor's assessed level of control risk. In this case, the auditor has assessed control risk too high. The risk of assessing control risk too high is the risk that the assessed level of control risk based on the sample is greater (*the deviation rate in the auditor's sample exceeds the tolerable rate,...*) than the true operating effectiveness of the control (*...but the deviation rate in the population is less than the tolerable rate*). The situation described in answer a. would result in assessing control risk too low. Answers c. and d. would support the auditor's assessment of control risk. (ID: 8827)

13. (b) The risk of incorrect acceptance is the risk that the sample supports the conclusion that the recorded account balance is not materially misstated when it is materially misstated. The risk of incorrect rejection is the risk that the sample supports the conclusion that the recorded account balance is materially misstated when it is not materially misstated. These are sampling risks related to substantive tests of details. The risk of assessing control risk too low is the risk that the assessed level of control risk based on the sample is less than the true operating effectiveness of the control. The risk of assessing control risk too high is the risk that the assessed level of control risk based on the sample is greater than the true operating effectiveness of the control. (ID: 9945)

14. (a) When planning a particular sample for a substantive test of details, such as subsequent cash receipts, the auditor should consider (1) the relationship of the sample to the relevant audit objective; (2) *preliminary judgments about materiality levels*; (3) the auditor's allowable risk of incorrect acceptance; and (4) characteristics of the population, i.e., the items comprising the account balance or class of transactions of interest. The amount of bad debt write-offs from the prior year would not be appropriate to consider to detect information about subsequent cash receipts. The size of the intercompany receivable balance is not related to subsequent cash receipts. The risk of assessing control risk too low (the risk that the assessed level of control risk based on the sample is less than the true operating effectiveness of the control) relates to sampling risk in performing tests of controls rather than a substantive test of details as described in this question. (ID: 9361)

15. (b) When an auditor is supplied with copies of vendor invoices instead of originals and told the originals have been misplaced, the auditor should *reevaluate the risk of fraud and design alternate tests for the related transactions*. Audit procedures that are appropriate to the particular audit objective should be applied to each sample item. If considering those unexamined items (the originals) to be misstated would lead to a conclusion that the balance or class contains material misstatement, the auditor should consider alternative audit procedures that would provide sufficient appropriate audit evidence to form a conclusion. The auditor should also consider whether the reasons for the lack of availability of the items have implications in relation to assessing

risks of material misstatement due to fraud, the assessed level of control risk that the auditor expects to be supported, or the degree of reliance on management representations. (ID: 9370)

16. (d) The risk of assessing control risk too high is the risk that the assessed level of control risk based on the sample is greater than the true operating effectiveness of the control. If a control activity is unrelated to the client's assertions, the assessment could have been either too low or too high. The auditor's decisions reduce the extent of substantive testing, not the control activity itself. (ID: 8393)

Statistical Sampling

17. (c) Both statistical and nonstatistical sampling plans can provide sufficient audit evidence if properly applied. The distinguishing feature of statistical sampling methods as opposed to nonstatistical methods is that the user is able to provide a mathematical measurement of the degree of uncertainty that results from examining only part of a population. Statistical sampling, as well as nonstatistical sampling, is subject to nonsampling errors (procedural mistakes or human error). Both methods of sampling may be used to reduce audit risk, but neither would affect the level of materiality. Both can be used to reduce the risk of failing to detect errors and fraud, which is the risk of incorrect acceptance. (ID: 5991)

18. (b) Stratified sampling can be particularly useful in reducing the overall sample size on populations that have a wide range of dollar values (or highly variable recorded amounts). The primary objective is to decrease the effect of variance in the total population, thereby reducing sample size. PPS sampling insures items with large amounts all make it into the sample, but not by stratifying the population. The estimated tolerable misstatement and standard deviation are irrelevant to a decision to stratify. (ID: 5668)

19. (b) Under the ratio estimation technique, the auditor uses sample results to estimate the ratio of audited value to book value. The ratio is then applied to the population book value to estimate the audited value of the population. The sample "audited value/book value" ratio equals 1.2:1 ($150,000 ÷ $125,000). When this ratio is applied to the population book balance of $5,000,000, an estimated $6,000,000 audited value results. (ID: 7496)

20. (d) Attribute sampling provides evidence of the rate of occurrence of a specified characteristic in a population at auditor-specified levels of precision and reliability. Variable sampling is used by the auditor to estimate the total dollar amount of a population at auditor-specified levels of precision and reliability. Discovery sampling is a form of attribute sampling that is designed to locate at least one exception if the rate of occurrence in the population is at or above a specified rate. This method is used to search for critical occurrences that may indicate the existence of an irregularity, and is appropriate when the expected occurrence rate is quite low (usually near zero) and the auditor wants a sample that will provide a specified chance to observe one occurrence. Answer a. is incorrect, as the population is not divided into groups according to a common characteristic. (ID: 0266)

21. (c) Substantive tests of details are performed by the auditor to either detect misstatements or obtain evidence about the validity and propriety of the accounting treatment of transactions and balances. In substantive testing, the auditor is primarily interested in dollar amounts, and the traditional method of performing substantive tests is by variables sampling. (ID: 5127)

22. (a) The auditor would increase the preliminary assessment of control risk because the achieved upper precision limit of 8% (sample error rate plus an allowance for sampling risk) exceeded the tolerable error rate of 7% (determined by professional judgment). Therefore, the results of the test did not allow the auditor to conclude with 99% confidence that the error rate in the population did not exceed 7%. All other answers describe comparisons that are meaningless. (ID: 0250)

23. (b) The allowance for sampling risk is the difference between the observed sample rate and the achieved upper precision limit. The observed sample rate was 3.5% (7/200). Therefore, the allowance for sampling risk would be 4.5% (8% − 3.5%). (ID: 0251)

24. (d) The auditor should modify her/his planned assessed level of control risk when the sample deviation rate plus the allowance for sampling risk exceeds the tolerable rate. In this question, the deviation rate of 6% (3 deviations among 50 documents) plus the allowance for sampling risk of 2% is greater than the given tolerable rate of 7%. (ID: 2807)

25. (d) When the sample rate of deviation plus the allowance for sampling risk, which is the upper deviation limit, exceeds the tolerable rate, the sample results do not support the assessed level of control risk and the auditor should reduce the planned reliance on a prescribed control. Answers a., b., and c. represent results that support planned reliance. (ID: 5972)

26. (a) An increase in the tolerable rate of deviation would allow a reduction in sample size. As the likely deviation rate decreases, the auditor may *decrease* the planned sample size. The allowable risk of assessing control risk too low has an *inverse* effect on the sample size. Of all the factors to be considered, the population size has the *least* effect on the sample size. (ID: 8134)

27. (a) The factors affecting sample size when using classical variables sampling are (1) desired precision, (2) desired sample reliability, (3) variability among item values in the population (the estimate of the population's standard deviation) and (4) population size. PPS is a non-parametric method that does not assume a normal distribution. PPS plans require special design to deal with negative balances and zero balances because sample selection is based on the *cumulative sum* of dollars of the population. Negative figures distort the cumulative sum and zero balances would not be considered without special adjustments in a PPS plan. Classical variables techniques are unaffected by either zero balances or negative balances. (ID: 0265)

28. (d) The population size has little effect on the sample size. To determine the number of items to be selected for a particular sample for a test of controls, the auditor should consider the tolerable rate of deviation from the controls being tested, the likely rate of deviations, and the allowable risk of assessing control risk too low. An auditor applies professional judgment to relate these factors in determining the appropriate sample size. As the tolerable deviation rate increases, the sample size can be decreased, not increased. (ID: 9930)

29. (b) Deviations from pertinent control procedures at a given rate ordinarily would be expected to result in misstatements at a lower rate. The sufficiency of audit sample sizes is determined by factors such as the assessments of control risk, inherent risk, and risk for other substantive tests related to a given assertion. Population size is not a determining factor. The relationship between the expected population deviation rate and sample size is direct, not inverse. In determining tolerable rate, an auditor should consider control risk and the degree of assurance desired by the audit evidence. (ID: 5100)

Attributes Sampling

30. (a) The net of projected actual misstatements [($3,700 − $200) × 20 =] is $70,000, which is larger than the tolerable misstatement of $60,000. If the tolerable misstatement exceeds the sum of actual overstatements and understatements, the auditor may consider the account fairly stated. (ID: 6938)

31. (a) The risk of assessing control risk *too high* is the risk that the assessed level of control risk based on the sample is greater than the true operating effectiveness of the control structure policy or procedure. Answer b. is incorrect because fewer errors or deviations would be discovered; therefore, the auditor would not identify those misstatements. Answer c. is incorrect because the true operating effectiveness of internal control would not support such an assessment; the auditor would find fewer errors or deviations. Answer d. is incorrect because the sample would support the tolerable error for misstatements because the sample would reveal fewer errors or deviations than exist in the balance or class of transactions. (ID: 5106)

32. (b) In performing tests of controls, the auditor is frequently interested in determining the rate of deviation from prescribed internal control policies and procedures. The sampling plan generally used in this situation is attribute sampling. (ID: 6236)

33. (d) In an auditor's test of transactions, if a random number matches the number of a voided voucher, that voucher ordinarily should be replaced by another voucher in the random sample if the voucher has been properly voided. The voucher would be counted as an error and would not be replaced if it could not be located or constituted a deviation. The materiality of the dollar amount is irrelevant because the focus in a test of controls is whether or not procedures are properly performed, not the dollar value of the transaction being tested. (ID: 7636)

34. (a) Rather than using the sample to estimate an unknown, the auditor's objective is generally to corroborate the accuracy of certain client data, such as data about account balances or classes of transactions, or to evaluate the internal accounting controls over the processing of data. Thus, the auditor is concerned with whether

the control procedures are operating effectively. Answers b. and c. relate to substantive tests rather than to tests of controls. Materiality is based on the auditor's judgment, not on sampling procedures.   (ID: 0246)

35. (c) Check authorization is an internal control. In tests of internal controls, the auditor is determining the rate of occurrence of a deviation from the control procedure, not testing the dollar amounts reported in the financial statements. The allowable risk of assessing control risk too low affects the degree of assurance desired by the auditor. If a high degree of assurance is sought, sampling risk must be low. Sample size and risk are inversely related.   (ID: 6833)

36. (a) Both the expected (likely) deviation rate and the tolerable deviation rate are considerations in determining the sample size for a test of controls.   (ID: 5980)

37. (a) When determining sample size, the auditor gives consideration to assessing control risk too low and the tolerable deviation rate. The "allowable risk of assessing control risk too high" is a distracter.   (ID: 6579)

38. (d) When performing tests of controls, the auditor is looking for the deviation rate from established control procedures set by the client. Thus, the auditor performs attributes sampling procedures. Answers a. and c. represent substantive sampling procedures. Answer b. describes a selection method that is not relevant to attribute sampling.   (ID: 3921)

39. (a) Attributes sampling involves the determination of the rate of occurrence of some characteristic (attribute) in a population. In an audit, the attribute of interest is frequently a deviation from a particular control procedure. Identifying entries posted to incorrect accounts is an example of testing compliance with the use of correct accounts. In estimating the amount in an expense account, evaluating the reasonableness of depreciation expense, and selecting receivables for confirmation of balances, a CPA is testing for dollar amounts which would involve variables sampling.   (ID: 8406)

40. (b) The *number of items in the population* has virtually no effect on the sample size unless the population is very small.   (ID: 8848)

Variables Sampling

41. (c) A disadvantage of PPS sampling to classical variables sampling is that special consideration must be given to zero and negative balance accounts because they are usually excluded from the PPS sample. Answers a., b., and d. are advantages of PPS sampling.   (ID: 3939)

42. (a) In classical variables sampling for estimation, precision represents the range within which the sample result is expected to be accurate. Hence, it provides a calculation of the maximum acceptable error in either direction. Reliability varies inversely with the assessed level of control risk and is a measure of the probability the sample result will fall within the precision range as mentioned above. Projected error is the anticipated deviation rate, based on the sample, in the entire population. The standard deviation is a measure of the dispersion among the relative values of a particular characteristic.   (ID: 0244)

43. (a) The use of the ratio estimation sampling technique is most effective when the calculated audit amounts are approximately proportional to the client's book amounts. The auditor uses sample results to estimate the ratio of audited value to book value, which is then applied to the population to estimate the actual value. Ratio estimation should be used when each population item *has a book value,* an audited value may be ascertained for each sample item, and *differences occur frequently.* Large overstatement or understatement differences would reduce the effectiveness of this technique.   (ID: 5669)

44. (c) Tolerable misstatement is a planning concept and is related to the auditor's determination of materiality for planning the financial statement audit in such a way that tolerable misstatement, combined for all of the tests in the entire audit, does not exceed materiality for the financial statements. Materiality judgments (tolerable misstatements) are not affected by the auditor's business risk. Judgments about materiality (tolerable misstatements) are subjective and do involve consideration of qualitative as well as quantitative factors and ordinarily will change during the process of conducting an audit as the auditor develops new evidence.   (ID: 0255)

45. (b) Generally, variables sampling involves the determining of proper dollar value of the sampled items and makes inferences about the fairness of the amounts reported in the financial statements. Variables sam-

pling typically involves deciding whether the dollar value of an account is reasonable. Generally, attributes sampling involves the determination of the rate of occurrence of some characteristic in a population. Proper prices, the number of misstatements, or proper recording are attributes. (ID: 7816)

46. (a) Special consideration must be given to zero and negative balance accounts which usually are excluded from a probability-proportional-to-size (PPS) sample. For both classical variables sampling and PPS sampling, the sampling process may begin before the complete population is available and the auditor must consider the preliminary judgments about materiality. If few errors are expected, the sample will result in a smaller sample size using PPS sampling than if classical variables sampling is used. (ID: 8404)

PPS Sampling

47. (d) This is one of several approaches that can be used to determine sample size when errors are expected, but it is the only approach possible with the information given. (ID: 7497)

$$\text{Sampling Interval} = \frac{\textit{Tolerable Misstatement}}{\textit{Reliability Factor for Misstatement of Overstatement}}$$

$$= \frac{\$48,000}{3.00} = \$16,000$$

$$\text{Sample Size} = \frac{\textit{Recorded Amount}}{\textit{Sample Interval}}$$

$$= \frac{\$480,000}{\$16,000} = 30$$

48. (c) In PPS sampling, the auditor achieves control over the risk of incorrect acceptance by specifying the level of risk the auditor is willing to assume. PPS sampling does not require direct consideration of the standard deviation of dollar amounts to determine the appropriate sample. The book value of the unit determines how probable it is that it will be included in the sample, not whether it is over or understated. The sampling interval is calculated by dividing the book value of the population by the sample size. (ID: 0243)

49. (a) In PPS sampling, because the sample is selected proportional to size, larger dollar amounts have a higher probability of being selected, thus *overstatements* (*errors*) are more likely to be selected than understatements. An auditor will normally use PPS sampling when testing for material overstatements. For the reason just stated, PPS sampling is unlikely to select smaller-value items and these amounts may be significantly understated in the sample, not increased. PPS sampling is a form of variables sampling which is normally used in substantive testing where the auditor is usually interested in the selection of dollar amounts, not attributes as is usually the case in tests of controls. Additionally, samples taken to test the operating effectiveness of controls (to provide a basis for the auditor to conclude whether the controls are being properly applied) should be selected in a manner such that the sample is representative of the population, thus all items in the population should have an opportunity to be selected which is not the case with PPS sampling. Zero balances are not subject to PPS selection and negative balances would have to be segregated into a separate population for testing. (ID: 8840)

PERFORMANCE BY TOPICS

Each category below parallels a topic covered in Chapter 6. Record the number and percentage of questions you answered correctly in each topic.

Audit Sampling		
Question #	Correct	√
1		
2		
3		
4		
5		
6		
7		
8		
9		
10		
11		
12		
13		
14		
15		
16		
# Questions	16	
# Correct	_____	
% Correct	_____	

Statistical Sampling		
Question #	Correct	√
17		
18		
19		
20		
21		
22		
23		
24		
25		
26		
27		
28		
29		
# Questions	13	
# Correct	_____	
% Correct	_____	

Attributes Sampling		
Question #	Correct	√
30		
31		
32		
33		
34		
35		
36		
37		
38		
39		
40		
# Questions	11	
# Correct	_____	
% Correct	_____	

Variables Sampling		
Question #	Correct	√
41		
42		
43		
44		
45		
46		
# Questions	6	
# Correct	_____	
% Correct	_____	

PPS Sampling		
Question #	Correct	√
47		
48		
49		
# Questions	3	
# Correct	_____	
% Correct	_____	

Solution 6-2 SIMULATION ANSWER: PPS Sampling Interval & Sample Size

$$\text{Sampling Interval} = \frac{\textit{Tolerable Misstatement}}{\textit{Reliability Factor for Misstatement of Overstatement}}$$

$$= \frac{\$15,000}{3.00} = \$5,000$$

$$\text{Sample Size} = \frac{\textit{Recorded Amount}}{\textit{Sample Interval}}$$

$$= \frac{\$300,000}{\$5,000} = \$60$$

(ID: 9209)

Solution 6-3 SIMULATION ANSWER: Projected Misstatement in a PPS Sample

	Recorded amount	Audit amount	Tainting	Sampling Interval	Projected misstatement
1st misstatement	$ 400	$ 320	20%	$1,000	$ 200
2nd misstatement	500	0	100%	1,000	1,000
3rd misstatement	3,000	2,500	*	1,000	500
Total projected misstatement					$1,700

* The recorded amount is greater than the sampling interval; therefore, the projected misstatement equals the actual misstatement.

(ID: 9210)

Solution 6-4 SIMULATION ANSWER: Research

AU	§	350	46

.46   Statistical sampling helps the auditor (a) to design an efficient sample, (b) to measure the sufficiency of the audit evidence obtained, and (c) to evaluate the sample results. By using statistical theory, the auditor can quantify sampling risk to assist himself [*sic*] in limiting it to a level he [*sic*] considers acceptable. However, statistical sampling involves additional costs of training auditors, designing individual samples to meet the statistical requirements, and selecting the items to be examined. Because either nonstatistical or statistical sampling can provide sufficient audit evidence, the auditor chooses between them after considering their relative cost and effectiveness in the circumstances.

(ID: 9211)

CHAPTER 7

AUDITING IT SYSTEMS

CHAPTER 7

AUDITING IT SYSTEMS

I. IT-Based Systems

A. Electronic Data Processing

An IT-based, or EDP-based, system includes (1) hardware, (2) software, (3) documentation, (4) personnel, (5) data, and (6) controls. There can be significant differences between IT-based activities and non-IT activities.

1. Considerations

a. **Documentation** Many control procedures in IT systems do not leave documentary evidence of performance.

b. **Electronic Information** Files and records are usually in machine-readable form and cannot be read without using a computer.

c. **Reduced Human Involvement** Computers may obscure errors that a human would notice while handling the transaction.

d. **Reliability** IT systems are more reliable than manual systems because all of the data are subjected to the same controls. Manual systems are subject to human error on a random basis. Computer processing virtually eliminates computational errors associated with manual processing.

e. **Knowledge** An auditor may need specialized IT knowledge to perform an audit.

f. **Difficulty of Change** It is harder to change an IT system once it is implemented than it is to change a manual system. Therefore, the auditor will want to become familiar with a new IT system at an early stage of the development process so that the auditor can anticipate possible future audit problems.

2. Processing Methodology

a. **Transaction Processing Modes** Transactions may be processed either in batches or online.

(1) **Batch Processing** Transactions to be processed are accumulated in groups (batches) before processing and are then processed as a batch. Batch processing frequently involves sequential access to the data files. For example, a company may accumulate a day's charge sales before processing them against the master file during the night. Before they are processed, the transactions would be sorted into the order of the records on the master file. One disadvantage of batch processing is that, because of the time delays, errors may not be detected immediately. The file updating process is most efficient when the transaction file has been sorted into the same order as the master file. There are four basic steps in the process of updating a batch of records in a master file that is kept on a magnetic disk. First, a transaction enters the CPU. Second, the record to be updated is read from its location on the disk into the CPU. Third, the record is updated in the CPU. Fourth, the updated record is written onto the disk in the same location as the original record. The result is that the original record is replaced by the updated record. This results in the original record being erased.

(2) **Online Processing** Transactions are processed and the file is updated as the transactions occur. Online processing usually involves files that can be accessed directly. For example, a cash register terminal may update the inventory file automatically when a sale is made.

(3) **Real-Time Processing** An online system is operating in real time if the data is processed fast enough to get the response back in time to influence the process. For example, an airline reservation system is an online, real-time (OLRT) system because the customer receives reservations after waiting only a few moments.

(4) **Integrated System** All files affected by a transaction are updated in one transaction-processing run, rather than having a separate run for each file. For example, in an integrated system, a sales transaction may update the sales summary file, the accounts receivable master file, and the inventory file during one processing run.

b. **Processing External to Client** While many companies have their own equipment to do their processing within the company (i.e., in-house), others utilize outside processors. Several common arrangements are as follows:

(1) **Block Time** Client rents a certain block of computer time from an outside party. For example, a company may rent time from a bank that does not utilize its computer system 24 hours per day.

(2) **Time-Sharing** A number of users share a computer system. Each may have a terminal that it can use to access a CPU located outside of the client. Each user can access the system whenever it wishes.

(3) **Service Bureau** An outside organization that provides a wide range of data processing services for a fee.

(4) **Cloud Computing** The delivery of computing as a service rather than a product. Shared resources, software, and information are provided to computers as a metered service over the Internet. Computing clouds provide computation, software, data access, and storage resources without requiring cloud users to know the location and other details of the computing infrastructure.

3. **Development & Implementation** A CPA sometimes becomes involved in the development and implementation of a computer-based application system. The CPA may do the work or may work with client personnel (systems analysts, programmers, etc.). The development and implementation process involves the following phases:

a. **Systems Analysis (Feasibility Study)** The system's overall objectives and requirements are clearly determined. The existing system then is studied to see if it is meeting them adequately. Broad alternative approaches also are considered.

b. **Systems Design** In general systems design, the alternative approaches are evaluated in more detail and a specific proposal is developed for implementing the alternative that is felt to be best. In detailed systems design, the recommended system is designed in detail. This includes designing files, determining resource requirements, and developing plans for the following phases.

c. **Program Specifications & Implementation Planning** Detailed specifications are developed for the computer programs that will be required, and plans are made for testing the program and implementing the system. This involves (1) hardware installation; (2) coding and debugging programs; (3) training users; (4) systems testing; and (5) conversion and volume testing. Coding and debugging involves programmers writing and testing the required programs. In systems testing, the system is tested thoroughly. The results of the tests are compared with the specifications and requirements of the system to determine whether it does what it is supposed to do. Conversion is done from the old system to the new system. This involves such things as converting and verifying files and data. Conversion may involve parallel processing (i.e., parallel operations) in which the old system and the new system are run at the same time with the actual data for the period and the results compared. This checks the new system and avoids disaster if the new system fails the first time it is used. Volume testing involves testing the capacity of the system to handle expected volumes of information and transactions.

    d.   **Implementation** The system is released to the user.

    e.   **Monitoring** Once the system is operating routinely, it is reviewed to be sure it is attaining the original objectives set for it, and to correct any problems.

B.   **Client Documentation**

Documentation is an important aspect of control and communication. It generally provides (1) an understanding of the system's objectives, concepts, and output, (2) a source of information for systems analysts and programmers when involved in program maintenance and revision, (3) information that is needed for a supervisory review, (4) a basis for training new personnel, (5) a means of communicating common information, (6) a source of information about accounting controls, and (7) a source of information that will aid in providing continuity in the event experienced personnel leave. If reliable documentation is not available, the auditor must find other sources of information. There are several types of documentation.

Exhibit 1 ▶ IT System Documentation Mnemonic

O	Operations documentation
P	Problem definition documentation
S	Systems documentation
O	Operator documentation
U	User documentation
P	Program documentation

    1.   **Problem Definition Documentation** Permits the auditor to gain a general understanding of the system without having to become involved in the details of the programs. Contents include the following:

        a.   Description of the reasons for implementing the system

        b.   Description of the operations performed by the system

        c.   Project proposals

        d.   Evidence of approval of the system and subsequent changes (for example, a particular individual may have to sign a form to indicate these)

        e.   A listing of the assignment of project responsibilities

    2.   **Systems Documentation** Provides sufficient information to trace accounting data from its original entry to system output. Contents include the following:

        a.   A description of the system

        b.   A systems flowchart shows the flow of data through the system and the interrelationships between the processing steps and computer runs.

  c. Input descriptions

  d. Output descriptions

  e. File descriptions

  f. Descriptions of controls

  g. Copies of authorizations and their effective dates for systems changes that have been implemented

3. **Program Documentation** Primarily used by systems analysts and programmers to provide a control over program corrections and revisions. However, it may be useful to the auditor to determine the current status of a program. Contents include the following:

  a. Brief description of the program

  b. Program flowchart, decision table, or detailed logic narrative

    (1) **Program Flowchart** Shows the steps followed by the program in processing the data

    (2) **Decision Table** This describes a portion of the logic used in the program. Although it is not always used, it can replace or supplement the program flowchart.

    (3) **Detailed Logic Narrative** Narrative description of the logic followed by a program

  c. Source statements (i.e., a listing of the program instructions) or parameter listings

  d. List of control features

  e. Detailed description of file formats and record layouts

  f. Table of code values used to indicate processing requirements

  g. Record of program changes, authorizations, and effective dates

  h. Input and output formats

  i. Operating instructions

  j. Descriptions of any special features

4. **Operations Documentation** Information provided to the computer operator; it can be used by the auditor to obtain an understanding of the functions performed by the operator and to determine how data is processed; contents include the following:

  a. A brief description of the program

  b. Description of the inputs and outputs that are required (e.g., the forms used)

  c. Sequence of cards, tapes, disks, and other files

  d. Setup instructions and operating system requirements

  e. Operating notes listing program messages, halts, and action necessary to signal the end of jobs

       f.   Control procedures to be performed by operations

       g.   Recovery and restart procedures (to be used for hardware or software malfunctions)

       h.   Estimated normal and maximum run time

       i.   Instructions to the operator in the event of an emergency

5. **User Documentation** This is a description of the input required for processing and an output listing. The auditor may use it to gain an understanding of the functions performed by a user and the general flow of information. Contents include a description of the system, description of the input and output, list of control procedures and an indication of the position of the person performing the procedures, error correction procedures, cutoff procedures for submitting the data to the IT Department, and a description of how a user department should check reports for accuracy.

6. **Operator Documentation** Documentation should be prepared that will indicate the jobs run and any operator interaction.

   a. **Daily Computer Log** This may be prepared manually by the computer operator. It indicates the jobs run, the time required, who ran them, etc.

   b. **Console Log** This is a listing of all interactions between the console and the CPU. Prepared by the computer as messages are entered from the console, it can be a valuable control for detecting unauthorized intervention of the computer operator during the running of a program. It also shows how the operator responded to processing problems.

II. Effects of IT-Based Systems on Audits

A. **Engagement Planning**
An auditor's objectives do not change when auditing the financial statements of a company using an IT system. The ultimate objective is still to express an opinion on the fairness of presentation of the financial statements. While the audit objectives do not change, the audit procedures used to accomplish them may change. The auditor should consider the following matters:

1. **Extent** The extent to which the computer is used in each significant accounting application.

2. **Complexity** The complexity of the entity's computer operations, including the use of an outside service center.

3. **Organization** The organizational structure of the computer processing activities.

4. **Availability of Data** Some data may only be available for a limited time.

5. **Analytics** An additional factor in the use of analytics is the increased availability of data that is used by management. Such computer-prepared data and analyses, although not necessarily a part of the basic accounting records, may be valuable sources of information (e.g., budget and variance information).

6. **CAAT** The use of computer-assisted audit techniques (CAAT) to increase the efficiency of performing audit procedures. If specific skills are needed, and a specialist is used, the auditor should have sufficient computer-related knowledge to (a) communicate the objectives of the other professional's work; (b) evaluate whether the specified procedures will meet the auditor's objectives; and (c) evaluate the results of the procedures applied as they relate to the nature, timing, and extent of other planned audit procedures. The auditor's responsibilities with respect to using such a professional are equivalent to those for other assistants.

B.   Consideration of IT Controls

1.   **Only Reasonable Assurance** All internal control systems, regardless of how well designed, face certain inherent limitations which make the achievement of absolute assurance an impossibility. In an IT system, errors can occur in designing, maintaining, or monitoring automated controls. For example, IT personnel may not understand how an IT system processes sales transactions which could result in incorrect changes to the system which processes sales for a new product line. Additionally, errors can occur in the use of the information produced by the IT system.

2.   **Basic Concepts** The characteristics that distinguish computer processing from manual processing include the following:

a.   **Transaction Trails** Some computer systems are designed so that a complete transaction trail that is useful for audit purposes might exist for only a short period of time or only in computer-readable form. This trail is used to monitor the system, answer queries, and deter fraud.

b.   **Uniform Processing of Transactions** Computer processing uniformly subjects like transactions to the same processing instructions. Consequently, computer processing virtually eliminates the occurrence of clerical error normally associated with manual processing. Conversely, errors will result in all like transactions being processed incorrectly.

c.   **Segregation of Functions** Many internal control procedures once performed by separate individuals in manual systems may be concentrated in systems that use computer processing. Therefore, an individual who has access to the computer may be in a position to perform incompatible functions. As a result, other control procedures may be necessary in computer systems to achieve the control objectives ordinarily accomplished by segregation of functions in manual systems.

d.   **Potential for Errors & Fraud** Decreased human involvement in handling transactions processed by computers can reduce the potential for observing errors and fraud. Errors or fraud occurring during the design or changing of application programs can remain undetected for long periods of time.

e.   **Potential for Increased Management Supervision** Computer systems offer management a wide variety of analytical tools that may be used to review and supervise the operations of the company. The availability of these additional controls may serve to enhance the entire internal control structure on which the auditor may wish to assess control risk at below the maximum level. For example, comparisons by management of budget to actual results and the response by management to unusual fluctuations indicate management's monitoring of the ongoing operations as a prevention of unfavorable crisis situations.

f.   **Initiation or Subsequent Execution of Transactions by Computer** The authorization of "automatic" transactions or procedures might not be documented in the same way as those initiated in a manual accounting system, and management's authorization of those transactions may be implicit in its acceptance of the design of the computer system.

g.   **Dependence of Other Controls on Controls Over Computer Processing** Computer processing may produce reports and other output that are used in performing manual control procedures. The effectiveness of these manual control procedures can be dependent on the effectiveness of controls over the completeness and accuracy of computer processing.

3. **Accounting Control Procedures** Internal accounting control procedures sometimes are defined by classifying control procedures into two types: general and application control procedures.

    a. **General Controls** Those controls that relate to all or many computerized accounting applications and often include control over the development, modification, and maintenance of computer programs and control over the use of and changes to data maintained on computer files. When an auditor anticipates assessing control risk at a low level, the auditor would focus initially on these general controls.

    b. **Application Controls** Those controls that relate to specific computerized accounting applications, i.e., input, processing, and output controls for an accounts payable application.

4. **Review of Internal Control** Due to the increased concentration of functions within the computer processing operation, the auditor's concern over the interdependence of control procedures is generally greater than it is in a manual system. In fact, application controls often are dependent upon general controls. Accordingly, it may be more efficient to review the design of general controls before reviewing the specific application controls.

C. **Audit Evidence**
The auditor can use either manual audit procedures, computer-assisted audit techniques, or a combination of both to obtain sufficient appropriate audit evidence.

1. **Substantive Procedures Only** During the risk assessment process, the auditor may determine that it is not possible or practicable to reduce detection risk at the relevant assertion level to an acceptably low level with audit evidence obtained from substantive procedures alone. In these circumstances, the auditor should perform tests of controls to obtain audit evidence about the operating effectiveness of relevant controls. For example, the auditor may find it impossible to design effective substantive procedures that by themselves provide sufficient appropriate audit evidence when an entity uses IT to conduct its business and no documentation of transactions is produced or maintained, other than through the IT system.

2. **Information Availability** Sometimes information and corroborating audit evidence are available in electronic form only. Source documents (purchase orders, bills of lading, invoices, and checks) may be in the form of electronic messages. Certain electronic evidence might not be accessible after a specified period of time if files are changed, unless backup files are created. The auditor should consider the time when information is available in determining the nature, timing, and extent of substantive tests and tests of controls.

    a. **Electronic Data Interchange (EDI)** With EDI, an entity and its customers or vendors conduct business electronically. EDI transactions must be formatted using uniform standards, and transmitted such that they are both secure and private. Purchasing, shipping, billing, cash receipt, and cash disbursement functions may be achieved through electronic exchanges, ordinarily without paper documents.

    b. **Image Processing** With image processing systems, paper documents are scanned into electronic images for electronic storage and retrieval. The entity might keep paper documents only for a limited time after this conversion.

3. **Internal Consistency** Auditors test accounting information by analysis and review, retracing, recalculation, and reconciliation. By performing these procedures, auditors may evaluate the internal consistency of information. Normally, internally consistent information provides evidence about the fairness of financial statement presentations.

4. **Data Mining** Data mining (also known as relationship mapping, data interrogation, or knowledge discovery) is the distillation of previously unknown information from raw data. The largest strength of data mining is identification of unexpected relationships. Manual review may

be inefficient for entities with a high number of transactions. Data mining is used for many purposes (streamlining operations, marketing analysis), although this discussion focuses on auditing. Data mining tools can assist auditors to perceive patterns in mountainous data-bases in a timely manner. By quickly discovering a fraudulent scheme, auditors could prevent future fraud and facilitate asset recovery.

Exhibit 2 ▶ Fraud Profile Examples for Accounts Payable

Vendor records that list more than one payment address. (Vendors may have multiple branches, or payments to a legitimate vendor may have been redirected fraudulently.)

Vendor records showing only post office box addresses. (While payments are frequently sent to lock boxes, usually there is one address—for instance, shipping or purchasing—that is a street address.)

In a large organization, records for one vendor showing the same authorized signer on every check and/or the same receiving clerk accepting every delivery connected with that vendor. (In an organization with several possible signers and receiving clerks for any given transaction, this circumstance is an unlikely coincidence.)

Matching employee and vendor addresses. (It is rare that an employee's home-based business is a legitimate vendor.)

Mailing addresses that are shared by vendors. (Several false vendors may share the same address or payments may be redirected to the same address for a perpetrator's convenience.)

Payments close to payment-review thresholds. (Management review is not necessary up to the threshold. Employees may aim to commit fraud for the largest amount possible per transaction.)

Invoice numbers from the same vendor that are close in sequence. (Legitimate vendors typically have many customers.)

a. A data-mining tool is like a sieve, allowing an auditor to sift through large amounts of data quickly, providing an overview of an entity. These preliminary procedures can be performed on entire populations, instead of relatively small samples.

b. For example, a bank may have the same employees who authorized a loan to a debtor named Jones being named on checks drawn on the account that Jones opened with the loan proceeds. This coincidence might escape manual detection and yet warrant extra auditor scrutiny.

c. Analysis tools also can highlight individual transactions that fit a fraud profile. A fraud profile is a summary of expected data characteristics that an auditor expects to find in a particular type of fraudulent transaction, based on an understanding of a given entity's internal control weaknesses.

5. **Electronic vs. Paper Evidence** The term electronic evidence relates to information that is transmitted, processed, maintained, and/or accessed by electronic means (e.g., using a computer, scanner, sensor, and/or magnetic media). Many of the issues related to electronic evidence also are applicable to evidence in the form of computer-printed documents and reports, particularly if there is no way to review or validate the printed information independently. The attributes of audit evidence (paper versus electronic) are:

a. **Difficulty of Alteration** Easily-altered evidence lacks credibility and has reduced value to the auditor. Paper evidence is difficult to alter without detection. An auditor has a reasonable likelihood of detecting significant alterations that have been made to paper documents. This quality provides auditors with some assurance that the evidence represents original information. Alterations due to the operation of a IT system may not be detected, unless specifically-designed tests are performed.

b.   ***Prima Facie* Credibility** Credibility of evidence is enhanced when the source of the evidence is independent in relation to the client and the auditor has the ability to corroborate that evidence. Paper documents (e.g., incoming purchase orders) usually have a high degree of credibility. However, a purchase order transmitted electronically from a customer derives its credibility primarily from the controls within the electronic environment. A fraudulent or altered electronic purchase order exhibits no apparent difference, compared to a valid purchase order, when extracted from the electronic environment of the entity.

c.   **Completeness of Documents** Appropriate audit evidence includes the essential terms of a transaction so that an auditor can verify the validity of the transaction. Paper evidence typically includes all of the essential terms of a transaction. Paper evidence also includes information regarding other parties to the transaction (e.g., customer name and address, or preferred shipping methods), on the face of the document. Work on the completeness assertion for paper documents often includes review of acknowledgments of data entry and postings. An electronic environment may mask this evidence with codes or by cross-references to other data files that may not be visible to the users of the data.

d.   **Evidence of Approvals** Approvals integrated into the evidence add to the completeness of the evidence. Paper documents typically show approvals on their face. For example, incoming purchase orders may have Marketing Department price approvals and Credit Department approvals written on the face of each original document. The same treatment may apply to electronic approvals by integrating approvals into the electronic record. Electronic elements may require additional interpretation.

e.   **Ease of Use** This factor relates to evaluating and understanding evidence. Auditors use traditional paper evidence without additional tools or expert analysis. Electronic evidence often requires extraction of the desired data by an auditor knowledgeable in electronic data extraction techniques or through use of a specialist.

f.   **Clarity** Appropriate audit evidence should allow the same conclusions to be drawn by different auditors performing the same tasks. The nature of electronic evidence is not always clear.

D.   Fundamental Change

Auditors may need to consider the implications of IT in evaluating any of the five components of internal control as they relate to the achievement of the entity's objectives. For example, in today's business world, it is not uncommon to find entities which have complex, highly integrated IT systems that share data and that are used to support all aspects of the entity's financial reporting, operations, and compliance objectives. As enterprise resource planning (ERP) systems become more comprehensive and more widely in use, this issue becomes more prevalent—even for small and mid-sized entities. The use of IT often changes the fundamental manner in which transactions are initiated, recorded, processed, and reported from paper-based systems that rely primarily on manual controls to electronic systems using a combination of manual and automated controls.

1.   **Manual** In a manual system, an entity uses manual procedures and records in paper format (e.g., to enter sales orders, authorize credit, prepare shipping reports and invoices, and maintain accounts receivable records). Controls in a "traditional" system also are manual, and may include procedures such as approvals and reviews of activities, and reconciliations and follow-up of reconciling items. Manual controls are performed by people, and therefore pose specific risks to the entity's internal control. Manual controls may be less reliable than automated controls because they can be more easily bypassed, ignored, or overridden; they are also more prone to errors and mistakes. Therefore, consistent application of a manual control

cannot be assumed. However, manual controls may be more appropriate when judgment is required, such as in the following circumstances:

    a. Large, unusual, or nonrecurring transactions

    b. Circumstances where misstatements are difficult to define, anticipate, or predict

    c. In changing circumstances that require a control response outside the scope of an existing automated control

    d. In monitoring the effectiveness of automated controls

  2. **Automated** Alternatively, an entity may have complex IT systems that use automated procedures to initiate, record, process, and report transactions, in which case records in electronic format replace paper documents such as purchase orders, invoices, and shipping documents. Controls in systems that use IT consist of a combination of automated controls (e.g., controls embedded in computer programs) and manual controls. Further, manual controls may be independent of the IT system and may use information produced by the IT system, or may be limited to monitoring the effective functioning of the system and the automated controls and handling exceptions. An entity's mix of manual and automated controls varies with the nature and complexity of the entity's use of IT.

  3. **Benefits** An IT environment provides benefits to the auditor related to effectiveness and efficiency because it enables the entity to perform the following:

    a. Consistently apply predefined business rules and perform complex calculations in processing large volumes of transactions or data

    b. Enhance the timeliness, availability, and accuracy of information

    c. Facilitate the additional analysis of information

    d. Enhance the ability to monitor the performance of the entity's activities and its policies and procedures

    e. Reduce the risk that controls will be circumvented, especially if controls over changes to the IT system are effective

  4. **Risks** Some of the risks that an auditor faces when working within an IT environment include the following:

    a. Overreliance on information provided by the IT system that could be incorrectly processing data or consistently processing inaccurate data

    b. Unauthorized access to data that may result in destruction of data or improper changes to data including the recording of unauthorized or nonexistent transactions or inaccurate recording of transactions

    c. Unauthorized changes to computer programs

    d. Failure to make necessary changes to computer programs

    e. Inappropriate manual intervention

    f. Potential loss of data

E. **Procedures**
In understanding a reporting entity's financial reporting process, the auditor must understand procedures utilized for entering transaction totals into the general ledger, procedures utilized for initiating, recording, and processing journal entries in the general ledger (both standard and

non-standard journal entries), and procedures utilized for recording recurring and nonrecurring adjustments to financial statements that are not reflected in formal journal entries (e.g., consolidating adjustments, report combinations, and reclassifications).

F.   Tests of Controls

1.   **Design** In designing tests of controls, the auditor should consider indirect controls on which direct controls depend. For example, the auditor should consider controls related to the accuracy and completeness of information when other controls depend on that information to operate effectively.

2.   **Automated Controls** Due to the inherent consistency of IT processing, audit evidence concerning the implementation of an automated application control combined with audit evidence concerning the operating effectiveness of general IT controls, particularly security and change controls, may provide substantial audit evidence about the operating effectiveness of the application control.

3.   **No Tests of Controls** When the auditor is not performing tests of controls, the auditor needs to be satisfied that performing substantive tests alone would be effective in restricting detection risk to an acceptable level. For example, the auditor may determine that performing substantive tests alone would be effective and more efficient than performing tests of controls for assertions related to fixed assets and to long-term debt in an entity where a limited number of transactions are related to those financial statement elements and when the auditor can readily obtain corroborating evidence in the form of documents and confirmations.

4.   **Combined With Substantive Tests** In complex situations—especially where there is a large volume of transactions processed within the complex IT environment—the auditor may determine that performing tests of controls for certain assertions would be effective and more efficient than performing only substantive tests. Alternatively, the auditor may determine that it is not practical or even possible to restrict detection risk to an acceptable level by performing only substantive tests. In making the determination as to whether tests of controls are mandatory, factors an auditor considers include the following:

   a.   The nature of the financial statement assertion

   b.   The volume of transactions or data related to the financial statement assertion

   c.   The nature and complexity of the systems, including the use of IT, by which the entity processes and controls information supporting the financial statement assertions

   d.   The nature of the available audit evidence, including audit evidence that is available only in electronic form

5.   **Examples** Examples of situations where the auditor may determine that tests of controls are necessary include the following:

   a.   An entity that conducts business using a system in which the computer initiates orders for goods based on predetermined rules and pays the related payables based on electronic information in transactions regarding receipt of goods. No other documentation of orders or goods received is produced or maintained.

   b.   An entity that provides electronic services to customers (e.g., an Internet service provider or a telephone company) and uses computer applications to log services provided to users, initiate bills for the services, process the billing transactions, and automatically record such amounts in electronic accounting records that are used to produce the financial statements.

G.   Special Systems

1.   **Online, Real-Time (OLRT) Systems** Because of the technical complexity of OLRT systems, the auditor will need more technical expertise to consider internal control. Care also must be exercised not to disrupt the system. Techniques such as test data (integrated test facility) and tagging may be used. Generalized audit software may be used to perform substantive tests on the data files.

2.   **Personal Computer Systems** The basic control and audit considerations in a small computer environment are the same as those in a larger and more complex IT system. However, the specific procedures the auditor uses needs to be adapted to fit the personal computer environment. The number of records that can be stored in a minicomputer system is limited, so audit trails often are retained for a limited period of time. Therefore, the auditor must plan the audit steps to take place when sufficient supporting information is available.

   a.   **Segregation of Functions** Often, segregation of functions within the IT Department and between the IT Department and user departments does not exist to a significant extent in a small business system. Users even may perform IT functions. The most desirable segregation controls in this environment would include (1) segregation between data entry and processing and (2) segregation between IT and user transaction authorization. The auditor should assist management in identifying and implementing alternative or compensating controls where separation of functions does not exist. When the auditor finds weaknesses in segregation, the audit program generally should include more substantive tests.

   b.   **System Design & Documentation** Users should be involved in the selection of both hardware and software because the choice of software in small systems is influenced by the hardware. Although access to program documentation should be limited, it is difficult to enforce in many small computer environments where the data processing group is small. Regardless, there may be times when the auditor may not be able to rely upon the documentation in such an environment.

   c.   **File Conversion & System Testing** Frequently, an organization's initial IT applications include the use of a small business computer system. File conversion and system testing are particularly important in these initial applications and, therefore, should influence the auditor in the audit. Before relying on the contents of converted files, the auditor should evaluate the controls used to ensure against lost or distorted data during conversion. If the auditor determines that sufficient user system testing has not been performed by the client, the auditor should perform procedures that will allow for sufficient testing of the system.

   d.   **Hardware Control** Limiting access to computer hardware is difficult in the small computer environment. Often, these systems lack controls that would prevent access to the actual hardware. Such a situation may cause the auditor to reduce reliance on stored data records. However, good application controls usually can compensate for problems caused by the absence or ineffectiveness of hardware controls.

   e.   **Software Control** All program changes should be authorized, tested, and documented. However, in some small data processing environments, the auditor will not be able to rely on program change controls. Thus, the auditor may find it appropriate to obtain a copy of the original software directly from the manufacturer. It is also important to control disks with stored data when not in use. Files should be copied or backed up to ensure against loss of data. The use of hard disk drives calls for access protection with the use of passwords, IDs, and the like.

   f.   **Application Controls** Many of the protection controls available in large systems to prohibit file manipulation or processing errors are not available in minicomputer systems.

(1) Limit (reasonableness) checks generally are not adapted to specific situations because most small system software is purchased off the shelf.

(2) The auditor should look for the existence of external labels on software. Review of the client's storage and use procedures is also appropriate.

(3) Most data is **not** converted into machine-readable form before input into the personal computer system. This should cause the auditor to be more concerned with data input controls and less concerned with data conversion controls.

(4) In small organizations or situations that generally characterize these environments, there is usually less movement of data between departments. Also, data processing personnel are familiar with system output users. Therefore, the auditor may be concerned less with controls over movement of data between departments and the distribution of output to authorized users than if the auditor was in a large IT environment.

g. **Small IT Environment Audit Impact** In a small environment, many of the computer personnel functions are combined for a small number of employees. In these situations, two key functions that should be segregated are the applications programmer and the operator. When these functions are not segregated, fraud can be perpetrated and concealed because the programmer knows exactly what the IT system is capable of performing.

3. **Distributed Systems** Distributed systems are a network of remote computer sites where small computers are connected to the main computer system. Access at each location should be well controlled and audited separately to verify the integrity of the data processed. Also, because users may have both authorization and recording duties, compensating controls should exist for this lack of segregation of duties.

4. **Service Center (Service Bureau)** Certain controls are particularly important because of the nature of the client-IT service center relationship.

Exhibit 3 ▶ IT Service Center Controls Mnemonic

T	Transmission
E	Error correction
A	Audit trail
M	Master file changes
O	Output
S	Security

a. **Transmission** Document counts, hash totals, financial totals, etc., may be used to control the transmission of data to and from the client's office.

b. **Error Correction** Client should receive an error listing that identifies all of the errors that occurred in the system. Correction, review, and approval procedures should be established and used.

c. **Audit Trail** An audit trail must be maintained. This may be done through proper filing and sequencing of original transaction documents, and also through periodic printouts of journal and ledger balances.

d. **Master File Changes** Printout of all master file changes should be sent to the client. Control counts of master file records and control totals of items within master file records may be used.

e. **Output** Output must be restricted to the client. An output distribution list (indicating who should receive the output) and control tests on samples of output may be used.

f. **Security** Service center must have adequate controls to protect the client's data (while being stored and during processing). Further, there must be adequate reconstruction procedures so that the client's data files can be reconstructed (i.e., recreated) if all or part of them are destroyed. A service center sometimes hires a CPA to issue a report on its internal control and security. An auditor whose client uses the service center may rely on this report, or if the auditor feels it is inadequate, the auditor may visit the service center to observe the operations.

5. **Time-Sharing Systems** Audit considerations are primarily the same as discussed for online, real-time systems. Additionally, the auditor may decide to visit the time-sharing center to review its controls if the auditor (a) feels that a large amount of the client's important financial data is processed there and (b) is not able to determine from other sources (such as a review by another auditor) the quality of the center's control and compliance procedures.

III. General Controls (GC)

A. Organization & Operation Controls

1. **GC 1:** Segregation of functions between the IT Department and users

2. **GC 2:** Provision for general authorization over the execution of transactions (prohibiting the IT Department from initiating or authorizing transactions)

3. **GC 3:** Part of proper internal control is the segregation of functions within the IT Department. Among the various functions that should be segregated are the following:

Exhibit 4 ▶ IT Department Functions Segregation Mnemonic

C	Control group	Responsible for internal control within IT Department
O	Operators	Convert data into machine readable form
P	Programmer	Develops and writes the computer programs; responsible for debugging of programs; writes the run manual
A	Analyst	Designs the overall system and prepares the system flowchart
L	Librarian	Keeps track of program and file use; maintains storage of all data and backups; controls access to programs

a. **Input Preparation** Process of converting the input data into machine-readable form. Input methods include key-to-tape (i.e., keying the information directly onto the magnetic tape), key-to-disk, and optical character recognition (OCR).

b. **Computer Operations** Computer operators physically run the equipment. This includes loading (i.e., entering) the program and data into the computer at the correct time, mounting tapes and disks on the appropriate tape and disk drives, and dealing with problems that occur during processing.

c. **Programming**

(1) Applications programmers write, test, and debug the application programs from the specifications provided by the systems analyst.

(2) Systems programmers implement, modify, and debug the software necessary to make the hardware operate.

      d.   **Systems Analysis** Systems analysts investigate a business system and decide how the computer can be applied. This includes designing the system, deciding what the programs will do, and determining how the outputs should appear.

      e.   **Librarians** Librarians provide control over the various programs, data tapes, disks, and documentation (manuals, etc.) when they are not in use; also, librarians are responsible for restricting access to IT materials to authorized personnel only. Library-control software may be used in some systems to keep control over programs, data, etc., that is kept online.

      f.   **Data Integrity** Data must be safeguarded for maximum control. To this end, users are given passwords or IDs to ensure that only authorized persons can access selected data. These passwords and IDs are changed frequently to further ensure the integrity of the system and its data. Passwords can be used to limit access to the entire system and to limit what the individual can access and/or change once in the system.

      g.   **Database Administrator** The database administrator is responsible for maintaining the database and restricting its access to authorized personnel.

B.   **Systems Development & Documentation Controls**
A weakness in systems development and documentation controls means that an auditor usually will have to spend more time in order to understand the system and evaluate the controls. Because application controls often are dependent on the quality of general controls, the absence of effective system development controls may weaken the accounting application controls.

    1.   **GC 4:**   The procedures for system design, including the acquisition of software packages, should require active participation by representatives of the users and, as appropriate, the Accounting Department and internal auditors.

    2.   **GC 5:**   Each system should have written specifications that are reviewed and approved by an appropriate level of management and users in applicable departments.

    3.   **GC 6:**   Systems testing should be a joint effort of users and IT personnel and should include both the manual and computerized phases of the system.

    4.   **GC 7:**   Final approval should be obtained prior to placing a new system into operation.

    5.   **GC 8:**   All master file and transaction file conversions should be controlled to prevent unauthorized changes and to provide accurate and complete results.

    6.   **GC 9:**   After a new system has been placed in operation, all program changes should be approved before implementation to determine whether they have been authorized, tested, and documented.

    7.   **GC 10:**   Management should require various levels of documentation and establish formal procedures to define the system at appropriate levels of detail.

C.   **Hardware & Systems Software Controls**
Hardware controls are controls that are built into the computer. A weakness in hardware and systems software controls may affect the auditor's assessed level of control risk.

    1.   **Parity Bit (Redundant Character Check)** In odd parity, an odd number of magnetized dots (on tape, disk, etc.) always should represent each character. When recording data, the computer automatically checks this. Then, when reading the data, the computer checks to see if there is still an odd number. In even parity, an even number of magnetized dots is used to represent each character. For example, the use of a parity bit probably would discover a distortion caused by dust on a tape or a distortion caused by sending data over telephone lines.

2. **Echo Check** CPU sends a signal to activate an input or output device in a certain manner. The device then sends a signal back to verify activation. The CPU then compares the signals.

3. **Hardware Check** Computer checks to make sure the equipment is functioning properly. For example, periodically the computer may search for circuits that are going bad.

4. **Boundary Protection** Keeps several files or programs separate when they share a common storage. For example, in time-sharing, several users may share primary storage. Boundary protection would prevent their data and/or programs from becoming mixed and the different users from accessing each other's data.

5. **GC 11:** The control features inherent in the computer hardware, operating system, and other supporting software should be utilized to the maximum possible extent to provide control over operations and to detect and report hardware malfunctions.

6. **GC 12:** Systems software should be subjected to the same control procedures as those applied to the installation of, and changes to, application programs.

D. **Access Controls**
A weakness in access controls increases the opportunity for unauthorized modifications of files and programs and misuse of the system; thereby decreasing the integrity of the system.

1. **Physical Access Controls** Only authorized personnel should have access to the facilities housing IT equipment, files and documentation.

2. **Electronic Access Controls** Access control software and other sophisticated devices are available to limit system access.

3. **GC 13:** Access to program documentation should be limited to those persons who require it in the performance of their duties.

4. **GC 14:** Access to data files and programs should be limited to those individuals authorized to process or maintain particular systems.

5. **GC 15:** Access to computer hardware should be limited to authorized individuals.

E. **Data & Procedural Controls**
Serious weaknesses in data and procedural controls can affect the auditor's assessment of control risk when establishing the scope of the substantive testing.

1. **File Labels**

   a. **External Labels** Human-readable labels attached to the outside of a secondary storage device, indicating the name of the file, expiration date, etc.

   b. **Internal Labels** Labels in machine-readable form.

      (1) **Header Label** Appears at the beginning of the file and contains such information as the file name, identification number, and the tape reel number.

      (2) **Trailer Label** Appears at the end of the file and contains such information as a count of the number of the records in the file and an end-of-file code.

2. **File Protection Ring:** A plastic ring that must be attached to a reel of magnetic tape before the tape drive will write on the tape. Writing on magnetic tape automatically erases the data already there, so the file protection ring guards against the inadvertent erasure of the information on the tape.

3. **File Protection Plans**

    a. **Duplicate Files** The most important data files are duplicated and the duplicates are safely stored away from the computer center.

    b. **Disk Reconstruction Plan** In updating a record in a disk file, the record is read from the disk into the CPU, altered, and then written back to its previous location on the disk, thereby erasing the preupdated record. Therefore, a "disk dump" is used in which a copy of the contents of the disk is made on magnetic tape periodically, say each morning. Then, as the day's transactions are processed against the disk file, copies of the transactions are recorded on another tape. If it becomes necessary to reconstruct the disk file at any time during the day, the old file can be read from the tape to the disk and reupdated with the transactions from the transaction tape.

    c. **Grandparent-Parent-Child (or Vice Versa) Retention Concept** This is also known as Grandfather-Father-Son Retention. The master file is updated at the end of each day by the day's transaction file, illustrated in Exhibit 5. After updating on Thursday, the Thursday updated master file (TUMF) is the child, the Wednesday updated master file (WUMF) is the parent, and the Tuesday updated master file (TSUMF) is the grandparent. These three files plus Wednesday's and Thursday's transaction files (WTF and TTF, respectively) are retained. If there is a problem during Friday's update run, the TUMF can be regenerated by running the copy of the WUMF with Thursday's transaction file. If necessary the WUMF could be reconstructed by processing TSUMF with Wednesday's transaction file. Once updating is completed on Friday, Friday's updated master file (FUMF) becomes the child, TUMF becomes the parent and WUMF becomes the grandparent. Therefore, at that time, TSUMF and Wednesday's transaction file can be erased.

Exhibit 5 ▶ Grandparent-Parent-Child Retention Concept

4. **Physical Safeguards**

    a. **Proper Physical Environment** Consider extreme temperature, humidity, dust, etc.

    b. **Environment Free From Possibility of Disasters** Includes proper fireproofing and locating the computer in a safe place (for example, not in the basement if there is a danger of flooding).

    c. **Backup Facilities** Arrangements should be made to use other equipment in the case of disasters or other serious problems. Backup arrangements are frequently made with service bureaus or with computer installations of subsidiaries. Backup facilities are referred to as "hot" or "cold" sites, depending on their state of readiness.

    d. **Control Access to Computer Room** Only authorized personnel should have access. For example, computer operators would be authorized to be in the computer room, but programmers would not be. Further, there should be at least two people in the computer room at all times. A weakness in internal control exists when a client uses microcomputers, because these computers rarely are isolated in a limited-access location and operators may remove hardware and software components and modify them at home more readily.

5.   **GC 16:**   A control function should be responsible for receiving all data to be processed, for ensuring that all data are recorded, for following up on errors detected during processing to see that the transactions are corrected and resubmitted by the proper party, and for verifying the proper distribution of output.

6.   **GC 17:**   A written manual of systems and procedures should be prepared for all computer operations and should provide for management's general or specific authorizations to process transactions.

7.   **GC 18:**   Internal auditors or other independent groups within an organization should review and evaluate proposed systems at critical stages of development.

8.   **GC 19:**   On a continuing basis, internal auditors or other independent groups within an organization should review and test computer processing activities.

IV. Application Controls (AC)

A. Input Controls

Input controls are designed to provide reasonable assurance that data received by IT have been authorized, converted into machine sensible form, and identified properly. Further, they assure that data have not been lost, suppressed, added, duplicated, or otherwise changed improperly. Basic categories of input to be controlled are (1) transaction entry, (2) file maintenance transactions (e.g., changing sales prices on a product master file), (3) inquiry transactions (e.g., how many units of a particular inventory item are on hand), and (4) error correction transactions.

1.   **AC 1:**   Only properly authorized and approved input, prepared in accordance with management's general or specific authorization, should be accepted for processing by IT.

2.   **AC 2:**   The system should verify all significant codes used to record data.

3.   **AC 3:**   Conversion of data into machine-sensible form should be controlled.

4.   **Common Errors in Conversion** Keying errors and the losing or dropping of records.

5.   **Input Control Techniques**

    a.   **Control Totals** A total is computed and then recomputed at a later time. The totals are compared and should be the same. Control totals can be used as input, processing, and output controls.

        (1)   **Financial Total** This has financial meaning in addition to being a control. For example, the dollar amount of accounts receivable to be updated can be compared with a computer-generated total of the dollar amount of updates read from the tape.

        (2)   **Hash Total** This has meaning only as a control. For example, a total of the account numbers of those accounts that should have been updated can be compared with a computer-generated total of those account numbers actually entered.

        (3)   **Record Count (Document Count)** This is a count of the number of transactions processed. For example, the computer can be programmed to print the total number of A/R records actually inputted.

b. **Computer Editing** Computers can be programmed to perform a wide range of edit tests (i.e., edit checks) on records as they are being entered into the system. If a particular record does not meet the test, it is not processed. Edit tests include the following:

(1) **Limit (Reasonableness) Test** A particular field of an input transaction record is checked to be sure it is not greater (or smaller) than a prespecified amount, or that it is within a prespecified range of acceptable values. For example, "hours worked" on a payroll record may be checked to be sure it does not exceed 50 hours in one week.

(2) **Valid Field and/or Character Test** The particular field is examined to be sure it is of the proper size and composition. For example, if a customer account number should be numeric digits appearing in the first 7 spaces of the record, the first 7 spaces can be examined to be sure that there are numbers there.

(3) **Valid Number or Code Test** Verifies that a particular number or code is one of those that is recognized by the system. For example, if a company has 5 retail outlets and records sales by using a location code of 1-5, the computer can check to be sure the code digit on the transaction record is a 1, 2, 3, 4, or 5.

(4) **Sequence Check** If the input records should be in some particular sequence, the computer can be programmed to verify the sequence. For example, after sorting, the day's transaction file that is being entered should be in ascending order by customer account number.

(5) **Missing Data Test** This verifies that all of the data fields actually contain data. For example, a point-of-sale terminal may be programmed not to accept a transaction unless the clerk has entered 10 pieces of required data.

(6) **Valid Transaction Test** There are only a certain number of transaction types that would be expected for most files, so the computer can be programmed to verify that a particular transaction is an appropriate type for a particular file. For example, in the case of inventory, the only valid transaction may be to debit the inventory account when inventory is added and credit the account when inventory is taken away.

(7) **Valid Combination of Fields** This is a check to be sure a certain combination of fields is reasonable. For example, a large retail outlet may program its computer to check the reasonableness of the product code field and the quantity-sold field. This would disclose a clerical error that resulted in a sale being entered for 11 television sets when only 1 was sold; i.e., it is not reasonable that one retail customer would purchase 11 television sets.

(8) **Check Digit (Self-Checking Digit)** This is a digit (determined according to a prespecified mathematical routine) that is added to the same place in a piece of numeric data to permit the numeric data to be checked for accuracy during input, processing, or output. For example, a customer account number may be 1234. A check digit could be formed by adding the first and third digits and using the sum. The sum of the two digits is 4 (i.e., 1 + 3), so the check digit is 4. It is added to the end of the number that is assigned to the customer. The new customer account number becomes 12344. The computer can be programmed to verify the check digit at appropriate times. For instance, if the number is accidentally entered as 13244, the check digit would not match and the transaction would not be accepted. In practice, the mathematical routine generally is more complex than the one illustrated here.

(9)   Valid Sign Test A particular field can be checked to be sure it has the proper sign. For example, the quantity received in an inventory record should not be negative.

c.   Error Log (Error Listing) This is a computer-prepared list of those transactions that were not processed because of some error condition (e.g., an invalid customer account number). When an error is encountered, the usual procedure is for the computer to not process the erroneous transaction, but to skip it and continue processing the valid transactions rather than to halt processing altogether. A control function should be responsible for following up on errors detected during processing to see that the transactions are corrected and resubmitted by the proper party. This control function ideally should be delegated to a special IT control group that is independent from system analysis, programming, and operation.

6.   **AC 4:**   Movement of data between one processing step and another, or between departments, should be controlled.

7.   **AC 5:**   The correction of all errors detected by the application system and the resubmission of corrected transactions should be reviewed and controlled.

B.   Processing Controls
Many input controls are also valid processing controls.

1.   **AC 6:**   Control totals should be produced and reconciled with input control totals.

2.   **AC 7:**   Controls should prevent processing the wrong file, detect errors in file manipulation, and highlight operator-caused errors.

3.   **AC 8:**   Limit and reasonableness checks should be incorporated within programs.

4.   **AC 9:**   Run-to-run controls should be verified at appropriate points in the processing cycle.

C.   Output Controls
Primarily balancing, visual scanning or verification, and distribution.

1.   **AC 10:**   Output control totals should be reconciled with input and processing controls.

2.   **AC 11:**   Output should be scanned and tested by comparison to original source documents.

3.   **AC 12:**   Systems output should be distributed only to authorized users.

D.   Audit Effect of Weakness in Application Controls
This must be considered in relation to the particular application and to the total audit. Controls in the categories of input, processing, and output must be considered in relation to each other; i.e., a strong control in processing may compensate for a weakness in input.

V.   General Auditing Approaches

A.   Around (Without) the Computer
The computer is treated as a "black box" that is ignored for all practical purposes. The auditor concentrates on input and output; i.e., if the inputs are correct and the outputs are correct, what went on within the computer also must be correct. The auditor does **not** test or directly examine the computer program, nor use the computer to perform the tests. Rather, the auditor relies on computer-prepared documents and printouts, which provide a visible audit trail that can be used in performing the audit procedures.

1. **Type of System** Auditing around the computer is appropriate for simple systems that provide extensive printouts of processing, i.e., systems that provide a good audit trail.

2. **Testing of Controls** Extensive use is made of the error listing (error log) to verify the existence and functioning of the control procedures. For example, if the error listing shows that a payroll transaction was not processed because the "hours-worked" field exceeded the limit allowed, the auditor has evidence that the limit test exists and is functioning. The auditor also will trace transactions from the source documents (for example, a sales slip) through processing to their final place in the accounts and reports. Note that while computer-generated output is being used, the computer is not being used as an audit tool.

3. **Substantive Testing** The computer-prepared output is used as a basis for substantive testing. For example, the auditor may select a sample of accounts receivable to be confirmed from a computer-prepared listing of all the individual accounts receivable.

B. **Through (With) the Computer**
    The computer is used to perform tests of controls and substantive testing. The auditor places emphasis on the input data and the processing of the data. While output is not ignored, the auditor reasons that if the input is correct and the processing is correct, then the output must be correct. As a system becomes more complex, more processing is done within the computer and more data files are kept only in machine-readable form. This causes the audit trail to disappear. When this happens, auditing through the computer is really the only alternative open to the auditor. The following techniques are available to the auditor:

    Exhibit 6 ▶ Auditing Through the Computer Mnemonic

W	Writing own program
E	Embedded audit modules
T	Tagging
C	Client-prepared program
U	Utility programs (utility routines)
P	Program comparison
T	Test data (test deck)
R	Review of program logic
I	Integrated test facility (ITF, minicompany approach)
P	Parallel simulation
P	Program tracing

1. **Writing Own Program** The auditor writes a program for the specific substantive test to be performed. The major drawback is the time and effort required to get the program operational.

2. **Embedded Audit Modules** Sections of program code are included in the client's application program to collect audit data for the auditor. For example, at the auditor's direction, a file may be created of all sales transactions that are for more than $100. This monitors the client's system as transactions are actually processed. It can be hard to install once the application program is operational. Thus, it may be most efficiently included during system design.

3. **Tagging** Selected transactions are "tagged" (i.e., specially marked) at the auditor's direction. Then, as they are processed, additional documentation is generated so that the auditor can see how the transactions are handled as they are processed, i.e., it allows the auditor to

examine the transactions at the intermediate steps in processing that normally are done within the computer but not displayed.

4.   **Client-Prepared Program**   Often the internal audit staff has programs to do the same things the auditor would like to do. Therefore, the auditor may be able to use the programs. However, first the auditor must test them to make sure that they do what they are supposed to do and that their integrity can be relied on.

5.   **Utility Programs (Utility Routines)**   Standard programs are furnished by the computer manufacturer for performing common data processing functions such as (a) changing the media a file is stored on (e.g., tape-to-disk, disk-to-tape, tape-to-paper), (b) modifying the data by changing or deleting records within a file, (c) creating or destroying a file, (d) changing the name or password of a file, (e) printing the contents of a file so it may be inspected visually, (f) sorting a file, and (g) merging two or more files. Utility programs may be more technical than GAS (see V., C.). Therefore, the auditor may have to be more technically proficient with IT to use them efficiently. The auditor also must be sure the utility program has not been altered. Consideration should be given as to whether the use of a utility routine will decrease the audit time or if GAS may be more appropriate.

6.   **Program Comparison**   The auditor-controlled copy of the program is compared with the program the client is using currently (usually done on a surprise basis). The idea behind this technique is that the comparison will disclose unauthorized changes made in the program. While the auditor may do this manually, there is software available to do it. A major drawback is the problem of the auditor maintaining a current copy of the program. Routine maintenance (updating) by programmers may mean that the auditor's copy does not agree with the copy being used, and it is the auditor's copy that is wrong.

7.   **Test Data (Test Deck)**   The auditor prepares a series of fictitious transactions (test data), some of which are valid and some of which contain errors that should be detected by the controls the auditor wants to test. The auditor uses the client's programs to process the test data and then examines the output to check processing, including the computer-prepared error listing.

   a.   For example, if the payroll program is not supposed to process payroll data for employees whose employee time cards indicate they have worked more than 60 hours per week, the auditor's test data would contain at least one time card with more than 60 hours worked on it. If the control is working, the particular transaction should not be processed but should appear on the computer-prepared error listing.

   b.   There are at least three potential problems with using test data: (1) Care must be exercised to prevent the fictitious data from becoming part of the client's real data files. (2) Time and care are required to prepare the test data so that it will test for the things that could go wrong and that are of interest to the auditor. (3) The auditor must take steps to make sure that the program being tested (i.e., the program testing the fictitious data) is the one that actually is used in routine processing.

8.   **Review of Program Logic**   The auditor reviews the application program's documentation, including the flowcharts and possibly the program listing, to obtain a sufficient understanding of the logic of the program in order to evaluate it. This may be time consuming. Unless the auditor specifically believes there is a logic error in the program, other audit techniques probably will be more efficient.

9.   **Integrated Test Facility (ITF), Minicompany Approach**   The auditor creates a fictitious entity within the client's actual data files. The fictitious data then is processed for the entity as part of the client's regular data processing. For example, if the auditor wants to test the accounts receivable update program, the auditor could create a fictitious customer's account receivable in the client's actual accounts receivable master file. During the period under audit, the auditor occasionally would introduce transactions for the fictitious customer. For

instance, the "customer" would make credit purchases, would overpay the account, would not pay the account, would make purchase returns, etc. These transactions would be processed as part of the client's normal processing. The auditor knows what effect the various transactions should have on the accounts receivable, so the auditor can check the status of the account at any time to verify that transactions are being processed correctly, i.e., that the application programs are working as they should.

a. **Advantage Over Test Data** Two of the main advantages of ITF over the use of test data are that the auditor introduces fictitious data throughout the period (approaches continuous auditing) and it is processed along with the client's other "live" (i.e., actual) data.

b. **Problems** Several potential problems relating to the use of ITF are as follows:

(1) The data is part of the client's data files, so it accidentally may be included in the financial statements and reports that are prepared. To avoid this, the auditor may wish to introduce reversing entries to reverse the effects of the fictitious transactions (for example, to remove the "sales" made to the fictitious customer from the sales account) or the auditor may have the statement preparation program modified to skip the fictitious account when preparing the financial statements. Or, the auditor may decide to use small dollar amounts so that even if they are not removed, they will not have a material effect.

(2) Time, effort, and skill are required to make the fictitious entity operational and make sure the transactions processed against it will test the conditions and controls of interest to the auditor.

(3) There is also the problem of secrecy because the auditor's confidence in the technique will decrease if the client's data preparation and computer operations personnel know that the entity is fictitious and that the transactions for it are being introduced by the auditor in order to audit compliance.

10. **Parallel Simulation** Once the auditor has checked a program, the auditor must determine that the client continues to use it. Parallel simulation involves processing actual client data through an auditor's software program, possibly using the client's computer. After processing the data, the auditor compares the output with output obtained from the client. Two techniques that can be used to help the auditor verify that the program being used for routine processing is the one that has been checked are as follows:

a. **Controlled Processing** The auditor observes (i.e., controls) an actual processing run and compares the results against those expected.

b. **Controlled Reprocessing** The auditor tests a program and keeps a copy of the program. At some future point in time, the auditor has the client use the auditor's control copy of the program to process some actual transactions. The results are compared with those from the client's routine processing run. For example, the auditor may have a control copy of the payroll program. The auditor would select the time cards and payroll data for several employees and have them processed using the control copy. The auditor would then compare the results of gross pay, net pay, withholding, etc., from the program with those that were attained by the payroll program the client had just used. A major problem is for the auditor to keep the control copy of the program current.

11. **Tracing (Program Tracing, Tracing Software)** This prints a listing of the program instructions (steps) that were executed in processing a transaction. The auditor must be familiar with the programming language in which the client's application program is written. Even then, it may be time consuming to follow through the program listing.

C.   Generalized Audit Software

This is a set of programs or routines (i.e., a software package) specifically designed to perform certain data processing functions that are useful to the auditor. The auditor can use generalized audit software (GAS) on the data files of a variety of clients. The auditor only need describe the organization of each client's files to GAS briefly, rather than write computer programs. Also known as General Purpose Audit Software or General Purpose Computer Audit Software, this is the computer-assisted audit technique used most prevalently.

1.   Reasons

    a.   Use of Large Variety of Data Much of a client's data is retained only in machine-readable form. GAS makes it possible for the auditor to access the data, analyze it, and present the results in a meaningful and convenient form.

    b.   Effectively Deal With Large Quantities of Data GAS lets the auditor examine more data in more detail. For example, given an insurance company that has a policy file maintained on disk, the auditor can use GAS to perform mathematical tests on each of the policy records in the file. If auditing the file manually, the auditor could examine only a sample of the policies.

    c.   Lessens Dependence on Client Personnel The auditor can do much of the computerized testing; i.e., the auditor does not need to rely as much on client personnel.

    d.   Economy GAS produces economies in the audit while increasing audit quality.

    e.   Access to Data GAS enables the auditor to gain access and test information stored in the client's files without having to acquire a complete understanding of the client's IT system.

2.   Audit Tasks Performed by GAS While the exact procedures performed will vary among software packages, audit software is used to accomplish six basic types of audit tasks.

    a.   Examining Records for Quality, Completeness, Consistency & Correctness GAS can be instructed to scan the records in a file and print those that are exceptions to auditor-specified criteria. Examples include (1) reviewing accounts receivable balances for amounts that are over the credit limit, (2) reviewing inventory quantities for negative or unreasonably large balances, (3) reviewing payroll files for terminated employees, and (4) reviewing bank demand deposit files for unusually large deposits or withdrawals.

    b.   Testing Calculations & Making Computations GAS can test the accuracy of mathematical computations and can perform quantitative analyses to evaluate the reasonableness of client representations. Examples include (1) recalculating the extensions of inventory items, depreciation amounts, the accuracy of sales discounts, and interest, and (2) determining the accuracy of the net pay computations for employees.

    c.   Comparing Data on Separate Files GAS can be used to determine if identical information on separate files agrees. Examples include (1) comparing changes in accounts receivable balances between two dates with details of sales and cash receipts on transaction files, (2) comparing payroll details with personnel records, and (3) comparing current and prior-period inventory files to assist in locating obsolete or slow-moving items.

    d.   Selecting, Printing & Analyzing Audit Samples GAS can select statistical samples (random, stratified, etc.), print the items for the auditor's working papers or on special confirmation forms, and then, when the results are known (for example, when the confirmations are returned), analyze the data statistically. Examples include (1) select and print accounts receivable confirmations, (2) select inventory items for observation, and (3) select fixed asset additions for vouching.

e. **Summarizing or Resequencing Data & Performing Analyses** GAS can reformat and aggregate data in a variety of ways. Examples include (1) refooting account files, (2) testing accounts receivable aging, (3) preparing general ledger trial balances, (4) summarizing inventory turnover statistics for obsolescence analysis, and (5) resequencing inventory items by location to facilitate physical observations.

f. **Comparing Data Obtained Through Other Audit Procedures With Company Records** Manually gathered audit evidence can be converted to machine-readable form and then GAS can compare it to other machine-readable data. Examples include (1) comparison of inventory test counts with perpetual records and (2) comparison of creditor statements with accounts payable files.

Example 1 ▶ Potential Applications of GAS in Audit of Inventory

1. Determine the inventory items that should be reduced for quick sale, according to company policy.

2. Merge last year's inventory file with this year's and list those items that have unit costs of more than $100 that have increased by more than 10 percent.

3. Test for quantities on hand in excess of units sold during a period and list possible obsolete inventory items.

4. Select a sample of inventory items for a physical count and reconcile to the perpetual records.

5. Scan the sequence of inventory tag numbers and print a list of any missing numbers.

6. Select a random sample of inventory items for price testing and test the price.

7. Perform a net-realizable value test on year-end inventory quantities, using unit selling price data, and list any items where inventory cost exceeds net realizable value.

Example 2 ▶ Potential Applications of GAS in Audit of Accounts Receivable

1. Select and list accounts according to auditor-defined past-due conditions (e.g., over $5,000 and more than 90 days past-due).

2. List a random sample of past-due accounts to use in determining if follow-up procedures conform to company policy.

3. Select a sample of customer accounts for confirmation and have the computer print the confirmation requests.

4. Determine if the accounts receivable master file balance agrees with the general ledger and independently prove a company-prepared aging of accounts.

5. Match subsequent cash collections with accounts receivable records and independently age receivables not yet paid several weeks after the trial balance date.

6. Compare amounts due from individual customers with their approved credit limits and print a list of customers with balances in excess of their authorized amounts.

7. Print, for review and follow-up, a list of accounts for which collection efforts have been temporarily suspended.

3. **Feasibility** When deciding whether to use GAS, the auditor should consider the following:

a. **Nature of the Audit Area & Audit Approach** In some cases, the use of GAS may be the only feasible approach to attain the audit objective, for example, in complex systems with invisible audit trails. Additionally, the client may support or oppose the use of GAS.

b. **Significance of Audit Effort & Timing** GAS may permit the auditor to complete an audit procedure quicker than any other alternative.

c. **Availability of Data** Some data is available only in machine-readable form. Other data is not in machine-readable form and therefore, would have to be converted before GAS could be applied to it.

d. **Availability of Qualified Staff Personnel** Does the auditor or staff possess the necessary technical expertise to use GAS on the system being audited? For example, an auditor may be experienced in using GAS on relatively simple systems, but not on complex systems.

e. **Economic Considerations** While GAS can accomplish many things for the auditor, it has costs associated with its use such as staff hours, technical review hours, and mechanical assistance hours.

4. **Planning GAS Applications** The following steps should be followed in planning:

a. Set the objectives of the GAS application.

b. Determine the reports and other output requirements.

c. Review the content, accessibility, etc., of client data files.

d. Identify client personnel who may provide administrative or technical assistance.

e. Determine the need for equipment and supplies.

f. Determine the degree of audit control needed so that the auditor will have confidence that the GAS is processed correctly.

g. Prepare application budgets and timetables.

5. **Steps in Using GAS** The auditor goes through a series of steps in applying GAS.

a. **Determine Routines** Determine the specific GAS routines to be used and the particular order in which to use them for the particular application. The auditor does not have to use all of the routines available. Any routine can be used as many times as the auditor wishes.

b. **Complete Coding Sheets** The auditor describes the routines to use, the order in which to use them, the client's system, and data files to GAS.

c. **Processing** The GAS, the auditor's instructions, and the client's data files are entered into a computer and processed. The auditor should maintain physical control over the GAS (i.e., it should be kept in the auditor's possession) and should be present when it is run. The auditor should also be present to receive the output directly from the computer.

d. **Use Output** The auditor uses the GAS output in the audit.

6. **Statistical Sampling** Computer programs have been developed to assist the auditor in planning and evaluating sampling procedures. These programs overcome the limitations of tables and perform calculations, such as a standard deviation computation, that are difficult and time consuming to perform manually.

a. **Flexibility** Computer programs are flexible. For example, they can calculate sample sizes for different sampling techniques. They can help the auditor select a random sample. They can evaluate samples covering single or multiple locations and can offer many more options for the auditor's planning considerations. These programs generally have built-in controls over human errors. For example, programs can be designed to include controls to identify unreasonable input.

b. **Documentation** The printed output generally is written in nontechnical language that can be understood easily by an auditor. The printout can be included in the auditor's working papers as documentation of the sampling procedure.

c. **Programs** Programs offered by vendors generally are developed by vendors, by third parties for the vendor, or by CPA firms. In selecting a program, the auditor should obtain reasonable assurance that the program is suitable. The auditor should determine whether the statistical theory used to develop the program is appropriate for the auditor's purpose. It is important for the auditor to test a program adequately before use or to determine that the vendor did so. Statistical sampling software should contain basic control features that, for example, reject negative numbers where inapplicable or alert the auditor to inappropriately high risk levels or tolerable rates.

VI. Appendix: IT Terms

ad hoc **report** Nonstandardized report composed when the need arises. Frequently developed by users, rather than programmers with extensive training, for limited use.

application program Designed to perform the processing of a specific application. For example, an accounts receivable update program is an application program that processes accounts receivable data to update the accounts receivable master file.

bit A binary digit (0 or 1, on or off, etc.), representing the smallest unit of data possible.

byte A group of bits that represents a single character, whether alphabetic or numeric.

characters Letters, numbers, and special symbols (e.g., periods, commas, and hyphens).

central processing unit (CPU, mainframe) Primary hardware component. The actual processing of data occurs in the CPU. It contains primary storage, a control unit, and an arithmetic/logic unit.

> **primary storage (main memory)** Portion of the CPU that holds the program, data, and results (intermediate and final) during processing; therefore, this includes only temporary storage. The primary storage contains the data and program steps that are being processed by the CPU and is divided into RAM (random-access memory) and ROM (read-only memory).
>
> **control unit** Portion of the CPU that controls and directs the operations of the computer. It interprets the instructions from the program and directs the computer system to carry them out.
>
> **arithmetic/logic unit** Portion of the CPU that has special circuitry for performing arithmetic calculations and logical operations. This may be combined with the control unit.

cloud computing The delivery of computing resources as a metered service over the Internet.

cold site Location where equipment and power is available in the event of disaster at the primary location, but requiring considerable effort to get an operational system functioning. (Compare to hot site.)

collaborative computing applications (groupware, shareware) A program that allows several people to have access to the same information and attempts to track the authors of changes.

CPA SysTrust An attestation service developed in part by the AICPA, that is designed to provide assurance on whether a system's controls are operating effectively and allow the system to function reliably.

CPA WebTrust A symbol appearing on a Web site that indicates that the organization meets joint Canadian Institute of Chartered Accountants and AICPA business practice disclosures, transaction integrity, and information protection criteria.

database A structured set of interrelated files combined to eliminate redundancy of data items within the files and to establish logical connections between data items. For example, within personnel and payroll files, some of the data in the two records will be the same; in a database system, these files would be combined to eliminate the redundant data.

database management system (DBMS) A set of programs (software) that manages the database (i.e., creates, accesses, and maintains the database).

decision tables Decision tables emphasize the relationships among conditions and actions, and present decision choices. Decision tables often supplement systems flowcharts.

decode Convert data from an encoded state to its original form.

digital signature Encryption feature used to authenticate the originator of a document and insure that the message is intact.

disaster recovery Restoration of data and business function after loss.

document management Electronic document storage and retrieval.

downtime Time when the computer is not functioning. This may be scheduled or unscheduled.

edit Refers to the addition, deletion, and/or rearrangement of data. **Input editing** refers to editing before processing and **output editing** refers to editing after processing.

electronic commerce (e-commerce) Business via the Internet, including EDI.

electronic data interchange (EDI) Electronic communication among entities such as financial institutions and customer-vendor partners (typically involving order placement, invoicing, and payment and may involve inventory monitoring and automatic restocking). ANSI X12 is a domestic EDI format. EDIFACT is an international EDI format.

electronic document submission Submission of documents such as federal tax returns and securities reports in electronic form, usually over the Internet.

e-mail Electronic messages, typically delivered through the Internet. The messages may have attached files, including documents and programs.

encode, encrypt Scrambling data to prevent unauthorized use.

enterprise resource planning software Large multimodule applications that manage a business' different aspects, from traditional accounting to inventory management and advanced planning and forecasting.

extranet A password-protected intranet, usually for established vendors and customers. (Compare to internet.)

field Group of related characters. For example, a customer name.

file Group of related records. For example, a customer file. (Also see master file and transaction file.)

firewall Software designed to prevent unauthorized access to data by separating one segment from another.

gateway Software or hardware that links two or more computer networks.

groupware A program designed to allow several people to work on a single project. While this allows for greater flexibility, there is a loss of accountability. (Also see collaborative computing applications.)

hardware maintenance Involves equipment service. Routine service is scheduled. Unscheduled maintenance arises when there are unanticipated problems.

heuristic In computing, the adjective *heuristic* signifies *able to change;* it is used to describe a computer program that can modify itself in response to the user, for example, a spell check program.

hot site Location where a functioning system is planned for use with minimal preparation in the event of a disaster at the primary work location. (Compare to cold site.)

input/output devices Devices for transferring data in and out of the CPU. Examples include:

> **bar code reader** An input device to scan bar codes, such as universal product codes on merchandise.

> **keyboard** Typewriterlike device to allow the user to type information into the computer.

> **magnetic ink character recognition (MICR)** Sensing information recorded in special magnetized ink. MICR is commonly used by the banking industry for check processing.

> **magnetic tape reader** A device to sense information recorded as magnetized spots on magnetic tape (e.g., the magnetic strips used on credit cards and ATM cards).

> **modem** A device to allow users to transfer files over telephone lines to distant computers.

> **monitor, screen** A televisionlike screen to display information, providing feedback to the user.

> **mouse, trackball** A pointing device to manipulate representations displayed on a screen.

> **optical character recognition (OCR) scanner** A device to sense printed information through the use of light-sensitive devices.

> **printer** A device to produce output on paper, including invoices and checks.

Internet A network of networks. The Internet is a public network of many networks. (Compare to intranet.)

intranet A network generally restricted to employee access. LANs are typically intranets. (Compare to internet and extranet.)

inventory control system A system that tracks the quantity of inventory bought and sold.

library program (library routine) Programs that are frequently used by other programs. They are kept within the system and "called up" whenever necessary. One example is generating random numbers.

local area network (LAN) A network of computers within a small area (i.e., a building) to transmit information electronically and share files and peripheral equipment among members (compare to wide area network).

management information system (MIS) An information system within an organization that provides management with the information needed for planning and control. This involves an integration of the functions of gathering and analyzing data, and reporting (i.e., communicating) the results to management in a meaningful form.

mapping Converting data between application format and a standard format, such as EDI.

master file Contains relatively permanent data. For example, an accounts receivable master file would contain a record for each customer and each record would include fields for customer number, name, address, credit limit, amount owed, etc. (Compare to transaction file.)

network An arrangement of computers to allow users access to common data, hardware, and/or software.

operating system (OS) Manages the coordinating and scheduling of various application programs and computer functions. Examples include the following:

> **multiprocessing** Allows the execution of two or more programs at the same time and requires the utilization of more than one CPU.

> **multiprogramming** A program is processed until some type of input or output is needed. The OS then delegates the process to a piece of peripheral equipment, and the CPU begins executing other programs. Processing speed is enhanced considerably, making it appear as if more than one program is being processed concurrently, while utilizing only one CPU.

> **virtual storage** The OS divides a program into segments (called pages) and brings only sections of the program into memory as needed to execute the instructions. This saves memory and processing cost because the majority of the program remains in less expensive secondary storage.

pass (run) A complete cycle of input, processing, and output in the execution of a computer program.

patch Addition of a new part to a program. It may be added to correct or update a program. For example, if a new government regulation affecting withholding tax becomes effective, a patch may be added to the payroll program to provide for this. A patch may also be added for a fraudulent purpose. For example, an employee might insert a patch into a payroll program to print an extra check.

peripheral equipment Equipment that is **not** part of the CPU but that may be placed under the control of the CPU, i.e., which may be accessed directly by the CPU. Input/output devices and secondary storage devices are peripheral equipment.

point-of-sale (POS) system A system that records goods sold and figures the amount due at the cash register, frequently also verifying credit cards or checks.

program Set of instructions that the computer follows to accomplish a specified task (e.g., accounts receivable update program, inventory management program, and payroll program).

program maintenance Refers to making changes in the program in order to keep it current and functioning properly. For example, maintenance of the payroll program may involve modifying it because of changes in the social security law or to provide for a greater number of employees.

record Group of related fields. For example, a customer record would include ID number, name, address, etc.

router Switches that transfer incoming messages to outgoing links via the most efficient route possible, for example, over the Internet.

secondary storage Devices external to the CPU that store data.

> **disk, diskette** Randomly accessible data is represented in concentric circles called "tracks." A magnetic disk is a platter coated on both sides with a material on which data can be represented as magnetized dots according to a predetermined code. Diskettes are more common than disks, as they hold more data. Still more data can be stored on CDs (also called laser disks). A disk drive is used to read data from the disk into the CPU and to write data from the CPU onto the disk. A hard drive is more permanently fixed than a disk or diskette, with faster retrieval. Disks are usually more easily moved than a hard drive.

> **magnetic tape** Plastic tape that is coated with a material on which data can be represented as magnetized dots according to a predetermined code. It resembles audio tape.

> **off-line storage** Not in direct communication with the CPU. Human intervention is needed for the data to be processed. For example, a disk must be inserted in a disk drive before it can be accessed.

online storage In direct communication with the CPU without human intervention. For example, a hard drive ordinarily is accessed by the CPU without human intervention.

randomly accessible (direct access) Data records can be accessed directly. Disks are an example. For example, if the customer records are stored in a file on a disk, the disk drive could go directly to a specific customer's record without having to read any of the other customer records.

sequentially accessible Requires the reading of all data between the starting point and the information sought. Magnetic tape is sequentially accessible. For example, if alphabetized records are on magnetic tape and none are read, most of the tape must be read to get to a specific customer's data.

self-service applications Software that allows customers to provide much of their own customer service.

software Programs, routines, documentation, manuals, etc., that make it possible for the computer system to operate and process data. (Compare to hardware.)

systems programs (supervisory programs) Perform the functions of coordinating and controlling the overall operation of the computer system.

telecommuting Working outside of a traditional office, remaining connected by the Internet, phone, etc. Usually implies a office in the employee's home, although a sales agent or insurance adjuster might also work from a vehicle and/or customer sites.

transaction (detail) file Contains current, temporary data. A transaction file is used to update a master file. For example, the day's charge sales would be accumulated on a transaction file that would be used to update the accounts receivable master file during an update run.

Trojan horse A seemingly legitimate program that operates in an unauthorized manner, usually causing damage.

universal in-box A system to collect email and voice mail in one "place," accessible by either regular phone or computer.

utility program (utility routine) Standard program for performing routine functions, e.g., sorting and merging.

value-added network (VAN) A network service that provides additional services beyond mere connections to the Internet, particularly services enabling EDI.

video conference Real-time meeting over the Internet.

virus A program that replicates and attaches itself to other programs. The effects of a virus can be a merely annoying message or malicious activity, such as reformatting a hard drive or flooding an e-mail system.

virus hoax An e-mail message with a false warning. Its originator tries to get it circulated as widely as possible.

voice mail A system that records, directs, stores, and replays telephone messages.

web crawler A program used to search the World Wide Web for files meeting user criteria.

wide area network (WAN) A computer network encompassing a large area (i.e., citywide or globally) to transmit information electronically and share files among members (typically companywide only). (Compare to local area network).

CHAPTER 7—AUDITING IT SYSTEMS

Problem 7-1 MULTIPLE-CHOICE QUESTIONS

1. Which of the following computer documentations would an auditor most likely utilize in obtaining an understanding of internal control?

   a. Systems flowcharts
   b. Record counts
   c. Program listings
   d. Record layouts   (5/90, AUD, #27, amended, ID: 0278)

2. One of the major problems in an IT system is that incompatible functions may be performed by the same individual. One compensating control for this is the use of

   a. Echo checks
   b. A self-checking digit system
   c. Computer-generated hash totals
   d. A computer log   (Editors, ID: 0297)

3. Which of the following is a general control that would most likely assist an entity whose systems analyst left the entity in the middle of a major project?

   a. Grandfather-father-son record retention
   b. Input and output validation routines
   c. Systems documentation
   d. Check digit verification   (ID: 2300)

4. A retail entity uses electronic data interchange (EDI) in executing and recording most of its purchase transactions. The entity's auditor recognizes that the documentation of the transactions will be retained for only a short period of time. To compensate for this limitation, the auditor most likely would

   a. Increase the sample of EDI transactions to be selected for cutoff tests
   b. Perform tests several times during the year, rather than only at year-end
   c. Plan to make a 100% count of the entity's inventory at or near the year-end
   d. Decrease the assessed level of control risk for the existence or occurrence assertion
                                                                      (R/00, AUD, #9, ID: 6934)

5. Which of the following is an engagement attribute for an audit of an entity that processes most of its financial data in electronic form without any paper documentation?

   a. Discrete phases of planning, interim, and year-end fieldwork
   b. Increased effort to search for evidence of management fraud
   c. Performance of audit tests on a continuous basis
   d. Increased emphasis on the completeness assertion   (R/99, AUD, #22, ID: 6838)

6. An auditor anticipates assessing control risk at a low level in a computerized environment. Under these circumstances, on which of the following procedures would the auditor initially focus?

   a. Programmed control procedures
   b. Application control procedures
   c. Output control procedures
   d. General control procedures   (5/92, AUD, #36, ID: 2789)

7. A retailing entity uses the Internet to execute and record its purchase transactions. The entity's auditor recognizes that the documentation of details of transactions will be retained for only a short period of time. To compensate for this limitation, the auditor most likely would

    a. Compare a sample of paid vendors' invoices to the receiving records at year-end
    b. Plan for a large measure of tolerable misstatement in substantive tests
    c. Perform tests several times during the year, rather than only at year-end
    d. Increase the sample of transactions to be selected for cutoff tests   (R/07, AUD, #2, ID: 8374)

8. Which of the following is an example of how specific internal controls in a database environment may differ from controls in a nondatabase environment?

    a. Controls should exist to ensure that users have access to and can update only the data elements that they have been authorized to access.
    b. Controls over data sharing by diverse users within an entity should be the same for every user.
    c. The employee who manages the computer hardware should also develop and debug the computer programs.
    d. Controls can provide assurance that all processed transactions are authorized, but cannot verify that all authorized transactions are processed.   (R/00, AUD, #8, ID: 6933)

9. Misstatements in a batch computer system caused by incorrect programs or data may **not** be detected immediately because

    a. Errors in some transactions may cause rejection of other transactions in the batch.
    b. The identification of errors in input data typically is not part of the program.
    c. There are time delays in processing transactions in a batch system.
    d. The processing of transactions in a batch system is not uniform.   (11/94, AUD, #37, ID: 5110)

10. Which of the following most likely represents a significant deficiency in internal control?

    a. The systems programmer designs systems for computerized applications and maintains output controls.
    b. The systems analyst reviews applications of data processing and maintains systems documentation.
    c. The control clerk establishes control over data received by the IT department and reconciles control totals after processing.
    d. The accounts payable clerk prepares data for computer processing and enters the data into the computer.   (Editors, ID: 2304)

11. When evaluating internal control of an entity that processes sales transactions on the Internet, an auditor would be most concerned about the

    a. Lack of sales invoice documents as an audit trail
    b. Potential for computer disruptions in recording sales
    c. Inability to establish an integrated test facility
    d. Frequency of archiving and data retention   (R/99, AUD, #10, ID: 6826)

12. Which of the following statements is correct concerning internal control in an electronic data interchange (EDI) system?

    a. Preventive controls generally are more important than detective controls in EDI systems.
    b. Control objectives for EDI systems generally are different from the objectives for other information systems.
    c. Internal controls in EDI systems rarely permit control risk to be assessed at below the maximum.
    d. Internal controls related to the segregation of duties generally are the most important controls in EDI systems.   (R/99, AUD, #11, ID: 6827)

13. Which of the following would most likely be a weakness in internal control of a client that utilizes micro-computers rather than a larger computer system?

   a. Employee collusion possibilities are increased because microcomputers from one vendor can process the programs of a system from a different vendor.
   b. The microcomputer operators may be able to remove hardware and software components and modify them at home.
   c. Programming errors result in all similar transactions being processed incorrectly when those transactions are processed under the same conditions.
   d. Certain transactions may be automatically initiated by the microcomputers and management's authorization of these transactions may be implicit in its acceptance of the system design.   (Editors, ID: 7500)

14. Which of the following statements most likely represents a disadvantage for an entity that keeps microcomputer-prepared data files rather than manually prepared files?

   a. Attention is focused on the accuracy of the programming process rather than errors in individual transactions.
   b. It is usually easier for unauthorized persons to access and alter the files.
   c. Random error associated with processing similar transactions in different ways is usually greater.
   d. It is usually more difficult to compare recorded accountability with physical count of assets.
                                                          (5/94, AUD, #16, ID: 4681)

15. Which of the following characteristics distinguishes computer processing from manual processing?

   a. Computer processing virtually eliminates the occurrence of computational error normally associated with manual processing.
   b. The potential for systematic error is ordinarily greater in manual processing than in computerized processing.
   c. Errors or fraud in computer processing will be detected soon after their occurrences.
   d. Most computer systems are designed so that transaction trails useful for audit purposes do not exist.
                                                          (Editors, ID: 0289)

16. Which of the following control procedures most likely could prevent IT personnel from modifying programs to bypass programmed controls?

   a. Periodic management review of computer utilization reports and systems documentation
   b. Segregation of duties within IT for computer programming and computer operations
   c. Participation of user department personnel in designing and approving new systems
   d. Physical security of IT facilities in limiting access to IT equipment
                                                          (11/95, AUD, #14, amended, ID: 5961)

17. When an accounting application is processed by computer, an auditor cannot verify the reliable operation of programmed control procedures by

   a. Constructing a processing system for accounting applications and processing actual data from through-out the period through both the client's program and the auditor's program
   b. Manually comparing detail transaction files used by an edit program to the program's generated error listings to determine that errors were properly identified by the edit program
   c. Manually reperforming, as of a point in time, the processing of input data and comparing the simulated results to the actual results
   d. Periodically submitting auditor-prepared test data to the same computer process and evaluating the results
                                                          (Editors, ID: 0279)

18. Which of the following outcomes is a likely benefit of information technology used for internal control?

   a. Processing of unusual or nonrecurring transactions
   b. Enhanced timeliness of information
   c. Potential loss of data
   d. Recording of unauthorized transactions   (R/10, AUD, #28, ID: 9378)

19. In which of the following circumstances would an auditor expect to find that an entity implemented automated controls to reduce risks of misstatement?

    a. When errors are difficult to predict
    b. When misstatements are difficult to define
    c. When large, unusual, or nonrecurring transactions require judgment
    d. When transactions are high-volume and recurring   (R/10, AUD, #35, ID: 9385)

20. In an environment that is highly automated, an auditor determines that it is not possible to reduce detection risk solely by substantive tests of transactions. Under these circumstances, the auditor most likely would

    a. Perform tests of controls to support a lower level of assessed control risk
    b. Increase the sample size to reduce sampling risk and detection risk
    c. Adjust the materiality level and consider the effect on inherent risk
    d. Apply analytical procedures and consider the effect on control risk   (R/05, AUD, #44, ID: 7839)

21. Which of the following is **not** a major reason for maintaining an audit trail for a computer system?

    a. Deterrent to fraud
    b. Monitoring purposes
    c. Analytical procedures
    d. Query answering   (11/91, AUD, #24, ID: 2292)

22. Which of the following is an essential element of the audit trail in an electronic data interchange (EDI) system?

    a. Disaster recovery plans that ensure proper back-up of files
    b. Encrypted hash totals that authenticate messages
    c. Activity logs that indicate failed transactions
    d. Hardware security modules that store sensitive data   (R/99, AUD, #13, ID: 6829)

23. Which of the following activities most likely would detect whether payroll data were altered during processing?

    a. Monitor authorized distribution of data control sheets
    b. Use test data to verify the performance of edit routines
    c. Examine source documents for approval by supervisors
    d. Segregate duties between approval of hardware and software specifications
    (R/00, AUD, #14, ID: 6939)

24. Matthews Corp. has changed from a system of recording time worked on clock cards to a computerized payroll system in which employees record time in and out with magnetic cards. The EDP system automatically updates all payroll records. Because of this change

    a. A generalized computer audit program must be used.
    b. Part of the audit trail is altered.
    c. Transactions must be processed in batches.
    d. The potential for payroll-related fraud is diminished.   (Editors, ID: 0296)

25. An auditor who is testing IT controls in a payroll system would most likely use test data that contain conditions such as

    a. Deductions not authorized by employees
    b. Overtime not approved by supervisors
    c. Payroll checks with unauthorized signatures
    d. Time tickets with invalid job numbers   (Editors, ID: 0286)

26. In a computerized payroll system environment, an auditor would be **least** likely to use test data to test controls related to

    a. Missing employee numbers
    b. Proper approval of overtime by supervisors
    c. Time tickets with invalid job numbers
    d. Agreement of hours per clock cards with hours on time tickets   (5/91, AUD, #31, ID: 0049)

27. Which of the following could be difficult to determine because electronic evidence may **not** be retrievable after a specific period?

    a. The acceptance level of detection risk
    b. The timing of control and substantive tests
    c. Whether to adopt substantive or reliance test strategies
    d. The assessed level of inherent risk   (R/09, AUD, #16, ID: 8816)

28. An auditor would most likely be concerned with which of the following controls in a distributed data processing system?

    a. Hardware controls
    b. Systems documentation controls
    c. Access controls
    d. Disaster recovery controls   (5/91, AUD, #16, ID: 0273)

29. To obtain evidence that on-line access controls are properly functioning, an auditor most likely would

    a. Create checkpoints at periodic intervals after live data processing to test for unauthorized use of the system
    b. Examine the transaction log to discover whether any transactions were lost or entered twice due to a system malfunction
    c. Enter invalid identification numbers or passwords to ascertain whether the system rejects them
    d. Vouch a random sample of processed transactions to assure proper authorization   (5/93, AUD, #41, ID: 3937)

30. A client that recently installed a new accounts payable system assigned employees a user identification code (UIC) and a separate password. Each UIC is a person's name, and the individual's password is the same as the UIC. Users are not required to change their passwords at initial log-in nor do passwords ever expire. Which of the following statements does **not** reflect a limitation of the client's computer-access control?

    a. Employees can easily guess fellow employees' passwords.
    b. Employees are not required to change passwords.
    c. Employees can circumvent procedures to segregate duties.
    d. Employees are not required to take regular vacations.   (R/05, AUD, #42, ID: 7837)

31. Which of the following would an auditor ordinarily consider the greatest risk regarding an entity's use of electronic data interchange (EDI)?

    a. Authorization of EDI transactions
    b. Duplication of EDI transmissions
    c. Improper distribution of EDI transactions
    d. Elimination of paper documents   (6/99, AUD, #3, ID: 6850)

32. Which of the following controls is a processing control designed to ensure the reliability and accuracy of data processing?

	Limit test	Validity check test
a.	Yes	Yes
b.	No	No
c.	No	Yes
d.	Yes	No

    (11/94, AUD, #38, ID: 5111)

Items 33 and 34 are based on the following:

Invoice #	Product	Quantity	Unit price
201	F10	150	$ 5.00
202	G15	200	$10.00
203	H20	250	$25.00
204	K35	300	$30.00

33. Which of the following numbers represents the record count?

   a. 1
   b. 4
   c. 810
   d. 900   (5/98, AUD, #3, ID: 6620)

34. Which of the following most likely represents a hash total?

   a. FGHK80
   b. 4
   c. 204
   d. 810   (5/98, AUD, #4, ID: 6621)

35. Which of the following is usually a benefit of using electronic funds transfer for international cash transactions?

   a. Improvement of the audit trail for cash receipts and disbursements
   b. Creation of self-monitoring access controls
   c. Reduction of the frequency of data entry errors
   d. Off-site storage of source documents for cash transactions   (R/99, AUD, #8, ID: 6824)

36. Which of the following statements is correct concerning the security of messages in an electronic data interchange (EDI) system?

   a. When the confidentiality of data is the primary risk, message authentication is the preferred control rather than encryption.
   b. Encryption performed by physically secure hardware devices is more secure than encryption performed by software.
   c. Message authentication in EDI systems performs the same function as segregation of duties in other information systems.
   d. Security at the transaction phase in EDI systems is not necessary because problems at that level will usually be identified by the service provider.   (R/99, AUD, #12, ID: 6828)

37. The completeness of IT-generated sales figures can be tested by comparing the number of items listed on the daily sales report with the number of items billed on the actual invoices. This process uses

   a. Check digits
   b. Control totals
   c. Process tracing data
   d. Validity tests   (Editors, ID: 0292)

38. An IT input control is designed to ensure that

   a. Only authorized personnel have access to the computer area.
   b. Machine processing is accurate.
   c. Data received for processing are properly authorized and converted to machine readable form.
   d. Electronic data processing has been performed as intended for the particular application.
                                                               (Editors, ID: 0306)

39. A customer intended to order 100 units of product Z96014, but incorrectly ordered nonexistent product Z96015. Which of the following controls most likely would detect this error?

    a. Check digit verification
    b. Record count
    c. Hash total
    d. Redundant data check   (5/98, AUD, #5, ID: 6622)

40. Which of the following input controls is a numeric value computed to provide assurance that the original value has not been altered in construction or transmission?

    a. Hash total
    b. Parity check
    c. Encryption
    d. Check digit   (5/98, AUD, #8, ID: 6625)

41. When an auditor tests a computerized accounting system, which of the following is true of the test data approach?

    a. Several transactions of each type must be tested.
    b. Test data are processed by the client's computer programs under the auditor's control.
    c. Test data must consist of all possible valid and invalid conditions.
    d. The program tested is different from the program used throughout the year by the client.
                                                                 (5/95, AUD, #72, ID: 5690)

42. Which of the following is the primary reason that many auditors hesitate to use embedded audit modules?

    a. Embedded audit modules cannot be protected from computer viruses.
    b. Auditors are required to monitor embedded audit modules continuously to obtain valid results.
    c. Embedded audit modules can easily be modified through management tampering.
    d. Auditors are required to be involved in the system design of the application to be monitored.
                                                                 (R/02, AUD, #20, ID: 7110)

Item 43 is based on the following flowchart:

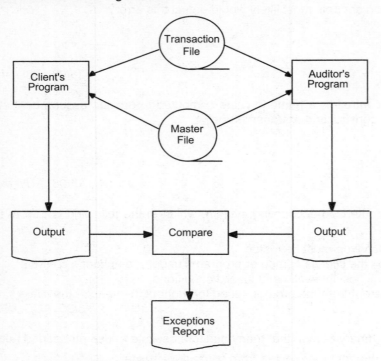

43. The preceding flowchart depicts
    a. Program code checking
    b. Parallel simulation
    c. Controlled reprocessing
    d. Integrated test facility
    (Editors, ID: 0308)

44. An auditor most likely would test for the presence of unauthorized IT program changes by running
    a. A program with test data
    b. A check digit verification program
    c. A source code comparison program
    d. A program that computes control totals
    (11/92, AUD, #37, amended, ID: 2971)

45. Which of the following computer-assisted auditing techniques allows fictitious and real transactions to be processed together without client operating personnel being aware of the testing process?
    a. Integrated test facility
    b. Input controls matrix
    c. Parallel simulation
    d. Data entry monitor
    (11/94, AUD, #70, ID: 5143)

46. Which of the following computer-assisted auditing techniques processes client input data on a controlled program under the auditor's control to test controls in the computer system?
    a. Test data
    b. Review of program logic
    c. Integrated test facility
    d. Parallel simulation
    (R/01, AUD, #17, ID: 7032)

47. An auditor would **least** likely use computer software to

    a. Construct parallel simulations
    b. Access client data files
    c. Prepare spreadsheets
    d. Assess IT control risk   (5/93, AUD, #40, amended, ID: 3936)

48. Processing data through the use of simulated files provides an auditor with information about the operating effectiveness of control policies and procedures. One of the techniques involved in this approach makes use of

    a. Controlled reprocessing
    b. An integrated test facility
    c. Input validation
    d. Program code checking   (11/92, AUD, #36, ID: 2970)

49. An auditor who wishes to capture an entity's data as transactions are processed and continuously test the entity's computerized information system most likely would use which of the following techniques?

    a. Snapshot application
    b. Embedded audit module
    c. Integrated data check
    d. Test data generator   (R/01, AUD, #15, ID: 7030)

50. In parallel simulation, actual client data are reprocessed using an auditor software program. An advantage of using parallel simulation, instead of performing tests of controls without a computer, is that

    a. The test includes all types of transaction errors and exceptions that may be encountered.
    b. The client's computer personnel do not know when the data are being tested.
    c. There is no risk of creating potentially material errors in the client's data.
    d. The size of the sample can be greatly expanded at relatively little additional cost.
                                                (R/05, AUD, #17, ID: 7812)

51. When an auditor tests the internal controls of a computerized accounting system, which of the following is true of the test data approach?

    a. Test data are coded to a dummy subsidiary so they can be extracted from the system under actual operating conditions.
    b. Test data programs need not be tailor-made by the auditor for each client's computer applications.
    c. Test data programs usually consist of all possible valid and invalid conditions regarding compliance with internal controls.
    d. Test data are processed with the client's computer and the results are compared with the auditor's predetermined results.   (R/07, AUD, #17, ID: 8389)

52. In auditing an entity's computerized payroll transactions, an auditor would be **least** likely to use test data to test controls concerning

    a. Overpayment of employees for hours not worked
    b. Control and distribution of unclaimed checks
    c. Withholding of taxes and Social Security contributions
    d. Missing employee identification numbers   (R/09, AUD, #44, ID: 8844)

53. Which of the following is a computer-assisted audit technique that permits an auditor to insert the auditor's version of a client's program to process data and compare the output with the client's output?

    a. Test data module
    b. Frame relay protocol
    c. Remote node router
    d. Parallel simulation   (R/10, AUD, #14, ID: 9364)

54. A primary advantage of using generalized audit software packages to audit the financial statements of a client is that the auditor may

    a. Access information stored on computer files while having a limited understanding of the client's hardware and software features
    b. Consider increasing the use of substantive tests of transactions in place of analytical procedures
    c. Substantiate the accuracy of data through self-checking digits and hash totals
    d. Reduce the level of required tests of controls to a relatively small amount

(11/95, AUD, #52, amended, ID: 5999)

55. When conducting fieldwork for a physical inventory, an auditor can**not** perform which of the following steps using a generalized audit software package?

    a. Observing inventory
    b. Selecting sample items of inventory
    c. Analyzing data resulting from inventory
    d. Recalculating balances in inventory reports

(R/06, AUD, #49, ID: 8167)

56. Using personal computers in auditing may affect the methods used to review the work of staff assistants because

    a. Supervisory personnel may not have an understanding of the capabilities and limitations of personal computers.
    b. Working paper documentation may not contain readily observable details of calculations.
    c. Documenting the supervisory review may require assistance of management services personnel.
    d. The audit fieldwork standards for supervision may differ.

(Editors, ID: 0196)

57. When companies use information technology (IT) extensively, evidence may be available only in electronic form. What is an auditor's best course of action in such situations?

    a. Assess the control risk as high
    b. Use audit software to perform analytical procedures
    c. Use generalized audit software to extract evidence from client databases
    d. Perform limited tests of controls over electronic data

(R/07, AUD, #29, ID: 8401)

58. Which of the following is a term for an attest engagement in which a CPA assesses a client's commercial Internet site for predefined criteria that are designed to measure transaction integrity, information protection, and disclosure of business practices?

    a. ElectroNet
    b. EDIFACT
    c. TechSafe
    d. WebTrust

(R/99, AUD, #2, ID: 6818)

59. Which of the following is a professional engagement that a CPA may perform to provide assurance on a system's reliability?

    a. MAS AssurAbility
    b. CPA WebMaster
    c. MAS AttestSure
    d. CPA SysTrust

(R/06, AUD, #10, ID: 8128)

———————————————

Problem 7-2 SIMULATION: Flowchart

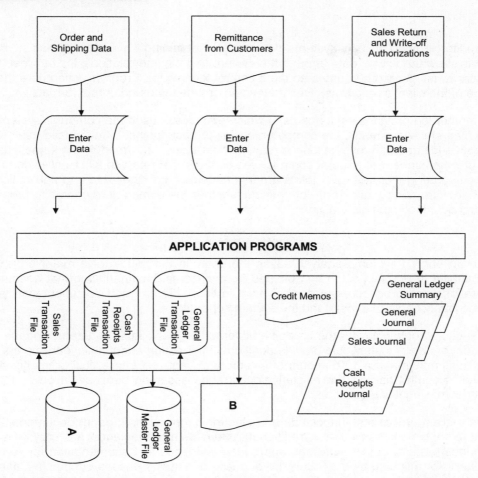

Based on the accompanying flowchart of a client's revenue cycle, what do the symbols marked A and B most likely represent?

Answer List

1. Accounts receivable master file
2. Cash disbursements transaction file
3. Customer checks
4. Customer orders
5. Receiving reports
6. Receiving report file
7. Remittance advice file
8. Sales invoices

(ID: 9207)

_____

Problem 7-3 SIMULATION: Research

IT poses specific risks to an entity's internal control. What section of the professional literature lists some of these risks?

	§			

(ID: 9208)

_____

Solution 7-1 MULTIPLE-CHOICE ANSWERS

Documentation

1. (a) An auditor is likely to use systems flowcharts in obtaining an understanding of internal control. Systems flowcharts show the flow of data through the system and the interrelationships between the processing steps and computer runs. A record count is an input control technique. Program listings are the source statements or language of the client's programs. Record layouts are the input and output formats. (ID: 0278)

2. (d) A computer log provides evidence as to which employees used the computer system and the operations performed by them. As a result, the computer log will protect against unauthorized use of the IT system, and it will provide an audit trail with respect to incompatible operations performed by the same individual. Incompatible functions are the concern of general controls, i.e., controls that relate to all IT activities. A self-checking digit system and computer-generated hash totals are input controls, i.e., they relate to application controls. An echo check is a hardware control aimed at determining whether the computer is operating properly. It has no effect on the control over incompatible functions. (ID: 0297)

Planning

3. (c) When an entity's systems analyst leaves the entity in the middle of a major project, the greatest assistance in continuing the project could be obtained from systems documentation that adequately describes the systems operations and procedures up to that point in time. Given good documentation, a new systems analyst could immediately begin to understand the systems operations. (ID: 2300)

4. (b) The auditor should consider the time when information is available in determining the timing of tests. Increasing the extent of cut-off tests would provide additional information about only year-end transactions. The nature of the business may make a 100% count of inventory at year-end impractical or insufficient. Increasing the assessed level of control risk for the existence/occurrence assertion because records are unavailable is unduly harsh, but decreasing it is unjustified. (ID: 6934)

5. (c) When a client processes financial data in electronic form without paper documentation, the auditor may audit on a more continuous basis than a traditional system, as a convenience, and may be required to audit on a more continuous basis to obtain sufficient, appropriate evidence as documentation for some transactions may only be available for a limited time. This is the opposite of discrete phases of planning, interim, and year-end fieldwork. The level of effort to search for management fraud and emphasis on the completeness assertion would likely not be significantly affected. (ID: 6838)

6. (d) When an auditor anticipates assessing control risk at a low level in a computerized environment, generally, the auditor would initially focus on general control procedures, which are those controls that relate to all or many computerized accounting activities and often include control over the development, modification, and maintenance of computer programs and control over the use of and changes to data maintained on computer files. (ID: 2789)

7. (c) When documentation is only retained for a short period of time, the auditor most likely would compensate for this limitation by performing tests several times during the year, rather than only at year-end. (ID: 8374)

Internal Control

8. (a) Controls in a database environment can be very specific as to which elements of a record can be accessed or changed, resulting in a more detailed set of authorizations. [Note: The examiners say to select the best answer.] Controls over data sharing should be appropriate for each user, usually resulting in diverse controls. Preferably, hardware management and software development are segregated. The relationship between authorization and processing usually is the same within a database and a non-database environment. (ID: 6933)

9. (c) There are time delays when data is processed in batches, so errors may not be detected immediately. The identification of errors in input data would be identified through various means such as the use of batch totals and normally would be part of the program. The processing of transactions in a batch system is uniform. (ID: 5110)

10. (a)   A weakness in internal control exists where an individual is in a position to both perpetrate and conceal an error or fraud. Hence, a systems programmer should not be given any control over the review or distribution of the output of the IT system. (ID: 2304)

11. (b)   Computer disruptions could destroy the only record of an online transaction. By their nature, sales transactions processed on the Internet don't involve sales invoice documents. Integrated test facilities, archiving, and data retention are issues that arise whether sales are on the Internet or entered into a computer system by the entity. (ID: 6826)

12. (a)   Preventive controls are generally more important than detective controls in EDI systems because of the speed with which goods and services are delivered. Objectives remain the same as for other information systems. Internal controls in EDI systems must be strong to minimize losses. Segregation of duties is not as important as protection of assets in an EDI system. (ID: 6827)

13. (b)   Both large computer systems and microcomputers are vulnerable to employee collusion and programming errors. Microcomputer hardware and software could more readily be removed from a place of business than large computer systems. (ID: 7500)

14. (b)   Many internal control procedures once performed by separate individuals in manual systems may be concentrated in systems that use computer processing. Therefore, an individual who has access to the computer may be in a position to perform incompatible functions. Answers (a) and (c) are false statements. Detailed ledger accounts may be maintained as easily with microcomputer data files as with manually prepared files. (ID: 4681)

15. (a)   An advantage of computer processing is that it virtually eliminates computational errors. Errors or fraud are not detected more quickly when computer processing is used. The potential for systematic errors is greater in computer processing than in manual processing. Transaction trails useful for audit purposes are created but the data may be available for only a short period of time. (ID: 0289)

16. (b)   A control procedure for preventing employees from modifying programs to bypass programmed controls is to segregate the functions of programming and computer operations. Answers (a), (c), and (d) are all appropriate IT controls but by themselves would not prevent IT employees from modifying programs. (ID: 5961)

17. (c)   The auditor would not be able to verify the reliable operation of programmed control procedures by the reperformance of the processing of the *client's* input data through the *client's* computer program as it would produce the same output as that created by the client. The auditor would be able to verify the reliable operation of control procedures when s/he is submitting auditor-prepared test data to the client's computer process, submitting actual data to the auditor's computer program, or utilizing an edit program, as these would allow the auditor to make comparisons between the client's expected output, using the client's data and computer program, and the auditor's expected results using auditor-prepared data, the auditor's computer program, and the auditor's edit program. (ID: 0279)

18. (b)   A likely benefit of IT used for internal control is *enhanced timeliness*, availability, and accuracy *of information*. Processing of large, unusual, or nonrecurring transactions is an example of a circumstance where manual controls of systems may be more suitable. Potential loss of data or inability to access data as required as well as recording of unauthorized or nonexistent transactions or inaccurate recording of transactions are examples of specific risks that IT poses to an entity's internal control. (ID: 9378)

19. (d)   An auditor would expect to find that an entity implemented automated controls to reduce risks of misstatement *when transactions are high-volume and recurring*; in situations where errors can be anticipated or predicted; or for control activities where the specific ways to perform the control can be adequately designed and automated. The other answer alternatives describe circumstances where judgment and discretion are required and thus manual controls of systems may be more suitable. (ID: 9385)

Evidence

20. (a)   When the auditor has determined that it is not possible or practicable to reduce the detection risks at the relevant assertion level to an acceptably low level with audit evidence obtained only from substantive procedures, s/he should perform tests of controls to obtain audit evidence about their operating effectiveness. The

auditor may find it impossible to design effective substantive procedures that by themselves provide sufficient appropriate audit evidence at the relevant assertion level when an entity conducts its business using information technology (IT) and no documentation of transactions is produced or maintained, other than through the IT system. Increasing the sample size for substantive tests in this circumstance would be ineffective as the question states that it is not possible to reduce detection risk solely by substantive tests of transactions. Changing the materiality level would be inappropriate. Further, changing the materiality level does not have an effect on inherent risk, which is the susceptibility of an assertion to misstatement without any internal controls. Analytics performed by the auditor do not have an effect on control risk, which is the risk that the entity's internal controls will not detect material misstatements in the financial statements. (ID: 7839)

21. (c) Analytical procedures involve the analysis of the plausible relationship among both financial and nonfinancial data. A lack of an accounting audit trail for a computer system would not preclude the auditor from performing analytical procedures. The purpose of an audit trail would be to monitor the system, answer queries, and deter fraud. (ID: 2292)

22. (c) Logs with failed transactions are examined to determine whether the corrected transactions were eventually executed and to detect attempts of unauthorized system use. Proper file backup is a recovery issue. Message authentication and hardware security modules are security issues. (ID: 6829)

23. (b) With test data, the auditor can readily compare actual results to anticipated results. Monitoring distribution wouldn't detect data alteration. Source documents could be correctly approved and data could be later altered in processing without impact on the source documents. Segregation of duties discourages fraud, but not unintentional mistakes. Further, approval of hardware and software specifications are not necessarily the most critical functions to segregate in the IT area. (ID: 6939)

24. (b) When time clock cards are used, they constitute a form of physical evidence that can be examined in determining the proper amount of wage expense. By changing to an IT system, part of the audit trail is altered—although not necessarily destroyed. The IT system can be audited in numerous ways that don't require the use of a generalized audit program. The potential for payroll fraud may or may not change depending on the internal controls incorporated into the new payroll system. The system automatically updates the payroll records whenever anyone punches in or out. Batch processing is eliminated in this system. (ID: 0296)

25. (d) An auditor testing IT controls in a payroll system would most likely use test data containing time tickets with invalid job numbers. The computer should be programmed to compare job numbers on the time tickets with a list of valid, authorized job numbers. Answers (a) and (b) relate to preparation of data before it enters the IT system. Answer (c) relates to controls after data processing has taken place. (ID: 0286)

26. (b) Proper approval of overtime would most likely be made by inspection of the related documents and reports to assess whether the authorization policy was applied. The computerized system would be unable to make such a judgment. The computerized payroll system could be utilized to test controls related to missing employee numbers, time tickets with invalid job numbers, and agreement of hours per clock cards with hours on time tickets. (ID: 0049)

27. (b) *The timing of control and substantive tests* could be difficult to determine because electronic evidence may not be retrievable after a specific period if files are changed and if backup files do not exist. The auditor must consider the entity's data retention policies when determining the timing of some procedures. The determination of the other answer alternatives is not made more difficult because electronic evidence may not be retrievable after a specific period. (ID: 8816)

General Controls

28. (c) A distributed data processing system is one in which many different users have access to the main computer through various computer locations. Thus, access controls, which restrict access to the main computer, are necessary to maintain a strong internal control structure, because those with access to the computer are in a position to perform incompatible functions. Hardware controls, systems documentation controls, and disaster recovery controls would not be as important in assessing control risk and would not likely present unusual problems in a distributed system. (ID: 0273)

29. (c)   Password controls, used in restricting access to computers, are designed to preclude access capabilities of those employees whose regular functions are incompatible with computer use. To obtain evidence that user identification and password controls are functioning as designed, an auditor would most likely examine a sample of invalid passwords or numbers to determine whether the computer is recognizing the invalid passwords and rejecting access. Answer (a) checks the level of authorization an employee has once within the system rather than access to the online system. Answer (b) is a procedure for determining the completeness of transaction processing. Answer (d) does not address whether the online access is being limited or circumvented.
(ID: 3937)

30. (d)   The question asks for a response that is not a limitation of the computer-access control. While not requiring employees to take regular vacations is a poor practice from an internal control standpoint, it does not reflect a limitation of the *computer-access* control. The ability to guess fellow employees' passwords easily, the lack of a requirement to change passwords, and the ability to circumvent procedures to segregate duties reflect limitations of the computer-access controls.
(ID: 7837)

Application Controls

31. (c)   Improper transactions, regardless of the media, are usually the greatest risk. Appropriate authorization of EDI transactions doesn't present a risk. Duplication of EDI transactions would likely be found by one of the involved parties upon reconciliation. Elimination of paper documents is a goal of EDI.
(ID: 6850)

32. (a)   Computers can be programmed to perform a wide range of edit tasks on records as they are being inputted into the system. If a particular record does not meet the test, it would not be processed. Edit tests include limit tests, validity check tests, check digit tests, etc.
(ID: 5111)

33. (b)   A record count is a count of the number of records in a batch or file or similar group.
(ID: 6620)

34. (d)   A hash total is a numeric total with meaning only as a control. Because of the alpha characters in the product codes, a hash total cannot be derived from product codes without a conversion of letters into numeric amounts. Totals of quantities have meaning beyond a control.
(ID: 6621)

35. (c)   With EDI, information is entered into a system once and transmitted to other parties. These other parties do not have to re-enter the information into their systems, eliminating an opportunity for errors to occur. Using EDI, audit trails typically are less clear, if anything. Creation of self-monitoring access controls and off-site storage of source documents for cash transactions could occur with or without EDI.
(ID: 6824)

36. (b)   Physically secure hardware devices are less likely to be compromised than software. Message authentication provides assurance about messages' sources. Encryption provides assurance about privacy. Message authentication performs similarly to control duties in non-IT systems, but not the segregation of duties aspect. Service providers usually do not provide security at the transaction level.
(ID: 6828)

37. (b)   The use of control totals is an example of a processing control which is designed to provide reasonable assurances that EDP has been performed as intended for the particular application, i.e., that all transactions are processed as authorized, that no authorized transactions were omitted, and that no unauthorized transactions were added. A *check digit* is a number that is added at the end of a numerical entry to check its accuracy. A *validity test,* is designed to ensure that only data meeting specific criteria are allowed. Answer (c) apparently refers to "tagging" of data, a technique used by auditors to follow a transaction through the processing cycle.
(ID: 0292)

38. (c)   Input controls are designed to provide reasonable assurance that data received by IT have been properly authorized, converted into machine readable form and identified as well as that data has not been lost, added, duplicated, or otherwise improperly changed. Answer (a) describes an access control. Answer (b) describes an output control. Answer (d) describes a processing control.
(ID: 0306)

39. (a)   A check digit is a digit that is appended to a piece of numeric data following a pre-specified routine. A record count is a count of the number of records in a batch or file or similar group. A hash total is a numeric total with meaning only as a control. A redundant data check would check one piece of data against another, not the elements of a product code label against each other.
(ID: 6622)

40. (d) A check digit is a digit that is appended to a piece of numeric data following a pre-specified routine. A hash total is a numeric total with meaning only as a control. A parity check is an extra bit attached to the end of a string of bits to detect errors resulting from electronic interference when transmitting the string. Encryption is the conversion of a message into a coded message. (ID: 6625)

CAAT

41. (b) In the test data approach to testing a computerized accounting system, test data are processed by the client's computer programs under the auditor's control. The auditor will determine how many transactions and what types of transactions to test which may or may not include several transactions of each type. The auditor need not include test data for all possible valid and invalid conditions. The object is to test the client's program that is used throughout the year and the auditor must take steps to make sure that the program being tested is the one that is actually used in routine processing; thus, a different program would not be tested. (ID: 5690)

42. (d) Embedded audit modules can be difficult to install once the application program is operational, but efficiently included during system design. Embedded audit modules can be protected from viruses as well as other applications. Sporadic or occasional monitoring of embedded audit modules can produce valid results. Management tampering can modify other applications as easily as embedded audit modules. (ID: 7110)

43. (b) In parallel simulation, the auditor compares the results of the client's processing with results obtained by using the client's input and files and the auditor's own program. In program code checking, the auditor reviews the client's program documentation, including a narrative description and the source code. An integrated test facility includes processing of dummy records with the client's records using the client's program. In controlled reprocessing, the auditor maintains control over the reprocessing of previously processed results using a version of the program the auditor has tested and compares the computer output of the original processing and reprocessing. (ID: 0308)

44. (c) A source code comparison program could be used to compare the original code written for a specific program to the current code in use for that program. Thus, it would make note of any differences in the program from the time it was originally written. Test data would generally be used to test the output of the program but would provide no evidence as to whether the program code had been changed. A check digit program involves the use of a digit that is added to the end of a piece of numeric data to permit the data to be checked for accuracy during input, processing, or output. Control totals are totals computed at different times in the computer process and are used as input, processing, and output controls. They would not provide evidence as to whether any changes were made to the original program code. (ID: 2971)

45. (a) An integrated test facility (ITF) processes fictitious data with real data in order to test computer controls; client personnel are unaware of the testing. An input control matrix documents controls and their presence. Parallel simulation processes client input data on an auditor-controlled program to test controls; test data is not utilized. The term "data entry monitor" is not commonly used. (ID: 5143)

46. (d) Parallel simulation processes actual client data through an auditor-controlled program. Test data and integrated test facilities run fictitious data through the client's programs. A review of program logic does not test any data. (ID: 7032)

47. (d) After obtaining an understanding of the client's IT controls, the auditor must assess control risk for the IT portion of the client's internal control. Assessing control risk is the process of evaluating the effectiveness of an entity's internal control policies and procedures in preventing or detecting material misstatements in the financial statements. Procedures to judge the effectiveness of internal control design would include inquiries, observations, and inspections. One would not need computer software to accomplish this task. Gaining access to client data files, preparing spreadsheets, and constructing parallel simulations would all make use of computer software. (ID: 3936)

48. (b) Processing data through the use of simulated files makes use of an integrated test facility. Using this method, the auditor creates a fictitious entity within the client's actual data files. The auditor then processes fictitious data for the entity as part of the client's regular data processing. Controlled reprocessing involves the processing of the client's actual data through the auditor's controlled copy of the client's program. Input validation is concerned only that the inputted data is accurate. Program code checking involves analysis of the client's actual program. (ID: 2970)

49. (b)   Embedded audit modules are coded into a client's application to collect data for the auditor. Integrated data checks and test data generators involve auditor-controlled fictitious data. Snapshot applications capture screen images. (ID: 7030)

50. (d)   Compared to auditing without a computer, the size of the sample can be greatly expanded at little cost using a computer. Parallel simulation might not include all types of transaction errors and exceptions that may be encountered. Using parallel simulation is no guarantee that the client's personnel are unaware that the data is being tested. As there is little risk of creating material errors in the client's data with a non-computer audit procedure, this hardly can be said to be an advantage of parallel simulation using a computer over not using a computer at all. (ID: 7812)

51. (d)   In the test data approach to testing a computerized accounting system, test data are processed by the client's computer programs under the auditor's control. No dummy subsidiary is involved. Test data must be customized to each audit. The auditor need not include test data for all possible valid and invalid conditions. (ID: 8389)

52. (b)   In auditing an entity's computerized payroll transactions, an auditor would be least likely to use test data to test controls concerning control and distribution of unclaimed checks. The other answer alternatives are examples of data that can be accessed and tested via computer applications while controls over unclaimed checks are more likely to be manual. (ID: 8844)

53. (d)   A parallel simulation is a computer-assisted audit technique that permits an auditor to insert the auditor's version of a client's program to process data and compare the output with the client's output. (ID: 9364)

Generalized Audit Software

54. (a)   One of the reasons for using generalized audit software (GAS) is that it enables the auditor to gain access and test information stored in the client's files without having to acquire a complete understanding of the client's IT system. Although the use of GAS enables the auditor to deal more effectively with large quantities of data and produces economies in the audit while increasing the quality of the audit, it cannot replace analytical procedures. Self-checking digits and hash totals are controls in the client system. Reducing the level of required tests of controls to a relatively small amount is the result of assessing control risk and applying preliminary tests of controls, not a result of using a GAS package. (ID: 5999)

55. (a)   While the exact procedures performed will vary among software packages, generalized audit software is used to accomplish six basic types of audit tasks: (1) examining records for quality, completeness, consistency and correctness; (2) testing calculations and making computations; (3) comparing data on separate files; (4) selecting, printing and analyzing audit samples; (5) summarizing or resequencing data and performing analyses; and (6) comparing data obtained through other audit procedures with company records. (ID: 8167)

56. (b)   Working paper documentation may not contain readily observable details of calculations because these calculations would be performed by the computer. If supervisory personnel do not have an understanding of the capabilities and limitations of personal computers, the auditor should seek the assistance of a professional possessing such skills, who may be either on the auditor's staff or an outside professional. The auditor's responsibilities with respect to using such a professional are equivalent to those for other assistants. The audit fieldwork standards for supervision do not differ when personal computers are used in an audit. (ID: 0196)

57. (c)   Generalized audit software (GAS) makes it possible for an auditor to access data in electronic form; typical GAS will analyze data and present results in a meaningful and convenient form. Assessing control risk as high may result in unnecessary additional audit procedures; an IT system may have strong internal control, and consequently, low control risk. Analytics cannot be performed if the information is available only in electronic form and there is no means to access it. If data is available only in electronic form, tests of controls over that data likely should be extensive, rather than limited. (ID: 8401)

Definitions

58. (d)   The CPA WebTrust symbol on a web site indicates that the organization meets AICPA business practice disclosures, transaction integrity, and information protection criteria. A specially trained and licensed

CPA reviews compliance with these criteria every 90 days. EDIFACT is an international EDI format. (ANSI X12 is a domestic EDI format.) ElectroNet and TechSafe are not widely used terms. (ID: 6818)

59. (d) CPA SysTrust is an attestation service developed in part by the AICPA, that is designed to provide assurance on whether a system's controls are operating effectively and allow the system to function reliably. Answers (a), (b), and (c) are nonsense answer choices. (ID: 8128)

PERFORMANCE BY TOPICS

Each category below parallels a topic covered in Chapter 7. Record the number and percentage of questions you answered correctly in each topic.

Documentation

Question #	Correct	√
1		
2		
# Questions	2	
# Correct		
% Correct		

Planning

Question #	Correct	√
3		
4		
5		
6		
7		
# Questions	5	
# Correct		
% Correct		

Internal Control

Question #	Correct	√
8		
9		
10		
11		
12		
13		
14		
15		
16		
17		
18		
19		
# Questions	12	
# Correct		
% Correct		

Evidence

Question #	Correct	√
20		
21		
22		
23		
24		
25		
26		
27		
# Questions	8	
# Correct		
% Correct		

General Controls

Question #	Correct	√
28		
29		
30		
# Questions	3	
# Correct		
% Correct		

Application Controls

Question #	Correct	√
31		
32		
33		
34		
35		
36		
37		
38		
39		
40		
# Questions	10	
# Correct		
% Correct		

CAAT

Question #	Correct	√
41		
42		
43		
44		
45		
46		
47		
48		
49		
50		
51		
52		
53		
# Questions	13	
# Correct		
% Correct		

Generalized Audit Software

Question #	Correct	√
54		
55		
56		
57		
# Questions	4	
# Correct		
% Correct		

Definitions

Question #	Correct	√
58		
59		
# Questions	2	
# Correct		
% Correct		

Solution 7-2 SIMULATION ANSWER: Flowchart

A. 1

This symbol represents a file. In the revenue cycle application process, the most likely output among the choices given is an accounts receivable master file, especially since there is a cash receipts transaction file. A remittance file (G) is not typically a separately constructed file. Answers F and B are not part of the revenue cycle.

B. 8

This symbol represents some sort of printed output. Sales invoices are the most likely output from the system at this point. The customer orders would most likely be at the beginning of the revenue cycle. Receiving reports are not part of the revenue cycle. Customer checks are not created by the system but are received from the customer.

(ID: 9207)

Solution 7-3 SIMULATION ANSWER: Research

AU	§	314	60

.60   IT also poses specific risks to an entity's internal control, including:

- Reliance on systems or programs that are processing data inaccurately, processing inaccurate data, or both.

- Unauthorized access to data that may result in destruction of data or improper changes to data, including the recording of unauthorized or nonexistent transactions or inaccurate recording of transactions.

- Unauthorized changes to data in master files.

- Unauthorized changes to systems or programs.

- Failure to make necessary changes to systems or programs.

- Inappropriate manual intervention.

- Potential loss of data or inability to access data as required.   (ID: 9208)

_____

Wondering how to allocate your study time?

In your excitement to answer multiple choice questions, don't forget that the examiners ask questions in simulation format as well!

The first pass through a chapter:

1. Strive to answer **all** the multiple choice questions and the objective elements of the simulations, except for research elements.

2. Choose one or more of the simulations to answer completely. Read the questions and responses for the simulation elements that you don't answer.

3. At the very beginning of your review, don't worry about whether you finish questions within the time allocated. As you become more familiar with the content and the way the examiners ask questions, your speed will increase. Start concerning yourself about time when you are on the first pass through your fourth or fifth chapter.

When you review the chapter later:

1. Answer **at least** those objective questions that you did not understand the first time. (If you had a lucky guess, did you really understand?)

2. Select a new simulation to answer completely. Read the questions and responses for the simulation elements that you don't answer.

When you review the chapter for the final time (for some chapters, the second time may **be** the final time):

1. Answer the questions "cold turkey" (without reviewing the text materials just before answering questions). Before answering questions, only review the notes you would review just before the exam. For a whole exam section, this should take less than five minutes.

2. Answer **at least** those objective questions that you did not understand the first time.

3. Select a new simulation, if available, to answer completely. Read the questions and responses for the simulation elements that you don't answer.

Remember, with the techniques and information in your material,

A passing score is well within reach!

———————

STUDY TIP: STANDARD AUDIT REPORT

You need to know the three paragraphs of the standard audit report by name, in order, and word for word. Learning the modifications for various situations is considerably easier than learning dozens of reports. These modifications are summarized in Exhibit 26, *Most Common Conditions Requiring Modification of Report.*

FAQ

The following issue is an apparent (but not an actual) contradiction. For a more complete discussion, see the related material in the text and explanations to questions.

Q: Why is it that the standards state that an auditor can express an unqualified opinion on one of the financial statements and express a qualified or adverse opinion or disclaim an opinion on another; and also include guidance that, generally, piecemeal opinions should not be expressed when the auditor has disclaimed an opinion or has expressed an adverse opinion on the financial statements taken as a whole?

A: An auditor may express an unqualified opinion on the balance sheet and a disclaimer of opinion on the income statement. These statements are at the same level. The balance sheet is not part of the income statement. However, if an auditor disclaims an opinion on the income statement and expresses an opinion on revenue in the income statement, this might overshadow the disclaimer of opinion on the income statement. The difference from the first situation is that revenue is a part of the income statement. The opinion on revenue is known as a piecemeal opinion.

CHAPTER 8

REPORTS ON AUDITED FINANCIAL STATEMENTS

CHAPTER 8

REPORTS ON AUDITED FINANCIAL STATEMENTS

I. **Reporting Standards**

A. **Adherence to GAAP (AU 410)**

1. **Definitions**

a. **GAAP** The term *generally accepted accounting principles* (GAAP) as used in reporting standards includes not only accounting principles and practices but also the methods of applying them. The first reporting standard (see below) does not require a statement of fact by the auditor but rather an opinion as to whether the financial statements are presented in conformity with such principles.

b. **GAAP Hierarchy** GAAP hierarchy identifies the sources of accounting principles and the framework for selecting principles to be used in the preparation of financial statements.

2. **First Standard of Reporting**

Exhibit 1 ▶ The First Standard of Reporting

> The auditor must state in the auditor's report whether the financial statements are presented in accordance with generally accepted accounting principles.
>
> Editor note: An identification of the country of origin of those generally accepted accounting principles is also required.

The American Institute of Certified Public Accountants' (AICPA) Code of Professional Conduct (ET 203) provides that an unqualified opinion should not be expressed if the financial statements contain a material departure from accounting principles promulgated by bodies they have designated unless, due to unusual circumstances, adherence to the principles would make the statements misleading. Therefore, ET 203 implies that application of officially established accounting principles results in the fair presentation of financial position, results of operations, and cash flows in conformity with GAAP.

Editor note: When an auditor reports on financial statements prepared in accordance with a comprehensive basis of accounting other than GAAP, the first standard of reporting is satisfied by stating in the auditor's report that the basis of presentation is a comprehensive basis of accounting other than GAAP and by expressing an opinion (or disclaiming an opinion) on whether the financial statements are presented in conformity with the comprehensive basis of accounting used.

3. **Regulated Companies (AU 544)** The basic principles of accounting encompassed by the term *GAAP* which pertain to business enterprises in general also apply to companies whose accounting practices are prescribed by governmental regulatory authorities or commissions, for example, public utilities and insurance companies. Thus, the first reporting standard is equally applicable to opinions on financial statements of such regulated companies presented for purposes *other than* filings with their respective supervisory agencies; and material variances from GAAP, and their effects, should be dealt with in the independent auditor's report in the same manner followed for companies which are not regulated.

4. **Professional Judgment** Professional judgment determines which accounting principles should be used in any situation. The auditor's judgment should be applied within the framework of GAAP.

    The auditor's opinion that financial statements present fairly an entity's financial position, results of operations, and cash flows in conformity with GAAP should be based on the auditor's judgment as to whether the

    a. Accounting principles selected and applied have general acceptance;

    b. Accounting principles are appropriate in the circumstances;

    c. Financial statements, including the related notes, are informative of matters that may affect their use, understanding, and interpretation;

    d. Information presented in the financial statements is classified and summarized in a reasonable manner, that is, neither too detailed nor too condensed; and

    e. Financial statements reflect the underlying transactions and events in a manner that presents the financial position, results of operations, and cash flows stated within a range of acceptable limits that are reasonable and practicable to attain in financial statements.

5. **Sources of GAAP** The AICPA is authorized under ET 203 to designate bodies to establish accounting principles. These designated bodies and their respective accounting principles are:

    a. **FASB** The Financial Accounting Standards Board (FASB) with respect to the *FASB Accounting Standards Codification*™ (ASC or Codification). The Codification is the official source of authoritative US GAAP for nongovernmental entities.

    b. **GASB** The Governmental Accounting Standards Board (GASB), with respect to Statements of Governmental Accounting Standards issued in July 1984 and thereafter. The GASB establishes accounting principles for state and local governmental entities.

    c. **FASAB** Federal Accounting Standards Advisory Board (FASAB), with respect to Statements of Federal Accounting Standards adopted and issued in March 1993 and subsequently. The FASAB establishes accounting principles for federal government entities.

    d. **IASB** International Accounting Standards Board, with respect to International Financial Reporting Standards (IFRS)

6. **Nongovernmental GAAP** The FASB's Codification organizes US GAAP into various accounting topics. For reference by public companies, the relevant SEC guidance is also included—it is displayed below the related topical content. The content contained in the SEC sections of the Codification is provided for convenience and related only to SEC registrants. The SEC sections of the Codification are not the authoritative sources of such content and do not contain the entire population of SEC rules, regulations, interpretive releases, and staff guidance.

    a. **GAAP Hierarchy** With the Codification, only two levels of US GAAP exist:

        (1) Authoritative represented by the Codification

             Any literature not included in the Codification is nonauthoritative with one exception—rules and interpretive releases of the SEC under authority of federal securities laws are also authoritative sources of GAAP for public companies, also known as issuers (public companies) or SEC registrants.

(2) Nonauthoritative represented by all other literature

Sources of nonauthoritative accounting guidance and literature include, for example, practices that are widely recognized and prevalent either generally or in the industry, FASB Concepts Statements, AICPA Issues Papers, International Financial Reporting Standards of the International Accounting Standards Board (IASB), pronouncements of professional associations or regulatory agencies, Technical Information Service Inquiries and Replies included in AICPA Technical Practice Aids, and accounting textbooks, handbooks, and articles.

b. **Unspecified Treatment** If the guidance for a transaction or event is not specified within a source of authoritative GAAP for that entity, an entity shall first consider accounting principles for similar transactions or events within a source of authoritative GAAP for that entity and then consider nonauthoritative guidance from other sources. The appropriateness of other sources of accounting guidance depends on its relevance to particular circumstances, the specificity of the guidance, the general recognition of the issuer or author as an authority, and the extent of its use in practice.

7. **State & Local Governments GAAP Hierarchy** The hierarchy for sources of GAAP for state and local government entities is composed of four categories, or levels of authority, as follows.

a. Level one: consists of GASB Statements and Interpretations, as well as AICPA and FASB pronouncements made applicable to state and local governmental entities by GASB Statements or Interpretations.

b. Level two: consists of GASB Technical Bulletins and when cleared by the GASB, AICPA Statements of Position and Industry Auditing and Accounting Guides, to the extent the AICPA makes these latter documents applicable to state and local government entities.

c. Level three: consists of AICPA Practice Bulletins to the extent these bulletins are made applicable to state and local governmental entities and cleared by the GASB. Also included are consensus positions of a group of accountants organized by the GASB that attempt to reach consensus positions on accounting issues applicable to state and local governmental entities.

d. Level four: consists of questions and answers published by the GASB staff, as well as practices that are widely recognized and prevalent in state and local government.

8. **Federal Government GAAP Hierarchy** The hierarchy for sources of GAAP for federal government units is also composed of four categories, or levels of authority. These are:

a. Level one: consists of Federal Accounting Standards Advisory Board (FASAB) Statements and Interpretations, as well as AICPA and FASB pronouncements made applicable to federal governmental entities by FASAB Statements or Interpretations.

b. Level two: consists of FASAB Technical Bulletins and, if specifically made applicable to federal entities by the AICPA and cleared by the FASAB, AICPA Industry Audit and Accounting Guides and AICPA SOP.

c. Level three: consists of AICPA Practice Bulletins, if specifically made applicable to federal governmental entities and cleared by the FASAB, as well as Technical Releases of the Accounting and Auditing Policy Committee of the FASAB.

    d.   Level four: includes implementation guides published by the FASAB staff, as well as practices that are widely recognized and prevalent in the federal government.

9.   **Conflicts / Unspecified Treatment (Governmental Entities)**

    a.   **Conflicts** If there is a conflict between accounting principles relevant to the circumstances from sources in different categories, the auditor should follow the treatment specified by the source in the higher category. For example, category (B) should be followed before categories (C) or (D).

    b.   **Unspecified Treatment** If the accounting treatment of a transaction or event is not specified by a pronouncement covered by ET 203 or another source of established accounting principles, the auditor should consider other accounting literature. The appropriateness of other accounting literature depends on its relevance to particular circumstances, the specificity of the guidance, and the general recognition of the issuer or author as an authority.

Exhibit 2 ▶ Governmental GAAP Hierarchy

<u>State and Local Governments</u>	<u>Federal Governmental Units</u>
CATEGORY A (LEVEL ONE)	
GASB Statements	FASAB Statements
GASB Interpretations	FASAB Interpretations
AICPA and FASB Pronouncements if made applicable to state and local governments by GASB Statements or Interpretations	AICPA and FASB pronouncements made applicable to federal governmental entities by FASAB Statements or Interpretations
CATEGORY B (LEVEL TWO)	
GASB Technical Bulletins	FASAB Technical Bulletins
AICPA Industry Audit and Accounting Guides and Statements of Position*	AICPA Industry Audit and Accounting Guides and AICPA SOP**
CATEGORY C (LEVEL THREE)	
GASB EITF Consensuses (not yet organized by GASB)	AICPA Practice Bulletins**
AICPA Practice Bulletins*	Technical Releases of the Accounting and Auditing Policy Committee of the FASAB
CATEGORY D (LEVEL FOUR)	
"Qs and As" published by GASB staff	Implementation guides published by the FASAB staff
Prevalent practice	Practices that are widely recognized and prevalent in the federal government
* If made applicable to state and local governments by AICPA	**If specifically made applicable to federal governmental entities and cleared by the FASAB.

B.   Consistency (AU 420)

Exhibit 3 ▶ The Second Standard of Reporting—the Consistency Standard

> The auditor must identify in the auditor's report those circumstances in which such principles [GAAP] have not been consistently observed in the current period in relation to the preceding period.

1.   **Consistency Is Implied in Standard Report** Consistency in application of accounting principles is implied in the standard auditor's report, i.e., *if satisfied*, the auditor does **not** refer to consistency in the audit report.

2.   **Objective of Consistency Standard** The objective of the second standard of reporting is to provide assurance that if comparability has been materially affected by changes in accounting principles that it will be reported appropriately by the auditor.

3.   **Explanatory Paragraph Required** If there has been a change in accounting principles or in their method of application that has a material effect on the comparability of the company's financial statements (and the auditor determines it has been handled appropriately), the auditor should refer to the change in an explanatory paragraph in the report. The explanatory paragraph (**after** the opinion paragraph) should identify the nature of the change and make reference to the note in the financial statements that describes the change. This is not a qualification of the audit opinion hence the auditor's concurrence with the change is implied in the report.

Editor Note: According to the guidance (PCAOB AS 6) for issuers (public companies), both a change in accounting principle *and an adjustment to correct a misstatement (error) in previously issued financial statements* are matters relating to consistency that the auditor should recognize in the audit report if they have a material effect on the financial statements. Note that this makes the evaluation of consistency for issuers broader than the second standard of reporting because it includes *errors not involving an accounting principle*. Additionally, the explanatory paragraph added to audit reports of issuers must clearly indicate whether an adjustment to previously issued financial statements was due to a change in accounting principal or the correction of a misstatement.

4.   **Accounting Changes Affecting Consistency** The following are accounting changes that affect consistency and if evaluated by the auditor as having been handled appropriately, require the addition of an explanatory paragraph (**after** the opinion paragraph) to the auditor's report.

Editor note: If the auditor finds that an accounting change is not justified or has not been made according to GAAP (the new principle is not GAAP; the method of accounting for the effect of the change is not GAAP, or disclosure is inadequate) the change should be treated as a departure from GAAP, resulting in either a qualified or adverse opinion.

a.   **Change in Accounting Principle** A change in accounting principle arises (1) from the use of a generally accepted accounting principle that is different from the one previously used (both apply and are GAAP); (2) when the accounting principle formerly used is no longer GAAP; or (3) from the use of a different method of applying a generally accepted accounting principle.

The standard setters make special note that the following cases involve changes in principles:

(1)   **Change in Reporting Entity** A change in reporting entity **not** resulting from a transaction or event.

A change in reporting entity that *does* result from a transaction or event, such as the creation, cessation, or complete or partial purchase or disposition of a subsidiary or other business unit, does *not* require recognition in the auditor's report.

(2) **Changes in Presentation of Cash Flows** An entity should disclose its policy for determining which items are treated as cash equivalents. Any change to that policy is a change in accounting principle that is reported by restating financial statements for earlier years presented for comparative purposes.

(3) **Investment Accounted for by the Equity Method** If a company's financial statements contain an investment accounted for by the equity method, the auditor's evaluation of consistency should include consideration of the investee. If the investee makes a change in accounting principle that is material to the investing company's financial statements, the auditor should add an explanatory paragraph (**after** the opinion paragraph) to the auditor's report.

b. **Correction of an Error in Principle** This involves changing from an accounting principle that is not generally accepted to one that is generally accepted (including correcting a mistake in the application of a principle).

Editor note: Although guidance for both issuers and nonissuers consider this a consistency issue, PCAOB AS 6 categorizes it as the correction of a misstatement, thus it must be identified as a misstatement in the explanatory paragraph of an audit report for an issuer.

c. **Change in Principle Inseparable From Change in Estimate** When the effect of a change in accounting estimate is inseparable from the effect of a related change in accounting principle, although the *accounting* for the change is handled as a change in estimate, a change in principle is involved.

5. **Changes *Not* Affecting Consistency** The following changes do **not** affect consistency *if no element of accounting principles or their application is involved*. Therefore, they do **not** require recognition in the auditor's report. *However, if material, they may require disclosure in the financial statements and the opinion must be qualified or adverse if disclosure is inadequate.*

a. **Changes in Accounting Estimates** Accounting estimates will be changed as circumstances change. Estimates such as expected salvage values and service lives of fixed assets are a normal part of doing business.

b. **Error Correction That Does Not Involve an Accounting Principle** This is the correction of an error in previously issued financial statements that resulted from mathematical mistakes, oversight, or misuse of facts.

Editor note: As previously mentioned, this *is* a consistency issue for public companies if the adjustment has a material effect on the previously issued financial statements.

c. **Changes in Classification & Reclassification** These are changes in classifications made in previously issued financial statements to enhance comparability with current financial statements.

Editor note: PCAOB AS 6 includes expanded guidance for auditors of issuers concerning the evaluation of whether such reclassifications involve corrections of material misstatements or changes in accounting principles. For example, if items were incorrectly classified in previously issued financial statements, the reclassification should be recognized in the auditor's report as the correction of a misstatement.

d. **Substantially Different Transactions or Events** A consistency problem does not arise when the use of a different accounting principle is required because the transactions and events being processed are clearly different from those in the previous period.

e. **Current Change Expected to Have a Material Future Effect** A consistency problem does not arise when an accounting change does not affect the current year's financial statements but is expected to have a substantial effect in later years. (It should be disclosed in the notes to the financial statements whenever the statements of the period of change are presented.)

6. **Current Year** When reporting only on the current period's financial statements, the auditor should obtain sufficient appropriate audit evidence about the consistency of the application of accounting principles even though the prior period financial statements are not presented.

When the auditor has not audited the financial statements of the preceding year, the auditor should adopt procedures that are practicable and reasonable in the circumstances to be assured that the accounting principles are consistent between the current and the preceding year.

7. **Multiple Years** When reporting on the financial statements of two or more years that are presented for comparative purposes, the auditor should report on a lack of consistency between the years. The auditor should also report on a lack of consistency between the years and the year prior to the earliest year presented.

Exhibit 4 ▶ Consistency of Financial Statements

Do these changes affect comparability? (require recognition in the auditor's report by the addition of an explanatory paragraph **after** the opinion paragraph)	Yes	No
Change in accounting principle or method of applying it	✓	
Change in reporting entity		
Not resulting from a transaction or event	✓	
Resulting from a transaction or event		✓
Changes in presentation of cash flows	✓	
Investment accounted for by the equity method; investee makes a change in accounting principle	✓	
Correction of an error in principle	✓	
Misstatement in previously issued financial statements—**not** involving a principle		
Nonissuer		✓
Issuer (public entity)	✓	
Change in principle inseparable from a change in estimate	✓	
Change in accounting estimate		✓
Changes in classification and reclassification		✓
Different events & transactions from previously issued financial statements		✓
Changes expected to have a material future effect, but no substantial effect on current financial statements		✓

C.   **Adequacy of Disclosure in Financial Statements (AU 431)**

Exhibit 5 ▶ The Third Standard of Reporting

> When the auditor determines that informative disclosures are not reasonably adequate, the auditor must so state in the auditor's report.

1.   **Material Matters** Financial statements presented in conformity with GAAP must contain adequate disclosure of material matters. Adequate disclosure includes the form, arrangement, and content of the statements and notes, including the terminology used, amount of detail, classification of items, and the bases of amounts set forth. In determining whether a particular matter should be disclosed, the auditor should consider the circumstances and facts that the auditor is aware of at the time.

      a.   Failure by management to include information required by GAAP in the financial statements will result in the auditor expressing a qualified or adverse opinion on the statements.

      b.   If practicable, the auditor should provide such information in the report, unless its omission from the report is sanctioned by a specific auditing standard. "Practicable" means that the information can reasonably be obtained from the client's accounts and records, and that providing it in the report does **not** require the auditor to assume the position of *preparer* of financial information. For instance, an auditor is **not** expected to provide a basic financial statement or segment information omitted by management.

2.   **Confidential Information** In conducting an audit of financial statements and in other areas of work with the client, the auditor uses confidential information provided by the client. Thus, the auditor should **not** disclose—without management's consent—information **not** required to be disclosed in financial statements to comply with GAAP.

D.   **Overall Opinion & Association With Financial Statements**

Exhibit 6 ▶ The Fourth Standard of Reporting

> The auditor must either express an opinion regarding the financial statements, taken as a whole, or state that an opinion cannot be expressed, in the auditor's report. When the auditor cannot express an overall opinion, the auditor should state the reasons therefor in the auditor's report. In all cases where an auditor's name is associated with financial statements, the auditor should clearly indicate the character of the auditor's work, if any, and the degree of responsibility the auditor is taking, in the auditor's report.

1.   **Overall Opinion** Reference to the financial statements *taken as a whole* applies equally to a complete set of financial statements and to an individual financial statement (such as a balance sheet) for one or more periods presented. Thus, an auditor may express an unqualified opinion on one of the financial statements and express a qualified or adverse opinion or disclaim an opinion on another if the circumstances warrant. For example, when an auditor of a new client cannot become satisfied with the accuracy of opening inventory balances, this scope limitation affects the income, retained earnings, and cash flow statements, but not the balance sheet. (This is because cost of goods sold cannot be verified.) Thus, an unqualified opinion could be issued on the balance sheet and a disclaimer of opinion should be issued on the other financial statements. See Exhibit 21 in this chapter.

2.   **Association With Financial Statements** The objective of the fourth standard is to prevent any misinterpretation of the degree of responsibility the auditor is assuming when the auditor's name is associated with financial statements.

3.   **Piecemeal Opinions** The auditor should not express an opinion on specified elements, accounts, or items included in financial statements on which the auditor has expressed an

adverse opinion or disclaimed an opinion on the financial statements taken as a whole, *if* such reporting would be tantamount to expressing a piecemeal opinion on the financial statements. Piecemeal opinions are expressions of opinion as to certain identified items in financial statements and tend to overshadow or contradict a disclaimer of opinion or an adverse opinion. However, an auditor is able to express an opinion on one or more certain identified items of a financial statement, provided the identified items and the scope of the related audit do not encompass so many elements as to constitute a major portion of the financial statements. For example, it may be appropriate for an auditor to express an opinion on an entity's accounts receivable even if the auditor disclaimed an opinion on the financial statements taken as a whole. However, the report on the certain identified item should be presented separately from the report on the financial statements. (See Chapter 11 for further explanation.)

II. Types of Opinions (AU 508)

A. Unqualified Opinion, Standard Report
The standard report is issued when the auditor feels the financial statements fairly present, in all material respects, the financial position, results of operations, and cash flows in conformity with US GAAP or OCBOA (including adequate disclosure). The audit must have been conducted in accordance with US GAAS.

Editor note: Auditors of public companies (issuers) must state that the audit was conducted in accordance with the standards of the Public Company Accounting Oversight Board (United States) rather than GAAS. An auditor must also include the city and state (or city and country, in the case of non-US auditors) from which the auditor's report has been issued.

Exhibit 7 ▶ Conditions for Unqualified Opinion, Standard Report

1.	No departures from US GAAP
2.	Disclosures in financial statements (notes to the financial statements) are adequate and complete
3.	No unusual uncertainties surrounding the financial statements
4.	No scope limitations
5.	GAAP must be consistently followed between periods
6.	Independent auditor

B. Modified Unqualified Opinion
Certain circumstances, while not affecting the auditor's unqualified opinion on the financial statements, may require that the auditor add an explanatory paragraph (or other explanatory language) to the report. These circumstances include: part of the audit is performed by other auditors; a justified departure from GAAP (very rare); substantial doubt about the entity's ability to continue as a going concern; a material lack of consistency; certain circumstances related to reports on comparative financial statements; certain circumstances related to interim financial information; RSI accompanies the financial statements; and other information in documents containing the financial statements is materially inconsistent with the financial statements.

Additionally, the auditor may add an explanatory paragraph to emphasize a matter regarding the financial statements, but this is not required. Emphasis paragraphs are added solely at the auditor's discretion.

C. Qualified Opinion
A qualified opinion states that, "except for" the effects of the matter to which the qualification relates, the financial statements present fairly, in all material respects, the financial position, results of operations, and cash flows of the entity in conformity with GAAP. A qualification may exist due to a scope limitation (and the auditor has decided not to express an unqualified opinion or disclaim

an opinion) or a material departure from GAAP (and the auditor has decided not to express an adverse opinion).

D.   Adverse Opinion
An adverse opinion states that the financial statements do not present fairly the financial position, results of operations, or cash flows of the entity in conformity with GAAP. It is expressed when the financial statements taken as a whole are not presented fairly in conformity with GAAP.

E.   Disclaimer of Opinion
A disclaimer of opinion states that the auditor does not express an opinion on the financial statements. Usually an opinion is disclaimed due to scope limitations. It should **not** be expressed when there is a material departure from GAAP.

III.   Unqualified Opinions & the Standard Report (AU 508 continued)

A.   Implications of the Standard Report
The auditor's standard report states that the financial statements present fairly, in all material respects, an entity's financial position, results of operations, and cash flows in conformity with US GAAP. The auditor may express this opinion only when an audit conducted according to US GAAS has been completed and the necessary conditions are met. The auditor's standard report identifies the financial statements audited in an opening, introductory paragraph, describes the nature of an audit in a scope paragraph, and expresses the auditor's opinion in a separate opinion paragraph. The United States of America should be identified as the country of the origin of the GAAS and GAAP.

B.   Components of the Standard Report
The basic elements of the report are:

1.   Title A title that includes the word "independent."

2.   Address Addressed to the company, to its board of directors, or to its stockholders (**not to management**). If the auditor is retained to audit the financial statements of a company that is **not** the auditor's client, the report would be addressed to the client and **not** to the directors or stockholders of the company being audited.

3.   Introductory Paragraph

   a.   A statement that identifies the financial statements that were audited.

   b.   A statement that the financial statements are the responsibility of the company's management and that the auditor's responsibility is to express an opinion on the financial statements based on the audit.

4.   Scope Paragraph

   a.   A statement that the audit was conducted in accordance with US GAAS.

   b.   A statement that GAAS requires that the auditor plan and perform the audit to obtain reasonable assurance about whether the financial statements are free of material misstatement.

   c.   Statements that an audit includes:

      (1)   Examining, on a test basis, evidence supporting the amounts and disclosures in the financial statements.

      (2)   Assessing the accounting principles used and significant estimates made by management.

(3)   Evaluating the overall financial statement presentation.

d.   A statement that the auditor believes that the audit provides a reasonable basis for the auditor's opinion.

5.   **Opinion Paragraph** An opinion as to whether the financial statements present fairly, in all material respects, the financial position of the company as of the balance sheet date and the results of its operations and its cash flows for the period then ended in conformity with US GAAP.

6.   **Signature** The manual or printed signature of the auditor's firm.

7.   **Date** The date of the report should be no earlier than the date on which the auditor has obtained sufficient appropriate audit evidence to support the opinion.

Exhibit 8 ▶ The Form of the Auditor's Standard Report for a Single Year

---

<u>Independent Auditor's Report</u>

Address (The title and address should be included in all letters, but is not reproduced in all subsequent exhibits.)

(Introductory paragraph)

We have audited the accompanying balance sheet of X Company as of December 31, 20XX, and the related statements of income, retained earnings, and cash flows for the year then ended. These financial statements are the responsibility of the Company's management. Our responsibility is to express an opinion on these financial statements based on our audit.

(Scope paragraph)

We conducted our audit in accordance with US generally accepted auditing standards. Those standards require that we plan and perform the audit to obtain reasonable assurance about whether the financial statements are free of material misstatement. An audit includes examining, on a test basis, evidence supporting the amounts and disclosures in the financial statements. An audit also includes assessing the accounting principles used and significant estimates made by management, as well as evaluating the overall financial statement presentation. We believe that our audit provides a reasonable basis for our opinion.

(Opinion paragraph)

In our opinion, the financial statements referred to above present fairly, in all material respects, the financial position of X Company as of (at) December 31, 20XX, and the results of its operations and its cash flows for the year then ended in conformity with US generally accepted accounting principles.

Signature & Date (These should be included in all letters, but are not reproduced in all subsequent exhibits.)

C.   Modified Unqualified Opinion
There are certain circumstances which, while **not** affecting the auditor's unqualified opinion, may require that the auditor add explanatory language to the standard report. These circumstances include the following:

1.   **Part of Audit Performed by Other Independent Auditors (AU 543)** Sometimes the auditor will be in a position where other independent auditors have audited the financial statements of subsidiaries, divisions, branches, components, or investments that are included in the financial statements the auditor is auditing. The auditor must first decide whether he or she has participated sufficiently to be the principal auditor, i.e., to report on the financial statements.

   a.   **Whether Principal Auditor Makes Reference to Other Auditor** As principal auditor, the auditor must decide whether to assume responsibility for the work of the other auditor as it relates to the expression of an opinion on the financial statements taken as a whole.

      (1)   **Decision Not to Make Reference / Principal Auditor Assumes Responsibility** The principal auditor must be satisfied of the other auditor's independence, professional reputation, and the quality and scope of the audit performed. This position is usually appropriate when (a) the other auditor is an associated or correspondent firm, (b) the other auditor was retained by the principal auditor, (c) the principal auditor takes steps necessary to be satisfied with the other auditor's work, or (d) the other auditor audited an immaterial portion of the financial statements.

      No reference should be made to the other auditor's work or report. If all other conditions for an unqualified opinion are met, a standard report can be issued.

      (2)   **Decision to Make Reference / Principal Auditor Decides *Not* to Assume Responsibility** The principal auditor's report should clearly indicate, in the introductory, scope, and opinion paragraphs, the division of responsibility between the portion of the financial statements covered by the principal auditor's own audit and that covered by the audit of the other auditor. The portion examined by the other auditor should be indicated (e.g., dollar amounts or percentages of total assets, total revenues, etc.). The other auditor may be named only if (a) the other auditor has given permission, and (b) the other auditor's report is included.

   Exhibit 9 ▶ Report Indicating Division of Responsibility

Independent Auditor's Report

(Introductory paragraph)

We have audited the consolidated balance sheets of ABC Company and subsidiaries as of December 31, 20X2 and 20X1, and the related consolidated statements of income, retained earnings, and cash flows for the years then ended. These financial statements are the responsibility of the Company's management. Our responsibility is to express an opinion on these financial statements based on our audits. We did not audit the financial statements of B Company, a wholly owned subsidiary, which statements reflect total assets of $_____ and $_____ as of December 31, 20X2 and 20X1, respectively, and total revenues of $_____ and $_____ for the years then ended. Those statements were audited by other auditors whose report has been furnished to us, and our opinion, insofar as it relates to the amounts included for B Company, is based solely on the report of other auditors.

(Scope paragraph)

We conducted our audits in accordance with US generally accepted auditing standards. Those standards require that we plan and perform the audit to obtain reasonable assurance about whether the financial statements are free of material misstatements. An audit includes examining on a test basis, evidence supporting the amounts and disclosures in the financial statements. An audit also includes assessing the accounting principles used and significant estimates made by management, as well as evaluating the overall financial statements presentation. We believe that our audits and the report of other auditors provide a reasonable basis for our opinion.

(Opinion paragraph)

In our opinion, based on our audits and the report of other auditors, the consolidated financial statements referred to above present fairly, in all material respects, the financial position of ABC Company and subsidiaries as of December 31, 20X2 and 20X1, and the results of their operations and their cash flows for the years then ended in conformity with US generally accepted accounting principles.

---

b. **Other Procedures** Regardless of whether or not reference is made, the principal auditor should inquire as to the professional reputation and independence of the other auditors and should attempt to achieve a proper coordination of their activities.

2. **Justifiable Departure From Promulgated Accounting Principle (Ethics Rule 203)** In the rare circumstance where the auditor can demonstrate that, due to unusual circumstances, the financial statements would be misleading if promulgated GAAP were applied, the auditor must describe the departure, its approximate effects, if practicable, and the reasons why compliance would result in a misleading statement. In this situation, it is appropriate for the auditor to express an unqualified opinion on the financial statements with an explanatory paragraph.

3. **Lack of Consistency** The auditor's standard report implies that the accounting principles have been consistently applied between periods. In these cases, the auditor should **not** refer to consistency in the report. If there has been a change affecting consistency, the auditor should refer to the change in an explanatory paragraph of the report. The explanatory paragraph, **after** the opinion paragraph, should identify the nature of the change and refer the reader to the note in the financial statements that discusses the change in detail. An unqualified opinion would be expressed. The auditor's concurrence with a change is implicit unless the auditor takes exception to the change.

Exhibit 10 ▶ Change in Accounting Principle (*after* opinion paragraph)

As discussed in Note X to the financial statements, the Company changed its method of computing depreciation in 20X1.

4. **Going Concern Doubt** The audit report should include an explanatory paragraph **after** the opinion paragraph if the auditor concludes that substantial doubt about the entity's ability to continue as a going concern does exist. This paragraph should **not** include any conditional language and should include the terms *substantial doubt* and *going concern*.

Exhibit 11 ▶ Going Concern Doubt: Explanatory Paragraph (*after* opinion paragraph)

The accompanying financial statements have been prepared assuming that the Company will continue as a going concern. As discussed in Note X to the financial statements, the Company has suffered recurring losses from operations and has a net capital deficiency, raising substantial doubt about its ability to continue as a going concern. Management's plans in regard to these matters are also described in Note X. The financial statements do not include any adjustments that might result from the outcome of this uncertainty.

Editor note: If disclosure is inadequate, a qualified or adverse opinion should be expressed (GAAP departure).

5. **Emphasis of a Matter** The auditor may wish to emphasize a matter regarding the financial statements even though the auditor intends to express an unqualified opinion. For example, the auditor may wish to emphasize that the entity is a component of a larger business enterprise or that it has had significant transactions with related parties. The auditor may wish to mention an important subsequent event. This should be presented in a separate paragraph in the auditor's report **after** the opinion paragraph.

IV. Departures From Unqualified Opinions (AU 508 continued)

A. Qualified Opinions
When the auditor expresses a qualified opinion, the auditor should disclose all of the substantive reasons in one or more separate explanatory paragraph(s) **before** the opinion paragraph of the report. A qualified opinion should include the word *except* or *exception* in a phrase such as *except for* or *with the exception of.* Phrases such as *subject to* and *with the foregoing explanation* are **not** clear or forceful enough and should **not** be used.

1. **Scope Limitations** Restrictions on the scope of an audit, whether imposed by the client or by circumstances, may require the auditor to express a qualified opinion. The decision depends upon the auditor's assessment of the importance of the omitted procedure(s) in relation to the financial statements. When a significant scope limitation is imposed by the client, the auditor normally would disclaim an opinion on the financial statements.

Exhibit 12 ▶ Scope Limitations

<u>Independent Auditor's Report</u>

(Same first paragraph as the standard report)

Except as discussed in the following paragraph, we conducted our audits in accordance with US generally accepted auditing standards. Those standards require that we plan and perform the audit to obtain reasonable assurance about whether the financial statements are free of material misstatement. An audit includes examining, on a test basis, evidence supporting the amounts and disclosures in the financial statements. An audit also includes assessing the accounting principles used and significant estimates made by management, as well as evaluating the overall financial statement presentation. We believe that our audits provide a reasonable basis for our opinion.

We were unable to obtain audited financial statements supporting the Company's investment in a foreign affiliate stated at $_____ and $_____ at December 31, 20X2 and 20X1, respectively, or its equity in earnings of that affiliate of $_____ and $____, which is included in net income for the years then ended as described in Note X to the financial statements; nor were we able to satisfy ourselves as to the carrying value of the investment in the foreign affiliate or the equity in its earnings by other auditing procedures.

In our opinion, except for the effects of such adjustments, if any, as might have been determined to be necessary had we been able to examine evidence regarding the foreign affiliate investment and earnings, the financial statements referred to in the first paragraph above present fairly, in all material respects, the financial position of X Company as of December 31, 20X2 and 20X1, and the results of its operations and its cash flows for the years then ended in conformity with US generally accepted accounting principles.

---

a.   **Qualified Opinion** If a qualified opinion is expressed, the reasons should be explained in the audit report in an explanatory paragraph (**before** the opinion paragraph) and referred to in both the scope and opinion paragraphs.   The wording in the opinion paragraph should indicate that the qualification pertains to the possible effects on the financial statements and **not** to the scope limitation itself.

b.   **Scope Limitation Examples**

   (1)   The auditor is unable to observe physical inventories or apply alternative procedures to verify their balances.

   (2)   The client refuses to permit its attorney to furnish information requested in a letter of audit inquiry.

c.   **Uncertainties & Scope Limitations**

   (1)   A matter involving an uncertainty is one that is expected to be resolved at a future date, at which time conclusive audit evidence concerning its outcome would be expected to become available.   Uncertainties include, but are not limited to, contingencies and matters related to estimates.

   (2)   Conclusive audit evidence concerning the ultimate outcome of uncertainties cannot be expected to exist at the time of the audit because the outcome and related audit evidence are prospective.   In these circumstances, management is responsible for estimating the effect of future events on the financial statements, or determining that a reasonable estimate cannot be made and making the required disclosures.   An audit includes an assessment of whether the audit evidence is sufficient to support management's analysis and estimate.

   (3)   Absence of the existence of information related to the outcome of an uncertainty does not necessarily lead to a conclusion that the audit evidence supporting management's assertion is not sufficient.   Rather, the auditor's judgment regarding the sufficiency of the audit evidence is based on the audit evidence that is, or should be, available.   An unqualified opinion is appropriate if sufficient audit evidence supports management's assertions about the nature of a matter involving an uncertainty and its presentation or disclosure in the financial statements.

   (4)   If the auditor is unable to obtain sufficient audit evidence to support management's assertions, the auditor should consider the need to express a qualified opinion or to disclaim an opinion because of a scope limitation.   A qualification or disclaimer of opinion because of a scope limitation is appropriate if sufficient audit evidence related to an uncertainty does or did exist but was not available to the auditor for reasons such as management's record retention policies or a restriction imposed by management.

    d.   **Limited Reporting Engagements** The auditor is **not** precluded from reporting on only one of the basic financial statements and not the others. A scope limitation would **not** exist if the auditor is able to apply all the procedures to the one financial statement the auditor considers necessary. Such engagements involve limited reporting objectives.

2.   **Departure From GAAP**

    a.   When financial statements are materially affected by a departure from GAAP, the auditor should express a qualified or an adverse opinion. Materiality, significance of an item to the entity, pervasiveness of the misstatement, and the effect of the misstatement on the financial statements as a whole, must be considered in deciding whether to express a qualified or an adverse opinion.

    b.   When the auditor expresses a qualified opinion, the auditor should disclose, in a separate explanatory paragraph(s) **before** the opinion paragraph, the substantive reasons that have led the auditor to conclude that there is a departure from GAAP. The opinion paragraph should include appropriate qualifying language and should refer to the explanatory paragraph(s). The explanatory paragraph(s) also should disclose the principal effects of the matter on the financial position, results of operations and cash flows, if practicable. If the effects cannot be determined, the report should so state.

Exhibit 13 ▸ Departure From GAAP

<u>Independent Auditor's Report</u>

(Same first and second paragraphs as the standard report)

The company has excluded, from property and debt in the accompanying balance sheets, certain lease obligations that, in our opinion, should be capitalized in order to conform with US generally accepted accounting principles. If these lease obligations were capitalized, property would be increased by $_____ and $_____, long-term debt by $_____ and $_____, and retained earnings by $_____ and $_____ as of December 31, 20X2 and 20X1, respectively. Additionally, net income would be increased (decreased) by $_____ and $_____, and earnings per share would be increased (decreased) by $_____ and $_____, respectively, for the years then ended.

In our opinion, except for the effects of not capitalizing certain lease obligations as discussed in the preceding paragraph, the financial statements referred to above present fairly, in all material respects, the financial position of X Company as of December 31, 20X2 and 20X1, and the results of its operations and its cash flows for the years then ended in conformity with US generally accepted accounting principles.

---

    c.   **Inadequate Disclosure**

        (1)   If information that is essential for a fair presentation of financial statements in conformity with GAAP is **not** disclosed in the financial statements or accompanying notes, the auditor should express a qualified or an adverse opinion, and should provide the information in the report if practicable, unless its omission from the auditor's report is recognized as appropriate by a specific auditing standard.

        Exhibit 14 ▸ Report Qualified for Inadequate Disclosure (Not Practicable to Present)

<u>Independent Auditor's Report</u>

(Same first and second paragraphs as the standard report)

The Company's financial statements do not disclose [*describe the nature of the omitted information that is not practicable to present in the auditor's report*]. In our opinion, disclosure of this information is required by US generally accepted accounting principles.

> In our opinion, except for the omission of the information discussed in the preceding paragraph,...

(2) The auditor is **not** required to prepare a basic financial statement and include it in the report if the company's management declines to present the statement. In the case of, for example, the omission of a cash flow statement, a qualified opinion would be appropriate, with an explanatory paragraph added **before** the opinion paragraph.

Exhibit 15 ▶ Report Qualified: Lacking Basic Financial Statement

---

<u>Independent Auditor's Report</u>

We have audited the accompanying balance sheets of X Company as of December 31, 20X2 and 20X1, and the related statements of income and retained earnings for the years then ended. These financial statements are the responsibility of the Company's management. Our responsibility is to express an opinion on these financial statements based on our audit.

(Same second paragraph as the standard report)

The Company declined to present a statement of cash flows for the years ended December 31, 20X2 and 20X1. Presentation of such statement summarizing the Company's operating, investing, and financing activities is required by US generally accepted accounting principles.

In our opinion, except that the omission of a statement of cash flows results in an incomplete presentation as explained in the preceding paragraph, the financial statements referred to above present fairly, in all material respects, the financial position of X Company as of December 31, 20X2 and 20X1, and the results of its operations for the years then ended in conformity with US generally accepted accounting principles.

---

d. **Uncertainties or Risks** Departures from GAAP involving uncertainties or risks (and related materiality considerations) generally fall into one of the following categories which result in the expression of an unqualified or adverse opinion:

(1) **Inadequate Disclosure** The auditor should consider materiality in evaluating the adequacy of disclosure of matters involving risks or uncertainties in the financial statements in the context of the financial statements taken as a whole. The auditor should evaluate the materiality of reasonably possible losses that may be incurred upon the resolution of uncertainties both individually and in the aggregate without regard to an evaluation of the materiality of known and likely misstatements in the financial statements.

(2) **Inappropriate Accounting Principles** In preparing financial statements, management estimates the outcome of certain types of future events. For example, estimates ordinarily are made about the useful lives of depreciable assets, the collectability of accounts receivable, the realizable value of inventory items, and the provision for product warranties. The inability to make a reasonable estimate may raise questions about the appropriateness of the accounting principles used. In those or other situations, the auditor may conclude that the accounting principles used cause the financial statements to be materially misstated.

(3) **Unreasonable Accounting Estimates** The auditor concludes that management's estimate is unreasonable and that its effect is to cause the financial statements to be materially misstated.

e. **Accounting Changes** The auditor should evaluate a change in accounting principle to be satisfied that (a) the newly adopted accounting principle is a generally accepted accounting principle, (b) the method of accounting for the effect of the change is in conformity with GAAP, and (c) management's justification for the change is reasonable. If a change in accounting principle does **not** meet these conditions, the auditor should express a qualified opinion, or if the effect of the change is sufficiently material, an adverse opinion should be expressed.

Exhibit 16 ▶ Report Qualified: Accounting Change Not Justified by Management

> Independent Auditor's Report
>
> (Same first and second paragraphs as the standard report)
>
> As disclosed in Note X to the financial statements, the Company adopted, in 20X2, the first-in, first-out method of accounting for its inventories, whereas it previously used the last-in, first-out method. Although use of the first-in, first-out method is in conformity with US generally accepted accounting principles, in our opinion, the Company has not provided reasonable justification for making this change as required by those principles.
>
> In our opinion, except for the change in accounting principle discussed in the preceding paragraph, the financial statements referred to above present fairly, in all material respects, the financial position of X Company as of December 31, 20X2 and 20X1, and the results of its operations and its cash flows for the years then ended in conformity with US generally accepted accounting principles.

B. **Adverse Opinions**
State that financial statements do **not** present fairly the financial position, the results of operations, or cash flows in conformity with GAAP.

Exhibit 17 ▶ Adverse Opinion

> Independent Auditor's Report
>
> (Same first and second paragraphs as the standard report)
>
> As discussed in Note X to the financial statements, the Company carries its property, plant and equipment accounts at appraisal values, and provides depreciation on the basis of such values. Further, the Company does not provide for income taxes with respect to differences between financial income and taxable income arising because of the use, for income tax purposes, of the installment method of reporting gross profit from certain types of sales. US generally accepted accounting principles require that property, plant, and equipment be stated at an amount not in excess of cost, reduced by depreciation based on such amount, and that deferred income taxes be provided.
>
> Because of the departures from US generally accepted accounting principles identified above, as of December 31, 20X2 and 20X1, inventories have been increased $_____ and $_____ by inclusion in manufacturing overhead of depreciation in excess of that based on cost; property, plant, and equipment, less accumulated depreciation, is carried at $_____ and $_____ in excess of an amount based on the cost to the Company; and deferred income taxes of $_____ and $_____ have not been recorded, resulting in an increase of $_____ and $_____ in retained earnings and in appraisal surplus of $_____ and $_____, respectively. For the years ended December 31, 20X2 and 20X1, cost of goods sold has been increased $_____ and $_____, respectively, because of the effects of the depreciation accounting referred to above and deferred income taxes of $_____ and $_____ have not been provided, resulting in an increase in net income of $_____ and $_____, respectively.
>
> In our opinion, because of the effects of the matters discussed in the preceding paragraphs, the financial statements referred to above do not present fairly, in conformity with US generally accepted accounting principles, the financial position of X Company as of December 31, 20X2 and 20X1, or the results of its operations or its cash flows for the years then ended.

1. **Explanatory Paragraph** The auditor should disclose in a separate explanatory paragraph(s) **before** the opinion paragraph of the report (a) all the substantive reasons for the adverse opinion, and (b) the principal effects of the subject matter of the adverse opinion on financial position, results of operations, and cash flows, if practicable. If the effects are not reasonably determinable, the report should so state.

2. **Opinion Paragraph** The opinion paragraph should include a direct reference to a separate paragraph that discloses the basis for the adverse opinion.

C. **Disclaimer of Opinion**
States that the auditor does **not** express an opinion on the financial statements. It is appropriate when the auditor has **not** performed an audit sufficient in scope to enable the auditor to form an opinion on the financial statements.

Exhibit 18 ▶ Disclaimer of Opinion Due to Scope Limitation

<u>Independent Auditor's Report</u>

We were engaged to audit the accompanying balance sheets of X Company as of December 31, 20X2 and 20X1, and the related statements of income, retained earnings, and cash flows for the years then ended. These financial statements are the responsibility of the Company's management.

[Second (scope) paragraph of standard report should be omitted.]

The Company did not make a count of its physical inventory in 20X2 or 20X1, stated in the accompanying financial statements at $_____ as of December 31, 20X2, and at $_____ as of December 31, 20X1. Further, evidence supporting the cost of property and equipment acquired prior to December 31, 20X1, is no longer available. The Company's records do not permit the application of other auditing procedures to inventories or property and equipment.

The Company did not take physical inventories and we were not able to apply other auditing procedures to satisfy ourselves as to inventory quantities and the cost of property and equipment, thus, the scope of our work was not sufficient to enable us to express, and we do not express, an opinion on these financial statements.

---

1. **Scope Limitation** If a scope limitation is the reason for the disclaimer, the auditor should indicate in a separate paragraph the reasons for the disclaimer. The auditor should state that the scope of the audit was not sufficient to warrant the expression of an opinion, but the auditor should **not** identify the procedures that were performed nor include the paragraph describing the characteristics of an audit, i.e., the scope paragraph. In addition any other reservations regarding fair presentation in conformity with GAAP should be disclosed.

2. **Material GAAP Departures** A disclaimer of opinion should **not** be expressed when the auditor believes, on the basis of the audit, that there are material departures from GAAP.

V. **Reports on Comparative Financial Statements (AU 508 continued)**

A. **Standard Report**
An auditor's standard report covers statements of the current period and those of one or more prior periods that are presented on a comparative basis. Therefore, a continuing auditor, an auditor who has audited the current period's financial statements and those of one or more immediately preceding periods, will update the report (re-express an opinion) on the individual financial statements of those prior periods. The updated opinion may differ from that previously given if circumstances warrant a change. During the audit of the current period financial statements, the auditor should be alert for circumstances or events that affect the prior period financial statements. Generally, the date of the report should be no earlier than the date on which the auditor has obtained sufficient appropriate audit evidence to support the opinion.

Exhibit 19 ▶ Auditor's Standard Report: Comparative Financial Statements

---

<u>Independent Auditor's Report</u>

We have audited the accompanying balance sheets of X Company as of December 31, 20X2 and 20X1, and the related statements of income, retained earnings, and cash flows for the years then ended. These financial statements are the responsibility of the Company's management. Our responsibility is to express an opinion on these financial statements based on our audits.

We conducted our audits in accordance with US generally accepted auditing standards. Those standards require that we plan and perform the audit to obtain reasonable assurance about whether the financial statements are free of material misstatement. An audit includes examining, on a test basis, evidence supporting the amounts and disclosures in the financial statements. An audit also includes assessing the accounting principles used and significant estimates made by management, as well as evaluating the overall financial statement presentation. We believe that our audits provide a reasonable basis for our opinion.

In our opinion, the financial statements referred to above present fairly, in all material respects, the financial position of X Company as of December 31, 20X2 and 20X1, and the results of its operations and its cash flows for the years then ended in conformity with US generally accepted accounting principles.

B.   Differing Opinions

The auditor's report on the comparative statements applies to the individual financial statements that are presented. Therefore, the same type of opinion is **not** required (qualified, unqualified, etc.) on all of the statements. When it is **not** the same, the auditor should (1) disclose all of the substantive reasons for the modified opinion (or for disclaiming an opinion) in a separate explanatory paragraph of the report, and (2) in the opinion paragraph, include an appropriate modification (or disclaimer of opinion) along with a reference to the explanation.

Exhibit 20 ▶ Different Opinions for Financial Statements Presented—Qualified Opinion on Current Year Financial Statements and an Unqualified Opinion on Prior Year Financial Statements

---

<u>Independent Auditor's Report</u>

(Same first and second paragraphs as the standard report)

The Company has excluded, from property and debt in the accompanying 20X2 balance sheet, certain lease obligations that were entered into in 20X2 which, in our opinion, should be capitalized in order to conform with US generally accepted accounting principles. If these lease obligations were capitalized, property would be increased by $_____, long-term debt by $_____, and retained earnings by $_____ as of December 31, 20X2, and net income and earnings per share would be increased (decreased) by $_____ and $_____, respectively, for the year then ended.

In our opinion, except for the effects on the 20X2 financial statements of not capitalizing certain lease obligations as described in the preceding paragraph, the financial statements referred to above present fairly, in all material respects, the financial position of ABC Company as of December 31, 20X2 and 20X1, and the results of its operations and its cash flows for the years then ended in conformity with US generally accepted accounting principles.

Exhibit 21 ▶ Different Opinions for Financial Statements Presented—Unqualified Opinion on Current Year Financial Statements and a Disclaimer of Opinion on Prior Year Statements of Income, Retained Earnings & Cash Flows

<u>Independent Auditor's Report</u>

(Same first paragraph as the standard report)

Except as explained in the following paragraph, we conducted our audits in accordance with auditing standards generally accepted in the United States of America. Those standards require that we plan and perform our audit to obtain reasonable assurance about whether the financial statements are free of material misstatement. An audit includes examining, on a test basis, evidence supporting the amounts and disclosures in the financial statements. An audit also includes assessing the accounting principles used and significant estimates made by management, as well as evaluating the overall financial statement presentation. We believe that our audits provide a reasonable basis for our opinion.

We did not observe the taking of the physical inventory as of December 31, 20X0, since that date was prior to our appointment as auditors for the Company, and we were unable to satisfy ourselves regarding inventory quantities by means of other auditing procedures. Inventory amounts as of December 31, 20X0, enter into the determination of net income and cash flows for the year ended December 31, 20X1.

Because of the matter discussed in the preceding paragraph, the scope of our work was not sufficient to enable us to express, and we do not express, an opinion on the results of operations and cash flows for the year ended December 31, 20X1.

In our opinion, the balance sheets of ABC Company as of December 31, 20X2 and 20X1, and the related statements of income, retained earnings, and cash flows for the year ended December 31, 20X2, present fairly, in all material respects, the financial position of ABC Company as of December 31, 20X2 and 20X1, and the results of its operations and its cash flows for the year ended December 31, 20X2, in conformity with accounting principles generally accepted in the United States of America.

C.   **Subsequent Restatement of Prior Period Statements to Conform With GAAP**
      If the auditor, during the current audit, becomes aware of circumstances or events that affect the financial statements of a prior period, the auditor should consider such matters when updating the report.

Exhibit 22 ▶ Changed Opinion

<u>Independent Auditor's Report</u>

(Same first and second paragraphs as the standard report)

In our report dated March 1, 20X2, we expressed an opinion that the 20X1 financial statements did not fairly present financial position, results of operations, and cash flows in conformity with US generally accepted accounting principles because of two departures from such principles: (1) the Company carried its property, plant and equipment at appraisal values, and provided for depreciation on the basis of such values, and (2) the Company did not provide for deferred income taxes with respect to differences between income for financial reporting purposes and taxable income. As described in Note X, the Company has changed its method of accounting for these items and restated its 20X1 financial statements to conform with US generally accepted accounting principles. Accordingly, our present opinion on the 20X1 financial statements, as presented herein, is different from that expressed in our previous report.

In our opinion, the financial statements referred to above present fairly, in all material respects, the financial position of X Company as of December 31, 20X2 and 20X1, and the results of its operations and its cash flows for the years then ended in conformity with US generally accepted accounting principles.

1. **Unqualified Opinion** If an auditor previously had qualified the opinion on the financial statements of a prior period because of a departure from GAAP, and the prior period financial statements are restated in the current period to conform with GAAP, the updated report of the prior period should indicate that the statements have been restated and should express an unqualified opinion with respect to the restated financial statements.

2. **Different Opinion From Previous** If the auditor decides to express a different opinion than that previously expressed, the auditor should disclose all the substantive reasons for the different opinion in a separate explanatory paragraph(s) **before** the opinion paragraph of the report. The explanatory paragraph should disclose (a) the date of the auditor's previous report, (b) the type of opinion previously expressed, (c) the circumstances or events that caused the auditor to express a different opinion, and (d) that the auditor's updated opinion on the financial statements of the prior period is different from the auditor's previous opinion on those statements.

D.   Report of Predecessor Auditor

1. **Reissued** The predecessor auditor should consider whether the opinion previously issued on the financial statements of the prior period is still appropriate. This should include (a) reading the financial statements of the current period, (b) comparing the statements reported on with those that are being presented for comparative purposes, (c) obtaining a letter of representation from the successor auditor as to whether the successor's audit found anything that might have a material effect on (or require disclosure in) the prior period's statements, and (d) obtaining an updating representation letter from management.

   a. **Procedures** If the predecessor becomes aware of circumstances that may affect the predecessor's own previous opinion, the predecessor should inquire about the event and may want to perform tests such as reviewing the working papers of the successor auditor in regard to the matter. The predecessor must then decide whether to revise the opinion.

   b. **Report** When the predecessor reissues the report, the predecessor should use the same date as that of the predecessor's own previous report to avoid any implication that the predecessor examined any records, transactions, or events after that date. The predecessor should **not** refer to the work or report of the successor auditor. If the predecessor revises the report or if the financial statements are restated, the report should be dual dated.

2. **Not Presented** If the financial statements of a prior period are presented for comparative purposes, but the report of the predecessor auditor is **not** presented, the successor auditor should modify the introductory paragraph of the report to indicate (a) that another auditor audited the prior period financial statements, (b) the date of the predecessor's report, (c) the type of report issued by the predecessor auditor, and (d) if the report was other than standard, and the substantive reasons therefore.

Exhibit 23 ▶ Report When Predecessor's Report Is Not Presented

We have audited the balance sheet of ABC Company as of December 31, 20X2, and the related statements of income, retained earnings, and cash flows for the year then ended. These financial statements are the responsibility of the Company's management. Our responsibility is to express an opinion on these financial statements based on our audit. The financial statements of ABC Company as of December 31, 20X1, were audited by other auditors whose report dated March 31, 20X2, expressed an unqualified opinion on those statements.

(Same second paragraph as the standard report)

In our opinion, the 20X2 financial statements referred to above present fairly, in all material respects, the financial position of ABC Company as of December 31, 20X2, and the results of its operations and its cash flows for the year then ended in conformity with US generally accepted accounting principles.

a. If the predecessor auditor's opinion was other than a standard report, the successor auditor should describe the nature of and the reasons for the report modifications.

Exhibit 24 ▶ Predecessor Auditor's Report Not Standard

> …were audited by other auditors whose report, dated March 1, 20X2, on those statements included an explanatory paragraph that described the change in the Company's method of computing depreciation discussed in Note X to the financial statements.

b. If the financial statements of the prior period have been restated, the introductory paragraph should indicate that a predecessor auditor reported on the financial statements of the prior period before restatement. In addition, if the successor auditor applies sufficient procedures to satisfy the appropriateness of the restatement adjustments, the successor may also state this in the report.

Exhibit 25 ▶ Prior Period Is Restated

> We also audited the adjustments described in Note X that were applied to restate the 20X1 financial statements. In our opinion, such adjustments are appropriate and have been properly applied.

VI. Summary of Various Audit Opinions & Corresponding Reports

A. Unqualified

1. **Standard Report** When all of the necessary conditions for an unqualified opinion are met and none of the situations described under the section below (modified unqualified) exist, the auditor may issue a standard report.

2. **Modified Unqualified**

    a. **Doubt About Ability to Continue as a Going Concern** Add an explanatory paragraph **after** the opinion paragraph to describe the conclusion using the terms *substantial doubt* and *going concern*, referring the reader to the related note in the financial statements.

    b. **Lack of Consistency Resulting in a Material Effect on the Comparability of Financial Statements** Add an explanatory paragraph **after** the opinion paragraph to describe the change, referring the reader to the related note in the financial statements.

    Editor note: If the change is **not** properly accounted for and disclosed, this should be treated as a GAAP departure.

    c. **Principal Auditor Does *Not* Take Responsibility for an Other Auditor's Work** The principal auditor should make reference to an other auditor (the other auditor should not be named unless the other auditor gives permission and the other's report is included) and clearly indicate the division of responsibility. The introductory, scope, and opinion paragraphs should all be changed to reflect the division of responsibility; however, no explanatory paragraph is required.

    Editor note: If the principal auditor *does* take responsibility for the other auditor's work, no reference should be made to the other auditor's work or report. If all other conditions for an unqualified opinion are met, a standard report can be issued.

    d. **Prior Period Opinion Changed to Unqualified** If a qualified or adverse opinion was expressed on a prior period and those financial statements have been restated to conform to GAAP, an explanatory paragraph should be added **before** the opinion paragraph to update the prior report, describing the reason for the different opinion. The standard opinion paragraph should be used.

e.   **RSI Included** Add an explanatory paragraph **after** the opinion paragraph to refer to the RSI and explain the relevant circumstances.

f.   **Other Information Inconsistent With Financial Statements** Add an explanatory paragraph **after** the opinion paragraph to describe the inconsistency.

g.   **Justifiable Departure From GAAP (Rare)** Add an explanatory paragraph **after** the opinion paragraph describing the departure, the approximate effects, and the reasons why compliance would result in a misleading statement.

h.   **Emphasis of a Matter** An explanatory paragraph may be added **after** the opinion paragraph to emphasize a matter regarding the financial statements. This is solely at the auditor's discretion—it is never required.

B.   Qualified
An explanatory paragraph should be added **before** the opinion paragraph and words such as *except for* or *with the exception of* should be used in the opinion paragraph to refer to the added paragraph, thus qualifying the opinion.

1.   **Scope Limitation** The added paragraph should be referred to in the scope and opinion paragraphs.

The auditor may, instead, choose to disclaim an opinion.

2.   **Material Departure From GAAP** The auditor may, instead, choose to issue an adverse opinion. This decision is based on materiality, significance of the item to the entity, pervasiveness of the misstatement, and the effect of the misstatement on the financial statements taken as a whole.

Editor note: Inadequate disclosure and inappropriate accounting changes are examples of departures from GAAP.

C.   Adverse
An explanatory paragraph should be added **before** the opinion paragraph and referred to in the opinion paragraph.

D.   Disclaimer
The introductory paragraph is modified and an explanatory paragraph should be added **before** the disclaimer paragraph and referred to in the disclaimer of opinion paragraph. If the disclaimer is due to a scope limitation, the scope paragraph should be omitted.

E.   Comparative
If there are different opinions for comparative financial statements presented, an explanatory paragraph should be added **before** the opinion paragraph and referred to in the opinion paragraph with "except for…" language.

F.   Predecessor Auditor
If a predecessor's report is **not** presented with comparative statements, the successor auditor should modify the introductory paragraph of his or her report and only express an opinion on current year financial statements (audited by the successor). The standard scope and opinion paragraphs should be used.

Exhibit 26 ▶ Most Common Conditions Requiring Modification of Audit Report

Reasons for Modification*	Opinion Expressed	Explanatory Paragraph	Opinion Paragraph
GAAP Departure	Qualified or Adverse	**Before** opinion paragraph to explain the departure and amount(s)	**Modified** to provide qualifying language and refer to explanatory paragraph(s)
Inadequate Disclosure (type of GAAP departure)	Qualified or Adverse	**Before** opinion paragraph to explain missing disclosure	**Modified** to provide qualifying language and refer to explanatory paragraph(s)
Scope Limitation	Qualified or Disclaimer	**Before** opinion paragraph to explain scope limitation and potential monetary effects	**Modified** to provide qualifying language or to provide disclaimer**
Going Concern Doubt	Modified unqualified (disclaimer is allowed)	**After** opinion paragraph to describe conclusion and referring reader to the note in the financial statements	**Not** modified
Lack of Consistency	Modified unqualified	**After** opinion paragraph describing change and referring reader to the note in the financial statements	**Not** modified
Reliance on Report of Another Auditor	Modified unqualified	NA	**Modified** to refer to report of other auditor ***
Prior Period Opinion Changed to Unqualified	Modified unqualified	**Before** opinion paragraph to describe reason	**Not** modified
RSI included	Modified unqualified	**After** opinion paragraph to refer to RSI & explain relevant circumstances	**Not** modified
Other information inconsistent; management refuses to change	Modified unqualified	**After** opinion paragraph to describe inconsistency****	**Not** modified

NOTE: When **not** qualifying an opinion, an explanatory paragraph generally (but not always) comes **after** the opinion paragraph (which is **not** modified). When the opinion is other than unqualified and an explanatory paragraph is included, it comes **before** the opinion.

---

*   Assuming item is material
**   Qualified opinion requires modification of scope paragraph (using "except for" language). Disclaimer requires modification of introductory paragraph and the scope paragraph is OMITTED.
*** Division of responsibility indicated in introductory paragraph; scope paragraph is also modified to refer to report of other auditor—all 3 paragraphs modified
**** Auditor also has option to withhold report or, if not illegal or prohibited, to withdraw from engagement

VII. Timing Issues

A.   Dating the Audit Report (AU 530)

1.   **General Rule** The date of the report should be no earlier than the date on which the auditor has obtained sufficient appropriate audit evidence to support the opinion. Sufficient evidence includes evidence that the audit documentation has been reviewed and that the entity's financial statements, including disclosures, have been prepared and that management has asserted that it has taken responsibility for them. This will ordinarily result in a report date that is close to the report release date. The auditor does **not** have responsibility to make any inquiries or to conduct any audit procedures after this date (with the exception of filings under the Securities Act of 1933).

2.   **Subsequent Events**

a.   **Adjustment** If the auditor becomes aware of an event requiring adjustment (Type I subsequent event) of the financial statements that occurred after the date of the audit report but before it is issued, the statements should be adjusted or the opinion should be qualified. If the adjustment is made without any disclosure in the financial statements, the auditor's original report date is still used. If the adjustment is made and disclosed in the financial statements, or if the audit report is qualified due to lack of adjustment, the auditor may dual date the report by using the original report date except for the subsequent event which is dated later.

b. **Disclosure** The auditor may become aware of a new event requiring disclosure (Type II subsequent event) (such as a lawsuit filed after the balance sheet date but before the financial statements are issued). If disclosure is **not** made, the audit opinion would be qualified. If disclosure is made, the auditor may dual date the report. If dual dating is used, the responsibility for any events that occurred after the report date is limited to the particular subsequent event that is dual dated. If the auditor chooses, the later date may be used for the entire report. However, the auditor's responsibility for events occurring after the original report date will then extend to the later date.

3. **Reissuance** When an auditor reissues a report, the original report date should be used. This implies that there has been no audit past this date. When events that occurred subsequent to the date of the report require modification of the statements or the opinion, a dual date is appropriate. If events that occurred subsequent to the date of the report only require disclosure in the financial statements, the events may be disclosed in a note to the statements and the date of the original report may be used.

B. **Subsequent Events (AU 560)**
Subsequent events are events or transactions having a material effect on the financial statements that occur after the balance sheet date, but before the date the financial statements are issued.

1. **Types**

a. **Require Adjustment (Type 1)** Subsequent events that provide additional evidence about conditions that existed at the date of the balance sheet and affect the estimates used in preparing the financial statements require adjustment of the financial statements. Examples include a loss on an uncollectible trade account because a customer went bankrupt shortly after the end of the period (this indicates that the customer's financial position at the balance sheet date was not adequate to meet obligations), and the settlement of litigation for an amount different from the amount recorded in the accounts (as long as the reason for the litigation occurred prior to the balance sheet date).

b. **Require Only Disclosure (Type 2)** Subsequent events that provide evidence about conditions that did **not** exist at the balance sheet date but arose after that date, do **not** require adjustment of the financial statements. The conditions should be disclosed if their disclosure is required to keep the financial statements from being misleading. In some cases, *pro forma* statements may be prepared. Occasionally, the auditor may decide to include an explanatory paragraph in the report to draw the attention of the reader to the event. Examples of events requiring disclosure (but **not** adjustment) include (a) sale of a bond or capital stock issue, (b) purchase of a business, (c) settlement of litigation arising from events that occurred subsequent to the balance sheet date, (d) loss of plant or inventories as a result of a fire or flood, and (e) losses on receivables resulting from conditions that arose after the balance sheet date (such as a customer's major casualty loss).

2. **Reissuance of Financial Statements** Events that occur between the time of the original issuance of the statements and the time of reissuance of the statements (for example, in reports filed with a regulatory agency) should **not** result in an adjustment of the financial statements unless the adjustment would meet the criteria for the correction of an error or the criteria for prior period adjustments.

3. **Auditing Procedures in Subsequent Period** The subsequent period extends from the balance sheet date to the date of the auditor's report.

    a. Certain audit procedures should be performed after the balance sheet date to assure a proper cutoff and to evaluate the balances of certain asset and liability accounts.

    b. Additional auditing procedures should be applied to the period after the balance sheet date to identify subsequent events that may require adjustment or disclosure. These generally include (1) reading the latest interim financial statements and comparing them with the financial statements being reported on, (2) discussing with management having responsibility for financial and accounting matters the existence of substantial contingent liabilities, any significant change in stockholders' equity items, the current status of financial statement items that were accounted for on a tentative basis, and the existence of any unusual adjustments made after the balance sheet date, (3) reading the minutes of the board of directors' and stockholders' meetings, (4) inquiring of the client's legal counsel about litigation, claims, and assessments, (5) obtaining a letter of representation from management, dated as of the date of the auditor's report, as to whether any subsequent events occurred that would require adjustment to or disclosure in the statements, and (6) making any additional inquiries and performing any procedures that are considered necessary by the auditor.

C. **Subsequent Discovery of Facts Existing at Date of Audit Report (AU 561)**
    The auditor may, after the date of the report, become aware of facts that existed at that date and that might have affected the report had the auditor been aware of them.

    1. **Responsibility** The auditor does **not** have any obligation to perform auditing procedures or make inquiries after the report date unless the auditor becomes aware of this type of information. When the auditor becomes aware of information that relates to financial statements previously reported on by the auditor, but that was **not** known at the date of the report, and that is of such a nature and from such a source that the auditor would have investigated it, had the auditor been aware of it during the audit, the auditor should, as soon as practicable, determine whether the information is reliable and whether the facts existed at the date of the report.

        a. The auditor should discuss the matter with the appropriate level of the client's management, and request cooperation in the investigation into the matter.

        b. The auditor should consult an attorney when encountering these circumstances because of legal implications that may be involved, including the confidentiality of auditor-client communications.

    2. **Preventing Future Reliance on Report** When the subsequently discovered information is found both to be reliable and to have existed at the report date, the auditor should take action if the nature and effect of the matter are such that the report would have been affected by the information had it been known, and such that the auditor believes there are persons currently relying on, or likely to rely on, the financial statements. To prevent future reliance on the report, the auditor should advise the client to make appropriate disclosure of the newly discovered information, and the effect of the facts to the persons relying on, or likely to rely on, the statements.

        a. **Client Cooperates** If the client cooperates, the method used will depend on the circumstances.

            (1) **Revise & Reissue** The statements should be revised and reissued if the effect of the subsequently discovered information can be determined promptly. The reasons for the revision usually will be described in a note to the statements and referred to in the auditor's report.

(2) **Statements of a Subsequent Period** If the issuance of financial statements and the auditor's report for a subsequent period is imminent, appropriate revision can be made in such statements.

(3) **Notification by Client** If the effect on the statements cannot be determined promptly, but it appears the statements will be revised after investigation, the client should notify persons who are relying (or are likely to rely) on the statements and report that they should not do so, and that revised statements and the report will be issued when the investigation is complete.

b. **Client Does Not Cooperate** If the client does **not** cooperate, the auditor should notify the board of directors that unless the client cooperates, the auditor will (1) notify the client that the auditor's report cannot be associated with the financial statements, (2) notify regulatory agencies that the auditor's report should not be relied upon, and (3) notify each person that the auditor knows is relying on the statements and report that they should no longer do so.

3. **Disclosure to Other Parties**

a. When the auditor must make a disclosure and the auditor has been able to make a satisfactory investigation and determine that the information is reliable, the disclosure should include a description of the nature of the subsequently acquired information and describe the effect of the information on the financial statements and the report. The disclosure should be as factual and precise as possible, but it should **not** contain any comment on the conduct or motive of any person.

b. When the auditor has been prevented from making a satisfactory investigation, the auditor need **not** provide detailed information but can indicate that additional information, that the client has not helped substantiate, has come to the auditor's attention, and if true, the auditor believes the report should no longer be relied upon. No such disclosure should be made unless the auditor believes that the financial statements are likely to be misleading.

D. **Consideration of Omitted Procedures After Report Date (AU 390)**
The auditor may conclude, after the date of the report, that one or more auditing procedures considered necessary at that date were omitted from the audit, even though there is **no** indication that the financial statements are not fairly presented in conformity with GAAP or another comprehensive basis of accounting.

1. **Responsibility** Although the auditor does **not** have any responsibility to perform a retrospective review of the work performed, the omission of a necessary auditing procedure may be disclosed when the reports and working papers relating to the engagement are subjected to post-issuance review (e.g., a firm's internal inspection program or peer review).

2. **Assessment** Upon concluding that a necessary auditing procedure has been omitted, the auditor should assess the importance of the omitted procedure to the auditor's present ability to support a previously expressed opinion regarding the financial statements in question. This assessment can be aided by (a) reviewing the working papers, (b) discussing the audit circumstances with engagement personnel and others, and (c) reevaluating the overall scope of the audit. The results of other procedures that were applied may tend to compensate for, or make less important, the omitted procedure.

3. **Course of Action** If the auditor concludes that the omission of the necessary procedure impairs the present ability to support the previously expressed opinion, and the auditor believes that there are persons currently relying, or likely to rely, on the report, the auditor should proceed as follows:

a. **Previously Omitted Procedures Can Be Applied** The auditor should promptly apply the omitted procedure(s) or alternative procedures that would provide a satisfactory basis for the auditor's opinion. If, as a result, the auditor becomes aware of facts existing at the date of the report that would have affected that report had the auditor been aware of them, then the auditor should take steps to prevent future reliance on the report.

b. **Previously Omitted Procedures Can *Not* Be Applied** The auditor should consult an attorney to determine an appropriate course of action concerning responsibilities to the client, regulatory authorities, if any, having jurisdiction over the client, and persons relying, or likely to rely, on the report.

VIII. Association With Financial Statements (AU 504)

A. Association
The fourth standard of reporting seeks to avoid any misunderstanding as to the responsibility a CPA is assuming when a CPA's name is associated with financial statements.

Exhibit 27 ▶ From the Fourth Standard of Reporting

> "…In all cases where an auditor's name is associated with financial statements, the auditor should clearly indicate the character of the auditor's work, if any, and the degree of responsibility the auditor is taking in the auditor's report."

1. The CPA is associated with an entity's financial statements when the CPA (1) has agreed to the use of his or her name in a report, document, or written communication that contains the financial statements and/or (2) submits financial statements that the CPA has prepared (or assisted in preparing) to the client or to others (even if the CPA does not append his or her name to the financial statements).

2. Association does **not** occur when the CPA prepares data, such as tax returns, solely for submission to taxing authorities because these do not constitute financial statements.

B. Disclaimer of Opinion on Unaudited Financial Statements
When associated with a public entity's financial statements that the CPA has not audited or reviewed, the CPA should issue the disclaimer shown in Exhibit 28. Note that this disclaimer is different from a disclaimer of opinion due to a scope limitation discussed earlier.

Exhibit 28 ▶ Disclaimer

> The accompanying balance sheet of X Company as of December 31, 20X1, and the related statements of income, retained earnings, and cash flows for the year then ended were not audited by us and, accordingly, we do not express an opinion on them.

1. **Location** Disclaimer may accompany, or may be placed directly on, the unaudited financial statements.

2. **Markings** Each page of the statement should be marked as *unaudited.*

3. **Responsibility** CPA's only responsibility is to read the financial statements for obvious material misstatements.

4. **Procedures** The CPA should **not** describe any procedures that may have been applied, because to do so might give the impression that the CPA audited or reviewed the financial statements.

5. **Inclusion of Name** When a CPA learns that a client who is a public entity plans to include the CPA's name in a client-prepared written communication that will contain financial

statements that the CPA has **not** audited or reviewed, the CPA should ask (a) that his or her name **not** be used or (b) that the client clearly mark the financial statements as *unaudited* and that a notation be made that the auditor does **not** express an opinion on them. If the client refuses, the CPA may need to consult legal counsel as to appropriate actions.

C.   Disclaimer of Opinion on Unaudited OCBOA Financial Statements

Exhibit 29 ▶ OCBOA Financial Statements

> The accompanying statement of assets and liabilities resulting from cash transactions of XYZ Corporation as of December 31, 20X1, and the related statement of revenues collected and expenses paid during the year then ended were not audited by us and, accordingly, we do not express an opinion on them.

1. **Modification of Disclaimer** The unaudited disclaimer applies except that the identification of the financial statements should be modified to conform to AU 623, *Special Reports.*

2. **Note to Financial Statements** Should describe the difference between the basis of presentation and GAAP. The monetary effect of such differences does **not** need to be stated.

D.   Disclaimer of Opinion When CPA Is Not Independent
The second general standard requires independence in mental attitude. The CPA cannot be in accordance with GAAS if the CPA is not independent, so the CPA should disclaim an opinion and clearly state that he or she is not independent (the CPA should **not** give the reasons for this lack of independence).

Exhibit 30 ▶ Lack of Independence

> We are not independent with respect to XYZ Company, and the accompanying balance sheet as of December 31, 20X1, and the related statements of income, retained earnings, and cash flows for the year then ended were not audited by us and, accordingly, we do not express an opinion on them.

1. **Nonpublic Entity** The CPA should follow SSARS when the financial statements are those of a nonpublic entity.

2. **Public Entity** Paragraphs 1. through 2. of C., above, should be followed except that the disclaimer should be modified so that it clearly indicates the CPA is **not** independent. The reasons for lack of independence should **not** be described.

E.   Modified Disclaimer
If the CPA feels the unaudited financial statements do not conform to GAAP (which includes adequate disclosure), the CPA should ask the client to revise the statements. If the client refuses, the CPA should describe the departure in a disclaimer by (1) specifically referring to the nature of the departure and (2) if practicable, stating the effects of the departure on the financial statements or including the information that is needed in order to provide adequate disclosure.

1. **Indeterminable or Impracticable** If the effects of the departure cannot be reasonably determined, the CPA should state this in the disclaimer. In the case of inadequate disclosure, it may not be practicable for the CPA to include the omitted disclosures in the disclaimer.

2. **Withdrawal** If the client refuses to revise the statements or accept the disclaimer describing the departure, the CPA should refuse to be associated with the statements. The CPA may find it necessary to withdraw from the engagement.

3. **Negative Assurance** The CPA should **not** include statements in the disclaimer that would give negative assurance except as specifically permitted by the AICPA. (One permissible area is letters for underwriters.)

F.   Comparative Financial Statements

1.   Documents Filed With the SEC Unaudited financial statements presented in comparative form with audited financial statements should be clearly marked "unaudited." The auditor's report should **not** refer to the unaudited statements.

2.   Documents Other Than Those Filed With the SEC The unaudited financial statements should be clearly marked to indicate they have **not** been audited and either (a) the report on the prior period should be reissued or (b) the current period's report should contain a separate paragraph that describes the responsibility assumed for the financial statements of the prior period. In either case, the CPA should consider any information that has come to his or her attention during the CPA's current engagement that would help in evaluating the current form and presentation of the prior period information.

a.   Current Period Financial Statements Unaudited, Prior Period Financial Statements Audited If a separate paragraph is to be used, it should state (1) the prior period's statements were previously audited, (2) the date of the previous report, (3) the type of opinion that was previously expressed, (4) if it was **not** unqualified, the substantive reasons for this, and (5) that no auditing procedures have been performed after the date of the previous report.

Exhibit 31 ▶ Prior Audited, Current Unaudited

> The financial statements for the year ended December 31, 20X1, were audited by us (other accountants) and we (they) expressed an unqualified opinion on them in our (their) report dated March 1, 20X2, but we (they) have not performed any auditing procedures since that date.

b.   Prior Period Financial Statements Were Not Audited If a separate paragraph is to be used, it should (1) state the service that was performed in the prior period, (2) state the date of the report on that service, (3) describe any material modifications noted in that report, and (4) state that the scope of the service was less than that of an audit and, therefore, does **not** provide a basis for the expression of an opinion on the financial statements taken as a whole. When the financial statements are those of a public entity, the separate paragraph should include a disclaimer of opinion or a description of a review. When the prior period statements are for a nonpublic entity and were compiled or reviewed, the separate paragraph should contain an appropriate description of the compilation or review. The unaudited financial statements should be clearly marked to indicate their status.

Exhibit 32 ▶ Review Performed on Prior Period Financial Statements & Current Year's Statements Audited

> The 20X1 financial statements were reviewed by us (other accountants) and our (their) report thereon, dated March 1, 20X2, stated we (they) were not aware of any material modifications that should be made to those statements for them to be in conformity with generally accepted accounting principles. However, a review is substantially less in scope than an audit and does not provide a basis for the expression of an opinion on the financial statements taken as a whole.

Exhibit 33 ▶ Compiled Prior Period Financial Statements

> The 20X1 financial statements were compiled by us (other accountants) and our (their) report thereon, dated March 1, 20X2, stated we (they) did not audit or review those financial statements and, accordingly, express no opinion or other form of assurance on them.

IX. **Consideration of an Entity's Ability to Continue as a Going Concern (AU 341)**

A. **Responsibility**
Continuation of an entity as a going concern is assumed in financial reporting in the absence of significant information to the contrary. The auditor is responsible for evaluating information gathered during the audit to determine whether there is substantial doubt about the entity's ability to continue as a going concern for a reasonable period of time. A reasonable period of time is defined as a period **not** to exceed one year from the date of the financial statements.

1. **Scope** The auditor's evaluation is based on knowledge of events and relevant conditions that exist at or have occurred prior to the date of the auditor's report.

2. **Nature** Key information to be considered includes the entity's inability to meet its obligations in a timely manner without substantial disposal of assets outside the normal course of business, restructuring of debt, externally forced revisions of operations, or similar actions. Some examples of nonfinancial factors include the possible loss of key personnel, suppliers, and/or major customers.

3. **Future** The auditor is **not** expected to predict future conditions or events. If an entity ceases to exist within a year of receiving an audit report which does **not** refer to substantial doubt about the entity's ability to continue as a going concern, it does **not** necessarily indicate an inadequate performance by the auditor. The absence of a reference to substantial doubt should **not** be interpreted as an assurance of the entity's ability to continue as a going concern.

B. **Audit Procedures**
Audit procedures do **not** need to be designed specifically to identify conditions and events that, when considered in the aggregate, may indicate substantial doubt about the entity's ability to continue as a going concern. The results of auditing procedures designed and performed to achieve other audit objectives should be sufficient for that purpose. The following are examples of procedures that may identify such conditions and events:

1. Analytics

2. Review of subsequent events

3. Review of compliance with the terms of debt and loan agreements

4. Reading of minutes of meetings of stockholders, board of directors, and major committees of the board

5. Inquiry of an entity's legal counsel about litigation, claims, and assessments

6. Confirmation with related and third parties of the details of arrangements to provide or maintain financial support

C. **Indications**
Procedures such as those listed above may identify conditions and events that, when considered in the aggregate, indicate that substantial doubt may exist. Such conditions and events include the following:

1. **Negative Trends** For example, working capital deficiencies, recurring operating losses, negative cash flows from operating activities, or adverse key financial ratios.

2. **Other Indications of Possible Financial Difficulties** For example, default on loan or similar agreements, arrearages in dividends, denial of usual trade credit from suppliers, restructuring of debt, noncompliance with statutory capital requirements, need to seek new sources or methods of financing, or to dispose of substantial assets.

3. **Internal Matters** For example, work stoppages or other labor difficulties, substantial dependence on the success of a particular project, uneconomic long-term commitments, or need to significantly revise operations.

4. **External Matters That Have Occurred** For example, legal proceedings, legislation, or similar matters that might jeopardize an entity's ability to operate; loss of a key franchise, license, or patent; loss of a principal customer or supplier; or uninsured or underinsured catastrophe such as a drought, earthquake, or flood.

D. **Conclusions**

If, after completing the audit, the auditor finds that conditions and events exist that, when considered in the aggregate, indicate that there could be substantial doubt about the entity's ability to continue as a going concern for a reasonable period of time, the following steps should be taken:

1. **Mitigating Factors** The auditor should obtain any additional information available about the conditions and events or about mitigating factors including management's plans.

2. **Management Plans** The auditor must consider management's plans in order to evaluate the likelihood of successful implementation. The auditor should obtain information about the plans and decide whether it is likely the adverse effects will be mitigated for a reasonable period of time and that such plans can be implemented effectively. The auditor's consideration relating to management's plans may include the following:

    a. **Dispose of Assets**

        (1) Restrictions on disposal of assets, such as covenants limiting such transactions in loan or similar agreements or encumbrances against assets

        (2) Apparent marketability of assets that management plans to sell

        (3) Possible direct or indirect effects of disposal of assets

    b. **Borrow Money or Restructure Debt**

        (1) Availability of debt financing, including existing or committed credit arrangements, such as lines of credit or arrangements for factoring receivables or sale-leaseback of assets

        (2) Existing or committed arrangements to restructure or subordinate debt or to guarantee loans to the entity

        (3) Existing restrictions on additional borrowing or the sufficiency of available collateral

    c. **Reduce or Delay Expenditures**

        (1) Apparent feasibility of plans to reduce overhead or administrative expenditures, to postpone maintenance or research and development projects, or to lease rather than purchase assets

        (2) Possible direct or indirect effects of reduced or delayed expenditures

    d. **Increase Ownership Equity**

        (1) Apparent feasibility of plans to increase ownership equity, including existing or committed arrangements to raise additional capital

        (2) Existing or committed arrangements to reduce current dividend requirements or to accelerate cash distributions from affiliates or other investors

e. **Prospective Financial Information** When prospective financial information is significant to management's plans, the auditor should request management to provide that information and should consider the adequacy of support for significant assumptions underlying that information. The auditor should give particular attention to assumptions that are (1) material to the prospective financial statements, (2) especially sensitive or susceptible to change, or (3) inconsistent with historical trends. The auditor's consideration should include reading the information and the underlying assumptions, comparing the prospective information in prior periods with actual results, and comparing prospective information for the current period with actual results to date.

3. **Disclosure of Doubt** The auditor should consider the adequacy of the disclosure of the doubt about the entity's ability to continue and include an explanatory paragraph **after** the opinion paragraph in the audit report. If the auditor concludes that substantial doubt about the entity's ability to continue as a going concern exists, the auditor must consider disclosure of the conditions or events in the financial statements. Information that might be disclosed include the following:

a. Pertinent conditions and events giving rise to the assessment of substantial doubt about the entity's ability to continue as a going concern for a reasonable period of time

b. The possible effects of such conditions and events

c. Management's evaluation of the significance of those conditions and events and any mitigating factors

d. Possible discontinuance of operations

e. Management's plans (including relevant prospective financial information)

f. Information about the recoverability or classification of recorded asset amounts or the amounts or classification of liabilities

4. **Disclosure of Trigger** If the auditor concludes that substantial doubt does **not** exist, the auditor should consider the disclosure of the information that triggered concern about the entity's ability to continue as a going concern for a reasonable period of time and outline mitigating circumstances, including management's plans.

E. **Audit Report**

1. **Explanatory Paragraph for Modified Unqualified Opinion** The audit report should include an explanatory paragraph **after** the opinion paragraph if the auditor concludes that substantial doubt about the entity's ability to continue as a going concern exists.

a. **Required Terms** The explanatory paragraph should include the phrase "substantial doubt about its (the entity's) ability to continue as a going concern" or similar wording that includes the terms *substantial doubt* **and** *going concern*. The use of conditional language regarding the entity's ability to continue as a going concern is prohibited.

b. **Inappropriate Statement** "If XYZ Company is unable to renegotiate the labor contract, there may be substantial doubt about XYZ Company's ability to continue as a going concern."

c. **Appropriate Statement** "The accompanying financial statements have been prepared assuming that the Company will continue as a going concern. As discussed in Note X to the financial statements, the Company has suffered recurring losses from operations and has a net capital deficiency that raise substantial doubt about its ability to continue as a going concern. Management's plans in regard to these matters are also described in Note X. The financial statements do not include any adjustments that might result from the outcome of this uncertainty."

2. **Inadequate Disclosure** If the auditor concludes that the entity's disclosures with respect to the entity's ability to continue as a going concern for a reasonable period of time are inadequate, a departure from generally accepted accounting principles exists. This may result in either a qualified (except for) or an adverse opinion.

F. **Comparison With Prior Financial Statements**
Substantial doubt about an entity's ability to continue as a going concern that arose in the current period should **not** affect the auditor's report on the financial statements of prior periods used for comparison with current financial statements. If substantial doubt existed in the prior period, but has been alleviated in the current period, the explanatory paragraph after the opinion paragraph in the auditor's report should **not** be repeated.

G. **Communications**
The auditor should communicate with those charged with governance when there is substantial doubt about the entity's ability to continue as a going concern for a reasonable period of time after the consideration of identified conditions and events in the aggregate as well as management's plans. This communication should include:

1. The nature of the events or conditions identified

2. The possible effect on the financial statements and the adequacy of related disclosures in the financial statements

3. The effects on the auditor's report

H. **Documentation**
The auditor should document:

1. The conditions or events that led the auditor to believe that there is substantial doubt about the entity's ability to continue as a going concern for a reasonable period of time.

2. The elements of management's plans that the auditor considered to be particularly significant to overcoming the adverse effects of the conditions or events.

3. The auditing procedures performed and evidence obtained to evaluate the significant elements of management's plans.

4. The auditor's conclusion as to whether substantial doubt about the entity's ability to continue as a going concern for a reasonable period of time remains or is alleviated. If substantial doubt remains, the auditor also should document the possible effects of the conditions or events on the financial statements and the adequacy of the related disclosures. If substantial doubt is alleviated, the auditor also should document the conclusion as to the need for disclosure of the principal conditions and events that initially caused the auditor to believe there was substantial doubt.

5. The auditor's conclusion as to whether an explanatory paragraph should be included in the audit report. If disclosures with respect to an entity's ability to continue as a going concern are inadequate, the auditor also should document the conclusion as to whether to express a qualified or adverse opinion for the resultant departure from generally accepted accounting principles.

X. Other Information in Documents Containing Audited Financial Statements (AU 550)

A. Auditor's Overall Responsibilities

Generally, the auditor's opinion on the financial statements does **not** cover other information in documents containing audited financial statements and the audit report. Additionally, the auditor has **no** responsibility for determining whether such information is properly stated. (The exception being when there is a separate requirement to do so in the particular circumstances of an engagement.)

1. **Read the Other Information Prior to Report Release Date** However, the auditor should read the other information. The auditor should make appropriate arrangements with management or those charged with governance to obtain the other information prior to the report release date. If this is not possible, the auditor should read such other information as soon as practicable. The auditor may also decide to delay the release of the report until the information is provided.

2. **Objective** The auditor's purpose is to identify and attempt to resolve possible material *inconsistencies* and apparent material *misstatements of facts* (see definitions below) that could undermine the credibility of the audited financial statements and the audit report. Failing a resolution on the revisions needed, the auditor should respond in a manner that is appropriate for the particular circumstances.

3. **Communication** The auditor should communicate with those charged with governance:

   a. **Auditor's Responsibilities** The auditor's responsibility with respect to the other information

   b. **Procedures & Results** Any procedures performed relating to the other information and the results

Editor note: The auditor's responsibility for other information presented in a document containing audited financial statements that is *required* to be included per an accounting standard is covered in AU 558, *Required Supplementary Information*. However, if the other information is prepared according to an accounting standard's guidance and is presented *voluntarily*, then it is addressed by this standard—AU 550.

B. Audit Report

1. **Audit Report Reference Not Required** The auditor is **not** required to reference the other information in the audit report.

2. **Optional Disclaimer** However, the auditor may include an explanatory paragraph disclaiming an opinion on the other information. For example, an auditor may choose to do so when the auditor could be associated with the information and the user may infer a level of assurance that is not intended. An example of such an explanatory paragraph is:

   Our audit was conducted for the purpose of forming an opinion on the basic financial statements as a whole. The [*identify the other information*] is presented for purposes of additional analysis and is not a required part of the basic financial statements. Such information has not been subjected to the auditing procedures applied in the audit of the basic financial statements, and accordingly, we do not express an opinion or provide any assurance on it.

C. Definitions

1. **Other Information** Financial and nonfinancial information (other than the financial statements and the audit report) that is included in a document containing audited financial statements and the audit report, excluding required supplementary information.

   a. **Examples**

      - A report by management or those charged with governance on operations

      - Financial summaries or highlights

      - Employment data

      - Planned capital expenditures

      - Financial ratios

      - Names of officers and directors

      - Selected quarterly data

   b. **Items Not Considered to be *Other Information*** Per GAAS, other information does **not**, for example, include a press release or similar memorandum or a cover letter accompanying the document containing audited financial statements and the audit report; information contained in analyst briefings; or information contained on the entity's website.

2. **Documents Containing Audited Financial Statements**

   a. Annual reports (or similar documents) that are issued to owners (or similar stakeholders)

   b. Annual reports of governments and organizations for charitable or philanthropic purposes that are available to the public that contain audited financial statements and the audit report

   c. Other documents to which the auditor, at the client's request, devotes attention

3. **Inconsistency (With Financial Statements)** An inconsistency is other information that conflicts with information contained in the audited financial statements. A material inconsistency may raise doubt about the audit conclusions drawn from audit evidence previously obtained and, possibly, about the basis for the auditor's opinion.

4. **Misstatement of Fact (Unrelated to Financial Statements)** A misstatement of fact is other information that is unrelated to matters appearing in the audited financial statements that is incorrectly stated or presented. A material misstatement of fact may undermine the credibility of the document containing audited financial statements.

D. Procedures for Material Inconsistencies Identified Prior to Report Release Date

1. **Revision of Financial Statements Needed** If the auditor determines the financial statements should be revised and management refuses, the auditor should modify the auditor's opinion in accordance with AU 508, *Reports on Audited Financial Statements*.

2. **Revision of Other Information Needed** If the auditor determines the other information should be revised and management refuses, the auditor should respond as follows.

   a. The auditor should communicate this matter to those charged with governance.

b. Depending on the circumstances and the significance of the inconsistency, the auditor should do one of the following.

    (1) Add Explanatory Language to Standard Report Include in the audit report an explanatory paragraph describing the material inconsistency (this does not affect the auditor's unqualified opinion);

    (2) Withhold the Audit Report; or

    (3) Withdraw From the Engagement

    When management refuses to revise the other information, the auditor may base any decision on what further action to take on advice from legal counsel.

    Editor note: In audits of governmental entities, withdrawal from the engagement or withholding the audit report may not be options. In such cases, the auditor may issue a report to those charged with governance and the appropriate statutory body, if applicable, giving details of the inconsistency.

E. Procedures for Material Inconsistencies Identified Subsequent to Report Release Date

1. Revision of Financial Statements Needed The auditor should apply the relevant requirements in AU 561, *Subsequent Discovery of Facts Existing at the Date of the Auditor's Report*. (See the section on timing issues in this chapter.)

2. Revision of Other Information Needed

    a. Management Makes Revision The auditor should carry out the procedures necessary under the circumstances. These may include reviewing the steps taken by management to ensure that individuals in receipt of the previously issued financial statements, the audit report, and the other information are informed of the need for revision.

    b. Management Refuses to Revise The auditor should notify those charged with governance of the auditor's concerns regarding the other information and take any further appropriate action. This may include obtaining advice from legal counsel.

F. Procedures for Material Misstatements of Fact Identified

1. Discussion With Management If, on reading the other information for the purpose of identifying material inconsistencies, the auditor becomes aware of an apparent material misstatement of fact, the auditor should discuss the matter with management.

2. Consultation With Third Party If the discussion with management does not resolve the auditor's concerns, the auditor should request that management consult with a qualified third party, such as the entity's legal counsel, and the auditor should consider the advice received by the entity.

3. Management Refuses to Revise If the auditor concludes there is a material misstatement of fact and management refuses to revise the other information, the auditor should notify those charged with governance and take any further appropriate action. This may include obtaining advice from legal counsel, withholding the audit report, or withdrawing from the engagement.

XI. Required Supplementary Information (AU 558)

A. Overview / Objective
When a designated accounting standard setter requires information to accompany an entity's basic financial statements, the auditor's objective is to perform limited procedures in order to describe (1) the degree of completeness of the required supplementary information (RSI) and (2) its

adherence with prescribed guidelines in an explanatory paragraph added to the audit report on the financial statements **after** the opinion paragraph.

No opinion is expressed nor is any assurance provided on the RSI.

Editor note: The auditor's responsibility for financial and nonfinancial information (other than the financial statements and the audit report) that is included in a document containing audited financial statements and the audit report that is **not** required by a designated accounting standard setter, but is presented *voluntarily* by the entity, is addressed in AU 550, *Other Information in Documents Containing Audited Financial Statements*.

B. Definitions

1. **Required Supplementary Information** Information that a designated accounting standard setter requires to accompany an entity's basic financial statements. RSI is **not** part of the basic financial statements; however, a designated accounting standard setter considers the information to be an essential part of financial reporting for placing the basic financial statements in an appropriate operational, economic, or historical context. In addition, authoritative guidelines for the methods of measurement and presentation of the information have been established.

   Generally, the auditor's opinion on the basic financial statements does **not** cover RSI. (The exception being when there is a separate requirement to do so in the particular circumstances of an engagement.)

2. **Designated Accounting Standard Setter** The following bodies have been designated by the AICPA Council to establish GAAP pursuant to ET 202, *Compliance With Standards*, and ET 203, *Accounting Principles*:

   • Financial Accounting Standards Board (FASB)

   • Governmental Accounting Standards Board (GASB)

   • Federal Accounting Standards Advisory Board (FASAB)

   • International Accounting Standards Board (IASB)

3. **Basic Financial Statements** Financial statements presented in accordance with an applicable financial reporting framework as established by a designated accounting standard setter, excluding RSI.

4. **Applicable Financial Reporting Framework** The financial reporting framework adopted by management and those charged with governance in the preparation of the financial statements that is acceptable in view of the nature of the entity and the objective of the financial statements, or that is required by law or regulation.

5. **Prescribed Guidelines** The authoritative guidelines established by the designated accounting standard setter for the methods of measurement and presentation of the RSI.

C. Written Management Representations
The auditor should obtain written representations from management:

1. That it acknowledges its responsibility for the RSI

2. About whether the RSI is measured and presented in accordance with prescribed guidelines

3. About whether the methods of measurement or presentation have changed from those used in the prior period and, if so, the reasons for such changes

4. About any significant assumptions or interpretations underlying the measurement or presentation of the RSI

D. Procedures

In addition to obtaining the written representations from management just described, the auditor should apply the following procedures to RSI. If the auditor is unable to complete these procedures due to significant difficulties encountered in dealing with management, the auditor should inform those charged with governance.

1. Inquire of management about the methods of preparing the information, including whether:

    a. It has been measured and presented in accordance with prescribed guidelines

    b. Methods of measurement or presentation have been changed from those used in the prior period and the reasons for any such changes

    c. There were any significant assumptions or interpretations underlying the measurement or presentation of the information

2. Compare the information for consistency with

    a. Management's responses to the foregoing inquiries

    b. The basic financial statements

    c. Other knowledge obtained during the audit of the basic financial statements

E. Reporting

The auditor should include an explanatory paragraph in the audit report on the financial statements, **after** the opinion paragraph, to refer to the RSI. It should explain the following circumstances, as applicable.

1. The RSI is included and the auditor has applied the required procedures.

2. Some RSI is missing and some is presented in accordance with the prescribed guidelines.

3. The auditor has identified material departures from the prescribed guidelines.

4. The auditor is unable to complete the required procedures.

5. The auditor has unresolved doubts about whether the RSI is presented in accordance with prescribed guidelines.

6. The RSI is omitted.

Editor note: Because the RSI accompanies the basic financial statements, the audit report on the financial statements includes a discussion of the responsibility taken by the auditor on that information. However, because the RSI is **not** part of the basic financial statements, the auditor's opinion on the fairness of presentation of such financial statements in accordance with the applicable financial reporting framework is **not** affected by the presentation by the entity of the RSI or the failure to present some or all of it. Furthermore, if the RSI is omitted by the entity, the auditor does **not** have a responsibility to present it.

F. Reporting Elements of Explanatory Paragraph When All or Some of the RSI Is Presented

1. A statement that [*identify the applicable financial reporting framework (for example, accounting principles generally accepted in the United States of America)*] require that the [*identify the required supplementary information*] be presented to supplement the basic financial statements.

2. A statement that such information, although not a part of the basic financial statements, is required by [*identify designated accounting standard setter*], who considers it to be an essential part of financial reporting for placing the basic financial statements in an appropriate operational, economic, or historical context.

3. If the auditor is able to complete the required procedures:

    a. A statement that the auditor has applied certain limited procedures to the required supplementary information in accordance with auditing standards generally accepted in the United States of America, which consisted of inquiries of management about the methods of preparing the information and comparing the information for consistency with management's responses to the auditor's inquiries, the basic financial statements, and other knowledge the auditor obtained during the audit of the basic financial statements.

    b. A statement that the auditor does not express an opinion or provide any assurance on the information because the limited procedures do not provide the auditor with sufficient evidence to express an opinion or provide any assurance.

Exhibit 34 ▶ The RSI Is Included, the Auditor Has Applied the Specified Procedures, and No Material Departures From Prescribed Guidelines Have Been Identified

[*Identify the applicable financial reporting framework (for example, accounting principles generally accepted in the United States of America)*] require that the [*identify the required supplementary information*] on page XX be presented to supplement the basic financial statements. Such information, although not a part of the basic financial statements, is required by [*identify designated accounting standard setter*] who considers it to be an essential part of financial reporting for placing the basic financial statements in an appropriate operational, economic, or historical context. We have applied certain limited procedures to the required supplementary information in accordance with auditing standards generally accepted in the United States of America, which consisted of inquiries of management about the methods of preparing the information and comparing the information for consistency with management's responses to our inquiries, the basic financial statements, and other knowledge we obtained during our audit of the basic financial statements. We do not express an opinion or provide any assurance on the information because the limited procedures do not provide us with sufficient evidence to express an opinion or provide any assurance.

4. If the auditor is **not** able to complete the required procedures:

    a. A statement that the auditor was unable to apply certain limited procedures to the required supplementary information in accordance with auditing standards generally accepted in the United States because [*state the reasons*]

    b. A statement that the auditor does not express an opinion or provide any assurance on the information

Exhibit 35 ▶ Specified Procedures Not Completed

[*Identify the applicable financial reporting framework (for example, accounting principles generally accepted in the United States of America)*] require that the [*identify the supplementary information*] on page XX be presented to supplement the basic financial statements. Such information, although not a part of the basic financial statements, is required by [*identify designated accounting standard setter*] who considers it to be an essential part of financial reporting for placing the basic financial statements in an appropriate operational, economic, or historical context. We were unable to apply certain limited procedures to the required supplementary information in accordance with auditing standards generally accepted in the United States of America because [*state the reasons*]. We do not express an opinion or provide any assurance on the information.

5. If some of the RSI is omitted:

    a. A statement that management has omitted [*description of the missing required supplementary information*] that [*identify the applicable financial reporting framework (for example, accounting principles generally accepted in the United States of America)*] require to be presented to supplement the basic financial statements

    b. A statement that such missing information, although not a part of the basic financial statements, is required by [*identify designated accounting standard setter*], who considers it to be an essential part of financial reporting for placing the basic financial statements in an appropriate operational, economic, or historical context

    c. A statement that the auditor's opinion on the basic financial statements is not affected by the missing information

Editor note: These elements are in addition to the elements in F.1. through 3 above.

Exhibit 36 ▶ Some RSI Is Omitted and Some Is Presented in Accordance With the Prescribed Guidelines

[*Identify the applicable financial reporting framework (for example, accounting principles generally accepted in the United States of America)*] require that [*identify the included supplementary information*] be presented to supplement the basic financial statements. Such information, although not a part of the basic financial statements, is required by [*identify designated accounting standard setter*] who considers it to be an essential part of financial reporting for placing the basic financial statements in an appropriate operational, economic, or historical context. We have applied certain limited procedures to the required supplementary information in accordance with auditing standards generally accepted in the United States of America, which consisted of inquiries of management about the methods of preparing the information and comparing the information for consistency with management's responses to our inquiries, the basic financial statements, and other knowledge we obtained during our audit of the basic financial statements. We do not express an opinion or provide any assurance on the information because the limited procedures do not provide us with evidence sufficient to express an opinion or provide any assurance.

Management has omitted [*describe the missing required supplementary information*] that [*identify the applicable financial reporting framework*] require to be presented to supplement the basic financial statements. Such missing information, although not a part of the basic financial statements, is required by [*identify designated accounting standard setter*] who considers it to be an essential part of financial reporting for placing the basic financial statements in an appropriate operational, economic, or historical context. Our opinion on the basic financial statements is not affected by this missing information.

6.   If the measurement or presentation of the RSI departs materially from the prescribed guidelines, a statement that although the auditor's opinion on the basic financial statements is not affected, material departures from prescribed guidelines exist [*describe the material departures from the applicable financial reporting framework*]

Exhibit 37 ▶ Material Departures From Prescribed Guidelines Identified

[*Identify the applicable financial reporting framework (for example, accounting principles generally accepted in the United States of America)*] require that the [*identify the supplementary information*] on page XX be presented to supplement the basic financial statements. Such information, although not a part of the basic financial statements, is required by [*identify designated accounting standard setter*] who considers it to be an essential part of financial reporting for placing the basic financial statements in an appropriate operational, economic, or historical context. We have applied certain limited procedures to the required supplementary information in accordance with auditing standards generally accepted in the United States of America, which consisted of inquiries of management about the methods of preparing the information and comparing the information for consistency with management's responses to our inquiries, the basic financial statements, and other knowledge we obtained during our audit of the basic financial statements. Although our opinion on the basic financial statements is not affected, the following material departures from the prescribed guidelines exist [*identify the required supplementary information and describe the material departures from the prescribed guidelines*]. We do not express an opinion or provide any assurance on the information.

7.   If the auditor has unresolved doubts about whether the RSI is measured or presented in accordance with prescribed guidelines, a statement that although the auditor's opinion on the basic financial statements is not affected, the results of the limited procedures have raised doubts about whether material modifications should be made to the required supplementary information for it to be presented in accordance with guidelines established by [*identify designated accounting standard setter*]

Exhibit 38 ▶ Unresolved Doubts About Whether the RSI Is in Accordance With Prescribed Guidelines

[*Identify the applicable financial reporting framework (for example, accounting principles generally accepted in the United States of America)*] require that the [*identify the supplementary information*] on page XX be presented to supplement the basic financial statements. Such information, although not a part of the basic financial statements, is required by [*identify designated accounting standard setter*] who considers it to be an essential part of financial reporting for placing the basic financial statements in an appropriate operational, economic, or historical context. We have applied certain limited procedures to the required supplementary information in accordance with auditing standards generally accepted in the United States of America, which consisted of inquiries of management about the methods of preparing the information and comparing the information for consistency with management's responses to our inquiries, the basic financial statements, and other knowledge we obtained during our audit of the basic financial statements. We do not express an opinion or provide any assurance on the information because the limited procedures do not provide us with sufficient evidence to express an opinion or provide any assurance. Although our opinion on the basic financial statements is not affected, the results of the limited procedures have raised doubts about whether material modifications should be made to the required supplementary information for it to be presented in accordance with guidelines established by [*identify designated accounting standard setter*]. [*The auditor may consider including in the report the reason(s) the auditor was unable to resolve the doubts.*]

G.   Reporting Elements of Explanatory Paragraph When All of the RSI Is Omitted

1.   A statement that management has omitted [description of the missing required supplementary information] that [identify the applicable financial reporting framework (for example, accounting principles generally accepted in the United States of America)] require to be presented to supplement the basic financial statements

2.   A statement that such missing information, although not a part of the basic financial statements, is required by [*identify designated accounting standard setter*], who considers it to be an essential part of financial reporting for placing the basic financial statements in an appropriate operational, economic, or historical context

3.   A statement that the auditor's opinion on the basic financial statements is not affected by the missing information

Exhibit 39 ▶ All RSI Omitted

Management has omitted [*describe the missing required supplementary information*] that [*identify the applicable financial reporting framework (for example, accounting principles generally accepted in the United States of America)*] require to be presented to supplement the basic financial statements. Such missing information, although not a part of the basic financial statements, is required by [*identify designated accounting standard setter*] who considers it to be an essential part of financial reporting for placing the basic financial statements in an appropriate operational, economic, or historical context. Our opinion on the basic financial statements is not affected by this missing information.

CHAPTER 8—REPORTS ON AUDITED FINANCIAL STATEMENTS

Problem 8-1 MULTIPLE-CHOICE QUESTIONS

1. When issuing an unqualified opinion, the auditor who evaluates the audit findings should be satisfied that the

   a. Amount of known misstatement is documented in the management representation letter.
   b. Estimate of the total likely misstatement is less than a material amount.
   c. Amount of known misstatement is acknowledged and recorded by the client.
   d. Estimate of the total likely misstatement includes the adjusting entries already recorded by the client.

   (11/98, AUD, #21, ID: 6712)

2. The fourth standard of reporting requires the auditor's report to contain either an expression of opinion regarding the financial statements taken as a whole or an assertion to the effect that an opinion cannot be expressed. The objective of the fourth standard is to prevent

   a. An auditor from expressing different opinions on each of the basic financial statements
   b. Restrictions on the scope of the audit, whether imposed by the client or by the inability to obtain evidence
   c. Misinterpretations regarding the degree of responsibility the auditor is assuming
   d. An auditor from reporting on one basic financial statement and not the others

   (11/95, AUD, #68, ID: 6015)

3. Field is an employee of Gold Enterprises. Hardy, CPA, is asked to express an opinion on Field's profit participation in Gold's net income. Hardy may accept this engagement only if

   a. Hardy also audits Gold's complete financial statements.
   b. Gold's financial statements are prepared in conformity with GAAP.
   c. Hardy's report is available for distribution to Gold's other employees.
   d. Field owns controlling interest in Gold.

   (11/95, AUD, #83, ID: 6030)

4. The first standard of reporting requires that the auditor state in the auditor's report whether the financial statements are presented in accordance with generally accepted accounting principles. This should be construed to require

   a. A statement of fact by the auditor
   b. An implied measure of fairness
   c. An objective measure of compliance
   d. An opinion by the auditor

   (Editors, ID: 7507)

5. The phrase *generally accepted accounting principles* is an accounting term that

   a. Includes broad guidelines of general application but not detailed practices and procedures
   b. Encompasses the conventions, rules, and procedures necessary to define accepted accounting practice at a particular time
   c. Provides a measure of conventions, rules, and procedures governed by the AICPA
   d. Is included in the audit report to indicate that the audit has been conducted in accordance with generally accepted auditing standards (GAAS)

   (R/08, AUD, #19, ID: 8625)

6. When single year financial statements are presented, an auditor ordinarily would express an unqualified opinion in an unmodified report if the

   a. Auditor is unable to obtain audited financial statements supporting the entity's investment in a foreign affiliate.
   b. Entity declines to present a statement of cash flows with its balance sheet and related statements of income and retained earnings.
   c. Auditor wishes to emphasize an accounting matter affecting the comparability of the financial statements with those of the prior year.
   d. Prior year's financial statements were audited by another CPA whose report, which expressed an unqualified opinion, is not presented.

   (5/94, AUD, #74, ID: 4739)

7. If a company issues financial statements that purport to present its financial position and results of operations but omits the statement of cash flows, the auditor ordinarily will express a(an)

    a. Disclaimer of opinion
    b. Qualified opinion
    c. Review report
    d. Unqualified opinion with a separate explanatory paragraph   (5/93, AUD, #46, amended, ID: 3942)

8. Restrictions imposed by a client prohibit the observation of physical inventories, which account for 35% of all assets. Alternative audit procedures cannot be applied, although the auditor was able to examine satisfactory evidence for all other items in the financial statements. The auditor should issue a(an)

    a. "Except for" qualified opinion
    b. Unqualified opinion with an explanation in the scope paragraph
    c. Unqualified opinion with a separate explanatory paragraph
    d. Disclaimer of opinion   (Editors, ID: 7501)

9. In which of the following circumstances would an auditor **not** express an unqualified opinion?

    a. There has been a material change between periods in accounting principles.
    b. Quarterly financial data required by the SEC has been omitted.
    c. The auditor wishes to emphasize an unusually important subsequent event.
    d. The auditor is unable to obtain audited financial statements of a consolidated investee.
    (11/95, AUD, #69, ID: 6016)

10. An explanatory paragraph following the opinion paragraph of an auditor's report describes an uncertainty as follows:

As discussed in Note X to the financial statements, the Company is a defendant in a lawsuit alleging infringement of certain patent rights and claiming damages. Discovery proceedings are in progress. The ultimate outcome of the litigation cannot presently be determined. Accordingly, no provision for any liability that may result upon adjudication has been made in the accompanying financial statements.

What type of opinion should the auditor express under these circumstances?

    a. Adverse
    b. Qualified due to a scope limitation
    c. Qualified due to a GAAP violation
    d. Unqualified   (11/95, AUD, #70, ID: 6017)

11. Park, CPA, was engaged to audit the financial statements of Tech Co., a new client, for the year ended December 31, year 1. Park obtained sufficient audit evidence for all of Tech's financial statement items except Tech's opening inventory. Due to inadequate financial records, Park could not verify Tech's January 1, year 1, inventory balances. Park's opinion on Tech's year 1 financial statements most likely will be

	Balance sheet	*Income statement*
a.	Disclaimer	Disclaimer
b.	Unqualified	Disclaimer
c.	Disclaimer	Adverse
d.	Unqualified	Adverse

    (5/94, AUD, #76, amended, ID: 4741)

12. In which of the following situations would an auditor ordinarily choose between expressing a qualified opinion or an adverse opinion?

    a. The auditor did not observe the entity's physical inventory and is unable to become satisfied about its balance by other auditing procedures.

    b. Conditions that cause the auditor to have substantial doubt about the entity's ability to continue as a going concern are inadequately disclosed.

    c. There has been a change in accounting principles that has a material effect on the comparability of the entity's financial statements.

    d. The auditor is unable to apply necessary procedures concerning an investor's share of an investee's earnings recognized on the equity method. (R/00, AUD, #17, ID: 6942)

13. If a client makes a change in accounting principle that is inseparable from the effect of a change in estimate, this material event should be handled in the accounting records as a change in

    a. Estimate and the auditor would report a consistency exception

    b. Estimate and the auditor would not modify the report

    c. Principle and the auditor would report a consistency exception

    d. Principle and the auditor would not modify the report (Editors, ID: 7502)

14. In which of the following situations would an auditor ordinarily choose between expressing an "except for" qualified opinion or an adverse opinion?

    a. The auditor did not observe the entity's physical inventory and is unable to become satisfied as to its balance by other auditing procedures.

    b. The financial statements fail to disclose information that is required by generally accepted accounting principles.

    c. The auditor is asked to report only on the entity's balance sheet and not on the other basic financial statements.

    d. Events disclosed in the financial statements cause the auditor to have substantial doubt about the entity's ability to continue as a going concern. (5/93, AUD, #58, ID: 3954)

15. Digit Co. uses the FIFO method of costing for its international subsidiary's inventory and LIFO for its domestic inventory. Under these circumstances, the auditor's report on Digit's financial statements should express an

    a. Unqualified opinion

    b. Opinion qualified because of a lack of consistency

    c. Opinion qualified because of a departure from GAAP

    d. Adverse opinion (11/95, AUD, #67, ID: 6014)

16. An auditor concludes that a client's illegal act, which has a material effect on the financial statements, has **not** been properly accounted for or disclosed. Depending on the materiality of the effect on the financial statements, the auditor should express either a(an)

    a. Adverse opinion or a disclaimer of opinion

    b. Qualified opinion or an adverse opinion

    c. Disclaimer of opinion or an unqualified opinion with a separate explanatory paragraph

    d. Unqualified opinion with a separate explanatory paragraph or a qualified opinion (5/95, AUD, #13, ID: 5631)

17. A client decides **not** to make an auditor's proposed adjustments that collectively are **not** material and wants the auditor to issue the report based on the unadjusted numbers. Which of the following statements is correct regarding the financial statement presentation?

    a. The financial statements are free from material misstatement, and no disclosure is required in the notes to the financial statements.

    b. The financial statements do not conform with generally accepted accounting principles (GAAP).

    c. The financial statements contain unadjusted misstatements that should result in a qualified opinion.

    d. The financial statements are free from material misstatement, but disclosure of the proposed adjustments is required in the notes to the financial statements. (R/08, AUD, #44, ID: 8650)

18. Which of the following statements is a basic element of the auditor's standard report?

    a. The disclosures provide reasonable assurance that the financial statements are free of material misstatement.
    b. The financial statements are consistent with those of the prior period.
    c. An audit includes assessing significant estimates made by management.
    d. The auditor evaluated the overall internal control. (11/95, AUD, #62, amended, ID: 6009)

19. The existence of audit risk is recognized by the statement in the auditor's standard report that the

    a. Auditor is responsible for expressing an opinion on the financial statements, which are the responsibility of management.
    b. Financial statements are presented fairly, in all material respects, in conformity with GAAP.
    c. Audit includes examining, on a test basis, evidence supporting the amounts and disclosures in the financial statements.
    d. Auditor obtains reasonable assurance about whether the financial statements are free of material misstatement. (11/94, AUD, #9, ID: 5082)

20. An auditor's responsibility to express an opinion on the financial statements is

    a. Explicitly represented in the opinion paragraph of the auditor's standard report
    b. Explicitly represented in the opening paragraph of the auditor's standard report
    c. Explicitly represented in the scope paragraph of the auditor's standard report
    d. Implicitly represented in the auditor's standard report (5/92, AUD, #11, amended, ID: 7503)

21. For an entity that does **not** receive governmental financial assistance, an auditor's standard report on financial statements generally would **not** refer to

    a. Significant estimates made by management
    b. The entity's internal control
    c. Management's responsibility for the financial statements
    d. An assessment of the entity's accounting principles (5/94, AUD, #71, amended, ID: 4736)

22. Which paragraphs of an auditor's standard report on financial statements should refer to generally accepted auditing standards (GAAS) and generally accepted accounting principles (GAAP) in which paragraphs?

	GAAS	GAAP
a.	Opening	Scope
b.	Scope	Scope
c.	Scope	Opinion
d.	Opening	Opinion

    (5/94, AUD, #77, ID: 4742)

23. March, CPA, is engaged by Monday Corp., a client, to audit the financial statements of Wall Corp., a company that is not March's client. Monday expects to present Wall's audited financial statements with March's auditor's report to 1st Federal Bank to obtain financing in Monday's attempt to purchase Wall. In these circumstances, March's auditor's report would usually be addressed to

    a. Monday Corp., the client that engaged March
    b. Wall Corp., the entity audited by March
    c. 1st Federal Bank
    d. Both Monday Corp. and 1st Federal Bank (11/95, AUD, #78, ID: 6025)

24. A CPA's standard report on audited financial statements would be inappropriate if it referred to

    a. Management's responsibility for the financial statements
    b. An assessment of the entity's accounting principles
    c. Significant estimates made by management
    d. The CPA's assessment of sampling risk factors (R/06, AUD, #47, ID: 8165)

25. Which of the following representations does an auditor make explicitly and which implicitly when issuing an unqualified opinion?

	Conformity with GAAP	*Adequacy of disclosure*
a.	Implicitly	Implicitly
b.	Explicitly	Explicitly
c.	Implicitly	Explicitly
d.	Explicitly	Implicitly

(Editors, ID: 363)

26. In which of the following circumstances would an auditor most likely add an explanatory paragraph to the standard report while **not** affecting the auditor's unqualified opinion?

   a. The auditor is asked to report on the balance sheet, but not on the other basic financial statements.
   b. There is substantial doubt about the entity's ability to continue as a going concern.
   c. Management's estimates of the effects of future events are unreasonable.
   d. Certain transactions cannot be tested because of management's records retention policy.

(5/93, AUD, #47, ID: 3943)

27. An auditor would express an unqualified opinion with an explanatory paragraph added to the auditor's report for

	An unjustified accounting change	*A material weakness in internal control*
a.	Yes	Yes
b.	Yes	No
c.	No	Yes
d.	No	No

(11/95, AUD, #65, amended, ID: 6012)

28. In which of the following situations would an auditor ordinarily issue an unqualified audit opinion without an explanatory paragraph?

   a. The auditor wishes to emphasize that the entity had significant related-party transactions.
   b. The auditor decides to make reference to the report of another auditor as a basis, in part, for the auditor's opinion.
   c. The entity issues financial statements that present financial position and results of operations, but omits the statement of cash flows.
   d. The auditor has substantial doubt about the entity's ability to continue as a going concern, but the circumstances are fully disclosed in the financial statements.   (11/90, AUD, #6, ID: 324)

29. The introductory paragraph of an auditor's report contains the following sentences:

We did not audit the financial statements of EZ Inc., a wholly owned subsidiary, which statements reflect total assets and revenues constituting 27 percent and 29 percent, respectively, of the related consolidated totals. Those statements were audited by other auditors whose report has been furnished to us, and our opinion, insofar as it relates to the amounts included for EZ Inc., is based solely on the report of the other auditors.

These sentences

   a. Indicate a division of responsibility
   b. Assume responsibility for the other auditor
   c. Are an improper form of reporting
   d. Require a departure from an unqualified opinion   (11/95, AUD, #77, amended, ID: 6024)

30. Pell, CPA, decides to serve as principal auditor in the audit of the financial statements of Tech Consolidated, Inc. Smith, CPA, audits one of Tech's subsidiaries. In which situation(s) should Pell make reference to Smith's audit?

    I. Pell reviews Smith's working papers and assumes responsibility for Smith's work, but expresses a qualified opinion on Tech's financial statements.
    II. Pell is unable to review Smith's working papers; however, Pell's inquiries indicate that Smith has an excellent reputation for professional competence and integrity.

  a. I only
  b. II only
  c. Both I and II
  d. Neither I nor II
                                (5/97, AUD, #5, ID: 6394)

31. Delta Life Insurance Co. prepares its financial statements on an accounting basis insurance companies use pursuant to the rules of a state insurance commission. If Wall, CPA, Delta's auditor, discovers that the statements are **not** suitably titled, Wall should

  a. Disclose any reservations in an explanatory paragraph and qualify the opinion
  b. Apply to the state insurance commission for an advisory opinion
  c. Issue a special statutory basis report that clearly disclaims any opinion
  d. Explain in the notes to the financial statements the terminology used   (5/93, AUD, #57, ID: 3953)

32. When financial statements contain a departure from GAAP because, due to unusual circumstances, the statements would otherwise be misleading, the auditor should explain the unusual circumstances in a separate paragraph and express an opinion that is

  a. Unqualified
  b. Qualified
  c. Qualified or adverse, depending on materiality
  d. Adverse   (5/94, AUD, #75, amended, ID: 4740)

33. Eagle Company's financial statements contain a departure from generally accepted accounting principles because, due to unusual circumstances, the statements would otherwise be misleading. The auditor should express an opinion that is

  a. Unqualified but not mention the departure in the auditor's report
  b. Unqualified and describe the departure in a separate paragraph
  c. Qualified and describe the departure in a separate paragraph
  d. Qualified or adverse, depending on materiality, and describe the departure in a separate paragraph
                                (11/90, AUD, #12, ID: 329)

34. The following explanatory paragraph was included in an auditor's report to indicate a lack of consistency:

"As discussed in note T to the financial statements, the company changed its method of accounting for long-term contracts in year 2."

How should the auditor report on this matter if the auditor concurred with the change?

	Type of opinion	Location of explanatory paragraph
a.	Unqualified	Before opinion paragraph
b.	Unqualified	After opinion paragraph
c.	Qualified	Before opinion paragraph
d.	Qualified	After opinion paragraph (11/91, AUD, #18, amended, ID: 2286)

35. For which of the following events would an auditor issue a report that omits any reference to consistency?

  a. A change in the method of accounting for inventories
  b. A change from an accounting principle that is not generally accepted to one that is generally accepted
  c. A change in the useful life used to calculate the provision for depreciation expense
  d. Management's lack of reasonable justification for a change in accounting principle
                                (11/96, AUD, #15, ID: 6367)

36. When an entity changes its method of accounting for income taxes, which has a material effect on comparability, the auditor should refer to the change in an explanatory paragraph added to the auditor's report. This paragraph should identify the nature of the change and

   a. Explain why the change is justified under generally accepted accounting principles
   b. Describe the cumulative effect of the change on the audited financial statements
   c. State the auditor's explicit concurrence with or opposition to the change
   d. Refer to the financial statement note that discusses the change in detail   (5/93, AUD, #49, ID: 3945)

37. In the first audit of a client, an auditor was not able to gather sufficient evidence about the consistent application of accounting principles between the current and the prior year, as well as the amounts of assets or liabilities at the beginning of the current year. This was due to the client's record retention policies. If the amounts in question could materially affect current operating results, the auditor would

   a. Be unable to express an opinion on the current year's results of operations and cash flows
   b. Express a qualified opinion on the financial statements because of a client-imposed scope limitation
   c. Withdraw from the engagement and refuse to be associated with the financial statements
   d. Specifically state that the financial statements are not comparable to the prior year due to an uncertainty   (5/98, AUD, #15, ID: 6632)

38. When there has been a change in accounting principle, but the effect of the change on the comparability of the financial statements is **not** material, the auditor should

   a. Refer to the change in an explanatory paragraph
   b. Explicitly concur that the change is preferred
   c. Not refer to consistency in the auditor's report
   d. Refer to the change in the opinion paragraph   (5/94, AUD, #73, ID: 4738)

39. In the first audit of a new client, an auditor was able to extend auditing procedures to gather sufficient evidence about consistency. Under these circumstances, the auditor should

   a. Not report on the client's income statement
   b. Not refer to consistency in the auditor's report
   c. State that the consistency standard does not apply
   d. State that the accounting principles have been applied consistently   (11/95, AUD, #74, ID: 6021)

40. An auditor includes a separate paragraph in an otherwise unmodified report to emphasize that the entity being reported on had significant transactions with related parties. The inclusion of this separate paragraph

   a. Is considered an "except for" qualification of the opinion
   b. Violates generally accepted auditing standards if this information is already disclosed in the notes to the financial statements
   c. Necessitates a revision of the opinion paragraph to include the phrase "with the foregoing explanation"
   d. Is appropriate and would not negate the unqualified opinion   (5/94, AUD, #69, ID: 4734)

41. Which of the following phrases should be included in the opinion paragraph when an auditor expresses a qualified opinion?

	When read in conjunction with Note X	*With the foregoing explanation*
a.	Yes	No
b.	No	Yes
c.	Yes	Yes
d.	No	No (11/92, AUD, #46, ID: 2980)

42. An auditor may **not** issue a qualified opinion when

   a. An accounting principle at variance with GAAP is used.
   b. The auditor lacks independence with respect to the audited entity.
   c. A scope limitation prevents the auditor from completing an important audit procedure.
   d. The auditor's report refers to the work of a specialist.   (11/95, AUD, #63, ID: 6010)

43. When qualifying an opinion because of an insufficiency of audit evidence, an auditor should refer to the situation in the

	Opening (introductory) paragraph	Scope paragraph
a.	No	No
b.	Yes	No
c.	Yes	Yes
d.	No	Yes

(5/94, AUD, #88, ID: 4753)

44. An auditor may reasonably issue an "except for" qualified opinion for a(an)

	Scope limitation	Unjustified accounting change
a.	Yes	No
b.	No	Yes
c.	Yes	Yes
d.	No	No

(11/91, AUD, #16, ID: 2284)

45. An auditor decides to issue a qualified opinion on an entity's financial statements because a major inadequacy in its computerized accounting records prevents the auditor from applying necessary procedures. The opinion paragraph of the auditor's report should state that the qualification pertains to

a. A client-imposed scope limitation
b. A departure from generally accepted auditing standards
c. The possible effects on the financial statements
d. Inadequate disclosure of necessary information

(11/93, AUD, #49, ID: 4286)

46. When qualifying an opinion because of an insufficiency of audit evidence, an auditor should refer to the situation in the

	Scope paragraph	Notes to the financial statements
a.	Yes	Yes
b.	Yes	No
c.	No	Yes
d.	No	No

(R/10, AUD, #22, ID: 9372)

47. Due to a scope limitation, an auditor disclaimed an opinion on the financial statements taken as a whole, but the auditor's report included a statement that the current asset portion of the entity's balance sheet was fairly stated. The inclusion of this statement is

a. Not appropriate because it may tend to overshadow the auditor's disclaimer of opinion
b. Not appropriate because the auditor is prohibited from reporting on only one basic financial statement
c. Appropriate provided the auditor's scope paragraph adequately describes the scope limitation
d. Appropriate provided the statement is in a separate paragraph preceding the disclaimer of opinion paragraph

(5/94, AUD, #72, ID: 4737)

48. A limitation on the scope of an audit sufficient to preclude an unqualified opinion will usually result when management

a. Is unable to obtain audited financial statements supporting the entity's investment in a foreign subsidiary
b. Refuses to disclose in the notes to the financial statements related-party transactions authorized by the board of directors
c. Does not sign an engagement letter specifying the responsibilities of both the entity and the auditor
d. Fails to correct a significant deficiency communicated to the audit committee after the prior year's audit

(5/93, AUD, #56, amended, ID: 3952)

49. When a qualified opinion results from a limitation on the scope of the audit, the situation should be described in an explanatory paragraph

    a. Preceding the opinion paragraph and referred to only in the scope paragraph of the auditor's report
    b. Following the opinion paragraph and referred to in both the scope and opinion paragraphs of the auditor's report
    c. Following the opinion paragraph and referred to only in the scope paragraph of the auditor's report
    d. Preceding the opinion paragraph and referred to in both the scope and opinion paragraphs of the auditor's report
          (5/90, AUD, #22, ID: 340)

50. A limitation on the scope of an audit sufficient to preclude an unqualified opinion will usually result when management

    a. States that the financial statements are not intended to be presented in conformity with generally accepted accounting principles
    b. Presents financial statements that are prepared in accordance with the cash receipts and disbursements basis of accounting
    c. Does not make the minutes of the board of directors' meetings available to the auditor
    d. Asks the auditor to report on the balance sheet and not on the other basic financial statements
          (Editors, ID: 345)

51. When disclaiming an opinion due to a client-imposed scope limitation, an auditor should indicate in a separate paragraph why the audit did not comply with generally accepted auditing standards. The auditor should also omit the

	Scope paragraph	Opinion paragraph
a.	No	Yes
b.	Yes	Yes
c.	No	No
d.	Yes	No

          (11/93, AUD, #46, ID: 4283)

52. Restrictions imposed by a retail entity that is a new client prevent an auditor from observing any physical inventories. These inventories account for 40% of the entity's assets. Alternative auditing procedures cannot be applied due to the nature of the entity's records. Under these circumstances, the auditor should express a(an)

    a. Disclaimer of opinion
    b. Qualified opinion
    c. Adverse opinion
    d. Unqualified opinion with an explanatory paragraph
          (R/03, AUD, #19, ID: 7641)

53. As a condition of obtaining a loan from First National Bank, Maxim Co. is required to submit an audited balance sheet but not the related statements of income, retained earnings, or cash flows. Maxim would like to engage a CPA to audit only its balance sheet. Under these circumstances, the CPA

    a. May not audit only Maxim's balance sheet if the amount of the loan is material to the financial statements taken as a whole
    b. May not audit only Maxim's balance sheet if Maxim is a nonissuer
    c. May audit only Maxim's balance sheet if the CPA disclaims an opinion on the other financial statements
    d. May audit only Maxim's balance sheet if access to the information underlying the basic financial statements is not limited
          (R/11, AUD, #28, ID: 9928)

54. Which of the following phrases would an auditor most likely include in the auditor's report when expressing a qualified opinion because of inadequate disclosure?

    a. Subject to the departure from generally accepted accounting principles, as described above
    b. With the foregoing explanation of these omitted disclosures
    c. Except for the omission of the information discussed in the preceding paragraph
    d. Does not present fairly in all material respects
          (11/95, AUD, #71, ID: 6018)

55. When an auditor qualifies an opinion because of inadequate disclosure, the auditor should describe the nature of the omission in a separate explanatory paragraph and modify the

	Introductory paragraph	Scope paragraph	Opinion paragraph
a.	Yes	No	No
b.	Yes	Yes	No
c.	No	Yes	Yes
d.	No	No	Yes

(5/91, AUD, #46, ID: 317)

56. In which of the following circumstances would an auditor be most likely to express an adverse opinion?

a. The chief executive officer refuses the auditor access to minutes of board of directors' meetings.
b. Tests of controls show that the entity's internal control structure is so poor that it cannot be relied upon.
c. The financial statements are not in conformity with GAAP regarding the capitalization of leases.
d. Information comes to the auditor's attention that raises substantial doubt about the entity's ability to continue as a going concern. (5/94, AUD, #87, ID: 4752)

57. An auditor most likely would issue a disclaimer of opinion because of

a. Inadequate disclosure of material information
b. The omission of the statement of cash flows
c. A material departure from generally accepted accounting principles
d. Management's refusal to furnish written representations (5/91, AUD, #53, ID: 319)

58. Under which of the following circumstances would a disclaimer of opinion **not** be appropriate?

a. The auditor is unable to determine the amounts associated with an employee fraud scheme.
b. Management does not provide reasonable justification for a change in accounting principles.
c. The client refuses to permit the auditor to confirm certain accounts receivable or apply alternative procedures to verify their balances.
d. The chief executive officer is unwilling to sign the management representation letter.

(11/95, AUD, #66, ID: 6013)

59. Under which of the following circumstances would the expression of a disclaimer of opinion be inappropriate?

a. The auditor is unable to obtain the audited financial statements of a consolidated investee.
b. Management does not provide reasonable justification for a change in accounting principles.
c. The company failed to make a count of its physical inventory during the year and the auditor was unable to apply alternative procedures to verify inventory quantities.
d. Management refuses to allow the auditor to have access to the company's canceled checks and bank statements. (R/09, AUD, #29, ID: 8829)

60. When comparative financial statements are presented, the fourth standard of reporting, which refers to financial statements *taken as a whole*, should be considered to apply to the financial statements of

a. The current period and other periods presented
b. One period immediately preceding the current period
c. One period immediately preceding the earliest periods presented
d. No other periods (Editors, ID: 7504)

61. A registration statement filed with the SEC contains the reports of two independent auditors on their audits of financial statements for different periods. The predecessor auditor who audited the prior period financial statements generally should obtain a letter of representation from the

a. Successor independent auditor
b. Client's audit committee
c. Principal underwriter
d. Securities and Exchange Commission (11/95, AUD, #86, ID: 6033)

62. A former client requests a predecessor auditor to reissue an audit report on a prior period's financial statements. The financial statements are **not** restated and the report is **not** revised. What date(s) should the predecessor auditor use in the reissued report?

    a. The date of the prior period report
    b. The date of the client's request
    c. The dual dates
    d. The date of reissue   (Editors, ID: 352)

63. The predecessor auditor, who is satisfied after properly communicating with the successor auditor, has reissued a report because the audit client desires comparative financial statements. The predecessor auditor's report should make

    a. Reference to the report of the successor auditor only in the scope paragraph
    b. Reference to the work of the successor auditor in the scope and opinion paragraphs
    c. Reference to both the work and the report of the successor auditor only in the opinion paragraph
    d. No reference to the report or the work of the successor auditor   (5/90, AUD, #13, ID: 334)

64. Comparative financial statements include the prior year's statements that were audited by a predecessor auditor whose report is **not** presented. If the predecessor's report was unqualified, the successor should

    a. Add an explanatory paragraph that expresses only limited assurance concerning the fair presentation of the prior year's financial statements
    b. Express an opinion only on the current year's financial statements and make no reference to the prior year's financial statements
    c. Indicate in the auditor's report that the predecessor auditor expressed an unqualified opinion on the prior year's financial statements
    d. Obtain a letter of representations from the predecessor auditor concerning any matters that might affect the successor's opinion   (R/03, AUD, #13, ID: 7635)

65. Jewel, CPA, audited Infinite Co.'s prior year financial statements. These statements are presented with those of the current year for comparative purposes without Jewel's auditor's report, which expressed a qualified opinion. In drafting the current year's auditor's report, Crain, CPA, the successor auditor, should

        I. Not name Jewel as the predecessor auditor
        II. Indicate the type of report issued by Jewel
        III. Indicate the substantive reasons for Jewel's qualification

    a. I only
    b. I and II only
    c. II and III only
    d. I, II, and III   (11/95, AUD, #76, ID: 6023)

66. An entity's comparative financial statements include the financial statements of the prior year that were audited by a predecessor auditor whose report is not presented. If the predecessor's report was qualified, the successor should

    a. Issue an updated comparative audit report indicating the division of responsibility.
    b. Explain to the client that comparative financial statements may not be presented under these circumstances.
    c. Express an opinion only on the current year's financial statements and make no reference to the prior year's statements.
    d. Indicate the substantive reasons for the qualification in the predecessor auditor's opinion.

        (R/11, AUD, #26, ID: 9926)

67. How does an auditor make the following representations when issuing the standard auditor's report on comparative financial statements?

	Consistent application of accounting principles	Examination of evidence on a test basis
a.	Implicitly	Explicitly
b.	Explicitly	Implicitly
c.	Implicitly	Implicitly
d.	Explicitly	Explicitly

(R/11, AUD, #27, ID: 9927)

68. An auditor issued an audit report that was dual dated for a subsequent event occurring after the original report date but before issuance of the auditor's report. The auditor's responsibility for events occurring subsequent to the original report date was

a. Limited to include only events occurring up to the date of the last subsequent event referenced
b. Limited to the specific event referenced
c. Extended to subsequent events occurring through the date of issuance of the report
d. Extended to include all events occurring since the original report date

(11/94, AUD, #67, amended, ID: 5140)

69. In May year 3, an auditor reissues the auditor's report on the year 1 financial statements at a continuing client's request. The year 1 financial statements are **not** restated and the auditor does **not** revise the wording of the report. The auditor should

a. Dual date the reissued report
b. Use the release date of the reissued report
c. Use the current period auditor's report date on the reissued report
d. Use the original report date on the reissued report   (5/94, AUD, #66, amended, ID: 4731)

70. Samson, CPA, obtained sufficient appropriate audit evidence to support an opinion on Coco's December 31, year 1, financial statements on March 6, year 2. A subsequent event requiring adjustment to the year 1 financial statements occurred on April 10, year 2, and came to Samson's attention on April 24, year 2. If the adjustment is made without disclosure of the event, Samson's report ordinarily should be dated

a. March 6, year 2
b. April 10, year 2
c. April 24, year 2
d. Using dual dating   (Editors, ID: 2765)

71. The auditor's report should be dated no earlier than when the auditor has

a. Delivered the report to the client
b. Completed the review of the working papers
c. Obtained sufficient appropriate audit evidence to support the opinion
d. Completed the fieldwork   (Editors, ID: 386)

72. On August 13, a CPA obtained sufficient appropriate audit evidence to support an opinion on a client's financial statements for the year ended June 30. On August 27, an event came to the CPA's attention that should be disclosed in the notes to the financial statements. The event was properly disclosed by the entity, but the CPA decided **not** to dual date the auditor's report and dated the report August 27. Under these circumstances, the CPA was taking responsibility for

a. All subsequent events that occurred through August 27
b. Only the specific subsequent event disclosed by the entity
c. All subsequent events that occurred through August 13 and the specific subsequent event disclosed by the entity
d. Only the subsequent events that occurred through August 13   (R/03, AUD, #3, amended, ID: 7625)

73. On February 25, a CPA issued an auditor's report expressing an unqualified opinion on financial statements for the year ended January 31. On March 2, the CPA learned that on February 11 the entity incurred a material loss on an uncollectible trade receivable as a result of the deteriorating financial condition of the entity's principal customer that led to the customer's bankruptcy. Management then refused to adjust the financial statements for this subsequent event. The CPA determined that the information is reliable and that there are creditors currently relying on the financial statements. The CPA's next course of action most likely would be to

   a. Notify the entity's creditors that the financial statements and the related auditor's report should no longer be relied on
   b. Notify each member of the entity's board of directors about management's refusal to adjust the financial statements
   c. Issue revised financial statements and distribute them to each creditor known to be relying on the financial statements
   d. Issue a revised auditor's report and distribute it to each creditor known to be relying on the financial statements   (R/99, AUD, #32, ID: 6848)

74. Which of the following procedures would an auditor most likely perform to obtain evidence about the occurrence of subsequent events?

   a. Confirming a sample of material accounts receivable established after year-end
   b. Comparing the financial statements being reported on with those of the prior period
   c. Investigating personnel changes in the Accounting Department occurring after year-end
   d. Inquiring as to whether any unusual adjustments were made after year-end

   (11/95, AUD, #56, ID: 6003)

75. Zero Corp. suffered a loss that would have a material effect on its financial statements on an uncollectible trade account receivable due to a customer's bankruptcy. This occurred suddenly due to a natural disaster ten days after Zero's balance sheet date, but one month before the issuance of the financial statements and the auditor's report. Under these circumstances,

	The financial statements should be adjusted	The event requires financial statement disclosure but no adjustment	The auditor's report should be modified for a lack of consistency
a.	Yes	No	No
b.	Yes	No	Yes
c.	No	Yes	Yes
d.	No	Yes	No

   (5/94, AUD, #53, ID: 4718)

76. A client acquired 25% of its outstanding capital stock after year-end and prior to the audit report date. The auditor should

   a. Advise management to adjust the balance sheet to reflect the acquisition
   b. Disclose the acquisition in the opinion paragraph of the auditor's report
   c. Advise management to disclose the acquisition in the notes to the financial statements
   d. Issue pro forma financial statements giving effect to the acquisition as if it had occurred at year-end

   (Editors, ID: 372)

77. An auditor is concerned with completing various phases of the audit after the balance sheet date. This "subsequent period" extends to the date of the

   a. Final review of the audit working papers
   b. Delivery of the auditor's report to the client
   c. Public issuance of the financial statements
   d. Auditor's report   (Editors, ID: 381)

78. Which of the following procedures would an auditor most likely perform in obtaining evidence about subsequent events?

    a. Examine a sample of transactions that occurred since the year-end to verify the effectiveness of computer controls
    b. Inquire of management whether there have been significant changes in working capital since the year-end
    c. Recompute depreciation charges for plant assets sold for substantial gains since the year-end
    d. Reperform the tests of controls that indicated significant deficiencies in the operation of internal control
    (R/05, AUD, #23, ID: 7818)

79. Which of the following items would most likely require an adjustment to the financial statements for the year ended December 31, year 1?

    a. Uninsured loss of inventories purchased in year 1 as a result of a flood in year 2
    b. Settlement of litigation in year 2 over an event that occurred in year 2
    c. Loss on an uncollectible trade receivable recorded in year 1 from a customer that declared bankruptcy in year 2
    d. Proceeds from a capital stock issuance in year 2 which was being approved by the board of directors in year 1
    (R/08, AUD, #48, ID: 8654)

80. Which of the following procedures would an auditor most likely perform in obtaining evidence about subsequent events?

    a. Examine changes in the quoted market prices of investments purchased since the year-end.
    b. Compare the latest available interim financial information with the financial statements being reported upon.
    c. Apply analytical procedures to the details of the balance sheet accounts that were tested at interim dates.
    d. Inquire about payroll checks that were recorded before the year-end but cashed after the year-end.
    (R/08, AUD, #50, ID: 8656)

81. An auditor should be aware of subsequent events that provide evidence concerning conditions that did not exist at year-end but arose after year-end. These events may be important to the auditor because they may

    a. Require adjustments to the financial statements as of the year-end
    b. Have been recorded based on preliminary accounting estimates
    c. Require disclosure to keep the financial statements from being misleading
    d. Have been recorded based on year-end tests for asset obsolescence
    (R/10, AUD, #40, ID: 9390)

82. Which of the following procedures would an auditor most likely perform to obtain evidence about the occurrence of subsequent events?

    a. Determine whether inventory ordered before the year-end was included in the physical count.
    b. Inquire about payroll checks that were recorded before year-end but cashed after year-end.
    c. Investigate changes in capital stock recorded after year-end.
    d. Review tax returns prepared by management after year-end.
    (R/11, AUD, #6, ID: 9906)

83. In auditing contingent liabilities, which of the following procedures would an auditor most likely perform?

    a. Confirm the details of outstanding purchase orders.
    b. Apply analytical procedures to accounts payable.
    c. Read the minutes of the board of directors' meetings.
    d. Perform tests of controls on the cash disbursement activities.
    (R/11, AUD, #35, ID: 9935)

84. Which of the following events occurring after the issuance of an auditor's report most likely would cause the auditor to make further inquiries about the previously issued financial statements?

a. A lawsuit is resolved that is explained in a separate paragraph of the prior year's auditor's report.
b. New information is discovered concerning undisclosed related-party transactions of the prior year.
c. A technological development occurs that affects the entity's ability to continue as a going concern.
d. The entity sells a subsidiary that accounts for 35% of the entity's consolidated sales.

(R/05, AUD, #24, ID: 7819)

85. After issuing a report, an auditor has no obligation to make continuing inquiries or perform other procedures concerning the audited financial statements, unless

a. Information, which existed at the report date and may affect the report, comes to the auditor's attention.
b. Management of the entity requests the auditor to reissue the auditor's report.
c. Information about an event that occurred after the audit report date comes to the auditor's attention.
d. Final determinations or resolutions are made of contingencies that had been disclosed in the financial statements. (11/91, AUD, #20, amended, ID: 2288)

86. Subsequent to the issuance of an auditor's report, the auditor became aware of facts existing at the report date that would have affected the report had the auditor then been aware of such facts. After determining that the information is reliable, the auditor should next

a. Determine whether there are persons relying or likely to rely on the financial statements who would attach importance to the information
b. Request that management disclose the newly discovered information by issuing revised financial statements
c. Give public notice that the auditor is no longer associated with financial statements
d. Issue revised pro forma financial statements taking into consideration the newly discovered information (11/94, AUD, #89, amended, ID: 5162)

87. After issuing an auditor's report, an auditor has no obligation to make continuing inquiries concerning audited financial statements unless

a. Information about a material transaction that occurred just after the auditor's report was issued is deemed to be reliable.
b. A final resolution is made of a contingent liability that had been disclosed in the financial statements.
c. Information that existed at the report date and may affect the report comes to the auditor's attention.
d. An event occurs just after the auditor's report was issued that affects the entity's ability to continue as a going concern. (R/09, AUD, #24, ID: 8824)

88. After issuing an auditor's report, an auditor becomes aware of facts that existed at the report date that would have affected the report had the auditor known of the facts at the time. What is the first thing the auditor should do?

a. Notify each member of the board of directors that the auditor's report may not be associated with the financial statements from this point forward.
b. Issue revised financial statements and auditor's report describing the reason for the revision in a note to the financial statements.
c. Determine whether there are persons currently relying on, or likely to rely on, the financial statements and whether those persons would attach importance to the information.
d. Notify regulatory agencies having jurisdiction over the client that the auditor's report should not be relied upon from this point forward. (R/11, AUD, #38, ID: 9938)

89. On March 15, year 2, Kent, CPA, issued an unqualified opinion on a client's audited financial statements for the year ended December 31, year 1. On May 4, year 2, Kent's internal inspection program disclosed that engagement personnel failed to observe the client's physical inventory. Omission of this procedure impairs Kent's present ability to support the unqualified opinion. If the stockholders are currently relying on the opinion, Kent should first

   a. Advise management to disclose to the stockholders that Kent's unqualified opinion should not be relied on
   b. Undertake to apply alternative procedures that would provide a satisfactory basis for the unqualified opinion
   c. Compensate for the omitted procedure by performing tests of controls to reduce audit risk to a sufficiently low level
   d. Reissue the auditor's report and add an explanatory paragraph describing the departure from generally accepted auditing standards   (5/94, AUD, #70, amended, ID: 4735)

90. An auditor concludes that an audit procedure considered necessary at the time of the audit had been omitted. The auditor should assess the importance of the omitted procedure to the ability to support the previously expressed opinion. Which of the following would be **least** helpful in making that assessment?

   a. A discussion with the client about whether there are persons relying on the auditor's report
   b. A discussion of the circumstances with engagement personnel
   c. A reevaluation of the overall scope of the audit
   d. A review of the other audit procedures that were applied that might compensate for the one omitted
   (Editors, ID: 371)

91. An auditor is considering whether the omission of a substantive procedure considered necessary at the time of an audit may impair the auditor's present ability to support the previously expressed opinion. The auditor need **not** apply the omitted procedure if the

   a. Financial statements and auditor's report were not distributed beyond management and the board of directors.
   b. Auditor's previously expressed opinion was qualified because of a departure from GAAP.
   c. Results of other procedures that were applied tend to compensate for the procedure omitted.
   d. Omission is due to unreasonable delays by client personnel in providing data on a timely basis.
   (5/95, AUD, #85, ID: 5703)

92. An auditor concludes that a substantive auditing procedure considered necessary during the prior period's audit was omitted. Which of the following factors would most likely cause the auditor promptly to apply the omitted procedure?

   a. There are no alternative procedures available to provide the same evidence as the omitted procedure.
   b. The omission of the procedure impairs the auditor's present ability to support the previously expressed opinion.
   c. The source documents needed to perform the omitted procedure are still available.
   d. The auditor's opinion on the prior period's financial statements was unqualified.
   (5/92, AUD, #33, ID: 2786)

93. Six months after issuing an unqualified opinion on audited financial statements, an auditor discovered that the engagement personnel failed to confirm several of the client's material accounts receivable balances. The auditor should first

   a. Request the permission of the client to undertake the confirmation of accounts receivable
   b. Perform alternative procedures to provide a satisfactory basis for the unqualified opinion
   c. Assess the importance of the omitted procedures to the auditor's ability to support the previously expressed opinion
   d. Inquire whether there are persons currently relying, or likely to rely, on the unqualified opinion
   (11/90, AUD, #35, ID: 332)

94. On February 9, Brown, CPA, expressed an unqualified opinion on the financial statements of Web Co. On October 9, during a peer review of Brown's practice, the reviewer informed Brown that engagement personnel failed to perform a search for subsequent events for the Web engagement. Brown should first

a. Request Web's permission to perform substantive procedures that would provide a satisfactory basis for the opinion
b. Inquire of Web whether there are persons currently relying, or likely to rely, on the financial statements
c. Take no additional action because subsequent events have no effect on the financial statements that were reported on
d. Assess the importance of the omitted procedures to Brown's present ability to support the opinion

(R/05, AUD, #28, ID: 7823)

95. On March 1, Green, CPA, expressed an unqualified opinion on the financial statements of Ajax Co. On July 1, Green's internal inspection program discovered that engagement personnel failed to observe Ajax's physical inventory. Green believes that this omission impairs Green's ability to support the unqualified opinion. If Ajax's creditors are currently relying on Green's opinion, Green should first

a. Request Ajax's management to communicate to its creditors that Green's opinion should not be relied on.
b. Reissue Green's auditor's report with an explanatory paragraph describing the departure from GAAS.
c. Undertake to apply the alternative procedures that would provide a satisfactory basis for Green's opinion.
d. Advise Ajax's board of directors to disclose this development in its next interim report.

(R/08, AUD, #1, ID: 8607)

96. After an audit report is issued, an auditor discovers that an important audit procedure was not performed. Which of the following procedures is acceptable in this situation?

a. No further action is necessary if the audit report can still be supported.
b. Let the current report stand and correct material errors on the next audit report.
c. Immediately notify known users of the omitted audit procedure.
d. Require that the client notify financial statements users of the omitted procedures.

(R/11, AUD, #15, ID: 9915)

97. When an independent CPA assists in preparing the financial statements of a publicly held entity, but has not audited or reviewed them, the CPA should issue a disclaimer of opinion. In such situations, the CPA has no responsibility to apply any procedures beyond

a. Ascertaining whether the financial statements are in conformity with generally accepted accounting principles
b. Determining whether management has elected to omit substantially all required disclosures
c. Documenting that the client's internal control is not being relied on
d. Reading the financial statements for obvious material misstatements

(5/92, AUD, #2, amended, ID: 2755)

98. When an independent CPA is associated with the financial statements of a publicly held entity but has **not** audited or reviewed such statements, the appropriate form of report to be issued must include a(an)

a. Regulation S-X exemption
b. Report on pro forma financial statements
c. Unaudited association report
d. Disclaimer of opinion

(11/94, AUD, #76, ID: 5149)

99. If an accountant concludes that unaudited financial statements on which the accountant is disclaiming an opinion also lack adequate disclosure, the accountant should suggest appropriate revision. If the client does **not** accept the accountant's suggestion, the accountant should

 a. Issue an adverse opinion and describe the appropriate revision in the report
 b. Accept the client's inaction because the statements are unaudited and the accountant has disclaimed an opinion
 c. Describe the appropriate revision to the financial statements in the accountant's disclaimer of opinion
 d. Make reference to the appropriate revision and issue a modified report expressing limited assurance

(Editors, ID: 7505)

100. A CPA concludes that the unaudited financial statements on which the CPA is disclaiming an opinion are not in conformity with generally accepted accounting principles (GAAP) because management has failed to capitalize leases. The CPA suggests appropriate revisions to the financial statements, but management refuses to accept the CPA's suggestions. Under these circumstances, the CPA ordinarily would

 a. Express limited assurance that no other material modifications should be made to the financial statements.
 b. Restrict the distribution of the CPA's report to management and the entity's board of directors.
 c. Issue a qualified opinion or adverse opinion depending on the materiality of the departure from GAAP.
 d. Describe the nature of the departure from GAAP in the CPA's report and state the effects on the financial statements, if practicable.

(R/08, AUD, #31, ID: 8637)

101. Which of the following procedures most likely would assist an auditor in identifying conditions and events that may indicate substantial doubt about an entity's ability to continue as a going concern?

 a. Performing cutoff tests of sales transactions with customers with long-standing receivable balances
 b. Evaluating the entity's procedures for identifying and recording related-party transactions
 c. Inspecting title documents to verify whether any real property is pledged as collateral
 d. Inquiring of the entity's legal counsel about litigation, claims, and assessments

(R/06, AUD, #35, ID: 8153)

102. After considering an entity's negative trends and financial difficulties, an auditor has substantial doubt about the entity's ability to continue as a going concern. The auditor's considerations relating to management's plans for dealing with the adverse effects of these conditions most likely would include management's plans to

 a. Increase current dividend distributions
 b. Reduce existing lines of credit
 c. Increase ownership equity
 d. Purchase assets formerly leased

(R/01, AUD, #11, ID: 7026)

103. An auditor concludes that there is substantial doubt about an entity's ability to continue as a going concern for a reasonable period of time. If the entity's financial statements adequately disclose its financial difficulties, the auditor's report is required to include an explanatory paragraph that specifically uses the phrase(s)

	Reasonable period of time, not to exceed one year	*Going concern*
a.	Yes	Yes
b.	Yes	No
c.	No	Yes
d.	No	No

(5/98, AUD, #14, ID: 6631)

104. Mead, CPA, had substantial doubt about Tech Co.'s ability to continue as a going concern when reporting on Tech's audited financial statements for the year ended June 30, year 1. That doubt has been removed in year 2. What is Mead's reporting responsibility if Tech is representing its financial statements for the year ended June 30, year 2, on a comparative basis with those of year 1?

   a. The explanatory paragraph included in the year 1 auditor's report should not be repeated.
   b. The explanatory paragraph included in the year 1 auditor's report should be repeated in its entirety.
   c. A different explanatory paragraph describing Mead's reasons for the removal of doubt should be included.
   d. A different explanatory paragraph describing Tech's plans for financial recovery should be included.

   (11/95, AUD, #73, amended, ID: 6020)

105. Which of the following statements is correct with respect to the auditor's consideration of an entity's ability to continue as a going concern?

   a. The auditor's workpapers must include audit evidence which provides assurance that the entity will continue as a going concern.
   b. If there is absence of reference to substantial doubt in the auditor's report, this should be viewed as assurance as to an entity's ability to continue as a going concern.
   c. It is not necessary for the auditor to design audit procedures solely to identify conditions and events that, when considered in the aggregate, indicate there could be substantial doubt about the entity's ability to continue as a going concern for a reasonable period of time.
   d. The auditor has a responsibility to evaluate whether there is substantial doubt about the entity's ability to continue as a going concern for a reasonable period of time, not to exceed the date of the financial statements being audited.

   (Editors, ID: 7506)

106. Which of the following auditing procedures most likely would assist an auditor in identifying conditions and events that may indicate substantial doubt about an entity's ability to continue as a going concern?

   a. Inspecting title documents to verify whether any assets are pledged as collateral
   b. Confirming with third parties the details of arrangements to maintain financial support
   c. Reconciling the cash balance per books with the cutoff bank statement and the bank confirmation
   d. Comparing the entity's depreciation and asset capitalization policies to other entities in the industry

   (5/94, AUD, #55, ID: 4720)

107. An auditor believes that there is substantial doubt about an entity's ability to continue as a going concern for a reasonable period of time. In evaluating the entity's plans for dealing with the adverse effects of future conditions and events, the auditor most likely would consider, as a mitigating factor, the entity's plans to

   a. Repurchase the entity's stock at a price below its book value
   b. Issue stock options to key executives
   c. Lease rather than purchase operating facilities
   d. Accelerate the due date of an existing mortgage

   (R/06, AUD, #11, ID: 8129)

108. When an auditor has substantial doubt about an entity's ability to continue as a going concern because of the probable discontinuance of operations, the auditor most likely would express a qualified opinion if

   a. The effects of the adverse financial conditions likely will cause a bankruptcy filing.
   b. Information about the entity's ability to continue as a going concern is not disclosed.
   c. Management has no plans to reduce or delay future expenditures.
   d. Negative trends and recurring operating losses appear to be irreversible.

   (R/06, AUD, #5, ID: 8123)

109. Which of the following conditions or events most likely would cause an auditor to have substantial doubt about an entity's ability to continue as a going concern?

   a. Significant related-party transactions are pervasive.
   b. Usual trade credit from suppliers is denied.
   c. Arrearages in preferred stock dividends are paid.
   d. Restrictions on the disposal of principal assets are present.

   (5/98, AUD, #13, ID: 6630)

110. Which of the following audit procedures most likely would assist an auditor in identifying conditions and events that may indicate substantial doubt about an entity's ability to continue as a going concern?

    a. Reading the minutes of meetings of the stockholders and the board of directors
    b. Comparing the market value of property to amounts owed on the property
    c. Reviewing lease agreements to determine whether leased assets should be capitalized
    d. Inspecting title documents to verify whether any assets are pledged as collateral
                                                                                    (R/05, AUD, #12, ID: 7807)

111. Which of the following conditions or events most likely would cause an auditor to have substantial doubt about an entity's ability to continue as a going concern?

    a. Cash flows from operating activities are negative
    b. Research and development projects are postponed
    c. Significant related-party transactions are pervasive
    d. Stock dividends replace annual cash dividends   (11/94, AUD, #71, ID: 5144)

112. Kane, CPA, concludes that there is substantial doubt about Lima Co.'s ability to continue as a going concern for a reasonable period of time. If Lima's financial statements adequately disclose its financial difficulties, Kane's auditor's report is required to include an explanatory paragraph that specifically uses the phrase(s)

	Possible discontinuance of operations	*Reasonable period of time, not to exceed one year*
a.	Yes	Yes
b.	Yes	No
c.	No	Yes
d.	No	No

                                                                                    (11/95, AUD, #72, ID: 6019)

113. A CPA firm is completing the fieldwork for an audit of Swenson Co. for the current year ended December 31. The manager in charge of the audit is performing the final steps in the evidence accumulation phase of the audit and notes that there have been several changes in Swenson during the year under audit. Which of the following items would indicate there could be substantial doubt about Swenson's ability to continue as a going concern for a reasonable period of time?

    a. Cash infusion by a venture capital firm
    b. Recurring working capital shortages
    c. A lack of significant contracts with new customers
    d. Term debt refinanced with a new bank   (R/09, AUD, #4, ID: 8804)

114. An auditor believes that there is substantial doubt about an entity's ability to continue as a going concern for a reasonable period of time. In evaluating the entity's plans for dealing with the adverse effects of future conditions and events, the auditor most likely would consider, as a mitigating factor, the entity's plans to

    a. Extend the due dates of existing loans.
    b. Operate at increased levels of production.
    c. Accelerate expenditures for research and development projects.
    d. Issue stock options to key executives.   (R/08, AUD, #17, ID: 8623)

115. Which of the following conditions or events most likely would cause an auditor to have substantial doubt about an entity's ability to continue as a going concern?

    a. Significant related-party transactions are pervasive.
    b. Usual trade credit from suppliers is denied.
    c. Arrearages in preferred stock dividends are paid.
    d. Restrictions on the disposal of principal assets are present.   (R/11, AUD, #2, ID: 9902)

116. After considering management's plans, an auditor concludes that there is substantial doubt about a client's ability to continue as a going concern for a reasonable period of time. The auditor's responsibility includes

    a. Disclaiming an opinion on the financial statements due to the indications of possible financial difficulties
    b. Indicating to the client's audit committee whether management's plans for dealing with the adverse effects of the financial difficulties can be effectively implemented
    c. Considering the adequacy of disclosure about the client's possible inability to continue as a going concern
    d. Issuing a qualified or adverse opinion, depending upon materiality, due to the possible effects on the financial statements   (R/11, AUD, #5, ID: 9905)

117. An auditor believes there is substantial doubt about an entity's ability to continue as a going concern for a reasonable period of time. In evaluating the entity's plans for dealing with the adverse effects of future conditions and events, the auditor most likely would consider, as a mitigating factor, the entity's plans to

    a. Purchase production facilities currently being leased from a third party.
    b. Postpone expenditures to upgrade its information technology system.
    c. Pay cash dividends that are in arrears to the preferred stockholders.
    d. Increase the useful lives of plant assets for depreciation purposes.   (R/11, AUD, #36, ID: 9936)

118. An auditor concludes that there is substantial doubt about an entity's ability to continue as a going concern for a reasonable period of time. The entity's financial statements adequately disclose its financial difficulties. Under these circumstances, the auditor's report is required to include an explanatory paragraph that specifically uses the phrase(s)

	"Except for the effects of such adjustments"	*"Possible discontinuance of the entity's operations"*
a.	Yes	Yes
b.	Yes	No
c.	No	Yes
d.	No	No

    (R/11, AUD, #37, ID: 9937)

119. An auditor concludes, prior to the audit report release date, that there is a material inconsistency in the other information in an annual report to shareholders containing audited financial statements. If the auditor concludes that the financial statements do **not** require revision, but the client refuses to revise the other information to eliminate the inconsistency, the auditor should communicate the matter to those charged with governance and may

    a. Revise the auditor's report to include a separate explanatory paragraph describing the material inconsistency
    b. Issue an "except for" qualified opinion after discussing the matter with the client's board of directors
    c. Consider the matter closed, because the other information is not in the audited financial statements
    d. Disclaim an opinion on the financial statements after explaining the material inconsistency in a separate explanatory paragraph   (11/94, AUD, #86, amended, ID: 5159)

120. An auditor concludes that there is a material inconsistency in the other information in an annual report to shareholders containing audited financial statements. The auditor believes that the financial statements do **not** require revision, but the client is unwilling to revise or eliminate the material inconsistency in the other information. Under these circumstances, what action would the auditor most likely take?

    a. Consider the situation closed because the other information is not in the audited financial statements
    b. Issue an "except for" qualified opinion after discussing the matter with the client's audit committee
    c. Disclaim an opinion on the financial statements after explaining the material inconsistency in a separate explanatory paragraph
    d. Revise the auditor's report to include a separate explanatory paragraph describing the material inconsistency   (R/06, AUD, #29, ID: 8147)

121. When there is other information in documents containing audited financial statements and the auditor's report, the auditor should

   a. Perform inquiry and analytical procedures to ascertain whether the other information is reasonable
   b. Add an explanatory paragraph to the auditor's report referencing the other information
   c. Perform the appropriate substantive auditing procedures to corroborate the other information
   d. Read the other information to identify material inconsistencies, if any, with the audited financial statements
   (11/92, AUD, #57, amended, ID: 2991)

122. An auditor reads the cover letter accompanying the document containing the audit report and audited financial statements and identifies a material inconsistency with the financial statements. The auditor determines that the financial statements do **not** require revision. Which of the following actions should the auditor take?

   a. No action is required
   b. Include an explanatory paragraph in the auditor's report
   c. Consider withdrawing from the engagement
   d. Request a client representation letter acknowledging the inconsistency
   (Editors, ID: 8399)

123. If management declines to present supplementary information required by the Governmental Accounting Standards Board (GASB), the auditor should issue a(an)

   a. Adverse opinion
   b. Qualified opinion with an explanatory paragraph
   c. Unqualified opinion
   d. Unqualified opinion with an additional explanatory paragraph
   (5/90, AUD, #25, ID: 399)

124. What is an auditor's responsibility for supplementary information, such as the disclosure of pension information, which is outside the basic financial statements but required by the GASB?

   a. The auditor should apply substantive tests of transactions to the supplementary information and verify its conformity with the GASB requirement.
   b. The auditor should apply certain limited procedures to the supplementary information and include an explanatory paragraph in the audit report to refer to the RSI.
   c. The auditor's only responsibility for the supplementary information is to determine that such information has not been omitted.
   d. The auditor has no responsibility for such supplementary information as long as it is outside the basic financial statements.
   (R/03, AUD, #20, ID: 7642)

Problem 8-2 SIMULATION: Types of Opinions

- The auditor is independent.
- The auditor previously expressed an unqualified opinion on the prior year's financial statements.
- Only single year (not comparative) statements are presented for the current year.
- The conditions for an unqualified opinion exist unless contradicted in the factual situations.
- The conditions stated in the factual situations are material.
- No report modifications are to be made except in response to the factual situation.

The following items present various independent factual situations an auditor might encounter in conducting an audit. The list represents the types of opinions the auditor ordinarily would issue. For each situation, select one response—the action the auditor normally would take based on the information above and in each situation. A selection may be used once, more than once, or not at all.

Situation	Type of Opinion
1. In auditing the long-term investments account, an auditor is unable to obtain audited financial statements for an investee located in a foreign country. The auditor concludes that sufficient appropriate audit evidence regarding this investment cannot be obtained.	
2. Due to recurring operating losses and working capital deficiencies, an auditor has substantial doubt about an entity's ability to continue as a going concern for a reasonable period of time. However, the financial statement disclosures concerning these matters are adequate.	
3. A principal auditor decides to take responsibility for the work of another CPA who audited a wholly owned subsidiary of the entity and issued an unqualified opinion. The total assets and revenues of the subsidiary represent 17% and 18%, respectively, of the total assets and revenues of the entity being audited.	
4. An entity issues financial statements that present financial position and results of operations but omits the related statement of cash flows. Management discloses in the notes to the financial statements that it does not believe the statement of cash flows to be a useful financial statement.	
5. An entity changes its method of inventory pricing from LIFO to FIFO. The auditor concurs with the change although it has a material effect on the comparability of the entity's financial statements.	
6. An entity is a defendant in a lawsuit alleging infringement of certain patent rights. However, the ultimate outcome of the litigation cannot be reasonably estimated by management. The auditor believes there is a reasonable possibility of a significant material loss, but the lawsuit is adequately disclosed in the notes to the financial statements.	
7. An entity discloses in the notes to the financial statements certain lease obligations. The auditor believes that the failure to capitalize these leases is a departure from generally accepted accounting principles.	

Types of Opinions

A. "Except for" qualified opinion

B. Unqualified opinion

C. Adverse opinion

D. Disclaimer of opinion

E. Modified unqualified opinion

(ID: 9236)

———————————

Problem 8-3 SIMULATION: Audit Report

Webb & Weber, CPAs, audited the consolidated financial statements of Quest Co. and all but one of its subsidiaries for the year ended September 30, year 1, and expressed a qualified opinion because Quest capitalized certain research and development expenditures that should have been expensed.

Webb & Weber also audited Quest's consolidated financial statements and all but one of its subsidiaries for the year ended September 30, year 2. These consolidated financial statements are being presented on a comparative basis with those of the prior year and an unqualified opinion is being expressed.

Webb, the engagement partner, instructed Perry, an assistant on the engagement, to draft the auditor's report on November 4, year 2, the date of completion of the audit. In drafting the report, Perry considered the following:

- In preparing its year 2 financial statements, Quest changed its method of accounting for research and development costs and properly expensed these amounts. Quest also restated its year 1 financial statements to conform with GAAP. Consequently, Webb & Weber's present opinion on the year 1 financial statements is different (unqualified) from the opinion expressed on November 5, year 1.

- Hill & Hall, CPAs, audited the financial statements of Biotherm, Inc., a consolidated subsidiary of Quest, for the years ended September 30, year 2 and year 1. The subsidiary's financial statements reflect total assets constituting 23% and 22% at September 30, year 2 and year 1, respectively, and total revenues constituting 21% and 20% in year 2 and year 1, respectively, of the consolidated totals. Hill & Hall expressed an unqualified opinion each year and furnished Webb & Weber with a copy of each year's audit report. Webb & Weber have decided not to assume responsibility for the work of Hill & Hall insofar as it relates to the expression of an opinion on the consolidated financial statements taken as a whole because of the materiality of Biotherm's financial statements to the consolidated financial statements. Hill & Hall's report will not be presented together with that of Webb & Weber.

- Quest is the subject of a grand jury investigation into possible violations of federal antitrust laws and possible related crimes. Related civil class actions are pending. This is adequately disclosed in Note 12 to Quest's consolidated financial statements. Because of the early stage of the investigation, the ultimate outcome of these matters cannot presently be determined. Therefore, no provision for any liability that may result has been recorded.

- Quest experienced a net loss in year 2 and is currently in default under substantially all of its debt agreements. Management's plans in regard to these matters are adequately disclosed in Note 14 to Quest's consolidated financial statements, although the financial statements do not include any adjustments that might result from the outcome of this uncertainty. These matters raise substantial doubt about Quest's ability to continue as a going concern.

<u>Independent Auditor's Report</u>

We have audited the consolidated financial statements of Quest Co. and subsidiaries as of September 30, year 2 and year 1, and the related consolidated statements of income, changes in stockholders' equity, and cash flows for the years then ended. These financial statements are the responsibility of the Company's management. Our responsibility is to express an opinion on these financial statements based on our audits. We did not audit the financial statements of Biotherm, Inc., a wholly owned subsidiary, which statements reflect total assets constituting 23% and 22% at September 30, year 2 and year 1, respectively, and total revenues constituting 21% and 20% in year 2 and year 1, respectively, of the consolidated totals. Those statements were audited by Hill & Hall, CPAs, whose reports have been furnished to us, and our opinion, insofar as it relates to the amounts included for Biotherm, Inc., is based solely on their reports.

We conducted our audits in accordance with generally accepted auditing standards. Those standards require that we plan and perform the audit to obtain reasonable assurance about whether the financial statements are free of material misstatement. An audit includes examining, on a test basis, evidence supporting the amounts and disclosures in the financial statement. An audit also includes assessing the accounting principles used, as well as assessing control risk. We believe that our audits provide a reasonable basis for our opinion.

In our previous report dated November 5, year 1, we expressed a qualified opinion that, except for the effects on the year 1 financial statements of not expensing certain research and development costs, the year 1 financial statements present fairly, in all material respects, the financial position of Quest Co. and subsidiaries as of September 30, year 1, and the results of its operations and its cash flows for the year then ended in conformity with generally accepted accounting principles. As described in Note 10, the Company has changed its method of accounting for these items and restated its year 1 financial statements to conform with generally accepted accounting principles. Accordingly, our present opinion on the year 1 financial statements, as presented herein, is different from that expressed in our previous report.

In our opinion, based on our audits and the reports of the other auditors, the consolidated financial statements referred to above present fairly, in all material respects, the financial position of Quest Co. as of September 30, year 2 and year 1, in conformity with generally accepted accounting principles, except for the uncertainty, which is discussed in Note 12 to the consolidated financial statements.

The accompanying consolidated financial statements have been prepared assuming that the Company will continue in existence for a reasonable period of time. As discussed in Note 14 to the consolidated financial statements, the Company suffered a net loss in year 2 and is currently in default under substantially all of its debt agreements. Management's plans in regard to these matters are also described in Note 14. The consolidated financial statements do not include any adjustments that might result from the outcome of this uncertainty.

Webb & Weber, CPAs
November 4, year 2

Webb reviewed Perry's draft and indicated there were many deficiencies in Perry's draft. The following items are the deficiencies noted by Webb. For each deficiency indicate whether:
- W—Webb's review note is correct.
- P—Perry's draft is correct.
- B—Both Webb's review note and Perry's draft are incorrect.

Webb's Review Notes	W / P / B
1. The reference to the subsidiary, Biotherm, and the magnitude of its financial statements should be in the scope paragraph rather than in the opening (introductory) paragraph.	
2. The other independent auditors, Hill & Hall, should be named in the scope paragraph rather than in the opening (introductory) paragraph.	
3. The reference in the scope paragraph to "the financial statements are free of material misstatement" should be followed by the phrase "whether caused by error or fraud."	
4. The required reference in the scope paragraph to assessing "significant estimates made by management" has been omitted.	
5. The reference in the scope paragraph to "assessing control risk" is inappropriate and should be omitted from the report.	
6. The required reference in the scope paragraph to "evaluating the overall financial statement presentation" has been omitted.	
7. A separate explanatory paragraph describing the grand jury investigation into possible violations of federal antitrust laws is required to be placed between the scope and opinion paragraphs.	
8. The reference in the first explanatory paragraph (between the scope and opinion paragraphs) to the qualified opinion on the year 1 financial statements is not properly placed. It should be placed in the opinion paragraph.	

(ID: 9237)

Problem 8-4 SIMULATION: Audit Report Modifications

- The auditor is independent.
- The auditor previously expressed an unqualified opinion on the prior year's financial statements.
- Only single year (not comparative) statements are presented for the current year.
- The conditions for an unqualified opinion exist unless contradicted in the factual situations.
- The conditions stated in the factual situations are material.
- No report modifications are to be made except in response to the factual situation.

The following items present various independent factual situations an auditor might encounter in conducting an audit. The list represents the report modifications (if any) that would be necessary. For each situation, select one response—the action the auditor normally would take, based on the information above and in each situation.

Situation	Report Modification
1. In auditing the long-term investments account, an auditor is unable to obtain audited financial statements for an investee located in a foreign country. The auditor concludes that sufficient appropriate audit evidence regarding this investment cannot be obtained.	
2. Due to recurring operating losses and working capital deficiencies, an auditor has substantial doubt about an entity's ability to continue as a going concern for a reasonable period of time. However, the financial statement disclosures concerning these matters are adequate.	
3. A principal auditor decides to take responsibility for the work of another CPA who audited a wholly owned subsidiary of the entity and issued an unqualified opinion. The total assets and revenues of the subsidiary represent 17% and 18%, respectively, of the total assets and revenues of the entity being audited.	
4. An entity issues financial statements that present financial position and results of operations but omits the related statement of cash flows. Management discloses in the notes to the financial statements that it does not believe the statement of cash flows to be a useful financial statement.	
5. An entity changes its method of inventory pricing from LIFO to FIFO. The auditor concurs with the change although it has a material effect on the comparability of the entity's financial statements.	
6. An entity is a defendant in a lawsuit alleging infringement of certain patent rights. However, the ultimate outcome of the litigation cannot be reasonably estimated by management. The auditor believes there is a reasonable possibility of a significant material loss, but the lawsuit is adequately disclosed in the notes to the financial statements.	
7. An entity discloses in the notes to the financial statements certain lease obligations. The auditor believes that the failure to capitalize these leases is a departure from generally accepted accounting principles.	

Q&A
8-72

Report Modifications

A. Describe the circumstances in an explanatory paragraph preceding the opinion paragraph without modifying the three standard paragraphs.

B. Describe the circumstances in an explanatory paragraph following the opinion paragraph without modifying the three standard paragraphs.

C. Describe the circumstances in an explanatory paragraph preceding the opinion paragraph and modify the opinion paragraph.

D. Describe the circumstances in an explanatory paragraph following the opinion paragraph and modify the opinion paragraph.

E. Describe the circumstances in an explanatory paragraph preceding the opinion paragraph and modify the scope and opinion paragraphs.

F. Describe the circumstances in an explanatory paragraph following the opinion paragraph and modify the scope and opinion paragraphs.

G. Describe the circumstances within the scope paragraph without adding an explanatory paragraph.

H. Describe the circumstances within the opinion paragraph without adding an explanatory paragraph.

I. Describe the circumstances within the scope and opinion paragraphs without adding an explanatory paragraph.

J. Issue the standard auditor's report without modification.   (ID: 9238)

Problem 8-5 SIMULATION: Audit Report

Webb & Weber, CPAs, audited the consolidated financial statements of Quest Co. and all but one of its subsidiaries for the year ended September 30, year 1, and expressed a qualified opinion because Quest capitalized certain research and development expenditures that should have been expensed.

Webb & Weber also audited Quest's consolidated financial statements and all but one of its subsidiaries for the year ended September 30, year 2. These consolidated financial statements are being presented on a comparative basis with those of the prior year and an unqualified opinion is being expressed.

Webb, the engagement partner, instructed Perry, an assistant on the engagement, to draft the auditor's report on November 4, year 2, the date of completion of the audit. In drafting the report, Perry considered the following:

- In preparing its year 2 financial statements, Quest changed its method of accounting for research and development costs and properly expensed these amounts. Quest also restated its year 1 financial statements to conform with GAAP. Consequently, Webb & Weber's present opinion on the year 1 financial statements is different (unqualified) from the opinion expressed on November 5, year 1.

- Hill & Hall, CPAs, audited the financial statements of Biotherm, Inc., a consolidated subsidiary of Quest, for the years ended September 30, year 2 and year 1. The subsidiary's financial statements reflect total assets constituting 23% and 22% at September 30, year 2 and year 1, respectively, and total revenues constituting 21% and 20% in year 2 and year 1, respectively, of the consolidated totals. Hill & Hall expressed an unqualified opinion each year and furnished Webb & Weber with a copy of each year's auditor's report. Webb & Weber have decided not to assume responsibility for the work of Hill & Hall insofar as it relates to the expression of an opinion on the consolidated financial statements taken as a whole because of the materiality of Biotherm's financial statements to the consolidated financial statements. Hill & Hall's report will not be presented together with that of Webb & Weber.

- Quest is the subject of a grand jury investigation into possible violations of federal antitrust laws and possible related crimes. Related civil class actions are pending. This is adequately disclosed in Note 12 to Quest's consolidated financial statements. Because of the early stage of the investigation, the ultimate outcome of these matters cannot presently be determined. Therefore, no provision for any liability that may result has been recorded.

- Quest experienced a net loss in year 2 and is currently in default under substantially all of its debt agreements. Management's plans in regard to these matters are adequately disclosed in Note 14 to Quest's consolidated financial statements, although the financial statements do not include any adjustments that might result from the outcome of this uncertainty. These matters raise substantial doubt about Quest's ability to continue as a going concern.

Independent Auditor's Report

We have audited the consolidated financial statements of Quest Co. and subsidiaries as of September 30, year 2 and year 1, and the related consolidated statements of income, changes in stockholders' equity, and cash flows for the years then ended. These financial statements are the responsibility of the Company's management. Our responsibility is to express an opinion on these financial statements based on our audits. We did not audit the financial statements of Biotherm, Inc., a wholly owned subsidiary, which statements reflect total assets constituting 23% and 22% at September 30, year 2 and year 1, respectively, and total revenues constituting 21% and 20% in year 2 and year 1, respectively, of the consolidated totals. Those statements were audited by Hill & Hall, CPAs, whose reports have been furnished to us, and our opinion, insofar as it relates to the amounts included for Biotherm, Inc., is based solely on their reports.

We conducted our audits in accordance with generally accepted auditing standards. Those standards require that we plan and perform the audit to obtain reasonable assurance about whether the financial statements are free of material misstatement. An audit includes examining, on a test basis, evidence supporting the amounts and disclosures in the financial statements. An audit also includes assessing the accounting principles used, as well as assessing control risk. We believe that our audits provide a reasonable basis for our opinion.

In our previous report dated November 5, year 1, we expressed a qualified opinion that, except for the effects on the year 1 financial statements of not expensing certain research and development costs, the year 1 financial statements present fairly, in all material respects, the financial position of Quest Co. and subsidiaries as of September 30, year 1, and the results of its operations and its cash flows for the year then ended in conformity with generally accepted accounting principles. As described in Note 10, the Company has changed its method of accounting for these items and restated its year 1 financial statements to conform with generally accepted accounting principles. Accordingly, our present opinion on the year 1 financial statements, as presented herein, is different from that expressed in our previous report.

In our opinion, based on our audits and the reports of the other auditors, the consolidated financial statements referred to above present fairly, in all material respects, the financial position of Quest Co. as of September 30, year 2 and year 1, in conformity with generally accepted accounting principles, except for the uncertainty, which is discussed in Note 12 to the consolidated financial statements.

The accompanying consolidated financial statements have been prepared assuming that the Company will continue in existence for a reasonable period of time. As discussed in Note 14 to the consolidated financial statements, the Company suffered a net loss in year 2 and is currently in default under substantially all of its debt agreements. Management's plans in regard to these matters are also described in Note 14. The consolidated financial statements do not include any adjustments that might result from the outcome of this uncertainty.

Webb & Weber, CPAs
November 4, year 2

Webb reviewed Perry's draft and indicated there were many deficiencies in Perry's draft. The following items are the deficiencies noted by Webb. For each deficiency, indicate whether:

- W—Webb's review note is correct.
- P—Perry's draft is correct.
- B—Both Webb's review note and Perry's draft are incorrect.

Webb's Review Notes	W / P / B
1. The reference in the first explanatory paragraph (between the scope and opinion paragraphs) to Note 10 does not express our concurrence with Quest's change in accounting principle. Our concurrence should be specifically expressed in this paragraph.	
2. The reference to the other auditors in the opinion paragraph is incomplete. It should specifically include the words "unqualified opinion" to describe the type of opinion expressed by Hill & Hall.	
3. The opinion paragraph should extend the auditor's opinion beyond financial position to include the results of Quest's operations and its changes in stockholders' equity.	
4. The reference to the uncertainty in the opinion paragraph is incomplete. It should describe the nature of the uncertainty as pertaining to the grand jury investigation into possible violations of federal antitrust laws.	
5. The explanatory paragraph following the opinion paragraph does not include the term "substantial doubt." This term is required to be used in this paragraph under these circumstances.	
6. The explanatory paragraph following the opinion paragraph does not include the term "going concern." This term is required to be used in this paragraph under these circumstances.	
7. The explanatory paragraph following the opinion paragraph includes an inappropriate statement that "the consolidated financial statements do not include any adjustments that might result from the outcome of this uncertainty." This statement is misleading and should be omitted.	
8. The auditor's report is not correctly dated. It should be dual dated because of Note 12, the grand jury investigation, and also because of Note 14, the going concern uncertainty.	

(ID: 9239)

Problem 8-6 SIMULATION: Research

What authoritative reference provides guidance on an engagement to report on only one basic financial statement and not the others, when the auditor's access to information and application of procedures is not limited in scope?

	§			(ID: 9240)

Solution 8-1 MULTIPLE-CHOICE ANSWERS

Reporting Standards

1. (b) An unqualified opinion should be issued only when the auditor is satisfied that the financial statements present fairly, in all material respects, the financial position of the entity as of the balance sheet date and the results of its operations and its cash flows in conformity with GAAP. Documentation, acknowledgment, or recording of the amount of known misstatements are insufficient to accomplish this goal. Adjusting entries already recorded by the client would correct misstatements, not be a part of the total misstatement. (ID: 6712)

2. (c) The objective of the fourth reporting standard is to prevent misinterpretation of the degree of responsibility the auditor is assuming when associated with financial statements. The auditor may express different opinions on the statements presented. Material scope restrictions result in a qualification or disclaimer of opinion. An auditor is not precluded from reporting on only one of the basic financial statements and not the others. (ID: 6015)

3. (a) If the specified item is based upon an entity's net income, the auditor should have audited the complete financial statements to express an opinion on the specified item. Hardy could express an opinion even if Gold's financial statements are not prepared in conformity with GAAP or if Field does not own controlling interest in Gold. There is no requirement that Hardy's report be available for distribution to Gold's other employees; such disclosure might actually conflict with client confidentiality requirements. Also see the text discussion of piecemeal opinions. (ID: 6030)

4. (d) The first reporting standard is construed to require an opinion by the auditor as to whether the financial statements are presented in accordance with GAAP rather than a statement of fact. The auditor must also judge whether the financial statements are presented fairly within the framework of GAAP, not some implied measure of fairness. The audit report contains the auditor's subjective opinion concerning the financial statement presentation. (ID: 7507)

5. (b) The phrase generally accepted accounting principles is a technical accounting term that encompasses the conventions, rules, and procedures necessary to define accepted accounting practice at a particular time. It includes not only broad guidelines of general application, but also detailed practices and procedures. No single reference source, such as the AICPA, exists for all of GAAP. The first sentence of the scope paragraph of the standard report explicitly states that the audit was conducted in accordance with GAAS; the inclusion of a phrase about adherence to GAAP in the opinion paragraph of the report is not an indirect reference to GAAS. (ID: 8625)

Types of Opinions

6. (d) Since single year financial statements are presented, an auditor need not modify the audit report to indicate that the prior year statements were audited by other auditors. The inability to obtain audited financial statements supporting an entity's investment in a foreign affiliate represents a scope limitation resulting in a qualified opinion or a disclaimer of opinion. The entity's omission of the statement of cash flows would result in a qualified opinion. While emphasis of a matter does not preclude the issuance of an unqualified opinion, the report must be modified to include a separate paragraph discussing the matter. (ID: 4739)

7. (b) If a company issues financial statements that purport to present financial position and results of operations but omits the related statement of cash flows, the auditor will normally issue a qualified opinion. (ID: 3942)

8. (d) When restrictions that significantly limit the scope of the audit are imposed by the client, ordinarily the auditor should disclaim an opinion on the financial statements. (ID: 7501)

9. (d) The inability to obtain audited financial statements of a consolidated investee represents a scope limitation resulting in a qualified opinion or a disclaimer of opinion. The circumstances in answers a., b., and c. may require an explanatory paragraph, but they do not preclude an unqualified opinion. (ID: 6016)

10. (d) If, after considering the existing conditions and available evidence, the auditor concludes that sufficient audit evidence supports management's assertions about the nature of a matter involving an uncertainty an

unqualified opinion is ordinarily appropriate. When an explanatory paragraph does not affect an opinion, it comes after the opinion paragraph. (ID: 6017)

11. (b) The auditor may express differing opinions on the balance sheet and income statement. The opinion on the balance sheet is unqualified because the ending inventory is fairly stated. The opinion on the income statement is a disclaimer because of an inability to obtain sufficient audit evidence (a scope limitation) regarding cost of goods sold (because beginning inventory has a significant impact on cost of goods sold). (ID: 4741)

12. (b) When inadequately disclosed conditions exist that cause an auditor to have substantial doubt about the entity's ability to continue as a going concern, the statements are not in accordance with GAAP. An adverse opinion generally is not an option when a scope limitation is present. An inability to apply procedures (including not observing physical inventory) is a scope limitation. A change in accounting principles, if adequately disclosed, would not result in an adverse opinion. (ID: 6942)

13. (a) The effect of a change in accounting principle may be inseparable from the effect of a change in estimate. Although the accounting for such a change is the same as that accorded a change only in estimate, a change in principle is involved. Accordingly, this type of change requires recognition in the auditor's report through the addition of an explanatory paragraph. (ID: 7502)

14. (b) When financial statements are materially affected by a departure from GAAP and the auditor has audited the statements in accordance with GAAS, the auditor should express a qualified or an adverse opinion. Answer a. describes a scope limitation which would ordinarily result in a qualified opinion or a disclaimer of opinion. Answer c. describes a limited reporting engagement and could result in any of the reporting opinions. Answer d. is an example of a situation where the auditor is required to add an explanatory paragraph to an unqualified opinion (as long as adequate disclosure is made) or may disclaim an opinion. (ID: 3954)

15. (a) The auditor's standard report implies that the auditor is satisfied that the statements are consistent with respect to GAAP, and such principles have been consistently applied between periods. Use of different cost principles for different inventories is not inherently inconsistent. (ID: 6014)

16. (b) Whenever an auditor concludes that an illegal act has a material effect on the financial statements, and the act has not been properly accounted for or disclosed, the auditor should express a qualified or an adverse opinion, depending on the materiality of the effect on the financial statements. An unqualified opinion with an explanatory paragraph is not appropriate. A disclaimer of opinion generally would be appropriate if the auditor is precluded by the client from obtaining sufficient appropriate audit evidence to determine if such an illegal act has occurred or is likely to have occurred—this is not the case described. (ID: 5631)

17. (a) In the situation described, the financial statements are free from material misstatement, and no disclosure is required in the notes to the financial statements. An unqualified opinion states that the financial statements present fairly, in all material respects, the financial position, results of operations, and cash flows of the entity in conformity with GAAP. (ID: 8650)

Standard Report

18. (c) The scope paragraph of an auditor's standard report includes a statement that an audit also includes assessing the accounting principles used and significant estimates made by management, as well as evaluating the overall financial statement presentation. Answers a. and d. are not mentioned in the report. Consistency is only mentioned when it is absent and requires explanatory language be added to the standard report after the opinion paragraph. (ID: 6009)

19. (d) The statement that the auditor obtains reasonable assurance about whether the financial statements are free of material misstatement recognizes the existence of audit risk. Answers a., b., and c. do not recognize the existence of audit risk. (ID: 5082)

20. (b) The basic elements of the introductory paragraph of the auditor's standard report are a statement that financial statements identified in the report were audited and a statement that the financial statements are the responsibility of the company's management and that the auditor's responsibility is to express an opinion on the financial statements based on the audit. (ID: 7503)

21. (b)   The basic elements of the standard audit report on financial statements do not include a reference to the entity's internal control. The other answers are included in the report.   (ID: 4736)

22. (c)   GAAS is referred to in the scope paragraph; GAAP is referred to in the opinion paragraph.   (ID: 4742)

23. (a)   If the auditor is engaged to audit the financial statements of a company that is not the auditor's client, the report should be addressed to the client and not to the directors or stockholders of the company being audited.   (ID: 6025)

24. (d)   A CPA's assessment of sampling risk factors should not be referred to in an audit report. Management's responsibility for the financial statements is always mentioned in the introductory paragraph. "An audit also includes assessing the accounting principles used and significant estimates made by management..." is stated in the scope paragraph.   (ID: 8165)

25. (d)   An unqualified opinion states that the financial statements present fairly, in all material respects, the financial position, results of operations, and cash flows in conformity with GAAP. Disclosure, per the third standard of reporting, is not explicitly mentioned unless it is found to be inadequate.   (ID: 363)

Explanatory Language

26. (b)   An explanatory paragraph may be added to the standard report because of a matter involving the uncertainty as to an entity's ability to continue as a going concern. The other answers are examples of when a qualified or adverse opinion or a disclaimer of an opinion should be issued.   (ID: 3943)

27. (d)   A material unjustified accounting change would require that the auditor express a qualified or adverse opinion on the financial statements. If one or more material weaknesses in internal control exist, the auditor would express an adverse opinion on internal control over financial reporting.   (ID: 6012)

28. (b)   If reference is made to the report of another auditor as a basis, in part, for the opinion, this divided responsibility is indicated in the introductory, scope, and opinion paragraphs of the report. In some circumstances, the auditor may wish to emphasize a matter regarding the financial statements, but nevertheless intends to express an unqualified opinion. For example, he may wish to emphasize that the entity has had significant transactions with related parties. Such explanatory information should be presented in a separate paragraph (following the opinion paragraph) of the auditor's report. If a company issues financial statements that purport to present financial position and results of operations but omits the related statement of cash flows, the auditor will normally conclude that the omission requires qualification of his opinion. An explanatory paragraph would be added before the opinion paragraph. If the auditor concludes that substantial doubt about the entity's ability to continue as a going concern for a reasonable period of time remains, the audit report should include an explanatory paragraph (following the opinion paragraph) to reflect that conclusion.   (ID: 324)

Another Auditor

29. (a)   When the auditor decides to make reference to the report of another auditor as a basis, in part, for the opinion, the auditor should disclose this fact in the introductory paragraph of the audit report and should refer to the report of the other auditor in expressing the opinion. These references indicate division of responsibility for performance of the audit.   (ID: 6024)

30. (b)   Situation I is incorrect because Pell is satisfied and assumes responsibility for the work of the Smith. If the principal auditor is satisfied as to the independence and professional reputation of the other auditor, the auditor may be able to express an opinion on the financial statements taken as a whole without making reference in the report to the audit of the other auditor. Only situation II is correct because Pell cannot review the workpapers, therefore cannot assume responsibility; thus, Pell should make reference to Smith's audit in the audit report.   (ID: 6394)

Departure From GAAP

31. (a)   If the auditor believes that the financial statements are not suitably titled, the auditor should disclose these reservations in an explanatory paragraph of the report and qualify the opinion. The auditor should not rely on someone else for the opinion. The opinion should be qualified; a disclaimer of opinion would be inappropriate

under these circumstances. Terms such as balance sheet, statement of financial position, statement of income, statement of operations, and statement of cash flows or similar titles are generally understood to be applicable only to financial statements that are intended to present financial position, results of operations, or cash flows in conformity with GAAP. Therefore, explanatory language in the notes to the financial statements is insufficient.

(ID: 3953)

32. (a) If the financial statements contain a departure from the GAAP and the auditor can demonstrate that due to unusual circumstances the financial statements would otherwise have been misleading, the auditor can express an unqualified opinion (with respect to the conformity of the financial statements with GAAP) if a separate paragraph is added to the report describing the departure, its approximate effects, if practicable, and the reasons why compliance with the principle would result in a misleading statement. (ID: 4740)

33. (b) Rule 203 of the AICPA Code of Professional Conduct requires members to follow GAAP whenever possible. However, if the statements contain a departure from GAAP and it can be shown that due to unusual circumstances the financial statements would otherwise be misleading, the member can comply with the rule by describing the departure, its approximate effects, if practicable, and the reasons why compliance with the principle would result in a misleading statement. This should be done in a separate paragraph, or paragraphs, of the auditor's report, and it is appropriate for an unqualified opinion to be expressed. (ID: 329)

Consistency

34. (b) If there has been a change in accounting principles or in the method of their application that has a material effect on the comparability of the company's financial statements, the auditor should refer to the change in an explanatory paragraph of the report. Such explanatory paragraph (following the opinion paragraph) should identify the nature of the change and refer the reader to the note in the financial statements that discusses the change in detail. The lack of consistency would not require that the auditor qualify the opinion if the auditor concurs with the change. (ID: 2286)

35. (c) Consistency is only mentioned when it is absent in the financial statements. A change in the useful life used to calculate the provision for depreciation expense is merely a change in estimate and does not require comment by the auditor. The other answers would require explanations regarding consistency. (ID: 6367)

36. (d) If there has been a change in accounting principles or in the method of their application that has a material effect on the comparability of the company's financial statements, the auditor should refer to the change in an explanatory paragraph, identify the nature of the change, and refer the reader to the note in the financial statements that discussed the change in detail. The justification of the change should not be given, the justification is implied by the statement in the auditor's report that the financial statements are presented fairly. The auditor would not describe the effect of the change in the audit report or state concurrence because this is also implied in the auditor's opinion. (ID: 3945)

37. (a) A disclaimer is appropriate when the auditor has not performed an audit sufficient in scope (in this case, was unable to gather sufficient evidence) to be able to form an opinion on the financial statements. (ID: 6632)

38. (c) An auditor would not refer to consistency in the auditor's report if no change in accounting principles or in the method of their application had occurred or if the effect of a change on comparability of the financial statements was not material. (ID: 4738)

39. (b) In this case, the auditor was able to extend auditing procedures to gather sufficient evidence about consistency, so an unqualified opinion can be expressed and there should be no reference to consistency in the auditor's report. Per the second reporting standard, the standard report implies that the auditor is satisfied that the comparability of financial statements between periods has not been materially affected by changes in accounting principles and that such principles have been consistently applied. There is no reason to exclude the income statement. The consistency standard does apply in first-year audits. When the independent auditor has not audited the financial statements of a company for the preceding year, the auditor should adopt procedures that are practicable and reasonable in the circumstances to assure the auditor that the accounting principles employed are consistent between the current and the preceding year. When adequate records have been maintained by the client, it is usually practicable to gather sufficient appropriate audit evidence about consistency. (ID: 6021)

Emphasis of a Matter

40. (d)   In some circumstances, the auditor may wish to emphasize a matter regarding the financial state-ments, but intends to express an unqualified opinion. Examples of matters the auditor may wish to emphasize include that the entity has had significant transactions with related parties; that the entity is a component of a larger business enterprise; unusually important subsequent events; or accounting matters, other than those involving a changes in accounting principles, affecting the comparability of the financial statements with those of the preceding period. As just explained, these circumstances would not require an "except for" qualified report. The information may be included in the emphasis paragraph and the notes to the financial statements. Typi-cally, more detail regarding the matter is provided in the notes to the financial statements. Phrases such as "with the foregoing explanation" should not be used in the opinion paragraph if an emphasis paragraph is included in the auditor's report. (ID: 4734)

Qualified Opinion

41. (d)   Neither phrase should be used when the auditor is expressing a qualified opinion. Phrases such as *subject to* and *with the foregoing explanation* are not clear or forceful enough and should not be used. Because accompanying notes are part of the financial statements, wording such as *fairly presented, in all material respects, when read in conjunction with Note 1* is likely to be misunderstood and should not be used. (ID: 2980)

42. (b)   A CPA cannot be in accordance with GAAS if the CPA is not independent, so the CPA must disclaim an opinion and should state specifically the lack of independence. A qualified opinion may be issued when there is a material departure from GAAP. When there are scope limitations, the auditor should qualify or disclaim an opinion. Reference may be made to the work of a specialist when there is a departure from an unqualified opinion and such reference will help to clarify the reason for the qualification. (ID: 6010)

43. (d)   In a qualified opinion resulting from a scope limitation, the scope and opinion paragraphs are modified and an explanatory paragraph is added preceding the opinion paragraph. The introductory paragraph is the same as in a standard unqualified report. (ID: 4753)

44. (c)   Restrictions on the scope of an audit, whether imposed by the client or by circumstances, such as the timing of procedures, the inability to obtain sufficient appropriate audit evidence, or an inadequacy in the accounting records, may require the auditor to qualify the opinion or to disclaim an opinion. If management has not provided reasonable justification for a change in accounting principle, the auditor should express a qualified opinion or, if the effect of the change is sufficiently material, the auditor should express an adverse opinion on the financial statements. (ID: 2284)

45. (c)   When an auditor qualifies an opinion because of a scope limitation; the opinion paragraph should indicate that the qualification pertains to the possible effects on the financial statements rather than to the scope limitation itself. Reference in the opinion paragraph to a client-imposed scope limitation or to inadequate dis-closure of necessary information are examples of incorrectly basing the exception on the restriction. The auditor was unable to apply audit procedures; the auditor did not depart from GAAS. (ID: 4286)

46. (b)   When qualifying an opinion because of an insufficiency of audit evidence, an auditor should refer to the situation in the scope paragraph. Restrictions on the scope of the audit such as the inability to obtain sufficient appropriate audit evidence may require the auditor to qualify the opinion or to disclaim an opinion. When a qualified opinion results from a limitation on the scope of the audit or an insufficiency of audit evidence, the situation should be described in an explanatory paragraph preceding the opinion paragraph and referred to in both the scope and opinion paragraphs of the auditor's report. It is not appropriate for the scope of the audit to be explained in a note to the financial statements, because the description of the audit scope is the auditor's responsibility, not the client's. (ID: 9372)

Scope Limitation

47. (a)   Piecemeal opinions (expressions of opinion as to certain identified items in financial statements) should not be expressed when the auditor has disclaimed an opinion because piecemeal opinions tend to overshadow or contradict a disclaimer of opinion. The auditor may issue an audit report on only one basic finan-cial statement; this is a limited reporting engagement and does not involve scope limitations if the auditor's access to information is not limited and the auditor is able to apply all necessary procedures. When disclaiming

an opinion due to a scope limitation, the scope paragraph is omitted from the audit report. The inclusion of the statement is inappropriate in any paragraph of an audit report that disclaims an opinion. (ID: 4737)

48. (a)   The auditor can determine that the expression of an unqualified opinion is appropriate only if the audit has been conducted in accordance with GAAS and if the auditor has, therefore, been able to apply all the procedures necessary in the circumstances. Restrictions on the scope of work, the inability to obtain sufficient appropriate audit evidence, or an inadequacy in the accounting records may require the auditor to qualify or disclaim an opinion. If management refused to sign an engagement letter, the engagement would be rejected. The other answers do not describe scope limitations. (ID: 3952)

49. (d)   When a qualified opinion results from a limitation on the scope of the audit or an insufficiency of audit evidence, the situation should be described in an explanatory paragraph preceding the opinion paragraph and referred to in both the scope and opinion paragraphs of the auditor's report. (ID: 340)

50. (c)   When restrictions that significantly limit the scope of the audit are imposed by the client, ordinarily the auditor should disclaim an opinion on the financial statements. The auditor should review the minutes of board of director's meetings for information about material transactions authorized or discussed at the meetings. Answer a. contemplates a departure from GAAP, not a scope limitation. The auditor is not precluded from reporting on financial statements prepared in accordance with the cash receipts and disbursements basis of accounting. Answer b. is simply an example of an other comprehensive basis of accounting and would require a special report. The auditor is not precluded from reporting on one basic financial statement and not on the others. This is a limited reporting engagement and does not involve a scope limitation if the auditor's access to information underlying the basic financial statements is not limited and if the auditor is able to apply all necessary procedures. (ID: 345)

51. (d)   When disclaiming an opinion because of a scope limitation, the auditor should not identify the procedures that were performed nor include the paragraph describing the characteristics of an audit, i.e., the scope paragraph; to do so may tend to overshadow the disclaimer. The disclaimer of opinion paragraph replaces the opinion paragraph. (ID: 4283)

52. (a)   A disclaimer is appropriate when the auditor has not performed an audit sufficient in scope to enable the auditor to form an opinion on the financial statements. The only viable alternative answer would be a qualified opinion; however, common restrictions on the scope of the audit include those applying to the observation of physical inventories and the confirmation of accounts receivable by direct communication with debtors. Restrictions on the application of these or other audit procedures to important elements of the financial statements require the auditor to decide whether sufficient appropriate audit evidence has been examined to permit the expression of an unqualified or qualified opinion, or whether an opinion should be disclaimed. When restrictions that significantly limit the scope of the audit are imposed by the client, ordinarily the auditor should disclaim an opinion on the financial statements. Inventories that account for 40% of a retail entity's assets are sufficiently significant to warrant a disclaimer. (ID: 7641)

53. (d)   The auditor may be asked to report on one basic financial statement and not on the others. Such an engagement does not involve a scope limitation if the auditor's access to information underlying the basic financial statements is not limited and if the auditor applies all the procedures necessary in the circumstances. Such an engagement involves a limited reporting objective. Materiality is not a factor nor is whether the client is a nonissuer. The auditor is not required to disclaim an opinion on the other financial statements. For this type of engagement the auditor's report only refers to the statement audited. Reference in the 4th reporting standard to the financial statements *taken as a whole* applies equally to a complete set of financial statements and to an individual financial statement for one or more periods presented. (ID: 9928)

Inadequate Disclosure

54. (c)   The language generally used in this circumstance is *except for the omission of the information* discussed *in the preceding paragraph*. *Subject to* and *with the foregoing explanation* are unacceptable language because they are not clear or forceful enough. The language in answer d. is for an adverse opinion. (ID: 6018)

55. (d)   The opinion paragraph should be modified. The scope and introductory paragraphs are not affected. (ID: 317)

Adverse Opinion

56. (c)   If the financial statements are not in conformity with GAAP and the departure has a material, pervasive effect, an adverse opinion is appropriate. A client-imposed restriction to the auditor's access to the minutes of the board of directors' meetings is a scope limitation and could result in a qualified opinion or more likely, a disclaimer of an opinion. An internal control structure that cannot be relied on will result in expanding substantive tests or determining that the entity is not auditable. Substantial doubt about the entity's ability to continue as a going concern will result in the addition of an explanatory paragraph (following the opinion paragraph) to the standard unqualified report assuming the entity's disclosure of the situation is adequate.

(ID: 4752)

Disclaimer of Opinion

57. (d)   Management's refusal to furnish written representations constitutes a scope limitation that is sufficient to preclude an unqualified opinion and is ordinarily sufficient to cause an auditor to disclaim an opinion or withdraw from the engagement. The other answers are departures from GAAP and would result in a qualified or an adverse opinion.   (ID: 319)

58. (b)   An unjustified accounting change would require that the auditor express a qualified or adverse opinion. Answers a., b., and c. represent various restrictions on the scope of the audit. A restriction on the scope of the audit, whether imposed by the client or circumstances, may require the auditor to express a qualified opinion or a disclaimer of opinion.   (ID: 6013)

59. (b)   If management does not provide reasonable justification for a change in accounting principle, the auditor should express a qualified opinion or, if the effect of the change is sufficiently material, the auditor should express an adverse opinion. A disclaimer of opinion should not be expressed because there are material departures from GAAP. The other answers are examples of scope limitations. Restrictions on the scope of an audit, whether imposed by the client or by circumstances, may require the auditor to qualify the opinion or to disclaim an opinion.   (ID: 8829)

Comparative Financial Statements

60. (a)   Reference in the fourth reporting standard to the financial statements *taken as a whole* applies not only to the financial statements of the current period, but also to those of one or more prior periods that are presented on a comparative basis with those of the current period.   (ID: 7504)

61. (a)   The letter of representation should be obtained from the successor auditor. An auditor who has audited the financial statements for prior periods, but has not audited the statements for the most recently audited period included in the registration statement has a responsibility relating to events subsequent to the date of the prior period financial statements, and extending to the effective date, that bear materially on the prior period financial statements on which that auditor reported. Generally the auditor should obtain a letter of representation from the successor auditor regarding whether the successor's audit (including the procedures with respect to subsequent events) revealed any matters that might have a material effect on the financial statements reported on by the predecessor or would require disclosure.   (ID: 6033)

62. (a)   The date of the prior period report should be used. A predecessor auditor's knowledge of the current affairs of a former client is obviously limited in the absence of a continuing relationship. Consequently, when reissuing a report on prior period financial statements, a predecessor should use the date of the previous report to avoid any implication that the predecessor has examined any records, transactions, or events after that date. If the predecessor revises that report or if the financial statements are restated, the predecessor should dual date the report.   (ID: 352)

63. (d)   A predecessor auditor who reissues a report because the client desires comparative statements should not refer in the reissued report to the report or work of the successor auditor.   (ID: 334)

64. (c)   If the financial statements of a prior period have been audited by a predecessor auditor whose standard report is not presented, the successor auditor should indicate in the introductory paragraph of the successor's report that the financial statements of the prior period were audited by another auditor, the date of the predecessor's report, and that an unqualified opinion was expressed. If the predecessor's report was other than a standard (unqualified) report, the nature of and reasons for the explanatory paragraph that was part of

the predecessor's report or the predecessor's opinion qualification should also be included in the introductory paragraph of the successor's report. An explanatory paragraph is not required and no assurance on the prior year's statements is given. The predecessor auditor's knowledge of the current affairs of a former client is obviously limited so a letter of representation as described in answer d. is nonsensical. If the predecessor's report was reissued (not the case here), the predecessor auditor would obtain a letter from the successor auditor as to whether the successor's audit revealed any issues that might materially affect the prior year's financial statements. (ID: 7635)

65. (d)   If the financial statements of a prior period have been audited by a predecessor auditor whose report is not presented, the successor auditor should indicate in the introductory paragraph of the report that the financial statements of the prior period were audited by another auditor, the date of that report, the type of report issued by the predecessor auditor, and if the report was other than a standard report, the substantive reasons. The successor auditor should not name the predecessor auditor in the report. (ID: 6023)

66. (d)   If the financial statements of a prior period have been audited by a predecessor auditor whose report is not presented, the successor auditor should indicate in the introductory paragraph of the audit report (1) that the financial statements of the prior period were audited by another auditor; (2) the date of that report; (3) the type of report issued by the predecessor auditor; and (4) if the report was other than a standard report, the substantive reasons. The successor auditor does not have the option to issue an updated report on the audit conducted by the predecessor. (An auditor indicates division of responsibility in an audit report when an auditor's opinion on financial statements is based in part on the report of another auditor regarding those same financial statements.) Comparative statements can be presented under the circumstances described in this question as long as the successor auditor includes the information just described about the prior period financial statements and audit report or if the predecessor reissues the audit report on the financial statements of the prior period at the request of the former client and performs the required procedures to determine if the report is still appropriate. (The predecessor should use the date of the previous report on the reissued report unless the report is revised, in which case it should be dual-dated.) The successor auditor should not express an opinion only on the current year's financial statements and make no reference to the prior year's statements. To do so would be a violation of the 4th standard of reporting: *The auditor must either express an opinion regarding the financial statements, taken as a whole, or state that an opinion cannot be expressed, in the auditor's report. When the auditor cannot express an overall opinion, the auditor should state the reasons therefor in the auditor's report. In all cases where an auditor's name is associated with financial statements, the auditor should clearly indicate the character of the auditor's work, if any, and the degree of responsibility the auditor is taking, in the auditor's report.* Reference in the 4th reporting standard to the financial statements taken as a whole applies not only to the financial statements of the current period but also to those of one or more prior periods that are presented on a comparative basis with those of the current period. (ID: 9926)

67. (a)   The answer is the same for the standard auditor's report for both comparative and single-year financial statements. Consistency is implied (implicit) in the standard report, i.e., if satisfied, the auditor does not refer to consistency in the audit report. The standard audit report states (explicitly) in the scope paragraph that an audit includes examining, on a test basis, evidence supporting the amounts and disclosures in the financial statements. (ID: 9927)

Dating of Audit Report

68. (b)   When using dual dating, the auditor's responsibility for events occurring subsequent to the original report date is limited to the specific event disclosed. (ID: 5140)

69. (d)   Use of the original report date in a reissued report removes any implication that records, transactions, or events after that date have been examined or reviewed. (ID: 4731)

70. (a)   When the financial statements are adjusted without disclosure for a subsequent event that occurs after the date of the auditor's report but before its issuance, the report should ordinarily be dated no earlier than when the auditor has obtained sufficient appropriate audit evidence to support the opinion. If adjustment and disclosure are made or if adjustment is not made (and the auditor qualifies the opinion), the auditor can either dual date or use the later date (of the subsequent event). If the later date is used, the auditor's responsibility for subsequent events extends to this date and thus the auditor should extend / perform "subsequent period" audit procedures to that date. (ID: 2765)

71. (c) The auditor's report should not be dated earlier than the date on which the auditor has obtained sufficient appropriate audit evidence to support the opinion. (ID: 386)

72. (a) The auditor may use dual dating, for example, February 16, 20__, except for Note __, as to which the date is March 1, 20__, or may date the report as of the later date. In the former instance, the responsibility for events occurring subsequent to the original report date is limited to the specific event referred to in the note (or otherwise disclosed). In the latter instance, the independent auditor's responsibility for subsequent events extends to the date of the report. (ID: 7625)

Subsequent Events

73. (b) Informing third parties is appropriate only when the audit committee (a committee of the board of directors) fails to take appropriate action. (ID: 6848)

74. (d) One of the auditor's procedures to determine the occurrence of subsequent events that may require adjustment or disclosure is asking management if any unusual adjustments were made after year-end. Confirming a sample of accounts receivable established after year-end is usually done to determine if proper cutoff was made. Comparison between the current and the prior year financial statements is unlikely to uncover evidence about the occurrence of subsequent events—rather a comparison of the current statements to the latest interim statements and an analysis those interim statements should be done. Investigating personnel changes in the Accounting Department occurring after year-end would be more likely when possible misconduct, rather than a subsequent event, is being considered. (ID: 6003)

75. (d) Two types of subsequent events require consideration by management and evaluation by the auditor. This is an example of the second type which does not result in adjustment of the current financial statements because the condition did not exist at the balance sheet date. However, as it is described as "material", it should be disclosed to keep the current financial statements from being misleading. Consistency refers to changes in accounting principles or adjustments to correct misstatements rather than the occurrence of subsequent events. (ID: 4718)

76. (c) This is an example of a type II subsequent event which do not result in adjustment of the current financial statements because the condition did not exist at the balance sheet date. However, because of its nature, the auditor should advise management to disclose it in the notes to the current financial statements so they are not misleading. The opinion paragraph should not be modified—the auditor may include an explanatory paragraph if the auditor wishes to emphasize it by directing attention to the disclosure in the notes to the financial statements. Management, not the auditor, is responsible for issuing the financial statements (and *pro forma* financial statements), including appropriate disclosures. (ID: 372)

77. (d) This "subsequent period" extends to the date of the auditor's report. (ID: 381)

78. (b) Certain procedures are performed after the balance sheet date: (1) check for proper cutoff; (2) confirm balances that were unknown until after the balance sheet date; and (3) obtain a management representation letter. Although other procedures are performed if warranted, additional procedures generally include inquiries and reading interim statements and minutes of meetings. Examining internal controls in the next fiscal period and recomputing amounts applicable to the next fiscal period typically are beyond the scope of this work. If tests of controls indicate significant deficiencies in internal controls, those tests are unlikely to be performed again. (ID: 7818)

79. (c) A loss on an uncollectible trade receivable recorded in year 1 from a customer that declared bankruptcy in year 2 would most likely require an adjustment to the financial statements. Auditors must consider two types of subsequent events. The first type requires adjustment of the financial statements because it provides evidence about conditions that existed at the balance sheet date. A loss on an uncollectible trade account receivable as a result of a customer's deteriorating financial condition leading to bankruptcy subsequent to the balance sheet date would be indicative of conditions existing at the balance sheet date. A bankruptcy after the balance sheet date is the classic example of an event that represents the culmination of conditions that existed over a relatively long period of time as opposed to a sudden event like a fire or flood that occurred after the balance sheet date. The second type of subsequent event provides evidence about conditions that did **not** exist at the balance sheet date and does **not** require adjustment of the financial statements, however due to their nature; some of them may require disclosure to keep the financial statements from being misleading. The other

answers are examples of the second type of subsequent event. They are also examples of events that would require disclosure. (ID: 8654)

80. (b) The auditor generally should compare the latest available interim financial information with the financial statements being reported upon. This is an example of a procedure to find events occurring in the period subsequent to the balance sheet date, but prior to the issuance of the audit report, which may require adjustment to or disclosure in the financial statements. Changes in the market prices of investments purchased and recorded after the year-end are not relevant because the investments are appropriately not a part of the current year's financial statements. The application of analytical procedures to the details of balance sheet accounts that were tested at interim dates is done so that evidence can be obtained for the extension of the conclusions made at the time of the interim tests to the period end—it is not part of the subsequent period testing. When payroll checks (appropriately recorded as expense in the current year) were cashed does not affect the financial statements. (ID: 8656)

81. (c) Subsequent events that provide evidence concerning conditions that did not exist at year-end but arose after year-end may be important to the auditor because they may require disclosure to keep the financial statements from being misleading. Subsequent events that provide evidence concerning conditions that did exist at the balance sheet date require adjustments to the financial statements. (ID: 9390)

82. (c) An auditor should perform auditing procedures with respect to the period after the balance sheet date for the purpose of ascertaining the occurrence of subsequent events that may require adjustment or disclosure. These procedures should be performed at or near the date of the audit report. For example, the auditor generally should inquire of and discuss with officers and other executives having responsibility for financial and accounting matters as to whether there was any significant change in the capital stock, long-term debt, or working capital to the date of inquiry. The determination of whether inventory ordered before the year-end was included in the physical count as well as inquiries about payroll checks recorded before year-end, but cashed after year-end are examples of procedures to determine proper cutoff, not the occurrence of subsequent events. A review of tax returns prepared after year-end would generally not be as likely to reveal the occurrence of subsequent events as would changes in capital stock after year-end. (ID: 9906)

83. (c) Contingent liabilities arise from events or circumstances occurring before the balance sheet date, the resolution of which is contingent upon a future event or circumstance. Examples include pending or threatened litigation; actual or possible claims and assessments; obligations related to product defects; obligations related to product warranties; and obligations related to product coupons and premiums. The primary concern of an auditor regarding contingent liabilities is discovering their existence. The minutes would be likely to have information about the events or circumstances (lawsuits) that give rise to them. Outstanding purchase orders generally relate to accounts payable for normal operations, not contingent liabilities. Analytical procedures would not be nearly as likely (as effective) a procedure as reading the minutes. Tests of controls regarding cash disbursements would be an ineffective procedure because contingent liabilities are appropriately unpaid. (ID: 9935)

Subsequent Discovery of Facts

84. (b) Management represents that it has informed the auditor of all related parties in its representation letter to the auditor and that it has disclosed all material related-party transactions in financial statements by claiming those statements to be in accordance with GAAP. To discover that related-party transactions existed at the date of the audit report that the auditor did not know about calls into question either the thoroughness of the audit or management's integrity. The postreport resolution of a lawsuit properly reported in the financial statements, technological advancements, and subsidiary sales occurring after the date of the auditor's report generally require no action by the auditor. (ID: 7819)

85. (a) After the date of the report, the auditor has no obligation to make any further or continuing inquiry or perform any other auditing procedures with respect to the audited financial statements covered by that report, unless new information which may affect the report becomes known by the auditor. (ID: 2288)

86. (a) After determining that information regarding subsequent discovery of facts is reliable, the auditor next determines if people are relying on the information who would believe the information is important. (ID: 5162)

87. (c)   After the date of the report, the auditor has no obligation to make any further inquiry or perform any other auditing procedures concerning audited financial statements, unless new information that existed at the report date and may affect the report comes to the auditor's attention.   (ID: 8824)

88. (c)   When the subsequently discovered information is found both to be reliable and to have existed at the date of the auditor's report, the auditor should first determine if there are persons currently relying or likely to rely on the financial statements who would attach importance to the information. The auditor would only notify each member of the board of directors that the auditor's report may no longer be associated with the financial statements or regulatory agencies that the auditor's report should no longer be relied upon if the client does not take action to make the appropriate disclosures. The client, not the auditor, would issue revised financial statements. (The disclosure by the client to users would include the revised statements and audit report. The reasons for the revision would ordinarily be described in a note to the financial statements and referred to in the auditor's report.)   (ID: 9938)

Omitted Procedures

89. (b)   If the auditor concludes that the omission of a procedure considered necessary at the time of the audit in the circumstances then existing impairs the auditor's present ability to support the previously expressed opinion regarding the financial statements, and the auditor believes there are persons currently relying on the report, the auditor should promptly undertake to apply the omitted procedure or alternative procedures that would provide a satisfactory basis for the opinion. Answer a. is a procedure to be followed when the auditor determines, after attempting to perform procedures, that an unqualified opinion is inappropriate. Answer c. would not be feasible and would not eliminate the need to perform some auditing procedures beyond tests of controls. Answer d. would not be an alternative in any situation.   (ID: 4735)

90. (a)   When an auditor concludes that an audit procedure considered necessary has been omitted, the first concern should be to determine whether the previously issued opinion can still be supported. A review of the working papers, discussion of the circumstances with engagement personnel and others, and a reevaluation of the overall scope of the audit may be helpful in making this assessment. If the opinion can still be supported, no further action is necessary. Otherwise, if the auditor believes there are persons relying on the report, then the auditor must promptly undertake the omitted procedures or alternative procedures. A determination of whether or not there are persons relying on the report would provide no evidence to the auditor in assessing the importance of the omitted procedure.   (ID: 371)

91. (c)   The results of other procedures that were applied during the audit may tend to compensate for the one omitted or make its omission less important. The distribution of the report, the type of the opinion, or client delays do not reduce the auditor's responsibility to perform omitted procedures if the auditor's present ability to support the previously expressed opinion is impaired.   (ID: 5703)

92. (b)   If the auditor concludes that the omission of a procedure considered necessary at the time of the audit in the circumstances then existing impairs the auditor's present ability to support the previously expressed opinion regarding the financial statements taken as a whole, and the auditor believes there are persons currently relying, or likely to rely, on the report, the auditor should promptly undertake to apply the omitted procedure or alternative procedures that would provide a satisfactory basis for the opinion.   (ID: 2786)

93. (c)   When the auditor concludes that an auditing procedure considered necessary at the time of the audit in the circumstances then existing was omitted from the audit of financial statements, the auditor should assess the importance of the omitted procedure to the auditor's present ability to support the previously expressed opinion regarding those financial statements taken as a whole. Answers a., b., and d. are steps that can be performed after the required assessment.   (ID: 332)

94. (d)   Upon concluding that an auditing procedure was omitted, the auditor should first assess the importance of the omitted procedure to the auditor's present ability to support the previously expressed opinion. Procedures that were performed may compensate for the omitted procedure. If the auditor can support the previously expressed opinion without the omitted procedure, further procedures are unnecessary. If the auditor's ability to support the previously expressed opinion is impaired and the auditor believes there are persons currently relying, or likely to rely, on the report, the auditor should apply the omitted procedures or alternative procedures. The auditor, not management, determines whether there are persons currently relying, or likely to rely, on the report.   (ID: 7823)

95. (c)   If the auditor concludes that the omission of a procedure considered necessary at the time of the audit impairs the auditor's present ability to support the previously expressed opinion and there are persons currently relying (such as Ajax's creditors), or likely to rely, on the report, the auditor should promptly apply the omitted procedure or alternative procedures that would provide a satisfactory basis for the opinion.   Only if the auditor discovers, after performing these procedures, that the audit report cannot be supported, would other actions such as the other answers come into play, depending on the circumstances.   (ID: 8607)

96. (a)   When an auditor concludes that an auditing procedure considered necessary at the time of the audit was omitted (after an audit report is issued), the auditor should assess the importance of the omitted procedure to the auditor's present ability to support the audit report. For example, the results of other procedures that were applied may tend to compensate for the one omitted or make its omission less important. Also, subsequent audits may provide audit evidence in support of the previously expressed opinion. No further action is necessary if the audit report can still be supported. Letting the current report stand and correcting material errors on the next audit report is not an option. The auditor should first determine if the report can still be supported and if it cannot, the omitted or alternative procedures should be applied that would provide a satisfactory basis for the opinion; thus, the auditor would not immediately notify known users. Only when as a result of the subsequent application of the omitted procedure or alternative procedures, the auditor becomes aware that facts regarding the financial statements existed at the date of the audit report that would have affected that report had the auditor been aware of them and the auditor believes there are persons currently relying or likely to rely on the financial statements who would attach importance to the information, would the auditor advise the client to make the appropriate disclosure of the facts (not the omitted procedure) and the impact on the financial statements to such users. If the client refuses to do so, the auditor should take steps to prevent future reliance on the audit report. (If the auditor is unable to apply the previously omitted procedure or alternative procedures, the auditor should consult an attorney to determine an appropriate course of action concerning the auditor's responsibilities to the client, regulatory authorities, if any, having jurisdiction over the client, and persons relying, or likely to rely, on the audit report.)   (ID: 9915)

Association With Financial Statements

97. (d)   When an accountant is associated with the financial statements of a public entity, but has not audited or reviewed them and thus disclaims an opinion, the auditor has no responsibility to apply any procedures beyond reading the financial statements for obvious material misstatements.   (ID: 2755)

98. (d)   A disclaimer of opinion is the appropriate report in this situation.   (ID: 5149)

99. (c)   If the accountant concludes that the unaudited financial statements on which the auditor is disclaiming an opinion are not in conformity with GAAP in that they do not include adequate disclosure, the auditor should suggest appropriate revision; failing that, the auditor should describe the departure in the disclaimer of opinion. This description should refer specifically to the lack of disclosure and include the necessary information for adequate disclosure. The auditor cannot accept the client's inaction. When a disclaimer of opinion is appropriate, it cannot be replaced with another type of opinion.   (ID: 7505)

100. (d)   If the accountant concludes that the unaudited financial statements on which the accountant is disclaiming an opinion are **not** in conformity with GAAP, the accountant should suggest appropriate revision; failing that, the accountant should describe the nature of the departure in the report and, if practicable, state the effects on the financial statements or include the necessary information for adequate disclosure. When disclaiming an opinion, no assurance can be expressed. Restricting the distribution of the report is not an adequate remedy. The accountant cannot issue a qualified or adverse opinion on unaudited financial statements.   (ID: 8637)

Going Concern

101. (d)   The entity's legal counsel may provide information about the probability of litigation, claims, and assessments that could possibly cause the company to cease to exist. The procedures in answers a., b., and c. would not provide evidence of an entity's inability to continue as a going concern. Performing cutoff tests provides evidence about whether account balances are stated accurately. Evaluating procedures concerning related-party transactions would provide evidence of proper disclosure of such transactions. Real property pledged as collateral does not necessarily indicate a cause for concern.   (ID: 8153)

102. (c)   In this situation, an auditor's consideration of management's plans may include plans to dispose of assets, restructure debt, reduce expenditures, and increase ownership equity. (ID: 7026)

103. (c)   The terms *substantial doubt* and *going concern* are required. (ID: 6631)

104. (a)   If substantial doubt about the entity's ability to continue as a going concern existed at the date of prior period financial statements that are presented on a comparative basis, and that doubt has been removed in the current period, the explanatory paragraph included in the auditor's report (following the opinion paragraph) should not be repeated. A different explanatory paragraph is not required. (ID: 6020)

105. (c)   It is not necessary to design audit procedures solely to identify conditions and events that, when considered in the aggregate, indicate there could be substantial doubt about the entity's ability to continue as a going concern for a reasonable period of time. The results of auditing procedures designed and performed to achieve other audit objectives should be sufficient for that purpose. There is no requirement that the auditor's workpapers include evidence which provides assurance that the entity will continue as a going concern. The fact that the entity may cease to exist as a going concern subsequent to receiving a report from the auditor that does not refer to substantial doubt, even within one year following the date of the financial statements, does not, in itself, indicate inadequate performance by the auditor. Accordingly, the absence of reference to substantial doubt in an auditor's report should not be viewed as providing assurance as to an entity's ability to continue as a going concern. (The auditor is not responsible for predicting future conditions or events.) *A reasonable period of time* is defined as not to exceed one year beyond the date of the financial statements. (ID: 7506)

106. (b)   Confirmation with related and third parties of the details of arrangements to provide or maintain financial support is an audit procedure which may identify conditions and events that may indicate substantial doubt about the entity's ability to continue as a going concern. Pledging assets as collateral does not indicate an inability to continue as a going concern. The other two auditing procedures described (c. and d.) would not provide evidence about an entity's ability to continue as a going concern. (ID: 4720)

107. (c)   Possible plans to mitigate the adverse effects of future conditions and events may include: reducing or delaying expenditures such as leasing instead of purchasing operating facilities; increasing ownership equity; and borrowing money or restructuring debt. Issuing stock options would only cost the company money if they were exercised rather than mitigate the situation. (ID: 8129)

108. (b)   Going concern issues alone do not affect an unqualified opinion. However, if the auditor concludes that the entity's disclosures regarding its ability to continue as a going concern are inadequate, misleading, or depart from GAAP, a qualified or an adverse opinion should be issued. Answers a. and d. are conditions that cause doubt about an entity's ability to continue as a going concern. Management does not need to have plans to reduce or delay future expenditures; this also may be a cause for concern, but does not require a qualified opinion. (ID: 8123)

109. (b)   Denial of usual trade credit from suppliers may drive a business into bankruptcy, even if it wasn't floundering previously. As suppliers have the conflicting goals of selling as much as possible, but extending credit only to creditworthy customers, they remain cognizant of the recent payment history of their debtors. Related-party transactions and restrictions on the disposal of assets are commonly encountered in healthy businesses. The payment of arrearages in preferred stock dividends are generally made only when "surplus" money is available. (ID: 6630)

110. (a)   The minutes of meetings of stockholders and the board of directors are likely to contain clear indications of doubts about the entity's ability to continue as a going concern. Comparisons of market value of property and related loans don't focus on the financial condition of the entity as a whole; many assets—such as relationships with customers and suppliers—are very valuable, and yet do not appear on the balance sheet. Lease agreements rarely highlight financial distress. Assets often are pledged as collateral by entities in strong financial condition. (ID: 7807)

111. (a)   Negative cash flows from operating activities is an example of a condition that, when considered with other events, may indicate there is substantial doubt about an entity's ability to continue as a going concern. (ID: 5144)

112. (d)   The terms *substantial doubt* and *going concern* should be used in a phrase similar to *substantial doubt about its* [the entity's] *ability to continue as a going concern.* Neither phrase given as an answer is required.   (ID: 6019)

113. (b)   Ordinarily, information that significantly contradicts the going concern assumption relates to the entity's inability to continue to meet its obligations (recurring working capital shortages) as they become due without substantial disposition of assets outside of the ordinary course of business, restructuring of debt, externally forced revisions of its operations, etc. As this definition indicates, some items (all of the other answers) are usually a concern only when considered in conjunction with other financial difficulties or negative trends and depending on the circumstances. Recurring working capital shortages is a stand-alone indication that there could be a going concern issue, thus it is the best answer. The cash infusion would be a concern if was needed to meet current obligations. Lack of new customers would be a concern if the company needed to maintain a certain rate of growth to meet its current obligations. Term debt refinanced with a new bank would be reviewed by an auditor for other reasons, but on the surface, is not an indicator of a going concern problem. It would be if the refinancing was done under less favorable terms due to working capital shortages.   (ID: 8804)

114. (a)   The auditor would most likely consider, as a mitigating factor, the entity's plans to extend the due dates of existing loans. The extension would immediately allow the entity more time to raise cash and more flexibility in planning expenditures. The auditor would need to conclude that it would be granted by the lender and would provide enough of an increase in available funds to be effective. The auditor would be less likely to consider increased levels of production as a mitigating factor. This would definitely mean an increase of expenditures which might not result in increased profitability. Accelerating expenditures for R & D is even more risky especially when the auditor considers that the benefit would need to occur soon enough to meet the reasonable period criteria, i.e., not to exceed one year beyond the date of the financial statements being audited. Although issuing stock options to key executives is often used to attract talent and motivate management (aligning their interests with those of the shareholders), it is unlikely this would be considered a mitigating factor even though upon their granting the options involve no cash outlay and if exercised, generally produce tax savings. Most plans do not allow the employee to exercise the options for at least a year and then often only a portion of them.   (ID: 8623)

115. (b)   The auditor may identify information about certain conditions or events that, when considered in the aggregate, indicate there could be substantial doubt about the entity's ability to continue as a going concern for a reasonable period of time. The significance of such conditions and events will depend on the circumstances, and some may have significance only when viewed in conjunction with others. The denial of usual trade credit from suppliers is an example of an indicator of possible financial difficulties. Significant and pervasive related—party transactions may be motivated by the lack of sufficient working capital or credit to continue the business or other adverse conditions; however, this is not as strong an indicator as the denial of trade credit from suppliers. (In the absence of evidence to the contrary, transactions with related parties should not be assumed to be outside the ordinary course of business.) Generally, payment of arrearages in preferred stock dividends would be a positive indicator of financial health. The presence of restrictions on the disposal of principal assets may be due to contractual or regulatory requirements or simply a part of an entity's internal control policies—it is not an indicator of doubt about an entity's ability to continue as a going concern.   (ID: 9902)

116. (c)   When, after considering management's plans, the auditor concludes there is substantial doubt about the entity's ability to continue as a going concern for a reasonable period of time, the auditor should consider the possible effects on the financial statements and the adequacy of the related disclosure. The auditor may choose to disclaim an opinion, but it is not a requirement, i.e., a responsibility. It is also not the auditor's responsibility to indicate to the client's audit committee whether management's plans for dealing with adverse effects of the financial difficulties can be effectively implemented. (The auditor does consider whether such plans can be effectively implemented for the purposes of determining if disclosure is adequate and the effect on the audit report.) The auditor should communicate with those charged with governance (1) the nature of the events or conditions identified; (2) the possible effect on the financial statements and the adequacy of related disclosures in the financial statements; and (3) the effects on the auditor's report. The audit report should include an explanatory paragraph (following the opinion paragraph) to reflect the conclusion that there is substantial doubt; i.e., issue a modified unqualified opinion; not a qualified or adverse opinion. A qualified or adverse opinion, depending on the materiality, should be issued if the related disclosure is inadequate. The question did not indicate that was the case.   (ID: 9905)

117. (b) In evaluating the entity's plans for dealing with the adverse effects of future events, the auditor would most likely consider the entity's plans to postpone expenditures to upgrade its IT system as a mitigating factor for a going concern problem. Regarding management's plans, the auditor should consider whether it is likely the adverse effect will be mitigated for a reasonable period of time and that such plans can be effectively implemented. The purchase of production facilities currently being leased are not as likely as the postponement of a major expense (upgrade of the IT system) to provide lower expenditures—the near future impact of a purchase instead of lease decision could be the same or higher expenditures. Payment of cash dividends that are in arrears would intensify, not mitigate, cash flow problems. The increase of the useful lives of plant assets for depreciation purposes, if justifiable, could increase tax payments. Even if one infers this also means that the purchase of new assets would be postponed, this is not clearly stated as was the better answer, postponement of expenditures for the upgrade to the IT system. (ID: 9936)

118. (d) The auditor's conclusion about the entity's ability to continue as a going concern should be expressed (in an explanatory paragraph following the opinion paragraph) through the use of the phrase "substantial doubt about its (the entity's) ability to continue as a going concern" or similar wording that includes the terms *substantial doubt* and *going concern*. Neither of the question's phrases contains these terms and both use language that is not as strong. Additionally, the auditor should **not** use conditional language in expressing a conclusion, such as: "If the Company continues to suffer recurring losses from operations and continues to have a net capital deficiency, there may be substantial doubt about its ability to continue as a going concern" or "The Company has been unable to renegotiate its expiring credit agreements. Unless the Company is able to obtain financial support, there is substantial doubt about its ability to continue as a going concern." (ID: 9937)

Other Information in Documents Containing Audited Financial Statements

119. (a) One of the auditor's alternatives in this situation is to include an explanatory paragraph in the audit report describing the material inconsistency. The addition of this paragraph would not affect the auditor's opinion. The auditor may also decide to withhold the audit report or withdraw from the engagement, if withdrawal is possible under applicable law or regulation. The auditor should not consider the matter closed. A qualified opinion or a disclaimer of opinion would not be appropriate. (ID: 5159)

120. (d) When the auditor concludes that a material inconsistency exists, the auditor must decide whether the financial statements, the other information, or both require revision. If the auditor decides that the financial statements do not, but that the other information does require revision, the client should be requested to revise the other information. If the client refuses, the auditor should consider revising the audit report to describe the material inconsistency, withholding the audit report, or possibly withdrawing from the engagement. (ID: 8147)

121. (d) The auditor's opinion on the financial statements does not cover other information and the auditor has no responsibility to determine whether such information is properly stated. (The auditor has no obligation to perform inquiry, analytical procedures, or other substantive auditing procedures to corroborate other information in a document.) However, the auditor should read the other information to identify material inconsistencies, if any, with the audited financial statements. (The objective of the auditor is to respond appropriately when the auditor becomes aware that the other information could undermine the credibility of the audited financial statements and the audit report.) An explanatory paragraph should be added if the auditor concludes that there is a material inconsistency in the other information, and the other information is not revised by management to eliminate the material inconsistency. (The auditor should also communicate the matter to those charged with governance.) If no inconsistencies are identified, the auditor is not required to reference the other information in the audit report. However, the auditor may include an explanatory paragraph disclaiming on opinion on the other information when the auditor believes the auditor could be associated with the information and the user may infer a level of assurance that is not intended. (ID: 2991)

122. (a) For purposes of GAAS, other information does not encompass a cover letter accompanying the document containing audited financial statements and the audit report. (ID: 8399)

Required Supplementary Information

123. (d) Because the RSI is not part of the entity's basic financial statements, the auditor's opinion on the fairness of presentation of such financial statements in conformity with GAAP is **not** affected. The auditor should issue an unqualified opinion with an additional explanatory paragraph that includes a discussion of the responsibility taken by the auditor on that information because the RSI accompanies the basic financial

statements. If all of the RSI is omitted, the explanatory paragraph should include a statement that management has omitted it; a description of the missing information including the identification of the applicable financial reporting framework; a statement that identifies the standard setter and explains that the standard setter considers it essential; and a statement that the auditor's opinion on the basic financial statements is not affected by the missing information.   (ID: 399)

124. (b)   RSI differs from other types of information outside the basic financial statements because an accounting standard setter (FASB, GASB, FASAB, or IASB) designated by the AICPA to establish GAAP considers the information an essential part of the financial reporting of certain entities and because authoritative guidelines for the measurement and presentation of the information have been established. Accordingly, the auditor should apply certain limited procedures to the RSI and should include an explanatory paragraph after the opinion paragraph in the audit report to explain that the RSI is included and that audit procedures were applied. If there are problems with the RSI, the explanatory paragraph should describe whether some or all of the information has been omitted or has not been presented in accordance with the applicable guidelines; and whether the auditor was unable to complete the audit procedures or has unresolved doubts about whether the information is presented in accordance with prescribed guidelines.   (ID: 7642)

—————————————

PERFORMANCE BY TOPICS

Each category below parallels a topic covered in Chapter 8. Record the number and percentage of questions you answered correctly in each topic.

Reporting Standards

Question #	Correct	√
1		
2		
3		
4		
5		
# Questions	5	

Correct _____
% Correct _____

Types of Opinions

Question #	Correct	√
6		
7		
8		
9		
10		
11		
12		
13		
14		
15		
16		
17		
# Questions	12	

Correct _____
% Correct _____

Standard Report

Question #	Correct	√
18		
19		
20		
21		
22		
23		
24		
25		
# Questions	8	

Correct _____
% Correct _____

Explanatory Language

Question #	Correct	√
26		
27		
28		
# Questions	3	

Correct _____
% Correct _____

Another Auditor

Question #	Correct	√
29		
30		
# Questions	2	

Correct _____
% Correct _____

Departure From GAAP

Question #	Correct	√
31		
32		
33		
# Questions	3	

Correct _____
% Correct _____

Consistency

Question #	Correct	√
34		
35		
36		
37		
38		
39		
# Questions	6	

Correct _____
% Correct _____

Emphasis of a Matter

Question #	Correct	√
40		
# Questions	1	

Correct _____
% Correct _____

Qualified Opinion

Question #	Correct	√
41		
42		
43		
44		
45		
46		
# Questions	6	

Correct _____
% Correct _____

Scope Limitation

Question #	Correct	√
47		
48		
49		
50		
51		
52		
53		
# Questions	7	

Correct _____
% Correct _____

Inadequate Disclosure

Question #	Correct	√
54		
55		
# Questions	2	

Correct _____
% Correct _____

Adverse Opinion

Question #	Correct	√
56		
# Questions	1	

Correct _____
% Correct _____

Disclaimer of Opinion

Question #	Correct	√
57		
58		
59		
# Questions	3	

Correct _____
% Correct _____

Comparative Financial Statements

Question #	Correct	√
60		
61		
62		
63		
64		
65		
66		
67		
# Questions	8	

Correct _____
% Correct _____

Dating of Audit Report

Question #	Correct	√
68		
69		
70		
71		
72		
# Questions	5	

Correct _____
% Correct _____

Subsequent Events

Question #	Correct	√
73		
74		
75		
76		
77		
78		
79		
80		
81		
82		
83		
# Questions	11	

Correct _____
% Correct _____

Subsequent Discovery of Facts

Question #	Correct	√
84		
85		
86		
87		
88		
# Questions	5	

Correct _____
% Correct _____

Omitted Procedures

Question #	Correct	√
89		
90		
91		
92		
93		
94		
95		
96		
# Questions	8	

Correct _____
% Correct _____

PERFORMANCE BY TOPICS (*continued*)

Association With Financial Statements

Question #	Correct	√
97		
98		
99		
100		
# Questions	4	

Correct _____
% Correct _____

Going Concern

Question #	Correct	√
101		
102		
103		
104		
105		
106		
107		
108		
109		
110		
111		
112		
113		
114		
115		
116		
117		
118		
# Questions	18	

Correct _____
% Correct _____

_____

Other Information in Documents Containing Audited Financial Statements

Question #	Correct	√
119		
120		
121		
122		
# Questions	4	

Correct _____
% Correct _____

Required Supplementary Information

Question #	Correct	√
123		
124		
# Questions	2	

Correct _____
% Correct _____

Solution 8-2 SIMULATION ANSWER: Types of Opinions

1. A. "Except for" qualified opinion

Restrictions on the scope of an audit, whether imposed by the client or by the circumstances, such as an inability to obtain sufficient appropriate audit evidence, or an inadequacy in the accounting records, may require the auditor to qualify the opinion, if material, or to disclaim an opinion, if *very* material. The problem stated that the conditions in all the situations were material, not very material.

2. E. Modified unqualified opinion

Substantial doubt about an entity's ability to continue as a going concern is one of the circumstances which does not affect the auditor's unqualified opinion (if financial statement disclosure is adequate), but does require the addition of an explanatory paragraph after the opinion paragraph.

3. B. Unqualified opinion

If the principal auditor is satisfied as to the independence and professional reputation of the other auditor and the audit performed by the other auditor, the principal auditor may express an unqualified opinion on the financial statements taken as a whole.

4. A. "Except for" qualified opinion

The auditor is not required to prepare a basic financial statement and include it in the report if the company's management declines to present the statement. Accordingly, the auditor should issue an "except for" qualified opinion.

5. E. Modified unqualified opinion

The auditor concurs with the change in accounting principle. Therefore, the auditor may express an unqualified opinion; however, the addition of an explanatory paragraph, following the opinion paragraph, is required.

6. B. Unqualified opinion

If, after considering existing conditions and available evidence, the auditor concludes that sufficient audit evidence supports management's assertions about an uncertainty and its presentation or disclosure, an unqualified opinion ordinarily is appropriate. An emphasis paragraph may be added, after the opinion paragraph, but it is not required—emphasis paragraphs are added solely at the auditor's discretion.

7. A. "Except for" qualified opinion

When financial statements are affected by a departure from generally accepted accounting principles the auditor should express a qualified opinion (if it's material) or an adverse opinion (if it's *very* material). Factors to consider when deciding which of these opinions to issue include the dollar magnitude of the effect; the qualitative and quantitative aspects of the departure; the pervasiveness of the misstatement; and the effects on the other financial statements. In this case, the problem stated that the conditions in all the situations were material, not very material.

(ID: 9236)

_____

Solution 8-3 SIMULATION ANSWER: Audit Report

1. P

A division of responsibility is indicated in the introductory paragraph including the significance of the portion of the entity audited by another auditor. Either the amount or the percentage of total assets and revenues that are reflected in the subsidiary's statements are adequate.

2. B

A division of responsibility is indicated in the introductory paragraph including the significance of the portion of the entity audited by another auditor. The scope and opinion paragraphs are also modified to refer to the other auditor.

3. P

The phrase, "whether caused by error or fraud," is not part of the standard auditor's report.

4. W

The phrase, "significant estimates made by management," is included in the scope paragraph of the standard report.

5. W

Control risk is not mentioned in the standard report on financial statements. The scenario did not describe this as an examination of internal control that was integrated with an audit of financial statements.

6. W

The phrase, "evaluating the overall financial statement presentation" is included in the scope paragraph of the standard report.

7. P

As the investigation is adequately disclosed in the notes to the financial statements, it need not be mentioned in the auditor's report. If the auditor wanted to emphasize this matter and yet still issue an unqualified opinion, the auditor would mention it in an explanatory paragraph following the opinion paragraph.

8. P

If an auditor had previously qualified the opinion on the financial statements of a prior period because of a departure from GAAP, and the prior period financial statements are restated in the current period, the updating report should indicate that the statements have been restated in a paragraph preceding the opinion paragraph.

(ID: 9237)

Solution 8-4 SIMULATION ANSWER: Audit Report Modifications

1. E

When a qualified opinion results from a limitation on the scope of the audit or an insufficiency of audit evidence, the situation should be described in an explanatory paragraph preceding the opinion paragraph and referred to in both the scope and opinion paragraphs of the auditor's report.

2. B

If, after considering identified conditions and events and management's plans, the auditor concludes that substantial doubt about the entity's ability to continue as a going concern for a reasonable period of time remains, the audit report should include an explanatory paragraph (following the opinion paragraph) to reflect that conclusion. Inadequate disclosure with respect to an entity's ability to continue as a going concern is a departure from GAAP, resulting in either an "except for" qualified opinion or an adverse opinion. In this case, however, because it was concluded that financial statement disclosures were adequate, an unqualified opinion with an explanatory paragraph is appropriate.

3. J

If the auditor decides that it is appropriate to serve as the principal auditor, the auditor must then decide whether to make reference in the report to the audit performed by another auditor. If the principal auditor decides to assume responsibility for the work of the other auditor insofar as that work relates to the principal auditor's expression of an opinion taken as a whole, no reference should be made to the other auditor's work or report.

4. C

The auditor is not required to prepare a basic financial statement and include it in the audit report if the company's management declines to present the statement. Accordingly, the auditor should issue an "except for" qualified opinion. The circumstances surrounding the qualification are to be reported in a separate paragraph preceding the opinion paragraph. The opinion paragraph should then be modified using the appropriate "except for" wording, making reference to the separate explanatory paragraph.

5. B

Changes in accounting principle having a material effect on the financial statements require recognition in the independent auditor's report through the addition of an explanatory paragraph (following the opinion paragraph). Such an explanatory paragraph should identify the nature of the change and refer the reader to the note in the financial statements that discusses the change in detail.

6. J

Circumstances that may require the auditor to add an explanatory paragraph to a standard report, while not precluding an unqualified opinion, do not include an uncertainty. An emphasis paragraph may be added; however, emphasis paragraphs are never required—they are added solely at the auditor's discretion.

7. C

The auditor should disclose, in a separate explanatory paragraph preceding the opinion paragraph, all the substantive reasons for a departure from generally accepted accounting principles and the opinion paragraph should include appropriate qualifying language. (ID: 9238)

Solution 8-5 SIMULATION ANSWER: Audit Report

   1. P

Concurrence with a change in accounting principle is implicit and need not be explicitly stated. If management does not provide reasonable justification for a change, the auditor's opinion would be qualified.

   2. P

Such a reference is not required.

   3. B

The opinion paragraph should extend the auditor's opinion beyond the statement of financial position to include the results of operations and cash flows, not changes in stockholders' equity.

   4. B

If an auditor elects to emphasize an uncertainty, it should be in a paragraph following the opinion paragraph. No reference should be made to the uncertainty in the introductory, scope, or opinion paragraphs.

   5. W

If the auditor concludes that substantial doubt about the entity's ability to continue as a going concern exists, the terms *substantial doubt* and *going concern* are required to be used in an explanatory paragraph.

   6. W

If the auditor concludes that substantial doubt about the entity's ability to continue as a going concern exists, the terms *substantial doubt* and *going concern* are required to be used in an explanatory paragraph.

   7. P

This sentence is the last sentence in the standard going concern explanatory paragraph.

   8. P

Auditors use dual dates when subsequent events, not going concern uncertainties, are mentioned.   (ID: 9239)

——————————

Solution 8-6 SIMULATION ANSWER: Research

AU	§	508	.33	(ID: 9240)

.33   *Limited reporting engagements.* The auditor may be asked to report on one basic financial statement and not on the others. For example, he or she may be asked to report on the balance sheet and not on the statements of income, retained earnings or cash flows. These engagements do not involve scope limitations if the auditor's access to information underlying the basic financial statements is not limited and if the auditor applies all the procedures he [*sic*] considers necessary in the circumstances; rather, such engagements involve limited reporting objectives.

STUDY TIP

Government Auditing

Candidates studying governmental auditing should realize that the applicability of AU 801, *Compliance Audits* and governmental auditing guidance overlap. AU 801 is the AICPA's guidance. *Government Auditing Standards* and OMB Circular A-133, *Audits of States, Local Governments, and Non-Profit Organizations*, are issued by the federal government. *Government Auditing Standards* are also referred to as the "Yellow Book" because they are published in a book with a yellow cover. Currently, the complete text is available on the U.S. Government Accountability Office's Web site at www.gao.gov/govaud/iv2011gagas.pdf.

CHANGE ALERT

Government Auditing Standards, 2011 Revision; issued 12/2011

The portions of this revision that are applicable to performance audits will become eligible to be tested **beginning with the July-August 2012 exam window. At that time, only the new guidance will be testable**. The remainder of the revision (applicable to financial audits and attestation engagements) will become eligible to be tested beginning with the July-August 201<u>3</u> exam window—our coverage of this content will be included in a Bisk Education updating supplement to the 42nd edition of our textbook. (This supplement updates the 41st edition of our textbook and corresponding version 14.3 or higher series software.) A release date has not yet been set for the 42 series updating supplement that will include it, but it will probably be available for download from our website during mid-June 201<u>3</u>.

In December 2011 the Comptroller General of the United States and the head of the U.S. Government Accountability Office (GAO) issued the 2011 revision of *Government Auditing Standards.* It is effective for financial audits and attestation engagements for periods ending on or after December 15, 201<u>2</u>, and for performance audits beginning on or after December 15, 201<u>1</u>. Early implementation is <u>not</u> permitted.

This revision supersedes the 2007 revision.

Validity Appropriateness is the measure of the quality of evidence that encompasses the relevance, validity, and reliability of evidence. Validity as an aspect of the quality of evidence refers to the extent to which evidence represents what it is purported to represent.

Significant internal control deficiencies Auditors should include in the audit report (1) the scope of their work on internal control and (2) any deficiencies in internal control that are significant within the context of the audit objectives and based upon the audit work performed.

Fraud reporting requirements When auditors conclude, based on sufficient, appropriate evidence, that fraud, noncompliance with provisions of laws, regulations, contracts or grant agreements, or abuse either has occurred or is likely to have occurred which is significant within the context of the audit objectives, they should report the matter as a finding.

CHAPTER 9

GOVERNMENT AUDITING

CHAPTER 9

GOVERNMENT AUDITING

I. Compliance Auditing Considerations in Governmental Audits (AU 801)

Governments normally establish audit requirements for entities to undergo an audit of their compliance with applicable compliance requirements. Compliance audits usually are performed in conjunction with a financial statement audit. AU 801 does **not** apply to the financial statement audit component of such engagements.

A. Applicability

AU 801, *Compliance Audits*, is applicable when an auditor is engaged, or required by law or regulation, to perform a compliance audit in accordance with *both* GAAS and *Government Auditing Standards and* express an opinion on compliance. An example of an engagement to which this section is applicable is an audit performed in accordance with the provisions of Office of Management and Budget (OMB) Circular A-133, *Audits of States, Local Governments and Non-Profit Organizations*.

1. **Generally Accepted Auditing Standards (GAAS)** AU 801 requires the adaption and application of many of the AU sections (GAAS) to a compliance audit; however, some AU sections generally cannot be adapted because they are not relevant to a compliance audit. For the most part, these include standards in sections 400, 600, 700, and 900. (An appendix to AU 801 lists the specific AU sections/paragraphs that are not applicable. Some of these standards are listed as not applicable because AU 801 provides specific guidance for their subject matter.) Standards in sections 100, 200, 300 and 500 generally can be adapted to the objectives of a compliance audit. This can be done with relative ease for some standards, for example, by simply replacing the word *misstatement* with the word *noncompliance*. Others are more difficult to adapt and apply—AU 801 provides more specific guidance for these sections. That said, an auditor is not required, in planning and performing a compliance audit, to make a literal translation of each procedure that might be performed in a financial statement audit, but rather to obtain sufficient appropriate audit evidence to support the auditor's opinion on compliance.

2. *Government Auditing Standards* The standards for financial audits under *Government Auditing Standards*, often referred to as generally accepted government auditing standards (GAGAS) or the "Yellow Book"

3. **Opinion on Compliance Required** A governmental audit requirement that requires an auditor to express an opinion on compliance

    AU 801 is **not** applicable when the governmental audit requirement calls for an examination in accordance with Statements on Standards for Attestation Engagements of an entity's compliance with specified requirements or an examination of an entity's internal control over compliance. Statement on Standards for Attestation Engagements AT 601, *Compliance Attestation*, is applicable to these engagements. Laws or regulations will not always indicate which standards to follow. In such cases, auditor judgment will be needed to determine, based on the circumstances, the appropriate standards to follow.

    Editor note: GAGAS and governmental audit requirements usually contain certain standards and requirements that are supplementary to those in GAAS.

B. Compliance Is Management's Responsibility

Management is responsible for ensuring that an entity complies with the compliance requirements. This includes identifying the entity's government programs and understanding the compliance requirements of each program's administration. Management should establish internal controls to provide reasonable assurance of compliance. Corrective action should be taken when instances of noncompliance are identified by management's evaluation and monitoring of controls or as the result of an audit finding.

C. Auditor's Objectives

1. **Sufficient Appropriate Audit Evidence** The auditor should obtain sufficient appropriate audit evidence to form an opinion and report at the level specified in the governmental audit requirement—most specify that the auditor's opinion be at the program level—on whether the entity complied in all material respects with the applicable compliance requirements.

2. **Perform Procedures to Address Audit & Reporting Requirements** The auditor should identify audit and reporting requirements specified in the governmental audit requirement that are supplementary to GAAS and GAGAS, if any, and perform procedures to address those requirements.

D. Definitions
The standard defines the following terms:

1. **Applicable Compliance Requirements** Compliance requirements that are subject to the compliance audit.

2. **Audit** refers to financial audits, attestation engagements, and performance audits conducted in accordance with GAGAS.

3. **Audit Findings** The matters that are required to be reported by the auditor in accordance with the governmental audit requirement.

4. **Audit Organization** refers to government audit organizations as well as public accounting or other firms that perform audits and attestation engagements using GAGAS.

5. **Audit Risk of Noncompliance** The risk that the auditor expresses an inappropriate audit opinion on the entity's compliance when material noncompliance exists. Audit risk of non-compliance is a function of the risks of material noncompliance and detection risk of noncompliance.

6. **Auditor** describes individuals performing work under GAGAS (including audits and attestation engagements) regardless of job title. Therefore, individuals who may have the titles auditor, analyst, practitioner, evaluator, inspector, or other similar titles are considered auditors in GAGAS.

7. **Compliance Audit** A program-specific audit or an organization-wide audit of an entity's compliance with applicable compliance requirements.

8. **Compliance Requirements** Laws, regulations, rules, and provisions of contracts or grant agreements applicable to government programs with which the entity is required to comply.

9. **Deficiency in Internal Control Over Compliance** A deficiency in internal control over compliance exists when the design or operation of a control over compliance does not allow management or employees, in the normal course of performing their assigned functions, to prevent, or detect and correct, noncompliance on a timely basis.

    a. **Deficiency in Design** This exists when a control necessary to meet the control objective is missing or an existing control is not properly designed so that, even if the control operates as designed, the control objective would not be met.

    b. **Deficiency in Operation** This exists when a properly designed control does not operate as designed or the person performing the control does not possess the necessary authority or competence to perform the control effectively.

10. **Detection Risk of Noncompliance** The risk that the procedures performed by the auditor to reduce audit risk of noncompliance to an acceptably low level will not detect noncompliance that exists and that could be material, either individually or when aggregated with other instances of noncompliance.

11. **Governmental Audit Requirement** A government requirement established by law, regulation, rule, or provision of contracts or grant agreements requiring that an entity undergo an audit of its compliance with applicable compliance requirements related to one or more government programs that the entity administers. Governmental audit requirements also may set forth specific supplementary requirements of the compliance audit, for example, procedures to be performed by the auditor, documentation requirements, the form of reporting, and continuing professional education requirements with which the auditor is required to comply.

12. *Government Auditing Standards* Standards and guidance issued by the Comptroller General of the United States, U.S. Government Accountability Office for financial audits, attestation engagements, and performance audits (also known as generally accepted government auditing standards (GAGAS) or the "Yellow Book").

13. **Government Program** The means by which governmental entities achieve their objectives. For example, one of the objectives of the U.S. Department of Agriculture is to provide nutrition to individuals in need. Examples of government programs designed to achieve that objective are the Supplemental Nutrition Assistance Program and the National School Lunch Program. Government programs that are relevant to this section are those in which a grantor or pass-through entity provides an award to another entity, usually in the form of a grant, contract, or other agreement. Not all government programs provide cash assistance; sometimes noncash assistance is provided (for example, a loan guarantee, commodities, or property).

14. **Grantor** A government agency from which funding for the government program originates.

15. **Known Questioned Costs** Questioned costs specifically identified by the auditor; known questioned costs are a subset of likely questioned costs.

16. **Likely Questioned Costs** The auditor's best estimate of total questioned costs, not just the known questioned costs. Likely questioned costs are developed by extrapolating from audit evidence obtained, for example, by projecting known questioned costs identified in an audit sample to the entire population from which the sample was drawn.

17. **Material Noncompliance** In the absence of a definition of material noncompliance in the governmental audit requirement, a failure to follow compliance requirements or a violation of prohibitions included in the applicable compliance requirements that results in noncompliance that is quantitatively or qualitatively material, either individually or when aggregated with other noncompliance, to the affected government program.

18. **Material Weakness in Internal Control Over Compliance** A deficiency, or combination of deficiencies, in internal control over compliance, such that there is a reasonable possibility that material noncompliance with a compliance requirement will not be prevented, or detected and corrected, on a timely basis. In this section, a reasonable possibility exists when the likelihood of the event is either reasonably possible or probable as defined as follows:

Reasonably Possible The chance of the future event or events occurring is more than remote but less than likely.

    a.   **Remote** The chance of the future event or events occurring is slight.

    b.   **Probable** The future event or events are likely to occur.

19. **Organization-Wide Audit** An audit of an entity's financial statements and an audit of its compliance with the applicable compliance requirements as they relate to one or more government programs that the entity administers.

20. **Pass-Through Entity** An entity that receives an award from a grantor or other entity and distributes all or part of it to another entity to administer a government program.

21. **Program-Specific Audit** An audit of an entity's compliance with applicable compliance requirements as they relate to one government program that the entity administers. The compliance audit portion of a program-specific audit is performed in conjunction with either an audit of the entity's or the program's financial statements.

22. **Questioned Costs** Costs that are questioned by the auditor due to:

    a. **Violations** A violation or possible violation of the applicable compliance requirements

    b. **Inadequate Documentation** The costs are not supported by adequate documentation

    c. **Unreasonableness** The incurred costs appear unreasonable and do not reflect the actions that a prudent person would take in the circumstances.

23. **Risk of Material Noncompliance** The risk that material noncompliance exists prior to the audit. This consists of two components, described as follows:

    a. **Inherent Risk of Noncompliance** The susceptibility of a compliance requirement to noncompliance that could be material, either individually or when aggregated with other instances of noncompliance, before consideration of any related controls over compliance.

    b. **Control Risk of Noncompliance** The risk that noncompliance with a compliance requirement that could occur and that could be material, either individually or when aggregated with other instances of noncompliance, will not be prevented, or detected and corrected, on a timely basis by the entity's internal control over compliance.

24. **Significant Deficiency in Internal Control Over Compliance** A deficiency, or a combination of deficiencies, in internal control over compliance that is less severe than a material weakness in internal control over compliance, yet important enough to merit attention by those charged with governance.

E. **Compliance Audit Requirements**

1. **Adapting & Applying GAAS** When performing a compliance audit, the auditor, using professional judgment, should adapt and apply the AU sections that are relevant and necessary to meet the objectives.

2. **Materiality Levels** The auditor should establish and apply materiality levels for the compliance audit based on the governmental audit requirement.

Generally, the auditor's consideration of materiality is in relation to the government program taken as a whole. However, the governmental audit requirement may specify a different level of materiality for one or more of the purposes listed below.

The auditor's determination of materiality usually is influenced by the needs of the grantors because the governmental audit requirement usually is established by them and the auditor's report on compliance is primarily for their use; however, the auditor also considers the needs of users as a group, including grantors.

The auditor's purpose for establishing materiality levels is to:

a. Determine the nature and extent of risk assessment procedures.

b. Identify and assess the risks of material noncompliance.

c. Determine the nature, extent, and timing of further audit procedures.

d. Evaluate whether the entity complied with the applicable compliance requirements.

e. Report findings of noncompliance and other matters required to be reported by the governmental audit requirement.

3. **Identifying Government Programs & Applicable Compliance Requirements** The auditor should determine which of the entity's government programs and compliance requirements to test, i.e., the *applicable compliance requirements*, in accordance with the governmental audit requirement. Some governmental audit requirements specifically identify the applicable compliance requirements. Other governmental audit requirements provide a framework for the auditor to determine the applicable compliance requirements.

    a. **Sources of Information About Applicable Compliance Requirements**

        (1) *The Compliance Supplement* Issued by the OMB, and used in OMB Circular A-133 audits, it contains the compliance requirements that typically are applicable to federal government programs, as well as suggested audit procedures when compliance requirements are applicable and have a direct and material effect on the entity's compliance.

        (2) **Program-Specific Audit Guides** The applicable program-specific audit guide issued by the grantor agency, which contains the compliance requirements pertaining to the government program and suggested audit procedures to test for compliance with the applicable compliance requirements.

    b. **Procedures to Obtain Additional Information**

        (1) Reading laws, regulations, rules, and provisions of contracts or grant agreements that pertain to the government program

        (2) Making inquiries of management and other knowledgeable entity personnel

        (3) Making inquiries of appropriate individuals outside the entity, such as the office of the federal, state, or local program official or auditor, or other appropriate audit oversight organizations or regulators, about the laws and regulations applicable to entities within their jurisdiction, including statutes and uniform reporting requirements

        (4) Making inquiries of a third-party specialist, such as an attorney

        (5) Reading the minutes of meetings of the governing board of the entity being audited

        (6) Reading audit documentation about the applicable compliance requirements prepared during prior years' audits or other engagements

        (7) Discussing the applicable compliance requirements with auditors who performed prior years' audits or other engagements

4. **Risk Assessment Procedures** For each of the government programs and applicable compliance requirements selected for testing, the auditor should perform risk assessment procedures to obtain a sufficient understanding of the applicable compliance requirements and the entity's related internal controls. This understanding establishes a frame of reference within

which the auditor plans the compliance audit and exercises professional judgment about assessing risks of material noncompliance and responding to those risks throughout the compliance audit.

a. **Management's Response to Other Engagements' Findings** The auditor should inquire of management about whether there are findings and recommendations in reports or other written communications resulting from previous audits, attestation engagements, and internal or external monitoring that directly relate to the objectives of the compliance audit. The auditor should gain an understanding of management's response to findings and recommendations that could have a material effect on the entity's compliance with the applicable compliance requirements, for example, taking corrective action. The auditor should use this information to assess risk and determine the nature, extent, and timing of the audit procedures for the compliance audit, including determining the extent to which testing the implementation of any corrective actions is applicable to the audit objectives.

b. **Other Factors That Influence Nature & Extent of Risk Assessment Procedures**

   (1) The newness and complexity of the applicable compliance requirements

   (2) The nature of the applicable compliance requirements

   (3) The services provided by the entity and how they are affected by external factors

   (4) The level of oversight by the grantor or pass-through entity

c. **Evaluation of Controls** Performing risk assessment procedures to obtain an understanding of the entity's internal control over compliance includes an evaluation of the design of controls and whether the controls have been implemented.

5. **Assessing the Risks of Material Noncompliance** The auditor should assess the risks of material noncompliance whether due to fraud or error for each applicable compliance requirement.

   a. **Pervasive Risk** The auditor should consider whether any of those risks are pervasive to the entity's compliance because they may affect the entity's compliance with many compliance requirements. Examples of situations in which there may be a pervasive risk are an entity's history of poor record keeping for its government programs or an entity that is experiencing financial difficulty and for which there is an increased risk that grant funds will be diverted for unauthorized purposes.

   b. **Inherent Risk & Control Risk** In assessing the risks of material noncompliance, the auditor may evaluate inherent risk of noncompliance and control risk of noncompliance individually or in combination.

   c. **Factors to Consider** Factors the auditor may consider in assessing the risks of material noncompliance are as follows:

      (1) The complexity of the applicable compliance requirements

      (2) The susceptibility of the applicable compliance requirements to noncompliance

      (3) The length of time the entity has been subject to the applicable compliance requirements

      (4) The auditor's observations about how the entity has complied with the applicable compliance requirements in prior years

      (5)   The potential effect on the entity of noncompliance with the applicable compliance requirements

      (6)   The degree of judgment involved in adhering to the compliance requirements

      (7)   The auditor's assessment of the risks of material misstatement in the financial statement audit

6.   **Performing Further Audit Procedures in Response to Assessed Risks**

    a.   **Overall Response** If the auditor identifies risks of material noncompliance that are pervasive to the entity's compliance, the auditor should develop an overall response to such risks.

    b.   **Tests of Details** The auditor should design and perform further audit procedures, including tests of details to obtain sufficient appropriate audit evidence about the entity's compliance with each of the applicable compliance requirements in response to the assessed risks of material noncompliance. Risk assessment procedures, tests of controls, and analytical procedures *alone* are **not** sufficient to address a risk of material noncompliance.

      (1)   **Areas to Test** Examples of areas where tests of details may be performed include grant disbursements or expenditures; eligibility files; cost allocation plans; and periodic reports filed with grantor agencies.

      (2)   **Intentional and Unintentional Noncompliance** A compliance audit includes designing procedures to detect both intentional and unintentional material noncompliance.

      (3)   **Sampling** An auditor may decide to use audit sampling to obtain sufficient appropriate audit evidence in a compliance audit.

    c.   **Tests of Operating Effectiveness of Controls** If *any* of the following conditions are met, the auditor should test the operating effectiveness of controls over each applicable compliance requirement to which the conditions apply in each compliance audit. The use of audit evidence about the operating effectiveness of controls obtained in prior audits is **not** applicable to a compliance audit.

      (1)   The auditor's risk assessment includes an expectation of the operating effectiveness of controls over compliance related to the applicable compliance requirements.

      (2)   Substantive procedures alone do not provide sufficient appropriate audit evidence.

      (3)   Such tests of controls over compliance are required by the governmental audit requirement.

7.   **Supplementary Audit Requirements** The auditor should determine whether audit requirements are specified in the governmental audit requirement that are supplementary to GAAS and GAGAS and perform procedures to address those requirements, if any.

8.   **Written Representations** The auditor should request from management written representations that are tailored to the entity and the governmental audit requirement. In some cases, management may include qualifying language to the effect that representations are made to the best of management's knowledge and belief. However, such qualifying language is **not** appropriate for the representations in the first, second and last of the following statements:

a. Acknowledging management's responsibility for understanding and complying with the compliance requirements;

b. Acknowledging management's responsibility for establishing and maintaining controls that provide reasonable assurance that the entity administers government programs in accordance with the compliance requirements;

c. Stating that management has identified and disclosed to the auditor all of its government programs and related activities subject to the governmental audit requirement;

d. Stating that management has made available to the auditor all contracts and grant agreements, including amendments, if any, and any other correspondence relevant to the programs and related activities subject to the governmental audit requirement;

e. Stating that management has disclosed to the auditor all known noncompliance with the applicable compliance requirements or stating that there was no such noncompliance;

f. Stating whether management believes that the entity has complied with the applicable compliance requirements (except for noncompliance it has disclosed to the auditor);

g. Stating that management has made available to the auditor all documentation related to compliance with the applicable compliance requirements;

h. Identifying management's interpretation of any applicable compliance requirements that are subject to varying interpretations;

i. Stating that management has disclosed to the auditor any communications from grantors and pass-through entities concerning possible noncompliance with the applicable compliance requirements, including communications received from the end of the period covered by the compliance audit to the date of the auditor's report;

j. Stating that management has disclosed to the auditor the findings received and related corrective actions taken for previous audits, attestation engagements, and internal or external monitoring that directly relate to the objectives of the compliance audit, including findings received and corrective actions taken from the end of the period covered by the compliance audit to the date of the auditor's report;

k. Stating that management has disclosed to the auditor all known noncompliance with the applicable compliance requirements subsequent to the period covered by the auditor's report or stating that there were no such known instances; and

l. Stating that management is responsible for taking corrective action on audit findings of the compliance audit.

The auditor should request any additional representations needed, if any.

9. Subsequent Events The auditor should perform audit procedures up to the date of the auditor's report to obtain sufficient appropriate audit evidence that all subsequent events related to the entity's compliance during the period covered by the auditor's report on compliance have been identified. The nature and extent of these procedures should take the auditor's risk assessment into account.

a. Procedures Audit procedures should include, but are not limited to, inquiring of management about and considering:

(1) Relevant **internal** auditors' reports issued during the subsequent period;

(2) Other auditors' reports identifying noncompliance that were issued during the **subsequent** period;

(3) Reports from grantors and pass-through entities on the entity's noncompliance that were issued during the subsequent period; and

(4) Information about the entity's noncompliance obtained through other professional engagements performed for that entity.

b. **Period Subsequent to Auditor's Report** The auditor has no obligation to perform any audit procedures related to the entity's compliance during the period subsequent to the period covered by the auditor's report. However, if before the report release date, the auditor becomes aware of noncompliance in the period subsequent to the period covered by the auditor's report that is of such a nature and significance that its disclosure is needed to prevent report users from being misled, the auditor should discuss the matter with management and, if appropriate, those charged with governance, and should include an explanatory paragraph in the audit report describing the nature of the noncompliance. For example, disclosure would be warranted if the discovery of noncompliance in the subsequent period was of such magnitude that it caused the grantor to stop funding the program.

10. **Evaluating Sufficiency & Appropriateness of Audit Evidence and Forming an Opinion** The auditor should evaluate the sufficiency and appropriateness of the audit evidence obtained. The auditor should form an opinion, at the level specified by the governmental audit requirement, on whether the entity complied in all material respects with the applicable compliance requirements, and report appropriately. When determining if the entity materially complied with applicable compliance requirements, noncompliance identified by the auditor should be considered even if the entity corrected it once the auditor brought it to management's attention. In forming an opinion, the auditor should evaluate likely questioned costs, not just known questioned costs, as well as other material noncompliance that, by its nature, may not result in questioned costs. Factors to consider in the determination of whether the entity materially complied with the applicable compliance requirements may include:

a. The frequency of noncompliance with the applicable compliance requirements identified during the compliance audit;

b. The nature of the noncompliance with the applicable compliance requirements identified;

c. The adequacy of the entity's system for monitoring compliance with the applicable compliance requirements and the possible effect of any noncompliance on the entity; and

d. Whether any identified noncompliance with the applicable compliance requirements resulted in likely questioned costs that are material to the government program.

11. **Reporting & Communication Requirements**

a. **Elements of a Report on Compliance Only** The auditor's report on compliance should include the following elements:

(1) A title that includes the word *independent*

(2) Identification of the one or more government programs covered by the compliance audit or reference to a separate schedule containing that information

(3) Identification of the applicable compliance requirements or a reference to where they can be found

(4) Identification of the period covered by the report

(5)   A statement that compliance with the applicable compliance requirements is the responsibility of the entity's management

(6)   A statement that the auditor's responsibility is to express an opinion on the entity's compliance with the applicable compliance requirements based on the compliance audit

(7)   A statement that the compliance audit was conducted in accordance with auditing standards generally accepted in the United States of America, the standards applicable to financial audits contained in *Government Auditing Standards*, and the governmental audit requirement

(8)   A statement that the compliance audit included examining, on a test basis, evidence about the entity's compliance with those requirements and performing such other procedures as the auditor considered necessary in the circumstances

(9)   A statement that the auditor believes the compliance audit provides a reasonable basis for her/his opinion

(10) A statement that the compliance audit does not provide a legal determination of the entity's compliance

(11) The auditor's opinion, at the level specified by the governmental audit requirement, on whether the entity complied, in all material respects, with the applicable compliance requirements

(12) If noncompliance that results in an opinion modification is identified, a description of such noncompliance, or a reference to a description of such noncompliance in an accompanying schedule

(13) If other noncompliance that is required to be reported by the governmental audit requirement is identified (that is, noncompliance that does not result in an opinion modification), a description of such noncompliance or a reference to a description of such noncompliance in an accompanying schedule

(14) If the criteria used to evaluate compliance are established or determined by contractual agreement or regulatory provisions that are developed solely for the parties to the agreement or regulatory agency responsible for the provisions or are available only to the specified parties, a separate paragraph should be prepared at the end of the report that includes a statement indicating that the report is intended solely for the information and use of the specified parties, an identification of the specified parties to whom use is restricted, and a statement that the report is not intended to be and should not be used by anyone other than the specified parties

(15) The manual or printed signature of the auditor's firm

(16) The date of the auditor's report

b.   **Elements of a Combined Report on Compliance & Internal Control Over Compliance** (See Exhibit 1 for an example of this report.) If the governmental audit requirement requires the auditor to report on internal control over compliance and the auditor combines the auditor's report on compliance with a report on internal control over compliance, the elements listed below should be *added* to the report elements listed above.

(1)   A statement that management is responsible for establishing and maintaining effective internal control over compliance with the requirements of laws, regulations, rules, and provisions of contracts or grant agreements applicable to government programs.

(2) A statement that in planning and performing the compliance audit, the auditor considered the entity's internal control over compliance with the applicable compliance requirements to determine the auditing procedures for the purpose of expressing an opinion on compliance, but not for the purpose of expressing an opinion on the effectiveness of internal control over compliance.

(3) A statement that the auditor is not expressing an opinion on internal control over compliance.

(4) A statement that the auditor's consideration of the entity's internal control over compliance was not designed to identify all deficiencies in internal control that might be significant deficiencies or material weaknesses in internal control over compliance.

(5) The definition of *deficiency in internal control over compliance* and *material weakness in internal control over compliance*.

(6) A description of any identified material weaknesses in internal control over compliance or a reference to an accompanying schedule containing such a description.

(7) If significant deficiencies in internal control over compliance were identified, the definition of *significant deficiency in internal control over compliance* and a description of the deficiencies or a reference to an accompanying schedule containing such a description.

(8) If no material weaknesses in internal control over compliance were identified, a statement to that effect.

(9) The restricted use paragraph should be included in all combined reports on the entity's compliance and internal control over compliance.

c. **Elements of a Separate Report on Internal Control Over Compliance** If the governmental audit requirement requires the auditor to report on internal control over compliance and the auditor chooses to issue a separate report on internal control over compliance, the auditor should include in that separate report the elements listed above and the following additional elements:

(1) A title that includes the word *independent*

(2) A statement that the auditor audited the entity's compliance with applicable compliance requirements pertaining to [*identify the government program(s) and the period audited*] and a reference to the auditor's report on compliance

(3) A statement that the compliance audit was conducted in accordance with auditing standards generally accepted in the United States of America, the standards applicable to financial audits contained in *Government Auditing Standards*, and the governmental audit requirement

(4) The manual or printed signature of the auditor's firm

(5) The date of the auditor's report

Exhibit 1 ▶ Combined Report on Compliance With Applicable Requirements and Internal Control Over Compliance

---

<u>Independent Auditor's Report</u>

[*Addressee*]

Compliance

We have audited Example Entity's compliance with the [*identify the applicable compliance requirements or refer to the document that describes the applicable compliance requirements*] applicable to Example Entity's [*identify the government program(s) audited or refer to a separate schedule that identifies the program(s)*] for the year ended June 30, 20X1. Compliance with the requirements referred to above is the responsibility of Example Entity's management. Our responsibility is to express an opinion on Example Entity's compliance based on our audit.

We conducted our audit of compliance in accordance with auditing standards generally accepted in the United States of America; the standards applicable to financial audits contained in *Government Auditing Standards* issued by the Comptroller General of the United States; and [*insert the name of the governmental audit requirement or program-specific audit guide*]. Those standards and [*insert the name of the governmental audit requirement or program-specific audit guide*] require that we plan and perform the audit to obtain reasonable assurance about whether noncompliance with the compliance requirements referred to above that could have a material effect on [*identify the government program(s) audited or refer to a separate schedule that identifies the program(s)*] occurred. An audit includes examining, on a test basis, evidence about Example Entity's compliance with those requirements and performing such other procedures as we considered necessary in the circumstances. We believe that our audit provides a reasonable basis for our opinion. Our audit does not provide a legal determination of Example Entity's compliance with those requirements.

In our opinion, Example Entity complied, in all material respects, with the compliance requirements referred to above that are applicable to [*identify the government program(s) audited*] for the year ended June 30, 20X1.

Internal Control Over Compliance

Management of Example Entity is responsible for establishing and maintaining effective internal control over compliance with the compliance requirements referred to above. In planning and performing our audit, we considered Example Entity's internal control over compliance to determine the auditing procedures for the purpose of expressing our opinion on compliance, but not for the purpose of expressing an opinion on the effectiveness of internal control over compliance. Accordingly, we do not express an opinion on the effectiveness of Example Entity's internal control over compliance.

A *deficiency in internal control over compliance* exists when the design or operation of a control does not allow management or employees, in the normal course of performing their assigned functions, to prevent, or detect and correct, noncompliance on a timely basis. A *material weakness in internal control over compliance* is a deficiency, or combination of deficiencies in internal control over compliance, such that there is a reasonable possibility that material noncompliance with a compliance requirement will not be prevented, or detected and corrected, on a timely basis.

Our consideration of internal control over compliance was for the limited purpose described in the first paragraph of this section and was not designed to identify all deficiencies in internal control that might be deficiencies, significant deficiencies, or material weaknesses in internal control over compliance. We did not identify any deficiencies in internal control over compliance that we consider to be material weaknesses, as defined above.

This report is intended solely for the information and use of management, [*identify the body or individuals charged with governance*], others within the entity, [*identify the legislative or regulatory body*], and [*identify the grantor agency(ies)*] and is not intended to be and should not be used by anyone other than these specified parties.

[*Signature*]
[*Date*]

d. **Other Reporting Requirements** The auditor should report noncompliance as well as other matters that are required to be reported by the governmental audit requirement in the manner specified by the governmental audit requirement. If the other matters required to be reported by the governmental audit requirement are not appropriate for the auditor to report on, the auditor should attach a separate report.

e. **Material Noncompliance or Scope Restriction** The auditor should modify her/his opinion on compliance in accordance with AU 508, *Reports on Audited Financial Statements*, if any of the following conditions exist:

(1) The compliance audit identifies noncompliance with the applicable compliance requirements that the auditor believes has a material effect on the entity's compliance.

(2) A restriction on the scope of the compliance audit

f. **Reference to Another Auditor** The auditor should modify the report when the auditor makes reference to the report of another auditor as the basis, in part, for the auditor's report.

g. **Printed Forms** Printed forms, schedules, or reports designed or adopted by government agencies with which they are to be filed sometimes contain prescribed wording. If these require the auditor to make a statement that the auditor has no basis to make, the auditor should accordingly reword the form, schedule, or report or attach an appropriately worded separate report.

h. **Reissuance of a Compliance Report** If an auditor reissues a report, it should include an explanatory paragraph stating that the report is replacing a previously issued report and describing the reasons why it is being reissued, and any changes from the previously issued report. Reissuance of an auditor-prepared document required by the governmental audit requirement that is incorporated by reference into the auditor's report is considered to be a reissuance of the report.

(1) **Additional Procedures Performed for All Programs** If additional procedures are performed for all of the government programs being reported on, the auditor's report date should be updated to reflect the date the auditor obtained sufficient appropriate audit evidence regarding the events that caused the auditor to perform the new procedures.

(2) **Additional Procedures Performed for Only Some Programs** If additional procedures are performed for only some of the government programs, the auditor should dual date the report with the updated report date reflecting the date the auditor obtained sufficient appropriate audit evidence regarding the government programs affected by the circumstances and referencing the government programs for which additional audit procedures have been performed.

i. **Communication Requirements**

(1) In the absence of a governmental audit requirement to report on internal control over compliance, the auditor should, nevertheless, communicate in writing to management and those charged with governance identified significant deficiencies and material weaknesses in internal control over compliance. *Government Auditing Standards* require the auditor to obtain a response from responsible officials, preferably in writing.

(2) The auditor also should communicate to those charged with governance of the entity the auditor's responsibilities under GAAS, GAGAS, and the governmental audit requirement; an overview of the planned scope and timing of the compliance audit; and significant findings from the compliance audit.

12. **Documentation Requirements** The auditor should document:

   a. The risk assessment procedures performed, including those related to gaining an understanding of internal control over compliance

   b. The auditor's responses to the assessed risks of material noncompliance

   c. The procedures performed to test compliance with the applicable compliance requirements and the results of those procedures, including any tests of controls over compliance

   d. The materiality levels and the basis on which they were determined

   e. How the auditor complied with the specific governmental audit requirements that are supplementary to GAAS and GAGAS

   Editor note: The auditor is **not** expected to prepare specific documentation of how the auditor adapted and applied each of the applicable AU sections to the objectives of a compliance audit. The documentation of the audit strategy, audit plan, and work performed cumulatively demonstrate whether the auditor has complied with this requirement.

II. Governmental Auditing Standards

A. **Overview**
GAGAS apply to audits and attestation engagements of government entities, programs, activities, and functions and of government assistance administered by nongovernmental organizations (including nonprofit entities and business enterprises). The ethical principles that provide the overall framework for application of GAGAS and, thus, guide the work of auditors are the public interest, integrity, objectivity, proper use of government information, resources, and position, and professional behavior. The concept of accountability underlies decision makers' need to know whether resources are managed properly and used in compliance with laws and regulations, programs achieve their objectives and desired outcomes, services are provided effectively, efficiently, economically, ethically, and equitably, and managers are held accountable for their use of public resources. Auditors may use GAGAS in conjunction with professional standards issued by other authoritative bodies and may cite their use in their reports.

B. **Professional Requirements**
GAGAS identify professional requirements with specific language (consistent with GAAS) to indicate the degree of responsibility imposed on auditors and audit organizations. The two categories of requirements are: *unconditional requirements* (in which the words *must* or *is required* are used) and *presumptively mandatory requirements* (in which the word *should* is used). Explanatory material intended to provide guidance or to be descriptive rather than required is also included in the standards in which the words *may, might* and *could* are used.

C. **Engagement Types**

1. **Financial Audits** Financial audits are concerned primarily with providing reasonable assurance as to whether financial statements are presented fairly in all material respects in conformity with GAAP or with an other comprehensive basis of accounting (OCBOA). Other objectives include providing special reports for portions of financial statements; reviewing interim financial information; issuing letters for underwriters and certain other requesting parties; reporting on the controls over transaction processing by service organizations; and auditing compliance with regulations relating to federal award expenditures and other government financial assistance in conjunction with a financial statement audit.

2. **Attestation Engagements** Attestation engagements concern examining, reviewing or performing agreed-upon procedures on a subject matter or an assertion about a subject matter and reporting on the results. They may be concerned with either financial or nonfinancial

matters and may provide different levels of assurance about the subject matter or assertion depending on the user's needs.

3.   **Performance Audits**   Performance audits provide assurance or conclusions based on an evaluation of sufficient, appropriate evidence to assess program performance against stated criteria.   Their objectives include assessments of program effectiveness, economy and efficiency; internal control; compliance; and prospective analyses.

D.   General Standards
These general standards apply to financial audits, attestation engagements and performance audits performed in accordance with GAGAS.

1.   **Independence**   In all matters relating to the audit work, the audit organization and the individual auditor, whether government or public, must be free from personal, external, and organizational impairments to independence, and must avoid the appearance of such impairments of independence.   GAGAS do not provide standards for other services, thus auditors must not report that nonaudit services were conducted in accordance with GAGAS.   Audit organizations need to ensure that their independence is not impaired by any nonaudit services they provide. Auditors should evaluate threats to independence using the conceptual framework when the facts and circumstances under which the auditors perform their work may create or augment threats to independence.   Auditors should evaluate threats both individually and in the aggregate because threats can have a cumulative effect on an auditor's independence.   Facts and circumstances that create threats to independence can result from events such as the start of a new audit; assignment of new staff to an ongoing audit; and acceptance of a nonaudit service at an audited entity.   Many other events can result in threats to independence.   Auditors use professional judgment to determine whether the facts and circumstances created by an event warrant use of the conceptual framework.   Whenever relevant new information about a threat to independence comes to the attention of the auditor during the audit, the auditor should evaluate the significance of the threat.   Auditors should determine whether identified threats to independence are at an acceptable level or have been eliminated or reduced to an acceptable level.

2.   **Professional Judgment**   Auditors must use professional judgment in planning and performing audits and attestation engagements and in reporting the results.

3.   **Competence**   The staff assigned to perform the audit or attestation engagement must collectively possess adequate professional competence for the tasks required.

4.   **Quality Control**   Each audit organization performing audits or attestation engagements in accordance with GAGAS must:

a.   Establish a system of quality control that is designed to provide the audit organization with reasonable assurance that the organization and its personnel comply with professional standards and applicable legal and regulatory requirements

b.   Have an external peer review at least once every 3 years; external audit organizations should make their most recent peer review report publicly available; internal audit organizations should share the report with those charged with governance; government audit organizations should communicate the results of their reviews and availability of the report with appropriate oversight bodies

E.   Standards Common to GAGAS Engagements
The following standards apply to financial audits, attestation engagements, and performance audits conducted in accordance with GAGAS.   In detail, there are variations among them; however, to the depth of this coverage, these standards are very similar.

1.   **Documentation**   Documentation must contain sufficient information to enable an experienced auditor with no previous connection to the engagement to obtain a clear understanding of

the work performed and ascertain that the evidence supports the auditors' significant judgments and conclusions. Documentation must be complete before auditors issue their reports.

2. **Reporting Compliance With GAGAS** Reports should state that the engagements were performed in accordance with GAGAS.

3. **Reporting Officials' Views** If the auditors' report on the engagement discloses deficiencies in internal control, fraud, illegal acts, violations of provisions of contracts or grant agreements, or abuse, auditors should obtain and report the views of responsible officials concerning the findings, conclusions, and recommendations, as well as planned corrective actions. Auditors should also include in the report an evaluation of the comments.

4. **Reporting Confidential or Sensitive Information** If certain pertinent information is prohibited from public disclosure or is excluded from a report due to the confidential or sensitive nature of the information, auditors should disclose in the report that certain information has been omitted and the reason or other circumstances that makes the omission necessary. When audit organizations are subject to public records laws, auditors should determine whether public records laws could impact the availability of classified or limited-official-use reports and determine whether other means of communicating with management and those charged with governance would be more appropriate.

5. **Report Issuance & Distribution** If the subject of the audit involves material that is classified for security purposes or contains confidential or sensitive information, auditors may limit the report distribution. Auditors should document any limitation on report distribution. Distribution of reports depends on the relationship of the auditors to the audited organization and the nature of the information contained in the report.

F. **Standards Common to Financial Audits & Attestation Engagements**
The following standards apply to financial audits and attestation engagements in accordance with GAGAS. To the depth of this coverage, these standards are similar for both types of engagements.

1. **Communication During Planning** Auditors should communicate their understanding of the services to be performed for each engagement, in writing, to management, those charged with governance, and to the individuals contracting for or requesting the audit or engagement.

2. **Results of Previous Engagements** Auditors should evaluate whether the entity has taken appropriate corrective action to address findings and recommendations from previous engagements that could have a material effect on the financial statements or the subject matter.

3. **Elements of Findings** The elements needed for a finding depend on the particular audit or engagement objectives. Thus, a finding or set of findings is complete to the extent that the objectives are satisfied. When deficiencies are identified auditors should plan and perform procedures to develop the elements of a finding to achieve those objectives.

4. **Reporting Internal Control Deficiencies, Fraud, Illegal Acts, Violations & Abuse** For all financial audit and attestation engagements, auditors must report, as applicable to the engagement objectives, all instances of fraud and illegal acts unless clearly inconsequential and violations of provisions of contracts or grant agreements and abuse that could have a material effect on the financial statements or the subject matter of the engagement. When auditors detect violations of provisions of contracts or grant agreements or abuse that have an effect on the financial statements or the subject matter that is less than material but more than inconsequential, they should communicate those findings in writing to entity officials. Also, auditors should report significant deficiencies and material weaknesses in internal control.

G.   Financial Audit Standards

GAGAS incorporate the AICPA fieldwork and reporting standards and the related SASs unless specifically excluded or modified by GAGAS and outline the following additional fieldwork and reporting standards for financial audits performed in accordance with GAGAS.

1.   **Communication During Planning** Auditors should communicate in writing the nature of planned work and level of assurance to be provided related to internal control over financial reporting and compliance with laws, regulations, and provisions of contracts or grant agreements and any potential restriction on the auditors' reports, in order to reduce the chance of any misunderstanding.

2.   **Detecting Misstatements Resulting From Violations or Abuse** Auditors should design the audit to provide reasonable assurance of detecting misstatements resulting from violations of provisions of contracts or grant agreements that could have a direct and material effect on the determination of financial statement amounts or other financial data significant to the audit objectives. If specific information comes to the auditors' attention that provides evidence of such possible violations, the auditors should apply procedures to ascertain whether such violations have, or are likely to have, occurred.

3.   **Reporting on Internal Control & Compliance** When providing an opinion or a disclaimer on financial statements, auditors must also report on internal control over financial reporting and on compliance with laws, regulations, and provisions of contracts or grant agreements. Auditors should include either in the same or in separate report(s) a description of the scope of this testing of internal control. If the auditor issues separate reports, the auditors' report on the financial statements should include in a reference to these separate reports that these reports are an integral part of a GAGAS audit and are important for assessing the results of the audit.

4.   **Communicating Significant Matters** Due to the public interest in the operations of government entities and entities that receive or administer government awards, in GAGAS audits there may be situations in which certain types of information in addition to the examples presented in AICPA standards would help facilitate the readers' understanding of the financial statements and the auditors' report. The determination of whether to include such information is a matter of professional judgment.

5.   **Restated Financial Statements** Auditors should advise management to make appropriate disclosures when the auditors become aware that it is likely that previously issued financial statements are materially misstated. Auditors also should evaluate the timeliness and appropriateness of management's disclosure and actions to determine and correct misstatements; report on restated financial statements; and report directly to appropriate officials when the audited entity does not take the necessary steps.

H.   Attestation Engagement Standards

GAGAS incorporate the AICPA general attestation standard on criteria, its fieldwork and reporting standards for attestation engagements plus the Statements on Standards for Attestation Engagements (SSAEs), unless specifically excluded or modified by GAGAS, as well as outline additional government attestation standards. Of course, the GAGAS general standards also apply.

1.   **Communication During Planning** Auditors should obtain written acknowledgment or other evidence of the entity's responsibilities for the subject matter or the written assertion as it relates to the objectives of the engagement. Auditors should communicate the nature, extent, and timing of planned testing and reporting; the level of assurance the auditor will provide; and any potential restriction on the auditors' reports, in order to reduce the chance of any misunderstanding.

2.   **Internal Control** In planning examination-level attestation engagements, auditors should obtain a sufficient understanding of internal control that is material to the subject matter or assertion to plan the engagement and design procedures to achieve the engagement objectives.

3.   **Detecting Fraud, Illegal Acts, Violations & Abuse** If auditors become aware of abuse that could be quantitatively or qualitatively material, auditors should apply procedures specifically directed to ascertain the potential effect on the subject matter or other data significant to the engagement objectives.

   a.   **Examination** In planning, auditors should design the engagement to provide reasonable assurance of detecting fraud, illegal acts, or violations of provisions of contracts or grant agreements that could have a material effect on the subject matter of the attestation engagement.

   b.   **Review or Agreed-Upon Procedures** If during the course of the engagement, information comes to the auditors' attention indicating that fraud, illegal acts, or violations of provisions of contracts or grant agreements that could have a material effect on the subject matter may have occurred, auditors should perform procedures as necessary to determine if fraud, illegal acts, or violations of provisions of contracts or grant agreements are likely to have occurred and, if so, determine their effect on the results of the attestation engagement.

I.   **Performance Audit Standards**

1.   **Planning & Supervision** Work must be planned adequately and staff must be supervised properly. In planning the audit, auditors should assess significance and audit risk and apply these assessments in defining the audit objectives and the scope and methodology to address those objectives. Auditors must plan the audit to reduce audit risk to an appropriate level for the auditors to provide reasonable assurance that the evidence is sufficient and appropriate to support the auditors' findings and conclusions. Auditors must prepare a written audit plan for each audit.

2.   **Evidence** Sufficient, appropriate evidence must be obtained to provide a reasonable basis for the auditor's findings and conclusions.

3.   **Form** Auditors must prepare audit reports communicating the results of each audit. Auditors should use a form of the audit report that is appropriate for its intended use and is in writing or in another retrievable form.

4.   **Report Contents** The report should include the objectives, scope, and methodology; and the audit results, including findings, conclusions, and recommendations, as appropriate.

5.   **Report Quality Elements** The report should be as timely, complete, accurate, objective, convincing, clear, and concise as the subject permits.

6.   **Validity** Appropriateness is the measure of the quality of evidence that encompasses the relevance, validity, and reliability of evidence. Validity as an aspect of the quality of evidence refers to the extent to which evidence represents what it is purported to represent.

7.   **Significant internal control deficiencies** Auditors should include in the audit report the scope of their work on internal control and any deficiencies in internal control that are significant within the context of the audit objectives and based upon the audit work performed.

8.   **Fraud reporting requirements** When auditors conclude, based on sufficient, appropriate evidence, that fraud, noncompliance with provisions of laws, regulations, contracts or grant agreements, or abuse either has occurred or is likely to have occurred which is significant within the context of the audit objectives, they should report the matter as a finding.

III. **Single Audit Act**

A.   **Purpose**
OMB Circular A-133, *Audits of States, Local Governments, and Nonprofit Organizations,* sets forth requirements for audits in accordance with the Single Audit Act and the Single Audit Act Amendments of 1996.

B.   Threshold
The amount of federal awards expended by a nonfederal entity (as opposed to receipts) within a fiscal year determines whether an entity meets the threshold. The threshold is $500,000.

1.   Entities that expend total federal awards equal to or in excess the threshold in a fiscal year require an audit performed in accordance with the Single Audit Act and OMB Circular A-133. Those that equal or exceed the threshold, but receive awards under only one program, have the option of having an audit performed in accordance with A-133 or having an audit made of the one program.

2.   Institutions expending less than the threshold annually in federal awards are exempt from federal audit requirements, but records must be available for review by appropriate officials of the grantor agency or sub-granting agency.

C.   Compliance Reporting
Compliance should be tested for those requirements that relate to the allowability of program expenditures as well as the eligibility of the individual or groups to which federal award is provided. The auditor should test and report on the following matters pertaining to compliance with laws and regulations:

1.   Laws and regulations that may have a material effect on the financial statements.

2.   General requirements applicable to federal financial assistance.

3.   Specific requirements that may have a material effect on each major program, as defined by the Single Audit Act.

4.   Certain laws and regulations applicable to nonmajor federal award programs.

D.   Compliance Requirements
OMB Circular A-133 identifies compliance requirements. For each federal program, the auditor reports whether there are audit findings for each of 14 types of compliance requirements and the total amount of questioned costs.

1.   **Activities Allowed or Unallowed** Specifies the types of goods or services entities may purchase with financial assistance.

2.   **Allowable Costs / Cost Principles** Prescribes the direct and indirect costs allowable for federal reimbursement.

3.   **Cash Management** Requires recipients of federal awards to minimize the time lapse between receipt and disbursement of that assistance.

4.   **Davis-Bacon Act** Requires that laborers working on federally financed construction projects be paid a wage not less than the prevailing regional wage established by the Secretary of Labor.

5.   **Eligibility** Specifies the characteristics of individuals or groups to whom entities may give financial assistance.

6.   **Equipment & Real Property Management**

7.   **Matching, Level of Effort, Earmarking** Specifies the amounts entities should contribute from their own resources toward projects for which financial assistance is provided.

8.   **Period of Availability of Federal Funds**

9.   **Procurement & Suspension & Debarment**

10.   **Program Income**

11. **Real Property Acquisition & Relocation Assistance** Prescribes how real property should be acquired with federal awards and how recipients must help relocate people displaced when that property is acquired.

12. **Reporting** Specifies reports entities must file in addition to those required by the general requirements.

13. **Subrecipient Monitoring**

14. **Special Tests & Provisions** Other provisions for which federal agencies have determined that noncompliance could materially affect the program (for example, some programs require recipients to hold public hearings on the proposed use of federal awards; other programs set a deadline for the expenditure of federal awards).

E. **Management Responsibilities**
Management is required to prepare a schedule of major and nonmajor federal award programs.

F. **Materiality**
In auditing an entity's compliance with requirements governing each major federal award program in accordance with the Single Audit Act, the auditor considers materiality in relation to each program. (This differs from audits in accordance with GAAS.)

G. **Risk**
OMB Circular A-133 prescribes a risk-based approach to determine major programs, requiring the auditor to consider a combination of materiality, internal control, and other factors in determining whether a program must be tested as major. It also allows federal agencies to designate certain programs as major, requiring the auditor to test them as major, even though they may not satisfy the risk-based criteria. The auditor must perform procedures that assess inherent and control risk and restrict detection risk. The auditor must obtain an understanding of internal control over federal programs sufficient to plan the audit to support a low assessed level of control risk for major programs.

1. **Inherent Risk** In assessing inherent risk, the auditor considers the results of any procedures performed as part of the audit of the financial statements, and of any tests of compliance with the general requirements.

2. **Detection Risk** In determining an acceptable level of detection risk, the auditor considers the level to which s/he seeks to restrict audit risk related to the major federal award program and the assessed levels of inherent risk and control risk.

3. **Cluster of Programs** A cluster of programs is a group of closely related programs that share common compliance requirements. The auditor must consider a cluster of programs as one program for determining major programs, with some exceptions.

H. **Consistency With Financial Statements**
Auditors must determine whether financial reports and claims for advances and reimbursement contain information supported by the records from which the basic financial statements were prepared, and that amounts claimed or used for matching purposes were determined in accordance with OMB Circulars A-87 and A-102.

I. **Noncompliance**
To evaluate the effects of questioned costs on the opinion on compliance properly, the best estimate of total costs questioned for each major federal award program is considered, not just those questioned costs that were identified specifically. The auditor must report any instances of noncompliance found and resulting questioned costs.

J. **Subrecipients**
In a single year, if a primary recipient passes $25,000 or more of federal award through to a subrecipient, that primary recipient becomes responsible for determining that the assistance is spent in accordance with applicable laws and regulations. The primary recipient should:

1. Determine that subrecipients met the audit requirements of OMB Circular A-133, if applicable.

2. Determine if the assistance was spent in accordance with applicable laws and regulations.

3. Ensure that corrective action is taken within six months after receipt of a report that identifies instances of noncompliance.

4. Consider the need for an adjustment to the records of the primary recipient.

5. Require each subrecipient to permit independent auditors to have access to their records and financial statements as necessary to comply with OMB Circular A-133.

K. Nonmajor Programs
The Single Audit Act requires that transactions selected from federal assistance programs, other than major federal assistance programs be tested for compliance with applicable federal laws and regulations.

L. Reporting
The auditor must summarize the results of the audit concerning internal control, financial statements, and compliance with laws and regulations. The audit report must be issued within 9 months after the entity's year-end.

1. Auditees and recipient entities must complete their respective parts of a data collection form. This form states whether the audit was completed in accordance with Circular A-133 and provides information about the entity, its federal programs, and the results of the audit.

2. Auditors must report findings and questioned costs in a single schedule, using prescribed criteria for reporting. The schedule of findings and questioned costs must include a summary of the auditor's results, the auditor's findings relating to the financial statements, and findings and questioned costs for federal awards.

3. Recipient entities must prepare a summary schedule of prior audit findings. Auditees must report the status of all audit findings included in the prior audit's schedule of findings and questioned costs relative to federal awards.

M. Conflict of Interest
The auditor who prepares the indirect cost proposal or cost allocation plan may not also perform the audit when the indirect costs recovered by the client during the prior year exceeded $1,000,000. The auditor should not audit her/his own work.

IV. Other Compliance Auditing Responsibilities

A. Program-Specific Audits
The Single Audit Act and OMB Circular A-133 permit certain recipients of federal awards to have program-specific audits. When engaged to conduct such an audit, the auditor should first obtain an understanding of the audit requirements for that particular program from an agreement with the grantor agency, from an audit guide published by the grantor agency, or through contact with the grantor agency.

B. Compliance Testing
An auditor may be engaged to test and report on compliance with laws and regulations other than those previously discussed.

1. **Procedures** Auditors should consider performing the following procedures:

    a. Inquire of management about additional compliance auditing requirements applicable to the entity.

    b.   Inquire of the office of the state or local auditor or other appropriate audit oversight organization about audit requirements applicable to the entity.

    c.   Review information about governmental audit requirements available from state societies of CPAs or associations of governments.

2.   **Noncompliance** When the audit of an entity's compliance with requirements governing a major federal award program detects noncompliance with those requirements that the auditor believes have a material effect on the program, the auditor should express a qualified or adverse opinion.

_____

CPA Exam Week Checklist

What to pack for exam week:

1. CPA exam registration material (Notice to Schedule and **two** proper forms of ID).

2. Hotel confirmation.

3. Cash and/or a major credit card.

4. Alarm clock—Don't rely on a hotel wake-up call.

5. Comfortable clothing that can be layered to suit varying temperatures.

6. An inexpensive watch (to leave in a testing site locker).

7. Appropriate review materials (don't take to exam site).

8. Healthy snack foods.

Evenings before exam sections:

1. Read through your Bisk Education chapter outlines for the next day's section(s).

2. Eat lightly and monitor your intake of alcohol and caffeine. Get a good night's rest.

3. Do not try to cram. A brief review of your notes will help to focus your attention on important points and remind you that you are well prepared, but too much cramming can shatter your self-confidence. If you have reviewed conscientiously, you already are well-prepared for the CPA exam.

The morning of each exam section:

1. Eat a satisfying breakfast. It will be several hours before your next meal. Eat enough to ward off hunger, but not so much that you feel uncomfortable.

2. Dress appropriately. Wear layers you can take off to suit varying temperatures in the room.

3. Arrive at the exam center at least 30 minutes early. Check in as soon as you are allowed to do so.

More helpful exam information is included in the **Practical Advice** appendix in this volume.

––––––––––––––––

CHAPTER 9—GOVERNMENT AUDITING

Problem 9-1 MULTIPLE-CHOICE QUESTIONS

1. Although the scope of audits of recipients of federal financial assistance in accordance with federal audit regulations varies, these audits generally have which of the following elements in common?

   a. The auditor is to determine whether the federal financial assistance has been administered in accordance with applicable laws and regulations.
   b. The materiality levels are lower and are determined by the government entities that provided the federal financial assistance to the recipient.
   c. The auditor should obtain written management representations that the recipient's internal auditors will report their findings objectively without fear of political repercussion.
   d. The auditor is required to express both positive and negative assurance that illegal acts that could have a material effect on the recipient's financial statements are disclosed to the inspector general.

   (5/98, AUD, #1, ID: 7597)

2. The scope of audits of recipients of federal financial assistance in accordance with federal audit regulations varies. Which of the following elements do these audits have in common?

   a. The auditor is required to disclose all situations and transactions that could be indicative of fraud, abuse, and illegal acts to the federal inspector general.
   b. The materiality levels are higher and are determined by the government entities that provide the federal financial assistance to the recipients.
   c. The auditor is required to document an understanding of internal control established to ensure compliance with the applicable laws and regulations.
   d. The accounts should be 100% verified by substantive tests because certain statistical sampling applications are not permitted.

   (R/06, AUD, #31, ID: 8149)

3. In reporting under *Government Auditing Standards*, an auditor most likely would be required to report a falsification of accounting records directly to a federal inspector general when the falsification is

   a. Discovered after the auditor's report has been made available to the federal inspector general and to the public
   b. Reported by the auditor to the audit committee as a significant deficiency in internal control
   c. Voluntarily disclosed to the auditor by low-level personnel as a result of the auditor's inquiries
   d. Communicated by the auditor to the auditee and the auditee fails to make a required report of the matter

   (R/99, AUD, #31, ID: 6847)

4. An auditor was engaged to conduct a performance audit of a governmental entity in accordance with *Government Auditing Standards*. These standards do **not** require, as part of this auditor's report

   a. A statement of the audit objectives and a description of the audit scope
   b. Indications or instances of illegal acts that could result in criminal prosecution discovered during the audit
   c. The pertinent views of the entity's responsible officials concerning the auditor's findings
   d. A concurrent opinion on the financial statements taken as a whole

   (11/94, AUD, #90, ID: 5163)

5. In reporting under *Government Auditing Standards,* an auditor most likely would be required to communicate management's misappropriation of assets directly to a federal inspector general when the fraudulent activities are

   a. Concealed by management by circumventing specific internal controls designed to safeguard those assets
   b. Reported to the entity's governing body and the governing body fails to make a required report to the federal inspector general
   c. Accompanied by fraudulent financial reporting that results in material misstatements of asset balances
   d. Perpetrated by several levels of management in a scheme that is likely to continue in future years

   (ID: 6715)

6. When auditing an entity's financial statements in accordance with *Government Auditing Standards* (the "Yellow Book"), an auditor is required to report on

      I. Noteworthy accomplishments of the program
     II. The scope of the auditor's testing of internal controls

  a. I only
  b. II only
  c. Both I and II
  d. Neither I nor II   (R/00, AUD, #18, ID: 6943)

7. Because of the pervasive effects of laws and regulations on the financial statements of governmental units, an auditor may consider obtaining written management representations acknowledging that management has

  a. Identified and disclosed all laws and regulations that have a direct and material effect on its financial statements
  b. Implemented internal control policies and procedures designed to detect all illegal acts
  c. Expressed both positive and negative assurance to the auditor that the entity complied with all laws and regulations
  d. Employed internal auditors who can report their findings, opinions, and conclusions objectively without fear of political repercussion   (5/94, AUD, #84, amended, ID: 4749)

8. In performing a financial statement audit in accordance with *Government Auditing Standards,* an auditor is required to report on the entity's compliance with laws and regulations. This report should

  a. State that compliance with laws and regulations is the responsibility of the entity's management
  b. Describe the laws and regulations that the entity must comply with
  c. Provide an opinion on overall compliance with laws and regulations
  d. Indicate that the auditor does not possess legal skills and cannot make legal judgments   (11/93, AUD, #58, ID: 4295)

9. In auditing a not-for-profit entity that receives governmental financial assistance, the auditor has a responsibility to

  a. Issue a separate report that describes the expected benefits and related costs of the auditor's suggested changes to the entity's internal control
  b. Render an opinion concerning the entity's continued eligibility for the governmental financial assistance
  c. Notify the governmental agency providing the financial assistance that the audit is not designed to provide any assurance of detecting errors and fraud
  d. Assess whether management has identified laws and regulations that have a direct and material effect on the entity's financial statements   (11/95, AUD, #88, amended, ID: 6035)

10. Reporting on internal control under *Government Auditing Standards* differs from reporting under generally accepted auditing standards in that *Government Auditing Standards* requires a

  a. Statement of positive assurance that internal control procedures designed to detect material errors and fraud were tested
  b. Written report describing each significant deficiency observed including identification of those considered material weaknesses
  c. Statement of negative assurance that internal control procedures not tested have an immaterial effect on the entity's financial statements
  d. Written report describing the entity's internal control procedures specifically designed to prevent fraud, abuse, and illegal acts   (5/93, AUD, #24, amended, ID: 3920)

11. In an audit in accordance with *Government Auditing Standards,* an auditor is required to report on the auditor's tests of the entity's compliance with applicable laws and regulations. This requirement is satisfied by designing the audit to provide

    a. Positive assurance that the internal control policies and procedures tested by the auditor are operating as prescribed
    b. Reasonable assurance of detecting misstatements that are material to the financial statements
    c. Negative assurance that significant deficiencies communicated during the audit do not prevent the auditor from expressing an opinion
    d. Limited assurance that the internal controls designed by management will prevent or detect errors, fraud, and illegal acts (5/92, AUD, #32, amended, ID: 2785)

12. In reporting on compliance with laws and regulations during a financial statement audit in accordance with *Government Auditing Standards,* an auditor should include in the auditor's report

    a. A statement of assurance that all controls over fraud and illegal acts were tested
    b. Material instances of fraud and illegal acts that were discovered
    c. The materiality criteria used by the auditor in considering whether instances of noncompliance were significant
    d. An opinion on whether compliance with laws and regulations affected the entity's goals and objectives (5/95, AUD, #89, ID: 5707)

13. Which of the following bodies promulgates standards for audits of federal financial assistance recipients?

    a. Governmental Accounting Standards Board
    b. Financial Accounting Standards Board
    c. Governmental Auditing Standards Board
    d. Government Accountability Office (Editors, ID: 7513)

14. Which of the following statements is a standard applicable to financial statement audits in accordance with *Government Auditing Standards* (the "Yellow Book")?

    a. An auditor should report on the scope of the auditor's testing of compliance with laws and regulations.
    b. An auditor should assess whether the entity has reportable measures of economy and efficiency that are valid and reliable.
    c. An auditor should report recommendations for actions to correct problems and improve operations.
    d. An auditor should determine the extent to which the entity's programs achieve the desired results. (R/99, AUD, #28, ID: 6844)

15. Which of the following statements is a standard applicable to financial statement audits in accordance with *Government Auditing Standards* (the "Yellow Book")?

    a. An auditor should report on the scope of the auditor's testing of internal controls.
    b. All instances of abuse, waste, and mismanagement should be reported to the audit committee.
    c. An auditor should report the views of responsible officials concerning the auditor's findings.
    d. Internal control activities designed to detect or prevent fraud should be reported to the inspector general. (R/99, AUD, #29, ID: 6845)

16. An enterprise engaged a CPA to audit its financial statements in accordance with *Government Auditing Standards* (the "Yellow Book") because of the provisions of government grant funding agreements. Under these circumstances, the CPA is required to report on the enterprise's internal controls either in the report on the financial statements or in

    a. The report on the performance audit
    b. The notes to the financial statements
    c. A letter to the government funding agency
    d. A separate report (R/07, AUD, #13, ID: 8385)

17. Reporting standards for financial audits under *Government Auditing Standards* (the "Yellow Book") differ from reporting under generally accepted auditing standards in that *Government Auditing Standards* require the auditor to

    a. Provide positive assurance that control activities regarding segregation of duties are consistent with the entity's control objectives
    b. Present the results of the auditor's tests of controls
    c. Provide negative assurance that the auditor discovered no evidence of intentional override of internal controls
    d. Describe the scope of the auditor's principal substantive tests   (R/07, AUD, #45, ID: 8417)

18. An auditor notes significant deficiencies in a financial statement audit conducted in accordance with *Government Auditing Standards.* In reporting on internal control, the auditor should state that

    a. Expressing an opinion on the entity's financial statements provides no assurance on internal control.
    b. The auditor obtained an understanding of the design of relevant policies and procedures, and determined whether they have been placed in operation.
    c. The specified government funding or legislative body is responsible for reviewing internal control as a condition of continued funding.
    d. The auditor has not determined whether any of the significant deficiencies described in the report are so severe as to be material weaknesses.   (5/94, AUD, #85, amended, ID: 4750)

19. For financial statement audits, generally accepted government auditing standards (GAGAS) incorporate the *Statements on Auditing Standards* (SAS) that are issued by the AICPA. GAGAS prescribe additional standards on

	Direct reporting of illegal acts	Reporting on internal controls
a.	Yes	Yes
b.	Yes	No
c.	No	Yes
d.	No	No

                                                                        (R/03, AUD, #4, ID: 7626)

20. The GAO standards of reporting for governmental financial audits incorporate the AICPA standards of reporting and prescribe supplemental standards to satisfy the unique needs of governmental audits. Which of the following is a supplemental reporting standard for governmental financial audits?

    a. Auditors should report the scope of their testing of compliance with laws and regulations and of internal controls.
    b. Material indications of illegal acts should be reported in a document distributed only to the entity's senior officials.
    c. All changes in the audit program from the prior year should be reported to the entity's audit committee.
    d. Any privileged or confidential information discovered should be reported to the organization that arranged for the audit.   (R/06, AUD, #3, ID: 8121)

21. When auditing an entity's financial statements in accordance with *Government Auditing Standards* (the "Yellow Book"), an auditor is required to report on

    I. Recommendations for actions to improve operations
    II. The scope of the auditor's tests of compliance with laws and regulations

    a. I only
    b. II only
    c. Both I and II
    d. Neither I nor II   (R/00, AUD, #19, ID: 6944)

22. Wolf is auditing an entity's compliance with requirements governing a major federal financial assistance program in accordance with *Government Auditing Standards.* Wolf detected noncompliance with requirements that have a material effect on the program. Wolf's report on compliance should express

    a. No assurance on the compliance tests
    b. An adverse or disclaimer of opinion
    c. A qualified or adverse opinion
    d. Reasonable assurance on the compliance tests   (11/94, AUD, #85, amended, ID: 5158)

23. The auditor's report on internal controls and compliance with laws and regulations in accordance with *Government Auditing Standards* (the "Yellow Book"), is required to include

    I. The scope of the auditor's testing of internal controls
    II. Uncorrected misstatements that were determined by management to be immaterial

    a. I only
    b. II only
    c. Both I and II
    d. Neither I nor II   (R/02, AUD, #16, ID: 7106)

24. Hill, CPA, is auditing the financial statements of Helping Hand, a not-for-profit organization that receives financial assistance from governmental agencies. To detect misstatements in Helping Hand's financial statements resulting from violations of laws and regulations, Hill should focus on violations that

    a. Could result in criminal prosecution against the organization
    b. Involve significant deficiencies to be communicated to the organization's trustees and the funding agencies
    c. Have a direct and material effect on the amounts in the organization's financial statements
    d. Demonstrate the existence of material weaknesses in the organization's internal control
                     (11/92, AUD, #56, amended, ID: 2990)

25. Tell, CPA, is auditing the financial statements of Youth Services Co. (YSC), a not-for-profit organization, in accordance with *Government Auditing Standards.* Tell's report on YSC's compliance with laws and regulations is required to contain statements of

	Positive assurance	*Negative assurance*
a.	Yes	Yes
b.	Yes	No
c.	No	Yes
d.	No	No

                     (5/93, AUD, #60, ID: 3956)

26. In auditing compliance with requirements governing major federal financial assistance programs under the Single Audit Act, the auditor's consideration of materiality differs from materiality under generally accepted auditing standards. Under the Single Audit Act, materiality is

    a. Calculated in relation to the financial statements taken as a whole
    b. Determined separately for each major federal financial assistance program
    c. Decided in conjunction with the auditor's risk assessment
    d. Ignored, because all account balances, regardless of size, are fully tested   (11/95, AUD, #89, ID: 6036)

Problem 9-2 SIMULATION: GAGAS Engagement—Audit Risk

Toxic Waste Disposal Co., Inc. (TWD), a continuing audit client, has engaged your firm to audit its financial statements for the year ended July 31, Year 5, in accordance with *Government Auditing Standards.* TWD is a nonprofit organization that contracts with municipal governments to remove environmental wastes.

You are considering audit risk at the financial statement level in planning the audit of TWD's financial statements for the year ended July 31, Year 5. Audit risk at the financial statement level is influenced by the risks of material misstatement, which may be indicated by a combination of factors related to management, the industry, and the entity.

Indicate whether each of the following factors would most likely increase audit risk (I), decrease audit risk (D), or have no effect on audit risk (N).

Factors	Effect on Audit Risk
1. The internal auditor reports to the controller.	
2. The accounting department has experienced a high rate of turnover of key personnel.	
3. TWD's bank has a loan officer who meets regularly with TWD's CEO and controller to monitor TWD's financial performance.	
4. TWD's employees are paid biweekly.	
5. Your firm has audited TWD for five years.	
6. During Year 5, litigation filed against TWD in Year 1 alleging that TWD discharged pollutants into state waterways was dropped by the state. Loss contingency disclosures that TWD included in prior years' financial statements are being removed for the Year 1 financial statements.	
7. During July, TWD completed a barter transaction with a municipality. TWD removed waste from a municipally-owned site and acquired title to another contaminated site at below market price. TWD intends to service this new site in Year 6.	
8. During July, TWD increased its casualty insurance coverage on several pieces of sophisticated machinery from historical cost to replacement cost.	
9. Inquiries about the substantial increase in revenue TWD recorded in the fourth quarter of Year 5 disclosed a new policy. TWD guaranteed to several municipalities that it would refund the federal and state funding paid to TWD if any municipality fails federal or state site clean-up inspection in Year 6.	

(ID: 9212)

Problem 9-3 SIMULATION: Report on Compliance With Laws & Regulations

The auditors' separate report on compliance with laws and regulations that was drafted by a staff accountant of your firm at the completion of the engagement contained the statements below. The criteria used to evaluate compliance were determined by regulatory provisions that were developed solely for the regulatory agency responsible for the provisions. It was submitted to the engagement partner who reviewed matters thoroughly and properly concluded that no material instances of noncompliance were identified. For each of the statements below, indicate whether each is an appropriate (A) or inappropriate (I) element within the report on compliance with laws and regulations.

Report Elements	Appropriate (A) or Inappropriate (I)
1. A statement that the compliance audit was conducted in accordance with auditing standards generally accepted in the United States of America, the standards applicable to financial audits contained in *Government Auditing Standards*, and the governmental audit requirement.	
2. A statement that the compliance audit included examining, on a test basis, evidence about the entity's compliance with those requirements and performing such other procedures as the auditor considered necessary in the circumstances.	
3. A statement that it is the auditor's responsibility is to express an opinion on management's assertion that the entity is in compliance with the applicable compliance requirements based on the compliance audit.	
4. A statement that compliance with the applicable compliance requirements is the responsibility of the entity's management.	
5. Identification of the applicable compliance requirements or a reference to where they can be found.	
6. The auditor's opinion, at the level specified by the governmental audit requirement, on whether the entity complied, in all respects, with the applicable compliance requirements.	
7. A statement that the compliance audit provides a legal determination of the entity's compliance.	
8. A separate paragraph at the end of the report that includes (a) a statement indicating that the report is intended solely for the information and use of the specified parties (b) an identification of the specified parties to whom use is restricted, and (c) a statement that the report is not intended to be and should not be used by anyone other than the specified parties.	

(ID: 9213)

_____

Problem 9-4 SIMULATION: Research

What authoritative reference describes the auditor's objectives in a compliance audit?

[　　　] § [　　　] [　　　]   (ID: 9214)

_____

Solution 9-1 MULTIPLE-CHOICE ANSWERS

GAGAS—Responsibilities

1. (a)   The auditor must design the audit to provide reasonable assurance that the financial statements are free of material misstatements resulting from violations of law and regulations that have a direct and material effect on the determination of financial statement amounts. Materiality levels are determined by the auditor in relation to an entity's federal programs. An auditor generally does not obtain representations regarding internal auditors' reports. An auditor usually does not express assurance on disclosures to an inspector general.   (ID: 7597)

2. (c)   All audits of recipients of federal financial assistance require the auditor to obtain and document an understanding of internal control established to ensure compliance with the laws and regulations applicable to the federal award.   (ID: 8149)

3. (d)   Generally, the auditor need report a falsification of accounting records only to the audit committee (or equivalent). If auditors have communicated such irregularities or illegal acts to the auditee, and it fails to report them, then the auditors should communicate their awareness of that failure to the auditee's governing body. If the auditee does not make the required report as soon as practicable after the auditors' communication with its governing body, then the auditors should report the irregularities or illegal acts directly to the external party specified.   (ID: 6847)

4. (d)   *Governmental Auditing Standards* do not require an opinion on the financial statements taken as a whole, when the engagement is a *performance* audit. GAGAS does require a statement of the audit scope, indications of illegal acts discovered during the audit, and—if the auditor's report on the engagement discloses deficiencies in internal control, fraud, illegal acts, violations of contracts or grant agreement provisions, or abuse— the views of the responsible officials concerning the auditor's findings in the auditor's report.   (ID: 5163)

5. (b)   It is the audit committee's (or its equivalent) responsibility to take appropriate action regarding fraudulent activities that are perpetrated or concealed by management. Only when the audit committee fails to take appropriate action (such as not filing a required report), is the auditor responsible to do so. The other responses are failings by management, not omissions of the governing body (the audit committee equivalent).   (ID: 6715)

6. (b)   GAGAS require a written report on the consideration of internal control in all audits; whereas GAAS require communication only when the auditor has noted significant deficiencies. Reporting on program accomplishments is not required of the auditor.   (ID: 6943)

7. (a)   The auditor should assess whether management has identified laws and regulations that have a direct and material effect on the determination of amounts in the entity's financial statements. The auditor may consider obtaining written representation from management regarding the completeness of management's identification of applicable laws and regulations. The items in (b), (c) and (d) are not required.   (ID: 4749)

8. (a)   The basic elements of a report on compliance should include a statement that management is responsible for compliance with laws, regulations, contracts, and grants. The items in (b), (c) and (d) are not required.   (ID: 4295)

9. (d)   The auditor, when auditing a nonprofit organization that receives governmental financial assistance should assess whether management has identified laws and regulations that have a direct and material effect on the entity's financial statements.   (ID: 6035)

10. (b)   GAGAS require a written report on the consideration of internal control in all audits; whereas GAAS require communication only when the auditor has noted significant deficiencies. The auditor is not required to report on the description of the entity's internal control procedures. The auditor should not issue the representations in answer (c) or give positive assurance because of the potential for misinterpretation of the limited degree of assurance associated with the auditor's written report representing that no significant deficiencies were noted.   (ID: 3920)

11. (b)   In an audit in accordance with GAGAS, an auditor is required to report on the entity's compliance with applicable laws and regulations. The standards require that the auditor plan and perform the audit to obtain reasonable assurance about whether the financial statements are free of material misstatement. Answers (a),

(c), and (d) relate to internal control; the auditor does not give any form of assurance on the entity's internal control in this type of audit.   (ID: 2785)

12. (b)   AICPA standards and GAGAS require auditors to address the effect fraud or illegal acts may have on the audit report and to determine that the audit committee or others with equivalent authority and responsibility are adequately informed about the fraud or illegal acts. GAGAS further require that this information be in writing and also include reporting on significant violations of provisions of contracts or grant agreements and significant abuse. Therefore, when auditors conclude, on the basis of evidence obtained, that fraud, an illegal act, a significant violation of a contract or grant agreement, or significant abuse either has occurred or is likely to have occurred, they should include in their audit report the relevant information. Answer (c) is the second best answer; GAGAS require auditors to place their findings in proper perspective and identify the condition, criteria, cause, and effect of noncompliance. There is no requirement that all controls be tested. Answer (d) is not required in a financial statement audit.   (ID: 5707)

13. (d)   The standards for audits of federally assisted programs may be found in the publication of the U.S. Government Accountability Office (GAO) entitled *Government Auditing Standards*. The Governmental Accounting Standards Board (GASB) establishes financial accounting principles for state and local government entities. The Financial Accounting Standards Board (FASB) establishes GAAP. The Governmental Auditing Standards Board does not exist.   (ID: 7513)

14. (a)   The auditor must report on the scope of tests of compliance with laws and regulations. An auditor may report recommendations to correct problems and improve operations, but this is not the purpose of an audit. The auditor expresses an opinion on whether the information is correct; users of the report determine whether the measures of economy and efficiency are valid and reliable as well as the extent to which programs achieve the desired results.   (ID: 6844)

15. (a)   The auditor must summarize the audit results concerning internal control, financial statements, and compliance with laws and regulations. Immaterial amounts are not necessarily reported to the audit committee. Officials may report their own views—it is the auditor's duty to do so only if the auditor's report on the engagement discloses deficiencies in internal control, fraud, illegal acts, violations of provisions of contracts or grant agreements, or abuse. A report on all internal control activities designed to detect or prevent fraud is far more than need be reported to the inspector general or other parties.   (ID: 6845)

16. (d)   *Government Auditing Standards* require that when providing an opinion or a disclaimer on financial statements, auditors must also report on internal control over financial reporting and on compliance with laws, regulations, and provisions of contracts or grant agreements. Auditors should include either in the same or in a separate report(s) a description of the scope of the auditors' testing of internal control over financial reporting and compliance with laws, regulations, and provisions of contracts or grant agreements. An auditor sends a letter to a funding agency in certain circumstances; while the auditor may include this information in such a letter, the auditor still must include this information in an audit report.   (ID: 8385)

17. (b)   When providing an opinion or a disclaimer of opinion on financial statements in accordance with GAGAS, the audit must include in the report either a description of the scope of the auditor's testing of internal control over financial reporting and compliance with laws, regulations, and contractual provisions and the results of those tests (negative assurance) or, if sufficient work was performed, an opinion (positive assurance); or refer to a separate report containing that information. The auditor does not necessarily assure that no evidence of intentional override of controls was found. The auditor doesn't report the scope of the principal substantive tests.   (ID: 8417)

GAGAS—Internal Control

18. (b)   The auditor should obtain a sufficient understanding by performing risk assessment procedures to evaluate the design of controls relevant to an audit of financial statements and to determine whether they have been implemented. This includes governmental audits. GAGAS requires that the auditor include in their report on the financial statements either a description of the scope of the auditors' testing of internal control and the results of those tests or an opinion, if sufficient work was performed; or reference to the separate report(s) containing that information. GAGAS requires that auditors identify those significant deficiencies that are individually or in the aggregate considered to be material weaknesses.   (ID: 4750)

19. (a) According to GAGAS, when providing an opinion or a disclaimer on financial statements, auditors should include in their report on the financial statements either a description of the scope of the auditors' testing of internal control over financial reporting and compliance with laws, regulations, and provisions of contracts or grant agreements and the results of those tests or an opinion, if sufficient work was performed; or reference to the separate report(s) containing that information. In some circumstances, auditors should report fraud and illegal acts directly to parties external to the audited entity. (ID: 7626)

20. (a) In addition to GAAS, GAGAS require auditors to include in their report either a description of the scope of the auditors' testing of internal control over financial reporting and compliance with laws, regulations, and provisions of contracts or grant agreements and the results of those tests or, if sufficient work was performed, an opinion; or a reference to the separate report(s) containing that information. In some circumstances, auditors must report illegal acts directly to parties external to the audited entity. Auditors are not required to disclose all changes in the audit program. Certain privileged or confidential information may be prohibited from disclosure; the report should state the nature of the omitted information and the requirement that makes the omission necessary. (ID: 8121)

GAGAS—Compliance

21. (b) In an audit in accordance with GAGAS, an auditor is required to report on the auditor's test of the entity's compliance with applicable laws and regulations. Among the basic elements of such a report is a statement that the standards require that the auditor plan and perform the audit to obtain reasonable assurance about whether the financial statements are free of material misstatement. Recommendations for actions to improve operations are a side-benefit of an audit and are not required. (ID: 6944)

22. (c) When an auditor detects noncompliance with requirements that have a material effect on a program, the auditor should express a qualified or adverse opinion. A disclaimer is appropriate only when an audit has not been completed. Reasonable assurance on tests is implicit, not explicit. (ID: 5158)

23. (a) GAGAS require that the auditor include in their report on the financial statements either a description of the scope of the auditors' testing of internal control and the results of those tests or an opinion, if sufficient work was performed; or reference to the separate report(s) containing that information. Material misstatements in the financial statements impact the audit report, not the report on internal control. Uncorrected misstatements that are immaterial have no impact on the audit report or the report on internal control. (ID: 7106)

24. (c) Due to their acceptance of financial assistance from government agencies, not-for-profit organizations may be subject to laws and regulations. The audit should be designed to give reasonable assurance that the financial statements are free of misstatements resulting from violations of laws and regulations that have a direct and material effect on the determination of financial statement amounts. The audit should not be restricted to the consideration of violations that result in the conditions described in (a), (b), and (d). (ID: 2990)

25. (a) Reports on compliance with laws and regulations, in accordance with GAGAS, should contain positive assurance consisting of a statement by the auditor that the tested items were in compliance with applicable laws and regulations, and negative assurance stating that nothing came to the auditor's attention as a result of specified procedures that caused the auditor to believe the untested items were not in compliance with applicable laws and regulations. (ID: 3956)

26. (b) In auditing an entity's compliance with requirements governing each major federal financial assistance program in accordance with the Single Audit Act, the auditor considers materiality in relation to each program. (ID: 6036)

PERFORMANCE BY TOPICS

Each category below parallels a topic covered in Chapter 9. Record the number and percentage of questions you answered correctly in each topic.

GAGAS—Responsibilities

Question #	Correct	√
1		
2		
3		
4		
5		
6		
7		
8		
9		
10		
11		
12		
13		
14		
15		
16		
17		

\# Questions   17

\# Correct   _____
% Correct   _____

GAGAS—Internal Control

Question #	Correct	√
18		
19		
20		

\# Questions   3

\# Correct   _____
% Correct   _____

GAGAS—Compliance

Question #	Correct	√
21		
22		
23		
24		
25		
26		

\# Questions   6

\# Correct   _____
% Correct   _____

Solution 9-2 SIMULATION ANSWER: GAGAS Engagement—Audit Risk

   1. I

Audit risk is increased when the internal auditors report to the person they are evaluating (i.e., controller). The internal auditor should report to the audit committee.

   2. I

High turnover of accounting personnel increases the potential for errors due to poorly trained personnel and, thus, increases audit risk.

   3. D

The monitoring of financial performance decreases audit risk.

   4. N

The pay period has no effect on audit risk since it has no effect on the possibility for error or fraud.

   5. D

Audit risk is decreased due to familiarity with the audit history, client industry, and client procedures.

   6. D

The settlement of a loss contingency reduces audit risk.

   7. I

Difficult-to-audit transactions, such as the barter transaction, increase audit risk.

   8. N

The increase in casualty insurance coverage has no effect on the possibility of errors and fraud and, therefore, does not affect audit risk.

   9. I

The guarantee represents a loss contingency which could result in revenue not being realized. Therefore, audit risk is increased.
(ID: 9212)

_____

Solution 9-3 SIMULATION ANSWER: Report on Compliance With Laws & Regulations

1. A

2. A

3. I

The report should include a statement that the auditor's responsibility is to express an opinion [directly] on the entity's compliance with the applicable compliance requirements based on the compliance audit; not on management's assertion.

4. A

5. A

6. I

The report should contain the auditor's opinion, at the level specified by the governmental audit requirement, on whether the entity complied, in all *material* respects, with the applicable compliance requirements.

7. I

The report should include a statement that the compliance audit does *not* provide a legal determination of the entity's compliance.

8. A

This paragraph is required if the criteria used to evaluate compliance are (a) established or determined by contractual agreement or regulatory provisions that are developed solely for the parties to the agreement or regulatory agency responsible for the provisions or (b) available only to the specified parties.   (ID: 9213)

―――――――――――

Solution 9-4 SIMULATION ANSWER: Research

AU	§	801	10

.10   The auditor's objectives in a compliance audit are to

a.   obtain sufficient appropriate audit evidence to form an opinion and report at the level specified in the governmental audit requirement on whether the entity complied in all material respects with the applicable compliance requirements; and

b.   identify audit and reporting requirements specified in the governmental audit requirement that are supplementary to GAAS and *Government Auditing Standards*, if any, and perform procedures to address those requirements.   (ID: 9214)

_____

Boards of Accountancy

Certified Public Accountants are licensed to practice by Boards of Accountancy in 54 jurisdictions. Application forms and requirements to sit for the CPA exam should be requested from your particular board. IT IS EXTREMELY IMPORTANT THAT YOU COMPLETE THE APPLICATION FORM CORRECTLY AND RETURN IT TO YOUR STATE BOARD BEFORE THE SPECIFIED DEADLINE. Errors or delays may result in the rejection of your application. Be extremely careful in filling out the application and be sure to enclose all required materials. In many jurisdictions, complete applications must be received by the board at least **ninety** days before the examination date. Requirements as to education, experience, internship, and other matters vary. If you have not done so already, take a moment to contact the appropriate board for specific current requirements. Complete the application in a timely manner.

It may be possible to sit for the exam in another state as an out-of-state candidate. Candidates wishing to do so should contact the Board of Accountancy in their home jurisdiction as well as the other jurisdiction.

Approximately one month before the exam, check to see that your application to sit for the exam has been processed. DON'T ASSUME THAT YOU ARE PROPERLY REGISTERED UNLESS YOU HAVE RECEIVED YOUR NOTICE TO SCHEDULE.

The AICPA publishes a booklet entitled *The Uniform CPA Examination Candidate Bulletin: Information for Applicants*. You may download a copy from the AICPA's exam website.

Addresses of State Boards are in the **Exam Preparation Tips** section of this volume and on the site of the National Association of the State Boards of Accountancy (http://www.nasba.org).

———————————

STUDY TIP

PCAOB Standards

PCAOB requirements tend to be similar to GAAS in nature, but generally more stringent. PCAOB standards are in addition to GAAS requirements. The editors recommend that candidates thoroughly review GAAS first, and then review PCAOB standards once GAAS are well understood.

CHAPTER 10

OTHER AUDITING STANDARDS

CHAPTER 10

OTHER AUDITING STANDARDS

I. **Sarbanes-Oxley Act of 2002**

A. **Public Company Accounting Oversight Board**
The Sarbanes-Oxley Act of 2002 established the Public Company Accounting Oversight Board (PCAOB) and charged it with the responsibility of overseeing the audit firms of public companies. The Securities and Exchange Commission (SEC) has oversight and enforcement authority over the PCAOB. The term "public companies" refers to issuers of publicly traded securities.

1. **Responsibilities** The PCAOB's duties include registering public accounting firms; establishing auditing, quality control, ethics, independence and other standards relating to public company audits; conducting inspections, investigations and disciplinary proceedings of registered accounting firms; and enforcing compliance with the Act.

2. **Registration** Public accounting firms that perform or participate in audits of public companies, or their subsidiaries, must be registered with the PCAOB; registrations must be updated annually.

3. **Interim Guidance** The PCAOB adopted interim (or transitional) professional standards of auditing, attestation, independence, quality control, and ethics issued by the AICPA that were in existence on April 16, 2003. In doing so, the PCAOB adopted the existing body of audit and attest literature as its interim standards. Each of the interim standards set forth remain in effect until modified or superseded, either by PCAOB action approved by the SEC, or by SEC action.

4. **SEC-Approved PCAOB Standards** The SEC approves auditing standards (AS) adopted by the PCAOB. These are discussed in the following sections of this chapter.

B. **Prohibited Services**
The Sarbanes-Oxley Act of 2002 prohibits any registered public accounting firm from providing the following nonaudit services to its audit clients that are issuers: (1) bookkeeping or other services related to the accounting records of financial statements of the audit client; (2) financial information system design and implementation; (3) appraisal or valuation services, fairness opinions, or contribution-in-kind reports; (4) actuarial services; (5) internal audit outsourcing services; (6) management functions or human resources; (7) broker, dealer, investment advisor, or investment banking services; (8) legal services and expert services unrelated to the audit; and (9) any other service that the Board determines, by regulation, is impermissible. A CPA may perform these services for clients that are issuers, if the CPA is not that client's auditor. An auditor may perform other nonaudit services not listed above, such as tax preparation services, for audit clients that are issuers only with advance approval from the audit committee.

C. **Rotation**
The Sarbanes-Oxley Act of 2002 prohibits a registered public accounting firm from providing audit services to an issuer if the lead audit partner, or the audit partner responsible for reviewing the audit, has performed audit services for that issuer in each of the five previous fiscal years of that issuer.

D. **Conflicts of Interest**
It is prohibited for a firm to provide audit services to an issuer if the issuer's CEO, controller, CFO, CAO, or other person serving in an equivalent capacity, was employed in the audit firm and participated in the audit of that issuer during the previous fiscal year of that issuer.

E.   Audit Committee Responsibilities

In addition to normal responsibilities, the Sarbanes-Oxley Act of 2002 requires that audit committees be directly responsible for appointing, compensating and overseeing the external audit firm. This includes resolving any disagreements between the external auditor and management. Audit committees are also responsible for preapproving any allowed nonaudit services. If these permissible nonaudit services are related to internal control over financial reporting, the registered public accounting firm must provide, in writing, to the audit committee a description of the scope of the service and discuss with the audit committee the potential effects of the service on the independence of the firm. The firm must then document this discussion.

II.   PCAOB Audit Documentation Standards

A.   Report Reference (AS 1)

PCAOB AS 1 requires auditors' reports on engagements conducted in accordance with the PCAOB's standards to include a reference that the engagement was performed in accordance with the standards of the PCAOB, rather than US GAAS.

B.   Audit Documentation (AS 3)

PCAOB AS 3, *Audit Documentation,* presents many of the same requirements as AU 339 of the same title (Chapter 4) with the exception of the following major differences:

1.   **Documentation Completion Date**   The auditor should complete the final audit file within 45 days following the report release date.

2.   **Retention**   Workpapers must be retained for 7 years from the report release date.

3.   **Significant Findings or Issues**   In addition to AU 339, *Audit Documentation*, requirements pertaining to significant findings or issues, PCAOB AS 3 requires that all significant findings or issues be identified in an *engagement completion document.* This document may include all information necessary to understand the significant findings/issues or it may consist of cross-references to the supporting audit documentation.

4.   **Workpapers of Other Auditors**   All supporting documentation prepared by other auditors must be retained by or accessible to the office issuing the auditor's report. In addition, the following specific documentation must be obtained, reviewed and retained by the office issuing the audit report (unless reference is made to the other auditor):

   a.   An engagement completion document including any cross-referenced documentation

   b.   A list of significant risks and results of related audit procedures

   c.   Sufficient information concerning significant findings/issues that contradict or are inconsistent with final conclusions

   d.   Any findings affecting the consolidating or combining of accounts in the consolidated financial statements

   e.   Sufficient information to show that financial statement amounts audited by other auditors reconcile to the information underlying the consolidated financial statements

   f.   A schedule of accumulated misstatements, including descriptions of the nature and cause of each misstatement, and an evaluation of uncorrected misstatements, including the quantitative and qualitative factors

   g.   All significant deficiencies and material weaknesses in internal control over financial reporting, including a clear distinction between the two

   h.   Management representation letters

   i.   All matters to be communicated to the audit committee

III. Audit of Internal Control Over Financial Reporting (AS 5)

A. Overview

AS 5, PCAOB *An Audit of Internal Control Over Financial Reporting That Is Integrated with An Audit of Financial Statements,* establishes requirements and provides guidance for auditors engaged to audit management's assessment of the effectiveness of internal control over financial reporting (ICFR) that is integrated with an audit of the financial statements. Effective ICFR provides reasonable assurance that the financial reporting process and the preparation of the financial statements are reliable for external purposes.

B. Auditor's Objective in an Audit of ICFR

The objective of the auditor for this type of engagement is to express an opinion on the effectiveness of the company's ICFR as of a point in time and taken as a whole. To express an opinion as of a point in time, the auditor must obtain evidence that ICFR has operated effectively for a sufficient period of time which may be less than the period covered by the company's financial statements. To express an opinion on ICFR as a whole, the auditor must obtain evidence about the effectiveness of selected controls over *all* relevant assertions. This involves testing the design and operating effectiveness of controls that in most cases would **not** be required if *only* expressing an opinion on the financial statements. During an audit of financial statements, when the auditor's risk assessment of specific financial statement assertions includes an expectation of the operating effectiveness of the relevant controls, evidence must be obtained that these controls were effective for a particular time (or throughout the period) upon which the auditor plans to rely on them. The auditor's risk assessment, during a financial statement audit, would ordinarily **not** include an expectation of the operating effectiveness of controls for *all* relevant assertions.

1. Material Weaknesses If one or more material weaknesses exist, a company's ICFR is not effective. Therefore, the auditor must plan and perform the audit to obtain evidence that is sufficient to obtain reasonable assurance about whether material weaknesses exist as of the date of management's assessment. There may be a material weakness in ICFR even when financial statements are not materially misstated. Indicators of material weaknesses include:

a. Identification of fraud on the part of senior management, whether or not material

b. Restatement of previously issued financial statements to reflect the correction of a material misstatement

c. Auditor identification of a material misstatement of current period financial statements that would not have been detected by the company's ICFR

d. Ineffective oversight by the company's audit committee of external financial reporting and ICFR

2. Standards & Criteria The three GAAS general standards are applicable to an audit of ICFR. PCAOB AS 5 establishes the applicable fieldwork and reporting standards. The auditor should use the same appropriate, established control framework to perform an audit of ICFR as the company's management uses in its annual evaluation of the effectiveness of ICFR.

C. Definitions

This standard defines the following terms:

1. Control Objective A *control objective* provides a specific target against which to evaluate the effectiveness of controls. A control objective for internal control over financial reporting generally relates to a relevant assertion and states a criterion for evaluating whether the company's control procedures in a specific area provide reasonable assurance that a misstatement or omission in that relevant assertion is prevented or detected by controls on a timely basis.

2. **Deficiency** A *deficiency* in internal control over financial reporting exists when the design or operation of a control does not allow management or employees, in the normal course of performing their assigned functions, to prevent or detect misstatements on a timely basis.

    a. A deficiency in *design* exists when

        (1) A control necessary to meet the control objective is missing or

        (2) An existing control is not properly designed so that, even if the control operates as designed, the control objective would not be met.

    b. A deficiency in *operation* exists when a properly designed control does not operate as designed, or when the person performing the control does not possess the necessary authority or competence to perform the control effectively.

3. **Financial Statements & Related Disclosures** *Financial statements and related disclosures* refers to a company's financial statements and notes to the financial statements as presented in accordance with generally accepted accounting principles (GAAP). References to financial statements and related disclosures do not extend to the preparation of management's discussion and analysis or other similar financial information presented outside a company's GAAP-basis financial statements and notes.

4. **Internal Control Over Financial Reporting** *Internal control over financial reporting* is a process designed by, or under the supervision of, the company's principal executive and principal financial officers, or persons performing similar functions, and effected by the company's board of directors, management, and other personnel, to provide reasonable assurance regarding the reliability of financial reporting and preparation of financial statements for external purposes in accordance with GAAP and includes those policies and procedures that:

    a. Pertain to the maintenance of records that, in reasonable detail, accurately and fairly reflect the transactions and dispositions of the assets of the company;

    b. Provide reasonable assurance that transactions are recorded as necessary to permit preparation of financial statements in accordance with generally accepted accounting principles, and that receipts and expenditures of the company are being made only in accordance with authorizations of management and directors of the company; and

    c. Provide reasonable assurance regarding prevention or timely detection of unauthorized acquisition, use, or disposition of the company's assets that could have a material effect on the financial statements.

        Note: The auditor's procedures as part of either the audit of internal control over financial reporting or the audit of the financial statements are not part of a company's internal control over financial reporting.

        Note: Internal control over financial reporting has inherent limitations. Internal control over financial reporting is a process that involves human diligence and compliance and thus, is subject to lapses in judgment and breakdowns resulting from human failures. Internal control over financial reporting also can be circumvented by collusion or improper management override. Because of such limitations, there is a risk that material misstatements will not be prevented or detected on a timely basis by internal control over financial reporting. However, these inherent limitations are known features of the financial reporting process. Therefore, it is possible to design into the process safeguards to reduce, though not eliminate, this risk.

5. **Management's Assessment** *Management assessment* is the assessment described in Item 308(a)(3) of Regulations S-B and S-K that is included in management's annual report on internal control over financial reporting." It is described therein as "Management's assessment of the effectiveness of the registrant's internal control over financial reporting as of the end of the registrant's most recent fiscal year, including a statement as to whether or not internal control over financial reporting is effective. This discussion must include disclosure of any material weakness in the registrant's internal control over financial reporting identified by management. Management is not permitted to conclude that the registrant's internal control over financial reporting is effective if there are one or more material weaknesses in the registrant's internal control over financial reporting.

6. **Material Weakness** A *material weakness* is a deficiency, or a combination of deficiencies, in internal control over financial reporting, such that there is a reasonable possibility that a material misstatement of the company's annual or interim financial statements will not be prevented or detected on a timely basis.

    Note: There is a reasonable possibility of an event, as used in this standard, when the likelihood of the event is either *reasonably possible* or *probable*, as those terms are defined in the Financial Accounting Standards Board *Accounting Standards Codification* glossary. *Reasonably possible* is defined therein as "...more than remote but less than likely." *Probable* is defined therein as "...likely to occur."

7. **Preventive or Detective Controls** Controls over financial reporting may be preventive controls or detective controls. Effective internal control over financial reporting often includes a combination of preventive and detective controls.

    a. Preventive controls have the objective of preventing errors or fraud that could result in a misstatement of the financial statements from occurring.

    b. Detective controls have the objective of detecting errors or fraud that has already occurred that could result in a misstatement of the financial statements.

8. **Relevant Assertion** A *relevant assertion* is a financial statement assertion that has a reasonable possibility of containing a misstatement or misstatements that would cause the financial statements to be materially misstated. The determination of whether an assertion is a relevant assertion is based on inherent risk, without regard to the effect of controls.

9. **Significant Account or Disclosure** An account or disclosure is a *significant account or disclosure* if there is a reasonable possibility that the account or disclosure could contain a misstatement that, individually or when aggregated with others, has a material effect on the financial statements, considering the risks of both overstatement and understatement. The determination of whether an account or disclosure is significant is based on inherent risk, without regard to the effect of controls.

10. **Significant Deficiency** A *significant deficiency* is a deficiency, or a combination of deficiencies, in internal control over financial reporting that is less severe than a material weakness, yet important enough to merit attention by those responsible for oversight of the company's financial reporting.

D. **Integrating Audits of ICFR & Financial Statements**
Although an audit of ICFR and an audit of financial statements have distinct objectives, the auditor must plan an integrated approach and perform the work so that the objectives of both are achieved.

1. **Test of Controls** The tests of controls should be designed to simultaneously meet the objectives of both audits—to obtain sufficient evidence to support both the auditor's opinion on ICFR as of year-end and the auditor's control risk assessments during the audit of financial statements. During an audit of the financial statements, when making a determination of the effectiveness of controls to assess control risk, the auditor should consider the results of the additional tests of controls that were performed in order to express an opinion on ICFR. Likewise, during an audit of ICFR, the results of any additional tests of controls performed to support the opinion on the financial statements should be considered. And although the absence of misstatements verified by substantive procedures in an audit of financial statements is no substitute for the direct testing of controls required by an audit of ICFR, their absence should be taken into consideration by the auditor when making risk assessments that underlie the decisions about the testing needed to determine the effectiveness of controls in an audit of ICFR.

2. **Substantive Procedures** Although some procedures performed in an audit of ICFR may reduce the work needed during an audit of financial statements, the auditor must perform substantive procedures for all relevant assertions. This requirement for an audit of financial statements is **not** diminished by the procedures performed during an audit of ICFR.

E. **Planning**

1. **Audit Procedure Considerations** The following matters should be considered to determine if and if so, how, they will impact the auditor's procedures and risk assessment.

   a. **Previous Engagements** Knowledge of the company's ICFR obtained during previous engagements

   b. **Industry Issues** Industry issues such as financial reporting practices, economic conditions, laws and regulations, and technological changes

   c. **Company-Specific Issues** Company-specific issues such as its organization; operating system characteristics and degree of complexity; capital structure; ongoing legal or regulatory matters; any recent changes in the company and its operations or its ICFR; and public information about the company that is relevant to the evaluation of the likelihood of material financial statement misstatements and the effectiveness of its ICFR

   d. **Auditor's Preliminary Judgments** The auditor's preliminary judgments about the effectiveness of ICFR; and materiality, risk, and other factors related to the identification of material weaknesses

   e. **Auditor's Client Acceptance & Retention Evaluation** Consideration of any risks analyzed as part of the auditor's client acceptance and retention evaluation

   f. **Identified Control Deficiencies** Control deficiencies previously communicated to the audit committee or management

   g. **Other Available Evidence** Type and extent of available other evidence that is relevant to the effectiveness of the company's ICFR

2. **Role of Risk Assessment** The assessment of risk affects all the auditor's decisions. In assessing risk, the auditor should focus on the areas of highest risk—there is no need to test controls when their failure would not result in the reasonable possibility of a material misstatement to the financial statements. The risk that a company's ICFR will fail to prevent or detect a misstatement caused by fraud is usually greater than the risk that it will fail to prevent or detect an error.

3. **Scaling the Audit** The audit should be adjusted to fit the size and complexity of the company. Smaller and/or less complex companies may address the risks of misstatement and the needed controls differently than more complex companies.

4. **Risk of Fraud & Management Override** When selecting controls to test, the auditor should consider whether the company's controls sufficiently address the risk of material misstatement due to fraud and improper management override of other controls.

5. **Using the Work of Others** Assistance can be obtained from internal auditors, other company personnel and third parties. The auditor's decision to use others and the extent to use them should be based on an evaluation of their competence and objectivity. The auditor should also consider the risk associated with the control being tested—the higher the risk, the more important it becomes for the auditor to perform the work.

6. **Materiality** The standard directs the auditor of ICFR to use the same guidance for materiality considerations used in planning an audit of financial statements.

F. **Selection of Controls to Test**
The auditor should use a "top-down" approach to identify risks and select controls. The auditor should begin at the financial statement level and gain an understanding of the overall risks to ICFR. Then the auditor should evaluate the entity-level controls. Next, the auditor should identify the significant accounts and disclosures and their relevant assertions. The auditor should then verify his or her understanding of the risks in the company's processes and select for testing those controls that sufficiently address the assessed risk of misstatement to each relevant assertion.

1. **Entity-Level Controls** Entity-level controls that are important to the auditor's determination of the effectiveness of the company's ICFR must be tested. Depending on their nature and precision, the degree of effectiveness of the entity-level controls can impact both the selection of other controls to be tested as well as the nature, timing and extent of the testing of other controls. The entity-level controls include:

   a. Controls related to the control environment

   b. Controls over management override of other controls

   c. The company's risk assessment processes

   d. Centralized processing and controls, including shared service environments

   e. Controls to monitor results of operations

   f. Controls to monitor other controls, including activities of the internal audit function, the audit committee, and self-assessment programs

   g. Controls over the period-end financial reporting process

   h. Policies that address significant business control and risk management practices

2. **Assessment of Control Environment** The auditor must determine whether management's philosophy and operating style promote effective ICFR by reflecting their sound integrity and ethical values. The auditor must also determine if the board or audit committee understands and exercises oversight responsibility over ICFR.

3. **Evaluation of Period-End Financial Reporting Process** The period-end financial reporting process evaluation by the auditor should include assessing:

   a. Inputs, procedures performed, and outputs of the processes the company uses to produce its annual and quarterly financial statements

   b. Types of adjusting and consolidating entries

   c. Effect of and the degree to which information technology (IT) is used

   d. Who participates from management

   e. Locations involved

   f. Nature and extent of the oversight by management, the board of directors, and the audit committee

4. **Identification of Significant Accounts & Disclosures and Their Relevant Assertions** The auditor should evaluate both the qualitative and quantitative risk factors related to the financial statement line items and disclosures in order to identify significant accounts and disclosures and their relevant assertions. These risk factors are the same for both an audit of ICFR and an audit of the financial statements as are the significant accounts and disclosures and their relevant assertions—however for various reasons, the audit of financial statements may also involve performing substantive procedures on items that are not identified as part of this significant group. The components of an account or disclosure might be subject to different risks and thus may require different controls to address these separate risks. As part of this process, the auditor should also determine the likely sources of potential misstatements that would cause the financial statements to be materially misstated. The auditor should reflect on scenarios of what could go wrong.

5. **Multiple Locations or Business Units** Tests should only be performed at locations that present a reasonable possibility of material misstatement to the consolidated financial statements. For other locations or business units, the testing of entity-level controls may be sufficient to provide the needed assurance. Entities that are acquired on or before the date of management's assessment and operations that are accounted for as discontinued operations on the date of management's assessment should be included in the auditor's considerations. Testing of controls over the reporting of equity method investments would ordinarily **not** extend to the investee's controls.

6. **Understanding Likely Sources of Misstatement** The auditor should continue to develop a further understanding of the likely sources of misstatement which he or she started while identifying significant accounts and disclosures and their relevant assertions.

   a. **Auditor's Objectives** The auditor's objectives are to:

      (1) Understand the flow of transactions (including the effect of IT) related to the relevant assertions, including how these transactions are initiated, authorized, processed, and recorded

      (2) Confirm that all the points within the company's processes at which a material (individually or combined with other misstatements) misstatement could arise have been identified

      (3) Identify the controls that management has implemented over the prevention or timely detection of unauthorized acquisition, use, or disposition of the company's assets that could result in a material misstatement of the financial statements

b. **Procedures** The procedures used to achieve these objectives should either be performed by the auditor or under his or her direct supervision due to the degree of judgment required.

c. **Walk-Throughs** An effective method to achieve these objectives is to perform walk-throughs. The auditor follows a transaction from its origin to its reflection in the financial statements, step-by-step, using the same documents and information technology that a company's personnel use. Walk-throughs usually involve a combination of procedures, including inquiry, observation, inspections of documentation and reperformance.

7. **Selection of Controls** The decision for selection is based on whether a control by itself (or in combination with other controls) sufficiently addresses the assessed risk of misstatement to a given relevant assertion. It is not necessary to test all the controls that address an assertion.

G. **Testing Controls**

1. **Testing Design Effectiveness** The auditor should test the design of a control by determining whether the control, if performed correctly by persons with the necessary authority and competence, meets the company's control objectives and can be expected to prevent or detect errors or fraud that could result in material misstatements in the financial statements. Walk-throughs that include inquiries of appropriate people, observation of the company's operations, and inspection of documentation will usually suffice.

2. **Testing Operating Effectiveness** The auditor should test the operating effectiveness of a control by determining if the control is operating as designed and confirming that it is being performed by a person with the necessary authority and competence. Procedures for this test would include reperformance of the control in addition to inquiries of appropriate people, observation of the company's operations, and inspection of documentation.

3. **Evidence to Be Obtained** The evidence obtained is dependent on the nature, timing, and extent of audit procedures performed. Generally, more evidence is required to support the conclusion that a control is operating effectively than is needed when a control is deemed ineffective. The auditor should increase the amount of evidence gathered as the risk associated with a control increases. The following factors affect the risk associated with a control:

    a. The nature and materiality of misstatements that the control is intended to prevent or detect

    b. The inherent risk associated with the related account(s) and assertion(s)

    c. Whether there have been changes in the volume or nature of transactions that might adversely affect control design or operating effectiveness

    d. Whether the account has a history of errors

    e. The effectiveness of entity-level controls, especially controls that monitor other controls

    f. The nature of the control and the frequency with which it operates

    g. The degree to which the control relies on the effectiveness of other controls

    h. The competence of the personnel who perform the control or monitor its performance and whether there have been changes in these key personnel

    i. Whether the control relies on performance by an individual or is automated, i.e., an automated control would generally be expected to be lower risk if relevant information technology general controls are effective

j. The complexity of the control and the significance of the judgments that must be made in connection with its operation

4. **Deviations From Controls** When deviations from controls are discovered, the auditor should determine the impact on the assessment of the risk associated with the control, the evidence being gathered, and the operating effectiveness of the control. Any *one* control does not necessarily have to operate without any deviation to be considered effective because effective ICFR does **not** provide absolute assurance.

5. **Special Considerations to Reduce Testing for Subsequent Years' Audits** The auditor should incorporate knowledge gained in prior years' audits of ICFR into the determination of the nature, timing, and extent of audit procedures selected to test controls.

    a. **Risk Factors** After taking into account various risk factors, the additional information provided in subsequent years' audits may allow the auditor to assess the risk as lower than in the first year and thus reduce the testing in the subsequent audits. The factors affecting the risk associated with a control in subsequent years' audits includes those listed in the previous "Evidence to Be Obtained" section of this topic plus the following factors:

        (1) The nature, extent, and timing of procedures performed in previous audits

        (2) The results of the previous years' testing of the control

        (3) Whether there have been changes in the control or the process in which it operates since the previous audit

    b. **Benchmarking** The standard specifically allows the use of a benchmarking strategy (establishment of a baseline) under certain conditions for automated (IT) application controls in subsequent years' audits because of their inherent reliability. If the auditor is able to obtain evidence that general controls over program changes, access to programs, and computer operations are effective and continue to be tested; and that there have been no changes to the automated application controls since they were last tested, the auditor may conclude that the automated application controls continue to be effective.

6. **Vary the Testing** The auditor should vary the nature, timing, and extent of the testing of controls from one year to another to allow for changes in circumstances as well as to make the audit unpredictable.

7. **Service Organizations** The relevant concepts in AU 324, *Service Organizations,* (concerning a company that obtains services from another organization that are part of the company's information system) are applicable to ICFR audits. If, as described in AU 324, the services provided are part of the company's information system, then it follows that they are part of the information and communications component of the company's ICFR. Thus, the auditor should include the activities of the service organization in the determination of what evidence is needed to support his or her opinion. The auditor should gain an understanding of both the controls of the service organization that are relevant to the company's internal control and the controls of the company over the activities of the service organization. Then the auditor should obtain evidence that the relevant controls are operating effectively. The auditor may use a service auditor's report on controls placed in operation and tests of operating effectiveness if the auditor judges that the report provides sufficient evidence and is satisfied as to the professional reputation, competence and independence of the service auditor. However, the auditor should **not** refer to the service auditor's report in his or her opinion of ICFR.

8. **Superseded Controls** Sometimes management changes controls during the period being audited. The auditor must use professional judgment to determine if testing of the superseded controls is needed.

H. **Evaluating Identified Deficiencies**

1. **Severity of the Deficiency** The auditor must determine if each control deficiency identified, either individually or in combination, is a material weakness as of the date of management's assessment by evaluating its severity. However, the auditor is **not** required to search for deficiencies that do not constitute a material weakness. The severity of a deficiency is dependent on whether there is a reasonable possibility that the company's controls will fail to prevent or detect a misstatement and the magnitude of the potential misstatement. Severity is not dependent on whether a misstatement has actually occurred. What matters is the lack of effectiveness of a company's controls, i.e., if there is a reasonable possibility that a deficiency, or a combination of deficiencies, will result in a misstatement of an account balance or disclosure.

2. **Prudent Official Standard** The auditor should set and use a *prudent official* standard to help evaluate the severity of a deficiency, or combination of deficiencies. To do so, the auditor must determine the level of detail and degree of assurance that would satisfy prudent officials in the conduct of their own affairs that they have reasonable assurance that transactions are recorded as necessary to permit the preparation of financial statements in conformity with GAAP. If this standard is not met, the auditor should consider the deficiency, or combination of deficiencies, to be an indicator of a material weakness.

3. **Compensating Controls** The auditor should consider the effect of compensating controls when determining if a deficiency, or combination of deficiencies, constitutes a material weakness. The compensating control should be judged effective enough to prevent or detect a misstatement that could be material in order to be considered to have a mitigating effect.

I. **Management's Written Representations**
The standard refers the auditor to AU 333, *Management Representations,* for further guidance on the management representation letter such as who should sign it, the period it covers, and when to obtain an updated letter as these are the same as for an audit of the financial statements. The auditor should obtain the following written representations from management:

1. Acknowledgment of management's responsibility for establishing and maintaining effective ICFR

2. Statement that management has performed an evaluation and made an assessment of the effectiveness of the company's ICFR and specifying the control criteria

3. Statement that management did not use the auditor's procedures performed during either the audit of ICFR or the financial statements as part of the basis for management's assessment of the effectiveness of the company's ICFR

4. Statement of management's conclusion, as set forth in its assessment, about the effectiveness of the company's ICFR based on the control criteria as of a specified date

5. Statement that management disclosed to the auditor all deficiencies in the design or operation of ICFR identified as part of management's evaluation, including separately disclosing all such deficiencies that it believes to be significant deficiencies or material weaknesses in ICFR

6. Description of any fraud resulting in a material misstatement to the company's financial statements and any other fraud that involves senior management or management or other employees who have a significant role in the company's ICFR

7. Statement of whether control deficiencies identified and communicated to the audit committee during previous engagements have been resolved, and specifically identifying any that have not

8. Statement whether there were, subsequent to the date being reported on, any changes in ICFR or other factors that might significantly affect ICFR, including any corrective actions taken by management with regard to significant deficiencies and material weaknesses

J. Communications

1. **Ineffective Oversight** In the case where the auditor concludes that oversight by the company's audit committee of external financial reporting and ICFR is ineffective, the auditor must communicate that conclusion, in writing, to the board of directors.

2. **Material Weaknesses** The auditor must communicate, in writing, to management and the audit committee all material weaknesses identified during the audit. This should be done prior to the issuance of the audit report on ICFR. If a material weakness has **not** been included in management's assessment, the auditor should also communicate this fact, in writing, to the audit committee.

3. **Significant Deficiencies** The auditor must also communicate, in writing, all significant deficiencies to the audit committee.

4. **Deficiencies** The auditor should communicate, in writing, all deficiencies in ICFR to management of which he or she is *aware*—the auditor is **not** required to perform procedures that are sufficient to identify *all* control deficiencies. The audit committee should be informed by the auditor when this communication to management has been made.

5. **Scope Limitation** If the auditor concludes that he or she cannot express an opinion because there has been a scope limitation, the auditor should communicate, in writing, to management and the audit committee that the audit of ICFR cannot be completed. See the "Disclaiming an Opinion or Withdrawing From the Engagement" section of this topic for further information.

6. **Material Misstatement in Additional Information Included With Management's Report** If the auditor determines that the other information included with management's annual report on ICFR contains a material misstatement of fact and if after a discussion with management, management does not remedy it, the auditor should communicate his or her concerns, in writing, to management and the audit committee. See the "Report Modifications" section of this topic for additional information.

7. **Fraud & Illegal Acts** The standard refers the auditor to AU 316, *Consideration of Fraud in a Financial Statement Audit,* AU 317, *Illegal Acts by Clients,* and §10A of the Securities Exchange Act of 1934 for guidance regarding the auditor's responsibilities if he or she becomes aware of fraud or possible illegal acts.

8. **Management's Annual Certification Is Misstated** The standard refers the auditor to AU 722, *Interim Financial Information,* for guidance as to communication responsibilities in this instance.

9. **Auditor Disagrees With Management's Exclusion of Certain Entities** The auditor may disagree with management's application of the SEC's criteria for exclusion of certain entities from the assessment of ICFR or find their disclosure of the exclusion inadequate. The standard refers the auditor to AU 722, *Interim Financial Information,* for guidance as to communication responsibilities in this instance.

K.   Reporting

1.   Forming an Opinion The auditor should form an opinion of the effectiveness of ICFR after considering the evidence obtained from all sources. In addition to the evidence from the auditor's testing of controls and identification of control deficiencies, this would include misstatements identified during the financial statement audit and the evidence in current reports on ICFR issued by internal auditors or others. The auditor should **not** issue a report stating that no deficiencies exist because an audit of ICFR does not provide assurance that all deficiencies less severe than a material weakness have been identified.

2.   Required Elements of Audit Report The following must be included in the auditor's report on ICFR:

a.   A title that includes the word *independent*

b.   A statement that management is responsible for maintaining effective ICFR and for assessing the effectiveness of ICFR

c.   An identification of management's report on internal control

d.   A statement that the auditor's responsibility is to express an opinion on the company's ICFR based on his or her audit

e.   A definition of ICFR as stated in paragraph A5 of the standard (see the "Definitions" section of this topic)

f.   A statement that the audit was conducted in accordance with the standards of the PCAOB (United States)

g.   A statement that the standards of the PCAOB require that the auditor plan and perform the audit to obtain reasonable assurance about whether effective ICFR was maintained in all material respects

h.   A statement that an audit includes obtaining an understanding of ICFR, assessing the risk that a material weakness exists, testing and evaluating the design and operating effectiveness of internal control based on the assessed risk, and performing such other procedures as the auditor considered necessary in the circumstances

i.   A statement that the auditor believes the audit provides a reasonable basis for his or her opinion

j.   A paragraph stating that because of inherent limitations, ICFR may not prevent or detect misstatements and that projections of any evaluation of effectiveness to future periods are subject to the risk that controls may become inadequate because of changes in conditions, or that the degree of compliance with the policies or procedures may deteriorate

k.   The auditor's opinion on whether the company maintained, in all material respects, effective ICFR as of the specified date, based on the control criteria

l.   The manual or printed signature of the auditor's firm

m.   The city, and state (or city and country, in the case of non-US auditors) from which the auditor's report has been issued

n.   The date of the audit report

3. **Separate or Combined Reports** The auditor may choose to issue separate reports on the company's financial statements and ICFR or to issue a combined report containing both opinions. If the auditor issues separate reports, a separate paragraph should be added to each report that cross-references the other report, giving the date and nature of its opinion. The reference in the financial statement report to the ICFR report should also identify the control criteria on which the ICFR opinion is based.

4. **Date of Report** The auditor should date the audit report(s) no earlier than the date on which the auditor has obtained sufficient competent evidence to support the auditor's opinion. If separate reports on the financial statements and ICFR are issued, the date of the reports should be the same, as the auditor cannot audit ICFR without also auditing the financial statements.

5. **Audit Report on ICFR Included With Filings Under Federal Securities Statutes** AU 711, *Filings Under Federal Securities Statutes,* is applicable when the auditor's report is included in registration statements, proxy statements, or periodic reports filed under federal securities statutes.

6. **Report Modifications** The auditor should modify the report if any of the following conditions exist:

   a. **Elements of Management's Annual Report on ICFR Are Incomplete or Improperly Presented** After forming an opinion on the effectiveness of ICFR, the auditor should review management's presentation on the elements that is required by the SEC to be included in the company's annual report on ICFR. If the auditor determines that any of these elements are incomplete or not properly presented the auditor should add an explanatory paragraph that describes the reasons why the auditor found management's report unsatisfactory.

   b. **Scope Limitation** See the "Disclaiming an Opinion or Withdrawing From the Engagement" section of this topic.

   c. **Auditor Decides to Refer to the Report of Other Auditors** When another auditor has audited the financial statements and ICFR of one or more components of a company, the auditor needs to determine whether he or she may serve as the principal auditor and use the work and reports of another auditor as a basis, in part, for his or her opinion on ICFR. The standard states that AU 543, *Part of Audit Performed by Other Independent Auditors*, is applicable to this determination by the auditor. If the auditor decides that he or she should be the principal auditor of the financial statements, then he or she must also be the principal auditor for ICFR. The principal auditor's decision whether to make reference in the report on ICFR to the audit of ICFR performed by another auditor is similar to the same decision for financial reporting, so again, AU 543 is applicable. When the auditor decides to make this reference, the auditor should refer to the report of the other auditor when describing the scope of the audit and when expressing the opinion.

   d. **Other Information in Management's Annual Report on ICFR** If the additional information included by management appears to be part of management's annual report on ICFR, then the auditor should disclaim an opinion on the other information. If the auditor determines that the other information contains a material misstatement of fact and if after a discussion with management, management does not remedy it, the auditor should communicate his or her concerns, in writing, to management and the audit committee. This standard also refers the auditor to AU 317, *Illegal Acts by Clients,* and §10A of the Securities Exchange Act of 1934 for further direction because in some circumstances additional action may be required.

e. **Management's Annual Certification Is Misstated** The standard refers the auditor to AU 722, *Interim Financial Information,* for guidance as to communication requirements if matters come to the auditor's attention that convince the auditor that modifications to the disclosures about changes in ICFR are needed for the annual certifications to be accurate and to be in compliance with either the requirements of §302 of Sarbanes-Oxley Act of 2002 or Securities Exchange Act rules for any interim period. If management and the audit committee fail to respond satisfactorily, the auditor (in addition to the requirements described in AU 722) should add an explanatory paragraph to his or her report on ICFR which explains the reasons he or she believes management's disclosures should be modified.

f. **Assessment of ICFR Excludes Certain Entities** The SEC allows management to limit its assessment of ICFR by excluding certain entities and the auditor may choose to do likewise. This situation is **not** considered a scope limitation. However, the auditor should include, either in an additional explanatory paragraph or as part of the scope paragraph in his or her report, a disclosure similar to management's concerning the exclusion of an entity from both the scope of management's assessment and the auditor's audit of ICFR. If the auditor considers management's application of the SEC's exclusion criteria to be unreasonable or management's disclosure inadequate, the auditor should follow the guidance in AU 722, *Interim Financial Information,* as to communication requirements. In addition, the auditor should add in explanatory paragraph to his or her report on ICFR which describes the reasons why the auditor believes management's disclosures should be modified.

g. **Subsequent Events** The auditor may obtain knowledge about subsequent events with respect to conditions that did *not* exist at the date of the assessment, but arose subsequent to that date and before issuance of the auditor's report and had a material effect on the company's ICFR. The auditor should add an explanatory paragraph to his or her report describing the event and its effects or a reference to the disclosure in management's report. (If the effect cannot be determined, the auditor should disclaim an opinion. For additional information see the "Subsequent Events" section of this topic.)

7. **Adverse Opinion** If there are one or more material weaknesses, the auditor must express an adverse opinion on the company's ICFR unless the scope of the audit has been limited. (The auditor must either withdraw from the engagement or disclaim an opinion if there are restrictions on the scope of the engagement. See the "Disclaiming an Opinion or Withdrawing From the Engagement" section of this topic.)

    a. **Disclosure** The auditor should include a disclosure in the report as to whether the opinion on the financial statements was affected by the adverse opinion on ICFR.

    b. **Material Weakness** An adverse opinion report resulting from a material weakness must include the definition of a material weakness (see the "Definitions" section of this topic). The remaining modifications to the report and required actions depend on if the material weakness was also included in management's assessment, and if so, how it was included:

        (1) When a material weakness was identified and was included in management's assessment, the report must include a statement that a material weakness was identified and an identification of the material weakness described in management's assessment. If the auditor finds that the disclosure is not fairly presented in all material respects, the auditor's report should describe this conclusion and the information needed to fairly describe the material weakness.

        (2) When a material weakness was identified, but was **not** included in management's assessment the following items must be included in the auditor's report:

            (a) A statement that a material weakness was identified, but not included in management's assessment

            (b) A description of the material weakness that includes specific information about its nature plus the actual and potential effect on the financial statements issued during its existence

            (c) Additionally, the auditor should communicate, in writing, to the audit committee that the material weakness was not identified or disclosed in management's assessment.

8. **Disclaiming an Opinion or Withdrawing From the Engagement**

    a. **Scope Limitation** The auditor may not form an opinion on the effectiveness of ICFR if there have been restrictions on the scope of the auditor's work to the degree that the auditor was unable to apply the procedures necessary under the circumstances. If there has been such a scope limitation the auditor is required to disclaim an opinion or withdraw from the engagement. One example of a scope limitation is when the auditor is unable to obtain written representations from management. In this case, the auditor should also consider the effects of management's refusal on his or her ability to rely on other representations made by management, including those made in conjunction with the audit of the financial statements. The auditor may issue a disclaimer as soon as he or she determines that a scope limitation will prevent the attainment of evidence sufficient to gain the reasonable assurance needed to express an opinion. No additional work is required by the auditor at this point. The report date is the date that the auditor has gained sufficient competent evidence to support the representations contained in his or her report. The auditor should communicate, in writing, to management and the audit committee that he or she is unable to satisfactorily complete the audit of ICFR. When disclaiming an opinion due to a scope limitation, the auditor's report should:

        (1) Include a statement that the scope of the audit was not sufficient to warrant the expression of an opinion

(2) Include a separate paragraph(s) that gives the substantive reasons for the disclaimer

(3) **Not** identify the procedures that were performed **nor** include the description of the characteristics of an audit of ICFR to avoid overshadowing the disclaimer

(4) Include a description of any material weakness that was identified in the company's ICFR (if the auditor was able to conclude it existed based on the limited procedures applied); this should include specifics about the nature of the material weakness and its actual and potential effect on the presentation of the company's financial statements issued during the existence of the material weakness—this description should conform to the requirements of the standard for the issuance of an adverse opinion due to a material weakness (covered in the previous "Adverse Opinion" section of this topic); the definition of the term material weakness per the standard (see the "Definitions" section of this topic) should also be included

b. **Effect of Subsequent Event Not Determinable** The auditor should disclaim an opinion when he or she cannot determine the effect that a subsequent event (with respect to conditions that existed at the date of the assessment) had on a company's ICFR. For additional information see the "Subsequent Events" section of this topic.

L. **Subsequent Events**

1. **Procedures to Identify Subsequent Events** Changes in ICFR or other factors that have a material impact on ICFR may occur subsequent to the date that ICFR is being audited but before the date of the auditor's report. AU 560, *Subsequent Events,* provides direction on subsequent events for a financial statement audit that may also be helpful during an audit of ICFR. As previously covered, the auditor should attain written representations from management relating to subsequent events. The auditor should review, for this subsequent period, the following:

a. Internal audit reports

b. Other independent auditor reports of deficiencies in internal control

c. Regulatory agency reports on the company's ICFR

d. Information about the company's ICFR obtained via other engagements.

2. **When the Subsequent Event Became Known or Arose** *Before* **the Issuance of the Auditor's Report:**

a. **And** *Did* **Exist As of the Date of Management's Assessment** If the auditor becomes aware of subsequent events that materially and adversely affect ICFR as of the date of the assessment, the auditor should issue an adverse opinion. If management's assessment states that ICFR is effective, the auditor should follow the guidance described previously under "Adverse Opinion" in this topic. If the auditor cannot determine the effect of the event on the company's ICFR, the auditor should disclaim an opinion.

b. **And Did** *Not* **Exist As of the Date of Management's Assessment** The auditor may become aware of a subsequent event with respect to conditions that did **not** exist as of the date specified in management's assessment, but arose subsequent to that date and before issuance of the auditor's report. If the subsequent event had a material effect on ICFR, the auditor should add an explanatory paragraph to his or her report that either describes the event and its effect or includes a referral to the disclosure in management's report.

3. **When the Subsequent Event Became Known *After* the Issuance of the Auditor's Report**
    If after the auditor issues the report, he or she becomes aware of a subsequent event that existed as of the report date and that might have affected his or her opinion, the auditor should follow the guidance in AU 561, *Subsequent Discovery of Facts Existing at the Date of the Auditor's Report.*

IV. **Reporting on Whether a Previously Reported Material Weakness Continues to Exist (AS 4)**

A. **Overview**
    PCAOB AS 4, *Reporting on Whether a Previously Reported Material Weakness Continues to Exist*, applies when an auditor is engaged to report on whether a previously reported material weakness in ICFR continues to exist as of a date specified by management. The PCAOB does not require this type of engagement. A *previously reported material weakness* means a material weakness that was described previously in an auditor's report on ICFR as required by PCAOB AS 5. The auditor may report on more than one previously reported material weakness in a single engagement.

B. **Conditions**
    There may be certain material weaknesses that are not suitable for this type of engagement; that is, if identifying *all* stated control objectives affected by the material weakness is difficult, then the material weakness should be addressed, instead, in the annual audit of ICFR. The following conditions must all be met for an auditor to complete this type of engagement:

    1. Management has accepted responsibility for the effectiveness of ICFR.

    2. Management has evaluated the effectiveness of the specific control(s) using the same stated control objectives and control criteria it used for its most recent annual assessment of ICFR.

    3. Management has asserted that the specific control(s) identified is/are effective in achieving the stated control objective.

    4. Management has supported its assertion with sufficient evidence, including documentation.

    5. Management has presented a written report that will accompany the audit report that contains all required elements.

C. **Opinion**
    In order to render an *unqualified opinion, the auditor must have (1) obtained evidence about the design and operating effectiveness of the specifically identified controls, (2) determined that the material weakness no longer exists, and (3) determined that there were no scope limitations. If a scope limitation exists, the auditor is required to either disclaim an opinion or withdraw from the engagement.

    *Editor's note: The auditor's opinion on whether a previously reported material weakness continues to exist may be expressed as *the material weakness no longer exists* or *the material weakness exists*. The PCAOB's guidance does **not** use the terms *unqualified opinion* or *adverse opinion*; instead, it refers simply to "an opinion" or "the auditor's opinion." However, it does explicitly state that a qualified opinion is **not** permitted.

D. **Material Weakness Continues to Exist**
    If an auditor determines that a material weakness continues to exist, the following should be considered:

    1. If the auditor issues a report, it must state that the material weakness continues to exist as of the date specified by management.

    2. If the auditor does not issue a report (which is not required), he or she must communicate to the audit committee, in writing, his or her conclusion that the material weakness continues to exist. If another material weakness is discovered during the engagement, it must also be communicated to the audit committee in writing.

3.	The auditor must consider the conclusion that the material weakness continues to exist as part of his or her evaluation of management's quarterly disclosures about ICFR, as required by PCAOB AS 5.

4.	If an auditor is engaged to report on two previously reported material weaknesses and only one of them continues to exist, the auditor can report in either of two ways: (1) the auditor can issue one report that contains two different opinions on each material weakness; or (2) the auditor can issue a report that contains a single opinion on the material weakness that no longer exists if management modifies its assertion to address only that material weakness. The auditor will still need to communicate in writing to the audit committee, the conclusion regarding the second material weakness that continues to exist.

## V.	Evaluating Consistency of Financial Statements (AS 6)

### A.	Consistency & the Audit Report

1.	**Objective** PCAOB Auditing Standard (AS) 6 establishes requirements and provides direction for the auditor's evaluation of the consistency of the financial statements, including changes to previously issued financial statements, and the effect of that evaluation on the auditor's report on the financial statements.

2.	**Comparability of Financial Statements Between Periods** To identify consistency matters that might affect the report, the auditor should evaluate whether the comparability of the financial statements between periods has been materially affected by changes in accounting principles or by material adjustments to previously issued financial statements for the relevant periods.

3.	**Periods to Evaluate** The periods covered in the auditor's evaluation of consistency depend on the periods covered by the auditor's report on the financial statements. When reporting only on the current period, the auditor should evaluate whether the current period financial statements are consistent with those of the preceding period. When reporting on two or more periods, the auditor should evaluate consistency between such periods and the consistency of such periods with the period prior thereto if such prior period is presented with the financial statements being reported upon.

4.	**Recognition in Audit Report** The auditor should recognize the following matters relating to the consistency of the company's financial statements in the auditor's report if those matters have a material effect on the financial statements.

   a.	A change in accounting principle

   b.	An adjustment to correct a misstatement in previously issued financial statements

   An explanatory paragraph should be added, following the opinion paragraph, as discussed in the following topics.

### B.	Change in Accounting Principle

1.	**Definition** A change in accounting principle is a change from one generally accepted accounting principle to another generally accepted accounting principle when

   (a)	There are two or more generally accepted accounting principles that apply

   (b)	The accounting principle formerly used is no longer generally accepted

   (c)	A change in the method of applying an accounting principle has occurred

2. **Change in Accounting Estimate Effected by a Change in Accounting Principle** The auditor should evaluate and report on a change in accounting estimate effected by a change in accounting principle like other changes in accounting principles.

3. **Change in Reporting Entity** The auditor should recognize a change in the reporting entity like other changes in accounting principles unless the change in reporting entity results from a transaction or event. (A change in reporting entity that results from a transaction or event, such as the creation, cessation, or complete or partial purchase or disposition of a subsidiary or other business unit does not require recognition in the auditor's report.)

4. **Investee's Change in Accounting Principle** If a company's financial statements contain an investment accounted for by the equity method, the auditor's evaluation of consistency should include consideration of the investee. If the investee makes a change in accounting principle that is material to the investing company's financial statements, the auditor should add an explanatory paragraph (following the opinion paragraph) to the auditor's report.

5. **Auditor's Evaluation** The auditor should evaluate a change in accounting principle to determine whether

   a. The newly adopted accounting principle is a generally accepted accounting principle

   b. The method of accounting for the effect of the change is in conformity with generally accepted accounting principles

   c. The disclosures related to the accounting change are adequate

   d. The company has justified that the alternative accounting principle is preferable

   Editor note: If the above criteria are not met, the auditor should consider the matter to be a departure from GAAP and, if the effect of the change in accounting principle is material, issue a qualified or adverse opinion.

6. **Explanatory Paragraph** If the auditor concludes that the above criteria have been met, the auditor should add an explanatory paragraph to the auditor's report, through the addition of an explanatory paragraph **following** the opinion paragraph. The explanatory paragraph should include identification of the nature of the change and a reference to the note disclosure describing the change.

   a. **Adoption of a New Pronouncement Example** "As discussed in Note X to the financial statements, the company has changed its method of accounting for [*describe accounting method change*] in [*year(s) of financial statements that reflect the accounting method change*] due to the adoption of [*name of accounting pronouncement*]."

   b. **Change in Accounting Principle Not Involving a New Pronouncement Example** "As discussed in Note X to the financial statements, the company has elected to change its method of accounting for [*describe accounting method change*] in [*year(s) of financial statements that reflect the accounting method change*]."

   c. **Report Recognition Periods Required** The explanatory paragraph relating to a change in accounting principle should be included in reports on financial statements in the year of the change and in subsequent years until the new accounting principle is applied in all periods presented. If the accounting change is accounted for by retrospective application to the financial statements of all prior periods presented, the additional paragraph is needed only in the year of the change.

C.   Correction of a Material Misstatement in Previously Issued Financial Statements

    1.   Explanatory Paragraph The correction of a material misstatement in previously issued financial statements should be recognized in the auditor's report through the addition of an explanatory paragraph **following** the opinion paragraph. The explanatory paragraph should include the following.

        a.   A statement that the previously issued financial statements have been restated for the correction of a misstatement in the respective period

        b.   A reference to the company's disclosure of the correction of the misstatement.

        c.   Example "As discussed in Note X to the financial statements, the 20X2 financial statements have been restated to correct a misstatement."

    2.   Report Recognition Periods Required This type of explanatory paragraph in the auditor's report should be included in reports on financial statements when the related financial statements are restated to correct the prior material misstatement. The paragraph need not be repeated in subsequent years.

Editor note: A change from an accounting principle that is not generally accepted to one that is generally accepted is a correction of a misstatement.

D.   Change in Classification
Changes in classification in previously issued financial statements do **not** require recognition in the auditor's report, unless the change represents the correction of a material misstatement or a change in accounting principle. Accordingly, the auditor should evaluate a material change in financial statement classification and the related disclosure to determine whether such a change also is a change in accounting principle or a correction of a material misstatement. For example, certain reclassifications in previously issued financial statements, such as reclassifications of debt from long-term to short-term or reclassifications of cash flows from the operating activities category to the financing activities category, might occur because those items were incorrectly classified in the previously issued financial statements. In such situations, the reclassification also is the correction of a misstatement.

VI. Review of Interim Financial Information of Issuers

A.   Overview

    1.   Objective The objective of the guidance covered by the PCAOB's adopted and amended AU 722, *Interim Financial Information*, is to provide the CPA with a basis for communicating whether material modifications are needed to make the information conform with GAAP.

    2.   Period Covered The term *interim financial information* means financial information or statements covering a period less than a full year or for a 12-month period ending on a date other than the entity's fiscal year-end.

    3.   SEC Filing Requirements The Securities and Exchange Commission (SEC) requires a registrant to engage an independent accountant to review the registrant's interim financial information, in accordance with AU 722, before the registrant files its quarterly report on Form 10-Q or Form 10-QSB. The SEC also requires management, with the participation of the principal executive and financial officers (the certifying officers) to make certain quarterly and annual certifications with respect to the company's internal control over financial reporting. Although AU 722 does not require an accountant to issue a written report on a review of interim financial information, the SEC requires that an accountant's review report be filed with the interim financial information if, in any filing, the entity states that the interim financial information has been reviewed by an independent public accountant.

4. **Review vs. Audit**   The objective of a review of interim financial information differs significantly from that of an audit conducted in accordance with GAAP. A review of interim financial information does not provide a basis for expressing an opinion about whether the financial statements are presented fairly, in all material respects, in conformity with generally accepted accounting principles. A review consists principally of performing analytical procedures and making inquiries of persons responsible for financial and accounting matters, and does not contemplate (a) tests of accounting records through inspection, observation, or confirmation; (b) tests of controls to evaluate their effectiveness; (c) obtaining corroborating evidence in response to inquiries; or (d) performing certain other procedures ordinarily performed in an audit. A review may bring to the accountant's attention significant matters affecting the interim financial information, but it does not provide assurance that the accountant will become aware of all significant matters that would be identified in an audit. Also, a review is not designed to provide assurance on internal control or to identify significant deficiencies. However, the accountant is responsible for communicating with the audit committee or others with equivalent authority or responsibility, regarding any significant deficiencies that come to the auditor's attention.

The auditor's responsibility as it relates to management's quarterly certifications on internal control over financial reporting is also different from the auditor's responsibility as it relates to management's annual assessment of internal control over financial reporting. The auditor should perform limited procedures quarterly to provide a basis for determining whether he or she has become aware of any material modifications that, in the auditor's judgment, should be made to the disclosures about changes in internal control over financial reporting.

B. **Procedures**

1. **Inquiries & Other Review Procedures**

   a. **Reading Minutes**   Reading the available minutes of meetings of stockholders, directors, and appropriate committees, and inquiring about matters dealt with at meetings for which minutes are not available, to identify matters that may affect the interim financial information.

   b. **Obtaining Reports From Other Accountants**   Obtaining reports from other accountants, if any, who have been engaged to perform a review of the interim financial information of significant components of the reporting entity, its subsidiaries, or its other investees, or inquiring of those accountants if reports have not been issued.

   c. **Inquiring of Members of Management**   Inquiring of members of management who have responsibility for financial and accounting matters concerning

   (1) Whether the interim financial information has been prepared in conformity with generally accepted accounting principles consistently applied

   (2) Unusual or complex situations that may have an effect on the interim financial information

   (3) Significant transactions occurring or recognized in the last several days of the interim period

   (4) The status of uncorrected misstatements identified during the previous audit and interim review (that is, whether adjustments had been recorded subsequent to the prior audit or interim period and, if so, the amounts recorded and period in which such adjustments were recorded)

   (5) Matters about which questions have arisen in the course of applying the review procedures

(6) Events subsequent to the date of the interim financial information that could have a material effect on the presentation of such information

(7) Their knowledge of any fraud or suspected fraud affecting the entity involving (a) management, (b) employees who have significant roles in internal control, or (c) others where the fraud could have a material effect on the financial statements

(8) Whether they are aware of allegations of fraud or suspected fraud affecting the entity, for example, received in communications from employees, former employees, analysts, regulators, short sellers, or others

(9) Significant journal entries and other adjustments

(10) Communications from regulatory agencies

(11) Significant deficiencies, including material weaknesses, in the design or operation of internal controls which could adversely affect the issuer's ability to record, process, summarize, and report financial data

d. **Accounting Records** Obtaining evidence that the interim financial information agrees or reconciles with the accounting records. For example, the accountant may compare the interim financial information to

(1) The accounting records, such as the general ledger

(2) A consolidating schedule derived from the accounting records

(3) Other supporting data in the entity's records

In addition, the accountant should consider inquiring of management as to the reliability of the records to which the interim financial information was compared or reconciled.

e. **Reading Interim Financial Information** To determine whether it conforms to GAAP.

f. **Other Information** Reading other information that accompanies the interim financial information and is contained in reports (to consider whether such information or the manner of its presentation is materially inconsistent with the interim financial information)

(1) To holders of securities or beneficial interests

(2) Filed with regulatory authorities under the Securities Exchange Act of 1934 (such as Form 10-Q or 10-QSB)

If the accountant concludes that there is a material inconsistency, or becomes aware of information that he or she believes is a material misstatement of fact, the action taken will depend on his or her judgment in the particular circumstances.

g. **Management's Quarterly Certifications About Internal Control** Evaluating management's quarterly certifications about internal control over financial reporting by performing the following procedures:

(1) Inquiring of management about significant changes in the design or operation of internal control over financial reporting as it relates to the preparation of annual as well as interim financial information that could have occurred subsequent to the preceding annual audit or prior review of interim financial information

(2) Evaluating the implications of misstatements identified by the auditor as part of the auditor's other interim review procedures as they relate to effective internal control over financial reporting

(3) Determining, through a combination of observation and inquiry, whether any change in internal control over financial reporting has materially affected, or is reasonably likely to materially affect, the company's internal control over financial reporting

h. **Analytics** Applied to interim financial information to provide a basis for inquiring about unusual items. These procedures consist of

(1) Comparing the financial information with the immediately preceding interim period and with the corresponding previous period(s)

(2) Comparing actual results with anticipated results

(3) Studying the relationships of those elements that can be expected to conform to predictable patterns. The CPA should consider the types of matters that required accounting adjustments in the preceding year or quarters.

i. **Obtaining Management's Written Representations** Management's responsibility for the financial information, completeness of the minutes, subsequent events, etc.

2. **Required Procedures** AU 722 specifically requires the following procedures:

a. **Disaggregated Comparison** Comparing disaggregated revenue data, for example, comparing revenue reported by month and by product line or business segment for the current interim period with that of comparable prior periods.

b. **Reconciliation** Obtaining evidence that the interim financial information agrees or reconciles with the accounting records.

c. **Fraud Inquiry** Inquiring of members of management who have responsibility for financial and accounting matters as to their knowledge of any fraud or suspected fraud affecting the entity, and whether they are aware of allegations of fraud or suspected fraud, affecting the entity received in communications from employees, former employees, analysts, regulators, short sellers, or others.

If the auditor becomes aware of information indicating that fraud or an illegal act has or may have occurred, the auditor must also determine his or her responsibilities under AU 316, *Consideration of Fraud in a Financial Statement Audit*, AU 317, *Illegal Acts by Clients*, and Section 10A of the Securities Exchange Act of 1934.

3. **Timing** Performing some of the work before the end of the interim period (a) usually permits the work to be carried out more efficiently, and (b) permits early consideration of accounting matters that affect the interim financial information.

4. **Extent**   The extent to which the CPA applies procedures depends on the accountant's knowledge of changes in accounting practices or in the nature or volume of business activity; inquiry concerning litigation, claims, and assessments; questions raised in performing other procedures; and modification of review procedures.

5. **Understanding With Client**   AU 722 requires an accountant to establish an understanding with his or her client regarding the services to be performed in an engagement to review interim financial information. This understanding is usually in the form of an engagement letter that includes: a general description of the procedures; a statement that the procedures are substantially less in scope than an audit performed in accordance with GAAS; an explanation that the financial information is the responsibility of the company's management; and a description of the form of the report, if any.

6. **Knowledge of the Entity's Business & Internal Control**   AU 722 requires that, for an accountant to perform a review of interim financial information, there must exist a sufficient knowledge of the client's business and internal control policies and procedures as they relate to the preparation of both annual and interim financial information to: (a) identify types of potential material misstatements in the interim financial information and consider the likelihood of their occurrence; and (b) select the inquiries and analytics that will provide the accountant with a basis for reporting whether material modifications should be made for such information to conform with GAAP.

7. **Subsequent Events**   Subsequent discovery of facts that existed at the date of the auditor's report should be handled in accordance with AU 561.

8. **Quality of Principles & Estimates**   AU 722 requires an auditor to discuss the quality of accounting principles and accounting estimates, but limited to the impact of transactions, events, and changes considered in performing review procedures. The auditor should attempt a discussion with those charged with governance prior to filing the Form 10-Q. The discussion should occur before the filing or as soon thereafter as practicable.

C. **Communications to Management, Audit Committee & Others**
    As a result of conducting a review of interim financial information, the accountant may become aware of matters that cause him or her to believe that

    1. Material modification should be made to the interim financial information for it to conform with generally accepted accounting principles

    2. Modification to the disclosures about changes in internal control over financial reporting is necessary for the certifications to be accurate and to comply with the requirements of Section 302 of the Act and Securities Exchange Act Rule 13a-14(a) or 15d-14(a), whichever applies

    3. The entity filed the Form 10-Q or Form 10-QSB before the completion of the review

In such circumstances, the accountant should communicate the matter(s) to the appropriate level of management as soon as practicable.

When conducting a review of interim financial information, the accountant may become aware of matters relating to internal control that may be of interest to the audit committee. Matters that should be reported to the audit committee are referred to as significant deficiencies. A significant deficiency is a deficiency, or a combination of deficiencies, in internal control over financial reporting, that is less severe than a material weakness yet important enough to merit attention by those responsible for oversight of the company's financial reporting.

D. Report

The report should consist of: (1) a statement that the review conformed to the standards for a review of interim financial information; (2) an identification of the information reviewed; (3) a description of the procedures for a review; (4) a statement that the scope of a review is substantially less than that of an audit and that an opinion on the financial statements, taken as a whole, is **not** expressed; and (5) a statement as to whether the CPA is aware of any material modifications needed to make the financial information conform with GAAP.

1. **Report Form** The report is addressed to the company, its board of directors, or its stockholders and is dated as of the completion of the review. Each page of the interim financial information should be clearly marked "unaudited." The CPA may use and make reference to the report of another accountant, such reference indicates a division of responsibility for performing the review.

Exhibit 1 ▶ Report on Interim Financial Information

> We have reviewed the accompanying [*describe the interim financial information or statements reviewed*] of X Company as of September 30, 20X3 and 20X2, and for the three-month and nine-month periods then ended. This (these) interim financial information (statements) is (are) the responsibility of the Company's management.
>
> We conducted our review in accordance with the standards of the Public Company Accounting Oversight Board (United States). A review of interim financial information consists principally of applying analytical procedures and making inquiries of persons responsible for financial and accounting matters. It is substantially less in scope than an audit conducted in accordance with the standards of the Public Company Accounting Oversight Board, the objective of which is the expression of an opinion regarding the financial statements taken as a whole. Accordingly, we do not express such an opinion.
>
> Based on our review, we are not aware of any material modifications that should be made to the accompanying interim financial statement(s) for it (them) to be in conformity with US generally accepted accounting principles.

2. **Modification of CPA's Report** Neither an uncertainty **nor** a lack of consistency in applying accounting principles would result in a modified report as long as the matters are disclosed adequately in the interim financial information or statements. However, a modification is required if a change in accounting principle is **not** in conformity with GAAP.

   a. **Departure From GAAP** Report should be modified when the interim financial information is affected materially by a departure from GAAP. The nature of the departure and, if practicable, its effects should be disclosed.

Exhibit 2 ▶ Departure From GAAP

> (Explanatory third paragraph)
>
> Based on information furnished to us by management, we believe that the Company has excluded from property and debt in the accompanying balance sheet certain lease obligations that should be capitalized to conform with generally accepted accounting principles. This information indicates that if these lease obligations were capitalized at September 30, 20X1, property would be increased by $_____, long-term debt by $_____, and net income and earnings per share would be increased (decreased) by $_____, $_____, $_____, and $_____, respectively, for the three-month and nine-month periods then ended.
>
> (Concluding paragraph)
>
> Based on our review, with the exception of the matter(s) described in the preceding paragraph(s), we are not aware of any material modifications that should be made to the accompanying financial (information or statements) for them (it) to be in conformity with US generally accepted accounting principles.

b.   **Inadequate Disclosure** Report should be modified and, if practicable, the needed information should be included.

Exhibit 3 ▶ Inadequate Disclosure

> (Explanatory third paragraph)
>
> Management has informed us that the Company is presently contesting deficiencies in federal income taxes proposed by the Internal Revenue Service for the years 20X1 through 20X3 in the aggregate amount of approximately $_____, and that the extent of the company's liability, if any, and the effect on the accompanying (information or statements) are (is) not determinable at this time. The (information or statements) fail to disclose these matters, which we believe are required to be disclosed in conformity with generally accepted accounting principles.
>
> (Concluding paragraph)
>
> Based on our review, with the exception of the matter(s) described in the preceding paragraph(s), we are not aware of any material modifications that should be made to the accompanying financial (information or statements) for them (it) to be in conformity with US generally accepted accounting principles.

E.   Presented in Note to Audited Financial Statements

SEC Regulation S-K requires some companies to include a note containing selected quarterly financial information in their audited financial statements. In addition, other companies may choose to do so. If the quarterly data is presented voluntarily, the auditor should review it or the auditor should expand the report to state the data has not been reviewed. The interim financial information is **not** required by GAAP and has not been audited; therefore, the auditor ordinarily will **not** modify the report on the audited financial statements to refer to the quarterly data.

1.   **Omission** If the CPA has audited the annual financial statements for which the quarterly information required by Regulation S-K is presented, the CPA should review the quarterly information. If unable to perform such review, the report on the audited financial statements may need to be modified. If the quarterly data either has been omitted **or** has not been reviewed, the auditor's report on the annual statements should be modified.

2.   **Other** The auditor's report also should be expanded when the following occurs: the interim financial information is not marked "unaudited;" the interim information is presented voluntarily, but has not been reviewed and is not appropriately marked as such; the interim information does not conform to GAAP; or the information, although reviewed, fails to indicate that a review is substantially less in scope than an audit performed per GAAS.

VII. PCAOB Risk Assessment Standards vs. GAAS & ISA

A.   PCAOB AS 8, *Audit Risk*

1.   **Overview** This standard discusses the auditor's consideration of audit risk in an audit of financial statements as part of an integrated audit or an audit of financial statements only. It describes the components of audit risk and the auditor's responsibilities for reducing audit risk to an appropriately low level in order to obtain reasonable assurance that the financial statements are free of material misstatement.

2.   **Inverse Relationship of Detection Risk & Substantive Procedures** PCAOB standards include an explicit requirement that as the appropriate level of detection risk decreases, the evidence from substantive procedures that the auditor should obtain increases.

GAAS and ISA include a discussion about the inverse relationship and guidance that the auditor can act accordingly. Put another way, GAAS and ISA include an implicit rather than an explicit requirement regarding this matter because risk assessment is required and its purpose is to allow auditors to vary the amount of audit attention related to particular areas based on the risks presented by them.

Editor note: Detection risk relates to the substantive audit procedures and is managed by the auditor's response to the risk of material misstatement (RMM). As the assessed RMM increases, the evidence from substantive procedures that the auditor should obtain also increases. The auditor reduces detection risk through the nature, extent, and timing of substantive procedures performed. However, the auditor should perform substantive procedures for all relevant assertions related to material classes of transactions, account balances, and disclosures.

B.   PCAOB AS 9, *Audit Planning*

1.   Overview This standard establishes requirements regarding planning an audit, including assessing matters that are important to the audit, and establishing an appropriate audit strategy and audit plan.

2.   Development of the Audit Strategy & Audit Plan PCAOB standards include a requirement to evaluate whether the following matters are important to the company's financial statements and internal control over financial reporting and, if so, how they will affect the auditor's procedures. These matters were adapted from PCAOB AS 5, *An Audit of Internal Control Over Financial Reporting That Is Integrated with An Audit of Financial Statements.*

   a.   Knowledge of the company's internal control over financial reporting obtained during other engagements performed by the auditor

   b.   Matters affecting the industry in which the company operates, such as financial reporting practices, economic conditions, laws and regulations, and technological changes

   c.   Matters relating to the company's business, including its organization, operating characteristics, and capital structure

   d.   The extent of recent changes, if any, in the company, its operations, or its internal control over financial reporting

   e.   The auditor's preliminary judgments about materiality, risk, and, in integrated audits, other factors relating to the determination of material weaknesses

   f.   Control deficiencies previously communicated to the audit committee or management

   g.   Legal or regulatory matters of which the company is aware

   h.   The type and extent of available evidence related to the effectiveness of the company's internal control over financial reporting

   i.   Preliminary judgments about the effectiveness of internal control over financial reporting

   j.   Public information about the company relevant to the evaluation of the likelihood of material financial statement misstatements and the effectiveness of the company's internal control over financial reporting

   k.   Knowledge about risks related to the company evaluated as part of the auditor's client acceptance and retention evaluation

   l.   The relative complexity of the company's operations

GAAS and ISA advise the auditor to consider similar matters with less emphasis on internal control.

3. **Documentation of the Audit Plan & Audit Strategy** PCAOB standards do not include the phrase *at the relevant assertion level for each material class of transactions, account balance, and disclosure* when describing the documentation requirements for audit procedures as do GAAS and ISA. This is not a difference between the standards regarding documentation of audit procedures. GAAS and ISA use the phrase to indicate the level of detail of the coverage while the PCAOB omits it for clarity reasons because not all audit procedures relate to the assertion level, i.e., some are performed at the entity level.

4. **Multilocation Engagements** PCAOB standards state that the auditor should determine the extent to which auditing procedures should be performed at selected locations or business units to obtain sufficient appropriate evidence to obtain reasonable assurance about whether the consolidated financial statements are free of material misstatement. This includes determining the locations or business units at which to perform audit procedures, as well as the nature, extent, and timing of the audit procedures to be performed at those individual locations or business units. The auditor should assess the RMM to the consolidated financial statements associated with the location or business unit and correlate the amount of audit attention devoted to the location or business unit with the degree of RMM associated with that location or business unit.

    Factors that are relevant to the assessment of the RMM associated with a particular location or business unit and the determination of the necessary audit procedures include:

    a. The nature and amount of assets, liabilities, and transactions executed at the location or business unit, including, e.g., significant transactions executed at the location or business unit that are outside the normal course of business for the company, or that otherwise appear to be unusual given the auditor's understanding of the company and its environment

    b. The materiality of the location or business unit

    c. The specific risks associated with the location or business unit that present a reasonable possibility of material misstatement to the company's consolidated financial statements

    d. Whether the RMM associated with the location or business unit apply to other locations or business units such that, in combination, they present a reasonable possibility of material misstatement to the company's consolidated financial statements

    e. The degree of centralization of records or information processing

    f. The effectiveness of the control environment, particularly with respect to management's control over the exercise of authority delegated to others and its ability to effectively supervise activities at the location or business unit

    g. The frequency, timing, and scope of monitoring activities by the company or others at the location or business unit

    GAAS advise consideration of different locations and business components when establishing the scope of an audit, but do not include a detailed discussion like the PCAOB standards. ISA address some of the same aspects of this matter in a separate standard on audits of group financial statements (including the work of component auditors) mainly in relation to the impact on the scope of the audit. The focus in ISA is on the determination of whether a component is significant (mainly based on materiality) and, if so, the applicable audit procedures. Risk assessment is an important factor but not to the degree or specificity as described in the PCAOB approach.

C.   **PCAOB AS 10, *Supervision of the Audit Engagement***

1.   **Overview**   This standard sets forth requirements for supervision of the audit engagement, including, in particular, supervising the work of engagement team members. It applies to the engagement partner and to other engagement team members who assist the engagement partner with supervision.

2.   **Supervision by Other Engagement Team Members**   PCAOB standards state that the engagement partners may seek assistance from appropriate engagement team members in fulfilling their responsibilities. GAAS and ISA mention delegation of review responsibilities only.

3.   **Extent of Supervision Needed Factors**   Per PCAOB standards, to determine the extent of supervision necessary for engagement team members to perform their work as directed and form appropriate conclusions, the engagement partner and other engagement team members performing supervisory activities should take into account:

a.   The nature of the company, including its size and complexity

b.   The nature of the assigned work for each engagement team member, including the procedures to be performed, and the controls or accounts and disclosures to be tested

c.   The knowledge, skill, and ability of each engagement team member.

ISA list essentially the same factors. GAAS explain that many factors are involved in determining the extent of the supervision that is appropriate and give two examples: the complexity of the subject matter and the qualifications of the persons performing the work, including knowledge of the client's business and industry.

D.   **PCAOB AS 11, *Consideration of Materiality in Planning and Performing an Audit***

1.   **Overview**   This standard describes the auditor's responsibilities for consideration of materiality in planning and performing an audit.

2.   **Materiality for Financial Statements as a Whole**   PCAOB standards require the auditor to establish a materiality level for the financial statements as a whole that is appropriate in light of the particular circumstances, including consideration of the company's earnings and other relevant factors.

GAAS and ISA have essentially the same requirement. GAAS and ISA state that the determination of what is material to the users is a matter of professional judgment. The auditor often may apply a percentage to a chosen benchmark as a step in determining materiality for the financial statements taken as a whole. To identify an appropriate benchmark, factors, e.g., earnings should be considered.

3.   **Definition of Materiality**   The PCAOB's requirement for establishing a materiality level for the financial statements as a whole is based on the concept of materiality that is articulated by the courts in interpreting the federal securities laws. In interpreting the federal securities laws, the Supreme Court of the United States has held that a fact is material if there is "a substantial likelihood that the…fact would have been viewed by the reasonable investor as having significantly altered the 'total mix' of information made available." As the Supreme Court has noted, determinations of materiality require "delicate assessments of the inferences a 'reasonable shareholder' would draw from a given set of facts and the significance of those inferences to him [*sic*]."

The GAAS requirement is based on the definition of materiality similarly articulated by the FASB: "…the magnitude of an omission or misstatement of accounting information that, in the light of surrounding circumstances, makes it probable that the judgment of a reasonable person relying on the information would have been changed or influenced by the omission or misstatement."

4.   **Tolerable Misstatement** PCAOB standards contain a requirement to take into account the nature, cause (if known), and amount of misstatements that were accumulated in audits of the financial statements of prior periods when determining tolerable misstatement and planning and performing audit procedures.

GAAS and ISA do not have such a requirement.

Editor note: *Tolerable misstatement* is the maximum error in a population (e.g., the class of transactions, account balance, or disclosure) that the auditor is willing to accept. When assessing the RMM and designing and performing further audit procedures to respond to the assessed risks, the auditor should allow for the possibility that some misstatements of lesser amounts than the materiality levels could, in the aggregate, result in a material misstatement of the financial statements.

E.   **PCAOB AS 12, *Identifying and Assessing Risks of Material Misstatement***

1.   **Overview** This standard establishes requirements regarding the process of identifying and assessing RMM of the financial statements. The risk assessment process discussed in the standard includes information-gathering procedures to identify risks and an analysis of the identified risks.

2.   **Additional Procedures for Obtaining an Understanding** PCAOB standards require the auditor to consider performing certain procedures as part of obtaining an understanding of the company. These procedures include reading public information about the company, observing or reading transcripts of earnings calls, obtaining an understanding of compensation arrangements with senior management, and obtaining information about trading activity in the company's securities and holdings in the company's securities by significant holders.

With the exception of the first item, GAAS and ISA do not have such a requirement.

3.   **Disclosures** PCAOB standards require the auditor to develop expectations about the disclosures that are necessary for the company's financial statements to be presented fairly in conformity with the applicable financial reporting framework to identify and assess the RMM related to omitted, incomplete, or inaccurate disclosures. Additionally, the engagement team members should discuss how fraud might be perpetrated or concealed by omitting or presenting incomplete or inaccurate disclosures. The auditor's evaluation of fraud risk factors should include how fraud could be perpetrated or concealed by presenting incomplete or inaccurate disclosures or by omitting disclosures that are necessary for the financial statements to be presented fairly in conformity with the applicable financial reporting framework.

Although consideration of appropriate disclosure is included throughout the GAAS and ISA, they do not include a risk assessment requirement similar to this for disclosures.

4.   **Control Deficiencies Identified** PCAOB standards state that if the auditor identifies a control deficiency in the company's control environment, the auditor should evaluate the extent to which this control deficiency is indicative of a fraud risk factor.

GAAS and ISA do not have such a requirement.

5. **Relationship of Understanding of Internal Control to Tests of Controls** PCAOB standards require the auditor to take into account the evidence obtained from understanding internal control when assessing control risk and, in the audit of internal control, forming conclusions about the effectiveness of controls. The auditor should also take into account the evidence obtained from understanding internal control when determining the nature, extent, and timing of procedures necessary to support the auditor's conclusions about the effectiveness of entity-level controls in the audit of internal control.

GAAS and ISA do not have such a requirement linking tests of controls to the audit of internal control.

6. **Review of Interim Financial Information** When the auditor has performed a review of interim financial information in accordance with AU 722, *Interim Financial Information,* PCAOB standards require the auditor to evaluate whether information obtained during the review is relevant to identifying RMM in the year-end audit.

GAAS and ISA do not have such a requirement.

7. **Analytical Procedures** Per PCAOB standards, when the auditor has performed a review of interim financial information in accordance with AU 722, *Interim Financial Information*, the auditor should take into account the analytical procedures applied in that review when designing and applying analytical procedures as risk assessment procedures.

GAAS and ISA do not have such a requirement.

8. **Discussion Among Engagement Team** Per PCAOB standards, communication among the engagement team members about significant matters affecting the RMM should continue throughout the audit, including when conditions change.

GAAS and ISA do not have such a requirement to continue the discussion throughout the audit. GAAS state that depending on the circumstances of the audit, there *may* be multiple discussions in order to facilitate the ongoing exchange of information between audit team members regarding the susceptibility of the entity's financial statements to material misstatements. The purpose is for audit team members to communicate and share information obtained throughout the audit that may affect the assessment of the RMM due to fraud or error or the audit procedures performed to address the risks.

F. **PCAOB AS 13, *The Auditor's Responses to the Risks of Material Misstatement***

1. **Overview** This standard establishes requirements for responding to the RMM in financial statements through the general conduct of the audit and performing audit procedures regarding significant accounts and disclosures.

2. **Determination of Need for Pervasive Changes** PCAOB standards require the auditor to determine whether it is necessary to make pervasive changes to the nature, timing, or extent of audit procedures to adequately address the assessed RMM. Examples of such pervasive changes include modifying the audit strategy to:

   a. Increase the substantive testing of the valuation of numerous significant accounts at year-end because of significantly deteriorating market conditions

   b. Obtain more persuasive audit evidence from substantive procedures due to the identification of pervasive weaknesses in the company's control environment

GAAS and ISA require the adjustment of the audit strategy and plan to changes in circumstances which would cover the events described above, but they do not have this specific requirement.

3. **More Persuasive Evidence Required** PCAOB standards require the auditor to obtain more persuasive evidence about the effectiveness of controls for each relevant assertion for which the audit approach consists primarily of tests of controls.

    GAAS and ISA do not have such a requirement.

4. **Evaluating Operating Effectiveness of Controls** PCAOB standards and GAAS require the auditor to determine whether the person performing the control possesses the necessary authority and competence to perform the control effectively.

    ISA do not have such a requirement.

5. **Tests of Controls in an Integrated Audit** PCAOB standards require the auditor to perform tests of controls in integrated audits to meet the objectives of both the audit of financial statements and the audit of internal control.

    GAAS and ISA do not have such a requirement.

6. **Testing of Controls That Have Not Changed** When the auditor is relying on controls, GAAS and ISA allow the testing of the operating effectiveness of controls that have not changed to be performed at least every third annual audit.

    PCAOB standards require the auditor to test controls during the period of reliance, i.e., the period covered by the financial statements or the portion of that period for which the auditor plans to rely on them in order to modify the nature, extent, and timing of substantive procedures—they do **not** allow rotational testing.

7. **Assessment of Control Risk** PCAOB standards require the assessment of control risk.

    GAAS and ISA do not require the separate specific assessment of control risk—how to consider the components of audit risk is left up to the auditor's judgment.

8. **Substantive Procedures** PCAOB standards require the auditor to perform substantive procedures for each relevant assertion of each significant account and disclosure, regardless of the assessed level of control risk.

    GAAS and ISA have essentially the same requirement; however, they require it regardless of the assessed RMM rather than the assessed level of control risk and require it for each material class of transactions, account balance, and disclosure.

9. **Confirmation Procedures** PCAOB standards and GAAS do not specifically address confirmation procedures in their risk assessment standards; however, in their respective standards dedicated to confirmations, an auditor who has not requested confirmations in the examination of accounts receivable is required to document the justification for not doing so.

    ISA address confirmation procedures in their risk assessment standards, requiring the auditor to consider whether confirmation procedures are to be performed as substantive audit procedures.

10. **Interim Substantive Procedures** PCAOB standards and GAAS list various factors the auditor is required to consider when determining whether to perform substantive procedures at an interim date.

    ISA do not have such a requirement; however, they do provide a list of similar factors that may influence the auditor's decision.

11. **Substantive Procedures to Cover Remaining Period if Interim Testing Performed** All three sets of standards include requirements to cover the remaining period. PCAOB standards require that such procedures include comparing relevant information about the account balance at the interim date with comparable information at the end of the period to identify amounts that appear unusual and investigating such amounts; and performing audit procedures to test the remaining period. GAAS and ISA contain essentially the same guidance; however, they use the term *may*, i.e., specific procedures are not required for covering the remaining period.

12. **Dual-Purpose Tests** PCAOB standards define a dual-purpose test as a substantive test of a transaction and a test of a control relevant to that transaction that are performed concurrently, e.g., a substantive test of sales transactions performed concurrently with a test of controls over those transactions. PCAOB standards state that when dual-purpose tests are performed, the auditor should design the dual-purpose test to achieve the objectives of both the test of the control and the substantive test. Also, when performing a dual-purpose test, the auditor should evaluate the results of the test in forming conclusions about both the assertion and the effectiveness of the control being tested.

GAAS and ISA do not have such requirements.

G. **PCAOB AS 14, *Evaluating Audit Results***

1. **Overview** This standard establishes requirements regarding the auditor's evaluation of audit results and determination of whether the auditor has obtained sufficient appropriate audit evidence. The evaluation process set forth in this standard includes, among other things, evaluation of misstatements identified during the audit; the overall presentation of the financial statements, including disclosures; and the potential for management bias in the financial statements.

2. **Analytical Procedures Regarding Revenue** All three sets of standards require the auditor to perform analytical procedures relating to revenue; however only the PCAOB standards require them to be performed through the end of the period.

3. **Timely Communication of Accumulated Misstatements** All three sets of standards require the auditor to communicate misstatements accumulated during the audit to management and follow up on their correction; however, PCAOB standards do not include a specific requirement for the auditor to request their correction as GAAS and ISA do.

4. **Evaluation of Effect of Misstatements on Assessed RMM** PCAOB standards require the auditor to evaluate the nature and effects of the individual misstatements accumulated during the audit on the assessed risks of material misstatement.

GAAS and ISA do not have an explicit requirement to evaluate the effect of accumulated misstatements on risk assessment; however, GAAS and ISA do have a requirement for the auditor to consider whether the overall audit strategy and audit plan need to be revised if the nature of identified misstatements and the circumstances of their occurrence are indicative that other misstatements may exist that, when aggregated with identified misstatements, could be material.

5. **Misstatements Indicative of Fraud** PCAOB standards and GAAS require the auditor to perform procedures to obtain additional audit evidence to determine whether fraud has occurred or is likely to have occurred, and, if so, its effect on the financial statements and the auditor's report if the auditor believes that a misstatement is or might be intentional, and if the effect on the financial statement cannot be readily determined.

ISA have similar requirements; however, they do not explicitly require the auditor to perform audit procedures to obtain additional audit evidence to determine the effect of the misstatement on the financial statements.

6. **Communications Regarding Fraud** If the auditor becomes aware of information indicating that fraud or another illegal act has occurred or might have occurred, PCAOB standards require the auditor to determine the auditor's responsibility for communications under their adopted interim standards on (a) fraud and (b) illegal acts by clients; and federal securities laws and regulations. The auditor is required, whenever the auditor has determined that there is evidence that fraud may exist, to bring the matter to the attention of an appropriate level of management.

GAAS and ISA have essentially the same requirement for communication with management and those charged with governance. As for communication outside the entity, their guidance requires the auditor to determine when the auditor should communicate. GAAS state that the auditor may wish to consult with legal counsel beforehand.

7. **Adjusting Entries by Management That Offset Accumulated Misstatements** If management identifies adjusting entries that offset misstatements accumulated by the auditor, PCAOB standards require the auditor to perform procedures to determine why the misstatements were not identified previously and to evaluate the implications on the integrity of management and the auditor's risk assessments, including fraud risk assessments. The auditor should also perform additional procedures as necessary to address the risk of further undetected misstatements.

GAAS and ISA do not have such a requirement.

H. **PCAOB AS 15,** *Audit Evidence*
This standard explains what constitutes audit evidence and establishes requirements for designing and performing audit procedures to obtain sufficient appropriate audit evidence to support the opinion expressed in the auditor's report.

There are no substantive differences between the three sets of standards regarding audit evidence.

VIII. **International Standards on Auditing**

A. **Overview**
The International Auditing and Assurance Standards Board (IAASB) of the International Federation of Accountants (IFAC) issues International Standards on Auditing (ISA) and assurance standards.

A CPA practicing in the United States may be engaged to audit the financial statements of a client in accordance with the ISA. In those circumstances where the auditor's report states that the audit was conducted in accordance with International Auditing Standards, the US auditor should comply with both the ISA and, as required by the AICPA Code of Professional Conduct, auditing standards generally accepted in the United States of America for a nonissuer or the standards of the Public Company Accounting Oversight Board (United States) for an issuer. An engagement of this nature is normally conducted by performing an audit in accordance with auditing standards generally accepted in the United States of America or the PCAOB standards plus performing the additional procedures required by the ISA.

B. **ISA vs. US Auditing Standards**
The substantive differences between the standards include the following.

1. **Nonissuers**

   a. **ISA 210,** *Agreeing the Terms of Audit Engagements* **vs. AU 311,** *Planning and Supervision*

      ISA 210 states that if the terms of the audit engagement are changed, the auditor and management shall agree on and record the new terms of the engagement in an engagement letter or other suitable form of written agreement.

ISA 210 states that if the auditor is unable to agree to the change of the terms of the engagement and is not permitted by management to continue the original engagement, the auditor should withdraw where possible under applicable law or regulation and determine whether there is any obligation, either contractual or otherwise, to report the circumstances to other parties, such as the those charged with governance, owners, or regulators.

Auditing standards generally accepted in the United States of America do not include this requirement.

Editor note: The following particular differences discussed for nonissuers are also applicable to the PCAOB standards because they relate to interim standards adopted by the PCAOB.

b.   **ISA 240, *The Auditor's Responsibilities Relating to Fraud in an Audit of Financial Statements*, vs. AU 333, *Management Representations***

ISA 240 states that the auditor should obtain a written representation from management that it has disclosed to the auditor the results of its assessment of the risk that the financial statements may be materially misstated as a result of fraud.

AU 333 does not require this representation.

c.   **ISA 250, *Consideration of Laws and Regulations in an Audit of Financial Statements*, vs. AU 317, *Illegal Acts by Clients***

Editor note: ISA 250 uses the term *noncompliance with laws and regulations* while AU 317 uses the term *illegal acts*.

If the auditor suspects there may be noncompliance AU 317 requires the auditor to apply additional procedures; ISA 250 does not.

AU 317 lists specific circumstances where a duty to notify outside parties of an illegal act may exist; ISA 250 does not—it only requires the auditor to determine whether a responsibility to report to outside parties exists.

AU 317 requires the auditor to withdraw from the engagement if the client refuses to accept a modified audit report (caused by the auditor's determination that an illegal act had a material effect on the financial statements and has not been properly accounted for or disclosed); ISA 250 does not.

d.   **ISA 510, *Initial Audit Engagements—Opening Balances*, vs. AU 315, *Communications Between Predecessor and Successor Auditors***

Per ISA 510, if the auditor is unable to obtain sufficient appropriate audit evidence regarding opening balances, the auditor shall express a qualified opinion or disclaim an opinion. AU 315 does not include an explicit requirement; however, it includes implicit guidance that the auditor should disclaim an opinion if sufficient appropriate evidence cannot be obtained.

e.   **ISA 560, *Subsequent Events*, vs. AU 530, *Dating of the Independent Auditor's Report***

Per ISA 560, when management amends the financial statements for facts discovered after the date of the auditor's report but before the date the financial statements are issued, the auditor would provide management with a new report on the amended statements. The new auditor's report would be dated no earlier than the date of approval of the amended financial statements and, accordingly, the additional procedures performed would be extended to the date of the new auditor's report. In contrast, AU 530 states that the date of the report ordinarily is not changed when the subsequent event requiring an adjustment to the financial statements is made without disclosure. In situations when the subsequent event requires disclosure, AU 530 permits the auditor to dual-date the report or date the report as of the later date. In the former instance, the auditor's responsibility for events occurring subsequent to the original report date is limited to the specific event referred to in the note. In the latter instance, the independent auditor's responsibility for subsequent events extends to the date of the report and, accordingly, the additional procedures performed should be extended to that date.

f.   **ISA 570, *Going Concern*, vs. AU 341, *The Auditor's Consideration of an Entity's Ability to Continue as a Going Concern***

AU 341 does not require the auditor to design audit procedures solely to identify events and conditions that indicate there could be substantial doubt. It requires the auditor to consider whether the results of other procedures performed during the course of the engagement identify conditions and events that, when considered in the aggregate, indicate there could be substantial doubt about the entity's ability to continue as a going concern. ISA 570 does recommend specific procedures.

One of the procedures required by ISA 570 is the evaluation of management's assessment of the entity's ability to continue as a going concern. AU 341 does not require the assessment of management's plan except when the auditor believes there is substantial doubt about the entity's ability to continue as a going concern. Then the auditor is required to consider management's plans for dealing with the adverse effects of the conditions and events that led to the auditor's belief.

ISA 570 requires the auditor to consider the same period as that used by management in making its assessment, a period at least, but not limited to, twelve months from the date of the financial statements. ISA 570 also requires the auditor to inquire of management as to its knowledge of events or conditions beyond the period of assessment used by management that may cast significant doubt on the entity's ability to continue as a going concern. AU 341 requires the auditor to evaluate whether there is substantial doubt about the entity's ability to continue as a going concern for a reasonable period of time, not to exceed one year beyond the date of the financial statements. AU 317 does not require inquiries of management beyond this period about events or conditions that may cast doubt.

When events or conditions have been identified which may cast significant doubt on the entity's ability to continue as a going concern, ISA 570 requires the auditor to seek written representations from management regarding its plans for future action. AU 341 contains no such requirement; however, an illustrative going concern representation is included in Appendix B of AU 333, *Management Representations*.

If there is significant delay in the approval of the financial statements by management or those charged with governance after the date of the financial statements, ISA 570 states that the auditor shall inquire as to the reasons for the delay. If the auditor believes the delay could be related to the going concern issue, the auditor should perform additional audit procedures and consider the effect on the auditor's conclusion regarding the existence of a material uncertainty. AU 341 does not speak to the issue of such a delay.

The terminology in the explanatory paragraph is different. AU 341 requires the use of the phrases *substantial doubt* and *going concern*. The ISA's illustrative explanatory paragraph includes the term *going concern*, but it uses the phrase *significant* doubt.

g. **ISA 600,** *Special Considerations—Audits of Group Financial Statements (Including the Work of Component Auditors),* **vs. AU 543,** *Part of Audit Performed by Other Independent Auditors*

Editor note: As the difference between the titles indicates, the scope of these two standards is different; however, they cover some of the same issues.

ISA 600 states that the auditor's report on the group financial statements shall not refer to a component auditor unless required by law or regulation to include such reference. The "group" engagement partner is required to take responsibility for the audit opinion. AU 543 allows the auditor to decide whether to serve as the principal auditor. The auditor must then decide whether or not to divide the responsibility.

h. **ISA 610,** *Using the Work of Internal Auditors,* **vs. AU 322,** *The Auditor's Consideration of the Internal Audit Function in an Audit of Financial Statements*

The two standards have different guidance when determining the effect of the work of the internal auditors on the external auditor's procedures. ISA 610 does not require consideration of the materiality of financial statement amounts while AU 322 does.

In evaluating specific work done by internal auditors, ISA 610 requires the evaluation of the resolution of any exceptions or unusual matters disclosed by the internal auditors. AU 322 does not have such a requirement.

i. **ISA 620,** *Using the Work of an Auditor's Expert,* **vs. AU 336,** *Using the Work of a Specialist*

Per ISA 620, in some circumstances, it may be appropriate to refer to the auditor's expert in an auditor's report containing a modified opinion, to explain the nature of the modification. In these circumstances, the auditor may need the permission of the expert before making such a reference. AU 336 discusses situations in which it is appropriate for the auditor to reference the specialist in the auditor's report; however, the auditor is not required to obtain the specialist's permission.

2. **Issuers** The substantive differences between ISA and PCAOB auditing standards (also see the section in this chapter on PCAOB risk assessment standards vs. GAAS and ISA) are as follows:

a. **Audit of Internal Control Over Financial Reporting That Is Integrated With an Audit of Financial Statements** The ISA do not have a similar requirement.

b. **Principal Auditor / Shared Responsibility** As mentioned in the preceding section, the ISA do not allow the principal auditor to share responsibility with another auditor and accordingly do not allow a reference in the audit report to another auditor.

c. **Period for Going Concern Evaluation** Also as previously mentioned, PCAOB standards limit the period to 12 months while the ISA set 12 months as the minimum.

Editor note: The individual ISA or the entire handbook of pronouncements can be viewed or downloaded for no charge on IFAC's website (http://www.ifac.org/publications-resources /2012-handbook-international-quality-control-auditing-review-other-assurance-a).

CHAPTER 10—OTHER AUDITING STANDARDS

Problem 10-1 MULTIPLE-CHOICE QUESTIONS

1. Which of the following statements is correct concerning the Sarbanes-Oxley Act of 2002 and publicly traded audit clients?

   a. The lead engagement and reviewing audit partners must change every seven years.
   b. An audit firm may not perform an audit for a client whose controller was previously employed by the audit firm and participated in the audit of the client within the client's previous fiscal year.
   c. The audit firm may not also provide tax services to an audit client.
   d. The audit firm may also provide tax services to an audit client without the preapproval of the audit committee. (Editors, ID: 8065)

2. Under the Sarbanes-Oxley Act of 2002, a registered public accounting firm may perform which of the following services with pre-approval from the audit committee for an audit client that is a publicly traded company?

   a. Internal audit outsourcing services
   b. Tax services
   c. Bookkeeping services
   d. Financial information systems design (Editors, ID: 8063)

3. The Sarbanes-Oxley Act of 2002 requires audit committees to be directly responsible for which of the following activities?

	Hiring Auditor	*Negotiating Fees*	*Overseeing Audit Work*
a.	Yes	No	Yes
b.	Yes	Yes	No
c.	No	Yes	Yes
d.	Yes	Yes	Yes

   (Editors, ID: 8064)

4. Which of the following is **not** a documentation requirement for an engagement conducted pursuant to the standards of the PCAOB?

   a. The auditor must identify all significant findings or issues in an engagement completion document.
   b. The auditor must retain audit documentation for at least seven years from the report release date.
   c. Audit documentation must contain sufficient information to enable an experienced auditor, having no previous connection with the engagement, to understand the nature, extent, timing, and results of procedures performed; evidence obtained; and conclusions reached.
   d. A complete and final set of audit documentation should be assembled for retention not more than 60 days after the report release date. (Editors, ID: 8268)

5. The office issuing the auditor's report on a public company must obtain, and review and retain, prior to the report release date, the following documentation related to the work performed by other auditors, **except for**

   a. Any findings affecting the consolidating or combining of accounts in the consolidated financial statements
   b. All internal controls over financial reporting found to be ineffective by other auditors
   c. Letters of representations from management
   d. Sufficient information to allow the reconciliation of the financial statement amounts audited by the other auditors to the information underlying the consolidated financial statements (Editors, ID: 89470)

6. The Public Company Accounting Oversight Board (PCAOB) uses the term *internal control over financial reporting* to describe a process that does **not** include which of the following?

   a. Procedures performed by the auditor
   b. Procedures that pertain to the maintenance of reasonably detailed records that accurately and fairly reflect the transactions and dispositions of the company's assets
   c. Procedures that provide reasonable assurance that transactions are recorded as necessary to permit preparation of the financial statements in accordance with GAAP and that receipts and expenditures are made only in accordance with company management and director authorization
   d. Procedures that provide reasonable assurance regarding prevention or timely detection of unauthorized acquisition, use, or disposition of company assets that could have a material effect on the financial statements
   (Editors, ID: 7938)

7. The Public Company Accounting Oversight Board's auditing standards recognize that effective internal control over financial reporting (ICFR) cannot, and does not, provide absolute assurance of achieving the company's reporting objectives in large part due to inherent limitations. Which of the following is **not** such an inherent limitation?

   a. Lapses in judgment and breakdowns resulting from human failures
   b. Circumvention by collusion
   c. Circumvention by improper management override
   d. Lack of controls over information technology
   (Editors, ID: 7941)

8. Which of the following statements apply to an audit of internal control over financial reporting conducted in accordance with the standards of the Public Company Accounting Oversight Board (PCAOB)?

   I. The auditor should consider the effect of compensating controls in assessing whether the objectives of internal control over financial reporting have been achieved.
   II. While management is responsible for the company's internal control, the auditor should also assess the effectiveness of the board of directors' and audit committee's oversight as part of evaluating the control environment.

   a. I only
   b. II only
   c. Both I and II
   d. Neither I nor II
   (Editors, ID: 7943)

9. Mammoth Co. plans to present comparative financial statements for the years ended December 31, year 5, and year 6, respectively. Brown, CPA, audited Mammoth's financial statements for both years and plans to report on the comparative financial statements on March 1, year 7. Brown's audit is subject to the requirements of the Public Company Accounting Oversight Board (PCAOB). Mammoth's current management team was not present until January 1, year 6. What period of time should be covered by Mammoth's management representation letter?

   a. January 1, year 5, through December 31, year 6
   b. January 1, year 5, through March 1, year 7
   c. January 1, year 6, through December 31, year 6
   d. January 1, year 6, through March 1, year 7
   (Editors, ID: 7944)

10. Wale Company plans to present comparative financial statements for the years ended December 31, year 7, and year 8, respectively. Dauphin, CPA, audited Wale's financial statements for both years and plans to report on the comparative financial statements on March 1, year 9. Dauphin's audit is subject to the requirements of the Public Company Accounting Oversight Board (PCAOB). What time is covered by Dauphin's opinion on internal control over financial reporting (ICFR)?

    a. The end of year 7 and the end of year 8
    b. The end of year 8
    c. Year 7 and year 8
    d. Year 8
    (Editors, ID: 7947)

11. In an audit of internal control over financial reporting conducted in accordance with the standards of the Public Company Accounting Oversight Board (PCAOB), the auditor must communicate in writing to the audit committee

    a. Significant deficiencies only
    b. Material weaknesses only
    c. All deficiencies in internal control over financial reporting
    d. Significant deficiencies and material weaknesses   (Editors, ID: 7949)

12. What is the term for an internal control deficiency such that there is a reasonable possibility that a material misstatement of the company's financial statements will not be prevented or detected on a timely basis?

    a. Deficiency in internal control
    b. Material deficiency
    c. Material weakness
    d. Significant deficiency   (Editors, ID: 7950)

13. The conceptual definition of materiality that applies to an audit of a public company's internal control over financial reporting includes which of the following considerations?

	Qualitative	*Quantitative*
a.	Yes	Yes
b.	Yes	No
c.	No	Yes
d.	No	No

                                                                            (Editors, ID: 7951)

14. In an audit of internal control over financial reporting conducted in accordance with the standards of the Public Company Accounting Oversight Board (PCAOB), which procedure is insufficient by itself to test the effectiveness of a control?

    a. Inquiries of appropriate personnel
    b. Inspection of relevant documents
    c. Observation of operations
    d. Reperformance of the control procedure   (Editors, ID: 7953)

15. Which of the following statements is **false** in regard to an audit of internal control over financial reporting conducted in accordance with the standards of the Public Company Accounting Oversight Board (PCAOB)?

    a. The auditor may rely upon the judgments of others regarding the sufficiency of evidence.
    b. The auditor may use the work of others to alter the nature, timing, or extent of the work that the auditor performs.
    c. The extent to which the auditor may use the work of others depends on their objectivity.
    d. As the risk associated with a control increases, the need for the auditor to perform his or her own work on the control increases.   (Editors, ID: 7954)

16. Each of the following types of controls is considered to be an entity-level control, **except** those

    a. Relating to the control environment
    b. Pertaining to the company's risk assessment process
    c. Regarding the company's annual stockholder meeting
    d. Addressing policies over significant risk management practices   (R/11, AUD, #20, ID: 9920)

17. In accordance with the standards of the PCAOB, which of the following conditions must be met in order for an auditor to report on whether a previously reported material weakness continues to exist?

    I. Management supports its assertion with sufficient evidence, including documentation.
    II. Management accepts responsibility for the effectiveness of internal control over operations.
    III. Management evaluates the effectiveness of the specific control(s) that address the material weakness using the same control criteria management used for its most recent annual assessment of internal control over financial reporting and its stated control objective(s).

    a. Only I
    b. Only II
    c. Only I and III
    d. I, II, and III   (Editors, ID: 8269)

18. Which of the following statements is **false** in regard to an engagement conducted in accordance with the standards of the PCAOB to report on whether a previously reported material weakness continues to exist?

    a. The auditor may report on more than one previously reported material weakness as part of a single engagement.
    b. This type of engagement is voluntary, i.e., the standards of the PCAOB do not require an auditor to undertake an engagement to report on whether a previously reported material weakness continues to exist.
    c. A qualified opinion is not permitted.
    d. The auditor's opinion on whether a previously reported material weakness continues to exist may be expressed as "the material weakness exists" or "the material weakness has been eliminated".

                                                                            (Editors, ID: 89465)

19. Which of the following circumstances does **not** describe when a change in accounting principle is a change from one generally accepted accounting principle to another generally accepted accounting principle?

    a. There are two or more generally accepted accounting principles that apply.
    b. The accounting principle formerly used is no longer generally accepted.
    c. There is a change in accounting estimate.
    d. There is a change in the method of applying an accounting principle.   (Editors, ID: 9282)

20. The auditor should evaluate a change in accounting principle to determine whether the newly adopted accounting principle is a generally accepted accounting principle. All of the following conditions must also be met **except for**

    a. The method of accounting for the effect of the change is in conformity with generally accepted accounting principles.
    b. The disclosures related to the accounting change are adequate.
    c. The company has justified that the alternative accounting principle is preferable.
    d. The company has prepared *pro forma* financial statements with and without the change.

                                                                            (Editors, ID: 9283)

21. The correction of a material misstatement in the previously issued financial statements of an issuer

    a. Should be recognized in the auditor's report through the addition of an explanatory paragraph following the opinion paragraph
    b. Should be recognized in the auditor's report through the addition of an explanatory paragraph preceding the opinion paragraph
    c. Should be recognized in the auditor's report through the addition of an explanatory paragraph following the opinion paragraph if the correction involved an error in accounting principle
    d. Should be recognized in the auditor's report through the addition of an explanatory paragraph preceding the opinion paragraph if the correction involved an error in accounting principle (Editors, ID: 9281)

22. Which of the following statements is **not** true of both an engagement to review interim financial statements according to PCAOB auditing standards and SSARS?

    a. The objective of a review differs significantly from that of an audit.
    b. A review includes primarily applying analytical procedures and making inquiries.
    c. A review requires obtaining an understanding of the entity's internal control over financial reporting.
    d. The CPA should possess an understanding of the entity's industry, including the accounting principles and practices generally used. (Editors, ID: 9284)

23. During an engagement to review the interim financial statements of a public entity, a CPA becomes aware that several leases that should be capitalized are not capitalized. The CPA considers these leases to be material to the financial statements. The CPA decides to modify the standard review report because management will not capitalize the leases. Under these circumstances, the CPA should

    a. Issue an adverse opinion because of the departure from GAAP.
    b. Express no assurance of any kind on the entity's financial statements.
    c. Disclose the departure from GAAP in a separate paragraph after the limited assurance paragraph of the review report.
    d. Disclose the departure from GAAP in a separate paragraph before the limited assurance paragraph of the review report. (Editors, ID: 9285)

24. When developing the audit strategy and audit plan for an issuer, the auditor should evaluate whether the following matters are important to the company's financial statements and internal control over financial reporting and, if so, how they will affect the auditor's procedures, **except for**

    a. The relative complexity of the company's operations
    b. The response to the auditor's letter of audit inquiry to the client's lawyer for the current audit
    c. Matters relating to the company's business, including its organization, operating characteristics, and capital structure
    d. The extent of recent changes, if any, in the company, its operations, or its internal control over financial reporting (Editors, ID: 89466)

25. When the auditor is relying on controls in a financial statement audit, GAAS and ISA allow the testing of the operating effectiveness of controls that have not changed to be performed at least every third annual audit. How do PCAOB auditing standards differ?

    a. Such controls must be tested every other annual audit.
    b. The auditor should not rely on the testing of controls; substantive procedures alone provide sufficient, appropriate evidence.
    c. Evidence must be obtained that such controls were effective during the entire period of reliance.
    d. The every third annual audit rule only applies to automated controls. (Editors, ID: 89467)

26. Which of the following boards is responsible for promulgating International Standards on Auditing?

    a. International Accounting Standards Board
    b. International Auditing and Assurance Standards Board
    c. International Ethics Standards Board for Accountants
    d. International Auditing and Attestation Standards Board (Editors, ID: 9286)

27. Primary differences between International Standards on Auditing (ISA) and Public Company Accounting Oversight Board (PCAOB) auditing standards include all of the following **except**

    a. PCAOB auditing standards, unlike ISA, do not include a requirement to put changes to the terms of an engagement in writing.
    b. ISA do not have a requirement similar to PCAOB auditing standards for an audit of internal control over financial reporting that is integrated with an audit of financial statements.
    c. ISA, unlike PCAOB auditing standards, do not allow the principal auditor to share responsibility with another auditor and accordingly, do not allow a reference in the audit report to another auditor
    d. There are significant differences per PCAOB auditing standards vs. ISA regarding requirements for written representations from management. (Editors, ID: 9287)

28. Both the AICPA's Statements on Auditing Standards and the PCAOB's auditing standards limit the period of evaluation by an auditor of an entity's ability to continue as a going concern to 12 months from the date of the financial statements. The International Standards on Auditing differ in that they

   a. Require that it be at least 12 months from the date of the release of the audit report
   b. Require that it be at least 12 months from the date of the financial statements, but do not limit it to 12 months
   c. Require that it be at least 12 months from the date of the management representation letter
   d. Require that it be at least 12 months from the date of the financial statements if the previous audit report contained an unqualified opinion, otherwise the evaluation should be for at least 18 months from the date of the financial statements   (Editors, ID: 9288)

   _____

Problem 10-2 SIMULATION: Management Representations in an Audit of Internal Control Over Financial Reporting

The table below lists possible management representations that should be obtained in an audit of internal control over financial reporting. For each item, indicate whether it is appropriate (A) or inappropriate (I).

Management Representations	A / I
1. Acknowledgment of management's responsibility for establishing and maintaining effective internal control over financial reporting.	
2. A statement that management has performed an evaluation and made an assessment of the effectiveness of the company's internal control over financial reporting and specifying the control criteria.	
3. A statement that management agreed to and relied on the auditor's procedures performed during the audits of internal control over financial reporting or the financial statements as part of the basis for management's assessment of the effectiveness of internal control over financial reporting.	
4. Management's conclusion, as set forth in its assessment, about the effectiveness of the company's internal control over financial reporting based on the control criteria for the same period covered by audit.	
5. A statement that management has disclosed to the auditor all deficiencies in the design or operation of internal control over financial reporting identified as part of management's evaluation, including separately disclosing to the auditor all such deficiencies that it believes to be significant deficiencies or material weaknesses in internal control over financial reporting.	
6. A description of any fraud resulting in a material misstatement to the company's financial statements and any other fraud that does not result in a material misstatement to the company's financial statements but involves senior management or management or other employees who have a significant role in the company's internal control over financial reporting.	
7. A statement as to whether control deficiencies identified and communicated to management during previous engagements have been resolved, and specifically identifying any that have not.	
8. A statement as to whether there were, subsequent to the date being reported on, any changes in internal control over financial reporting or other factors that might significantly affect internal control over financial reporting, including any corrective actions taken by management with regard to significant deficiencies and material weaknesses.	

(ID: 89468)

Problem 10-3 SIMULATION: Research

Which citation in the professional standards explains why the audit report on internal control over financial reporting should be dated the same as the audit report on the financial statements for a public company?

[   ]   [   ]   [   ]   (ID: 89469)

Solution 10-1 MULTIPLE-CHOICE ANSWERS

Sarbanes-Oxley Act of 2002

1. (b) It is prohibited for a firm to provide audit services to an issuer if the issuer's CEO, controller, CFO, CAO, or other person serving in the equivalent capacity, was employed in the audit firm and participated in the audit of that issuer during the one-year fiscal period prior to the current audit. The Sarbanes-Oxley Act of 2002 also prohibits a registered public accounting firm from providing audit services to an issuer if the lead audit partner, or the audit partner responsible for reviewing the audit, has performed audit services for that issuer in each of the five previous fiscal years. An auditor may perform other services, such as tax preparation services, for audit clients that are issuers of public securities only with advance approval from the audit committee.

(ID: 8065)

2. (b) The Sarbanes-Oxley Act of 2002 prohibits any registered public accounting firm from providing bookkeeping, financial information system design, and internal audit outsourcing services as well as many other non-audit services to a publicly traded audit client. A firm may, however, perform tax services, for a publicly traded audit client only with the advance approval of the audit committee.

(ID: 8063)

3. (d) The Sarbanes-Oxley Act of 2002 requires that audit committees be directly responsible for appointing, compensating and overseeing the external audit firm.

(ID: 8064)

PCAOB Audit Documentation

4. (d) A complete and final set of audit documentation should be assembled for retention not more than 45, not 60, days after the report release date. According to GAAS, not PCAOB auditing standards, the assembly of the final audit file should be completed within 60 days following the report release date. The alternative answers are all audit documentation requirements for public companies.

(ID: 8268)

5. (b) The office issuing the auditor's report on a public company is not required to obtain records of all internal controls over financial reporting found to be ineffective by other auditors; however, documentation regarding all significant deficiencies and material weaknesses in internal control over financial reporting, including a clear distinction between those two categories is required. In addition to this and the items in the other three answer alternatives, the following documentation related to the work performed by other auditors must be obtained, and reviewed and retained, prior to the report release date by the office issuing the auditor's report: an engagement completion document; a list of significant risks, the auditor's responses, and the results of the auditor's related procedures; sufficient information relating to any significant findings or issues that are inconsistent with or contradict the final conclusions; a schedule of accumulated misstatements, including a description of the nature and cause of each accumulated misstatement, and an evaluation of uncorrected misstatements, including the quantitative and qualitative factors the auditor considered to be relevant to the evaluation; and all matters to be communicated to the audit committee.

(ID: 89470)

PCAOB Audit of ICFR

6. (a) An auditor's procedures performed during either an audit of ICFR or an audit of financial statements are not part of a company's internal control over financial reporting (ICFR). The term *internal control over financial reporting* is defined as a process designed by, or under the supervision of, the company's principal executive and principal financial officers, or persons performing similar functions, and effected by the company's board of directors, management, and other personnel, to provide reasonable assurance regarding the reliability of financial reporting and the preparation of financial statements for external purposes in accordance with GAAP. Answers b, c, and d describe what its policies and procedures pertain to or provide.

(ID: 7938)

7. (d) Lack of information technology (IT) controls is not an inherent limitation of an internal control system. A combination of manual and automated controls may be designed for systems that use IT. All of the other answers are examples of inherent limitations of ICFR. However, because these inherent limitations are known features of the financial reporting process, it is possible to design into the process safeguards to reduce, though not eliminate, this risk.

(ID: 7941)

8. (c) The auditor should consider the effect of compensating controls when determining if a deficiency constitutes a material weakness. The compensating control should be judged effective enough to prevent or detect a material misstatement in order to be considered to have a mitigating effect. Ineffective oversight by the

audit committee of the company's external financial reporting and internal control over financial reporting (ICFR) should be regarded as an indication of a material weakness in ICFR. (ID: 7943)

9. (b)   Issues such as who should sign the letter, the period to be covered by the letter, and when an updated letter should be obtained are the same as in a financial statement audit under GAAS. If comparative financial statements are reported on, the written representations obtained at the completion of the most recent audit should address all periods being reported on. The representations should be made as of the date of the auditor's report. If current management was not present during all periods covered by the auditor's report, the auditor should nevertheless obtain written representations from current management on all such periods.
(ID: 7944)

10. (b)   The auditor's opinion on ICFR is as of a specified date rather than a period of time. When the auditor elects to issue a combined report, the audit opinion will address multiple periods for the financial statements presented, but only the end of the most recent fiscal year for the effectiveness of ICFR. (ID: 7947)

11. (d)   The auditor must communicate, in writing, to the audit committee, all significant deficiencies and material weaknesses identified during the audit. (ID: 7949)

12. (c)   A *material weakness* is a deficiency or combination of deficiencies, in internal control over financial reporting such that there is a reasonable possibility that a material misstatement of the company's financial statements will not be prevented or detected on a timely basis. A *significant deficiency* is a deficiency or a combination of deficiencies, in internal control that is less severe than a material weakness, yet important enough to merit attention by those responsible for oversight of the company's financial reporting. A *deficiency in internal control* exists when the design or operation of a control does not allow management or employees, in the normal course of performing their assigned functions, to prevent or detect misstatements on a timely basis. The various standards don't use the term material deficiency. (ID: 7950)

13. (a)   In planning the audit of ICFR, the auditor should use the same materiality considerations used in planning the audit of a entity's annual financial statements. Materiality judgments are made in the light of surrounding circumstances and necessarily involve both quantitative and qualitative considerations. (ID: 7951)

14. (a)   Inquiry alone does not provide sufficient evidence to support a conclusion about the effectiveness of a control. Some tests, by their nature, provide greater evidence than others. The following tests that an auditor might perform are listed in the order of least to most evidence that they ordinarily produce: inquiry, observation, inspection of relevant documentation, and reperformance of a control. Auditors normally use a mix of these procedures. (ID: 7953)

15. (a)   Judgments about evidence sufficiency and other factors affecting the opinion must be the auditor's. The other statements are true. (ID: 7954)

16. (c)   Controls regarding the company's annual stockholder meeting are not entity-level. Entity-level controls include: controls related to the control environment; controls over management override of other controls; the company's risk assessment processes; centralized processing and controls, including shared service environments; controls to monitor results of operations; controls to monitor other controls, including activities of the internal audit function, the audit committee, and self-assessment programs; controls over the period-end financial reporting process; and policies that address significant business control and risk management practices. (ID: 9920)

PCAOB Previously Reported Material Weakness

17. (c)   According to PCAOB standards, *all* of the following conditions must be met for an auditor to complete this type of engagement: (1) management accepts responsibility for the effectiveness of internal control over financial reporting (ICFR); not over operations; (2) management evaluates the effectiveness of the specific control(s) that it believes addresses the material weakness using the same control criteria that management used for its most recent annual assessment of ICFR and management's stated control objective(s); (3) management asserts that the specific control(s) identified is effective in achieving the stated control objective; (4) management supports its assertion with sufficient evidence, including documentation; and (5) management presents a written report that will accompany the auditor's report that contains all the required elements. (ID: 8269)

18. (d)   The auditor's opinion on whether a previously reported material weakness continues to exist may be expressed as *the material weakness no longer exists*, not *has been eliminated*, or *the material weakness exists*. The PCAOB's guidance does not use the terms *unqualified* opinion and *adverse* opinion, instead, it refers simply to "an opinion" or "the auditor's opinion." The other answer alternatives are true.   (ID: 89465)

PCAOB Consistency

19. (c)   A change in accounting estimate is not a change in accounting principle. Editor note: However, the auditor should evaluate and report on a change in accounting estimate effected by a change in accounting principle like other changes in accounting principle. (A change in accounting estimate effected by a change in accounting principle is a change in accounting estimate that is inseparable from the effect of a related change in accounting principle.) This guidance is the same for issuers (PCAOB audit standards) and nonissuers (GAAS).
(ID: 9282)

20. (d)   Preparation of *pro forma* financial statements is not required.   (ID: 9283)

21. (a)   The correction of a material misstatement in the previously issued financial statements of an *issuer* should be recognized in the auditor's report through the addition of an explanatory paragraph following the opinion paragraph. If the entity was a *non*issuer, the correction should be recognized in the auditor's report through the addition of an explanatory paragraph following the opinion paragraph *if the correction involved an error in accounting principle*. If no element of a principle or its application is included in the error, then its correction would *not* be recognized in the auditor's report for a nonissuer. Examples of such errors are mathematical mistakes, oversights, or misuse of facts that existed at the time the financial statements were originally prepared.
(ID: 9281)

Reviews for Issuers

22. (c)   A review performed in accordance with SSARS does **not** contemplate obtaining an understanding of the entity's internal control.   (ID: 9284)

23. (d)   If the CPA becomes aware that the interim financial information of a public entity is materially affected by a departure from GAAP, the CPA should modify the report. The modification should describe the nature of the departure and, if practicable, should state the effects on the interim financial information. It should *precede* the limited assurance paragraph. If the client was a *non*issuer and the CPA was following the SSARS, the separate paragraph should *follow* the limited assurance paragraph.   (ID: 9285)

PCAOB Risk Assessment Standards

24. (b)   The auditor should evaluate legal or regulatory matters of which the company is aware; however, the response to the auditor's letter of inquiry to the client's lawyer would not be available in the planning stage; it should be dated as close as possible to the date of the audit report. Additional matters for evaluation during the planning stage are knowledge of the company's internal control over financial reporting obtained during other engagements performed by the auditor; matters affecting the industry in which the company operates, such as financial reporting practices, economic conditions, laws and regulations, and technological changes; the auditor's preliminary judgments about materiality, risk, and, in integrated audits, other factors relating to the determination of material weaknesses; control deficiencies previously communicated to the audit committee or management; the type and extent of available evidence related to the effectiveness of the company's internal control over financial reporting; preliminary judgments about the effectiveness of internal control over financial reporting; public information about the company relevant to the evaluation of the likelihood of material financial statement misstatements and the effectiveness of the company's internal control over financial reporting; and knowledge about risks related to the company evaluated as part of the auditor's client acceptance and retention evaluation.   (ID: 89466)

25. (c)   If the auditor plans to assess control risk at less than the maximum by relying on controls, and the nature, extent, and timing of planned substantive procedures are based on that lower assessment, the auditor must obtain evidence that the controls selected for testing are designed effectively and operated effectively during the entire *period of reliance*, i.e., the period being covered by the company's financial statements, or the portion of that period, for which the auditor plans to rely on controls in order to modify the nature, timing, and extent of planned substantive procedures. Rotational testing is not allowed.   (ID: 89467)

ISA

26. (b)   The International Auditing and Assurance Standards Board (IAASB) of the International Federation of Accountants issues International Standards on Auditing (ISA).   (ID: 9286)

27. (d)   There are no substantive differences per PCAOB auditing standards vs. ISA regarding requirements for written representations from management.   (ID: 9287)

28. (b)   The International Standards on Auditing require that the period of the auditor's evaluation of an entity's ability to continue as a going concern be at least 12 months from the date of the financial statements, but do not limit it to 12 months.   (ID: 9288)

_____

PERFORMANCE BY TOPICS

Each category below parallels a topic covered in Chapter 10. Record the number and percentage of questions you answered correctly in each topic.

Sarbanes-Oxley Act of 2002

Question #	Correct	√
1		
2		
3		
# Questions	3	
# Correct		
% Correct		

PCAOB Audit Documentation

Question #	Correct	√
4		
5		
# Questions	2	
# Correct		
% Correct		

PCAOB Audit of ICFR

Question #	Correct	√
6		
7		
8		
9		
10		
11		
12		
13		
14		
15		
16		
# Questions	11	
# Correct		
% Correct		

PCAOB Previously Reported Material Weakness

Question #	Correct	√
17		
18		
# Questions	2	
# Correct		
% Correct		

PCAOB Consistency

Question #	Correct	√
19		
20		
21		
# Questions	3	
# Correct		
% Correct		

Reviews for Issuers

Question #	Correct	√
22		
23		
# Questions	2	
# Correct		
% Correct		

PCAOB Risk Assessment Standards

Question #	Correct	√
24		
25		
# Questions	2	
# Correct		
% Correct		

ISA

Question #	Correct	√
26		
27		
28		
# Questions	3	
# Correct		
% Correct		

_____

Solution 10-2 SIMULATION ANSWER: Management Representations in an Audit of Internal Control Over Financial Reporting

Management Representations	A / I
1. Acknowledgment of management's responsibility for establishing and maintaining effective internal control over financial reporting.	A
2. A statement that management has performed an evaluation and made an assessment of the effectiveness of the company's internal control over financial reporting and specifying the control criteria.	A
3. A statement that management agreed to and relied on the auditor's procedures performed during the audits of internal control over financial reporting or the financial statements as part of the basis for management's assessment of the effectiveness of internal control over financial reporting.	I
4. Management's conclusion, as set forth in its assessment, about the effectiveness of the company's internal control over financial reporting based on the control criteria for the same period covered by audit.	I
5. A statement that management has disclosed to the auditor all deficiencies in the design or operation of internal control over financial reporting identified as part of management's evaluation, including separately disclosing to the auditor all such deficiencies that it believes to be significant deficiencies or material weaknesses in internal control over financial reporting.	A
6. A description of any fraud resulting in a material misstatement to the company's financial statements and any other fraud that does not result in a material misstatement to the company's financial statements but involves senior management or management or other employees who have a significant role in the company's internal control over financial reporting.	A
7. A statement as to whether control deficiencies identified and communicated to management during previous engagements have been resolved, and specifically identifying any that have not.	I
8. A statement as to whether there were, subsequent to the date being reported on, any changes in internal control over financial reporting or other factors that might significantly affect internal control over financial reporting, including any corrective actions taken by management with regard to significant deficiencies and material weaknesses.	A

1. A

Self-explanatory

2. A

Self-explanatory

3. I

A statement that management *did not use*, not *agreed to and relied on*, the auditor's procedures performed during the audits of internal control over financial reporting or the financial statements as part of the basis for management's assessment of the effectiveness of internal control over financial reporting should be included.

4. I

Management's conclusion, as set forth in its assessment, about the effectiveness of the company's internal control over financial reporting based on the control criteria *as of a specified date*, not *for the same period covered by audit* should be included.

5. A

Self-explanatory

6. A

Self-explanatory

7. I

A statement as to whether control deficiencies identified and communicated to *the audit committee*, not *management*, during previous engagements have been resolved, and specifically identifying any that have not.

8. A

Self-explanatory

(ID: 89468)

_____

Solution 10-3 SIMULATION ANSWER: Research

PCAOB	AS	5	89

(ID: 89469)

.89   The auditor should date the audit report no earlier than the date on which the auditor has obtained sufficient appropriate evidence to support the auditor's opinion. Because the auditor cannot audit internal control over financial reporting without also auditing the financial statements, the reports should be dated the same.

_____

CHAPTER 11

OTHER TYPES OF REPORTS

CHAPTER 11

OTHER TYPES OF REPORTS

I. **Engagement to Report on Supplementary Information (AU 551)**

  A.   **Overview**

        1.   **Definition of Supplementary Information** Supplementary information is defined as information presented outside the basic financial statements, excluding required supplementary information. It is not considered necessary for the financial statements to be fairly presented in accordance with the applicable financial reporting framework. Such information may be presented in a document containing the audited financial statements or separate from the financial statements. Examples include:

            • Additional details or explanations of items in or related to the basic financial statements

            • Consolidating information

            • Historical summaries of items extracted from the basic financial statements

            • Statistical data

            • Other material, some of which may be from sources outside the accounting system or outside the entity

        2.   **Engagement Objective** Evaluate the presentation of the supplementary information and report on whether it is fairly stated, in all material respects, in relation to the financial statements as a whole.

        3.   **Required Conditions** The auditor should determine that all of the following conditions are met.

           a.   The supplementary information was derived from, and relates directly to, the underlying accounting and other records used to prepare the financial statements.

           b.   The supplementary information relates to the same period as the financial statements.

           c.   The financial statements were audited, and the auditor served as the principal auditor in that engagement.

           d.   Neither an adverse opinion nor a disclaimer of opinion was issued on the financial statements.

           e.   The supplementary information will accompany the entity's audited financial statements, or such audited financial statements will be made readily available by the entity.

               Editor note: Audited financial statements are deemed to be readily available if a third-party user can obtain the audited financial statements without any further action by the entity. For example, financial statements on an entity's website may be considered readily available, but being available upon request is not considered readily available.

B.   Management's Responsibilities
The auditor should obtain the agreement of management that it acknowledges and understands its responsibility:

1.   For the preparation of the supplementary information in accordance with the applicable criteria

2.   To provide the auditor with certain written representations

3.   To include the audit report on the supplementary information in any document that contains the supplementary information and that indicates that the auditor has reported on such supplementary information

4.   To present the supplementary information with the audited financial statements or, if the supplementary information will not be presented with the audited financial statements, to make the audited financial statements readily available to the intended users of the supplementary information no later than the date of issuance by the entity of the supplementary information and the audit report thereon.

C.   Procedures

1.   **Written Management Representations**   The auditor should obtain written representations from management:

   a.   That it acknowledges its responsibility for the presentation of the supplementary information in accordance with the applicable criteria

   b.   That it believes the supplementary information, including its form and content, is fairly presented in accordance with the applicable criteria

   c.   That the methods of measurement or presentation have not changed from those used in the prior period or, if they have, the reasons for such changes

   d.   About any significant assumptions or interpretations underlying the measurement or presentation of the supplementary information

   e.   That when the supplementary information is not presented with the audited financial statements, management will make the audited financial statements readily available to the intended users of the supplementary information no later than the date of issuance by the entity of the supplementary information and the audit report thereon

2.   **Other Procedures**   In addition to the procedures performed during the audit of the financial statements and obtaining the preceding written representations from management, the auditor should perform the following procedures using the same materiality level used in the audit of the financial statements:

   a.   Inquire of management about the purpose of the supplementary information and the criteria used by management to prepare it, such as an applicable financial reporting framework, criteria established by a regulator, a contractual agreement, or other requirements.

   b.   Determine whether the form and content of the supplementary information complies with the applicable criteria.

   c.   Obtain an understanding about the methods of preparing the supplementary information and determine whether these methods have changed from those used in the prior period and, if so, the reasons for such changes.

      d.   Compare and reconcile the supplementary information to the underlying accounting and other records used in preparing the financial statements or to the financial statements themselves.

      e.   Inquire of management about any significant assumptions or interpretations underlying the measurement or presentation of the supplementary information.

      f.   Evaluate the appropriateness and completeness of the supplementary information.

    Editor note: With respect to the supplementary information, the auditor is **not** required to obtain a separate understanding of the entity's internal control or to assess fraud risk.

3.   **Subsequent Events** The auditor has no responsibility for the consideration of subsequent events with respect to the supplementary information. However, if information comes to the auditor's attention prior to the release of the audit report on the financial statements regarding subsequent events that affect the financial statements, the auditor should apply the relevant requirements in AU 560, *Subsequent Events*. If information comes to the auditor's attention subsequent to the release of the audit report on the financial statements regarding facts that may have existed at that date, which might have affected the report had the auditor been aware of such facts, the auditor should apply the relevant requirements in AU 561, *Subsequent Discovery of Facts Existing at the Date of the Auditor's Report*.

D.   **Reporting**

1.   **Reporting When Supplementary Information Presented With Financial Statements** The auditor should report on the supplementary information in either

- An explanatory paragraph **following** the opinion paragraph in the audit report on the financial statements or

- A separate report on the supplementary information

The explanatory paragraph or separate report should include the following elements:

      a.   A statement that the audit was conducted for the purpose of forming an opinion on the financial statements as a whole.

      b.   A statement that the supplementary information is presented for purposes of additional analysis and is not a required part of the financial statements.

      c.   A statement that the supplementary information is the responsibility of management and was derived from, and relates directly to, the underlying accounting and other records used to prepare the financial statements.

      d.   A statement that the supplementary information has been subjected to the auditing procedures applied in the audit of the financial statements and certain additional procedures, including comparing and reconciling such information directly to the underlying accounting and other records used to prepare the financial statements or to the financial statements themselves and other additional procedures, in accordance with auditing standards generally accepted in the United States of America.

      e.   If the auditor issues an unqualified opinion on the financial statements and has concluded that the supplementary information is fairly stated, in all material respects, in relation to the financial statements as a whole, a statement (in the form of an opinion) to that effect.

Exhibit 1 ▶ Supplementary Information Explanatory Paragraph / Unqualified Opinion Issued on Financial Statements & Supplementary Information Fairly Stated

Our audit was conducted for the purpose of forming an opinion on the financial statements as a whole. The [*identify accompanying supplementary information*] is presented for purposes of additional analysis and is not a required part of the financial statements. Such information is the responsibility of management and was derived from and relates directly to the underlying accounting and other records used to prepare the financial statements. The information has been subjected to the auditing procedures applied in the audit of the financial statements and certain additional procedures, including comparing and reconciling such information directly to the underlying accounting and other records used to prepare the financial statements or to the financial statements themselves, and other additional procedures in accordance with auditing standards generally accepted in the United States of America. In our opinion, the information is fairly stated in all material respects in relation to the financial statements as a whole.

    f.   If the auditor issues a qualified opinion on the financial statements and the qualification has an effect on the supplementary information, a statement that, in the auditor's opinion, except for the effects on the supplementary information of [*describe reason for qualification of the auditor's opinion on the financial statements and reference the explanatory paragraph*], such information is fairly stated, in all material respects, in relation to the financial statements as a whole

2.   **Separate Report on Supplementary Information When Supplementary Information Is Not Presented With Financial Statements** When the audited financial statements are not presented with the supplementary information, the auditor should report on the supplementary information in a separate report. This report should include, in addition to the preceding elements:

- A reference to the report on the financial statements

- The date of that report

- The nature of the opinion expressed on the financial statements

- Any report modifications

The auditor may consider restricting the use of a separate report on supplementary information to the appropriate specified parties to avoid potential misinterpretation or misunderstanding of the supplementary information that is not presented with the financial statements.

Exhibit 2 ▶ Supplementary Information Separate Report / Unqualified Opinion Issued on Financial Statements & Supplementary Information Fairly Stated

We have audited the financial statements of XYZ Entity as of and for the year ended June 30, 20X1, and have issued our report thereon dated [*date of the audit report on the financial statements*] which contained an unqualified opinion on those financial statements. Our audit was performed for the purpose of forming an opinion on the financial statements as a whole. The [*identify supplementary information*] is presented for the purposes of additional analysis and is not a required part of the financial statements. Such information is the responsibility of management and was derived from and relates directly to the underlying accounting and other records used to prepare the financial statements. The information has been subjected to the auditing procedures applied in the audit of the financial statements and certain additional procedures, including comparing and reconciling such information directly to the underlying accounting and other records used to prepare the financial statements or to the financial statements themselves, and other additional procedures in accordance with auditing standards generally accepted in the United States of America. In our opinion, the information is fairly stated in all material respects in relation to the financial statements as a whole.

3. **Adverse Opinion or Disclaimer of Opinion on Financial Statements Precludes Reporting on Supplementary Information** When the audit report on the financial statements contains an adverse opinion or a disclaimer of opinion, the auditor is precluded from expressing an opinion on whether supplementary information is fairly stated. When permitted by law or regulation, the auditor may withdraw from an engagement to report on the supplementary information. If the auditor does not withdraw, the audit report on the supplementary information should state that because of the significance of the matter disclosed in the audit report, it is inappropriate to, and the auditor does not, express an opinion on the supplementary information.

    Exhibit 3 ▶ Explanatory Paragraph for No Opinion on Supplementary Information Due to Adverse Opinion or Disclaimer of Opinion Issued on Financial Statements

    > We were engaged for the purpose of forming an opinion on the basic financial statements as a whole. The [*identify accompanying supplementary information*] is presented for the purposes of additional analysis and is not a required part of the financial statements. Because of the significance of the matter described above [*the auditor may describe the basis for the adverse opinion or disclaimer of opinion*], it is inappropriate to and we do not express an opinion on the supplementary information referred to above.

4. **Date of Audit Report on Supplementary Information** The date of the audit report on the supplementary information should not be earlier than the date on which the auditor completed the procedures required to render an opinion on it.

5. **Supplementary Information Materially Misstated** The auditor should discuss the matter with management and propose appropriate revision of the supplementary information.

    If management does **not** revise the supplementary information, the auditor should either:

    a. Modify the auditor's opinion on the supplementary information and describe the misstatement in the audit report (this does not affect the opinion on the financial statements) or

    b. If a separate report is being issued on the supplementary information, withhold the audit report on the supplementary information

II. Special Reports (AU 623)

A.   Special Purpose Reports
Auditor's reports that apply only to (1) financial statements prepared in conformity with OCBOA; (2) specified elements, accounts, or items of a financial statement; (3) compliance with aspects of contractual agreements or regulatory requirements related to audited financial statements; (4) financial presentations to comply with contractual agreements or regulatory provisions that result in either incomplete presentations or a presentation that is not in conformity with GAAP or OCBOA; or (5) financial information presented in prescribed forms or schedules that require a prescribed form of auditor's report.

B.   Reports on Financial Statements Prepared in Conformity With OCBOA
GAAS applies whenever an auditor conducts an audit of and reports on any financial statement.

Exhibit 4 ▶ Auditor's Report on Cash Basis Financial Statements

---

Independent Auditor's Report*

We have audited the accompanying statements of assets and liabilities arising from cash transactions of XYZ Company as of December 31, 20X2 and 20X1, and the related statements of revenue collected and expenses paid for the years then ended. These financial statements are the responsibility of the company's management. Our responsibility is to express an opinion on these financial statements based on our audits.

We conducted our audits in accordance with US generally accepted auditing standards. Those standards require that we plan and perform the audit to obtain reasonable assurance about whether the financial statements are free of material misstatement. An audit includes examining, on a test basis, evidence supporting the amounts and disclosures in the financial statements. An audit also includes assessing the accounting principles used and significant estimates made by management, as well as evaluating the overall financial statement presentation. We believe that our audits provide a reasonable basis for our opinion.

As described in Note X, these financial statements were prepared on the basis of cash receipts and disbursements, which is a comprehensive basis of accounting other than generally accepted accounting principles.

In our opinion, the financial statements referred to above present fairly, in all material respects, the assets and liabilities arising from cash transactions of XYZ Company as of December 31, 20X2 and 20X1, and the revenue collected and expenses paid during the years then ended, on the basis of accounting described in Note X.

*   This report should be addressed, signed, and dated as previously discussed. For the sake of brevity, these <u>elements</u> are omitted from this and most other exhibits of reports in this chapter.

---

1.   **OCBOA** A comprehensive basis other than GAAP is (a) a basis that is used to comply with the requirements or financial provisions of a government regulatory agency, but only for filing with that agency (e.g., state insurance commission rules for insurance companies); (b) a basis used (or expected to be used) for filing the client's income tax return for the period covered by the financial statements; (c) the cash receipts and disbursements basis (including modifications to cash basis that have substantial support); and (d) a definite set of criteria having substantial support that is applied to all material financial statement items, (e.g., price-level basis of accounting).

2.   **Statement Titles** "Balance sheet," "statement of financial position," "statement of income," "statement of operations," "statement of cash flows," etc., apply only to statements prepared in conformity with GAAP. Suitable titles should be given to financial statements prepared in conformity with a comprehensive basis of accounting other than GAAP. For example, an appropriate title for a cash basis financial statement might be "statement of assets and liabilities arising from cash transactions," and an appropriate title for a financial statement prepared on a statutory basis might be "statement of income—statutory basis."

If the financial statement titles are inappropriate, the auditor should express a qualified opinion, referencing an explanatory paragraph added before the opinion paragraph.

3.   **OCBOA Report**

    a.   **Similarities With Standard Audit Report** Elements the same as the standard audit report are: (1) a title that includes the word "independent"; (2) paragraph one, an introductory paragraph; (3) paragraph two, a scope paragraph; (4) the firm's signature; and (5) a date.

    b.   **Paragraph Three** States: (1) the basis of presentation, and refers to the note that describes the basis, and (2) that the basis of presentation is a comprehensive basis of accounting other than GAAP.

    c.   **Paragraph Four** Expresses the auditor's opinion on the financial statements in accordance with the OCBOA basis.

    d.   **Restrictive Paragraph** This paragraph is used when the financial statements are prepared in conformity with the requirements of a government regulatory agency. It states that the distribution of the report is restricted to those within the entity and for filing with the regulatory agency.

C.   **Reports on Specified Elements, Accounts, or Items of a Financial Statement**
Examples include rentals, royalties, a profit participation, or a provision for income taxes.

Exhibit 5 ▶ Report Relating to Royalties

<u>Independent Auditor's Report</u>

We have audited the accompanying schedule of royalties applicable to engine production of the Q Division of XYZ Corporation for the year ended December 31, 20X2, under the terms of a license agreement dated May 14, 20X0, between ABC Company and XYZ Corporation. This schedule is the responsibility of XYZ Corporation's management. Our responsibility is to express an opinion on this schedule based on our audit.

We conducted our audit in accordance with US generally accepted auditing standards. Those standards require that we plan and perform the audit to obtain reasonable assurance about whether the schedule of royalties is free of material misstatement. An audit includes examining, on a test basis, evidence supporting the amounts and disclosures in the schedule. An audit also includes assessing the accounting principles used and significant estimates made by management, as well as evaluating the overall schedule presentation. We believe that our audit provides a reasonable basis for our opinion.

We have been informed that, under XYZ Corporation's interpretation of the agreement referred to in the first paragraph, royalties were based on the number of engines produced after giving effect to a reduction for production retirements that were scrapped, but without a reduction for field returns that were scrapped, even though the field returns were replaced with new engines without charge to customers.

In our opinion, the schedule of royalties referred to above presents fairly, in all material respects, the number of engines produced by the Q Division of XYZ Corporation during the year ended December 31, 20X2, and the amount of royalties applicable thereto, under the license agreement referred to above.

This report is intended solely for the information and use of the boards of directors and management of XYZ Corporation and ABC Company and should not be used for any other purpose.

---

1. **GAAS** The ten GAAS are applicable with the exception of the first standard of reporting which is applicable only when the specified elements, accounts, or items are intended to be presented in conformity with GAAP.

2. **Materiality** An engagement to express an opinion on one or more specified elements, accounts, or items (specified items) may be undertaken as a separate engagement or in conjunction with an audit of the financial statements. An opinion is being expressed on each of the specified items encompassed by the auditor's report, so materiality must be related to each of them. Therefore, the audit will usually be more extensive in regard to the specified items than it would be if the only objective were to express an opinion on the financial statements taken as a whole. The auditor must consider any interrelationships among the specified items being reported on and other items in the financial statements.

3. **Piecemeal Opinion** When the auditor has expressed an adverse opinion or disclaimed an opinion on the financial statements taken as a whole, the auditor should **not** report on specified items that are included in those statements if the effect is to express a piecemeal opinion. The auditor is able to report on one or more specified items provided that a major portion of the financial statements is not involved. This report should be presented separately from the report on the financial statements.

4. **Conditions for Report Restriction** If the presentation of the specified items is not in conformity with GAAP or OCBOA due to compliance with a contract or agreement, a separate paragraph should be added to the report restricting its use.

D. **Reports on Compliance With Contracts or Regulations Related to Audited Financial Statements**

Contractual agreements sometimes require entities to furnish compliance reports prepared by independent auditors (e.g., a loan agreement may contain provisions relating to payments made to a sinking fund and maintenance of a specified current ratio).

Exhibit 6 ▶ Compliance With Contractual Provisions Given in a Separate Report

We have audited, in accordance with auditing standards generally accepted in the United States of America, the balance sheet of XYZ Company as of December 31, 20X2, and the related statements of income, retained earnings, and cash flows for the year then ended, and have issued our report thereon dated February 16, 20X3.

In connection with our audit, nothing came to our attention that caused us to believe that the company failed to comply with the terms, covenants, provisions or conditions of Sections XX to XX, inclusive, of the Indenture dated July 21, 20X0, with ABC Bank. However, it should be noted that our audit was not directed primarily toward obtaining knowledge of such noncompliance.

This report is intended solely for the information and use of the board of directors and management of XYZ Company and ABC Bank and is not intended to be and should not be used by anyone other than those specified parties.

1. **Negative Assurance** The auditor normally gives negative assurance regarding compliance with agreements. This may be done by using a separate report or it may be added to the report accompanying the financial statements. Negative assurance should be given only when the auditor has audited the financial statements to which the agreements or requirements relate and the report's use will be restricted to the named parties. The assurance should not extend to covenants that relate to matters that have not been subjected to audit procedures during the audit of the financial statements. Also, if the auditor has expressed an adverse opinion or disclaimed an opinion on the financial statements, no such assurance should be given.

2. **Report** The auditor's report includes the following:

   a. **Title, Signature & Date** A title that includes the word "independent."

b. **Paragraph One** The financial statements were audited in accordance with GAAS and includes the date of the auditor's report on those financial statements. Any departure from the standard report should also be disclosed.

c. **Paragraph Two** A reference to the specific covenants or paragraphs of the agreement, provides negative assurance relative to the compliance with the applicable covenants insofar as they relate to accounting matters, and specifies that the negative assurance is being given in connection with the audit of the financial statements.

d. **Paragraph Three** A description and source of significant interpretations, if any, made by the company's management relating to the provisions of a relevant agreement.

e. **Paragraph Four** Restricts the use of the report to those within the entity and the parties to the contract or agreement or for filing with the regulatory agency.

E. **Incomplete Presentation Otherwise in Conformity With GAAP or OCBOA**
This might include a situation where a buy-sell agreement requires that assets and liabilities be presented in accordance with GAAP, but it only includes those items that will be sold and transferred under the agreement rather than all the entity's assets and liabilities. This situation constitutes a financial statement in the limited circumstances addressed by AU 623.

1. **Presentation** The presentation should be titled appropriately so that no confusion exists (terms such as *balance sheet, income statement, statement of cash flows,* should **not** be used). Disclosures should be made similar to those provided in a complete set of financial statements.

2. **Materiality** Materiality is in relation to the presentation taken as a whole.

3. **Report** The audit report includes an introductory paragraph, a scope paragraph, an explanatory paragraph, an opinion paragraph, and a paragraph restricting the use of the report.

   a. The introductory paragraph identifies the financial information being reported on and states the responsibilities of management and the auditor.

   b. The explanatory paragraph (1) explains what the financial presentation is intended to present and refers the reader to a note that describes the basis of the financial presentation, and (2) states that the financial presentation is not intended to be a complete set of financial information in accordance with GAAP.

F. **Statements Prepared on a Prescribed Basis Not in Conformity With GAAP or OCBOA**
An auditor can be associated with financial statements using specified reporting requirements. For example, a loan application may call for financial statements, with the inventory to be valued at sales price; or in an acquisition agreement, the financial statements may request that fixed assets and inventories be measured at their liquidation values.

1. **Materiality** The auditor considers the adequacy of the disclosures associated with the financial statements. Materiality is considered at the financial statement level.

2. **Report** The auditor's report includes the following:

   a. A responsibility paragraph

   b. A scope paragraph

   c. An explanatory paragraph similar to an incomplete presentation otherwise in conformity with GAAP

   d. A paragraph that includes a description and the source of significant interpretations made by management

e. An opinion paragraph

f. A paragraph restricting the distribution of the report

G. Financial Information Presented in Prescribed Forms or Schedules
Regulatory bodies, government agencies, and others sometimes use printed forms or schedules that prescribe the form of the auditor's report. A problem arises if the prescribed report does not conform to the applicable professional reporting standards of the public accounting profession (e.g., calling for assertions that are not consistent with the auditor's function).

1. Procedures Insertion of additional wording can make some report forms acceptable; other report forms require complete revision.

2. Assertions If a printed report calls for an assertion the auditor believes is not justified, the auditor should either reword the form or attach a separate report.

III. Letters for Underwriters

A. **Filings Under Federal Securities Statutes (AU 711)**
The financial representations contained in documents filed with the SEC are the responsibility and representations of management. However, the Securities Act of 1933 imposes responsibility on an auditor for false or misleading financial statements (or for omissions that make them misleading) in an effective registration statement prepared or certified by the CPA.

1. **Auditor's Defense** The auditor must prove that (a) there were reasonable grounds to believe (and the auditor did believe) that the statements in the registration statement were true and that there was no omission of a material fact at the date of the registration statement or (b) that the part of the registration statement that is in question did not fairly represent the auditor's statement as an expert or was not fairly copied or extracted from the report or valuation.

- **Reasonableness Standard** The standard of reasonableness is that standard which would be used by a prudent person in the management of his or her own property.

2. **Date** The auditor's responsibility extends to the effective date of the registration statement.

3. **Use of Name** The auditor should be sure his or her name is not used in a way that may indicate that the auditor's responsibility is greater than it really is.

4. **Subsequent Events Procedures in 1933 Act Filings** The auditor should extend subsequent event procedures from the date of the report to the effective date of the registration statement. The auditor can rely, for the most part, on inquiries of responsible officials and employees. The auditor should perform the auditing procedures used to assess the existence of subsequent events (e.g., inquiry of management, reading of minutes, etc.) and, in addition, should (a) read the entire prospectus and other pertinent portions of the registration statement, and (b) obtain written confirmation from officers and other executives regarding subsequent events that have a material effect on the audited financial statements included in the registration statement or which require disclosure in order to keep the statements from being misleading.

5. **Response to Subsequent Events & Subsequently Discovered Facts** If the auditor discovers either (a) subsequent events requiring adjustment or disclosure or (b) facts existing at the time of the report which might have affected the report had the auditor known about them, the auditor should do the following:

a. Ask management to revise the statements and/or add the required disclosures.

b. If management refuses, the auditor should modify the report accordingly and consider obtaining advice from legal counsel.

6. **Reports Based on a Review of Interim Financial Information** The SEC requires that when a report based on a review of interim financial information is presented or incorporated in a registration statement by reference, a clarification should be made that the review report is not a "report" or "part" of the registration statement within the meaning of Sections 7 and 11 of the Securities Act of 1933.

7. **Two or More Auditors** A registration statement filed with the SEC may contain the reports of two or more auditors for different periods. An auditor who has not audited the financial statements for the most recent period has a responsibility for events that have a material effect on the financial statements the auditor reported on that occurred during the period running from the date of the report until the effective date of the registration statement. The auditor generally should (a) read the pertinent portions of the prospectus and registration statement and (b) obtain a letter of representation from the successor auditor about subsequent events which the successor has become aware.

B. **Letters for Underwriters & Certain Other Requesting Parties (AU 634)**
AU 634 provides guidance to accountants for reporting on the results of and performing engagements to issue letters for underwriters and certain other requesting parties, commonly referred to as comfort letters, in connection with financial statements and financial statement schedules contained in registration statements filed with the SEC under the Securities Act of 1933. Comfort letters are not required under the Act, and copies are not filed with the SEC. It is nonetheless a common condition of an underwriting agreement in connection with the offering for sale of securities registered with the SEC under the Act that the accountants are to furnish a comfort letter.

1. **Purpose** Section 11 of the Act provides that underwriters, among others, could be liable if any part of a registration statement contains material omissions or misstatements. The Act also provides for an affirmative defense for underwriters if it can be demonstrated that, after an investigation, the underwriter has reasonable grounds to believe that there were no material omissions or misstatements. An accountant's issuance of a comfort letter is one procedure used to establish that an underwriter has conducted a reasonable investigation.

2. **Representations** Using a statutory due diligence defense under Section 11 of the Act, a comfort letter may be addressed to parties other than a named underwriter, only when a law firm or attorney for the requesting party issues a written opinion to the accountants that states that such party has a due diligence defense under Section 11 of the Act. AU 634 precludes the accountant from providing a comfort letter if an appropriate representation letter is not provided. An attorney's letter indicating that a party "may" be deemed to be an underwriter, or has liability substantially equivalent to that of an underwriter under the securities laws, would not meet this requirement. If the requesting party, in a securities offering registered pursuant to the Act, other than a named underwriter, cannot provide such a letter, he or she must provide a representation letter for the accountant to provide him or her with a comfort letter. The letter should be addressed to the accountants, signed by the requesting party, and contain a due diligence process paragraph.

Exhibit 7 ▶ Representation Letter Excerpt

> This review process, applied to the information relating to the issuer, is substantially consistent with the due diligence review process that we would perform if this placement of securities were being registered pursuant to the Securities Act of 1933. We are knowledgeable with respect to the due diligence review process that would be performed if this placement of securities were being registered pursuant to the Act.

3. **Limitations** In requesting comfort letters, underwriters generally are seeking assistance on matters of importance to them. They wish to perform a "reasonable investigation," as a defense against possible claims under Section 11, of financial and accounting data that has not been "expertized." Accountants normally are willing to assist underwriters, but the assistance accountants can provide by way of comfort letters is subject to limitations. One limitation is that independent accountants properly can comment in their professional capacity only on matters to which their professional expertise is substantially relevant. Another limitation is that procedures short of an audit, such as those contemplated in a comfort letter, provide the accountants with a basis for expressing, at the most, negative assurance.

4. **Draft** Because the underwriter will expect the accountants to furnish a comfort letter of a scope to be specified in the underwriting agreement, a draft of that agreement should be furnished to the accountants so that they can indicate whether they will be able to furnish a letter in acceptable form. It is a desirable practice for the accountants, promptly after they have received the draft of the agreement, to prepare a draft of the form of the letter they expect to furnish. The draft should deal with all matters to be covered in the final letter.

5. **Prohibited** Accountants should not comment on matters merely because they are capable of reading, counting, measuring, or performing other functions that might be applicable. Examples of matters that, unless subjected to the controls over financial reporting, should not be commented on by accountants include the square footage of facilities and backlog

information. Accountants should not comment on tables, statistics, and other financial information relating to an unaudited period, unless they have obtained knowledge of the client's internal control over financial reporting (comparable to that obtained during an audit). In addition, accountants should not comment on information subject to legal interpretation.

6. **Additional Letters** Accountants may not issue any additional letters or reports to the underwriter or the other requesting parties, in connection with the offering or placement of securities, in which the accountants comment on items for which commenting is otherwise precluded by AU 634, such as square footage of facilities.

7. **Format & Content**

   a.   **Permissible Topics** Generally, accountants may comment only with respect to information (1) obtained from accounting records that are subject to the entity's controls over financial reporting and that is expressed in dollars (or percentages derived from such dollar amounts), or (2) derived directly from accounting records by analysis or computation.

      Accountants also may comment on quantitative information that has been obtained from an accounting record, if the information is subject to the same controls over financial reporting as the dollar amounts. Permissible topics include the following:

      (1)   The independence of the accountants

      (2)   Whether the audited financial statements and financial statement schedules included in the registration statement comply as to form in all material respects with the applicable accounting requirements of the Act and the related published rules and regulations

      (3)   Unaudited financial statements, condensed interim financial information, capsule financial information, pro forma financial information, financial forecasts, and changes in selected financial statement items during a period subsequent to the date and period of the latest registration statement

      (4)   Tables, statistics, and other financial information included in the registration statement

      (5)   Negative assurance as to whether certain nonfinancial statement information complies as to form with Regulation S-K, if the information is (a) derived from the accounting records subject to the entity's controls over financial reporting and (b) capable of evaluation against SEC criteria; accountants may perform procedures and report findings with respect to conformity with Regulation S-K

   b.   **Date** The letter ordinarily is dated on or shortly before the date on which the registration statement becomes effective.

   c.   **Addressee** The letter should not be addressed or given to any parties other than the client and the named underwriter, broker-dealer, financial intermediary, or buyer or seller. The appropriate addressee is the intermediary who has negotiated the agreement with the client, and with whom the accountants will deal in discussions regarding the scope and sufficiency of the letter.

   d.   **Explanatory Paragraph** When the report on the audited financial statements and financial statement schedules included in the registration statement departs from the standard report, the accountants should refer to that fact in the comfort letter and discuss the subject matter of the paragraph.

   e.   **Reiterate Audit Opinion** The underwriter occasionally requests the accountants to repeat in the comfort letter their report on the audited financial statements included in the registration statement. Because of the special significance of the date of the accountants' report, the accountants should **not** repeat their opinion. The underwriter sometimes requests negative assurance regarding the accountants' report. Because accountants have a statutory responsibility with respect to their opinion as of the effective date of a registration statement, and because the additional significance, if any, of negative assurance is unclear and such assurance may therefore give rise to misunderstanding, accountants should **not** give negative assurance.

f. **Optional** Accountants may refer (in the introductory paragraphs of the comfort letter) to the fact that they have issued reports on (1) condensed financial statements that are derived from audited financial statements; (2) selected financial data; (3) interim financial information; (4) pro forma financial information; (5) a financial forecast; and (6) management's discussion and analysis. Any optional references should be to previously-issued accountants' reports. If the reports were not included (or incorporated by reference) in the registration statement, they may be attached to the comfort letter. The accountants should not repeat previously-issued reports, otherwise imply that they are reporting as of the date of the comfort letter, or imply that they assume responsibility for the sufficiency of the procedures for the underwriter's purposes. For certain information on which they have reported, accountants may agree to comment regarding compliance with SEC criteria. Accountants should not mention reports issued in accordance with AU 325, *Communicating Internal Control Related Matters Identified in an Audit,* or any restricted-use reports issued in connection with procedures performed on the client's internal control in accordance with AT 501.

g. *Pro Forma* **Information** Accountants should **not** comment in a comfort letter on *pro forma* financial information unless they have an appropriate level of knowledge of the accounting and financial reporting practices of the entity. This ordinarily would have been obtained by the accountant's audit or review of historical financial statements of the entity for the most recent annual or interim period for which the pro forma financial information is presented.

h. **Compliance** Accountants may be requested to express an opinion on whether the financial statements covered by their report comply as to form with the pertinent SEC accounting requirements. Accountants may provide positive assurance on compliance as to form with SEC requirements only with respect to those rules and regulations applicable to the form and content of financial statements and financial statement schedules that they have audited. Accountants are limited to providing negative assurance on compliance as to form on unaudited statements or schedules. If there is a material departure from SEC criteria, it must be disclosed.

Exhibit 8 ▶ Sample Paragraph Regarding Compliance With SEC Criteria

> In our opinion (include the phrase *except as disclosed in the registration statement,* if applicable) the (*identify the financial statements and financial statement schedules*) audited by us and included (incorporated by reference) in the registration statement comply as to form in all material respects with the applicable accounting requirements of the Act and the related rules and regulations adopted by the SEC.

8. **Subsequently Discovered Matters** Accountants who discover matters that are not mentioned in the draft letter, that may require mention in the final comfort letter, (e.g., changes, increases, or decreases in specified items not disclosed in the registration statement) will need to discuss them with their client so that consideration can be given to whether disclosure should be made in the registration statement. If disclosure is not to be made, the accountants should inform the client that the matters will be mentioned in the comfort letter and should suggest that the underwriter be informed promptly.

IV. Review of Interim Financial Information of Nonissuers (AU 722)

    A. Overview

        1. Definitions

            a. Interim Financial Information *Interim financial information* means financial information or statements covering a period less than a full year or for a 12-month period ending on a date other than the entity's fiscal year-end. Interim financial information may be condensed or in the form of a complete set of financial statements.

            b. Applicable Financial Reporting Framework *Applicable financial reporting framework* means a set of criteria used to determine measurement, recognition, presentation, and disclosure of all material items appearing in the financial statements; for example, US GAAP, International Financial Reporting Standards or comprehensive bases of accounting other than GAAP.

        2. Modified GAAS The three general standards of GAAS are applicable to reviews of interim financial information conducted in accordance with AU 722, *Interim Financial Information*. AU 722 provides guidance on the application of the fieldwork and reporting standards to a review of interim financial information, to the extent those standards are relevant.

        3. Applicability AU 722 is applicable to the review of interim financial information of nonissuers. (Guidance for the review of public companies' interim financial information resides in the auditing standards of the Public Company Accounting Oversight Board.) An accountant may conduct, in accordance with AU 722, a review of interim financial information if the following conditions are met.

            a. The entity's latest annual financial statements have been audited;

            b. The CPA has either

                (1) Been engaged to audit the entity's current year financial statements or

                (2) Audited the latest annual financial statements and although an audit of the current year financial statements is expected, the appointment of another auditor to audit them is not effective prior to the beginning of the period to be reviewed; and

            c. The same financial reporting framework used to prepare the annual financial statements is used for the interim financial information.

Editor note: The preceding conditions are an acknowledgement of the difference between a review performed by an accountant with an audit base of knowledge versus that performed by an accountant who is not the entity's auditor. Further, when these conditions are met, generally the review engagement is intended to provide a periodic update to the year-end reporting and is considered an extension of the annual audit. Thus, the standard setters decided the requirements and guidance should reside in the auditing literature. Accordingly, if these conditions are *not* met, reviews of interim financial information of nonissuers should be performed in accordance with Statements on Standards for Accounting and Review Services.

            d. When the interim financial information is condensed information, all of the following conditions are met:

                (1) The condensed interim financial information purports to conform with an appropriate financial reporting framework, which includes appropriate form and content of interim financial statements.

(2) The condensed interim financial information includes a note that the financial information does not represent complete financial statements and should be read in conjunction with the entity's latest annual audited financial statements.

(3) The condensed interim financial information accompanies the entity's latest audited annual financial statements or such audited annual financial statements are made readily available by the entity.

4. **Condition for Engagement Acceptance** Prior to accepting the engagement, the accountant should assess management's ability to acknowledge their responsibility to establish and maintain controls that are sufficient to provide a reasonable basis for the preparation of reliable interim financial information in accordance with the applicable financial reporting framework. If management does not have the ability to make such an acknowledgement of its responsibility, the independent accountant should not accept the engagement.

5. **Establishing an Understanding With the Client** The understanding established with the client should be documented in a written communication. It should include:

a. **Objective** The objective of a review of interim financial information is to provide the accountant with a basis for communicating whether there are any material modifications that should be made to the interim financial information for it to conform with the applicable financial reporting framework

b. **Limitations**

(1) A review does **not** provide a basis for expressing an opinion about whether the financial information is presented fairly, in all material respects, in conformity with the applicable financial reporting framework.

(2) A review does not provide assurance that the accountant will become aware of all significant matters that would be identified in an audit.

(3) A review is not designed to provide assurance on internal control or to identify significant deficiencies and material weaknesses in internal control; however, the accountant is responsible for communicating to management and those charged with governance any significant deficiencies or material weaknesses in internal control that the accountant identified.

c. **Management's Responsibilities**

(1) The entity's interim financial information

(2) Establishing and maintaining effective internal control over financial reporting

(3) Identifying and ensuring that the entity complies with the laws and regulations applicable to its activities

(4) Making all financial records and related information available to the accountant

(5) Providing the accountant, at the conclusion of the engagement, with a letter confirming certain representations made during the review

(6) Adjusting the interim financial information to correct material misstatements— although a review of interim financial information is not designed to obtain reasonable assurance that the interim financial information is free from material misstatement, management also is responsible for affirming in its representation letter to the accountant that the effects of any uncorrected misstatements aggregated by the accountant during the current engagement and pertaining to the current-year period(s) under review are immaterial, both individually and in the aggregate, to the interim financial information taken as a whole.

d.   Accountant's Responsibilities

(1)   Conducting the review in accordance with AICPA standards

(2)   Performing analytical procedures and making inquiries of persons responsible for financial and accounting matters

(3)   A review is substantially less in scope than an audit conducted in accordance with auditing standards generally accepted in the United States of America, the objective of which is the expression of an opinion regarding the financial information taken as a whole. Accordingly, the accountant will not express an opinion on the interim financial information

e.   Form of the Communication   The understanding with the client should include whether the expected form of the communication upon completion of the engagement, is to be written or oral.

f.   Report Required to Be Included If Accountant Associated With Review   A statement should also be included in the understanding that if the entity states in any report, document, or written communication containing the interim financial information that the information has been reviewed by the accountant or makes other reference to the accountant's association, that the accountant's review report will be included in the document.

6.   Knowledge of the Entity's Business & Its Internal Control   The accountant must have a sufficient knowledge of the client's business and internal control to:

a.   Knowledge Required   The accountant must have a sufficient knowledge of the client's business and internal control to:

(1)   Identify the types of potential material misstatements in the interim financial information and consider the likelihood of their occurrence

(2)   Select the inquiries and analytics that will provide the accountant with a basis for reporting whether material modifications should be made for such information to conform with the applicable financial reporting framework

b.   Procedures to Update Knowledge   In planning the review, the following procedures should be performed to update the accountant's knowledge:

(1)   Reading documentation of the preceding year's audit and of reviews of prior interim periods to identify matters that may be relevant to the current review, for example, the accountant should specifically consider:

(a)   Corrected material misstatements

(b)   Matters identified in any summary of uncorrected misstatements

(c)   Identified risks of material misstatement due to fraud, including the risk of management override of controls

(d)   Significant financial accounting and reporting matters that may be of continuing significance, such as significant deficiencies and material weaknesses

(2) Reading the most recent annual and comparable prior interim period financial information

(3) Considering the results of any audit procedures performed with respect to the current year's financial statements

(4) Inquiring of management about changes in the entity's business activities

(5) Inquiring of management about whether relevant significant changes in internal control have occurred subsequent to the preceding annual audit or prior review of interim financial information, including changes in the entity's policies, procedures, and personnel, as well as the nature and extent of such changes

B. Procedures

1. **Analytical Procedures & Related Inquiries** The accountant should apply analytical procedures to the interim financial information to identify and provide a basis for inquiry about the relationships and individual items that appear to be unusual and that may indicate a material misstatement. This should include comparing

   a. Interim financial information with comparable information for the immediately preceding interim period, if applicable, and with the corresponding period(s) in the previous year

   b. Plausible relationships among both financial and, where relevant, nonfinancial information

   c. Recorded amounts, or ratios developed from recorded amounts, to expectations developed by the accountant

   d. Disaggregated revenue data

   Expectations developed by the accountant in performing analytical procedures in connection with a review of interim financial information ordinarily are less precise than those developed in an audit. Also, in a review the accountant ordinarily is not required to corroborate management's responses with other evidence. However, the accountant should consider the reasonableness and consistency of management's responses in light of the results of other review procedures and the accountant's knowledge of the entity's business and its internal control.

2. **Other Procedures & Inquiries** The following are inquiries the accountant should make and other review procedures the accountant should perform when conducting a review of interim financial information. If, as a result, the accountant believes that the interim financial information may not be in conformity with the applicable financial reporting framework in all material respects, the accountant should make additional inquiries or perform other procedures.

   a. Reading the available minutes of meetings of stockholders, directors, and appropriate committees, and inquiring about matters dealt with at meetings for which minutes are not available, to identify matters that may affect the interim financial information

   b. Obtaining reports from other accountants, if any, who have been engaged to perform a review of the interim financial information of significant components of the reporting entity, its subsidiaries, or its other investees, or inquiring of those accountants if reports have not been issued

c. Inquiring of members of management who have responsibility for financial and accounting matters concerning:

(1) Whether the interim financial information has been prepared in conformity with the applicable financial reporting framework consistently applied

(2) Unusual or complex situations that may have an effect on the interim financial information

(3) Significant transactions occurring or recognized in the last several days of the interim period

(4) The status of uncorrected misstatements identified during the previous audit and interim review

(5) Matters about which questions have arisen in the course of applying the review procedures

(6) Events subsequent to the date of the interim financial information that could have a material effect on the presentation of such information

(7) Their knowledge of any fraud or suspected fraud affecting the entity involving management, employees who have significant roles in internal control, or others where the fraud could have a material effect on the financial information

(8) Whether they are aware of allegations of fraud or suspected fraud affecting the entity

(9) Significant journal entries and other adjustments

(10) Communications from regulatory agencies

(11) Significant deficiencies, including material weaknesses, in the design or operation of internal control as it relates to the preparation of both annual and interim financial information

d. Obtaining evidence that the interim financial information agrees or reconciles with the accounting records

e. Reading the interim financial information to consider whether, based on the results of the review procedures performed and other information that has come to the accountant's attention, the information to be reported conforms with the applicable financial reporting framework

f. Reading other information in documents containing the interim financial information to consider whether such information or the manner of its presentation is materially inconsistent with the interim financial information.

3. **Written Management Representations** Written representations from management should be obtained for all interim financial information presented and for all periods covered by the review.

4. **Evaluation of Results of Procedures** Misstatements identified by the accountant or brought to the accountant's attention, including inadequate disclosure, should be evaluated individually and in the aggregate to determine whether material modification should be made to the interim financial information for it to conform with the applicable financial reporting framework.

The accountant should use his or her professional judgment in evaluating the materiality of any likely misstatements that the entity has not corrected. The accountant should consider matters such as (a) the nature, cause and amount of the misstatements; (b) whether the misstatements originated in the preceding year or interim periods of the current year; (c) materiality judgments made in conjunction with the current or prior year's annual audit; and (d) the potential effect of the misstatements on future interim or annual periods.

C. **Communications to Management & Those Charged With Governance**

1. **Material Modification** If the accountant determines that a material modification should be made to the interim financial information for it to conform with the applicable financial reporting framework, the accountant should communicate this to the appropriate level of management as soon as practicable. If management does not respond appropriately, the accountant should inform those charged with governance as soon as practicable. If done orally, the communication should be documented. If those charged with governance do not respond appropriately, the accountant should evaluate whether to resign from the engagement and as the entity's auditor, in which case consultation with an attorney may be advisable.

2. **Fraud or Illegal Acts** Possible fraud or illegal acts discovered should be brought to the attention of the appropriate level of management. If a matter involves possible fraud on the part of senior management or the fraud results in a material misstatement, the accountant should communicate directly with those charged with governance.

3. **Significant Deficiencies or Material Weaknesses in Internal Control** Significant deficiencies or material weaknesses in internal control discovered should be communicated to management and those charged with governance.

D. **Report on a Review of Interim Financial Information**
Although the guidance generally does not require an accountant to issue a written report on a review of interim financial information, an accountant's review report should accompany the interim financial information if, in a report; document; or written communication containing the reviewed interim financial information, the entity states that the interim financial information has been reviewed by an independent public accountant or makes other reference to the accountant's association. In other situations, the accountant may determine it appropriate to issue a written report to address the risk that a user of interim financial information may associate the accountant with the interim financial information and, in the absence of a review report, inappropriately assume a higher level of assurance than that obtained.

1. **Standard Report** Each page of the interim financial information should be clearly marked as unaudited. The report should contain these elements:

   a. A title that includes the word independent.

   b. A statement that the interim financial information identified in the report was reviewed.

   c. A statement that the interim financial information is the responsibility of the entity's management.

   d. A statement that the review of interim financial information was conducted in accordance with standards established by the AICPA.

   e. A description of the procedures for a review of interim financial information.

   f. A statement that a review of interim financial information is substantially less in scope than an audit conducted in accordance with auditing standards generally accepted in the United States, the objective of which is an expression of an opinion regarding the financial information taken as a whole, and accordingly, no such opinion is expressed.

g. A statement about whether the accountant is aware of any material modifications that should be made to the accompanying interim financial information for it to conform with the applicable financial reporting framework. The statement should include an identification of the country of origin of those accounting principles (for example, accounting principles generally accepted in the United States of America or US generally accepted accounting principles).

h. The manual or printed signature of the accountant's firm.

i. The date of the review report. (Generally, the report should be dated as of the date of completion of the review procedures.)

Exhibit 9 ▶ Standard Review Report (for Interim Financial Information for a Nonissuer When the Review is in Essence an Extension of an Annual Audit)

Independent Accountant's Report

We have reviewed the accompanying [*describe the interim financial information or statements reviewed*] of ABC Company and consolidated subsidiaries as of September 30, 20X1, and for the three-month and nine-month periods then ended. This interim financial information is the responsibility of the company's management.

We conducted our review in accordance with standards established by the American Institute of Certified Public Accountants. A review of interim financial information consists principally of applying analytical procedures and making inquiries of persons responsible for financial and accounting matters. It is substantially less in scope than an audit conducted in accordance with auditing standards generally accepted in the United States, the objective of which is the expression of an opinion regarding the financial information taken as a whole. Accordingly, we do not express such an opinion.

Based on our review, we are not aware of any material modifications that should be made to the accompanying interim financial information for it to be in conformity with [*identify the applicable financial reporting framework; for example, accounting principles generally accepted in the United States of America*].

---

2. **Modification of Review Report** The accountant's report should be modified for departures from the applicable financial reporting framework, which include inadequate disclosure and changes in accounting principles that are not in conformity with the applicable financial reporting framework. The modification to the report for such a departure should describe its nature in an explanatory paragraph and, if practicable, should state the effects on the interim financial information. The final paragraph should be modified as follows: "Based on our review, *with the exception of the matter described in the preceding paragraph*, we are not aware…"

The existence of substantial doubt about the entity's ability to continue as a going concern or a lack of consistency in the application of accounting principles would not require the addition of a paragraph to the report, provided that the interim financial information appropriately discloses such matters. Although not required, the accountant may wish to emphasize such matters in a separate explanatory paragraph.

V. Reporting on Condensed Financial Statements & Selected Financial Data (AU 552)

A.   Condensed Financial Statements

AU 552 provides guidance on reporting in a client-prepared document on condensed financial statements derived from audited financial statements of a public entity that are required to be filed with a regulatory agency. Condensed financial statements are presented in considerably less detail than statements presented in conformity with GAAP. Therefore, they should be read in conjunction with the entity's most recent complete financial statements.

Exhibit 10 ▶ Condensed Financial Statements With Audited Financial Statements

---

We have audited, in accordance with US generally accepted auditing standards, the consolidated balance sheet of X Company and subsidiaries as of December 31, 20X0, and the related consolidated statements of income, retained earnings, and cash flows for the year then ended (not presented herein); and in our report dated February 15, 20X1, we expressed an unqualified opinion on those consolidated financial statements.

In our opinion, the information set forth in the accompanying condensed consolidated financial statements is fairly stated, in all material respects, in relation to the consolidated financial statements from which it has been derived.

---

1.   **Not GAAP** Because condensed financial statements do not constitute a fair presentation of financial position, results of operations, and cash flows in conformity with GAAP, an auditor engaged to report on such statements should not report in the same manner as an auditor reporting on the complete financial statements from which the condensed statements are derived.

2.   **Report** The report on condensed financial statements that are derived from financial statements that the auditor has audited should indicate the following:

   a.   That the auditor has audited and expressed an opinion on the complete financial statements

   b.   The date of the auditor's report on the complete financial statements, thereby removing any implication that records, transactions, or events after that date have been audited

   c.   The type of opinion expressed

   d.   Whether, in the auditor's opinion, the information set forth in the condensed financial statements is fairly stated in all material respects in relation to the complete financial statements from which it has been derived

3.   **Optional Reporting** If a client makes a statement in a client-prepared document that both names the auditor and states that condensed financial statements have been derived from audited financial statements, the auditor is **not** required to report on the condensed financial statements provided that they are included in a document that either contains the audited financial statements or incorporates such statements by reference to information filed with a regulatory agency.

   a.   If such a statement is included in a client-prepared document of a public entity, and that document neither contains the audited financial statements nor incorporates such statements by reference, the auditor should request the client to either delete the auditor's name from the document or include the auditor's report on the condensed financial statements as described in 2., above.

   b.   If the client does not comply with the auditor's request, the auditor should consider other appropriate actions, such as consulting legal counsel.

4.   **Comparative Statements** Condensed financial statements derived from audited financial statements of a public entity may be presented on a comparative basis with interim financial information as of a subsequent date that is accompanied by the auditor's review report. In such a case, the auditor should report on the condensed financial statements of each period in a manner appropriate for the type of service rendered in each period

B.   **Selected Financial Data**

AU 552 also provides guidance for selected financial data that are derived from audited financial statements and are presented in a document that either includes audited financial statements or incorporates such statements by reference to information filed with a regulatory agency.

Exhibit 11 ▶ Selected Financial Data With Audited Financial Statements

We have audited the accompanying consolidated balance sheets of ABC Company and subsidiaries as of December 31, 20X2 and 20X1, and the related consolidated statements of income, retained earnings, and cash flows for each of the three years in the period ended December 31, 20X2. These financial statements are the responsibility of the company's management. Our responsibility is to express an opinion on these financial statements based on our audits.

We conducted our audits in accordance with US generally accepted auditing standards. Those standards require that we plan and perform the audit to obtain reasonable assurance about whether the financial statements are free of material misstatement. An audit includes examining, on a test basis, evidence supporting the amounts and disclosures in the financial statements. An audit also includes assessing the accounting principles used and significant estimates made by management, as well as evaluating the overall financial statement presentation. We believe that our audits provided a reasonable basis for our opinion.

In our opinion, the consolidated financial statements referred to above present fairly, in all material respects, the financial position of the ABC Company and subsidiaries as of December 31, 20X2 and 20X1, and the results of its operations and their cash flows for each of the three years in the period ended December 31, 20X2, in conformity with US generally accepted accounting principles.

We have also previously audited, in accordance with US generally accepted auditing standards, the consolidated balance sheets as of December 31, 20X3, 20X2, and 20X1, and the related consolidated statements of income, retained earnings, and cash flows for the years ended December 31, 20X2 and 20X1 (none of which are presented herein); and we expressed unqualified opinions on those consolidated financial statements.

In our opinion, the information set forth in the selected financial data for each of the five years in the period ended December 31, 20X2, appearing on page XX is fairly stated in all material respects in relation to the consolidated financial statements from which it has been derived.

1.   **SEC Requirements** Selected financial data are not a required part of the basic financial statements, and the entity's management is responsible for determining the specific selected financial data to be presented. However, certain reports must include, for each of the last five fiscal years, selected financial data in accordance with SEC Regulation S-K. (There is no SEC requirement for the auditor to report on such selected financial data.)

2.   **Limit Report Scope** If the auditor is engaged to report on the selected financial data, the report should be limited to data that are derived from financial statements audited by that auditor.

a.   If the selected data includes both data derived from audited statements and other information (such as the number of employees or square footage of facilities), the report should identify specifically the data on which the auditor is reporting and should indicate the same items as mentioned in A.2., above.

 b. The auditor is not precluded from expressing an opinion on one or more of the specified elements, accounts, or items of a financial statement in accordance with the provisions of AU 623, *Special Reports.*

 c. If the selected financial data are derived from financial statements that were audited by another independent auditor, the report on the selected financial data should state so, and the auditor should not express an opinion on that data.

3. **Optional Reporting** In situations where the client names the independent auditor in a client-prepared document and states that the selected financial data are derived from financial statements audited by the named auditor, the auditor is not required to report on the selected financial data provided that the document either contains audited financial statements or incorporates such statements by reference to information filed with a regulatory agency.

 a. If the client document is lacking these characteristics, the auditor should either:

  (1) Request that neither the auditor's name nor reference to the auditor be associated with the information.

  (2) Disclaim an opinion on the selected information and request that the disclaimer be included in the document.

 b. If the client does not comply, the client should be advised that there is no consent to either the use of the auditor's name or the reference to the auditor, and the auditor should consider a consultation with legal counsel.

VI. Reports on Application of Accounting Principles (AU 625)

    A.   General

    AU 625 provides guidance for CPAs, who have not been engaged to report on the financial statements of a specific entity, who either prepare a report or give oral advice to management or those charged with governance on either:

        1.   The application of accounting principles to specified transactions, either completed or proposed, involving facts and circumstances of a specific entity or

        2.   The type of opinion that may be rendered on a specific entity's financial statements

    B.   Exceptions

    Exceptions include engagements to report on financial statements, assist in litigation involving accounting matters, provide expert testimony in accounting-related litigation, give advice to another accountant in public practice, and communications such as position papers. Position papers include newsletters, articles, speeches or lectures, and text of speeches or lectures. Position papers do not include communications intended to provide guidance on the application of accounting principles to a specific transaction.

    C.   Procedures

    The accountant should be capable of making reasonable professional judgments. The general standards of training and due care must be followed. The work must be planned adequately and assistants must be supervised properly. Sufficient information must be gathered to provide a reasonable basis for a professional judgment. Prior to making a judgment, the accountant should (1) obtain an understanding of the form and substance of the transactions involved; (2) review applicable generally accepted accounting principles; (3) perform research to ascertain and consider the existence of creditable precedents or analogies; and (4) consult with other professionals or experts, if necessary.

        1.   **Hypothetical Transaction** AU 625 prohibits an accountant in public practice (a reporting accountant) from issuing a written report on the application of accounting principles or the type of opinion that may be expressed on financial statements not involving facts and circumstances of a specific entity and transaction, in other words, a hypothetical transaction.

        2.   **Management** Rather than arranging the engagement through, or inquiring of, a principal or intermediary, the accountant contacts the entity's management.

    D.   Reporting Standards

    AU 625 does not prohibit oral reports. It is as applicable to oral advice as to a written report, if the reporting accountant believes the principal to a transaction intends to use the advice as an important factor in decision making.

        1.   **Type of Opinion** When preparing the report and the included opinion, the accountant should consider the requester of the report, the circumstances under which the request is made, the purpose of the request, and the intended use of the report.

            a.   The reporting accountant (one who has been engaged to give advice) has the responsibility to consult with the continuing accountant who prepares or audits the financial statements to determine the form and substance of transactions, how the management applied accounting principles to similar transactions, if management disputes the method of accounting recommended by the continuing accountant, and if the continuing accountant has reached a different conclusion on the application of accounting principles or type of opinion.

            b.   The responsibilities of the continuing accountant to respond to the reporting accountant are the same as the responsibilities of a predecessor auditor to a successor auditor.

2. **Address** The accountant's written report is addressed to the requesting entity and ordinarily includes identification of the specific entity and the country of origin of the appropriate accounting principles.

3. **Description** The first part of the report should describe the engagement.

    a. Include a brief description of the nature of the engagement and state that the engagement was performed in accordance with acceptable AICPA standards.

    b. Describe the transactions, relevant facts, circumstances, assumptions, and sources of information. This includes identifying principals to specific transactions, describing hypothetical transactions, describing nonspecific principals such as Company A and Company B.

    c. Describe the appropriate accounting principles or the type of opinion, and the reasons for the reporting accountant's conclusion.

4. **Concluding Comments** The report should state that (a) responsibility for proper accounting rests with the preparers of the financial statements who should consult with their continuing accountants; and (b) any difference in the facts, circumstances, or assumptions presented may change the report.

5. **Restrictions** The accountant's written report includes a final paragraph stating the following restrictions: (a) a restriction of the report for the information and use of specified parties; (b) identification of the specified parties; and (c) a statement that the report is not intended to be, and should not be, used by other than the specified parties.

Exhibit 12 ▶ Report on Application of Accounting Principles or Type of Opinion

---

(Introduction)

We have been engaged to report on the appropriate application of accounting principles generally accepted in [country of origin of such principles] to the specific transaction described below. This report is being issued to the ABC Company for assistance in evaluating accounting principles for the described specific transaction. Our engagement has been conducted in accordance with standards established by the American Institute of Certified Public Accountants.

(Description of transaction)

The facts, circumstances, and assumptions relevant to the specific transaction as provided to us by the management of ABC Company are as follows: [text describing transaction].

(Appropriate accounting principles)

[Text discussing generally accepted accounting principles]

(Concluding comments)

The ultimate responsibility for the decision on the appropriate application of accounting principles generally accepted in [country of origin of such principles] for an actual transaction rests with the preparers of financial statements, who should consult with their continuing accountants. Our judgment on the appropriate application of accounting principles generally accepted in [country of origin of such principles] for the described specific transaction is based solely on the facts provided to us as described above. Should these facts and circumstances differ, our conclusion may change.

(Restricted Use)

This report is intended solely for the information and use of the board of directors and management of ABC Company and is not intended to be, and should not be, used by anyone other than those specified parties.

VII. Reporting on Financial Statements Prepared for Use in Other Countries (AU 534)

A.   Applicability
AU 534 provides guidelines for an independent auditor engaged to report on financial statements of a US entity for use outside the United States, given the following conditions:

1.   **Foreign GAAP** Financial statements are prepared in conformity with GAAP of another country.

2.   **US Entity** The entity is organized or domiciled in the United States

3.   **US Auditor** The auditor practices in the United States.

B.   Purpose of Statements
Such financial statements may be prepared, for example, when: (1) the statements will be included in the financial statements of a non-US parent; (2) the entity has substantial non-US investors; and (3) capital is to be raised in another country.

C.   General & Fieldwork Standards
The auditor should comply with the general and fieldwork standards of US GAAS. However, the US procedures may need to be modified to apply when there are differences between accounting principles generally accepted in the other country and US GAAP.

1.   **Examples**

a.   **Valuation** Accounting principles generally accepted in another country may require that certain assets be revalued to adjust for the effects of inflation—in which case, the auditor should perform procedures to test the revaluation adjustments.

b.   **Recognition** Another country's accounting principles may not require or permit recognition of deferred taxes—consequently, procedures for testing deferred tax balances would not be applicable.

2.   **Auditor's Understanding & Knowledge** The auditor should understand the accounting principles and auditing standards generally accepted in the other country and the legal responsibilities involved.

a.   **References** The auditor may obtain such knowledge by reading the applicable statutes, professional literature, and codification of accounting principles and auditing standards generally accepted in that country. The auditor should consider consulting with persons having expertise in the accounting principles and auditing standards of the other country.

b.   **No GAAP** If the accounting principles of another country are not established with sufficient authority or by general acceptance, the auditor may report on the financial statements if both the following criteria are met:

(1)   The auditor judges the client's principles and practices to be appropriate.

(2)   The client's principles and practices are disclosed in a clear and comprehensive manner.

c.   **International Standards** International Financial Reporting Standards established by the International Accounting Standards Board may be used.

D.   Reporting Standards
The auditor may prepare either a US-style or foreign-style report, or both.

1.   **Modified US Report** A US-style report that is modified to the accounting principles is preferred. Recall that the standard US-style report includes that the US GAAP is used.

Exhibit 13 ▶ Financial Statements Prepared in Conformity With Accounting Principles Generally Accepted in Another Country in a US-Style Report

We have audited the balance sheet of the International Company as of December 31, 20X1, and the related statements of income, retained earnings, and cash flows for the year then ended, which, as described in Note X, have been prepared on the basis of accounting principles generally accepted in (name of country). These financial statements are the responsibility of the Company's management. Our responsibility is to express an opinion on these financial statements based on our audit.

We conducted our audit in accordance with auditing standards generally accepted in the United States (and in [name of country]). US standards require that we plan and perform the audit to obtain reasonable assurance about whether the financial statements are free of material misstatement. An audit includes examining, on a test basis, evidence supporting the amounts and disclosures in the financial statements. An audit also includes assessing the accounting principles used and significant estimates made by management, as well as evaluating the overall financial statement presentation. We believe that our audit provides a reasonable basis for our opinion.

In our opinion, the financial statements referred to above present fairly, in all material respects, the financial position of the International Company at December 31, 20X1, and the results of its operations and cash flows for the year then ended, in conformity with accounting principles generally accepted in (name of country).

a. The report should include (in addition to standard required items) the following:

(1) A reference to the note to the financial statements that describes the basis of preparation, including the nationality of the accounting principles.

(2) A note that says the audit was made in accordance with GAAS and the auditing standards of the other country, if appropriate.

b. Although the report is intended for use only outside the United States, this is not intended to preclude limited use of the financial statements to parties (such as banks) within the United States that deal directly with the entity.

2. **Foreign Report** The standard report of another country may be used, provided that the following is evident:

a. The standard report is used by auditors in the other country, given similar circumstances.

b. The auditor understands the meaning and implications of the report with respect to different customs and different word interpretations.

c. The auditor is in the position to make the attestations contained in the report.

d. When using a standard report of a foreign country that is similar to the one used in the United States, the country name should be added to the report to avoid erroneous interpretation due to a different custom or culture.

3. **Dual Report** Use of both a US-style and a foreign-style report also is allowed. The auditor should include a note such as the one in Exhibit 14.

Exhibit 14 ▶ Note Describing Differences Between US & Foreign GAAP

We also have reported separately on the financial statements of International Company for the same period presented in conformity with accounting principles generally accepted in (name of country). (The significant differences between the accounting principles accepted in [name of country] and those generally accepted in the United States are summarized in Note X.)

VIII. Restricting Use of Audit Report (AU 532)

    A. Applicability

    AU 532, *Restricting the Use of an Auditor's Report,* provides guidance in determining whether an engagement necessitates a restricted-use report and the language to use. This guidance is **not** applicable to reports issued under the provisions of AU 634, *Letters for Underwriters and Certain Other Requesting Parties.*

    B. Guidance

    General use signifies that the report is not restricted to specified parties. Auditor's reports on financial statements prepared in conformity with GAAP or certain bases of accounting other than GAAP (OCBOA) ordinarily are **not** restricted as to use. (However, nothing in AU 532 precludes an auditor from restricting the use of any report.) *Restricted use* signifies that reports are intended only for specified parties. Reports are restricted as to use for a variety of reasons, including the purpose of the report, the nature of the procedures applied or assumptions used in its preparation, and its potential for being misunderstood when taken out of context.

        1. Restrictions Auditors should restrict the use of a report when the:

            a. Subject matter of the report or the presentation being reported on is based on measurement or disclosure criteria contained in contractual agreements or regulatory provisions that are **not** in conformity with GAAP or an OCBOA. This type of report is restricted as to use because the basis, assumptions, or purpose of such presentations are developed for and directed only to the parties to the agreement or regulatory agencies responsible for the provisions. Auditors can exercise professional judgment as to whether to add others as specified parties to this type of restricted-use report.

            b. Report is issued as a by-product of a financial statement audit. The use of a by-product report is restricted because as it is not the primary objective of the engagement. The potential for misunderstanding exists due to the limited degree of assurance associated with it—because generally only limited procedures were directed toward its subject matter. Auditors should **not** add other parties (other than management, those charged with governance, other internal users, specified regulatory agencies, or contractual parties) as specified parties.

        2. Combined Report If an auditor issues a single combined report covering subject matter that requires a restriction on use as well as material that is not restricted, the combined report should be restricted.

        3. Distribution Auditors are not responsible for their client's distribution of their reports; however, they should consider informing their clients about a restricted-use report's limited distribution, i.e., that the reports are not intended for distribution to nonspecified parties.

        4. Report Language An auditor's restricted-use report should contain a separate paragraph at the end of the report that includes:

            a. A statement that the report is intended solely for the information and use of the specified parties

            b. An identification of the specified parties

            c. A statement that the report is not intended to be and should not be used by anyone other than the specified parties

---

CHAPTER 11—OTHER TYPES OF REPORTS

Problem 11-1 MULTIPLE-CHOICE QUESTIONS

1. When an auditor is engaged to report on whether supplementary information is fairly stated, in all material respects, in relation to the financial statements as a whole and the audited financial statements are **not** presented with the supplementary information, the auditor should

   a. Include a copy of the audit report on the financial statements
   b. Report on the accompanying information only if the auditor participated in its preparation
   c. Determine a materiality level that is appropriate for the subject of the supplementary information
   d. Report on the supplementary information in a separate report.   (Editors, ID: 9270)

2. In order to opine on whether supplementary information is fairly stated, in all material respects, in relation to the financial statements, as a whole, all of the following conditions must be met **except for**

   a. The supplementary information was derived from, and relates directly to, the underlying accounting and other records used to prepare the financial statements and relates to the same period.
   b. The financial statements were audited, and the auditor served as the principal auditor in that engagement.
   c. Neither an adverse opinion nor a disclaimer of opinion was issued on the financial statements.
   d. The supplementary information will accompany the entity's audited financial statements, or such audited financial statements will be made available upon request.   (Editors, ID: 9271)

3. An accountant who is **not** independent of a client is precluded from issuing a

   a. Report on consulting services
   b. Compilation report on historical financial statements
   c. Compilation report on prospective financial statements
   d. Special report on compliance with contractual agreements   (11/90, AUD, #37, ID: 393)

4. Helpful Co., a nonprofit entity, prepared its financial statements on an accounting basis prescribed by a regulatory agency solely for filing with that agency. Green audited the financial statements in accordance with generally accepted auditing standards and concluded that the financial statements were fairly presented on the prescribed basis. Green should issue a

   a. Qualified opinion
   b. Standard three paragraph report with reference to footnote disclosure
   c. Disclaimer of opinion
   d. Special report   (11/91, AUD, #17, ID: 2285)

5. When an auditor reports on financial statements prepared on an entity's income tax basis, the auditor's report should

   a. Disclaim an opinion on whether the statements were examined in accordance with generally accepted auditing standards
   b. Not express an opinion on whether the statements are presented in conformity with the comprehensive basis of accounting used
   c. Include an explanation of how the results of operations differ from the cash receipts and disbursements basis of accounting
   d. State that the basis of presentation is a comprehensive basis of accounting other than GAAP
                                                                        (5/94, AUD, #83, ID: 4748)

6. An auditor is engaged to report on selected financial data that are included in a client-prepared document containing audited financial statements. Under these circumstances, the report on the selected data should

   a. Be limited to data derived from the audited financial statements
   b. Be distributed only to senior management and the board of directors
   c. State that the presentation is a comprehensive basis of accounting other than GAAP
   d. Indicate that the data are not fairly stated in all material respects   (11/95, AUD, #87, ID: 6034)

7. Which of the following titles would be considered suitable for financial statements that are prepared on a cash basis?

    a. Income statement
    b. Statement of operations
    c. Statement of revenue collected and expenses paid
    d. Statement of cash flows

    (R/09, AUD, #15, ID: 8815)

8. A CPA is permitted to accept a separate engagement (**not** in conjunction with an audit of financial statements) to audit an entity's schedule of

	Accounts receivable	*Royalties*
a.	Yes	Yes
b.	Yes	No
c.	No	Yes
d.	No	No

    (11/93, AUD, #56, ID: 7694)

9. An auditor may express an opinion on an entity's accounts receivable balance even if the auditor has disclaimed an opinion on the financial statements taken as a whole provided the

    a. Report on the accounts receivable discloses the reason for the disclaimer of opinion on the financial statements.
    b. Distribution of the report on the accounts receivable is restricted to internal use only.
    c. Auditor also reports on the current asset portion of the entity's balance sheet.
    d. Report on the accounts receivable is presented separately from the disclaimer of opinion on the financial statements.

    (5/96, AUD, #8, ID: 6240)

10. Which of the following would be an appropriate title for a statement of revenue and expenses prepared using an other comprehensive basis of accounting (OCBOA)?

    a. Statement of operations
    b. Statement of income—statutory basis
    c. Income statement
    d. Statement of activities

    (R/10, AUD, #1, amended, ID: 9351)

11. Reports are considered special reports when issued in conjunction with

    a. Interim financial information reviewed to determine whether material modifications should be made to conform with GAAP
    b. Feasibility studies presented to illustrate an entity's results of operations
    c. Compliance with aspects of regulatory requirements related to audited financial statements
    d. Pro forma financial presentations designed to demonstrate the effects of hypothetical transactions

    (R/10, AUD, #25, ID: 9375)

12. Comfort letters ordinarily are

	Addressed to the client's	*Signed by the client's*
a.	Audit committee	Independent auditor
b.	Underwriter of securities	Senior management
c.	Audit committee	Senior management
d.	Underwriter of securities	Independent auditor

    (R/07, AUD, #15, ID: 8387)

13. When an accountant issues to an underwriter a comfort letter containing comments on data that have **not** been audited, the underwriter most likely will receive

    a. Negative assurance on capsule information
    b. Positive assurance on supplementary disclosures
    c. A limited opinion on "pro forma" financial statements
    d. A disclaimer on prospective financial statements

    (5/92, AUD, #8, ID: 2761)

14. Which of the following statements is correct concerning letters for underwriters, commonly referred to as comfort letters?

   a. Letters for underwriters are required by the Securities Act of 1933 for the initial public sale of registered securities.
   b. Letters for underwriters typically give negative assurance on unaudited interim financial information.
   c. Letters for underwriters usually are included in the registration statement accompanying a prospectus.
   d. Letters for underwriters ordinarily update auditors' opinions on the prior year's financial statements.
   (5/95, AUD, #86, ID: 5704)

15. When an independent accountant's report based on a review of interim financial information is presented in a registration statement, a prospectus should include a statement about the accountant's involvement. This statement should clarify that the

   a. Accountant is not an "expert" within the meaning of the Securities Act of 1933.
   b. Accountant's review report is not a "part" of the registration statement within the meaning of the Securities Act of 1933.
   c. Accountant performed only limited auditing procedures on the interim financial statements.
   d. Accountant's review was performed in accordance with standards established by the American Institute of CPAs.
   (5/90, AUD, #24, ID: 398)

16. Comfort letters ordinarily are signed by the client's

   a. Independent auditor
   b. Underwriter of securities
   c. Audit committee
   d. Senior management
   (11/92, AUD, #58, ID: 2992)

17. When issuing letters for underwriters, commonly referred to as comfort letters, an accountant may provide negative assurance concerning

   a. The absence of any significant deficiencies in internal control
   b. The conformity of the entity's unaudited condensed interim financial information with generally accepted accounting principles (GAAP)
   c. The results of procedures performed in compiling the entity's financial forecast
   d. The compliance of the entity's registration statement with the requirements of the Securities Act of 1933
   (R/08, AUD, #21, ID: 8627)

18. The objective of a review of interim financial information of a nonissuer is to provide an accountant with a basis for communicating whether

   a. Material modifications should be made to conform with the applicable financial reporting framework
   b. A reasonable basis exists for expressing an updated opinion regarding the financial statements that were previously audited
   c. Condensed financial statements or *pro forma* financial information should be included in a registration statement
   d. The financial information is presented fairly in accordance with generally accepted accounting principles
   (5/95, AUD, #83, amended, ID: 5701)

19. Which of the following procedures ordinarily should be applied when an independent accountant conducts a review of interim financial information of a nonissuer?

   a. Verify changes in key account balances
   b. Read the minutes of the board of directors' meeting
   c. Inspect the open purchase order file
   d. Perform cutoff tests for cash receipts and disbursements
   (11/92, AUD, #51, ID: 2985)

20. Which of the following circumstances requires modification of the accountant's report on a review of interim financial information of a nonissuer?

	An uncertainty	Inadequate disclosure
a.	No	No
b.	Yes	Yes
c.	Yes	No
d.	No	Yes

(Editors, ID: 410)

21. When planning a review of an audit client's interim financial statements, which of the following procedures should the accountant perform to update the accountant's knowledge about the entity's business and its internal control?

   a. Perform analytical procedures on selected accounts by comparing the interim amounts to the amounts for the previous audited fiscal year-end.
   b. Inquire of the entity's outside legal counsel about the status of any previous pending litigation and any new litigation involving the entity.
   c. Select a sample of material revenue transactions occurring during the interim period and examine supporting documentation.
   d. Consider the results of audit procedures performed with respect to the current year's financial statements.

(R/11, AUD, #47, ID: 9947)

22. An auditor may report on condensed financial statements that are derived from a complete set of audited financial statements only if the auditor

   a. Expresses an unqualified opinion on the audited financial statements from which the condensed financial statements are derived
   b. Indicates whether the information is fairly stated in all material respects in relation to the complete financial statements
   c. Determines that the condensed financial statements include all the disclosures necessary for the complete set of financial statements
   d. Presents the condensed financial statements in comparative form with the prior year's condensed financial statements

(R/10, AUD, #50, ID: 9400)

23. In connection with a proposal to obtain a new audit client, a CPA in public practice is asked to prepare a report on the application of accounting principles to a specific transaction. The CPA's report should include a statement that

   a. The engagement was performed in accordance with Statements on Standards for Accounting and Review Services.
   b. Responsibility for the proper accounting treatment rests with the preparers of the financial statements.
   c. The evaluation of the application of accounting principles is hypothetical and may not be used for opinion-shopping.
   d. The report is based solely on communications with a specified intermediary, if that is the case.

(R/00, AUD, #20, amended, ID: 6945)

24. The financial statements of KCP America, a US entity, are prepared for inclusion in the consolidated financial statements of its non-US parent. These financial statements are prepared in conformity with the accounting principles generally accepted in the parent's country and are for use only in that country. How may KCP America's auditor report on these financial statements?

   I. A US-style report (unmodified)
   II. A US-style report modified to report on the accounting principles of the parent's country
   III. The report form of the parent's country

	I	II	III
a.	Yes	No	No
b.	No	Yes	No
c.	Yes	No	Yes
d.	No	Yes	Yes

(5/91, AUD, #49, ID: 389)

25. Before reporting on the financial statements of a US entity that have been prepared in conformity with another country's accounting principles, an auditor practicing in the United States should

    a. Understand the accounting principles generally accepted in the other country
    b. Be certified by the appropriate auditing or accountancy board of the other country
    c. Notify management that the auditor is required to disclaim an opinion on the financial statements
    d. Receive a waiver from the auditor's state board of accountancy to perform the engagement

    (11/94, AUD, #88, ID: 5161)

26. A US entity prepares its financial statements in conformity with accounting principles generally accepted in another country. These financial statements will be included in the consolidated financial statements of its non-US parent. Before reporting on the financial statements of the US entity, the auditor practicing in the United States should

    a. Notify management of the US entity that the auditor is required to disclaim an opinion on the financial statements
    b. Receive a waiver to report on the US entity from the appropriate accountancy authority in the other country
    c. Obtain written representations from management of the US entity regarding the purpose and uses of the financial statements
    d. Communicate with the auditor of the non-US parent regarding the level of assurance to be provided

    (R/03, AUD, #17, ID: 7639)

———————————

Problem 11-2 SIMULATION: Report on Financial Statements Prepared in Conformity with an OCBOA

The auditors' report on financial statements prepared in conformity with an OCBOA was drafted by a staff accountant of your firm at the completion of the engagement. It contained the elements below. Indicate whether each item is an appropriate (A) or an inappropriate (I) element within the report.

Report Elements	Appropriate (A) or Inappropriate (I)
1. A title that includes the word independent.	
2. A statement that the financial statements are the responsibility of the company's management.	
3. A statement that the audit was conducted in accordance with standards established by the American Institute of Certified Public Accountants and includes an identification of the United States of America as the country of origin of those standards.	
4. A statement that the auditor is responsible for expressing an opinion on the financial statements based on the audit.	
5. A statement that those standards require that the auditor plan and perform the audit to obtain reasonable assurance about whether the financial statements are free of material misstatement.	
6. A statement that an audit includes: (a) Examining, on a test basis, evidence supporting the amounts and disclosures in the financial statements; (b) Assessing the accounting principles used and significant estimates made by management; and (c) Evaluating the company's system of internal control.	
7. A paragraph that describes the basis of the presentation.	

(ID: 9246)

_____

Problem 11-3 SIMULATION: Research

What authoritative reference provides guidance on who a comfort letter may be addressed to?

[gray box] § [gray box] [gray box]   (ID: 9247)

_____

Solution 11-1 MULTIPLE-CHOICE ANSWERS

Supplementary Information

1. (d)   When an auditor is engaged to report on whether supplementary information is fairly stated, in all material respects, in relation to the financial statements as a whole, and the audited financial statements are **not** presented with the supplementary information, the auditor should report on the supplementary information in a separate report. The supplementary information is the responsibility of management. The materiality level should be the same level used in the audit of the financial statements. A copy of the audit report on the financial statements would not be included. (ID: 9270)

2. (d)   One of the conditions that must be met is that the supplementary information will accompany the entity's audited financial statements, or such audited financial statements will be made readily available by the entity. Audited financial statements are deemed to be readily available if a third party user can obtain the audited financial statements without any further action by the entity. For example, financial statements on an entity's website may be considered readily available, but being available upon request is not considered readily available. (ID: 9271)

Special Reports

3. (d)   Entities may be required by contractual agreements, such as certain bond indentures and loan agreements, or by regulatory agencies to furnish compliance reports by independent auditors. A lack of independence would not preclude an accountant from issuing compilation reports or a report on consulting services. (ID: 393)

4. (d)   Special reports include those that are related to financial statements prepared on an accounting basis prescribed by a regulatory agency solely for filing with that agency. (ID: 2285)

5. (d)   The auditor's report should include a paragraph that refers to the note to the financial statements that describes the basis of accounting. The auditor utilized GAAS in the examination; thus, there is no need for a disclaimer. Answer b. is incorrect because an opinion is presented. The auditor is not required to include the explanation described in answer c. (ID: 4748)

6. (a)   An auditor's report on information accompanying the basic financial statements should include either an opinion on whether the accompanying information is fairly stated in all material respects in relation to the basic financial statements taken as a whole or as a disclaimer of opinion. The report should be limited to data that are derived from financial statements audited by that auditor. There is no restriction on the distribution. The basis of accounting is not necessarily other than GAAP. The data generally are indicated as fairly stated in all material respects. (ID: 6034)

7. (c)   Titles such as *balance sheet, statement of financial position, statement of income* (or *income statement*), *statement of operations,* and *statement of cash flows* are generally understood to be applicable only to financial statements that are presented in accordance with GAAP. Financial statements prepared in conformity with a comprehensive basis of accounting other than GAAP (OCBOA) should **not** use these GAAP titles. Examples of suitable titles for cash basis financial statements are *statement of assets and liabilities arising from cash transactions,* or *statement of revenues collected and expenses paid.* (ID: 8815)

8. (a)   An engagement to express an opinion on one or more specified elements, accounts, or items of a financial statement may be undertaken either as a separate engagement or in conjunction with an audit of financial statements. (ID: 7694)

9. (d)   The auditor should not express an opinion on specified elements, accounts, or items included in financial statements on which the auditor has expressed an adverse opinion or disclaimed an opinion based on an audit, if such reporting would be tantamount to expressing a piecemeal opinion on the financial statements. However, an auditor would be able to express an opinion on one or more specified elements provided the matters were not intended to and did not encompass so many elements as to constitute a major portion of the financial statements. However, the report on the specified element(s) should be presented separately from the report on the financial statements of the entity. (ID: 6240)

10. (b) *Statement of income—statutory basis* is an example of an appropriate format for a title of a financial statement prepared on a statutory basis, i.e., an other comprehensive basis of accounting (OCBOA). Terms such as statement of operations and income statement are generally understood to be applicable only to financial statements that are intended to present results of operations in conformity with GAAP. A statement of activities is a financial statement prepared in accordance with GAAP by a not-for-profit organization. Note: If OCBOA financial statements are not suitably titled, the auditor should qualify the opinion, disclosing the auditor's reservations in an explanatory paragraph added to the report. (ID: 9351)

11. (c) Reports are considered special reports when issued in conjunction with compliance with aspects of regulatory requirements related to audited financial statements (AU 623, *Special Reports*). Interim financial information reviewed to determine whether material modifications should be made to conform with GAAP are review reports (AR 90, *Review of Financial Statements* or AU 722, *Interim Financial Information*). Reports on feasibility studies could be examination or compilation reports, or reports on results of applying agreed-upon procedures (AT 301, *Financial Forecasts and Projections*). Reports on *pro forma* financial presentations designed to demonstrate the effects of hypothetical transactions can be either examination or review reports (AT 401, *Reporting on Pro forma Financial Information*). (ID: 9375)

Letters for Underwriters

12. (d) In connection with audited financial statements and schedules included in a registration statement to be filed with the SEC, underwriters may request accountants to provide them with a comfort letter. The comfort letter is addressed to the underwriter and signed by the auditor. (ID: 8387)

13. (a) When an accountant issues to an underwriter a comfort letter containing comments on data that have not been audited, the underwriter most likely will receive negative assurance on capsule information. Negative assurance should not be given, with respect to capsule information, unless the accountants have obtained knowledge of the client's internal control policies and procedures relating to the preparation of financial statements. This problem gave no indication that such knowledge was not obtained. (ID: 2761)

14. (b) A typical comfort letter includes a statement regarding the accountant's independence, an opinion regarding whether the audited financial information included or incorporated by reference complies to the Securities Act of 1933, negative assurance on unaudited condensed interim financial information included or incorporated by reference, and negative assurance on whether there has been any later changes in specified accounts in the financial statement items included in the registration statement. Comfort letters are not required under the Act and copies are not filed with the SEC. Comfort letters ordinarily express an opinion regarding the audited financial statements' compliance with the Act, which is not an "update" of the audit opinion. (ID: 5704)

15. (b) The Securities and Exchange Commission requires that, when an independent accountant's report based on a review of interim financial information is presented or incorporated by reference in a registration statement, a prospectus that includes a statement about the independent accountant's involvement should clarify that his or her review report is not a report or part of the registration statement within the meaning of Sections 7 and 11 of the Securities Act of 1933. (ID: 398)

16. (a) In connection with audited financial statements and schedules included in a registration statement to be filed with the SEC, a client may request the services of an independent auditor. One of these services is the issuance of comfort letters for underwriters. The underwriter of securities receives the comfort letter. The client and senior management do not sign the comfort letter. (ID: 2992)

17. (b) An accountant may give negative assurance as to whether any material modifications should be made to an entity's unaudited condensed interim financial information for it to be in conformity with GAAP when the accountant has conducted a review of the interim financial information in accordance with AU 722, *Interim Financial Information*. Accountants should not mention reports related to internal control in a comfort letter, thus, negative assurance regarding the absence of any significant deficiencies in internal control should not be made. Accountants may not provide negative assurance on the results of procedures performed in compiling an entity's financial forecast. Accountants provide assistance regarding the financial information contained in a registration statement, not the compliance of the registration statement with the Securities Act of 1933. (ID: 8627)

Review of Interim Financial Information

18. (a)   The objective of a review of interim financial information of a nonissuer is to provide the accountant with a basis for communicating whether material modifications should be made for such information to conform with the applicable financial reporting framework. It is not to update the opinion on the previously audited financial statements nor to determine whether condensed statements or *pro forma* information should be included. In a review, the accountant supplies only limited assurance and would not provide an opinion stating the financial information is presented fairly.

(ID: 5701)

19. (b)   The procedures for a review of interim financial information should include reading the minutes of meetings of stockholders, board of directors, and committees of the board of directors to identify actions that may affect the interim financial information. Answers a., c., and d. are not among the procedures normally applied in a review of interim financial information.

(ID: 2985)

20. (d)   The accountant's report on a review of interim financial information should be modified for departures from the applicable financial reporting framework, which include inadequate disclosure and changes in accounting principles that are not in conformity with the applicable financial reporting framework. The existence of an uncertainty or a lack of consistency in the application of accounting principles affecting interim financial information would not require the accountant to include an additional paragraph in the report, provided that the interim financial information appropriately discloses such matters.

(ID: 410)

21. (d)   An interim review performed for an issuer requires knowledge of the entity's internal control. Knowledge of the entity's internal control is required for an interim review of a nonissuer only when conditions exist such that the interim review is considered to be an extension of the annual audit. In planning such a review, to update the CPA's knowledge about the entity's business and internal control, the CPA should consider the results of audit procedures performed with respect to the current year's financial statements. Other procedures of equal importance, according to the guidance, that should be performed include: (1) reading documentation of the preceding year's audit and of reviews of prior interim periods to identify matters that may be relevant to the current review, for example, the CPA should specifically consider (a) corrected material misstatements, (b) matters identified in any summary of uncorrected misstatements, (c) identified risks of material misstatement due to fraud, including the risk of management override of controls, and (d) significant financial accounting and reporting matters that may be of continuing significance, such as significant deficiencies and material weaknesses; (2) reading the most recent annual and comparable prior interim period financial information; (3) inquiring of management about changes in the entity's business activities; and (4) inquiring of management about whether relevant significant changes in internal control have occurred subsequent to the preceding annual audit or prior review of interim financial information, including changes in the entity's policies, procedures, and personnel, as well as the nature and extent of such changes. Performing analytical procedures on selected accounts would more likely be a review procedure used to gather review evidence rather than to update the CPA's knowledge about the entity's business and internal control. Inquiry of the entity's legal counsel is generally not a review procedure nor is the testing of revenue transactions—these are audit procedures. Reviews do not contemplate the obtainment of corroborating evidence or tests of accounting records. Reviews consist principally of performing analytical procedures and making inquiries of persons within the entity responsible for financial and accounting matters.

(ID: 9947)

Condensed Statements & Selected Data

22. (b)   The auditor's report on condensed financial statements that are derived from financial statements that the CPA has audited should indicate (1) that the auditor has audited and expressed an opinion on the complete financial statements; (2) the date of the auditor's report on the complete financial statements; (3) the type of opinion expressed; and (4) whether, in the auditor's opinion, the information set forth in the condensed financial statements is fairly stated in all material respects in relation to the complete financial statements from which it has been derived. A qualified opinion on the complete set of audited financial statements is not required. The condensed financial statements will not include all the disclosures necessary for the complete set of financial statements. For this reason, they should be read in conjunction with the entity's most recent complete financial statements. A comparative presentation is not required.

(ID: 9400)

Accounting Principles

23. (b) The CPA's report should include a statement that the responsibility for the proper accounting treatment rests with the preparers of the financial statements, who should consult with their continuing accountant, i.e., the accountant who has been engaged to report on the financial statements. The report should also state the engagement was conducted in accordance with standards established by the AICPA; not in accordance with SSARS. There should not be a statement in the report that the application of accounting principles is hypothetical—the CPA should not undertake an engagement to provide a report on the application of accounting principles to a hypothetical transaction. Nor should the CPA accept an engagement to prepare a report based solely on communications with an intermediary. (ID: 6945)

For Use in Other Countries

24. (d) If financial statements prepared in conformity with accounting principles generally accepted in another country are prepared for use *only* outside the United States, the auditor may report using either a US-style report modified to report on the accounting principles of another country, or if appropriate, the report form of the other country. An unmodified US-style report would be inappropriate in this situation. (ID: 389)

25. (a) The auditor must understand the accounting principles of the other country. The auditor does not have to be certified in the other country, disclaim an opinion, or receive a waiver from a board of accountancy. (ID: 5161)

26. (c) A US entity ordinarily prepares financial statements for use in the United States in conformity with accounting principles generally accepted in the United States, but it may also prepare financial statements that are intended for use outside the United States and are prepared in conformity with accounting principles generally accepted in another country. Before reporting on financial statements prepared in conformity with the accounting principles of another country, the auditor should have a clear understanding of, and obtain written representations from management regarding, the purpose and uses of such financial statements. (ID: 7639)

PERFORMANCE BY TOPICS

Each category below parallels a topic covered in Chapter 11. Record the number and percentage of questions you answered correctly in each topic.

Supplementary Information

Question #	Correct	√
1		
2		

\# Questions   2

\# Correct   _____
% Correct   _____

Special Reports

Question #	Correct	√
3		
4		
5		
6		
7		
8		
9		
10		
11		

\# Questions   9

\# Correct   _____
% Correct   _____

Letters for Underwriters

Question #	Correct	√
12		
13		
14		
15		
16		
17		

\# Questions   6

\# Correct   _____
% Correct   _____

Review of Interim Financial Information

Question #	Correct	√
18		
19		
20		
21		

\# Questions   4

\# Correct   _____
% Correct   _____

Condensed Statements & Selected Data

Question #	Correct	√
22		

\# Questions   1

\# Correct   _____
% Correct   _____

Accounting Principles

Question #	Correct	√
23		

\# Questions   1

\# Correct   _____
% Correct   _____

For Use in Other Countries

Question #	Correct	√
24		
25		
26		

\# Questions   3

\# Correct   _____
% Correct   _____

Solution 11-2 SIMULATION ANSWER: Report on Financial Statements Prepared in Conformity with an OCBOA

Report Elements	**Appropriate (A) or Inappropriate (I)**
1. A title that includes the word independent.	A
2. A statement that the financial statements are the responsibility of the company's management.	A
3. A statement that the audit was conducted in accordance with standards established by the American Institute of Certified Public Accountants and includes an identification of the United States of America as the country of origin of those standards.	I
4. A statement that the auditor is responsible for expressing an opinion on the financial statements based on the audit.	A
5. A statement that those standards require that the auditor plan and perform the audit to obtain reasonable assurance about whether the financial statements are free of material misstatement.	A
6. A statement that an audit includes: (a) Examining, on a test basis, evidence supporting the amounts and disclosures in the financial statements; (b) Assessing the accounting principles used and significant estimates made by management; and (c) Evaluating the company's system of internal control.	I
7. A paragraph that describes the basis of the presentation.	I

1. A

2. A

3. I

The report should include a statement that the audit was conducted in accordance with *generally accepted auditing standards* (not standards established by the American Institute of Certified Public Accountants) and includes an identification of the United States of America as the country of origin of those standards.

4. A

5. A

6. I

This statement is correct except for part (c); instead of evaluating the company's system of internal control, it should state that the audit includes *evaluating the overall financial statement presentation*.

7. I

The report should include a paragraph that states the basis of presentation and *refers to the note to the financial statements that describes the basis*.

(ID: 9246)

Solution 11-3 SIMULATION ANSWER: Research

AU	§	634		25	

(ID: 9247)

.25   The letter should not be addressed or given to any parties other than the client and the named underwriters, broker-dealer, financial intermediary or buyer or seller. The appropriate addressee is the intermediary who has negotiated the agreement with the client, and with whom the accountants will deal in discussions regarding the scope and sufficiency of the letter. When a comfort letter is furnished to other accountants, it should be addressed in accordance with the guidance in this paragraph and copies should be furnished to the principal accountants and their client.

———————————

CHAPTER 12

ACCOUNTING & REVIEW SERVICES

CHAPTER 12

ACCOUNTING & REVIEW SERVICES

I. **Compilation & Review Engagements for Nonissuers**

A. **Framework (AR 60)**

1. **Authoritative Guidance Hierarchy**

a. **SSARS** Statements on Standards for Accounting and Review Services (SSARS) are issued by the AICPA and provide performance and reporting guidance for compilations and reviews of unaudited financial statements or other unaudited financial information of nonissuers.

(1) **Exception for Certain Interim Reviews** There is one exception for certain reviews of interim financial information. When all of the following conditions are met, interim reviews should be performed in accordance with GAAS (AU 722, *Interim Financial Information*) instead of SSARS:

- The entity's latest annual financial statements have been audited;

- The CPA has either been engaged to audit the entity's current year financial statements or audited the latest annual financial statements and although an audit of the current year financial statements is expected, the appointment of another auditor to audit them is not effective prior to the beginning of the period to be reviewed; and

- The same financial reporting framework used to prepare the annual financial statements is used for the interim financial information.

(2) **Interim Review Is Extension of Annual Audit** When these conditions are met, the review engagement is generally intended to provide a periodic update to the year-end reporting and is considered an extension of the annual audit. Thus, the standard setters decided the guidance should reside in the auditing literature. (See Chapter 11 for more information on this topic.)

b. **Interpretative Publications** Interpretative publications provide guidance on the application of SSARS. They consist of Interpretations of SSARS; appendices to SSARS; and compilation and review guidance included in AICPA Audit and Accounting Guides and Statements of Position. CPAs should be aware of and consider applicable interpretive publications. Interpretations are recommendations, not standards; however, if a CPA does not apply the applicable interpretative guidance, the CPA should be prepared to justify the departure.

c. **Other Publications** Other compilation and review publications have no authoritative status. A CPA is **not** expected to be aware of the full body of other publications. A CPA should be satisfied that the guidance is both relevant and appropriate. Other publications include AICPA compilation and review publications not listed above; the AICPA annual *Compilation and Review Alert;* compilation and review articles in the *Journal of Accountancy, The CPA Letter,* and other professional journals; and other instructional materials.

2. **Ethical Principles & Quality Control Standards** In addition to SSARS, AICPA members performing compilation and review engagements are governed by the AICPA's Code of Professional Conduct and Statements on Quality Control Standards.

3.   **Definitions**

a.   **Financial Reporting Framework** A set of criteria used to determine measurement, recognition, presentation, and disclosure of all material items appearing in the financial statements.

b.   **Applicable Financial Reporting Framework** The financial reporting framework adopted by management and used in the preparation of the financial statements that is acceptable in view of the nature of the entity and the objective of the financial statements, or that is required by law or regulation. The financial reporting framework encompasses financial accounting standards established by an authorized or recognized standards setting organization.

c.   **Submission of Financial Statements** Presenting to management financial statements that a CPA has prepared.

d.   **Review Evidence** Information used by a CPA to provide a reasonable basis for obtaining limited assurance.

e.   **Third Party** All persons, including those charged with governance, except for members of management.

f.   **Professional Requirements** SSARS use two categories of professional requirements, identified by specific terms to describe the degree of responsibility they impose on CPAs—*unconditional requirements and presumptively mandatory requirements*—which have essentially the same meaning as defined in GAAS covered in Chapter 1.

g.   **Compilation** Assisting management in presenting financial information in the form of financial statements without undertaking to provide any assurance on the statements.

h.   **Review** Obtaining review evidence to provide a limited level of assurance that there are no material modifications that should be made to the financial statements for them to be in conformity with the applicable financial reporting framework.

(1)   **Compilation vs. Review** A compilation does not involve making inquiries or performing analytical or other review procedures. A compilation does not provide any level of assurance. The objective of a review is to provide limited assurance. A CPA need not be independent to perform a compilation; however, the lack of independence must be stated in the report. Independence is required for a review.

(2)   **Review vs. Audit** A review provides only limited assurance that there are no material modifications that should be made to the financial statements for them to be in conformity with the applicable financial reporting framework. An audit provides a high level of assurance (reasonable assurance) that the financial statements are free of material misstatement.

(3)   **Compilation & Review vs. Audit** Neither a review nor a compilation involves obtaining an understanding of internal control, assessing fraud risk, testing accounting records, examining source documents, or other procedures ordinarily performed in an audit.

4.   **Elements of a Compilation or Review Engagement**

a.   **Three-Party Relationship**   A compilation or review engagement involves three parties: management (or the responsible party); a CPA; and intended users, who may be from different entities or the same entity. Sometimes management is the intended user.

(1)   **Management (Responsible Party)**   Management is responsible for the preparation and fair presentation of the financial statements in accordance with the applicable financial reporting framework and for internal control. A CPA is precluded from issuing an unmodified compilation or review report unless management accepts these responsibilities. The CPA may make suggestions about the form or content of the financial statements or prepare them, in whole or in part; however this service is based on information that is the representation of management.

(2)   **CPA**   A CPA (an accountant in the practice of public accounting) should possess a level of knowledge of the accounting principles and practices of the entity's industry needed to compile or review financial statements that are appropriate in form.

(3)   **Intended Users**   The intended users are the person(s) who understand the limitations of the compilation or review engagement and financial statements or financial information. The CPA has no responsibility to identify the intended users. Sometimes intended users (for example, bankers or regulators) will impose additional requirements. The CPA may perform these additional services as long as the CPA adheres to professional standards.

b.   **Applicable Financial Reporting Framework**   Management is responsible for the selection of the entity's applicable financial reporting framework, as well as individual accounting policies when the reporting framework contains acceptable alternatives. Examples of financial reporting frameworks include US GAAP as promulgated by the FASB, GASB, or FASAB; IFRS issued by the IASB; and OCBOA.

c.   **Financial Statements or Financial Information**   A CPA may be engaged to compile or review a complete set of financial statements or an individual financial statement. The financial statements may be for an annual period or for a shorter or longer period, depending on management's needs. The applicable financial reporting framework determines what constitutes a complete set of financial statements.

d.   **Evidence**   When performing a compilation engagement, the CPA has no responsibility to obtain any evidence about the accuracy or completeness of the financial statements. In a review engagement, the CPA should apply professional judgment in determining the specific nature, extent, and timing of review procedures which are deliberately limited relative to an audit. Review evidence obtained through the performance of analytical procedures and inquiries ordinarily will provide the CPA with a reasonable basis for obtaining limited assurance.

e.   **Written Report Objective**   The CPA's objective in reporting is to prevent misinterpretation of the degree of responsibility the CPA is assuming when the CPA's name is associated with the financial statements.

5. **Materiality** The concept of materiality is ordinarily addressed by the applicable financial reporting framework. If not, then the CPA should be guided by the following:

- Misstatements, including omissions, are considered to be material if they, individually or in the aggregate, could reasonably be expected to influence the economic decisions of users taken on the basis of the financial statements;

- Judgments about materiality are made in light of surrounding circumstances and are affected by the size or nature of a misstatement or a combination of both; and

- Judgments about matters that are material to users of the financial statements are based on a consideration of the common financial information needs of users as a group. The possible effect of misstatements on specific individual users, whose needs may vary widely, is **not** considered.

A CPA's determination of materiality is a matter of professional judgment and is affected by the CPA's perception of the financial information needs of users of the financial statements. Appropriate assumptions about users are essentially the same as for GAAS covered in Chapter 2.

B.   Compilation of Financial Statements (AR 80)

1.   **Applicability** A CPA is required to comply with this guidance whenever the CPA is engaged to report on compiled financial statements or submits financial statements to a client or to third parties.

2.   **Objective / Limitation** A compilation is a service, the objective of which is limited to assisting management in presenting financial information in the form of financial statements without undertaking to obtain or provide any assurance that there are no material modifications that should be made to the financial statements in order for the statements to be in conformity with the applicable financial reporting framework.

3.   **Independence Not Required** Independence is **not** required to perform a compilation engagement; however, the lack of it must be stated in the compilation report. See the reporting section of this topic for more information.

4.   **Engagement Letter**

   a.   **Establish & Document an Understanding With the Client** The CPA should establish an understanding with the client regarding the services to be performed and should document the understanding through a written communication with management, i.e., an engagement letter.

   b.   **Contents** The engagement letter should include the objectives and limitations of the engagement as well as management's and the CPA's responsibilities. Thus, the understanding should address the following items:

   - *The objective of a compilation is to assist management in presenting financial information in the form of financial statements.

   - *The CPA utilizes information that is the representation of management without undertaking to obtain or provide any assurance that there are no material modifications that should be made to the financial statements in order for the statements to be in conformity with the applicable financial reporting framework.

   - *Management is responsible for the preparation and fair presentation of the financial statements in accordance with the applicable financial reporting framework.

   - *Management is responsible for designing, implementing, and maintaining internal control relevant to the preparation and fair presentation of the financial statements.

   - Management is responsible for preventing and detecting fraud.

   - Management is responsible for identifying and ensuring that the entity complies with the laws and regulations applicable to its activities.

   - Management is responsible for making all financial records and related information available to the CPA.

   - *The CPA is responsible for conducting the engagement in accordance with SSARS issued by the AICPA.

   - A compilation differs significantly from a review or an audit of financial statements. A compilation does not contemplate performing inquiry, analytical procedures, or other procedures performed in a review. Additionally, a compilation does not contemplate obtaining an understanding of the entity's internal control; assessing fraud risk; testing accounting records by obtaining sufficient appropriate audit evidence through inspection, observation, confirmation, or the examination of source documents (for example, cancelled checks or bank images); or other procedures ordinarily performed in an audit. *Accordingly, the CPA will not express an opinion or provide any assurance regarding the financial statements.

- The engagement cannot be relied upon to disclose errors, fraud, or illegal acts.

- The CPA will inform the appropriate level of management of any material errors and of any evidence or information that comes to the CPA's attention during the performance of compilation procedures that fraud or an illegal act may have occurred. The CPA need not report any matters regarding illegal acts that may have occurred that are clearly inconsequential and may reach agreement in advance with the entity on the nature of any such matters to be communicated.

- The effect of any independence impairments on the expected form of the CPA's compilation report.

*These statements or words to the same effect are also included in the CPA's compilation report.

c. **Additional Matters If Applicable** The engagement letter should also address the following additional matters if applicable:

- Material departures from the applicable financial reporting framework may exist, and the effects of those departures, if any, on the financial statements may not be disclosed.

- Substantially all disclosures (and statement of cash flows, if applicable) required by the applicable financial reporting framework may be omitted.

- Reference to supplementary information

d. **Optional Matters** The letter may also include other matters, for example, fees and billings.

e. **If Report Not Issued** If the compiled financial statements are **not** expected to be used by a third party and the CPA does **not** expect to issue a compilation report, the CPA should include in the engagement letter an acknowledgment of management's representation and agreement that the financial statements are not to be used by a third party.

5. **Performance Requirements**

a. **Understanding of the Industry** To compile financial statements that are appropriate in form for a particular industry, a CPA should understand the accounting principles and practices of that industry. A CPA can accept an engagement for an entity in an industry in which the CPA has no previous experience as long as the CPA can acquire the knowledge by consulting AICPA guides, industry publications, financial statements of other entities in the industry, textbooks and periodicals, appropriate continuing professional education, or individuals knowledgeable about the industry.

b. **Knowledge of the Client**

(1) **Business** A CPA should obtain a general understanding of the client's organization; operating characteristics; and the nature of its assets, liabilities, revenues, and expenses. This knowledge is usually acquired through experience with the client or its industry and inquiry of its personnel.

(2) **Accounting Principles & Practices** The CPA should obtain an understanding of the accounting principles and practices used by the client in measuring, recognizing, recording, and disclosing all significant accounts and disclosures in the financial statements. The CPA should be alert to accounting policies and

procedures that are unusual as compared with normal practices within the industry.

    c.   **Read the Financial Statements** Before submission, the CPA should read the financial statements to consider if they

- Appear to be appropriate in form; and

- Are free from obvious material errors.

This would encompass detection of math or clerical errors and misapplication of accounting principles, including inadequate disclosure.

    d.   **Problems With Information or Fraud / Illegal Acts** Although a CPA is not required to verify information supplied by the client, a CPA may become aware that information is unsatisfactory or that fraud or an illegal act may have occurred. The CPA should request that management consider the effect of these matters on the financial statements. The CPA should then consider the effect of management's conclusions on the CPA's compilation report. If the financial statements may be materially misstated and the client refuses to supply additional or revised information, the CPA should withdraw from the engagement.

6.   **Documentation**

    a.   **Purpose** The documentation is the CPA's primary support that the engagement was performed in accordance with SSARS as stated in the report.

    b.   **Content** The CPA should prepare documentation in sufficient detail to provide a clear understanding of the work performed. It should include

- The engagement letter;

- Significant findings or issues and their resolution; and

- Communications, oral or written, to management about fraud or illegal acts.

7.   **Reporting**

    a.   **When a Report Is Not Required** When a CPA submits compiled financial statements to a client that are **not** expected to be used by a third party, a report is not required; however, each page of the financial statements should include a reference restricting their use, such as *Restricted for Management's Use Only*.

    b.   **When a Report Is Required** When a CPA is engaged to report on compiled financial statements or submits financial statements that are to be used by a third party, the statements should be accompanied by a written report. Procedures that may have been performed as part of the compilation engagement should **not** be described in the report.

    c.   **Standard Compilation Report Structure** The standard report is comprised of three paragraphs:

- Introductory paragraph

- Management's responsibilities paragraph

- Accountant's responsibilities paragraph

Exhibit 1 ▶ Standard Compilation Report

> Accountant's Compilation Report
>
> We have compiled the accompanying balance sheet of XYZ Company as of December 31, 20XX, and the related statements of income, retained earnings, and cash flows for the year then ended. We have not audited or reviewed the accompanying financial statements and, accordingly, do not express an opinion or provide any assurance about whether the financial statements are in accordance with accounting principles generally accepted in the United States of America.
>
> Management is responsible for the preparation and fair presentation of the financial statements in accordance with accounting principles generally accepted in the United States of America and for designing, implementing, and maintaining internal control relevant to the preparation and fair presentation of the financial statements.
>
> Our responsibility is to conduct the compilation in accordance with Statements on Standards for Accounting and Review Services issued by the American Institute of Certified Public Accountants. The objective of a compilation is to assist management in presenting financial information in the form of financial statements without undertaking to obtain or provide any assurance that there are no material modifications that should be made to the financial statements.

Note that the management's responsibilities paragraph is the same as for a review report (AR 90) covered in this chapter.

d.   **Title** If applicable, the title may be Independent's Accountant's Compilation Report.

e.   **Date** The date of completion of the compilation should be the date of the report.

f.   **Financial Statements' Reference to Report** Each page of the financial statements should include a reference, such as *See Accountant's Compilation Report*.

g.   **Financial Statements That Omit Substantially All Disclosures** A CPA may be requested to compile financial statements that omit substantially all disclosures required by an applicable financial reporting framework. This is permissible as long as the intent is not to mislead. An explanatory paragraph should be added **after** the accountant's responsibilities paragraph.

Exhibit 2 ▶ Substantially All Disclosures Omitted Explanatory Paragraph

> Management has elected to omit substantially all of the disclosures required by accounting principles generally accepted in the United States of America. If the omitted disclosures were included in the financial statements, they might influence the user's conclusions about the company's financial position, results of operations, and cash flows. Accordingly, the financial statements are not designed for those who are not informed about such matters.

h.   **Financial Statements That Include Only a Few Disclosures** When the entity wishes to include disclosures about only a few matters in the form of notes to the financial statements, such disclosures should be labeled *Selected Information—Substantially All Disclosures Required by* [identify the applicable financial reporting framework] *Are Not Included*.

i.   **Reporting When Not Independent** A CPA is **not** required to be independent of an entity to issue a compilation report; however, the report must be modified.

    (1)   **Report Modification** The report should be modified by adding a final paragraph that specifically discloses the lack of independence, such as: *We are not independent with respect to XYZ Company.*

    (2)   **Disclosure of Reasons Is Permitted** The CPA may disclose the reason(s) the CPA's independence is impaired in the same final paragraph. If the CPA elects to do this, *all* the reasons should be included. An example of a final paragraph disclosing the reason for the impairment of independence is *We are not independent with respect to XYZ Company as of and for the year ended December 31, 20XX, because a member of the engagement team had a direct financial interest in XYZ Company.*

j.   **Emphasis of a Matter Paragraph** As long as the matter is disclosed in the financial statements (emphasis paragraphs should not be used in lieu of management disclosures), a CPA may add a separate explanatory paragraph to the report to emphasize a matter. Emphasis paragraphs are never required.

Note that this guidance is essentially the same for a review engagement (AR 90) covered in this chapter.

k.   **Material Departures From Applicable Financial Reporting Framework / Financial Statements Not Revised**

    (1)   **When Modification of the Report Is Adequate** The departure should be disclosed in a separate paragraph of the report, including disclosure of the effects on the financial statements. If the effects have not been determined by management or are not known as the result of the CPA's procedures, the CPA is not required to determine them; however, the report should include a statement that such determination has not been made.

Exhibit 3 ▶ Compilation Report Disclosing a Departure From Applicable Financial Reporting Framework

---

Accountant's Compilation Report
Introductory & Management's Responsibilities Paragraphs
Same as standard compilation report
Accountant's Responsibilities Paragraph
Same, except the following is added as the last sentence:

During our compilation, we did become aware of a departure from accounting principles generally accepted in the United States of America that is described in the following paragraph.

Explanatory Paragraph Added

As disclosed in Note X to the financial statements, accounting principles generally accepted in the United States of America require that land be stated at cost. Management has informed us that the company has stated its land at appraised value and that, if accounting principles generally accepted in the United States of America had been followed, the land account and stockholders' equity would have been decreased by $500,000.

---

    (2)   **When Modification of the Report Is Not Adequate** If modification of the report is not adequate to indicate the deficiencies in the financial statements as a whole, the CPA should withdraw from the engagement and provide no further

services with respect to those financial statements. The CPA may wish to consult with legal counsel.

Note that, except for the report modifications, this guidance is essentially the same for a review engagement (AR 90) covered in this chapter.

l. **Restricted Use Reports**

(1) **General Use Reports** Reports on financial statements prepared in conformity with an applicable financial reporting framework ordinarily are not restricted regarding use. These are known as *general use* reports.

(2) **Restricted Use Reports** The term restricted use applies to reports intended only for one or more specified third parties. The need for restriction may result from the purpose of the report and the potential for the report to be misunderstood when taken out of the context. A CPA should restrict the use of a report when the subject matter or the presentation being reported on is based on measurement or disclosure criteria contained in contractual agreements or regulatory provisions that are not in conformity with an applicable financial reporting framework.

(3) **General & Restricted Subject Matter Combined in One Report** The combined report should be restricted.

(4) **Paragraph Added to Restrict Use of the Report** The paragraph should be added to the end of the report and should include:

- A statement that the report is intended solely for the use of the specified parties

- An identification of the specified parties

- A statement that the report is not intended to be and should not be used by anyone other than the specified parties

Note that this guidance is essentially the same for a review engagement (AR 90) covered in this chapter.

m. **Going Concern Problems** If disclosure about the uncertainty is excluded or inadequate it should be handled in the CPA's report like any other material departure from an applicable financial reporting framework. If disclosed, the CPA may elect to include an emphasis paragraph.

Note that this guidance is essentially the same for a review engagement (AR 90) covered in this chapter.

n. **Subsequent Events** If the subsequent event is not adequately accounted for in the financial statements or disclosed in the notes, it should be handled in the CPA's report like any other material departure from an applicable financial reporting framework. If disclosed, the CPA may elect to include an emphasis paragraph.

Note that this guidance is essentially the same for a review engagement (AR 90) covered in this chapter.

o. **Subsequent Discovery of Facts Existing at the Date of the Report** The guidance is essentially the same as for an audit engagement as covered in Chapter 8.

Note that this guidance is essentially the same for a review engagement (AR 90) covered in this chapter.

p. **Supplementary Information**

(1) **Degree of Responsibility** When the financial statements are accompanied by information presented for supplementary analysis purposes, the CPA should clearly indicate the degree of responsibility, if any, the CPA is taking with respect to such information.

(2) **Report Modification** When the CPA has compiled both the financial statements and other data presented only for supplementary analysis purposes, the report should refer to the other data, or the CPA can issue a separate report on the other data. If a separate report is issued, the report should state that the other data accompanying the financial statements is presented only for the purposes of additional analysis, and that it has been compiled from information that is the representation of management, without audit or review, and that the CPA does not express an opinion or provide any assurance on such data.

8. **Communications Regarding Fraud or Illegal Acts** When information comes to the CPA's attention that fraud or an illegal act may have occurred, it should be brought to the attention of the appropriate level of management. The CPA should also consider consulting with legal counsel.

a. **Inconsequential** The CPA need not report matters that are clearly inconsequential and may reach agreement in advance with the entity on the nature of such items to be communicated.

b. **Senior Management Implicated** When such matters involve senior management, the CPA should report the matter to an individual or group at a higher level, such as the owner or those charged with governance. Communication can be oral or written; if oral, the CPA should document it.

c. **Owner Implicated** When matters involve an owner of the business, the CPA should consider withdrawing from the engagement.

d. **Duty to Disclose to Outside Parties** The guidance is essentially the same as for an audit client as covered in Chapter 2.

Note that this guidance is essentially the same for a review engagement (AR 90) covered in this chapter.

9. **Change in Engagement** Before the completion of the audit or review, a CPA may be requested to change the engagement to a compilation.

a. **Considerations** Before the CPA agrees to change the engagement to a compilation, the following should be considered:

• The client's reason for the request, particularly the implications of a restriction on the scope of the audit or review

• The additional effort required to complete the audit or review

• The estimated additional cost to complete the audit or review

If the additional cost or effort to complete the audit or review is minimal, the CPA should consider the propriety of accepting a change in the engagement.

b. **Reasonable Bases for Change in Engagement**

(1) **Change in Circumstances** A change in circumstances affecting the entity's requirement for an audit or review

(2) **Misunderstanding** A misunderstanding regarding the nature of an audit, review, or compilation

c. **Scope Restriction of Audit or Review** If the reason for the request is due to a restriction on the scope of the audit or review, whether imposed by the client or caused by circumstance, the decision to change the engagement can be more problematic. The CPA should evaluate the possibility that information affected by the scope restriction may be incorrect, incomplete, or otherwise unsatisfactory.

Ordinarily, the CPA is precluded from issuing a compilation report when

- During an audit, the CPA has been prohibited by the client from corresponding with the entity's legal counsel; or

- During an audit or review, a management representation letter is not provided.

d. **When Change to a Compilation Occurs** The compilation report should **not** include reference to

- The original engagement;

- Any audit or review procedures that may have been performed; or

- Any scope limitations that resulted in the changed engagement.

Note that this guidance is essentially the same for a review engagement (AR 90) covered in this chapter.

C. **Review of Financial Statements (AR 90)**

1. **Applicability** A CPA is required to comply with this guidance whenever the CPA has been engaged to review financial statements, except for reviews of interim financial information if the following are true:

- The entity's latest annual financial statements have been audited;

- The CPA has been engaged to audit the entity's current year financial statements, or audited the latest annual statements and another CPA's appointment to audit the current year statements is not effective prior to the beginning of the period covered by the review; and

- The same financial reporting framework used to prepare the annual financial statements is used for the interim financial information.

When all of these conditions are met, interim reviews should be performed in accordance with GAAS (AU 722, *Interim Financial Information*) instead of SSARS. In this circumstance, the review engagement is generally intended to provide a periodic update to the year-end reporting and is considered an extension of the annual audit. Thus, the standard setters decided the guidance should reside in the auditing literature.

2. **Objective / Limitation** A review is a service, the objective of which is to obtain limited assurance that there are no material modifications that should be made to the financial statements in order for the statements to be in conformity with the applicable financial reporting framework.

3. **Independence** A CPA is precluded from performing a review engagement if the CPA's independence is impaired for any reason.

4. **Engagement Letter**

a. **Establish & Document an Understanding With the Client** The CPA should establish an understanding with the client regarding the services to be performed and should document the understanding through a written communication with management, i.e., an engagement letter.

b. **Contents** The engagement letter should include the objectives and limitations of the engagement as well as management's and the CPA's responsibilities. Thus, the understanding should address the following items:

- *The objective of a review is to obtain limited assurance that there are no material modifications that should be made to the financial statements in order for the statements to be in conformity with the applicable financial reporting framework.

- *Management is responsible for the preparation and fair presentation of the financial statements in accordance with the applicable financial reporting framework.

- *Management is responsible for designing, implementing, and maintaining internal control relevant to the preparation and fair presentation of the financial statements.

- Management is responsible for preventing and detecting fraud.

- Management is responsible for identifying and ensuring that the entity complies with the laws and regulations applicable to its activities.

- Management is responsible for making all financial records and related information available to the CPA.

- Management will provide the CPA, at the conclusion of the engagement, with a letter that confirms certain representations made during the review.

- *The CPA is responsible for conducting the engagement in accordance with SSARS issued by the AICPA.

- *A review includes primarily applying analytical procedures to management's financial data and making inquiries of company management.

- *A review is substantially less in scope than an audit, the objective of which is the expression of an opinion regarding the financial statements as a whole.

- A review does not contemplate obtaining an understanding of the entity's internal control; assessing fraud risk; testing accounting records by obtaining sufficient appropriate audit evidence through inspection, observation, confirmation, or the examination of source documents (for example, cancelled checks or bank images); or other procedures ordinarily performed in an audit. *Accordingly, the CPA will not express an opinion regarding the financial statements as a whole.

- The engagement cannot be relied upon to disclose errors, fraud, or illegal acts.

- The CPA will inform the appropriate level of management of any material errors and of any evidence or information that comes to the CPA's attention during the performance of review procedures that fraud or an illegal act may have occurred. The CPA need not report any matters regarding illegal acts that may have occurred that are clearly inconsequential and may reach agreement in advance with the entity on the nature of any such matters to be communicated.

*These statements or words to the same effect are also included in the CPA's review report.

c.   **Additional Matters If Applicable** The engagement letter should also address the following additional matters if applicable:

- Material departures from the applicable financial reporting framework may exist, and the effects of those departures, if any, on the financial statements may not be disclosed.

- Reference to supplementary information

d.   **Optional Matters** The letter may also include other matters, for example, fees and billings.

5.   **Performance Requirements** Review evidence obtained through the performance of analytical procedures and inquiries will ordinarily provide the CPA with a reasonable basis for expressing limited assurance; however, the CPA should perform additional procedures if necessary. The design and performance of review procedures should be based on the CPA's understanding of the industry and the client as well as awareness of the risk that the financial statements may be materially misstated. The CPA should focus the analytical procedures and inquiries in areas of increased risk of misstatement.

a.   **Understanding of the Industry** The CPA should possess an understanding of the industry in which the client operates, including the accounting principles and practices generally used in the industry sufficient to assist the CPA with determining the specific nature, timing, and extent of review procedures to be performed. A CPA can accept an engagement for an entity in an industry in which the CPA has no previous experience as long as the CPA can acquire the knowledge by consulting AICPA guides, industry publications, financial statements of other entities in the industry, textbooks and periodicals, appropriate continuing professional education, or individuals knowledgeable about the industry.

b.   **Knowledge of the Client** An understanding of the client's business and knowledge of the accounting principles and practices of the client's industry is needed so that the CPA can determine and apply appropriate inquiries and analytics.

(1) **Business** A CPA should obtain a general understanding of the client's organization; operating characteristics; and the nature of its assets, liabilities, revenues, and expenses. This knowledge is usually acquired through experience with the client or its industry and inquiry of its personnel.

(2) **Accounting Principles & Practices** The CPA should obtain an understanding of the accounting principles and practices used by the client in measuring, recognizing, recording, and disclosing all significant accounts and disclosures in the financial statements. The CPA can gain this understanding through inquiry, the review of client prepared documents, or experience with the client. The CPA should be alert to accounting policies and procedures that are unusual as compared with normal practices within the industry.

c.   **Analytical Procedures** If analytical procedures performed identify fluctuations or relationships that are inconsistent with other relevant information or that differ from expected values by a significant amount, the CPA should investigate these differences by inquiring of management and performing other procedures. Although the CPA is not required to corroborate management's responses with other evidence (as in an audit), the CPA may need to perform other procedures when, for example, management is unable to provide an explanation, or the explanation, together with review evidence obtained relevant to management's response, is not considered adequate. In other words, the CPA should consider the reasonableness and consistency of management's responses.

d. **Inquiries of Financial Management** The CPA should consider making the following inquiries of financial management:

- Whether the financial statements have been prepared in conformity with the applicable financial reporting framework

- The client's accounting principles and practices and the methods followed in applying them and procedures for recording, classifying, and summarizing transactions, and accumulating information for disclosure in the financial statements

- Unusual or complex situations that may have an effect on the financial statements

- Significant transactions occurring or recognized near the end of the reporting period

- The status of uncorrected misstatements identified during the previous engagement

- Questions that have arisen in the course of applying the review procedures

- Events subsequent to the date of the financial statements that could have a material effect on the financial statements

- Their knowledge of any fraud or suspected fraud affecting the entity involving management or others where the fraud could have a material effect on the financial statements

- Significant journal entries and other adjustments

- Communications from regulatory agencies

e. **Other Inquiries & Review Procedures** The CPA should also consider making these inquiries or performing these procedures:

- Inquiries concerning actions taken at meetings of stockholders, board of directors, committees of the board of directors, or comparable meetings that may affect the financial statements

- Reading the financial statements to consider whether they appear to conform with the applicable financial reporting framework

- Obtaining reports from other accountants, if any, who have been engaged to audit or review the financial statements of significant components of the entity, its subsidiaries and other investees

Again, the CPA is not required to corroborate management's responses with other evidence; however, the CPA should consider the reasonableness and consistency of management's responses in light of the results of other review procedures and the accountant's knowledge of the client's business and the industry in which it operates.

f. **Management Representations** The CPA must obtain representations from management for all financial statements and periods covered by the review report.

(1) **Content** The CPA should request that management provide written representations related to the following matters; however the representation letter ordinarily should be tailored to include additional appropriate representations relating to matters specific to the entity's business or industry.

- Management's acknowledgment of its responsibility for the preparation and fair presentation of the financial statements in accordance with the applicable financial reporting framework

- Management's belief that the financial statements are fairly presented in conformity with the applicable financial reporting framework

- Management's acknowledgement of its responsibility for designing, implementing, and maintaining internal control relevant to the preparation and fair presentation of the financial statements

- Management's acknowledgement of its responsibility to prevent and detect fraud

- Knowledge of any fraud or suspected fraud affecting the entity involving management or others where the fraud could have a material effect on the financial statements, including any communications received from employees, former employees, or others

- Management's full and truthful response to all inquiries

- Completeness of information

- Information concerning subsequent events

(2)   **Date**   The letter should be dated as of the date of the CPA's review report.

(3)   **Address**   The letter should be addressed to the CPA.

(4)   **Signatures**   The letter should be signed by members of management that are responsible for and knowledgeable about the matters covered. Current management must provide the representations for all periods covered by the financial statements and the review report even if they were not present for all periods. Normally, the chief executive officer and chief financial officer or others with equivalent positions in the entity should sign the representation letter.

(5)   **Updating Management Representations**   The guidance for obtaining an updated management representation letter is essentially the same as for an audit covered in Chapter 4.

6.   **Documentation**

a.   **Purpose**   The documentation is the CPA's primary support for both the representation in the CPA's review report that the engagement was performed in accordance with SSARS and for the limited assurance expressed in the report.

b.   **Content**   The CPA should prepare documentation in sufficient detail to provide a clear understanding of the work performed (including the nature, timing, extent, and results of review procedures performed); the review evidence obtained and its source; and the conclusions reached. Because of differing circumstances, it is not possible to specify the form, content, or extent of the documentation that a CPA should prepare for each engagement; however it should include the following:

- The engagement letter

- Analytical procedures performed, including:

  - The expectations and the factors considered in their development

  - The results of the comparison of the expectations to the recorded amounts or ratios

  - Management's responses to the CPA's inquiries regarding fluctuations or relationships that are inconsistent with other relevant information or that differ from expected values by a significant amount

- A description and the results of any additional procedures performed in response to significant unexpected differences arising from analytical procedures

- Significant matters covered by the CPA's inquiries and the responses

- Any significant findings or issues (for example, the results of review procedures that indicate the financial statements could be materially misstated) including actions taken and final conclusions

- Significant unusual matters that the CPA considered while performing the review procedures, including their disposition

- Communications (oral and written) to management about fraud or illegal acts

- Management's representation letter

c. **Oral Explanations** Oral explanations on their own do not represent sufficient support for the work performed or conclusions reached but may be used to clarify or explain information contained in the documentation.

7. **Incomplete Review** When the CPA is unable to perform the inquiry and analytical procedures necessary to obtain limited assurance or the client does not provide the CPA with a representation letter, the review will be incomplete and a review report should **not** be issued. In such a situation, the CPA should consider whether it is appropriate to issue a compilation report on the financial statements.

8. **Reporting** Financial statements reviewed by a CPA should be accompanied by a written report.

a. **Standard Review Report Structure** The standard report is comprised of four paragraphs:

- Introductory paragraph

- Management's responsibilities paragraph (same as for the standard compilation of financial statements report)

- Accountant's responsibilities paragraph

- Results of engagement paragraph

Exhibit 4 ▶ Standard Review Report

Independent Accountant's Review Report

We have reviewed the accompanying balance sheet of XYZ Company as of December 31, 20XX, and the related statements of income, retained earnings, and cash flows for the year then ended. A review includes primarily applying analytical procedures to management's financial data and making inquiries of company management. A review is substantially less in scope than an audit, the objective of which is the expression of an opinion regarding the financial statements as a whole. Accordingly, we do not express such an opinion.

Management is responsible for the preparation and fair presentation of the financial statements in accordance with accounting principles generally accepted in the United States of America and for designing, implementing, and maintaining internal control relevant to the preparation and fair presentation of the financial statements.

Our responsibility is to conduct the review in accordance with Statements on Standards for Accounting and Review Services issued by the American Institute of Certified Public Accountants. Those standards require us to perform procedures to obtain limited assurance that there are no material modifications that should be made to the financial statements. We believe that the results of our procedures provide a reasonable basis for our report.

Based on our review, we are not aware of any material modifications that should be made to the accompanying financial statements in order for them to be in conformity with accounting principles generally accepted in the United States of America.

---

b. **Date** The report should not be dated earlier than the date on which the CPA has accumulated review evidence sufficient to provide a reasonable basis for concluding that the CPA has obtained limited assurance that there are no material modifications that should be made to the financial statements in order for the statements to be in conformity with the applicable financial reporting framework.

c. **Financial Statements' Reference to Report** Each page of the financial statements should include a reference, such as *See Independent Accountant's Review Report.*

d. **Limited Reporting Engagement** A CPA may be asked to issue a review report on one financial statement, such as a balance sheet, and not on other related financial statements, such as the statements of income, retained earnings, and cash flows. The CPA may do so if the scope of the CPA's inquiries and analytical procedures has not been restricted.

e. **Emphasis of a Matter Paragraph** The guidance is the essentially the same as for a compilation engagement (AR 80) covered in this chapter.

f. **Material Departures From Applicable Financial Reporting Framework / Financial Statements Not Revised** Except for the report modifications shown in the next exhibit, the guidance is essentially the same as for a compilation engagement (AR 80) covered in this chapter.

Exhibit 5 ▶ Review Report Disclosing a Departure From Applicable Financial Reporting Framework

Independent Accountant's Review Report
Introductory & Management's Responsibilities Paragraphs *Same as standard review report*
Accountant's Responsibilities Paragraph *Modification shown in boldface*
Based on our review, **with the exception of the matter described in the following paragraph**, we are not aware of any material modifications that should be made to the accompanying financial statements in order for them to be in conformity with accounting principles generally accepted in the United States of America.
Explanatory Paragraph Added
As disclosed in Note X to the financial statements, accounting principles generally accepted in the United States of America require that land be stated at cost. Management has informed us that the company has stated its land at appraised value and that, if accounting principles generally accepted in the United States of America had been followed, the land account and stockholders' equity would have been decreased by $500,000.

g. **Restricted Use Reports** The guidance is essentially the same as for a compilation engagement (AR 80) covered in this chapter.

h. **Going Concern Problems** The guidance is essentially the same as for a compilation engagement (AR 80) covered in this chapter.

i. **Subsequent Events** The guidance is essentially the same as for a compilation engagement (AR 80) covered in this chapter.

j. **Subsequent Discovery of Facts Existing at the Date of the Report** As was the case for a compilation engagement, the guidance is essentially the same as for an audit engagement covered in Chapter 8.

k.   **Supplementary Information**   When the financial statements are accompanied by information presented for supplementary analysis purposes, the CPA should clearly indicate the degree of responsibility, if any, the CPA is taking with respect to such information.

When the CPA has reviewed the financial statements, an explanation should be included in the review report or in a separate report on the other data. The report should state that the review has been made for the purpose of expressing a conclusion that there are no material modifications that should be made to the statements in order for them to be in conformity with the applicable financial reporting framework and the other data accompanying the statements is presented only for purposes of additional analysis and that it either

- Has been subjected to the inquiry and analytical procedures applied in the review of the statements, and the CPA did not become aware of any material modifications that should be made to such data, *or*

- Has **not** been subjected to the inquiry and analytical procedures applied in the review of the statements, but was compiled from information that is the representation of management, without audit or review, and the CPA does not express an opinion or provide any assurance on such data.

9.   **Communications Regarding Fraud or Illegal Acts**   The guidance is essentially the same as for a compilation engagement (AR 80) covered in this chapter.

10.   **Change in Engagement From Audit to a Review**   The guidance is essentially the same as for a change in engagement from an audit or review to a compilation (AR 80) covered in this chapter.

D.   **Compilation Reports on Financial Statements in Certain Prescribed Forms (AR 300)**
A prescribed form is any standard preprinted form adopted by the body to which it is to be submitted, e.g., forms used by governmental and regulatory bodies other than those concerned with the sale or trading of securities, industry trade associations, etc. A form adopted by the entity whose financial statements are to be compiled is **not** considered to be a prescribed form.

1.   **Applicability**   SSARS guidance on compilations (AR 80) and reporting on comparative financial statements (AR 200) is applicable when the unaudited financial statements are included in a prescribed form.

This standard (AR 300) provides guidance when the prescribed form or related instructions call for a departure from the applicable financial reporting framework in a compilation engagement. The nature of the departure may be the specification of a nonconforming measurement principle or the failure to request the required presentation or disclosures.

This standard also provides additional guidance applicable to reports on financial statements included in a prescribed form.

2.   **Departures From the Reporting Framework Required by the Prescribed Form**   There is a presumption that the information required by a prescribed form is sufficient to meet the needs of the body that adopted the form; thus, there is no need to advise that body about departures from the applicable financial reporting framework required by the prescribed form or related instructions. However, note that the report should be a restricted use report.

Exhibit 6 ▶ Compilation Report for a Prescribed Form That Calls for a Departure From the Applicable Financial Reporting Framework

Accountant's Compilation Report

We have compiled the [*identification of financial statements, including period covered and the name of entity*] included in the accompanying prescribed form. We have not audited or reviewed the financial statements included in the accompanying prescribed form and, accordingly, do not express an opinion or provide any assurance about whether the financial statements are in accordance with accounting principles generally accepted in the United States of America.

Management is responsible for the preparation and fair presentation of the financial statements included in the form prescribed by [*name of body*] in accordance with accounting principles generally accepted in the United States of America and for designing, implementing, and maintaining internal control relevant to the preparation and fair presentation of the financial statements.

Our responsibility is to conduct the compilation in accordance with Statements on Standards for Accounting and Review Services issued by the American Institute of Certified Public Accountants. The objective of a compilation is to assist management in presenting financial information in the form of financial statements without undertaking to obtain or provide any assurance that there are no material modifications that should be made to the financial statements.

The financial statements included in the accompanying prescribed form are presented in accordance with the requirements of [*name of body*], and are not intended to be a presentation in accordance with accounting principles generally accepted in the United States of America.

This report is intended solely for the information and use of [*the specified parties*] and is not intended to be and should not be used by anyone other than these specified parties.

3. **Other Departures From the Reporting Framework or From the Requirements of the Prescribed Form** If a departure from the applicable financial reporting framework other than departures required by the prescribed form or a departure from the prescribed form's requirements exist, the CPA should follow SSARS guidance on compilations (AR 80) regarding departures from the applicable financial reporting framework.

4. **Preprinted Form Not Conforming With SSARS** A CPA should not sign a preprinted report form that does not conform with SSARS compilation guidance in AR 80 or this standard (AR 300), whichever is applicable. In such circumstances, the CPA should append an appropriate report to the prescribed form.

E. **Personal Financial Statements (AR 600)**

1. **Purpose** This standard allows a CPA to submit a written personal financial plan containing unaudited personal financial statements to a client without complying with SSARS guidance on compilations (AR 80) when certain conditions exist.

2. **Conditions for Exemption From SSARS** The CPA may elect to take the exemption if *all* of the following conditions are met:

   - The CPA establishes an understanding with the client and documents the understanding through a written communication with the client that the financial statements

     - Will be used solely to assist the client and the client's advisers to develop the client's personal financial goals and objectives; and

     - Will not be used to obtain credit or for any purposes other than developing these goals and objectives.

   - Nothing comes to the CPA's attention during the engagement that would cause the CPA to believe that the financial statements will be used to obtain credit or for any purposes other than developing the client's financial goals and objectives.

3.   **Report Required**   The issuance of a written report is required if this exemption is exercised. Note that the CPA states that the financial statement has not been audited, reviewed, *or compiled.*

Exhibit 7 ▶ Report When the CPA Submits a Written Financial Plan Containing Unaudited Personal Financial Statements That Are Exempt From AR 80

> The accompanying Statement of Financial Condition of X, as of December 31, 20XX, was prepared solely to help you develop your personal financial plan. Accordingly, it may be incomplete or contain other departures from accounting principles generally accepted in the United States of America and should not be used to obtain credit or for any purposes other than developing your financial plan. We have not audited, reviewed, or compiled the statement.

F.   **Communications Between Predecessor & Successor Accountants (AR 400)**

1.   **Purpose**   This standard provides guidance to a successor CPA who decides to communicate with a predecessor CPA about the acceptance or performance of a compilation or review engagement. The successor should bear in mind that the predecessor and the client may have disagreed about accounting principles, procedures applied by the predecessor, or similarly significant matters.

2.   **Definitions**

   a.   **Successor**   The successor is either considering making a proposal to compile or review financial statements or has accepted the engagement.

   b.   **Predecessor**   The predecessor may have reported on the most recent financial statements or been engaged to perform, but did not complete, a review or compilation and has either resigned or been terminated.

3.   **Client Consent**   As with an audit, a successor should obtain specific consent from a prospective client to make any inquiries of a predecessor and request that the client authorize the predecessor to respond fully. If the prospective client refuses to permit the predecessor to respond or limits the response, the successor should inquire about the reasons and consider the implications regarding the pursuance of the engagement.

   Upon acceptance, the successor may wish to review the predecessor's engagement documentation. The successor should also request the client to ask the predecessor to allow this access.

4.   **Communication With Predecessor Regarding Engagement Acceptance**

   a.   **Circumstances When Communication Is Recommended**   Unlike an audit, a successor is **not** required to communicate with a predecessor regarding the acceptance of a compilation or review engagement, but may deem it prudent to do so when, for example,

   •   Information obtained about the prospective client is limited or appears to require special attention;

   •   The change in CPAs takes place substantially after the end of the accounting period; or

   •   There have been frequent changes in CPAs.

   b.   **Inquiries**   The guidance regarding the inquiries is essentially the same as for an audit as covered in Chapter 1 with these differences:

   •   SSARS include an inquiry about the cooperation of management in providing additional or revised information, if necessary.

- SSARS do **not** include an inquiry about significant deficiencies and material weaknesses in internal control (because neither a review nor a compilation requires obtaining an understanding of the client's internal control).

    c.   **Responses** The guidance regarding the responses is essentially the same as for an audit as covered in Chapter 1.

5.   Other Inquiries

    a.   **Engagement Documentation** The guidance regarding inquiries involving engagement documentation is essentially the same as for an audit as covered in Chapter 1. SSARS provide a shorter list of documentation that would most likely be of interest: documentation relating to contingencies and other matters of continuing accounting significance.

    b.   **Reference** The successor should **not** refer to the report or work of the predecessor in the report, except as specifically permitted by AR 200 with respect to the financial statements of a prior period.

6.   Prior Financial Statements Require Revision

    a.   **Course of Action** If revisions to the financial statements reported on by the predecessor may be required, the successor should ask the client to contact the predecessor. The successor should follow the guidance on compilations (AR 80) and reviews (AR 90) regarding subsequent discovery of facts existing at the date of the report which is essentially the same as for an audit covered in Chapter 8.

    b.   **If Client Does Not Cooperate** The guidance is essentially the same as for an audit as covered in Chapter 1.

G.   Compilations of Presentations Other Than Financial Statements (AR 110 & 120)

1.   Compilation of Specified Elements, Accounts, or Items of a Financial Statement (AR 110)

    a.   **Applicability** A CPA is required to comply with this guidance whenever the CPA is engaged to report on one or more compiled specified elements, accounts, or items of a financial statement (items) or submits same to a client or to third parties. However, if the item is included as supplementary information, the CPA should refer to that topic (supplementary information) in AR 80.

    b.   **Definition** A compilation of an item is limited to assisting management in presenting financial information without undertaking to obtain or provide any assurance that there are no material modifications that should be made to that information. This may be undertaken as a separate engagement or in conjunction with a compilation, review, or audit of financial statements. Examples of items that a CPA may compile include schedules of rentals, royalties, profit participation, or provision for income taxes.

    c.   **Engagement Letter** This guidance is the essentially the same as for a compilation of financial statements (AR 80) covered in this chapter.

    d.   **Performance Requirements** This guidance is the essentially the same as for a compilation of financial statements (AR 80) covered in this chapter.

    e.   **Documentation** This guidance is the essentially the same as for a compilation of financial statements (AR 80) covered in this chapter.

      f.   **Reporting**

          (1)   **Whether to Issue a Report** A report is **not** required for this engagement unless the CPA has been engaged to report on the item. However, if it is likely that the CPA's name will be associated with the presentation and because of that a user may inappropriately infer an unintended level of assurance, the CPA should consider issuing a report. Procedures that the may have been performed as part of the compilation engagement should not be described in the report.

          (2)   **Report Structure**

          Exhibit 8 ▶ Standard Compilation Report on a Schedule of Accounts Receivable

Accountant's Compilation Report
All 3 Paragraphs *Same as for a compilation of financial statements* Except Replace the references to *financial statements* with *schedule of the item*

          (3)   **Title** This guidance is the essentially the same as for a compilation of financial statements (AR 80) covered in this chapter.

          (4)   **Date** This guidance is the essentially the same as for a compilation of financial statements (AR 80) covered in this chapter.

          (5)   **Financial Statements Reference to Report** This guidance is the essentially the same as for a compilation of financial statements (AR 80) covered in this chapter.

          (6)   **Engagement in Conjunction With a Compilation of Financial Statements** If this compilation was performed in conjunction with a compilation of financial statements, the introductory paragraph should so state and indicate the date of the compilation report on the financial statements. Any departure from the standard report on those statements should also be disclosed if considered relevant to the presentation of the item.

          (7)   **Reporting When Not Independent** This guidance is the essentially the same as for a compilation of financial statements (AR 80) covered in this chapter.

      g.   **Communications Regarding Fraud or Illegal Acts** This guidance is the essentially the same as for a compilation of financial statements (AR 80) covered in this chapter.

2.   **Compilation of *Pro Forma* Financial Information (AR 120)**

      a.   **Applicability** A CPA is required to comply with this guidance whenever the CPA is engaged to report on *pro forma* financial information or submits same to a client or to third parties. However, if the *pro forma* financial information is included as supplementary information, the CPA should refer to that topic (supplementary information) in AR 80.

      b.   **Definition** A compilation of *pro forma* financial information is limited to assisting management in presenting financial information without undertaking to obtain or provide any assurance that there are no material modifications that should be made to that information. This may be undertaken as a separate engagement or in conjunction with a compilation, review, or audit of financial statements.

c.   **Objective** The objective of *pro forma* financial information is to show what the significant effects on historical financial information might have been had a consummated or proposed transaction (or event) occurred at an earlier date. *Pro forma* financial information is commonly used to show the effects of transactions such as the following:

- Business combination

- Change in capitalization

- Disposition of a significant portion of the business

- Change in the form of business organization or status as an autonomous entity

- Proposed sale of securities and the application of the proceeds

This objective is achieved primarily by applying *pro forma* adjustments to historical financial information. *Pro forma* adjustments should be based on management's assumptions and give effect to all significant effects directly attributable to the transaction (or event).

d.   **Presentation**

   (1)   **Labeling** *Pro forma* financial information should be labeled as such to distinguish it from historical financial information.

   (2)   **Description** This presentation should describe:

- The transaction (or event) that is reflected in the *pro forma* financial information

- The source of the historical financial information on which it is based

- The significant assumptions used in developing the *pro forma* adjustments

- Any significant uncertainties about those assumptions

   (3)   **Cautions** The presentation should also indicate that the *pro forma* financial information should be read in conjunction with the related historical financial information and that the *pro forma* financial information is not necessarily indicative of the results (such as financial position and results of operations, as applicable) that would have been attained had the transaction (or event) actually taken place earlier.

e.   **Conditions for Compiling *Pro Forma* Financial Information**

   (1)   **Historical Financial Statements Included** A CPA may only compile *pro forma* financial information if the document that contains it includes (or incorporates by reference) the historical financial statements of the entity on which the *pro forma* financial information is based. Historical interim financial information may be presented in condensed form. In the case of a business combination, the document should include (or incorporate by reference) the appropriate historical financial information for the significant constituent parts of the combined entity.

   (2)   **Audit, Review, or Compilation of Historical Financial Statements Required** The historical financial statements of the entity (or, in the case of a business combination, of each significant constituent part of the combined entity) on which the *pro forma* financial information is based must have been compiled, reviewed, or audited.

   (3)   **Report on Historical Financial Statements Included** The CPA's compilation, review, or audit report on the historical financial statements should be included (or incorporated by reference) in the document containing the *pro forma* financial information.

f. **Engagement Letter** This guidance is the essentially the same as for a compilation of financial statements (AR 80) covered in this chapter.

g. **Performance Requirements** This guidance is the essentially the same as for a compilation of financial statements (AR 80) covered in this chapter. The requirement to read the *pro forma* financial information to consider if it appears to be appropriate in form and free of obvious material errors includes the summary of significant assumptions.

h. **Documentation** This guidance is the essentially the same as for a compilation of financial statements (AR 80) covered in this chapter.

i. **Reporting**

(1) **Whether to Issue a Report** This guidance is the same as for a compilation of specified elements, accounts, or items of a financial statement (AR 110) covered in this chapter.

(2) **Report Structure** The passages that differ from the standard report on a compilation of financial statements are shown in boldface.

Exhibit 9 ▶ Compilation Report on *Pro Forma* Financial Information (Reflecting a Business Combination)

Accountant's Compilation Report

We have compiled the accompanying ***pro forma* financial information** of XYZ Company as of December 31, 20XX, **reflecting the business combination of the Company and ABC Company. The historical condensed financial statements are derived from the historical unaudited financial statements of XYZ Company, which were compiled by us, and of ABC Company, which were compiled by other accountants.** We have not audited or reviewed the accompanying ***pro forma* financial information** and, accordingly, do not express an opinion or provide any assurance about whether the ***pro forma* financial information** is in accordance with accounting principles generally accepted in the United States of America.

Management's & Accountant's Responsibilities Paragraphs
Same as for a compilation of financial statements
Except replace
References to *financial statements* with *pro forma financial information*

Explanatory Paragraph Added
(Objective & limitations of pro forma financial information)

The objective of this *pro forma* financial information is to show what the significant effects on the historical financial information might have been had the transaction (or event) occurred at an earlier date. However, the *pro forma* financial information is not necessarily indicative of the results of operations or related effects on financial position that would have been attained had the transaction (or event) actually occurred earlier.

---

(3) **Title** This guidance is the essentially the same as for a compilation of financial statements (AR 80) covered in this chapter.

(4) **Date** This guidance is the essentially the same as for a compilation of financial statements (AR 80) covered in this chapter.

(5) **Financial Statements' Reference to Report** This guidance is the essentially the same as for a compilation of financial statements (AR 80) covered in this chapter.

(6)   Engagement in Conjunction With a Compilation of Financial Statements
This guidance is the same as for a compilation of specified elements, accounts, or items of a financial statement (AR 110) covered in this chapter.

(7)   Modifications in the Report on Historical Financial Statements The report on *pro forma* financial information should also refer (in the introductory paragraph) to any modifications in the CPA's report on the historical financial statements.

(8)   *Pro Forma* Financial Information That Omits Substantially All Disclosures
This guidance is the essentially the same as for a compilation of financial statements (AR 80) covered in this chapter. The explanatory paragraph required when management has elected to omit substantially all disclosures, but the *pro forma* financial information is otherwise in conformity with the applicable financial reporting framework should be added **after** the paragraph on the objectives and limitations of the *pro forma* financial information.

(9)   Reporting When Not Independent This guidance is the essentially the same as for a compilation of financial statements (AR 80) covered in this chapter.

j.   Communications Regarding Fraud or Illegal Acts This guidance is the essentially the same as for a compilation of financial statements (AR 80) covered in this chapter.

II. Compilations & Reviews for Nonissuers: Reporting on Comparative Financial Statements (AR 200)

A. Overview

Comparative financial statements are financial statements of two or more periods which are presented in a columnar format. AR 200 applies when reporting on comparative financial statements of a nonissuer when the financial statements of one or more periods presented have been compiled and reported on or reviewed per AR 80 or 90, respectively. The CPA should issue an appropriate report that covers each of the periods presented in the comparative financial statements.

1. **Report Structure** The same common report elements / paragraphs required for compilation and review reports on financial statements of a single period are applicable to comparative financial statements.

2. **Continuing Accountant** A CPA engaged to audit, review, or compile the current period's financial statements who has audited, reviewed, or compiled those of one or more consecutive periods immediately prior to the current period.

3. **Updated Report** A report issued by a continuing accountant. It takes into consideration information the continuing accountant becomes aware of during the current engagement. In it, depending on the circumstances, the continuing accountant will either re-express the previous conclusion on the prior period statements or express a different conclusion on the prior period statements as of the date of the current report.

4. **Reissued Report** A report issued after the date of the original report, but bearing the same date as the original report. If it must be revised because of the effects of specific events, it should be dual-dated, using the original date and a separate date that applies to the effects of such events.

5. **Client-Prepared Financial Statements Included on Separate Pages** It is permissible for the client to include client-prepared financial statements of some periods that have **not** been audited, reviewed, or compiled by the CPA on separate pages of a document containing financial statements of other periods on which the CPA has reported, if they are accompanied by an indication by the client that the CPA has not audited, reviewed, or compiled those statements and does not assume any responsibility for them.

   If financial statements of other periods that have not been audited, reviewed, or compiled are presented in columnar form in a document with financial statements on which a CPA has reported and the CPA's name has been used or the CPA's report has been included in the document, the CPA should advise the client that this is inappropriate. The CPA should consider what other actions might be appropriate, including consultation with an attorney.

6. **Modified & Unmodified Reports** A CPA may modify a report with respect to one or more financial statements for one or more periods while issuing an unmodified report on the other financial statements presented.

7. **Omission of Disclosures** Statements that omit substantially all disclosures are not comparable to financial statements that include such disclosures. Therefore, the CPA should **not** issue a report on comparative financial statements when statements for some, but not all, of the periods presented omit substantially all required disclosures.

8. **Financial Statements' Reference to Report** Each page of the comparative financial statements compiled or reviewed by the CPA should include a reference such as *See Accountant's Compilation Report* or *See Independent Accountant's Review Report*.

B. **Continuing Accountant's Standard Report**

1. **Same or Higher Level of Service in Current Period** A continuing accountant who performs the same or a higher level of service with respect to the financial statements of the current period should update the report on the prior period financial statements presented.

Exhibit 10 ▶ Compilation Report Both Periods

Accountant's Compilation Report
Introductory Paragraph *Same as standard report except for language change to cover more than 1 period*
Management's Responsibilities Paragraph *Same as standard report*
Accountant's Responsibilities Paragraph *Same as standard report except use of plural in:* "Our responsibility is to conduct the compilation**s** in accordance…"

Exhibit 11 ▶ Review Report Both Periods

Independent Accountant's Review Report
Introductory Paragraph *Same as standard report except for language change to cover more than 1 period*
Management's Responsibilities Paragraph *Same as standard report*
Accountant's Responsibilities Paragraph *Same as standard report except use of plural in:* "Our responsibility is to conduct the review**s** in accordance…"
Results of Engagement Paragraph *Same as standard report except use of plural in:* "Based on our review**s**, we are not aware…"

Exhibit 12 ▶ Current Period Reviewed / Prior Period Compiled

Independent Accountant's Review Report
First 3 Paragraphs *Same as standard report*
Results of Engagement Paragraph *Same as standard report except financial statements reviewed are designated year 2*
Updating Paragraph Added
The accompanying 20X1 financial statements of XYZ Company were compiled by us. The objective of a compilation is to assist management in presenting financial information in the form of financial statements without undertaking to obtain or provide any assurance that there are no material modifications that should be made to the financial statements. Accordingly, we do not express an opinion or provide any assurance about whether the financial statements are in accordance with accounting principles generally accepted in the United States of America.

2. **Lower Level of Service in Current Period** A continuing accountant who performs a lower level of service with respect to the financial statements of the current period should either (a) include as a separate paragraph of the report a description of the responsibility assumed for the financial statements of the prior period or (b) reissue the report on the financial statements of the prior period.

   a. **Compilation Report** The CPA should issue a compilation report on the current period financial statements that includes a description of the responsibility assumed for the financial statements of the prior period. The description should include the original date of the CPA's report and should also state that the CPA has not performed any procedures in connection with that review engagement after that date.

Exhibit 13 ▶ Current Period Compiled / Prior Period Reviewed

Accountant's Compilation Report

Introductory Paragraph
Same as standard report except disclaimer designates statements of year 2

Management's & Accountant's Responsibilities Paragraphs
Same as standard report

The accompanying 20X1 financial statements were previously reviewed by us and we stated that we were not aware of any material modifications that should be made to those financial statements in order for them to be in conformity with accounting principles generally accepted in the United States of America in our report dated March 31, 20X2, but we have not performed any procedures in connection with that review engagement since that date.

---

   b. **Combined Report** The CPA should combine the compilation report on the financial statements of the current period with the reissued review report on the financial statements of the prior period or present them separately. The combined report should state that the CPA has not performed any procedures in connection with that review engagement after the date of the review report.

C. **Continuing Accountant's Changed Reference to a Departure From the Applicable Financial Reporting Framework**
   When the CPA's report on the prior period financial statements contains a changed reference to a departure from the applicable financial reporting framework, the report should include a separate explanatory paragraph indicating:

   • The date of the CPA's previous report

   • The circumstances or events that caused the reference to be changed

   • That the prior period financial statements have been changed, when applicable

Exhibit 14 ▶ Explanatory Paragraph for Changed Reference to a GAAP Departure for a Compilation Report on Comparative Financial Statements

---

In our report dated March 1, 20X2 with respect to the 20X1 financial statements, we referred to a departure from accounting principles generally accepted in the United States of America because the company carried its land at appraised values. As described in Note X, the Company has changed its method of accounting for land and restated its 20X1 financial statements to conform with accounting principles generally accepted in the United States of America.

Exhibit 15 ▶ Explanatory Paragraph for Changed Reference to a GAAP Departure for a Review Report on Comparative Financial Statements

Same as the compilation report paragraph above with this additional sentence:

Accordingly, our present statement on the 20X1 financial statements, as presented herein, that we are not aware of any material modifications that should be made to the accompanying financial statements is different from that expressed in our previous report.

D. Predecessor's Compilation or Review Report

At the client's request, a predecessor CPA may reissue the compilation or review report on the prior period financial statements. However, a predecessor is not required to do so.

1. Predecessor's Report Not Presented (Not Reissued) When a predecessor has compiled or reviewed the financial statements of a prior period (that are presented for comparative purposes) but does not reissue the compilation or review report, the successor should either

a. Options

- Perform a compilation, review, or audit of the prior period financial statements and issue an appropriate report, or

- Include an additional paragraph in the current report that makes reference to the predecessor's report on the prior period financial statements.

b. Making Reference to Predecessor's Report The reference should *either be added to the end of the introductory paragraph or placed in a separate paragraph and should include:

- A statement that other accountants compiled or reviewed the prior period financial statements (generally, the predecessor should not be named);

- The date of the predecessor's report

- The disclaimer (for a compilation) or limited assurance (for a review) statement that appeared in the report

- A description of any modifications that were made to the standard report and of any paragraphs that were included to emphasize any matter in the financial statements

*Editor note: The guidance in AR 200.17 indicates an additional paragraph; however, the illustrations in Exhibits A and B of AR 200 show the reference added to the end of the introductory paragraph.

Exhibit 16 ▶ Reference in Compilation Report to the Predecessor's Report When It Is Not Presented (Not Reissued)

The financial statements of XYZ Company as of December 31, 20X1, were compiled by other accountants whose report dated February 1, 20X2 stated that they have not audited or reviewed the 20X1 financial statements and, accordingly, do not express an opinion or provide any assurance about whether the financial statements are in accordance with accounting principles generally accepted in the United States of America.

Exhibit 17 ▶ Reference in Review Report to the Predecessor's Report When It Is Not Presented (Not Reissued)

The financial statements of XYZ Company as of December 31, 20X1, were reviewed by other accountants whose report dated February 1, 20X2, stated that based on their procedures, they are not aware of any material modifications that should be made to the financial statements in order for them to be in conformity with accounting principles generally accepted in the United States of America.

2.   **Predecessor's Report Reissued** If a predecessor is unable to complete the procedures described below the predecessor should not reissue the report and may wish to consult with an attorney regarding the appropriate course of action.

   a.   **Considerations Prior to Reissue** Before reissuing a compilation or review report on the financial statements of a prior period, a predecessor should consider whether the report is still appropriate. The predecessor should consider:

   • The current form and manner of presentation of the prior period financial statements

   • Subsequent events not previously known

   • Changes in the financial statements that require the addition or deletion of modifications to the standard report

   b.   **General Procedures Prior to Reissue** A predecessor should perform the following procedures before reissuing a compilation or review report on the financial statements of a prior period:

   • Read the current period financial statements and the report of the successor.

   • Compare the prior period financial statements with those previously issued and with those of the current period.

   • Obtain a letter from the successor that indicates whether the successor is aware of any matter that might have a material effect on the financial statements, including disclosures, reported on by the predecessor. The predecessor should not refer in the reissued report to this letter or to the report of the successor.

   c.   **Directed Procedures Prior to Reissue** If the predecessor becomes aware of information that may affect the financial statements of the prior period or the report on them, the predecessor should make inquiries or perform analytics similar to the ones the predecessor would have performed at the date of the report on the prior period statements had the predecessor been aware of the information, and perform any other necessary procedures. Examples include discussion with the successor and review of the successor's engagement documentation on the matter.

   d.   **Date of Reissued Report** The date of the previous report should be used when reissuing a report. This avoids any implication that the predecessor performed any procedures (other than those described above) after that date.

   e.   **Dual Dating Reissued Report** Dual dating is appropriate if the predecessor revised the report or if the financial statements are restated. The predecessor should also obtain a written statement from the former client setting forth the information currently acquired and its effect on the prior period financial statements and, if applicable, expressing an understanding of its effect on the predecessor's reissued report.

3.   **Restated Prior Period Financial Statements** When prior period financial statements have been restated

   • The predecessor may reissue the report (normally, this is what should happen as covered above); or

   • The predecessor may **not** reissue the report and the successor may be engaged to report on the prior year financial statements; or

   • The predecessor may **not** reissue the report and the successor may **not** be engaged to report on the prior year financial statements.

a. **Predecessor's Report Not Presented (Not Reissued) / Successor Engaged to Report on Prior Year** The successor should indicate in the introductory paragraph of the compilation or review report that a predecessor reported on the financial statements of the prior period before restatement. The successor may also indicate in the report that the successor compiled or reviewed the adjustments that were applied to restate prior year financial statements.

Exhibit 18 ▶ Reference to the Predecessor's Report When It Is Not Presented (Not Reissued) and the Successor Is Engaged to Compile the Restatement Adjustment(s)

Added to the end of the introductory paragraph:

The financial statements prior to adjustment of XYZ Company as of and for the year ended December 31, 20X1, were compiled by other accountants whose report dated February 1, 20X2, stated that they have not audited or reviewed the 20X1 financial statements and, accordingly, do not express an opinion or provide any assurance about whether the financial statements are in accordance with accounting principles generally accepted in the United States of America.

Explanatory paragraph added to end of report

We also compiled the adjustments described in Note X that were applied to restate the 20X1 financial statements. We have not audited or reviewed the adjustments described in Note X that were applied to restate the 20X1 financial statements and, accordingly, do not express an opinion or provide any assurance about whether the adjustments described in Note X that were applied to restate the 20X1 financial statements are in accordance with accounting principles generally accepted in the United States of America.

Exhibit 19 ▶ Reference to the Predecessor's Report When It Is Not Presented (Not Reissued) and the Successor Is Engaged to Review the Restatement Adjustment(s)

Added to the end of the introductory paragraph:

The financial statements of XYZ Company as of December 31, 20X1 prior to adjustment were reviewed by other accountants whose report dated February 1, 20X2, stated that based on their procedures, they are not aware of any material modifications that should be made to the financial statements in order for them to be in conformity with accounting principles generally accepted in the United States of America.

Explanatory paragraph added to end of report

We also reviewed the adjustments described in Note X that were applied to restate the 20X1 financial statements. Based on our review, we are not aware of any material modifications that should be made to the adjustments described in Note X that were applied to restate the 20X1 financial statements in order for them to be in conformity with accounting principles generally accepted in the United States of America.

---

b. **Predecessor's Report Not Presented (Not Reissued) / Successor Not Engaged to Report on Prior Year** The successor should indicate in the introductory paragraph of the compilation or review report that a predecessor reported on the financial statements of the prior period before restatement.

E. Reporting When Prior Period Is Audited

1. **Options** When the current period financial statements of a nonissuer have been compiled or reviewed and those of the prior period have been audited, the CPA should issue an appropriate compilation or review report on the current period financial statements and either

   • The report on the prior period should be reissued; or

   • The report on the current period should include as a separate paragraph a description of the responsibility assumed for the financial statements of the prior period.

2.   **Separate Paragraph on Responsibility Assumed** The separate paragraph should indicate:

- That the financial statements of the prior period were audited previously

- The date of the previous report

- The type of opinion expressed previously

- If the opinion was other than unqualified, the substantive reasons

- That no auditing procedures were performed after the date of the previous report

Exhibit 20 ▶ Final Paragraph for Compilation or Review Report When Prior Period Was Audited

> The 20X1 financial statements were audited by (us) (other accountants) and (we) (they) expressed an unqualified opinion on them in (our) (their) report dated March 1, 20X2, but (we) (they) have not performed any auditing procedures since that date.

F.   Reporting on Financial Statements That Previously Did Not Omit Disclosures
Even though a CPA may have compiled, reviewed, or audited financial statements that did **not** omit substantially all required disclosures, the CPA may later be asked to compile financial statements for the same period that **do** omit substantially all the disclosures required by the applicable financial reporting framework so that the statements can be presented in comparative financial statements. In this case, the CPA may report on these statements as long as an additional paragraph is included in the report that indicates the nature of the previous service and the date of the previous report.

Exhibit 21 ▶ Prior Period Statements Omitting Substantially All Disclosures Compiled From Previously Reviewed Statements

> We have compiled the accompanying balance sheets of XYZ Company as of December 31, 20X2 and 20X1, and the related statements of income, retained earnings, and cash flows for the years then ended. We have not audited or reviewed the accompanying financial statements and, accordingly, do not express an opinion or provide any assurance about whether the financial statements are in accordance with accounting principles generally accepted in the United States of America.
>
> Management is responsible for the preparation and fair presentation of the financial statements in accordance with accounting principles generally accepted in the United States of America and for designing, implementing, and maintaining internal control relevant to the preparation and fair presentation of the financial statements.
>
> Our responsibility is to conduct the compilations in accordance with Statements on Standards for Accounting and Review Services issued by the American Institute of Certified Public Accountants. The objective of a compilation is to assist management in presenting financial information in the form of financial statements without undertaking to obtain or provide any assurance that there are no material modifications that should be made to the financial statements.
>
> Management has elected to omit substantially all of the disclosures required by accounting principles generally accepted in the United States of America. If the omitted disclosures were included in the financial statements, they might influence the user's conclusions about the company's financial position, results of operations, and cash flows. Accordingly, the financial statements are not designed for those who are not informed about such matters.
>
> The 20X1 financial statements were compiled by us from financial statements that did not omit substantially all of the disclosures required by accounting principles generally accepted in the United States of America and that we previously reviewed as indicated in our report dated March 1, 20X2.

CHAPTER 12—ACCOUNTING & REVIEW SERVICES

Problem 12-1 MULTIPLE-CHOICE QUESTIONS

1. A CPA is required to comply with the provisions of Statements on Standards for Accounting and Review Services when

	Processing financial data for clients of other CPA firms	_Consulting on accounting matters_
a.	Yes	Yes
b.	Yes	No
c.	No	Yes
d.	No	No

(11/93, AUD, #12, ID: 4249)

2. An accountant is required to comply with the provisions of Statements on Standards for Accounting and Review Services for compilations when

   I. Reproducing client-prepared financial statements, without modification, as an accommodation to a client
   II. Preparing standard monthly journal entries for depreciation and expiration of prepaid expenses

   a. I only
   b. II only
   c. Both I and II
   d. Neither I nor II

(5/96, AUD, #1, amended, ID: 6233)

3. The authoritative body designated to promulgate standards that provide performance and reporting guidance for compilations and reviews of the unaudited financial statements of a nonissuer is the

   a. Financial Accounting Standards Board
   b. Government Accountability Office
   c. American Institute of Certified Public Accountants
   d. Auditing Standards Board

(11/90, AUD, #40, amended, ID: 6)

4. SSARS consider which of the following to be a submission of financial statements when the accountant has?

   a. Typed client-prepared financial statements, without modification, as an accommodation to the client
   b. Provided a client with a financial statement format that does not include dollar amounts, to be used by the client in preparing financial statements
   c. Proposed correcting journal entries to be recorded by the client that change client-prepared financial statements
   d. Generated, through the use of computer software, financial statements prepared in accordance with a comprehensive basis of accounting other than GAAP

(11/94, AUD, #22, amended, ID: 5095)

5. SSARS guidance for compilations of unaudited financial statements establishes standards and procedures for which of the following engagements?

   a. Assisting in adjusting the books of account for a partnership
   b. Compiling an individual's personal financial statements which will be used solely to assist the client and the client's advisors to develop the clients' personal financial goals
   c. Processing financial data for clients of other accounting firms
   d. Compiling an individual's personal financial statements to be used to obtain a mortgage

(11/91, AUD, #13, amended, ID: 2281)

6. An accountant is required to comply with the provisions of the Statements on Standards for Accounting and Review Services for compilations when performing which of the following tasks?

   a. Preparing monthly journal entries
   b. Providing the client with software to generate financial statements
   c. Generating financial statements of a nonissuer
   d. Providing a blank financial statement format or template   (R/08, AUD, #22, amended, ID: 8628)

7. Reviews of interim financial information for nonissuers should be performed in accordance with auditing standards rather than Statements on Standards for Accounting and Review Services (SSARS) when

   a. The client intends to change from an other comprehensive basis accounting (OCBOA) to GAAP for its next annual reporting period
   b. The review report will be distributed to third parties
   c. Certain conditions are met that demonstrate the review is being performed by an accountant with an audit base of knowledge
   d. The entity's financial statements have audited for the two previous reporting periods

                                                                                        (Editors, ID: 8642)

8. An accountant is required to comply with the provisions of Statements on Standards for Accounting and Review Services (SSARS) when

	Compiling financial statements generated through the use of computer software	Reproducing client prepared financial statements, without modification, for the client
a.	Yes	Yes
b.	Yes	No
c.	No	Yes
d.	No	No

                                                                        (R/10, AUD, #26, ID: 9376)

9. The standard compilation report includes which statement or phrase?

   a. A compilation is substantially less in scope than a review or an audit.
   b. The accountant does not express an opinion but expresses only limited assurance on the compiled financial statements.
   c. The objective of a compilation is to assist management in presenting financial information in the form of financial statements.
   d. The accountant has compiled the financial statements in accordance with standards established by the Auditing Standards Board.   (5/94, AUD, #78, amended, ID: 4743)

10. Which of the following representations does an accountant make implicitly when issuing the standard report for the compilation of a nonissuer's financial statements?

   a. The accountant is independent with respect to the entity.
   b. The financial statements have not been audited.
   c. A compilation consists principally of inquiries and analytical procedures.
   d. The accountant does not express any assurance on the financial statements.
                                                                        (11/93, AUD, #54, amended, ID: 4291)

11. An accountant has compiled the financial statements of a nonissuer in accordance with Statements on Standards for Accounting and Review Services (SSARS). Does SSARS require that the compilation report be printed on the accountant's letterhead and that the report be manually signed by the accountant?

	Printed on the accountant's letterhead	*Manually signed by the accountant*
a.	Yes	Yes
b.	Yes	No
c.	No	Yes
d.	No	No

                                                                        (R/99, AUD, #1, amended, ID: 6817)

12. When the accountant is engaged to report on compiled financial statements or submits financial statements that are reasonably expected to be used by a third party, the financial statements should be accompanied by a written report stating that

    a. The scope of the accountant's procedures has not been restricted in testing the financial information that is the representation of management.
    b. The accountant assessed the accounting principles used and significant estimates made by management.
    c. The accountant does not express an opinion or any other form of assurance on the financial statements.
    d. A compilation consists principally of inquiries of entity personnel and analytical procedures applied to financial data. (11/95, AUD, #80, amended, ID: 6027)

13. The standard report on compiled financial statements includes which of the following statements or phrases?

    a. A compilation includes assessing the accounting principles used and significant management estimates, as well as evaluating the overall financial statement presentation.
    b. The accountant compiled the financial statements in accordance with Statements on Standards for Accounting and Review Services.
    c. A compilation is substantially less in scope than an audit, the objective of which is the expression of an opinion.
    d. The accountant is not aware of any material modifications that should be made to the accompanying financial statements in order for them to be in conformity with GAAP. (5/95, AUD, #78, amended, ID: 5696)

14. When compiling the financial statements of a nonissuer, an accountant should

    a. Review agreements with financial institutions for restrictions on cash balances
    b. Understand the accounting principles and practices of the entity's industry
    c. Inquire of key personnel concerning related parties and subsequent events
    d. Perform ratio analyses of the financial data of comparable prior periods (11/92, AUD, #44, amended, ID: 2978)

15. How does an accountant make the following representations when issuing the standard report for the compilation of a nonissuer's financial statements?

	The financial statements have not been audited	The accountant has compiled the financial statements
a.	Implicitly	Implicitly
b.	Explicitly	Explicitly
c.	Implicitly	Explicitly
d.	Explicitly	Implicitly

    (11/91, AUD, #26, amended, ID: 2294)

16. Which of the following procedures is ordinarily performed by an accountant during an engagement to compile financial statements?

    a. Make inquiries of the employees and senior management regarding transactions with related parties.
    b. Determine whether there is substantial doubt about the entity's ability to continue as a going concern.
    c. Scan the entity's records for the period just after the balance sheet date to identify subsequent events requiring disclosure.
    d. Consider whether the financial statements are free from obvious material mistakes in the application of accounting principles. (R/08, AUD, #5, ID: 8611)

17. Which of the following statements is correct regarding a compilation report on financial statements issued in accordance with Statements on Standards for Accounting and Review Services (SSARS)?

    a. The report should not be issued if the accountant is not independent from the entity.
    b. The report should include a statement indicating that the information is the representation of the accountant.
    c. The report should include a description of other procedures performed during the compilation.
    d. The date on the report should be the date of completion of the compilation.

    (R/08, AUD, #18, ID: 8624)

18. Which of the following statements would be appropriate in an accountant's report on compiled financial statements of a nonissuer prepared in accordance with Statements on Standards for Accounting and Review Services (SSARS)?

    a. We are not aware of any material modifications that should be made to the accompanying financial statements.
    b. A compilation is substantially less in scope than an audit, the objective of which is the expression of an opinion regarding the financial statements as a whole.
    c. The objective of a compilation is to assist management in presenting financial information in the form of financial statements.
    d. A compilation is performed to obtain reasonable assurance about whether the financial statements are free from material misstatement.

    (R/08, AUD, #23, ID: 8629)

19. Which of the following actions should an accountant take when engaged to compile a company's financial statements in accordance with Statements on Standards for Accounting and Review Services (SSARS)?

    a. Perform analytical procedures.
    b. Express negative assurance on the financial statements.
    c. Make management inquiries and examine internal controls.
    d. Perform the engagement even though independence is compromised.

    (R/08, AUD, #41, ID: 8647)

20. When an accountant is **not** independent with respect to an entity, which of the following types of compilation reports may be issued?

    a. The standard compilation report may be issued, regardless of independence.
    b. A compilation report with negative assurance may be issued.
    c. A compilation report with special wording that notes the accountant's lack of independence may be issued.
    d. A compilation report may be issued if the engagement is upgraded to a review.

    (R/08, AUD, #47, ID: 8653)

21. Independence is **not** required on which of the following types of engagements?

    a. Audit
    b. Review
    c. Compilation
    d. Agreed-upon procedures

    (R/09, AUD, #19, ID: 8819)

22. An accountant compiled the financial statements of a nonissuer in accordance with Statements on Standards for Accounting and Review Services (SSARS). If the accountant has an ownership interest in the entity, which of the following statements is correct?

    a. The accountant should refuse the compilation engagement.
    b. A report need **not** be issued for a compilation of a nonissuer.
    c. The accountant should include the disclaimer "I am an owner of the entity" in the report.
    d. The accountant should include the statement "I am **not** independent with respect to the entity" in the compilation report.

    (R/10, AUD, #23, ID: 9373)

23. General Retailing, a nonissuer, has asked Ford, CPA, to compile its financial statements that omit substantially all disclosures required by GAAP. Ford may comply with General's request provided the omission is clearly indicated in Ford's report and the

    a. Distribution of the financial statements and Ford's report is restricted to internal use only.
    b. Reason for omitting the disclosures is acknowledged in the notes to the financial statements.
    c. Omitted disclosures would not influence any potential creditor's conclusions about General's financial position.
    d. Omission is not undertaken with the intention of misleading the users of General's financial statements. (R/11, AUD, #32, ID: 9932)

24. What type of analytical procedure would an auditor most likely use in developing relationships among balance sheet accounts when reviewing the financial statements of a nonissuer?

    a. Trend analysis
    b. Regression analysis
    c. Ratio analysis
    d. Risk analysis (5/95, AUD, #74, amended, ID: 5692)

25. Which of the following should be the first step in reviewing the financial statements of a nonissuer?

    a. Comparing the financial statements with statements for comparable prior periods and with anticipated results
    b. Completing a series of inquiries concerning the entity's procedures for recording, classifying, and summarizing transactions
    c. Obtaining a general understanding of the entity's organization, its operating characteristics, and its products or services
    d. Applying analytical procedures designed to identify relationships and individual items that appear to be unusual (R/05, AUD, #13, amended, ID: 7808)

26. When performing an engagement to review a nonissuer's annual financial statements, an accountant most likely would

    a. Obtain an understanding of the entity's internal control
    b. Limit the distribution of the accountant's report
    c. Confirm a sample of significant accounts receivable balances
    d. Ask about actions taken at board of directors' meetings (R/05, AUD, #8, amended, ID: 7803)

27. Each page of a nonissuer's financial statements reviewed by an accountant should include the following reference:

    a. See Accompanying Accountant's Footnotes
    b. Reviewed, No Material Modifications Required
    c. See Accountant's Review Report
    d. Reviewed, No Accountant's Assurance Expressed (5/95, AUD, #81, amended, ID: 5699)

28. Which of the following would be performed during a review engagement?

    a. Examination of board minutes
    b. Confirmation of cash and accounts receivable
    c. Comparison of current-year to prior-year account balances
    d. Recalculation of depreciation expense (R/06, AUD, #50, ID: 8168)

29. During an engagement to review the financial statements of a nonissuer, an accountant becomes aware that several leases that should be capitalized are not capitalized. The accountant considers these leases to be material to the financial statements. The accountant decides to modify the standard review report because management will not capitalize the leases. Under these circumstances, the accountant should

    a. Issue an adverse opinion because of the departure from GAAP
    b. Express no assurance of any kind on the entity's financial statements
    c. Emphasize that the financial statements are for limited use only
    d. Disclose the departure from GAAP in a separate paragraph of the accountant's report

    (5/96, AUD, #7, amended, ID: 6239)

30. Moore, CPA, has been asked to issue a review report on the balance sheet of Dover Co., a nonissuer. Moore will **not** be reporting on Dover's statements of income, retained earnings, and cash flows. Moore may issue the review report provided the

    a. Balance sheet is presented in a prescribed form of an industry trade association.
    b. Scope of the inquiry and analytical procedures has not been restricted.
    c. Balance sheet is not to be used to obtain credit or distributed to creditors.
    d. Specialized accounting principles and practices of Dover's industry are disclosed.

    (5/95, AUD, #79, amended, ID: 5697)

31. An accountant is asked to issue a review report on the balance sheet, but **not** on other related statements. The scope of the inquiry and analytical procedures has not been restricted, but the client failed to provide a representation letter. Which of the following should the accountant issue under these circumstances?

    a. Review report with a qualification
    b. Review report with a disclaimer
    c. Review report and footnote exceptions
    d. Compilation report with the client's consent

    (R/05, AUD, #49, ID: 7844)

32. Financial statements of a nonissuer that have been reviewed by an accountant should be accompanied by a report stating that a review

    a. Provides only limited assurance that the financial statements are fairly presented
    b. Includes examining, on a test basis, information that is the representation of management
    c. Includes primarily applying analytical procedures to management's financial data and making inquiries of company management
    d. Does not contemplate obtaining corroborating evidential matter or applying certain other procedures ordinarily performed during an audit

    (11/95, AUD, #79, amended, ID: 6026)

33. In reviewing the annual financial statements of a nonissuer, an accountant is required to modify the standard review report for which of the following matters?

	Inability to assess the risk of material misstatement due to fraud	*Discovery of significant deficiencies in the design of the entity's internal control*
a.	Yes	Yes
b.	Yes	No
c.	No	Yes
d.	No	No

    (R/01, AUD, #8, amended, ID: 7023)

34. If requested to perform a review engagement for a nonissuer in which an accountant has an immaterial direct financial interest, the accountant is

    a. Not independent and, therefore, may not be associated with the financial statements
    b. Not independent and, therefore, may not issue a review report
    c. Not independent and, therefore, may issue a review report, but may not issue an auditor's opinion
    d. Independent because the financial interest is immaterial and, therefore, may issue a review report

    (5/95, AUD, #20, amended, ID: 5638)

35. Which of the following procedures is usually the first step in reviewing the annual financial statements of a nonissuer?

    a. Make preliminary judgments about risk and materiality to determine the scope and nature of the procedures to be performed
    b. Obtain a general understanding of the entity's organization, its operating characteristics, and its products or services
    c. Assess the risk of material misstatement arising from fraudulent financial reporting and the misappropriation of assets
    d. Perform a preliminary assessment of the operating efficiency of the entity's internal control activities
    (R/06, AUD, #33, amended, ID: 8151)

36. When providing limited assurance that the financial statements of a nonissuer require no material modifications to be in accordance with generally accepted accounting principles, the accountant should

    a. Assess the risk that a material misstatement could occur in a financial statement assertion
    b. Confirm with the entity's lawyer that material loss contingencies are disclosed
    c. Understand the accounting principles of the industry in which the entity operates
    d. Develop audit programs to determine whether the entity's financial statements are fairly presented
    (5/95, AUD, #58, amended, ID: 5676)

37. Under which of the following circumstances would an accountant most likely conclude that it is necessary to withdraw from an engagement to review a nonissuer's financial statements?

    a. The entity does not have reasonable justification for making a change in accounting principle.
    b. The entity prepares its financial statements on the income tax basis of accounting.
    c. The entity requests the accountant to report only on the balance sheet, and not on the other financial statements.
    d. The entity declines to provide the accountant with a signed representation letter.
    (R/03, AUD, #5, amended, ID: 7627)

38. Which of the following procedures would an accountant **least** likely perform during an engagement to review the financial statements of a nonissuer?

    a. Observing the safeguards over access to and use of assets and records
    b. Comparing the financial statements with anticipated results in budgets and forecasts
    c. Inquiring of management about actions taken at the board of directors' meetings
    d. Studying the relationships of financial statement elements expected to conform to predictable patterns
    (11/94, AUD, #74, amended, ID: 5147)

39. An accountant has been engaged to review a nonissuer's financial statements that contain several departures from GAAP. If the financial statements are **not** revised and modification of the standard review report is **not** adequate to indicate the deficiencies, the accountant should

    a. Withdraw from the engagement and provide no further services concerning these financial statements
    b. Inform management that the engagement can proceed only if distribution of the accountant's report is restricted to internal users
    c. Determine the effects of the departures from GAAP and issue a modified report on the financial statements
    d. Issue a modified review report provided the entity agrees that the financial statements will not be used to obtain credit
    (11/94, AUD, #20, amended, ID: 5093)

40. An accountant has been asked to issue a review report on the balance sheet of a nonissuer without reporting on the related statements of income, retained earnings, and cash flows. The accountant may issue the requested review report only if

    a. The balance sheet is not to be used to obtain credit or distributed to the entity's creditors.
    b. The balance sheet is part of a comprehensive personal financial plan developed to assist the entity.
    c. There have been no material changes during the year in the entity's accounting principles.
    d. The scope of the accountant's inquiry and analytical procedures has not been restricted.
    (R/05, AUD, #30, amended, ID: 7825)

41. Which of the following statements is correct regarding both a compilation and a review engagement of a nonpublic company's financial statements performed in accordance with SSARS?

    a. The CPA should assess fraud risk.
    b. The CPA must obtain an understanding of the client's internal control.
    c. The CPA must establish an understanding with the client regarding the services to be performed and document it in an engagement letter.
    d. The reports contain a statement that the engagement is substantially less in scope than an audit.

    (R/07, AUD, #6, amended, ID: 8378)

42. Which of the following procedures does a CPA normally perform first in a review engagement in accordance with Statements on Standards for Accounting and Review Services (SSARS)?

    a. Inquiry regarding the client's principles and practices and the method of applying them
    b. Inquiry concerning the effectiveness of the client's system of internal control
    c. Inquiry to identify transactions between related parties and management
    d. Inquiry of the client's professional advisors, including bankers, insurance agents, and consultants

    (R/07, AUD, #7, ID: 8379)

43. The standard report issued by an accountant after reviewing the financial statements of a nonissuer according to SSARS should state that

    a. The objective of a review is to assist management in presenting financial information in the form of financial statements.
    b. A review includes primarily applying analytical procedures to management's financial data and making inquiries of company management.
    c. The accountant does not express an opinion or any other form of assurance on the financial statements.
    d. The accountant did not obtain an understanding of the entity's internal control or assess fraud risk.

    (R/07, AUD, #38, amended, ID: 8410)

44. When providing limited assurance that the annual financial statements of a nonissuer require no material modifications to be in accordance with the applicable financial reporting framework, the accountant should

    a. Assess the risk of material misstatement in the financial statements due to fraud.
    b. Perform tests of controls to evaluate the effectiveness of the controls.
    c. Understand the accounting principles of the industry in which the entity operates.
    d. Communicate with the audit committee regarding material weaknesses in internal control.

    (R/08, AUD, #7, ID: 8613)

45. In an engagement to review the annual financial statements of a nonissuer, the accountant most likely would perform which of the following procedures?

    a. Physical inspection of inventory
    b. Vouching of inventory purchase transactions
    c. Analysis of inventory turnover
    d. Evaluation of internal control over inventory

    (R/08, AUD, #13, ID: 8619)

46. Which of the following statements is true regarding analytical procedures in a review engagement?

    a. Analytical procedures are not required to be used as a substantive test.
    b. Analytical procedures do not involve comparisons of recorded amounts to expected amounts.
    c. Analytical procedures are required to be used in the final review stage.
    d. Analytical procedures involve the use of both financial and nonfinancial data.

    (R/08, AUD, #28, ID: 8634)

47. To obtain a reasonable basis for the expression of limited assurance in a review engagement, the accountant is required to do all of the following **except**

    a. Apply analytical procedures to the financial statements
    b. Make inquiries of management and, when deemed appropriate, other company personnel
    c. Send a letter of inquiry to the client's attorney
    d. Obtain representations from management for all financial statements and periods covered by the accountant's review report   (Editors, ID: 8635)

48. Which of the following procedures would an accountant most likely perform during an engagement to review the annual financial statements of a nonissuer?

    a. Review the predecessor accountant's working papers.
    b. Inquire of management about related-party transactions.
    c. Corroborate litigation information with the entity's attorney.
    d. Communicate internal control deficiencies to senior management.   (R/08, AUD, #39, ID: 8645)

49. Which of the following procedures would a CPA most likely perform when reviewing the annual financial statements of a nonissuer?

    a. Verify that the accounting estimates that could be material to the financial statements have been developed.
    b. Obtain an understanding of the entity's internal control components.
    c. Assess the entity's ability to continue as a going concern for a reasonable period of time.
    d. Make inquiries about actions taken at the board of directors meetings.   (R/08, AUD, #42, ID: 8648)

50. Which of the following procedures is an accountant required to perform when reviewing the financial statements of a nonpublic entity in accordance with Statements on Standards for Accounting and Review Services (SSARS)?

    a. Assess control risk
    b. Obtain a management representation letter
    c. Confirm account balances
    d. Perform a physical inventory observation   (R/09, AUD, #3, ID: 8803)

51. Which of the following statements is correct regarding a review of a nonpublic entity's financial statements in accordance with Statements on Standards for Accounting and Review Services (SSARS)?

    a. The accountant is required to assess the risk of fraud.
    b. It is not necessary for the accountant to obtain a management representation letter.
    c. An opinion is expressed in the review report.
    d. The accountant must be independent to issue the review report.   (R/09, AUD, #25, ID: 8825)

52. An accountant has been engaged to review a nonissuer's financial statements that contain several departures from GAAP. Management is unwilling to revise the financial statements, and the accountant believes that modification of the standard review report is inadequate to communicate the deficiencies. Under these circumstances, the accountant should

    a. Determine the effects of the departures from GAAP and issue a special report on the financial statements
    b. Express a disclaimer of opinion on the financial statements and advise the board of directors that the financial statements should **not** be relied on
    c. Inform management that a review of the financial statements **cannot** be completed and request a change from a review to a compilation engagement
    d. Withdraw from the engagement and provide **no** further services concerning these financial statements
                                                                              (R/10, AUD, #2, ID: 9352)

53. Which of the following procedures would a CPA ordinarily perform when reviewing the financial statements of a nonissuer in accordance with Statements on Standards for Accounting and Review Services (SSARS)?

    a. Apply year-end cutoff tests for the sales and purchasing functions
    b. Compare the financial statements with budgets or forecasts
    c. Obtain an understanding of the entity's internal control components
    d. Document whether control risk is assessed at or below the maximum level

    (R/10, AUD, #18, ID: 9368)

54. Which of the following is required of an accountant in reviewing a company's financial statements under Statements on Standards for Accounting and Review Services (SSARS)?

    a. Obtain knowledge of the client's industry
    b. Send bank confirmations
    c. Corroboration of management's responses to inquiries
    d. Observe client's physical inventory   (R/10, AUD, #42, amended, ID: 9392)

55. Which of the following situations would preclude an accountant from issuing a review report on a company's financial statements in accordance with Statements on Standards for Accounting and Review Services (SSARS)?

    a. The owner of a company is the accountant's father.
    b. The accountant was engaged to review only the balance sheet.
    c. Land has been recorded at appraisal value instead of historical cost.
    d. Finished-goods inventory does **not** include any overhead amounts.   (R/10, AUD, #48, ID: 9398)

56. Which of the following statements would **not** normally be included in a representation letter for a review of interim financial information?

    a. To the best of our knowledge and belief, no events have occurred subsequent to the balance sheet and through the date of this letter that would require adjustment to or disclosure in the interim financial information.
    b. We acknowledge our responsibility for the design and implementation of programs and controls to prevent and detect fraud.
    c. We understand that a review consists principally of performing analytical procedures and making inquiries about the interim financial information.
    d. We have made available to you all financial records and related data.   (R/11, AUD, #21, ID: 9921)

57. When performing a review of interim financial information, an accountant would typically do each of the following, **except**

    a. Consider the results from the latest audit
    b. Test controls related to the preparation of annual financial information
    c. Perform analytical procedures
    d. Make inquiries of management   (R/11, AUD, #22, ID: 9922)

58. In an accountant's review of interim financial information, the accountant typically performs each of the following, **except**

    a. Reading the available minutes of the latest stockholders' meeting
    b. Applying financial ratios to the interim financial information
    c. Inquiring of the Accounting Department's management
    d. Obtaining corroborating external evidence   (R/11, AUD, #49, ID: 9949)

59. May an accountant accept an engagement to compile or review the financial statements of a not-for-profit entity if the accountant is unfamiliar with the specialized industry accounting principles, but plans to obtain the required level of knowledge before compiling or reviewing the financial statements?

	Compilation	*Review*
a.	No	No
b.	Yes	No
c.	No	Yes
d.	Yes	Yes

(5/94, AUD, #46, ID: 4711)

60. An accountant should perform analytical procedures during an engagement to

	Compile a nonissuer's financial statements	*Review a nonissuer's financial statements*
a.	No	No
b.	Yes	Yes
c.	Yes	No
d.	No	Yes

(5/94, AUD, #59, amended, ID: 4724)

61. Which of the following describes how the objective of a review of financial statements differs from the objective of a compilation engagement?

a. The primary objective of a review engagement is to test the completeness of the financial statements prepared, but a compilation tests for reasonableness.

b. The primary objective of a review engagement is to provide positive assurance that the financial statements are fairly presented, but a compilation provides no such assurance.

c. In a review engagement, accountants provide limited assurance, but a compilation expresses no assurance.

d. In a review engagement, accountants provide reasonable or positive assurance that the financial statements are fairly presented, but a compilation provides limited assurance.

(R/07, AUD, #9, ID: 8381)

62. An accountant has been engaged to compile the financial statements of a nonpublic entity. The financial statements contain many departures from GAAP because of inadequacies in the accounting records. The accountant believes that modification of the compilation report is not adequate to indicate the deficiencies. Under these circumstances, the accountant should

a. Inform management that the engagement can proceed only if distribution of the accountant's report is restricted to internal use

b. Withdraw from the engagement and provide no further service concerning these financial statements

c. Quantify the effects of the departures from GAAP and describe the departures from GAAP in a special report

d. Obtain written representations from management that the financial statements will not be used to obtain credit from financial institutions   (R/09, AUD, #28, ID: 8828)

63. Which of the following services, if any, may an accountant who is **not** independent provide?

a. Compilations, but **not** reviews

b. Reviews, but **not** compilations

c. Both compilations and reviews

d. No services

(R/10, AUD, #47, ID: 9397)

64. An accountant who had begun an audit of the financial statements of a nonissuer was asked to change the engagement to a review because of a restriction on the scope of the audit. If there is reasonable justification for the change, the accountant's review report should include reference to the

	Scope limitation that caused the changed engagement	*Original engagement that was agreed to*
a.	Yes	No
b.	No	Yes
c.	No	No
d.	Yes	Yes

(11/94, AUD, #78, amended, ID: 5151)

65. An accountant had begun to audit the financial statements of a nonissuer. Which of the following circumstances most likely would be considered a reasonable basis for agreeing to the entity's request to change the engagement to a compilation?

a. The entity's management does not provide the accountant with a signed representation letter.
b. The accountant is prohibited from corresponding with the entity's legal counsel.
c. The entity's principal creditors no longer require the entity to furnish audited financial statements.
d. The accountant is prevented from examining the minutes of the board of directors' meetings.

(R/05, AUD, #27, amended, ID: 7822)

66. While auditing the financial statements of a nonissuer, a CPA was requested to change the engagement to a review in accordance with Statements on Standards for Accounting and Review Services (SSARS) because of a scope limitation. If the CPA believes the client's request is reasonable, the CPA's review report should

    I. Refer to the scope limitation that caused the change
    II. Describe the auditing procedures that have already been applied

a. I only
b. II only
c. Both I and II
d. Neither I nor II

(R/07, AUD, #44, amended, ID: 8416)

67. An accountant agrees to the client's request to change an engagement from a review to a compilation of financial statements. The compilation report should include

a. No reference to the original engagement
b. Reference to a departure from GAAS
c. Scope limitations that may have resulted in the change of engagement
d. Information about review procedures already performed

(R/09, AUD, #6, ID: 8806)

68. A CPA started to audit the financial statements of a nonissuer. After completing certain audit procedures, the client requested the CPA to change the engagement to a review because of a scope limitation. The CPA concludes that there is reasonable justification for the change. Under these circumstances, the CPA's review report should include a

a. Statement that a review is substantially less in scope than an audit
b. Reference to the scope limitation that caused the changed engagement
c. Description of the auditing procedures that were completed before the engagement was changed
d. Reference to the CPA's justification for agreeing to change the engagement

(R/11, AUD, #9, ID: 9909)

69. Financial information is presented in a printed form that prescribes the wording of the independent auditor's report. The form is not acceptable to the auditor because the form calls for statements that are inconsistent with the auditor's responsibility. Under these circumstances, the auditor most likely would

a. Withdraw from the engagement
b. Reword the form or attach a separate report
c. Express a qualified opinion with an explanation
d. Limit distribution of the report to the party who designed the form

(11/96, AUD, #16, ID: 6368)

70. Kell engaged March, CPA, to submit to Kell a written personal financial plan containing unaudited personal financial statements. March anticipates omitting certain disclosures required by GAAP because the engagement's sole purpose is to assist Kell in developing a personal financial plan. For March to be exempt from complying with the requirements of AR 80, *Compilation of Financial Statements*, Kell is required to agree that the

    a. Financial statements will not be presented in comparative form with those of the prior period.
    b. Omitted disclosures required by GAAP are not material.
    c. Financial statements will not be disclosed to a non-CPA financial planner.
    d. Financial statements will not be used to obtain credit.   (5/95, AUD, #21, ID: 5639)

71. Must a CPA in public practice be independent in fact and appearance when providing the following services?

	Compilation of personal financial statements	Preparation of a tax return	Compilation of a financial forecast
a.	No	No	No
b.	No	No	Yes
c.	Yes	No	No
d.	No	Yes	No

(5/92, AUD, #56, ID: 2809)

72. Clark, CPA, compiled and properly reported on the financial statements of Green Co., a nonissuer, for the year ended March 31, year 1. These financial statements omitted substantially all disclosures required by generally accepted accounting principles (GAAP). Green asked Clark to compile the statements for the year ended March 31, year 2, and to include all GAAP disclosures for year 2 statements only, but otherwise present both years' financial statements in comparative form. What is Clark's responsibility concerning the proposed engagement?

    a. Clark may not report on the comparative financial statements because the year 1 statements are not comparable to the year 2 statements that include the GAAP disclosures.
    b. Clark may report on the comparative financial statements provided Clark updates the report on the year 1 statements that do not include the GAAP disclosures.
    c. Clark may report on the comparative financial statements provided an explanatory paragraph is added to Clark's report on the comparative financial statements.
    d. Clark may report on the comparative financial statements provided the year 1 statements do not contain any obvious material misstatements.   (5/92, AUD, #4, amended, ID: 2757)

73. Gole, CPA, is engaged to review the year 4 financial statements of North Co., a nonissuer. Previously, Gole audited North's year 3 financial statements and expressed an unqualified opinion. Gole decides to include a separate paragraph in the year 4 review report because North plans to present comparative financial statements for year 4 and year 3. This separate paragraph should indicate that

    a. The year 4 review report is intended solely for the information of management and the board of directors.
    b. There are justifiable reasons for changing the level of service from an audit to a review.
    c. No auditing procedures were performed after the date of the year 3 auditor's report.
    d. The year 3 auditor's report may no longer be relied on.   (11/94, AUD, #79, amended, ID: 5152)

74. When unaudited financial statements are presented in comparative form with audited financial statements in a document filed with the Securities and Exchange Commission, such statements should be

	Marked as "unaudited"	Withheld until audited	Referred to in the auditor's report
a.	Yes	No	No
b.	Yes	No	Yes
c.	No	Yes	Yes
d.	No	Yes	No

(11/93, AUD, #50, ID: 4287)

75. When unaudited financial statements of a nonissuer are presented in comparative form with audited financial statements in the subsequent year, the unaudited financial statements should be clearly marked to indicate their status and

    I. The report on the unaudited financial statements should be reissued.
    II. The report on the audited financial statements should include a separate paragraph describing the responsibility assumed for the unaudited financial statements.

    a. I only
    b. II only
    c. Both I and II
    d. Either I or II   (5/94, AUD, #89, amended, ID: 4754)

76. Before reissuing a compilation report on the financial statements of a nonissuer for the prior year, the predecessor accountant is required to

    a. Obtain an updated management representation letter from the entity's management.
    b. Compare the prior year's financial statements with those of the current year.
    c. Review the successor accountant's working papers for matters affecting the prior year.
    d. Make inquiries of the entity's lawyers concerning continuing litigation.   (R/08, AUD, #38, ID: 8644)

77. Before reissuing a compilation report on the financial statements of a nonissuer for the prior year, the predecessor accountant is required to

    a. Make inquiries about actions taken at meetings of the board of directors during the current year
    b. Verify that the reissued report will **not** be used to obtain credit from a financial institution
    c. Review the successor accountant's working papers for matters affecting the prior year
    d. Compare the prior year's financial statements with those of the current year
                           (R/10, AUD, #17, ID: 9367)

78. A CPA is reporting on comparative financial statements of a nonissuer. The CPA audited the prior year's financial statements and reviewed those of the current year in accordance with Statements on Standards for Accounting and Review Services (SSARS). The CPA has added a separate paragraph to the review report to describe the responsibility assumed for the prior year's audited financial statements. This separate paragraph should indicate

    a. The type of opinion expressed previously
    b. That the CPA did not update the assessment of control risk
    c. The reasons for the change from an audit to a review
    d. That the audit report should no longer be relied on   (R/11, AUD, #8, ID: 9908)

Problem 12-2 SIMULATION: Compilation & Review Requirements

Each of the following items represents a series of unrelated procedures that an accountant may consider performing in separate engagements to review the financial statements of a nonissuer (a review) and to compile the financial statements of a nonissuer (a compilation) according to SSARS. Select, as the best answer for each item, whether the procedure is required (R) or not required (N) for **both** review and compilation engagements.

Procedures	Required / Not Required	
	Compilation	Review
1. The accountant should establish an understanding with the entity regarding the nature and limitations of the services to be performed.		
2. The accountant should make inquiries concerning actions taken at the board of directors' meetings.		
3. The accountant, as the entity's successor accountant, should communicate with the predecessor accountant to obtain access to the predecessor's working papers.		
4. The accountant should obtain a level of knowledge of the accounting principles and practices of the entity's industry.		
5. The accountant should obtain an understanding of the entity's internal control structure.		
6. The accountant should perform analytical procedures designed to identify relationships that appear to be unusual.		
7. The accountant should make an assessment of the fraud risk.		

(ID: 9243)

———————————

Problem 12-3 SIMULATION: Review Report

Wallace & Wallace, CPAs, audited the financial statements of West Co., a nonissuer, for the year ended September 30, 20X1, and expressed an unqualified opinion. For the year ended September 30, 20X2, West issued comparative financial statements. Wallace & Wallace reviewed West's year 2 financial statements and Gordon, an assistant on the engagement, drafted the review report below. Martin, the engagement supervisor, decided not to reissue the prior year's audit report, but instructed Gordon to include a separate paragraph in the current year's review report describing the responsibility assumed for the prior year's audited financial statements.

Martin reviewed Gordon's draft and indicated that there were many deficiencies in Gordon's draft.

Accountant's Review Report

We have reviewed the accompanying balance sheet of West Company as of September 30, 20X2, and the related statements of income and cash flows for the year then ended. A review includes primarily applying analytical procedures to management's financial data and making inquiries of company management. A review also includes assessing the accounting principles used and significant estimates made by management, as well as evaluating the overall financial statement presentation.

Management is responsible for the preparation and fair presentation of the financial statements in accordance with accounting principles generally accepted in the United States of America.

Our responsibility is to conduct the review in accordance with standards issued by the American Institute of Certified Public Accountants. Those standards require us to perform procedures to obtain limited assurance that there are no material modifications that should be made to the financial statements. We believe that the results of our procedures provide a reasonable basis for our report.

Based on our review, we are not aware of any material modifications that should be made to the accompanying financial statements. Accordingly, the accompanying financial statements have been prepared assuming that the company will continue as a going concern. Furthermore, we have no responsibility to update this report for events and circumstances occurring after the date of this report.

The financial statements for the year ended September 30, 20X1, were audited by us and we expressed an unqualified opinion on them in our report dated November 7, 20X1, but we have not performed any auditing procedures since that date. In our opinion, the financial statements referred to above are presented fairly, in all material respects, for the year then ended in conformity with generally accepted accounting principles.

Wallace & Wallace, CPAs
November 6, 20X2

Each of the following items represents a deficiency noted by Martin. For each deficiency, indicate whether Martin is correct (M); Gordon is correct (G); or both Martin and Gordon are incorrect (B).

Report Deficiencies Noted by Martin	M / G / B
1. There should be a reference to the prior year's audited financial statements in the first (introductory) paragraph.	
2. All of the current year's basic financial statements are not properly identified in the first (introductory) paragraph.	
3. The standards referred to in the third (accountant's responsibilities) paragraph should not be standards issued by the American Institute of Certified Public Accountants, but should be Standards for the Compilation and Review of Financial Statements.	
4. The title of the report should be *Independent Accountant's Review Report*.	
5. The statement in the third paragraph that the accountant is required to perform procedures to obtain limited assurance that there are no material modifications that should be made to the financial statements should be in the introductory paragraph following the description of a review.	
6. There should be a statement in the second (management's responsibilities) paragraph that describes management's responsibilities relative to internal control.	
7. There should be a comparison of the scope of a review to an audit in the introductory paragraph.	
8. There should be no reference to "assessing the accounting principles used," "significant estimates made by management," and "evaluating the overall financial statement presentation" in the introductory paragraph.	

(ID: 9241)

Problem 12-4 SIMULATION: Review Report

Wallace & Wallace, CPAs, audited the financial statements of West Co., a nonissuer, for the year ended September 30, 20X1, and expressed an unqualified opinion. For the year ended September 30, 20X2, West issued comparative financial statements. Wallace & Wallace reviewed West's year 2 financial statements and Gordon, an assistant on the engagement, drafted the review report below. Martin, the engagement supervisor, decided not to reissue the prior year's audit report, but instructed Gordon to include a separate paragraph in the current year's review report describing the responsibility assumed for the prior year's audited financial statements.

Martin reviewed Gordon's draft and indicated that there were many deficiencies in Gordon's draft.

Accountant's Review Report

We have reviewed the accompanying balance sheet of West Company as of September 30, 20X2, and the related statements of income and cash flows for the year then ended. A review includes primarily applying analytical procedures to management's financial data and making inquiries of company management. A review also includes assessing the accounting principles used and significant estimates made by management, as well as evaluating the overall financial statement presentation.

Management is responsible for the preparation and fair presentation of the financial statements in accordance with accounting principles generally accepted in the United States of America.

Our responsibility is to conduct the review in accordance with standards issued by the American Institute of Certified Public Accountants. Those standards require us to perform procedures to obtain limited assurance that there are no material modifications that should be made to the financial statements. We believe that the results of our procedures provide a reasonable basis for our report.

Based on our review, we are not aware of any material modifications that should be made to the accompanying financial statements. Accordingly, the accompanying financial statements have been prepared assuming that the company will continue as a going concern. Furthermore, we have no responsibility to update this report for events and circumstances occurring after the date of this report.

The financial statements for the year ended September 30, 20X1, were audited by us and we expressed an unqualified opinion on them in our report dated November 7, 20X1, but we have not performed any auditing procedures since that date. In our opinion, the financial statements referred to above are presented fairly, in all material respects, for the year then ended in conformity with generally accepted accounting principles.

Wallace & Wallace, CPAs
November 6, 20X2

Each of the following items represents a deficiency noted by Martin. For each deficiency, indicate whether Martin is correct and Gordon is incorrect (M); Gordon is correct and Martin is incorrect (G); or both Martin and Gordon are incorrect (B).

Report Deficiencies Noted by Martin	M / G / B
1. There should be a reference to "conformity with generally accepted accounting principles" in the fourth paragraph.	
2. There should be a reference to consistency in the fourth paragraph.	
3. There should be a restriction on the distribution of the accountant's review report in the fourth paragraph.	
4. The reference to "going concern" in the fourth paragraph should be in the first paragraph.	
5. The accountant's lack of responsibility to update the report in the fourth paragraph should be in the first paragraph.	
6. There should be no mention of the type of opinion expressed on the prior year's audited financial statements in the fifth paragraph.	
7. All of the prior year's basic financial statements are not properly identified in the fifth paragraph.	
8. The reference in the fifth paragraph to the fair presentation of the prior year's audited financial statements in accordance with generally accepted accounting principles should be omitted.	
9. The report should be dual dated to indicate the date of the prior year's auditor's report.	

(ID: 9245)

_____

Problem 12-5 SIMULATION: Compilation & Review Requirements

Each of the following items represents a series of unrelated procedures that an accountant may consider performing in separate engagements to review the financial statements of a nonissuer (a review) and to compile the financial statements of a nonissuer (a compilation) according to SSARS. Select, as the best answer for each item, whether the procedure is required (R) or not required (N) for **both** review and compilation engagements.

Procedures	Required / Not Required	
	Compilation	Review
1. The accountant should send a letter of inquiry to the entity's attorney to corroborate the information furnished by management concerning litigation.		
2. The accountant should obtain a management representation letter from the entity.		
3. The accountant should compare recorded amounts, or ratios developed from recorded amounts, to expectations developed by the accountant.		
4. The accountant should communicate to the entity's senior management illegal employee acts discovered by the accountant that are clearly inconsequential.		
5. The accountant should make inquiries about events subsequent to the date of the financial statements that would have a material effect on the financial statements.		
6. The accountant should modify the accountant's report if there is a change in accounting principles that is adequately disclosed.		
7. The accountant should submit a hard copy of the financial statements and accountant's report when the financial statements and accountant's report are submitted on a computer disk.		
8. The accountant should perform specific procedures to evaluate whether there is substantial doubt about the entity's ability to continue as a going concern.		

(ID: 9244)

Problem 12-6 SIMULATION: Research

Before submission of compiled financial statements, the accountant should read the financial statements and consider whether such financial statements appear to be appropriate in form and free from obvious material errors. In this context, which citation in the professional standards defines the term *error*?

| | § | | | (ID: 89463) |

Solution 12-1 MULTIPLE-CHOICE ANSWERS

Authoritative Guidance—SSARS

1. (d)   SSARS do not establish standards or procedures for other accounting services such as consulting on accounting, tax, and similar matters, or processing financial data for clients of other accounting firms.

(ID: 4249)

2. (d)   Neither I nor II.   The accountant is required to comply with the provisions of SSARS for compilations whenever he or she is engaged to report on compiled financial statements or submits financial statements to a client or to third parties.   *Submission of financial statements* is defined as presenting to management financial statements that an accountant has prepared.   Neither I nor II meets this definition.   (ID: 6233)

3. (c)   Statements on Standards for Accounting and Review Services (SSARS) are issued by the AICPA's Accounting and Review Services Committee, the senior technical committee of the Institute designated to issue pronouncements in connection with the unaudited financial statements or other unaudited financial information of a nonissuer.   (ID: 6)

4. (d)   The submission of financial statements is defined by SSARS as presenting to management financial statements that an accountant has prepared.   The other three answers do not meet this definition.   (ID: 5095)

5. (d)   An engagement to compile an individual's personal financial statements to be used to obtain a mortgage must be performed in compliance with AR 80, *Compilations of Financial Statements*.   AR 600, *Reporting on Personal Financial Statements Included in Written Personal Financial Plans* provides an exemption from AR 80 for such personal financial statements and guidance on reporting if the statements will not be used to obtain credit or for any other purpose than developing the client's personal financial goals.   (However, AR 600 does not preclude an accountant from complying with AR 80 in such engagements.)   Answers a. and c. do not meet the SSARS definition of submission of financial statements.   (ID: 2281)

6. (c)   The accountant is required to comply with the provisions of SSARS for compilations whenever he or she is engaged to report on compiled financial statements or submits financial statements to a client or to third parties.   *Submission of financial statements* is defined as presenting to management financial statements that an accountant has prepared.   Only answer c. meets this definition.   (ID: 8628)

7. (c)   Reviews of interim financial information should be performed in accordance with auditing standards covered in AU 722, *Interim Financial Information*, (not SSARS) when the following conditions are met: (1) the entity's latest annual financial statements have been audited; (2) the accountant has been engaged to audit the entity's current year financial statements, or audited the latest annual statements and another accountant's appointment to audit the current year statements is not effective prior to the beginning of the period covered by the review; and (3) the client prepares its interim financial information in accordance with the same financial reporting framework as that used to prepare the annual financial statements.   This is in acknowledgement of the difference between a review performed by an accountant with an audit base of knowledge versus that performed by an accountant who is not the entity's auditor.   Further, if these conditions are met, generally the review engagement to provide limited assurance on interim financial reporting is intended to provide a periodic update to the year-end reporting and is considered an extension of the annual audit.   The other answers are not part of the criteria to determine which set of standards should be followed.   (ID: 8642)

8. (b)   The accountant is required to comply with the provisions of SSARS for compilations whenever he or she is engaged to report on compiled financial statements or submits financial statements to a client or to third parties.   *Submission of financial statements* is defined as presenting to management financial statements that an accountant has prepared.   Reproducing client-prepared financial statements, without modification, for the client is not considered a submission of financial statements.   (ID: 9376)

Compilations

9. (c)   The only phrase (of the alternatives) that is included in the standard compilation report is: The objective of a compilation is to assist management in presenting financial information in the form of financial statements.

(ID: 4743)

10. (a) An accountant would discuss independence explicitly in a compilation report only when the accountant lacks independence. When the accountant is independent, it is implicit. Financial statements compiled by an accountant should be accompanied by a report stating that the financial statements have not been audited or reviewed and, accordingly, the accountant does not express an opinion or any other form of assurance on them; thus, answers b. and d. are explicitly stated. Inquiries and analytics are performed during a review engagement, but generally not in a compilation engagement. (ID: 4291)

11. (d) There is no requirement that a compilation report be printed on letterhead or that it be signed manually. (ID: 6817)

12. (c) When the accountant is engaged to report on compiled financial statements or submits financial statements that are reasonably expected to be used by a third party, the financial statements should be accompanied by a written report that states that the accountant does not express an opinion or any other form of assurance on the financial statements. No reference to testing the financial information or to assessing the principles and estimates used is made in the report nor is testing the information supplied required in a compilation. A review consists primarily of inquiries of entity personnel and analytics. (ID: 6027)

13. (b) The compilation report should include a statement that the accountant's responsibility is to conduct the compilation in accordance with Statements on Standards for Accounting and Review Services issued by the AICPA. A compilation report does not include a statement that the accounting principles and significant estimates were assessed and an evaluation of the overall financial statement presentation was done; this statement is part of the standard audit report. The other answer alternatives are both statements, in part, that should be included in a review report rather than a compilation report. (ID: 5696)

14. (b) The accountant should possess a level of knowledge of the accounting principles and practices of the industry in which the entity operates that will enable the accountant to compile financial statements that are appropriate in form for an entity operating in that industry. Answers a., c., and d. represent procedures beyond the scope of a compilation. (ID: 2978)

15. (b) Both are explicitly stated in the introductory paragraph of the standard compilation report. The introductory paragraph begins: *We have compiled the accompanying balance sheet of XYZ Company …* and includes this statement: *We have not audited or reviewed the accompanying financial statements….* (ID: 2294)

16. (d) When engaged to compile the financial statements of a nonissuer, an accountant should read the financial statements and consider whether they appear to be appropriate in form and free from obvious material errors. This would include mistakes in the compilation of the financial statements, including arithmetical or clerical mistakes; and mistakes in the application of accounting principles, including inadequate disclosure. A compilation does not contemplate performing inquiries, analytical procedures or other procedures performed in a review. Accordingly, it would not include performing procedures regarding related-party transactions, going concern issues, or subsequent events. (A compilation does not provide a basis for expressing any level of assurance on the financial statements.) Note: Even though an accountant is not required to perform these procedures, if going concern or subsequent event issues come to the accountant's attention, the accountant should request that management consider the possible effects on the financial statements. The accountant should then evaluate management's response and consider its effect on the compilation report. (ID: 8611)

17. (d) The date on the report should be the date of completion of the compilation. An accountant need not be independent with respect to an entity to issue a compilation report; however, the report should be modified. The accountant should specifically disclose the lack of independence in the last paragraph of the report. The accountant is not precluded from including a description of the reasons(s) that the accountant's independence is impaired; however, if the accountant elects to do so, all the reasons should be included. The accountant utilizes information that is the representation of management. Any other procedures that the accountant might have performed as part of the compilation engagement should not be described in the report. (ID: 8624)

18. (c) One of the basic elements of a report on compiled financial statements is a statement that the objective of a compilation is to assist management in presenting financial information in the form of financial statements without undertaking to obtain or provide any assurance that there are no material modifications that should be made to the financial statements. A statement that a review is substantially less in scope than an audit, the objective of which is the expression of an opinion regarding the financial statements taken as a whole

is an element of a review report rather than a compilation report. The last answer is similar to the statement included in the scope paragraph of the standard audit report rather than a compilation report. (ID: 8629)

19. (d) An accountant need not be independent with respect to an entity to issue a compilation report. In such a case, the accountant should specifically disclose the lack of independence in the last paragraph of the report. The accountant is not precluded from disclosing the reason(s) for the impairment. If this election is made, all reasons should be included. A compilation does not include performing analytical procedures. A compilation does not provide a basis for expressing any level of assurance on the financial statements being compiled. A compilation does not include making management inquiries nor does it contemplate gaining an understanding of an entity's internal control. (ID: 8647)

20. (c) When an accountant is not independent with respect to an entity, a compilation report with special wording that notes the accountant's lack of independence may be issued. The accountant should specifically disclose the lack of independence in the last paragraph of the report. The accountant is not precluded from disclosing the reason(s) for the impairment. If this election is made, all reasons should be included. Regardless of the accountant's independence, a compilation does not provide a basis for expressing any level of assurance on the financial statements being compiled. There is no point in upgrading the engagement when the accountant lacks independence. An accountant is precluded from issuing a review report for an entity with respect to which the accountant is not independent. (ID: 8653)

21. (c) An accountant is not required to be independent to perform a compilation engagement. The lack of independence should be specifically disclosed by adding a statement in the final paragraph of the report. The accountant is not precluded from disclosing the reason(s) for the impairment. If this election is made, all reasons should be included. Independence is required for the other answers. (ID: 8819)

22. (d) If an accountant compiles the financial statements of a nonissuer in accordance with SSARS for a client with which the accountant has an ownership interest, the accountant should include the statement "I am not independent with respect to the entity." in the compilation report. An accountant is not precluded from issuing a compilation report for an entity with respect to which the accountant is not independent. The accountant is also not precluded from disclosing the reason(s) that independence is impaired—in this case ownership—however, there is no requirement to disclose the reasons for the lack of independence as indicated by answer c. (ID: 9373)

23. (d) An entity may request the accountant to compile financial statements that omit substantially all the disclosures required by an applicable financial reporting framework, including disclosures that might appear in the body of the financial statements. The accountant may compile such financial statements, provided that the omission of substantially all disclosures is not undertaken with the intention of misleading those who might reasonably be expected to use such financial statements. Distribution is not restricted to internal use; however, the compilation report should include a paragraph, after the accountant's responsibilities paragraph, that states that management has elected to omit the disclosures; that if the disclosures were included, they might influence the user's conclusions about the company's financial position, results of operations, and cash flows (or equivalent presentations for OCBOA statements); and that, accordingly, the statements are not designed for those who are not informed about such matters. Acknowledgement in the notes to the financial statements is not sufficient. Whether the omission would influence a creditor is not a consideration. (ID: 9932)

Reviews

24. (c) In reviewing the financial statements of a nonissuer, the auditor would most likely use ratio analysis as an analytic for developing relationships among balance sheet accounts. Ratios are useful in evaluating an entity's solvency. Ratio analysis that includes relationships between income statement and balance sheet accounts are useful in evaluating operational efficiency and profitability. Ratio analysis provides an indication of the firm's financial strengths and weaknesses. (ID: 5692)

25. (c) Obtaining a general understanding of the entity's organization, operating characteristics, and products or services allows the accountant to plan the engagement effectively. Without a general understanding of the entity, the accountant would not be able to: anticipate results; develop appropriate questions about procedures for recording, classifying, and summarizing transactions; or determine whether relationships and individual items appear unusual. (ID: 7808)

26. (d) In an engagement to review a nonissuer's financial statements, a CPA uses inquiries and analytics to provide a basis for expressing limited assurance that the financial statements do not contain material deviations from GAAP or OCBOA. Inquiries about actions taken at board of directors' meetings fall within this scope. A review of a nonissuer's financial statements does not require the CPA to obtain an understanding of internal control, assess control risk, or test account records. A review report is appropriate for general use. (ID: 7803)

27. (c) Each page of the financial statements reviewed by the accountant should include a reference, such as "See Accountant's Review Report." (ID: 5699)

28. (c) Review engagement procedures generally are limited to inquiries and analytics. Comparison of current-year to prior-year account balances is an analytical procedure. Answers a., b., and d. are audit procedures. (ID: 8168)

29. (d) When a CPA becomes aware of a departure from the applicable financial reporting framework that is material to the financial statements, if the financial statements are not revised, the CPA should consider whether modification of the standard report is adequate to disclose the departure. If the CPA concludes that modification of the standard report is appropriate, the departure should be disclosed in a separate paragraph, including disclosure of the effects of the departure on the financial statements, if such effects have been determined by management or are known as the result of the CPA's procedures. The CPA is not required to determine the effects of a departure if management has not done so, provided the CPA states in the report that such determination has not been made. If modification of the report is not adequate to indicate the deficiencies in the financial statements as a whole, the CPA should withdraw from the engagement and provide no further services with respect to those financial statements. The CPA may also wish to consult with legal counsel. (ID: 6239)

30. (b) A CPA may be asked to issue a review report on one financial statement, such as a balance sheet, and not on other related financial statements, such as the statements of income, retained earnings, and cash flows. This is allowed if the scope of the inquiry and analytical procedures has not been restricted. (ID: 5697)

31. (d) Failure by the client's management to provide a representation letter covering all of the periods under review precludes the completion of a review. The accountant may issue a compilation report as an accountant is not required to verify, corroborate, or review information supplied for a compilation. (ID: 7844)

32. (c) The report should include a statement that a review includes primarily applying analytical procedures to management's financial data and making inquiries of company management. (ID: 6026)

33. (d) A review does not include assessing fraud risk nor does it contemplate obtaining an understanding of the entity's internal control, so the report would not speak to these matters. (ID: 7023)

34. (b) An accountant is precluded from performing a review engagement if the accountant's independence is impaired for any reason. (ID: 5638)

35. (b) Obtaining a general understanding of the entity's organization, operating characteristics, and products or services allows the accountant to plan the engagement effectively. The other answers contemplate procedures beyond the scope of a review engagement according to SSARS. (ID: 8151)

36. (c) In a review of financial statements, where the CPA expresses limited assurance that the financial statements do not contain material deviations from GAAP, the accountant is required to obtain a knowledge of the accounting principles and practices of the industry in which the entity operates. This is required so that the CPA can determine and apply proper inquiries and analytics. The CPA does not need to apply the procedures listed in the other answers for a review. (ID: 5676)

37. (d) A CPA must obtain a representation letter from management to complete a review. If a CPA becomes aware of a departure from GAAP (such as a lack of justification for a change in accounting principles) in the financial statements, the CPA should consider whether the departure can be adequately disclosed by modifying the standard report. If it can, a separate paragraph should be used to disclose the departure. An accountant may review financial statements prepared in accordance with a basis of accounting other than GAAP, such as the income tax basis. A CPA may issue a review report on one financial statement and not on

other related financial statements if the scope of the CPA's inquiries and analytical procedures has not been restricted. (ID: 7627)

38. (a) Procedures for conducting a review of financial statements generally are limited to analytical procedures and inquiries. The practitioner does not need to observe internal controls. (ID: 5147)

39. (a) If the accountant believes that modification of the standard report is not adequate to indicate the deficiencies in the financial statements taken as a whole, the accountant should withdraw from the review (or compilation) engagement and not provide any further services regarding those financial statements. The accountant would follow the procedures in answer c. if modification of the standard report was considered adequate. (ID: 5093)

40. (d) The accountant may be asked to issue a review report on one financial statement, such as a balance sheet, and not on other related financial statements, such as the statements of income, retained earnings, and cash flows. The accountant may do so if the scope of his or her inquiry and analytical procedures has not been restricted. (ID: 7825)

41. (c) The CPA must establish an understanding with the client regarding the services to be performed and document it in an engagement letter for both engagements. Neither engagement contemplates obtaining an understanding of internal control or assessing fraud risk. Only the review report includes a statement that a review is substantially less in scope than an audit, the objective of which is the expression of an opinion regarding the financial statements as a whole. (ID: 8378)

42. (a) A review provides an accountant with a basis for expressing limited assurance on financial statements. Inquiries should be made regarding the client's principles and practices, including the methods used in applying them. In performing a review, it is not intended that the CPA will obtain an understanding of internal control; assess fraud risk; test accounting records; or other procedures normally performed during an audit (such as identifying related-party transactions). (ID: 8379)

43. (b) The standard review report states that a review includes primarily applying analytical procedures to management's financial data and making inquiries of company management. The objective of a compilation is to assist management in presenting financial information in the form of financial statements. In a review, a CPA expresses limited assurance on the financial statements. A CPA is not required to obtain an understanding of the entity's internal control or assess fraud risk in a SSARS review so it would not be included in the report. (ID: 8410)

44. (c) This question states the objective of a review engagement. For a review engagement, an accountant should possess a level of knowledge of the accounting principles and practices of the industry in which the entity operates and an understanding of the entity's business that will provide through the performance of inquiry and analytical procedures, a reasonable basis for expressing limited assurance that there are no material modifications that should be made to the financial statements in order for them to be in conformity with the applicable financial reporting framework. A review according to SSARS does not include assessing fraud risk or evaluating the effectiveness of controls—a review does not even contemplate obtaining an understanding of the entity's internal control. The accountant is not required to communicate the existence of material weaknesses in internal control to the entity's audit committee. (ID: 8613)

45. (c) In a review, the accountant must apply analytical procedures, such as the analysis of inventory turnover. A review does not include tests of accounting records through inspection, observation, confirmation, or examination of source documents; or other procedures ordinarily performed in an audit. So the accountant would not perform a physical inspection of inventory or vouch inventory purchase transactions. Nor does a review according to SSARS include obtaining an understanding of the entity's internal control, so the accountant would not evaluate internal control over inventory. (ID: 8619)

46. (d) The analytical procedures the accountant may consider performing when conducting a review of financial statements include comparing current financial information with relevant nonfinancial information. In order to obtain a reasonable basis for the expression of limited assurance, the accountant must apply analytical procedures to the financial statements, as well as make inquiries and obtain representations from management. Analytical procedures include comparing recorded amounts, or ratios developed from recorded amounts, to

expectations developed by the accountant. Although analytical procedures are required by GAAS to be included in the both the planning and the final review stage of an audit, this is not a requirement of a review.
(ID: 8634)

47. (c) The attainment of corroborating evidence, such as sending a letter of inquiry to the client's attorney, is not a requirement of a review. The other answers make up the performance requirements of a review.
(ID: 8635)

48. (b) A review does include making inquiries of management which should include asking about related-party transactions. The successor accountant may wish to review the predecessor's working papers relating to matters of continuing accounting significance and those relating to contingencies. As this is not a requirement, as are inquiries of management, it is not as likely to be performed. In a review the accountant is ordinarily not required to corroborate management's responses with other evidence, so it is not likely that the accountant would contact the entity's attorney. A review according to SSARS does not contemplate obtaining an understanding of the entity's internal control, thus communication of internal control deficiencies to senior management would not be likely.
(ID: 8645)

49. (d) When reviewing the financial statements of a nonissuer, an accountant should make inquiries about actions taken at the board of directors meetings. Making inquiries of management along with applying analytical procedures and obtaining representations from management are required in order to obtain a reasonable basis for the expression of limited assurance. A review does not include verification of accounting estimates or tests of accounting records and procedures ordinarily performed in an audit. A review according to SSARS does not contemplate obtaining an understanding of an entity's internal control. A review does not include the assessment of an entity's ability to continue as a going concern; however, during the performance of a review (or a compilation) it may come to the attention of the accountant that there may be such an uncertainty. If so, the accountant should request that management consider the possible effects on the financial statements, including related disclosures.
(ID: 8648)

50. (b) When reviewing the financial statements of a nonpublic entity in accordance with SSARS, the accountant is required to obtain a management representation letter. A review differs significantly from an audit of financial statements in which the auditor provides reasonable assurance that the financial statements, taken as a whole, are free of material misstatement. The objective of a review is to express limited assurance that there are no material modifications that should be made to the financial statements in order for them to be in conformity with the applicable financial reporting framework. A review does not contemplate obtaining an understanding of the entity's internal control, thus assessing control risk is not required. Nor does it involve tests of accounting records by obtaining sufficient, appropriate audit evidence via inspection, observation, confirmation or examination of source documents or other procedures usually performed in an audit, so confirmation of account balances and observation of the physical inventory would also not be required.
(ID: 8803)

51. (d) The accountant must be independent to issue the review report because although the accountant is not expressing an opinion, limited assurance is being given. The other answers are not true.
(ID: 8825)

52. (d) If modification of the standard review (or compilation) report is inadequate to communicate the deficiencies in the financial statements due to departures from GAAP, the accountant should withdraw from the engagement and provide no further services concerning these financial statements. The accountant may wish to consult with legal counsel. Under these circumstances it would not be an option for the accountant to determine the effects of the departures and issue a special report; disclaim an opinion; or change from a review engagement to a compilation engagement because the accountant is precluded from providing further services with respect to these financial statements.
(ID: 9352)

53. (b) When reviewing the financial statements of a nonissuer in accordance with SSARS, a CPA would ordinarily compare the financial statements with budgets or forecasts. A review does not contemplate obtaining an understanding of the entity's internal control or assessing control risk; assessing fraud risk; tests of accounting records by obtaining sufficient appropriate audit evidence through inspection, observation, confirmation, or the examination of source documents or other procedures ordinarily performed in an audit.
(ID: 9368)

54. (a) An accountant reviewing a company's financial statements in accordance with SSARS is required to obtain knowledge of the client's industry. Sending bank confirmations, observing a client's physical inventory,

and corroboration of management's responses to inquiries with other evidence are audit procedures which are not required in a review engagement. (ID: 9392)

55. (a)   If the owner of a company is the accountant's father, the accountant would be precluded from issuing a review report on a company's financial statements in accordance with SSARS because independence is required. The other answers would not preclude an accountant from performing a review. Note: The accountant engaged to review only the balance sheet may do so if the scope of the accountant's inquiry and analytical procedures has not been restricted. (ID: 9398)

56. (c)   The statement that a review consists principally of performing analytical procedures and making inquiries about the interim financial information is not appropriate for inclusion in a management representation letter; rather, it should be included in the engagement letter to provide information about the CPA's responsibilities. Written representations from management ordinarily confirm representations explicitly or implicitly given to the auditor; indicate and document the continuing appropriateness of such representations; and reduce the possibility of misunderstanding concerning the matters that are the subject of the representations. The other answers are appropriate statements for inclusion in a management representation letter for all reviews.

(ID: 9921)

57. (b)   No review, interim or annual, performed according to the SSARS contemplates obtaining an understanding of the client's internal controls, much less testing controls to evaluate their effectiveness. An interim review performed according to GAAS for a nonissuer or PCAOB audit standards for an issuer does require obtaining an understanding of the client's internal control as it relates to the preparation of both annual and interim financial information, but does not involve testing controls. The other answers would typically be done during a review engagement which consists principally of performing analytical procedures and making inquiries of person responsible for financial and accounting matters. (ID: 9922)

58. (d)   Reviews consist principally of performing analytical procedures and making inquiries of persons within the entity responsible for financial and accounting matters. Reviews do not contemplate the obtainment of corroborating evidence. The other answers describe procedures typically performed during a review engagement. (ID: 9949)

Compilations & Reviews

59. (d)   For a compilation or review engagement, the requirement that the CPA possess a level of knowledge of the accounting principles and practices of the industry in which the entity operates does not prevent a CPA from accepting a compilation or review engagement for an entity. However, it does place upon the CPA a responsibility to obtain the required level of knowledge. (ID: 4711)

60. (d)   For a financial statement compilation, the accountant is not required to make inquiries or perform other procedures to verify, corroborate, or review information supplied by the entity. A financial statement review involves performing inquiries and analytics that provide a reasonable basis for expressing limited assurance that there are no material modifications that should be made to the statements in order for them to be in conformity with the applicable financial reporting framework. (ID: 4724)

61. (c)   The objective of a review differs significantly from the objective of a compilation. The inquiry and analytical procedures performed in a review should provide the accountant with a reasonable basis for expressing limited assurance that there are no material modifications that should be made to the financial statements. No expression of assurance is contemplated in a compilation. (ID: 8381)

62. (b)   If the accountant believes that modification of the standard report is not adequate to indicate the deficiencies in the financial statements, taken as whole, the accountant should withdraw from the compilation (or review) engagement and provide no further services concerning those financial statements. It may also be advisable for the accountant to consult with an attorney. (ID: 8828)

63. (a)   An accountant who is not independent may perform compilations, but not reviews. (ID: 9397)

Change in Engagement Type

64. (c)   When there is reasonable justification to change the engagement because of scope restrictions, the report should not include reference to the original engagement, any auditing procedures that were performed, or the scope limitation.   (ID: 5151)

65. (c)   Before an audit engagement has been completed, the client may ask the CPA to change the engagement to a compilation. In reaching a decision, the CPA should consider the client's reasons for making the request, especially if either the client or circumstance has imposed a restriction on the scope of the audit. A change in the circumstances that caused the client to require an audit usually is considered an acceptable reason for change of an audit to a review or compilation engagement. The CPA should consider whether the information affected by the scope restriction may be incorrect, incomplete, or otherwise unsatisfactory. When correspondence with the client's legal counsel is prohibited in an audit engagement, the CPA ordinarily is prohibited from issuing a compilation report as well as an audit report.   (ID: 7822)

66. (d)   When the CPA decides that a change in engagement is appropriate and the requirements of the new engagement type are met, the CPA should issue an appropriate report, without including any reference to the original engagement, any auditing procedures that may have been performed, or any scope limitations that resulted in the changed engagement.   (ID: 8416)

67. (a)   The compilation report should not include a reference to the original engagement, any review procedures that may have been performed, or scope limitations that resulted in the changed engagement. A reference to a departure from GAAS is not related to the question because an accountant must perform a compilation or review of a nonpublic entity in accordance with SSARS, not GAAS.   (ID: 8806)

68. (a)   When a CPA concludes that there is reasonable justification to change the engagement, the CPA should comply with the standards applicable to a review engagement and issue an appropriate review report which would include a statement that a review is substantially less in scope than an audit, the objective of which is the expression of an opinion regarding the financial statements as a whole, and that, accordingly, the CPA does not express such an opinion. The report should not include a reference to: the scope limitation that caused the changed engagement; any description of audit procedures that may have been performed before the engagement was changed; nor the original engagement—reference to the CPA's justification for agreeing to change the engagement would constitute a reference to the original engagement.   (ID: 9909)

Prescribed Forms

69. (b)   When a printed report form calls upon an independent auditor to make a statement that the auditor is not justified in making, the auditor should reword the form or attach a separate report.   (ID: 6368)

Personal Financial Statements

70. (d)   One condition of exemption from AR 80 is an understanding with the client that the financial statements will not be used to obtain credit. The statements may be presented in comparative form and in conformity with GAAP or OCBOA. The certification of the user financial planner is irrelevant to the issuance of the report.   (ID: 5639)

71. (a)   A CPA need not be independent to perform compilation services or prepare tax returns.   (ID: 2809)

Comparative Financial Statements

72. (a)   Compiled financial statements that omit substantially all of the disclosures required by GAAP are not comparable to financial statements that include such disclosures. Accordingly, the accountant should not issue a report on the comparative financial statements when statements for one or more, but not all, of the periods presented omit substantially all of the disclosures required by GAAP.   (ID: 2757)

73. (c)   When the current period financial statements of a nonissuer have been compiled or reviewed and those of the prior period have been audited, the accountant should issue an appropriate compilation or review report on the current period financial statements and **either** the report on the prior period should be reissued **or** the report on the current period should include as a separate paragraph an appropriate description of the responsibility assumed for the financial statements of the prior period. In the latter case, the separate paragraph

should indicate (a) that the financial statements of the prior period were audited previously, (b) the date of the previous report, (c) the type of opinion expressed previously, (d) if the opinion was other than unqualified, the substantive reasons therefor, and (e) that no auditing procedures were performed after the date of the previous report. (ID: 5152)

74. (a) When unaudited financial statements are presented in comparative form with audited financial statements in documents filed with the Securities and Exchange Commission, such statements should be clearly marked as "unaudited" but not referred to in the auditor's report. (ID: 4287)

75. (d) Either reissuance or reference in a separate paragraph is acceptable. (ID: 4754)

76. (b) Before reissuing a compilation (or a review report) of a nonissuer on the financial statements of a prior period, the predecessor accountant should read the financial statements of the current period and the successor's report; compare the prior period financial statements with those previously issued and with those of the current period; and obtain a letter from the successor that indicates whether the successor is aware of any matter that might have a material effect on the financial statements, including disclosures, reported on by the predecessor. The other answers are not required. Note: The predecessor should not refer to the letter from the successor or the successor's report in the reissued report. (ID: 8644)

77. (d) Before reissuing a compilation (or review) report on the financial statements of a nonissuer for the prior year, the predecessor accountant is required to (1) read the financial statements of the current period and the successor's report; (2) compare the prior period financial statements with those previously issued and with those of the current period; and (3) obtain a letter from the successor that indicates whether the successor is aware of any matter that might have a material effect on the financial statements, including disclosures, reported on by the predecessor—the predecessor should not refer in the reissued report to this letter or to the report of the successor. In a compilation engagement the accountant is not required to make inquiries or perform other procedures to verify, corroborate, or review information supplied by the entity. The predecessor is not required to review the successor's working papers for matters affecting the prior year—the predecessor may rely on a review of the financial statements of the current period and the successor's report as well as the letter from the successor just described in (3) to identify any matters affecting the prior year. The predecessor is not required to verify that the reissued report will not be used to obtain credit from a financial institution. (ID: 9367)

78. (a) When the current period financial statements of a nonissuer have been compiled or reviewed and those of the prior period have been audited, the CPA should issue an appropriate compilation or review report on the current period financial statements and either the report on the prior period should be reissued or the report on the current period should include, as a separate paragraph, an appropriate description of the responsibility assumed for the financial statements of the prior period. In the latter case, the separate paragraph should indicate (1) that the financial statements of the prior period were audited previously; (2) the date of the previous report; (3) the type of opinion expressed previously; (4) if the opinion was other than unqualified, the substantive reasons; and (5) that no auditing procedures were performed after the date of the previous report. The reasons for a review in the current period vs. the audit in the prior period should not be included and neither should the fact that the assessment of control risk (an audit procedure) was not updated. There is nothing in the question that indicates that the prior year's audit report should no longer be relied on. (ID: 9908)

PERFORMANCE BY TOPICS

Each category below parallels a topic covered in Chapter 12. Record the number and percentage of questions you answered correctly in each topic.

Authoritative Guidance—SSARS

Question #	Correct √
1	
2	
3	
4	
5	
6	
7	
8	
# Questions	8
# Correct	
% Correct	

Compilations

Question #	Correct √
9	
10	
11	
12	
13	
14	
15	
	15

Reviews

Question #	Correct √
24	
25	
26	
27	
28	
29	
30	
31	
32	
33	
34	
35	
36	
37	
38	
39	
40	
41	
42	
43	
44	
45	
46	
47	
48	
49	
50	
51	
52	
53	
54	
55	
56	
57	
58	
# Questions	35
# Correct	
% Correct	

Compilations & Reviews

Question #	Correct √
59	
60	
61	
62	
63	
# Questions	5
# Correct	
% Correct	

Change in Engagement Type

Question #	Correct √
64	
65	
66	
67	
68	
# Questions	5
# Correct	
% Correct	

Prescribed Forms

Question #	Correct √
69	
# Questions	1
# Correct	
% Correct	

Personal Financial Statements

Question #	Correct √
70	
71	
# Questions	2
# Correct	
% Correct	

Comparative Financial Statements

Question #	Correct √
72	
73	
74	
75	
76	
77	
78	
# Questions	7
# Correct	
% Correct	

Solution 12-2 SIMULATION ANSWER: Compilation & Review Requirements

Procedures	Required / Not Required	
	Compilation	Review
1. The accountant should establish an understanding with the entity regarding the nature and limitations of the services to be performed.	R	R
2. The accountant should make inquiries concerning actions taken at the board of directors' meetings.	N	R
3. The accountant, as the entity's successor accountant, should communicate with the predecessor accountant to obtain access to the predecessor's working papers.	N	N
4. The accountant should obtain a level of knowledge of the accounting principles and practices of the entity's industry.	R	R
5. The accountant should obtain an understanding of the entity's internal control structure.	N	N
6. The accountant should perform analytical procedures designed to identify relationships that appear to be unusual.	N	R
7. The accountant should make an assessment of the fraud risk.	N	N

1. R, R

The accountant should establish an understanding with management regarding the services to be performed for both engagements and should document the understanding through a written communication (in the form of an engagement letter) with management.

2. N, R

The accountant is not required to make inquiries about information supplied by the client in a compilation engagement. Inquiries concerning actions taken at meetings of stockholders, board of directors, committees of the board of directors, or comparable meetings that may affect the financial statements should be made in a review engagement.

3. N, N

The successor accountant may wish to review the predecessor's working papers. This step is not required in either a compilation or a review.

4. R, R

For both engagements, the accountant should possess a level of knowledge of the accounting principles and practices of the industry in which the entity operates.

5. N, N

Neither engagement contemplates obtaining an understanding of the entity's internal control structure.

6. N, R

The accountant is not required to perform such procedures for a compilation; however, such analytics are required for a review.

7. N, N

Neither engagement contemplates assessing fraud risk.

(ID: 9243)

Solution 12-3 SIMULATION ANSWER: Review Report

Report Deficiencies Noted by Martin	M / G / B
1. There should be a reference to the prior year's audited financial statements in the first (introductory) paragraph.	G
2. All of the current year's basic financial statements are not properly identified in the first (introductory) paragraph.	M
3. The standards referred to in the third (accountant's responsibilities) paragraph should not be standards issued by the American Institute of Certified Public Accountants, but should be Standards for the Compilation and Review of Financial Statements.	B
4. The title of the report should be *Independent Accountant's Review Report*.	B
5. The statement in the third paragraph that the accountant is required to perform procedures to obtain limited assurance that there are no material modifications that should be made to the financial statements should be in the introductory paragraph following the description of a review.	G
6. There should be a statement in the second (management's responsibilities) paragraph that describes management's responsibilities relative to internal control.	M
7. There should be a comparison of the scope of a review to an audit in the introductory paragraph.	M
8. There should be no reference to "assessing the accounting principles used," "significant estimates made by management," and "evaluating the overall financial statement presentation" in the introductory paragraph.	M

1. **G**

Gordon is correct. The first paragraph of the report should not include a reference to the prior year's audited financial statements. The standard review report should be issued on the current period statements and the prior period report should be reissued or a separate paragraph should be added to the current period report which describes the responsibility assumed for the financial statements of the prior period.

2. **M**

Martin is correct. The statement of retained earnings should be listed in the first paragraph.

3. **B**

Both are incorrect. The review should be conducted in accordance with Statements on Standards for Accounting and Review Services which are issued by the AICPA.

4. **B**

Both are incorrect. The title should clearly indicate that it is the accountant's review repot and should include the word *independent*.

5. **G**

Gordon is correct. The statement should be in the third (accountant's responsibilities) paragraph.

6. **M**

Martin is correct. The following should be part of the statement regarding management's responsibilities: "…and for designing, implementing, and maintaining internal control relevant to the preparation and fair presentation of the financial statements."

7. M

Martin is correct. The introductory paragraph of the review report should include the following comparison of the scope of a review to an audit: "A review is substantially less in scope than an audit, the objective of which is the expression of an opinion regarding the financial statements as a whole."

8. M

Martin is correct. These phrases are part of the scope paragraph of the standard audit report. This is a review report.   (ID: 9241)

Solution 12-4 SIMULATION ANSWER: Review Report

Report Deficiencies Noted by Martin	M / G / B
1. There should be a reference to "conformity with generally accepted accounting principles" in the fourth paragraph.	M
2. There should be a reference to consistency in the fourth paragraph.	G
3. There should be a restriction on the distribution of the accountant's review report in the fourth paragraph.	G
4. The reference to "going concern" in the fourth paragraph should be in the first paragraph.	B
5. The accountant's lack of responsibility to update the report in the fourth paragraph should be in the first paragraph.	B
6. There should be no mention of the type of opinion expressed on the prior year's audited financial statements in the fifth (separate) paragraph.	G
7. All of the prior year's basic financial statements are not properly identified in the fifth (separate) paragraph.	G
8. The reference in the fifth (separate) paragraph to the fair presentation of the prior year's audited financial statements in accordance with generally accepted accounting principles should be omitted.	M
9. The report should be dual dated to indicate the date of the prior year's auditor's report.	G

1. M

Martin is correct. The fourth paragraph should include a reference to "conformity with generally accepted accounting principles."

2. G

Gordon is correct. The standard review report does not refer to consistency.

3. G

Gordon is correct. The standard review report does not contain a restriction on distribution.

4. B

Both are incorrect. The standard review report does not contain a reference to a "going concern."

5. B

Both are incorrect. The statement regarding responsibility to update the report should be omitted.

6. G

Gordon is correct. The fifth paragraph should describe the responsibility the CPA is assuming for the financial statements of the prior period. Specifically, it should indicate (1) that the prior period's financial statements were audited previously; (2) the date of the previous report; (3) the type of opinion that was previously expressed; (4) if the opinion was other than qualified, the reasons; and (5) that no auditing procedures have been performed since the date of the previous report.

7. G

Gordon is correct. A list of the basic financial statements is not required in the fifth paragraph.

8. M

Martin is correct. The reference in the fifth paragraph to the fair presentation of the prior year's audited financial statements in accordance with generally accepted accounting principles should be omitted.

9. G

Gordon is correct. The report should be dated as of the completion of the inquiry and analytical procedures; the report should not be dual dated. The fifth paragraph correctly indicates the date of the audit report for the prior year's financial statements. (ID: 9245)

———————————

Solution 12-5 SIMULATION ANSWER: Compilation & Review Requirements

Procedures	Required / Not Required	
	Compilation	Review
1. The accountant should send a letter of inquiry to the entity's attorney to corroborate the information furnished by management concerning litigation.	N	N
2. The accountant should obtain a management representation letter from the entity.	N	R
3. The accountant should compare recorded amounts, or ratios developed from recorded amounts, to expectations developed by the accountant.	N	R
4. The accountant should communicate to the entity's senior management illegal employee acts discovered by the accountant that are clearly inconsequential.	N	N
5. The accountant should make inquiries about events subsequent to the date of the financial statements that would have a material effect on the financial statements.	N	R
6. The accountant should modify the accountant's report if there is a change in accounting principles that is adequately disclosed.	N	N
7. The accountant should submit a hard copy of the financial statements and accountant's report when the financial statements and accountant's report are submitted on a computer disk.	N	N
8. The accountant should perform specific procedures to evaluate whether there is substantial doubt about the entity's ability to continue as a going concern.	N	N

1. N, N

Neither engagement requires sending a letter of inquiry to the entity's attorney.

2. N, R

An accountant is not required to make inquiries or perform other procedures to verify, corroborate, or review information supplied by the entity in a compilation engagement. An accountant is required to obtain a written representation from members of management in a review engagement.

3. N, R

Analytical procedures such as this are required for a review, but not for a compilation.

4. N, N

When evidence comes to the accountant's attention during the performance of compilation or review procedures that fraud or an illegal act may have occurred, that matter should be brought to the attention of the appropriate level of management. The accountant need not report matters regarding illegal acts that are clearly inconsequential.

5. N, R

A compilation does not require inquiries about subsequent events. A review includes inquiries to members of management who have responsibility for financial and accounting matters concerning events subsequent to the date of the financial statements that could have a material effect on the financial statements.

6. N, N

As long as the change is appropriate and is appropriately disclosed in the financial statements, there is no requirement to alter the report for a compilation or review.

7. N, N

There is no professional requirement that the accountant submit a hard copy of financial statements or the accountant's report for a review or a compilation.

8. N, N

During the performance of compilation or review procedures, evidence *may* come to the accountant's attention indicating there may be an uncertainty about the entity's ability to continue as a going concern. Specific procedures for the evaluation of an entity's ability to continue as a going concern are not required for either type of engagement. (ID: 9244)

_____

Solution 12-6 SIMULATION ANSWER: Research

AR	§	80		12	

(ID: 89463)

.12   Before submission, the accountant should read the financial statements and consider whether such financial statements appear to be appropriate in form and free from obvious material errors. In this context, the term *error* refers to mistakes in the preparation of financial statements, including arithmetical or clerical mistakes, and mistakes in the application of accounting principles, including inadequate disclosure.

CHAPTER 13

ATTESTATION ENGAGEMENTS

CHAPTER 13

ATTESTATION ENGAGEMENTS

I. **Overview of Attestation Standards (AT 101)**

A. **Attestation Engagements**

1. **Definition** Statements on Standards for Attestation Engagements (SSAE) define an attest engagement as one in which a CPA in public practice (or practitioner) is engaged to, or does, issue an examination, review, or agreed-upon procedures report on subject matter, or an assertion about subject matter, that is the responsibility of another party.

   Editor note: In our coverage, guidelines for AT 101 are applicable to all attest engagements, unless otherwise stated; guidelines in other sections are applicable only to the subject matter in that particular section, unless otherwise stated.

2. **Background** For years, attest services generally were limited to expressing a positive opinion on historical financial statements on the basis of an audit in accordance with generally accepted auditing standards (GAAS). However, CPAs increasingly were requested to provide assurance on representations other than historical financial statements and in forms other than the positive opinion. In responding to these needs, CPAs were generally able to apply the basic concepts underlying GAAS to these attest services. However, as the range of attest services grew it became increasingly difficult to do so. Consequently, the main objective of issuing SSAE was to provide a general framework for and set reasonable boundaries around the attest function.

3. **Hierarchy** The AICPA Code of Professional Conduct requires an AICPA member who performs an attestation engagement to comply with SSAE. SSAE are codified within the framework of the 11 attestation standards. Attestation interpretations consist of Interpretations of SSAE, appendixes to SSAE, attestation guidance included in AICPA Audit and Accounting Guides, and AICPA attestation Statements of Position. Attestation interpretations are recommendations on the application of SSAE in specific circumstances. The practitioner should be aware of and consider attestation interpretations applicable to the attestation engagement. If the practitioner does not apply the attestation guidance included in an applicable attestation interpretation, the practitioner should be prepared to explain how he or she complied with SSAE provisions addressed by such attestation guidance.

4. **Practitioner** Throughout this discussion of attest standards, unless otherwise stated, the terms "CPA" and "practitioner" signify an independent CPA in public practice.

5. **Degrees of Responsibility** AT 20 defines two kinds of requirements that describe the practitioner's degrees of responsibility.

   a. **Unconditional Requirements** The practitioner is required to comply with an unconditional requirement in all cases in which the requirement applies. The words must or is required indicate an unconditional requirement.

   b. **Presumptively Mandatory Requirements** The practitioner is also required to comply with a presumptively mandatory requirement in all cases in which the requirement applies. However, in rare circumstances, the practitioner may depart from such a requirement provided the practitioner documents the justification in the workpapers and the alternative procedures performed to achieve the objectives of that requirement. The word should indicates a presumptively mandatory requirement.

6. **Other Engagements** When the practitioner performs an attest engagement for a government and agrees to follow specified governmental standards, the practitioner must follow those standards in addition to SSAE. An attest engagement may be part of a larger engagement, for example, a feasibility study or business acquisition study that includes an examination of prospective financial information. In such circumstances, these standards apply only to the attest portion of the engagement. Any report issued by a practitioner under other professional standards should be clearly distinguishable from attest reports.

7. **Inapplicable Engagements** A CPA may perform several services outside the scope of the attestation standards, including engagements: (a) performed in accordance with GAAS, (b) performed in accordance with SSARS, (c) performed in accordance with Standards for Consulting Services, (d) client advocacy engagements (e.g., as before the IRS), and (e) tax advice and return preparation services.

8. **Subject Matter** The subject matter of an attest engagement may take many forms, including: (a) historical or prospective performance or condition (e.g., historical or prospective financial information, performance measurements, backlog data); (b) physical characteristics (e.g., descriptions, square footage of facilities); (c) historical events (e.g., the market price of products or services at a specific time); (d) analyses (e.g., break-even analyses, target profit levels); (e) systems and processes (e.g., internal control); and (f) behavior (e.g., corporate governance, compliance with laws and regulations, human resource practices).

9. **Written Assertion** An assertion is any declaration(s) about whether subject matter is based on, or in conformity with, selected criteria. A CPA may attest to a written assertion or directly on the subject matter. In either situation, the CPA typically obtains a written assertion in an examination or a review engagement. A written assertion may be presented to the CPA in several ways, including: a narrative description, a schedule, or as part of a representation letter which clearly identifies what is being presented and the point in time or period of time covered. Without a written assertion, the CPA still may report on the subject matter; however, the CPA needs to exercise caution and ensure that interested parties clearly understand the subject matter in question, including restricting use of the report, when appropriate.

10. **Subsequent Events** Subsequent events are defined by AT 101 in the same manner as for audits. While the practitioner has no responsibility to detect subsequent events, the practitioner should inquire of the responsible party (and the client, if different) as to whether they are aware of any subsequent events through the report date. The representation letter ordinarily contains a representation about subsequent events. The practitioner may later become aware of conditions that existed at that date that might have affected the report had the practitioner been aware of them. In this situation, the practitioner considers the guidance in the auditing standards (AU 561).

11. **Quality Control Standards** Attest standards relate to the conduct of individual engagements; quality control standards relate to the conduct of a firm's attest practice as a whole. Attestation standards and quality control standards are related and the quality control policies and procedures that a firm adopts may affect both the conduct of individual attest engagements and the conduct of a firm's attest practice. AT 101 clarifies that although an effective quality control system is conducive to compliance with attestation standards, deficiencies in, or noncompliance with, a firm's quality control system do not, in and of themselves, indicate that an engagement was not performed in accordance with the applicable professional standards.

B.   Responsible Party
The CPA attests to either a written assertion or subject matter that is the representation of a responsible party. The responsible party is the person or persons who are responsible for the subject matter. The responsible party may be the management of the client entity or it may be another party (such as the management of an entity seeking to sell a property to the client).

1.   **No Responsible Party** Due to the nature of the subject matter, there may be no obvious responsible party. In that situation, a party who has a reasonable basis for making a written assertion about the subject matter becomes the responsible party. Practitioners may be engaged to gather information to enable the responsible party to evaluate the subject matter in connection with providing a written assertion. Regardless of the procedures performed by the CPA, the responsible party must accept responsibility for the assertion and the subject matter and must not base that assertion solely on procedures performed by the CPA. Because of the CPA's attest role, the CPA may **not** assume the role of the responsible party in an attest engagement.

2.   **Prerequisite** The identification of a responsible party is a prerequisite for an attest engagement. A CPA may accept an engagement to perform an examination, a review, or an agreed-upon procedures engagement on subject matter or a written assertion provided that *one* of the following conditions is met:

a.   The party wishing to engage the CPA is responsible for the subject matter, or has a reasonable basis for providing a written assertion about the subject matter if the nature of the subject matter is such that a responsible party does not otherwise exist.

b.   The party wishing to engage the CPA is not responsible for the subject matter but is able to (or have a third party who is responsible for the subject matter) provide the CPA with evidence of the third party's responsibility for the subject matter.

3.   **Acknowledgment** The CPA should obtain written acknowledgment or other evidence of the responsible party's responsibility for the subject matter or the written assertion, as it relates to the engagement. The responsible party can acknowledge that responsibility in a number of ways including in an engagement letter, a representation letter, the presentation of the subject matter, or a written assertion. If the CPA is not able to obtain direct written acknowledgment, the CPA should obtain other evidence of the responsible party's responsibility for the subject matter (e.g., by reference to legislation, regulation, or contract).

C.   General Standards
Note that three of the five general standards parallel the three auditing general standards.

1.   **Training** The practitioner must have adequate technical training and proficiency to perform the attestation engagement.

2.   **Knowledge** The practitioner must have adequate knowledge in the subject matter. The CPA may use specialists, provided that the CPA has enough knowledge of the subject matter (1) to communicate to the specialist the objectives of the work, and (2) to evaluate the specialist's work to determine if the objectives were achieved.

3.   **Criteria** The practitioner must have reason to believe that the subject matter is capable of evaluation against criteria that are suitable and available to users. Suitable criteria must be objective, measurable, complete, and relevant.

a.   Criteria promulgated by a body designated by AICPA Governing Council under the AICPA Code of Professional Conduct are considered suitable criteria by definition. Criteria issued by regulatory agencies and other bodies of experts that follow due-process procedures also are considered suitable. Criteria issued by industry associations or other groups should be examined critically for suitability. Such criteria should be described clearly in the presentation.

      b.   Competent persons using the same or similar criteria ordinarily should be able to obtain materially similar estimates or measurements. However, competent persons will not always reach the same conclusions because: (1) measurements often require exercise of considerable professional judgment, and (2) a slightly different evaluation of the facts could yield a significant difference in the conclusion.

      c.   Criteria may be available to users in several ways. If criteria availability is limited, the practitioner's report must be restricted to those who have access.

    4.   **Independence** The practitioner must maintain independence in mental attitude in all matters relating to the engagement.

    5.   **Due Professional Care** The practitioner must exercise due professional care in the planning and performance of the engagement and the preparation of the report.

D.   **Fieldwork Standards**
Note that these two standards are similar to two of the three auditing fieldwork standards.

    1.   **Planning & Supervision** The practitioner must adequately plan the work and must properly supervise any assistants. An understanding with the client as to the services to be performed must be reached.

    2.   **Evidence** The practitioner must obtain sufficient evidence to provide a reasonable basis for the conclusion that is expressed in the report.

      a.   **Documentation** The quantity, type, and content of workpapers will vary with the situation. (An examination will require more evidence than a review.) A CPA prepares and retains workpapers during attest engagements that are appropriate to the situation and the CPA's needs. (The guidance regarding attest workpapers is similar to that for audit workpapers.) Workpapers should be sufficient to document that: (1) work was adequately planned and supervised; and (2) the CPA obtained evidential matter providing a reasonable basis for the conclusion expressed in the CPA's report.

      b.   **Representations** If the client or responsible party refuses to furnish appropriate written representations, the CPA should consider the effects of this refusal on his or her ability to rely on other representations. If the representation letter is necessary evidence for reporting, this refusal constitutes a scope limitation on the examination sufficient to require a qualified opinion, a disclaimer of an opinion, or withdrawal from the engagement.

E.   **Reporting Standards**
AT 101 provides for three types of attestation engagements: examinations, reviews, and applications of agreed-upon procedures. Reports on examination or review engagements may be used by the general public. Use of reports on agreed-upon procedures are restricted to the use of parties who have agreed to the specified procedures.

    1.   **Identification** The practitioner must identify the subject matter or the assertion being reported on and state the character of the engagement in the report. If the attestation is on an assertion, the assertion must accompany, or be restated within, the CPA's report. The statement of the character of an attest engagement designed to result in a general-use report (i.e., an examination or a review) includes two elements: (a) a description of the nature and scope of the work performed, and (b) a reference to the professional (AICPA) standards governing the engagement.

2. **Conclusion** The practitioner must state the practitioner's conclusion about the subject matter or the assertion in relation to the criteria against which the subject matter was evaluated in the report.

    a. **Misstatements** If deviations from the criteria or material misstatements exist, the practitioner should modify the report, directly expressing an opinion on the subject matter, rather than the assertion.

    b. **Materiality** The CPA should consider the idea of materiality in applying this standard. Materiality is determined by the relative size of a misstated or omitted fact, rather than by its absolute amount. Materiality considerations include whether a reasonable person relying on the presentation of assertions would be influenced by the inclusion or correction of an individual assertion.

    c. **Use** General-use attest reports are limited to two levels of assurance: one based on a reduction of attestation risk to an appropriately low level (an "examination") and the other based on a reduction of attestation risk to a moderate level (a "review").

        (1) **Examinations** A practitioner selects, from all available procedures, any combination that restricts attest risk to an appropriately low level. A conclusion is expressed in the form of an opinion.

        (2) **Reviews** Procedures typically are limited to inquiries and analytical procedures. The conclusion is expressed in the form of negative assurance.

3. **Reservations** The practitioner must state all of the practitioner's significant reservations about the engagement subject matter and, if applicable, the assertion related thereto in the report.

    a. **Unresolved Problem** "Reservations about the engagement" refers to any unresolved problem the CPA had in complying with the standards and guidance applicable to attestation services or procedures agreed to by the specified parties. An unqualified conclusion should not be expressed if the CPA has been unable to apply all the procedures considered necessary to comply with attestation standards.

    b. **Scope Restrictions** Restrictions on the scope of the engagement, whether imposed by the client or by other circumstances, may require the CPA to qualify the report, to disclaim any assurance, or to withdraw from the engagement. The decision as to the appropriate course of action depends on the effect of the omitted procedure(s) on the CPA's ability to express assurance on the presentation of assertions. When restrictions that significantly limit the scope of the engagement are imposed by the client, the CPA generally should either withdraw from the engagement or disclaim any assurance on the subject matter, assertions, or presentation. An incomplete review engagement requires the CPA to withdraw.

4. **Restrictions** AT 101 does **not** prohibit a practitioner from restricting the use of any report. The fourth standard of reporting is as follows: The practitioner must state in the report that the report is intended solely for the information and use of the specified parties under the following circumstances:

    • When the criteria used to evaluate the subject matter are determined by the practitioner to be appropriate only for a limited number of parties who either participated in their establishment or can be presumed to have an adequate understanding of the criteria

    • When the criteria used to evaluate the subject matter are available only to specified parties

- When reporting on subject matter and a written assertion has not been provided by the responsible party

- When the report is on an attestation engagement to apply agreed-upon procedures to the subject matter

When a report is restricted as to use, it contains a separate final paragraph that includes the following types of statements: (a) indicate the report is intended solely for the use of the specified parties, (b) identify the specified parties, and (c) indicate the report is not intended to be, and should not be, used by anyone other than the specified parties.

5. **Other Information in Client-Prepared Document** The client may publish documents containing information in addition to the practitioner's attest report and the related assertion. This guidance is inapplicable if the practitioner or another practitioner is engaged to issue an opinion on the other information or when the other information appears in a registration statement filed under the Securities Act of 1933.

   a. The practitioner's responsibility doesn't extend beyond the information identified in the practitioner's report or by the report of another practitioner. The practitioner should read the other information in the document and consider whether it, or the manner of its presentation, is materially inconsistent with the information appearing in the practitioner's report.

   b. If the practitioner is aware of inconsistencies with the other information, either the practitioner's report or the other information should be revised. If the practitioner believes the other information must be changed, and it is not, the practitioner should consider other actions: adding an explanatory paragraph to the practitioner's report, withholding the use of the report in the document, or withdrawal.

   c. If the practitioner is aware of an apparent material misstatement of fact in the other information, the practitioner should discuss such concerns with the client. If a valid basis for concern remains, the practitioner should propose the client consult with another party whose advice may be useful (for example, legal counsel). If a valid basis for concern remains after discussion, the practitioner should consider consulting legal counsel and notifying the client's management and audit committee of the practitioner's views.

6. **Common Report Components** Standard reports for examinations and reviews share some elements:

   a. **Title** The title includes the word *independent.*

   b. **Responsible Party's Responsibility** A statement that the *subject matter* [or, assertion] is the responsible party's responsibility.

   c. **Identification** An identification of the *subject matter* [or, assertion] and the responsible party. When reporting on the assertion, if the assertion doesn't accompany the practitioner's report, the first paragraph of the report also contains a statement of the assertion.

   d. **Restriction** A statement restricting the report use to specified parties under the following situations:

      (1) **Suitability** When the practitioner determines the criteria used to evaluate the subject matter are appropriate only for a limited number of parties who either participated in criteria development or can be inferred to have an adequate understanding of the criteria.

      (2) **Availability** When the criteria used to evaluate the subject matter are available only to specified parties.

      (3)   **Written Assertion** When a written assertion was not provided by the responsible party.

    e.   **Signature & Date** The practitioner's manual or printed signature. The date of the completion of the procedures.

F.   Examinations

Examinations represent the highest level of assurance. When CPAs are engaged to express an opinion as the result of an attestation engagement, they should state clearly whether: (1) management's assertion is presented (or fairly stated), in all material respects, based on (or in conformity with) the established/stated criteria, or (2) the subject matter of the assertion is based on (or in conformity with) the established or stated criteria in all material respects. Nothing precludes a practitioner from examining an assertion but providing an opinion on the subject matter.

Exhibit 1 ▶ Examination Report on Subject Matter

<u>Independent Accountant's Report</u>

We have examined the [*identify the subject matter—for example, the accompanying schedule of investment returns of XYZ Company for the year ended December 31, 20XX*]. XYZ Company's management is responsible for the schedule of investment returns. Our responsibility is to express an opinion based on our examination.

Our examination was conducted in accordance with attestation standards established by the American Institute of Certified Public Accountants and, accordingly, included examining, on a test basis, evidence supporting [*identify the subject matter—for example, XYZ Company's schedule of investment returns*] and performing such other procedures as we considered necessary in the circumstances. We believe that our examination provides a reasonable basis for our opinion.

[*Additional paragraph(s) may be added to emphasize certain matters relating to the attest engagement or the subject matter.*]

In our opinion, the schedule referred to above presents, in all material respects, [*identify the subject matter—for example, the investment returns of XYZ Company for the year ended December 31, 20XX*] based on [*identify criteria—for example, the ABC criteria set forth in Note 1*].

---

1.   **Modifications** Reports expressing a positive opinion on the reliability of an assertion may be qualified or modified for an aspect of the subject matter, assertion, or the engagement. In addition, examination reports may emphasize certain matters relating to the attest engagement, subject matter, or assertion. Remember, if deviations from the criteria or material misstatements exist, the practitioner should modify the report, directly expressing an opinion on the subject matter, rather than the assertion.

2.   **Report Components** The practitioner reports on either the subject matter or the assertion. The practitioner's examination report includes the following:

    a.   **Responsibility** A statement that the practitioner's responsibility is to express an opinion on the *subject matter* [or, assertion] based on the practitioner's examination.

    b.   **Standards** A statement that the examination was performed in accordance with attestation standards established by the AICPA, and, accordingly, included procedures that the practitioner considered necessary in the situation.

    c.   **Basis** A statement that the practitioner believes the examination provides a reasonable basis for his or her opinion.

    d.   **Conclusion** The practitioner's opinion on whether the *subject matter is based on (or in conformity with)* [or, the assertion is presented (or fairly stated) based on] the criteria in all material respects.

G. Reviews

A review report provides limited assurance. The CPA's report states whether any information came to the CPA's attention on the basis of the work performed that indicates that the subject matter is materially misstated or divergent from criteria; or that assertions are **not** presented in all material respects in conformity with criteria. The report: (1) indicates that the work performed was less in scope than an examination, (2) disclaims a positive opinion on the assertions, and (3) contains a statement of limitations on the use of the report when it has been prepared in conformity with specified criteria that have been agreed upon by the specified parties because it is intended solely for specified parties. The practitioner reports on either the subject matter or the assertion. The practitioner's review report includes the following:

1. **Standards** A statement that the review was performed in accordance with attestation standards established by the AICPA.

2. **Disclaimer** A statement that a review is substantially less in scope than an examination, the objective of which is an expression of an opinion on the subject matter [or, assertion], and accordingly, no such opinion is expressed.

3. **Conclusion** A statement about whether the practitioner is aware of any material modifications that should be made to the *subject matter in order for it to be based on (or in conformity with), in all material respects,* [or, assertion in order for it to be presented (or fairly stated) in all material respects, based on (or in conformity with)] the criteria, other than those modifications, if any, indicated in the practitioner's report. The conclusion is expressed in the form of negative assurance: *Nothing came to our attention…*

Exhibit 2 ▶ Restricted Review Report on an Assertion

<u>Independent Accountant's Report</u>

We have reviewed management's assertion that [*identify the assertion—for example, the accompanying schedule of investment returns of XYZ Company for the year ended December 31, 20XX is presented in accordance with the ABC criteria referred to in Note 1*]. XYZ Company's management is responsible for the assertion.

Our review was conducted in accordance with attestation standards established by the American Institute of Certified Public Accountants. A review is substantially less in scope than an examination, the objective of which is the expression of an opinion on management's assertion. Accordingly, we do not express such an opinion.

[*Additional paragraph(s) may be added to emphasize certain matters relating to the attest engagement or the assertion.*]

Based on our review, nothing came to our attention that caused us to believe that management's assertion referred to above is not fairly stated, in all material respects, based on [*identify the criteria—for example, the ABC criteria referred to in the investment management agreement between XYZ Company and DEF Investment Managers, Ltd., dated November 15, 20X1*].

This report is intended solely for the information and use of XYZ Company and [*identify other specified parties—for example, DEF Investment Managers, Ltd.*] and is not intended to be and should not be used by anyone other than these specified parties.

Editor note: Although suitable criteria exist for the subject matter, the report in Exhibit 2 is restricted as to use because the criteria are available only to specified parties; otherwise, the paragraph restricting the use of the report would be omitted.

II. Guidance for Particular Attest Engagements

A. Agreed-Upon Procedures (AT 201)

An agreed-upon procedures engagement is one in which a practitioner is engaged to issue a report of findings based on specific procedures performed on subject matter. A client engages the practitioner to assist specified parties in evaluating subject matter or an assertion as a result of needs of specified parties. The specified parties and the practitioner agree upon procedures to be performed by the practitioner that the specified parties believe are appropriate. The nature, extent, and timing of procedures may vary widely. The specified parties assume responsibility for the sufficiency of the procedures since they best understand their own needs. The practitioner does not provide an opinion or negative assurance. Instead, the practitioner's report on agreed-upon procedures should be in the form of procedures and findings. A practitioner's report on such engagements should indicate clearly that its use is restricted to those specified parties. A written assertion is **not** required for engagements covered by AT 201, unless required by another attest standard section.

1. **Required Conditions for Engagements** To satisfy the agreement and responsibility requirements enumerated here, the practitioner ordinarily communicates directly with, and obtains affirming acknowledgments from, each specified party. If there is no such communication, the practitioner may find other procedures adequate, such as: (a) comparing proposed procedures to written requirements from specified parties; (b) discussing procedures with appropriate representatives of specified parties; or (c) reviewing relevant contracts with, or correspondence from, specified parties.

   a. **Independence** The practitioner is independent,

   b. **Responsibility** The specified parties take responsibility for the sufficiency of the agreed-upon procedures for their purpose, plus a party responsible for the subject matter (either the client or third party, see AT 101 coverage) exists.

   c. **Procedures & Criteria** The specified parties and the practitioner agree upon procedures to be performed by the practitioner and the criteria to be used in the determination of findings.

   d. **Suitability** The specific subject matter is subject to reasonably consistent measurement. The procedures are expected to result in reasonably consistent findings using the criteria. Evidential matter related to the specific subject matter is expected to exist to provide a reasonable basis for expressing findings in the practitioner's report.

   e. **Materiality** Where applicable, the practitioner and the specified parties agree on any materiality limits; these are described in the practitioner's report.

   f. **Restricted Report** Use of the report is restricted to the specified parties.

   g. **Disclosure** For engagements involving prospective financial information, the prospective financial statements must include a summary of significant assumptions.

2. **Nature** The requirements of the attest standards, except the second reporting standard, are applicable. A management representation letter is optional.

   a. **Specialist** The specified parties and the practitioner must agree explicitly on the involvement of a specialist.

   b. **Internal Auditors & Other Personnel** The agreed-upon procedures are to be performed entirely by the practitioner and any assisting specialists; however, internal auditors or other client personnel may prepare schedules or provide other information for the practitioner's use in performing the procedures.

3. **Findings** The practitioner reports all findings from applying the agreed-upon procedures. The concept of materiality is inapplicable unless the specified parties and the practitioner have established a definition of materiality.

4. **Report Components** In addition to elements listed in paragraph I., E., 6., the practitioner's report contains the following:

   a. **Nature** An identification of the character of the engagement.

   b. **Responsibility** A statement that the sufficiency of the procedures is solely the specified parties' responsibility. A disclaimer of responsibility on the part of the practitioner for the sufficiency of the procedures.

   c. **Description** A list of, or reference to, the procedures performed and related findings.

   d. **Materiality** Where applicable, a description of any agreed-upon materiality limits.

   e. **Disclaimer** A statement that the practitioner did not conduct an examination of the subject matter, the objective of which would be the expression of an opinion on the subject matter, and a statement that if the practitioner had performed additional procedures, other matters might have come to his or her attention that would have been reported.

   f. **Restriction** A statement restricting the report use because it is intended solely for the use of specified parties (see the fourth reporting standard).

   g. **Limitations** Where applicable, reservations or restrictions concerning procedures or findings.

   h. **Prospective Financial Information** Where applicable, items required by AT 301.

   i. **Specialist** Where applicable, a description of the assistance provided by a specialist.

Exhibit 3 ▶ Report on Agreed-Upon Procedures

Independent Accountant's Report
on Applying Agreed-Upon Procedures

To the Board of Directors and Management of X Company:

We have performed the procedures enumerated below, which were agreed to by the Board of Directors and Management of X Company, solely to assist you in connection with the proposed acquisition of Y Company as of December 31, 20XX. Y Company is responsible for its cash and accounts receivable records. This agreed-upon procedures engagement was conducted in accordance with attestation standards established by the American Institute of Certified Public Accountants. The sufficiency of these procedures is solely the responsibility of the parties specified in this report. Consequently, we make no representation regarding the sufficiency of the procedures described below either for the purpose for which this report has been requested or for any other purpose.

The procedures and the associated findings are as follows:

Cash

1. We obtained confirmation of the cash on deposit from the following banks, and we agreed the confirmed balance to the amount shown on the bank reconciliations maintained by Y Company. We mathematically checked the bank reconciliations and compared the resultant cash balances per book to the respective general ledger account balances.

Bank	General Ledger Account Balances December 31, 20XX
ABC National Bank	$ 5,000
DEF State Bank	3,776
XYZ Trust Company—regular account	86,912
XYZ Trust Company—payroll account	5,000
	$110,688

We found no exceptions as a result of the procedures.

Accounts Receivable

2. We added the individual customer account balances shown in an aged trial balance of accounts receivable (identified as Exhibit A) and compared the resultant total with the balance in the general ledger account.

We found no difference.

3. We compared the individual customer account balances shown in the aged trial balance of accounts receivable (Exhibit A) as of December 31, 19XX, to the balances shown in the accounts receivable subsidiary ledger.

We found no exceptions as a result of the comparisons.

4. We traced the aging (according to invoice dates) for 50 customer account balances shown in Exhibit A to the details of outstanding invoices in the accounts receivable subsidiary ledger. The balances selected for tracing were determined by starting at the eighth item and selecting every fifteenth item thereafter.

We found no exceptions in the aging of the amounts of the 50 customer account balances selected. The sample size traced was 9.8 percent of the aggregate amount of the customer account balances

5. We mailed confirmations directly to the customers representing the 150 largest customer account balances selected from the accounts receivable trial balance, and we received responses as indicated below. We also traced the items constituting the outstanding customer account balance to invoices and supporting shipping documents for customers from which there was no reply. As agreed, any individual differences in a customer account balance of less than $300 were to be considered minor, and no further procedures were performed.

Of the 150 customer balances confirmed, we received responses from 140 customers; 10 customers did not reply. No exceptions were identified in 120 of the confirmations received. The differences disclosed in the remaining 20 confirmation replies were either minor in amount (as defined above) or were reconciled to the customer account balance without proposed adjustment thereto. A summary of the confirmation results according to the respective aging categories is as follows.

		Accounts Receivable December 31, 20XX	
Aging Categories	Account Balances	Confirmations Requested	Confirmations Received
Current:	$156,000	$ 76,000	$ 65,000
Past due:			
Less than one month	60,000	30,000	19,000
One to three months	36,000	18,000	10,000
Over three months	48,000	48,000	8,000
	$300,000	$172,000	$102,000

We were not engaged to and did not conduct an audit, the objective of which would be the expression of an opinion on cash and accounts receivable. Accordingly, we do not express such an opinion. Had we performed additional procedures, other matters might have come to our attention that would have been reported to you.

This report is intended solely for the information and use of the board of directors and management of X Company and is not intended to be and should not be used by anyone other than these specified parties.

5. **Explanatory Language** The practitioner may include explanations about issues such as the following: (a) disclosures of stipulated facts, assumptions, or interpretations used in applying procedures; (b) condition of records, controls, or data; (c) a statement that the practitioner has no responsibility to update the report.

6. **Scope Limitations** When the situation imposes restrictions on the performance of procedures, the practitioner should obtain agreement from the specified parties to modify the agreed-upon procedures, describe any restrictions in the report, or withdraw from the engagement.

7. **Additional Specified Parties** After completing an engagement, a practitioner may add another party as a specified party, considering such factors as used in determining the original specified parties. If the report is reissued, the practitioner does not change the date.

8. **Outside Knowledge** The practitioner need not perform additional procedures, but if a matter comes to the practitioner's attention that significantly contradicts the subject matter, the practitioner should include this matter in the report.

9. **Request to Change Engagement Type** If the practitioner concludes, based on professional judgment, that there is reasonable justification to change the engagement, and provided the practitioner complies with the standards applicable to that engagement, the practitioner issues the report appropriate to the new engagement type. This report should not include reference to either the original engagement or performance limitations that resulted in a different engagement. If the original engagement procedures are substantially complete or the effort to do so is relatively insignificant, the practitioner should evaluate the propriety of an engagement change.

10. **Combined Reports** The reports on applying agreed-upon procedures may be combined with reports on other services, provided the types of services can be distinguished clearly and applicable guidance for each service is followed.

B. **Financial Forecasts & Projections (AT 301)**
AT 301 establishes guidance concerning performance and reporting for engagements to examine, compile, or apply agreed-upon procedures to prospective financial statements (PFS).

1. **Applicability** The guidance applies to a CPA who submits (to the client or others) PFS that the CPA has assembled or assisted in assembling, or reports on PFS, if such statements are (or reasonably might be) expected to be used by a third party. In deciding whether the PFS are (or reasonably might be) expected to be used by a third party, the CPA may rely on either the written or oral representation of the responsible party, unless contradictory information comes to his or her attention. An exception to this guidance exists for litigation support services, because the practitioner's work is subject to detailed analysis and challenge by parties to the dispute. This exception is inapplicable when either all third parties do not have opportunity for analysis and challenge or if the practitioner is engaged specifically to issue a report on PFS.

2. **Preparation** The practitioner's work may not be described as including *preparation* of the PFS. The practitioner may assist the responsible party in identifying assumptions, gathering information, or assembling the statements. The responsible party still has sole responsibility for the preparation and presentation of the PFS, because the PFS are dependent on the responsible party's actions, plans, and assumptions. A practitioner may prepare a financial analysis, including collecting information, forming assumptions, and assembling a presentation. Such an analysis is inappropriate for general use and is not a forecast or projection. If the responsible party reviews and adopts the assumptions and presentation, or bases assumptions and a presentation on the analysis, the practitioner may perform an AT 301 engagement and issue a report appropriate for general use.

3. **Definitions**

   a. **Prospective Financial Statements (PFS)** Either financial forecasts or financial projections that include summaries of significant assumptions and accounting policies (does not include *pro forma* financial statements or partial presentations).

b. **Partial Presentation** A presentation of prospective financial information omitting required elements of PFS.

c. **Financial Forecast** PFS that present, to the best of the responsible party's knowledge and belief, an entity's expected financial position, results of operations, and cash flows. A financial forecast may be expressed in specific monetary amounts as a single-point estimate of forecasted results or as a range, where the responsible party selects key assumptions to form a range within which it reasonably expects, to the best of its knowledge and belief, the item or items subject to the assumptions actually to fall.

d. **Financial Projection** PFS that present, to the best of the responsible party's knowledge and belief, given one or more hypothetical assumptions, an entity's expected financial position, results of operations, and cash flows. A financial projection sometimes is prepared to present one or more hypothetical courses of action for evaluation. It answers the question, "What would happen if...?" A financial projection is based on the responsible party's assumptions reflecting conditions it expects would exist and the course of action it expects would be taken, given one or more hypothetical assumptions. It may also contain a range.

e. **Entity** Any unit, existing or to be formed, for which financial statements could be prepared in conformity with GAAP or OCBOA.

f. **Hypothetical Assumption** An assumption used in a financial projection to present a condition or course of action that is not necessarily expected to occur, but is consistent with the purpose of the projection.

g. **Responsible Party** The person or persons who are responsible for the assumptions underlying the prospective financial statements, usually management. It can be persons outside the entity who currently do not have authority to direct operations.

h. **Assembly** Processing related to the presentation of prospective financial statements.

i. **Key Factors** The significant matters on which an entity's future results are expected to depend. Key factors are the bases for assumptions.

j. **Materiality** Materiality is a concept that is judged in the light of the expected range of reasonableness of the information. Users should not expect prospective information to be as precise as historical information.

4. **Uses of PFS**

a. **General Use** Refers to the use of PFS by persons with whom the responsible party is not negotiating directly. Since users are unable to ask questions of the responsible party, the presentation most useful to them is one that portrays, to the best of the responsible party's knowledge and belief, the expected results. Only a financial forecast is appropriate for general use.

b. **Limited Use** Refers to the use of PFS by the responsible party alone or by the responsible party and third parties with whom the responsible party is negotiating directly. Third-party recipients of PFS intended for limited use can ask questions of the responsible party and directly negotiate terms with it. Any type of PFS that would be useful in the circumstances normally is appropriate for limited use. The presentation may be a financial forecast or a financial projection.

5. **Partial Presentations** The practitioner's procedures in an engagement connected with a partial presentation is affected by the nature of the information presented. The scope for an examination or compilation of some partial presentations may be similar to that for the examination or compilation of a presentation of PFS. Reports on partial presentations of both

forecasted and projected information should include a description of any limitations of the usefulness of the presentation.

6. **Common Report Elements** Standard reports for the three engagements share some elements: (a) a caveat that the prospective results might **not** be achieved; (b) a statement that the CPA assumes no responsibility to update the report for events and circumstances occurring after the date of the report; (c) the practitioner's signature; and (d) the date of the completion of the CPA's procedures.

7. **Compilation of PFS** A compilation of PFS involves (a) assembling, to the extent necessary, the PFS based on the responsible party's assumptions, (b) performing the required compilation procedures, including reading the statements and considering whether they are appropriate and are presented in conformity with AICPA presentation guidelines, and (c) issuing a compilation report. Independence is **not** necessary for a compilation engagement.

    a. **Limited Procedures** A compilation is not intended to provide assurance on the PFS or the assumptions underlying such statements. Because of the limited nature of the CPA's procedures, a compilation does not provide assurance that the CPA will become aware of significant matters that might be disclosed by more extensive procedures.

    b. **Assumptions** Since this summary is essential to the reader's understanding of PFS, the CPA should not compile PFS that exclude disclosure of the summary of significant assumptions. Also, the CPA should not compile a financial projection that omits (1) an identification of the hypothetical assumptions or (2) a description of the limitations on the usefulness of the presentation.

    c. **Obviously Inappropriate** The practitioner should consider when representations or other information appear to be obviously inappropriate, incomplete, etc., and if so, should attempt to clarify the matter. If the matter is not clarified, the practitioner ordinarily withdraws from the engagement.

8. **Compilation Reports** In addition to the previously discussed elements, the standard compilation report includes: (a) identification of the PFS presented by the responsible party; (b) a statement that the CPA has compiled the PFS in accordance with attestation standards established by the AICPA; and (c) a statement that a compilation is limited in scope and does not enable the CPA to express an opinion or any other form of assurance on the PFS or the assumptions.

Exhibit 4 ▶ Compilation Report on a Forecast (Projection)

We have compiled the accompanying forecasted [*projected*] balance sheet, statements of income, retained earnings, and cash flows of XYZ Company as of December 31, 20X1, and for the year then ending, in accordance with attestation standards established by the American Institute of Certified Public Accountants. [*If for a projection add: The accompanying projection was prepared for (state special purpose, for example, "the purpose of negotiating a loan to expand XYZ Company's plant").*]

A compilation is limited to presenting in the form of a forecast [*projection*] information that is the representation of management and does not include evaluation of the support for the assumptions underlying the projection. We have not examined the forecast [*projection*] and, accordingly, do not express an opinion or any other form of assurance on the accompanying statements or assumptions. Furthermore, [*If for a projection, add: even if (describe hypothetical assumption, for example, "the loan is granted and the plant is expanded,"*)] there will usually be differences between the forecasted [*projected*] and actual results, because events and circumstances frequently do not occur as expected, and those differences may be material. We have no responsibility to update this report for events and circumstances occurring after the date of this report.

> **<Additional paragraph for a projection report>**
>
> The accompanying projection and this report are intended solely for the information and use of [*identify specified parties, for example, "XYZ Company and DEF National Bank"*] and is not intended to be and should not be used by anyone other than these specified parties.

a. **Projection Presentation** The practitioner's report should include a separate paragraph that describes the limitations on the usefulness of the presentation.

b. **Range** When the PFS contain a range, the practitioner's report also should include a separate paragraph that states that the responsible party has elected to portray the expected results of one or more assumptions as a range.

Exhibit 5 ▶ Separate Paragraph for Forecast Containing Range

> As described in the summary of significant assumptions, management of XYZ company has elected to portray forecasted [*describe financial statement element or elements for which the expected results of one or more assumptions fall within a range, and identify the assumptions expected to fall within a range, for example, "revenue at the amounts $X,XXX and $Y,YYY, which is predicated upon occupancy rates of XX percent and YY percent of available apartments,"*] rather than as a single point estimate. Accordingly, the accompanying forecast presents forecasted financial position, results of operations, and cash flows [*describe one or more assumptions expected to fall within a range, for example, "at such occupancy rates"*]. However, there is no assurance that the actual results will fall within the range [*describe one or more assumptions expected to fall within a range, for example, "occupancy rates"*] presented.

c. **Emphasis** In some circumstances, a CPA may wish to expand the report to emphasize a matter regarding the PFSs. Such information may be presented in a separate paragraph of the CPA's report. However, the CPA should exercise care that emphasizing such a matter does not give the impression that the CPA is expressing assurance or expanding the degree of responsibility the CPA is taking regarding such information.

d. **Historical Financial Information** PFS may be included in a document that also includes historical financial statements (HFS) with a related practitioner's report. Additionally, HFS may be summarized and presented with PFS for comparative purposes.

Exhibit 6 ▶ Paragraph for Forecast Presented With Historical Information

> The historical financial statements for the year ended December 31, 20X1, and our report thereon are set forth on pages XX-YY of this document.

e. **Independence Not Required** A CPA may compile PFS for an entity with respect to which a CPA is not independent. When the CPA is not independent, the CPA should include the following as a separate paragraph in the report, "We are not independent with respect to XYZ Company." The CPA is permitted, but not required, to disclose (in the same paragraph) the reason(s) for the independence impairment. If the CPA elects to do this, *all* the reasons should be included.

f. **Omitted Information** An entity may request a CPA to compile PFS that contain presentation deficiencies or omit disclosures other than those relating to significant assumptions. The CPA may compile such PFS provided the deficiency or omission is indicated clearly in the report and is not, to the CPA's knowledge, undertaken with the intention of misleading those who reasonably might be expected to use such statements. In particular, if the PFS are presented in conformity with OCBOA and do not disclose the basis of accounting, the basis should be disclosed in the CPA's report.

Exhibit 7 ▶ Paragraph for Forecast With Omitted Information

Management has elected to omit the summary of significant accounting policies required by the guidelines for presentation of a forecast established by the American Institute of Certified Public Accountants. If the omitted disclosures were included in the forecast, they might influence the user's conclusions about the Company's financial position, results of operations, and cash flows for the forecast period. Accordingly, this forecast is not designed for those who are not informed about such matters.

9. **Examination of PFS** An examination of PFS is a professional service that involves (a) evaluating the preparation of the PFS, (b) evaluating the support underlying the assumptions, (c) evaluating the presentation of the PFS for conformity with AICPA presentation guidelines, and (d) issuing an examination report. The practitioner follows the general, fieldwork, and reporting standards outlined in AT 101 as applicable to examination engagements.

10. **Examination Reports** As a result of the examination, the CPA has a basis for reporting on whether, in the CPA's opinion, (a) the assumptions provide a reasonable basis for the responsible party's forecast or projection, given the hypothetical assumptions, and (b) whether the PFS are presented in accordance with AICPA guidelines.

    a. **Standard Report** In addition to the previously listed elements, the CPA's standard report on an examination of PFS includes the following: (1) an identification of the PFS presented; (2) a statement that the practitioner's responsibility is to express an opinion on the PFS based on an examination; (3) a brief description of the nature of an examination of PFS; and (4) the CPA's opinion that the PFS are presented in accordance with AICPA presentation guidelines and that the underlying assumptions provide a reasonable basis for the forecast (or projection, given the hypothetical assumptions).

    b. **Projection** When a CPA examines a projection, the CPA's opinion regarding the assumptions should be conditioned on the hypothetical assumptions; that is, the CPA should express an opinion on whether the assumptions provide a reasonable basis for the projection given the hypothetical assumptions. Also, the report should include a separate paragraph that limits the use to specified parties.

Exhibit 8 ▶ Standard Report on Examination of Forecast (Projection)

We have examined the accompanying forecasted [*projected*] balance sheet, statements of income, retained earnings, and cash flows of XYZ Company as of December 31, 20X1, and for the year then ending. XYZ Company is responsible for the forecast [*projection*]. Our responsibility is to express an opinion on the forecast [*projection*] based on our examination.

Our examination was made in accordance with attestation standards established by the American Institute of Certified Public Accountants and, accordingly, included such procedures as we considered necessary to evaluate both the assumptions used by management and the preparation and presentation of the forecast [*projection*]. We believe our examination provides a reasonable basis for our opinion.

<Opinion paragraph for a forecast report>

In our opinion, the accompanying forecast is presented in conformity with guidelines for presentation of a forecast established by the American Institute of Certified Public Accountants, and the underlying assumptions provide a reasonable basis for management's forecast. However, there will usually be differences between the forecasted and actual results, because events and circumstances frequently do not occur as expected, and those differences may be material. We have no responsibility to update this report for events and circumstances occurring after the date of this report.

<Opinion paragraph for a projection report>

In our opinion, the accompanying projection is presented in conformity with guidelines for presentation of a projection established by the American Institute of Certified Public Accountants, and the underlying assumptions provide a reasonable basis for management's projection [*describe the hypothetical assumption, for example, "assuming the granting of the requested loan to expand XYZ Company's plant as described in the summary of significant assumptions."*]. However, even if [*describe hypothetical assumption, for example, "the loan is granted and the plant is expanded,"*] there will usually be differences between the projected and actual results, because events and circumstances frequently do not occur as expected, and those differences may be material. We have no responsibility to update this report for events and circumstances occurring after the date of this report.

<Additional paragraph for a projection report>

The accompanying projection and this report were prepared for [*identify specified parties, for example, "XYZ Company and DEF National Bank"*] and are not intended to be and should not be used by anyone other than these specified parties.

---

c.   **Range** Ranges should be handled as discussed for compilations.

d.   **Historical Financial Information** Comparative historical financial information is handled as discussed for a compilation.

e.   **Emphasis** The practitioner may wish to emphasize a matter regarding the PFS, but issue an unqualified opinion. The practitioner may present other information and comments, such as explanatory comments or other informative material, in a separate paragraph of the report.

f.   **Evaluation Based in Part on Report of Another Accountant** When the principal practitioner decides to refer to the report of another CPA as a basis, in part, for the principal's own opinion, the principal practitioner should disclose that fact in stating the scope of the examination and refer to the report of the other CPA in expressing the opinion. Such a reference indicates the division of responsibility for the performance of the examination.

g.   **Part of Larger Engagement** When the practitioner's examination of PFS is part of a larger engagement, for example, a financial feasibility study or business acquisition study, it is appropriate to expand the report on the examination of the PFS to describe the entire engagement.

h.   **Qualified Opinion** In a qualified report, the CPA states, in a separate paragraph, all the substantive reasons for modifying the opinion, and describes the departure from AICPA presentation guidelines. The opinion includes the words "except" or "exception" as the qualifying language and refers to the separate explanatory paragraph.

Exhibit 9 ▶ Qualifying Language for Forecast (Examination Report)

The forecast does not disclose the significant accounting policies. Disclosure of such policies is required by guidelines for presentation of a forecast established by the American Institute of Certified Public Accountants.

In our opinion, except for the omission of the disclosure of the significant accounting policies as discussed in the preceding paragraph, the accompanying forecast is presented in conformity with…

i. **Adverse Opinion** In an adverse opinion, the CPA states, in a separate paragraph, all the substantive reasons for the adverse opinion. The opinion should state that the presentation is not in conformity with presentation guidelines and should refer to the explanatory paragraph. When applicable, the opinion paragraph also should state that, in the accountant's opinion, the assumptions do not provide a reasonable basis for the prospective financial statements.

    (1) If the presentation, including the summary of significant assumptions, fails to disclose assumptions that, at the time, appear to be significant, the CPA should describe the assumptions in the report and issue an adverse opinion.

    (2) The CPA should not examine a presentation that omits all disclosures of assumptions. Also, the CPA should not examine a financial projection that omits: (a) an identification of the hypothetical assumptions or (b) a description of the limitations on the usefulness of the presentation.

Exhibit 10 ▶ Adverse Opinion for Forecast (Examination Report)

We have examined the accompanying forecasted balance sheet, statements of income, retained earnings, and cash flows of XYZ Company as of December 31, 20X1, and for the year then ending. XYZ Company is responsible for the forecast. Our responsibility is to express an opinion on the forecast based on our examination.

Our examination was made in accordance with attestation standards established by the American Institute of Certified Public Accountants and, accordingly, included such procedures as we considered necessary to evaluate both the assumptions used by management and the preparation and presentation of the forecast. We believe our examination provides a reasonable basis for our opinion.

As discussed under the caption "Sales" in the summary of significant forecast assumptions, the forecasted sales include, among other things, revenue from the Company's federal defense contracts continuing at the current level. The Company's present federal defense contracts will expire in March 20X1. No new contracts have been signed and no negotiations are under way for new federal defense contracts. Furthermore, the federal government has entered into contracts with another company to supply the items being manufactured under the Company's present contracts.

In our opinion, the accompanying forecast is not presented in conformity with guidelines for presentation of a financial forecast established by the American Institute of Certified Public Accountants because management's assumptions, as discussed in the preceding paragraph, do not provide a reasonable basis for management's forecast. We have no responsibility to update this report for events or circumstances occurring after the date of this report.

j. **Disclaimer of Opinion** In a disclaimer of opinion, the CPA's report should indicate, in a separate paragraph, the respects in which the examination did not comply with standards for an examination. The CPA should state that the scope of the examination was not sufficient to enable an opinion to be expressed concerning the presentation or the underlying assumptions, and the CPA's disclaimer of opinion should include a direct reference to the explanatory paragraph. When there is a scope limitation and the CPA also believes there are material departures from the presentation guidelines, those departures should be described in the CPA's report.

Exhibit 11 ▶ Disclaimer of Opinion for Forecast (Examination Report)

We were engaged to examine the accompanying forecasted balance sheet, statements of income, retained earnings, and cash flows of XYZ Company as of December 31, 20X1, and for the year then ending. XYZ Company is responsible for the forecast

As discussed under the caption "Income From Investee" in the summary of significant forecast assumptions, the forecast includes income from an equity investee constituting 23 percent of forecasted net income, which is management's estimate of the Company's share of the investee's income to be accrued for 20X1. The investee has not prepared a forecast for the year ending December 31, 20X1, and we were therefore unable to obtain suitable support for this assumption.

Because, as described in the preceding paragraph, we are unable to evaluate management's assumption regarding income from an equity investee and other assumptions that depend thereon, we express no opinion concerning the presentation of or the assumptions underlying the accompanying forecast. We have no responsibility to update this report for events and circumstances occurring after the date of this report.

11. **Agreed-Upon Procedures**

    a.   **Standards** The guidance in AT 101 (including general, fieldwork, and reporting standards) and AT 201 applies to engagements to apply agreed-upon procedures to PFS. This includes the extent of procedures and agreement among the parties regarding the procedures.

    b.   **Conditions** A practitioner may accept an engagement to apply agreed-upon procedures to PFS provided that: (1) the practitioner is independent; (2) the practitioner and the specified users agree upon the procedures and criteria; (3) the specified users take responsibility for the sufficiency of the agreed-upon procedures for their purposes; (4) the PFS include a summary of significant assumptions; (5) the PFS are subject to reasonably consistent evaluation against criteria that are suitable and available to the specified parties; (6) the procedures are expected to result in reasonably consistent findings using the criteria; (7) evidential matter related to the PFS is expected to exist to provide a reasonable basis for expressing the findings in the practitioner's report; (8) where applicable, the practitioner and the specified user agree on any materiality limits for reporting purposes; and (9) use of the report is restricted to the specified parties.

12. **Reports on Results of Applying Agreed-Upon Procedures** When the CPA reports on the results of applying agreed-upon procedures, the CPA should **not** express any form of negative assurance on the PFS. In addition to the previously discussed elements, the practitioner's report must include:

    a.   A title that includes the word *independent*

    b.   Identification of the specified parties

    c.   Reference to the PFS and the character of the engagement

    d.   A statement that the procedures performed were those agreed to by the specified parties identified in the report

    e.   Identification of the responsible party and a statement that the PFS are the responsible party's responsibility

    f.   A statement that the engagement was conducted in accordance with attestation standards established by the AICPA

g. A statement that the sufficiency of the procedures is solely the responsibility of the specified parties and a disclaimer of responsibility for the sufficiency of those procedures

h. A list of (or reference to) procedures performed and related findings

i. Where applicable, a description of any agreed-upon materiality limits

j. A statement that the practitioner was not engaged to and did not conduct an examination of PFS

k. A disclaimer of opinion on whether the presentation of the PFS is in conformity with AICPA presentation guidelines and on whether the underlying assumptions provide a reasonable basis for the forecast or a reasonable basis for the projection given the hypothetical assumptions

l. A statement that if the practitioner had performed additional procedures, other matters might have come to his or her attention that would have been reported

m. A restriction on the use of the report, because it is intended to be used solely by the specified parties, and should not be used by others

n. Where applicable, reservations or restrictions concerning procedures or findings

o. Where applicable, a description of assistance provided by a specialist

C. ***Pro Forma* Financial Information (AT 401)**
Pro forma financial information is used to show what the significant effects on historical financial information *might have been* if a consummated or proposed transaction or event had occurred at an earlier date. *Pro forma* financial information generally is used to show the effects of transactions such as a business combination, a change in capitalization, the disposition of a significant portion of a business, a change in the form of business organization, or the proposed sale of securities and the application of proceeds. Engagements to report on an examination or review of *pro forma* financial information are covered by AT 101 and AT 401. When *pro forma* financial information is presented outside the basic financial statements but within the same document, and the CPA is not engaged to report on the *pro forma* financial information, the CPA's responsibilities are described in AU 550, *Other Information in Documents Containing Audited Financial Statements* and in AU 711, *Filings Under Federal Securities Statutes*).

1. **Requirements** A CPA may agree to report on an examination or a review of *pro forma* financial information if the following conditions are met.

    a. *Pro forma* adjustments should be based on management's assumptions and should consider all significant effects directly attributable to the transaction or event. The transaction or event reflected in the *pro forma* information should be described, as well as the source of the historical information upon which it is based, the significant assumptions used, and any significant uncertainties about those assumptions. The presentation should indicate that the *pro forma* information should be read in conjunction with the historical data. The presentation also should state that the *pro forma* financial information does not necessarily indicate the results that would have been attained had the transaction actually taken place earlier.

    b. The document containing *pro forma* information includes (or incorporates by reference), complete historical financial statements (HFS) of the entity for the most recent year, or for the preceding year, if financial statements for the most recent year are not yet available. Interim *pro forma* financial information must include (or incorporate by reference), historical interim financial information, which may be condensed, for that period. In the case of a business combination, the document must include (or incorporate by reference) the appropriate historical financial information for the significant constituent parts of the combined entity.

c. The HFS of the entity (or, of each significant constituent part of the combined entity) on which the *pro forma* financial information is based must have been audited or reviewed. The practitioner's attestation risk relating to the *pro forma* financial information is affected by the scope of the engagement providing the practitioner with assurance about the underlying historical financial information to which the *pro forma* adjustments are applied.

(1) The level of assurance given by the CPA on the *pro forma* financial information is limited to the lowest level of assurance provided on the underlying HFS of any significant constituent part of the combined entity. For example, if the underlying HFS of each significant constituent part of the combined entity have been audited at year-end and reviewed at an interim date, the CPA may perform an examination or a review of the *pro forma* financial information at year-end, but is limited to performing a review of the *pro forma* financial information at the interim date.

(2) The practitioner must have an appropriate level of knowledge of the accounting and financial reporting practices of each significant constituent part of the combined entity.

2. **Examination Objective** Examination procedures applied to *pro forma* financial information are to provide reasonable assurance as to whether the following exists: (a) management's assumptions provide a reasonable basis for presenting the significant effects directly attributable to the underlying transaction or event; (b) the related *pro forma* adjustments give appropriate effect to those assumptions; and (c) the *pro forma* column reflects the proper application of those adjustments to the HFS.

3. **Review Objective** Review procedures are to provide negative assurance as to whether any information came to the CPA's attention to cause a belief that: (a) management's assumptions do **not** provide a reasonable basis for presenting the significant effects directly attributable to the transaction or event; (b) the related *pro forma* adjustments do **not** give appropriate effect to those assumptions; and (c) the related *pro forma* column does **not** reflect the proper application of those adjustments to the HFS.

4. **Procedures** The procedures the CPA applies to the assumptions and *pro forma* adjustments for either an examination or a review engagement, other than those applied to the HFS, are as follows:

a. Obtain an understanding of the underlying transaction or event, for example, by reading relevant contracts and minutes of meetings of the board of directors, and by making inquiries of appropriate officials.

b. Obtain a level of knowledge of each significant constituent part of the combined entity in a business combination. Matters to consider include accounting principles and financial reporting practices followed, transactions between the entities, and material contingencies.

c. Discuss with management its assumptions regarding the effects of the transaction or event.

d. Evaluate whether *pro forma* adjustments are included for all significant effects directly attributable to the transaction or event.

e. Obtain sufficient evidence in support of adjustments. The evidence required to support the level of assurance given is a matter of professional judgment. The CPA typically would obtain more evidence in an examination engagement than in a review engagement. Examples of evidence are purchase, merger, or exchange agreements;

appraisal reports; debt agreements; employment agreements; actions of the board of directors; and existing or proposed legislation or regulatory actions.

f. Evaluate whether management's assumptions that underlie the *pro forma* adjustments are presented in a sufficiently clear and comprehensive manner. Also, evaluate whether the *pro forma* adjustments are consistent with each other and with the data used to develop them.

g. Determine that computations of *pro forma* adjustments are mathematically correct, and that the *pro forma* column reflects the proper application of those adjustments to the HFS.

h. Obtain written representations from management acknowledging responsibility for the assumptions used in determining the *pro forma* adjustments and concerning management's belief that: (1) the assumptions provide a reasonable basis for presenting all the significant effects directly attributable to the transaction or event; (2) the related *pro forma* adjustments give appropriate effect to those assumptions; (3) the *pro forma* column reflects the proper application of those adjustments to the historical financial statements; and (4) the significant effects directly attributable to the transaction or event are appropriately disclosed in the *pro forma* financial information.

i. Read the *pro forma* financial information and evaluate whether: (1) the underlying transaction or event, the *pro forma* adjustments, the significant assumptions, and the significant uncertainties, if any, about those assumptions have been appropriately described; and (2) the source of the historical financial information on which the *pro forma* financial information is based has been appropriately identified.

5. **Report** The report on *pro forma* financial information may be added to the CPA's report on historical financial information, or it may appear separately.

a. **Contents** In addition to the previously listed items, a report on *pro forma* financial information includes the following:

(1) **Limitation** A separate paragraph explaining the objective of *pro forma* financial information and its limitations.

(2) **Reference** A reference to the financial statements from which the historical financial information is derived and any modification in the practitioner's report on the historical financial information.

(3) **Date** The practitioner's report on *pro forma* financial information should be dated as of the completion of the appropriate procedures. If the reports are combined and the date of completion of the procedures for the examination or review of the *pro forma* financial information is after the date of completion of the fieldwork for the audit or review of the historical financial information, the combined report should be dual-dated.

b. **Modifications** Restrictions on the scope of the engagement, significant uncertainties about the assumptions that could affect the transaction or event materially, reservations about the propriety of the assumptions and the conformity of the presentation with those assumptions (including inadequate disclosure of significant matters), or other reservations may require the CPA to qualify the opinion, render an adverse opinion, disclaim an opinion, or withdraw from the engagement. The CPA should disclose all substantive reasons for any report modifications. Uncertainty as to whether the transaction or event will be consummated ordinarily would not require a report modification.

Exhibit 12 ▶ Report on Examination of *Pro Forma* Financial Information

We have examined the *pro forma* adjustments reflecting the transaction [*or event*] described in Note 1 and the application of those adjustments to the historical amounts in [*the assembly of*] the accompanying *pro forma* condensed balance sheet of X Company as of December 31, 20X1, and the *pro forma* condensed statement of income for the year then ended. The historical condensed financial statements are derived from the historical financial statements of X Company, which were audited by us, and of Y Company, which were audited by other accountants, appearing elsewhere herein [*or incorporated by reference*]. Such *pro forma* adjustments are based upon management's assumptions described in Note 2. X Company's management is responsible for the *pro forma* financial statements. Our responsibility is to express an opinion on the *pro forma* financial information based on our examination.

Our examination was made in accordance with attestation standards established by the American Institute of Certified Public Accountants and, accordingly, included such procedures as we considered necessary under the circumstances. We believe our examination provides a reasonable basis for our opinion.

The objective of this *pro forma* financial information is to show what the significant effects on the historical financial information might have been had the transaction [*or event*] occurred at an earlier date. However, the *pro forma* condensed financial statements are not necessarily indicative of the results of operations or related effects on financial position that would have been attained had the above-mentioned transaction [*or event*] occurred earlier.

[*Additional paragraph(s) may be added to emphasize certain matters relating to the engagement.*]

In our opinion, management's assumptions provide a reasonable basis for presenting the significant efforts directly attributable to the above-mentioned transaction [*or event*] described in Note 1, the related *pro forma* adjustments give appropriate effect to those assumptions, and the *pro forma* column reflects the proper application of those adjustments to the historical financial statement amounts in the *pro forma* condensed balance sheet as of December 31, 20X1, and the *pro forma* condensed statement of income for the year then ended.

c. **Examination** In addition to the previously listed elements, an examination report also includes the following:

(1) **Reference** A statement that the historical financial statements were audited.

(2) **Responsibility** A statement that the practitioner's responsibility is to express an opinion on the *pro forma* financial information based on his or her examination.

(3) **Standards** A statement that the examination was made in accordance with attestation standards established by the AICPA, and accordingly, included such procedures as the practitioner considered necessary in the circumstances.

(4) **Basis** A statement that the practitioner believes the examination provides a reasonable basis for his or her opinion.

(5) **Opinion** The practitioner's opinion as to whether management's assumptions provide a reasonable basis for presenting the significant effects directly attributable to the transaction or event, whether the related *pro forma* adjustments give appropriate effect to those assumptions, and whether the *pro forma* column reflects the proper application of those adjustments to the historical financial statements.

d. **Review** In addition to the previously listed elements, a review report also includes the following:

(1) **Reference** A statement as to whether the historical financial statements were audited or reviewed.

(2) **Disclaimer** A statement that a review is substantially less in scope than an examination, the objective of which is the expression of an opinion on the *pro forma* financial information, and accordingly, the practitioner does not express such an opinion.

(3) **Conclusion** The practitioner's conclusion as to whether any information came to the CPA's attention to cause a belief that management's assumptions do not provide a reasonable basis for presenting the significant effects directly attributable to the transaction or event, or that the related *pro forma* adjustments do not give appropriate effect to those assumptions, or that the *pro forma* column does not reflect the proper application of those adjustments to the historical financial statements.

Exhibit 13 ▶ Report on Review of *Pro Forma* Financial Information

We have reviewed the *pro forma* adjustments reflecting the transaction [*or event*] described in Note 1 and the application of those adjustments to the historical amounts in [*the assembly of*] the accompanying *pro forma* condensed balance sheet of X Company as of March 31, 20X2, and the *pro forma* condensed statement of income for the three months then ended. These historical condensed financial statements are derived from the historical unaudited financial statements of X Company, which were reviewed by us, and of Y Company, which were reviewed by other accountants, appearing elsewhere herein [*or incorporated by reference*]. Such *pro forma* adjustments are based on management's assumptions as described in Note 2. X Company's management is responsible for the *pro forma* financial statements.

Our review was conducted in accordance with attestation standards established by the American Institute of Certified Public Accountants. A review is substantially less in scope than an examination, the objective of which is the expression of an opinion on management's assumptions, the *pro forma* adjustments, and the application of those adjustments to historical financial information. Accordingly, we do not express such an opinion.

<Same third paragraph as in an examination report.>

[*Additional paragraph(s) may be added to emphasize certain matters relating to the engagement.*]

Based on our review, nothing came to our attention that caused us to believe that management's assumptions do not provide a reasonable basis for presenting the significant effects directly attributable to the above-mentioned transaction [*or event*] described in Note 1, that the related *pro forma* adjustments do not give appropriate effect to those assumptions, or that the *pro forma* column does not reflect the proper application of those adjustments to the historical financial statement amounts in the *pro forma* condensed balance sheet as of March 31, 20X2, and the *pro forma* condensed statement of income for the three months then ended.

D. **Examination of Internal Control Over Financial Reporting (AT 501)**
AT 501 establishes requirements and provides guidance for the performance of an examination of a nonissuer's internal control over financial reporting (internal control) that is integrated with an audit of financial statements. (An auditor should **not** accept an engagement to *review* an entity's internal control or a written assertion thereon.) It aligns the definitions and related guidance for evaluating deficiencies in internal control with PCAOB AS 5, *An Audit of Internal Control Over Financial Reporting That is Integrated with an Audit of Financial Statements.*

1. **Applicability** AT 501 does **not** provide guidance for the following engagements:

   a. As covered under AT 101, *Attest Engagements:*

      (1) Examining the suitability of design of an entity's internal control

      (2) Examining controls over the effectiveness and efficiency of operations

   b. Performance of agreed-upon procedures on controls covered under AT 201, *Agreed-Upon Procedures Engagements*

   c. Examining controls over compliance with laws and regulations covered under AT 601, *Compliance Attestation*

   d. Reporting on controls at a service organization covered under AU 334, *Service Organizations*

2. **Objective** The auditor's objective is to form an opinion on the effectiveness of an entity's internal control as of a point in time and taken as a whole. To express an opinion as of a point in time, the auditor should obtain evidence that internal control has operated effectively for a sufficient period of time which may be less than the period covered by the company's financial statements. To express an opinion on internal control taken as a whole, the auditor should obtain evidence about the effectiveness of selected controls over *all* relevant assertions. This involves testing the design and operating effectiveness of controls that in most cases would **not** be required if *only* expressing an opinion on the financial statements.

   a. **Material Weaknesses** If one or more material weaknesses exist, an entity's internal control *cannot* be considered effective, thus the auditor must obtain sufficient appropriate evidence to obtain reasonable assurance about whether material weaknesses exist as of the date specified in management's assertion. There may be a material weakness in internal control even when financial statements are **not** materially misstated. An auditor is **not** required to search for deficiencies that are less severe than a material weakness.

   b. **Standards and Criteria** An auditor should comply with the general, fieldwork, and reporting attestation standards required for all attestation engagements and the specific requirements covered in this statement. An auditor should use the same suitable and available criteria to perform an examination as management uses for its evaluation.

3. **Definitions**

   a. **Control Objective** The aim or purpose of specified controls. Control objectives ordinarily address the risks that the controls are intended to mitigate. In the context of internal control, a control objective generally relates to a relevant assertion for a significant account or disclosure and addresses the risk that the controls in a specific area will not provide reasonable assurance that a misstatement or omission in that relevant assertion is prevented, or detected and corrected on a timely basis.

   b. **Deficiency** A deficiency in internal control exists when the design or operation of a control does not allow management or employees, in the normal course of performing their assigned functions, to prevent, or detect and correct misstatements on a timely basis.

(1) A deficiency in *design* exists when

    (a) A control necessary to meet the control objective is missing or

    (b) An existing control is not properly designed so that, even if the control operates as designed, the control objective would not be met.

(2) A deficiency in *operation* exists when a properly designed control does not operate as designed, or when the person performing the control does not possess the necessary authority or competence to perform the control effectively.

c. **Detective Control** A control that has the objective of detecting and correcting errors or fraud that have already occurred that could result in a misstatement of the financial statements.

d. **Financial Statements and Related Disclosures** An entity's financial statements and notes to the financial statements as presented in accordance with the applicable financial reporting framework. References to financial statements and related disclosures do **not** extend to the preparation of other financial information presented outside an entity's basic financial statements and notes.

e. **Internal Control Over Financial Reporting** A process effected by those charged with governance, management, and other personnel, designed to provide reasonable assurance regarding the preparation of reliable financial statements for external purposes in accordance with the applicable financial reporting framework and includes those policies and procedures that

(1) Pertain to the maintenance of records that, in reasonable detail, accurately and fairly reflect the transactions and dispositions of the assets of an entity

(2) Provide reasonable assurance that transactions are recorded as necessary to permit preparation of financial statements in accordance with the applicable financial reporting framework, and that receipts and expenditures of an entity are being made only in accordance with authorizations of management and those charged with governance

(3) Provide reasonable assurance regarding prevention, or timely detection and correction of unauthorized acquisition, use, or disposition of an entity's assets that could have a material effect on the financial statements

Note: Internal control has *inherent limitations*. Internal control is a process that involves human diligence and compliance and is subject to lapses in judgment and breakdowns resulting from human failures. Internal control also can be circumvented by collusion or improper management override. Because of such limitations, there is a risk that material misstatements will not be prevented, or detected and corrected on a timely basis by internal control. However, these inherent limitations are known aspects of the financial reporting process.

f. **Management's Assertion** Management's conclusion about the effectiveness of an entity's internal control that is included in management's report on internal control.

g. **Material Weakness** A deficiency, or a combination of deficiencies, in internal control such that there is a *reasonable possibility* (per the FASB's definition regarding accounting for contingencies) that a material misstatement of an entity's financial statements will not be prevented, or detected and corrected on a timely basis.

h.   **Preventive Control** A control that has the objective of preventing errors or fraud that could result in a misstatement of the financial statements.

i.   **Relevant Assertion** A financial statement assertion that has a reasonable possibility of containing a misstatement or misstatements that would cause the financial statements to be materially misstated. The determination of whether an assertion is a relevant assertion is made without regard to the effect of controls.

j.   **Significant Account or Disclosure** An account balance or disclosure that has a reasonable possibility that it could contain a misstatement that, individually or when aggregated with others, has a material effect on the financial statements, considering the risks of both overstatement and understatement. The determination of whether an account balance or disclosure is a significant account or disclosure is made without regard to the effect of controls.

k.   **Significant Deficiency** A deficiency, or a combination of deficiencies, in internal control that is less severe than a material weakness, yet important enough to merit attention by those charged with governance.

4.   **Required Conditions for Performance of Examination**

   a.   Management accepts responsibility for the effectiveness of the entity's internal control.

   b.   Management evaluates the effectiveness of the entity's internal control using suitable and available criteria.

   c.   Management supports its assertion about the effectiveness of the entity's internal control with sufficient appropriate evidence. This includes documentation of the controls and their objectives and evidence of monitoring activities.

   d.   Management provides its assertion about the effectiveness of the entity's internal control in a report that accompanies the auditor's report.

5.   **Integrating the Examination With the Financial Statement Audit**

   a.   **Significant Accounts and Disclosures and Their Relevant Assertions** The significant accounts and disclosures and their relevant assertions and the risk factors used to identify them are the same in the examination of internal control (examination) as in an audit of financial statements (audit).

   b.   **Tests of Controls** The tests of controls should be designed to achieve the objectives of both engagements simultaneously, i.e., to obtain sufficient appropriate evidence to support the auditor's opinion on internal control as well as the auditor's risk assessment for purposes of the audit. As previously mentioned, for the purposes of the audit, the auditor is **not** required to test the controls of *all* relevant assertions as is required in the examination. Consideration of the results of the additional tests of controls performed for the purposes of the examination may affect the auditor's decisions about the nature, timing and extent of substantive procedures and further tests of controls for the purposes of the audit. Obviously, this would be particularly true if deficiencies were identified in the examination.

   c.   **Substantive Procedures** Likewise, the results of substantive procedures performed for purposes of the audit should be evaluated to determine their effect on the auditor's risk assessments regarding the testing necessary to form a conclusion about the effectiveness of a control in the examination. Results of substantive tests of particular interest include those related to fraud, illegal acts, related-party transactions, and those that detect misstatements or indicate management bias in making accounting estimates or selecting accounting principles.

d. **Period End Reporting Process** As part of the examination, the auditor should evaluate the procedures that make up the period end reporting process because of its importance to financial reporting and the integrated approach.

e. **Risk Assessment and Materiality** The same materiality should be used for planning and performing both engagements and the same risk assessment process supports both.

f. **Fraud Risk Assessment** The results of the fraud risk assessment for the purposes the audit should be incorporated into the examination. The auditor should consider whether the identified risks due to fraud and inappropriate management override of other controls are sufficiently addressed by the internal control system.

g. *As of* **Date or Period Covered** The date specified in management's assertion (the *as of* date of the examination) should correspond to the balance sheet date of the period covered by the financial statements. If management chooses an *as of* date for the examination that is different than the end of the entity's fiscal year, the examination and the audit should still be integrated. If the auditor is engaged to examine the effectiveness of internal control for a period of time (rather than an *as of* date), the examination should be integrated with an audit that covers the same period.

h. **Auditor's Report Date** Because the examination is integrated with the audit, the dates of the reports should be the same.

6. **Planning**

a. **Role of Risk Assessment** Risk assessment underlies all phases of the examination process. Obviously, the auditor should focus on areas with the highest risk. It is **not** necessary to test controls that, even if deficient, do not present a reasonable possibility of a material misstatement to the financial statements. The auditor should bear in mind that an entity's internal control is *less* likely to prevent or detect and correct a misstatement caused by fraud than one due to error. Additionally, the size and complexity of an organization affects the auditor's risk assessment, allowing scaling of the examination for smaller or less complex entities.

b. **Using the Work of Others** In an examination, the auditor may use the work of others within the entity (in addition to internal auditors) and third parties working under the direction of management or those charged with governance. The auditor should consider their objectivity and competence in the same manner as that of internal auditors for purposes of the audit. As the risk associated with a control increases, so does the need for the auditor to perform the work.

c. **Control Environment** The auditor should evaluate the control environment because of its importance to effective internal control.

7. **Selection of Controls to Test** The auditor should use a top-down approach, starting with the financial statements and then focusing on the entity-level controls; working down to the identification of the significant accounts, disclosures and their relevant assertions that present a reasonable possibility of material misstatement of the financial statements. The auditor can then select the controls that sufficiently address the assessed risk of material misstatement to each relevant assertion.

8. **Testing Controls** As the risk associated with a control increases, the evidence the auditor should obtain also increases. As previously mentioned, the auditor is expressing an opinion on internal control *taken as whole.* The risk-based approach allows the auditor to vary the amount of evidence obtained for individual controls.

In order of *least* evidence produced to most, these are the tests an auditor might perform: inquiry, observation, inspection of documentation, recalculation, and reperformance of a control. Inquiry alone does **not** provide sufficient appropriate evidence to support a conclusion about the effectiveness of a control. The quality of evidence is enhanced by testing controls over a longer period of time and closer to the *as of* date of the examination.

    a.   **Design Effectiveness** Walk-throughs (following a transaction from origination through the entity's processes until it is reflected in the financial statements, using the same documents and information technology that entity personnel use) are usually sufficient to evaluate design effectiveness.

    b.   **Operating Effectiveness** Procedures include a mix of inquiry, observation, inspection of documentation, recalculation, and reperformance of the control. Because only reasonable rather than absolute assurance is provided by effective internal control, an individual control does **not** have to operate without any deviation to be considered effective.

9. **Evaluation of Identified Deficiencies**

    a.   **Severity** The auditor should evaluate the severity of each deficiency to determine whether it, individually or in combination, is a material weakness. The severity does **not** depend on whether a misstatement actually occurred. A compensating control can limit the severity of a deficiency and prevent it from being a material weakness. Severity depends on

        (1)   The magnitude of the potential misstatement

        (2)   Whether there is a reasonable possibility that the entity's controls will fail to prevent, or detect and correct a misstatement

    b.   **Indicators of a Material Weakness**

        (1)   Identification of fraud, whether or not material, on the part of senior management

        (2)   Restatement of previously issued financial statements to reflect the correction of a material misstatement due to error or fraud

        (3)   Identification by the auditor of a material misstatement of financial statements under audit in circumstances that indicate that the misstatement would not have been detected and corrected by the entity's internal control

        (4)   Ineffective oversight of the entity's financial reporting and internal control by those charged with governance

    c.   **Prudent Official Standard** If a determination is made that a deficiency is **not** a material weakness, the auditor should consider whether prudent officials, having knowledge of the same facts and circumstances, would likely reach the same conclusion.

10. **Evaluation of Management's Report** The auditor should determine if management's report appropriately includes the following:

    a.   A statement regarding management's responsibility for internal control

b. A description of the subject matter of the examination

c. An identification of the criteria against which internal control is measured

d. Management's assertion about the effectiveness of internal control

e. A description of the material weaknesses, if any

f. The date as of which management's assertion is made

11. **Management's Written Representations** The auditor should obtain representations from management:

a. Acknowledging management's responsibility for establishing and maintaining effective internal control

b. Stating that management has performed an evaluation of the effectiveness of the entity's internal control and specifying the control criteria

c. Stating that management did not use the auditor's procedures performed during the integrated audit as part of the basis for management's assertion

d. Stating management's assertion about the effectiveness of the entity's internal control based on the control criteria as of a specified date

e. Stating that management has disclosed to the auditor all deficiencies in the design or operation of internal control, including separately disclosing to the auditor all such deficiencies that it believes to be significant deficiencies or material weaknesses in internal control

f. Describing any fraud resulting in a material misstatement to the entity's financial statements and any other fraud that does not result in a material misstatement to the entity's financial statements, but involves senior management or management or other employees who have a significant role in the entity's internal control

g. Stating whether the significant deficiencies and material weaknesses identified and communicated to management and those charged with governance during previous engagements have been resolved and specifically identifying any that have not

h. Stating whether there were, subsequent to the date being reported on, any changes in internal control or other factors that might significantly affect internal control, including any corrective actions taken by management with regard to significant deficiencies and material weaknesses

12. **Communications**

a. Significant deficiencies and material weaknesses should be communicated, in writing by the auditor's report release date, to the entity's management and those charged with governance, including those previously communicated, but **not** remediated. In the case where the nature of some matters directs their early communication, even if such significant deficiencies or material weaknesses are remediated during the audit, they should still be included in this formal written communication. (At the time of their initial early communication, they are not required to be in writing.)

b. If the auditor concludes that the oversight of the entity's financial reporting and internal control by the entity's audit committee (or similar subgroup) is inadequate, the auditor should communicate this, in writing by the auditor's report release date, to the board of directors (or similar governing body if one exists).

c. The auditor should also communicate to management, in writing, all identified deficiencies which are not significant deficiencies or material weaknesses, no later than 60 days following the report release date and inform those charged with governance when this communication has been made. As previously mentioned, the auditor is **not** required to search for deficiencies that are less severe than a material weakness, thus this communication would only include deficiencies of which the auditor is *aware.*

d. If one or more material weaknesses are identified which are **not** disclosed or identified in management's report, the auditor should communicate this, in writing, to those charged with governance.

e. If the auditor cannot express an opinion because there has been a limitation on the scope of the examination, the auditor should communicate, in writing, to management and those charged with governance that the examination cannot be satisfactorily completed.

f. If the auditor concludes that additional information contained in management's report contains a material misstatement of fact that management refuses to revise, the auditor should notify management and those charged with governance, in writing, of the auditor's views.

13. **Reporting on Internal Control**

a. The auditor's report on an examination should include these elements:

(1) A title that includes the word *independent*

(2) A statement that management is responsible for maintaining effective internal control and for evaluating the effectiveness of internal control

(3) An identification of management's assertion on internal control that accompanies the auditor's report, including a reference to management's report

(4) A statement that the auditor's responsibility is to express an opinion on the entity's internal control (or on management's assertion) based on the auditor's examination

(5) A statement that the examination was conducted in accordance with attestation standards established by the American Institute of Certified Public Accountants

(6) A statement that such standards require that the auditor plan and perform the examination to obtain reasonable assurance about whether effective internal control was maintained in all material respects

Editor's note: An examination provides the same level of assurance as an audit.

(7) A statement that an examination includes obtaining an understanding of internal control, assessing the risk that a material weakness exists, testing and evaluating the design and operating effectiveness of internal control based on the assessed risk, and performing such other procedures as the auditor considers necessary in the circumstances

(8) A statement that the auditor believes the examination provides a reasonable basis for the auditor's opinion

(9) A definition of internal control (the auditor should use the same description of the entity's internal control as management uses in its report)

(10) A paragraph stating that, because of inherent limitations, internal control may not prevent, or detect and correct misstatements and that projections of any evaluation of effectiveness to future periods are subject to the risk that controls may become inadequate because of changes in conditions, or that the degree of compliance with the policies or procedures may deteriorate

(11) The auditor's opinion on whether the entity maintained, in all material respects, effective internal control as of the specified date, based on the control criteria; or, the auditor's opinion on whether *management's assertion* about the effectiveness of the entity's internal control as of the specified date is fairly stated, in all material respects, based on the control criteria

(12) The manual or printed signature of the auditor's firm

(13) The date of the report which should be no earlier than the date on which the auditor has obtained sufficient appropriate evidence to support the auditor's opinion.

b. The auditor should **not** issue a report stating that **no** deficiencies were identified.

c. The auditor should **not** issue a report indicating that **no** material weaknesses were identified.

d. The auditor may issue a combined report or separate reports on the entity's financial statements and on internal control.

e. **Report Modifications**

(1) **Defects in Management's Report** If the elements of management's report are incomplete or improperly presented and management refuses to revise their report, the auditor should add an explanatory paragraph to the auditor's report describing the reasons for this determination.

(2) **Opinion Based, in Part, on the Report of Another Auditor** When the auditor has examined the internal control of one or more components of an entity, the auditor should determine whether to serve as the principal auditor and use the work and report of another auditor as the basis, in part, for the his or her own opinion. The attest standard states that AU 543, *Part of Audit Performed by Other Independent Auditors*, is applicable to this determination by the auditor. When the auditor decides to make reference to the report of another auditor, the scope and opinion paragraphs of the principal auditor's report should be modified accordingly.

(3) **Additional Information in Management's Report** If management's report includes additional information (beyond the elements previously described) that appear to be part of management's report, the auditor should add an explanatory paragraph as the last paragraph in the auditor's report that disclaims an opinion on the additional information. If the auditor believes the additional information contains a material misstatement of fact the auditor should refer to the guidance in AT 101 on the same issue with information contained in a client-prepared document containing a practitioner's attest report. In some instances, the auditor may also need to apply the guidance in AU 317, *Illegal Acts by Clients*.

(4) **Subsequent Event** If the auditor obtains knowledge about conditions that did **not** exist at the date specified in management's assertion, but arose subsequent to that date and before the release of the auditor's report that had a material effect on the entity's internal control, the auditor should include an explanatory paragraph in the auditor's report that describes the event and its effects or refers the reader to the same information in management's report.

f.   **Adverse Opinion** If there is more than one material weakness, the auditor should express an adverse opinion. (This also applies when the auditor discovers a material weakness subsequent to the *as of* date of the examination, but before the date of the auditor's report that existed as of the date in management's assertion and whose effect on internal control can be determined. If this type of subsequently discovered material weakness's effect cannot be determined, the auditor should disclaim an opinion.) Under these circumstances, the auditor is prohibited from expressing an opinion on management's assertion and should report *directly* on the effectiveness of internal control. (See the eleventh element of the auditor's report.) The auditor should determine the effect of an adverse opinion on the auditor's opinion on the financial statements and disclose whether the auditor's opinion on the financial statements was affected by the material weakness. This adverse report on internal control should include

(1)   A definition of material weakness

(2)   A statement that one or more material weaknesses have been identified and an identification of the material weaknesses described in management's report; the auditor's report does **not** need to include a description of the material weaknesses *as long as* each material weakness is included and fairly presented in all material respects in management's report

(3)   If management's report does **not** include a fair presentation of all material weaknesses, the auditor's report should include

(a)   A statement that one or more material weaknesses have been identified and not included in management's report

(b)   A description of all such material weaknesses which contains specific information about the nature of each, and its actual and potential effect on the presentation of the entity's financial statements

(c)   In the case where one or more material weaknesses have been included in management's report, but not fairly presented, the auditor's report should state this conclusion and include the information needed for a fair presentation

g.   **Disclaimer of Opinion or Withdrawal From an Engagement**

(1)   Management's refusal to furnish an assertion about the effectiveness of the entity's internal control in a report that accompanies the auditor's report should cause the auditor to withdraw from the engagement. If a law or regulation prohibits the auditor's withdrawal, the auditor should disclaim an opinion on internal control.

(2)   If there are restrictions on the scope of an engagement, for example, if management refuses to provide written representations, the auditor should either withdraw from the engagement or disclaim an opinion. The auditor may issue the disclaimer of opinion as soon as the auditor concludes that the scope limitation will prevent the auditor from obtaining the reasonable assurance necessary to express an opinion. No additional work is required.

(3)   The auditor should disclaim an opinion when the auditor discovers a material weakness subsequent to the *as of* date of the examination, but before the date of the auditor's report that existed as of the date in management's assertion and whose effect on internal control can **not** be determined. (If its effect can be determined, the auditor should issue an adverse opinion.)

(4) A disclaimer of opinion should include:

(a) A statement that the auditor does not express an opinion on the effectiveness of internal control

(b) In a separate paragraph or paragraphs, an explanation that includes the substantive reasons for the disclaimer

(c) The auditor should **not** identify the procedures that were performed **nor** include the statements describing the characteristics of an examination

(d) If the limited procedures performed allowed the auditor to conclude that one or more material weaknesses exist, the auditor's report should also include the definition of a material weakness and a description of any material weakness identified that includes specific information about the nature of any material weakness and its actual and potential effect on the entity's financial statements. The auditor should also determine the effect the material weakness has on the auditor's opinion of the financial statements and should disclose whether the auditor's opinion was affected by the material weaknesses.

E. **Compliance Attestation (AT 601)**
AT 601 provides guidance for engagements related to an entity's compliance with requirements of specified laws, regulations, rules, contracts, or grants, as well as the effectiveness of an entity's internal control (IC) over compliance with specified requirements. The subject matter may be financial or nonfinancial compliance requirements. IC over compliance may include parts of (but is not the same as) IC over financial reporting. An attest engagement must comply with the general, fieldwork, and reporting standards delineated in AT 101 as well as specific standards established in AT 601.

1. **Appropriate Engagements** CPAs may be engaged to perform agreed-upon procedures to assist users in evaluating compliance with specified requirements (or related assertions) and/or the effectiveness of an entity's IC over compliance. These engagements also are subject to the requirements of AT 201. CPAs also may be engaged to examine, but not review, an entity's compliance with specified requirements, or related written assertions. CPAs may provide nonattest services connected with compliance; however, these services adhere to professional consulting standards, rather than SSAE.

2. **Responsibilities** The responsible party is responsible for ensuring that the entity complies with the requirements applicable to its activities.

3. **Conditions for Engagement Performance** For both types of engagements, the responsible party must accept responsibility for the entity's compliance with specified requirements and the effectiveness of IC over compliance, and provide a written assertion about compliance with specified requirements or IC over compliance in either: (a) a separate report to accompany the practitioner's report; or (b) a representation letter to the practitioner.

a. **Agreed-Upon Procedures** The responsible party evaluates compliance with specified requirements or the effectiveness of the entity's IC over compliance.

b. **Examinations** The responsible party evaluates compliance with specified requirements, and sufficient evidential matter exists, or could be developed, to support that evaluation.

4. **Written Assertion** In an examination, the responsible party's refusal to provide a written assertion requires the practitioner to withdraw unless the engagement is mandated legally.

In that case, the practitioner must either express an adverse opinion in a restricted-use report or disclaim an opinion. In an agreed-upon procedures engagement where the client is the responsible party, absence of a written assertion requires the practitioner to withdraw, unless the engagement is mandated legally. In an agreed-upon procedures engagement where the client is not the responsible party, absence of a written assertion does not force the practitioner to withdraw, but the practitioner should consider the effects of the refusal on the engagement and report.

5. **Representations** When the practitioner's client is not the responsible party, the practitioner also may obtain written representations from the client. A responsible party's refusal to provide a written representation letter is a limitation on the scope of an examination or agreed-upon procedures engagement sufficient to preclude an unqualified opinion. Based on the nature of the representations not received or the refusal, the practitioner may determine that a qualified opinion is appropriate. When the practitioner's client is the responsible party, the refusal constitutes a limitation on the engagement scope sufficient to require the practitioner to withdraw. When the practitioner's client is not the responsible party, the practitioner is not required to withdraw. The practitioner should consider the effects of the responsible party's refusal on his or her ability to rely on other representations by the responsible party.

6. **Modifications** The practitioner modifies the report if: (a) material noncompliance with specified requirements exists; (b) a restriction on the engagement scope exists; or (c) the practitioner refers to another practitioner's report as the basis, in part, for the report.

7. **Agreed-Upon Procedures Engagement** The objective of this engagement is to present specific findings to assist users in evaluating an entity's assertion about compliance with specified requirements or about the effectiveness of an entity's IC over compliance based on procedures agreed-upon by the report users. The CPA's procedures generally may be as limited or as extensive as the specified parties desire as long as the specified users participate in establishing the procedures to be performed, and take responsibility for the adequacy of such procedures for their purposes. Prior to performing procedures, the practitioner should obtain an understanding of the specified compliance requirements.

Exhibit 14 ▶ Standard Report on Agreed-Upon Compliance Procedures

---

<u>Independent Accountant's Report</u>

We have performed the procedures enumerated below, which were agreed to by [*list specified parties*], solely to assist the specified parties in evaluating W Company's internal control over compliance with [*list specified compliance requirements*] during the three months ending December 31, 20X1. Management is responsible for W Company's compliance with those requirements. This agreed-upon procedures engagement was conducted in accordance with attestation standards established by the American Institute of Certified Public Accountants. The sufficiency of the procedures is solely the responsibility of those parties specified in this report. Consequently, we make no representation regarding the sufficiency of the procedures described below either for the purpose for which this report has been requested or for any other purpose.

[*List the procedures performed and related findings.*]

We were not engaged to and did not conduct an examination, the objective of which would be the expression of an opinion on compliance. Accordingly, we do not express such an opinion. Had we performed additional procedures, other matters might have come to our attention that would have been reported to you.

This report is intended solely for the information and use of [*list or refer to specified parties*] and is not intended to be and should not be used by anyone other than these specified parties.

---

a. When a situation imposes restrictions on the engagement scope, the practitioner attempts to obtain agreement to modify the procedures. If such agreement is not obtained, the practitioner should describe the restrictions in the report or withdraw from the engagement.

b. The practitioner has no obligation to perform beyond the agreed-upon procedures and no responsibility to perform procedures to detect noncompliance in the subsequent period, beyond obtaining the responsible party's representation about noncompliance in the subsequent period (the period starting at the end of the period addressed by the practitioner's report and ending on the date of completion of the procedures, also the report date). However, if noncompliance is found by other means or in the subsequent period, it typically is reported.

c. If the practitioner is engaged to report on both compliance with specified requirements and the effectiveness of IC over compliance, the practitioner may issue one report.

d. The practitioner's report should **not** provide negative assurance about whether management's assertion is fairly stated.

8. **Examination Engagement** The objective of an examination is to express an opinion on an entity's compliance with specified requirements (or related assertion) based on specified criteria. To express such an opinion, the practitioner accumulates sufficient evidence regarding the entity's compliance with specified requirements, thereby limiting attestation risk to an appropriately low level. Among other procedures, the practitioner considers subsequent events. The practitioner considers issues that parallel those in a financial statement audit, but the perspective may be different. Some of these issues are risk, materiality, planning, professional skepticism, relevant internal controls and internal audit functions, use of specialists, and obtaining sufficient evidence.

Exhibit 15 ▶ Standard Report on Examination of Compliance

<u>Independent Accountant's Report</u>

We have examined W Company's internal control over compliance with [*list specified compliance requirements*] during the three months ending December 31, 20X1. W Company's management is responsible for W Company's compliance with those requirements. Our responsibility is to express an opinion on W Company's compliance based on our examination.

Our examination was conducted in accordance with attestation standards established by the American Institute of Certified Public Accountants and, accordingly, included examining, on a test basis, evidence about W Company's compliance with those requirements and performing such other procedures as we considered necessary in the circumstances. We believe that our examination provides a reasonable basis for our opinion. Our examination does not provide a legal determination on W Company's compliance with specified requirements.

In our opinion, W Company complied, in all material respects, with the aforementioned requirements for the three months ended December 31, 20X1.

F. **Management's Discussion & Analysis (AT 701)**
Management is responsible for MD&A preparation. AT 701 provides specific guidance to CPAs related to the performance of an attest engagement with respect to MD&A prepared pursuant to Securities and Exchange Commission (SEC) regulations. This guidance does not change an auditor's responsibility in a financial statement audit, or apply to situations where CPAs provide recommendations rather than assurance. (SSAE require an auditor to read the MD&A and consider whether it is materially inconsistent with information appearing in the financial statements.) A practitioner engaged to examine or review MD&A complies with AT 101 plus the specific standards in AT 701. A practitioner engaged to perform agreed-upon procedures on MD&A follows the guidance in AT 201.

1. **Objectives** The objective is to report on MD&A taken as a whole. An examination of MD&A provides users with an independent opinion regarding whether: (a) the presentation meets SEC criteria, (b) the historical financial information is derived accurately from the financial statements, and (c) the underlying information and assumptions provide a reasonable basis for the disclosures contained therein. A review of MD&A provides users and preparers with negative assurance concerning such matters.

2. **Engagement Acceptance** A CPA may perform an examination or review of MD&A for an annual period, an interim period, or a combined annual and interim period. A base knowledge of the entity gained through a financial statement audit is necessary to provide the CPA with sufficient knowledge to evaluate the results of procedures. For nonpublic entities, the CPA also must receive a written assertion from management that MD&A was prepared using SEC criteria.

   a. **Annual Period** A CPA may accept an engagement to examine or review MD&A of an entity for an annual period, provided the practitioner audits the financial statements for at least the latest period to which MD&A relates and the financial statements for the other periods covered by MD&A have been audited.

   b. **Review of Interim Period** A CPA may accept an engagement to review MD&A for an interim period provided that MD&A for the most recent fiscal year has been (or will be) examined or reviewed (by either the CPA or a predecessor) and the CPA performs either an audit of the interim financial statements or a review for either of the following:

      (1) **Public Entity** A review of the financial statements for the related comparative interim periods and issues a review report in accordance with AU 722.

      (2) **Nonpublic Entity** A review of either (a) the financial statements for the related interim periods under SSARSs and issues a review report, or (b) the related condensed interim financial information in accordance with AU 722 and issues a review report, and such information is accompanied by complete financial statements for the most recent audited fiscal year.

   c. **Predecessor** If a predecessor audited prior period financial statements, the successor must acquire sufficient knowledge of the entity and apply appropriate procedures relating to prior years included in the MD&A presentation.

3. **Scope** The practitioner considers the following as well as historical financial information:

   a. *Pro Forma* **Information** The guidance in AT 401 when performing procedures with respect to any *pro forma* information, even if MD&A indicates that certain information is derived from unaudited financial statements.

   b. **External Information** For example, debt ratings of a rating agency.

   c. **Forward-Looking Information** Tested only for the purpose of expressing an opinion or providing limited assurance on MD&A taken as a whole. The CPA considers whether cautionary language concerning achievability is included.

d. **Voluntary Information** When the entity includes other information in MD&A required by other SEC regulations, the CPA also considers those other SEC criteria in subjecting such information to procedures.

4. **Engagement Procedures** The CPA obtains an understanding of the SEC criteria for MD&A and management's MD&A preparation method; plans the engagement; considers materiality; considers relevant portions of the entity's internal control; considers subsequent events; and obtains appropriate written representations from management. The misstatement of an individual assertion is material if the magnitude of the misstatement (individually or aggregated) is such that a reasonable person would be influenced by its correction. A practitioner also considers whether management (and any assistants) has appropriate knowledge of rules and regulations of the SEC to prepare MD&A.

a. **Examination** The CPA obtains sufficient evidence, including testing completeness, and forms an opinion consistent with examination objectives. The CPA considers the results of financial statement audits for the periods covered by MD&A, including the possible impact on the examination engagement scope of a modified auditor's report.

b. **Review** Procedures generally are limited to inquiries and analytics concerning factors that have a material effect on financial condition, results of operations, and cash flows. The CPA also forms a conclusion consistent with review objectives.

5. **Examination Performance** The CPA applies procedures to obtain reasonable assurance of detecting material misstatements. In a financial statement audit, the auditor applies procedures to some information included in MD&A. Because the objective of an audit is different from that of an examination of MD&A, additional procedures typically are performed in an examination.

6. **Review Performance** The CPA develops an overall strategy for analytics and inquiries. The CPA considers factors such as matters affecting the entity's industry; matters relating to the entity's business; the types of relevant information that management reports to external analysts; the extent of management's knowledge of, and experience with, SEC criteria for MD&A; if the entity is a nonpublic entity, the intended use of MD&A; matters identified during other engagements; and, the nature of complex or subjective matters that may require special skill or knowledge.

7. **Reports** A report on a examination or review of MD&A includes the date of the completion of the CPA's procedures, which should not precede the date of the audit (or review) report on the latest historical financial statements covered by the MD&A. If the entity is a nonpublic entity, the following sentence is added to the beginning of the explanatory paragraph: "Although W Company is not subject to the rules and regulations of the Securities and Exchange Commission, the accompanying Management's Discussion and Analysis is intended to be a presentation in accordance with the rules and regulations adopted by the Securities and Exchange Commission."

Exhibit 16 ▶ Standard Report on Examination of MD&A

<u>Independent Accountant's Report</u>

We have examined W Company's Management's Discussion and Analysis taken as a whole, included [*incorporated by reference*] in the company's [*insert description of registration statement or document*]. Management is responsible for the preparation of the company's Management's Discussion and Analysis, pursuant to rules and regulations adopted by the Securities and Exchange Commission. Our responsibility is to express an opinion on the presentation based on our examination. We have audited, in accordance with auditing standards generally accepted in the United States of America, the financial statements of W Company as of December 31, 20X2 and 20X1, and for each of the years in the three-year periods ended December 31, 20X2, and in our report dated March 31, 20X3, we expressed an unqualified opinion on those financial statements.

The preparation of Management's Discussion and Analysis requires management to interpret the criteria, make determinations as to the relevancy of information to be included, and make estimates and assumptions that affect reported information. Management's Discussion and Analysis includes information regarding the estimated future impact of transactions and events that have occurred or are expected to occur, expected sources of liquidity and capital resources, operating trends, commitments, and uncertainties. Actual results in the future may differ materially from management's present assessment of this information because events and circumstances frequently do not occur as expected.

Our examination of Management's Discussion and Analysis was conducted in accordance with attestation standards established by the American Institute of Certified Public Accountants and, accordingly, included examining, on a test basis, evidence supporting the historical amounts and disclosures in the presentation. An examination also includes assessing the significant determinations made by management as to the relevancy of information to be included and the estimates and assumptions that affect reported information. We believe that our examination provides a reasonable basis for our opinion.

In our opinion, the company's presentation of Management's Discussion and Analysis includes, in all material respects, the required elements of the rules and regulations adopted by the Securities and Exchange Commission; the historical financial amounts included therein have been accurately derived, in all material respects, from the company's financial statements; and the underlying information, determinations, estimates, and assumptions of the company provide a reasonable basis for the disclosures contained therein.

Exhibit 17 ▶ Standard Report on Review of MD&A

Independent Accountant's Report

We have reviewed W Company's Management's Discussion and Analysis taken as a whole, included [*incorporated by reference*] in the company's [*insert description of registration statement or document*]. Management is responsible for the preparation of the company's Management's Discussion and Analysis, pursuant to rules and regulations adopted by the Securities and Exchange Commission. We have audited, in accordance with auditing standards generally accepted in the United States of America, the financial statements of W Company as of December 31, 20X2 and 20X1, and for each of the years in the three-year periods ended December 31, 20X2, and in our report dated March 31, 20X3, we expressed an unqualified opinion on those financial statements.

We conducted our review of Management's Discussion and Analysis in accordance with attestation standards established by the American Institute of Certified Public Accountants. A review of Management's Discussion and Analysis consists principally of applying analytical procedures and making inquiries of persons responsible for financial, accounting, and operational matters. It is substantially less in scope than an examination, the objective of which is the expression of an opinion on the presentation. Accordingly, we do not express such an opinion.

<Same explanatory paragraph as in an examination report>

Based on our review, nothing came to our attention that caused us to believe that the company's presentation of Management's Discussion and Analysis does not include, in all material respects, the required elements of the rules and regulations adopted by the Securities and Exchange Commission; that the historical financial amounts included therein have not been accurately derived, in all material respects, from the company's financial statements; or that the underlying information, determinations, estimates, and assumptions of the company do not provide a reasonable basis for the disclosures contained therein.

This report is intended solely for the information and use of [*list or refer to specified parties*] and is not intended to be and should not be used by anyone other than the specified parties.

---

8. **Review Presentation** In order for a CPA to issue a report on a review of MD&A, the financial statements for the periods covered by MD&A and the related auditor's or practitioner's report(s) should accompany MD&A (or be incorporated by reference to information filed with a regulatory agency). There are additional requirements in the following circumstances:

   a. **Interim Periods** The comparative financial statements for the most recent annual period and the related MD&A should accompany the interim MD&A (or be incorporated by reference). Generally, this requirement is satisfied by a public entity that has filed its annual financial statements and MD&A in its annual Form 10-K.

   b. **Nonpublic Entity** The MD&A should include a statement that it was prepared using SEC criteria or a separate written assertion should accompany MD&A.

G. **Reporting on Controls at a Service Organization (AT 801)**

   1. **Overview** This standard addresses examination engagements undertaken by a service auditor to report on controls at organizations that provide services to user entities when those controls are likely to be relevant to user entities' internal control over financial reporting. (It complements AU 324, *Service Organizations*, in that reports prepared in accordance with this standard may provide appropriate evidence per AU 324.)

   For engagements conducted under this standard, the service auditor is required to report directly on the subject matter; not on management's assertion.

2. **Objective**   The objectives of the service auditor are to:

    a.   Obtain reasonable assurance about whether, in all material respects, based on suitable criteria,

        (1)   Management's description of the service organization's system fairly presents the system that was designed and implemented throughout the specified period (or in the case of a type 1 report, as of a specified date—see the following definitions regarding type 1 and 2 reports)

        (2)   The controls related to the control objectives stated in management's description of the service organization's system were suitably designed throughout the specified period (or in the case of a type 1 report, as of a specified date)

        (3)   When included in the scope of the engagement, the controls operated effectively to provide reasonable assurance that the control objectives stated in management's description of the service organization's system were achieved throughout the specified period

    b.   Report on the preceding matters in accordance with the service auditor's findings

3. **Definitions**

    a.   **Carve-out Method**   Method of addressing the services provided by a subservice organization whereby management's description of the service organization's system identifies the nature of the services performed by the subservice organization and excludes from the description and from the scope of the service auditor's engagement, the subservice organization's relevant control objectives and related controls. Management's description of the service organization's system and the scope of the service auditor's engagement include controls at the service organization that monitor the effectiveness of controls at the subservice organization, which may include management of the service organization's review of a service auditor's report on controls at the subservice organization.

    b.   **Complementary User Entity Controls**   Controls that management of the service organization assumes, in the design of the service provided by the service organization, will be implemented by user entities, and which, if necessary to achieve the control objectives stated in management's description of the service organization's system, are identified as such in that description.

    c.   **Control Objectives**   The aim or purpose of specified controls at the service organization. Control objectives address the risks that controls are intended to mitigate.

    d.   **Controls at a Service Organization**   The policies and procedures at a service organization likely to be relevant to user entities' internal control over financial reporting. These policies and procedures are designed, implemented, and documented by the service organization to provide reasonable assurance about the achievement of the control objectives relevant to the services covered by the service auditor's report.

    e.   **Controls at a Subservice Organization**   The policies and procedures at a subservice organization likely to be relevant to internal control over financial reporting of user entities of the service organization. These policies and procedures are designed, implemented, and documented by a subservice organization to provide reasonable assurance about the achievement of control objectives that are relevant to the services covered by the service auditor's report.

    f.   **Criteria**   The standards or benchmarks used to measure and present the subject matter and against which the service auditor evaluates the subject matter.

g. **Inclusive Method** Method of addressing the services provided by a subservice organization whereby management's description of the service organization's system includes a description of the nature of the services provided by the subservice organization as well as the subservice organization's relevant control objectives and related controls.

h. **Internal Audit Function** The service organization's internal auditors and others, for example, members of a compliance or risk department, who perform activities similar to those performed by internal auditors.

i. **Report on Management's Description of a Service Organization's System and the Suitability of the Design of Controls** (referred to in this section as a type 1 report). A report that comprises the following:

   (1) Management's description of the service organization's system

   (2) A written assertion by management of the service organization about whether, in all material respects, and based on suitable criteria,

   (a) Management's description of the service organization's system fairly presents the service organization's system that was designed and implemented as of a specified date

   (b) The controls related to the control objectives stated in management's description of the service organization's system were suitably designed to achieve those control objectives as of the specified date

   (3) A service auditor's report that expresses an opinion on the preceding matters

j. **Report on Management's Description of a Service Organization's System and the Suitability of the Design and Operating Effectiveness of Controls** (referred to in this section as a type 2 report). A report that comprises the following:

   (1) Management's description of the service organization's system

   (2) A written assertion by management of the service organization about whether in all material respects, and based on suitable criteria,

   (a) Management's description of the service organization's system fairly presents the service organization's system that was designed and implemented throughout the specified period

   (b) The controls related to the control objectives stated in management's description of the service organization's system were suitably designed throughout the specified period to achieve those control objectives

   (c) The controls related to the control objectives stated in management's description of the service organization's system operated effectively throughout the specified period to achieve those control objectives

   (3) A service auditor's report that:

   (a) Expresses an opinion on the preceding matters

   (b) Includes a description of the tests of controls and the results thereof

k. **Service Auditor** A practitioner who reports on controls at a service organization

l. **Service Organization** An organization or segment of an organization that provides services to user entities, which are likely to be relevant to those user entities' internal control over financial reporting.

m. **Service Organization's Assertion** A written assertion about the matters referred to in the definitions in either the type 1 or type 2 report.

n. **Service Organization's System** The policies and procedures designed, implemented, and documented, by management of the service organization to provide user entities with the services covered by the service auditor's report. Management's description of the service organization's system identifies the services covered, the period to which the description relates (or in the case of a type 1 report, the date to which the description relates), the control objectives specified by management or an outside party, the party specifying the control objectives (if not specified by management), and the related controls.

o. **Subservice Organization** A service organization used by another service organization to perform some of the services provided to user entities that are likely to be relevant to those user entities' internal control over financial reporting.

p. **Test of Controls** A procedure designed to evaluate the operating effectiveness of controls in achieving the control objectives stated in management's description of the service organization's system.

q. **User Auditor** An auditor who audits and reports on the financial statements of a user entity.

r. **User Entity** An entity that uses a service organization.

4. **Conditions Required to Accept / Continue the Engagement**

a. The service auditor has the capabilities and competence to perform the engagement.

b. The service auditor's preliminary knowledge of the engagement circumstances indicates that the

    (1) Criteria to be used will be suitable and available to the intended user entities and their auditors

    (2) Service auditor will have access to sufficient appropriate evidence to the extent necessary; and

    (3) Scope of the engagement and management's description of the service organization's system will not be so limited that they are unlikely to be useful to user entities and their auditors.

c. Management agrees to the terms of the engagement by acknowledging and accepting its responsibility for the following:

    (1) Preparing its description of the service organization's system and its assertion, including the completeness, accuracy, and method of presentation of the description and assertion

    (2) Having a reasonable basis for its assertion

    (3) Selecting the criteria to be used and stating them in the assertion

    (4) Specifying the control objectives, stating them in the description of the service organization's system, and, if the control objectives are specified by law, regulation, or another party (for example, a user group or a professional body), identifying in the description the party specifying the control objectives

(5) Identifying the risks that threaten the achievement of the control objectives stated in the description and designing, implementing, and documenting controls that are suitably designed and operating effectively to provide reasonable assurance that the control objectives stated in the description of the service organization's system will be achieved

(6) Providing the service auditor with:

(a) Access to all information, such as records and documentation, including service level agreements, of which management is aware that is relevant to the description of the service organization's system and the assertion

(b) Additional information that the service auditor may request from management for the purpose of the examination engagement

(c) Unrestricted access to personnel within the service organization from whom the service auditor determines it is necessary to obtain evidence relevant to the service auditor's engagement

(d) Written representations at the conclusion of the engagement

(7) Providing a written assertion that will be included in, or attached to management's description of the service organization's system, and provided to user entities.

Editor note: Management's subsequent refusal to provide a written assertion represents a scope limitation and consequently, the service auditor should withdraw from the engagement. If law or regulation does not allow the service auditor to withdraw from the engagement, the service auditor should disclaim an opinion.

5. **Suitability of the Criteria** The service auditor should assess whether management has used suitable criteria in:

a. Preparing its description of the service organization's system

b. Evaluating whether controls were suitably designed to achieve the control objectives stated in the description

c. Evaluating whether controls operated effectively throughout the specified period to achieve the control objectives stated in the description of the service organization's system

6. **Materiality** In an engagement to report on controls at a service organization, the concept of materiality relates to the information being reported on, not the financial statements of user entities. The service auditor plans and performs procedures to determine whether management's description of the service organization's system is fairly presented, in all material respects; whether controls at the service organization are suitably designed in all material respects to achieve the control objectives stated in the description; and in the case of a type 2 report, whether controls at the service organization operated effectively throughout the specified period in all material respects to achieve the control objectives stated in the description.

The concept of materiality is not applied when disclosing, in the description of the tests of controls, the results of those tests when deviations have been identified. This is because, in the particular circumstances of a specific user entity or user auditor, a deviation may have significance beyond whether or not, in the opinion of the service auditor, it prevents a control from operating effectively.

7. **Understanding of System** The service auditor should obtain an understanding of the service organization's system, including controls that are included in the scope of the engagement.

8. **Evidence of Management's Description** The service auditor should obtain and read management's description of the service organization's system and should evaluate whether those aspects of the description that are included in the scope of the engagement are presented fairly, including whether:

    a. The control objectives stated in management's description of the service organization's system are reasonable in the circumstances

    b. Controls identified in management's description of the service organization's system were implemented

    c. Complementary user entity controls, if any, are adequately described

    d. Services performed by a subservice organization, if any, are adequately described, including whether the inclusive method or the carve-out method has been used in relation to them

9. **Evidence of Design of Controls** The service auditor should determine which of the controls at the service organization are necessary to achieve the control objectives stated in management's description of the service organization's system and should assess whether those controls were suitably designed to achieve the control objectives by

    a. Identifying the risks that threaten the achievement of the control objectives stated in management's description of the service organization's system

    b. Evaluating the linkage of the controls identified in management's description of the service organization's system with those risks

10. **Evidence of Operating Effectiveness of Controls**

    a. **Achievement of Control Objectives** When performing a type 2 engagement, the service auditor should test those controls that the service auditor has determined are necessary to achieve the control objectives stated in management's description of the service organization's system and should assess their operating effectiveness throughout the period. Evidence obtained in prior engagements about the satisfactory operation of controls in prior periods does not provide a basis for a reduction in testing, even if it is supplemented with evidence obtained during the current period.

    b. **Changes to Controls** When performing a type 2 engagement, the service auditor should inquire about changes in the service organization's controls that were implemented during the period covered by the service auditor's report. If significant, the service auditor should determine whether those changes are included in management's description of the service organization's system. If such changes are not included in the description, the service auditor should describe the changes in the service auditor's report and determine the effect on the service auditor's report.

    c. **Test of Controls** When designing and performing tests of controls, the service auditor should:

        (1) Perform other procedures in combination with inquiry to obtain evidence about how the control was applied; the consistency with which the control was applied; and by whom or by what means the control was applied

        (2) Determine whether the controls to be tested depend on other controls, and if so, whether it is necessary to obtain evidence supporting the operating effectiveness of those other controls

        (3) Determine an effective method for selecting the items to be tested to meet the objectives of the procedure

    d.   **Deviations** The service auditor should investigate the nature and cause of any deviations identified, and should determine whether:

        (1)   Identified deviations are within the expected rate of deviation and are acceptable—if so, the testing that has been performed provides an appropriate basis for concluding that the control operated effectively throughout the specified period

        (2)   Additional testing of the control or of other controls is necessary to reach a conclusion about whether the controls related to the control objectives stated in management's description of the service organization's system operated effectively throughout the specified period

        (3)   The testing that has been performed provides an appropriate basis for concluding that the control did not operate effectively throughout the specified period

11.   **Internal Audit** If the service organization has an internal audit function, the service auditor should obtain an understanding of the nature of the responsibilities of the internal audit function and of the activities performed in order to determine whether the internal audit function is likely to be relevant to the engagement.

When the service auditor intends to use the work of the internal audit function, the service auditor should determine whether the work of the internal audit function is likely to be adequate for the purposes of the engagement.

If the work of the internal audit function has been used, the service auditor should not make reference to that work in the service auditor's *opinion*; however, in the case of a type 2 report, if the work of the internal audit function has been used in performing tests of controls, that part of the service auditor's report that describes the service auditor's tests of controls and results thereof should include a description of the internal auditor's work and of the service auditor's procedures with respect to that work.

12.   **Written Management Representations** The written representations should be in the form of a representation letter addressed to the service auditor and should be as of the same date as the date of the service auditor's report. The service auditor should request management to provide written representations that:

    a.   Reaffirm its assertion included in or attached to the description of the service organization's system

    b.   It has provided the service auditor with all relevant information and access agreed to

    c.   It has disclosed to the service auditor any of the following of which it is aware

        (1)   Instances of noncompliance with laws and regulations or uncorrected errors attributable to the service organization that may affect one or more user entities

        (2)   Knowledge of any actual, suspected, or alleged intentional acts by management or the service organization's employees, that could adversely affect the fairness of the presentation of management's description of the service organization's system or the completeness or achievement of the control objectives stated in the description

        (3)   Design deficiencies in controls

        (4)   Instances when controls have not operated as described

        (5)   Any events subsequent to the period covered by management's description of the service organization's system up to the date of the service auditor's report that could have a significant effect on management's assertion

13. **Other Information** The service auditor should read other information, if any, included in a document containing management's description of the service organization's system and the service auditor's report to identify material inconsistencies, if any, with that description.

If the service auditor becomes aware of a material inconsistency or an apparent misstatement of fact in the other information, the service auditor should discuss the matter with management. If the service auditor concludes that there is a material inconsistency or a misstatement of fact in the other information that management refuses to correct, the service auditor should take further appropriate action.

14. **Subsequent Events** The service auditor should inquire whether management is aware of any events subsequent to the period covered by management's description of the service organization's system up to the date of the service auditor's report that could have a significant effect on management's assertion. If the service auditor becomes aware, through inquiry or otherwise, of such an event, or any other event that is of such a nature and significance that its disclosure is necessary to prevent users of a type 1 or type 2 report from being misled, and information about that event is not disclosed by management in its description, the service auditor should disclose such event in the service auditor's report.

The service auditor has no responsibility to keep informed of events subsequent to the date of the service auditor's report; however, after the release of the service auditor's report, the service auditor may become aware of conditions that existed at the report date that might have affected management's assertion and the service auditor's report had the service auditor been aware of them. The evaluation of such subsequent information is similar to the evaluation of information discovered subsequent to the date of the report on an audit of financial statements, as described in AU 561, *Subsequent Discovery of Facts Existing at the Date of the Auditor's Report*, and therefore, the service auditor should adapt and apply that guidance.

15. **Documentation** The service auditor should prepare documentation that is sufficient to enable an experienced service auditor, having no previous connection with the engagement, to understand the following:

a. The nature, extent, and timing of the procedures performed to comply with this section and with applicable legal and regulatory requirements

b. The results of the procedures performed and the evidence obtained

c. Significant findings or issues arising during the engagement, the conclusions reached thereon, and significant professional judgments made in reaching those conclusions

In documenting the nature, extent, and timing of procedures performed, the service auditor should record identifying characteristics of the specific items or matters being tested; who performed the work and the date such work was completed; and who reviewed the work performed and the date and extent of such review.

If the service auditor uses specific work of the internal audit function, the service auditor should document the conclusions reached regarding the evaluation of the adequacy of the work of the internal audit function and the procedures performed by the service auditor on that work.

The service auditor should document discussions of significant findings or issues with management and others, including the nature of the significant findings or issues, when the discussions took place, and with whom.

If the service auditor has identified information that is inconsistent with the service auditor's final conclusion regarding a significant finding or issue, the service auditor should document how the service auditor addressed the inconsistency.

The service auditor should assemble the engagement documentation in an engagement file and complete the administrative process of assembling the final engagement file on a timely basis, no later than 60 days following the service auditor's report release date.

16. **Reporting & Communications**

a. **Report Date** The service auditor should date the service auditor's report no earlier than the date on which the service auditor has obtained sufficient appropriate evidence to support the service auditor's opinion.

b. **Elements of a Type 2 Report**

(1) A title that includes the word i*ndependent*

(2) An addressee

(3) Identification of:

(a) Management's description of the service organization's system and the function performed by the system

(b) Any parts of management's description of the service organization's system that are not covered by the service auditor's report

(c) Any information included in a document containing the service auditor's report that is not covered by the service auditor's report

(d) The criteria

(e) Any services performed by a subservice organization and whether the carve-out method or the inclusive method was used in relation to them; depending on which method is used, the following should be included:

• If the carve-out method was used, a statement that management's description of the service organization's system excludes the control objectives and related controls at relevant subservice organizations, and that the service auditor's procedures do not extend to the subservice organization

• If the inclusive method was used, a statement that management's description of the service organization's system includes the subservice organization's specified control objectives and related controls, and that the service auditor's procedures included procedures related to the subservice organization

(4) If management's description of the service organization's system refers to the need for complementary user entity controls, a statement that the service auditor has not evaluated the suitability of the design or operating effectiveness of complementary user entity controls, and that the control objectives stated in the description can be achieved only if complementary user entity controls are suitably designed and operating effectively, along with the controls at the service organization.

(5) A reference to management's assertion and a statement that management is responsible for:

(a) Preparing the description of the service organization's system and the assertion, including the completeness, accuracy, and method of presentation of the description and assertion

(b) Providing the services covered by the description of the service organization's system

(c) Specifying the control objectives unless the control objectives are specified by law, regulation, or another party, and stating them in the description of the service organization's system

(d) Identifying the risks that threaten the achievement of the control objectives

(e) Selecting the criteria

(f) Designing, implementing, and documenting controls that are suitably designed and operating effectively to achieve the related control objectives stated in the description of the service organization's system

(6) A statement that the service auditor's responsibility is to express an opinion on the fairness of the presentation of management's description of the service organization's system and on the suitability of the design and operating effectiveness of the controls to achieve the related control objectives stated in the description, based on the service auditor's examination.

(7) A statement that the examination was conducted in accordance with attestation standards established by the American Institute of Certified Public Accountants and that those standards require the service auditor to plan and perform the examination to obtain reasonable assurance about whether management's description of the service organization's system is fairly presented and the controls are suitably designed and operating effectively throughout the specified period to achieve the related control objectives.

(8) A statement that an examination of management's description of a service organization's system and the suitability of the design and operating effectiveness of the service organization's controls to achieve the related control objectives stated in the description involves performing procedures to obtain evidence about the fairness of the presentation of the description and the suitability of the design and operating effectiveness of those controls to achieve the related control objectives stated in the description.

(9) A statement that the examination included assessing the risks that management's description of the service organization's system is not fairly presented and that the controls were not suitably designed or operating effectively to achieve the related control objectives.

(10) A statement that the examination also included testing the operating effectiveness of those controls that the service auditor considers necessary to provide reasonable assurance that the related control objectives stated in management's description of the service organization's system were achieved.

(11) A statement that an examination engagement of this type also includes evaluating the overall presentation of management's description of the service organization's system and suitability of the control objectives stated in the description.

(12) A statement that the service auditor believes the examination provides a reasonable basis for his or her opinion.

(13) A statement about the inherent limitations of controls, including the risk of projecting to future periods any evaluation of the fairness of the presentation of management's description of the service organization's system or conclusions about the suitability of the design or operating effectiveness of controls.

(14) The service auditor's opinion on whether, in all material respects, based on the criteria described in management's assertion.

    (a) Management's description of the service organization's system fairly presents the service organization's system that was designed and implemented throughout the specified period

    (b) The controls related to the control objectives stated in management's description of the service organization's system were suitably designed to provide reasonable assurance that those control objectives would be achieved if the controls operated effectively throughout the specified period

    (c) The controls the service auditor tested, which were those necessary to provide reasonable assurance that the control objectives stated in management's description of the service organization's system were achieved, operated effectively throughout the specified period

    (d) If the application of complementary user entity controls is necessary to achieve the related control objectives stated in management's description of the service organization's system, a reference to this condition

(15) A reference to a description of the service auditor's tests of controls and the results thereof, that includes:

    (a) Identification of the controls that were tested, whether the items tested represent all or a selection of the items in the population, and the nature of the tests in sufficient detail to enable user auditors to determine the effect of such tests on their risk assessments

    (b) If deviations have been identified in the operation of controls included in the description, the extent of testing performed by the service auditor that led to the identification of the deviations (including the number of items tested), and the number and nature of the deviations noted (even if, on the basis of tests performed, the service auditor concludes that the related control objective was achieved)

(16) A statement restricting the use of the service auditor's report to management of the service organization, user entities of the service organization's system during some or all of the period covered by the service auditor's report, and the independent auditors of such user entities

(17) The date of the service auditor's report

(18) The name of the service auditor and the city and state where the service auditor maintains the office that has responsibility for the engagement

c. **Elements of a Type 1 Report**

(1) A title that includes the word *independent*

(2) An addressee

(3) Identification of

    (a) Management's description of the service organization's system prepared by the management, and the function performed by the system

    (b) Any parts of management's description of the service organization's system that are not covered by the service auditor's report

(c) Any information included in a document containing the service auditor report that is not covered by the service auditor's report

(d) The criteria

(e) Any services performed by a subservice organization and whether the carve-out method or the inclusive method was used in relation to them; depending on which method is used, the following should be included:

- If the carve-out method was used, a statement that management's description of the service organization's system excludes the control objectives and related controls at relevant subservice organizations, and that the service auditor's procedures do not extend to the subservice organization

- If the inclusive method was used, a statement that management's description of the service organization's system includes the subservice organization's specified control objectives and related controls, and that the service auditor's procedures included procedures related to the subservice organization

(4) If management's description of the service organization's system refers to the need for complementary user entity controls, a statement that the service auditor has not evaluated the suitability of the design or operating effectiveness of complementary user entity controls, and that the control objectives stated in the description can be achieved only if complementary user entity controls are suitably designed and operating effectively, along with the controls at the service organization

(5) A reference to management's assertion and a statement that management is responsible for:

(a) Preparing the description of the service organization's system and assertion, including the completeness, accuracy, and method of presentation of the description and assertion

(b) Providing the services covered by the description of the service organization's system

(c) Specifying the control objectives, unless the control objectives are specified by law, regulation, or another party, and stating them in the description of the service organization's system

(d) Identifying the risks that threaten the achievement of the control objectives

(e) Selecting the criteria

(f) Designing, implementing, and documenting controls that are suitably designed and operating effectively to achieve the related control objectives stated in the description of the service organization's system

(6) A statement that the service auditor's responsibility is to express an opinion on the fairness of the presentation of management's description of the service organization's system and on the suitability of the design of the controls to achieve the related control objectives stated in the description, based on the service auditor's examination.

(7) A statement that the examination was conducted in accordance with attestation standards established by the American Institute of Certified Public Accountants, and that those standards require the service auditor to plan and perform the examination to obtain reasonable assurance about whether management's description of the service organization's system is fairly presented and the controls are suitably designed as of the specified date to achieve the related control objectives.

(8)   A statement that the service auditor has not performed any procedures regarding the operating effectiveness of controls and, therefore, expresses no opinion thereon.

(9)   A statement that an examination of management's description of a service organization's system and the suitability of the design of the service organization's controls to achieve the related control objectives stated in the description involves performing procedures to obtain evidence about the fairness of the presentation of the description and the suitability of the design of those controls to achieve the related control objectives stated in the description.

(10)   A statement that the examination included assessing the risks that management's description of the service organization's system is not fairly presented and that the controls were not suitably designed to achieve the related control objectives.

(11)   A statement that an examination engagement of this type also includes evaluating the overall presentation of management's description of the service organization's system and suitability of the control objectives stated in the description.

(12)   A statement that the service auditor believes the examination provides a reasonable basis for his or her opinion.

(13)   A statement about the inherent limitations of controls, including the risk of projecting to future periods any evaluation of the fairness of the presentation of management's description of the service organization's system or conclusions about the suitability of the design of the controls to achieve the related control objectives.

(14)   The service auditor's opinion on whether, in all material respects, based on the criteria described in management's assertion:

    (a)   Management's description of the service organization's system fairly presents the service organization's system that was designed and implemented as of the specified date

    (b)   The controls related to the control objectives stated in management's description of the service organization's system were suitably designed to provide reasonable assurance that those control objectives would be achieved if the controls operated effectively as of the specified date

    (c)   If the application of complementary user entity controls is necessary to achieve the related control objectives stated in management's description of the service organization's system, a reference to this condition

(15)   A statement restricting the use of the service auditor's report to management of the service organization, user entities of the service organization's system as of the end of the period covered by the service auditor's report, and the independent auditors of such user entities.

(16)   The date of the service auditor's report.

(17)   The name of the service auditor and the city and state where the service auditor maintains the office that has responsibility for the engagement

d. **Modified Opinion** The service auditor's opinion should be modified and the service auditor's report should contain a clear description of all the reasons for the modification, if the service auditor concludes that:

(1) Management's description of the service organization's system is not fairly presented, in all material respects;

(2) The controls are not suitably designed to provide reasonable assurance that the control objectives stated in management's description of the service organization's system would be achieved if the controls operated as described;

(3) In the case of a type 2 report, the controls did not operate effectively throughout the specified period to achieve the related control objectives stated in management's description of the service organization's system; or

(4) The service auditor is unable to obtain sufficient appropriate evidence

e. **Disclaimer** If the service auditor plans to disclaim an opinion because of the inability to obtain sufficient appropriate evidence, and, based on the limited procedures performed, has concluded that:

(1) Certain aspects of management's description of the service organization's system are not fairly presented, in all material respects;

(2) Certain controls were not suitably designed to provide reasonable assurance that the control objectives stated in management's description of the service organization's system would be achieved if the controls operated as described; or

(3) In the case of a type 2 report, certain controls did not operate effectively throughout the specified period to achieve the related control objectives stated in management's description of the service organization's system

The service auditor should identify these findings in his or her report.

The service auditor should not identify the procedures that were performed nor include statements describing the characteristics of a service auditor's engagement in the service auditor's report; to do so might overshadow the disclaimer.

f. **Communications** If the service auditor becomes aware of incidents of noncompliance with laws and regulations, fraud, or uncorrected errors attributable to management or other service organization personnel that are not clearly trivial and that may affect one or more user entities, the service auditor should determine the effect of such incidents on management's description of the service organization's system, the achievement of the control objectives, and the service auditor's report.

Additionally, the service auditor should determine whether this information has been communicated appropriately to affected user entities. If the information has not been so communicated, and management of the service organization is unwilling to do so, the service auditor should take appropriate action.

CHAPTER 13—ATTESTATION ENGAGEMENTS

Problem 13-1 MULTIPLE-CHOICE QUESTIONS

1. A nonissuer engaged a CPA to determine whether the client's websites meet defined criteria for standard business practices and controls over transaction integrity and information protection. In performing this engagement, the CPA should comply with the provisions of

   a. Statements on Assurance Standards
   b. Statements on Standards for Attestation Engagements
   c. Statements on Standards for Management Consulting Services
   d. Statements on Auditing Standards   (R/99, AUD, #3, amended, ID: 6819)

2. A CPA is required to comply with the provisions of Statements on Standards for Attestation Engagements (SSAE) when engaged to

   a. Report on financial statements that the CPA generated through the use of computer software
   b. Review management's discussion and analysis (MD&A) prepared pursuant to rules and regulations adopted by the SEC
   c. Provide the client with a financial statement format that does not include dollar amounts
   d. Audit financial statements that the client prepared for use in another country
                                                                          (R/02, AUD, #13, ID: 7103)

3. Which of the following activities would most likely be considered an attestation engagement?

   a. Consulting with management representatives of a firm to provide advice
   b. Issuing a report about a firm's compliance with laws and regulations
   c. Advocating a client's position on tax matters that are being reviewed by the IRS
   d. Preparing a client's tax returns   (R/05, AUD, #40, ID: 7835)

4. Which of the following is a conceptual difference between the attestation standards and generally accepted auditing standards?

   a. The attestation standards provide a framework for the attest function beyond historical financial statements.
   b. The requirement that the practitioner be independent in mental attitude is omitted from the attestation standards.
   c. The attestation standards do not permit an attest engagement to be part of a business acquisition study or a feasibility study.
   d. None of the standards of fieldwork in generally accepted auditing standards are included in the attestation standards.   (5/94, AUD, #10, ID: 4675)

5. Which of the following is **not** an attestation standard?

   a. The practitioner must obtain sufficient evidence to provide a reasonable basis for the conclusion that is expressed in the report.
   b. The practitioner must identify the subject matter or the assertion being reported on and state the character of the engagement in the report.
   c. The practitioner must adequately plan the work and must properly supervise any assistants.
   d. A sufficient understanding of internal control shall be obtained to plan the engagement.
                                                                          (5/93, AUD, #4, amended, ID: 3900)

6. A CPA in public practice is required to comply with the provisions of the Statements on Standards for Attestation Engagements (SSAE) when

	Testifying as an expert witness in accounting and auditing matters given stipulated facts	Compiling a client's financial projection that presents a hypothetical course of action
a.	Yes	Yes
b.	Yes	No
c.	No	Yes
d.	No	No

(R/01, AUD, #1, ID: 7016)

7. Which of the following professional services would be considered an attestation engagement?

a. Advocating on behalf of a client about trust tax matters under review by the Internal Revenue Service
b. Providing financial analysis, planning, and capital acquisition services as a part-time, in-house controller
c. Advising management in the selection of a computer system to meet business needs
d. Preparing the income statement and balance sheet for one year in the future based on client expectations and predictions   (R/05, AUD, #43, ID: 7838)

8. Which of the following procedures would be most effective in reducing attestation risk?

a. Discussion with responsible individuals
b. Examination of evidence
c. Inquiries of senior management
d. Analytical procedures   (R/07, AUD, #4, ID: 8376)

9. A CPA is engaged to examine management's assertion that the entity's schedule of investment returns is presented in accordance with specific criteria. In performing this engagement, the CPA should comply with the provisions of

a. Statements on Standards for Accounting and Review Services (SSARS)
b. Statements on Auditing Standards (SAS)
c. Statements on Standards for Consulting Services (SSCS)
d. Statements on Standards for Attestation Engagements (SSAE)   (R/07, AUD, #43, ID: 8415)

10. Which of the following is a conceptual similarity between generally accepted auditing standards and the attestation standards?

a. Both sets of standards require the CPA to report on the adequacy of disclosure in the financial statements.
b. All of the standards of fieldwork in generally accepted auditing standards are included in the attestation standards.
c. The requirement that the CPA be independent in mental attitude is included in both sets of standards.
d. Both sets of standards are applicable to engagements regarding financial forecasts and projections.   (R/09, AUD, #49, ID: 8849)

11. What type of evidence would provide the highest level of assurance in an attestation engagement?

a. Evidence secured solely from within the entity
b. Evidence obtained from independent sources
c. Evidence obtained indirectly
d. Evidence obtained from multiple internal inquiries   (R/10, AUD, #19, ID: 9369)

12. An accountant's standard report on a compilation of a projection should **not** include a

a. Statement that a compilation of a projection is limited in scope
b. Disclaimer of responsibility to update the report for events occurring after the report's date
c. Statement that the accountant expresses only limited assurance that the results may be achieved
d. Caveat that the prospective results may not be achieved   (11/93, AUD, #57, amended, ID: 4294)

13. An accountant may accept an engagement to apply agreed-upon procedures to prospective financial statements provided that

    a. Use of the report is restricted to the specified users.
    b. The prospective financial statements are also examined.
    c. Responsibility for the adequacy of the procedures performed is taken by the accountant.
    d. Negative assurance is expressed on the prospective financial statements taken as a whole.

    (11/94, AUD, #23, amended, ID: 5096)

14. When an accountant examines a financial forecast that fails to disclose several significant assumptions used to prepare the forecast, the accountant should describe the assumptions in the accountant's report and issue a(an)

    a. Unqualified opinion with a separate explanatory paragraph
    b. "Subject to" qualified opinion
    c. "Except for" qualified opinion
    d. Adverse opinion

    (Editors, ID: 432)

15. When a CPA examines a client's projected financial statements, the CPA's report should

    a. Explain the principal differences between historical and projected financial statements
    b. State that the CPA performed procedures to evaluate management's assumptions
    c. Refer to the CPA's auditor's report on the historical financial statements
    d. Include the CPA's opinion on the client's ability to continue as a going concern

    (R/02, AUD, #1, ID: 7091)

16. When an accountant compiles a financial forecast, the accountant's report should include a(an)

    a. Explanation of the differences between a financial forecast and a financial projection
    b. Caveat that the prospective results of the financial forecast may not be achieved
    c. Statement that the accountant's responsibility to update the report is limited to one year
    d. Disclaimer of opinion on the reliability of the entity's internal controls   (R/06, AUD, #32, ID: 8150)

17. Which of the following is a prospective financial statement for general use upon which an accountant may appropriately report?

    a. *Pro forma* financial statement
    b. Partial presentation
    c. Financial projection
    d. Financial forecast

    (Editors, ID: 7511)

18. When an accountant examines projected financial statements, the accountant's report should include a separate paragraph that

    a. Restricts the use of the report because it is intended to be used solely by specified parties
    b. Provides an explanation of the differences between an examination and an audit
    c. States that the accountant is responsible for events and circumstances up to one year after the report's date
    d. Disclaims an opinion on whether the assumptions provide a reasonable basis for the projection

    (11/95, AUD, #82, amended, ID: 6029)

19. Which of the following statements concerning prospective financial statements is correct?

    a. Only a financial forecast would normally be appropriate for limited use.
    b. Only a financial projection would normally be appropriate for general use.
    c. Any type of prospective financial statement would normally be appropriate for limited use.
    d. Any type of prospective financial statement would normally be appropriate for general use.

    (5/90, AUD, #23, ID: 424)

20. An accountant's compilation report on a financial forecast should include a statement that

    a. The forecast should be read only in conjunction with the audited historical financial statements.
    b. The accountant expresses only limited assurance on the forecasted statements and their assumptions.
    c. There will usually be differences between the forecasted and actual results.
    d. The hypothetical assumptions used in the forecast are reasonable in the circumstances.

    (11/94, AUD, #83, ID: 5156)

21. Accepting an engagement to examine an entity's financial projection most likely would be appropriate if the projection were to be used by

    a. All employees who work for the entity
    b. Potential stockholders who request a prospectus or a registration statement
    c. All stockholders of record as of the report date
    d. A bank with which the entity is negotiating for a loan   (5/94, AUD, #14, amended, ID: 4679)

22. An examination of a financial forecast is a professional service that involves

    a. Compiling or assembling a financial forecast that is based on management's assumptions
    b. Evaluating the preparation of a financial forecast and the support underlying management's assumptions
    c. Assuming responsibility to update management on key events for one year after the report's date
    d. Limiting the distribution of the accountant's report to management and the board of directors

    (5/95, AUD, #22, amended, ID: 5640)

23. An accountant's standard report on a compilation of a projection should **not** include a statement that

    a. There will usually be differences between the forecasted and actual results.
    b. The hypothetical assumptions used in the projection are reasonable in the circumstances.
    c. The accountant has no responsibility to update the report for future events and circumstances.
    d. The compilation of a projection is limited in scope.   (R/05, AUD, #19, ID: 7814)

24. When an accountant compiles projected financial statements, the accountant's report should include a separate paragraph that

    a. Explains the difference between a compilation and a review
    b. Documents the assessment of the risk of material misstatement due to fraud
    c. Expresses limited assurance that the actual results may be within the projected range
    d. Describes the limitations on the projection's usefulness   (R/07, AUD, #39, ID: 8411)

25. An accountant may accept an engagement to apply agreed-upon procedures to prospective financial statements provided the

    a. Provisions of Statements on Standards for Accounting and Review Services (SSARS) are followed.
    b. Accountant also examines the prospective financial statements.
    c. Distribution of the report is restricted to the specified users.
    d. The accountant takes responsibility for the adequacy of the procedures performed.

    (R/07, AUD, #49, ID: 8421)

26. Accepting an engagement to compile an entity's financial projection most likely would be inappropriate if the projection is to be included in a(an)

    a. Mortgage application for the purpose of expanding the entity's facilities
    b. Offering statement of the entity's initial public offering of common stock
    c. Comprehensive document to be used in negotiating a new labor contract
    d. Report to the audit committee that is not sent to the stockholders   (R/09, AUD, #2, ID: 8802)

27. A practitioner has been engaged to apply agreed-upon procedures in accordance with Statements on Standards for Attestation Engagements (SSAE) to prospective financial statements. Which of the following conditions must be met for the practitioner to perform the engagement?

    a. The prospective financial statement includes a summary of significant accounting policies.
    b. The practitioner takes responsibility for the sufficiency of the agreed-upon procedures.
    c. The practitioner and specified parties agree upon the procedures to be performed by the practitioner.
    d. The practitioner reports on the criteria to be used in the determination of findings.

    (R/09, AUD, #11, ID: 8811)

28. An accountant's compilation report on a financial forecast should include a statement that

    a. The hypothetical assumptions used in the forecast are reasonable in the circumstances.
    b. The forecast should be read only in conjunction with the audited historical financial statements.
    c. The accountant expresses only limited assurance on the forecasted statements and their assumptions.
    d. There will usually be differences between the forecasted and actual results.

    (R/09, AUD, #20, ID: 8820)

29. A CPA is engaged to examine an entity's financial forecast. The CPA believes that several significant assumptions do **not** provide a reasonable basis for the forecast. Under these circumstances, the CPA should issue a(an)

    a. Adverse opinion
    b. *Pro forma* opinion
    c. Qualified opinion
    d. Unqualified opinion with an explanatory paragraph

    (R/09, AUD, #35, ID: 8835)

30. Which of the following prospective financial statements is(are) appropriate for general use?

	Financial forecast	*Financial projection*
a.	Yes	Yes
b.	Yes	No
c.	No	Yes
d.	No	No

    (R/09, AUD, #38, ID: 8838)

31. Which of the following procedures should an accountant perform during an engagement to compile prospective financial statements?

    a. Test the entity's internal controls to determine if adequate controls exist so that financial projections can be reasonably achieved
    b. Make inquiries prior to the date of the report about possible future transactions that may impact the forecast once the report is issued
    c. Make inquiries about the accounting principles used in the preparation of the prospective financial statements
    d. Compare the prospective financial statements with the entity's historical results for the prior year

    (R/10, AUD, #43, ID: 9393)

32. Accepting an engagement to compile a financial projection most likely would be inappropriate if the projection is to be distributed to

    a. The entity's principal stockholder, to the exclusion of the other stockholders
    b. Potential stockholders in an offering statement
    c. A financial institution in a loan application
    d. A state or federal regulatory agency

    (R/11, AUD, #3, ID: 9903)

33. In reporting on a nonissuer's internal control over financial reporting, an auditor should include a paragraph that describes the

    a. Documentary evidence regarding the control environment factors
    b. Changes in internal control since the prior report
    c. Potential benefits from the auditor's suggested improvements
    d. Inherent limitations of any internal control structure   (5/95, AUD, #84, amended, ID: 5702)

34. Brown, CPA, has accepted an engagement to examine the effectiveness of internal control over financial reporting of Crow Company (a nonissuer). Crow Company's written assertion about the effectiveness of internal control should be presented

        I. In a separate report that will accompany Brown's report
       II. In a representation letter to Brown

    a. Neither I nor II
    b. Either I or II
    c. I only
    d. II only   (11/95, AUD, #36, amended, ID: 5983)

35. How do the scope, procedures, and objective of an engagement to examine the design and operating effectiveness of an entity's internal control over financial reporting compare to those for obtaining an understanding of internal control and assessing control risk as part of an audit?

	Scope	Procedures	Objective
a.	Similar	Different	Similar
b.	Different	Similar	Similar
c.	Different	Different	Different
d.	Different	Similar	Different

    (5/90, AUD, #40, amended, ID: 400)

36. Mill, CPA, was engaged by a group of royalty recipients to apply agreed-upon procedures to financial data supplied by Modern Co. regarding Modern's written assertion about its compliance with contractual requirements to pay royalties. Mill's report on these agreed-upon procedures should contain a (an)

    a. Disclaimer of opinion about the fair presentation of Modern's financial statements
    b. List of the procedures performed (or reference thereto) and Mill's findings
    c. Opinion about the effectiveness of Modern's internal control activities concerning royalty payments
    d. Acknowledgment that the sufficiency of the procedures is solely Mill's responsibility

    (R/01, AUD, #13, ID: 7028)

37. A CPA's report on agreed-upon procedures related to management's assertion about an entity's compliance with specified requirements should contain

    a. A statement of restrictions on the use of the report
    b. An opinion about whether management's assertion is fairly stated
    c. Negative assurance that control risk has not been assessed
    d. An acknowledgment of responsibility for the sufficiency of the procedures (11/95, AUD, #81, ID: 6028)

38. A practitioner's report on agreed-upon procedures that is in the form of procedures and findings should contain

    a. Negative assurance that the procedures did not necessarily disclose all reportable conditions
    b. An acknowledgment of the practitioner's responsibility for the sufficiency of the procedures
    c. A statement of restrictions on the use of the report
    d. A disclaimer of opinion on the entity's financial statements   (R/06, AUD, #14, ID: 8132)

39. An accountant's report on a review of *pro forma* financial information should include a

    a. Statement that the entity's internal control was not relied on in the review
    b. Disclaimer of opinion on the financial statements from which the *pro forma* financial information is derived
    c. Caveat that it is uncertain whether the transaction or event reflected in the *pro forma* financial information will ever occur
    d. Reference to the financial statements from which the historical financial information is derived

    (5/94, AUD, #68, amended, ID: 4733)

40. Which of the following components is appropriate in a practitioner's report on the results of applying agreed-upon procedures?

    a. A list of the procedures performed, as agreed to by the specified parties identified in the report.
    b. A statement that management is responsible for expressing an opinion.
    c. A title that includes the phrase "independent audit."
    d. A statement that the report is unrestricted in its use.

    (R/10, AUD, #49, ID: 9399)

41. An accountant has been engaged to examine *pro forma* adjustments that show the effects on previously audited historical financial statements due to a proposed disposition of a significant portion of an entity's business. Other than the procedures previously applied to the historical financial statements, the accountant is required to

	Reevaluate the entity's internal control over financial reporting	*Determine that the computations of the pro forma adjustments are mathematically correct*
a.	Yes	Yes
b.	Yes	No
c.	No	Yes
d.	No	No (R/03, AUD, #6, ID: 7628)

Problem 13-2 SIMULATION: Attestation Standards Terminology

The items in the table below are definitions of terms used in the attestation standards. Select, from the accompanying list of terms, the term each item defines. A term may be used once, more than once, or not at all.

Definitions	Terms
1. Any declaration or set of declarations about whether the subject matter is based on or in conformity with the criteria selected.	
2. Any unresolved problem that the practitioner had in complying with the attestation standards, interpretive standards, or the specific procedures agreed to by the specified parties.	
3. A presentation that shows, given one or more hypothetical assumptions, an entity's expected financial position, results of operations, and cash flows.	
4. A deficiency, or a combination of deficiencies, in internal control such that there is a reasonable possibility that a material misstatement of the entity's financial statements will not be prevented, or detected and corrected on a timely basis.	
5. A financial statement assertion that has a reasonable possibility of containing a misstatement or misstatements that would cause the financial statements to be materially misstated.	
6. Exists when the design or operation of a control does not allow management or employees, in the normal course of performing their assigned functions, to prevent, or detect and correct misstatements on a timely basis.	
7. A presentation that shows an entity's expected financial position, results of operations, and cash flows.	
8. The person or persons, either as individuals or representatives of the entity, responsible for the subject matter.	
9. A presentation that shows what the significant effects on historical financial information might have been had a consummated or proposed transaction (or event) occurred at an earlier date.	
10. A deficiency, or a combination of deficiencies, in internal control that is important enough to merit attention by those charged with governance.	

Selection List of Terms

A.	Responsible party	L.	Assertion
B.	Deficiency in internal control	M.	Weakness
C.	Affirmation	N.	Assurance
D.	Significant deficiency	O.	Accountable party
E.	Client	P.	Assessment
F.	Material weakness	Q.	Material limitation
G.	Exception	R.	Material assertion
H.	Financial projection	S.	Evaluation
I.	Reservation	T.	Finding
J.	Relevant assertion	U.	Financial forecast
K.	*Pro forma* financial information	V.	Significant limitation

(Editors, ID: 89464)

Problem 13-3 SIMULATION: Research

What authoritative reference provides guidance for the date of a practitioner's report on agreed-upon procedures?

	§			(ID: 9242)

Solution 13-1 MULTIPLE-CHOICE ANSWERS

Attestation Standards

1. (b)   Attestation engagements involve the issuance of a report on a subject matter or an assertion about a subject matter that is the responsibility of another party. Statements on Auditing Standards apply to financial statement audits of nonissuers. The other two answers do not exist. (ID: 6819)

2. (b)   An attest engagement is one in which a CPA in public practice (or practitioner) is engaged to, or does, issue an examination, review, or agreed-upon procedures report on subject matter or an assertion about subject matter that is the responsibility of another party. Reports on financial statements are subject to the guidance of Statements on Auditing Standards (SAS) and Statements on Standards for Accounting & Review Services (SSARS). Supplying a client with a blank financial statement format is a service exempt from SAS and SSARS; SSAE do not apply to financial statements. (ID: 7103)

3. (b)   An attest engagement is one in which a CPA in public practice is engaged to issue an examination, review, or agreed-upon procedures report on subject matter or an assertion about subject matter that is the responsibility of another party. AT 600 established guidance concerning attest engagements on an entity's compliance with requirements of specified laws, regulations, rules, contracts, etc. AT 100 specifically lists, as engagements to which attest standards are inapplicable, engagements performed in accordance with Statements on Standards for Consulting Services, client advocacy engagements, and tax return preparation services. (ID: 7835)

4. (a)   The attestation standards provide guidance and establish a broad framework for a variety of attest services than include providing assurance on representations that are not limited to historical financial statements and are in forms other than the positive opinion. The fourth general attestation standard requires that the practitioner maintain independence in mental attitude in all matters relating to the engagement. An attest engagement may be part of a larger engagement, such as a feasibility study, that may include an examination of prospective financial information. The two attestation fieldwork standards are very similar to the first and third standards of fieldwork for audits. (ID: 4675)

5. (d)   A sufficient understanding of internal control for planning an engagement is not an attestation standard. The other answers are attestation standards. Answer a. is the second standard of fieldwork; answer b. is the first standard of reporting; and answer c. is the first standard of fieldwork. (ID: 3900)

6. (c)   SSAE do not apply to client advocacy engagements, but they do apply to engagements to examine, compile, or apply agreed-upon procedures to financial forecasts and projections. (ID: 7016)

7. (d)   The SSAEs provide guidance concerning attest engagements on prospective financial statements. The other answers would not be considered attest engagements. (ID: 7838)

8. (b)   Examination of evidence is the most effective procedure. In the hierarchy of available attest procedures, those that involve search and verification (for example, inspection, confirmation, or observation), particularly when using independent sources outside the entity, are generally more effective in restricting attestation risk than those involving internal inquiries and comparisons of internal information (for example, analytical procedures and discussions with individuals responsible for the subject matter or the assertion). (ID: 8376)

9. (d)   SSAE apply when a CPA in public practice is engaged to issue an examination, review, or agreed-upon procedures report on subject matter or an assertion about subject matter that is the responsibility of another party. SSARS apply to compilations and reviews of financial statements. SAS apply to audits to financial statements. SSCS apply to consulting engagements. (ID: 8415)

10. (c)   The requirement that the CPA be independent in mental attitude is included in both sets of standards. Only GAAS require the CPA to report on the adequacy of disclosure in the financial statements. The attestation standards do not include a standard similar the GAAS second standard of fieldwork: "The auditor must obtain a sufficient understanding of the entity and its environment, including its internal control, to assess the risk of material misstatement of the financial statements whether due to error or fraud, and to design the nature, timing, and extent of further audit procedures." Only the attestation standards are applicable to engagements regarding financial forecasts and projections. (ID: 8849)

11. (b) Evidence obtained from independent sources outside an entity provides the highest level of assurance. Evidence obtained from independent sources outside an entity provides greater assurance about the subject matter or the assertion than evidence secured solely from within the entity even if it is obtained from multiple inquiries. Information obtained from the independent attester's direct personal knowledge (such as through physical examination, observation, computation, operating tests, or inspection) is more persuasive than information obtained indirectly. (ID: 9369)

Financial Forecasts & Projections

12. (c) The practitioner's standard report on a compilation of prospective financial statements should include a statement that a compilation is limited in scope and does not enable the practitioner to express an opinion or any other form of assurance on the prospective financial statements or the assumptions; a statement that the practitioner assumes no responsibility to update the report for events and circumstances occurring after the date of the report; and a caveat that the prospective results may not be achieved. It should also include an identification of the prospective financial statements presented by the responsible party and a statement that the practitioner compiled the prospective financial statements in accordance with attestation standards established by the AICPA. (ID: 4294)

13. (a) A practitioner may perform an agreed-upon procedures attestation engagement on prospective financial statements provided that use of the report is to be restricted to the specified parties. SSAE 10 merely requires the subject matter to be subject to reasonably consistent estimation or measurement. Responsibility for adequacy for the procedures performed is taken by the specified users, not the accountant. The practitioner should not provide negative assurance. (ID: 5096)

14. (d) When a CPA examines a financial forecast that fails to disclose several assumptions that appear to be significant, the CPA should describe the assumptions in the report and issue an adverse opinion. (ID: 432)

15. (b) When a CPA examines a projection, the CPA should express an opinion on whether the assumptions provide a reasonable basis for the projection given the hypothetical assumptions. The standard report includes the following in the scope paragraph, "…included such procedures as we considered necessary to evaluate both the assumptions used by management and the preparation and presentation of the projection. (ID: 7091)

16. (b) A standard compilation report of prospective financial statements requires a caveat that the prospective results may not be achieved. An explanation of the difference between a financial forecast and a financial projection is not needed. The practitioner assumes no responsibility to update the report for events and circumstances occurring after the date of the report. A compilation does not consider the entity's internal controls. (ID: 8150)

17. (d) Prospective financial statements are for either general use or limited use. General use of prospective financial statements refers to use of the statements by persons with whom the responsible party is not negotiating directly, for example, in an offering statement of an entity's debt or equity interests. Because recipients of prospective financial statements distributed for general use are unable to ask the responsible party directly about the presentation, the presentation most useful to them is one that portrays, to the best of the responsible party's knowledge and belief, the expected results. Thus, only a financial forecast is appropriate for general use. (ID: 7511)

18. (a) The report should contain a separate paragraph that restricts the use of the report because it is intended to be used solely by specified parties. The report does not provide an explanation of the differences between an examination and an audit. The accountant is not responsible for events occurring after the date of the report. The standard report contains the practitioner's opinion that the prospective financial statements are presented in conformity with AICPA presentation guidelines and that the underlying assumptions provide a reasonable basis for the forecast or a reasonable basis for the projection given the hypothetical assumptions. (ID: 6029)

19. (c) Any type of prospective financial statements that would be useful in the circumstances would normally be appropriate for limited use. Thus, the presentation may be a financial forecast or a financial projection. Only the financial forecast is appropriate for general use. (ID: 424)

20. (c) The standard report in includes a statement that there will usually be differences between the forecasted and actual results. The items in answers a., b., and d. are not in the standard report. (ID: 5156)

21. (d) A projection, since it is not meant for general use, would be inappropriate for all stockholders of record and employees, as it would be unreasonable to expect these groups to be familiar with the basis of the projection or to be involved closely with those preparing it. (ID: 4679)

22. (b) An examination of prospective financial statements...involves evaluating the preparation of the prospective financial statements, evaluating the support underlying the assumptions, evaluating the presentation of the prospective financial statements for conformity with AICPA presentation guidelines, and issuing an examination report. This service does not include compiling the forecast, or assuming responsibility to update management on key events afterwards. The report may be for general use, in which case the distribution need not be limited. (ID: 5640)

23. (b) A report on a compilation of a financial projection must include a statement that a compilation is limited in scope and does not enable the accountant to express an opinion or any other form of assurance on the prospective financial statements or the assumptions. As a compilation report should provide no assurance, a statement that that the assumptions used are reasonable is inappropriate. Reports for all types of engagements involving financial projections must include a caveat that the prospective results may not be achieved and a statement that the accountant assumes no responsibility to update the report for events and circumstances occurring after the date of the report. (ID: 7814)

24. (d) An accountant's report on a compilation of projected financial statements should include a description of the limitations on the projection's usefulness. It does not express an opinion or any other form of assurance, nor does it mention fraud or the difference between a compilation and a review. (ID: 8411)

25. (c) Among other things, a report on the results of applying agreed-upon procedures to financial forecasts and projections must include a restriction on the use of the report. The Statements on Standards for Attestation Engagements (SSAE) apply to engagements to apply agreed-upon procedures to prospective financial statements, not SSARS. A CPA may perform agreed-upon procedures without examining or compiling the related prospective financial statements. The client must accept responsibility for the adequacy of the procedures performed in an agreed-upon procedures engagement. (ID: 8421)

26. (b) Inclusion of an entity's compiled financial projection in an offering statement of the entity's initial public offering of common stock would be inappropriate because this is an example of a general use distribution. A financial forecast is the only type of prospective financial statement appropriate for general use. The other three answers are examples of limited use distributions and could appropriately include either a financial projection or a financial forecast. A financial projection, unlike a financial forecast, is not confined to the presentation of (to the best of the responsible party's knowledge and belief) the expected results. Instead, a projection incorporates one or more hypothetical assumptions. A general use distribution will include parties who will not be able to directly ask the responsible parties questions about the presentation and were not involved in negotiating the terms of the engagement for its preparation. Deprived of this type of involvement, it is best that they receive prospective financial statements that contain only the expected results, i.e., a financial forecast. (ID: 8802)

27. (c) One of the conditions that must be met by a practitioner who accepts an engagement to apply agreed-upon procedures in accordance with SSAE to prospective financial statements is that the practitioner and specified parties agree upon the procedures to be performed by the practitioner. The prospective financial statements must include a summary of significant assumptions, not account ting policies. The specified parties, not the practitioner, must take responsibility for the sufficiency of the agreed-upon procedures for their purpose. The practitioner does not report on the criteria to be used in the determination of findings, rather the criteria must be agreed upon between the practitioner and the specified parties. (ID: 8811)

28. (d) An accountant's compilation report on a financial forecast should include a caveat that the prospective results may not be achieved, such as there will usually be differences between the forecasted and actual results because events and circumstances frequently do not occur as expected, and those differences may be material. Answers a. and c. are not correct because the report should also include a statement that a compilation is limited in scope and does not enable the accountant to express an opinion or any other form of assurance

on the prospective financial statements or the assumptions. There is no requirement that the forecast be read in conjunction with the audited historical financial statements. (ID: 8820)

29. (a) If the CPA believes the assumptions do not provide a reasonable basis for the forecast, the CPA should issue an adverse opinion. The opinion paragraph should include a statement to that effect. (ID: 8835)

30. (b) A financial forecast is the only type of prospective financial statement appropriate for general use. General use refers to use of the statements by parties who are not negotiating directly with the responsible party. Because recipients of prospective financial statements distributed for general use are unable to ask the responsible party directly about the presentation, the presentation most useful to them is one that portrays, to the best of the responsible party's knowledge and belief, the expected results, i.e., a financial forecast. Any type of prospective financial statements that would be useful in the circumstances would normally be appropriate for limited use. Thus, a limited use distribution could include either a financial forecast or a projection. (ID: 8838)

31. (c) During an engagement to compile prospective financial statements, an accountant should make inquiries about the accounting principles used in the preparation of the prospective financial statements. The other answers are not required procedures. (ID: 9393)

32. (b) A CPA should not accept an engagement if the CPA's name will be used in conjunction with a financial projection that will be distributed to those who will not be negotiating directly with the responsible party (unless the projection is used to supplement a financial forecast which was not indicated by this question). The responsible party is the person(s) who are responsible for the assumptions underlying the prospective financial information. The responsible party is usually management, but it can be persons outside the entity, for example, a party considering acquiring the entity. The attestation standards for prospective financial statements distinguish between forecasts and projections. Relevant to this question, a financial projection is not appropriate for general use. General use refers to the use of the statements by persons with whom the responsible party is not negotiating directly, for example, in an offering statement of an entity's debt or equity interests. Because recipients of prospective financial statements distributed for general use are unable to ask the responsible party directly about the presentation, the presentation most useful to them is one that portrays, to the best of the responsible party's knowledge and belief, the expected results. Thus, only a financial forecast is appropriate for general use. Limited use refers to the use of the statements by the responsible party alone or by the responsible party and third parties with whom the responsible party is negotiating directly. Examples include use in negotiations for a bank loan, submission to a regulatory agency (submission to a regulatory agency is considered limited use even though, by law or regulation, it may be a matter of public record), and use solely within the entity. Thus, the other answers describe acceptable engagements as long as the report includes an appropriately worded restriction limiting its use. (ID: 9903)

Reporting on Internal Control

33. (d) A paragraph describing the inherent limitations of any internal control structure is one of required elements of the auditor's report on the examination of internal control. The other answers are not required elements. (ID: 5702)

34. (c) Management must present its written assertion about the effectiveness of the entity's internal control in a report that accompanies the auditor's report. (ID: 5983)

35. (d) Although the examination of an entity's internal control over financial reporting should be integrated with the audit of financial statements, the two engagements have different objectives and generally differ in scope. However, the procedures are similar in nature. (ID: 400)

Other Attestation Engagements

36. (b) A list of or reference to procedures performed, and related findings, are required elements of a report on agreed-upon procedures. No references to fairness of presentation, effectiveness of internal control, or acknowledgement of sufficiency of procedures are required. (ID: 7028)

37. (a) A report on an engagement consisting of applying agreed-upon procedures should include a statement of restrictions on the use of the report because it is intended to be used solely by the specified parties. In an agreed-upon procedures engagement, the practitioner does not provide an opinion; instead the report should

be presented in the form of procedures and findings. Negative assurance is not allowed. The sufficiency of the procedures is solely the responsibility of the specified parties who agreed to those procedures; the practitioner should disclaim responsibility for the sufficiency of the procedures. (ID: 6028)

38. (c)   In an agreed-upon procedures engagement, a client engages the practitioner to assist specified parties in evaluating subject matter or an assertion as a result of needs of the specified parties. The specified parties and the practitioner agree upon procedures to be performed by the practitioner that the specified parties believe are appropriate. Therefore, the specified parties assume responsibility for the sufficiency of the procedures since they best understand their own needs. The practitioner does not provide an opinion or negative assurance. Instead, the practitioner's report on agreed-upon procedures should be in the form of procedures and findings. A practitioner's report on such engagements should indicate clearly that its use is restricted to those specified parties. (ID: 8132)

39. (d)   The practitioner's report on *pro forma* financial information should include reference to the financial statements from which the historical financial information is derived. The statement in answer a. should not be made in any review engagement. Answer b. is incorrect because the report on *pro forma* information is a different engagement from reporting on the financial statements from which the *pro forma* information was derived; thus, the practitioner would not issue an opinion or disclaimer of opinion on those statements. No reference to uncertainty should be made as that is assumed, based upon the nature of the engagement, and the accountant need only provide a conclusion as to whether any information came to the accountant's attention to cause the accountant to believe management's assumptions do not provide a reasonable basis for the effects directly attributable to the transaction or event or that the *pro forma* column does not reflect the proper application of those adjustments to the historical financial statements. (ID: 4733)

40. (a)   A list of the procedures performed (or reference thereto) and related findings is an appropriate component of a practitioner's report on the results of applying agreed-upon procedures. Neither management nor the practitioner is responsible for expressing an opinion. The report includes a disclaimer of opinion on the subject matter. An appropriate title for the report is *Independent Accountant's Report on Applying Agreed-Upon Procedures*; it would not include the term *audit*. The report should include a statement of restrictions on the use of the report because it is intended to be used solely by the specified parties, not a statement that it is unrestricted in its use. (ID: 9399)

41. (c)   Other than the procedures applied to the historical financial statements, the procedures the practitioner should apply to the assumptions and *pro forma* adjustments for either an examination or a review engagement include the determination that computations of *pro forma* adjustments are mathematically correct and that the *pro forma* column reflects the proper application of those adjustments to the historical financial statements. However, the practitioner is not required to reevaluate the entity's internal control over financial reporting. (ID: 7628)

———————————

PERFORMANCE BY TOPICS

Each category below parallels a topic covered in Chapter 13. Record the number and percentage of questions you answered correctly in each topic.

Attestation Standards		
Question #	Correct	√
1		
2		
3		
4		
5		
6		
7		
8		
9		
10		
11		
# Questions	11	
# Correct		
% Correct		

Financial Forecasts & Projections		
Question #	Correct	√
12		
13		
14		
15		
16		
17		
18		
19		
20		
21		
22		
23		
24		
25		
26		
27		
28		
29		
30		
31		
32		
# Questions	21	
# Correct		
% Correct		

Reporting on Internal Control		
Question #	Correct	√
33		
34		
35		
# Questions	3	
# Correct		
% Correct		

Other Attestation Engagements		
Question #	Correct	√
36		
37		
38		
39		
40		
41		
# Questions	6	
# Correct		
% Correct		

Solution 13-2 SIMULATION ANSWER: Attestation Standards Terminology

Definitions	Terms
1. Any declaration or set of declarations about whether the subject matter is based on or in conformity with the criteria selected.	L. Assertion
2. Any unresolved problem that the practitioner had in complying with the attestation standards, interpretive standards, or the specific procedures agreed to by the specified parties.	I. Reservation
3. A presentation that shows, given one or more hypothetical assumptions, an entity's expected financial position, results of operations, and cash flows.	H. Financial projection
4. A deficiency, or a combination of deficiencies, in internal control such that there is a reasonable possibility that a material misstatement of the entity's financial statements will not be prevented, or detected and corrected on a timely basis.	F. Material weakness
5. A financial statement assertion that has a reasonable possibility of containing a misstatement or misstatements that would cause the financial statements to be materially misstated.	J. Relevant assertion
6. Exists when the design or operation of a control does not allow management or employees, in the normal course of performing their assigned functions, to prevent, or detect and correct misstatements on a timely basis.	B. Deficiency in internal control
7. A presentation that shows an entity's expected financial position, results of operations, and cash flows.	U. Financial forecast
8. The person or persons, either as individuals or representatives of the entity, responsible for the subject matter.	A. Responsible party
9. A presentation that shows what the significant effects on historical financial information might have been had a consummated or proposed transaction (or event) occurred at an earlier date.	K. *Pro forma* financial information
10. A deficiency, or a combination of deficiencies, in internal control that is important enough to merit attention by those charged with governance.	D. Significant deficiency

(Editors, ID: 89464)

Solution 13-3 SIMULATION ANSWER: Research

AT	§	201	.34	(ID: 9242)

.34   The date of completion of the agreed-upon procedures should be used as the date of the practitioner's report.

CHANGE ALERT

QCS 8 (QC 10A), *A Firm's System of Quality Control (Redrafted)*; issued 11/2010

This statement will become eligible to be tested beginning with the July-August 2012 exam window. At that time, only the new guidance will be testable.

In November 2010 the Auditing Standards Board (ASB) of the American Institute of Certified Public Accountants (AICPA) issued Statement on Quality Control Standards (SQCS) 8. It is effective and applicable to a CPA firm's system of quality control for its accounting and auditing practice as of January 1, 2012.

This standard supersedes SQCS 7.

Overview SQCSs use two categories of professional requirements, identified by specific terms, to describe the degree of responsibility they impose on firms, as follows:

- *Unconditional requirements.* The firm is required to comply with an unconditional requirement in all cases in which such a requirement is relevant. SQCSs use the word *must* to indicate an unconditional requirement.

- *Presumptively mandatory requirements.* The firm is also required to comply with a presumptively mandatory requirement in all cases in which such a requirement is relevant; however, in rare circumstances, the firm may depart from a presumptively mandatory requirement, provided that the firm documents the justification for the departure and how the alternative policies established, or procedures performed, in the circumstances were sufficient to achieve the objectives of the presumptively mandatory requirement. SQCSs use the word *should* to indicate a presumptively mandatory requirement.

Definitions The following definitions have been added:

- **Network** An association of entities.

- **Network Firm** A firm or other entity that belongs to a network.

Engagement Quality Control Review—Differences of Opinion

The firm should establish policies and procedures for addressing and resolving differences of opinion within the engagement team; with those consulted; and, when applicable, between the engagement partner and the engagement quality control reviewer.

Engagement Quality Control Review—Engagement Documentation

- The firm should establish policies and procedures designed to maintain the confidentiality, safe custody, integrity, accessibility, and retrieveability of engagement documentation.

- The firm should establish policies and procedures for the retention of engagement documentation for a period sufficient to meet the needs of the firm, professional standards, laws, and regulations.

CHAPTER 14

ACCOUNTANTS' PROFESSIONAL RESPONSIBILITIES

CHAPTER 14

ACCOUNTANTS' PROFESSIONAL RESPONSIBILITIES

I. AICPA Code of Professional Conduct

A. Background
The AICPA recognizes that a distinguishing mark of a profession is its acceptance of a high degree of responsibility to the public. The Code of Professional Conduct requires an unswerving commitment to honorable behavior even if it means sacrificing personal advantages.

1. **AICPA Membership** Membership in the American Institute of Certified Public Accountants (AICPA) is voluntary, and assumes an obligation of self-discipline above and beyond the requirements of laws and regulations. Reference to "member" in this chapter means a member or international associate of the AICPA.

2. **Uniform Accountancy Act** The AICPA and NASBA (National Association of State Boards of Accountancy) have a history of working together to enhance the regulation of the accounting profession to benefit the public and to promote uniformity of regulation among the U.S. jurisdictions. In 1992, the AICPA/NASBA Uniform Accountancy Act (UAA) became effective and subsequently was revised. Uniform Accountancy Rules were added to assist states in implementing the UAA's provisions.

3. **Compliance With All Applicable Regulations & Standards** The AICPA Professional Standards are summarized in this chapter. Regulations, however, vary from state to state and often differ from the AICPA Professional Standards. CPAs, as members of the AICPA, are required to comply with the AICPA Professional Standards, and also must comply with the regulations effective in the states in which they practice.

B. Principles of Conduct
Six articles compose the Principles of Conduct section of the AICPA Code of Professional Conduct. They stress the CPA's responsibility to the public, to clients, and to colleagues. Their purpose is to provide a level of conduct toward which CPAs should strive, and to provide a basis for the Rules of Conduct.

1. **Code Components**

   a. **Rules of Conduct** The rules of conduct govern the performance of professional services by members, within the framework provided by the Principles of Conduct.

   b. **Interpretations of Rules of Conduct** The Interpretations provide guidelines as to the scope and application of the Rules of Conduct. A CPA who departs from these guidelines shall have the burden of justifying such departures in any disciplinary hearing.

   c. **Ethics Rulings** The Ethics Rulings are formal rulings that summarize the application of the Rules of Conduct and Interpretations to particular circumstances. A CPA who departs from these rulings in similar circumstances may be requested to justify such departure. Note: Although there are numerous ethics rulings, only the more heavily tested ones are summarized in the Exhibits included in this chapter. Rather than memorizing a long list of situations, many quite complex, in which rulings have established precedents, knowing the more heavily tested situations and using judgment in the case of any other questions, has proven to be the most effective approach considering the amount of material to cover in preparation for the exam.

2. **Responsibilities (Article I)** In carrying out their responsibilities as professionals, members should exercise sensitive professional and moral judgments in all their activities. Members have responsibilities to all who use their professional services. Members also have a responsibility to cooperate with each other to continually improve the art of accounting, maintain the public's confidence, and carry out the responsibilities of self-governance.

3. **Public Interest (Article II)** Members should accept the obligation to act in a way that will **serve the public interest,** honor the public trust, and demonstrate a commitment to professionalism. A distinguishing mark of a profession is acceptance of its **responsibility to the public**. Members have a duty to discharge their responsibilities with integrity, objectivity, due professional care, and a genuine interest in serving the public. The public relies on the integrity and objectivity of certified public accountants to maintain the orderly functioning of commerce.

4. **Integrity (Article III)** To maintain and broaden public confidence, members should perform all professional responsibilities with the highest sense of integrity. Integrity requires a member to be honest and candid within the constraints of client confidentiality. Integrity also requires a member to observe the principles of objectivity and independence and of due care. **Service and the public trust** should not be subordinated to personal gain and advantage.

5. **Objectivity & Independence (Article IV)** Independence is required for audit and attest services only. Objectivity always is required.

   a. **Maintain Objectivity & Independence** A member should maintain objectivity and be free of conflicts of interest in discharging professional responsibilities.

   b. **Independence in Fact & Appearance** A member in public practice should be independent in fact and appearance when providing auditing and other attestation services. It is of utmost importance to the profession that the general public maintain confidence in the auditor's independence. Public confidence would be impaired by evidence that independence was actually impaired and it might also be impaired by the existence of circumstances that reasonable people might believe likely to influence independence.

   c. **Objectivity** Members in public practice providing services other than auditing and attestation, and members not in public practice have the responsibility to maintain objectivity in rendering professional services.

6. **Due Care (Article V)** A member should observe the profession's technical and ethical standards, strive continually to improve competence and the quality of services, and discharge professional responsibility to the best of the member's ability.

   a. **Quest for Excellence** The essence of due care is the quest for excellence. Members are required to carry out their professional responsibilities with competence and diligence, with concern for the best interest of those for whom the services are performed and the public. Services should be rendered promptly, carefully, thoroughly, and in accordance with applicable technical and ethical standards.

   b. **Competence** The maintenance of competence requires a commitment to learning and professional improvement throughout a member's professional life.

   c. **Plan & Supervise** A member is required to plan and supervise adequately all professional activities for which the member has responsibility.

7. **Scope & Nature of Services (Article VI)** A member in public practice should observe the Principles of the Code of Professional Conduct in determining the scope and nature of services to be provided. Members of the AICPA should practice in **firms** that maintain adequate internal quality control procedures, determine whether the scope and nature of other

services provided to an audit client would create a conflict of interest, and assess whether an activity is consistent with their role as professionals.

C.   Independence (Rule 101)
A member in public practice shall be independent in the performance of professional services. In the performance of professional services requiring independence, a member should consult the rules of the appropriate state board of accountancy; state CPA society; the Public Company Accounting Oversight Board (PCAOB) and the U.S. Securities and Exchange Commission (SEC), if the member's report will be filed with the SEC; the U.S. Department of Labor (DOL), if the report will be filed with the DOL; the Government Accountability Office (GAO), if law, regulation, agreement, policy, or contract requires the member's report to be filed under GAO regulations; and any organization that issues or enforces standards of independence applicable to the engagement. Such organizations may have independence requirements or rulings that differ from (and may be more restrictive than) those of the AICPA.

Exhibit 1 ▶ Ethics Rulings on Independence Not Impaired

Independence is **not** considered to be impaired in these following situations:
- A member provides extensive advisory services to a client. (ET 191-8)
- A member holds a membership in a social club, providing the membership is essentially a social matter and the member does not take part in its management. (ET 191-17)
- A member has a checking or savings account, or a certificate of deposit or money market accounts at a client financial institution, providing the accounts are fully insured by the appropriate state or federal government deposit insurance agencies, or the amount uninsured is immaterial to the member or the member's firm. (ET 191-70)
- A member leases property to or from a client and the lease qualifies as an operating lease under GAAP, providing the lease is comparable to other similar leases and all the terms of the lease are currently met. (ET 191-91)

1.   Independence Impaired (Interpretation 101-1) Certain transactions, interests, or relationships are considered to impair independence.

   a.   Transactions & Interest During the period of the professional engagement, or at the time of expressing an opinion, the following are considered to impair independence.

   (1)   Financial Interest Direct or material indirect financial interest in the client. A direct financial interest will impair independence even if it is immaterial. This applies also to a situation where the member or the member's firm is trustee, executor, or administrator of any estate that had acquired or was committed to acquire any direct or material indirect financial interest in the client and

   (a)   Member (individually or with others) had investment decision authority for the trust or estate or

   (b)   Trust or estate owned or was committed to acquire more than 10 percent of the client's outstanding equity securities or other ownership interests or

   (c)   Trust's or estate's holdings value in the client exceeded 10 percent of the total assets of the trust or estate.

   (2)   Business Investment Business investment with the client, any of its officers, directors, or principal stockholders that is material in relation to the member's net worth or to the net worth of the member's firm.

   (3)   Loans Loan to or from the client or any officer, director, or principal stockholder of the client except in the case of certain grandfathered loans and certain other permitted loans.

Exhibit 2 ▶ Ethics Rulings on Impaired Independence

Independence is considered to be impaired in the following situations:

- Fees for professional services rendered for more than one year prior to the date of the current year's report are not collected before the current year's report is issued. This includes billed and unbilled fees and notes receivable arising from such fees. It does not include fees outstanding from a client in bankruptcy. (ET 191-52)
- A member leases property to or from a client and the lease qualifies as a capital lease under GAAP. Independence would be considered impaired because the lease would be considered to be a loan. (ET 191-91)
- A member is an officer, director, or principal shareholder of an entity that has a loan to or from the member's client and the member has control over the entity, unless the loan is a permitted loan under Interpretation 101-5. (ET 191-110)
- A member serves as an executor or trustee of the estate of an individual who owns the majority of a client's stock. (ET 191-11)
- A member who is a partner or professional employee of the firm served as an elected legislator for a city at the same time his or her firm was engaged to perform the city's attest engagement, even though the city manager is an elected official rather than an appointee of the legislature. (ET 191-10)
- A member serves as a trustee of a charitable foundation and the foundation is the sole beneficiary of the estate of the foundation's deceased organizer—independence would be considered to be impaired with respect to both the foundation and the estate. (ET 191-12)
- Any partner or professional employee of the firm serves on a committee that administers a client's deferred compensation program because such service constitutes participation in the client's management functions. The partner or professional employee could however render consulting assistance without joining the committee. (ET 191-19)

b. **Relationship** During the period covered by the financial statements, in addition to the time periods covered (see a., above), the following also are considered to impair independence.

   (1) **Management** Director, officer, or employee, or in any capacity equivalent to that of a member of management.

   (2) **Client** A relationship with the client as a promoter, underwriter, voting trustee.

   (3) **Trustee** Trustee for any pension or profit-sharing trust of the client.

c. **Application of Independence Rules** A key position is a position in which an individual has: primary responsibility for significant accounting functions that support material components of the financial statements; primary responsibility for the preparation of the financial statements; or the ability to exercise influence over the contents of the financial statements, including when the individual is a member of the board of directors or similar governing body, chief executive officer, president, chief financial officer, chief operating officer, general counsel, chief accounting officer, controller, director of internal audit, director of financial reporting, treasurer, or any equivalent position. For purposes of attest engagements not involving a client's financial statements, a key position is one in which an individual is primarily responsible for, or able to influence, the subject matter of the attest engagement.

   (1) **Members Formerly Employed by, or Otherwise Associated With, Client** An individual who formerly was employed by a client or associated with a client as an officer, director, promoter, underwriter, voting trustee, or trustee for a pension or profit-sharing trust of the client would impair the firm's independence if the individual:

(a) Participated on the attest engagement team or was an individual in a position to influence the attest engagement for the client when the attest engagement covers any period that includes the former employment or association with that client; or

(b) Was otherwise a member with respect to the client, unless the individual first dissociates from the client by: (1) terminating any relationships with the client; (2) disposing of any direct or material indirect financial interest in the client; (3) collecting or repaying any loans to or from the client, except for loans specifically permitted or grandfathered; (4) ceasing to participate in all employee benefit plans sponsored by the client, unless the client is legally required to allow the individual to participate in the plan (for example, COBRA) and the individual pays 100% of the cost of the participation on a current basis; and (5) liquidating or transferring all vested benefits in the client's defined benefit plans, defined contribution plans, deferred compensation plans, and other similar arrangements at the earliest date permitted under the plan. (However, liquidation or transfer is not required if a penalty significant to the benefits is imposed upon liquidation or transfer.)

(2) **Member's Immediate Family** A member's immediate family (spouse, spousal equivalent, or dependent) is subject to Rule 101, Independence (and its interpretations and rulings), but with some exceptions. The exceptions are that independence would not be considered impaired solely as a result of the following.

(a) An individual in a member's immediate family was employed by the client in a position other than a key position.

(b) In connection with her/his employment, an individual in the immediate family of one of the following members participated in a retirement, savings, compensation, or similar plan that is a client, is sponsored by a client, or that invests in a client (provided such plan normally is offered to all employees in similar positions): (1) a partner or manager who provides ten or more hours of nonattest services to the client; or (2) any partner in the office in which the lead attest engagement partner primarily practices in connection with the attest engagement.

(3) **Close Relatives** Independence would be considered impaired with respect to close relatives (parent, sibling, or nondependent child) if:

(a) An individual participating on the attest engagement team has a close relative who had a key position with the client, or a financial interest in the client that was material to the close relative and of which the individual has knowledge or enabled the close relative to exercise significant influence over the client.

(b) An individual in a position to influence the attest engagement or any partner in the office in which the lead attest engagement partner primarily practices in connection with the attest engagement has a close relative who had a key position with the client, or a financial interest in the client that was material to the close relative and of which the individual or partner has knowledge and enabled the close relative to exercise significant influence over the client.

2. **Employment or Association With Attest Clients (Interpretation 101-2)** If a partner or professional employee leaves the firm and subsequently is employed by or associated with that client in a key position, then the firm's independence would be impaired, unless these conditions are met.

    a. **Payments for Prior Services** Payment of amounts owed to a former partner or professional employee for a prior interest in the firm or for unfunded, vested retirement benefits. The amounts may not be material to the firm and the formula used to calculate the payments should be fixed during the payout period.

    b. **No Influence in Firm's Operations** The former partner and professional employee is not in a position to influence the accounting firm's operations or financial policies.

    c. **No Participation With Former Firm** The former partner and professional employee may not participate or appear to participate, and is not associated with the firm. An appearance of participation includes: individual provides consultation to the firm; firm provides the individual with an office and related amenities (for example, secretarial and telephone services); individual's name is included in the firm's office directory or as a member of the firm in other membership lists of business, professional, or civic organizations unless the individual clearly is designated as retired.

    d. **Engagement Procedure Modification** The ongoing attest engagement team considers the appropriateness or necessity of engagement procedures modification to adjust for the risk that audit effectiveness could be reduced as a result of the former partner or professional employee's prior knowledge of the audit plan. Procedures adopted will depend on several factors, including whether the former partner or professional employee was a member of the engagement team, the positions held at the firm and accepted with the client, the time that lapsed since the professional left the firm, and circumstances of the departure. When the former professional will have significant interaction with the attest engagement team, the firm should perform the following.

        (1) Assessment of existing attestation engagement team members to determine their effectiveness in dealing with the former partner or professional employee.

        (2) Review of subsequent attestation engagement to determine whether the engagement team members maintained the appropriate level of skepticism when evaluating the representations and work of the former partner or professional employee, when the person joins the client in a key position within one year of disassociating from the firm.

    e. **Considering Employment or Association With Client** When a covered member becomes aware that a member of the attest engagement team or an individual in a position to influence the attest engagement is considering employment or association with a client, the covered member should notify an appropriate person in the firm.

        (1) Independence will be impaired for an attest engagement team member or an individual in a position to influence the attest engagement who seeks, discusses, or is in receipt of potential employment or association with an attest client, unless the person promptly reports such consideration or offer to an appropriate person in the firm and removes her/himself from the engagement until the employment offer is rejected or employment is no longer being sought.

        (2) A member should notify an appropriate person in the firm when that member becomes aware of a member of or an individual in a position to influence the attest engagement team who is considering employment or association with a client.

3. **Performance of Nonattest Services (Interpretation 101-3)** A member in public practice or the member's firm who performs attest services for a client (which requires independence) also may perform other nonattest services for the same client. The member must evaluate the effect of such services on the member's independence, including compliance with independence regulations of authoritative regulatory bodies.

a. **General Requirements**

   (1) **Management Functions** A member may provide advice, research materials, and recommendations to assist the client's management in performing its functions and making decisions.

   (2) **Understanding of Client's Responsibility** An understanding with the client, preferably documented in an engagement letter, should be established regarding the objectives of the engagement and the client's responsibility to:

   (a) Make all management decisions and perform all management functions;

   (b) Designate an individual who possesses suitable skill, knowledge, and/or experience, preferably within senior management, to oversee the services;

   (c) Evaluate the adequacy and results of the services performed;

   (d) Accept responsibility for the result of the services; and

   (e) Establish and maintain internal controls that include monitoring ongoing activities.

   (3) **Prior to Nonattest Services** Before performing nonattest services, the member should establish and document in writing the understanding with the client (board of directors, audit committee, or management, or appropriate in the circumstances) concerning the: objectives of the engagement; services to be performed; client's acceptance of responsibilities; member's responsibilities; and any engagement limitations. The documentation requirement does not apply to nonattest services performed prior to the client becoming an attest client.

   (4) **Routine Responsibilities** The understanding of client's responsibilities and prior to nonattest services requirements do not apply to certain routine activities performed by the member such as providing advice and responding to the client's questions as part of the normal client-member relationship.

b. **General Activities** Activities that would impair a member's independence include the following.

   (1) Having or exercising authority on behalf of the client to authorize, execute or consummate a transaction.

   (2) Preparing source documents in electronic form evidencing the occurrence of a transaction.

   (3) Having custody of client assets.

   (4) Supervising client employees in the performance of their normal recurring activities.

   (5) Determining which recommendations of the member should be implemented.

   (6) Reporting to the board of directors on behalf of management.

(7)   Serving as a client's stock transfer or escrow agent, registrar, general counsel or its equivalent.

(8)   Establishing or maintaining internal controls, including performing ongoing monitoring activities for a client.

c.   Bookkeeping

(1)   Independence would be impaired if the CPA did any of the following.

(a)   Determined or changed journal entries, account codings or classification for transactions or other client records without obtaining client approval.

(b)   Authorized or approved transactions.

(c)   Prepared source documents.

(d)   Made changes to source documents without client approval.

(2)   Independence would **not** be impaired if the CPA did the following.

(a)   Posted client-approved entries to a client's trial balance.

(b)   Prepared financial statements based on information in the trial balance.

(c)   Proposed standards, adjusting, or correcting journal entries or other changes affecting the financial statements to the client, provided the client reviews the entries and the member is satisfied that management understands the nature of the proposed entries and the impact the entries have on the financial statements.

(d)   Recorded transactions for which management determined or approved the appropriate account classifications, or posted coded transactions to a client's general ledger.

d.   Payroll & Other Disbursement

(1)   Independence would be impaired if the CPA did any of the following.

(a)   Accepted responsibility to authorize payment of client funds.

(b)   Accepted responsibility to sign or cosign client checks, even if only in emergency situations.

(c)   Maintained a client's bank account or had custody of a client's funds or made credit or banking decisions for the client.

(d)   Signed payroll tax returns on behalf of client management.

(e)   Approved vendor invoices for payment.

(2)   Independence would **not** be impaired if the CPA did the following.

(a)   Generated unsigned checks or processed client's payroll using payroll time records provided and approved by the client.

(b)   Transmitted client-approved payroll or other disbursement information to a financial institution, as long as the CPA was authorized to do so by the client and the client had appropriately authorized the financial institution to process that information.

    (c)   Made electronic payroll tax payments in accordance with U.S. Treasury Department or comparable guidelines as long as the client made arrangements for its financial institution to limit such payments to a named payee.

e.   **Benefit Plan Administration** (Note: Department of Labor regulations, which may be more restrictive, must be followed when auditing plans subject to ERISA, the Employee Retirement Income Security Act.)

    (1)   Independence would be impaired if the CPA did any of the following: made policy decisions on behalf of client management, interpreted plan documents on behalf of management to plan participants without first obtaining management's concurrence, made disbursements on behalf of the plan, had custody of assets of a plan, or served as a fiduciary to a plan as defined by ERISA.

    (2)   Independence would **not** be impaired if the CPA did the following.

        (a)   Communicated summary plan data to the plan trustee.

        (b)   Advised client management regarding the application or impact of provisions of the plan document.

        (c)   Processed transactions initiated by plan participants through the member's electronic medium, such as an interactive voice response system or Internet connection or other media.

        (d)   Prepared account valuations for plan participants using data collected through the member's electronic or other media.

        (e)   Prepared and transmitted participant statements to plan participants based on data collected through the member's electronic or other media.

f.   **Investment—Advisory or Management**

    (1)   Independence would be impaired if the CPA did any of the following: made investment decisions on behalf of client management or otherwise had discretionary authority over a client's investments; executed a transaction to buy or sell a client's investments; or had custody of client assets, such as taking temporary possession of securities purchased by a client.

    (2)   Independence would **not** be impaired if the CPA did the following.

        (a)   Recommended the allocation of funds that a client should invest in various asset classes, depending upon the client's desired rate of return, risk tolerance, etc.

        (b)   Performed recordkeeping and reporting of a client's portfolio balances including providing a comparative analysis of the client's investments to third-party benchmarks.

        (c)   Reviewed the manner in which a client's portfolio is being managed by investment account managers, including determining whether the managers are following the client's investment policy statement guidelines, are meeting the client's investment objectives and are conforming to the client's stated investment styles.

        (d)   Transmitted a client's investment selection to a broker-dealer or equivalent provided the client had authorized the broker-dealer or equivalent to execute the transaction.

g. **Corporate Finance—Consulting or Advisory**

(1) Independence would be impaired if the CPA did any of the following: committed the client to the terms of a transaction or consummated a transaction on behalf of the client; acted as a promoter, underwriter, broker, dealer, or guarantor of client securities, or distributor of private placement memoranda or offering documents; or maintained custody of client securities.

(2) Independence would **not** be impaired if the CPA did the following.

(a) Assisted in developing corporate strategies.

(b) Assisted in identifying or introducing the client to possible sources of capital that meet the client's specifications or criteria.

(c) Assisted in analyzing the effects of proposed transactions including providing advice to a client during negotiations with potential buyers, sellers, or capital sources.

(d) Assisted in drafting an offering document or memorandum.

(e) Participated in transaction negotiations in an advisory capacity.

(f) Was named as a financial adviser in a client's private placement memoranda or offering documents.

h. **Executive or Employee Search**

(1) Independence would be impaired if the CPA either: committed the client to employee compensation or benefit arrangements or hired or terminated client employees.

(2) Independence would **not** be impaired if the CPA did the following: recommended a position description or candidate specifications, solicited and performed screening of candidates, and recommended qualified candidates to a client based on the client-approved criteria, or participated in employee hiring or compensation discussions in an advisory capacity.

i. **Business Risk Consulting**

(1) Independence would be impaired if the CPA either made or approved business risk decisions or presented business risk considerations to the board or others on behalf of management.

(2) Independence would **not** be impaired if the CPA either provided assistance in assessing the client's business risks and control processes or recommended a plan for making improvements to a client's control processes and assisted in implementing these improvements.

j. **Information Systems—Design, Installation or Integration**

(1) Independence would be impaired if the CPA did any of the following: designed or developed a client's financial information system, made other than insignificant modifications to source code underlying a client's existing financial information system, supervised client personnel in the daily operation of a client's information system, or operated a client's local area network (LAN) system.

(2) Independence would **not** be impaired if the CPA did the following.

(a) Installed or integrated a client's financial information system that was not designed or developed by the member (e.g., an off-the-shelf accounting package).

(b) Assisted in setting up the client's chart of accounts and financial statement format with respect to the client's financial information statement.

(c) Designed, developed, installed, or integrated a client's information system that is unrelated to the client's financial statements or accounting records.

(d) Provided training and instruction to client employees on an information and control system.

k. **Appraisal, Valuation, or Actuarial Service**

(1) Independence would be impaired if the CPA performed services, individually or in the aggregate, that:

(a) Would be material to an attest client's financial statements.

(b) Involve a significant degree of subjectivity (for example, employee stock ownership plans, business combinations, or appraisals of assets or liabilities).

(2) Independence would **not** be impaired if the CPA either performed valuation of a client's pension or postemployment benefit liabilities or performed services for nonfinancial statement purposes.

l. **Internal Audit Assistance Services**

(1) Independence would be impaired if the CPA did any of the following.

(a) Performed ongoing monitoring or control activities that affect the execution of transactions or ensure that transactions are properly executed, accounted for, or both, and performed routine activities in connection with the client's operating or production processes that are equivalent to those of an ongoing compliance or quality control function.

(b) Determined which, if any, recommendations for improving the internal control system should be implemented.

(c) Reported to the board of directors or audit committee on behalf of management or the individual responsible for the internal audit function.

(d) Approved or responsible for the overall internal audit work plan, including the determination of the internal audit risk and scope, project priorities, and frequency of performance of audit procedures.

(e) Connected with the client as an employee or in any capacity equivalent to a member of client management.

(2) Independence would **not** be impaired if the CPA did the following.

(a) Performed services involving an extension of the procedures that are generally of the type considered to be extensions of the member's audit scope applied in the audit of the client's financial statements (for example, confirming of accounts receivable and analyzing fluctuations in account balances).

    (b)   Performed engagements under the attestation standards.

(3)   The member should be satisfied that the client's board of directors, audit committee, or other governing body is informed about the member's and management's respective roles and responsibilities in connection with the engagement. The member also should ensure that client management:

    (a)   Designates a competent individual or individuals, preferably within senior management, to be responsible for the internal audit function;

    (b)   Determines the scope, risk, and frequency of internal audit activities, including those to be performed by the member providing internal audit assistance services;

    (c)   Evaluates the findings and results arising from the internal audit activities, including those performed by the member providing internal audit assistance services; and

    (d)   Evaluates the adequacy of the audit procedures performed and the findings resulting from the performance of those procedures by, among other things, obtaining reports from the member.

4.   **Honorary Directorships & Trusteeships of NPOs (Interpretation 101-4)** A not-for-profit organization that limits its activities to performing charitable, religious, civic, or similar functions may seek to gain the prestige of a member's name by asking the member to serve on its board of directors or trustees. The member may do so and be associated with the organization's financial statements as long as the position is purely honorary, all letterheads and material circulated to outside parties that identify the member as a director or trustee clearly indicate that the position is honorary, and the member does not vote or in any other way participate in management functions.

5.   **Permitted Loans From Financial Institution Clients (Interpretation 101-5)** Generally, independence is considered to be impaired if, after May 2002, a member obtains a loan from an entity that is a client requiring independence at the time of obtaining the loan.

    a.   **Grandfathered Loans** Certain loans are grandfathered in the interpretations and are not considered to impair independence. The grandfathered loans must have been obtained from a financial institution under its normal lending procedures, terms, and requirements, and be current as to all terms. The types of grandfathered loans include home mortgages, other fully collateralized, secured loans and unsecured loans that are immaterial to the member's net worth. Grandfathered loans include loans that were obtained: (1) from a financial institution prior to its becoming a client requiring independence, (2) from a financial institution client not requiring independence, or (3) after May 2002, from a financial institute client requiring independence by a borrower prior to becoming a member in respect to the client.

    b.   **Other Permitted Loans** Only the following personal loans are permitted from a financial institution client for which independence is required. These loans and leases must be obtained under normal lending procedures, terms, and requirements, and must be kept current as to all terms, at all times.

    (1)   Car loans and leases collateralized by the vehicles.

    (2)   Loans fully collateralized by the cash surrender value of an insurance policy.

    (3)   Loans fully collateralized by cash deposits at the same financial institute.

   (4) Aggregate outstanding balances from credit cards and overdraft reserve accounts that are reduced to $10,000 or less on a current basis, taking into consideration the payment due date and any grace period.

6. **Actual or Threatened Litigation (Interpretation 101-6)** When the auditor concludes that independence is impaired, the auditor should either resign from the engagement or cease any audit work then in progress until the issues can be resolved between the parties, or disclaim an opinion because of a lack of independence. Independence is no longer impaired when a resolution is reached and the matters at issue no longer have any effect on the relationship between the auditor and the client.

  a. **Client & Member** Threatened or actual litigation may create an adverse relationship between the client and the CPA. This situation may affect management's willingness to disclose data to the CPA, as well as the CPA's objectivity in regard to the client. Since this is a complex area, it is impossible to pinpoint where independence becomes impaired. However, the Interpretation offers the following guidelines.

   (1) Independence would be impaired when:

    (a) Current management begins litigation alleging deficiencies in the audit work the CPA performed for the client.

    (b) The auditor begins litigation against current management alleging management fraud or deceit.

    (c) Current management has expressed the intention to begin litigation against the auditor alleging deficiencies in the audit work the CPA performed for the client as long as the CPA feels that it is probable that the claim will be filed.

   (2) Independence usually will not be impaired in the case of threatened or actual litigation that is not related to the audit performed for the client for an amount that is not material to the CPA's firm or to the financial statements of the client. Examples include disputes over billings for services or results of tax or consulting advice.

  b. **Security Holders** Independence is not impaired solely because of primary litigation in which the CPA and the client are defendants, for example, in the case of a *class action* suit. However, if there are cross-claims alleging that the auditor is responsible for the deficiencies that gave rise to the suit or alleging fraud or deceit by current management, the issue of independence should be examined carefully. The Interpretation provides the following guidelines. Independence usually is not impaired by:

   (1) Cross-claims filed to protect a right to legal redress in the event of a future adverse decision in the primary litigation. However, if there is a significant risk that the cross-claim will result in a settlement or judgment that is material to either the CPA's firm or the financial statements, independence is impaired.

   (2) The assertion of cross-claims against the auditor by underwriters if no such claims are asserted by the company or its current management.

   (3) A cross-claim filed against the auditor by someone who is also an officer or director of one of the auditor's other clients.

  c. **Third Parties** Independence usually will not be impaired because of third-party litigation against the auditor by a lending institution, other creditor, security holder, or insurance company alleging reliance on the financial statements examined by the auditor as a basis for extending credit or insurance coverage to the client. In cases where the real party in interest in the litigation (e.g., the other creditor) is also a client of the auditor (*the plaintiff client*), independence with respect to the plaintiff client may be impaired if the litigation involves an amount that would be material to either the CPA's firm or the plaintiff client's financial statements.

7. **Financial Interests in Nonclients (Interpretation 101-8)**

   a. **Client Parent/Nonclient Subsidiary** A member's independence is considered impaired when the member owns any direct or material indirect financial interest in a nonclient subsidiary that is material to the client parent. If the nonclient subsidiary is immaterial to the client, a member's material investment that allows the member to exercise significant influence over the nonclient subsidiary impairs independence.

   b. **Client Subsidiary/Nonclient Parent** Where a client investee (subsidiary) is material to nonclient investor (parent), any direct or material indirect financial interest of a member in the nonclient investor would be considered to impair the member's independence. If the client investee is immaterial to the nonclient investor, and if a member's financial interest in the nonclient investor allows the member to exercise significant influence over the actions of the nonclient investor, the member's independence would be considered impaired.

   c. **Other** Other relationships, such as those involving brother-sister common control or client-nonclient joint ventures, may affect the appearance of independence. Considerations include materiality of financial interest, the degree of influence the member may exercise, and the degree of influence to which the member may be subject.

8. **Governmental Financial Statements (Interpretation 101-10)** A financial reporting entity's basic financial statements, issued in conformity with U.S. GAAP (generally accepted accounting principles) include the government-wide financial statements, the fund financial statements and other entities disclosed in the notes to the basic financial statements. Entities that should be disclosed in the notes to the basic financial statements include, but are not limited to, related organizations, joint ventures, jointly governed organizations, and component units of another government with characteristics of a joint venture or jointly governed organization.

   a. **Auditor of Financial Reporting Entity** A member issuing a report on the basic financial statements of the financial reporting entity must be independent of the financial reporting entity. A member and her/his immediate family should not hold a key position with a major fund, nonmajor fund, internal service fund, fiduciary fund, or component unit of the financial reporting entity or other entity that should be disclosed in the notes to the basic financial statements. Independence is not required with respect to:

      (1) Any major or nonmajor fund, internal service fund, fiduciary fund, or component unit or other entities disclosed in the financial statements, where the primary auditor explicitly states reliance on other auditors reports thereon.

      (2) An entity disclosed in the notes to the basic financial statements, if the financial reporting entity is not financially accountable for the organization and the required disclosure does not include financial information.

   b. **Auditor of Fund or Component Unit**

      (1) A member who is auditing the financial statements of a fund or component unit of the financial reporting entity that should be disclosed in the notes to the basic financial statements of the financial reporting entity, but is not auditing the primary government, should be independent with respect to those financial statements that the member is reporting upon.

(2)   The member is not required to be independent of the primary government or other funds or component units of the reporting entity or entities that should be disclosed in the notes to the basic financial statements.

(3)   The member and her/his immediate family should not hold a key position within the primary government.

9.   **Cooperative Arrangements With Clients (Interpretation 101-12)** Independence will be considered to be impaired if a member's firm had any cooperative arrangement with the client that was material to the member's firm or to the client.

a.   **Examples** Examples of cooperative arrangements are a prime contractor/subcontractor agreement to provide services or products to a third party, and a joint venture to develop or market production services.

b.   **Joint Participation** Joint participation is not ordinarily a cooperative arrangement, if the participation of the firm and the client are governed by separate agreements or arrangements **and** they assume no responsibility for each other **and** neither party has the authority to act as the representative or agent of the other party.

10.   **Alternative Practice Structures (Interpretation 101-14)** The Professional Ethics Executive Committee has issued additional independence rules for alternative practice structures (APSs) which are intended to be conceptual and applicable, in spirit and in substance, to all structures where the "traditional firm" engaged in attest services is aligned closely with another organization, public or private, that performs other professional services.

a.   In many nontraditional structures, a substantial (the nonattest) portion of a CPA's practice is conducted under public or private ownership, and the attest portion of the practice is conducted through a separate firm owned and controlled by the CPA. All such structures must comply with applicable state laws and regulations and Rule 505 of the Code of Professional Conduct (*Form of Organization and Name*) and the elements of quality control are required to ensure that the public interest is protected adequately. This means that all services performed by CPAs and persons over whom they have control must be in compliance with applicable standards, and all other firms providing attest services must be enrolled in an AICPA-approved practice-monitoring program. Most importantly, the CPAs are responsible, financially and otherwise, for all the attest work performed.

b.   Additional rules specified in this interpretation apply to direct superiors and indirect superiors and other entities. Direct superiors are those persons that can directly control the activities of the owner or managerial employee involved in the alternative practice structure. Persons considered direct superiors and entities over whose activities such persons can exercise significant influence are subject to all the same independence requirements as a member.

c.   Indirect superiors and other entities are those persons who are one or more levels above the persons included in the category of direct superior, and includes the spouses, cohabitants, and dependent persons of the indirect superior. Indirect superiors and other entities may not have a relationship with an attest client of a member that is material or allows such persons or entities to exercise significant influence over the attest client. Further, the other entities may not be connected with an attest client as a promoter, underwriter, voting trustee, director or officer. Otherwise, the indirect superiors and other entities may provide services to an attest client of the member that would impair independence if performed by the member.

D.   **Independence Standards Board Statements**
The ISB dissolved in 2001, after the SEC revised independence rules applicable to auditors of SEC-registered entities. Three ISB pronouncements remain in effect; however, only two are relevant to the CPA exam.

1. **Independence Discussions With Audit Committees (ISB 1)** ISB 1 is applicable to any auditor intending to be considered an independent accountant with regard to an entity according to the securities acts administered by the SEC (the Acts). Annually, an independent accountant must perform three duties.

    a. The auditor must disclose, in writing, to the audit committee (or replacement), all relationships between the auditor and its related entities and the client entity and its related entities that, in the auditor's judgment, may be considered to bear on independence.

    b. The auditor must confirm in writing that, in the auditor's judgment, it is independent of the client entity according to the Acts.

    c. The auditor must discuss the auditor's independence with the audit committee.

2. **Employment With Audit Clients (ISB 3)** ISB 3 was issued as a result of concern that independence may be or appear to be threatened when an audit professional leaves the audit firm to join an audit client. The audit professional may not have exercised an appropriate level of skepticism during the audit process prior to leaving the audit firm. The professional may be familiar enough with the audit approach and testing strategy to be able to circumvent the audit process as an employee of the audit client. The remaining members of the audit team may be reluctant to challenge the decision of former colleagues and may not exercise appropriate skepticism or maintain objectivity. ISB 3 describes the following safeguards that firms should implement when their professionals join firm audit clients.

    a. Prior to a professional leaving the audit firm:

        (1) The professional is required to report promptly to the audit firm conversations with the audit client about possible employment. Any professional negotiating possible employment with an audit client must be removed immediately from the audit engagement.

        (2) After the professional has been removed from the audit engagement, the audit firm must review the professional's work to assess whether the professional on the audit engagement exercised appropriate skepticism.

    b. After a professional is employed by the audit client:

        (1) The on-going engagement team must consider the appropriateness or necessity of modifying the audit plan to adjust for risk of circumvention.

        (2) If the professional will have significant interaction with the audit team, the audit firm must take appropriate steps to provide that the existing audit team members have the stature and objectivity to deal effectively with the professional and the professional's work.

    c. When a professional joins an audit client within one year of disassociating from the audit firm and the professional has significant interaction with the audit team, the next annual audit must be reviewed separately by an audit firm professional uninvolved in the audit. This review should be tailored based on the position that the former audit firm professional has assumed with the audit client and any other facts and circumstances that might threaten independence.

E.   Integrity & Objectivity (Rule 102)
In the performance of any professional service, a member shall maintain objectivity and integrity, shall be free of conflicts of interest, and shall not knowingly misrepresent facts or subordinate her/his judgment to others.

Exhibit 3 ▶ Ethics Ruling on Use of CPA Designation by Member Not in Public Practice

> A member not in public practice may use the CPA designation in connection with financial statements and correspondence of the member's employer and also use the designation along with employment title on business cards. However, the member should be careful not to imply that the member is independent of the employer or it would be considered as knowingly misrepresenting facts in violation of Rule 102. (ET 191-65)

1.   Knowing Misrepresentations in Preparation (Interpretation 102-1) Knowingly making, permitting, or directing another to make materially false and misleading entries in an entity's financial statements or records is in violation of Rule 102. In addition, knowingly failing to correct materially false and misleading financial statements or records while having the authority to do so is in violation of Rule 102. Knowingly signing, or permitting or directing another to sign a document containing materially false and misleading information violates Rule 102.

2.   Conflicts of Interest (Interpretation 102-2) A conflict of interest may occur if a member performs a professional service for a client or employer and the member or the member's firm has a relationship that could be viewed as impairing the member's objectivity.

Exhibit 4 ▶ Ruling on Connection With Client Debtor or Creditor

> A member is an officer, director, or principal shareholder of an entity, but does not control the entity that has a loan to or from the member's client. If the member believes that the professional service can be performed with objectivity, and the relationship is disclosed to the client and consent is obtained from the client and other appropriate parties, the rule shall not prohibit the performance of the professional service. (ET 191-110)

a.   Objectivity If the member believes that objectivity can be maintained, discloses the relationship to the client, and obtains consent from the client, the rule shall not prohibit the performance of the professional service.

b.   Independence Independence impairments cannot be eliminated by such disclosure and consent in audits, reviews, and attest engagements requiring independence.

3.   Obligations to Employer's External Accountant (Interpretation 102-3) A member must be candid and not knowingly misrepresent facts or knowingly fail to disclose material facts in dealing with her/his employer's external accountant.

4.   Subordination of Judgment (Interpretation 102-4) If a member and the member's supervisor have a disagreement or dispute relating to the preparation of financial statements or the recording of transactions, the member should take the following steps to ensure that the situation does not constitute a subordination of judgment.

a.   Acceptable Statements If, upon consideration, the member concludes the financial statements, as proposed, represent an acceptable alternative and do not misrepresent the facts materially, the member need do nothing further.

b.   Materially Misstated Statements If the member concludes that the financial statements or records could be materially misstated, the member should make her/his concerns known to the appropriate level of management within the organization. The member should consider preparing appropriate documentation.

c.   **Further Action** If appropriate action is not taken, the member should consider her/his continuing relationship with the employer, and any responsibility to communicate to third parties, such as regulatory authorities. The member may wish to consult with legal counsel.

5.   **Educational Services (Interpretation 102-5)** Educational services are professional services and are subject to the rules of objectivity and integrity. This includes teaching at a university, teaching a continuing professional education course, and engaging in research and scholarship.

6.   **Client Advocacy (Interpretation 102-6)** A member may be requested by a client to perform a tax or consulting services engagement that involves acting as an advocate for the client or the client's position on accounting or financial reporting issues, either within the firm or outside the firm with standard setters, regulators or others.

a.   **Objectivity and Integrity** These services are considered professional services and the member shall comply with the rules of objectivity and integrity.

b.   **Standards** If the client advocacy appears to stretch the bounds of performance standards, the member should consider whether it is appropriate to perform the service.

II. General & Technical Standards

A.   General Standards (Rule 201)

1.   **Professional Competence** A member will undertake only those professional services that the CPA or the CPA's firm has reasonable expectations of being able to complete with professional competence. The member does not assume responsibility for infallibility of knowledge or judgment.

a.   Competence involves the technical knowledge of the CPA and the staff, the ability to apply this knowledge to the particular engagement, and the ability to supervise and evaluate the work performed.

b.   In some cases, additional research and/or consultation with others may be necessary as a normal part of the performance of professional services, and ordinarily does not represent a lack of competence. If the CPA cannot acquire the knowledge, the client should be advised that a competent individual must be engaged to perform the service either independently or as an associate.

2.   **Due Professional Care** A member must exercise due professional care in the performance of professional services.

3.   **Planning & Supervision** A member will adequately plan and supervise the performance of professional services.

Exhibit 5 ▶ Ethics Rulings on General & Technical Standards

Supervision of Technical Specialist on Management Consulting Services Engagements—A member must be qualified to supervise and evaluate the work of specialists employed by the member. The member need not be qualified to perform each of the specialist's tasks, however, the member should be able to define the tasks and evaluate the end product. (ET 291-9)

4.   **Sufficient Relevant Data** A member must obtain sufficient relevant data to provide a reasonable basis for reaching conclusions or making recommendations in relation to any professional services performed.

B.   Compliance With Standards (Rule 202)

A member who performs auditing, review, compilation, management consulting, tax, or other professional services shall comply with standards promulgated by bodies designated by Council of the AICPA.

C.   Accounting Principles (Rule 203)

A member will not express an opinion that financial statements are presented in conformity with GAAP or state that the member is not aware of any material modifications that should be made to such statements or data in order for them to be in conformity with GAAP, if the statements contain a deviation from GAAP that has a material effect on the financial statements taken as a whole, unless the CPA can demonstrate that because of unusual circumstances the financial statements would have been misleading.

1. **Departures From GAAP (Interpretation 203-1)** Proper accounting treatment is that which will render the financial statements not misleading. The member must use professional judgment in deciding when a deviation from GAAP is appropriate. Circumstances justifying a departure include new legislation or the evolution of a new form of business transaction.

2. **Status of FASB & GASB Interpretations (Interpretation 203-2)** The Financial Accounting Standards Board (FASB) has been designated as the body to establish accounting principles. FASB Statements of Financial Accounting Standards and those Accounting Research Bulletins and APB Opinions that have not been superseded by the FASB constitute accounting principles. The Governmental Accounting Standards Board (GASB) has been designated as the body to establish accounting principles for state and local governmental entities.

3. **Employees' Responsibility for Conformity With GAAP (Interpretation 203-4)** A member shall not state affirmatively that financial statements or other financial data are presented in conformity with GAAP if the statements or data contain any departure from a promulgated accounting principle that has a material effect on the statements or data taken as a whole. Representation regarding GAAP conformity included in a letter or other communication from a client may be considered an affirmative statement within the meaning of this rule.

III. Responsibilities to Clients

A.   Confidential Client Information (Rule 301)

A member in public practice will not disclose confidential information obtained in the course of the professional engagement without the consent of the client.

1. **Without Consent** Confidential client information that may be disclosed without the client's permission include the following.

    a.   To comply with a validly issued and enforceable subpoena or summons.

    b.   To comply with applicable laws and government regulations.

    c.   To comply with professional practice review procedures under AICPA or state CPA society or Board of Accountancy authorization.

    d.   To initiate a complaint with the professional ethics division or trial board of the AICPA or other appropriate investigative or disciplinary body. The members of these bodies may not use to their advantage or disclose any member's confidential client information obtained in these activities.

    e.   To initiate, pursue, or defend against in an actual or threatened lawsuit or alternative dispute resolution proceeding relating to the client.

2. **Purchase, Sale, or Merger of Practice (Interpretation 301-3)** A review of a member's professional practice is authorized in conjunction with a prospective purchase, sale, or merger of all or part of a member's practice. The member must take appropriate precautions, such

as through a written confidentiality agreement, so that the prospective purchaser does not disclose any confidential client information obtained in the course of the review. Members reviewing a practice in such a case shall not use to their advantage or disclose any confidential client information obtained in the review.

B.   Contingent Fees (Rule 302)
A member in public practice shall not offer or render services under an agreement whereby the fee is contingent upon the findings or results. Specified services that a member in public practice or the member's firm shall not perform for a contingent fee include an audit or review of a financial statement, a compilation of a financial statement when the member reasonably might expect that a third party will use the statement, or an examination of prospective financial information. A member also is precluded from preparing an original or amended tax return or claim for a tax refund for a contingent fee.

1.   Dependent on Complexity of Service A CPA's fees may depend on the complexity of the service rendered. Fees that are fixed by the courts or public authorities or which are determined in tax matters by judicial proceedings or governmental agency findings are not considered contingent and, therefore, are permitted.

2.   Certain Tax Matters (Interpretation 302-1) In some cases, contingent fees in certain tax matters are permitted. A contingent fee would be permitted when a member represents a client in an examination by a revenue agent of the client's federal or state income tax return, when the member represents a client in connection with obtaining a private letter ruling, when filing an amended return claiming a refund that exceeds the threshold for review by the appropriate taxing authority, or when filing an amended return based on a tax issue that is the subject of a test case involving a different taxpayer or on which the taxing authority is developing a position.

IV. Quality Control Standards (QC 10)

A.   Overview

1.   Applicability of Standard This Statement on Quality Control Standards (SQCS) applies to quality control for a CPA firm's accounting and auditing practice. It describes the elements of a quality control system and provides guidance for the design, implementation, and maintenance of the system.

Purpose A firm must establish a system of quality control to provide the firm with reasonable assurance that the firm and its personnel comply with professional standards and applicable regulatory and legal requirements and issue appropriate reports.

System of Quality Control A system of quality control consists of policies and procedures designed to meet these objectives and monitor compliance. The nature and extent of the policies and procedures depend on the firm's size and operating characteristics. A U.S. firm should have a system of quality control that provides reasonable assurance that work performed by its foreign offices or by its domestic or foreign affiliates meets U.S. professional standards.

Unconditional requirements A firm is required to comply with an unconditional requirement in all cases in which such a requirement is relevant. SQCSs use the word *must* to indicate an unconditional requirement.

Presumptively mandatory requirements A firm is also required to comply with a presumptively mandatory requirement in all cases in which such a requirement is relevant; however, in rare circumstances, the firm may depart from a presumptively mandatory requirement, provided that the firm documents the justification for the departure and how the alternative policies established, or procedures performed, in the circumstances were sufficient to achieve the objectives of the presumptively mandatory requirement. SQCSs use the word *should* to indicate a presumptively mandatory requirement.

2. **Relationship of GAAS & SQCS (AU 161)** GAAS relate to the conduct of individual audit engagements. Quality control relates to the conduct of a CPA firm's accounting and audit practice as a whole, thus GAAS and quality control are related. A firm's quality control system may affect the conduct of individual engagements as well as a firm's practice as a whole. However, deficiencies in individual engagements or instances of noncompliance with a firm's quality control system do not, in and of themselves, indicate that a particular audit engagement was not performed in accordance with GAAS.

3. **Definitions**

    a. **Accounting & Auditing Practice** A practice that performs engagements covered by the AICPA's SQCS, which are audit, attestation, compilation, review and any other services for which standards have been established by the AICPA Auditing Standards Board or the AICPA Accounting and Review Services Committee under Rules 201 or 202 of the AICPA Code of Professional Conduct (ET sections 201-202).

        Although standards for other engagements may be established by other AICPA technical committees, engagements performed in accordance with those standards are not encompassed in the definition of an accounting and auditing practice.

    b. **Engagement Documentation** The record of work performed, results obtained, and conclusions the practitioner reached, also known as working papers or workpapers.

    c. **Engagement Partner** An individual responsible for supervising the types of engagements covered by the AICPA's SQCS and for signing (or authorizing someone else to sign) the report on such engagements. Where required, this individual has the appropriate authority from a professional, legal or regulatory body. Firms may use different titles to refer to individuals with this authority.

    d. **Engagement Quality Control Review** A process designed to provide an objective evaluation, by an individual or individuals who are *not* members of the engagement team, of the significant judgments the engagement team made and the conclusions they reached in formulating the report.

    e. **Engagement Quality Control Reviewer** A partner, other person in the firm, qualified external person, or a team made up of such individuals, none of whom is part of the engagement team, with sufficient and appropriate experience and authority to perform the review.

    f. **Engagement Team** The engagement team includes all employees and contractors retained by the firm who perform engagement procedures.

        •   **Excluded** Specialists as discussed in AU section 336, *Using the Work of a Specialist,* and individuals who perform only routine clerical functions, such as word processing and photocopying, are excluded.

    g. **Firm** A form of organization permitted by law or regulation whose characteristics conform to resolutions of the Council of the AICPA that is engaged in the practice of public accounting.

    h. **Inspection** A retrospective evaluation of the adequacy of the firm's quality control policies and procedures; its personnel's understanding of those policies and procedures; and the extent of the firm's compliance with them. Inspection includes a review of completed engagements.

i.   **Monitoring** A process comprising an ongoing consideration and evaluation of the firm's system of quality control. Its objective is to enable the firm to obtain reasonable assurance that its system is designed appropriately and operating effectively.

j.   **Network** An Association of entities

k.   **Network Firm** A firm or other entity that belongs to a network

l.   **Partner** An individual with authority to bind the firm with respect to the performance of a professional services engagement. For purposes of this definition, partner may include an employee with this authority who has not assumed the risks and benefits of ownership. Firms may use different titles to refer to individuals with this authority.

m.   **Personnel** All individuals who perform professional services for which a firm is responsible, whether or not they are CPAs.

n.   **Professional Standards** Standards established by the AICPA Auditing Standards Board or the AICPA Accounting and Review Services Committee under Rules 201 or 202 of the AICPA Code of Professional Conduct or other standard setting bodies that set auditing and attest standards applicable to the engagement being performed.

o.   **Qualified External Person** An individual outside the firm with the capabilities and competence to act as an engagement partner.

p.   **Reasonable Assurance** The SQCS define reasonable assurance in a fashion similar to AU 230, i.e., a high, but not absolute level of assurance.

q.   **Relevant Ethical Requirements** Ethical requirements to which a firm and its personnel are subject, which consist of the AICPA Code of Professional Conduct together with rules of state boards of accountancy and applicable regulatory agencies, which may be more restrictive.

r.   **Staff** Personnel, other than partners and engagement partners, including any specialists who are employees of the firm.

4.   **Communication of Polices & Procedures** Although communication is enhanced if in writing, it is not required. In addition to the policies and procedures of the quality control system, the objectives they are designed to achieve should also be communicated. Feedback from personnel should be encouraged.

5.   **Documentation of Policies & Procedures** Quality control policies and procedures should be documented. The extent of the documentation depends on the size, structure, and nature of the firm's practice. Usually, it would be expected that a large firm would have more documentation than a small firm and that a multi-office firm's documentation would be more extensive than that of a single-office firm.

6.   **Engagement Quality Control Review—Differences of Opinion** The firm should establish policies and procedures for addressing and resolving differences of opinion within the engagement team; with those consulted; and, when applicable, between the engagement partner and the engagement quality control reviewer.

7.   **Engagement Quality Control Review—Engagement Documentation** The firm should establish policies and procedures designed to maintain the confidentiality, safe custody, integrity, accessibility, and retrieveability of engagement documentation. The firm should establish policies and procedures for the retention of engagement documentation for a period sufficient to meet the needs of the firm, professional standards, laws, and regulations.

B.   Elements of a Quality Control System
Each of the following interrelated elements should be included in quality control policies and procedures: leadership responsibilities for quality within the firm; relevant ethical requirements; acceptance & continuance of client relationships & specific engagements; human resources; engagement performance; and monitoring.

1.   **Leadership Responsibilities** A firm's quality control policies and procedures should require that a firm's leadership assume ultimate responsibility for the quality control system.

Culture of the Firm The policies and procedures should support a culture within the firm that recognizes that quality is essential and this should be reflected in the firm's business strategy. The standard refers to this as the *tone at the top.*

Operational Responsibilities Additionally, the person(s) assigned operational responsibility for quality control should be qualified and given the necessary authority.

Policies These policies should be established:

a.   Management responsibilities should be assigned so that commercial considerations do not override the quality of work performed.

b.   Performance evaluations, compensation (including incentives), and advancement of personnel should be geared to demonstrate the firm's commitment to the objectives of the quality control system.

c.   Sufficient and appropriate resources should be devoted to the development, communication, and support of its quality control procedures.

2.   **Relevant Ethical Requirements** Policies and procedures should be designed to obtain reasonable assurance that the firm and its personnel comply with relevant ethical requirements.

a.   **Fundamental Principles** The AICPA Code of Professional Conduct establishes these fundamental principles of professional ethics: responsibilities; the public interest; integrity; objectivity and independence; due care; scope and nature of services.

b.   **Independence**

(1)   **Objectives** The objectives of a firm's policies and procedures on independence should be:

(a)   Communication of the firm's independence requirements to its personnel and, as needed, to others

(b)   The identification and evaluation of circumstances and relationships that put independence at risk and the elimination of those risks with safeguards, if possible, and if not, withdrawal from the engagement

(2)   **Policies & Procedures** The firm's policies and procedures on independence and objectivity and should include processes in place or requirements that:

(a)   It is notified of any breaches of independence

(b)   Any regulatory requirements for rotation of personnel are met

(c)   At least annually, a firm should obtain written confirmation of compliance with its policies and procedures on independence from all personnel.

3.   **Acceptance & Continuance of Clients & Engagements**

a.   **Requirements** A firm should accept and continue relationships and engagements only when it

(1) Has considered the integrity of the client and the risks associated with providing services in the particular circumstances. Factors to consider include the nature of the client's operations, including its business practices and the attitude of the client's management and those charged with governance about internal control or such matters as the aggressive interpretation of accounting standards

(2) Is competent to perform the engagement and has the resources to do so

(3) Can comply with legal and ethical requirements

b. **Understanding With the Client** An understanding (oral or written per the requirements of other professional standards) with the client about the nature, scope, and limitations of the services to be provided should be obtained to minimize the risk of misunderstandings.

c. **Documentation** The resolution of significant issues that arise should be documented.

4. **Human Resources** A firm needs to have personnel who can accomplish the objectives of a system of quality control, i.e., perform its engagements in accordance with professional standards and regulatory and legal requirements, and issue appropriate reports. Accordingly, human resources policies and procedures should address: recruitment and hiring; determining capabilities and competencies; assigning personnel to engagements; professional development; and performance evaluation, compensation and advancement.

a. **Recruitment & Hiring** Processes should be in place that enable a firm to select individuals of integrity who have the competencies to perform the firm's work and the capacity for further development.

b. **Determining Capabilities & Competencies** Capabilities and competencies are measured in qualitative rather than quantitative terms and can be developed via a variety of methods.

(1) **Engagement Partner** Policies and procedures should provide reasonable assurance that the firm's engagement partners have the competencies needed to fulfill their responsibilities. Usually these competencies will be gained by experience in the types of engagements covered by this standard (in the practice of public accounting), but they can also be gained from other types of relevant experience. If needed, the experience of an engagement partner can be supplemented by continuing professional education and consultation.

Competency Requirements The competency requirements are broad, varied and interrelated. They include:

(a) An understanding of the role of a system of quality control and the Code of Professional Conduct

(b) An understanding of the service to be performed

(c) Technical proficiency

(d) Familiarity with the industry

(e) Professional judgment

(f) An understanding of the client's information technology systems

(2) **Uniform Accountancy Act (UAA)** CPAs are required to meet the legal requirements of the applicable licensing jurisdiction governing public accounting. The UAA is a model legislative statute and related administrative rules designed by the AICPA and the National Association of State Boards of Accountancy. Its purpose is to provide a uniform approach to the regulation of the accounting

profession. Many licensing jurisdictions have adopted the UAA in whole or in part. A firm's compliance with this SQCS is intended to meet the competency requirements of the UAA.

c. **Assignment of Personnel to Engagements**

   (1) **Engagement Partner** The firm should establish policies and procedures that require that the responsibilities of the engagement partner are clearly defined and communicated to that person and likewise, that the identity and role of the engagement partner are communicated to the client's management and those charged with governance. The SQCS includes a recommendation that systems be established to monitor the workload and availability of engagement partners to ensure that they have time to adequately perform their assignments.

   (2) **Staff** Consideration of the nature and extent of supervision is important—factors to consider for this as well as for the selection of the team are similar to the competency requirements of the engagement partner covered in the previous section. Teamwork and training are important so that less experienced members can be brought along.

d. **Professional Development** Policies and procedures should promote the need for all levels of personnel to participate in both general and industry-specific professional development activities in order to fulfill their responsibilities and meet the continuing professional education requirements of the AICPA and regulatory agencies. The importance of passing the CPA exam should be stressed.

e. **Performance Evaluation, Compensation & Advancement** Recognition and reward should be given to personnel who demonstrate a commitment to ethical principles as well as to professional development and maintenance of competence. The size and circumstances of the firm have a bearing on the degree of formality used to evaluate personnel. Policies and procedures should provide that personnel selected for advancement have the qualifications to assume their new responsibilities.

5. **Engagement Performance** Policies and procedures should be designed to provide the firm with reasonable assurance that engagements are consistently performed in accordance with professional standards and regulatory and legal requirements and that appropriate reports are issued. Engagement performance, supervision, and review responsibilities should be addressed.

   a. **Documentation** Policies and procedures should be established to ensure the confidentiality, safe custody, integrity, accessibility, retention, and retrievability of engagement documentation.

   b. **Consultation** Policies and procedures should ensure that consultation takes place when appropriate; sufficient resources are available to enable it to take place; all relevant facts are provided to those consulted; and the conclusions reached are documented and implemented.

   c. **Resolution of Differences of Opinion** A firm should have policies and procedures in place for resolving differences of opinion within the engagement team and between the team and others, including the engagement quality control reviewer. The resolution should be documented and implemented.

      Before Release of Report The engagement report should not be released until all issues are resolved.

   d. **Engagement Quality Control Review** Criteria should be developed to determine when an engagement quality control review should be performed. The review should be completed before the engagement report is released. Accordingly, the review should be conducted in a timely manner and may be done at appropriate stages during the engagement. The extent of the review may depend, among other things, on the complexity of the engagement and the degree of risk that the report may not be appropriate.

No Transfer of Responsibility The involvement of the quality control reviewer does not result in the transfer of any responsibility for the engagement from the engagement partner.

(1) Components of the Engagement Quality Control Review The review should include:

(a) An evaluation of the significant judgments made by the engagement team and the conclusions reached in formulating the report; this should include a selection of related engagement documentation for review

(b) The reading of the financial statements or other subject matter information to determine if the report is appropriate

(c) A discussion with the engagement partner regarding significant findings and issues

(2) Independence & Objectivity of the Review Even though the engagement quality control reviewer is not a member of the engagement team, the reviewer should also satisfy the independence requirements relating to the engagements reviewed. Additionally, when there are enough partners in a firm to make it practicable, the reviewer should not be selected by the engagement partner.

Impairment of Objectivity Consultation during the engagement with the quality control reviewer by the engagement team to assure the acceptability of a judgment or concerning other matters does not necessarily impair the quality control reviewer's objectivity. However, should the nature and extent of such consultations become significant, both parties need to exercise caution to preserve the reviewer's objectivity. The reviewer should be replaced by the firm if impairment does occur.

(3) Documentation of the Review There should be documentation that the:

(a) Firm's engagement quality control review procedures have been followed

(b) Review was completed before the engagement report was released

(c) Reviewer is not aware of any significant unresolved matters.

6. **Monitoring**

a. **Purpose** The purpose of monitoring procedures is to provide a comprehensive evaluation of adherence to all applicable professional standards and regulatory and legal requirements and the firm's quality control policies and procedures; and whether the quality control system has been appropriately designed and effectively implemented so that appropriate reports are issued.

b. **Assignment of Responsibility** Firms should assign responsibility for monitoring to a person of appropriate authority and experience and assign the performance of monitoring tasks to qualified personnel.

c. **Procedures**

(1) Monitoring procedures include:

      (a)   Review of selected administrative and personnel records pertaining to the quality control elements

      (b)   Review of engagement working papers, reports, and clients' financial statements

      (c)   Discussions with the firm's personnel

      (d)   Summarization of the findings from the monitoring procedures, at least annually, and consideration of the systemic causes of findings that indicate improvements are needed

      (e)   Determination of any corrective actions to be taken or improvements to be made with respect to the specific engagements reviewed or the firm's quality control policies and procedures

      (f)   Communication of the identified findings to appropriate firm management

      (g)   Consideration of findings by appropriate firm management who should also determine that any actions necessary, including necessary modifications to the quality control system, are taken on a timely basis

(2)   Monitoring procedures also include *assessment* of:

      (a)   Appropriateness of the firm's guidance materials and any practice aids

      (b)   New developments in professional standards and regulatory and legal requirements, and how they are reflected in the firm's policies and procedures

      (c)   Compliance with policies and procedures on independence

      (d)   Effectiveness of continuing professional development, including training

      (e)   Decisions related to acceptance and continuance of client relationships and specific engagements

      (f)   Firm personnel's understanding of the firm's quality control policies and procedures, and their implementation

(3)   Monitoring procedures can be accomplished through the performance of

      (a)   Engagement quality control reviews

      (b)   Postissuance reviews of engagement working papers, reports, and clients' financial statements for selected engagements

      (c)   Inspection procedures

d.   **Deficiencies** Any system of quality control has inherent limitations that can reduce its effectiveness. Deficiencies in individual engagements do not, in and of themselves, indicate that the firm's system of quality control is insufficient to provide it with reasonable assurance that its personnel comply with applicable standards.

Nature of Deficiencies The firm should determine if deficiencies identified by the monitoring activities are systemic, repetitive, or significant and thus merit prompt corrective action.

Communication The firm should communicate to relevant engagement partners and other appropriate personnel deficiencies noted as a result of the monitoring process and recommendations for remedial action.

Inappropriate Report or Omitted Engagement Procedures If the deficiencies resulted in an inappropriate report or procedures were omitted during an engagement, in addition to determining what further action is needed to comply with professional standards and regulatory and legal requirements, the firm may consider obtaining legal advice.

e. **Complaints & Allegations of Noncompliance** Policies and procedures should be established for dealing with complaints and allegations of noncompliance with professional standards or with the firm's system of quality control.

Clearly Defined Communication Channels There should be clearly defined channels for personnel to use to communicate concerns without fear of reprisal.

Documentation Complaints and allegations and the responses to them should be documented.

f. **Communication of Monitoring Results** At least annually, the firm should communicate the results of the monitoring of its quality control process to relevant engagement partners and other personnel, including the firm's leadership.

Basis for Reliance on System The communication should be thorough enough to provide a basis for their reliance on the system of quality control.

The information should include:

(1) A description of the monitoring procedures performed

(2) The conclusions drawn from the monitoring procedures

(3) A description of any systemic, repetitive, or other significant deficiencies and of the corrective actions taken

g. **Documentation** Policies and procedures should be established to document:

(1) Monitoring procedures, including the selection method of completed engagements to be inspected

(2) A record of the evaluation of adherence to professional standards and regulatory and legal requirements; whether the quality control system has been appropriately designed and effectively implemented; and whether as a result of the foregoing, that appropriate reports are issued

(3) Identification and evaluation of the deficiencies and the basis for determining if further action was needed

C. **Documentation of the Operation of a Quality Control System**
Documentation of the operation of quality control policies and procedures should be sufficient to provide evidence of the operation of each element of the quality control system.

The form and content of documentation is a matter of judgment and depends on a variety of factors, for example, the size of the firm and the nature and complexity of its practice and organization.

The retention period may be longer than that needed for monitoring and peer review activities if required by law or regulation.

V. Engagement Quality Review (AS 7)

A. Overview

1. **Applicability of Standard** An engagement quality review and concurring approval of issuance are required for each audit engagement and for each engagement to review interim financial information conducted pursuant to the standards of the PCAOB.

2. **Objective** The objective of the engagement quality reviewer is to perform an evaluation of the significant judgments made by the engagement team and the related conclusions reached in forming the overall conclusion on the engagement and in preparing the engagement report, if a report is to be issued, in order to determine whether to provide concurring approval of issuance.

B. Qualifications of an Engagement Quality Reviewer

1. **Associated Person** The engagement quality reviewer must be an associated person of a registered public accounting firm. An engagement quality reviewer from the firm that issues the engagement report (or communicates an engagement conclusion, if no report is issued) must be a partner or another individual in an equivalent position. The engagement quality reviewer may also be an individual from outside the firm.

2. **Competence, Independence, Integrity & Objectivity** An engagement quality reviewer must have competence, independence, integrity, and objectivity.

   a. The engagement quality reviewer must possess the level of knowledge and competence related to accounting, auditing, and financial reporting required to serve as the engagement partner on the engagement under review.

   b. The engagement quality reviewer must be independent of the company, perform the engagement quality review with integrity, and maintain objectivity in performing the review. To maintain objectivity, the engagement quality reviewer and others who assist the reviewer should not make decisions on behalf of the engagement team or assume any of the responsibilities of the engagement team. The engagement partner remains responsible for the engagement and its performance, notwithstanding the involvement of the engagement quality reviewer and others who assist the reviewer.

3. **"Cooling-Off" Period** The person who served as the engagement partner during either of the two audits preceding the audit subject to the engagement quality review may not be the engagement quality reviewer.

C. Engagement Quality Review for an Audit

1. **Process** In an audit engagement, the engagement quality reviewer should evaluate the significant judgments made by the engagement team and the related conclusions reached in forming the overall conclusion on the engagement and in preparing the engagement report. To evaluate such judgments and conclusions, the engagement quality reviewer should (a) hold discussions with the engagement partner and other members of the engagement team, and (b) review documentation. The engagement quality reviewer should:

   a. Evaluate the significant judgments that relate to engagement planning, including

      (1) The consideration of the firm's recent engagement experience with the company and risks identified in connection with the firm's client acceptance and retention process

      (2) The consideration of the company's business, recent significant activities, and related financial reporting issues and risks

        (3)   The judgments made about materiality and the effect of those judgments on the engagement strategy

    b.   Evaluate the engagement team's assessment of, and audit responses to

        (1)   Significant risks identified by the engagement team, including fraud risks

        (2)   Other significant risks identified by the engagement quality reviewer through performance of the procedures required by this standard

    c.   Evaluate the significant judgments made about (1) the materiality and disposition of corrected and uncorrected identified misstatements and (2) the severity and disposition of identified control deficiencies.

    d.   Review the engagement team's evaluation of the firm's independence in relation to the engagement.

    e.   Review the engagement completion document and confirm with the engagement partner that there are no significant unresolved matters.

    f.   Review the financial statements, management's report on internal control, and the related engagement report.

    g.   Read other information in documents containing the financial statements to be filed with the SEC and evaluate whether the engagement team has taken appropriate action with respect to any material inconsistencies with the financial statements or material misstatements of fact of which the engagement quality reviewer is aware.

    h.   Based on the procedures required by this standard, evaluate whether appropriate consultations have taken place on difficult or contentious matters. Review the documentation, including conclusions, of such consultations.

    i.   Based on the procedures required by this standard, evaluate whether appropriate matters have been communicated, or identified for communication, to the audit committee, management, and other parties, such as regulatory bodies.

2.   **Evaluation of Engagement Documentation** The engagement quality reviewer should evaluate whether the engagement documentation that s/he reviewed when performing the procedures described above

    a.   Indicates that the engagement team responded appropriately to significant risks

    b.   Supports the conclusions reached by the engagement team with respect to the matters reviewed

3.   **Concurring Approval of Issuance** The engagement quality reviewer may provide concurring approval of issuance only if, after performing with due professional care the review required by this standard, s/he is not aware of a significant engagement deficiency. The firm may grant permission to the client to use the engagement report only after the engagement quality reviewer provides concurring approval of issuance.

D.   **Engagement Quality Review for a Review of Interim Financial Information**

1.   **Process** The engagement quality reviewer should evaluate the significant judgments made by the engagement team and the related conclusions reached in forming the overall conclusion on the engagement and in preparing the engagement report, if a report is to be issued. To evaluate such judgments and conclusions, the engagement quality reviewer should, to the extent necessary to satisfy the requirements described below: (a) hold discussions with the engagement partner and other members of the engagement team, and (b) review documentation. The engagement quality reviewer should

a. Evaluate the significant judgments that relate to engagement planning, including the consideration of

(1) The firm's recent engagement experience with the company and risks identified in connection with the firm's client acceptance and retention process

(2) The company's business, recent significant activities, and related financial reporting issues and risks

(3) The nature of identified risks of material misstatement due to fraud

b. Evaluate the significant judgments made about (1) the materiality and disposition of corrected and uncorrected identified misstatements and (2) any material modifications that should be made to the disclosures about changes in internal control over financial reporting.

c. Perform the procedures described in paragraphs C.1.d. and e. above.

d. Review the interim financial information for all periods presented and for the immediately preceding interim period, management's disclosure for the period under review, if any, about changes in internal control over financial reporting, and the related engagement report, if a report is to be issued.

e. Read other information in documents containing interim financial information to be filed with the SEC and evaluate whether the engagement team has taken appropriate action with respect to material inconsistencies with the interim financial information or material misstatements of fact of which the engagement quality reviewer is aware.

f. Perform the procedures in C.1.h. and i. above.

2. **Evaluation of Engagement Documentation** The engagement quality reviewer should evaluate whether the engagement documentation that s/he reviewed when performing the required procedures supports the conclusions reached by the engagement team with respect to the matters reviewed.

3. **Concurring Approval of Issuance** The engagement quality reviewer may provide concurring approval of issuance only if, after performing with due professional care the review required by this standard, s/he is not aware of a significant engagement deficiency. In a review of interim financial information, the firm may grant permission to the client to use the engagement report (or communicate an engagement conclusion to its client, if no report is issued) only after the engagement quality reviewer provides concurring approval of issuance.

E. **Documentation of Engagement Quality Review**
Documentation of an engagement quality review should contain sufficient information to enable an experienced auditor, having no previous connection with the engagement, to understand the procedures performed by the engagement quality reviewer, and others who assisted the reviewer, to comply with the provisions of this standard, including information that identifies:

1. The engagement quality reviewer, and others who assisted the reviewer

2. The documents reviewed by the engagement quality reviewer, and others who assisted the reviewer

3. The date the engagement quality reviewer provided concurring approval of issuance or, if no concurring approval of issuance was provided, the reasons for not providing the approval

Documentation of an engagement quality review should be included in the engagement documentation. The requirements related to retention of and subsequent changes to audit documentation in PCAOB Auditing Standard No. 3, *Audit Documentation*, apply with respect to the documentation of the engagement quality review.

VI. Other Responsibilities & Practices

A. Acts Discreditable (Rule 501)
A member will not commit an act that is discreditable to the profession. (This and objectivity are two rules that a member who is not engaged in the practice of public accounting must follow.)

1. **Retention of Client's Records (Interpretation 501-1)** A member commits an act discreditable to the profession by refusing to return a client's records after the client has demanded them. A member's audit documentation, or working papers, including analyses and schedules prepared by the client at the request of the member, are the member's property, not client records, and need not be made available to the client. If the relationship of a member who is not the owner of a firm is terminated, the member may not take or retain originals or copies of the firm's client files or proprietary information unless permitted by a contractual arrangement. (ET 591-191)

   a. In some instances, workpapers contain information that is not reflected in the client's records, with the result that the client's financial information is incomplete. This would include, for example, adjusting, closing, combining, or consolidating journal entries, information normally contained in books of original entry and general or subsidiary ledgers, and tax and depreciation carryforward information.

   b. In those instances when an engagement has been completed, such information also should be made available to the client upon request. The information should be provided in the requested medium, provided it exists in that medium. The member is not required to convert information that is not in electronic form to an electronic form. Once the member has complied with the initial request, the member need not comply with subsequent requests to provide such information again.

   c. The member may require that all fees due the member, including the fees for the services (described in a., above), be paid before such information is provided.

2. **Discrimination & Harassment in Employment Practices (Interpretation 501-2)** Violation of any anti-discrimination law, including sexual and other forms of harassment, is presumed to be an act discreditable to the profession.

3. **Failure to Follow Standards and/or Procedures in Government Audits (Interpretation 501-3)** In audits of government grants, government units, or other recipients of government monies, the auditor is obligated to follow government audit standards, guides, procedures, statutes, rules, and regulations, in addition to GAAS. Failure to do so is an act discreditable to the profession unless the member discloses the fact that such requirements were not followed and includes the reasons in the report.

4. **Negligence in Preparation of Financial Statements or Records (Interpretation 501-4)** A member who negligently makes, or permits or directs another to make materially false and misleading entries in the financial statements or records of an entity or fails to correct an entity's materially false and misleading financial statements when having the authority to record an entry, or signs or permits or directs another to sign a document containing materially false and misleading information has committed an act discreditable to the profession.

5. **Failure to Follow Requirements of Governmental Bodies (Interpretation 501-5)** If a member prepares financial statements or related information for purposes of reporting to bodies, commissions, or regulatory agencies, the CPA must follow the requirements of the entity in addition to GAAP. If a member agrees to perform an attest or similar service for the

purpose of reporting to governmental bodies, commissions, or other regulatory agencies, the CPA should follow such requirements, in addition to applicable GAAS. A material departure from such requirements is an act discreditable to the profession, unless the CPA discloses that such requirements were not followed and includes the reasons in the report. Examples of governmental bodies, commissions, or other regulatory agencies include the SEC, Federal Communications Commission (FCC), state insurance commissions, and other regulatory agencies, such as the Public Company Accounting Oversight Board (PCAOB).

6. **Solicitation or Disclosure of CPA Examination Questions & Answers (Interpretation 501-6)** A member who solicits or knowingly discloses any May 1996 or later Uniform CPA Examination question and/or answer without the written authorization of the AICPA shall be considered to have committed an act discreditable to the profession.

7. **Failure to File Tax Return or Pay Tax Liability (Interpretation 501-7)** A member who fails to comply with applicable federal, state, or local laws regarding the timely filing of the member's personal tax returns or the member's firm's returns, or the timely remittance of payroll and other taxes collected on behalf of others, may be considered to have committed an act discreditable to the profession.

B. **Advertising & Other Forms of Solicitation (Rule 502)**
A member in public practice will not seek to obtain clients by advertising or other forms of solicitation in a manner that is false, misleading, or deceptive. Solicitation by the use of coercion, overreaching, or harassing conduct is prohibited.

1. **False, Misleading, or Deceptive Acts (Interpretation 502-2)** Advertising or other forms of solicitation that are false, misleading, or deceptive are prohibited since they are not in the public interest. Examples of such activities include those that

    a. Create false or unjustified expectations of favorable results;

    b. Imply the ability to influence any court, tribunal, regulatory agency, or similar body or official;

    c. Contain a representation that specific professional services will be performed for a stated fee, estimated fee, or fee range when it was likely at the time of representation that such fees would be substantially increased and the prospective client was not advised of that likelihood; or

    d. Contain any other representations that would be likely to cause a reasonable person to misunderstand or be deceived.

2. **Engagements Obtained Through Efforts of Third Parties (Interpretation 502-5)** Members are permitted to render professional services to clients or customers of third parties who were obtained through the advertising and solicitation efforts of the third parties. The member has the responsibility to determine that all promotional efforts are consistent with the Code of Professional Conduct. The reason is that the CPA will receive the benefits of the advertising and solicitation efforts of the third parties. Members cannot do through others what they are prohibited from doing.

C. **Commissions & Referral Fees (Rule 503)**
A member in public practice is prohibited from recommending or referring, for a commission, any product or service to a client or to be supplied by a client, when that member or member's firm provides certain services to the client. Specified services include an audit or review of a financial statement, a compilation of a financial statement when the member might reasonably expect that a third party will use the statement, or an examination of prospective financial information.

1. **Disclosure of Commissions** A member who receives or expects to receive a commission from a nonprohibited act should disclose that fact to the client.

2. **Referral Fees** Any member who accepts or pays a referral fee in relation to a client must disclose such acceptance or payment to the client.

D. **Form of Organization & Name (Rule 505)**
A member may practice public accounting in the form of organization permitted by law whose characteristics conform to resolutions of the Council of the AICPA. The name of the firm will not be misleading. The names of one or more past owners may be included in the firm name.

1. **AICPA Membership Designation** A firm cannot designate itself as *Members of the AICPA* unless all of its CPA owners are members of the AICPA.

2. **Separate Business (Interpretation 505-2)** A member in public practice also may own a controlling interest, as defined by GAAP, in a separate business offering to clients the type of services rendered by public accountants.

   a. In order for independence not to be considered impaired, the separate business, including the owners and the employees, must comply with all the provisions of the Code of Professional Conduct in the operation of the separate business.

   b. If a member owns an interest in such a business, but does not control the separate business, the provisions of the Code of Professional Conduct apply to the member, but not to the separate business or its other owners or employees.

3. **Application of Rule 505 to Alternative Practice Structures** The overriding focus is that CPAs remain responsible, financially and otherwise, for the attest work performed to protect the public interest.

   a. The Council Resolution requires that a majority of the financial interests in a firm engaged in attest services be owned by CPAs. Questions have arisen about alternative practice structures in which the majority of the financial interests in the attest firm is owned by CPAs and all or substantially all of the revenues are paid to another entity in return for services and the lease of employees, equipment, and office space.

   b. As long as the CPAs owning the attest firm remain financially responsible, and comply with the other provisions of the Code of Professional Conduct and bylaws (including compliance with state laws, enrollment in practice monitoring program, membership in SEC practice section if attest work is for SEC clients, compliance with independence rules, and compliance with other applicable standards), then the member is considered to be in compliance with the financial interests provision of the Resolution.

Exhibit 6 ▶ Ethics Rulings on Other Responsibilities & Practices

> - Fees: Collection of Notes Issued in Payment—A member may make arrangements with a bank to collect notes issued by a client in payment of a fee due. (ET 591-2)
> - Newsletters & Publications—A newsletter, booklet, or similar publication may be attributed to a member even if it was not prepared by the member provided the member has a reasonable basis to conclude that the information is not false, misleading, or deceptive. (ET 591-176)
> - Sale of Products to Clients—A member may purchase a product from a third-party and resell the product to a client at a profit. (ET 591-185)
> - Non-CPA Partner—A member in partnership with non-CPAs may sign reports with the firm name, the member's signature and the CPA designation, provided it is clear that the partnership itself is not being held out as composed entirely of CPAs. (ET 591-190)

VII. Consulting Services

A. **Overview**
Consulting services provided by CPAs have grown in the overall importance of the activity to the CPA profession and the scope of services performed. Services are no longer limited to advice on

accounting related matters, but now include a tremendous range of technical disciplines, industry knowledge, and consulting skills.

1. **Consulting Process** This process includes the analytical approach and process applied in a consulting service. It involves some combination of activities relating to a determination of client objectives, definition of problems and solutions, fact finding, evaluation of alternatives, formulation of proposed actions, communication of results, implementation, and follow-up.

2. **Consulting Services** These services are composed of professional services that use the CPA's technical skills, education, observations and experience, and knowledge of the consulting process. Such services include the following.

   a. **Consultations** The practitioner provides advice or information based mostly, if not entirely, on existing personal knowledge about the client, the circumstances, the technical matters involved, and the mutual intent of the parties. Examples of consultations include reviewing and commenting on a client-prepared business plan and making recommendations for computer software for further analysis by the client.

   b. **Advisory Services** The practitioner develops findings, conclusions, and recommendations for client consideration and decision making. Examples include operational review and improvement study, analysis of an accounting system, assistance with strategic planning, and defining requirements for an information system.

   c. **Implementation Services** The practitioner puts an action plan into effect. In an engagement of this type, client personnel may be pooled with those of the practitioners. The overall responsibility of all the activities rests with the practitioner. Examples include providing computer system installation and support, effecting steps to improve productivity, and assisting with the merger of organizations.

   d. **Transaction Services** The practitioner provides services concerning a specific client transaction, usually with a third party. Examples include insolvency services, valuation services, preparation of information to secure financing, analysis of a potential merger or acquisition, and litigation services.

   e. **Staff & Other Support Services** The practitioner provides staff and other support, as needed, to accomplish tasks specified by the client. Examples include the management of data processing facilities, computer programming, trustees in a bankruptcy situation, and controllership activities.

   f. **Product Services** The practitioner provides a product to the client along with professional services to support, use, or maintain the product provided. Examples of product services include the sale and delivery of a packaged training program or the sale and implementation of computer software.

B. **General Standards for Consulting Services**
The AICPA Management Consulting Services Executive Committee issues Statements on Standards for Consulting Services (SSCS). SSCS 1 supersedes the previous series of Statements on Standards for Management Advisory Services, and provides standards for practice for a wider variety of professional services.

1. **Applicability** The general standards of Professional Competence, Due Professional Care, Planning and Supervision, and Sufficient Relevant Data apply to all services performed by members of the AICPA and are contained in Rule 201 of the AICPA Code of Professional Conduct.

2. **Professional Judgment** Professional judgment is to be used in applying the Standards for Consulting Services to specific situations, since the understanding established with the client

may impose some constraints within which the services are to be performed. The CPA is not required to decline or withdraw from a consulting engagement when such limitations are imposed. An example is limitations on the CPA's efforts to gather relevant information.

C.   Additional General Standards
The following additional general standards address the distinctive nature of consulting services. These Standards are established under Rule 202 of the AICPA Code of Professional Conduct.

    1.   Client Interest The member shall serve the client's interest by seeking to accomplish the objectives established by the understanding with the client while maintaining integrity and objectivity. Independence is not required for consulting services.

    2.   Understanding With Client An oral or written understanding should be reached with the client concerning the nature, scope, and limitations of the services to be performed, and modifications should be made to the understanding if circumstances require a significant change during the engagement.

    3.   Communication With Client The client should be informed of the following.

        a.   Conflicts of interest that may occur that could be viewed as impairing the CPA's objectivity. The CPA may still perform the consulting services if the client consents

        b.   Significant reservations concerning the scope or benefits of the engagement

        c.   Significant engagement findings or events

D.   Consulting Services for Attest Clients
The performance of consulting services for an attest client does not impair independence. Members performing attest services for a client should comply with applicable independence standards, rules and regulations issued by the AICPA, the state boards of accountancy, state CPA societies, and other regulatory agencies.

VIII. International Federation of Accountants Code of Ethics for Professional Accountants

A.   Overview
The International Ethics Standards Board for Accountants (IESBA) of the International Federation of Accountants (IFAC) issues the Code of Ethics for Professional Accountants (Code). IFAC describes itself as a worldwide organization for the accountancy profession representing approximately 2.5 million accountants in 124 countries in public practice; industry and commerce; the public sector; and education.

    1.   The Code establishes ethical requirements for professional accountants. A member body of IFAC or firm shall not apply less stringent standards than those stated in the Code. However, if a member body or firm is prohibited from complying with certain parts of this **Code by law or regulation, they shall comply with all other parts of this Code.**

    2.   Some jurisdictions may have requirements and guidance that differ from those contained in this Code. Professional accountants in those jurisdictions need to be aware of those differences and comply with the more stringent requirements and guidance unless prohibited by law or regulation.

B.   Part A of the Code—General Application

    1.   Introduction and Fundamental Principles

        a.   Public Interest A distinguishing mark of the accountancy profession is its acceptance of the responsibility to act in the public interest rather than only satisfying the needs of an individual client or employer.

b. **Structure** The Code has three parts.

    (1) **Part A** Part A establishes the fundamental principles and provides a conceptual framework to use to identify and evaluate threats to compliance with the code (threats) and apply related safeguards or, if none are available, to avoid the threat.

    (2) **Parts B and C** Parts B and C describe how the conceptual framework applies in specific situations. Part B applies to professional accountants in public practice. Part C applies to professional accountants in business.

c. **Terminology** The Code uses the word *shall* to impose a requirement.

d. **Fundamental Principles** The Code requires accountants to adhere to five fundamental principles:

    (1) **Integrity** A professional accountant should be straightforward and honest in performing professional services.

    (2) **Objectivity** A professional accountant should not allow bias, conflict of interest or undue influence of others to override professional or business judgments.

    (3) **Professional Competence and Due Care** A professional accountant has a continuing duty to maintain professional knowledge and skill at the level required to ensure that a client or employer receives competent professional service based on current developments. A professional accountant should act diligently and in accordance with applicable technical and professional standards when providing professional services.

    (4) **Confidentiality** A professional accountant should respect the confidentiality of information acquired as a result of professional and business relationships and should not disclose any such information to third parties without proper and specific authority unless there is a legal or professional right or duty to disclose. Confidential information acquired as a result of professional and business relationships should not be used for the personal advantage of the professional accountant or third parties.

    (5) **Professional Behavior** A professional accountant should comply with relevant laws and regulations and should avoid any action that discredits the profession.

e. **Standard of a Reasonable Informed Party** To adhere to the Code accountants must exercise professional judgment and consider what a reasonable informed party would conclude in the same circumstances.

f. **Qualitative and Quantitative Factors** Both should be considered when evaluating the significance of a threat.

g. **When Safeguards Against Threats Are Not Available** If the threat is too significant or safeguards are not available or cannot be applied, the accountant should decline or discontinue the specific professional service or resign the engagement or organization.

h. **Threat Categories** Threats fall into one or more of these categories:

    (1) **Self-Interest** The threat that a financial or other interest will inappropriately influence the professional accountant's judgment or behavior

    (2) **Self-Review** The threat that a professional accountant will not appropriately evaluate the results of a previous judgment made or service performed by the professional accountant, or by another individual within the professional accountant's firm or employing organization, on which the accountant will rely when forming a judgment as part of providing a current service

(3) **Advocacy** The threat that a professional accountant will promote a client's or employer's position to the point that the professional accountant's objectivity is compromised

(4) **Familiarity** The threat that due to a long or close relationship with a client or employer, a professional accountant will be too sympathetic to their interests or too accepting of their work

(5) **Intimidation** The threat that a professional accountant will be deterred from acting objectively because of actual or perceived pressures, including attempts to exercise undue influence over the professional accountant

i. **Safeguards** Safeguards are actions or other measures that may eliminate threats or reduce them to an acceptable level. They fall into two broad categories:

(1) Safeguards created by the profession, legislation or regulation, such as:

- Educational, training and experience requirements for entry into the profession
- Continuing professional development requirements
- Corporate governance regulations
- Professional standards
- Professional or regulatory monitoring and disciplinary procedures
- External review by a legally empowered third party of the reports, returns, communications or information produced by a professional accountant

(2) Safeguards in the work environment

j. **Conflict Resolution** A professional accountant may be required to resolve a conflict in complying with the fundamental principles.

(1) **Factors** The following factors may be relevant to the resolution process.

(a) Relevant facts

(b) Ethical issues involved

(c) Fundamental principles related to the matter in question

(d) Established internal procedures

(e) Alternative courses of action

(2) **Conflict Within an Organization**

(a) Determine if those charged with governance should be consulted

(b) Document substance of the issue, discussion details and decisions

(3) **Unresolved Significant Conflicts** If a significant conflict cannot be resolved, a professional accountant may consider obtaining professional advice without breaching confidentiality from:

(a) The relevant professional body (anonymously)

(b) Legal advisors.(legal privilege)

(4) Resolution Not Achieved If, after exhausting all relevant possibilities, the ethical conflict remains unresolved, the accountant should refuse to remain associated with the matter and decide if it's appropriate to:

(a) Withdraw from the engagement team or specific assignment or

(b) Resign from the engagement, the firm or the employing organization.

2. **Integrity**

a. **Obligation** The principle of integrity imposes an obligation on all professional accountants to be straightforward and honest in all professional and business relationships. Integrity also implies fair dealing and truthfulness.

b. **No Association** A professional accountant shall not knowingly be associated with reports returns, communications or other information where the professional accountant believes that the information:

(1) Contains a materially false or misleading statement

(2) Contains statements or information furnished recklessly

(3) Omits or obscures information required to be included where such omission or obscurity would be misleading

3. **Objectivity**

a. **Obligation** The principle of objectivity imposes an obligation on all professional accountants not to compromise their professional or business judgment because of bias, conflict of interest or the undue influence of others.

b. **Professional Judgment Compromised** A professional accountant may be exposed to situations that may impair objectivity. A professional accountant shall not perform a professional service if a circumstance or relationship biases or unduly influences the accountant's professional judgment with respect to that service.

4. **Professional Competence and Due Care**

a. **Obligation** The principle of professional competence and due care imposes the following obligations on all professional accountants:

(1) To maintain professional knowledge and skill at the level required to ensure that clients or employers receive competent professional service

(2) To act diligently in accordance with applicable technical and professional standards when providing professional services

b. **Professional Competence** Professional competence may be divided into two separate phases:

(1) Attainment

(2) Maintenance Maintenance requires a continuing awareness and an understanding of relevant technical, professional and business developments.

c. **Diligence** Diligence encompasses the responsibility to act in accordance with the requirements of an assignment, carefully, thoroughly and on a timely basis.

d. **Training and Supervision** A professional accountant shall take reasonable steps to ensure that those working under the professional accountant's authority in a professional capacity have appropriate training and supervision.

e. **Inherent Limitations in Services** Where appropriate, a professional accountant shall make clients, employers or other users of the accountant's professional services aware of the limitations inherent in the services.

5. **Confidentiality**

a. **Obligation** The principle of confidentiality imposes an obligation on all professional accountants to refrain from:

(1) Disclosing outside the firm or employing organization confidential information acquired as a result of professional and business relationships without proper and specific authority or unless there is a legal or professional right or duty to disclose

(2) Using confidential information acquired as a result of professional and business relationships to their personal advantage or the advantage of third parties

b. Confidentiality shall be maintained:

(1) In a social environment and within a firm or employing organization

(2) When information is disclosed by prospective client or employer

(3) After business relationships end

c. **Staff** Reasonable steps should be taken to ensure that staff under the professional accountant's control and persons from whom advice and assistance is obtained respect the professional accountant's duty of confidentiality.

d. **Duty to Disclose** There is a professional duty or right to disclose, when not prohibited by law:

(1) To comply with the quality review of a member body or professional body

(2) To respond to an inquiry or investigation by a member body or regulatory body

(3) To protect the professional interests of a professional accountant in legal proceedings

(4) To comply with technical standards and ethics requirements

e. **Whether to Disclose Factors to Consider** In deciding whether to disclose confidential information, relevant factors to consider include:

(1) Whether the interests of all parties, including third parties whose interests may be affected, could be harmed if the client or employer consents to the disclosure of information

(2) Whether all the relevant information is known and substantiated, to the extent it is practicable; when the situation involves unsubstantiated facts, incomplete information or unsubstantiated conclusions, professional judgment shall be used in determining the type of disclosure to be made, if any

(3) The type of communication that is expected and to whom it is addressed;

(4) Whether the parties to whom the communication is addressed are appropriate recipients

6. **Professional Behavior**

   a. **Obligation** The principle of professional behavior imposes an obligation on all professional accountants to comply with relevant laws and regulations and avoid any action that the professional accountant knows or should know may discredit the profession. This includes actions that a reasonable and informed third party, weighing all the specific facts and circumstances available to the professional accountant at that time, would be likely to conclude adversely affects the good reputation of the profession.

   b. **Upholding the Profession's Reputation** In marketing and promoting themselves and their work, professional accountants shall not bring the profession into disrepute. Professional accountants shall be honest and truthful and *not*:

      (1) Make exaggerated claims for the services they are able to offer, the qualifications they possess, or experience they have gained

      (2) Make disparaging references or unsubstantiated comparisons to the work of others

C. **Part B of the Code—Professional Accountants in Public Practice**

1. **Scope** This Part of the Code describes how the conceptual framework contained in Part A applies in certain situations to professional accountants in public practice. This Part does not describe all of the circumstances and relationships that could be encountered by a professional accountant in public practice that create or may create threats to compliance with the fundamental principles. Therefore, the professional accountant in public practice is encouraged to be alert for such circumstances and relationships.

2. **Professional Appointment**

   a. **Client Acceptance** Before accepting a new client relationship, a professional accountant in public practice shall determine whether acceptance would create any threats to compliance with the fundamental principles. Potential threats to integrity or professional behavior may be created from, for example, questionable issues associated with the client (its owners, management or activities).

   b. **Engagement Acceptance** The fundamental principle of professional competence and due care imposes an obligation on a professional accountant in public practice to provide only those services that the professional accountant in public practice is competent to perform. Before accepting a specific client engagement, a professional accountant in public practice shall determine whether acceptance would create any threats to compliance with the fundamental principles. For example, a self-interest threat to professional competence and due care is created if the engagement team does not possess, or cannot acquire, the competencies necessary to properly carry out the engagement.

   c. **Changes in a Professional Appointment** A professional accountant in public practice who is asked to replace another professional accountant in public practice, or who is considering tendering for an engagement currently held by another professional accountant in public practice, shall determine whether there are any reasons, professional or otherwise, for not accepting the engagement, such as circumstances that create threats to compliance with the fundamental principles that cannot be eliminated or reduced to an acceptable level by the application of safeguards. For example, there may be a threat to professional competence and due care if a professional accountant in public practice accepts the engagement before knowing all the pertinent facts.

3. **Conflicts of Interest** A professional accountant in public practice shall take reasonable steps to identify circumstances that could pose a conflict of interest. Such circumstances may create threats to compliance with the fundamental principles. For example, a threat to

objectivity may be created when a professional accountant in public practice competes directly with a client or has a joint venture or similar arrangement with a major competitor of a client. A threat to objectivity of confidentiality may also be created when a professional accountant in public practice performs services for clients whose interests are in conflict or the clients are in dispute with each other in relation to the matter or transaction in question. Where a conflict of interest creates a threat to one or more of the fundamental principles, including objectivity, confidentiality, or professional behavior, that cannot be eliminated or reduced to an acceptable level through the application of safeguards, the professional accountant in public practice shall not accept a specific engagement or shall resign from one or more conflicting engagements.

4. **Second Opinions** Situations where a professional accountant in public practice is asked to provide a second opinion on the application of accounting, auditing, reporting or other standards or principles to specific circumstances or transactions by or on behalf of a company or an entity that is not an existing client may create threats to compliance with the fundamental principles. For example, there may be a threat to professional competence and due care in circumstances where the second opinion is not based on the same set of facts that were made available to the existing accountant or is based on inadequate evidence. When asked to provide such an opinion, a professional accountant in public practice shall evaluate the significance of any threats and apply safeguards when necessary to eliminate them or reduce them to an acceptable level.

5. **Fees and Other Types of Remuneration** When entering into negotiations regarding professional services, a professional accountant in public practice may quote whatever fee is deemed appropriate. The fact that one professional accountant in public practice may quote a fee lower than another is not in itself unethical. Nevertheless, there may be threats to compliance with the fundamental principles arising from the level of fees quoted. For example, a self-interest threat to professional competence and due care is created if the fee quoted is so low that it may be difficult to perform the engagement in accordance with applicable technical and professional standards for that price.

6. **Marketing Professional Services** When a professional accountant in public practice solicits new work through advertising or other forms of marketing, there may be a threat to compliance with the fundamental principles. For example, a self-interest threat to compliance with the principle of professional behavior is created if services, achievements, or products are marketed in a way that is inconsistent with that principle. A professional accountant in public practice shall not bring the profession into disrepute when marketing professional services. The professional accountant in public practice shall be honest and truthful, and not:

   a. Make exaggerated claims for services offered, qualifications possessed, or experience gained; or

   b. Make disparaging references or unsubstantiated comparisons to the work of another.

7. **Gifts and Hospitality** A professional accountant in public practice, or an immediate close family member, may be offered gifts and hospitality from a client. Such an offer may create threats to compliance with the fundamental principles. The existence and significance of any threat will depend on the nature, value, and intent of the offer. Where gifts or hospitality are offered that a reasonable and informed third party, weighing all the specific facts and circumstances, would consider trivial and inconsequential, a professional accountant in public practice may conclude that the offer is made in the normal course of business without the specific intent to influence decision making or to obtain information. In such cases, the professional accountant in public practice may generally conclude that any threat to compliance with the fundamental principles is at an acceptable level.

8. **Custody of Client Assets** A professional accountant in public practice shall not assume custody of client monies or other assets unless permitted to do so by law and, if so, in compliance with any additional legal duties imposed on a professional accountant in public

practice holding such assets. A professional accountant in public practice entrusted with money (or other assets) belonging to others shall therefore:

a. Keep such assets separately from personal or firm assets;

b. Use such assets only for the purpose for which they are intended;

c. At all times be ready to account for those assets and any income, dividends, or gains generated, to any persons entitled to such accounting; and

d. Comply with all relevant laws and regulations relevant to the holding of and accounting for such assets.

9. **Objectivity—All Services** A professional accountant in public practice shall determine when providing any professional service whether there are threats to compliance with the fundamental principle of objectivity resulting from having interests in, or relationships with, a client or its directors, officers or employees. A professional accountant in public practice who provides an assurance service shall be independent of the assurance client. Independence of mind and in appearance is necessary to enable the professional accountant in public practice to express a conclusion, and be seen to express a conclusion, without bias, conflict of interest, or undue influence of others.

10. **Independence—Audit and Review Engagements** This section addresses the independence requirements for audit engagements and review engagements, which are assurance engagements in which a professional accountant in public practice expresses a conclusion on financial statements. Such engagements comprise audit and review engagements to report on a complete set of financial statements and a single financial statement. In the case of audit engagements, it is in the public interest and, therefore, required by this Code, that members of audit teams, firms and network firms shall be independent of audit clients. Independence comprises:

a. **Independence of Mind** The state of mind that permits the expression of a conclusion without being affected by influences that compromise professional judgment, thereby allowing an individual to act with integrity and exercise objectivity and professional skepticism.

b. **Independence in Appearance** The avoidance of facts and circumstances that are so significant that a reasonable and informed third party would be likely to conclude, weighing all the specific facts and circumstances, that a firm's, or a member of the audit team's, integrity, objectivity or professional skepticism has been compromised.

11. **Independence—Other Assurance Engagements** This section addresses independence requirements for assurance engagements that are not audit or review engagements. Assurance engagements are designed to enhance intended users' degree of confidence about the outcome of the evaluation or measurement of a subject matter against criteria. In the case of assurance engagements, it is in the public interest and, therefore, required by this Code of Ethics, that members of assurance teams and firms be independent of assurance clients and that any threats that the firm has reason to believe are created by a network firm's interests and relationships be evaluated. In addition, when the assurance team knows or has reason to believe that a relationship or circumstance involving a related entity of the assurance client is relevant to the evaluation of the firm's independence from the client, the assurance team shall include that related entity when identifying and evaluating threats to independence and applying appropriate safeguards.

D. **Part C of the Code—Professional Accountants in Business**

1. **Scope** This Part of the Code describes how the conceptual framework contained in Part A applies in certain situations to professional accountants in business. This Part does not describe all of the circumstances and relationships that could be encountered by a professional accountant in business that create or may create threats to compliance with the

fundamental principles. Therefore, the professional accountant in business is encouraged to be alert for such circumstances and relationships.

2. **Potential Conflicts** A professional accountant in business shall comply with the fundamental principles. There may be times, however, when a professional accountant's responsibilities to an employing organization and professional obligations to comply with the fundamental principles are in conflict. A professional accountant in business is expected to support the legitimate and ethical objectives established by the employer and the rules and procedures drawn up in support of those objectives. As a consequence of responsibilities to an employing organization, a professional accountant in business may be under pressure to act or behave in ways that could create threats to compliance with the fundamental principles. Such pressure may be explicit or implicit; it may come from a supervisor, manager, director, or another individual within the employing organization. The significance of any threats arising from such pressures, such as intimidation threats, shall be evaluated and safeguards applied when necessary to eliminate them or reduce them to an acceptable level. Examples of such safeguards include:

    a. Obtaining advice, where appropriate, from within the employing organization, an independent professional advisor or a relevant professional body

    b. Using a formal dispute resolution process within the employing organization

    c. Seeking legal advice

3. **Preparation and Reporting of Information** Professional accountants in business are often involved in the preparation and reporting of information that may either be made public or used by others inside or outside the employing organization. Such information may include financial or management information; for example, forecasts and budgets, financial statements, management's discussion and analysis, and the management letter of representation provided to the auditors during the audit of the entity's financial statements. A professional accountant in business shall prepare or present such information fairly, honestly and in accordance with relevant professional standards so that the information will be understood in its context. A professional accountant in business shall take reasonable steps to maintain information for which the professional accountant in business is responsible in a manner that:

    a. Describes clearly the true nature of business transactions, assets, or liabilities;

    b. Classifies and records information in a timely and proper manner; and

    c. Represents the facts accurately and completely in all material respects.

4. **Acting With Sufficient Expertise** The fundamental principle of professional competence and due care requires that a professional accountant in business only undertake significant tasks for which the professional accountant in business has, or can obtain, sufficient specific training or experience. A professional accountant in business shall not intentionally mislead an employer as to the level of expertise or experience possessed, nor shall a professional accountant in business fail to seek appropriate expert advice and assistance when required. Circumstances that create a threat to a professional accountant in business performing duties with the appropriate degree of professional competence and due care include having:

    a. Insufficient time for properly performing or completing the relevant duties.

    b. Incomplete, restricted or otherwise inadequate information for performing the duties properly.

    c. Insufficient experience, training and/or education.

    d. Inadequate resources for the proper performance of the duties.

5. **Safeguards for Ensuring Sufficient Expertise** The significance of the threat shall be evaluated and safeguards applied when necessary to eliminate the threat or reduce it to an acceptable level. Examples of such safeguards include:

   a. Obtaining additional advice or training.

   b. Ensuring that there is adequate time available for performing the relevant duties.

   c. Obtaining assistance from someone with the necessary expertise.

   d. Consulting, where appropriate, with superiors within the employing organization, independent experts, or a relevant professional body.

6. **Financial Interests** Professional accountants in business may have financial interests, or may know of financial interests of immediate or close family members, that, in certain circumstances, may create threats to compliance with the fundamental principles. For example, self-interest threats to objectivity or confidentiality may be created through the existence of the motive and opportunity to manipulate price sensitive information in order to gain financially. Examples of circumstances that may create self-interest threats include situations where the professional accountant in business or an immediate or close family member:

   a. Holds a direct or indirect financial interest in the employing organization and the value of that financial interest could be directly affected by decisions made by the professional accountant in business;

   b. Is eligible for a profit related bonus and the value of that bonus could be directly affected by decisions made by the professional accountant in business;

   c. Holds, directly or indirectly, share options in the employing organization, the value of which could be directly affected by decisions made by the professional accountant in business;

   d. Holds, directly or indirectly, share options in the employing organization which are, or will soon be, eligible for conversion; or

   e. May qualify for share options in the employing organization or performance related bonuses if certain targets are achieved.

7. **Inducements** A professional accountant in business or an immediate or close family member may be offered an inducement. Inducements may take various forms, including gifts, hospitality, preferential treatment, and inappropriate appeals to friendship or loyalty. Offers of inducements may create threats to compliance with the fundamental principles. When a professional accountant in business or an immediate or close family member is offered an inducement, the situation shall be evaluated. Self-interest threats to objectivity or confidentiality are created when an inducement is made in an attempt to unduly influence actions or decisions, encourage illegal or dishonest behavior, or obtain confidential information. Intimidation threats to objectivity or confidentiality are created if such an inducement is accepted and it is followed by threats to make that offer public and damage the reputation of either the professional accountant in business or an immediate or close family member.

IX. Public Company Accounting Oversight Board (PCAOB) Standards

A. Overview
Section 103(a) of the Sarbanes-Oxley Act of 2002 (SOX) directs the Public Company Accounting Oversight Board (PCAOB) to establish "ethics standards to be used by registered public accounting firms in the preparation and issuance of audit reports". Moreover, §103(b) of SOX directs the PCAOB to establish rules on auditor independence "as may be necessary or appropriate in the public interest or for the protection of investors". SOX effectively eliminates self-regulation for the accounting profession. The PCAOB has assumed functions heretofore administered through the

AICPA for public companies that are required to register with the SEC (issuers of securities). In this regard the PCAOB approach is not unlike the AICPA conceptual framework. The AICPA is still the authoritative standard setting board for nonissuers in the areas of audit standards, ethics, independence and quality control standards.

B. **Provisions Affecting Public Accounting Firms**
Provisions that affect public accounting firms include:

1. Registered public accounting firms must prepare and maintain audit workpapers, and other information related to any audit report, in sufficient detail to support the conclusions reached in the report for a period not less than seven years.

2. Second partner review and approval of audit reports is required.

3. Registered public accounting firms must adopt quality control standards.

4. Registered public accounting firms must attest to, and report on, a required management assessment of internal controls to be disclosed in an "internal control report". The attestation is to be made in accordance with standards for attestation engagements issued or adopted by the PCAOB. The auditor should evaluate whether the internal control structure and procedures include records that accurately and fairly reflect the transactions of the issuer, provide reasonable assurance that the transactions are recorded in a manner that will permit the preparation of financial statements in accordance with GAAP, and a description of any material weaknesses in internal control.

5. The PCAOB must notify the SEC of pending investigations involving potential violations of the securities laws, and coordinate its investigation with the SEC Division of Enforcement as necessary to protect an ongoing SEC investigation.

6. The lead audit or coordinating partner and the reviewing partner must rotate off the audit every five years.

7. The accounting firm must report to the audit committee all critical accounting policies and practices to be used, all alternative treatments of financial information within GAAP that have been discussed with management, and the possible effects of the use of such alternative disclosures and treatments on the financial statements as well as the treatment preferred by the firm. In this regard the audit committee needs to include at least one member who is identified as a financial expert.

X. Government Accountability Office (GAO) Standards

A. **Overview**
The Government Accountability Office (GAO) issues independence and ethics rules that apply to auditors who perform attest services under Generally Accepted Government Auditing Standards (GAGAS). The GAO Independence Standards employ a principles-based approach to independence supplemented with certain safeguards for matters such as the performance of nonaudit services. In this regard the approach is not unlike the AICPA conceptual framework and the SEC's principles-based foundation for its independence standards.

B. **Primary Principles**
The standard for nonaudit services employs two primary principles as follows:

1. Audit organizations should not provide nonaudit services that involve performing management functions or making management decisions.

2. Audit organizations should not audit their own work or provide nonaudit services in situations where the nonaudit services are significant or material to the subject matter of the audits.

C.   Comparison of GAO and AICPA Independence Standards for Nonaudit Services
The GAO and AICPA independence standards are generally similar. Each set of rules relies on a principle-based approach to evaluate threats to independence and safeguards that should be built into the audit firm or audit organization to mitigate those threats. Each identifies certain nonaudit services that might create an impairment of independence when performed for an audit client or entity. One difference is an overall assessment of acceptability applies to all nonaudit services under GAO rules. That is, the nonaudit services must be immaterial and insignificant to the subject matter of the audit and must be performed by a separate engagement team. CPAs are advised to follow the more restrictive rules that typically exist under GAO standards. Two examples of where the standards differ are as follows:

1.   GAO Independence Standards prohibit the audit organization from maintaining or preparing the audited entity's basic financial statements and posting of transactions to the entity's financial records. The AICPA Independence Standards are more liberal and permit the recording of transactions for which management has determined or approved the appropriate account classification, or post coded transactions to a client's general ledger.

2.   GAO Independence Standards prohibit the audit organization from conducting an executive search or recruiting program for the audited entity when it leads to hiring or terminating a client employee. The AICPA Independence Standards allow such Human Resource Services when they assist the client in evaluating candidates for positions.

———————————

"On-Demand" Exam

There are four windows annually; the first one starts in January. A candidate may sit for any particular exam section only once during a window. Between windows there is a dark period of about a month when the exam is not administered. Once a candidate has a passing score for one section, that candidate has a certain length of time (typically 18 months) to pass the other three exam sections, or lose the credit for passing that first exam section. Candidates should check with the appropriate Board of Accountancy concerning details on the length of time to pass all four sections. Exam sites typically are open on Monday through Friday; some are open on Saturday as well.

January	February	March
April	May	June
July	August	September
October	November	December

More helpful exam information is included in the **Getting Started** foreword and **Practical Advice** appendix in this volume.

CHAPTER 14—ACCOUNTANTS' PROFESSIONAL RESPONSIBILITIES

Problem 14-1 MULTIPLE-CHOICE QUESTIONS

1. Which of the following is a correct statement regarding the nature and timing of communications between an accounting firm performing an initial audit of an issuer and the issuer's audit committee?

   a. Prior to accepting the engagement, the firm must orally affirm its independence to the audit committee with all members present.
   b. The firm must address all independence impairment issues on the date of the audit opinion.
   c. Communications related to independence may occur in any form prior to issuance of the financial statements.
   d. Prior to accepting the engagement, the firm should describe in writing all relationships that, as of the date of the communication, may reasonably be thought to bear on independence.   (ID: 9923)

2. Which of the following actions by a CPA most likely violates the profession's ethical standards?

   a. Using a records-retention agency to store confidential client records
   b. Retaining client records after the client has demanded their return
   c. Arranging with a financial institution to collect notes issued by a client in payment of fees due
   d. Compiling the financial statements of a client that employed the CPA's spouse as a bookkeeper
                                                                      (R/09, AUD-R, #1, ID: 8851)

3. According to the standards of the profession, which of the following activities may be required in exercising due care?

	Consulting with experts	Obtaining specialty accreditation
a.	Yes	Yes
b.	Yes	No
c.	No	Yes
d.	No	No

   (11/95, AUD-R, #3, ID: 5872)

4. Assuming appropriate disclosure is made, which of the following fee arrangements generally would be permitted under the ethical standards of the profession?

   a. A fee paid to the client's audit firm for recommending investment advisory services to the client
   b. A fee paid to the client's tax accountant for recommending a computer system to the client
   c. A contingent fee paid to the CPA for preparing the client's amended income tax return
   d. A contingent fee paid to the CPA for reviewing the client's financial statements
                                                                      (R/09, AUD-R, #25, ID: 8875)

5. According to the profession's standards, which of the following would be considered consulting services?

	Advisory services	Implementation services	Product services
a.	Yes	Yes	Yes
b.	Yes	Yes	No
c.	Yes	No	Yes
d.	No	Yes	Yes

   (11/94, AUD-R, #6, ID: 5184)

6. The concept of materiality would be **least** important to an auditor when considering the

   a. Adequacy of disclosure of a client's illegal act
   b. Discovery of weaknesses in a client's internal control structure
   c. Effects of a direct financial interest in the client on the CPA's independence
   d. Decision whether to use positive or negative confirmations of accounts receivable
                                                                      (5/91, AUD, #52, ID: 0003)

7. A CPA purchased stock in a client corporation and placed it in a trust as an educational fund for the CPA's minor child. The trust securities were not material to the CPA but were material to the child's personal net worth. Would the independence of the CPA be considered to be impaired with respect to the client?

   a. Yes, because the stock would be considered a direct financial interest and, consequently, materiality is not a factor
   b. Yes, because the stock would be considered an indirect financial interest that is material to the CPA's child
   c. No, because the CPA would not be considered to have a direct financial interest in the client
   d. No, because the CPA would not be considered to have a material indirect financial interest in the client
   (AUD, ID: 0029)

8. On June 1, Year 1, a CPA obtained a $100,000 personal loan from a financial institution client for whom the CPA provided compilation services. The loan was fully secured and considered material to the CPA's net worth. The CPA paid the loan in full on December 31, Year 1. On April 3, Year 2, the client asked the CPA to audit the client's financial statements for the year ended December 31, Year 2. Is the CPA considered independent with respect to the audit of the client's December 31, Year 2, financial statements?

   a. Yes, because the loan was fully secured
   b. Yes, because the CPA was not required to be independent at the time the loan was granted
   c. No, because the CPA had a loan with the client during the period of a professional engagement
   d. No, because the CPA had a loan with the client during the period covered by the financial statements
   (R/01, AUD-R, #2, amended, ID: 7037)

9. A CPA audits the financial statements of a client. The CPA has also been asked to perform bookkeeping functions for the client. Under the AICPA Code of Professional Conduct, which of the following activities would impair the CPA's independence with respect to the client?

   a. The CPA records transactions in accordance with classifications determined by management.
   b. The CPA prepares financial statements from a trial balance provided by management.
   c. The CPA posts adjusting journal entries prepared by management to the trial balance.
   d. The CPA authorizes client transactions and reports them to management.   (R/11, AUD, #13, ID: 9913)

10. In which of the following situations would a CPA's independence be considered to be impaired?

   I. The CPA maintains a checking account that is fully insured by a government deposit insurance agency at an audit-client financial institution.
   II. The CPA has a direct financial interest in an audit client, but the interest is maintained in a blind trust.
   III. The CPA owns a commercial building and leases it to an audit client. The lease qualifies as a capital lease.

   a. I and II
   b. II and III
   c. I and III
   d. I, II, and III
   (11/92, AUD, #2, amended, ID: 2936)

11. According to the profession's ethical standards, a CPA would be considered independent in which of the following instances?

   a. A client leases a warehouse from the CPA under a lease that qualifies as a capital lease.
   b. The CPA has a material direct financial interest in a client, but transfers the interest into a blind trust.
   c. The CPA owns an office building and the mortgage on the building is guaranteed by a client.
   d. The CPA belongs to a country club client in which membership requires the acquisition of a pro rata share of equity.
   (11/93, AUD, #46, amended, ID: 4238)

12. Under the ethical standards of the profession, which of the following positions would be considered a position of significant influence in an audit client?

    a. A marketing position related to the client's primary products
    b. A policy-making position in the client's finance division
    c. A staff position in the client's research and development division
    d. A senior position in the client's human resources division   (R/05, AUD-R, #17, ID: 7883)

13. A company hires one of its board members, a CPA, to issue accounting reports for the company. Assuming any required disclosures are made, which of the following reports may the CPA issue without violating independence rules?

    a. Compilations
    b. Reviews
    c. Audits
    d. Agreed-upon procedures   (R/11, AUD, #40, ID: 9940)

14. An accountant has been engaged to compile *pro forma* financial statements. During the accountant's acceptance procedures, it is discovered that the accountant is not independent with respect to the company. What action should the accountant take with regard to the compilation?

    a. The accountant should discuss the lack of independence with legal counsel to determine whether it is appropriate to accept the engagement.
    b. The accountant should disclose the lack of independence in the accountant's compilation report.
    c. The accountant should withdraw from the engagement.
    d. The accountant should compile the *pro forma* financial statements but should not provide a compilation report.   (R/11, AUD, #48, ID: 9948)

15. According to the profession's ethical standards, an auditor would be considered independent in which of the following instances?

    a. The auditor is the officially appointed stock transfer agent of a client.
    b. The auditor's checking account that is fully insured by a federal agency is held at a client financial institution.
    c. The client owes the auditor fees for more than two years prior to the issuance of the audit report.
    d. The client is the only tenant in a commercial building owned by the auditor. The lease qualifies as a capital lease under GAAP.   (5/94, AUD-R, #4, amended, ID: 4759)

16. Which of the following reports may be issued only by an accountant who is independent of a client?

    a. Standard report on an examination of a financial forecast
    b. Report on consulting services
    c. Compilation report on historical financial statements
    d. Compilation report on a financial projection   (AUD, ID: 4758)

17. According to the standards of the profession, which of the following circumstances will prevent a CPA performing audit engagements from being independent?

    a. Obtaining a collateralized automobile loan from a financial institution client
    b. Litigation with a client relating to billing for consulting services for which the amount is immaterial
    c. Employment of the CPA's spouse as a client's internal auditor
    d. Acting as an honorary trustee for a not-for-profit organization client   (5/95, AUD-R, #1, ID: 5335)

18. A person identified as an audit committee financial expert of an issuer generally must have acquired the attributes of a financial expert through any of the following experiences, **except**

    a. As a principal financial officer, principal accounting officer, controller, public accountant, or auditor
    b. Serving on at least one other issuer's audit committee or disclosure committee of the board of directors
    c. Actively supervising a principal financial officer or principal accounting officer
    d. Assessing the performance of public accountants with respect to preparation, auditing, or evaluation of financial statements   (ID: 9924)

19. According to the ethical standards of the profession, a CPA's independence would most likely be impaired if the CPA

    a. Accepted any gift from a client
    b. Became a member of a trade association that is a client
    c. Contracted with a client to supervise the client's office personnel
    d. Served, with a client bank, as a cofiduciary of an estate or trust   (R/07, AUD-R, #19, ID: 8443)

20. Under the ethical standards of the profession, which of the following investments by a CPA in a corporate client is an indirect financial interest?

    a. An investment held in a retirement plan
    b. An investment held in a blind trust
    c. An investment held through a regulated mutual fund
    d. An investment held through participation in an investment club   (R/08, AUD-R, #25, ID: 8682)

21. According to the AICPA Code of Professional Conduct, which of the following financial interests in the client during the period of the engagement impairs a CPA's independence?

    a. All direct and indirect financial interests
    b. Only direct financial interests
    c. Only direct and material indirect financial interests
    d. Only material financial interests   (R/09, AUD-R, #40, ID: 8890)

22. A CPA purchased stock in a client corporation and placed it in a trust as an educational fund for the CPA's minor child. The trust securities are not material to the CPA's wealth but are material to the child's personal net worth. According to the AICPA Code of Professional Conduct, would this action impair the CPA's independence with the client?

    a. No, because the CPA would not have a direct financial interest in the client.
    b. Yes, because the stock would be a direct financial interest and materiality is a factor.
    c. Yes, because the stock would be an indirect financial interest and materiality is not a factor.
    d. Yes, because the stock would be a direct financial interest and materiality is not a factor.
                                                                                  (R/11, AUD, #41, ID: 9941)

23. According to the profession's ethical standards, which of the following events may justify a departure from a Statement of Financial Accounting Standards?

	New legislation	Evolution of a new form of business transaction
a.	No	Yes
b.	Yes	No
c.	Yes	Yes
d.	No	No	(11/94, AUD-R, #2, ID: 5181)

24. A CPA is permitted to accept a separate engagement (not in conjunction with an audit of financial statements) to audit an entity's

	Schedule of accounts receivable	Schedule of royalties
a.	Yes	Yes
b.	Yes	No
c.	No	Yes
d.	No	No	(ID: 4293)

25. Which of the following best describes what is meant by the term generally accepted auditing standards?

   a. Rules acknowledged by the accounting profession because of their universal application
   b. Pronouncements issued by the Auditing Standards Board
   c. Measures of the quality of the auditor's performance
   d. Procedures to be used to gather evidence to support financial statements   (5/95, AUD-R, #2, ID: 5336)

26. One of a CPA firm's basic objectives is to provide professional services that conform with professional standards. Reasonable assurance of achieving this basic objective is provided through

   a. A system of quality control
   b. A system of peer review
   c. Continuing professional education
   d. Compliance with generally accepted reporting standards   (11/92, AUD, #3, ID: 2937)

27. Which of the following factors most likely would cause a CPA **not** to accept a new audit engagement?

   a. The prospective client's unwillingness to permit inquiry of its legal counsel
   b. The inability to review the predecessor auditor's working papers
   c. The CPA's lack of understanding of the prospective client's operations and industry
   d. The indications that management has not investigated employees in key positions before hiring them
   (R/03, AUD, #11, ID: 7633)

28. Which of the following is **not** a factor a CPA firm should take into consideration when deciding whether to undertake or continue client relationships and engagements?

   a. The possibility of the existence of related party transactions
   b. The client's integrity
   c. The firm's ability to perform the engagement
   d. The firm's ability to comply with legal and ethical requirements   (Editors, ID: 9046)

29. Would the following factors ordinarily be considered in planning an audit engagement's personnel requirements?

	Opportunities or on-the-job training	Continuity and periodic rotation of personnel
a.	Yes	Yes
b.	Yes	No
c.	No	Yes
d.	No	No

   (5/95, AUD, #6, ID: 5624)

30. Which of the following factors most likely would lead a CPA to conclude that a potential audit engagement should be rejected?

   a. The details of most recorded transactions are not available after a specified period of time.
   b. Internal control activities requiring the segregation of duties are subject to management override.
   c. It is unlikely that sufficient appropriate audit evidence is available to support an opinion on the financial statements.
   d. Management has a reputation for consulting with several accounting firms about significant accounting issues.   (R/00, AUD, #2, amended, ID: 6927)

31. Which of the following factors most likely would cause a CPA to **not** accept a new audit engagement?

   a. The prospective client has already completed its physical inventory count.
   b. The CPA lacks an understanding of the prospective client's operations and industry.
   c. The CPA is unable to review the predecessor auditor's working papers.
   d. The prospective client is unwilling to make all financial records available to the CPA.
   (R/01, AUD, #2, ID: 7017)

32. The nature and extent of a CPA firm's quality control policies and procedures will depend on various factors including its

	Size	Operating Characteristics
a.	Yes	Yes
b.	Yes	No
c.	No	Yes
d.	No	No

(5/95, AUD, #5, amended, ID: 5623)

33. Which of the following should be considered in establishing a CPA firm's quality control policies and procedures?

	Performance Evaluation, Compensation & Advancement	Professional Development	Recruitment & Hiring
a.	Yes	Yes	No
b.	Yes	Yes	Yes
c.	No	No	Yes
d.	Yes	No	Yes

(Editors, amended, ID: 0009)

34. Quality control policies and procedures that are established to decide whether to accept a new client should provide the CPA firm with reasonable assurance that

a. The CPA firm's duty to the public concerning the acceptance of new clients is satisfied.
b. The likelihood of associating with clients whose management lacks integrity is minimized.
c. Client-prepared schedules that are necessary for the engagement are completed on a timely basis.
d. Sufficient corroborating evidence to support the financial statement assertions is available.

(R/08, AUD, #24, ID: 8630)

35. Which of the following is an element of a CPA firm's quality control system that should be considered in establishing its quality control policies and procedures?

a. Complying with laws and regulations
b. Using statistical sampling techniques
c. Relevant ethical requirements
d. Considering audit risk and materiality

(5/94, AUD, #15, amended, ID: 4680)

36. Which of the following is an element of a CPA firm's quality control policies and procedures applicable to the firm's accounting and auditing practice?

a. Information processing
b. Engagement performance
c. Technology selection
d. Professional skepticism

(R/08, AUD, #49, ID: 8655)

37. The purpose of establishing quality control policies and procedures for deciding whether to accept or continue a client relationship is to

a. Monitor the risk factors concerning misstatements arising from the misappropriation of assets
b. Provide reasonable assurance that personnel are adequately trained to fulfill their responsibilities
c. Minimize the likelihood of associating with clients whose management lacks integrity
d. Document objective criteria for the CPA firm's responses to peer review comments

(R/09, AUD, #17, ID: 8817)

38. Which of the following conditions most likely would pose the greatest risk in accepting a new audit engagement?

a. Staff will need to be rescheduled to cover this new client.
b. There will be a client-imposed scope limitation.
c. The firm will have to hire a specialist in one audit area.
d. The client's financial reporting system has been in place for 10 years.

(R/10, AUD, #4, ID: 9354)

39. In an audit engagement, the engagement quality reviewer should evaluate the significant judgments made by the engagement team and the related conclusions reached in forming the overall conclusion on the engagement and in preparing the engagement report. To evaluate such judgments and conclusions, the engagement quality reviewer should

    a. Hold discussions with the engagement partner and other members of the engagement team and review documentation.
    b. Reperform audit procedures performed regarding significant risks identified during the audit.
    c. Interview members of the client's audit committee regarding the audit team's performance.
    d. Confirm material revenue account balances. (ID: 9274)

40. According to the PCAOB's *Engagement Quality Review* standard, an engagement quality reviewer must have competence, integrity, objectivity, and

    a. Impartiality.
    b. Independence.
    c. Critical thinking skills.
    d. Initiative. (ID: 9275)

41. An engagement quality review and concurring approval of issuance are required for engagements (conducted pursuant to the standards of the PCAOB) to perform audits and for engagements to

    a. Prepare tax returns.
    b. Prepare prospective financial statements.
    c. Provide consulting services.
    d. Review interim financial information. (ID: 9276)

42. Which of the following services may a CPA perform in carrying out a consulting service engagement for a client?

       I. Review of the client-prepared business plan
       II. Preparation of information for obtaining financing

    a. I only
    b. II only
    c. Both I and II
    d. Neither I nor II (5/96, AUD-R, #1, ID: 6257)

43. A CPA is permitted to disclose confidential client information without the consent of the client to

       I. Another CPA firm if the information concerns suspected tax return irregularities
       II. A state CPA society voluntary quality control review board

    a. I only
    b. II only
    c. Both I and II
    d. Neither I nor II (5/95, AUD-R, #5, ID: 5339)

44. The profession's ethical standards most likely would be considered to have been violated when a CPA represents that specific consulting services will be performed for a stated fee, and it is apparent at the time of the representation that the

    a. Actual fee would be substantially higher.
    b. Actual fee would be substantially lower than the fees charged by other CPAs for comparable services.
    c. CPA would not be independent.
    d. Fee was a competitive bid. (11/94, AUD-R, #1, ID: 5180)

45. Quality control, as referred to in Statements on Quality Control Standards (SQCS), applies to a CPA firm's responsibilities for its system of quality control for its

    a. Auditing services only
    b. Auditing and management advisory services
    c. Auditing and tax services
    d. Accounting and auditing practice (ID: 0033)

46. Which of the following fee arrangements generally would **not** be permitted under the ethical standards of the profession?

    a. A referral fee paid by a CPA to obtain a client
    b. A commission for compiling a client's internal-use financial statements
    c. A contingent fee for preparing a client's income tax return
    d. A contingent fee for representing a client in tax court   (R/03, AUD-R, #18, ID: 7660)

47. Under which of the following circumstances may a CPA charge fees that are contingent upon finding a specific result?

    a. For an examination of prospective financial statements
    b. For an audit or a review if agreed upon by both the CPA and the client
    c. For a compilation if a third party will use the financial statement and disclosure is not made in the report
    d. If fixed by courts, other public authorities, or in tax matters if based on the results of judicial proceedings
                                                                     (R/07, AUD-R, #18, ID: 8442)

48. According to the ethical standards of the profession, which of the following acts is generally prohibited?

    a. Purchasing a product from a third party and reselling it to a client
    b. Writing a financial management newsletter promoted and sold by a publishing company
    c. Accepting a commission for recommending a product to an audit client without informing the client's management
    d. Accepting engagements obtained through the efforts of third parties
                                                         (11/95, AUD-R, #1, amended, ID: 5870)

49. A CPA who is **not** in public practice is obligated to follow which of the following rules of conduct?

    a. Independence
    b. Integrity and objectivity
    c. Contingent fees
    d. Commissions   (R/05, AUD-R, #19, ID: 7885)

50. According to the AICPA Code of Professional Conduct, which of the following actions by a CPA most likely involves an act discreditable to the profession?

    a. Refusing to provide the client with copies of the CPA's workpapers
    b. Auditing financial statements according to governmental standards despite the client's preferences
    c. Accepting a commission from a nonattest function client
    d. Retaining client records after the client demands their return   (R/11, AUD, #46, ID: 9946)

51. Which of the following actions should a CPA firm take to comply with the AICPA's quality control standards?

    a. Establish procedures that comply with the standards of the Sarbanes-Oxley Act.
    b. Use attributes sampling techniques in testing internal controls.
    c. Consider inherent risk and control risk before determining detection risk.
    d. Establish policies to ensure that the audit work meets applicable professional standards.   (ID: 9914)

52. Which of the following actions by a CPA most likely violates the profession's ethical standards?

    a. Arranging with a financial institution to collect notes issued by a client in payment of fees due
    b. Compiling the financial statements of a client that employed the CPA's spouse as a bookkeeper
    c. Retaining client records after the client has demanded their return
    d. Purchasing a segment of an insurance company's business that performs actuarial services for post-employment benefit plans   (5/94, AUD-R, #1, amended, ID: 4756)

53. Which of the following acts by a CPA is a violation of professional standards regarding the confidentiality of client information?

    a. Releasing financial information to a local bank with the approval of the client's mail clerk
    b. Allowing a review of professional practice without client authorization
    c. Responding to an enforceable subpoena
    d. Faxing a tax return to a loan officer at the request of the client   (R/08, AUD-R, #18, ID: 8675)

54. A CPA in public practice may **not** disclose confidential client information regarding auditing services without the client's consent in response to which of the following situations?

a. A review of the CPA's professional practice by a state CPA society
b. A letter to the client from the IRS
c. An inquiry from the professional ethics division of the AICPA
d. A court-ordered subpoena or summons

(R/09, AUD-R, #19, ID: 8869)

55. Which of the following areas of professional responsibility should be observed by a CPA **not** in public practice?

	Objectivity	Independence
a.	Yes	Yes
b.	Yes	No
c.	No	Yes
d.	No	No

(R/08, AUD-R, #21, ID: 8678)

56. A pervasive characteristic of a CPA's role in a consulting services engagement is that of being a(n)

a. Objective advisor
b. Independent practitioner
c. Computer specialist
d. Confidential reviewer

(5/93, AUD, #5, amended, ID: 3901)

57. According to the standards of the profession, which of the following would be considered a part of a consulting services engagement?

I. Expressing a conclusion about the reliability of a client's financial statements
II. Reviewing and commenting on a client-prepared business plan

a. I only
b. II only
c. Both I and II
d. Neither I nor II

(5/98, AUD-R, #1, ID: 6618)

58. Nile, CPA, on completing an audit, was asked by the client to provide technical assistance in integrating a new IT system. The set of pronouncements designed to guide Nile in this engagement is the Statement(s) on

a. Quality Control Standards
b. Auditing Standards
c. Standards for Accountants' IT Services
d. Standards for Consulting Services

(5/94, AUD-R, #6, amended, ID: 4761)

59. Under the Statements on Standards for Consulting Services, which of the following statements best reflects a CPA's responsibility when undertaking a consulting services engagement? The CPA must

a. Not seek to modify any agreement made with the client
b. Not perform any attest services for the client
c. Inform the client of significant reservations concerning the benefits of the engagement
d. Obtain a written understanding with the client concerning the time for completion of the engagement

(11/95, AUD-R, #5, ID: 5874)

60. According to the standards of the profession, which of the following events would require a CPA performing a consulting services engagement for a nonaudit client to withdraw from the engagement?

I. The CPA has a conflict of interest that is disclosed to the client and the client consents to the CPA continuing the engagement.
II. The CPA fails to obtain a written understanding from the client concerning the scope of the engagement.

a. I only
b. II only
c. Both I and II
d. Neither I nor II

(5/95, AUD-R, #3, ID: 5337)

61. According to the profession's standards, which of the following is **not** required of a CPA performing a consulting engagement?

    a. Complying with Statements on Standards for Consulting Services
    b. Obtaining an understanding of the nature, scope, and limitations of the engagement
    c. Supervising staff who are assigned to the engagement
    d. Maintaining independence from the client   (11/94, AUD-R, #5, ID: 5183)

62. A member of the International Federation of Accountants (IFAC) may practice in a jurisdiction or belong to another professional organization that has less stringent requirements than the IESBA Code of Ethics for Professional Accountants (Code). Which set of requirements should the member follow under these circumstances?

    a. A member of IFAC shall not apply less stringent standards from those stated in the code under any circumstances.
    b. A member of IFAC shall not apply less stringent standards from those stated in the code unless prohibited from complying by law or regulation.
    c. A member of IFAC is allowed to comply with the less stringent requirements if these are imposed by an organization recognized by IFAC.
    d. A member of IFAC shall request a ruling from IESBA regarding a conflict between its standards and those of another organization.   (AUD, ID: 9298)

63. Which of the following is not one of the five fundamental principles of the International Federation of Accountant's Code of Ethics for Professional Accountants?

    a. Integrity
    b. Objectivity
    c. Professional behavior
    d. Independence   (AUD, ID: 9296)

64. The use of which of the following word(s) in the IESBA Code of Ethics for Professional Accountants imposes a requirement?

    a. Must
    b. Shall
    c. Should
    d. Is required   (AUD, ID: 9297)

65. According to the SEC, an auditor is **not** independent of its issuer audit client in which of the following situations?

    a. The auditor's cousin has an insurance policy obtained from the issuer before it became an audit client.
    b. The auditor has an automobile loan at standard terms from the audit client that is collateralized by the automobile.
    c. The auditor has an investment in an entity that has the ability to exercise significant influence over the audit client.
    d. The auditor's grandparent was in an accounting role at the audit client and ended employment before the period under audit began.   (ID: 9950)

———————————

Problem 14-2 SIMULATION: Request by Client for CPA's Workpapers

Poole & Sterns, CPAs, performed an audit of Flight, a privately held corporation. Poole & Sterns are AICPA members.

While performing the audit, Poole & Sterns, developed and included in its electronic working papers adjusting and closing journal entries, without which Flight's financial information is incomplete.

Flight's management requested copies of the adjusting and closing journal entries in XBRL format. Poole & Sterns' audit software prints adjusting and closing journal entries to *.txt files, but doesn't provide them in XBRL format.

Indicate whether the following statements are true or false.

Statement	True/False
1. Poole & Sterns, CPAs', working papers must be made available to Flight.	
2. Poole & Sterns, CPAs, should provide the adjusting and closing journal entries to Flight regardless of whether the fees related to the audit are unpaid.	
3. Poole & Sterns, CPAs, must provide the adjusting and closing journal entries to Flight regardless of whether any fees related to other work are unpaid.	
4. Poole & Sterns, CPAs, must provide the adjusting and closing journal entries to Flight in XBRL format.	
5. Once Poole & Sterns, CPAs, have provided the adjusting and closing journal entries to Flight, it need not comply with subsequent requests for the same information.	
6. If the engagement is ended before completion and fees incurred to that point are paid, Poole & Sterns, CPAs, must provide such adjusting and closing journal entries to Flight as are known to it at that point.	
7. As Flight is a privately held corporation, Poole & Sterns, CPAs, must keep working papers related to the audit for one year and no longer.	
8. Poole & Sterns, CPAs, may disclose information in the working papers without Flight's consent to comply with professional practice review procedures under AICPA authorization.	

(ID: 9248)

Problem 14-3 SIMULATION: Research

What authoritative reference permits a member in public practice to disclose confidential client information without the specific consent of the client during a review in conjunction with a prospective purchase, sale, or merger of all or part of a member's practice?

	§		

(ID: 9250)

Solution 14-1 MULTIPLE-CHOICE ANSWERS

Code of Professional Conduct

1. (d)   Under the Independence Standards Board Statement 1 (ISB 1) the auditor must disclose, in writing, to the audit committee, all relationships between the auditor and its related entities and the client entity and its related entities that, in the auditor's judgment, may be considered to bear on independence.   (ID: 9923)

2. (b)   Interpretation 501-1 generally requires an auditor to return a client's records after the client has demanded them.   With adequate assurance of non-disclosure by a records-retention agency, use of such an agency does not violate confidentiality requirements.   A CPA is not prohibited from collecting fees from clients. Compilation is a service that does not require the CPA's independence; also, the employment of the CPA's spouse as a bookkeeper (generally not considered a key employee) does not necessarily impair the CPA's independence.   (ID: 8851)

3. (b)   According to the standards of the profession, exercise in due care may require consulting with experts, but would not require obtaining specialty accreditation.   (ID: 5872)

4. (b)   A CPA may recommend a product to a tax client, provided the fee paid to the CPA is disclosed to the client.   A CPA may not recommend or refer any product or service to an audit client, for a fee.   A CPA may not accept a fee contingent upon the outcome of an original or amended tax return or claim for refund or an audit or review of financial statements.   (ID: 8875)

5. (a)   The Statement of Standards for Consulting Services (SSCS 1) defines advisory services, implementation services, and product services as consulting services.   (ID: 5184)

Independence

6. (c)   Independence will be considered to be impaired if during the period of the professional engagement, or at the time of expressing an opinion, the member or the member's firm had or was committed to acquire any direct or material indirect financial interest in the enterprise (ET 101-1).   In other words, if a direct financial interest exists, materiality is not a factor.   (ID: 0003)

7. (a)   Independence is impaired if the CPA or her/his firm has any direct or material indirect financial interest in the client enterprise.   For this purpose the term "CPA or her/his firm" includes a trust whose operating, financial, or accounting policies can be significantly influenced by the CPA.   As a result, the trust has a direct interest in the client, and independence is impaired regardless of materiality of the interest.   (ID: 0029)

8. (b)   Independence is impaired if a member obtains a loan from an entity that, at the time of obtaining the loan, is a client requiring independence, except for certain personal loans obtained under normal lending procedures, terms, and requirements, and kept current as to terms.   (ID: 7037)

9. (d)   Under the AICPA Code of Professional Conduct, Rule 101-3 states that the CPA's independence with respect to the client would be impaired if the CPA authorized or approved transactions.   The CPA's independence would not be impaired if they recorded transactions in accordance with classifications determined by management, prepared financial statements from a trial balance provided by management, or posted journal entries prepared by management to the trial balance.   (ID: 9913)

10. (b)   A CPA's independence would not be considered to be impaired by her/his maintaining a checking account that is fully insured by a government deposit insurance agency at an audit-client financial institution (ET 191-70).   Independence is considered impaired if a CPA has a direct financial interest, or a material indirect financial interest in a client, whether or not it is placed in a blind trust (ET 191-68).   Independence generally is considered impaired if a lease meets the criteria of a capital lease as defined by GAAP and independence is not considered impaired if a lease meets the criteria of an operating lease as long as the terms and conditions are comparable with other leases of a similar nature and all amounts are paid in accordance with the terms of the lease (ET 191-91).   (ID: 2936)

11. (d)   As long as membership in a club is essentially a social matter, independence of the member's firm would not be considered to be impaired because such equity or debt ownership is not considered to be a direct financial interest.   ET 191-91 states that independence is considered impaired if a lease meets the criteria of a

capital lease as defined by GAAP and independence is not considered impaired if a lease meets the criteria of an operating lease as long as the terms and conditions are comparable with other leases of a similar nature and all amounts are paid in accordance with the terms of the lease. The independence of the member would be considered impaired whether or not the direct financial interest is placed in a blind trust. The client's guarantee of the CPA's loan creates a material indirect financial relationship between the CPA and the client. (ID: 4238)

12. (b) Independence is considered impaired if a spouse or dependent person (immediate family) of the member is employed in a position that allows significant influence over the client's operating, financial, or accounting policies. Independence is considered impaired if the position with the client involves activities that are audit-sensitive, even though the position is not one that allows significant influence. A person's activities would be considered audit sensitive if such activities are normally an element of, or subject to, significant internal controls; for example, the positions of cashier, internal auditor, accounting or finance supervisor, purchasing agent, or inventory warehouse supervisor. (ID: 7883)

13. (a) Audit reports, audit reviews, and audit procedures all require a level of independence that would necessitate that they be done by an independent accountant outside of the organization. However, compilation reports do not require that high level of independence and could be prepared by a board member without violating independence rules. (ID: 9940)

14. (b) A CPA does not have to be independent to perform a compilation engagement, but a separate paragraph should be added to the report that discloses the lack of independence. Additionally, the CPA may include the reasons for the lack of independence in the same paragraph. The disclosure of the reason(s) is not required, but if the CPA elects to do so, all the reasons must be included. (ID: 9948)

15. (b) ET 191-70 states that the independence of an auditor with respect to a financial institution is not impaired if the accounts are fully insured by the appropriate state or federal insurance agency. General activities under ET 101-3 states that a member who serves as a client's stock transfer or escrow agent, registrar, general counsel or its equivalent would impair independence. ET 191-52 provides that independence is impaired when fees for professional services rendered for more than one prior year are not collected before the issuance of the report for the current year. ET 191-91 states that independence generally is considered impaired if a lease meets the criteria of a capital lease as defined by GAAP and independence is not considered impaired if a lease meets the criteria of an operating lease as long as the terms and conditions are comparable with other leases of a similar nature and all amounts are paid in accordance with the terms of the lease. (ID: 4759)

16. (a) Ruling ET 191-74 states that a CPA who is not independent with respect to the client may not issue an audit opinion or review report. The Rule also states that a CPA who is not independent may issue compilation reports for the client as long as the lack of independence is specifically disclosed without giving the reasons for the impairment of independence. (ID: 4758)

17. (c) ET 101-1 states that independence is impaired if a spouse's employment is in a position where the spouse's activities are audit sensitive, and specifically mentions *internal auditors.* Obtaining a collateralized car loan from an institutional client is a permitted loan (ET 101-5). Independence is usually not considered impaired in the case of threatened or actual litigation that is not related to the audit performed for the client for an amount that is immaterial (ET 101-6). Independence is also not considered impaired for a CPA to be an honorary trustee for a not-for-profit organization client (ET 101-4). (ID: 5335)

18. (b) The Sarbanes-Oxley Act of 2002 specifies that an audit committee must contain at least one financial expert. The attributes of a financial expert on the audit committee can be acquired in a number of ways, including: serving as a principal financial officer, principal accounting officer, controller, public accountant, or auditor; actively supervising a principal financial officer or principal accounting officer; or assessing the performance of public accountants with respect to preparation, auditing, or evaluation of financial statements. (ID: 9924)

19. (c) Serving in any capacity equivalent to that of a member of management during the period covered by the financial statements is considered to impair independence. A CPA ordinarily may accept a *de minimis* gift from a client, become a member of a trade association that is a client, or serve as a cofiduciary or an estate or trust with a client bank. (ID: 8443)

20. (c) If a member does not have the ability to direct investments, an investment in a client through a financial service product (such as a mutual fund) is considered an indirect financial interest and, hence, does not

necessarily impair independence. Independence is considered impaired if a covered member owns stock in a client through an investment club, where presumably the member has the ability to direct investments, whether or not exercised, resulting in a direct financial interest. Independence is considered impaired even if a CPA has a material indirect financial interest in a client, whether or not it is placed in a blind trust. (ID: 8682)

21. (c) Direct or material indirect financial interest in an audit client during the period of a professional engagement is held to impair a CPA's independence. (ID: 8890)

22. (d) According to the AICPA Code of Professional Conduct, any direct financial interest in a client corporation would impair a CPA's independence even if it is immaterial. (ID: 9941)

General & Technical Standards

23. (c) ET 203 provides that a CPA must use professional judgment in deciding when a deviation from GAAP is appropriate. Circumstances that may justify a departure include new legislation or the evolution of a new form of business. (ID: 5181)

24. (a) AU 623.13 states that an engagement to express an opinion on one or more specified elements, accounts, or items of a financial statement may be undertaken as a separate engagement (not in conjunction with an audit of financial statements). (ID: 4293)

25. (c) AU 150 states, "Auditing standards differ from auditing procedures in that *procedures* relate to acts to be performed, whereas *standards* deal with measures of the quality of the performance of those acts and the objectives to be attained by the use of the procedures undertaken." (ID: 5336)

Quality Control Standards

26. (a) A system of quality control should provide the firm with reasonable assurance that its personnel comply with professional standards and applicable regulatory and legal requirements, and that the reports issued are appropriate in the circumstances. A peer review provides information on whether a CPA firm is following an appropriate quality control system and would not by itself provide reasonable assurance that a CPA firm is providing professional services that conform with professional standards. Continuing professional education is only one of the policies and procedures concerned with the human resources element of quality control. Compliance with generally accepted reporting standards is only one part of the basic objective of providing professional services that conform with professional standards. (ID: 2937)

27. (a) Auditors typically inquire of the client's legal counsel regarding litigation, claims, and assessments. The prospective client's unwillingness to permit such inquiry casts doubt on the reliability of management representations. Further, such a scope limitation usually results in a disclaimer of opinion; ethics require auditors to accept only engagements they can reasonably expect to complete. There may be legitimate reasons why an auditor is unable to review a predecessor's working papers or why management doesn't investigate employees in key positions before hiring them. There is no need for the auditor to understand the prospective client's industry before the audit is begun as long as the auditor can reasonably expect to gain such understanding in a timely manner. (ID: 7633)

28. (a) The standards require that a firm's quality control policies and procedures regarding the acceptance and continuance of clients and engagements take answers b., c., and d. into consideration. In the absence of evidence to the contrary, related party transactions should not be assumed to be outside of the ordinary course of business. The auditor is concerned with complying with GAAS to identify related party transactions and determining that they are accounted for and disclosed according to GAAP. (ID: 9046)

29. (a) The auditor uses professional judgment in planning an audit engagement's personnel requirements; the auditor has final responsibility and may delegate portions of the audit functions to other firm personnel, referred to in the code as "assistants." Opportunities for on-the-job training as well as continuity and periodic rotation of personnel are all valid factors the auditor may consider in this task. (ID: 5624)

30. (c) If sufficient appropriate audit evidence is not available to support an opinion, an audit cannot be performed. In many online systems, most routine transaction details are not available after a specified period of

time. Internal control is usually subject to management override. Consultation with several accounting firms reflects management's concern over proper accounting and reporting. (ID: 6927)

31. (d) Unwillingness to make available all financial records heightens the risk associated with an audit client. Inventory assertions may be confirmed by alternative audit procedures. A CPA may gain an understanding of the client's operations and industry from audit guides and other publications. Review of the predecessor auditor's workpapers is not necessary prior to accepting an audit engagement. (ID: 7017)

32. (a) Factors which impact the nature and extent of a firm's quality control policies and procedures depend on various factors including its size and operating characteristics. (ID: 5623)

33. (b) A firm shall consider each of the elements of quality control, to the extent applicable to its practice, in establishing its quality control policies and procedures. Performance evaluation, compensation, and advancement; professional development: and recruitment and hiring decisions are part of the human resources element of a quality control system. The human resources element should also address the determination of capabilities and competencies and the assignment of personnel to engagements. (ID: 0009)

34. (b) One of the elements of a system of quality control is the *acceptance and continuance of client relationships and specific engagements*. Addressing this includes establishing policies and procedures designed to provide a firm with reasonable assurance that it will *accept or continue relationships with clients only when it has considered the integrity of the client*, including the identity and business reputation of the client's principal owners, key management, related parties, and those charged with its governance; and the risk associated with providing professional services in the particular circumstances. A firm's duty to the public may come into play within this element of quality control in the consideration of the withdrawal from an engagement under certain circumstances, but generally not in regard to the acceptance of a new client. However, the public interest is directly addressed in two other elements of a quality control system: *relevant ethical requirements* and *engagement performance*. Whether the client will meet any agreed-upon obligations such as the timely completion of schedules would probably not yet be known when the acceptance of a new client is being considered and is unlikely to be a factor in any event. Nor is it a quality control issue. Prior to the acceptance of a new client, the auditor can only try to ascertain if there will be sufficient corroborating evidence. Although this would be a consideration in whether to accept a new client and it could be posed that having personnel capable of making this judgment is part of this element of quality control, it is not as important an issue as the integrity of the client. (ID: 8630)

35. (c) Relevant ethical requirements is one of the elements that should be addressed by a firm's system of quality control. Answer a. is not an *element* of a system of quality control. Answers b. and d. would be associated with auditing requirements and procedures. (ID: 4680)

36. (b) *Engagement performance* is one of the elements of a firm's system of quality control. The firm's quality control system should include policies and procedures addressing it and the other elements which are: leadership responsibilities for quality within the firm; relevant ethical requirements; acceptance and continuance of client relationships and specific engagements; human resources; and monitoring. Information processing, technology selection, and professional skepticism are not defined elements of a firm's quality control system. (ID: 8655)

37. (c) One of the purposes of establishing quality control policies and procedures for deciding whether to accept or continue a client relationship is to *minimize the likelihood of associating with clients whose management lacks integrity*. Monitoring the risk factors concerning misstatements arising from the misappropriation of assets is not an aspect of a CPA's firm quality control system. Providing reasonable assurance that personnel are adequately trained to fulfill their responsibilities is part of both the human resources element and the engagement performance element of a quality control system rather than the acceptance and continuance of client relationships and specific engagements element. Documenting objective criteria for the CPA firm's responses to peer review comments is part of the engagement performance element of a firm's quality control system. (ID: 8817)

38. (b) A client-imposed scope limitation poses the greatest risk in accepting a new audit engagement. The other answer alternatives involve fairly routine planning considerations. Restrictions on the scope of the audit, whether imposed by the client or by circumstances, may require the auditor to qualify the opinion or to

disclaim an opinion. When restrictions that significantly limit the scope of the audit are imposed by the client, ordinarily the auditor should disclaim an opinion. (ID: 9354)

Engagement Quality Review

39. (a) To evaluate such judgments and conclusions, the engagement quality reviewer should hold discussions with the engagement partner and other members of the engagement team and review documentation. (ID: 9274)

40. (b) The engagement quality reviewer must be independent of the company, perform the engagement quality review with integrity, and maintain objectivity in performing the review. The engagement quality reviewer must possess the level of knowledge and competence related to accounting, auditing, and financial reporting required to serve as the engagement partner on the engagement under review. (ID: 9275)

41. (d) An engagement quality review and concurring approval of issuance are required for each audit engagement and for each engagement to review interim financial information conducted pursuant to the standards of the Public Company Accounting Oversight Board (PCAOB). (ID: 9276)

Other Professional Responsibilities

42. (c) In the standards for consulting services (SSCS 1), reviewing and commenting on a client-prepared business plan is cited as an example of a consultation service. An example of a transaction consulting service is the preparation of information for obtaining financing. (ID: 6257)

43. (b) ET 301 prohibits the disclosure of confidential information obtained in the course of the professional engagement without the consent of the client, but does not prohibit review of a CPA's professional practices (including pertinent information) as a part of an AICPA authorized voluntary quality review program. (ID: 5339)

44. (a) ET 502-2 provides, "Advertising or other forms of solicitation that are false, misleading, or deceptive are not in the public interest and are prohibited." A prohibited activity is one that contains a representation that specific professional services in current or future periods will be performed for a stated fee, estimated fee, or fee range when it is likely at the time of representation that such fees would be substantially increased and the prospective client was not advised of such likelihood. (ID: 5180)

45. (d) SQCS address a CPA's firm's responsibilities for its system of quality control for its accounting and auditing practice. (ID: 0033)

46. (c) A contingent fee for preparing a client's income tax return would not be permitted under the ethical standards of the profession. However, a contingent fee for representing a client in tax court would be permitted under the ethical standards, because the tax authority initiated the proceedings. A member who accepts or pays a referral fee in relation to a client must disclose such acceptance or payment to the client. A member is prohibited from recommending or referring, for a commission, any product or service to a client when that member or member's firm performs a financial statement compilation where the member might reasonably expect that a third party will use the statement. Since the financial statement compilation was for internal use only, it would be permitted under the ethical standards. (ID: 7660)

47. (d) An AICPA member in public practice shall not offer or render services under an agreement whereby the fee is contingent upon the findings or results, specifically including an examination of prospective financial information; an audit or review or financial statements; or a compilation of financial statements, when the member reasonably might expect that a third party will use the statement. Fees that are fixed by the courts or public authorities or which are determined in tax matters by judicial proceedings or governmental agency findings are not considered contingent and, therefore, are permitted. (ID: 8442)

48. (c) ET 503 prohibits a CPA from accepting a commission for recommending a product to a client, unless the CPA informs management. The other activities are not prohibited. (ID: 5870)

49. (b) A CPA who is not in public practice is obligated to integrity and objectivity, as well as the discreditable acts, rules of conduct. (ID: 7885)

50. (d) According to the AICPA Code of Professional Conduct, client records are the property of the client and cannot be retained by a CPA when the client demands their return. This is specifically identified as an act discreditable to the profession. (ID: 9946)

51. (d) The best answer is to establish policies to ensure that the audit work meets applicable professional standards. Compliance with the Sarbanes-Oxley Act is too limited; is not applicable to all firms; and does not encompass the AICPA's quality control standards. The other answers are not on point. GAAS require a firm of independent auditors to adopt a system of quality control in conducting an audit practice. Thus, a firm should establish quality control policies and procedures to provide it with reasonable assurance that its personnel comply with GAAS in its audit engagements. Further, the AICPA's quality control standards require that a CPA firm establish a system of quality control designed to provide the firm with reasonable assurance that the firm and its personnel comply with professional standards and applicable regulatory and legal requirements, and that the firm or engagement partners issue reports that are appropriate in the circumstances. A system of quality control consists of policies designed to achieve these objectives and the procedures necessary to implement and monitor compliance with those policies. (ID: 9914)

52. (c) ET 501 specifically states that a CPA would be in violation of ET 501 should the CPA refuse to return a client's records after the client has demanded them. ET 591-02 allows note collection for fees. ET 191-74 allows the issuance of a compilation report provided the report specifically discloses the lack of independence. The CPA's purchase of a segment of an insurance company's business that performs actuarial services for post employment benefit plans would not impair independence (ET 101-3). (ID: 4756)

53. (a) ET 301 prohibits the disclosure of confidential information obtained in the course of a professional engagement without consent of the client, but does not prohibit review of a CPA's professional practices (including pertinent information) as a part of an AICPA authorized voluntary quality review program. While disclosing information at a client's request is allowed, mail clerks typically do not have authority to approve releases of financial information. ET 301 shall not be construed to affect in any way the member's obligation to comply with a validly issued and enforceable subpoena or summons, or to prohibit a member's compliance with applicable laws and government regulations. (ID: 8675)

54. (b) A CPA may not disclose confidential client information regarding auditing services in a letter to the client from the IRS. A CPA's duty of nondisclosure does not apply when disclosure is made pursuant to a voluntary quality review, pursuant to a professional ethics division review, or in compliance with an enforceable subpoena or court order. (ID: 8869)

55. (b) A CPA who provides auditing and other attestation services should be independent in fact and appearance. In providing all other services, an CPA should maintain objectivity and avoid conflicts of interest. (ID: 8678)

Consulting Services

56. (a) The Bylaws of the AICPA include general definitions which state that in addition to furnishing advice in conjunction with their independent examinations of financial statements, CPAs are engaged to provide objective advice and consultation on various management problems (BL 921.09). Statements on Standards for Consulting Services (CS 100.07) state that the CPA is to serve the client interest by seeking to accomplish the objectives established by the understanding with the client while maintaining integrity and objectivity. (ID: 3901)

57. (b) According to the Statement on Standards for Consulting Services, consulting services include reviewing and commenting on a client-prepared business plan. Expressing a conclusion about the reliability of a client's financial statements is an attest engagement, not a consulting services engagement. (ID: 6618)

58. (d) Under the Standards for Consulting Services, advisory services are used to develop findings, conclusions and recommendations for client consideration and decision making. A stated example of advisory services is the defining of requirements for an information system. (ID: 4761)

59. (c) Under the Statements of Standards for Consulting Services, a CPA has the responsibility to inform the client of significant reservations concerning the benefits of the engagement. The Standards for Consulting Services do not require a CPA to obtain a written understanding with the client concerning the time for completion

of the engagement. Nor do the Standards prohibit a CPA from modifying a client agreement or from performing attest services.   (ID: 5874)

60. (d)   ET 202 requires that the client be informed of any conflict of interest or significant reservations concerning the scope or benefits of the engagement. However, independence is *not* required. This Rule also requires a written *or oral* understanding between consultant and client.   (ID: 5337)

61. (d)   ET 201 requires a CPA performing a consulting engagement to comply with Standards on Consulting Services and to supervise staff assigned to the engagement. ET 202 requires that the CPA obtain an understanding of the nature, scope, and limitations of the engagement. ET 202 also states that performing a consulting service does not, of itself, impair independence.   (ID: 5183)

IFAC Code of Ethics

62. (b)   A member of IFAC shall not apply less stringent standards from those stated in the code unless prohibited from complying by law or regulation. In this situation, the member shall comply with all other parts of the Code.   (ID: 9298)

63. (d)   The five fundamental principles that the International Ethics Standards Board for Accountants (IESBA) requires professional accountants to comply with per the IESBA Code of Ethics for Professional Accountants are integrity; objectivity; professional competence and due care; confidentiality; and professional behavior.   (ID: 9296)

64. (b)   The word *shall* is used to impose a requirement in the IESBA Code of Ethics for Professional Accountants.   (ID: 9297)

PCAOB Standards

65. (c)   According to the AICPA Code of Professional Conduct, a CPA's independence is considered impaired if the CPA has a financial interest in the audit client or has a financial interest in an entity that has the ability to exercise significant influence over the audit client. Having a relative who obtained an insurance policy from the issuer before it became an audit client or who was in an accounting role at the audit client and ended employment before the period under audit began would not be considered an impairment to independence. The auditor having an automobile loan at standard terms from the audit client that is collateralized by the automobile is not considered to have their independence impaired.   (ID: 9950)

––––––––––––––

PERFORMANCE BY TOPICS

Each category below parallels a topic covered in Chapter 14. Record the number and percentage of questions you answered correctly in each topic.

Code of Professional Conduct

Question #	Correct	√
1		
2		
3		
4		
5		
# Questions	5	
# Correct		
% Correct		

Independence

Question #	Correct	√
6		
7		
8		
9		
10		
11		
12		
13		
14		
15		
16		
17		
18		
19		
20		
21		
22		
# Questions	17	
# Correct		
% Correct		

General & Technical Standards

Question #	Correct	√
23		
24		
25		
# Questions	3	
# Correct		
% Correct		

Quality Control Standards

Question #	Correct	√
26		
27		
28		
29		
30		
31		
32		
33		
34		
35		
36		
37		
38		
# Questions	13	
# Correct		
% Correct		

Engagement Quality Review

Question #	Correct	√
39		
40		
41		
# Questions	3	
# Correct		
% Correct		

Other Professional Responsibilities

Question #	Correct	√
42		
43		
44		
45		
46		
47		
48		
49		
50		
51		
52		
53		
54		
55		
# Questions	14	
# Correct		
% Correct		

Consulting Services

Question #	Correct	√
56		
57		
58		
59		
60		
61		
# Questions	6	
# Correct		
% Correct		

IFAC Code of Ethics

Question #	Correct	√
62		
63		
64		
# Questions	3	
# Correct		
% Correct		

PCAOB Standards

Question #	Correct	√
65		
# Questions	1	
# Correct		
% Correct		

Solution 14-2 SIMULATION ANSWER: Request by Client for CPA's Workpapers

1. False

All of an auditor's working papers need not be made available to a client. Information in an auditor's working papers that completes the client's incomplete financial information need not be made available to the client in all circumstances.

2. False

Information in an auditor's workpapers that completes the client's incomplete financial information need not be made available to the client if any fees from that client are unpaid.

3. False

Information in an auditor's workpapers that completes the client's incomplete financial information need not be made available to the client if any fees from that client are unpaid.

4. False

Information in an auditor's workpapers that completes the client's incomplete financial information need not be converted into another medium when providing it to the client.

5. True

Once an AICPA member has complied with an initial request for information from an auditor's workpapers that completes the client's incomplete financial information, the member need not comply with subsequent requests to provide such information again.

6. False

If an engagement has been completed, ordinarily a member should provide information in the workpapers that completes the client's incomplete financial information to the client upon request. There is no requirement to do so for an incomplete engagement.

7. False

The auditor should adopt reasonable procedures to retain and access audit documentation for a period of time sufficient to meet the needs of the auditor's practice and to satisfy any applicable legal or regulatory requirements for records retention. Such retention period, however, should not be shorter than five years from the report release date. Statutes, regulations, or the audit firm's quality control policies may specify a longer retention period.

8. True

Auditors may disclose information in workpapers without the client's consent in select circumstances only; compliance with professional practice review procedures under AICPA authorization is one of these circumstances.

(ID: 9248)

————————————

Solution 14-3 SIMULATION ANSWER: Research

ET	§	301	.04

.04   301-3—Confidential information and the purchase, sale, or merger of a practice

Rule 301 prohibits a member in public practice from disclosing any confidential client information without the specific consent of the client. The Rule provides that it shall not be construed to prohibit the review of a member's professional practice under AICPA or state CPA society authorization.

For purposes of Rule 301, a review of a member's professional practice is hereby authorized to include a review in conjunction with a prospective purchase, sale, or merger of all or part of a member's practice. The member must take appropriate precautions (for example, through a written confidentiality agreement) so that the prospective purchaser does not disclose any information obtained in the course of the review, since such information is deemed to be confidential client information.

Members reviewing a practice in connection with a prospective purchase or merger shall not use to their advantage nor disclose any member's confidential client information that comes to their attention.   (ID: 9250)

_____

Don't forget the helpful hints in the material at the front and back of this text!

Once you have had a chance to become familiar with the text format, you may want to skim the **Getting Started** and **Writing Skills** sections of the book again. These provide:

- Information on how to integrate materials so they work best for you

- Helpful information on answering all question types

- Information on the heavily tested topics on exams

- Information on how to use your time wisely

- Exam-taking techniques that will earn extra points on the exam

Remember, with the techniques and information in your material,

A passing score is well within reach!

_____

APPENDIX A
PRACTICE EXAM

Editor note: There is only one practice (or final) exam. It's best to wait until you are ready before you take it.

Testlet 1 MULTIPLE-CHOICE QUESTIONS

1. A successor auditor ordinarily should request to review the predecessor's working papers relating to

	Contingencies	Internal control
a.	Yes	Yes
b.	Yes	No
c.	No	Yes
d.	No	No

(ID: 7092)

2. Holding other planning considerations equal, a decrease in the amount of misstatements in a class of transactions that an auditor could tolerate most likely would cause the auditor to

   a. Apply the planned substantive tests prior to the balance sheet date
   b. Perform the planned auditing procedures closer to the balance sheet date
   c. Increase the assessed level of control risk for relevant financial statement assertions
   d. Decrease the extent of auditing procedures to be applied to the class of transactions   (ID: 6574)

3. In a probability-proportional-to-size sample with a sampling interval of $10,000, an auditor discovered that a selected account receivable with a recorded amount of $5,000 had an audited amount of $4,000. If this were the only misstatement discovered by the auditor, the projected misstatement of this sample would be

   a. $ 1,000
   b. $ 2,000
   c. $ 5,000
   d. $10,000

(ID: 6935)

4. Morris, CPA, suspects that a pervasive scheme of illegal bribes exists throughout the operations of Worldwide Import-Export Inc., a new audit client. Morris notified the audit committee and Worldwide's legal counsel, but neither could assist Morris in determining whether the amounts involved were material to the financial statements or whether senior management was involved in the scheme. Under these circumstances, Morris should

   a. Express an unqualified opinion with a separate explanatory paragraph
   b. Disclaim an opinion on the financial statements
   c. Express an adverse opinion of the financial statements
   d. Issue a special report regarding the illegal bribes   (ID: 165)

5. An accountant may compile a nonissuer's financial statements that omit all of the disclosures required by GAAP only if the omission is

   I. Clearly indicated in the accountant's report
   II. Not undertaken with the intention of misleading the financial statement users

   a. I only
   b. II only
   c. Both I and II
   d. Either I or II

(ID: 4744)

6. Which of the following statements best explains why the CPA profession has found it essential to promulgate ethical standards and to establish means for ensuring their observance?

   a. A distinguishing mark of a profession is its acceptance of responsibility to the public.
   b. A requirement for a profession is to establish ethical standards that stress primary responsibility to clients and colleagues.
   c. Ethical standards that emphasize excellence in performance over material rewards establish a reputation for competence and character.
   d. Vigorous enforcement of an established code of ethics is the best way to prevent unscrupulous acts.

   (ID: 4757)

7. Quality control, as referred to in Statements on Quality Control Standards (SQCS), applies to a CPA firm's responsibilities for its system of quality control for its

   a. Auditing services only
   b. Auditing and management advisory services
   c. Auditing and tax services
   d. Accounting and auditing practice

   (ID: 33)

8. Which of the following statements is **not** correct about materiality?

   a. The concept of materiality recognizes that some matters are important for fair presentation of financial statements in conformity with GAAP, while other matters are not important.
   b. An auditor considers materiality for planning purposes in terms of the largest aggregate level of misstatements that could be material to any one of the financial statements.
   c. An auditor's consideration of materiality is influenced by the auditor's perception of the needs of a reasonable person who will rely on the financial statements.
   d. Materiality judgments are made in light of surrounding circumstances and necessarily involve both quantitative and qualitative judgments.

   (ID: 5084)

9. The theoretical distribution of means from all possible samples of a given size is a normal distribution and this distribution is the basis for statistical sampling. Which of the following statements is **not** true with respect to the sampling distribution of sample means?

   a. Approximately 68% of the sample means will be within one standard deviation of the mean for the normal distribution.
   b. The distribution is defined in terms of its mean and its standard error of the mean.
   c. An auditor can be approximately 95% confident that the mean for a sample is within two standard deviations of the population mean.
   d. The items drawn in an auditor's sample will have a normal distribution.

   (ID: 8973)

10. For audits of financial statements made in accordance with generally accepted auditing standards, the use of analytical procedures is required to some extent

	As a substantive test	In the final review stage
a.	Yes	Yes
b.	Yes	No
c.	No	Yes
d.	No	No

   (ID: 8952)

11. Miller, CPA, is engaged to compile the financial statements of Web Co., a nonissuer, in conformity with the income tax basis of accounting. If Web's financial statements do not disclose the basis of accounting used, Miller should

   a. Disclose the basis of accounting in the accountant's compilation report
   b. Clearly label each page "Distribution Restricted—Material Modifications Required"
   c. Issue a special report describing the effect of the incomplete presentation
   d. Withdraw from the engagement and provide no further services to Web

   (ID: 5154)

12. Kar, CPA, is a staff auditor participating in the audit engagement of Fort, Inc. Which of the following circumstances impairs Kar's independence?

    a. During the period of the professional engagement, Fort gives Kar tickets to a football game worth $25.
    b. Kar owns stock in a corporation that Fort's 401(k) plan also invests in.
    c. Kar's friend, an employee of another local accounting firm, prepares Fort's tax returns.
    d. Kar's sibling is an internal auditor employed part-time by Fort.   (ID: 7036)

13. Prior to the acceptance of an audit engagement with a client who has terminated the services of the predecessor auditor, the CPA should

    a. Contact the predecessor auditor without advising the prospective client and request a complete report of the circumstances leading to the termination, with the understanding that all information disclosed will be kept confidential
    b. Accept the engagement without contacting the predecessor auditor since the CPA can include audit procedures to verify the reason given by the client for the termination
    c. Not communicate with the predecessor auditor because this would violate the confidential relationship between auditor and client
    d. Advise the client of the intention to contact the predecessor auditor and request permission for the contact   (ID: 8947)

14. Which of the following statements best describes the auditor's responsibility regarding the detection of material errors and fraud?

    a. The auditor is responsible for the failure to detect material errors and fraud only when such failure results from the nonapplication of generally accepted accounting principles.
    b. Extended auditing procedures are required to detect material errors and fraud if the audit indicates that they may exist.
    c. The auditor is responsible for the failure to detect material errors and fraud only when the auditor fails to confirm receivables or observe inventories.
    d. Extended auditing procedures are required to detect unrecorded transactions even if there is no evidence that material errors and fraud may exist.   (ID: 8948)

15. According to the guidance in the attestation standards regarding using the work of others, in an engagement to examine a nonissuer's internal control over financial reporting that is integrated with an audit of its financial statements, the auditor may consider using the work of any of the following as evidence about the effectiveness of internal control, **except**

    a. Internal auditors
    b. Entity personnel who are not internal auditors
    c. Third parties working under the direction of management
    d. Previous auditors   (ID: 89456)

16. Analytical procedures used in the overall review stage of an audit generally include

    a. Gathering evidence concerning account balances that have not changed from the prior year
    b. Retesting control procedures that appeared to be ineffective during the assessment of control risk
    c. Considering unusual or unexpected account balances that were not previously identified
    d. Performing tests of transactions to corroborate management's financial statement assertions   (ID: 5665)

17. An accountant's standard report issued after compiling the financial statements of a nonissuer should state that

    a. I am not aware of any material modifications that should be made to the accompanying financial statements.
    b. A compilation includes primarily applying analytical procedures to management's financial data and making inquiries of company management.
    c. The objective of a compilation is to assist management in presenting financial information in the form of financial statements.
    d. A compilation is substantially less in scope than an audit, the objective of which is the expression of an opinion regarding the financial statements as a whole.　　(ID: 8154)

18. According to the ethical standards of the profession, which of the following acts generally is prohibited?

    a. Accepting a contingent fee for representing a client in connection with obtaining a private letter ruling from the Internal Revenue Service
    b. Retaining client records after the client has demanded their return
    c. Revealing client tax returns to a prospective purchaser of the CPA's practice
    d. Issuing a modified report explaining the CPA's failure to follow a governmental regulatory agency's standards when conducting an attest service for a client　　(ID: 7862)

19. The senior auditor responsible for coordinating the fieldwork usually schedules a pre-audit conference with the audit team primarily to

    a. Give guidance to the staff regarding both technical and personnel aspects of the audit
    b. Provide an opportunity to document staff disagreements regarding technical issues
    c. Establish the need for using the work of specialists and internal auditors
    d. Discuss staff suggestions concerning the establishment and maintenance of time budgets　　(ID: 5077)

20. Management's attitude toward aggressive financial reporting and its emphasis on meeting projected profit goals most likely would significantly influence an entity's control environment when

    a. External policies established by parties outside the entity affect its accounting practices.
    b. Management is dominated by one individual who is also a shareholder.
    c. Internal auditors have direct access to the board of directors and the entity's management.
    d. The audit committee is active in overseeing the entity's financial reporting policies.　　(ID: 6390)

21. A written representation from a client's management which, among other matters, acknowledges responsibility for the fair presentation of financial statements, should normally be signed by the

    a. Chief executive officer and the chief financial officer
    b. Chief financial officer and the chairman of the board of directors
    c. Chairman of the audit committee of the board of directors
    d. Chief executive officer, the chairman of the board of directors, and the client's lawyer　　(ID: 8954)

22. After issuing a report an auditor concludes that an auditing procedure considered necessary at the time of the audit was omitted from the audit. The auditor should first

    a. Undertake to apply the omitted procedure or alternative procedures that would provide a satisfactory basis for the auditor's opinion
    b. Assess the importance of the omitted procedure to the auditor's ability to support the opinion expressed on the financial statements taken as a whole
    c. Notify the audit committee or the board of director's that the auditor's opinion can no longer be relied upon
    d. Review the results of other procedures that were applied to compensate for the one omitted or to make its omission less important　　(ID: 8956)

23. Which of the following procedures is ordinarily performed by an accountant in a compilation engagement of a nonissuer?

    a. Reading the financial statements to consider whether they are free of obvious mistakes in the application of accounting principles
    b. Obtaining written representations from management indicating that the compiled financial statements will not be used to obtain credit
    c. Making inquiries of management concerning actions taken at meetings of the stockholders and the board of directors
    d. Applying analytical procedures designed to corroborate management's assertions that are embodied in the financial statement components
    (ID: 5693)

24. Under the ethical standards of the profession, which of the following business relationships would generally **not** impair an auditor's independence?

    a. Promoter of a client's securities
    b. Member of a client's board of directors
    c. Client's general counsel
    d. Advisor to a client's board of trustees
    (ID: 8175)

25. In the consideration of an entity's internal control, the auditor is basically concerned that the controls provide reasonable assurance that

    a. Operational efficiency has been achieved in accordance with management plans.
    b. Errors and fraud have been prevented or detected.
    c. Management cannot override the controls.
    d. Controls have not been circumvented by collusion.
    (ID: 7488)

26. The auditor is most likely to seek information from the plant manager with respect to the

    a. Adequacy of the provision for uncollectible accounts
    b. Appropriateness of physical inventory observation procedures
    c. Existence of obsolete machinery
    d. Deferral of procurement of certain necessary insurance coverage
    (ID: 8955)

27. The auditor concludes, prior to the report release date, that there is a material inconsistency that requires revision of the other information in an annual report to shareholders containing audited financial statements. If the client refuses to revise or eliminate the material inconsistency, the auditor should notify those charged with governance and

    a. Revise the auditor's report to include a separate explanatory paragraph describing the material inconsistency
    b. Consult with a party whose advice might influence the client, such as the client's legal counsel
    c. Issue a qualified opinion after discussing the matter with the client's board of directors
    d. Consider the matter closed since the other information is not in the audited financial statements
    (ID: 8957)

28. Under the ethical standards of the profession, which of the following investments in a client is **not** considered to be a direct financial interest?

    a. An investment held through a non-regulated mutual fund
    b. An investment held through a nonclient investment club
    c. An investment held in a blind trust
    d. An investment held by the trustee of a trust
    (ID: 7113)

29. An auditor would be most likely to consider expressing a qualified opinion if the client's financial statements include a footnote on related-party transactions that
   a. Lists the amounts due from related parties including the terms and manner of settlement
   b. Discloses compensating balance arrangements maintained for the benefit of related parties
   c. Represents that certain transactions with related parties were consummated on terms equally as favorable as would have been obtained in transactions with unrelated parties
   d. Presents the dollar volume of related-party transactions and the effects of any change in the method of establishing terms from that of the prior period   (ID: 8958)

30. May a CPA hire for the CPA's public accounting firm a non-CPA systems analyst who specializes in developing computer systems?
   a. Yes, provided the CPA is qualified to perform each of the specialist's tasks
   b. Yes, provided the CPA is able to supervise the specialist and evaluate the specialist's end product
   c. No, because non-CPA professionals are not permitted to be associated with CPA firms in public practice
   d. No, because developing computer systems is not recognized as a service performed by public accountants   (ID: 4240)

Testlet 2 MULTIPLE-CHOICE QUESTIONS

1. Which of the following factors most likely would cause an auditor to question the integrity of management?
   a. Management has an aggressive attitude toward financial reporting and meeting profit goals.
   b. Audit tests detect material fraud that was known to management, but not disclosed to the auditor.
   c. Managerial decisions are dominated by one person who is also a stockholder.
   d. Weaknesses in internal control reported to the audit committee are not corrected by management.
      (ID: 7631)

2. In planning an audit, the auditor's knowledge about the design of relevant internal control policies and procedures should be used to
   a. Identify the types of potential misstatements that could occur
   b. Assess the operational efficiency of the internal control structure
   c. Determine whether controls have been circumvented by collusion
   d. Document the assessed level of control risk   (ID: 5951)

3. A weakness in internal control over recording retirements of equipment may cause an auditor to
   a. Trace additions to the "other assets" account to search for equipment that is still on hand but no longer being used
   b. Select certain items of equipment from the accounting records and locate them in the plant
   c. Review the subsidiary ledger to ascertain whether depreciation was taken on each item of equipment during the year
   d. Inspect certain items of equipment in the plant and trace those items to the accounting records   (ID: 81)

4. An auditor's working papers serve mainly to
   a. Provide the principal support for the auditor's report
   b. Satisfy the auditor's responsibilities concerning the Code of Professional Conduct
   c. Monitor the effectiveness of the CPA firm's quality control procedures
   d. Document the level of independence maintained by the auditor   (ID: 5689)

5. When an accountant is engaged to compile a nonissuer's financial statements that omit substantially all disclosures required by GAAP, the accountant should indicate in the compilation report that the financial statements are

   a. Not designed for those who are uninformed about the omitted disclosures
   b. Prepared in conformity with a comprehensive basis of accounting other than GAAP
   c. Not compiled in accordance with Statements on Standards for Accounting and Review Services
   d. Special-purpose financial statements that are not comparable to those of prior periods   (ID: 5155)

6. Must a CPA, in public practice, be independent in fact and appearance when providing the following services?

	Compilation of personal financial statements	Preparation of a tax return	Compilation of a financial forecast
a.	Yes	No	No
b.	No	Yes	No
c.	No	No	Yes
d.	No	No	No

   (ID: 5182)

7. In developing a preliminary audit strategy, an auditor should consider

   a. Whether the allowance for sampling risk exceeds the achieved upper precision limit
   b. Findings from substantive tests performed at interim dates
   c. Whether the inquiry of the client's attorney identifies any litigation, claims, or assessments not disclosed in the financial statements
   d. The potential risks of material misstatement   (ID: 2276)

8. Which of the following conditions is necessary for an auditor to accept an engagement to examine the design and operating effectiveness of a nonissuer's internal control over financial reporting that is integrated with an audit of financial statements?

   a. The auditor anticipates relying on the entity's internal control in a financial statement audit.
   b. Management provides its assertion about the effectiveness of internal control in a report that accompanies the auditor's report.
   c. The auditor is a continuing auditor who previously has audited the entity's financial statements.
   d. Management agrees not to present the auditor's report in a general-use document to stockholders.

   (ID: 5091)

9. Independent internal verification of inventory occurs when employees who

   a. Issue raw materials obtain material requisitions for each issue and prepare daily totals of materials issued.
   b. Compare records of goods on hand with physical quantities do not maintain the records or have custody of the inventory.
   c. Are independent of issuing production orders update records from completed job cost sheets and production cost reports on a timely basis.
   d. Obtain receipts for the transfer of completed work to finished goods prepare a completed production report.   (ID: 89)

10. When qualifying an opinion because of an insufficiency of audit evidence, an auditor should refer to the situation in the

	Scope paragraph	Notes to the financial statements
a.	Yes	Yes
b.	Yes	No
c.	No	Yes
d.	No	No

    (ID: 7100)

11. Which of the following procedures should an accountant perform during an engagement to review the annual financial statements of a nonissuer?

 a. Communicating significant deficiencies discovered during the assessment of control risk
 b. Obtaining a representation letter from members of management
 c. Sending bank confirmation letters to the entity's financial institutions
 d. Examining cash disbursements in the subsequent period for unrecorded liabilities (ID: 5148)

12. The auditor with final responsibility for an engagement and one of the assistants have a difference of opinion about the results of an auditing procedure. If the assistant believes it is necessary to be disassociated from the matter's resolution, the CPA firm's procedures should enable the assistant to

 a. Refer the disagreement to the AICPA's Quality Review Committee
 b. Document the details of the disagreement with the conclusion reached
 c. Discuss the disagreement with the entity's management or its audit committee
 d. Report the disagreement to an impartial peer review monitoring team (ID: 4241)

13. In assessing the objectivity of internal auditors, an independent auditor should

 a. Evaluate the quality control program in effect for the internal auditors
 b. Examine documentary evidence of the work performed by the internal auditors
 c. Test a sample of the transactions and balances that the internal auditors examined
 d. Determine the organizational level to which the internal auditors report (ID: 5950)

14. Inherent risk and control risk differ from detection risk in that they

 a. Arise from the misapplication of auditing procedures
 b. May be assessed in either quantitative or nonquantitative terms
 c. Exist independently of the financial statement audit
 d. Can be changed at the auditor's discretion (ID: 5081)

15. An internal control questionnaire indicates that an approved receiving report is required to accompany every check request for payment of merchandise. Which of the following procedures provides the greatest assurance that this control is operating effectively?

 a. Select and examine canceled checks and ascertain that the related receiving reports are dated no earlier than the checks
 b. Select and examine canceled checks and ascertain that the related receiving reports are dated no later than the checks
 c. Select and examine receiving reports and ascertain that the related canceled checks are dated no earlier than the receiving reports
 d. Select and examine receiving reports and ascertain that the related canceled checks are dated no later than the receiving reports (ID: 8960)

16. When using the work of a specialist, the auditor may make reference to and identify the specialist in the auditor's report if the

 a. Auditor decides to express a qualified opinion.
 b. Specialist's reputation or professional certification is being emphasized.
 c. Auditor wishes to indicate a division of responsibility.
 d. Specialist's work provides the auditor greater assurance of reliability. (ID: 8968)

17. Baker, CPA, was engaged to review the financial statements of Hall Co., a nonissuer. During the engagement Baker uncovered a complex scheme involving client illegal acts and fraud that materially affect Hall's financial statements. If Baker believes that modification of the standard review report is not adequate to indicate the deficiencies in the financial statements, Baker should

 a. Disclaim an opinion
 b. Issue an adverse opinion
 c. Withdraw from the engagement
 d. Issue a qualified opinion (ID: 5698)

18. Under the Code of Professional Conduct of the AICPA, which of the following is required to be independent in fact and appearance when discharging professional responsibilities?

    a. A CPA in public practice providing tax and management advisory services
    b. A CPA in public practice providing auditing and other attestation services
    c. A CPA not in public practice
    d. All CPAs
    (ID: 8668)

19. Which of the following factors would **least** influence an auditor's consideration of the reliability of data for purposes of analytical procedures?

    a. Whether the data were processed in an IT system or in a manual accounting system
    b. Whether sources within the entity were independent of those who are responsible for the amount being audited
    c. Whether the data were subjected to audit testing in the current or prior year
    d. Whether the data were obtained from independent sources outside the entity or from sources within the entity
    (ID: 151)

20. A client erroneously recorded a large purchase twice. Which of the following internal control measures would be most likely to detect this error in a timely and efficient manner?

    a. Footing the purchases journal
    b. Reconciling vendors' monthly statements with subsidiary payable ledger accounts
    c. Tracing totals from the purchases journal to the ledger accounts
    d. Sending written quarterly confirmations to all vendors
    (ID: 8959)

21. In designing written audit programs, an auditor should establish specific audit objectives that relate primarily to the

    a. Timing of audit procedures
    b. Cost-benefit of gathering evidence
    c. Selected audit techniques
    d. Financial statement assertions
    (ID: 4673)

22. When comparative financial statements are presented but the predecessor auditor's report is **not** presented, the current auditor should do which of the following in the audit report?

    a. Disclaim an opinion on the prior year's financial statements
    b. Identify the predecessor auditor who audited the financial statements of the prior year
    c. Make no comment with respect to the predecessor audit
    d. Indicate the type of opinion expressed by the predecessor auditor
    (ID: 8969)

23. International standards on auditing require that if the terms of the audit engagement are changed

    a. The auditor and management shall agree on and record the new terms of the engagement in an engagement letter or other suitable form of written agreement.
    b. The auditor and management shall agree on the new terms of the engagement and the auditor should document their oral agreement.
    c. If the auditor is unable to agree to a change of the terms of the audit engagement and is not permitted by management to continue the original audit engagement, the auditor shall issue a disclaimer of opinion.
    d. If the auditor is unable to agree to a change of the terms of the audit engagement and is not permitted by management to continue the original audit engagement, the auditor shall withdraw from the audit engagement under any circumstances.
    (ID: 89458)

24. A violation of the profession's ethical standards most likely would have occurred when a CPA

    a. Issued an unqualified opinion on the Year 3 financial statements when fees for the Year 1 audit were unpaid
    b. Recommended a controller's position description with candidate specifications to an audit client
    c. Purchased a CPA firm's practice of monthly write-ups for a percentage of fees to be received over a three-year period
    d. Made arrangements with a financial institution to collect notes issued by a client in payment of fees due for the current year's audit
    (ID: 3897)

25. A successor auditor is required to attempt communication with the predecessor auditor prior to

    a. Performing tests of controls
    b. Testing beginning balances for the current year
    c. Making a proposal for the audit engagement
    d. Accepting the engagement
    (ID: 8137)

26. The Accounts Payable Department receives the purchase order form to accomplish all of the following **except**

    a. Compare invoice price to purchase order price
    b. Ensure the purchase had been properly authorized
    c. Ensure the goods had been received by the party requesting the goods
    d. Compare quantity ordered to quantity purchased
    (ID: 8967)

27. The auditor will most likely perform extensive tests for possible understatement of

    a. Revenues
    b. Assets
    c. Liabilities
    d. Capital
    (ID: 8962)

28. Which of the following is a documentation requirement that an auditor should follow when auditing in accordance with *Government Auditing Standards?*

    a. The auditor should obtain written representations from management acknowledging responsibility for correcting instances of fraud, abuse, and waste.
    b. The auditor's working papers should contain sufficient information so that supplementary oral explanations are not required.
    c. The auditor's working papers should contain a caveat that all instances of material errors and fraud may not be identified.
    d. The auditor should document the procedures that assure discovery of all illegal acts and contingent liabilities resulting from noncompliance.
    (ID: 4281)

29. According to the standards of the profession, which of the following activities would most likely **not** impair a CPA's independence?

    a. Providing extensive advisory services for a client
    b. Contracting with a client to supervise the client's office personnel
    c. Signing a client's checks in emergency situations
    d. Accepting a luxurious gift from a client
    (ID: 5873)

30. An auditor's independence is considered impaired if the auditor has

    a. An immaterial, indirect financial interest in a client
    b. An automobile loan from a client bank, collateralized by the automobile
    c. A joint, closely held business investment with the client that is material to the auditor's net worth
    d. A mortgage loan, executed with a financial institution client on March 1,1990, that is material to the auditor's net worth
    (ID: 7864)

Testlet 3 MULTIPLE-CHOICE QUESTIONS

1. According the PCAOB's auditing standard for engagement quality reviews, the reviewer should evaluate the significant judgments that relate to engagement planning, including all of the following **except**

   a. The consideration of the firm's recent engagement experience with the company and risks identified in connection with the firm's client acceptance and retention process
   b. The consideration of the company's business, recent significant activities, and related financial reporting issues and risks
   c. The judgments made about materiality and the effect of those judgments on the engagement strategy
   d. Review the engagement completion document and confirm with the engagement partner that there are no significant unresolved matters
   (ID: 89457)

2. Which of the following is intended to detect deviations from prescribed Accounting Department procedures?

   a. Substantive tests specified by a standardized audit program
   b. Tests of controls designed specifically for the client
   c. Analytical procedures as designed in the industry audit guide
   d. Computerized analytical procedures tailored for the configuration of IT equipment in use   (ID: 8970)

3. The date of the management representation letter should be as of the date of the

   a. Balance sheet
   b. Latest interim financial information
   c. Auditor's report
   d. Latest related-party transaction
   (ID: 5685)

4. Which of the following procedures would the principal auditor most likely perform after deciding to make reference to another CPA who audited a subsidiary of the entity?

   a. Review the working papers and the audit programs of the other CPA
   b. Visit the other CPA and discuss the results of the other CPA's audit procedures
   c. Make inquiries about the professional reputation and independence of the other CPA
   d. Determine that the other CPA has a sufficient understanding of the subsidiary's internal control
   (ID: 6831)

5. When engaged to compile the financial statements of a nonissuer, an accountant is required to possess a level of knowledge of the entity's accounting principles and practices. This requirement most likely will include obtaining knowledge of the

   a. Policies and procedures that are unusual as compared with normal accounting practices within the industry
   b. Design of the entity's internal controls placed in operation
   c. Risk factors relating to misstatements arising from illegal acts
   d. Internal control awareness of the entity's senior management
   (ID: 6823)

6. Under the ethical standards of the profession, which of the following situations involving nondependent members of an auditor's family is most likely to impair the auditor's independence?

   a. A parent's immaterial investment in a client
   b. A first cousin's loan from a client
   c. A spouse's employment with a client
   d. A sibling's loan to a marketing manager of a client
   (ID: 7112)

7. Which of the following strategies would a CPA most likely consider in auditing an entity that processes most of its financial data only in electronic form, such as a paperless system?

   a. Continuous monitoring and analysis of transaction processing with an embedded audit module
   b. Increased reliance on internal control activities that emphasize the segregation of duties
   c. Verification of encrypted digital certificates used to monitor the authorization of transactions
   d. Extensive testing of firewall boundaries that restrict the recording of outside network traffic   (ID: 6839)

8. The auditor would **least** likely be concerned about internal control as it relates to

   a. Land and buildings
   b. Common stock
   c. Shareholder meetings
   d. Minutes of board of directors meetings (ID: 8971)

9. Which of the following statements extracted from a client's lawyer's letter concerning litigation, claims, and assessments most likely would cause the auditor to request clarification?

   a. "I believe that the possible liability to the company is nominal in amount"
   b. "I believe that the action can be settled for less than the damages claimed"
   c. "I believe that the plaintiff's case against the company is without merit"
   d. "I believe that the company will be able to defend this action successfully" (ID: 6364)

10. When an auditor concludes there is substantial doubt about a continuing audit client's ability to continue as a going concern for a reasonable period of time, the auditor's responsibility is to

    a. Issue a qualified or adverse opinion, depending upon materiality, due to the possible effects on the financial statements
    b. Consider the adequacy of disclosure about the client's possible inability to continue as a going concern
    c. Report to the client's audit committee that management's accounting estimates may need to be adjusted
    d. Reissue the prior year's auditor's report and add an explanatory paragraph that specifically refers to "substantial doubt" and "going concern" (ID: 4727)

11. Which of the following statements is correct concerning both an engagement to compile and an engagement to review a nonissuer's annual financial statements?

    a. The accountant should obtain a written management representation letter.
    b. The accountant must be independent in fact and appearance.
    c. The accountant expresses no assurance on the financial statements.
    d. The accountant does not contemplate obtaining an understanding of internal control. (ID: 2327)

12. Which of the following is(are) a correct definition of professional standards?

    I. Procedures used by an auditor to gather evidence on which to base an opinion
    II. Measures of the quality of the auditor's performance

    a. I only
    b. II only
    c. Both I and II
    d. Neither I nor II (ID: 7645)

13. Harris, CPA, has been asked to audit and report on the balance sheet of Fox Co. but not on the statements of income, retained earnings, or cash flows. Harris will have access to all information underlying the basic financial statements. Under these circumstances, Harris may

    a. Not accept the engagement because it would constitute a violation of the profession's ethical standards
    b. Not accept the engagement because it would be tantamount to rendering a piecemeal opinion
    c. Accept the engagement because such engagements merely involve limited reporting objectives
    d. Accept the engagement, but should disclaim an opinion because of an inability to apply the procedures considered necessary (ID: 6008)

14. Sound internal control policies and procedures dictate that defective merchandise returned by customers should be presented to the

    a. Inventory control clerk
    b. Sales clerk
    c. Purchasing clerk
    d. Receiving clerk (ID: 8950)

15. "There have been no communications from regulatory agencies concerning noncompliance with, or deficiencies in, financial reporting practices that could have a material effect on the financial statements." The foregoing passage is most likely from a

    a. Report on internal control
    b. Special report
    c. Management representation letter
    d. Letter for underwriters   (ID: 6397)

16. An auditor's report on financial statements prepared on the cash receipts and disbursements basis of accounting should include all of the following **except**

    a. A reference to the note to the financial statements that describes the cash receipts and disbursements basis of accounting
    b. A statement that the cash receipts and disbursements basis of accounting is not a comprehensive basis of accounting
    c. An opinion as to whether the financial statements are presented fairly in conformity with the cash receipts and disbursements basis of accounting
    d. A statement that the audit was conducted in accordance with generally accepted auditing standards   (ID: 5700)

17. Which of the following procedures is **not** usually performed by the accountant during an annual review engagement of a nonissuer?

    a. Inquiring about actions taken at meetings of the board of directors that may affect the financial statements
    b. Issuing a report stating that the review was performed in accordance with standards issued by the AICPA
    c. Reading the financial statements to consider whether they conform with generally accepted accounting principles
    d. Communicating any material weaknesses discovered during the consideration of internal control   (ID: 2979)

18. Which of the following statements best describes the ethical standard of the profession pertaining to advertising and solicitation?

    a. All forms of advertising and solicitation are prohibited.
    b. There are no prohibitions regarding the manner in which CPAs may solicit new business.
    c. A CPA may advertise in any manner that is not false, misleading, or deceptive.
    d. A CPA may only solicit new clients through mass mailings.   (ID: 7111)

19. Which of the following relatively small misstatements most likely could have a material effect on an entity's financial statements?

    a. An illegal payment to a foreign official that was not recorded
    b. A piece of obsolete office equipment that was not retired
    c. A petty cash fund disbursement that was not properly authorized
    d. An uncollectible account receivable that was not written off   (ID: 5627)

20. A significant deficiency in internal control exists when

    a. The design or operation of a control does not allow management or employees, in the normal course of performing their assigned functions, to be able to prevent, or detect and correct misstatements on a timely basis.
    b. The person performing the control does not possess the necessary authority or competence to perform the control effectively.
    c. There is a deficiency, or a combination of deficiencies, that is less severe than a material weakness, yet important enough to merit attention by those charged with governance.
    d. The auditor finds evidence that a misstatement of the financial statements actually occurred as a direct result of a missing control.   (ID: 9036)

21. In the confirmation of accounts receivable, the auditor would most likely

    a. Request confirmation of a sample of the inactive accounts
    b. Seek to obtain positive confirmations for at least 50% of the total dollar amount of the receivables
    c. Require confirmation of all receivables from agencies of the federal government
    d. Require that confirmation requests be sent within one month of the fiscal year-end   (ID: 8963)

22. An auditor's report issued in connection with which of the following is generally **not** considered to be a special report?

    a. Compliance with requirements of government programs administered by an entity
    b. Specified elements, accounts, or items of a financial statement
    c. Financial statements prepared in accordance with an entity's income tax basis
    d. Financial information presented in a prescribed schedule that requires a prescribed form of auditor's report   (ID: 8977)

23. Which of the following procedures is usually performed by the accountant in an annual review engagement of a nonissuer?

    a. Sending a letter of inquiry to the entity's lawyer
    b. Comparing the financial statements with statements for comparable prior periods
    c. Confirming a significant percentage of receivables by direct communication with debtors
    d. Communicating significant deficiencies discovered during the study of internal control   (ID: 2787)

24. Burrow & Co., CPAs, have provided annual audit and tax compliance services to Mare Corp. for several years. Mare has been unable to pay Burrow in full for services Burrow rendered 19 months ago. Burrow is ready to begin fieldwork for the current year's audit. Under the ethical standards of the profession, which of the following arrangements will permit Burrow to begin the fieldwork on Mare's audit?

    a. Mare sets up a two-year payment plan with Burrow to settle the unpaid fee balance.
    b. Mare commits to pay the past due fee in full before the audit report is issued.
    c. Mare gives Burrow an 18-month note payable for the full amount of the past due fees before Burrow begins the audit.
    d. Mare engages another firm to perform the fieldwork, and Burrow is limited to reviewing the workpapers and issuing the audit report.   (ID: 7114)

25. Which of the following statements is correct concerning deficiencies in internal control identified in an audit of financial statements?

    a. An auditor is required to search for control deficiencies during an audit.
    b. All significant deficiencies are also considered to be material weaknesses.
    c. An auditor may communicate deficiencies during an audit or after the audit's completion.
    d. An auditor may report that no significant deficiencies were noted during an audit.   (ID: 5656)

26. Which of the following might be detected by an auditor's review of the client's sales cut-off?

    a. Excessive goods returned for credit
    b. Unrecorded sales discounts
    c. Lapping of year-end accounts receivable
    d. Inflated sales for the year   (ID: 8964)

27. When auditing an entity's financial statements in accordance with *Government Auditing Standards,* an auditor should prepare a written report on the auditor's

    a. Identification of the causes of performance problems and recommendations for actions to improve operations
    b. Understanding of internal control and assessment of control risk
    c. Field work and procedures that substantiated the auditor's specific findings and conclusions
    d. Opinion on the entity's attainment of the goals and objectives specified by applicable laws and regulations   (ID: 4282)

28. Which of the following inquiry or analytical procedures ordinarily is performed in a review engagement?

    a. Analytical procedures designed to test the accounting records by obtaining corroborating evidential matter
    b. Inquiries concerning the entity's procedures for recording and summarizing transactions
    c. Analytical procedures designed to test management's assertions regarding continued existence
    d. Inquiries of the entity's attorney concerning contingent liabilities   (ID: 2977)

29. The use of which of the following word(s) in the IESBA Code of Ethics for Professional Accountants imposes a requirement?

    a. Must.
    b. Shall
    c. Should
    d. Is required   (ID: 9297)

30. Which of the following boards is responsible for establishing requirements for professional accountants for the International Federation of Accountants?

    a. International Accounting Standards Board
    b. International Ethics Standards Board for Accountants
    c. International Code of Ethics for Accountants Board
    d. International Code of Professional Conduct Board   (ID: 9295)

———————————

Testlet 4 SIMULATIONS

Simulation 1 Accounts Receivable Confirmations

As part of the fieldwork on an engagement, the auditor obtained and documented an understanding of the company's internal controls relating to accounts receivable and assessed control risk related to accounts receivable at the maximum level. Susan, the staff person assigned to the engagement, requested and obtained from the company an aged accounts receivable schedule listing the total amount owed by each customer as of December 31, year 2, and sent the positive confirmation requests shown below to a sample of the company customers.

Confirmation Letters

February 1, year 3

Performance Marine Sales, Inc.
1284 River Road
Louisville, Kentucky 40059

Re: Balance at December 31, year 2 - $267,000

Dear Sirs:

As of December 31, year 2, our records indicate your balance with our company as the amount listed above. Please complete and sign the bottom portion of this letter and return the entire letter to our auditors, JS LLP, P.O. Box 100, Orlando, Florida 32806.

A stamped, self-addressed envelope is enclosed for your convenience.

Sincerely,

_____
Aquatic Jet Products, Inc.

The above balance is ☐ Correct

[X] Incorrect (show amount) *$325,000*

If incorrect, please provide information that could help to reconcile your account.

Response: We placed an order for $58,000 on December 26, year 2.

Signature   Title   Date

Susan's note to file:

Per discussion with the controller, the order for $58,000 was shipped f.o.b. shipping point on December 30, year 2, and was received by the customer on January 3, year 3. Therefore, no entry has been made to record the sale in year 2.

February 1, year 3

West Coast Ski Center, Inc.
163 Tide Avenue
Monterey, California 93940

Re: Balance at December 31, year 2 - $414,000

Dear Sirs:

As of December 31, year 2, our records indicate your balance with our company as the amount listed above. Please complete and sign the bottom portion of this letter and return the entire letter to our auditors, JS LLP, P.O. Box 100, Orlando, Florida 32806.

A stamped, self-addressed envelope is enclosed for your convenience.

Sincerely,

_____
Aquatic Jet Products, Inc.

The above balance is ☐ Correct

[X] Incorrect (show amount) *$320,000*

If incorrect, please provide information that could help to reconcile your account.

Response: We made a payment of $94,000 on December 12, year 2.

Signature   Title   Date

Susan's note to file:

Per discussion with the controller, the company received the payment of $94,000 on December 15, year 2, and posted it to "Other Income."

February 1, year 3

Fish & Ski World, Inc.
5660 Ocean Blvd
Port Arkansas, Texas 78373

Re: Balance at December 31, year 2 - $72,000

Dear Sirs:

As of December 31, year 2, our records indicate your balance with our company as the amount listed above. Please complete and sign the bottom portion of this letter and return the entire letter to our auditors, JS LLP, P.O. Box 100, Orlando, Florida 32806.

A stamped, self-addressed envelope is enclosed for your convenience.

Sincerely,

_____

Aquatic Jet Products, Inc.

_____

The above balance is ☐ Correct

☒ Incorrect
(show amount) *$163,000*

If incorrect, please provide information that could help to reconcile your account.

Response: Per our records, the following invoices are outstanding:

Invoice #4212 $72,000
Invoice #4593 $66,000
Invoice #4738 $25,000

Signature	Title	Date

Susan's note to file:

Invoices #4593 and 4738 are not on the A/R aging report at December 31, year 2.

February 1, year 3

NC Boating Center Inc.
110 Windward Blvd
Tierra Verde, Florida 33715

Re: Balance at December 31, year 2 - $239,000

Dear Sirs:

As of December 31, year 2, our records indicate your balance with our company as the amount listed above. Please complete and sign the bottom portion of this letter and return the entire letter to our auditors, JS LLP, P.O. Box 100, Orlando, Florida 32806.

A stamped, self-addressed envelope is enclosed for your convenience.

Sincerely,

_____

Aquatic Jet Products, Inc.

_____

The above balance is ☐ Correct

☐ Incorrect
(show amount) $_____

If incorrect, please provide information that could help to reconcile your account.

Response: We cannot determine the balance due at December 31, year 2.

Signature	Title	Date

Susan's note to file:

No amount was confirmed on the response letter.

Assume that all confirmations received have been appropriately signed, unless otherwise noted. For each customer in the table below, review the relevant confirmation letter and the comments at the bottom. Then select the best conclusion and/or follow-up procedure for each confirmation. Choose only one conclusion/procedure per confirmation. A conclusion/procedure may be used once, more than once, or not at all.

Customer	Conclusion/procedure
A. Performance Marine Sales, Inc.	
B. West Coast Ski Center, Inc.	
C. Fish & Ski World, Inc.	
D. NC Boating Center, Inc.	

Selection List

1.	Send a second request for confirmation to the customer.	4.	Verify that additional invoices noted on confirmation pertain to the subsequent year.
2.	Exception noted; propose adjustment and request that the controller post it to the accounting records.	5.	Not an exception, no further audit work deemed necessary.
3.	Verify by examining subsequent cash collections and/or shipping documents	6.	Not an exception, no adjustment necessary. Determine the sufficiency of allowance for doubtful accounts

(ID: 9252)

Simulation 2 Independence

Peirce & Hinds, CPAs, are reviewing issues of independence with regard to potential audit clients. Each of these potential clients are privately held companies. Peirce & Hinds are AICPA members. Except as noted, Peirce & Hinds do not have any other association with these potential clients.

Indicate whether Peirce & Hinds, CPAs, may accept an engagement to audit each potential client.

Statement	Yes/No
1. Hinds was the controller of Amos, Inc., resigning in January, Year 3, to partner with Peirce. Amos, Inc. is seeking an auditor for its Year 3 financial statements. Hinds no longer has any financial interest in Amos' pension plan.	
2. Worth, a former audit employee of Peirce & Hinds, quit last year and now is internal auditor at Claire Cosmetics. Worth is not owed any payments by Peirce & Hinds. Worth does not influence or participate in any of Peirce & Hinds, CPAs' activities. Peirce & Hinds, CPAs' ongoing attest engagement team plans to consider the appropriateness and necessity of engagement procedures modification to adjust for the risk that audit effectiveness could be reduced as a result of Worth's prior knowledge of the audit plan.	
3. Elegance, Inc. authorized Peirce & Hinds to sign payroll checks for it in emergency situations.	
4. Yost, a professional employee of Peirce & Hinds, is a motorcycle enthusiast. This year, he received the gift of a prototype motorcycle from Gremlin Motors, Inc. When he realized Gremlin was seeking a new auditor, Yost suggested Peirce & Hinds as auditors to Gremlin and promptly reported the gift to Peirce & Hinds.	
5. Peirce & Hinds operate a local area network for Ingot, Inc.	
6. Peirce's husband is Director of Marketing at Kelpie, Inc., but does not influence the financial reporting process in this position.	
7. Hinds interviewed applicants for controller and recommended qualified candidates to Mole, Inc.	
8. Within the last year, Peirce & Hinds performed an engagement to provide assistance in assessing business risks and control processes for Optimal Solutions, Inc.	

(ID: 9249)

Simulation 3 Errors and Fraud

Field, CPA, is auditing the financial statements of Miller Mailorder, Inc. (MMI) for the year ended January 31, 20X1. Field has compiled a list of possible errors and fraud that may result in the misstatement of MMI's financial statements.

For each possible error and fraud listed, select one internal control procedure from the answer list that, if properly designed and implemented, most likely could assist MMI in preventing or detecting the errors and fraud. A procedure may be used once, more than once, or not at all.

Possible Errors & Fraud	Internal Control Procedure
1. Customers' checks are received for less than the customers' full account balances, but the customers' full account balances are credited.	
2. Customers' checks are misappropriated before being forwarded to the cashier for deposit.	
3. Customers' checks are credited to incorrect customer accounts.	
4. Different customer accounts are each credited for the same cash receipt.	
5. Customers' checks are properly credited to customer accounts and are properly deposited, but errors are made in recording receipts in the cash receipts journal.	
6. Customers' checks are misappropriated after being forwarded to the cashier for deposit.	
7. Invalid transactions granting credit for sales returns are recorded.	

Internal Control Procedures

A. Shipping clerks compare goods received from the warehouse with the details on the shipping documents.

B. Approved sales orders are required for goods to be released from the warehouse.

C. Monthly statements are mailed to all customers with outstanding balances.

D. Shipping clerks compare goods received from the warehouse with approved sales orders.

E. Customer orders are compared with the inventory master file to determine whether items ordered are in stock.

F. Daily sales summaries are compared with control totals of invoices.

G. Shipping documents are compared with sales invoices when goods are shipped.

H. Sales invoices are compared with the master price file.

I. Customer orders are compared with an approved customer list.

J. Sales orders are prepared for each customer order.

K. Control amounts posted to the accounts receivable ledger are compared with control totals of invoices.

L. Sales invoices are compared with shipping documents and approved customer orders before invoices are mailed.

M. Prenumbered credit memos are used for granting credit for goods returned.

N. Goods returned for credit are approved by the supervisor of the Sales Department.

O. Remittance advices are separated from the checks in the mailroom and forwarded to the Accounting Department.

P. Total amounts posted to the accounts receivable ledger from remittance advices are compared with the validated bank deposit slip.

Q. The cashier examines each check for proper endorsement.

R. Validated deposit slips are compared with the cashier's daily cash summaries.

S. An employee, other than the bookkeeper, periodically prepares a bank reconciliation.

T. Sales returns are approved by the same employee who issues receiving reports evidencing actual return of goods.

(ID: 9254)

Simulation 4 Unrecorded Liabilities

Based on the company and its environment, including its internal control, the auditors assessed the risk of material misstatements to the financial statements, whether due to error or fraud, and designed the nature, timing, and extent of further audit procedures to be performed.

As a result of conducting the above risk assessment procedures, the audit program for year 2 includes the following changes from the audit program for year 1. The company has a calendar year-end and operates only on weekdays.

In conducting the audit procedures for the search for unrecorded liabilities, the materiality/scope for this area was assessed by the auditors at $6,000. Adjustments are only recorded for items equal to, or exceeding materiality.

For the items reflected in the following check register, which are **not** recorded in the accounts payable subsidiary ledger at December 31, year 2, determine if each potential liability is recorded in the proper accounting period and also determine the amount that should be journalized, if any.

Check Register				
Vendor	Check #	Check Date	Amount	Nature of Expense
Water World Distributors, Inc.	1333	1/6/year 3	$ 3,500	Water coolers in office and warehouse delivered 12/31/year 2
Daniel Breen, Esquire	1334	1/6/year 3	$ 6,000	Corporate legal services for December, year 2
Telephone Services, Inc.	1335	1/8/year 3	$ 6,500	December, year 2 telephone and computer services
Payroll processing— Paychecks	1336	1/10/year 3	$25,500	Biweekly payroll (12/25/year 2 -1/7/year 3)
Pitt Ohio Trucking Company	1337	1/10/year 3	$45,601	Trucking services 12/4/year 2 - 1/3/year 3, deliveries made evenly throughout the period
Petty cash	1338	1/17/year 3	$ 2,002	Replenish petty cash box
Smith's Forklift Repairs	1339	1/22/year 3	$11,000	Received new forklift on 12/29/year 2, ordered on 12/18/year 2
Glenn's Glass Distribution Center	1340	1/23/year 3	$12,230	Specialty goods ordered 12/20/year 2, delivered 12/31/year 2
Payroll processing— Paychecks	1341	1/24/year 3	$25,500	Biweekly payroll (1/8/year 3 -1/15/year 3)
Daniel Breen, Esquire	1342	2/6/year 3	$ 6,800	Corporate legal services for January, year 3

For each of the check numbers in the table below, indicate if an adjustment is required and if so, select its amount from the list below. Each selection may be used once, more than once, or not at all. If no adjustment is required, select $0.

Check #	Adjustment needed?		Amount
	Yes	No	
1333			
1334			
1335			
1336			
1337			
1338			
1339			
1340			
1341			
1342			

Selection List for Amount

$0	$7,650
$2,002	$9,900
$2,970	$11,000
$3,500	$12,230
$4,413	$12,750
$6,000	$25,500
$6,500	$41,188
$6,800	$45,601

(ID: 9255)

Simulation 5 Cutoff Procedures

For each of the potential December 31, year 2, sales cutoff problems listed below, select the appropriate adjustment for year 2 from the list provided. Each item in the list may be used once, more than once, or not at all.

Potential cutoff problem	Adjustment
A. The company shipped merchandise (f.o.b. destination) to a customer on December 29, year 2, and recorded the sale but not the relief of inventory. The customer received the merchandise on December 31, year 2.	
B. The company shipped merchandise (f.o.b. shipping point) on December 3, year 2, to a customer, and recorded the sale and relief of inventory. The customer, unhappy with the merchandise, returned the goods on December 29, year 2. The company records the following entry upon receipt of the goods: Inventory (dr.), Cost of Sales (cr.)	
C. The company shipped merchandise to a consignee on December 16, year 2, and did not record the transaction. The consignee returned the merchandise on December 28, year 2. Upon receipt of the goods, the company made the following entry: Inventory (dr.), Sales (cr.)	
D. The company shipped merchandise (f.o.b. shipping point) on December 29, year 2, and recorded relief of inventory, but not the sale, on that date. The customer has not received the merchandise and the company has not recorded the sale as of January 3, year 3.	

Selection List

1. No adjustment necessary.	6. Accounts Receivable (dr.) Inventory (cr.)

2. Accounts Receivable (dr.)
    Sales (cr.)
	7. Sales (dr.)
	    Accounts Receivable (cr.)
	Inventory (dr.)
	    Cost of Sales (cr.)

3. Sales (dr.)
    Accounts Receivable (cr.)
	8. Sales (dr.)
	    Inventory (cr.)

4. Inventory (dr.)
    Cost of Sales (cr.)
	9. Accounts Receivable (dr.)
	    Sales (cr.)
	Cost of Sales (dr.)
	    Inventory (cr.)

5. Cost of Sales (dr.)
    Inventory (cr.)
	10. Sales (dr.)
	    Cost of Sales (cr.)

(ID: 9253)

Simulation 6 Substantive Tests

An auditor determines that each of the following objectives will be part of a company's audit. For each objective, select **two** different substantive tests that provide the best support for the audit objective. A substantive test may be used once, more than once, or not at all.

Audit Objective	Substantive Tests
1. Receivables at the end of year 2 are properly cut off with respect to sales made in year 2.	
2. The aggregate of net receivables in the balance sheet is fairly stated at estimated net realizable value.	
3. Depreciation expense is fairly stated.	
4. Fixed assets included in the balance sheet exist.	

Selection List

A. Request positive confirmation directly from the customer of its balance owed to the company.	I. From the fixed assets subledger, trace a selection of fully depreciated assets from the ledger to the manufacturing floor and check the associated identification number.
B. Test that the income statement agrees to the change of assets minus liabilities and owner's equity.	J. Recalculate the year's depreciation expense.
C. Test the aging in the accounts receivable trial balance.	K. Review the process of assigning expected useful life to machinery with the controller and ask if any assumptions have changed.
D. Trace shipping documents to the related sales invoices and orders, and to entries in the sales journal and accounts receivable subsidiary ledger.	L. Foot the fixed asset subledger.
E. Analyze the historical relationship of bad debt write-offs in comparison with sales and accounts receivable.	M. Vouch additions to the property, plant and equipment subsidiary ledger.
F. Foot the accounts receivable trial balance.	N. Make a physical inspection of major property, plant and equipment acquisitions
G. Foot and cross-foot the sales journal.	O. Foot and cross-foot the purchases journal
H. Identify the last number used in year 2 and the first number used in year 3 for prenumbered shipping documents and prenumbered sales invoices. Trace the respective numbers to postings in the sales journal and accounts receivable subsidiary ledger.	P. Investigate and review cash receipts related to retirements and sales of property, plant and equipment during the year.

(ID: 9256)

Simulation 7 Research

You and your staff have completed an audit of a nonissuer for the calendar year ended December 31, year 2. The audit report date of the financial statement was March 11, year 3, and on March 26, year 3, the client issued the financial statements.

On April 15, year 3, as you are ascertaining that the workpapers and related audit programs are complete and properly signed off, you notice that the financial statements include a material misstatement subsequent to the issuance of an unqualified report. The misstatement was determined to be the inclusion of material nonexistent sales.

Your audit team issued the financial statements. Information regarding nonexistent sales was not known at the date of the audit report. The auditors find the subsequently discovered information is both reliable and existed at the date of the auditor's report. The team determines that the inclusion of the material nonexistent sales would have affected the audit report. The audit team believes there are persons currently relying on, or likely to rely on, the financial statements. Is the auditor's responsibility with respect to the nonexistent sales different if the auditor has resigned or been discharged prior to undertaking or completing the investigation than if he were the continuing auditor?

Reminder: On the actual exam, you will use an electronic database of authoritative literature to find and select the reference (appropriate section and paragraph of the relevant guidance). Please see the AICPA's tutorial and sample test on the exam section of their website.

	§			(ID: 9257)

MULTIPLE-CHOICE ANSWERS

Testlet 1 Answers

1. (a)   The predecessor auditor should ordinarily permit the successor auditor to review working papers, including documentation of planning, internal control, audit results, and other matters of continuing accounting and auditing significance, such as the working paper analysis of balance sheet accounts, and those relating to contingencies.   (ID: 7092)

2. (b)   If an auditor must decrease detection risk, the auditor should change the nature, extent, or timing of audit procedures. Performing procedures closer to the balance sheet date allows less opportunity for mis-statements due to roll-forward adjustments to the auditor's interim work. An increase in the assessed level of control risk will cause a decrease in the amount of misstatements that an auditor can tolerate. A decrease in the tolerable amount of misstatements would increase, not decrease, the extent of auditing procedures. (ID: 6574)

3. (b)   Book value less audit value divided by book value is the tainting percentage. [($5,000 – $4,000) / $5,000 = 0.2] The tainting percentage times the sampling interval is the projected error. 0.2 × $10,000 = $2,000 The sum of all the projected errors is the projected misstatement; there was only one error in this sample.
                                                                                                                                     (ID: 6935)

4. (b)   When an auditor is unable to conclude whether the financial statements are materially misstated due to an illegal act, the auditor generally should disclaim an opinion, or in some circumstances, issue a qualified opinion.   (ID: 165)

5. (c)   Both provisions are required by the SSARS.   (ID: 4744)

6. (a)   The AICPA's Code of Professional Conduct states that a distinguishing mark of a profession is its acceptance of responsibility to the general public.   (ID: 4757)

7. (d)   SQCS address a CPA's firm's responsibilities for its system of quality control for its accounting and auditing practice.   (ID: 33)

8. (b)   The auditor must determine a materiality level for the financial statements taken as a whole. The concept of materiality recognizes that some matters affect the fair presentation of financial statements, while others do not. Materiality judgments involve both quantitative and qualitative considerations. In making the assessment of materiality, an auditor should consider the needs of a reasonable person who would rely on the financial statements.   (ID: 5084)

9. (d)   Upon repeated random samples of a given size from a population, the distribution of the means of those samples will be a normal distribution. The mean of the distribution is equal to the population mean and the standard error of the mean of the distribution equals the population standard deviation divided by the square root of the sample size. Approximately 68% and 95% of the sample means will be within one and two standard deviations, respectively, of the mean of the distribution. All of these characteristics relate to the distribution of sample means that results from repeated samples of a given size from a population. However, the distribution of the items drawn by the auditor in a particular sample may take any form; such a sample does not necessarily have a normal distribution.   (ID: 8973)

10. (c)   Analytics should be applied to some extent to assist the auditor in planning the procedures to be performed and as an overall review in the final review stage.   (ID: 8952)

11. (a)   If financial statements compiled in conformity with OCBOA do not include disclosure of the basis, the accountant must modify the report by adding a separate paragraph that discloses the basis. Answers b., c., and d. are not options mentioned in the Standards.   (ID: 5154)

12. (d)   The independence of a member or firm may be impaired because of nondependent close relatives, which includes parent, sibling, or nondependent children that are in a position to influence the attest arrange-ment.   (ID: 7036)

13. (d)   The successor auditor should explain to the prospective client the need to make an inquiry of the predecessor and should request permission to do so. The predecessor should be contacted prior to final engagement acceptance. The predecessor may communicate with the successor provided that the client grants permission; such communication does not violate the auditor-client confidentiality. (ID: 8947)

14. (b)   The auditor has a responsibility to plan and perform the audit to obtain reasonable assurance about whether the financial statements are free of material misstatements, whether caused by error or fraud. The auditor satisfies this responsibility by exercising due care in the performance of procedures appropriate under the circumstances. If procedures indicate that material errors or fraud may exist, the auditor should extend procedures. (ID: 8948)

15. (d)   The auditor may use the work performed by, or receive direct assistance from, internal auditors, entity personnel (in addition to internal auditors), and third parties working under the direction of management or those charged with governance that provide evidence about the effectiveness of internal control. In the planning stage, the auditor may review the workpapers of the predecessor auditor to obtain knowledge of the entity's internal control; however, the information obtained is not considered to be evidence for the current audit. (ID: 89456)

16. (c)   The objective of analytical procedures used in the overall review stage of the audit is to assist the auditor in assessing the conclusions reached and in the evaluation of the overall financial statement presentation. The overall review would generally include reading the financial statements and notes and considering unusual or unexpected balances or relationships that were not previously identified. The other answers are done before the overall review stage. (ID: 5665)

17. (c)   A compilation report should state that the objective of a compilation is to assist management in presenting financial information in the form of financial statements without undertaking to obtain or provide any assurance that there are no material modifications that should be made to the financial statements. Answers a., b., and d. pertain to a review, not a compilation. (ID: 8154)

18. (b)   An auditor is required to return a client's records after the client has demanded them. Representing a client in connection with obtaining a private letter ruling is one of the specific tax matters for which an accountant may charge a contingent fee. Confidential client information may be disclosed without the client's permission in conjunction with a prospective purchase, sale, or merger of the accountant's practice. If an auditor does not follow requirements of government audits, this lapse must be disclosed in the auditor's report. (ID: 7862)

19. (a)   In a preaudit conference, a senior auditor would most likely discuss the technical and personnel aspects of a job. Feedback from the staff would occur later. Establishing the need for specialists and the use of internal auditors is done during the planning stage. Answer b. is done during fieldwork. (ID: 5077)

20. (b)   The control environment reflects the overall attitude, awareness, and actions of the board of directors, management, owners, and others concerning the importance of control and its emphasis in the entity. If management is dominated by one individual who is also a shareholder, aggressive reporting and the achievement of profit goals may be overemphasized to the detriment of proper reporting. Answers a., c., and d. represent examples of positive control environment influences. (ID: 6390)

21. (a)   The written representation letter should be signed by members of management who the auditor believes are responsible for and knowledgeable, directly or through others in the organization, about the matters covered by the representations. Normally, the chief executive officer and chief financial officer should sign the letter. (ID: 8954)

22. (b)   The omission of a procedure that was considered necessary at the time of the audit does not necessarily imply that the original opinion is faulty, or that not enough procedures were performed. Thus, the auditor should first assess the importance of the omitted procedure to the auditor's present ability to support the previously expressed opinion. The results of other procedures originally applied or the results of subsequent audits may provide evidence for the original audit opinion. If, at this point, the auditor concludes that the omitted procedure is indeed necessary to support the opinion, then the auditor should undertake to apply the omitted or an alternative procedure. (ID: 8956)

23. (a) Before submission, the accountant should read the compiled financial statements and consider whether such financial statements appear to be appropriate in form and free from obvious material errors. In this context, the term *error* refers to mistakes in the compilation of financial statements, including arithmetical or clerical mistakes, and mistakes in the application of accounting principles, including inadequate disclosure. A representation letter from members of management usually is not obtained in a compilation engagement. Inquiry of management concerning actions taken at meetings of the stockholders and the board of directors is a procedure normally used in a review engagement, and is not necessary in a compilation engagement. The accountant is not required to make inquiries or perform other procedures to verify, corroborate, or review information supplied by the entity. (ID: 5693)

24. (d) Several relationships impair independence, including being a member of management (including the board of directors) or promoter. Serving as a client's general counsel, stock transfer, escrow agent, or registrar also impairs independence. Under the ethical standards of the profession, an advisor relationship in and of itself doesn't impair an auditor's independence. (ID: 8175)

25. (b) The auditor's primary consideration is whether, and how, a specific control prevents, or detects and corrects, material misstatements in relevant assertions related to classes of transactions, account balances, or disclosures. An auditor is usually concerned with the operating effectiveness of controls as opposed to operating efficiency. Answers c. and d. are inherent limitations of internal control. (ID: 7488)

26. (c) The plant manager has a thorough knowledge of factory operations. This knowledge includes an awareness of the productive capability of the plant machinery, as well as new machinery on the market. As a result, the plant manager would know whether a particular machine is obsolete. The plant manager has no contact with accounts receivable and, thus, is not in a position to know about the adequacy of the provision for uncollectible accounts. The auditor determines the appropriateness of inventory observation procedures. The plant manager would be helpful in identifying the location of inventory. The plant manager is not responsible for procuring necessary insurance coverage and, therefore, would not be aware that such procurement was deferred. (ID: 8955)

27. (a) If the other information is not revised to eliminate the material inconsistency, the auditor should consider other actions such as revising the audit report to include an explanatory paragraph describing the material inconsistency; withholding the audit report; or withdrawing from the engagement, if not prohibited from doing so by law or regulation. The auditor should request that management consult with a qualified third party to help resolve the issue—an auditor should never consult with a client's legal counsel without first obtaining the client's permission. Issuing a qualified opinion would be misleading since the financial statements are presented fairly. (ID: 8957)

28. (a) If a member does not have the ability to direct investments, an investment in a client through a financial service product (such as a mutual fund) is considered an indirect financial interest and, hence, doesn't necessarily impair independence. Direct or material indirect financial interest in a client impairs independence. In addition, if a member has significant influence over the non-regulated mutual investment fund, independence would be considered to be impaired. Independence is considered impaired if a covered member owns stock in a client through an investment club, where presumably the member has the ability to direct investments, whether or not exercised, resulting in a direct financial interest. Accordingly, any of the club's investments in a client are deemed to impair independence regardless of materiality. Independence is considered impaired even if a CPA has a material indirect financial interest in a client, whether or not it is placed in a blind trust. Furthermore, the member should ensure that any blind trust that s/he is a beneficiary of does not hold a direct or material indirect financial interest in any of the member's client's. The requirements for independence with regard to ordinary trusts are not less restrictive. (ID: 7113)

29. (c) It is difficult to substantiate representations that a related-party transaction was consummated on terms equivalent to those that prevail in arm's-length transactions. Thus, if a footnote includes such a representation, the auditor should express a qualified or adverse opinion because of a departure from GAAP. Answers a., b., and d. are all appropriate disclosures with respect to related-party transactions. (ID: 8958)

30. (b) The service in question constitutes a type of service performed by public accountants, and the member may hire such an employee as long as the CPA is able to supervise the specialist and evaluate her/his results. The CPA is not required to be a specialist outside of the realm of accounting and tax services. The

CPA is permitted to be associated with non-CPA professionals, as long as the association is not misleading and the client is aware of the relationship. (ID: 4240)

_____

Testlet 2 Answers

1. **(b)** As management signs a representation letter that includes a statement that all known fraud has been reported to the auditor, if an auditor discovers fraud known to management, but undisclosed to the auditor, the auditor has evidence that management has lied regarding audit information at least once. This impairs reliance on other management statements. While an aggressive attitude toward meeting profit goals is suggestive of incentive and management decision dominated by one person may provide opportunity to commit fraud, they are not as important as actual known management deception. Some weaknesses in internal control may be knowingly left uncorrected due to cost-benefit considerations. (ID: 7631)

2. **(a)** The auditor should use the knowledge obtained in evaluating the design and implementation of controls to identify types of potential misstatements; consider factors that affect the risks of material misstatement; and design tests of controls, when applicable, and substantive procedures. (ID: 5951)

3. **(b)** The auditor may test controls over the recording of retirements by tracing certain items of equipment from the accounting records and locating them in the plant to make sure that they have not been retired. The "other assets" account has nothing to do with the recording of retired fixed assets. Tracing from the plant assets to the books does not consider assets which may appear on the books even though they have been retired. If retired equipment was not removed from the records, the related depreciation calculation would not reveal its retirement. (ID: 81)

4. **(a)** Audit documentation provides the principal support for the representation in the auditor's report that the auditor performed the audit in accordance with generally accepted auditing standards; and provides the principal support for the opinion expressed regarding the financial information or the assertion to the effect that an opinion cannot be expressed. (ID: 5689)

5. **(a)** When compiled financial statements omit substantially all disclosures, the accountant should indicate this in the report. The SSARS include the following as an example of an appropriate additional paragraph: "Management has elected to omit substantially all the disclosures required by accounting principles generally accepted in the United States of America. If the omitted disclosures were included in the financial statements, they might influence the user's conclusions about the company's financial position, results of operations, and cash flows. Accordingly, these financial statements are not designed for those who are not informed about such matters." The accountant must conclude that the omission was not made with the intention of misleading those who might reasonably be expected to use such financial statements. Answer b., indicating that the statements are prepared in conformity with OCBOA is an inappropriate remedy for the omission of disclosures required by GAAP. However, it should be noted that if financial statements compiled in conformity with a comprehensive basis of accounting other than GAAP do not include disclosure of the basis of accounting used, the basis should be disclosed in the accountant's report. Answers c. and d. are not acceptable statements for inclusion in the report. (ID: 5155)

6. **(d)** A CPA who provides auditing and other attestation services should be independent in fact and appearance. In providing all other services, an accountant should maintain objectivity and avoid conflicts of interest. Thus, an accountant need not be independent when providing compilation services or when preparing a tax return. (ID: 5182)

7. **(d)** In planning the scope of the audit, the auditor should consider, among other matters, the effect of the assessed risk of material misstatement at the overall financial statement level. When the auditor is developing a preliminary audit strategy, the auditor has not performed sampling procedures, interim tests, nor inquiry of the client's attorney. (ID: 2276)

8. **(b)** An auditor may perform an examination of internal control only if (1) management provides its assertion about the effectiveness of the entity's internal control in a report that accompanies the auditor's report; (2) management accepts responsibility for the effectiveness of the entity's internal control; (3) management

evaluates the effectiveness of the entity's internal control using suitable and available criteria; and (4) management supports its assertion about the effectiveness of the entity's internal control with sufficient appropriate evidence. The other answers are not required conditions for acceptance of the engagement. (ID: 5091)

9. (b) Incompatible functions are those that place any person in a position to both perpetrate and conceal errors or fraud in the normal course of her/his duties. A well-designed plan of organization separates the duties of authorization, recordkeeping, and custody of assets. Answers a. and d. do not separate custody and recordkeeping. Answer c. does not provide verification of inventory. (ID: 89)

10. (b) When qualifying an opinion because of insufficiency of audit evidence, an auditor refers to the situation in the scope and opinion paragraphs and includes an explanatory paragraph before the opinion paragraph. Management is responsible for the financial statements, including the notes; an auditor merely recommends changes. (ID: 7100)

11. (b) Obtaining a management representation letter is required by the SSARS. The procedures in the other answers are not required. (ID: 5148)

12. (b) A CPA firm's procedures should enable an assistant to document the details of the disagreement with the conclusion reached. If the assistant concludes that the financial statements could be materially misstated, the assistant should make the concerns known to the appropriate level of management within the organization and should consider preparing appropriate documentation. If appropriate action is not taken, the assistant should consider her/his continuing relationship with the employer and any responsibility to communicate to third parties, such as regulatory authorities. The assistant may wish to consult with legal counsel. (ID: 4241)

13. (d) When assessing the internal auditor's objectivity, the auditor should obtain information about the organizational status of the internal auditor including the organizational level to which the internal auditor reports. Answers a., b., and c. indicate competency, not objectivity. (ID: 5950)

14. (c) Inherent risk and control risk are present whether or not an audit is done. Detection risk is the risk that a material misstatement is present, and it is not detected during the audit. All three components of audit risk may be assessed in quantitative or qualitative terms. None of these types of risk arise from the misapplication of auditing standards; they are present in any audit. Inherent risk and control risk cannot be changed at the auditor's discretion; the auditor can only change the assessment of the level of inherent and control risk. (ID: 5081)

15. (b) The requirement is to determine the best test of controls for a procedure that calls for an approved receiving report to accompany every check. This control can be tested by selecting canceled checks and ascertaining that the related receiving reports are dated no later than the check. (In addition, the auditor probably would want to ascertain that the check amounts correspond to the price of the goods received.) If the auditor selects receiving reports (rather than checks) to test the control, the auditor will not become aware of instances of checks with no related receiving report. (ID: 8960)

16. (a) If the auditor decides to depart from an unqualified opinion as a result of the report or findings of a specialist, reference to and identification of the specialist may be made in the auditor's report if the auditor believes such reference will facilitate an understanding of the reason for the departure. (ID: 8968)

17. (c) When the accountant believes that modification of the standard report is not adequate to indicate the deficiencies in the financial statements as a whole, the accountant should withdraw from the review (or compilation) engagement and provide no further services with respect to those financial statements. (ID: 5698)

18. (b) A CPA who provides auditing and other attestation services should be independent in fact and appearance. In providing all other services, an accountant should maintain objectivity and avoid conflicts of interest. A CPA need not be independent when providing tax and management advisory services. A CPA need not be independent when not in public practice. (ID: 8668)

19. (a) Whether the data were processed in an IT system or in a manual accounting system generally would not influence the auditor's consideration of the reliability of data for purposes of analytics. Factors that do influence the reliability of data include whether the data was obtained from independent sources outside the entity or from sources within the entity; whether sources within the entity were independent of those who are

responsible for the amount being audited; whether the data was developed under a reliable system with adequate controls; whether the data was subjected to audit testing in the current or prior year; and whether the expectations were developed using data from a variety of sources. (ID: 151)

20. (b) By reconciling vendors' monthly statements with the subsidiary payable ledger accounts, the error would be corrected in at most a month's time. Footing the purchases journal only verifies its mathematical accuracy. Answer c. is incorrect because the erroneous purchase amount in the purchases journal was originally carried through from the client's ledger accounts. Vendors might not confirm the fact that the client is overstating its liability for purchases. (ID: 8959)

21. (d) Once the audit strategy has been established, the auditor is able to start the development of a more detailed audit plan to address the various matters identified in the audit strategy, taking into account the need to achieve the audit objectives. The audit program should include a description of the nature, timing, and extent of planned further audit procedures at the relevant assertion level for each material class of transactions, account balance, and disclosure. Answers a., b., and c. are all considerations of the substantive and analytical procedures necessary to satisfy the audit objectives. (ID: 4673)

22. (d) The current (successor) auditor should indicate in the introductory paragraph of the report (1) that the financial statements of the prior period were audited by another auditor, (2) the date of the prior report, (3) the type of report issued by the predecessor auditor, and (4) the reasons for any report other than a standard report. The successor expresses an opinion in the opinion paragraph only on the period which the successor audited. The successor does not disclaim or express an opinion on the prior-period statements. The successor should not name the predecessor in the report unless the predecessor's practice was acquired by, or merged with, that of the successor. (ID: 8969)

23. (a) International standards on auditing require that if the terms of the audit engagement are changed the auditor and management shall agree on and record the new terms of the engagement in an engagement letter or other suitable form of written (not oral) agreement. Note that auditing standards generally accepted in the United States do not include this requirement. If the auditor is unable to agree to a change of the terms of the audit engagement and is not permitted by management to continue the original audit engagement, the auditor shall withdraw from the audit engagement (not issue a disclaimer of opinion), where possible under applicable law or regulation (not withdraw under any circumstances) and determine whether there is any obligation, either contractual or otherwise, to report the circumstances to other parties, such as those charged with governance, owners or regulators. (ID: 89458)

24. (a) Independence is considered to be impaired if, when the report on the client's current year is issued, fees remain unpaid for professional services provided more than one year prior to the date of the report. Such amounts assume the characteristics of a loan within the meaning of Rule 101. Recommending a controller's position description is not a violation of the ethical standards as long as the final hiring decision is made by management of the client. Purchasing a CPA firm's practice of monthly write-ups does not violate any provisions of the Code or client confidentiality. A member firm may make arrangements with a bank to collect notes issued by a client in payment of fees due. (ID: 3897)

25. (d) A successor auditor should attempt certain communications before accepting the engagement. (ID: 8137)

26. (c) The A/P Department receives the vendor's invoice with quantities, descriptions, and prices of purchases. A copy of the purchase order enables the A/P Department to (1) compare the invoice and purchase order price, (2) ensure that the purchase was authorized, and (3) compare the quantity ordered and purchased. The A/P copy of the purchase order will not ensure that the goods were received by the party requesting the goods. (ID: 8967)

27. (c) The financial statements are the representations of management, who would like the financial position of the entity to appear as sound as possible. Thus, the auditor is concerned with possible overstatements of revenues, income, assets, and capital. Conversely, the auditor is concerned with the possible understatement of any losses, expenses, and liabilities. (ID: 8962)

28. (b) Included in the fieldwork standards of supplemental working paper requirements for financial audits is the statement that working papers should contain sufficient information so that supplementary oral explanations are not required. Written representations from management are not required. An audit does not ensure that all illegal acts and contingent liabilities resulting from noncompliance will be discovered by the auditor. The auditor's workpapers should include positive statements about the procedures applied and the results of those procedures; thus, there is no requirement that the working papers contain a caveat statement. (ID: 4281)

29. (a) According to the standards of the profession, providing extensive advisory services for a client would not impair the CPA's independence. Contracting with a client to supervise the client's office personnel, signing client checks, and accepting luxurious gifts would all impair a CPA's independence. (ID: 5873)

30. (c) A direct financial interest (business investment) always impairs an accountant's independence, regardless of materiality. Independence is impaired when a CPA holds a direct or material indirect financial interest. A loan to or from a client generally impairs independence; however, certain loans are permitted. These loans include car loans collateralized by the vehicles from financial institution clients when the loans are current as to all terms at all times and obtained under normal lending terms, requirements, and procedures. Grandfathered mortgages that are current as to all terms obtained under normal lending procedures, terms, and requirements before the institution became a client requiring independence are also permitted. With a twenty-first century question mentioning a 1990 date, the candidate may assume this loan meets these requirements. Candidates may have to make similar assumptions to answer other exam questions. (ID: 7864)

Testlet 3 Answers

1. (d) Reviewing the engagement completion document and confirming with the engagement partner that there are no significant unresolved matters is not a significant judgment related to engagement planning. (ID: 89457)

2. (b) Tests of controls are designed to obtain evidence about the operating effectiveness of internal controls. Deviations from prescribed procedures would be evidence of ineffectiveness. Answers a., c., and d. are substantive tests (tests of details and analytics) performed to detect material misstatements in the account balance, transaction class, and disclosure components of financial statements. (ID: 8970)

3. (c) The management representation letter should be dated as of the date of the auditor's report. (ID: 5685)

4. (c) When the principal auditor makes reference to another auditor, the principal auditor doesn't assume responsibility for the other auditor's work. At a minimum, the principal auditor should inquire about the professional reputation and independence of the other CPA. Reviewing the other CPA's work papers, discussing the results of the other CPA's procedures, and determining that the other CPA has a sufficient understanding of the subsidiary's controls are beyond the minimum requirements. (ID: 6831)

5. (a) When engaged to compile the financial statements of a nonissuer, the accountant should obtain an understanding of the accounting principles and practices used by the client in measuring, recognizing, recording, and disclosing all significant accounts and disclosures in the financial statements. The accountant's understanding also may include matters such as changes in accounting practices and principles and differences in the client's business model as compared with normal practices within the industry. The accountant should also be alert to unusual accounting policies and procedures that come to the accountant's attention as a result of this knowledge of the industry. Obtaining an understanding of the client's internal control and risk assessment are not part of a compilation engagement. (ID: 6823)

6. (c) Independence is considered impaired if a spouse or dependent person (immediate family) of the member is employed in a position that allows significant influence over the client's operating, financial, or accounting policies. Independence is considered impaired if the position with the client involves activities that are audit-sensitive, even though the position is not one that allows significant influence. A person's activities would be considered audit sensitive if such activities are normally an element of, or subject to, significant

internal controls; for example, the positions of cashier, internal auditor, accounting supervisor, purchasing agent, or inventory warehouse supervisor. (ID: 7112)

7. (a) When a client processes financial data in electronic form without paper documentation, the auditor may audit on a more continuous basis than a traditional system, as a convenience, and may be required to audit on a more continuous basis to obtain sufficient, competent evidence as documentation for some transactions may be available only for a limited time. An embedded audit module can facilitate this continuous auditing. If anything, an auditor may rely less on controls that emphasize segregation of duties. Digital certificate verification and testing of firewall boundaries are more concerned with security than internal control. (ID: 6839)

8. (c) The independent auditor is concerned primarily with those policies and procedures that are relevant to the audit. Generally, controls that are relevant to the audit pertain to an entity's objective of preparing financial statements for external purposes that are fairly presented in conformity with GAAP. Controls over land and buildings and common stock are of primary concern to the auditor because they relate directly to financial statement assertions. Control over meetings of shareholders and the minutes of BOD meetings are in the nature of administrative controls. Although these controls are of secondary concern to the auditor, the controls over the minutes of BOD meetings are more important than those over shareholder meetings because they relate directly to transaction authorization. Shareholder meetings have only an indirect impact on such authorization.

(ID: 8971)

9. (b) The response in answer b. is vague and probably would need clarification. The other answers indicate that the client probably doesn't have any material liability concerning the matters discussed. (ID: 6364)

10. (b) When the auditor concludes there is substantial doubt about the entity's ability to continue as a going concern for a reasonable period of time, the auditor should consider the possible effects on the financial statements and the adequacy of the related disclosure. The auditor would issue a qualified or adverse opinion if the auditor concludes that the entity's disclosure with respect to the ability to continue as a going concern is inadequate. The auditor may report adjustments to the audit committee, however, further action is required to deal specifically with the going concern issue, regardless of changes to accounting estimates. Substantial doubt about the entity's ability to continue as a going concern for a reasonable period of time that arose in the current period does not imply that a basis for such doubt existed in the prior period and should not affect the auditor's report on the prior-period statements presented on a comparative basis. (ID: 4727)

11. (d) Neither an annual review nor a compilation engagement contemplates obtaining an understanding of internal control or assessing control risk; testing of accounting records and of responses to inquiries by obtaining corroborating evidential matter; and certain other procedures ordinarily performed during an audit.

(ID: 2327)

12. (b) Auditing standards differ from auditing procedures in that procedures relate to acts to be performed, whereas standards deal with measures of the quality of the performance of those acts and the objectives to be attained by the use of the procedures undertaken. (ID: 7645)

13. (c) An auditor is not precluded from reporting on only one of the basic financial statements and not the others. A scope limitation would not exist if the auditor is able to apply all the procedures the auditor considers necessary. Such engagements involve limited reporting objectives. Acceptance of the engagement is not a violation of the profession's ethical standards, as the work can be expected to be accomplished. A piecemeal opinion is an opinion on specific elements of the financial statements when the auditor has disclaimed an opinion on the statements as a whole and is unacceptable. A disclaimer of opinion would be unnecessary because Harris will have access to all information underlying the basic financial statements and, thus, could apply all the procedures needed.

(ID: 6008)

14. (d) Sound control procedures dictate that an employee should not perform incompatible functions. Thus, all incoming shipments, including customer returns, should be processed by Receiving Department personnel. A receiving clerk should inspect the merchandise and prepare a receiving report. This employee should not have control over the inventory records because that would enable her/him to divert merchandise without recording it.

(ID: 8950)

15. (c) Whether there have been communications from regulatory agencies concerning noncompliance with or deficiencies in financial reporting practices should be addressed in a management representation letter. A report on internal control or another special report generally would not discuss communications from other entities. Letters for underwriters concentrate on financial statements more than internal control. (ID: 6397)

16. (b) The cash receipts and disbursements schedule is merely a comprehensive basis of accounting other than GAAP (OCBOA). The auditor's report should include a paragraph that refers to the note to the financial statements that describes the basis of accounting. The report should include a paragraph that expresses the auditor's opinion on whether the financial statements are presented fairly. The report should include a paragraph that states that the audit was conducted in accordance with GAAS. (ID: 5700)

17. (d) An annual review does *not* contemplate obtaining an understanding of the internal control or assessing control risk, tests of accounting records and of responses to inquiries by obtaining corroborating evidential matter, and certain other procedures ordinarily performed during an audit. Answers a., b., and c. are usually performed by the accountant in an annual review. (ID: 2979)

18. (c) Advertising or other forms of solicitation that are false, misleading, or deceptive are prohibited since they are not in the public interest. (ID: 7111)

19. (a) The auditor should consider the implications of an illegal act in relation to other aspects of the audit, particularly the reliability of representations of management. A relatively small misstatement of unretired fixed assets, improperly authorized petty cash fund disbursement, or uncollectible account receivable that was not written off have less impact on the financial statements taken as a whole and, by themselves, do not tend to place doubt on the integrity of management. (ID: 5627)

20. (c) A significant deficiency is a deficiency in internal control, or combination of deficiencies in internal control, that is less severe than a material weakness, yet important enough to merit attention by those charged with governance. Answer a. is the definition of a deficiency in internal control. Answer b. describes one of the conditions for a deficiency in the operation of a control to exist (the other condition is when a properly designed control does not operate as designed). Answer d. is false; the severity of a deficiency in internal control (taken into consideration by the auditor in the determination of whether a deficiency is either a significant deficiency or a material weakness) does not depend on whether a misstatement actually occurred. (ID: 9036)

21. (a) By requesting confirmation of a sample of inactive accounts, the auditor seeks to determine the accuracy of records relating to those accounts. Due to their inactive nature, defalcations could occur in these accounts, e.g., through lapping or an improper write-off. The cost of obtaining positive confirmations for at least 50% of the total dollar value of receivables generally would outweigh the benefits derived from such confirmations. The auditor does not treat receivables from federal agencies differently than other receivables, i.e., they are also subject to selective testing. Receivable confirmations can be sent as of any date. (ID: 8963)

22. (a) A report issued in connection with an entity's compliance with requirements of government programs it administers is not considered to be a special report. Answers b., c., and d. are special reports which include auditors' reports issued in connection with (1) financial statements that are prepared in conformity with a comprehensive basis of accounting other than GAAP (e.g., income tax basis), (2) specified elements, accounts, or items of a financial statement, (3) compliance with aspects of contractual agreements or regulatory requirements related to audited financial statements, (4) financial presentations to comply with contractual agreements or regulatory provisions, and (5) financial information presented in prescribed forms or schedules that require a prescribed form of auditor's report. (ID: 8977)

23. (b) An accountant's review procedures will include inquiry and analytical procedures. Analytics are designed to identify relationships and individual items that appear to be unusual, and consist of (1) comparison of the financial statements with statements for comparable prior period(s), (2) comparison of the statements with anticipated results, if available, and (3) study of the relationships of the elements of the statements that would be expected to conform with a predictable pattern based on the entity's experience. Answers a., c., and d. are procedures that should be performed in an audit. (ID: 2787)

24. (b)   Independence is considered impaired if fees for professional services rendered for more than one year prior are not collected before the issuance of the CPA's report for the current year. This includes billed and unbilled fees and notes receivable arising from such fees (ET 191-52).   (ID: 7114)

25. (c)   An auditor may communicate some deficiencies in internal control during an audit of financial statements in addition to after the audit's completion due to their significance and the need for timely corrective action. Such early communication is not required to be in writing. However, all significant deficiencies and material weaknesses should ultimately be reported in the required written communication to management and those charged with governance even if they were remediated during the audit. For a nonissuer, the required written communication is best made by the audit report release date, but should be made no later than 60 days following this date. For an issuer, it is required to be made prior to the issuance of the audit report. In an audit of financial statements, the auditor is not required to search for deficiencies in internal control. All material weaknesses are significant deficiencies, but not all significant deficiencies are material weaknesses. An auditor should not issue a written communication stating that no significant deficiencies were identified during the audit. (Management or those charged with governance may request that the auditor issue a communication indicating that no material weaknesses were identified to submit to a governmental authority. This is allowable.)   (ID: 5656)

26. (d)   The main objective of the sales cutoff test is to determine that sales are recorded in the proper period. The auditor would test for excessive sales returns and discounts from a sample encompassing the entire period, not just the year-end. Lapping of A/R would be detected by tracing payments received to postings in the appropriate receivable subsidiary ledger.   (ID: 8964)

27. (b)   In accordance with *Government Auditing Standards,* an auditor must also report on internal control over financial reporting and on compliance with laws, regulations, and provisions of contracts or grant agreements when providing an opinion or a disclaimer on financial statements. Answer a. represents procedures to be reported in a performance audit. Specific procedures performed are not included in the auditor's report. The auditor provides an opinion on the fairness of the presentation of the financial statements taken as a whole rather than an opinion on an entity's attainment of goals and objectives.   (ID: 4282)

28. (b)   Procedures ordinarily performed during a review include inquiries concerning the entity's procedures for recording and summarizing transactions. They are not concerned with corroborating evidential matter, management's assertions concerning continued existence, or the entity's attorney's opinion concerning contingent liabilities or other audit procedures.   (ID: 2977)

29. (b)   The word *shall* is used to impose a requirement in the IESBA Code of Ethics for Professional Accountants.   (ID: 9297)

30. (b)   The International Ethics Standards Board for Accountants (IESBA) of the International Federation of Accountants (IFAC) issues the Code of Ethics for Professional Accountants.   (ID: 9295)

———————————

PERFORMANCE BY TOPICS

The practice exam testlet and question numbers corresponding to each chapter of this textbook are listed below. To assess your preparedness for the exam, record the number and percentage of questions you answered correctly in each topic area.

Chapter 1:
Standards &
Related Topics

Question #	Correct √
1:1	
1:13	
2:25	
3:12	
# Questions	4

Correct _____
% Correct _____

Chapter 2: Planning

Question #	Correct √
1:2	
1:4	
1:8	
1:14	
1:19	
2:1	
2:2	
2:7	
3:19	
# Questions	9

Correct _____
% Correct _____

Chapter 3:
Internal Control

Question #	Correct √
1:20	
1:25	
2:3	
2:9	
2:14	
2:15	
2:20	
3:2	
3:8	
3:14	
3:20	
3:25	
# Questions	12

Correct _____
% Correct _____

Chapter 4:
Evidence & Procedures

Question #	Correct √
1:10	
1:16	
1:21	
1:26	
1:29	
2:4	
2:13	
2:16	
2:19	
3:3	
3:9	
3:15	
# Questions	12

Correct _____
% Correct _____

Chapter 5:
Audit Programs

Question #	Correct √
2:21	
2:26	
2:27	
3:21	
3:26	
# Questions	5

Correct _____
% Correct _____

Chapter 6:
Audit Sampling

Question #	Correct √
1:3	
1:9	
# Questions	2

Correct _____
% Correct _____

Chapter 7:
Auditing IT Systems

Question #	Correct √
3:7	
# Questions	1

Correct _____
% Correct _____

Chapter 8:
Reports on Audited
Financial Statements

Question #	Correct √
1:22	
1:27	
2:10	
2:22	
3:4	
3:10	
3:13	
# Questions	7

Correct _____
% Correct _____

Chapter 9:
Government Auditing

Question #	Correct √
2:28	
3:27	
# Questions	2

Correct _____
% Correct _____

Chapter 10:
Other Auditing Standards

Question #	Correct √
2:23	
3:1	
# Questions	2

Correct _____
% Correct _____

Chapter 11:
Other Types of Reports

Question #	Correct √
3:16	
3:22	
# Questions	2

Correct _____
% Correct _____

Chapter 12:
Accounting & Review
Services

Question #	Correct √
1:5	
1:11	
1:17	
1:23	
2:5	
2:6	
2:11	
2:17	
3:5	
3:11	
3:17	
3:23	
3:28	
# Questions	13

Correct _____
% Correct _____

Chapter 13:
Attestation Engagements

Question #	Correct √
1:15	
2:8	
# Questions	2

Correct _____
% Correct _____

Chapter 14:
Accountants' Professional
Responsibilities

Question #	Correct √
1:6	
1:7	
1:12	
1:18	
1:24	
1:28	
1:30	
2:12	
2:18	
2:24	
2:29	
2:30	
3:6	
3:18	
3:24	
3:29	
3:30	
# Questions	17

Correct _____
% Correct _____

PERFORMANCE BY AICPA CONTENT SPECIFICATION OUTLINE

The practice exam testlet and question numbers corresponding to each area of the AICPA content specification outline (CSO) are listed below. To assess your preparedness for the exam, record the number and percentage of questions you answered correctly in each CSO area.

CSO I Auditing and Attestation: Engagement Acceptance and Understanding the Assignment (12% - 16%)

Question #	Correct	√
1:1		
1:13		
1:15		
1:19		
2:8		
2:13		
2:23		
2:25		
3:1		
3:12		
3:13		
# Questions	11	
# Correct		
% Correct		

CSO II Auditing and Attestation: Understanding the Entity and Its Environment (including Internal Control) (16% - 20%)

Question #	Correct	√
1:2		
1:8		
1:20		
1:25		
2:1		
2:2		
2:7		
2:9		
2:14		
2:19		
2:20		
2:26		
3:2		
3:7		
3:8		
3:14		
3:19		
# Questions	17	
# Correct		
% Correct		

CSO III Auditing and Attestation: Performing Audit Procedures and Evaluating Evidence (16% - 20%)

Question #	Correct	√
1:3		
1:9		
1:14		
1:21		
1:26		
2:3		
2:15		
2:21		
2:27		
3:3		
3:9		
3:15		
3:20		
3:21		
3:25		
3:26		
# Questions	16	
# Correct		
% Correct		

CSO IV Auditing and Attestation: Evaluating Audit Findings, Communications, and Reporting (16% - 20%)

Question #	Correct	√
1:4		
1:10		
1:16		
1:22		
1:27		
1:29		
2:4		
2:10		
2:16		
2:22		
2:28		
3:4		
3:10		
3:16		
3:22		
3:27		
# Questions	16	
# Correct		
% Correct		

CSO V Accounting and Review Services Engagements (12% - 16%)

Question #	Correct	√
1:5		
1:11		
1:17		
1:23		
2:5		
2:6		
2:11		
2:17		
3:5		
3:11		
3:17		
3:23		
3:28		
# Questions	13	
# Correct		
% Correct		

CSO VI Professional Responsibilities (16% - 20%)

Question #	Correct	√
1:6		
1:7		
1:12		
1:18		
1:24		
1:28		
1:30		
2:12		
2:18		
2:24		
2:29		
2:30		
3:6		
3:18		
3:24		
3:29		
3:30		
# Questions	17	
# Correct		
% Correct		

TESTLET 4 SIMULATION ANSWERS

Simulation 1 Accounts Receivable Confirmations

Customer	Conclusion/procedure
A. Performance Marine Sales, Inc.	2
B. West Coast Ski Center, Inc.	2
C. Fish & Ski World, Inc.	4
D. NC Boating Center, Inc.	3

Selection List

1. Send a second request for confirmation to the customer.	4. Verify that additional invoices noted on confirmation pertain to the subsequent year.
2. Exception noted; propose adjustment and request that the controller post it to the accounting records.	5. Not an exception, no further audit work deemed necessary.
3. Verify by examining subsequent cash collections and/or shipping documents	6. Not an exception, no adjustment necessary. Determine the sufficiency of allowance for doubtful accounts

A. 2

The client should record the sale and relief of inventory because the title passed to the client's customer when the merchandise (order for $58,000) was delivered to the common carrier (f.o.b. shipping point) on December 30, year 2.

B. 2

The client should adjust the accounting records by debiting "other income" and crediting "accounts receivable."

C. 4

The auditor must confirm that the additional invoices (nos. 4593 and 4738) listed by the client's customer on the confirmation pertain to the subsequent year. If they do, it is not an exception and no adjustment to the accounting records is needed.

D. 3

The auditor should perform the additional audit procedures described, i.e., examining subsequent cash receipts and/or shipping documents to confirm the accounting records are correct. As an alternative (not included on this particular simulation's selection list) the auditor could decide to send a second confirmation request providing the individual invoice numbers and amounts or attaching copies of the individual unpaid invoices if in her/his judgment this would help the client's customer with the verification.

(ID: 9252)

Simulation 2 Independence

Statement	Yes/No
1. Hinds was the controller of Amos, Inc., resigning in January, Year 3, to partner with Peirce. Amos, Inc. is seeking an auditor for its Year 3 financial statements. Hinds no longer has any financial interest in Amos' pension plan.	No
2. Worth, a former audit employee of Peirce & Hinds, quit last year and now is internal auditor at Claire Cosmetics. Worth is not owed any payments by Peirce & Hinds. Worth does not influence or participate in any of Peirce & Hinds, CPAs' activities. Peirce & Hinds, CPAs' ongoing attest engagement team plans to consider the appropriateness and necessity of engagement procedures modification to adjust for the risk that audit effectiveness could be reduced as a result of Worth's prior knowledge of the audit plan.	Yes
3. Elegance, Inc. authorized Peirce & Hinds to sign payroll checks for it in emergency situations.	No
4. Yost, a professional employee of Peirce & Hinds, is a motorcycle enthusiast. This year, he received the gift of a prototype motorcycle from Gremlin Motors, Inc. When he realized Gremlin was seeking a new auditor, Yost suggested Peirce & Hinds as auditors to Gremlin and promptly reported the gift to Peirce & Hinds.	No
5. Peirce & Hinds operate a local area network for Ingot, Inc.	No
6. Peirce's husband is Director of Marketing at Kelpie, Inc., but does not influence the financial reporting process in this position.	Yes
7. Hinds interviewed applicants for controller and recommended qualified candidates to Mole, Inc.	Yes
8. Within the last year, Peirce & Hinds performed an engagement to provide assistance in assessing business risks and control processes for Optimal Solutions, Inc.	Yes

1. No

Independence would be impaired. An individual who formerly was employed by a client or associated with a client as an officer, director, promoter, underwriter, voting trustee, or trustee for a pension or profit-sharing trust of the client would impair the firm's independence if the individual was in a position to influence the attest engagement for the client when the attest engagement covers any period that includes the former employment or association with that client. By accepting this engagement, Hinds would be auditing her/his own work. A key position is a position in which an individual has: primary responsibility for significant accounting functions that support material components of the financial statements; primary responsibility for the preparation of the financial statements; or the ability to exercise influence over the contents of the financial statements, including when the individual is a controller or any equivalent position.

2. Yes

Independence would **not** be impaired. If a partner or professional employee leaves the firm and subsequently is employed by or associated with that client in a key position, then the firm's independence would be impaired, unless among other conditions, the ongoing attest engagement team considers the appropriateness or necessity of engagement procedures modification to adjust for the risk that audit effectiveness could be reduced as a result of the former partner or professional employee's prior knowledge of the audit plan.

3. No

Independence would be impaired if the CPA accepted responsibility to sign or co-sign client checks, even only in emergency situations.

4. No

Independence would be impaired if an employee or partner accepts more than a token gift from a client, even with the knowledge of the firm.

5. No

Independence would be impaired if the CPA designed or developed a client's financial information system, made other than insignificant modifications to source code underlying a client's existing financial information system, supervised client personnel in the daily operation of a client's information system, or operated a client's local area network (LAN) system.

6. Yes

Independence would **not** be impaired. A member's independence is not considered impaired solely as a result of the following: (1) an individual in a member's immediate family was employed by the client in a position other than a key position; or (2) in connection with her/his employment, an individual in the immediate family of one of the following members participated in a retirement, savings, compensation, or similar plan that is a client, is sponsored by a client, or that invests in a client, provided such plan normally is offered to all employees in similar positions: (a) a partner or manager who provides ten or more hours of nonattest services to the client; or (b) any partner in the office in which the lead attest engagement partner primarily practices in connection with the attest engagement.

7. Yes

Independence would **not** be impaired if the CPA recommended a position description or candidate specifications, solicited and performed screening of candidates, and recommended qualified candidates to a client based on the client-approved criteria, or participated in employee hiring or compensation discussions in an advisory capacity.

8. Yes

Independence would **not** be impaired if the CPA either provided assistance in assessing the client's business risks and control processes or recommended a plan for making improvements to a client's control processes and assisted in implementing these improvements. Independence would be impaired if the CPA either made or approved business risk decisions or presented business risk considerations to the board or others on behalf of management. (ID: 9249)

Simulation 3 Errors & Fraud

Possible Errors & Fraud	Internal Control Procedure
1. Customers' checks are received for less than the customers' full account balances, but the customers' full account balances are credited.	P
2. Customers' checks are misappropriated before being forwarded to the cashier for deposit.	C
3. Customers' checks are credited to incorrect customer accounts.	C
4. Different customer accounts are each credited for the same cash receipt.	P
5. Customers' checks are properly credited to customer accounts and are properly deposited, but errors are made in recording receipts in the cash receipts journal.	S
6. Customers' checks are misappropriated after being forwarded to the cashier for deposit.	P
7. Invalid transactions granting credit for sales returns are recorded.	N

1. P

The company would be able to detect errors in postings to customer accounts by placing certain control procedures in place. For example, by comparing the validated bank deposit slip total to the A/R posting total for the day, a difference in the amount posted from the remittance advices to the A/R ledger and the amount of checks actually received and deposited would be discovered.

2. C

Mailing monthly statements to all customers with outstanding balances would most likely detect customers' checks that are misappropriated before being forwarded to the cashier for deposit. The customers would be billed for invoices already paid and would let MMI know.

3. C

The company should implement control procedures to detect errors in postings to customer accounts. For example, mailing monthly statements to all customers with outstanding balances would detect errors as customers who had paid (but receive statements indicating a balance due) most likely would call the company to report the error.

4. P

By comparing the A/R postings to the validated deposit slip total, the difference resulting from posting one cash receipt remittance advice amount to two accounts in the A/R ledger would be detected.

5. S

Errors made in recording receipts in the cash receipts journal would most likely be detected if bank statements are reconciled periodically as the deposit amounts on the bank statements would be compared to the receipts as listed in the cash receipts journal. For internal control purposes, the person preparing the bank reconciliation should be someone other than the bookkeeper who is preparing the cash receipts journal.

6. P

The company should implement control procedures to prevent customer checks from being misappropriated before being deposited by the cashier. One procedure would compare the total amount posted to the accounts receivable ledger from the remittance advice to the validated deposit slip. Differences may indicate misappropriation of checks because they were not deposited or were deposited to incorrect bank accounts.

7. N

To prevent invalid transactions granting credit for sales returns from being recorded, control procedures should be implemented to require proper authorization of any sales returns. Authorization by the Sales Department supervisor would be appropriate, especially as the supervisor's goals are generally higher sales, and thus, the supervisor would not likely have a motivation for approving invalid sales returns.

(ID: 9254)

Simulation 4 Unrecorded Liabilities

		Check Register		
Vendor	**Check #**	**Check Date**	**Amount**	**Nature of Expense**
Water World Distributors, Inc.	1333	1/6/year 3	$ 3,500	Water coolers in office and warehouse delivered 12/31/year 2
Daniel Breen, Esquire	1334	1/6/year 3	$ 6,000	Corporate legal services for December, year 2
Telephone Services, Inc.	1335	1/8/year 3	$ 6,500	December, year 2 telephone and computer services
Payroll processing— Paychecks	1336	1/10/year 3	$25,500	Biweekly payroll (12/25/year 2 -1/7/year 3)
Pitt Ohio Trucking Company	1337	1/10/year 3	$45,601	Trucking services 12/4/year 2 - 1/3/year 3, deliveries made evenly throughout the period
Petty cash	1338	1/17/year 3	$ 2,002	Replenish petty cash box
Smith's Forklift Repairs	1339	1/22/year 3	$11,000	Received new forklift on 12/29/year 2, ordered on 12/18/year 2
Glenn's Glass Distribution Center	1340	1/23/year 3	$12,230	Specialty goods ordered 12/20/year 2, delivered 12/31/year 2
Payroll processing— Paychecks	1341	1/24/year 3	$25,500	Biweekly payroll (1/8/year 3 -1/15/year 3)
Daniel Breen, Esquire	1342	2/6/year 3	$ 6,800	Corporate legal services for January, year 3

Check # 1333: No adjustment needed

The amount of this check ($3,500) is lower than the $6,000 materiality level for adjustments set by the auditors for unrecorded liabilities; otherwise an adjustment would have been needed.

Check # 1334: Amount of adjustment: $6,000

This represents an expense for year 2, paid in year 3, which is equal to the materiality level; an adjustment (accrual of expense) is needed.

Check # 1335: Amount of adjustment: $6,500

This represents an expense for year 2, paid in year 3, which exceeds the materiality level; an adjustment (accrual of expense) is needed.

Check # 1336: Amount of adjustment: $12,750

The portion of this check that represents the salary expense for the period December 25 through December 31, year 2 is an expense for year 2, paid in year 3. The only information the problem gives you is that it is a biweekly payroll. Halving the amount of the check ($25,500/2 = $12,750) is a reasonable assumption to arrive at the amount of the adjustment (accrual of expense) needed.

Check # 1337: Amount of adjustment: $41,188

The portion of this check that represents the delivery expense for the period December 4 through December 31, year 2 is an expense for year 2, paid in year 3. The problem states that deliveries are made evenly throughout the period. The expense covers a period of 31 days (December 4, year 2 through January 3, year 3), 28 of which were part of year 2; thus, the calculation for the amount of the adjustment (accrual of expense) needed would be (($45,601 / 31) × 28) = $41,188.

Check # 1338: No adjustment is needed

This amount of this check ($2,002) is lower than the $6,000 materiality level for adjustments set by the auditors for unrecorded liabilities; no adjustment is needed.

Check # 1339: Amount of adjustment: $11,000

This represents an unrecorded liability for year 2 (when the forklift was ordered and received), which exceeds the materiality level; an adjustment (recording of the asset and related payable) is needed.

Check # 1340: Amount of adjustment: $12,230

This represents an unrecorded liability for year 2 (when the goods were ordered and received) which exceeds the materiality level; an adjustment (recording of the purchase and related payable) is needed.

Check # 1341: No adjustment needed

No adjustment is needed; this represents year 3 salary expense, paid in year 3.

Check # 1342: No adjustment needed

No adjustment is needed; this represents an expense for year 3, paid in year 3.

(ID: 9255)

Simulation 5 Cutoff Procedures

Potential cutoff problem	Adjustment
A. The company shipped merchandise (f.o.b. destination) to a customer on December 29, year 2, and recorded the sale but not the relief of inventory. The customer received the merchandise on December 31, year 2.	5
B. The company shipped merchandise (f.o.b. shipping point) on December 3, year 2, to a customer, and recorded the sale and relief of inventory. The customer, unhappy with the merchandise, returned the goods on December 29, year 2. The company records the following entry upon receipt of the goods: Inventory (dr.), Cost of Sales (cr.)	3
C. The company shipped merchandise to a consignee on December 16, year 2, and did not record the transaction. The consignee returned the merchandise on December 28, year 2. Upon receipt of the goods, the company made the following entry: Inventory (dr.), Sales (cr.)	8
D. The company shipped merchandise (f.o.b. shipping point) on December 29, year 2, and recorded relief of inventory, but not the sale, on that date. The customer has not received the merchandise and the company has not recorded the sale as of January 3, year 3.	2

Selection List

1. No adjustment necessary.	6. Accounts Receivable (dr.) Inventory (cr.)
2. Accounts Receivable (dr.) Sales (cr.)	7. Sales (dr.) Accounts Receivable (cr.) Inventory (dr.) Cost of Sales (cr.)
3. Sales (dr.) Accounts Receivable (cr.)	8. Sales (dr.) Inventory (cr.)
4. Inventory (dr.) Cost of Sales (cr.)	9. Accounts Receivable (dr.) Sales (cr.) Cost of Sales (dr.) Inventory (cr.)
5. Cost of Sales (dr.) Inventory (cr.)	10. Sales (dr.) Cost of Sales (cr.)

A. 5

The only adjustment needed is for the client to record the relief of inventory because the title passed to the client's customer when it received the merchandise from the common carrier (f.o.b. destination point) on December 31, year 2. The client has already recorded the sale.

B. 3

The only adjustment needed is for the client to reduce "sales" (dr.) and "accounts receivable" (cr.) for the merchandise that was returned on December 29, year 2. The client has already made the entry to include the merchandise in the inventory account.

C. 8

Merchandise out on consignment remains the property of the consignor, in this case, the client. The client handled the shipment correctly by **not** recording a sale or relief of inventory. However, they did not handle the subsequent return/receipt of the merchandise from the consignee correctly. The client needs to make an adjustment to reverse the entry it made, i.e., debit "accounts receivable" and credit "inventory."

D. 2

The only adjustment needed is for the client to record the sale because the title passed to the client's customer when the merchandise was delivered to the common carrier (f.o.b. shipping point) on December 29, year 2. The client has already recorded the relief of inventory. (ID: 9253)

Simulation 6 Substantive Tests

Audit Objective	Substantive Tests
1. Receivables at the end of year 2 are properly cut off with respect to sales made in year 2.	D, H
2. The aggregate of net receivables in the balance sheet is fairly stated at estimated net realizable value.	C, E
3. Depreciation expense is fairly stated.	J, K
4. Fixed assets included in the balance sheet exist.	N, M

1. D, H
   - Any shipping documents dated year 3 should not be invoiced (recorded as sales) in year 2; any shipping documents dated year 2 should be posted to the year 2 sales journal and accounts receivable subsidiary ledger.
   - Accounting for the prenumbered documents in each year's postings will determine if proper cutoff occurred.

2. C, E
   - If the aging of accounts receivable is not accurate, the allowance for uncollectible accounts receivable won't be either; thus, the net realizable value of receivables will not be fairly stated.
   - Comparison and the resulting analysis of the current year's relationship to prior years is a test of the reasonableness of the current year's relationship.

3. J, K
   - The recalculation of depreciation expense will confirm its mathematical accuracy and that the expense is allocated to the correct year.
   - This review will confirm that the methods and estimates are appropriate, reasonable, and consistently applied.

4. N, M
   - Testing (vouching) for existence by physically inspecting the acquisitions which are included in the balance sheet will confirm that fixed assets are not overstated.
   - This is another procedure to determine if the assets included in the balance sheet actually exist.

(ID: 9256)

_____

Simulation 7 Research

AU	§	9561	02	(ID: 9257)

.02   Interpretation—No. Section 561, *Subsequent Discovery of Facts Existing at the Date of the Auditor's Report,* requires the auditor to undertake to determine whether the information is reliable and whether the facts existed at the date of his [*sic*] report. This undertaking must be performed even when the auditor has resigned or been discharged.

_____

APPENDIX B
EXAM PREPARATION TIPS

Your first step toward an effective review program is to carefully read the material in this appendix. It contains essential information that will help you to succeed on the exam. Effective techniques and strategies for taking the exam are also included.

Video Cross-Reference to Chapters

The video programs are designed to supplement all our materials. They contain concise informative lectures as well as CPA exam tips and techniques to help you learn. The Hot•Spot™ videos concentrate on particular topics. Use them to study the areas that are most troubling for you. To round out your review, our Simulation Strategies videos focus on simulation-answering techniques using questions applicable to one exam section as opposed to concentrating on content. See the 6th and 7th steps in the foreword of this volume and the instructions at the beginning of any video viewer guide for a discussion on integrating videos into your study plan.

Hot•Spot™ Videos	Related Text Chapter	Hours: Minutes
FAR		
Cash, Receivables & Marketable Securities	2	2:15
Inventory, Fixed Assets & Intangibles	3, 4, 5	2:45
Bonds & Other Liabilities	6, 7	3:00
Leases & Pensions	8, 9	3:00
Owners' Equity & Miscellaneous Topics	10, 13	3:00
Revenue Recognition & Income Statement Presentation	1, 11, 12	3:55
Accounting for Income Taxes	14	1:55
Statement of Cash Flows	15	2:00
Consolidations	16	3:30
IFRS & SEC Reporting (available in early 2013)	17	TBD
Governmental Accounting	18, 19	3:50
Nonprofit Accounting	20	1:45
AUD		
Audit Standards & Planning	1, 2, 9, 10	3:30
Internal Control	3, 7	2:40
Audit Evidence	4, 5	2:30
Statistical Sampling	6	1:30
Standard Audit Reports	8	1:40
Other Reports, Reviews & Compilations	11, 12, 13	2:00
Professional Responsibilities	14	1:30
REG		
Contracts	1	3:00
Sales	2	2:20
Commercial Paper & Documents of Title	3	2:05
Secured Transactions	4	1:15
Bankruptcy & Suretyship	5	2:15
Fiduciary Relationships	6, 13	2:00
Business Entities	7	2:25
Government Regulation of Business	8, 9	1:10
Tax Ethics & Legal Duties	10	2:10
Individual Taxation	11	3:00
Gross Income, Tax Liabilities & Credits	11, 14	2:50
Property Taxation	12	2:20
Corporate Taxation	14	3:45
Partnerships & Other Tax Topics	12, 13, 15, 16	2:30
BEC		
Corporate Governance	1	3:30
Economics	2	3:25
Financial Management	3	3:00
Cost & Managerial Accounting	4, 5, 6	3:20
Information Technology	7	3:00

Simulation Strategies Videos	FAR	AUD	REG
Hours:minutes	2:40	2:15	2:15

SECTION ONE: GENERAL COMMENTS ON THE EXAM

OVERVIEW

It is to your advantage to take the exam as soon as possible after completing the formal education requirements because it is essentially an academic exam that tests the breadth of material covered by a good accounting curriculum.

One of the first things you should do is review the AUD content and skill specification outline (CSO/SSO) developed by the examiners (see the third section of this appendix). The outline identifies the topics covered by the exam. The CSO/SSO emphasizes the body of knowledge and entry-level skills required for the practice of public accounting.

Purpose of the Exam

The exam is one component of the CPA licensing requirement—it is designed to measure the technical competence of candidates.

Although licensing occurs at the state or territory level (usually by a board of accountancy), the exam is uniform at all sites and has national acceptance. Passing the exam in one jurisdiction generally allows you to obtain a reciprocal certificate or license in another jurisdiction if you meet that jurisdiction's other requirements.

Exam Partners

The exam is offered jointly by three organizations on behalf of the boards of accountancy:

- The American Institute of Certified Public Accountants (AICPA) develops and scores the exam.

- The National Association of the State Boards of Accountancy (NASBA) maintains a database of candidates' information.

- Prometric, a commercial testing center, delivers the exam to eligible candidates at its computer-based test centers across the United States and its territories as well as select international locations.

Exam Sections

The exam has four sections:

1. **Financial Accounting & Reporting (FAR)**—This section covers knowledge of generally accepted accounting principles and their application for business enterprises, government entities, and not-for-profit organizations. It consists of 3 multiple-choice question testlets containing a total of 90 questions and 1 simulation testlet containing 7 task-based simulations including at least 1 research question. (**4 hours**)

2. **Auditing & Attestation (AUD)**—This section covers knowledge and application of auditing procedures; generally accepted auditing standards; other standards and procedures for other types of engagements; and ethics, independence, and other professional responsibilities. It consists of 3 multiple-choice question testlets containing a total of 90 questions and 1 simulation testlet containing 7 task-based simulations including at least 1 research question. (**4 hours**)

3. **Regulation (REG)**—This section covers knowledge and application of federal taxation; ethics and responsibilities in tax practice; licensing and disciplinary systems; legal duties and responsibilities; and business law. It consists of 3 multiple-choice question testlets containing a total of 72 questions and 1 simulation testlet containing 6 task-based simulations including at least 1 research question. (**3 hours**)

4. **Business Environment & Concepts (BEC)**—This section covers knowledge and application of general business environment and concepts underlying the business reasons for and accounting implications of business transactions. It consists of 3 multiple-choice question testlets containing a total of 72 questions and 1 testlet containing 3 written communication tasks. It is the *only* section with written communication tasks and it does **not** include simulations. (**3 hours**)

Exam Availability—Testing Windows

There are four exam windows each year; the first one starts in January. Each window covers the first two months of each quarter except for international testing locations where the exam is only offered during the second month of the testing window. Between windows—during the third month of each quarter—the exam is not given.

Testing Windows	No Testing
January—February	March
April—May	June
July—August	September
October—November	December

You can take any or all sections (in any order) during any testing window; however, **you may *not* take the same exam section more than once during any one testing window**.

Time Limit for Passing All Four Sections

Generally, candidates must pass all four sections of the exam within a rolling time frame (typically 18 months), which begins on the date that the first section passed is taken. If all four sections are not passed within the required time frame, credit for the first section passed is lost and the time frame rolls to the date that the next section passed was taken and so on. Candidates should check with their board of accountancy regarding time limits.

Computer-Based Testing (CBT) / Tutorial and Sample Tests

The exam is offered only in English and only in a CBT format.

It is extremely important that you become familiar with the latest version of the exam's software. The AICPA provides a tutorial and sample tests (aicpa.org/becomeacpa/cpaexam/forcandidates/tutorialandsampletest) on their website. You must review these before the exam because neither is available at the test centers. Before the beginning of any exam session, candidates must attest to the fact that they have had the opportunity to review the tutorial and sample tests. This requirement is intended to ensure that *before* candidates report to the test centers, they are knowledgeable about the examination process and thoroughly familiar with examination functionality, format, and directions.

The AICPA recommends reviewing the tutorial before the sample tests. The time you spend with these materials will prevent you from losing any points on the exam due to unfamiliarity with the CBT system. The exam uses both a word processor and a spreadsheet program that are similar, but not identical, to common commercial applications. Even if you are completely comfortable with the commercial applications, you may find it unsettling to encounter different or missing functionalities on your exam day.

View the tutorial and take the sample test right before you begin studying for an exam section and then again a week before the exam.

Exam Confidentiality / Nondisclosure Policy

The Uniform CPA Examination is nondisclosed. This means that candidates are not allowed to receive a copy of their exam questions after taking the exam. Also, candidates are required to accept the terms of the exam which include a promise not to reveal questions or answers. The AICPA no longer discloses the exam in order to increase consistency, facilitate computer administration of the exam, and improve exam quality by pretesting questions. (See the "Exam Scoring" section of this appendix for more information about pretest questions.) Because the exam is no longer completely changed every year, statistical equating methods are more relevant and the usefulness of specific questions as indicators of candidates' knowledge can be tested.

Editor note: Only the AICPA has access to the exam questions and answers. For the past several years the AICPA has released (usually annually) a small number of questions with unofficial answers that it has removed from its pool of questions, i.e., it is their policy that released questions will not appear on future exams. The questions in Bisk Education materials are updated based upon content changes; items from previously disclosed exams and released questions; and the teaching expertise of our editors. Due to the nondisclosure requirements, our editors cannot address candidate's questions about specific exam questions.

Testing of New Pronouncements

Accounting and auditing pronouncements are eligible to be tested on the exam in the testing window beginning six months after a pronouncement's effective date, unless early application is permitted. When early application is permitted, a new pronouncement may be tested in the window beginning 6 months after the issue date. In this case, both the previous and the new pronouncement can be tested until the previous pronouncement has been superseded.

Reference Materials

All the content you need to review to pass the exam is in your Bisk Education *CPA Comprehensive Exam Review* texts; however, if you would like more detailed coverage in any area, you can consult the actual authoritative literature. Individual copies of recent pronouncements are available from the AICPA, FASB, PCAOB, IFAC, SEC, etc. To order materials from the AICPA, the Financial Accounting Standards Board (FASB), or International Federation of Accountants (IFAC) contact:

AICPA's Service Center	FASB Order Department	IFAC
220 Leigh Farm Road	P.O. Box 5116	545 Fifth Avenue, 14th Floor
Durham, NC 27707-8110	Norwalk, CT 06856-5116	New York, NY 10017
US telephone: (888) 777-7077	US telephone: (800) 748-0659	Telephone: (212) 286-9344
Outside United States:	Outside United States:	
(919) 402-4500	(203) 847-0700	
service@cpa2biz.com	fasbpubs@fasb.org	Communications@ifac.org
cpa2biz.com	fasb.org/store	ifac.org

The AICPA offers candidates with their notice to schedule (NTS) a **free six-month subscription to some of the databases of authoritative literature** used in the AUD section of the exam. Visit the AICPA's website (aicpa.org/becomeacpa/cpaexam/forcandidates/howtoprepare/pages/literature.aspx) for more information and to subscribe. IFAC makes the majority of their material available for download free of charge—hard copies must be purchased. The PCAOB's standards can be viewed on their website (pcaobus.org).

THE UNIFORM CPA EXAMINATION PROCESS

The information presented here is intended to give you an overall idea of what the exam will be like. It is **not** intended to take the place of *The Uniform CPA Examination Candidate Bulletin / Information for Applicants* (Candidate Bulletin). The Candidate Bulletin will provide you with more detailed instructions and information.

In addition to understanding the basic process as described in the Candidate Bulletin, **you need to know your board of accountancy's requirements for each step in the exam process**.

Candidate Bulletin

The Candidate Bulletin provides important general information about the entire process including the requirements for taking the exam. Read it. At the test center you will be required to affirm that you have had the opportunity to read it and that you agree to all of its terms and conditions. The Candidate Bulletin is available for download on the websites of both the AICPA (aicpa.org/becomeacpa/cpaexam/forcandidates/candidatebulletin) and NASBA (nasba.org).

Forty-five days before your exam, you should check one of the above websites to confirm you have the most recent Candidate Bulletin.

Contacting Your Board of Accountancy

Certified public accountants are licensed to practice by the individual boards of accountancy of the states and territories (jurisdictions) of the United States. The NASBA website (nasba.org) has links to all of the board sites.

Applying to Take the Exam

To sit for the exam, both US applicants and those from outside the United States must select the jurisdiction in which they wish to qualify.

In addition to the exam, boards of accountancy rely upon other means to ensure that candidates possess the necessary attributes including background checks, interviews, letters of reference, affidavits of employment, ethics exams, and educational requirements.

Depending on your jurisdiction, you should either apply online at cpacentral.nasba.org or contact your board of accountancy directly to apply—see the Candidate Bulletin for the approach required by your jurisdiction.

You must apply and submit any required documents and fees each time you want to take one or more exam sections. (Note: Some jurisdictions arrange for an exam administrator, such as CPA Examination Services, a division of NASBA, to handle the review of applications, collection of fees, etc.)

IT IS EXTREMELY IMPORTANT THAT YOU COMPLETE THE APPLICATION CORRECTLY AND SUBMIT IT BEFORE THE DEADLINE. Errors or omissions may result in the delay of approval or rejection of your application. Be sure to enclose all required materials. Requirements vary as to education, experience, and other matters, as do cutoff dates to apply to receive approval in time to sit for a particular testing window. If you have not already done so, call or visit the website of the appropriate board for their specific and current requirements.

PAY SPECIAL ATTENTION TO THE **FORM OF YOUR NAME ON YOUR APPLICATION**. YOUR APPLICATION INFORMATION WILL BE USED TO GENERATE YOUR NTS AND THE **ORDER** AND **SPELLING** OF YOUR NAME ON YOUR NTS MUST EXACTLY MATCH YOUR 2 IDs—THE 3 ITEMS YOU MUST BRING TO THE TEST CENTER TO GAIN ADMISSION. (See the following section on personal identification.)

International Applicants

The exam given at select international locations is offered only in English and is the same computerized test as the one administered in the United States. It is only offered during the months of February, May, August, and November. Please see the exam's website (aicpa.org/becomeacpa/cpaexam) for specific locations and schedules.

Applicants from countries other than the United States must follow the same basic steps as US applicants. They must select a US jurisdiction in which they wish to qualify (that participates in the International CPA Examination Administration Program) and file an application with its board of accountancy or designated agent. Any special instructions for candidates who have completed their education outside the United States are included in the board of accountancy requirements.

Regardless of which board of accountancy has declared you eligible for the exam, in addition to paying any domestic testing fees, you must pay additional nonrefundable fees for each exam section you plan to take internationally.

For more information on the international administration of the exam, visit the international section of the NASBA website (nasba.org/international/international-exam/).

Fees

The amount and types of fees as well as the timing for their payment vary by jurisdiction. You may be required to pay all or some of the fees when you submit your application. Your board or its agent may instruct you to pay portions of the fees to different entities. There are additional fees for taking the exam in Guam or international locations.

It is best not to apply for a section of the exam until you are ready to take it because refunds of fees are usually not available—check with your board or its exam administrator regarding their specific refund policy. Generally, if you fail to make an appointment during the period your NTS is valid or need to cancel your appointment and do not wish to reschedule it, you will not receive a refund or a credit; nor will you receive a refund or a credit if you fail to appear for your appointment at the test center or give less than 24 hours notice for a cancellation. In either case, you will probably have to reapply for the exam and pay the fees again.

Notice to Schedule (NTS)

Once a board or its exam administrator determines that a candidate is eligible to sit for the exam (and all fees are paid), they inform NASBA and NASBA adds the candidate to its database. (Thus, NASBA is able to ensure that no candidate can sit for the same exam section more than once during a single exam window.) When you receive your NTS from NASBA you can make your appointment to sit for the exam with Prometric. **You can *not* schedule an exam without an NTS**.

You should verify the accuracy of your NTS *before* making your appointment. You must present your NTS and proper identification to be admitted to the exam room at the testing center. Make sure that your name as it appears on your NTS **exactly** matches your name on the IDs you will be using to check in at the testing center. If your name on your NTS is different in any way (the order or spelling) from your IDs, you will not be permitted to test. If any information on your NTS is incorrect or your name doesn't match your IDs, immediately contact your board or its exam administrator to request a correction.

Your NTS will include an expiration date; it is only valid for a set period of time (determined by your board) during which you must schedule and take the exam section(s). (Many, *but not all*, boards have established a six-month validation period.) Cancelling an exam appointment does *not* change the expiration date of your NTS. If you do not take all sections for which you are registered before your NTS expires, you will **not** be able to extend it or receive a refund of any of the fees you have paid. Fees submitted for an expired NTS can **not** be applied to future exams.

You can **not** have more than one open NTS for the same exam section. You must receive the score or allow the NTS to expire before you can apply for the same exam section again and receive a new NTS for that exam section.

Your NTS contains your exam section identification number which is also your password to launch your exam once seated at a testing center. (The Candidate Bulletin includes a sample NTS.)

Personal Identification

See the Candidate Bulletin to review a list of examples of acceptable forms of *primary* and *secondary* identification—one of your IDs must appear on their *primary* list. (There is also a list of *un*acceptable forms of ID.)

You must have **two forms of identification. One of them must contain a recent photograph. Both must bear your signature. Neither can be expired. If you do not present acceptable identification, you will not be allowed to take the exam and you will forfeit all fees for that section.**

The middle initial can be substituted for the middle name, for example, the NTS reads Michael A. Smith, but the name on the candidate's ID reads Michael Albert Smith, or vice versa. Also, truncated (shortened) names are allowable on a candidate's driver's license (a *primary* form of ID), as long as the name on the signature [*secondary*] ID exactly matches the name on the NTS. Editor note: These exceptions / clarifications have recently been added to the Candidate Bulletin; however, the AICPA has not removed the "exactly match" language that appears in other sections of the Candidate Bulletin. If you can, it's best to select two acceptable (conforming) IDs with the identical form of your name and then enter your name on your application exactly as it appears on those IDs, as long as that form of your name complies with the requirements of the application. Otherwise, if you have any concerns, contact your board or its administrator.

If the test center staff has questions about the identification presented, you may be asked for additional proof of identity. Editor note: Bring an extra acceptable ID, just in case.

Note that there are separate requirements listed in the Candidate Bulletin for identification for international test centers.

Special Testing Accommodations

Special accommodations must be requested as part of the application process. If you need special testing accommodations, check with your board or its exam administrator and give them your information to request their approval. If approved, the type of accommodation needed will be sent to NASBA. NASBA will ensure that the information is included on your NTS and sent to Prometric.

When you receive your NTS, if the accommodations indicated are not correct, you will need to contact your board again *before* scheduling your appointment—changes to special accommodations can **not** be made by Prometric.

Candidates are advised that they may receive limited or no accommodations if they choose to test in an international location. The special accommodations on the NTS are applicable for testing in the United States and US territories only—approved special accommodations for international locations will be detailed in an e-mail from NASBA.

Scheduling Your Exam Appointment With Prometric if *No* Special Accommodations Are Needed

The exam is offered 5 days (and at some test centers, 6 days) per week.

Generally, you will be allowed to take the exam at any one of the authorized Prometric test centers in the United States and designated international locations, whether or not the test center is located in the jurisdiction where you are seeking your initial license. Check with your board of accountancy or their agent to find out if there are any restrictions on the location where you can take the examination.

No appointment can be made fewer than 5 days in advance of a desired test date. That said, candidates may select any available date during the open window.

If taking the exam on a particular day, time, and/or location is important to you, you should schedule it at least 45 days in advance to increase your chances of getting your first choice. Before contacting Prometric, know your second and third choices also.

You may schedule, confirm, reschedule, or cancel an exam appointment or change its location as well as find a preferred testing location online (**prometric.com/cpa**) or by calling **(800) 580-9648**—have your NTS in front of you before you begin. The AICPA recommends using the Internet option. See the Candidate Bulletin for deadlines and fees associated with changes to appointments—depending on when you notify Prometric of a change or cancellation, you may be required to pay a rescheduling fee or you may forfeit the exam fees.

If you schedule more than one exam section on the same day you must make sure the times don't overlap and that you have allowed enough time between exams to check in. Unfortunately, the online system will not warn you if your appointments overlap.

Remember, you must take each exam section by the expiration date on your NTS.

You should receive an e-mail confirmation of your appointment from Prometric whether you made your appointment via the website or phone. If you do not receive an e-mail, you should print a confirmation via the Prometric website. This is available to you even if you made the appointment using the phone.

Refer to the Candidate Bulletin for more detailed information about scheduling your appointment or if you are planning on taking the exam in Guam or an international location.

Scheduling Your Exam Appointment With Prometric if Special Accommodations Have Been Preapproved—United States and US Territories

Candidates with special testing accommodations preapproved by their board or exam administrator (and indicated on their NTS) **must schedule at least 10 days in advance** of the desired date **and must call (800) 967-1139 to schedule** their appointment. Changes to appointments must be made by calling this same number. You should receive an e-mail confirmation of your appointment from Prometric.

Candidates approved for special accommodations can **not** use the Prometric website to schedule or make changes to their appointments—if they use the website, they will **not** be provided with special accommodations. Refer to the Candidate Bulletin for more detailed information about scheduling your appointment.

See the Candidate Bulletin for more information about special accommodations in international testing locations—be aware that you must schedule the examination at least 30 days in advance of the date that you select.

Exam Appointment Time

The appointment time on the confirmation you receive from Prometric will reflect the exam testing time plus 30 minutes. The additional 30 minutes is **not** additional testing time—it is the time allowed to enter your password, respond to the introductory screens, and take the survey at the end of the exam. For example, the *testing* time for the AUD exam is 4 hours, thus the *appointment* time will be for 4½ hours.

You will also need to plan for *another* 30 minutes **before** your appointment time to allow time for check-in and seating procedures. This extra 30 minutes is **not** reflected in your appointment time.

Checking In on Exam Day

You must arrive at least 30 minutes before your scheduled appointment to allow enough time for check-in and seating procedures. (If you arrive late you may be denied permission to test and you will not receive a refund.)

You will not be admitted without your **NTS** and **2 acceptable forms of identification** and you will forfeit all fees for that exam section. Security measures include the following.

- A digital photograph of your face will be taken.

- Your ID will be scanned and swiped in a magnetic strip and barcode reader.

- Biometrics will be used to capture your fingerprint.

- You will be asked to turn your pockets out and then you will be scanned with a hand-held metal detector wand prior to each entry into the exam room, including returns from breaks.

You will be lent a key to a very *small* locker for storage of a few belongings, such as your purse / wallet or cell phone, because you are not allowed to take these items into the exam room. (You should only bring what is absolutely necessary to the test center. Test center staff will **not** be responsible for lost or stolen items.)

Pencils and scratch paper will be given to you.

	Time Allocation	Activity
Before exam appointment	At least 30 minutes	Check in & get seated
AUD exam appointment	10-minute limit enforced	Respond to introductory screens after log-in
4 ½ hours	4-hour limit enforced	Take AUD exam & discretionary break(s) between testlets— no more than 10 minutes for any break
	20 minutes or less	Complete voluntary survey

Exam Room Regulations

There are very strict rules for the exam room.

You must not communicate, orally or otherwise, with other candidates when in the exam room. To avoid even the appearance of cheating, you must not look at another candidate's materials or workstation.

During the exam, you must not read or process your thoughts out loud. Any conduct that unnecessarily disturbs other candidates is prohibited.

No food, beverages, or tobacco products are allowed.

You must not bring any paper or pencils (other than that provided to you by the test center staff) into the exam room. You will be directed to write your launch code (password from your NTS) on the scratch paper so that it can be accounted for, i.e., you will be required to exchange the original supply for a new supply should you request it, and you must turn it in after the exam.

See the Candidate Bulletin for a long list of prohibited items and other restrictions. Don't assume they will be what you may expect. For example, you are **not** allowed to have a watch (a countdown of the time remaining to complete the exam will display on your computer screen during the exam); jewelry—a pendant necklace or large earrings; an eyeglass case; or a container of any kind (including a plastic bag).

You *are* allowed to bring soft, foam earplugs with no strings attached, subject to an inspection by the test center staff.

If you require a separate sweater or a light jacket due to room temperature, it must be worn at all times.

All exam sessions are audio / videotaped to document any unusual activity.

After checking in, you will be escorted to your workstation (seating is assigned by Prometric) where you must remain seated during the exam except when given permission to leave the exam room for an authorized break.

Exam's Introductory Screens

After you enter your password (launch code from your NTS), you have only 10 minutes to read and respond to the introductory screens.

IF THE 10-MINUTE TIME LIMIT IS EXCEEDED, YOUR EXAM SESSION WILL AUTOMATICALLY TERMINATE AND YOU WILL **NOT** BE ALLOWED TO RESTART THE EXAM. You should move through these screens quickly—ten minutes is enough time to review them and respond, but there is not time to do anything else.

One of these screens presents the *Policy Statement and Agreement Regarding Exam Confidentiality and the Taking of Breaks*. A copy of this statement is included in the Candidate Bulletin so you can review it beforehand. If you do not accept it you will not be allowed to take the exam and your fees will be forfeited.

If you encounter a problem with your computer or the testing environment, you should immediately report it to the test center staff.

Exam Timer

The time remaining to complete the exam (displayed on the title bar of your computer screen) begins to count down after you have moved from the introductory screens to the first testlet. **The countdown does *not* pause while you are taking a break**.

Breaks

Breaks are only allowed between testlets—after a break, you can *not* return to a testlet you were working on prior to your break. If you leave the exam room at any other time, you will not be allowed to return, and the incident will be reported to your board of accountancy. (A testlet is a segment of the exam—see the "Exam Format" section of this appendix.)

You do **not** have to take a break. After each testlet, a candidate has the option to take a break, but the exam's countdown will continue so you should use any break time sparingly and judiciously. Also, breaks over 10 minutes may be reported to your board of accountancy.

If you choose to take a break, the test center staff will confirm that you have completed a testlet and you will be asked to provide a fingerprint prior to leaving and again on your return. You will also be scanned again with the metal detector wand.

When you return to your computer you will be required to enter your exam launch code (password) in order to continue the exam.

Checking Out

After you have completed your exam you will be asked to respond to a survey about your exam experience. When you finish, simply exit the room quietly. You must turn in your scratch paper, sign a log book, and complete other procedures as directed by the test center staff. They will then dismiss you. You will receive a *Confirmation of Attendance* which you should keep in case you need the contact information it provides if you have a question or concern.

Candidate Requests for Question Review

Candidates who believe they have identified a problem with an exam question should contact the AICPA Examinations Team in writing by fax or letter. See the Candidate Bulletin for the fax number or mailing address and the AICPA's specific instructions. Your fax or letter must be *received* within *four* days of taking the exam. The AICPA asks that you include your exam section identification number (exam launch code or password) and that you do **not** include the exact wording or attempt to outline the question—simply provide enough information for the examiners to identify the question, such as "question number 12 in the first testlet" or "the *Interest Expense* tab in the 1st simulation." They request that you include the nature of your concern, your rationale, and, if possible, references to support your position. According to the Candidate Bulletin, the AICPA is unable to respond directly to candidates, but reviews every fax or letter received by the deadline.

Receipt of Scores

The exam is scored by the AICPA. The AICPA does not have access to candidate identities—candidates' anonymity is preserved throughout the exam and scoring process. Exam responses are identified by exam section identification number only. (This is the same number as your exam launch code or password.)

Each exam section is scored separately.

The AICPA forwards the advisory scores to NASBA. NASBA matches the scores to the candidates and forwards the scores to the boards of accountancy.

Scores are approved and released to candidates by boards of accountancy. (Prometric, the AICPA, or NASBA do **not** provide score information to candidates.) Generally, boards of accountancy report scores on a numeric scale of 0-99, with 75 as a passing score.

Scores are generally released during regular business hours. See the Candidate Bulletin for NASBA's current score release timeline (estimated schedule). Be aware that some boards need at least a day to process and release the scores after they receive them from NASBA. Also note that scores for the BEC exam section may be delayed by approximately a week due to the additional analysis that might be required for the written communication tasks.

Postexam Diagnostics

If you fail an exam section you will receive a *Candidate Performance Report*. It will compare your performance by content area and by question type to those who scored between 75 and 80 (the "just passed" category). This is intended to serve as a study aid for retaking the exam. Contact your board or their agent about their specific re-examination policy.

Remember, you may only retake that section in a *future* testing window. You may **not** repeat any exam section within the same testing window.

Score Review and Appeal Processes

See the Candidate Bulletin for information about both of these separate processes. You will need to contact your board or its agent if you decide to apply for either. If you obtain their approval you must pay the required fees.

A score review is **not** a regrading. It is an independent verification of a candidate's score. You may only apply for a review for a short period of time after your score has been reported to you. The AICPA cautions candidates that a score change after a review is very unlikely due to the quality checks that take place prior to their reporting of scores.

An appeal is the opportunity to appeal a failing score because you would like to challenge an exam question. An appeal allows you to review the multiple-choice questions and simulations (written communication tasks are excluded) you answered incorrectly together with your responses and submit your comments online. It is conducted in an authorized location in the presence of a representative of your board or its agent. Be aware that some jurisdictions do **not** permit appeals and that the option to apply for an appeal in jurisdictions that allow it is only available for a short period of time after your score has been reported to you.

EXAM FORMAT

The exam is offered only in English and only in a computer-based testing format.

Reviewing the tutorial and taking the sample tests on the AICPA's website (aicpa.org/becomeacpa/cpaexam/forcandidates/tutorialandsampletest) will allow you to:

- Become familiar with the exam's directions and navigation system

- See how the questions are formatted

- Use the exam's software while answering a few practice questions

It is important for you to take advantage of this opportunity. Moreover, the Candidate Bulletin states that thorough familiarity with the exam's functionality, format, and directions is required before candidates report to test centers.

Four Testlets

Questions are grouped into 4 testlets. The testing software presents 3 multiple-choice testlets followed by 1 testlet of simulations (FAR, AUD, and REG) or written communication tasks (BEC). You can **not** pick the order of the testlets to answer, but *within* a testlet, you can answer the questions in any order and you can return to questions. **Once you indicate you have completed a testlet, you can *not* return to it**.

Multiple-Choice Questions

Each exam section has 3 multiple-choice testlets. The FAR and AUD multiple-choice testlets have 30 questions each (a total of 90 questions); the REG and BEC testlets have 24 questions each (a total of 72 questions). The questions in each testlet are in random order, i.e., they are not presented in the some order as an exam section's content specification outline (CSO). (The AUD CSO is in the third section of this appendix.)

Adaptive Testing Model for Multiple-Choice Questions

There are 2 levels of multiple-choice testlets, labeled *medium* and *difficult*. Within the testlets, questions often vary substantially in their level of difficulty, but across testlets, those labeled *difficult* contain more difficult questions than testlets labeled *medium*.

The first testlet is always at the *medium* level. After you finish a multiple-choice question testlet, the software will select the next testlet based on your performance on the previous testlet(s). If you do well, the next testlet will be *difficult*. Otherwise, you will receive another *medium* testlet. Thus, if you find the questions are becoming more challenging, you should be encouraged rather than discouraged—this is probably an indication that you are doing well.

The adaptive testing model is **not** used with the simulations. Nor are the simulations chosen based on your performance on the multiple-choice questions—they are preassigned.

The scoring procedures incorporate the difficulty of the testlets so candidates are scored fairly regardless of the difficulty of the testlets they take.

The examiners' intent is that analysis of adaptive testing statistics will eventually allow them to reduce the number of questions, resulting in more time for testing skills.

Simulations

The FAR and AUD sections have one simulation testlet containing 7 task-based simulations (TBS) including at least 1 research question. The REG section has 6 TBS including at least 1 research question. (BEC does **not** have simulations and it is the only exam section that has written communication tasks.)

A TBS is a condensed case study that tests accounting knowledge and skills using real life work-related situations. Each is expected to take approximately 8 to 15 minutes. All TBS are intended to assess knowledge and skills appropriate for an entry-level accountant. Accounting knowledge is tested through a variety of tasks, for example, you may be required to select answers from lists or enter numbers into worksheets.

See "Appendix C: Research Skills" in this text for information about the research questions.

Authoritative Literature

The AUD exam's fourth testlet of TBS includes access to a database of certain portions of the professional standards issued by the AICPA and PCAOB.

The financial accounting database for the FAR exam will include certain portions of the FASB and AICPA authoritative literature. The taxation database for the REG exam will include certain portions of the Internal Revenue Code, as well as certain portions of the professional standards issued by the AICPA and the PCAOB.

_____

SECTION TWO: EXAM STRATEGIES

OVERVIEW

The exam is more than a test of your knowledge and technical competence. It is also a test of your ability to function under psychological pressure. Your objective is to avoid surprises and eliminate hassles and distractions. You want to be in complete control so that you can concentrate on the exam material, rather than the exam situation. By taking charge of the exam, you will be able to handle pressure in a constructive manner. The keys to control are adequate preparation and an effective exam strategy.

Preparation

Advance preparation will arm you with the confidence you need to overcome the psychological pressure of the exam. As you complete your comprehensive review, you will cover most of the material that will be tested on the exam; it is unlikely that any question will deal with a topic you have not studied. But if an unfamiliar topic is tested, you will not be dismayed because you have learned to use the Solutions Approach™ to derive the best possible answer from the knowledge you possess.

The components of your advance preparation include the following.

- Comprehensive review materials such as your Bisk Education CPA Review program

- A study plan that enables you to review each subject area methodically and thoroughly

- A method for ongoing self-evaluation of your level of proficiency

- An understanding of the scoring process

- A Solutions Approach™ for each type of exam question

Exam Strategies

The second key to controlling the exam is to develop effective strategies for the days you take the exam. Your objective is to avoid surprises and frustrations so that you can focus your full concentration on the questions and your answers.

You should be familiar with the format of the exam and know exactly what you will do when you enter the exam room. Remember to read all instructions carefully, whether general or specific to a particular question. Disregarding the instructions may mean loss of points.

Knowing in advance what to expect while taking the exam and planning how you will spend your exam time will help you avoid any confusion and save you valuable time while answering questions. This will greatly enhance your probability of attaining a passing score.

EXAM SCORING

Generally, boards of accountancy report scores on a numeric scale of 0-99, with 75 as a passing score.

All questions on the AUD exam are scored electronically by the AICPA.

Each exam section is scored separately.

An understanding of the scoring procedure will help you maximize points on the exam. Remember that your objective is to pass the exam. You cannot afford to spend time on activities that will not affect your score or to ignore opportunities to increase it.

Pretest Questions

Any of the four testlets can include pretest questions which are used to develop future exams. **Pretest questions are *not* included in your score**. Instead, your response to a pretest question is used to evaluate the question's statistical performance.

You will **not** be able to distinguish the pretest questions from the questions that will be scored. On the AUD exam it is possible that as many as 15 of the 90 multiple-choice questions will be pretest questions and, likewise, 1 of the 7 simulations.

Scoring Weights

In AUD, the multiple-choice questions make up 60% of the total score and the simulations make up 40%. Thus, you can **not** pass AUD just by doing well on the multiple-choice questions.

Multiple-Choice Questions and Simulations

It is important to understand that your score for these questions is based solely on your *correct* answers. In other words, you receive credit for correct answers and **you are *not* penalized for incorrect responses**. Thus, **you should answer every question**. If you do not know the answer, make an intelligent guess.

You should avoid getting "bogged down" on any one question. Move along and answer all the questions in a testlet. This helps to avoid leaving any questions unanswered or answering in a panic due to poor budgeting of test time.

Scoring Implications

To summarize:

- Attempt an answer on every question.
- Respond directly to the requirements of the questions.
- Answer all requirements.
- Develop a Solutions Approach™ to questions.
- Allocate your exam time based on the exam's scoring weights.

More Information

If you would like more information on how the exam is scored, visit the AICPA's website to read "How Is the CPA Exam Scored?" (aicpa.org/becomeacpa/cpaexam/psychometricsandscoring/scoringinformation/pages /default.aspx).

EXAM TIME MANAGEMENT

You must plan how you will use your exam time and adhere to your schedule. If you budget your time carefully, you should be able to answer all questions. Work quickly but efficiently, i.e., use the Solutions Approach™ discussed in this appendix.

Remember, you must complete each testlet in the order it is presented—the 3 multiple-choice testlets are presented first, followed by the simulation testlet. This sample schedule for AUD has been prepared based on the AUD exam's scoring weights—60% for the multiple-choice questions and 40% for the simulations.

Be sure to adjust your time budget to accommodate your individual needs and strengths, for example, you may prefer a different allocation of time between the multiple-choice testlets and the simulation testlet; however, **under no circumstance should you allow yourself less than 1 hour for the final testlet**.

	Minutes
Answer first multiple-choice question testlet	46
Answer second multiple-choice question testlet	46
Answer third multiple-choice question testlet	46
Break	5
Review simulation titles to determine the first one to answer	1
Answer simulations	96
Total	240

You should use **all** the allotted time. If you finish a testlet ahead of your schedule, go back and reconsider the more difficult questions.

———————————

THE SOLUTIONS APPROACH™

The Bisk Education Solutions Approach™ is an efficient, systematic method of organizing and solving exam questions. Even a little knowledge can go a long way if you use a proper approach. Our approach, when properly developed and practiced, can make the difference between passing and failing.

Suggested Approach

We will suggest a number of steps for deriving a solution that will help maximize your score on the exam. Although you should remember the important steps in our suggested approach, don't be afraid to adapt these steps to your own taste and requirements. When you work the questions at the conclusion of each chapter, make sure to use your variation of the Solutions Approach™. It is very important that you attempt to answer a question and formulate your solution **before** looking at the answer. The worst thing you can do is look at a question and then turn to the answer without working it. This will build false confidence and will not help you to develop a Solutions Approach™.

Solutions Approach™ For Multiple-Choice Question Testlets

We recommend the following approach for the 3 multiple-choice question testlets. (The timing suggested is based on the exam's scoring weight of 60% for the multiple-choice questions.)

- Read the directions at the beginning of the testlet to ensure you know what is expected. You should have already become familiar with the format via the AICPA's tutorial and sample tests on their website (aicpa.org/becomeacpa/cpaexam/forcandidates/tutorialandsampletest).

- Answer the questions in order. This is a proven, systematic approach. You should limit yourself to a maximum of 1½ minutes per question for this first pass. Under no circumstances should you allow yourself to fall behind schedule. If a question is difficult or long, be sure to remain cognizant of the passage of time. If after a minute or so you feel that it is too costly to continue, select the answer you tentatively feel is the best, flag the question for review, and go on to the next question.

- Read each question carefully, so you know exactly what is being asked. Note key words. Be alert for negative requirements which are easily missed ("Which of the following does **not**...") and when the requirement is an exception ("...except for..."). The examiners usually use boldface type for "not" and "except," but you should not rely on that practice.

- Perform any intermediate calculations necessary for the determination of the correct answer.

- **Before looking at the possible responses**, anticipate the answer if you can. Many incorrect responses are based on the erroneous application of one or more items in the text of the question; thus, it is extremely helpful to anticipate the answer before you read the alternatives and are possibly led astray.

- Read the alternatives given.

- Select the best alternative. Very often, one or two possible responses will be clearly *in*correct. Of the other alternatives, be sure to select the one that best answers the question asked—sometimes more than one alternative is a correct statement, but *only one answers the question*. If there are two close possibilities, make sure you select the best one in light of the facts and requirements of the question.

- After you have completed your first pass, return to the questions you flagged for review and attempt to better answer them if you have time remaining from what you allocated for that testlet. If you cannot find a better answer, use your preliminary answer because your first impressions are often correct.

- After completing all of the individual questions in a testlet, go back and make sure that you have answered each question. Your score will be based on the number of correct answers with no penalty for incorrect responses. Double-check your answers if time permits—remember, you can **not** go back to a previously completed testlet.

Solutions Approach™ For the Final Testlet—Simulations

The final testlet in AUD consists of 7 simulations—usually 6 task-based simulations (TBS) and 1 research question.

A TBS is a group of objective questions, based on a hypothetical situation. What differentiates it from a multiple-choice question is the various formats that may be used to answer the TBS. The formats include, but are not limited to, the following: selecting the correct answer from a list of possible choices (somewhat like a multiple-choice question); typing a response into a designated area; or doing some spreadsheet calculations. The point is, no matter what type of format that may be used in a TBS; remember that it is merely an objective question that requires a correct response.

We recommend the following approach for the final testlet. (The timing suggested is based on the exam's scoring weight of 40% for the simulations.)

- Read the directions section at the beginning of the testlet to ensure you know what is expected. You should have already become familiar with the format of the exam via the AICPA's tutorial and sample tests on their website (aicpa.org/becomeacpa/cpaexam/forcandidates/tutorialandsampletest).

- Answer the research question first. Try to complete it within 5 or 6 minutes. (See "Appendix C: Research Skills" in this text for information about the research questions.)

- Read the titles (taking the AICPA's sample test will allow you to see how to locate the titles) to each of the TBS and go to the one with the subject matter you believe you are most knowledgeable about first. By doing the TBS you are most knowledgeable about first you will save time and become more confident as you proceed.

- Read all the information provided in the TBS and the requirements very carefully, noting exactly what is being asked.

- Perform any intermediate calculations necessary to the determination of the correct answers.

- Read the alternatives given and select the ones that **best answer the questions asked**.

- After completing all of the individual responses required, **go back** and double-check that you have, in fact, answered each question in the TBS. Your score will be based on the number of correct answers with no penalty for incorrect responses.

- Do **not** answer the rest of the TBS in order. After answering the first TBS with the subject matter that you felt most knowledgeable about, reread the titles for the remaining TBS and again go to the one with the subject matter that you believe you are most knowledgeable about. Continue this process until you've completed all of them. You generally should limit yourself to a maximum of 14 minutes per TBS. Under no circumstances should you allow yourself to fall behind schedule. If a TBS seems difficult or long, be sure to remain cognizant of the passage of time. If after a few minutes or so you feel that it is too costly to continue, answer all requirements with the response you tentatively feel is best, flag it for review, and go on to the next TBS.

- Return to any TBS you flagged and attempt to better answer them if you have time remaining for the exam. (Remember that you can **not** go back to any of the multiple-choice testlets.) If you cannot come up with any better answers, use your preliminary choices because your first impressions are often correct.

Scratch Paper

Identify and label your scratch paper to avoid confusing yourself during the stress of the exam.

Benefits of the Solutions Approach™

The Solutions Approach™ may seem cumbersome the first time you attempt it; however, you will find that it assists you in directing your thoughts toward the information required for the answer. Without a Solutions Approach™, you are apt to become distracted or confused by details that are irrelevant.

It may also seem time-consuming at first, but as you become comfortable using it, you will see that it actually saves time and results in a better answer choice.

We urge you to give the Solutions Approach™ a good try by using it throughout your review. As you practice, you may adapt it to your own preferences and requirements. **The important thing is to develop a system so that you do not approach exam questions with a storehouse of knowledge that you cannot express under exam conditions**.

_____

EXAM CHECKLISTS

What to have on hand for each exam section:

- Your NTS and 2 forms of acceptable matching identification; see the Candidate Bulletin

- Cash and/or a major credit card

- An inexpensive watch (not allowed in the exam room) to facilitate your timely arrival at the testing center

- Comfortable clothing that can be loosened to suit varying temperatures (What is worn into the exam room must be worn throughout the testing period; once at the testing center, you can remove a coat or sweater and place it in a small locker before entering the exam room.)

- Appropriate review materials and tools for final reviews during the last days before the exam

- Healthy snack foods (not allowed in exam room)

If you will be staying overnight:

- Make travel arrangements, including contingency plans, well in advance.

- Reserve a room for the preceding night so that you can check in, locate the testing center well before the exam, and get a good night's rest.

- Bring your hotel (and any other) confirmations.

- Use your own alarm device—don't rely on a hotel wake-up call.

- If crossing time zones, plan to compensate accordingly.

- International candidates should apply for passports and visas well in advance.

Evenings before exam sections:

- Briefly review your Bisk Education chapter outlines for the next day's exam section(s).

- Eat lightly and monitor your intake of alcohol and caffeine.

- Get a good night's rest.

- Do **not** try to cram. A brief review of your notes will help to focus your attention on important points and remind you that you are well prepared, but too much cramming can undermine your self-confidence.

The morning of each exam section:

- Eat a satisfying meal before your exam. It will be several hours before your next meal. Eat enough to ward off hunger, but not so much that you feel uncomfortable.

- Dress appropriately. Wear layers you can loosen to suit varying temperatures in the room. If you require a separate sweater or a jacket due to room temperature, it must be worn at all times.

- Arrive at the exam center at least 30 minutes early.

What to bring to the testing center:

- Your NTS and 2 forms of acceptable matching identification; see the Candidate Bulletin

- An inexpensive watch (to be left outside the exam room; the exam's computer screen displays the time remaining to complete the exam) to ensure you arrive **at least 30 minutes early**

- Take only those articles that you need to get to and from the testing center. Avoid taking any articles that are not allowed in the exam room, especially valuable ones (test center staff will **not** be held responsible for lost or stolen items). See the Candidate Bulletin for a list of prohibited items.

———————

TEN ATTRIBUTES OF EXAM SUCCESS

We believe that successful CPA candidates possess these ten characteristics that contribute to their ability to pass the exam.

1. Positive Mental Attitude

Preparation for the exam is a long, intense process. A positive mental attitude can be the difference between passing and failing.

2. Development of a Plan

The significant commitment involved in preparing for the exam requires a plan. A sample study plan is included in the foreword to this text. Whether you use our study plan or create your own, the importance of this attribute should not be overlooked.

3. Adherence to the Plan

You cannot expect to accomplish a successful and comprehensive review without adherence to your study plan.

4. Time Management

We all lead busy lives and the ability to budget study time is a key to success. We have outlined steps to budgeting study time in the foreword to this text.

5. Knowledge

There is a distinct difference between understanding material and knowing material. A superficial understanding of the exam content is not enough. You must know the material well. Your Bisk Education text is designed to help you acquire the knowledge that is essential to exam success.

6. Exam Strategies

You should be familiar with the exam format and know exactly what you will do in the exam room. In this appendix, we discuss the steps you should take from the time you enter the exam room until you hand in your scratch paper. Advance planning will save you time and confusion on exam day.

7. Exam Scoring

Remember that your objective is to score 75 points on each exam section. An understanding of the scoring procedures described in this appendix will help you to maximize points.

8. Solutions Approach™

The Solutions Approach™ is an efficient, systematic method of organizing and solving exam questions. This approach will permit you to organize your thinking and conclusions in a logical manner that will maximize your exam score. Many candidates have never developed an effective problem-solving methodology. Our approach teaches you to derive solutions independently and will help you avoid drawing "blanks" on the exam; with it, you always know where to begin.

9. Focus on the Ultimate Objective—Passing!

Your primary goal in preparing for the exam is to attain a score of 75 or better on all sections and, thus, pass the exam. Your review should be focused on this goal. Other objectives, such as learning new material or reviewing old material, are important only insofar as they assist you in passing the exam.

10. Exam Confidence

Exam confidence is actually a function of the other nine attributes. If you have acquired a good working knowledge of the material, an understanding of the grading system, a tactic for answering simulations, and a plan for taking the exam; you can go into the exam room confident that you are in control.

———————————

SECTION THREE:
AUD AICPA CONTENT & SKILL SPECIFICATION OUTLINE

The AICPA Board of Examiners (BOE) has developed a content specification outline (CSO) for each section of the exam. These outlines list the areas (Roman numerals), groups (capital letters), and topics (Arabic numerals) to be tested and indicate the approximate percentage of the total questions associated with each area. The AICPA does not provide percentages for groups or topics.

These are the six content areas covered by the AUD CSO (see the following pages for the complete outline):

Auditing and Attestation:

I.   Engagement acceptance and understanding the assignment (12%–16%)

II. Understanding the entity and its environment including internal control (16%–20%)

III. Performing audit procedures and evaluating evidence (16%–20%)

IV. Evaluating audit findings, communications, and reporting (16%–20%)

Other:

V.   Accounting and review services engagements (12%–16%)

VI. Professional responsibilities (16%–20%)

In October 2011, the BOE approved changes to the CSO for all four exam sections. This CSO is effective beginning with the January-February 2013 exam window. According to the AICPA, the changes include general improvements for clarity; the removal of redundancies; a reference review and update; and general editorial updates. The only substantive change for AUD is the transfer of a firm's system of quality control from the first area to the sixth area.

AUDITING & ATTESTATION

The AUD section tests knowledge and understanding of the following professional standards: auditing standards promulgated in the United States of America (related to audits of an *issuer* (a public company), a *nonissuer* (an entity that is not a public company), governmental entities, not-for-profit entities, and employee benefit plans; standards related to attestation and assurance engagements; and standards for performing accounting and review services.

Candidates are expected to demonstrate an awareness of: (1) the International Auditing and Assurance Standards Board (IAASB) and its role in establishing International Standards on Auditing (ISA), (2) the differences between ISA and US auditing standards, and (3) the audit requirements under US auditing standards that apply when they perform audit procedures on a US company that supports an audit report based upon the auditing standards of another country, or the ISA.

This section also tests knowledge of professional responsibilities of certified public accountants including ethics and independence.

Candidates are also expected to demonstrate an awareness of: (1) the International Ethics Standards Board for Accountants (IESBA) and its role in establishing requirements of the International Federation of Accountants (IFAC) *Code of Ethics for Professional Accountants*, and (2) the independence requirements that apply when they perform audit procedures on a US company that supports an audit report based upon the auditing standards of another country, or the ISA.

In addition to demonstrating knowledge and understanding of the professional standards, candidates are required to demonstrate the skills required to apply that knowledge in performing auditing and attestation tasks as certified public accountants.

Candidates are also expected to perform the following tasks:

- Demonstrate an awareness and understanding of the process by which standards and professional requirements are established for audit, attestation, and other services performed by CPAs, including the role of standard-setting bodies within the US and those bodies with the authority to promulgate international standards.

- Differentiate between audits; attestation and assurance services; compilations; and reviews.

- Differentiate between the professional standards for issuers and nonissuers.

- Identify situations that might be unethical or a violation of professional standards; perform research and consultations as appropriate; and determine the appropriate action.

- Recognize potentially unethical behavior of clients and determine the impact on the services being performed.

- Demonstrate the importance of identifying and adhering to requirements, rules, and standards that are established by licensing boards within their states and which may place additional professional requirements specific to their state of practice.

- Appropriately apply professional requirements in practice and differentiate between unconditional requirements and presumptively mandatory requirements.

- Exercise due care in the performance of work.

- Demonstrate an appropriate level of professional skepticism in the performance of work.

- Maintain independence in mental attitude in all matters relating to the audit.

- Research relevant professional literature.

The outline that follows specifies the tasks and related knowledge in which candidates are required to demonstrate proficiency.

I. **Auditing and Attestation: Engagement Acceptance and Understanding the Assignment (12% – 16%)**

   A. Determine nature and scope of engagement

   B. Consider the firm's policies and procedures pertaining to client acceptance and continuance

   C. Communicate with the predecessor auditor

   D. Establish an understanding with the client and document the understanding through an engagement letter or other written communication with the client

   E. Consider other planning matters

      1. Consider using the work of other independent auditors

      2. Determine the extent of the involvement of professionals possessing specialized skills

      3. Consider the independence, objectivity, and competency of the internal audit function

   F. Identify matters related to planning and prepare documentation for communications with those charged with governance

II. **Auditing and Attestation: Understanding the Entity and Its Environment (Including Internal Control) (16% – 20%)**

   A. Determine and document materiality levels for financial statements taken as a whole

   B. Conduct and document risk assessment discussions among audit team, concurrently with discussion on susceptibility of the entity's financial statement to material misstatement due to fraud

C.   Consideration of fraud

    1.   Identify characteristics of fraud

    2.   Document required discussions regarding risk of fraud

    3.   Document inquiries of management about fraud

    4.   Identify and assess risks that may result in material misstatements due to fraud

D.   Perform and document risk assessment procedures

    1.   Identify, conduct, and document appropriate inquiries of management and others within the entity

    2.   Perform appropriate analytical procedures to understand the entity and identify areas of risk

    3.   Obtain information to support inquiries through observation and inspection (including reading corporate minutes, etc.)

E.   Consider additional aspects of the entity and its environment including: industry, regulatory, and other external factors; strategies and business risks; financial performance

F.   Consider internal control

    1.   Perform procedures to assess the control environment including consideration of the Committee of Sponsoring Organizations of the Treadway Commission (COSO) framework and identifying entity-level controls

    2.   Obtain and document an understanding of business processes and information flows

    3.   Determine the effect of information technology (IT) on the effectiveness of an entity's internal control

    4.   Perform risk assessment procedures to evaluate the design and implementation of internal controls relevant to an audit of financial statements

    5.   Identify key risks associated with general controls in a financial IT environment including change management, backup/recovery, and network access (e.g., administrative rights)

    6.   Identify key risks associated with application functionality that supports financial transaction cycles including: application access control (e.g., administrative access rights); controls over interfaces, integrations, and e-commerce; significant algorithms, reports, validation, edit checks, error handling, etc.

    7.   Assess whether the entity has designed controls to mitigate key risks associated with general controls or application functionality

    8.   Identify controls relevant to reliable financial reporting and the period-end financial reporting process

    9.   Consider limitations of internal control

    10.   Consider the effects of service organizations on internal control

    11.   Consider the risk of management override of internal controls

G.   Document an understanding of the entity and its environment, including each component of the entity's internal control, in order to assess risks

H.   Assess and document the risk of material misstatements (RMM)

1.   Identify and document financial statement assertions and formulate audit objectives including significant financial statement balances, classes of transactions, disclosures, and accounting estimates

2.   Relate the identified risks to relevant assertions and consider whether the risks could result in a material misstatement to the financial statements

3.   Assess and document the RMM that relates to both financial statement level and specific assertions

4.   Identify and document conditions and events that may indicate the RMM

I.   Identify and document significant risks that require a special audit consideration

1.   Significant recent economic, accounting, or other developments

2.   Related parties and related party transactions

3.   Improper revenue recognition

4.   Nonroutine or complex transactions

5.   Significant management estimates

6.   Illegal acts

III.   **Auditing and Attestation: Performing Audit Procedures and Evaluating Evidence (16% – 20%)**

A.   Develop overall responses to risks

1.   Develop overall responses to risks identified and use the RMM to drive the nature, extent, and timing of further audit procedures

2.   Document significant risks identified, related controls evaluated, and overall responses to address assessed risks

3.   Determine and document level(s) of tolerable misstatement

B.   Perform audit procedures responsive to the RMM; obtain and document evidence to form a basis for conclusions

1.   Design and perform audit procedures whose nature, extent, and timing are responsive to the assessed RMM

2.   Integrating audits: in an integrated audit of internal control over financial reporting and the financial statements, design and perform testing of controls to accomplish the objectives of both audits simultaneously

3.   Design, perform, and document tests of controls to evaluate design effectiveness

4.   Design, perform, and document tests of controls to evaluate operating effectiveness

5.   Perform substantive procedures

6.   Perform audit sampling

7.   Perform analytical procedures

8.   Confirm balances and/or transactions with third parties

9.   Examine inventories and other assets

10.   Perform other tests of details, balances, and journal entries

11.   Perform computer-assisted audit techniques (CAAT), including data query, extraction, and analysis

12.   Perform audit procedures on significant management estimates

13.   Auditing fair value measurements and disclosures including the use of specialists in evaluating estimates

14.   Perform tests on unusual year-end transactions

15.   Audits performed in accordance with International Standards on Auditing (ISA) or auditing standards of another country: determine if differences exist and whether additional audit procedures are required

16.   Evaluate contingencies

17.   Obtain and evaluate lawyers' letters

18.   Review subsequent events

19.   Obtaining and placing reliance on representations from management

20.   Identify material weaknesses, significant deficiencies, and other control deficiencies

IV.   **Auditing and Attestation: Evaluating Audit Findings, Communications, and Reporting (16% – 20%)**

A.   Perform overall analytical procedures

B.   Evaluate the sufficiency and appropriateness of audit evidence and document engagement conclusions

C.   Evaluate whether audit documentation is in accordance with professional standards

D.   Review the work performed by others, including specialists and other auditors, to provide reasonable assurance that objectives are achieved

E.   Document the summary of uncorrected misstatements and related conclusions

F.   Evaluate whether financial statements are free of material misstatements

G.   Consider the entity's ability to continue as a going concern

H.   Consider other information in documents containing audited financial statements (e.g., supplemental information and management's discussion and analysis)

I.   Retain audit documentation as required by standards and regulations

J.   Prepare communications

1.   Reports on audited financial statements

2.   Reports required by government auditing standards

3.   Reports on compliance with laws and regulations

4.   Reports on internal control

5.   Reports on the processing of transactions by service organizations

6.   Reports on agreed-upon procedures

7.   Reports on financial forecasts and projections

8.   Reports on *pro forma* financial information

9.   Special reports

10.   Reissue reports

11.   Communicate internal control related matters identified in the audit

12.   Communications with those charged with governance

13.   Subsequent discovery of facts existing at the date of the auditor's report

14.   Consideration after the report date of omitted procedures

V.   Accounting and Review Services Engagements (12% – 16%)

    A.   Plan the engagement

       1.   Determine nature and scope of engagement

       2.   Decide whether to accept or continue the client and engagement including determining the appropriateness of the engagement to meet the client's needs and consideration of independence standards

       3.   Establish an understanding with the client and document the understanding through an engagement letter or other written communication with the client

       4.   Consider change in engagement

       5.   Determine if reports are to be used by third parties

    B.   Obtain and document evidence to form a basis for conclusions

       1.   Obtain an understanding of the client's operations, business, and industry

       2.   Obtain knowledge of accounting principles and practices in the industry and the client

       3.   Perform analytical procedures for review services

       4.   Obtain representations from management for review services

       5.   Perform other engagement procedures

       6.   Consider departures from generally accepted accounting principles (GAAP) or an other comprehensive basis of accounting (OCBOA)

       7.   Prepare documentation from evidence gathered

       8.   Retain documentation as required by standards

       9.   Review the work performed to provide reasonable assurance that objectives are achieved

    C.   Prepare communications

        1.   Reports on compilations

        2.   Reports on reviews

        3.   Restricted use of reports

        4.   Communicating to management and others

        5.   Subsequent discovery of facts existing at the date of the report

        6.   Consider degree of responsibility for supplementary information

VI.   **Professional Responsibilities (16% – 20%)**

    A.   Ethics and independence

        1.   Code of Professional Conduct (AICPA)

        2.   Requirements related to issuers including the Public Company Accounting Oversight Board (PCAOB); the US Securities and Exchange Commission (SEC); the Sarbanes-Oxley Act of 2002, Title II; and the Sarbanes-Oxley Act of 2002, Title III, Section 303

        3.   Government Accountability Office (GAO)

        4.   Department of Labor (DOL)

        5.   Code of Ethics for Professional Accountants (IFAC)

    B.   Other professional responsibilities

        1.   A firm's system of quality control

        2.   General role, structure, and requirements of the PCAOB (Sarbanes-Oxley Act of 2002, Titles I and IV)

SECTION FOUR:
AUD AUTHORITATIVE PRONOUNCEMENTS
CROSS-REFERENCE TO BISK CHAPTERS

Section No.	Bisk CPA Review Auditing & Attestation Chapter Number(s)	AU Section Title / Statements on Auditing Standards Nos.
AU 110	1	*Responsibilities and Functions of the Independent Auditor* SAS 1, 78, 82
AU 120	1	*Defining Professional Requirements in Statements on Auditing Standards* SAS 102
AU 150	1	*Generally Accepted Auditing Standards* SAS 95, 98, 102, 105, 113
AU 161	14	*The Relationship of Generally Accepted Auditing Standards to Quality Control Standards* SAS 25, 98
AU 201	1	*Nature of the General Standards* SAS 1
AU 210	1	*Training and Proficiency of the Independent Auditor* SAS 1, 5
AU 220	1	*Independence* SAS 1
AU 230	1	*Due Professional Care in the Performance of Work* SAS 1, 41, 82, 99, 104
AU 311	2	*Planning and Supervision* SAS 108, 114
AU 312	2	*Audit Risk and Materiality in Conducting an Audit* SAS 107
AU 314	2, 3	*Understanding the Entity and Its Environment and Assessing the Risks of Material Misstatement* SAS 109
AU 315	1	*Communications Between Predecessor and Successor Auditors* SAS 84, 93
AU 316	2	*Consideration of Fraud in a Financial Statement Audit* SAS 99, 113
AU 317	2	*Illegal Acts by Clients* SAS 54
AU 318	2, 3, 5	*Performing Audit Procedures in Response to Assessed Risks and Evaluating the Audit Evidence Obtained* SAS 110

Section No.	Bisk CPA Review Auditing & Attestation Chapter Number(s)	AU Section Title / Statements on Auditing Standards Nos.
AU 322	4	*The Auditor's Consideration of the Internal Audit Function in an Audit of Financial Statements* SAS 65
AU 324	2	*Service Organizations* SAS 70, 78, 88, 98 Editor note: See SSAE 16, *Reporting on Controls at a Service Organization*, for guidance for service auditors.
AU 325	3	*Communicating Internal Control Related Matters Identified in an Audit* SAS 115
AU 326	4	*Audit Evidence* SAS 106
AU 328	5	*Auditing Fair Value Measurements and Disclosures* SAS 101, 113
AU 329	4	*Analytical Procedures* SAS 56, 96
AU 330	5	*The Confirmation Process* SAS 67
AU 331	5	*Inventories* SAS 1, 43, 67
AU 332	5	*Auditing Derivative Instruments, Hedging Activities, and Investments in Securities* SAS 92
AU 333	4	*Management Representations* SAS 85, 89, 99, 113
AU 334	4	*Related Parties* SAS 45
AU 336	4	*Using the Work of a Specialist* SAS 73
AU 337	4	*Inquiry of a Client's Lawyer Concerning Litigation, Claims, and Assessments* SAS 12
AU 339	4	*Audit Documentation* SAS 103
AU 341	8	*The Auditor's Consideration of an Entity's Ability to Continue as a Going Concern* SAS 59, 64, 77, 96, 113, 114
AU 342	5	*Auditing Accounting Estimates* SAS 57, 113

Section No.	Bisk CPA Review Auditing & Attestation Chapter Number(s)	AU Section Title / Statements on Auditing Standards Nos.
AU 350	6	*Audit Sampling* SAS 39, 43, 45, 111
AU 380	2	*The Auditor's Communication With Those Charged With Governance* SAS 114
AU 390	8	*Consideration of Omitted Procedures After the Report Date* SAS 46
AU 410	8	*Adherence to Generally Accepted Accounting Principles* SAS 1, 62
AU 420	8	*Consistency of Application of Generally Accepted Accounting Principles* SAS 1, 43, 88
AU 431	8	*Adequacy of Disclosure in Financial Statements* SAS 32
AU 504	8	*Association With Financial Statements* SAS 26, 35, 72
AU 508	8	*Reports on Audited Financial Statements* SAS 58, 64, 79, 85, 93, 98
AU 530	8	*Dating of the Independent Auditor's Report* SAS 1, 29, 98, 103
AU 532	11	*Restricting the Use of an Auditor's Report* SAS 87
AU 534	11	*Reporting on Financial Statements Prepared for Use in Other Countries* SAS 51
AU 543	8	*Part of Audit Performed by Other Independent Auditors* SAS 1, 64
AU 544	8	*Lack of Conformity With Generally Accepted Accounting Principles* SAS 1, 2, 62, 77
AU 550	8	*Other Information in Documents Containing Audited Financial Statements* SAS 118
AU 551	11	*Supplementary Information in Relation to the Financial Statements as a Whole* SAS 119
AU 552	11	*Reporting on Condensed Financial Statements and Selected Financial Data* SAS 42, 71

Section No.	Bisk CPA Review Auditing & Attestation Chapter Number(s)	AU Section Title / Statements on Auditing Standards Nos.
AU 558	8	*Required Supplementary Information* SAS 120
AU 560	8	*Subsequent Events* SAS 1, 12, 98, 113
AU 561	8	*Subsequent Discovery of Facts Existing at the Date of the Auditor's Report* SAS 1, 98
AU 623	11	*Special Reports* SAS 62, 77
AU 625	11	*Reports on the Application of Accounting Principles* SAS 50, 97
AU 634	11	*Letters for Underwriters and Certain Other Requesting Parties* SAS 72, 76, 86
AU 711	11	*Filings Under Federal Securities Statutes* SAS 37
AU 722	11	*Interim Financial Information* SAS 100, 116, 121
AU 801	9	*Compliance Audits* SAS 117
AU 901	5	*Public Warehouses—Controls and Auditing Procedures for Goods Held* SAS 1, 43

	Bisk CPA Review Auditing & Attestation Chapter Number(s)	**AR Section Title / Statements on Standards for Accounting and Review Services Nos.**
AR 60	12	*Framework for Performing and Reporting on Compilation and Review Engagements* SSARS 19
AR 80	12	*Compilation of Financial Statements* SSARS 19
AR 90	12	*Review of Financial Statements* SSARS 19, 20
AR 110	12	*Specified Elements, Accounts, or Items of a Financial Statement* SSARS 13, 17
AR 120	12	*Compilation of Pro Forma Financial Information* SSARS 14, 17
AR 200	12	*Reporting on Comparative Financial Statements* SSARS 2, 3, 4, 5, 7, 11, 12 , 15, 17
AR 300	12	*Compilation Reports on Financial Statements Included in Certain Prescribed Forms* SSARS 3, 5, 7, 15, 17
AR 400	12	*Communications Between Predecessor and Successor Accountants* SSARS 4, 7, 9, 15, 17
AR 600	12	*Reporting on Personal Financial Statements Included in Written Personal Financial Plans* SSARS 6

———————————

Section No.	Bisk CPA Review Auditing & Attestation Chapter Number(s)	AT Section Title / Statements on Standards for Attestation Engagements Nos.
AT 20	13	*Defining Professional Requirements in Statements on Standards for Attestation Engagements* SSAE 13
AT 50	13	*SSAE Hierarchy* SSAE 14
AT 101	13	*Attest Engagements* SSAE 10, 11, 12, 14
AT 201	13	*Agreed-Upon Procedures Engagements* SSAE 10, 11
AT 301	13	*Financial Forecasts and Projections* SSAE 10, 11, 17
AT 401	13	*Reporting on Pro Forma Financial Information* SSAE 10
AT 501	13	*An Examination of an Entity's Internal Control Over Financial Reporting That Is Integrated With an Audit of Its Financial Statements* SSAE No. 15
AT 601	13	*Compliance Attestation* SSAE No. 10
AT 701	13	*Management's Discussion and Analysis* SSAE No. 10
AT 801	13	*Reporting on Controls at a Service Organization* SSAE No. 16

Section No.	Bisk CPA Review Auditing & Attestation Chapter Number(s)	QC Section Title / Statements on Quality Control Standards No.
QC 10A	14	*A Firm's System of Quality Control* SQCS 8

Reference	Bisk CPA Review Auditing & Attestation Chapter Number(s)	Other Standards
GAGAS	9	*Government Auditing Standards* ("Yellow Book")
PCAOB AS 1	10	*References in Auditors' Reports to the Standards of the Public Company Accounting Oversight Board*
PCAOB AS 3	10	*Audit Documentation*
PCAOB AS 4	10	*Reporting on Whether a Previously Reported Material Weakness Continues to Exist*
PCAOB AS 5	10	*An Audit of Internal Control Over Financial Reporting That Is Integrated with An Audit of Financial Statements*
PCAOB AS 6	10	*Evaluating Consistency of Financial Statements*
PCAOB AS 7	14	*Engagement Quality Review*
PCAOB AS 8	10	*Audit Risk*
PCAOB AS 9	10	*Audit Planning*
PCAOB AS 10	10	*Supervision of the Audit Engagement*
PCAOB AS 11	10	*Consideration of Materiality in Planning and Performing an Audit*
PCAOB AS 12	10	*Identifying and Assessing Risks of Material Misstatement*
PCAOB AS 13	10	*The Auditor's Responses to the Risks of Material Misstatement*
PCAOB AS 14	10	*Evaluating Audit Results*
PCAOB AS 15	10	*Audit Evidence*
ISA	10	International Standards on Auditing

———————

APPENDIX C
RESEARCH SKILLS

The final testlet in AUD consists of 7 simulations—usually 6 task-based simulations (TBS) and 1 research question.

For candidates familiar with researching electronic databases, this appendix contains several research questions for practice. Make sure your speed is sufficient for the exam's time constraints.

If you have not developed electronic database research skills, your first step is to study the material in this appendix.

SECTION ONE: GENERAL RESEARCH SKILLS

OVERVIEW

The final testlet in AUD consists of 7 simulations—usually 6 task-based simulations (TBS) and 1 research question.

Nature of Research Questions

A research question involves a search of an electronic database of authoritative literature for the guidance that supports the answer to the question posed. Your research is complete when you narrow your search down to a single paragraph in the authoritative literature. No analysis of the guidance is required. The *only* response accepted is the citation of a reference to the paragraph in the authoritative literature. You cannot avoid the research by writing a response that answers the question—**the examiners are testing your electronic database research skills**.

AUD Exam's Database of Authoritative Literature

The auditing exam's database of authoritative literature you will search to answer research questions includes certain portions of the professional standards issued by the American Institute of Certified Public Accountants (AICPA) and the Public Company Accounting Oversight Board (PCAOB).

Split Screen

The AICPA's testing software allows you to split the screen, so you can view the question / response and the authoritative literature database concurrently. You can search the authoritative literature and then enter the appropriate citation on the same split screen.

Search Method

The search can be made either by using the table-of-contents feature or the search engine with Boolean operators. Many candidates find that the table-of-contents approach is easier and more efficient than a Boolean search once they become familiar with the authoritative literature.

Additional Research Comments

Research skills are not something you can acquire overnight. You must become familiar with the authoritative literature and practice researching it to become proficient. It's best to do this well before you take the exam.

You should review the tutorial and take the sample test on the exam portion of the AICPA's website (aicpa.org /becomeacpa/cpaexam/forcandidates/tutorialandsampletest) to become familiar with the exam's most current research interface.

In many instances, research questions are relatively easy; however, should you get a difficult one on your exam, move on after a few minutes; answer a TBS; and then return. Often a simple break helps avoid frustration and allows you to start again with a fresh perspective.

In addition to the research questions in this textbook's chapters, this appendix contains AUD research questions for you to use to practice your skills.

BOOLEAN SEARCH APPROACH

The three Boolean operators are OR, AND, and NOT. Boolean operators can be combined to refine searches. For example, the following parameters would find information on letters to a client's attorney inquiring about litigation, claims, and assessments: (attorney OR lawyer) AND (letter OR inquiry). If you get too many or too few responses (hits) from a search, refine your search parameters until you find what you need. The exam doesn't limit candidates from repeating searches with refined parameters. A review of Boolean operators is provided here.

OR Operator

A search using "accounting OR auditing" will find all documents containing either the word *accounting* or the word *auditing*. OR typically is used to search for terms that are used as synonyms, such as *management* and *client*. As more terms are combined in an OR search, more documents are included in the results.

AND Operator

A search using "accounting AND auditing" will find all documents containing both the word *accounting* and the word *auditing*. All things being equal, a search using AND typically will find fewer documents than a search using OR, but more than a search using NOT. As more terms are combined in an AND search, fewer documents are included in the results.

NOT Operator

A search using "accounting NOT auditing" will find all documents containing the word *accounting* except those that also contain the word *auditing*. All things being equal, a search using NOT typically will find the fewest documents. As more terms are combined in a NOT search, fewer documents are included in the results.

Constructing Search Phrases

Avoid using a search phrase such as "guidance on materially false and misleading entries in records." Anything you find in the standards will be guidance; furthermore, the term *guidance* might not be in the reference that you seek. Also, eliminate words such as *on* and *in* unless you are seeking an exact phrase that you are sure includes them.

This leaves "materially false misleading entries records." Typically, search engines default to the Boolean search connector OR for all words, which probably would result in many irrelevant hits, so modify it to "materially AND false AND statements."

Why not include *misleading* in this search phrase? If *false* is in the reference, *misleading* probably will be there also; if *misleading* is in the reference without *materially*, that reference is likely irrelevant. In other words, the word *misleading* does little to narrow the search. However, if there are too few hits using "materially AND false AND statements," try "(material AND false AND statements) OR (materially AND misleading AND statements)." The standards are not always consistent with their use of words; the guidance might use both *material* and *materially*.

Answer Selection

Once you have narrowed the search response to a few hits, read through the most likely ones to determine which answers the research question.

———————————

SECTION TWO: AUD RESEARCH SKILLS

The AUD research questions test the ability to select the applicable set of standards; structure a search of it; navigate it; and select the relevant guidance.

Free Subscription to Authoritative Literature vs. Sample Tests

Candidates with their notice to schedule can visit the AICPA's website to get a free six-month subscription (aicpa.org/becomeacpa/cpaexam/forcandidates/howtoprepare/pages/literature.aspx) to authoritative literature used on the AUD exam. The AICPA offers this subscription so that candidates can become familiar with the use of online accounting resources; however, they caution candidates that **the interface used by the online package is _not_ exactly the same as that used in the exam**. Candidates must also review the tutorial and take the sample tests provided (aicpa.org/becomeacpa/cpaexam/forcandidates/tutorialandsampletest) because the sample tests reflect the functionality and interfaces used in the actual exam.

In other words, by all means, take advantage of the free subscription offered by the AICPA and use it to become familiar with the authoritative literature and to practice researching questions, but make sure you complement this by answering the sample test's research question so you know what to expect on the exam.

Entering Your Response

The response must be entered into three separate fields on the AUD exam: the abbreviation for the applicable set of standards (selected from a drop-down list); the section number within those standards; and the paragraph number within that section. Prompts are provided that define the fields and give examples of acceptable answer formats.

Search Method

As mentioned previously, many candidates find the table-of-contents approach easier and more efficient than a Boolean search once they become familiar with the AUD authoritative literature. If you are just beginning your review of AUD, you may find the most challenging aspect of this method to be the selection of the applicable set of standards. As your review progresses, you will find this becomes easier. (You may discover that practicing research questions provides more synergy with your preparation for the entire AUD exam than it does for the other exam sections. Becoming more comfortable with which set of standards is applicable is often an important aspect of successfully answering multiple-choice questions and TBS as well.)

How to Begin

First, obtain your free subscription to the AUD authoritative literature from the AICPA. Then become familiar with it by going online and locating the various sets of standards associated with the topics in our textbook (most of the individual chapter table-of-contents pages include these references). Then scroll through a particular section of a set of standards to locate the various concepts covered in our textbook. After you have gained some familiarity with the authoritative literature, review the AICPA's tutorial and practice the sample research question within the simulation portion of their sample test. Then practice answering research questions using the AICPA's online database until you are satisfied with your level of skill.

SECTION THREE: AUD RESEARCH PRACTICE

RESEARCH SIMULATION QUESTIONS

C-1

What authoritative reference provides guidance on fieldwork to a current year auditor who has not observed the physical count of the inventory in a prior year for a nonissuer?

| | § | | | (ID: 9259) |

C-2

What authoritative reference provides a minimum list of matters subject to inquiry of a predecessor auditor by a successor auditor for a nonissuer?

| | § | | | (ID: 9260) |

C-3

What authoritative reference requires a practitioner to prohibit the use of the practitioner's name in connection with a financial projection distributed to parties not negotiating directly with the party responsible for the projection?

| | § | | | (ID: 60532) |

C-4

What authoritative reference provides guidance on reporting when an accountant is engaged to compile financial statements that omit substantially all the disclosures required by GAAP, including disclosures that might appear in the body of the financial statements?

| | § | | | (ID: 9262) |

C-5

What authoritative reference provides guidance when an auditor's analytics for a nonissuer indicate that a misstatement in financial statements might exist, but not its amount?

| | § | | | (ID: 9263) |

C-6

What authoritative reference provides guidance for the manner of testing internal auditors' work for a nonissuer?

	§		

(ID: 9264)

_____

C-7

What authoritative reference provides guidance as to when a complete and final set of audit documentation should be assembled for the audit of the financial statements of a public company?

	§		

(ID: 9266)

_____

C-8

What authoritative reference describes the level of knowledge and competence the engagement quality reviewer must possess to perform an engagement quality review of a public company?

	§		

(ID: 9267)

_____

C-9

What authoritative reference provides guidance when an auditor decides to make reference to the report of another auditor as a basis, in part, for the auditor's opinion regarding where this fact should be disclosed in the audit report for a nonissuer?

	§		

(ID: 9268)

_____

C-10

What authoritative reference provides guidance as to when a member's independence shall be considered to be impaired if during the period of a professional engagement a covered member had or was committed to acquire a material indirect financial interest in the client?

	§		

(ID: 89890)

_____

C-11

What authoritative reference provides guidance as to how in the performance of any professional service, a member shall be free of conflicts of interest?

	§		

(ID: 89891)

_____

C-12

What authoritative reference provides guidance for a member in public practice to obtain clients by advertising or other forms of solicitation in a manner that is misleading?

[   ] § [   ] [   ]   (ID: 89892)

_____

C-13

What authoritative reference provides guidance if an auditor is asked to issue a written communication stating that no significant deficiencies were identified during an audit?

[   ] § [   ] [   ]   (ID: 89459)

_____

C-14

What authoritative reference provides guidance as to what the auditor's primary emphasis should be when reviewing related-party transactions?

[   ] § [   ] [   ]   (ID: 89460)

_____

C-15

What authoritative reference discusses the qualitative aspects of misstatements that an auditor should consider when misstatements are discovered in a sample during substantive tests?

[   ] § [   ] [   ]   (ID: 27792)

_____

RESEARCH SIMULATION ANSWERS

C-1

AU	§	331	13	(ID: 9259)

.13 The independent auditor may be asked to audit financial statements covering the current period and one or more periods for which he [*sic*] had not observed or made some physical counts of prior inventories. He [*sic*] may, nevertheless, be able to become satisfied as to such prior inventories through appropriate procedures, such as tests of prior transactions, reviews of the records of prior counts, and the application of gross profit tests, provided that he [*sic*] has been able to become satisfied as to the current inventory.

C-2

AU	§	315	09	(ID: 9260)

.09 The successor auditor should make specific and reasonable inquiries of the predecessor auditor regarding matters that will assist the successor auditor in determining whether to accept the engagement. Matters subject to inquiry should include—

- Information that might bear on the integrity of management.

- Disagreements with management as to accounting principles, auditing procedures, or other similarly significant matters.

- Communications to those charged with governance regarding fraud and illegal acts by clients.

- Communications to management and those charged with governance regarding significant deficiencies and material weaknesses in internal control.

- The predecessor auditor's understanding as to the reasons for the change of auditors.

The successor auditor may wish to consider other reasonable inquiries.

C-3

AT	§	301	11	(ID: 60532)

.11 Because a financial projection is not appropriate for general use, a practitioner should not consent to the use of his or her name in conjunction with a financial projection that he or she believes will be distributed to those who will not be negotiating directly with the responsible party, for example, in an offering statement of an entity's debt or equity interests, unless the projection is used to supplement a financial forecast.

C-4

AR	§	80		20	(ID: 9262)

.20 An entity may request the accountant to compile financial statements that omit substantially all the disclosures required by an applicable financial reporting framework, including disclosures that might appear in the body of the financial statements. The accountant may compile such financial statements, provided that the omission of substantially all disclosures is not, to his or her knowledge, undertaken with the intention of misleading those who might reasonably be expected to use such financial statements. When reporting on financial statements that omit substantially all disclosures, the accountant should include, after the paragraph describing the accountant's responsibility, a paragraph in the compilation report that includes the following elements:

a. A statement that management has elected to omit substantially all the disclosures (and the statement of cash flows, if applicable) required by the applicable financial reporting framework (or ordinarily included in the financial statements if the financial statements are prepared in accordance with an OCBOA)

b. A statement that if the omitted disclosures (and statement of cash flows, if applicable) were included in the financial statements, they might influence the user's conclusions about the company's financial position, results of operations, and cash flows (or equivalent for presentations other than accounting principles generally accepted in the United States of America)

c. A statement that, accordingly, the financial statements are not designed for those who are not informed about such matters

When the entity wishes to include disclosures about only a few matters in the form of notes to such financial statements, such disclosures should be labeled "Selected Information—Substantially All Disclosures Required by [*identify the applicable financial reporting framework (for example "Accepted Accounting Principles Generally Accepted in the United States of America"*)] Are Not Included."

See Compilation Exhibit B for examples of compilation reports when substantially all disclosures required by an applicable financial reporting framework are omitted.

C-5

AU	§	312		54	(ID: 9263)

.54 When the auditor tests relevant assertions related to an account balance or a class of transactions by a substantive analytical procedure, the auditor might not specifically identify misstatements but would obtain only an indication of whether misstatement might exist in the balance or class and possibly its approximate magnitude. If the substantive analytical procedure indicates that a misstatement might exist, but not its approximate amount, the auditor should request management to investigate and, if necessary, should expand his or her audit procedures to enable him or her to determine whether a misstatement exists in the account balance or class of transactions.

C-6

| AU | § | 322 | 26 | (ID: 9264) |

.26   In making the evaluation, the auditor should test some of the internal auditors' work related to the significant financial statement assertions. These tests may be accomplished by either (a) examining some of the controls, transactions, or balances that the internal auditors examined or (b) examining similar controls, transactions, or balances not actually examined by the internal auditors. In reaching conclusions about the internal auditors' work, the auditor should compare the results of his or her tests with the results of the internal auditors' work. The extent of this testing will depend on the circumstances and should be sufficient to enable the auditor to make an evaluation of the overall quality and effectiveness of the internal audit work being considered by the auditor.

_____

C-7

| PCAOB | AS | 3 | 15 | (ID: 9266) |

15.   Prior to the report release date, the auditor must have completed all necessary auditing procedures and obtained sufficient evidence to support the representations in the auditor's report. A complete and final set of audit documentation should be assembled for retention as of a date not more than 45 days after the report release date (*documentation completion date*). If a report is not issued in connection with an engagement, then the documentation completion date should not be more than 45 days from the date that fieldwork was substantially completed. If the auditor was unable to complete the engagement, then the documentation completion date should not be more than 45 days from the date the engagement ceased.

_____

C-8

| PCAOB | AS | 7 | 5 | (ID: 9267) |

5.   The engagement quality reviewer must possess the level of knowledge and competence related to accounting, auditing, and financial reporting required to serve as the engagement partner on the engagement under review.

_____

C-9

| AU | § | 508 | 12 | (ID: 9268) |

.12   When the auditor decides to make reference to the report of another auditor as a basis, in part, for his or her opinion, he or she should disclose this fact in the introductory paragraph of his or her report and should refer to the report of the other auditor in expressing his or her opinion. These references indicate division of responsibility for performance of the audit.

_____

C-10

ET	§	101-1	02	(ID: 89890)

.02 Independence shall be considered to be impaired if:

During the period of the professional engagement a covered member

1. Had or was committed to acquire any direct or material indirect financial interest in the client.

2. Was a trustee of any trust or executor or administrator of any estate if such trust or estate had or was committed to acquire any direct or material indirect financial interest in the client and

   (i) The covered member (individually or with others) had the authority to make investment decisions for the trust or estate; or

   (ii) The trust or estate owned or was committed to acquire more than 10 percent of the client's outstanding equity securities or other ownership interests; or

   (iii) The value of the trust's or estate's holdings in the client exceeded 10 percent of the total assets of the trust or estate.

3. Had a joint closely held investment that was material to the covered member.

4. Except as specifically permitted in interpretation 101-5, had any loan to or from the client, any officer or director of the client, or any individual owning 10 percent or more of the client's outstanding equity securities or other ownership interests.

C-11

ET	§	102-1	02	(ID: 89891)

.02 In the performance of any professional service, a member shall maintain objectivity and integrity, shall be free of conflicts of interest, and shall not knowingly misrepresent facts or subordinate his or her judgment to others.

A member shall be considered to have knowingly misrepresented facts in violation of rule 102 when he or she knowingly—

1. Makes, or permits or directs another to make, materially false and misleading entries in an entity's financial statements or records; or

2. Fails to correct an entity's financial statements or records that are materially false and misleading when he or she has the authority to record an entry; or

3. Signs, or permits or directs another to sign, a document containing materially false and misleading information.

C-12

ET	§	502-2	03	(ID: 89892)

.01 Advertising or other forms of solicitation that are false, misleading, or deceptive are not in the public interest and are prohibited. Such activities include those that—

1. Create false or unjustified expectations of favorable results.

2. Imply the ability to influence any court, tribunal, regulatory agency, or similar body or official.

3. Contain a representation that specific professional services in current or future periods will be performed for a stated fee, estimated fee or fee range when it was likely at the time of the representation that such fees would be substantially increased and the prospective client was not advised of that likelihood.

4. Contain any other representations that would be likely to cause a reasonable person to misunderstand or be deceived.

C-13

AU	§	325	25	(ID: 89459)

.25 The auditor should not issue a written communication stating that no significant deficiencies were identified during the audit.

C-14

AU	§	334	02	(ID: 89460)

.02 Financial Accounting Standards Board (FASB) *Accounting Standards Codification* (ASC) 850, *Related Party Disclosures*, gives the requirements for related party disclosures. Certain accounting pronouncements prescribe the accounting treatment when related parties are involved; however, established accounting principles ordinarily do not require transactions with related parties to be accounted for on a basis different from that which would be appropriate if the parties were not related. The auditor should view related party transactions within the framework of existing pronouncements, placing primary emphasis on the adequacy of disclosure. In addition, the auditor should be aware that the substance of a particular transaction could be significantly different from its form and that financial statements should recognize the substance of particular transactions rather than merely their legal form.

C-15

AU	§	350	27	(ID: 27792)

.27 In addition to the evaluation of the frequency and amounts of monetary misstatements, consideration should be given to the qualitative aspects of the misstatements. These include (a) the nature and cause of misstatements, such as whether they are differences in principle or in application, are errors or are caused by fraud, or are due to misunderstanding of instructions or to carelessness, and (b) the possible relationship of the misstatements to other phases of the audit. The discovery of fraud ordinarily requires a broader consideration of possible implications than does the discovery of an error.

APPENDIX D
FINANCIAL RATIOS

Analytical procedures consist of evaluations of financial information made by a study of plausible relationships among both financial and nonfinancial data. Plausible relationships among data may reasonably be expected to exist and continue in the absence of changes in conditions. Several common financial ratios are shown here for your reference.

Working Capital

$$Current\ Assets - Current\ Liabilities$$

Comments: Represents the liquid portion of resources or enterprise capital. The greater the amount of working capital, the greater the cushion of protection available to short-term creditors, and the greater assurance that short-term debts will be paid when due.

Current Ratio

$$\frac{Current\ Assets}{Current\ Liabilities}$$

Comments: This is a primary test of the overall solvency of the enterprise and its ability to meet current obligations from current assets. When the current ratio exceeds 1 to 1, an equal increase in current assets and current liabilities decreases the ratio. When the current ratio is less than 1 to 1, an equal increase in current assets and current liabilities increases the ratio.

Acid-Test or Quick Ratio

$$\frac{Cash + Marketable\ Securities + Net\ Receivables}{Current\ Liabilities}$$

Comments: This ratio provides a more severe test of immediate solvency by eliminating inventories and prepaid expenses (current assets that cannot be quickly converted into cash).

Defensive-Interval Ratio

$$\frac{Cash + Marketable\ Securities + Net\ Receivables}{Average\ Daily\ Cash\ Expenditures}$$

Comments: This ratio estimates the number of days that the company can meet its basic operational costs. The average daily cash expenditures can be approximated by reducing total expenses for the year by noncash charges (e.g., depreciation or amortization of intangibles) and dividing this amount by 365.

Debt to Equity

$$\frac{Total\ Liabilities}{Owners'\ Equity}$$

Comments: This ratio provides a measure of the relative amounts of resources provided by creditors and owners.

Times Interest Earned

$$\frac{\textit{Income Before Income Taxes and Interest Charges}}{\textit{Interest Charges}}$$

Comments: Measures the ability of the firm to meet its interest payments. Income taxes are added back to net income. (The ability to pay interest is not dependent on the amount of income taxes to be paid because interest is tax deductible.)

Times Preferred Dividends Earned

$$\frac{\textit{Net Income}}{\textit{Annual Preferred Dividend Requirement}}$$

Comments: Measures the adequacy of current earnings for the payment of preferred dividends.

Total Asset Turnover

$$\frac{\textit{Total Sales (Revenue)}}{\textit{Average Total Assets}}$$

Comments: This ratio is used to determine the amount of sales that are generated from each dollar of assets. Average total assets is generally determined by adding the beginning and ending total assets and dividing by two.

Receivables Turnover

$$\frac{\textit{Net Credit Sales}}{\textit{Average Net Receivables}}$$

Comments: This ratio provides an indication of the efficiency of credit policies and collection procedures, and the quality of the receivables. Average net receivables include trade notes receivable. Average net receivables is generally determined by adding the beginning and ending net receivables and dividing by two.

Number of Days' Sales in Average Receivables

$$\frac{360}{\textit{Receivables Turnover}}$$

Comments: Tests the average number of days required to collect receivables. Some analysts prefer to use 365, 300, or 250 as the number of business days in a year.

Inventory Turnover

$$\frac{\textit{Cost of Goods Sold}}{\textit{Average Inventory}}$$

Comments: Indicates the number of times inventory was acquired and sold (or used in production) during the period. It can be used to detect inventory obsolescence or pricing problems. Average inventory is generally determined by adding the beginning and ending inventories and dividing by two.

Gross Margin Percentage

$$\frac{\textit{Sales} - \textit{Cost of Goods Sold}}{\textit{Sales}}$$

Comments: Represents the percentage of sales revenue that the company retains after incurring the direct costs associated with producing the goods and services sold by a company. The higher the percentage, the more the company retains on each dollar of sales to cover its other costs and obligations.

Net Operating Margin Percentage

$$\frac{\textit{Operating Income}}{\textit{Sales}}$$

Comments: Represents the percentage of sales revenue that the company makes before interest and taxes on each dollar of sales.

Number of Days' Supply in Average Inventory

$$\frac{360}{\textit{Inventory Turnover}} \quad \text{or} \quad \frac{\textit{Average (Ending) Inventory}}{\textit{Average Daily Cost of Goods Sold}}$$

Comments: Indicates the number of days inventory is held before it is sold. Some analysts prefer to use 365, 300, or 250 as the number of business days in the year. Average daily cost of goods sold is determined by dividing cost of goods sold by the number of business days.

Length of Operating Cycle

$$\begin{array}{ccc} \textit{Number of days' sales} & & \textit{Number of days' supply} \\ \textit{in average receivables} & + & \textit{in average inventory} \end{array}$$

Comments: Measures the average length of time from the purchase of inventory to the collection of cash from its sale.

Book Value Per Common Share

$$\frac{\textit{Common Stockholders' Equity}}{\textit{Number of Common Shares Outstanding}}$$

To determine common stockholders' equity, preferred stock is subtracted from total stockholders' equity at the greater of its liquidation, par, or stated value. Cumulative preferred stock dividends in arrears are also similarly subtracted. Treasury stock affects the denominator as the number of common shares outstanding is reduced.

Comments: This ratio measures the amount that common shareholders would receive if all assets were sold at their carrying amounts and all creditors were paid. When balance sheet valuations do not approximate fair values, the importance of this ratio is diminished.

Book Value Per Preferred Share

$$\frac{\textit{Preferred Stockholders' Equity}}{\textit{Number of Preferred Shares Outstanding}}$$

Preferred stockholders' equity is comprised of (a) preferred stock at the greater of its liquidation, par, or stated value and (b) cumulative preferred stock dividends in arrears.

Comments: This ratio measures the amount that preferred shareholders would receive if the company were liquidated on the basis of the amounts reported on the balance sheet.

Return on Total Assets

$$\frac{\textit{Net Income + Interest Expense (Net of Tax)}}{\textit{Average Total Assets}}$$

Comments: This ratio provides a measure of the degree of efficiency with which resources (total assets) are used to generate earnings.

Return on Common Stockholders' Equity

$$\frac{\text{Net Income} - \text{Preferred Dividends}}{\text{Average Common Stockholders' Equity}}$$

Comments: Measures the rate of earnings on resources provided by common stockholders. Common stockholders' equity is measured as indicated in the explanation for the book value per common share calculation on the previous page. Average common stockholders' equity is generally determined by adding beginning and ending common stockholders' equity and dividing by two.

Successful use of leverage occurs when a company earns more by the use of borrowed money than it costs to use the borrowed funds. When compared to the return on total assets, the return on common stockholders' equity measures the extent to which leverage is being employed for or against the common stockholders. When the return on common stockholders' equity is greater than the return on total assets, leverage is positive and common stockholders benefit.

Return on Stockholders' Equity

$$\frac{\text{Net Income}}{\text{Average Stockholders' Equity}}$$

Comments: Measures the rate of earnings on resources provided by all stockholders, i.e., common and preferred. Average stockholders' equity is generally determined by adding beginning and ending stockholders' equity and dividing by two.

Earnings Per Share (EPS)

$$\frac{\text{Net Income} - \text{Preferred Dividends}}{\text{Average Number of Common Shares Outstanding}}$$

Comments: Measures the ability to pay dividends to common stockholders by measuring profit earned per share of common stock.

Price Earnings Ratio

$$\frac{\text{Market Price Per Common Share}}{\text{Earnings Per Common Share}}$$

Comments: A measure of whether a stock is relatively cheap or relatively expensive based on its present earnings.

Dividend Payout Ratio

$$\frac{\text{Cash Dividend Per Common Share}}{\text{Earnings Per Common Share}}$$

Comments: This ratio represents the percentage of earnings per share distributed to common stockholders in cash dividends. A low ratio would probably indicate the reinvestment of profits by a growth-oriented firm.

Yield on Common Stock

$$\frac{\text{Dividend Per Common Share}}{\text{Market Price Per Common Share}}$$

Comments: Measures cash flow return on common stock investment.

APPENDIX E
RECENTLY RELEASED AICPA QUESTIONS

In April 2012, the AICPA released fifty multiple-choice questions, two task-based simulations, and one research task related to the AUD section of the CPA Examination. These questions and their unofficial answers are reproduced here as received from the AICPA examiners, along with Bisk Education's explanations. The multiple-choice questions in Problems 1 and 2 were labeled *medium* and *hard*, respectively, by the AICPA examiners. The AICPA did not state if these questions ever appeared on any exam; whether they were assigned points or were merely being pretested (and earned no points) if they did appear on an exam; or if they were now obsolete for some reason. These questions are intended only as a study aid and should not be used to predict the content of future exams. It is the AICPA's policy that released questions will not appear on future exams.

Problem 1 MULTIPLE-CHOICE QUESTIONS

1. An accountant who accepts an engagement to compile a financial projection most likely would make the client aware that the

   a. Projection may not be included in a document with audited historical financial statements
   b. Accountant's responsibility to update the projection for future events and circumstances is limited to one year
   c. Projection omits all hypothetical assumptions and presents the most likely future financial position
   d. Engagement does not include an evaluation of the support for the assumptions underlying the projection
   (R/12, AUD, #1, ID: 89751)

2. Which of the following audit procedures most likely would assist an auditor in identifying conditions and events that may indicate there could be substantial doubt about an entity's ability to continue as a going concern?

   a. Confirmation of accounts receivable from principal customers
   b. Reconciliation of interest expense with debt outstanding
   c. Confirmation of bank balances
   d. Review of compliance with terms of debt agreements
   (R/12, AUD, #2, ID: 89752)

3. Which of the following would **not** be considered an analytical procedure?

   a. Converting dollar amounts of income statement account balances to percentages of net sales for comparison with industry averages
   b. Developing the current year's expected net sales based on the sales trend of similar entities within the same industry
   c. Projecting a deviation rate by comparing the results of a statistical sample with the actual population characteristics
   d. Estimating the current year's expected expenses based on the prior year's expenses and the current year's budget
   (R/12, AUD, #3, ID: 89753)

4. A principal auditor decides **not** to refer to the audit of another CPA who audited a subsidiary of the principal auditor's client. After making inquiries about the other CPA's professional reputation and independence, the principal auditor most likely would

   a. Document in the engagement letter that the principal auditor assumes no responsibility for the other CPA's work
   b. Obtain written permission from the other CPA to omit the reference in the principal auditor's report
   c. Contact the other CPA and review the audit programs and working papers pertaining to the subsidiary
   d. Add an explanatory paragraph to the auditor's report indicating that the subsidiary's financial statements are not material to the consolidated financial statements
   (R/12, AUD, #4, ID: 89754)

5. In auditing related-party transactions, an auditor ordinarily places primary emphasis on

   a. The probability that related-party transactions will recur
   b. Confirming the existence of the related parties
   c. Verifying the valuation of the related-party transactions
   d. The adequacy of the disclosure of the related-party transactions   (R/12, AUD, #5, ID: 89755)

6. The inability to complete which of the following activities most likely would prevent an accountant from accepting and completing an engagement for a review of financial statements performed in accordance with *Statements on Standards for Accounting and Review Services*?

   a. Performing tests of details of major account balances
   b. Performing inquiries and analytical procedures
   c. Obtaining an understanding of internal control to assess control risk
   d. Having previous experience in the client's industry   (R/12, AUD, #6, ID: 89756)

7. Obtaining an understanding of an internal control involves evaluating the design of the control and determining whether the control has been

   a. Authorized
   b. Implemented
   c. Tested
   d. Monitored   (R/12, AUD, #7, ID: 89757)

8. Which of the following procedures most likely would be performed in a review engagement of a nonissuer's financial statements in accordance with *Statements on Standards for Accounting and Review Services*?

   a. Making inquiries of management
   b. Observing a year-end inventory count
   c. Assessing the internal control system
   d. Examining subsequent cash receipts   (R/12, AUD, #8, ID: 89758)

9. An auditor should consider which of the following when evaluating the ability of a company to continue as a going concern?

   a. Audit fees
   b. Future assurance services
   c. Management's plans for disposal of assets
   d. A lawsuit for which judgment is not anticipated for 18 months   (R/12, AUD, #9, ID: 89759)

10. In which of the following should an auditor's report refer to the lack of consistency when there is a change in accounting principle that is significant?

    a. The scope paragraph
    b. The opinion paragraph
    c. An explanatory paragraph following the opinion paragraph
    d. An explanatory paragraph before the opinion paragraph   (R/12, AUD, #10, ID: 89760)

11. Which of the following is the best way to compensate for the lack of adequate segregation of duties in a small organization?

    a. Disclosing lack of segregation of duties to the external auditors during the annual review
    b. Replacing personnel every three or four years
    c. Requiring accountants to pass a yearly background check
    d. Allowing for greater management oversight of incompatible activities   (R/12, AUD, #11, ID: 89761)

12. Which of the following situations most likely represents the highest risk of a misstatement arising from misappropriations of assets?

    a. A large number of bearer bonds on hand
    b. A large number of inventory items with low sales prices
    c. A large number of transactions processed in a short period of time
    d. A large number of fixed assets with easily identifiable serial numbers   (R/12, AUD, #12, ID: 89762)

13. Which of the following procedures would an auditor most likely perform in the planning stage of an audit?

    a. Make a preliminary judgment about materiality
    b. Confirm a sample of the entity's accounts payable with known creditors
    c. Obtain written representations from management that there are no unrecorded transactions
    d. Communicate management's initial selection of accounting policies to the audit committee
    (R/12, AUD, #13, ID: 89763)

14. An auditor is required to confirm accounts receivable if the accounts receivable balances are

    a. Older than the prior year
    b. Material to the financial statements
    c. Smaller than expected
    d. Subject to valuation estimates   (R/12, AUD, #14, ID: 89764)

15. Under which of the following circumstances should an auditor consider confirming the terms of a large complex sale?

    a. When the assessed level of control risk over the sale is low
    b. When the assessed level of detection risk over the sale is high
    c. When the combined assessed level of inherent and control risk over the sale is moderate
    d. When the combined assessed level of inherent and control risk over the sale is high
    (R/12, AUD, #15, ID: 89765)

16. Of which of the following matters is a management representation letter required to contain specific representations?

    a. Length of a material contract with a new customer
    b. Information concerning fraud by the CFO
    c. Reason for a significant increase in revenue over the prior year
    d. The competency and objectivity of the internal audit department   (R/12, AUD, #16, ID: 89766)

17. In which of the following paragraphs of an auditor's report does an auditor communicate the nature of the engagement and the specific financial statements covered by the audit?

    a. Scope paragraph
    b. Opinion paragraph
    c. Introductory paragraph
    d. Explanatory paragraph   (R/12, AUD, #17, ID: 89767)

18. The understanding with the client regarding a financial statement audit generally includes which of the following matters?

    a. The expected opinion to be issued
    b. The responsibilities of the auditor
    c. The contingency fee structure
    d. The preliminary judgment about materiality   (R/12, AUD, #18, ID: 89768)

19. Under the Sarbanes-Oxley Act of 2002, exactly how many consecutive years may an audit partner lead an audit for an issuer?

    a. Four years
    b. Five years
    c. Six years
    d. Seven years

    (R/12, AUD, #19, ID: 89769)

20. A government internal audit function is presumed to be free from organizational independence impairments for reporting internally when the head of the organization

    a. Is **not** accountable to those charged with governance
    b. Performs auditing procedures that are consistent with generally accepted accounting principles
    c. Is a line-manager of the unit under audit
    d. Is removed from political pressures to conduct audits objectively, without fear of political reprisal

    (R/12, AUD, #20, ID: 89770)

21. Each of the following is a type of known misstatement, **except**

    a. An inaccuracy in processing data
    b. The misapplication of accounting principles
    c. Differences between management and the auditor's judgment regarding estimates
    d. A difference between the classification of a reported financial statement element and the classification according to generally accepted accounting principles

    (R/12, AUD, #21, ID: 89771)

22. An accountant can perform, with preapproval of the audit committee of the board of directors, which of the following nonaudit services during the audit of an issuer?

    a. Bookkeeping services
    b. Human resource services
    c. Tax planning services
    d. Internal audit outsourcing services

    (R/12, AUD, #22, ID: 89772)

23. The controller of a small utility company has interviewed audit firms proposing to perform the annual audit of their employee benefit plan. According to the guidelines of the Department of Labor (DOL), the selected auditor must be

    a. The firm that proposes the lowest fee for the work required
    b. Independent for purposes of examining financial information required to be filed annually with the DOL
    c. Included on the list of firms approved by the DOL
    d. Independent of the utility company and **not** relying on its services

    (R/12, AUD, #23, ID: 89773)

24. An accountant was asked by a potential client to perform a compilation of its financial statements. The accountant is not familiar with the industry in which the client operates. In this situation, which of the following actions is the accountant most likely to take?

    a. Request that management engage an independent industry expert to consult with the accountant
    b. Accept the engagement and obtain an adequate level of knowledge about the industry
    c. Decline the engagement
    d. Postpone accepting the engagement until the accountant has obtained an adequate level of knowledge about the industry

    (R/12, AUD, #24, ID: 89774)

25. To compile financial statements of a nonissuer in accordance with *Statements on Standards for Accounting and Review Services*, an accountant should

    a. Identify material misstatements in the financial statements
    b. Review bank statement reconciliations
    c. Make inquiries of significant customers, vendors, and creditors
    d. Obtain a general understanding of the client's business transactions   (R/12, AUD, #25, ID: 89775)

_____

Problem 2 MULTIPLE-CHOICE QUESTIONS

26. A CPA firm would best provide itself reasonable assurance of meeting its responsibility to offer professional services that conform with professional standards by

    a. Establishing an understanding with each client concerning individual responsibilities in a signed engagement letter
    b. Assessing the risk that errors and fraud may cause the financial statements to contain material misstatements
    c. Developing specific audit objectives to support management's assertions that are embodied in the financial statements
    d. Maintaining a comprehensive system of quality control that is suitably designed in relation to its organizational structure   (R/12, AUD, #26, ID: 89776)

27. An auditor who is unable to form an opinion on a new client's opening inventory balances may issue an unqualified opinion on the current year's

    a. Income statement only
    b. Statement of cash flows only
    c. Balance sheet only
    d. Statement of shareholders' equity only   (R/12, AUD, #27, ID: 89777)

28. Which of the following procedures would a CPA most likely perform in the planning phase of a financial statement audit?

    a. Make inquiries of the client's lawyer concerning pending litigation
    b. Perform cutoff tests of cash receipts and disbursements
    c. Compare financial information with nonfinancial operating data
    d. Recalculate the prior year's accruals and deferrals   (R/12, AUD, #28, ID: 89778)

29. Zag Co. issues financial statements that present financial position and results of operations but Zag omits the related statement of cash flows. Zag would like to engage Brown, CPA, to audit its financial statements without the statement of cash flows although Brown's access to all of the information underlying the basic financial statements will not be limited. Under these circumstances, Brown most likely would

    a. Add an explanatory paragraph to the standard auditor's report that justifies the reason for the omission
    b. Refuse to accept the engagement as proposed because of the client-imposed scope limitation
    c. Explain to Zag that the omission requires a qualification of the auditor's opinion
    d. Prepare the statement of cash flows as an accommodation to Zag and express an unqualified opinion   (R/12, AUD, #29, ID: 89779)

30. Under the ethical standards of the profession, which of the following is a "permitted loan" regardless of the date it was obtained?

    a. Home mortgage loan
    b. Student loan
    c. Secured automobile loan
    d. Personal loan   (R/12, AUD, #30, ID: 89780)

31. In confirming a client's accounts receivable in prior years, an auditor discovered many differences between recorded account balances and confirmation replies. These differences were resolved and were not misstatements. In defining the sampling unit for the current year's audit, the auditor most likely would choose

    a. Customers with credit balances
    b. Small account balances
    c. Individual overdue balances
    d. Individual invoices   (R/12, AUD, #31, ID: 89781)

32. An auditor is engaged to report on selected financial data that are included in a client-prepared document containing audited financial statements. Under these circumstances, the report on the selected data should

    a. State that the presentation is a comprehensive basis of accounting other than GAAP
    b. Restrict the use of the report to those specified users within the entity
    c. Be limited to data derived from the entity's audited financial statements
    d. Indicate that the data are subject to prospective results that may not be achieved
                                                                                     (R/12, AUD, #32, ID: 89782)

33. For which of the following audit tests would an auditor most likely use attribute sampling?

    a. Inspecting purchase orders for proper approval by supervisors
    b. Making an independent estimate of recorded payroll expense
    c. Determining that all payables are recorded at year end
    d. Selecting accounts receivable for confirmation of account balances   (R/12, AUD, #33, ID: 89783)

34. According to the Code of Professional Conduct of the AICPA, for which type of service may a CPA receive a contingent fee?

    a. Performing an audit of a financial statement
    b. Performing a review of a financial statement
    c. Performing an examination of prospective financial information
    d. Seeking a private letter ruling   (R/12, AUD, #34, ID: 89784)

35. Which of the following controls should prevent an invoice for the purchase of merchandise from being paid twice?

    a. The check signer accounts for the numerical sequence of receiving reports used in support of each payment.
    b. An individual independent of cash operations prepares a bank reconciliation.
    c. The check signer reviews and cancels the voucher packets.
    d. Two check signers are required for all checks over a specified amount.
                                                                                     (R/12, AUD, #35, ID: 89785)

36. A client has capitalizable leases but refuses to capitalize them in the financial statements. Which of the following reporting options does an auditor have if the amounts pervasively distort the financial statements?

    a. Qualified opinion
    b. Unqualified opinion
    c. Disclaimer opinion
    d. Adverse opinion   (R/12, AUD, #36, ID: 89786)

37. Which of the following items should be included in prospective financial statements issued in an attestation engagement performed in accordance with *Statements on Standards for Attestation Engagements*?

    a. All significant assertions used to prepare the financial statements
    b. All significant assumptions used to prepare the financial statements
    c. Pro forma financial statements for the past two years
    d. Historical financial statements for the past three years   (R/12, AUD, #37, ID: 89787)

38. A company employs three accounts payable clerks and one treasurer. Their responsibilities are as follows:

Employee	Responsibility
Clerk 1	Reviews vendor invoices for proper signature approval
Clerk 2	Enters vendor invoices into the accounting system and verifies payment terms
Clerk 3	Posts entered vendor invoices to the accounts payable ledger for payment and mails checks
Treasurer	Reviews the vendor invoices and signs each check

    Which of the following would indicate a weakness in the company's internal control?

    a. Clerk 1 opens all of the incoming mail.
    b. Clerk 2 reconciles the accounts payable ledger with the general ledger monthly.
    c. Clerk 3 mails the checks and remittances after they have been signed.
    d. The treasurer uses a stamp for signing checks.   (R/12, AUD, #38, ID: 89788)

39. Which of the following management assertions is an auditor most likely testing if the audit objective states that all inventory on hand is reflected in the ending inventory balance?

    a. The entity has rights to the inventory.
    b. Inventory is properly valued.
    c. Inventory is properly presented in the financial statements.
    d. Inventory is complete.   (R/12, AUD, #39, ID: 89789)

40. Which of the following activities is an accountant **not** responsible for in review engagements performed in accordance with *Statements on Standards for Accounting and Review Services*?

    a. Performing basic analytical procedures
    b. Remaining independent
    c. Developing an understanding of internal control
    d. Providing any form of assurance   (R/12, AUD, #40, ID: 89790)

41. Which of the following items should be included in an auditor's report for financial statements prepared in conformity with an other comprehensive basis of accounting (OCBOA)?

    a. A sentence stating that the auditor is responsible for the financial statements
    b. A title that includes the word "independent"
    c. The signature of the company controller
    d. A paragraph stating that the audit was conducted in accordance with OCBOA
      (R/12, AUD, #41, ID: 89791)

42. Which of the following statements best describes why an auditor would use only substantive procedures to evaluate specific relevant assertions and risks?

    a. The relevant internal control components are not well documented.
    b. The internal auditor already has tested the relevant controls and found them effective.
    c. Testing the operating effectiveness of the relevant controls would not be efficient.
    d. The cost of substantive procedures will exceed the cost of testing the relevant controls.
      (R/12, AUD, #42, ID: 89792)

43. Which of the following courses of action is the most appropriate if an auditor concludes that there is a high risk of material misstatement?

    a. Use smaller, rather than larger, sample sizes
    b. Perform substantive tests as of an interim date
    c. Select more effective substantive tests
    d. Increase of tests of controls

    (R/12, AUD, #43, ID: 89793)

44. Which of the following procedures would be generally performed when evaluating the accounts receivable balance in an engagement to review financial statements in accordance with *Statements on Standards for Accounting and Review Services*?

    a. Perform a reasonableness test of the balance by computing days' sales in receivables
    b. Vouch a sample of subsequent cash receipts from customers
    c. Confirm individually significant receivable balances with customers
    d. Review subsequent bank statements for evidence of cash deposits

    (R/12, AUD, #44, ID: 89794)

45. In which of the following circumstances would a covered member's independence be impaired with respect to a nonissuer client?

    a. The member is designated to serve as guardian of a friend's children if the need arises, and the friend's estate, which would be held in trust for the children, holds significant stock ownership in a client entity.
    b. The member's spouse qualifies because of geographical residence to belong to a client's credit union, and all transactions with the credit union are conducted under normal operating practices.
    c. The member owns municipal utility bonds issued by a client, and the bonds are **not** material to the member's wealth.
    d. The member belongs to a client golf club that requires members to acquire a share of the club's debt securities.

    (R/12, AUD, #45, ID: 89795)

46. According to the AICPA *Statements on Standards for Attestation Engagements*, a public accounting firm should establish quality control policies to provide assurance about which of the following matters related to agreed-upon procedures engagements?

    a. Use of the report is not restricted.
    b. The public accounting firm takes responsibility for the sufficiency of procedures.
    c. The practitioner is independent from the client and other specified parties.
    d. The practitioner sets the criteria to be used in the determination of findings.

    (R/12, AUD, #46, ID: 89796)

47. A cooling-off period of how many years is required before a member of an issuer's audit engagement team may begin working for the registrant in a key position?

    a. One year
    b. Two years
    c. Three years
    d. Four years

    (R/12, AUD, #47, ID: 89797)

48. A CPA is engaged to audit the financial statements of a nonissuer. After the audit begins, the client's management questions the extent of procedures and objects to the confirmation of certain contracts. The client asks the accountant to change the scope of the engagement from an audit to a review. Under these circumstances, the accountant should do each of the following, **except**

    a. Issue an accountant's review report with a separate paragraph discussing the change in engagement scope
    b. Consider the additional audit effort and cost required to complete the audit
    c. Evaluate the possibility that financial statement information affected by the limitation on work to be performed may be incorrect or incomplete
    d. Consider the reason given for the client's request and assess whether the request is reasonable

    (R/12, AUD, #48, ID: 89798)

49. Hart, CPA, is engaged to review the year 2 financial statements of Kell Co., a nonissuer. Previously, Hart audited Kell's year 1 financial statements and expressed a qualified opinion due to a scope limitation. Hart decides to include a separate paragraph in the year 2 review report because comparative financial statements are being presented for year 2 and year 1. This separate paragraph should indicate the

   a. Substantive reasons for the prior-year's qualified opinion
   b. Reason for changing the level of service from an audit to a review
   c. Consistency of application of accounting principles between year 2 and year 1
   d. Restriction on the distribution of the report for internal use only   (R/12, AUD, #49, ID: 89799)

50. Which of the following statements is generally correct about the sample size in statistical sampling when testing internal controls?

   a. As the population size doubles, the sample size should increase by about 67%.
   b. The sample size is inversely proportional to the expected error rate.
   c. There is **no** relationship between the tolerable error rate and the sample size.
   d. The population size has little or **no** effect on the sample size.   (R/12, AUD, #50, ID: 89800)

_____

Problem 3-1 SIMULATION: Internal Control Reporting

During audits of internal controls over financial reporting of various issuers, the auditors encountered the independent situations below. For each situation, select from the list provided the appropriate audit response. A response may be selected once, more than once, or not at all.

Situation	Response
1. The client did not furnish adequate evidence for the auditor to evaluate the internal controls over inventory. All other evidence was provided.	
2. The auditors examined the client's internal controls over cash receipts and concluded that they are operating exactly as designed. However, the design of the controls does not include control procedures to prevent misstatements and the potential omission of cash receipts.	
3. The auditors concluded that the ineffectiveness of the design of controls over accounts payable and cash disbursements represents a material weakness in internal control even though the financial statements are not materially misstated.	
4. Management has not provided assurance that there are no material weaknesses in controls. Subsequent tests revealed no material weaknesses.	
5. The auditor's prior-year report on internal control included an adverse opinion. The client has since modified internal controls. No material weaknesses were found in the current year.	

Response Selection List

A.	Assess control risk as low for the purpose of the financial statement audit	H.	Insist that management's assessment of internal control includes a description of the significant deficiency
B.	Consult legal counsel to explore reducing auditor liability	I.	Issue a disclaimer of opinion
C.	Determine if the control deficiency is a material weakness by obtaining further evidence	J.	Issue a report on internal controls stating that no deficiencies were noted
D.	Disclose in the notes to the financial statements that there are material weaknesses	K.	Issue a separate report on the client's internal control
E.	Express an adverse opinion on the internal controls	L.	Modify the report on internal controls for significant deficiencies
F.	Express an unqualified opinion on the internal controls	M.	Report matter only to the board of directors
G.	Express an unqualified opinion on the internal controls and add a paragraph on whether a previously reported material weakness in internal control continues to exist		

(R/12, AUD, ID: 89883)

Problem 3-2 SIMULATION: Bank Reconciliation

The auditor for Cubs Co. has obtained the following client-prepared bank reconciliation dated December 31, year 2, for detail testing.

Account 101—Cash account—First Bank of Munich
Bank reconciliation—December 31, Year 2
Prepared by: Joe Smith, January 10, year 3
Reviewed by: Evan Monroe, March 2, year 3

Balance per bank	$45,000	Note A
Add: deposits in transit		
10/25/year 2	12,000	
12/28/year 2	10,000	
Deduct: outstanding checks		
#8200 03/29/year 2	11,000	
#9003 11/30/year 2	14,000	
#9004 12/01/year 2	15,000	
Other reconciling items		
Balance per bank, adjusted	$27,000	
Balance per books before adjustments	$32,500	
Adjustments: bank fee and unrecorded items	(5,500)	
Balance per books, adjusted	$27,000	Note B

Notes
Note A: Agreed balance per bank to online account balance as of January 3, year 3
Note B: Agreed to general ledger on January 1, year 3

The following information is available:

- Evan Monroe was promoted to controller on December 15, year 2. His former position was assistant controller—fixed assets
- Evan Monroe has his personal bank accounts with First Bank of Munich
- Joe Smith was hired on December 1, year 2, as a staff accountant
- Joe Smith's prior job was with First Bank of Munich
- Cubs expects the year-end close to be complete on January 6, year 3
- The adjustments on the bank reconciliation were booked on January 30, year 3

In the table below, identify six potential issues that the auditor might have when examining the bank reconciliation prepared by Cubs by selecting the potential issues from the list provided. An issue may be used once or not at all.

Issues	Potential Issues
1. Issue #1	
2. Issue #2	
3. Issue #3	
4. Issue #4	
5. Issue #5	
6. Issue #6	

Issue Selection List

A. Reconciliation is not mathematically accurate	I. Reconciliation does not contain a proper title
B. Reconciliation balance was not properly agreed to the December 31 general ledger balance	J. Reconciliation does not agree to the cash disbursement subsidiary ledger
C. Reconciliation line item "Other reconciling items" is left blank	K. Reconciliation was not agreed to bank statement balance at the appropriate date
D. Reconciliation was not reviewed in a timely manner	L. Reconciliation does not include January, year 3, reconciliation items
E. Reconciliation was improperly approved as reviewer had a conflict of interest	M. Reconciliation was not prepared in a timely manner
F. Reconciliation has unsubstantiated unrecorded items	N. Reconciliation was prepared by an inexperienced individual
G. Reconciliation contains aged items that should have been added to the bank balance	O. Reconciliation contains stale checks
H. Reconciliation was improperly prepared by someone with a conflict of interest	

(R/12, AUD, ID: 89884)

Problem 3-3 SIMULATION: Research

Which citation in the professional standards provides an example of an appropriate opinion when the updated report on the financial statements of a prior period contains an opinion different from that previously expressed?

Reminder: On the actual exam, you will use an electronic database of authoritative literature to find and select the reference (appropriate section and paragraph of the relevant guidance). Please see the AICPA's tutorial and sample test on the exam section of their website.

[_____] § [_____] [_____]   (R/12, AUD, ID: 89885)

[_____]

Solution 1 MULTIPLE-CHOICE ANSWERS

1. (d) A compilation is not intended to provide assurance on the prospective financial statements or the assumptions underlying such statements; thus, an accountant who accepts an engagement to compile a financial projection most likely would make the client aware that the engagement does not include an evaluation of the support for the assumptions underlying the projection. Prospective financial statements may be included in a document that also contains audited historical financial statements. The standard report on a compilation of prospective financial statements includes a statement that the practitioner assumes no responsibility to update the report for events and circumstances occurring after the date of the report—it does not extend to one year. A financial forecast, not a projection, omits all hypothetical assumptions and presents the most likely future financial position. (Chapter 13-II-B; ID: 89751; CSO: I.D)

2. (d) A review of compliance with the terms of debt agreements is the audit procedure most likely to assist in the identification of conditions and events that may indicate there could be substantial doubt about an entity's ability to continue as a going concern. Ordinarily, information that significantly contradicts the going concern assumption relates to the entity's inability to continue to meet its obligations as they become due without substantial disposition of assets outside the ordinary course of business, restructuring of debt, externally forced revisions of its operations, or similar actions. (Chapter 8-IX-B; ID: 89752; CSO: IV.G)

3. (c) Analytical audit procedures consist of evaluations of financial information made by a study of plausible relationships among both financial and nonfinancial data. A basic premise underlying the application of analytical audit procedures is that plausible relationships among data may reasonably be expected to exist and continue in the absence of known conditions to the contrary. They are used to assist the auditor in planning the nature, timing, and extent of other auditing procedures; as a substantive test to obtain audit evidence about particular assertions related to account balances or classes of transactions; and as an overall review of the financial information in the final review stage of the audit. All of the answers describe analytical audit procedures performed for these purposes except for projecting a deviation rate by comparing the results of a statistical sample with the actual population characteristics. This is an audit sampling procedure. Audit sampling is the application of audit procedures to less than 100 percent of the population for the purpose of drawing conclusions about the population based on the results of the sample. (Chapter 4-IV-A; ID: 89753; CSO: III.B.7)

4. (c) Whether or not the principal auditor decides to make reference to the audit of the other auditor, the principal auditor should make inquiries concerning the professional reputation and independence of the other auditor. When the principal auditor decides *not* to make reference to the audit of the other auditor, i.e., to assume responsibility for the work of the other auditor insofar as that work relates to the principal auditor's expression of an opinion on the financial statements taken as a whole, the principal auditor should also consider whether to perform one or more of the following procedures: visit the other auditor and discuss the audit procedures followed and results; review the audit programs of the other auditor (in some cases, it may be appropriate to issue instructions to the other auditor as to the scope of his or her audit work); and review the working papers of the other auditor, including the understanding of internal control and the assessment of control risk. Regardless of the principal auditor's decision (whether or not to refer to the other auditor's work), the other auditor remains responsible for the performance of his or her own work, and for his or her own report; however this is not a matter ordinarily included in an engagement letter. The principal auditor is not required to obtain permission to omit the reference to the other auditor in the audit report. An explanatory paragraph should not be added to the auditor's report. If the principal auditor decides not to refer to the audit of another auditor, no reference should be made to the other auditor's work or report because to do so may cause a reader to misinterpret the degree of responsibility being assumed. (Chapter 8-III-C; ID: 89754; CSO: I.E.1)

5. (d) In auditing related-party transactions, an auditor ordinarily places primary emphasis on the adequacy of the disclosure of the related-party transactions. (Chapter 4-VIII-C; ID: 89755; CSO: II.I.2)

6. (b) When the accountant is unable to perform the inquiry and analytical procedures necessary to obtain limited assurance that there are no material modifications that should be made to the financial statements in order for them to be in conformity with the applicable financial reporting framework, or the client does not provide the accountant with a representation letter, the review will be incomplete. A SSARS review does not contemplate obtaining an understanding of the entity's internal control to assess control risk or for any reason; assessing fraud risk; testing accounting records by obtaining sufficient appropriate audit evidence through inspection, observation, confirmation, or the examination of source documents (for example, cancelled checks

or bank images); or other procedures ordinarily performed in an audit. Thus, the review does not include tests of details of major account balances. The accountant should possess an understanding of the industry in which the client operates, including the accounting principles and practices generally used in the industry sufficient to assist the accountant with determining the specific nature, timing, and extent of review procedures to be performed. This requirement does not prevent the accountant from accepting a review engagement for an entity in an industry with which the accountant has no previous experience. It does, however, place upon the accountant a responsibility to obtain the required level of knowledge. (Chapter 12-I-C; ID: 89756; CSO: V.A.2)

7. (b) Obtaining an understanding of an internal control involves evaluating the design of the control and determining whether the control has been implemented. (Chapter 3-II-C; ID: 89757; CSO: III.B.3)

8. (a) Making inquiries of management is the procedure most likely to be performed in a review engagement of a nonissuer's financial statements in accordance with SSARS. The accountant should perform procedures designed to accumulate review evidence that will provide a reasonable basis for obtaining limited assurance that there are no material modifications that should be made to the financial statements in order for them to be in conformity with the applicable financial reporting framework. Review evidence obtained through the performance of analytical procedures and inquiry will ordinarily provide the accountant with a reasonable basis for obtaining limited assurance; however, the accountant should perform additional procedures if necessary to obtain this limited assurance. (Written representations are also required from management for all financial statements and periods covered by the accountant's review report.) Observing a year-end inventory count and examining subsequent cash receipts are examples of testing accounting records by obtaining sufficient appropriate *audit* evidence through inspection, observation, confirmation, or the examination of source documents which are *not* required for a review. Also, a SSARS review does not contemplate assessing the internal control system. (Chapter 12-I-C; ID: 89758; CSO: V.B.5)

9. (c) An auditor should consider management's plans for disposal of assets when evaluating the ability of a company to continue as a going concern. Other examples the auditor should consider are the adequacy of support regarding plans to obtain additional financing by restructuring debt or borrowing money; reduce or delay expenditures; and/or to increase ownership equity. When evaluating management's plans, the auditor should identify those elements that are particularly significant to overcoming the adverse effects of the conditions and events and should plan and perform auditing procedures to obtain audit evidence about them. The auditor should consider whether it is likely the adverse effects will be mitigated for a reasonable period of time and that such plans can be effectively implemented. The fear of losing audit fees or future assurance service engagements (if the client does go bankrupt) should not be a consideration in whether to issue a "going-concern opinion." The auditor has a responsibility to evaluate whether there is substantial doubt about the entity's ability to continue as a going concern for a reasonable period of time, not to exceed one year beyond the date of the financial statements being audited. Thus, a lawsuit for which judgment is not anticipated for 18 months would not be relevant. Editor note: This question may have been released / dropped by the examiners due to the difference in the period an auditor is required to consider going concern issues according to U.S. auditing standards vs. International Standards of Auditing (ISA). ISA require a period of at least, but not limited to, 12 months, from the date of the financial statements. The period is extended if management's plan extends beyond 12 months and can be extended by the auditor when there is knowledge of events or conditions (beyond the period covered by management's plan) that may cast significant doubt about the entity's ability to continue as a going concern. (Chapter 8-IX-D; ID: 89759; CSO: IV.G)

10. (c) When there has been a change in an accounting principle or in the method of its application that has a material effect on the comparability of the company's financial statements, the auditor should refer to the change in an explanatory paragraph of the report following the opinion paragraph (if the auditor determines it has been handled appropriately). This is **not** a qualification of the auditor's opinion. The paragraph should identify the nature of the change and make reference to the note in the financial statements that discusses the change in detail. (Chapter 8-I-B; ID: 89760; CSO: IV.J.1)

11. (d) The best way to compensate for the lack of adequate segregation of duties in a small organization is to allow for greater management oversight of incompatible activities because it is the more constant control and a practical solution. Disclosing lack of segregation of duties to the external auditors during the annual review would not be effective because it could occur after the fact, moreover, establishing and maintaining effective internal control is the responsibility of management, not the auditors. Replacing personnel every three or four years is not effective because, again, it could occur after the fact, not to mention it is so draconian it could

actually motivate some individuals to commit a crime if they became aware of the policy. An issue discovered during a yearly background check of accountants is not as effective because it could also occur after the fact. (Chapter 3-II-A; ID: 89761; CSO: II.F.4)

12. (a) A large number of bearer bonds on hand most likely represents the highest risk of a misstatement arising from misappropriations of assets. Certain characteristics or circumstances may increase the susceptibility of assets to misappropriation, for example, large amounts of cash on hand or processed; inventory items that are small in size, of high value, or in high demand; easily convertible assets, such as bearer bonds, diamonds or computer chips; or fixed assets that are small in size, marketable, or lacking observable identification of ownership. A large number of inventory items with low sales prices or a large number of fixed assets with easily identifiable serial numbers would not be as attractive to a thief as bearer bonds. A large number of transactions processed in a short period of time is not a fraud risk factor. (Chapter 2-V-B; ID: 89762; CSO: II.C.4)

13. (a) An auditor would most likely make a preliminary judgment about materiality in the planning stage of an audit. Audit risk and materiality affect the application of generally accepted auditing standards; thus, they need to be considered together during the planning of an audit in designing the nature, timing, and extent of audit procedures and later, in evaluating the results of those procedures. The confirmation of a sample of the entity's accounts payable with known creditors is an example of an audit procedure that is not usually done unless evidence is uncovered that warrants it, so it would be unlikely to be performed early in the audit. The written representations from management should be made as of the date of the auditor's report because the auditor is concerned with events occurring through the date of the report that may require adjustment to or disclosure in the financial statements; thus, this would not be obtained during the planning stage. The communication of management's initial selection of accounting policies (the auditor's views about qualitative aspects of the entity's significant accounting practices, including accounting policies, accounting estimates, and financial statement disclosures) to the audit committee is an example of a required communication of a significant finding from the audit; thus, it is also unlikely to be communicated during the planning stage. (Chapter 2-II-F; ID: 89763; CSO: II.A)

14. (b) An auditor is required to confirm accounts receivable if the accounts receivable balances are material to the financial statements. Confirmation of accounts receivable is a generally accepted auditing procedure. It is generally presumed that evidence obtained from third parties will provide the auditor with higher-quality audit evidence than is typically available from within the entity. Thus, there is a presumption that the auditor will request the confirmation of accounts receivable during an audit unless one of the following is true: accounts receivable are immaterial to the financial statements; the use of confirmations would be ineffective; or the auditor's combined assessed level of inherent and control risk is low, and the assessed level, in conjunction with the evidence expected to be provided by analytical procedures or other substantive tests of details, is sufficient to reduce audit risk to an acceptably low level for the applicable financial statement assertions. (In many situations, both confirmation of accounts receivable and other substantive tests of details are necessary to reduce audit risk to an acceptably low level for the applicable financial statement assertions.) An auditor who has not requested confirmations in the examination of accounts receivable should document how he or she overcame this presumption. (Chapter 5-III-B; ID: 89764; CSO: III.B.8)

15. (d) Unusual or complex transactions may be associated with high levels of inherent risk and control risk. If the combined assessed level of inherent and control risk over the occurrence of revenue related to a large complex sale is high, the auditor should consider confirming the terms of that sale. (Chapter 5-III-B; ID: 89765; CSO: III.B.8)

16. (b) A management representation letter is required to contain specific representations about information concerning fraud by the CFO. (The specific representations should relate to knowledge of fraud or suspected fraud affecting the entity involving management; employees who have significant roles in internal control; or others where the fraud could have a material effect on the financial statements.) The other items are not appropriate for inclusion in the letter. (Chapter 4-III-B; ID: 89766; CSO: III.B.19)

17. (c) An auditor communicates the nature of the engagement and the specific financial statements covered by the audit in the introductory paragraph of the audit report: We have audited the accompanying balance sheet of X Company as of December 31, 20XX, and the related statements of income, retained earnings, and cash flows for the year then ended. These financial statements are the responsibility of the Company's management. Our responsibility is to express an opinion on these financial statements based on our audit.

Editor note: The examiners may have released / dropped this question because the scope paragraph also contains information about the nature of the engagement; however, it does not list the financial statements. (Chapter 8-III-B; ID: 89767; CSO: IV.J.1)

18. (b) The understanding with the client regarding a financial statement audit generally includes the responsibilities of the auditor. The other items are not appropriate for inclusion in the required engagement letter which documents the understanding. (Chapter 2-I-B; ID: 89768; CSO: I.D)

19. (b) Under the Sarbanes-Oxley Act of 2002, the lead audit or coordinating partner and the reviewing partner must rotate off the audit every five years. (Chapter 14-VII-B; ID: 89769; CSO: VI.A.2)

20. (d) A government internal audit function is presumed to be free from organizational independence impairments for reporting internally when the head of the organization is removed from political pressures to conduct audits objectively, without fear of political reprisal. (Chapter 9-I-B; ID: 89770; CSO: VI.A.3)

21. (c) *Known misstatements* are specific misstatements identified during the audit arising from the incorrect selection or misapplication of accounting principles or misstatements of facts identified, including, for example, those arising from mistakes in gathering or processing data and the overlooking or misinterpretation of facts. A difference between management and the auditor's judgment regarding [accounting] estimates is a *likely misstatement*. The other instance of a likely misstatement is a misstatement that the auditor considers likely to exist based on an extrapolation from audit evidence obtained, for example, the amount obtained by projecting known misstatements identified in an audit sample to the entire population from which the sample was drawn. (Chapter 2-II-C; ID: 89771; CSO: IV.E)

22. (c) Tax-planning services is an acceptable nonaudit service that an accountant can perform, with preapproval of the audit committee of the board of directors, during the audit of an issuer. (Chapter 14-I-C; ID: 89772; CSO: VI.A.2.)

23. (b) According to the guidelines of the Department of Labor (DOL), the selected auditor performing the annual audit of the company's employee benefit plan must be independent for purposes of examining financial information required to be filed annually with the DOL. The selected auditor may be a customer of the utility company, does not have to be on any approved list of firms, and does not have to be the lowest fee bidder for the work required. (Chapter 14-I-C; ID: 89773; CSO: VI.A.4.)

24. (b) When an accountant is asked to compile financial statements and the accountant is not familiar with the client's industry, the accountant most likely will accept the engagement and obtain an adequate level of knowledge about the industry. The requirement that the accountant possess a level of knowledge of the industry in which the client operates does not prevent the accountant from accepting a compilation engagement for an entity in an industry with which the accountant has no previous experience. It does, however, place upon the accountant a responsibility to obtain the required level of knowledge. Thus, the accountant is not required to decline or even postpone accepting the engagement. If the accountant decides to obtain the knowledge by consulting with an industry expert, the accountant, not management, should engage the expert. (Chapter 12-I-B; ID: 89774; CSO: V.B.1)

25. (d) To compile financial statements of a nonissuer in accordance with SSARS, an accountant should obtain a general understanding of the client's business transactions in order to compile financial statements that are appropriate in form for an entity operating in that industry. The accountant is not required to make inquiries or perform other procedures to verify, corroborate, or review information supplied by the entity. Thus, reviewing bank reconciliations or making inquiries of significant customers, vendors, and creditors is not required. Nor is the accountant compiling financial statements required to identify material misstatements in the financial statements. A compilation is a service, the objective of which is to assist management in presenting financial information in the form of financial statements without undertaking to obtain or provide any assurance that there are no material modifications that should be made to the financial statements in order for the statements to be in conformity with the applicable financial reporting framework. Editor note: Before submission, the accountant should read the financial statements and consider whether such financial statements appear to be appropriate in form and free from obvious material errors. In this context, the term *error* refers to mistakes in the preparation of financial statements, including arithmetical or clerical mistakes, and mistakes in the application of accounting

principles, including inadequate disclosure. This is a much narrower requirement than identifying material misstatements in the financial statements. (Chapter 12-I-B; ID: 89775; CSO: V.B.1)

Solution 2 MULTIPLE-CHOICE ANSWERS

26. (d)   The best way a CPA firm could best provide reasonable assurance of meeting its responsibility to offer professional services that conform with professional standards is by maintaining a comprehensive system of quality control that is suitably designed in relation to its organizational structure. (Chapter 14-IV-A; ID: 89776; CSO: VI.B.1.)

27. (c)   An auditor who is unable to form an opinion on a new client's opening inventory balances may issue an unqualified opinion on the current year's balance sheet only. When an auditor of a new client cannot become satisfied with the accuracy of opening inventory balances, this scope limitation affects the income, retained earnings, and cash flow statements, but not the balance sheet. (This is because cost of goods sold cannot be verified.) Thus, an unqualified opinion could be issued on the balance sheet and a disclaimer of opinion should be issued on the other financial statements. (Chapter 8-I-D; ID: 89777; CSO: IV.J.1)

28. (c)   During the planning phase of a financial statement audit a CPA would most likely compare financial information with nonfinancial operating data. This is an example of an analytical procedure. Analytical procedures are required during the planning phase. The latest date of the period coved by the lawyer's response to an auditor's inquiries should be as close as possible to the date of the auditor's report, thus, it is not likely these inquiries would be made during the planning phase. Cutoff tests of cash receipts and disbursements as well as the recalculation of the prior year's accruals and deferrals are procedures performed during the gathering-evidence phase of the audit rather than the planning phase. (Chapter 4-IV-A; ID: 89778; CSO: II.D.2)

29. (c)   The auditor (Brown) is not required to prepare a basic financial statement and include it in the report if the company's management declines to present the statement. In the case of the omission of a cash flow statement, a qualified opinion would be appropriate, with an explanatory paragraph added preceding the opinion paragraph. In accordance with a firm's system of quality control regarding the acceptance and continuance of client relationships and specific engagements, specifically those policies in place to minimize the risk of misunderstandings regarding the nature, scope, and limitations of the services to be performed, the auditor should explain to the client (Zag) that the omission requires a qualification of the auditor's opinion. (Chapter 8-IV-A; ID: 89779; CSO: I.D)

30. (c)   A car loan that is collateralized by the vehicle is a permitted loan which will not impair independence, regardless of the date it was obtained. (Chapter 14-I-C; ID: 89780; CSO: VI.A.1.)

31. (d)   When planning samples for tests of controls, the auditor will consider the relationship of the sample to the objective of the test of controls as well as the characteristics of the population. Confirmation replies relate directly to items appearing on individual invoices. (Chapter 6-I-F; ID: 89781; CSO: III.B.8.)

32. (c)   When an auditor is engaged to report on selected financial data that are included in a client-prepared document containing audited financial statements, the report on the selected data should be limited to data derived from [and relates directly to] the [underlying accounting and other records used to prepare] the entity's audited financial statements. None of the other answers are required report elements. Note that the question stipulates that the selected financial data is in a document containing the financial statements. The auditor *may consider* restricting the use of a separate report on supplementary information to the appropriate specified parties to avoid potential misinterpretation or misunderstanding of the supplementary information that is **not** presented with the financial statements. Editor note: When the entity presents the supplementary information with the financial statements, the auditor should report on the supplementary information in either an explanatory paragraph following the opinion paragraph in the auditor's report on the financial statements or in a separate report. When the audited financial statements are **not** presented with the supplementary information, the auditor should report on the supplementary information in a separate report. In this case, the report should include a reference to the report on the financial statements, the date of that report, the nature of the opinion expressed on the financial statements, and any report modifications. (Chapter 11-I-A; ID: 89782; CSO: IV.H)

33. (a)   Attribute sampling is used to test the effectiveness of internal control procedures. For example, the auditor may be concerned with estimating the percentage of purchase orders that do not have proper authorization. Variable sampling is utilized when testing details of transactions and account balances. (Chapter 6-III-A; ID: 89783; CSO: III.B.6.)

34. (d)   In some cases, contingent fees in certain tax matters are permitted. A contingent fee would be permitted when a member represents a client in an examination by a revenue agent of the client's tax return, or when a member represents a client with obtaining a private letter ruling. (Chapter 14-III-B; ID: 89784; CSO: VI.I.1.)

35. (c)   If the check signer reviews and cancels the voucher packets that should prevent an invoice from being paid twice. All of the other answers are valid controls, but not for the purpose of preventing an invoice from being paid twice. (Chapter 3-VII-E; ID: 89785; CSO: II.F.4)

36. (d)   If a client has capitalizable leases but refuses to capitalize them in the financial statements and the amounts pervasively distort the financial statements, the auditor should issue an adverse opinion. Such an opinion is expressed when the financial statements taken as a whole are not presented fairly in conformity with generally accepted accounting principles. The auditor could issue an "except for" qualified opinion if the effect was material, but not pervasive. (Chapter 8-IV-B; ID: 89786; CSO: IV.J.1)

37. (b)   [A summary of] all significant assumptions used to prepare the financial statements should be included in prospective financial statements issued in an attestation engagement performed in accordance with SSAE. The summary of significant assumptions is essential to the reader's understanding of prospective financial statements. Accordingly, the practitioner should not compile or perform an agreed-upon procedures engagement on prospective financial statements that exclude disclosure of the summary of significant assumptions. In an examination engagement if the presentation departs from the presentation guidelines because it fails to disclose assumptions that appear to be significant, the practitioner should express an adverse opinion. The other answers are not required to be included. (Chapter 13-II-B; ID: 89787; CSO: IV.J.7)

38. (c)   The mailing of the checks and remittances by clerk 3 after they have been signed indicates a weakness in the company's internal control due to improper segregation of duties. Incompatible functions place a person in the position to both perpetrate and conceal errors or fraud in the normal course of their duties. Therefore, a well-designed plan of organization separates the duties of authorization, record keeping, and custody of assets. Clerk 3 has duties that encompass both custody of assets and record keeping. Signed checks should be independently mailed directly after signing without being returned to persons involved in the invoice processing, check preparation, or recording functions. (Chapter 3-VII-E; ID: 89788; CSO: II.F.4)

39. (d)   If the audit objective states that all inventory on hand is reflected in the ending inventory balance an auditor is most likely testing the management assertion of completeness (*inventory is complete*): all assets, liabilities, and equity interests that should have been recorded have been recorded. Two of the other answers also are included in the category of assertions for account balances. *The entity has rights to the inventory* relates to the assertion of rights and obligations: the entity holds or controls the rights to assets, and liabilities are the obligations of the entity. The *inventory is properly valued* relates to the assertion of valuation and allocation: assets, liabilities, and equity interests are included in the financial statements at appropriate amounts and any resulting valuation or allocation adjustments are recorded appropriately. The *inventory is properly presented* in *the financial statements* relates to the assertion of classification and understandability: financial information is appropriately presented and described and disclosures are clearly expressed. This assertion is included in the category of presentation and disclosure. Chapter 5-III-C; ID: 89789; CSO: II.H.1)

40. (c)   An accountant is not responsible for developing an understanding of internal control in review engagements performed in accordance with SSARS. A review does require the CPA to perform analytical procedures and remain independent. The objective of a review is to provide limited assurance. (Chapter 12-I-C; ID: 89790; CSO: V.A.1)

41. (b)   A title that includes the word "independent" should be included in an auditor's report for financial statements prepared in conformity with an OCBOA. A statement that management, not the auditor, is responsible for the financial statements should be included. The manual or printed signature of the auditor's firm, not the signature of the company controller, is required. A paragraph that states that the audit was conducted in

accordance with generally accepted auditing standards, not with OCBOA, should also be included. (Chapter 11-II-B; ID: 89791; CSO: IV.J.9)

42. (c)   In some cases, the auditor may determine that performing only substantive procedures is appropriate to evaluate specific relevant assertions and risks. In those circumstances, the auditor may exclude the effect of controls from the relevant risk assessment. This may be because the auditor's risk assessment procedures have not identified any effective controls relevant to the assertion or because testing the operating effectiveness of controls would be not be efficient. However, the auditor needs to be satisfied that performing only substantive procedures for the relevant assertions would be effective in reducing detection risk to an acceptably low level. (A combined audit approach using both tests of the operating effectiveness of controls and substantive procedures is often most effective.) The quality of the documentation of the internal control components would not be a factor in the auditor's determination to use only substantive procedures. Because the auditor has the ultimate responsibility to express an opinion on the financial statements, judgments about assessments of inherent and control risks, the materiality of misstatements, the sufficiency of tests performed, the evaluation of significant accounting estimates, and other matters affecting the auditor's report should always be those of the auditor. The auditor may consider cost / benefit in the determination of an appropriate audit procedure; however, in this case, there is no information about a benefit, the answer only states nonsensically that the proposed action is more expensive. (Chapter 2-VII-B; ID: 89792; CSO: III.B.1)

43. (c)   When an auditor concludes that there is a high risk of material misstatement (RMM) the most appropriate course of action is to select more effective substantive tests. The auditor's selection of audit procedures is based on the RMM. The higher the auditor's assessment of risk, the more reliable and relevant is the audit evidence sought by the auditor from substantive procedures. When there is a high RMM, the auditor is more likely to use larger, rather than smaller, sample sizes. The higher the RMM, the more likely it is that the auditor may decide it is more effective to perform substantive procedures nearer to, or at, the period end rather than at an earlier date, or to perform audit procedures unannounced or at unpredictable times. The auditor should increase the extent of tests of controls the more the auditor relies on the operating effectiveness of controls in the assessment of risk. This reliance on controls by the auditor is due to an expectation of a low, not high, RMM because the auditor believes the entity has effective controls. (Chapter 2-VII-B; ID: 89793; CSO: III.A.1)

44. (a)   Performing a reasonableness test of the balance by computing days' sales in receivables would generally be performed when evaluating the accounts receivable balance in an engagement to review financial statements in accordance with SSARS. This is an example of an analytical procedure. Analytical procedures along with inquires will ordinarily provide the accountant with a reasonable basis for obtaining limited assurance which is the objective of a review. The other answers are examples of procedures ordinarily performed during an audit, not a review. A review according to SSARS does not contemplate obtaining an understanding of the entity's internal control; assessing fraud risk; testing accounting records by obtaining sufficient appropriate audit evidence through inspection, observation, confirmation, or the examination of source documents (for example, cancelled checks or bank images); or other procedures ordinarily performed in an audit. (Chapter 12-I-C.; ID: 89794; CSO: V.B.3)

45. (c)   Independence is impaired if the member has a direct or material indirect financial interest in the client. A direct financial interest will impair independence even if it is immaterial. (Chapter 14-I-C; ID: 89795; CSO: VI.I.1)

46. (c)   According to SSAE, a CPA may perform an agreed-upon procedures attest engagement provided that the CPA is independent. As a consequence of the role of the specified parties in agreeing upon the procedures performed, a practitioner's report on such engagements should clearly indicate that its use *is* restricted to those specified parties. The specified parties, not the public accounting firm, are required to take responsibility for the sufficiency of the agreed-upon procedures [for their purposes]. The criteria to be used in the determination of findings are agreed upon between the CPA (practitioner) and the specified parties, not set by the CPA. (Chapter 13-II-A; ID: 89796; CSO: I.B)

47. (a)   A cooling-off period of one year is required before a member of an issuer's audit engagement team may begin working for the registrant in a key position. (Chapter 14-I-C; ID: 89797; CSO: VI.A.2.)

48. (a)   If the accountant concludes that there is reasonable justification to change the engagement and if he or she complies with the standards applicable to a review engagement, the accountant should issue an

appropriate review report. The report should **not** include reference to the original engagement; any audit procedures that may have been performed; or scope limitations that resulted in the changed engagement. (Chapter 12-I-C; ID: 89798; CSO: V.A.4)

49. (a) The separate paragraph should indicate the substantive reasons for the prior-year's qualified opinion. When the current-period financial statements of a nonissuer have been compiled or reviewed and those of the prior period have been audited, the accountant should issue an appropriate compilation or review report on the current-period financial statements and either the report on the prior period should be reissued or the report on the current period should include, as a separate paragraph, an appropriate description of the responsibility assumed for the financial statements of the prior period. In the latter case, the separate paragraph should indicate that the financial statements of the prior period were audited previously; the date of the previous report; the type of opinion expressed previously; if the opinion was other than unqualified, the substantive reasons; and that no auditing procedures were performed after the date of the previous report. (Chapter 12-II-E; ID: 89799; CSO: V.C.2)

50. (d) When a sample is small in relation to the population, the population size has little or no effect on the determination of an appropriate sample size. (Chapter 6-III-C; ID: 89800; CSO: III.B.6)

———————————

Solution 3-1 SIMULATION ANSWER: Internal Control Reporting

Situation	Response
1. The client did not furnish adequate evidence for the auditor to evaluate the internal controls over inventory. All other evidence was provided.	I. Issue a disclaimer of opinion
2. The auditors examined the client's internal controls over cash receipts and concluded that they are operating exactly as designed. However, the design of the controls does not include control procedures to prevent misstatements and the potential omission of cash receipts.	C. Determine if the control deficiency is a material weakness by obtaining further evidence
3. The auditors concluded that the ineffectiveness of the design of controls over accounts payable and cash disbursements represents a material weakness in internal control even though the financial statements are not materially misstated.	E. Express an adverse opinion on the internal controls
4. Management has not provided assurance that there are no material weaknesses in controls. Subsequent tests revealed no material weaknesses.	F. Express an unqualified opinion on the internal controls
5. The auditor's prior-year report on internal control included an adverse opinion. The client has since modified internal controls. No material weaknesses were found in the current year.	F. Express an unqualified opinion on the internal controls

(ID: 89883)

1. I. Issue a disclaimer of opinion

The auditor can express an opinion on the company's internal control over financial reporting only if the auditor has been able to apply the procedures necessary in the circumstances. A scope limitation requires the auditor to disclaim an opinion or withdraw from the engagement. A disclaimer of opinion states that the auditor does not express an opinion on the effectiveness of internal control over financial reporting. The auditor should communicate, in writing, to management and the audit committee that the audit of internal control over financial reporting cannot be satisfactorily completed.

2. C. Determine if the control deficiency is a material weakness by obtaining further evidence

The auditor must evaluate the severity of each identified control deficiency to determine whether the deficiencies, individually or in combination, are material weaknesses as of the date of management's assessment.

3. E. Express an adverse opinion on the internal controls

A material weakness in internal control over financial reporting may exist even when financial statements are not materially misstated. If one or more material weaknesses exist, the company's internal control over financial reporting cannot be considered effective. Under these circumstances, the auditor must express an adverse opinion on the company's internal control over financial reporting, unless there is a restriction on the scope of the engagement. The auditor should determine the effect the adverse opinion on internal control has on the opinion on the financial statements. Additionally, the auditor should disclose whether the opinion on the financial statements was affected by the adverse opinion on internal control over financial reporting. The auditor must communicate, in writing, to management and the audit committee all material weaknesses identified during the audit. The written communication should be made prior to the issuance of the auditor's report on internal control over financial reporting.

4.   F.   Express an unqualified opinion on the internal controls

The auditor is required to express an opinion directly on the company's internal control over financial reporting rather than opining on management's assessment. Thus, even though management did not provide assurance that there were no material weaknesses in controls, the problem stated that tests revealed no material weaknesses. Editor note: The problem stated that management has not provided assurance that there are no material weaknesses. Apparently the examiners did not intend for this to be interpreted as a failure to obtain written representations from management which would constitute a scope limitation. A scope limitation should result in the auditor's withdrawal or issuance of a disclaimer of opinion. Apparently, the examiners also did not intend for this to be interpreted as a situation in which elements of management's annual report on internal control are incomplete or improperly presented which would require the auditor to modify the audit report by adding an explanatory paragraph. Perhaps this issue is why the examiners released / dropped this simulation.

5.   F.   Express an unqualified opinion on the internal controls

No material weaknesses were found in the current year, thus, the auditor can express an unqualified opinion.

Solution 3-2 SIMULATION ANSWER: Bank Reconciliation

Issues	Potential Issues
1. Issue #1	D. Reconciliation was not reviewed in a timely manner
2. Issue #2	K. Reconciliation was not agreed to bank statement balance at the appropriate date
3. Issue #3	O. Reconciliation contains stale checks
4. Issue #4	F. Reconciliation has unsubstantiated unrecorded items
5. Issue #5	G. Reconciliation contains aged items that should have been added to the bank balance
6. Issue #6	B. Reconciliation balance was not properly agreed to the December 31 general ledger balance

(ID: 89884)

1. D. Reconciliation was not reviewed in a timely manner

The year-end close was expected to be completed on January 6, year 3, yet the reconciliation was not reviewed until March 2, year 3.

2. K. Reconciliation was not agreed to bank statement balance at the appropriate date

The reconciliation should have been agreed to the bank statement balance as of December 31, year 2, not to the balance as of January 3, year 3, per Note A.

3. O. Reconciliation contains stale checks

Outstanding checks should have recent dates. Stale-dated checks should be resolved by attempting to contact the payee and then taking the appropriate action.

4. F. Reconciliation has unsubstantiated unrecorded items

The bank reconciliation should identify unrecorded items. They should be researched and resolved.

5. G. Reconciliation contains aged items that should have been added to the bank balance

The deposit dated 10/25/year 2 should have been received by the bank on the date of the deposit or very soon thereafter. This should have already been investigated, resolved, and, hopefully, included in the bank balance.

6. B. Reconciliation balance was not properly agreed to the December 31 general ledger balance

Per Note B, the balance was incorrectly agreed to the January 1, year 3, general ledger balance instead of the December 31, year 2, balance.

Solution 3-3 SIMULATION ANSWER: Research

AU	§	508		69	(ID: 89885)

.69   If, in an updated report, the opinion is different from the opinion previously expressed on the financial statements of a prior period, the auditor should disclose all the substantive reasons for the different opinion in a separate explanatory paragraph(s) preceding the opinion paragraph of his or her report. The explanatory paragraph(s) should disclose (a) the date of the auditor's previous report, (b) the type of opinion previously expressed, (c) the circumstances or events that caused the auditor to express a different opinion, and (d) that the auditor's updated opinion on the financial statements of the prior period is different from his or her previous opinion on those statements. The following is an example of an explanatory paragraph that may be appropriate when an auditor issues an updated report on the financial statements of a prior period that contains an opinion different from the opinion previously expressed:

<u>Independent Auditor's Report</u>

[Same first and second paragraphs as the standard report]

In our report dated March 1, 20X2, we expressed an opinion that the 20X1 financial statements did not fairly present financial position, results of operations, and cash flows in conformity with accounting principles generally accepted in the United States of America because of two departures from such principles: (1) the Company carried its property, plant, and equipment at appraisal values, and provided for depreciation on the basis of such values, and (2) the Company did not provide for deferred income taxes with respect to differences between income for financial reporting purposes and taxable income. As described in Note X, the Company has changed its method of accounting for these items and restated its 20X1 financial statements to conform with accounting principles generally accepted in the United States of America. Accordingly, our present opinion on the 20X1 financial statements, as presented herein, is different from that expressed in our previous report.

In our opinion, the financial statements referred to above, present fairly, in all material respects, the financial position of X Company as of December 31, 20X2 and 20X1, and the results of its operations and its cash flows for the years then ended in conformity with accounting principles generally accepted in the United States of America.

INDEX

A

S

Bisk Education
CPA REVIEW™

PASS THE CPA EXAM — GUARANTEED!*

GUARANTEED
SUCCESS
the First Time You Take the Exam

FREE
"How to Pass" DVD, Just for Calling

Offer is subject to change

CHOOSE YOUR FORMAT, ENSURE YOUR SUCCESS

Online, Videos and Books With Thousands of Review Questions and More Task-Based Simulations Than Any Other Provider

*Money-Back Guarantee — Call for details

▶▶▶ **PAYMENT PLANS ARE AVAILABLE!**

Call 888-CPA-BISK or Visit CPAexam.com/2013

Bisk Education
CPA REVIEW™

BISK CPA REVIEW VIDEOS

2 GREAT WAYS TO WATCH, LISTEN AND LEARN
TO PASS THE CPA EXAM

1 SIMULATION STRATEGIES DVDs

The Only CPA Review Prep That Targets Tough Simulations!

Master the simulation questions test takers fear most. Bisk CPA Review's one-of-a-kind Simulation Strategies DVDs guide you, step by step, through a variety of case studies and their unique solutions. You'll build the skills and self-assurance necessary to successfully recognize and react to these challenging test questions. Each DVD includes advanced review lectures vital to any CPA exam preparation. Choose from three DVDs: Financial Accounting & Reporting, Auditing & Attestation, and Regulation. Each DVD contains the following:

- Strategies for allocating time during the exam

- Tips on how to decide which simulations to tackle first

- Common pitfalls and techniques for problematic question types

- An accompanying viewer guide

- And more!

CPAexam.com/2013

2

HOT•SPOT™ DVDs

Weak in a specific area? Master it with your choice of topic-specific videos ... they're perfect for rounding out those rough spots before you sit for the exam!

These videos provide extensive coverage of the toughest, most challenging and most frequently tested topics within each of the four sections of the computer-based CPA exam – Financial Accounting & Reporting, Auditing & Attestation, Business Environment & Concepts, and Regulation.

Featuring America's best CPA review instructor – Bob Monette, JD, CPA, who uses humor to help you remember his problem-solving tips – each video is packed with valuable exam strategies and comes with a comprehensive viewer's guide for easy reference.

- Order just the titles you need (topic-specific videos available)

- Each video provides extensive coverage of a specific topic area

- Each video focuses on the toughest, most challenging and most frequently tested topics on the computer-based CPA exam

- Each video comes with a comprehensive viewer's guide

POWERFUL LAST-MINUTE STUDY TOOL

CALL NOW▶▶▶ 888-CPA-BISK

NO OTHER
VIDEO SERIES
IS THIS COMPREHENSIVE

DVDs: CHOOSE FROM THE FOLLOWING HOT•SPOT™ TITLES*

▶ ▶ ▶ Financial Accounting & Reporting Section
- Bonds & Other Liabilities
- Cash, Receivables & Marketable Securities
- Consolidations
- Statement of Cash Flows
- Accounting for Income Taxes
- Governmental Accounting
- Inventory, Fixed Assets & Intangible Assets
- Leases & Pensions
- Owners' Equity & Miscellaneous Topics
- Revenue Recognition & Income Statements
- Nonprofit Accounting
- IFRS & SEC Reporting

▶ ▶ ▶ Auditing & Attestation Section
- Audit Evidence
- Audit Standards & Planning
- Statistical Sampling
- Internal Control
- Standard Audit Reports
- Other Reports, Reviews & Compilations
- Professional Responsibilities

▶ ▶ ▶ Regulation Section
- Bankruptcy & Suretyship
- Business Entities
- Commercial Paper & Documents of Title
- Contracts
- Corporate Taxation
- Fiduciary Relationships
- Government Regulation of Business
- Gross Income, Tax Liabilities & Credits
- Individual Taxation
- Partnerships & Other Tax Topics
- Property Taxation
- Sales
- Secured Transactions
- Tax Ethics & Legal Duties

▶ ▶ ▶ Business Environment & Concepts Section
- Corporate Governance
- Cost & Managerial Accounting
- Economics
- Financial Management
- Information Technology

*Titles subject to change

"I am thrilled to let you know that I passed all four parts of the exam on the first try. I wanted to tell your company, 'Thanks for the great Hot•Spot DVDs.' The instructors were extremely knowledgeable and I believe their exam tips were the difference in passing or failing for me. Without your videos, I would not have been a success."

Tracy Wang
LOUISIANA

TARGETED TRAINING
THAT LETS YOU MASTER
ANY EXAM TOPIC
Bisk CPA Review Videos

SAVE ON YOUR PERSONAL CHOICE
OF INTERACTIVE FORMATS

$200 OFF

Bisk Education
CPA REVIEW
America's Best CPA Review Since 1971

▶▶▶ **DISCOUNT COUPON**

Source code 198970zbb1

Instructor-Led CPA Review ONLINE

BETTER THAN A LIVE CLASSROOM!

Features the hands-on guidance, structure and support of a live class review mixed with the flexibility, convenience and 24/7 access of online learning.

This coupon is good for $200 off the complete Bisk Instructor-Led CPA Review Online course.

To receive your discount, call **888-CPA-BISK**, fax **800-345-8273** or visit **www.CPAexam.com/2013** and be sure to include your source code number.

$100 OFF

Bisk Education
CPA REVIEW
America's Best CPA Review Since 1971

▶▶▶ **DISCOUNT COUPON**

Source code 198970zbb1

Hot•Spot DVDs

POWERFUL LAST-MINUTE STUDY TOOL

These videos feature America's leading CPA review experts who organize, prioritize and summarize key concepts vital to your exam success.

This coupon is good for $100 off the purchase of five or more Hot•Spot™ DVDs.

To receive your discount, call **888-CPA-BISK**, fax **800-345-8273** or visit **www.CPAexam.com/2013** and be sure to include your source code number.

$50 OFF

Bisk Education
CPA REVIEW
America's Best CPA Review Since 1971

▶▶▶ **DISCOUNT COUPON**

Source code 198970zbb1

Simulation Strategies DVDs

THE ONLY CPA REVIEW PREP THAT TARGETS TOUGH SIMULATIONS!

Master the simulation questions test takers fear most.

This coupon is good for $50 off the complete Bisk CPA Review Simulation Strategies DVD Series.

To receive your discount, call **888-CPA-BISK**, fax **800-345-8273** or visit **www.CPAexam.com/2013** and be sure to include your source code number.

SAVE ON YOUR PERSONAL CHOICE
OF INTERACTIVE FORMATS

$200 OFF

▶▶▶ **DISCOUNT COUPON**

Source code 198970zbb1

Instructor-Led CPA Review ONLINE

BETTER THAN A LIVE CLASSROOM!

Features the hands-on guidance, structure and support of a live class review mixed with the flexibility, convenience and 24/7 access of online learning.

This coupon is good for $200 off the complete Bisk Instructor-Led CPA Review Online course.

To receive your discount, call **888-CPA-BISK**, fax **800-345-8273** or visit **www.CPAexam.com/2013** and be sure to include your source code number.

$100 OFF

▶▶▶ **DISCOUNT COUPON**

Source code 198970zbb1

Hot•Spot DVDs

POWERFUL LAST-MINUTE STUDY TOOL

These videos feature America's leading CPA review experts who organize, prioritize and summarize key concepts vital to your exam success.

This coupon is good for $100 off the purchase of five or more Hot•Spot™ DVDs.

To receive your discount, call **888-CPA-BISK**, fax **800-345-8273** or visit **www.CPAexam.com/2013** and be sure to include your source code number.

$50 OFF

▶▶▶ **DISCOUNT COUPON**

Source code 198970zbb1

Simulation Strategies DVDs

THE ONLY CPA REVIEW PREP THAT TARGETS TOUGH SIMULATIONS!

Master the simulation questions test takers fear most.

This coupon is good for $50 off the complete Bisk CPA Review Simulation Strategies DVD Series.

To receive your discount, call **888-CPA-BISK**, fax **800-345-8273** or visit **www.CPAexam.com/2013** and be sure to include your source code number.

Are You *Sure* You Know What's on the Exam?

Get FREE Updating Supplements All Year Long!

Keep pace with the constantly changing CPA Exam. Register now at **www.CPAexam.com/2013** to automatically receive updating supplements covering new FASB and AICPA pronouncements, developments in Federal income taxation and more.

PLUS GET A FREE GIFT:

"How to Pass the CPA Exam" DVD

✓ Sure-fire techniques for avoiding the most common exam mistakes

✓ Proven strategies for making the most of your study time

✓ How to develop the characteristics that successful candidates share

✓ Key answer-writing tips that are sure to boost your score

✓ And much more!

Take a tour of 10 FREE classes at www.CPAexam.com/demo

Experience the Power of Our Instructor-Led Online Review.

Tour the Bisk CPA Review Online Classroom including sample lectures featuring America's top experts analyzing, simplifying and explaining must-know exam information.

Stay Up-To-Date All Year Long – FREE! | Visit **www.CPAexam.com/2013** or Complete the form on the reverse side and drop it in the mail.

FOLD CARD WITH ADDRESS LABEL OUT, THEN TAPE CLOSED

Bisk Education
CPA REVIEW
America's Best CPA Review Since 1971

NO POSTAGE
NECESSARY
IF MAILED
IN THE
UNITED STATES

BUSINESS REPLY MAIL
FIRST-CLASS MAIL   PERMIT NO. 7657   TAMPA, FL

POSTAGE WILL BE PAID BY ADDRESSEE

BISK CPA REVIEW
9417 PRINCESS PALM AVENUE
PO BOX 31028
TAMPA FL 33633-0295

STAY UP-TO-DATE WITH FREE UPDATING SUPPLEMENTS!

▶ ▶ ▶

PLUS, SEND IN THE FORM BELOW AND GET A FREE GIFT:

"HOW TO PASS THE CPA EXAM" DVD

BISK CPA REVIEW FREE REQUEST FORM

☑ **YES!** Please send the FREE information that I have checked below:

☐ FREE CPA Gift "How to Pass the CPA Exam" DVD
(CPA1565D)

☐ FREE Updating Supplements (Available to original purchasers only)
Check section(s) purchased:
☐ Financial Accounting & Reporting
☐ Auditing & Attestation
☐ Regulation
☐ Business Environment & Concepts
☐ Full Set (all four sections)

☐ I want to earn while I learn! Please send me FREE
information on how I can become a Bisk CPA Review
Representative on my campus. – (LNIA9002)

Please indicate the date you plan to take the exam sections
below (if you have already passed a section, please insert the letter "P"):
REG: _____ BEC: _____ FAR: _____ AUD: _____

How far in advance do you plan on beginning to prepare for
each section?
☐ 30 days ☐ 60 days ☐ 90 days
☐ Other: _____

What review format do you prefer?
☐ Live ☐ Online ☐ Video ☐ Text
☐ Other: _____

Where did you purchase your Bisk CPA Review textbook?
☐ Online ☐ Phone ☐ Bookstore

Name: _____
School (if applicable): _____
Company (if applicable): _____
Address: _____
City: _____ State: _____ ZIP: _____
Phone: ( ) _____
Email: _____
Place Purchased: _____
Date Purchased: _____

Phone numbers required for UPS delivery.
Orders without phone numbers and email address cannot be processed.
* Free shipping for U.S. orders only.   Edition #42

Source Code 197800zbb1 | MCID 18328

America's Best CPA Review Since 1971

Fill out the form and send in this page and you will automatically receive
updating supplements containing outlines of new FASB and AICPA
pronouncements and a review of new developments in Business Law and
Federal Income Taxation as they become available. Additionally, you'll be
informed of new subject areas or significant changes in the exam emphasis.

Bisk Education, Inc. | 9417 Princess Palm Avenue | Tampa, FL 33619-8313
888-CPA-BISK | 813-621-6200 | www.CPAexam.com/2013 | info@CPAexam.com